IRB WORLD RUGBY YEARBOOK 2008

EDITED BY PAUL MORGAN AND JOHN GRIFFITHS

Vision Sports Publishing
2 Coombe Gardens,
London, SW20 0QU
www.visionsp.co.uk

This First Edition Published by
Vision Sports Publishing in 2007

978-1-90536-33-4

Cover image: Martin Bureau, AFP/Getty Images
All other pictures by Getty Images unless otherwise stated
Illustrations by www.cakebreadillustrations.com

Typeset by Palimpsest Book Production Ltd, Grangemouth, Stirlingshire

Printed and bound in the UK by Cromwell Press Ltd, Trowbridge, Wiltshire

The IRB World Rugby Yearbook is an independent publication supported by the International Rugby Board but the views throughout, expressed by the different authors, do not necessarily reflect the policies and opinions of the IRB.

International Rugby Board
Huguenot House
35-38 St Stephen's Green
Dublin 2
Ireland

t +353-1-240-9200
f +353-1-240-9201
e irb@irb.com

www.irb.com

INTRODUCTION

FROM JOINT EDITOR – PAUL MORGAN

Welcome to the new edition of the IRB World Rugby Yearbook, the second since it was relaunched by the International Rugby Board and Vision Sports Publishing.

Of course this is a pretty special edition as it covers a momentous Rugby World Cup, where there were shocks around every corner and a worthy winner in South Africa.

To make sure we bring you the best of the Rugby World Cup we have added 64 pages, so it is now a whopping 640 pages. But we still managed to keep the price the same!

In addition to the Rugby World Cup section, which makes this edition a collector's item there is an informative look at referee's signals. I hope these will make the game I love a little easier to understand.

We have managed to keep chapters on each of the 20 sides that competed in the 2007 Rugby World Cup and all the old favourites are back again.

The journey to publication has once again been a long, and often arduous one, so there are a number of heartfelt thank yous I must make.

No Yearbook would be worth its salt without John Griffiths' statistics – which have graced the book for many years – and those of Hugh Copping, complemented them perfectly.

Of course to Jim Drewett and Toby Trotman at Vision Sports Publishing for sharing my vision for the book.

Principal writer Iain Spragg just keeps getting better and better, and more prolific.

The players who contributed including John Eales, Michael Lynagh and Will Greenwood, who joined our writing team and for the second year running my gratitude goes out to the best proofreader and fact-checker in the business, Howard Evans.

Chris Rhys, who brought his Major Tours section back this year, the correspondents from around the world, almost too numerous to mention, were a great source of inspiration, the great Frankie Deges playing a starring role.

Emirates were great partners again, so warm thanks go to them, and at the IRB nothing could have happened without Greg Thomas championing the project, along with Chris Thau and Alison Hughes...and last but not absolutely not least the many, many days and weeks spent on this book by the inexhaustible Dominic Rumbles.

The workload – as the Rugby World Cup took so much of his time – was far greater on Dom this year so I am very grateful for his help.

No statistically-based book would be published without a tireless typesetter and I was lucky to have a great team to work with at Palimpsest Book Production, led by Julie "that's no problem" Garvock.

Any comments are always gratefully received and any recommendations for future editions should come to me at Rugby World Magazine. Email me at paul_morgan@ipcmedia.com

INTRODUCTION

IRB INVESTMENT PAYING DIVIDENDS

FROM DR SYD MILLAR, CHAIRMAN OF THE INTERNATIONAL RUGBY BOARD

Alex Livesey/Getty Images

More than two million spectators went through the turnstiles at this Rugby World Cup, an incredible record!

The IRB set itself on a new course in 2005 with a new strategic plan and an unprecedented £30 million investment programme aimed at increasing the competitiveness of the game around the world.

The investment funds were a direct result of the success of the Rugby World Cup and we were perhaps a little conservative in thinking that we would not see any defined increase in competitiveness until RWC 2011.

How wrong we were. RWC 2007 in France revealed that our investment in new tournaments, player and coaching high performance programmes, union and facility infrastructures and key resources such as people with expertise on the ground is already reaping rewards.

RWC 2007 may have seen record ticket sales, crowds and TV audiences but the key feature of the tournament was undoubtedly the improved performance of the developing nations. Despite our proactive efforts to promote this strategic investment initiative that is changing the fortunes of the developing nations it has been somewhat disappointing how little information about the investment programme has been carried by the media.

For the record the IRB investment between late 2005 and the end of 2007 has seen: almost £16 million invested in Tonga, Samoa, Fiji, Canada, Japan, USA and Romania including the creation of four new tournaments to create new player pathways – Pacific Rugby Cup, Pacific Nations Cup, North America 4 and Nations Cup (all covered later in this book); £12 million invested in Tier 1 Unions to maintain standards at the top level including £2.25 million for Argentina; and £1.5 million in the Tier 3 Unions who gained RWC qualification.

The exciting thing is that the commercial success of RWC 2007 means we now have further significant funds to invest in the game and the Executive Committee will decide the way forward in April 2008.

Other challenges we are now addressing include the global playing calendar of the professional game as it is becoming severely congested. Understandably we are seeing increasing tension between different levels of the game which each require players to fulfil their various commitments in order to satisfy contractual, spectator and commercial demands.

The international rugby calendar is built around the four-year Rugby World Cup cycle. Every rugby union wants to win RWC and their strategic plans measure their success by how well they do at the tournament. Inevitably the tournament adds even more strain to the playing calendar regardless of what time of year it is played in, especially when you factor in the need for appropriate player rest periods and warm-up matches prior to a Rugby World Cup.

The IRB is taking the lead in this search for a better balanced programme of matches and our aim in 2008, in conjunction with the game's stakeholders, is to find the appropriate solutions for a better defined playing calendar that takes into account player welfare issues, relevance of the international match programme and the continued commercial appeal of the game.

Linked to the development of an integrated season is a review of Regulations 4 and 9 which govern player status, contracts and movement, and availability. The IRB has already started work on this and has begun consultation with the Member Unions. This move recognises that the existing Regulations were written to suit a game that no longer exists and new Regulations are needed to fit the modern professional game.

Another interesting part of this whole equation is the way the game is played. Presently the IRB is trialling a raft of experimental law variations (ELVs) around the world. I think most people associated with the game, including spectators, would agree that the game is in a very healthy state but that there are some fundamental problems creeping in. The game is quicker, players are stronger and faster, contact is more aggressive and physical, and the advancement of skill levels is putting strain on the Laws themselves in terms of the contest for possession.

There is an underlying consensus that rugby does need an overhaul in terms of the Laws of the Game. The IRB has been trialling the ELVs over the last two years around the world and it may well be that in 2008 they are implemented at all levels for a minimum of 12 months.

If successful and accepted they would then be adopted into the Laws of the Game in 2009.

An important issue to note is that the ELVs do not in any way change the basic fabric of the game in terms of its key elements - scrums, lineouts, the breakdown etc. And all through the project the IRB has adhered to one of the major elements of the Game's Charter – That Rugby is and must always be a game for all shapes and sizes.

CONTENTS

RUGBY WORLD CUP

INTERNATIONAL TOURNAMENTS

THE COUNTRIES

CROSS-BORDER TOURNAMENTS

INTRODUCTION

FROM GARY CHAPMAN – PRESIDENT GROUP SERVICES & DNATA, EMIRATES GROUP

What a year for rugby this year turned out to be! Emirates is incredibly proud to be associated with this great sport.

It was the year of the long awaited Rugby World Cup 2007, the most prestigious tournament of the year, and what a tournament it was. Who could have foreseen just how far some of the lesser talked about teams would progress; or how soon some of the big names would be packing their bags and heading home. The IRB put on a great show in front of record crowds in France, Cardiff and Edinburgh and the billions watching around the world.

Emirates came onboard for the first time as the Official Airline of Rugby World Cup 2007 and continued its sponsorship of the IRB's International Referees.

It was also the year that Dubai was named as the host of the IRB Rugby World Cup Sevens 2009, an event which Emirates will be closely involved in. We have a great deal of experience with Rugby Sevens having sponsored the highly successful Emirates Airline Dubai Rugby Sevens since 1988.

Emirates is also the sponsor of a further three tournaments in the IRB World Sevens Series, namely South Africa, London and Edinburgh, in addition to our shirt sponsorships of the England and Samoan sevens teams. Our Southern Hemisphere support of rugby extends to Australia where we have just signed a new two year contract as the title sponsor of Emirates Western Force.

Emirates has an extensive portfolio of top-class sports sponsorships around the world, from being official FIFA partner up until the 2014 FIFA World Cup™, to being Title Sponsor of the world's richest horse race, the Dubai World Cup; from the naming rights to the new home of Arsenal Football Club, the Emirates Stadium, to the sponsor of Australia's 2007 Cricket World Cup winning team and Official Airline of eleven major golf tournaments.

Emirates is very proud of its association with the IRB and hope that you enjoy this year's edition of the IRB Yearbook.

RUGBY WORLD CUP

BOKS ON TOP OF THE WORLD

France staged a magnificent Rugby World Cup. Here Iain Spragg looks back at the highs and lows of an event that took rugby to another level

Dave Rogers/Getty Images

Springboks captain John Smit and the President of South Africa, Thabo Mbeki, celebrate the win.

South Africa were crowned world champions for a second time in 12 years as France staged arguably the greatest Rugby World Cup in the history of the competition. The Springboks famously lifted the Webb Ellis Cup for a first time on a nation-defining day in Johannesburg in 1995 and they repeated the achievement in Paris after dethroning champions England in a titanic, nerve-jangling final that Jake White's side edged 15–6.

Although there were no tries at the Stade de France, the 2007 final still proved a fitting climax to a thoroughly absorbing tournament that repeatedly defied expectations and dented a few reputations along the way. Never before had the competition produced so many shocks and from the moment Argentina beat France in the first match in Saint Denis, the tone was set. The 2007 World Cup was going to be anything but prosaic.

It was not just the Pumas who enlivened the tournament. Fiji's thrilling progress to the quarter-finals was a joy to behold while both England and France electrified the competition with their triumphs over Australia and New Zealand respectively in the last eight. South Africa may have reclaimed the cup for the southern hemisphere but the widely predicted Tri-Nations procession failed to materialise. On the evidence of the results of the 48 games played over seven captivating weeks, the game was in rude health indeed.

The final itself was a heavyweight contest in every sense as the Springboks and the English pounded each other with bone-crunching ferocity in Paris and there was little to choose between the two sides. Expansive rugby was at a premium and although the likes of Bryan Habana and Jason Robinson had little opportunity to dazzle and dissect, the game was no less fascinating for it.

The Springboks struck first through a Percy Montgomery penalty and it was a lead they were to preserve for the whole 80 minutes. Jonny Wilkinson hit back for the English but two more booming kicks from Montgomery's left boot gave South Africa a 9–3 half-time advantage.

England emerged for the second-half breathing fire and almost found a way through the Springbok armour when Mark Cueto dived in at the corner but referee Alain Rolland went upstairs to the TMO for a ruling on whether Danie Rossouw had forced the England wing into touch. The verdict seemed to take an eternity but when it finally came it was no try.

With hindsight, it was to be England's best chance of the match. Brian Ashton's side probed and harried but just couldn't get within striking distance of the Springboks. A fourth penalty from Montgomery, a superb long-range effort from Francois Steyn and a constant flow of lineout ball from man-of-the-match Victor Matfield ensured White's side were out of reach and when the final whistle blew, they were world champions once again.

"This is awesome," Matfield said in the Stade de France. "We worked for four years for this. We knew we were going to have to take it to

England up front. The emotions are greater than I ever thought. I can't wait to get back home. I can't wait to see all the South Africans."

The tournament kicked-off with the Pool D opener in Paris between France and Argentina and the sense of the host nation's anticipation was as palpable as the Pumas' determination to prove to the global rugby fraternity they were no longer the game's poor relations. Argentina had a point to prove.

From the first whistle in the Stade de France, Marcelo Loffreda's side tore into Les Bleus with an unrelenting ferocity that the nervous home team simply had no answer to and when Ignacio Corleto provided the finishing touch to a rapier-like Argentina counter attack in the first half, the writing was on the wall. France were beaten 17–12 and the unpredictable tone for the rest of the competition had been set.

The Pumas however were far from finished and they set out to prove their triumph in Saint Denis was no mere flash in the pan. The gallant Georgians and outclassed Namibians were duly despatched and Argentina knew victory over Ireland would secure top spot in the group and condemn Eddie O'Sullivan's faltering side to an early flight home.

The Irish looked a shadow of the team they had been 12 months earlier while Loffreda's team were assured and with the impressive half-back pairing of Agustín Pichot and Juan Martín Hernández pulling the strings astutely, Argentina cruised to a 30–15 victory that sent the Pumas through. France claimed the runners-up place and Ireland's campaign lay in tatters.

The outcome of Pool B was no less dramatic – or demoralising for one of the northern hemisphere contingent. Australia and Wales were widely expected to book their perennial place in the last eight but as in Pool D, there was an impertinent gatecrasher lurking in the shadows to further enliven the tournament.

The Wallabies, the 2003 runners-up, had few problems in winning the group with a 100 per cent record but Wales' hopes of joining them were dashed by Fiji, who won themselves an army of new fans with a series of dashing displays that lit up the World Cup.

The two sides met in Nantes knowing victory would take them through to the quarter-finals and it was the Fijians who seized their chance in style. Wales outscored the South Sea Islanders five tries to four but it was Graham Dewes' score four minutes from time that proved decisive and Fiji were through to the last eight for the first time since the inaugural tournament in 1987.

There were to be no seismic shocks in Pool A. Both Tonga and Samoa acquitted themselves well but there was no stopping the heavyweights of South Africa and England reaching the knockout stages. The

Springboks' 36–0 mauling of the English in Paris eclipsed Tonga's surprise 19–15 triumph over Samoa but that result in Montpellier aside, the group went with the form book.

It was a similar story in Pool C as the All Blacks swept all before them, scored 309 points in their four outings and eased into the quarter-finals without breaking sweat.

The real issue was whether Scotland or Italy would join them. The Six Nations rivals met in the final group game in Saint Etienne and Frank Hadden's side were indebted to the unerring accuracy of Chris Paterson's boot in a tense 18–16 victory. The wing landed six penalties from six attempts and Scotland maintained their proud record of reaching the last eight in every World Cup.

There were more surprises to come in the quarter-finals.

The first of the four knockout games saw England tackle Australia in Marseille in a repeat of the 2003 final and if the men in white had been the marginal favourites in Sydney four years earlier, there was no doubt the Wallabies were universally expected to avenge their defeat in the Stade Velodrome in 2007.

The defending champions had looked toothless and tepid in their group games while Australia were the competition's second highest points scorers. But not for the first time in the tournament, events deviated dramatically from the pre-match script.

Wallabies coach John Connolly had spent the past two years attempting to overcome the perceived weakness in the Australian scrum but his side's Achilles heel came back to haunt them once again in Marseille and England's front row of Andy Sheridan, Mark Regan and Phil Vickery destroyed their counterparts in gold. Jonny Wilkinson landed four penalties, Stirling Mortlock missed a potential match-winner four minutes from time and England were 12–10 winners.

"The scrum was destroyed and England controlled the breakdown," Connolly conceded as he contemplated defeat. "Their scrum is world-class, but the breakdown is an issue for the whole team. I said before the tournament their scrum and lineout would be a massive threat to everyone."

But if the rugby world was surprised by England's triumph, they were left in a state of disbelief after the second quarter-final between France and New Zealand. Les Bleus had clearly been struggling with the burden of hosting the tournament while the All Blacks had been virtually invincible for the past four years and even the most optimistic French supporter could only recall their side's famous 1999 semi-final win over the Kiwis more in hope than expectation.

The vagaries of the organisation of the tournament saw the two sides cross swords in Cardiff's Millennium Stadium rather than back in France but Les Bleus seemed to relish the change of scenery and without the oppressive weight of expectation on their shoulders, Bernard Laporte's side blossomed.

The French refused to allow New Zealand to dominate proceedings and despite trailing 13–0 at the half hour mark, they fought back to level the game in the second-half with a try from Thierry Dusautoir. The All Blacks regained the advantage with a Rodney So'oialo score but Les Bleus hit back with a converted try from Yannick Jauzion to make it 20–18. The Kiwis had 10 minutes to redeem themselves but their World Cup hoodoo returned once again, their incisive attacking game deserted them and France were through.

"It is a great victory for all the players who gave everything on the field right until the end," French captain Raphael Ibanez said in the wake of one of greatest upsets in the tournament's history. "We keep a lot of respect for this New Zealand team, they remain exceptional players. But in such a great competition as the World Cup, courage and spirit make the difference and that's what happened today."

The third quarter-final the following day saw South Africa tackle Fiji in Marseille but the Springboks were in no mood to make it a hat-trick of southern hemisphere scalps for the underdogs and although the South Seas Islanders once again enthralled the crowd with some breathtaking and intuitive rugby, Jake White's side were just too strong and ran out winners.

The final 37–20 scoreline flattered the South Africans somewhat. Leading 20–6 in the second half, the Springboks appeared to be coasting to victory and when Fiji had Seru Rabeni sent to the sin bin for a late tackle on Butch James, the contest seemed over. But the 14-man Fijians had other ideas and scintillating tries from the impressive Vilimoni Delasau and Sireli Bobo, both of which were converted, levelled the match at 20–20. South Africa reverted to their forward power to get them out of the hole and although Fiji could find no answer, they departed the tournament with their heads held high.

"The two games yesterday, they were both upsets," said Fiji captain Mosese Rauluni. "We were hoping for a third upset today but couldn't pull it off. We had great belief when we were 13–3 down. We were finding holes in their defence. The boys were making the breaks but unfortunately we couldn't finish off. That's the way rugby goes."

The last quarter-final between Argentina and Scotland may have produced a less free-flowing spectacle but it was no less captivating in Saint Denis as the Pumas battled to make it to the last four for the first time and the Scots strived to emulate the achievement of their 1991 side.

The game was a war of attrition as both sides waited for the all-important mistake and it came when Gonzalo Longo charged down Dan Parks' clearance and pounced on the loose ball for the first try of the match after 32 minutes. Scotland hit back after the break with a score from substitute Chris Cusiter but the boot of Felipe Contepomi was the difference between the two sides and the Pumas won 19–13 to join England, France and South Africa in the semi-finals.

"We definitely did throw the kitchen sink at it," Scotland coach Frank Hadden said. "We knew Argentina, because of the energy they put into the breakdown, were going to tire at some stage and we nearly capitalised on that. Obviously, this isn't the position we wanted to be in at the end of the match but I'm very confident that our young side will learn from this."

The first of the semi-finals pitted England against France at the Stade de France in the 90th instalment of a cross Channel rivalry which had never been anything but acrimonious. It was a repeat of the 2003 semi-final between the two countries and Laporte's side were favourites to reach the final for the third time.

The English had failed to score a try four years earlier in their 24–7 win in Sydney but they crossed the whitewash inside the first 80 seconds in Paris. Andy Gomarsall's box kick bemused full-back Damien Traille and Josh Lewsey, a survivor from 2003, gleefully gobbled up the bouncing ball and powered his way through Traille's despairing tackle to give Brian Ashton's side a dream start. The Stade crowd were stunned and England led.

France however held their nerve and two penalties from Lionel Beauxis gave them a slender 6–5 half-time lead. It was 9–5 four minutes after the restart with another Beauxis penalty but the English were looking the stronger of the two and Wilkinson soon cut the advantage to a point with his first successful kick of the match.

You could now cut the atmosphere in the Stade de France with a knife and it remained 9–8 to Les Bleus until the final five minutes. The decisive moment came when Jason Robinson's mesmerising break was halted by a high tackle by replacement hooker Dimitri Szarzewski and Wilkinson obliged with three points from the resulting penalty. England had their noses in front for the first time since the first-half and when Wilkinson reminded the world of his drop goal prowess two minutes from time, the men in white were into a second successive final.

"At the start some didn't go over and I realised I had to give it my all," Wilkinson said after uncharacteristically missing three of six pots at goal. "It got better and they went over in the end. The fact that I get as many opportunities as I do is because the guys keep giving them to me. Every kick I miss they get me another one. With a bunch of guys like that you can't get disheartened."

Exactly 24 hours later, South Africa faced Argentina in the second semi-final. The Pumas had been the epitome of abrasive self-belief en route to the last four but against the Springboks in the Stade de France, their nerves finally showed in a error-strewn performance and the game was effectively over as a contest by half-time.

South Africa scored the first of their four tries when scrum-half Fourie du Preez intercepted Felipe Contepomi's pass and their second also came from a mistake. Schalk Burger stole possession from Longo and South Africa spread the ball to Habana, who chipped and chased for the second try. The third followed a fumble by fly-half Juan Martin Hernandez and ended with No 8 Danie Rossouw romping over and at half-time, the Springboks had established a commanding 24–6 lead.

Argentina briefly rallied soon after the break when Manuel Contepomi crashed over to cut the deficit but any hopes of a heroic fightback were extinguished when Habana intercepted a wayward Puma pass and accelerated away like a jet plane for his second try. South Africa were through to face England and Argentina's adventure was over.

"South Africa are a very dangerous team and when they had any spaces, when we made mistakes, they would take opportunities and score a try," a disappointed but proud Marcelo Loffreda said as he again made the case of for Argentina's inclusion in the Six Nation or Tri-Nations. "For us this has been something we have been preparing for some time. We don't have international competitions and for this reason we don't have the same facilities. Other teams are accustomed to playing more often. We were beaten by a great team. They were markedly better than us. We were victims of our own mistakes."

Argentina went on to win the much-maligned Bronze Medal match against the hosts 34–10 with another passionate and pulsating performance but eyes were already turning to the main event 24 hours later as the Springboks attempted to dethrone the English.

THE POOL MATCHES

POOL A

8 September, Stade Felix Bollaert, Lens

ENGLAND 28 (2G 3PG 1T)
UNITED STATES 10 (1G 1PG)

ENGLAND: M J Cueto; O J Lewsey, J D Noon, M J Catt, J T Robinson; O J Barkley, S Perry; A J Sheridan, M P Regan, P J Vickery (*captain*), S D Shaw, B J Kay, J P R Worsley, L B N Dallaglio, T Rees *Substitutions:* P C Richards for Perry (59 mins); G S Chuter for Regan (62 mins); M E Corry for Shaw (62 mins); M J H Stevens for Vickery (62 mins); A Farrell for Catt (62 mins); M Tait for Robinson (65 mins); L W Moody for Worsley (68 mins)

SCORERS *Tries*: Robinson, Barkley, Rees *Conversions:* Barkley (2) *Penalty Goals*: Barkley (3)

UNITED STATES: C Wyles; S Sika, P Emerick, V Esikia, T Ngwenya; M Hercus (*captain*), C Erskine; M MacDonald, O Lentz, C Osentowski, A Parker, M Mangan, L Stanfill, H Bloomfield, T Clever *Substitutions:* B Burdette for Lentz (51 mins); I Basauri for Bloomfield (54 mins); V Malifa for Sika (57 mins); M Moeakiola for MacDonald (59 mins); H Mexted for Mangan (68 mins)

SCORERS *Try*: Moeakiola *Conversion:* Hercus *Penalty Goal*: Hercus

REFEREE J I Kaplan (South Africa)

YELLOW CARDS: Esikia (29 mins), Dallaglio (73 mins), Emerick (80 mins)

9 September, Parc des Princes, Paris

SOUTH AFRICA 59 (5G 3PG 3T)
SAMOA 7 (1G)

SOUTH AFRICA: P C Montgomery; J-P R Pietersen, J Fourie, J de Villiers, B G Habana; A D James, P F du Preez; J P du Randt, J W Smit (*captain*), C J van der Linde, J P Botha, V Matfield, J H Smith, D J Rossouw, S W P Burger *Substitutions:* F P L Steyn for De Villiers (43 mins); B J Botha for Du Randt (51 mins); J L van Heerden for Rossouw (57 mins); A S Pretorius for James (57 mins); B W du Plessis for Smit (62 mins); E R Januarie for Du Preez (64 mins); G J Muller for J P Botha (64 mins); J P du Randt back for Van der Linde (66 mins)

SCORERS *Tries*: Habana (4), Montgomery (2), Fourie, Pietersen *Conversions:* Montgomery (5) *Penalty Goals*: Montgomery (3)

SAMOA: D Lemi; L Fa'atau, G Williams, J Meafou, Alesana Tuilagi; E Fuimaono-Sapolu, J Polu; J Va'a, M Schwalger, C Johnston, J Tekori, K Thompson, D Leo, H Tuilagi, S Sititi (*captain*) *Substitutions:* J Purdie for Tekori (55 mins); A Vaeluaga for H Tuilagi (56 mins); L Crichton for Fuimaono-Sapolu (56 mins); E Seveali'i for Meafou (60 mins); B P Lima for Fa'atau (60 mins); K Lealamanua for Va'a (62 mins); T Fuga for Lima (64 mins)

SCORER *Try*: Williams *Conversion:* Williams

REFEREE P G Honiss (New Zealand)

12 September, Stade de la Mosson, Montpellier

UNITED STATES 15 (1G 1PG 1T)
TONGA 25 (2G 2PG 1T)

UNITED STATES: C Wyles; S Sika, A Tuipulotu, V Esikia, T Ngwenya; M Hercus (*captain*), C Erskine; M MacDonald, O Lentz, C Osentowski, A Parker, M Mangan, L Stanfill, H Bloomfield, T Clever *Substitutions:* B Burdette for Lentz (49 mins); I Basauri for Bloomfield (53 mins); M Moeakiola for MacDonald (53 mins); P Eloff for Esikia (60 mins)

SCORERS *Tries*: MacDonald, Stanfill *Conversion:* Hercus *Penalty Goal*: Hercus

TONGA: V Lilo; T Tu'ifua, S Hufanga, E Taione, J Vaka; P Hola, S Havea; S Tonga'uiha, A Lutui, K Pulu, L Fa'aoso, P Hehea, H T-Pole, F Maka, N Latu (*captain*) *Substitutions:* S Tu'ipulotu for Havea (41 mins); A Havili for Vaka (60 mins); V Vaki for Latu (64 mins); L Filipine for Maka (64 mins); T Toke for Tonga'uiha (65 mins); I Tupou for Taione (70 mins); E Taukafa for Lutui (75 mins)

SCORERS *Tries*: Maka, Vaka, Vaki *Conversions:* Hola (2) *Penalty Goals*: Hola (2)

REFEREE S J Dickinson (Australia)

14 September, Stade de France, Paris

ENGLAND 0
SOUTH AFRICA 36 (3G 5PG)

ENGLAND: J T Robinson; O J Lewsey, J D Noon, A Farrell, P H Sackey; M J Catt, S Perry; A J Sheridan, M P Regan, M J H Stevens, S D Shaw, B J Kay, M E Corry (*captain*), N Easter, T Rees *Substitutions:* A C T Gomarsall for Perry (40 mins); L W Moody for Rees (52 mins); G S Chuter for Regan (55 mins); M Tait for Robinson (57 mins); S W Borthwick for Shaw (temp 54 to 58 mins and 77 mins); P T Freshwater for Sheridan (77 mins); P C Richards for Noon (79 mins)

SOUTH AFRICA: P C Montgomery; J-P R Pietersen, J Fourie, F P L Steyn, B G Habana; A D James, P F du Preez; J P du Randt, J W Smit (*captain*), B J Botha, J P Botha, V Matfield, J H Smith, D J Rossouw, J L van Heerden *Substitutions:* G J Muller for J P Botha (52 mins); C J van der Linde for Du Randt (60 mins); R Pienaar for Habana (temp 55 to 59 mins) and for Du Preez (66 mins); R B Skinstad for Smith (70 mins); B W du Plessis for Smit (70 mins); A S Pretorius for James (70 mins); W Olivier for Steyn (75 mins)

SCORERS *Tries*: Pietersen (2), Smith *Conversions:* Montgomery (3) *Penalty Goals*: Montgomery (4), Steyn

REFEREE J Jutge (France)

16 September, Stade de la Mosson, Montpellier

SAMOA 15 (5PG) TONGA 19 (1G 4PG)

SAMOA: G Williams; S Tagicakibau, E Seveali'i, S Mapusua, Alesana Tuilagi; L Crichton, S So'oialo; K Lealamanua, M Schwalger, C Johnston, J Tekori, K Thompson, D Leo, S Sititi (*captain*), U Ulia *Substitutions:* M Salanoa for Johnston (55 mins); D Lemi for Tagicakibau (55 mins); J Polu for So'oialo (55 mins); T Fuga for Schwalger (58 mins); L Lafaiali'i for Tekori (61 mins); J Purdie for Ulia (61 mins); L Lui for Williams (79 mins); C Johnston back for Salanoa (79 mins)

SCORER *Penalty Goals:* Williams (5)

TONGA: V Lilo; T Tu'ifua, S Hufanga, E Taione, J Vaka; P Hola, E Taufa; S Tonga'uiha, E Taukafa, K Pulu, I Afeaki, P Hehea, H T-Pole, F Maka, N Latu (*captain*) *Substitutions:* S Tu'ipulotu for Taufa (42 mins); A Lutui for Taukafa (50 mins); V Vaki for Afeaki (55 mins); I Tupou for Taione (72 mins); T Toke for S Tonga'uiha (72 mins); S Tonga'uiha back on for Maka (79 mins)

SCORERS *Try*: Taione *Conversion:* Hola *Penalty Goals*: Hola (4)

REFEREE J I Kaplan (South Africa)

YELLOW CARDS: Taione (28 mins); Toke (74 mins)

SENT OFF: T-Pole (71 mins)

22 September, Stade Félix Bollaert, Lens

SOUTH AFRICA 30 (2G 2PG 2T) TONGA 25 (2G 2PG 1T)

SOUTH AFRICA: R Pienaar; A K Willemse, W Olivier, W Julies, J-P R Pietersen; A S Pretorius, E R Januarie; G G Steenkamp, G van G Botha, C J van der Linde, J P Botha, P A van den Berg, D J Rossouw, R B Skinstad (*captain*), J L van Heerden *Substitutions:* J W Smit for G van G Botha (46 mins); B J Botha for Steenkamp (46 mins); V Matfield for Van den Berg (46 mins); B G Habana for Willemse (46 mins); F P L Steyn for Julies (46 mins); J H Smith for Rossouw (temp 24 to 30 mins and 49 mins); P C Montgomery for Pretorius (59 mins)

SCORERS *Tries*: Pienaar (2), Smith, Skinstad *Conversions:* Pretorius, Montgomery *Penalty Goals*: Montgomery, Steyn

TONGA: V Lilo; T Tu'ifua, S Hufanga, E Taione, J Vaka; P Hola, S Tu'ipulotu; S Tonga'uiha, A Lutui, K Pulu, P Hehea, E Kauhenga, V Vaki, F Maka, N Latu (*captain*) *Substitutions:* L Filipine for Latu (66 mins); E Taukafa for Lutui (66 mins); S Havea for Tu'ipulotu (66 mins); I Afeaki for Kauhenga (temp 50 to 66 mins) and for Hehea (66 mins); A Havili for Vaka (73 mins); I Tupou for Taione (75 mins)

SCORERS *Tries*: Pulu, Hufanga, Vaki *Conversions:* Hola (2) *Penalty Goals*: Hola (2)

REFEREE W Barnes (England)

YELLOW CARDS: Vaka (62 mins); Steyn (62 mins); Habana (68 mins)

22 September, Stade de la Beaujoire, Nantes

ENGLAND 44 (3G 4PG 2DG 1T) SAMOA 22 (1G 5PG)

ENGLAND: O J Lewsey; P H Sackey, M Tait, O J Barkley, M J Cueto; J P Wilkinson, A C T Gomarsall; A J Sheridan, G S Chuter, M J H Stevens, S D Shaw, B J Kay, M E Corry (*captain*), N Easter, J P R Worsley *Substitutions:* P T Freshwater for Sheridan (64 mins); S W Borthwick for S Shaw (64 mins); L W Moody for Worsley (69 mins); D Hipkiss for Tait (72 mins)

SCORERS *Tries*: Corry (2), Sackey (2) *Conversions:* Wilkinson (3) *Penalty Goals*: Wilkinson (4) *Dropped Goals:* Wilkinson (2)

SAMOA: L Crichton; D Lemi, S Mapusua, B P Lima, Alesana Tuilagi; E Fuimaono-Sapolu, J Polu; K Lealamanua, M Schwalger, C Johnston, J Tekori, K Thompson, D Leo, H Tuilagi, S Sititi (*captain*) *Substitutions:* F Palaamo for Lealamanua (61 mins); S So'oialo for Polu (65 mins); A Vaeluaga for H Tuilagi (69 mins); J Meafou for Mapusua (69 mins); L Lui for Lima (72 mins); J Purdie for Tekori (74 mins); K Lealamanua back on for Johnston (74 mins)

SCORERS *Try*: Polu *Conversion:* Crichton *Penalty Goals:* Crichton (5)

REFEREE A Lewis (Ireland)

26 September, Stade Geoffroy-Guichard, Saint Etienne

SAMOA 25 (2G 2PG 1T) UNITED STATES 21 (1G 3PG 1T)

SAMOA: L Crichton; L Fa'atau, E Seveali'i, S Mapusua, Alesana Tuilagi; E Fuimaono-Sapolu, J Polu; K Lealamanua, M Schwalger, C Johnston, L Lafaiali'i, K Thompson, S Sititi (*captain*), A Vaeluaga, J Purdie *Substitutions:* D Lemi for Fa'atau (59 mins); J Tekori for Thompson (63 mins); N Leleimalefaga for Lealamanua (69 mins); S So'oialo for Polu (69 mins); L Lui for Fuimaono-Sapolu (69 mins); S V Sefo for Schwalger (72 mins); Schwalger back for Purdie (77 mins); U Ulia for Vaeluaga (temp 66 to 69 mins); L Fa'atau back for Mapusua (temp 79 mins to end)

SCORERS *Tries*: Fa'atau, Alesana Tuilagi, Thompson *Conversions:* Crichton (2) *Penalty Goals:* Crichton (2)

UNITED STATES: C Wyles; T Ngwenya, P Eloff, V Esikia, S Sika; M Hercus (*captain*), C Erskine; M MacDonald, O Lentz, C Osentowski, A Parker, H Mexted, L Stanfill, F Mounga, T Clever *Substitutions:* B Burdette for Clever (44 mins); M Aylor for Mounga (63 mins); M Moeakiola for MacDonald (67 mins); A Tuipulotu for Esikia (71 mins)

SCORERS *Tries*: Ngwenya, Stanfill *Conversion:* Hercus *Penalty Goals*: Hercus (3)

REFEREE W Barnes (England)

YELLOW CARDS: Mounga (51 mins); Sefo (75 mins)

28 September, Parc des Princes, Paris

ENGLAND 36 (2G 2PG 2DG 2T)
TONGA 20 (2G 2PG)

ENGLAND: O J Lewsey; P H Sackey, M Tait, O J Barkley, M J Cueto; J P Wilkinson, A C T Gomarsall; A J Sheridan, G S Chuter, M J H Stevens, S W Borthwick, B J Kay, M E Corry (*captain*), N Easter, L W Moody *Substitutions:* A Farrell for Barkley (51 mins); P J Vickery for Stevens (56 mins); L B N Dallaglio for Corry (64 mins); D Hipkiss for Sackey (67 mins); L A Mears for Chuter (67 mins); P C Richards for Cueto (72 mins)

SCORERS *Tries*: Sackey (2), Tait, Farrell *Conversions:* Wilkinson (2) *Penalty Goals*: Wilkinson (2) *Dropped Goals:* Wilkinson (2)

TONGA: V Lilo; T Tu'ifua, S Hufanga, E Taione, J Vaka; P Hola, S Tu'ipulotu; S Tonga'uiha, A Lutui, K Pulu, V Vaki, L Fa'aoso, H T-Pole, F Maka, N Latu (*captain*) *Substitutions:* T Filise for S Tonga'uiha (45 mins); H Tonga'uiha for Hufanga (59 mins); M Molitika for Vaki (60 mins); E Taukafa for Lutui (64 mins); A Havili for Vaka (67 mins); S Havea for Tu'ipulotu (67 mins); I Afeaki for Fa'aoso (67 mins); S Tonga'uiha back for Filise (temp 49 to 54 mins)

SCORERS *Tries*: Hufanga, T-Pole *Conversions:* Hola (2) *Penalty Goals*: Hola (2)

REFEREE A C Rolland (Ireland)

30 September, Stade de la Mosson, Montpellier

SOUTH AFRICA 64 (8G 1PG 1T)
UNITED STATES 15 (1G 1PG 1T)

SOUTH AFRICA: P C Montgomery; A Z Ndungane, J Fourie, F P L Steyn, B G Habana; A D James, P F du Preez; J P du Randt, J W Smit (*captain*), B J Botha, P A van den Berg, V Matfield, J H Smith, S W P Burger, J L van Heerden *Substitutions:* C J van der Linder for B J Botha (24 mins); J-P R Pietersen for Habana (52 mins); J P Botha for Van den Berg (54 mins); R Pienaar for Montgomery (66 mins); A S Pretorius for Steyn (66 mins); R B Skinstad for Van Heerden (71 mins); B W du Plessis for Du Randt (71 mins); Van den Berg back for Matfield (temp 77 mins to end)

SCORERS *Tries*: Habana (2), Fourie (2), Burger, Steyn, Van der Linde, Du Preez, Smith *Conversions:* Montgomery (6), James (2) *Penalty Goal*: Montgomery

UNITED STATES: C Wyles; T Ngwenya, P Eloff, V Esikia, S Sika; M Hercus (*captain*), C Erskine; M MacDonald, O Lentz, C Osentowski, A Parker, M Mangan, L Stanfill, D Payne, T Clever *Substitutions:* M Moeakiola for MacDonald (49 mins); B Burdette for Lentz (74 mins); M Aylor for Clever (temp 42 to 54 mins) and for Stanfill (74 mins); H Bloomfield for Payne (74 mins); M Petri for Erskine (74 mins); V Malifa for Wyles (74 mins); T Palamo for Sika (74 mins)

SCORERS *Tries*: Ngwenya, Wyles *Conversion:* Hercus *Penalty Goal*: Hercus

REFEREE A J Spreadbury (England)

YELLOW CARD: Clever (23 mins)

POOL A

	P	W	D	L	PD	TD	PF	TF	BP	Pts
South Africa	4	4	0	0	142	18	189	24	3	19
England	4	3	0	1	20	4	108	11	2	14
Tonga	4	2	0	2	-7	-1	89	9	1	9
Samoa	4	1	0	3	-74	-10	69	5	1	5
USA	4	0	0	4	-81	-11	61	7	1	1

P=Played; **W**=Won; **D**=Draw; **L**=Lost; **PD**=Points Difference; **TD**=Tries Difference; **PF**=Points For; **TF**=Tries For; **BP**=Bonus Points; **PTS**=Points

POOL B

8 September, Stade Gerland, Lyons

AUSTRALIA 91 (10G 2PG 3T) JAPAN 3 (1PG)

AUSTRALIA: C E Latham; L D Tuqiri, S A Mortlock (*captain*), M J Giteau, A P Ashley-Cooper; S J Larkham, G M Gregan; M J Dunning, S T Moore, A K E Baxter, N C Sharpe, D J Vickerman, R D Elsom, W L Palu, G B Smith *Substitutions:* G T Shepherdson for Baxter (50 mins); H J McMeniman for Sharpe (50 mins); B Barnes for Larkham (54 mins); D A Mitchell for Ashley-Cooper (55 mins); A K E Baxter back for Dunning (67 mins); S A Hoiles for Palu (67 mins); M A Gerrard for Mortlock (67 mins); A L Freier for Moore (67 mins)

SCORERS *Tries*: Elsom (3), Latham (2), Barnes (2), Mitchell (2), Sharpe, Ashley-Cooper, Smith, Freier *Conversions:* Mortlock (7), Giteau (3) *Penalty Goals:* Mortlock (2)

JAPAN: T Kusumi; T Kitagawa, K Taira, N Oto, H Onozawa; K Ono, Y Yatomi; Masahito Yamamoto, T Inokuchi, R Yamamura, T Kumagae, L S Vatuvei, Y Watanabe, H Kiso, T Sasaki (*captain*) *Substitutions:* H Makiri for Watanabe (temp 8 to 11 mins) and for Sasaki (47 mins)

SCORER *Penalty Goal:* Ono

REFEREE A Lewis (Ireland)

9 September, Stade de la Beaujoire, Nantes

WALES 42 (4G 3PG 1T) CANADA 17 (1G 2T)

WALES: K A Morgan; S M Williams, T G L Shanklin, S T Parker, M A Jones; J Hook, D J Peel (*captain*); G D Jenkins, M Rees, A R Jones, I M Gough, A-W Jones, J Thomas, A J Popham, M E Williams *Substitutions:* S M Jones for Hook (48 mins); G Thomas for Morgan (48 mins); C L Charvis for M E Williams (temp 37 to 40 mins and 59 mins); M J Owen for Gough (63 mins); M Phillips for Peel (65 mins); T R Thomas for Rees (65 mins); D J Jones for A R Jones (68 mins)

SCORERS *Tries*: S M Williams (2), Parker, A-W Jones, Charvis *Conversions:* S M Jones (4) *Penalty Goals:* Hook (3)

CANADA: M Pyke; J Pritchard, C Culpan, D Spicer, D T H van der Merwe; A Monro, M Williams (*captain*); R G A Snow, P Riordan, J Thiel, L Tait, M James, J Cudmore, S-M Stephen, D Biddle *Substitutions:* M Pletch for Thiel (32 mins); D Pletch for Snow (56 mins); A Carpenter for Cudmore (60 mins); R Smith for Monro (63 mins); C Yukes for Biddle (63 mins); M Burak for Tait (68 mins); E Fairhurst for Williams (75 mins)

SCORERS *Tries:* Cudmore, Culpan, Williams *Conversions:* Pritchard

REFEREE A C Rolland (Ireland)

12 September, Stade Municipal, Toulouse

JAPAN 31 (2G 4PG 1T) FIJI 35 (3G 3PG 1T)

JAPAN: G Aruga; C Loamanu, Y Imamura, S Onishi, K Endo; B Robins, T Yoshida; T Nishiura, Y Matsubara, T Soma, H Ono, L Thompson, H Makiri, T Miuchi (*captain*), P O'Reilly *Substitutions:* Y Yatomi for Yoshida (57 mins); H Onozawa for Aruga (59 mins); K Taira for Yatomi (65 mins); R Yamamura for Soma (67 mins)

SCORERS *Tries:* Thompson (2), Soma *Conversions:* Onishi (2) *Penalty Goals:* Onishi (4)

FIJI: K Ratuvou; V Delasau, S Rabeni, S Bai, I Neivua; N Little, M Rauluni (*captain*); G Dewes, S Koto, H Qiodravu, K Leawere, W Lewaravu, S Naevo, S Koyamaibole, A Qera *Substitutions:* A Ratuva for Qera (57 mins); J Railomo for Qiodravu (67 mins); N Talei for Koyamaibole (67 mins); N Ligairi for Ratuvou (temp 3 to 9 mins) and for Delasau (69 mins)

SCORERS *Tries:* Qera (2), Rabeni, Leawere *Conversions:* Little (3) *Penalty Goals:* Little (3)

REFEREE M Jonker (South Africa)

YELLOW CARD: Delasau (39 mins)

15 September, Millennium Stadium, Cardiff

WALES 20 (2G 2PG) AUSTRALIA 32 (3G 1PG 1DG 1T)

WALES: G Thomas (*captain*); S M Williams, T G L Shanklin, S T Parker, M A Jones; S M Jones, D J Peel; G D Jenkins, M Rees, A R Jones, I M Gough, A-W Jones, C L Charvis, J Thomas, M E Williams *Substitutions:* K A Morgan for Parker (18 mins); J Hook for G Thomas (21 mins); D J Jones for A R Jones (65 mins); T R Thomas for Rees (65 mins); M J Owen for Gough (65 mins); M Phillips for Peel (70 mins); A J Popham for Charvis (temp 12 to 16 mins and 48 to 60 mins)

SCORERS *Tries*: J Thomas, S M Williams *Conversions:* Hook (2) *Penalty Goals:* S M Jones, Hook

AUSTRALIA: C E Latham; L D Tuqiri, S A Mortlock (*captain*), M J Giteau, D A Mitchell; B Barnes, G M Gregan; M J Dunning, S T Moore, G T Shepherdson, N C Sharpe, D J Vickerman, R D Elsom, W L Palu, G B Smith *Substitutions:* S N G Staniforth for Mortlock (40 mins); P R Waugh for Smith (62 mins); S A Hoiles for Palu (65 mins); A L Freier for Moore (67 mins); A K E Baxter for Shepherdson (72 mins); M D Chisholm for Elsom (75 mins); J L Huxley for Barnes (77 mins)

SCORERS *Tries*: Latham (2), Giteau, Mortlock *Conversions:* Mortlock (2), Giteau *Penalty Goal:* Mortlock *Dropped Goal:* Barnes

REFEREE S R Walsh (New Zealand)

YELLOW CARDS: Mitchell (65 mins); Sharpe (74 mins)

16 September, Millennium Stadium, Cardiff

FIJI 29 (3G 1PG 1T) CANADA 16 (1G 3PG)

FIJI: K Ratuvou; V Delasau, S Rabeni, S Bai, I Neivua; N Little, M Rauluni (*captain*); G Dewes, S Koto, J Railomo, K Leawere, I Rawaqa, S Naevo, S Koyamaibole, A Qera *Substitutions:* N Talei for Naevo (61 mins); H Qiodravu for Railomo (62 mins); M Kunavore for Rabeni (63 mins); V Sauturaga for Koto (69 mins); N Ligairi for Neivua (75 mins)

SCORERS *Tries:* Ratuvou (2), Leawere, Delasau *Conversions:* Little (3) *Penalty Goal:* Little

CANADA: M Pyke; J Pritchard, C Culpan, D Spicer, D T H van der Merwe; R Smith, M Williams (*captain*); R G A Snow, P Riordan, J Thiel, M Burak, M James, J Cudmore, S-M Stephen, D Biddle *Substitutions:* C Yukes for Stephen (60 mins); D Pletch for Snow (61 mins); L Tait for Burak (65 mins); A Carpenter for Biddle (67 mins)

SCORERS *Try:* Smith *Conversion:* Pritchard *Penalty Goals:* Pritchard (3)

REFEREE A J Spreadbury (England)

20 September, Millennium Stadium, Cardiff

WALES 72 (7G 1PG 4T) JAPAN 18 (1G 2PG 1T)

WALES: K A Morgan; S M Williams, J P Robinson, J Hook, D R James; S M Jones (*captain*), M Phillips; D J Jones, T R Thomas, C L Horsman, W James, A-W Jones, C L Charvis, A J Popham, M E Williams *Substitutions:* I Evans for A-W Jones (51 mins); C Sweeney for S M Jones (53 mins); G J Cooper for Phillips (53 mins); M J Owen for Popham (57 mins); H Bennett for Thomas (60 mins); G D Jenkins for Horsman (64 mins); T G L Shanklin for Robinson (72 mins)

SCORERS *Tries*: S M Williams (2), M E Williams (2), A-W Jones, Hook, Thomas, Morgan, Phillips, D R James, Cooper *Conversions:* S M Jones (5), Sweeney (2) *Penalty Goal:* S M Jones

JAPAN: C Loamanu; K Endo, Y Imamura, S Onishi, H Onozawa; B Robins, T Yoshida; T Nishiura, Y Matsubara, T Soma, H Ono, L Thompson, Y Watanabe, T Miuchi (*captain*), H Makiri *Substitutions:* K Taira for Imamura (50 mins); R Asano for Makiri (51 mins); T Kusumi for Onishi (51 mins); C-W Kim for Yoshida (65 mins); H Kiso for Thompson (65 mins); R Yamamura for Nishiura (65 mins); Nishiura back on for Soma (70 mins); T Inokuchi for Matsubara (74 mins)

SCORERS *Tries:* Endo, Onozawa *Conversion:* Robins *Penalty Goals:* Onishi (2)

REFEREE J Jutge (France)

23 September, Stade de la Mosson, Montpellier

AUSTRALIA 55 (4G 3PG 1DG 3T) FIJI 12 (1G 1T)

AUSTRALIA: C E Latham; L D Tuqiri, A P Ashley-Cooper, M J Giteau, D A Mitchell; B Barnes, G M Gregan (*captain*); M J Dunning, S T Moore, G T Shepherdson, M D Chisholm, D J Vickerman, R D Elsom, W L Palu, P R Waugh *Substitutions:* H J McMeniman for Elsom (57 mins); G S Holmes for Dunning (57 mins); A L Freier for Moore (57 mins); S J Cordingley for Gregan (57 mins); S N G Staniforth for Barnes (62 mins); S A Hoiles for Palu (65 mins); J L Huxley for Staniforth (67 mins)

SCORERS *Tries*: Mitchell (3), Giteau (2), Ashley-Cooper, Hoiles *Conversions:* Giteau (4) *Penalty Goals:* Giteau (3) *Dropped Goal:* Barnes

FIJI: N Ligairi; V Delasau, M Kunavore, S Bai (*captain*), I Neivua; W Luveniyali, J Daunivucu; A Yalayalatabua, V Sauturaga, H Qiodravu, I Domolailai, I Rawaqa, N Talei, J Qovu, A Ratuva *Substitutions:* M Rauluni for Daunivucu (40 mins); W Lewaravu for Domolailai (40 mins); S Rabeni for Luveniyali (40 mins); J Railomo for Yalayalatabua (59 mins); S Koyamaibole for Talei (62 mins); G Lovobalavu for Kunavore (64 mins)

SCORERS *Tries:* Neivua, Ratuva *Conversion:* Bai

REFEREE N Owens (Wales)

25 September, Stade Chaban-Delmas, Bordeaux

CANADA 12 (1G 1T) JAPAN 12 (1G 1T)

CANADA: M Pyke; J Pritchard, C Culpan, D Spicer, D T H van der Merwe; R Smith, M Williams (*captain*); R G A Snow, P Riordan, J Thiel, M Burak, M James, C Yukes, A Carpenter, A Kleeberger *Substitutions:* D Pletch for Snow (45 mins); M Webb for Carpenter (55 mins); S Franklin for Thiel (57 mins); M Pletch for Riordan (59 mins); J Mensah-Coker for Culpan (71 mins); J Jackson for Kleeberger (78 mins)

SCORERS *Tries:* Riordan, Van der Merwe *Conversion:* Pritchard

JAPAN: G Aruga; K Endo, Y Imamura, S Onishi, C Loamanu; B Robins, T Yoshida; T Nishiura, Y Matsubara, T Soma, H Ono, L Thompson, H Makiri, T Miuchi (*captain*), P O'Reilly *Substitutions:* C-W Kim for Yoshida (49 mins); R Yamamura for Soma (51 mins); L S Vatuvei for Ono (55 mins); K Taira for Imamura (68 mins); H Onozawa for Endo (71 mins); H Kiso for Miuchi (71 mins); T Soma back for Nishiura (74 mins)

SCORERS *Tries:* Endo, Taira *Conversion:* Onishi

REFEREE J I Kaplan (South Africa)

YELLOW CARD: Riordan (34 mins)

29 September, Stade Chaban-Delmas, Bordeaux

AUSTRALIA 37 (2G 1PG 4T) CANADA 6 (2PG)

AUSTRALIA: C E Latham; C B Shepherd, L D Tuqiri, A P Ashley-Cooper, D A Mitchell; J L Huxley, S J Cordingley; G S Holmes, A L Freier, A K E Baxter, N C Sharpe, M D Chisholm, H J McMeniman, D J Lyons, G B Smith (*captain*) *Substitutions:* S A Hoiles for Lyons (45 mins); S P Hardman for Freier (59 mins); P R Waugh for Sharpe (71 mins); G M Gregan for Cordingley (73 mins)

SCORERS *Tries*: Mitchell (2), Baxter, Freier, Smith, Latham *Conversions:* Shepherd (2) *Penalty Goal:* Huxley

CANADA: D T H van der Merwe; J Pritchard, M Pyke, D Daypuck, J Mensah-Coker; A Monro, M Williams (*captain*); R G A Snow, P Riordan, J Thiel, L Tait, M James, C Yukes, S-M Stephen, D Biddle *Substitutions:* A Carpenter for Riordan (45 mins); D Pletch for Snow (53 mins); M Webb for Stephen (53 mins); M Pletch for Yukes (63 mins); M Burak for James (63 mins); N Trenkel for Daypuck (66 mins); Snow back for D Pletch (72 mins); E Fairhurst for Van der Merwe (74 mins)

SCORER *Penalty Goals:* Pritchard (2)

REFEREE C White (England)

29 September, Stade de la Beaujoire, Nantes

WALES 34 (3G 1PG 2T) FIJI 38 (3G 4PG 1T)

WALES: G Thomas (*captain*); S M Williams, T G L Shanklin, J Hook, M A Jones; S M Jones, D J Peel; G D Jenkins, M Rees, C L Horsman, A-W Jones, I Evans, C L Charvis, A J Popham, M E Williams *Substitutions:* T R Thomas for Rees (46 mins); M Phillips for Peel (57 mins); D J Jones for Horsman (65 mins); I M Gough for Evans (65 mins); M J Owen for Popham (65 mins)

SCORERS *Tries*: Popham, S M Williams, G Thomas, M A Jones, M E Williams *Conversions:* S M Jones (2), Hook *Penalty Goal:* S M Jones

FIJI: K Ratuvou; V Delasau, S Rabeni, S Bai, I Neivua; N Little, M Rauluni (*captain*); G Dewes, S Koto, J Railomo, K Leawere, I Rawaqa, S Naevo, S Koyamaibole, A Qera *Substitutions:* S Bobo for Neivua (51 mins); H Qiodravu for Railomo (54 mins); N Ligairi for Rabeni (66 mins); A Ratuva for Qera (74 mins); V Sauturaga for Koto (77 mins); J Daunivucu for Little (80 mins)

SCORERS *Tries:* Qera, Delasau, Leawere, Dewes *Conversions:* Little (3) *Penalty Goals:* Little (4)

REFEREE S J Dickinson (Australia)

YELLOW CARD: Qera (39 mins)

POOL B

	P	W	D	L	PD	TD	PF	TF	BP	Pts
Australia	4	4	0	0	174	26	215	30	4	20
Fiji	4	3	0	1	-22	-2	114	14	3	15
Wales	4	2	0	2	63	10	168	23	4	12
Japan	4	0	1	3	-146	-23	64	7	1	3
Canada	4	0	1	3	-69	-11	51	6	0	2

P=Played; **W**=Won; **D**=Draw; **L**=Lost; **PD**=Points Difference; **TD**=Tries Difference; **PF**=Points For; **TF**=Tries For; **BP**=Bonus Points; **PTS**=Points

POOL C

8 September, Stade Vélodrome, Marseilles

NEW ZEALAND 76 (9G 1PG 2T) ITALY 14 (2G)

NEW ZEALAND: L R MacDonald; D C Howlett, J M Muliaina, C L McAlister, S W Sivivatu; D W Carter, B T Kelleher; T D Woodcock, K F Mealamu, C J Hayman, C R Jack, A J Williams, J Collins, R So'oialo, R H McCaw (*captain*) *Substitutions:* A D Oliver for Mealamu (51 mins); B G Leonard for Kelleher (51 mins); I Toeava for Muliaina (51 mins); N S Tialata for Collins (temp 45 to 51 mins) and for Woodcock (54 mins); S T Lauaki for Williams (54 mins); M C Masoe for McCaw (60 mins); A J D Mauger for Carter (60 mins)

SCORERS *Tries*: Howlett (3), McCaw (2), Sivivatu (2), Collins (2), Muliaina, Jack *Conversions*: Carter (7), McAlister (2) *Penalty Goal:* Carter

ITALY: D Bortolussi; K Robertson, A Masi, Mirco Bergamasco, M Stanojevic; R de Marigny, A Troncon; S Perugini, F Ongaro, M-L Castrogiovanni, S Dellapè, M Bortolami (*captain*), A Zanni, S Parisse, Mauro Bergamasco *Substitutions:* A Lo Cicero for Perugini (40 mins); M Vosawai for Zanni (41 mins); C Festuccia for Ongaro (52 mins); S Perugini back on for Castrogiovanni (53 mins); V Bernabò for Dellapè (57 mins); E Galon for Bortolussin (66 mins); P Griffen for Troncon (66 mins)

SCORERS *Tries:* Stanojevic, Mirco Bergamasco *Conversions:* Bortolussi, De Marigny

REFEREE W Barnes (England)

YELLOW CARDS: Hayman (41 mins); Perugini (60 mins)

9 September, Stade Geoffroy-Guichard, Saint Etienne

SCOTLAND 56 (8G) PORTUGAL 10 (1G 1PG)

SCOTLAND: R P Lamont; S F Lamont, M P di Rollo, R E Dewey, S L Webster; D A Parks, M R L Blair; A F Jacobsen, S Lawson, E A Murray, N J Hines, S Murray, J P R White (*captain*), S M Taylor, A Hogg *Substitutions:* G Kerr for Jacobsen (35 mins); H F G Southwell for Di Rollo (51 mins); C D Paterson for Parks (57 mins); K D R Brown for White (61 mins); S J MacLeod for S Murray (61 mins); R G M Lawson for Blair (65 mins); R W Ford for S Lawson (68 mins)

SCORERS *Tries*: R P Lamont (2), S Lawson, Dewey, Parks, Southwell, Brown, Ford *Conversions*: Parks (5), Paterson (3)

PORTUGAL: P Leal; David Mateus, F Sousa, Diogo Mateus, P Carvalho; D C Pinto, J Pinto; R Cordeiro, J Ferreira, R Spachuk, G Uva, D Penalva, J Severino Somoza, V Uva (*captain*), J Uva *Substitutions:* M Portela for Sousa (37 mins); J Correia for Ferreira (51 mins); P Murinello for Penalva (51 mins); J-M Muré for Cordeiro (59 mins); P Cabral for D C Pinto (61 mins); D Coutinho for J Uva (63 mins); L Pissarra for J Pinto (65 mins)

SCORERS *Try:* Carvalho *Conversion:* D C Pinto *Penalty Goal:* D C Pinto

REFEREE S R Walsh (New Zealand)

YELLOW CARD: J Uva (39 mins)

12 September, Stade Vélodrome, Marseilles

ITALY 24 (1G 4PG 1T) ROMANIA 18 (1G 2PG 1T)

ITALY: D Bortolussi; K Robertson, G-J Canale, Mirco Bergamasco, A Masi; R Pez, P Griffen; A Lo Cicero, C Festuccia, M-L Castrogiovanni, S Dellapè, M Bortolami (*captain*), J Sole, S Parisse, Mauro Bergamasco *Substitutions:* V Bernabò for Dellapè (7 mins); M Vosawai for Sole (48 mins); E Galon for Masi (temp 41 to 44 mins) and for Bortolussi (48 mins); A Troncon for Griffen (48 mins)

SCORERS *Tries:* Dellapè, penalty try *Conversion:* Pez *Penalty Goals:* Pez (3), Bortolussi

ROMANIA: I Dumitras; C Fercu, C Gal, R Gontineac, G Brezoianu; I Dimofte, L Sirbu; P Toderasc, M Tincu, B Balan, S Socol (*captain*), C Petre, F Corodeanu, O Tonita, A Manta *Substitutions:* C Popescu for Toderasc (63 mins); R Mavrodin for Tincu (temp 39 to 40 mins, 53 to 56 mins and 69 mins); C Ratiu for Tonita (71 mins); D Vlad for Dumitras (78 mins); V Calafeteanu for Sirbu (78 mins); A Tudori for Manta (80 mins)

SCORERS *Tries:* Manta, Tincu *Conversion:* Dimofte *Penalty Goals:* Dimofte (2)

REFEREE A J Spreadbury (England)

YELLOW CARD: Manta (52 mins)

15 September, Stade Gerland, Lyons

NEW ZEALAND 108 (14G 2T) PORTUGAL 13 (1G 1PG 1DG)

NEW ZEALAND: J M Muliaina; I Toeava, C G Smith, A J D Mauger, J T Rokocoko; N J Evans, B G Leonard; N S Tialata, A K Hore, G M Somerville, C R Jack, A J Williams, J Collins (*captain*), S T Lauaki, M C Masoe *Substitutions:* L R MacDonald for Muliaina (6 mins); C J Hayman for Jack (50 mins); A M Ellis for Leonard (53 mins); R So'oialo for Williams (53 mins); A D Oliver for Hore (56 mins); T D Woodcock for Somerville (60 mins); K F Mealamu for Collins (63 mins)

SCORERS *Tries*: Rokocoko (2), Mauger (2), Smith (2), Toeava, Williams, Collins, Masoe, Hore, Leonard, Evans, Ellis, MacDonald, Hayman *Conversions*: Evans (14)

PORTUGAL: P Leal; A Aguilar, M Portela, Diogo Mateus, P Carvalho; G Malheiro, L Pissarra; A Silva, J Correia, R Spachuk, M d'Orey, G Uva, D Coutinho, V Uva (*captain*), P Murinello *Substitutions:* D Penalva for D'Orey (26 mins); D C Pinto for Malheira (40 mins), J Pinto for Pissarra (40 mins); R Cordeiro for Silva (40 mins); T Gir?o for Coutinho (43 mins); J Uva for Murinello (50 mins); J Ferreira for V Uva ((53 mins)

SCORERS *Try:* Cordeiro *Conversion:* D C Pinto *Penalty Goal:* D C Pinto *Dropped Goal:* Malheiro

REFEREE C White (England)

18 September, Murrayfield

SCOTLAND 42 (6G) ROMANIA 0

SCOTLAND: R P Lamont; S F Lamont, S L Webster, R E Dewey, C D Paterson; D A Parks, M R L Blair; G Kerr, R W Ford, E A Murray, N J Hines, J L Hamilton, J P R White (*captain*), S M Taylor, A Hogg *Substitutions:* C J Smith for Kerr (50 mins); S J MacLeod for Hines (50 mins); C P Cusiter for Blair (58 mins); H F G Southwell for Dewey (58 mins); S Lawson for Ford (58 mins); K D R Brown for Hogg (64 mins); N Walker for Parks (67 mins); G Kerr back on for Murray (67 mins)

SCORERS *Tries*: Hogg (3), R P Lamont (2), Paterson *Conversions*: Paterson (6)

ROMANIA: I Dumitras; C Fercu, C Gal, R Gontineac, G Brezoianu; I Dimofte, L Sirbu; P Toderasc, M Tincu, B Balan, S Socol (*captain*), C Petre, F Corodeanu, O Tonita, A Manta *Substitutions:* R Mavrodin for Tincu (40 mins); I Tofan for Dimofte (44 mins); V Calafeteanu for Sirbu (44 mins); A Tudori for Manta (53 mins); C Ratiu for Corodeanu (60 mins); S Florea for Balan (68 mins); F Vlaicu for Gontineac (72 mins)

REFEREE N Owens (Wales)

19 September, Parc des Princes, Paris

ITALY 31 (2G 4PG 1T) PORTUGAL 5 (1T)

ITALY: D Bortolussi; P Canavosio, G-J Canale, A Masi, M Pratichetti; R de Marigny, A Troncon; A Lo Cicero, L Ghiraldini, M-L Castrogiovanni, C del Fava, M Bortolami (*captain*), S Parisse, M Vosawai, Mauro Bergamasco *Substitutions:* S Orlando for Vosawai (58 mins); S Perugini for Castrogiovanni (63 mins); M Aguero for Lo Cicero (63 mins); P Griffen for Troncon (79 mins)

SCORERS *Tries:* Masi (2), Mauro Bergamasco *Conversions:* Bortolussi (2) *Penalty Goals:* Bortolussi (4)

PORTUGAL: P Çabral; A Aguilar, F Sousa, Diogo Mateus, David Mateus; D C Pinto, J Pinto; R Cordeiro, J Correia, R Spachuk, G Uva, D Penalva, T Girão, V Uva (*captain*), J Uva *Substitutions:* D Gama for Diogo Mateus (30 mins); A Silva for Spachuk (60 mins); G Foro for David Mateus (60 mins); J-M Muré for Cordeiro (60 mins); P Murinello for J Uva (63 mins); L Pissarra for J Pinto (66 mins); D Figueirdo for Correia (69 mins)

SCORER *Try:* Penalva

REFEREE M Jonker (South Africa)

YELLOW CARD: Bortolami (7 mins)

23 September, Murrayfield

SCOTLAND 0 NEW ZEALAND 40 (2G 2PG 4T)

SCOTLAND: H F G Southwell; N Walker, M P di Rollo, A R Henderson, S L Webster; C D Paterson, C P Cusiter; A Dickinson, S Lawson, C J Smith, S J MacLeod, S Murray (*captain*), K D R Brown, D A Callam, J A Barclay *Substitutions:* D A Parks for Paterson (20 mins); G Kerr for Smith (50 mins); F M A Thomson for S Lawson (57 mins); R G M Lawson for Cusiter (58 mins); C J Smith back on for Dickinson (65 mins); R E Dewey for Henderson (68 mins); J L Hamilton for MacLeod (68 mins)

NEW ZEALAND: L R MacDonald; D C Howlett, C G Smith, C L McAlister, S W Sivivatu; D W Carter, B T Kelleher; T D Woodcock, A D Oliver, C J Hayman, R D Thorne, A J Williams, M C Masoe, R So'oialo, R H McCaw (*captain*) *Substitutions:* N J Evans for MacDonald (20 mins); A K Hore for Oliver (58 mins); B G Leonard for Kelleher (58 mins); S T Lauaki for McCaw (60 mins); N S Tialata for Hayman (65 mins); C R Jack for Williams (65 mins); I Toeava for C G Smith (65 mins)

SCORERS *Tries*: Howlett (2), McCaw, Kelleher, Williams, Carter *Conversions*: Carter (2) *Penalty Goals:* Carter (2)

REFEREE M Jonker (South Africa)

25 September, Stade Municipal, Toulouse

ROMANIA 14 (2G) PORTUGAL 10 (1G 1PG)

ROMANIA: I Dumitras; C Fercu, I Dimofte, R Gontineac, C Nicolae; D Dumbrava, V Calafeteanu; C Popescu, R Mavrodin, B Balan, C Ratiu, C Petre, A Tudori, O Tonita (*captain*), F Cordoeanu *Substitutions:* M Tincu for Mavrodin (40 mins); S Socol for Tudori (40 mins); P Ion for Balan (50 mins); B Balan back for Popescu (62 mins); L Sirbu for Calafeteanu (63 mins); V Ursache for Tonita (65 mins)

SCORERS *Tries:* Tincu, Cordoeanu *Conversions:* Calafeteanu, Dumbrava

PORTUGAL: P Leal; A Aguilar, M Portela, F Sousa, P Carvalho; D C Pinto, J Pinto; R Cordeiro, J Ferreira (*captain*), R Spachuk, G Uva, D Penalva, D Coutinho, T Girão, J Uva *Substitutions:* J Correia for Spachuk (50 mins); G Malheiro for D C Pinto (63 mins); J-M Muré for Ferreira (69 mins); L Pissarra for J Pinto (74 mins); P Murinello for J Uva (75 mins); S Palha for Penalva (78 mins)

SCORERS *Try:* Ferreira *Conversion:* D C Pinto *Penalty Goal:* Malheiro

REFEREE P G Honiss (New Zealand)

29 September, Stade Municipal, Toulouse

NEW ZEALAND 85 (10G 3T) ROMANIA 8 (1PG 1T)

NEW ZEALAND: N J Evans; J T Rokocoko, I Toeava, A J D Mauger, S W Sivivatu; C L McAlister, A M Ellis; N S Tialata, K F Mealamu, G M Somerville, R D Thorne, K J Robinson, J Collins (*captain*), S T Lauaki, M C Masoe *Substitutions:* R H McCaw for Masoe (54 mins); C R Jack for Robinson (54 mins); D C Howlett for McAlister (54 mins); B G Leonard for Ellis (59 mins); A K Hore for Mealamu (60 mins); C G Smith for Sivivatu (60 mins)

SCORERS *Tries*: Rokocoko (3), Sivivatu (2), Toeava (2), Masoe, Evans, Mauger, Hore, Smith, Howlett *Conversions*: Evans (6), McAlister (4)

ROMANIA: I Dumitras; S Ciuntu, C Gal, R Gontineac, G Brezoianu; I Dimofte, L Sirbu; B Balan, M Tincu, S Florea, S Socol (*captain*), C Petre, F Cordoeanu, O Tonita, A Manta *Substitutions:* C Ratiu for Corodeanu (47 mins); R Mavrodin for Tincu (52 mins); P Ion for Florea (52 mins); S Florea back for Balan (56 mins); F Vlaicu for Dumitras (60 mins); V Calafeteanu for Sirbu (61 mins); V Ursache for Manta (67 mins); C R Dascalu for Gontineac (69 mins)

SCORERS *Try:* Tincu *Penalty Goal:* Vlaicu

Referee J Jutge (France)

29 September, Stade Geoffroy-Guichard, Saint Etienne

SCOTLAND 18 (6PG) ITALY 16 (1G 3PG)

SCOTLAND: R P Lamont; S F Lamont, S L Webster, R E Dewey, C D Paterson; D A Parks, M R L Blair; G Kerr, R W Ford, E A Murray, N J Hines, J L Hamilton, J P R White (*captain*), S M Taylor, A Hogg *Substitutions:* H F G Southwell for R Lamont (24 mins); A R Henderson for Dewey (59 mins); C J Smith for Kerr (64 mins); K D R Brown for Hogg (69 mins); S J MacLeod for Hamilton (71 mins); C P Cusiter for Blair (71 mins)

SCORER *Penalty Goals:* Paterson (6)

ITALY: D Bortolussi; K Robertson, G-J Canale, Mirco Bergamasco, A Masi; R Pez, A Troncon (*captain*); S Perugini, C Festuccia, M-L Castrogiovanni, S Dellapè, C Del Fava, J Sole, S Parisse, Mauro Bergamasco *Substitutions:* A Lo Cicero for Perugini (48 mins); F Ongaro for Festuccia (52 mins); S Perugini back for Castrogiovanni (74 mins); E Galon for Masi (78 mins)

SCORERS *Try:* Troncon *Penalty Goals:* Bortolussi (3) *Conversion:* Bortolussi

REFEREE J I Kaplan (South Africa)

YELLOW CARDS: Mauro Bergamasco (7 mins); Hines (54 mins)

POOL C

	P	W	D	L	PD	TD	PF	TF	BP	Pts
New Zealand	4	4	0	0	274	42	309	46	4	20
Scotland	4	3	0	1	50	6	116	14	2	14
Italy	4	2	0	2	-32	-6	85	8	1	9
Romania	4	1	0	3	-121	-17	40	5	1	5
Portugal	4	0	0	4	-171	-25	38	4	1	1

P=Played; **W**=Won; **D**=Draw; **L**=Lost; **PD**=Points Difference; **TD**=Tries Difference; **PF**=Points For; **TF**=Tries For; **BP**=Bonus Points; **PTS**=Points

POOL D

7 September, Stade de France, Paris

FRANCE 12 (4PG) ARGENTINA 17 (4PG 1T)

FRANCE: C Heymans; A Rougerie, Y Jauzion, D Traille, C Dominici; D Skrela, P Mignoni; O Milloud, R Ibañez (*captain*), P de Villiers, F Pelous, J Thion, S Betsen, I Harinordoquy, R Martin *Substitutions:* F Michalak for Traille (temp 15 to 23 mins) and for Skrela (61 mins); S Chabal for Pelous (59 mins); D Szarzewski for Ibañez (59 mins); J Bonnaire for Martin (59 mins); J-B Elissalde for Mignoni (72 mins)

SCORER *Penalty Goals*: Skrela (4)

ARGENTINA: I Corleto; L Borges, M Contepomi, F Contepomi, H Agulla; J-M Hernández, A Pichot (*captain*); R Roncero, M E Ledesma, M Scelzo, C I Fernandez Lobbe, P Albacete, L Ostiglia, J M Leguizamon, J M Fernandez Lobbe *Substitutions:* R Alvarez Kairelis for C I Fernandez Lobbe (27 mins); S Gonzalez Bonorino for Scelzo (63 mins); M Durand for Ostiglia (72 mins); H Senillosa for M Contepomi (temp 47 to 49 mins and 72 mins)

SCORERS *Try:* Corleto *Penalty Goals:* F Contepomi (4)

REFEREE A J Spreadbury (England)

9 September, Stade Chaban-Delmas, Bordeaux

IRELAND 32 (2G 1PG 3T) NAMIBIA 17 (2G 1PG)

IRELAND: G T Dempsey; A D Trimble, B G O'Driscoll (*captain*), G M D'Arcy, D A Hickie; R J R O'Gara, P A Stringer; M J Horan, R Best, J J Hayes, D P O'Callaghan, P J O'Connell, S H Easterby, D P Leamy, D P Wallace *Substitutions:* S J Best for Horan (61 mins); J P Flannery for R Best (61 mins); N A Best for D P Wallace (68 mins); P W Wallace for O'Gara (79 mins); G E A Murphy for O'Driscoll (80 mins)

SCORERS *Tries*: O'Driscoll, Trimble, Easterby, pen try, Flannery *Conversions*: O'Gara (2) *Penalty Goal*: O'Gara

NAMIBIA: T C Losper; R C Witbooi, B C Langenhoven, W P van Zyl, J H Bock; E Wessels, E A Jantjies; G Lensing (*captain*), H Horn, J A du Toit, U Kazombiaze, N Esterhuize, J Nieuwenhuis, J Burger, J H Senekal *Substitutions:* M V MacKenzie for Senekal (21 mins); J H Redelinghuys for Lensing (49 mins); J H van Tonder for Jantjies (49 mins); G Lensing back for Redelinghuys (77 mins); J M Meyer for Horn (77 mins); M J Africa for Witbooi (80 mins); T du Plessis for Burger (temp 65 to 68 mins)

SCORERS *Tries:* Nieuwenhuis, Van Zyl *Conversions:* Wessels (2) *Penalty Goal:* Wessels

REFEREE J Jutge (France)

11 September, Stade Gerland, Lyons

ARGENTINA 33 (2G 3PG 2T) GEORGIA 3 (1PG)

ARGENTINA: I Corleto; L Borges, G Tiesi, F Contepomi (*captain*), F-M Aramburu; J-M Hernández, N Fernandez Miranda; M Ayerza, M E Ledesma, S Gonzalez Bonorino, R Alvarez Kairelis, P Albacete, M Durand, J M Leguizamon, J M Fernandez Lobbe *Substitutions:* O J Hasan Jalil for Gonzalez Bonorino (44 mins); M Schusterman for Leguizamon (60 mins); E Lozada for Alvarez Kairelis (temp 43 to 44 mins and 67 mins); A Vernet Basualdo for Ledesma (67 mins); H Senillosa for Tiesi (temp 43 to 44 mins) and for Borges (70 mins); F Todeschini for F Contepomi (73 mins)

SCORERS *Tries:* Borges (2), Albacete, Aramburu *Conversions:* F Contepomi, Hernandez *Penalty Goals:* F Contepomi (3)

GEORGIA: P Jimsheladze; B Khamashuridze, M Urjukashvili, I Giorgadze, I Machkhaneli; M Kvirikashvili, I Abuseridze; D Khinchagashvili, A Giorgadze, D Zirakashvili, I Zedginidze (*captain*), M Gorgodze, G Chkhaidze, B Udesiani, G Labadze *Substitutions:* A Kopaliani for Zirakashvili (40 mins); Z Maisuradze for Chkhaidze (49 mins); G Shkinin for Jimsheladze (58 mins); G Shvelidze for Khinchagashvili (62 mins); B Samkharadze for Abuseridze (63 mins); V Didebulidze for Udesiani (64 mins); R Gigauri for Urjukashvili

SCORER *Penalty Goal:* Kvirikashvili

REFEREE N Owens (Wales)

15 September, Stade Chaban-Delmas, Bordeaux

IRELAND 14 (2G) GEORGIA 10 (1G 1PG)

IRELAND: G T Dempsey; S P Horgan, B G O'Driscoll (*captain*), G M D'Arcy, D A Hickie; R J R O'Gara, P A Stringer; M J Horan, R Best, J J Hayes, D P O'Callaghan, P J O'Connell, S H Easterby, D P Leamy, D P Wallace *Substitutions:* J P Flannery for R Best (52 mins); S J Best for Hayes (65 mins); I J Boss for Stringer (69 mins); N A Best for Easterby (71 mins)

SCORERS *Tries*: R Best, Dempsey *Conversions*: O'Gara (2)

GEORGIA: O Barkalaia; G Elizbarashvili, M Urjukashvili, D Kacharava, G Shkinin; M Kvirikashvili, B Samkharadze; M Magrakvelidze, G Shvelidze, A Kopaliani, I Zedginidze (*captain*), M Gorgodze, I Maisuradze, G Chkhaidze, R Urushadze *Substitutions:* L Datunashvili for Zedginidze (31 mins); I Machkhaneli for Barkalai (33 mins); A Guigadze for Magrakvelidze (47 mins); D Khinchagashvili for Kopaliani (47 mins); O Eloshvili for Elizbarashvili (50 mins); Z Maisuradze for I Maisuradze (57 mins); I Abuseridze for Samkharadze (71 mins)

SCORERS *Try:* Shkinin *Conversion:* Kvirikashvili *Penalty Goal:* Kvirikashvili

REFEREE W Barnes (England)

YELLOW CARD: D Wallace (36 mins)

16 September, Stade Municipal, Toulouse

FRANCE 87 (11G 2T) NAMIBIA 10 (1G 1DG)

FRANCE: C Poitrenaud; V Clerc, D Marty, D Traille, C Heymans; F Michalak, J-B Elissalde (*captain*); J-B Poux, D Szarzewski, P de Villiers, S Chabal, L Nallet, Y Nyanga, J Bonnaire, T Dusautoir *Substitutions:* N Mas for De Villiers (40 mins); Y Jauzion for Traille (49 mins); I Harinordoquy for Nyanga (54 mins); R Ibañez for Szarzewski (57 mins); F Pelous for Chabal (57 mins); L Beauxis for Michalak (62 mins); A Rougerie for Poitrenaud (64 mins)

SCORERS *Tries:* Clerc (3), Nallet (2), Chabal (2), Heymans, Marty, Dusautoir, Bonnaire, Elissalde, Ibañez *Conversions:* Elissalde (11)

NAMIBIA: T C Losper; R C Witbooi, B C Langenhoven, W P van Zyl, J H Bock; E Wessels, J H van Tonder; G Lensing (*captain*), H Horn, J A du Toit, U Kazombiaze, N Esterhuize, J Burger, J Nieuwenhuis, M V MacKenzie *Substitutions:* L-W Botes for Wessels (11 mins); E A Jantjies for Van Tonder (40 mins); T du Plessis for MacKenzie; H D Lintvelt for Esterhuize (56 mins); J H Redelinghuys for Lensing (56 mins); J M Meyer for Horn (63 mins); M J Africa for Van Zyl (65 mins); K Lensing back on for Du Toit (67 mins)

SCORERS *Try:* Langenhoven *Conversion:* Losper *Dropped Goal:* Wessels

REFEREE A C Rolland (Ireland)

SENT OFF: Nieuwenhuis (18 mins)

21 September, Stade de France, Paris

FRANCE 25 (5PG 2T) IRELAND 3 (1DG)

FRANCE: C Poitrenaud; V Clerc, D Marty, D Traille, C Heymans; F Michalak, J-B Elissalde; O Milloud, R Ibañez (*captain*), P de Villiers, S Chabal, J Thion, S Betsen, J Bonnaire, T Dusautoir *Substitutions:* L Nallet for Chabal (45 mins); D Szarzewski for Ibañez (56 mins); Y Nyanga for Betsen (62 mins); A Rougerie for Poitrenaud (71 mins); Y Jauzion for Marty (73 mins); J-B Poux for Milloud (73 mins); L Beauxis for Elissalde (73 mins)

SCORERS *Tries:* Clerc (2) *Penalty Goals:* Elissalde (5)

IRELAND: G T Dempsey; S P Horgan, B G O'Driscoll (*captain*), G M D'Arcy, A D Trimble; R J R O'Gara, E G Reddan; M J Horan, J P Flannery, J J Hayes, D P O'Callaghan, P J O'Connell, S H Easterby, D P Leamy, D P Wallace *Substitutions:* M E O'Kelly for O'Callaghan (71 mins); N A Best for Easterby (72 mins); S J Best for Hayes (73 mins); F J Sheahan for Flannery (temp 49 to 54 mins and 78 mins)

SCORER *Dropped Goal:* O'Gara

REFEREE C White (England)

YELLOW CARDS: O'Connell (63 mins); Traille (75 mins)

22 September, Stade Vélodrome, Marseilles

ARGENTINA 63 (6G 2PG 3T) NAMIBIA 3 (1PG)

ARGENTINA: I Corleto; H Senillosa, G Tiesi, M Contepomi, H Agulla; F Contepomi, A Pichot (*captain*); R Roncero, A Vernet Basualdo, O J Hasan Jalil, C I Fernandez Lobbe, P Albacete, L Ostiglia, J M Leguizamon, J M Fernandez Lobbe *Substitutions:* N Fernandez Miranda for Pichot (55 mins); G Longo for Leguizamon (58 mins); F Todeschini for F Contepomi (58 mins); F Serra for Corleto (64 mins); M Scelzo for Roncero (65 mins); R Alvarez Kairelis for C I Fernandez Lobbe (65 mins)

SCORERS *Tries:* Leguizamon (2), Roncero, M Contepomi, F Contepomi, Tiesi, Corleto, penalty try, Todeschini *Conversions:* F Contepomi (4), Todeschini (2) *Penalty Goals:* F Contepomi (2)

NAMIBIA: J H Bock; A D Mouton, DuP Grobler, C Powell (*captain*), M J Africa; M Schreuder, E A Jantjies; J H Redelinghuys, J M Meyer, M Visser, U Kazombiaze, N Esterhuize, M V MacKenzie, T du Plessis, J Burger *Substitutions:* H D Lintvelt for MacKenzie (39 mins); G Lensing for Visser (40 mins); H Horn for Meyer (40 mins); W P van Zyl for Grobler (50 mins); B C Langenhoven for Mouton (52 mins); J H Senekal for Kazombiaze (59 mins); J H van Tonder for Schreuder (72 mins)

SCORER *Penalty Goal:* Schreuder

REFEREE S J Dickinson (Australia)

26 September, Stade Félix Bollaert, Lens

GEORGIA 30 (3G 3PG) NAMIBIA 0

GEORGIA: M Urjukashvili; G Shkinin, D Kacharava, I Giorgadze, I Machkhaneli; M Kvirikashvili, I Abuseridze (*captain*); G Shvelidze, A Giorgadze, D Zirakashvili, L Datunashvili, M Gorgodze, G Labadze, G Chkhaidze, R Urushadze *Substitutions:* V Didebulidze for Gorgodze (18 mins); B Khamashuridze for Shkinin (46 mins); B Udesiani for Urushadze (50 mins); B Samkharadze for Abuseridze (55 mins); D Khinchagashvili for A Giorgadze (55 mins); R Gigauri for Urjukashvili (68 mins); A Kopaliani for Khinchagashvili (71 mins)

SCORERS *Tries:* A Giorgadze, Machkhaneli, Kacharava *Conversions:* Kvirikashvili (3) *Penalty Goals:* Kvirikashvili (3)

NAMIBIA: J H Bock; R C Witbooi, W P van Zyl, C Powell, B C Langenhoven; M Schreuder, J H van Tonder; G Lensing (*captain*), H Horn, M Visser, U Kazombiaze, J H Senekal, J Nieuwenhuis, T du Plessis, J Burger *Substitutions:* J A du Toit for Visser (40 mins); N Esterhuize for Du Plessis (41 mins); J H Redelinghuys for Du Toit (51 mins); M J Africa for Schreuder (59 mins); J M Meyer for Horn (68 mins); E A Jantjies for Van Tonder (temp 43 to 54 mins) and for Bock (71 mins); D Kamonga for Senekal (71 mins)

REFEREE S R Walsh (New Zealand)

30 September, Stade Vélodrome, Marseilles

FRANCE 64 (5G 3PG 4T) GEORGIA 7 (1G)

FRANCE: C Poitrenaud; A Rougerie, D Marty, Y Jauzion, C Dominici; L Beauxis, P Mignoni; O Milloud, S Bruno, J-B Poux, L Nallet, J Thion, S Betsen (*captain*), J Bonnaire, Y Nyanga *Substitutions:* J-B Elissalde for Mignoni (21 mins); F Pelous for Thion (53 mins); D Skrela for Marty (58 mins); D Szarzewski for Bruno (58 mins); N Mas for Poux (58 mins); R Martin for Betsen (63 mins); V Clerc for Poitrenaud (72 mins); Poux back for Milloud (72 mins)

SCORERS *Tries:* Dominici (2), Poitrenaud, Nyanga, Beauxis, Bruno, Nallet, Martin, Bonnaire *Conversions:* Beauxis (5) *Penalty Goals:* Beauxis (3)

GEORGIA: O Barkalaia; B Khamashuridze, R Gigauri, I Giorgadze, M Urjukashvili; M Kvirikashvili, I Abuseridze (*captain*); M Magrakvelidze, A Giorgadze, D Zirakashvili, V Didebulidze, Z Mtchedlishvili, I Maisuradze, G Chkhaidze, R Urushadze *Substitutions:* B Samkharadze for Abuseridze (30 mins); L Datunashvili for Didebulidze (40 mins); G Shvelidze for Urushadze (temp 32 to 38 mins) and for Magrakvelidze (48 mins); Z Maisuradze for I Maisuradze (48 mins); A Kopaliani for Zirakashvili (53 mins); G Elizbarashvili for Khamashuridze (53 mins); O Eloshvili for Barkalaia (53 mins)

SCORERS *Try:* Z Maisuradze *Conversion:* Urjukashvili

REFEREE A Lewis (Ireland)

YELLOW CARDS: Magrakvelidze (28 mins); Gigauri (75 mins)

30 September, Parc des Princes, Paris

IRELAND 15 (1G 1PG 1T)
ARGENTINA 30 (1G 3PG 3DG 1T)

IRELAND: G E A Murphy; S P Horgan, B G O'Driscoll (*captain*), G M D'Arcy, D A Hickie; R J R O'Gara, E G Reddan; M J Horan, J P Flannery, J J Hayes, D P O'Callaghan, P J O'Connell, S H Easterby, D P Leamy, D P Wallace *Substitutions:* R Best for Flannery (65 mins); N A Best for Wallace (temp 24 to 27 mins and 65 mins); M E O'Kelly for O'Callaghan (65 mins); I J Boss for Reddan (66 mins); G W Duffy for Hickie (70 mins)

SCORERS *Tries:* O'Driscoll, Murphy *Conversion:* O'Gara *Penalty Goal:* O'Gara

ARGENTINA: I Corleto; L Borges, M Contepomi, F Contepomi, H Agulla; J-M Hernández, A Pichot (*captain*); R Roncero, M E Ledesma, M Scelzo, C I Fernandez Lobbe, P Albacete, L Ostiglia, G Longo, J M Fernandez Lobbe *Substitutions:* R Alvarez Kairelis for C I Fernandez Lobbe (54 mins); M Durand for Ostiglia (62 mins); H Senillosa for M Contepomi (70 mins); O J Hasan Jalil for Scelzo (76 mins); A Vernet Basualdo for Ledesma (79 mins)

SCORERS *Tries:* Borges, Agulla *Conversion:* F Contepomi *Penalty Goals:* F Contepomi (3) *Dropped Goals:* Hernández (3)

REFEREE P G Honiss (New Zealand)

POOL D

	P	W	D	L	PD	TD	PF	TF	BP	Pts
Argentina	4	4	0	0	110	14	143	16	2	18
France	4	3	0	1	151	21	188	24	3	15
Ireland	4	2	0	2	-18	2	64	9	1	9
Georgia	4	1	0	3	-61	-10	50	5	1	5
Namibia	4	0	0	4	-182	-27	30	3	0	0

P=Played; **W**=Won; **D**=Draw; **L**=Lost; **PD**=Points Difference; **TD**=Tries Difference; **PF**=Points For; **TF**=Tries For; **BP**=Bonus Points; **PTS**=Points

6 October, Stade Vélodrome, Marseilles

AUSTRALIA 10 (1G 1PG) ENGLAND 12 (4PG)

AUSTRALIA: C E Latham; L D Tuqiri, S A Mortlock (*captain*), M J Giteau, A P Ashley-Cooper; B Barnes, G M Gregan; M J Dunning, S T Moore, G T Shepherdson, N C Sharpe, D J Vickerman, R D Elsom, W L Palu, G B Smith *Substitutions:* P R Waugh for Smith (64 mins); A K E Baxter for Shepherdson (64 mins); H J McMeniman for Vickerman (temp 28 to 30 mins) and for Elsom (64 mins); D A Mitchell for Ashley-Cooper (64 mins); A L Freier for Moore (72 mins); S A Hoiles for Palu (75 mins)

SCORERS *Try*: Tuqiri *Conversion:* Mortlock *Penalty Goal:* Mortlock

ENGLAND: J T Robinson; P H Sackey, M Tait, M J Catt, O J Lewsey; J P Wilkinson, A C T Gomarsall; A J Sheridan, M P Regan, P J Vickery (*captain*), S D Shaw, B J Kay, M E Corry N Easter, L W Moody *Substitutions:* G S Chuter for Regan (51 mins); M J H Stevens for Vickery (58 mins); T Flood for Catt (63 mins); J P R Worsley for Moody (65 mins); L B N Dallaglio for Easter (68 mins); P C Richards for Gomarsall (temp 22 to 27 mins)

SCORER *Penalty Goals*: Wilkinson (4)

REFEREE A C Rolland (Ireland)

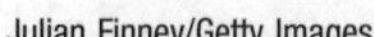
Julian Finney/Getty Images

That man Jonny Wilkinson knocked over the Aussies again, with his boot.

6 October, Millennium Stadium, Cardiff

NEW ZEALAND 18 (1G 2PG 1T)
FRANCE 20 (2G 2PG)

NEW ZEALAND: L R MacDonald; J T Rokocoko, J M Muliaina, C L McAlister, S W Sivivatu; D W Carter, B T Kelleher; T D Woodcock, A D Oliver, C J Hayman, K J Robinson, A J Williams, J Collins, R So'oialo, R H McCaw (*captain*) *Substitutions:* C R Jack for Robinson (49 mins); N J Evans for Carter (55 mins); B G Leonard for Kelleher (55 mins); A K Hore for Oliver (55 mins); M C Masoe for Collins (63 mins); I Toeava for Evans (70 mins)

SCORERS *Tries*: McAlister, So'oialo *Conversion*: Carter *Penalty Goals:* Carter (2)

FRANCE: D Traille; V Clerc, D Marty, Y Jauzion, C Heymans; L Beauxis, J-B Elissalde; O Milloud, R Ibañez (*captain*), P de Villiers, F Pelous, J Thion, S Betsen, J Bonnaire, T Dusautoir *Substitutions:* I Harinordoquy for Betsen (4 mins); J-B Poux for Milloud (40 mins); S Chabal for Pelous (51 mins); D Szarzewski for Ibañez (51 mins); F Michalak for Beauxis (67 mins); C Dominici for Heymans (69 mins)

SCORERS *Tries:* Dusautoir, Jauzion *Conversions:* Beauxis, Elissalde *Penalty Goals:* Beauxis (2)

REFEREE W Barnes (England)

YELLOW CARD: McAlister (45 mins)

Ross Land/Getty Images

France sprung the biggest shock of the tournament, knocking out red hot favourites New Zealand.

7 October, Stade Vélodrome, Marseilles

SOUTH AFRICA 37 (3G 2PG 2T) FIJI 20 (2G 2PG)

SOUTH AFRICA: P C Montgomery; J-P R Pietersen, J Fourie, F P L Steyn, B G Habana; A D James, P F du Preez; J P du Randt, J W Smit (*captain*), J N du Plessis, J P Botha, V Matfield, J H Smith, D J Rossouw, S W P Burger *Substitutions:* J L van Heerden for Rossouw (49 mins); G G Steenkamp for Du Randt (52 mins); G J Muller for J P Botha (temp 52 to 58 mins and 74 mins)

SCORERS *Tries*: Fourie, Smit, Pietersen, Smith, James *Conversions:* Montgomery (3) *Penalty Goals*: Montgomery, Steyn

FIJI: N Ligairi; V Delasau, K Ratuvou; S Rabeni, S Bobo; S Bai, M Rauluni (*captain*); G Dewes, S Koto, H Qiodravu, K Leawere, I Rawaqa, S Naevo, S Koyamaibole, A Qera *Substitutions:* J Railomo for Qiodravu (54 mins); G Lovobalavu for Ratuvou (63 mins); A Ratuva for Qera (70 mins); B Gadolo for Koto (70 mins); W Lewaravu for Leawere (72 mins)

SCORERS *Tries:* Delasau, Bobo *Conversions:* Bai (2) *Penalty Goals:* Bai (2)

REFEREE A Lewis (Ireland)

YELLOW CARD: Rabeni (50 mins)

Julian Finney/Getty Images

The Fijians lit up the quarter-finals with a stunning display of running rugby.

7 October, Stade de France, Paris

ARGENTINA 19 (1G 3PG 1DG) SCOTLAND 13 (1G 2PG)

ARGENTINA: I Corleto; L Borges, M Contepomi, F Contepomi, H Agulla; J-M Hernández, A Pichot (*captain*); R Roncero, M E Ledesma, M Scelzo, C I Fernandez Lobbe, P Albacete, L Ostiglia, G Longo, J M Fernandez Lobbe *Substitutions:* R Alvarez Kairelis for C I Fernandez Lobbe (50 mins); J-M Leguizamón for Ostiglia (54 mins); O J Hasan Jalil for Scelzo (56 mins); H Senillosa for M Contepomi (66 mins);

SCORERS *Try:* Longo *Conversion:* F Contepomi *Penalty Goals:* F Contepomi (3) *Dropped Goal:* Hernández

SCOTLAND: R P Lamont; S F Lamont, S L Webster, R E Dewey, C D Paterson; D A Parks, M R L Blair; G Kerr, R W Ford, E A Murray, N J Hines, J L Hamilton, J P R White (*captain*), S M Taylor, A Hogg *Substitutions:* A R Henderson for Dewey (40 mins); C J Smith for Kerr (56 mins); K D R Brown for Hogg (56 mins); S J MacLeod for Hamilton (56 mins); C P Cusiter for Blair (56 mins); S Lawson for Ford (67 mins); H F G Southwell for R Lamont (67 mins)

SCORERS *Try:* Cusiter *Conversion:* Paterson *Penalty Goals:* Paterson, Parks

REFEREE J Jutge (France)

Jamie McDonald

The Scots and their captain, Jason White, suffered quarter-final heartache in Paris.

13 October, Stade de France, Paris

FRANCE 9 (3PG) ENGLAND 14 (2PG 1DG 1T)

FRANCE: D Traille; V Clerc, D Marty, Y Jauzion, C Heymans; L Beauxis, J-B Elissalde; O Milloud, R Ibañez (*captain*), P de Villiers, F Pelous, J Thion, S Betsen, J Bonnaire, T Dusautoir *Substitutions:* S Chabal for Pelous (24 mins); F Michalak for Beauxis (50 mins); D Szarzewski for Ibañez (50 mins); C Dominici for Heymans (60 mins); J-B Poux for De Villiers (65 mins); I Harinordoquy for Betsen (66 mins)

SCORER *Penalty Goals:* Beauxis (3)

ENGLAND: J T Robinson; P H Sackey, M Tait, M J Catt, O J Lewsey; J P Wilkinson, A C T Gomarsall; A J Sheridan, M P Regan, P J Vickery (*captain*), S D Shaw, B J Kay, M E Corry N Easter, L W Moody *Substitutions:* D Hipkiss for Lewsey (39 mins); J P R Worsley for Moody (53 mins); M J H Stevens for Vickery (55 mins); G S Chuter for Regan (65 mins); T Flood for Catt (68 mins); L B N Dallaglio for Easter (69 mins); P C Richards for Gomarsall (70 mins)

SCORERS *Try:* Lewsey *Penalty Goals*: Wilkinson (2) *Dropped Goal:* Wilkinson

REFEREE J I Kaplan (South Africa)

Shaun Botterill/Getty Images

England stunned the hosts with a Josh Lewsey try in the second minute.

14 October, Stade de France, Paris

SOUTH AFRICA 37 (4G 3PG) ARGENTINA 13 (1G 2PG)

SOUTH AFRICA: P C Montgomery; J-P R Pietersen, J Fourie, F P L Steyn, B G Habana; A D James, P F du Preez; J P du Randt, J W Smit (*captain*), C J van der Linde, J P Botha, V Matfield, J H Smith, D J Rossouw, S W P Burger *Substitutions:* J N du Plessis for Du Randt (temp 43 to 48 mins and 71 mins); R B Skinstad for Rossouw (74 mins); W Olivier for Steyn (76 mins); G J Muller for J P Botha (temp 20 to 28 mins and 76 mins); B W du Plessis for Smit (76 mins); A S Pretorius for James (76 mins); R Pienaar for Pietersen (76 mins)

SCORERS *Tries*: Habana (2), Du Preez, Rossouw *Conversions:* Montgomery (4) *Penalty Goals*: Montgomery (3)

ARGENTINA: I Corleto; L Borges, M Contepomi, F Contepomi, H Agulla; J-M Hernández, A Pichot (*captain*); R Roncero, M E Ledesma, M Scelzo, C I Fernandez Lobbe, P Albacete, L Ostiglia, G Longo, J M Fernandez Lobbe *Substitutions:* O J Hasan Jalil for Scelzo (33 mins); R Alvarez Kairelis for C I Fernandez Lobbe (52 mins); J-M Leguizamón for Ostiglia (64 mins); G Tiesi for M Contepomi (64 mins)

SCORERS *Try:* M Contepomi *Conversion:* F Contepomi *Penalty Goals:* F Contepomi (2)

REFEREE S R Walsh (New Zealand)

YELLOW CARDS: Smith (77 mins); F Contepomi (78 mins)

Getty Images Sport

Bryan Habana was in breathtaking form in the semi-final, with two tries.

19 October, Parc des Princes, Paris

FRANCE 10 (1G 1PG)
ARGENTINA 34 (3G 1PG 2T)

FRANCE: C Poitrenaud; A Rougerie, D Marty, D Skrela, C Dominici; F Michalak, J-B Elissalde; J-B Poux, R Ibañez (captain), N Mas, L Nallet, J Thion, Y Nyanga, I Harinordoquy, T Dusautoir Substitutions: S Bruno for Dusautoir (temp 40 to 50 mins) and for Ibañez (50 mins); R Martin for Dusautoir (50 mins); P Mignoni for Elissalde (54 mins); V Clerc for Rougerie (59 mins); S Chabal for Thion (60 mins); L Beauxis for Skrela (66 mins)

SCORERS *Try:* Poitrennaud *Conversions:* Beauxis *Penalty Goal:* Elissalde

ARGENTINA: I Corleto; F M Aramburu, M Contepomi, F Contepomi, H Agulla; J-M Hernández, A Pichot (captain); R Roncero, A Vernet Basualdo, O J Hasan Jalil, R Alvarez Kairelis, P Albacete, M Durand, G Longo, J M Fernandez Lobbe Substitutions: J M Leguizamón for Durand (59 mins); H Senillosa for M Contepomi (59 mins); E Lozada for Alvarez Kairelis (69 mins); M Ayerza for Hasan Jalil (69 mins); F Todeschini for Corleto (73 mins); N Fernandez Miranda for Pichot (74 mins); E Guiñazu for Roncero (78 mins)

SCORERS *Tries:* F Contepomi (2), Hasan Jalil, Aramburu, Corleto *Conversions:* F Contepomi (3) *Penalty Goal:* F Contepomi

REFEREE P G Honiss (New Zealand)

YELLOW CARDS: Ibañez (40 mins); Alvarez Kairelis (40 mins); Leguizamón (62 mins)

Cameron Spencer/Getty Images

Argentina hit the heights with a stunning display against France to win the bronze medal.

THE FINAL

20 October, Stade de France, Paris

SOUTH AFRICA 15 (5PG) ENGLAND 6 (2PG)

SOUTH AFRICA: P C Montgomery; J-P R Pietersen, J Fourie, F P L Steyn, B G Habana; A D James, P F du Preez; J P du Randt, J W Smit (captain), C J van der Linde, J P Botha, V Matfield, J H Smith, D J Rossouw, S W P Burger Substitutions: J L van Heerden for Rossouw (72 mins); B W du Plessis for Smit (temp 71 to76 mins)

SCORERS *Penalty Goals:* Montgomery (4), Steyn

ENGLAND: J T Robinson; P H Sackey, M Tait, M J Catt, M J Cueto; J P Wilkinson, A C T Gomarsall; A J Sheridan, M P Regan, P J Vickery (captain), S D Shaw, B J Kay, M E Corry, N Easter, L W Moody Substitutions: M J H Stevens for Vickery (40 mins); D Hipkiss for Robinson (46 mins); T Flood for Catt (50 mins); G S Chuter for Regan (62 mins); J P R Worsley for Moody (62 mins); L B N Dallaglio for Easter (64 mins); P C Richards for Worsley (70 mins)

SCORER *Penalty Goals:* Wilkinson (2)

REFEREE A C Rolland (Ireland)

Dave Rogers/Getty Images

The unerring boot of Percy Montgomery separated the sides in the final.

Julian Finney/Getty Images

Springboks captain John Smit and coach Jake White with rugby's most prized possession.

RUGBY WORLD CUP TOURNAMENTS 1987-2003

FIRST TOURNAMENT: 1987 IN AUSTRALIA & NEW ZEALAND

POOL 1

Australia	19	**England**	6
USA	21	**Japan**	18
England	60	**Japan**	7
Australia	47	**USA**	12
England	34	**USA**	6
Australia	42	**Japan**	23

	P	W	D	L	F	A	Pts
Australia	3	3	0	0	108	41	6
England	3	2	0	1	100	32	4
USA	3	1	0	2	39	99	2
Japan	3	0	0	3	48	123	0

POOL 2

Canada	37	**Tonga**	4
Wales	13	**Ireland**	6
Wales	29	**Tonga**	16
Ireland	46	**Canada**	19
Wales	40	**Canada**	9
Ireland	32	**Tonga**	9

	P	W	D	L	F	A	Pts
Wales	3	3	0	0	82	31	6
Ireland	3	2	0	1	84	41	4
Canada	3	1	0	2	65	90	2
Tonga	3	0	0	3	29	98	0

POOL 3

New Zealand	70	**Italy**	6
Fiji	28	**Argentina**	9
New Zealand	74	**Fiji**	13
Argentina	25	**Italy**	16
Italy	18	**Fiji**	15
New Zealand	46	**Argentina**	15

	P	W	D	L	F	A	Pts
New Zealand	3	3	0	0	190	34	6
Fiji	3	1	0	2	56	101	2
Argentina	3	1	0	2	49	90	2
Italy	3	1	0	2	40	110	2

POOL 4

Romania	21	**Zimbabwe**	20
France	20	**Scotland**	20
France	55	**Romania**	12
Scotland	60	**Zimbabwe**	21
France	70	**Zimbabwe**	12
Scotland	55	**Romania**	28

	P	W	D	L	F	A	Pts
France	3	2	1	0	145	44	5
Scotland	3	2	1	0	135	69	5
Romania	3	1	0	2	61	130	2
Zimbabwe	3	0	0	3	53	151	0

QUARTER-FINALS

New Zealand	30	**Scotland**	3
France	31	**Fiji**	16
Australia	33	**Ireland**	15
Wales	16	**England**	3

SEMI-FINALS

France	30	**Australia**	24
New Zealand	49	**Wales**	6

THIRD PLACE MATCH

Wales	22	**Australia**	21

First World Cup Final, Eden Park, Auckland, 20 June 1987

NEW ZEALAND 29 (1G 4PG 1DG 2T)
FRANCE 9 (1G 1PG)

NEW ZEALAND: J A Gallagher; J J Kirwan, J T Stanley, W T Taylor, C I Green; G J Fox, D E Kirk (captain); S C McDowell, S B T Fitzpatrick, J A Drake, M J Pierce, G W Whetton, A J Whetton, W T Shelford, M N Jones

SCORERS TRIES : Jones, Kirk, Kirwan Conversion : Fox Penalty Goals : Fox (4) Drop Goal : Fox

FRANCE: S Blanco; D Camberabero, P Sella, D Charvet, P Lagisquet; F Mesnel, P Berbizier; P Ondarts, D Dubroca (captain), J-P Garuet, A Lorieux, J Condom, E Champ, L Rodriguez, D Erbani

SCORERS TRY : Berbizier Conversion : Camberabero Penalty Goal : Camberabero

REFEREE K V J Fitzgerald (Australia)

Ross Land/Getty Images

New Zealand captain David Kirk lifts the Rugby World Cup, and delights a nation.

SECOND TOURNAMENT: 1991 IN BRITAIN, IRELAND & FRANCE

POOL 1

New Zealand	18	England	12
Italy	30	USA	9
New Zealand	46	USA	6
England	36	Italy	6
England	37	USA	9
New Zealand	31	Italy	21

	P	W	D	L	F	A	Pts
New Zealand	3	3	0	0	95	39	9
England	3	2	0	1	85	33	7
Italy	3	1	0	2	57	76	5
USA	3	0	0	3	24	113	3

POOL 2

Scotland	47	Japan	9
Ireland	55	Zimbabwe	11
Ireland	32	Japan	16
Scotland	51	Zimbabwe	12
Scotland	24	Ireland	15
Japan	52	Zimbabwe	8

	P	W	D	L	F	A	Pts
Scotland	3	3	0	0	122	36	9
Ireland	3	2	0	1	102	51	7
Japan	3	1	0	2	77	87	5
Zimbabwe	3	0	0	3	31	158	3

POOL 3

Australia	32	Argentina	19
Western Samoa	16	Wales	13
Australia	9	Western Samoa	3
Wales	16	Argentina	7
Australia	38	Wales	3
Western Samoa	35	Argentina	12

	P	W	D	L	F	A	Pts
Australia	3	3	0	0	79	25	9
Western Samoa	3	2	0	1	54	34	7
Wales	3	1	0	2	32	61	5
Argentina	3	0	0	3	38	83	3

POOL 4

France	30	Romania	3
Canada	13	Fiji	3
France	33	Fiji	9
Canada	19	Romania	11
Romania	17	Fiji	15
France	19	Canada	13

	P	W	D	L	F	A	Pts
France	3	3	0	0	82	25	9
Canada	3	2	0	1	45	33	7
Romania	3	1	0	2	31	64	5
Fiji	3	0	0	3	27	63	3

QUARTER-FINALS

England	19	France	10
Scotland	28	Western Samoa	6
Australia	19	Ireland	18
New Zealand	29	Canada	13

SEMI-FINALS

England	9	Scotland	6
Australia	16	New Zealand	6

THIRD PLACE MATCH

New Zealand	13	Scotland	6

Second World Cup Final, Twickenham, 2 November 1991

AUSTRALIA 12 (1G 2PG)
ENGLAND 6 (2PG)

AUSTRALIA: M C Roebuck; D I Campese, J S Little, T J Horan, R H Egerton; M P Lynagh, N C Farr-Jones (captain); A J Daly, P N Kearns, E J A McKenzie, R J McCall, J A Eales, S P Poidevin, T Coker, V Ofahengaue

SCORERS TRY : Daly Conversion : Lynagh Penalty Goals : Lynagh (2)

ENGLAND: J M Webb; S J Halliday, W D C Carling (captain), J C Guscott, R Underwood; C R Andrew, R J Hill; J Leonard, B C Moore, J A Probyn, P J Ackford, W A Dooley, M G Skinner, M C Teague, P J Winterbottom

SCORER PENALTY GOALS : Webb (2)

REFEREE W D Bevan (Wales)

Russell Cheyne/Getty Images

Australia captain Nick Farr-Jones [left] lifts the Webb Ellis Cup – in 1991 – with David Campese

THIRD TOURNAMENT: 1995 IN SOUTH AFRICA

POOL A

South Africa	27	Australia	18
Canada	34	Romania	3
South Africa	21	Romania	8
Australia	27	Canada	11
Australia	42	Romania	3
South Africa	20	Canada	0

	P	W	D	L	F	A	Pts
South Africa	3	3	0	0	68	26	9
Australia	3	2	0	1	87	41	7
Canada	3	1	0	2	45	50	5
Romania	3	0	0	3	14	97	3

POOL B

Western Samoa	42	Italy	18
England	24	Argentina	18
Western Samoa	32	Argentina	26
England	27	Italy	20
Italy	31	Argentina	25
England	44	Western Samoa	22

	P	W	D	L	F	A	Pts
England	3	3	0	0	95	60	9
Western Samoa	3	2	0	1	96	88	7
Italy	3	1	0	2	69	94	5
Argentina	3	0	0	3	69	87	3

POOL C

Wales	57	Japan	10
New Zealand	43	Ireland	19
Ireland	50	Japan	28
New Zealand	34	Wales	9
New Zealand	145	Japan	17
Ireland	24	Wales	23

	P	W	D	L	F	A	Pts
New Zealand	3	3	0	0	222	45	9
Ireland	3	2	0	1	93	94	7
Wales	3	1	0	2	89	68	5
Japan	3	0	0	3	55	252	3

POOL D

Scotland	89	Ivory Coast	0
France	38	Tonga	10
France	54	Ivory Coast	18
Scotland	41	Tonga	5
Tonga	29	Ivory Coast	11
France	22	Scotland	19

	P	W	D	L	F	A	Pts
France	3	3	0	0	114	47	9
Scotland	3	2	0	1	149	27	7
Tonga	3	1	0	2	44	90	5
Ivory Coast	3	0	0	3	29	172	3

QUARTER-FINALS

France	36	Ireland	12
South Africa	42	Western Samoa	14
England	25	Australia	22
New Zealand	48	Scotland	30

SEMI-FINALS

South Africa	19	France	15
New Zealand	45	England	29

THIRD PLACE MATCH

France	19	England	9

Third World Cup Final, Ellis Park, Johannesburg, 24 June 1995

SOUTH AFRICA 15 (3PG 2DG)
NEW ZEALAND 12 (3PG 1DG) *

SOUTH AFRICA: A J Joubert; J T Small, J C Mulder, H P Le Roux, C M Williams; J T Stransky, J H van der Westhuizen; J P du Randt, C L C Rossouw, I S Swart, J J Wiese, J J Strydom, J F Pienaar (captain), M G Andrews, R J Kruger Substitutions: G L Pagel for Swart (68 mins); R A W Straeuli for Andrews (90 mins); B Venter for Small (97 mins)

SCORER PENALTY GOALS: Stransky (3) Drop Goals: Stransky (2)

NEW ZEALAND: G M Osborne; J W Wilson, F E Bunce, W K Little, J T Lomu; A P Mehrtens, G T M Bachop; C W Dowd, S B T Fitzpatrick (captain), O M Brown, I D Jones, R M Brooke, M R Brewer, Z V Brooke, J A Kronfeld Substitutions: J W Joseph for Brewer (40 mins); M C G Ellis for Wilson (55 mins); R W Loe for Dowd (83 mins); A D Strachan for Bachop (temp 66 to 71 mins)

SCORER PENALTY GOALS: Mehrtens (3) Drop Goal: Mehrtens

REFEREE E F Morrison (England)

* after extra time : 9-9 after normal time

Getty Images

Captain Francois Pienaar [middle, with cup] leads the celebrations after South Africa's victory

FOURTH TOURNAMENT: 1999 IN BRITAIN, IRELAND & FRANCE

POOL A

Spain	15	Uruguay	27
South Africa	46	Scotland	29
Scotland	43	Uruguay	12
South Africa	47	Spain	3
South Africa	39	Uruguay	3
Scotland	48	Spain	0

	P	W	D	L	F	A	Pts
South Africa	3	3	0	0	132	35	9
Scotland	3	2	0	1	120	58	7
Uruguay	3	1	0	2	42	97	5
Spain	3	0	0	3	18	122	3

POOL B

England	67	**Italy**	7
New Zealand	45	**Tonga**	9
England	16	**New Zealand**	30
Italy	25	**Tonga**	28
New Zealand	101	**Italy**	3
England	101	**Tonga**	10

	P	W	D	L	F	A	Pts
New Zealand	3	3	0	0	176	28	9
England	3	2	0	1	184	47	7
Tonga	3	1	0	2	47	171	5
Italy	3	0	0	3	35	196	3

POOL C

Fiji	67	**Namibia**	18
France	33	**Canada**	20
France	47	**Namibia**	13
Fiji	38	**Canada**	22
Canada	72	**Namibia**	11
France	28	**Fiji**	19

	P	W	D	L	F	A	Pts
France	3	3	0	0	108	52	9
Fiji	3	2	0	1	124	68	7
Canada	3	1	0	2	114	82	5
Namibia	3	0	0	3	42	186	3

POOL D

Wales	23	**Argentina**	18
Samoa	43	**Japan**	9
Wales	64	**Japan**	15
Argentina	32	**Samoa**	16
Wales	31	**Samoa**	38
Argentina	33	**Japan**	12

	P	W	D	L	F	A	Pts
Wales	3	2	0	1	118	71	7
Samoa	3	2	0	1	97	72	7
Argentina	3	2	0	1	83	51	7
Japan	3	0	0	3	36	140	3

POOL E

Ireland	53	**United States**	8
Australia	57	**Romania**	9
United States	25	**Romania**	27
Ireland	3	**Australia**	23
Australia	55	**United States**	19
Ireland	44	**Romania**	14

	P	W	D	L	F	A	Pts
Australia	3	3	0	0	135	31	9
Ireland	3	2	0	1	100	45	7
Romania	3	1	0	2	50	126	5
United States	3	0	0	3	52	135	3

PLAY-OFFS FOR QUARTER-FINAL PLACES

England	45	**Fiji**	24
Scotland	35	**Samoa**	20
Ireland	24	**Argentina**	28

QUARTER-FINALS

Wales	9	**Australia**	24
South Africa	44	**England**	21
France	47	**Argentina**	26
Scotland	18	**New Zealand**	30

SEMI-FINALS

South Africa	21	**Australia**	27
New Zealand	31	**France**	43

THIRD PLACE MATCH

South Africa	22	**New Zealand**	18

Fourth World Cup Final, Millennium Stadium, Cardiff Arms Park, 6 November 1999

AUSTRALIA 35 (2G 7PG) FRANCE 12 (4PG)

AUSTRALIA : M Burke; B N Tune, D J Herbert, T J Horan, J W Roff; S J Larkham, G M Gregan; R L L Harry, M A Foley, A T Blades, D T Giffin, J A Eales (captain), M J Cockbain, R S T Kefu, D J Wilson Substitutions J S Little for Herbert (46 mins); O D A Finegan for Cockbain (52 mins); M R Connors for Wilson (73 mins); D J Crowley for Harry (75 mins); J A Paul for Foley (85 mins); C J Whitaker for Gregan (86 mins); N P Grey for Horan (86 mins)

SCORERS TRIES : Tune, Finegan Conversions : Burke (2) Penalty Goals : Burke (7)

FRANCE : X Garbajosa; P Bernat Salles, R Dourthe, E Ntamack, C Dominici; C Lamaison, F Galthié; C Soulette, R Ibañez (captain), F Tournaire, A Benazzi, F Pelous, M Lièvremont, C Juillet, O Magne Substitutions O Brouzet for Juillet (HT); P de Villiers for Soulette (47 mins); A Costes for Magne (temp 19 to 22 mins) and for Lièvremont (67 mins); U Mola for Garbajosa (67 mins); S Glas for Dourthe (temp 49 to 55 mins and from 74 mins); S Castaignède for Galthié (76 mins); M Dal Maso for Ibañez (79 mins)

SCORER PENALTY GOALS : Lamaison (4)

REFEREE A J Watson (South Africa)

Getty Images

Australia captain John Eales [left] and George Gregan get their hands on the trophy in 1999.

FIFTH TOURNAMENT: 2003 IN AUSTRALIA

POOL A

Australia	24	**Argentina**	8
Ireland	45	**Romania**	17
Argentina	67	**Namibia**	14
Australia	90	**Romania**	8
Ireland	64	**Namibia**	7
Argentina	50	**Romania**	3
Australia	142	**Namibia**	0
Ireland	16	**Argentina**	15
Romania	37	**Namibia**	7
Australia	17	**Ireland**	16

	P	W	D	L	F	A	Pts
Australia	4	4	0	0	273	32	18
Ireland	4	3	0	1	141	56	14
Argentina	4	2	0	2	140	57	11
Romania	4	1	0	3	65	192	5
Namibia	4	0	0	4	28	310	0

POOL C

South Africa	72	**Uruguay**	6
England	84	**Georgia**	6
Samoa	60	**Uruguay**	13
England	25	**South Africa**	6
Samoa	46	**Georgia**	9
South Africa	46	**Georgia**	19
England	35	**Samoa**	22
Uruguay	24	**Georgia**	12
South Africa	60	**Samoa**	10
England	111	**Uruguay**	13

	P	W	D	L	F	A	Pts
England	4	4	0	0	255	47	19
South Africa	4	3	0	1	184	60	15
Samoa	4	2	0	2	138	117	10
Uruguay	4	1	0	3	56	255	4
Georgia	4	0	0	4	46	200	0

POOL B

France	61	**Fiji**	18
Scotland	32	**Japan**	11
Fiji	19	**United States**	18
France	51	**Japan**	29
Scotland	39	**United States**	15
Fiji	41	**Japan**	13
France	51	**Scotland**	9
United States	39	**Japan**	26
France	41	**United States**	14
Scotland	22	**Fiji**	20

	P	W	D	L	F	A	Pts
France	4	4	0	0	204	70	20
Scotland	4	3	0	1	102	97	14
Fiji	4	2	0	2	98	114	9
United States	4	1	0	3	86	125	6
Japan	4	0	0	4	79	163	0

POOL D

New Zealand	70	**Italy**	7
Wales	41	**Canada**	10
Italy	36	**Tonga**	12
New Zealand	68	**Canada**	6
Wales	27	**Tonga**	20
Italy	19	**Canada**	14
New Zealand	91	**Tonga**	7
Wales	27	**Italy**	15
Canada	24	**Tonga**	7
New Zealand	53	**Wales**	37

	P	W	D	L	F	A	Pts
New Zealand	4	4	0	0	282	57	20
Wales	4	3	0	1	132	98	14
Italy	4	2	0	2	77	123	8
Canada	4	1	0	3	54	135	5
Tonga	4	0	0	4	46	178	1

QUARTER-FINALS

New Zealand	29	**South Africa**	9
Australia	33	**Scotland**	16
France	43	**Ireland**	21
England	28	**Wales**	17

SEMI-FINALS

Australia	22	**New Zealand**	10
England	24	**France**	7

THIRD PLACE MATCH

New Zealand	40	**France**	13

Fifth World Cup Final, Telstra Stadium, Sydney, 22 November 2003

ENGLAND 20 (4PG 1DG 1T)
AUSTRALIA 17 (4PG 1T) *

ENGLAND: J Robinson; O J Lewsey, W J H Greenwood, M J Tindall, B C Cohen; J P Wilkinson, M J S Dawson; T J Woodman, S Thompson, P J Vickery, M O Johnson (captain), B J Kay, R A Hill, L B N Dallaglio, N A Back Substitutions: M J Catt for Tindall (78 mins); J Leonard for Vickery (80 mins); I R Balshaw for Lewsey (85 mins); L W Moody for Hill (93 mins)

SCORERS TRY: Robinson Penalty Goals: Wilkinson (4) Dropped Goal: Wilkinson

AUSTRALIA: M S Rogers; W J Sailor, S A Mortlock, E J Flatley, L Tuqiri; S J Larkham, G M Gregan (captain); W K Young, B J Cannon, A K E Baxter, J B Harrison, N C Sharpe, G B Smith, D J Lyons, P R Waugh Substitutions: D T Giffin for Sharpe (48 mins); J A Paul for Cannon (56 mins); M J Cockbain for Lyons (56 mins); J W Roff for Sailor (70 mins); M J Dunning for Young (92 mins); M J Giteau for Larkham (temp 18 to 30 mins; 55 to 63 mins; 85 to 93 mins)

SCORERS TRY: Tuqiri Penalty Goals: Flatley (4)

REFEREE A J Watson (South Africa)

* after extra time : 14-14 after normal time

Phil Walter/Getty Images

The alcohol flows as the England team celebrate their win in 2003.

RUGBY WORLD CUP RECORDS 1987–2007

(FINAL STAGES ONLY)

OVERALL RECORDS

MOST MATCHES WON IN FINAL STAGES

30	New Zealand
28	Australia
26	France
25	England

MOST OVERALL POINTS IN FINAL STAGES

249	J P Wilkinson	England	1999–2007
227	A G Hastings	Scotland	1987–95
195	M P Lynagh	Australia	1987–95
170	G J Fox	New Zealand	1987–91
163	A P Mehrtens	New Zealand	1995–99

MOST OVERALL TRIES IN FINAL STAGES

15	J T Lomu	New Zealand	1995–99
13	D C Howlett	New Zealand	2003–07
11	R Underwood	England	1987–95
11	J T Rokocoko	New Zealand	2003–07
11	C E Latham	Australia	1999–2007

MOST OVERALL CONVERSIONS IN FINAL STAGES

39	A G Hastings	Scotland	1987–95
37	G J Fox	New Zealand	1987–91
36	M P Lynagh	Australia	1987–95
29	D W Carter	New Zealand	2003–07
27	P J Grayson	England	1999–2003

MOST OVERALL PENALTIES IN FINAL STAGES

53	J P Wilkinson	England	1999–2007
36	A G Hastings	Scotland	1987–95
35	G Quesada	Argentina	1999–2003
33	M P Lynagh	Australia	1987–95
33	A P Mehrtens	New Zealand	1995–99

MOST OVERALL DROPPED GOALS IN FINAL STAGES

13	J P Wilkinson	England	1999–2007
6	J H de Beer	South Africa	1999
5	C R Andrew	England	1987–1995
5	G L Rees	Canada	1987–1999
4	J M Hernández	Argentina	2003–07

MOST MATCH APPEARANCES IN FINAL STAGES

22	J Leonard	England	1991–2003
20	G M Gregan	Australia	1995–2007
19	M J Catt	England	1995–2007
18	M O Johnson	England	1995–2003
18	B P Lima	Samoa	1991–2007
18	R Ibañez	France	1999–2007

MOST POINTS IN ONE COMPETITION

126	G J Fox	New Zealand	1987
113	J P Wilkinson	England	2003
112	T Lacroix	France	1995
105	P C Montgomery	South Africa	2007
104	A G Hastings	Scotland	1995
103	F Michalak	France	2003
102	G Quesada	Argentina	1999
101	M Burke	Australia	1999

MOST PENALTY GOALS IN ONE COMPETITION

31	G Quesada	Argentina	1999
26	T Lacroix	France	1995
23	J P Wilkinson	England	2003
21	G J Fox	New Zealand	1987
21	E J Flatley	Australia	2003
20	C R Andrew	England	1995

MOST TRIES IN ONE COMPETITION

8	J T Lomu	New Zealand	1999
8	B G Habana	South Africa	2007
7	M C G Ellis	New Zealand	1995
7	J T Lomu	New Zealand	1995
7	D C Howlett	New Zealand	2003
7	J M Muliaina	New Zealand	2003
7	D A Mitchell	Australia	2007

MOST DROPPED GOALS IN ONE COMPETITION

8	J P Wilkinson	England	2003
6	J H de Beer	South Africa	1999
5	J P Wilkinson	England	2007
4	J M Hernández	Argentina	2007

MOST CONVERSIONS IN ONE COMPETITION

30	G J Fox	New Zealand	1987
22	P C Montgomery	South Africa	2007
20	S D Culhane	New Zealand	1995
20	M P Lynagh	Australia	1987
20	L R MacDonald	New Zealand	2003
20	N J Evans	New Zealand	2007

MOST POINTS IN A MATCH

BY THE TEAM

145	New Zealand v Japan	1995
142	Australia v Namibia	2003
111	England v Uruguay	2003
108	New Zealand v Portugal	2007
101	New Zealand v Italy	1999
101	England v Tonga	1999

BY A PLAYER

45	S D Culhane	New Zealand v Japan	1995
44	A G Hastings	Scotland v Ivory Coast	1995
42	M S Rogers	Australia v Namibia	2003
36	T E Brown	New Zealand v Italy	1999
36	P J Grayson	England v Tonga	1999
34	J H de Beer	South Africa v England	1999
33	N J Evans	New Zealand v Portugal	2007
32	J P Wilkinson	England v Italy	1999

MOST TRIES IN A MATCH

BY THE TEAM

22	Australia v Namibia	2003
21	New Zealand v Japan	1995
17	England v Uruguay	2003
16	New Zealand v Portugal	2007
14	New Zealand v Italy	1999

BY A PLAYER

6	M C G Ellis	New Zealand v Japan	1995
5	C E Latham	Australia v Namibia	2003
5	O J Lewsey	England v Uruguay	2003
4	I C Evans	Wales v Canada	1987
4	C I Green	New Zealand v Fiji	1987
4	J A Gallagher	New Zealand v Fiji	1987
4	B F Robinson	Ireland v Zimbabwe	1991
4	A G Hastings	Scotland v Ivory Coast	1995
4	C M Williams	South Africa v Western Samoa	1995
4	J T Lomu	New Zealand v England	1995
4	K G M Wood	Ireland v United States	1999
4	J M Muliaina	New Zealand v Canada	2003
4	B G Habana	South Africa v Samoa	2007

MOST CONVERSIONS IN A MATCH

BY THE TEAM

20	New Zealand v Japan	1995
16	Australia v Namibia	2003
14	New Zealand v Portugal	2007
13	New Zealand v Tonga	2003
13	England v Uruguay	2003

BY A PLAYER

20	S D Culhane	New Zealand v Japan	1995
16	M S Rogers	Australia v Namibia	2003
14	N J Evans	New Zealand v Portugal	2007
12	P J Grayson	England v Tonga	1999
12	L R MacDonald	New Zealand v Tonga	2003

MOST PENALTY GOALS IN A MATCH

BY THE TEAM

8	Australia v South Africa	1999
8	Argentina v Samoa	1999
8	Scotland v Tonga	1995
8	France v Ireland	1995

BY A PLAYER

8	M Burke	Australia v South Africa	1999
8	G Quesada	Argentina v Samoa	1999
8	A G Hastings	Scotland v Tonga	1995
8	T Lacroix	France v Ireland	1995

MOST DROPPED GOALS IN A MATCH

BY THE TEAM

5	South Africa v England	1999
3	Fiji v Romania	1991
3	England v France	2003
3	Argentina v Ireland	2007

BY A PLAYER

5	J H de Beer	South Africa v England	1999
3	J P Wilkinson	England v France	2003
3	J M Hernández	Argentina v Ireland	2007

THE IRB 2007 AWARDS

THE GREAT AND THE GOOD

Emirates

By Iain Spragg

Dave Rogers/Getty Images

Clean sweep! Bryan Habana (left) the Player of the Year, Jake White the Coach of the Year and John Smit accepting South Africa's award as Team of the Year.

Bryan Habana was named the International Rugby Board Player of the Year for 2007 just 24 hours after helping South Africa claim the World Cup in Paris. The 24-year-old was an integral part of the Springbok side that dethroned England as world champions in the Stade de France and his outstanding performances in the build-up to and during the tournament made him the second South African after Schalk Burger in 2004 to be honoured with the annual award by the game's governing body.

The flying Blue Bulls wing scored eight tries in his seven appearances at the World Cup in France to equal Jonah Lomu's 1999 record for a single tournament and was one of the competition's shining lights as South Africa claimed a second world title after Francois Pienaar had led them to glory on home soil in 1995.

Habana was voted the world's best player by an independent panel of former internationals and every Test match played from the start of the 2007 Six Nations through to the World Cup final itself was taken into consideration. The panel was convened by Australia's 1999 World Cup-winning captain John Eales and featured Wales' Jonathan Davies, France's Fabien Galthie, England's Will Greenwood, Scotland's Gavin Hastings, America's Dan Lyle, Argentina's Federico Mendez, Pienaar and Ireland's Keith Wood, the inaugural IRB Player of the Year in 2001.

The Springbok speed merchant beat Argentinean duo Felipe Contepomi and Juan Hernandez, All Blacks flanker Richie McCaw and French centre Yannick Jauzion to the award on a night which is in association with Emirates Airline.

"I just wanted to help the team effort," Habana said after accepting his accolade at the sumptuous Pavillon d'Armenonville. "Everyone in the squad made a contribution – from number one to number 30."

South Africa captain John Smit led the tributes to his team-mate. "The thing I like about Bryan is, as good as he is on the field, he is as normal a South African as you would meet off the field," Smit said. "I think that is the beauty of his talent and how grateful he is for it."

Habana was first capped as a 21-year-old in 2004 and made a try-scoring debut against England at Twickenham. By the end of the World Cup campaign, he had scored 30 tries in 35 Test appearances for South Africa and was also instrumental in the Bulls' Super 14 final triumph over the Sharks – scoring a dramatic last-minute try that Derick Hougaard converted to win the match.

There was further recognition for South African rugby at the star-studded gala event in the French capital when Jake White was named the IRB Coach of the Year and the Springboks were unveiled as the IRB Team of the Year.

White succeeded New Zealand's Graham Henry as the world's leading coach and it was the second time in four years the 44-year-old had been acknowledged by his peers. White, who stepped down from his job after the World Cup final, was appointed Springboks coach in 2004 and guided the team to a first Tri-Nations title in six years in his first season in charge.

Other winners on the night were USA wing Takudzwa Ngwenya, who was awarded the IRPA Try of the Year award after beating Habana in a foot race in the Pool A clash between the Springboks and the States in Montpellier. A counter attack from the USA from inside their own 22 saw Ngwenya collect the ball just inside his own half and only Habana stood between him and the South African try line. The Springbok flyer known as 'Jet Shoes' had enjoyed the reputation as Test rugby's fastest player but the mantle passed to Ngwenya as the stepped in and then out and left Habana trailing in his wake for one of the tries of the World Cup.

There was also recognition in Paris for veteran France lock Fabien Pelous, who was awarded the IRPA Special Merit Award. The 33-year-old retired from international rugby after France's semi-final defeat to England and won 118 caps for his country, captaining Les Bleus with distinction on 42 occasions.

Meanwhile, the IRB Hall of Fame welcomed five new inductees in Paris. Rugby School and William Webb Ellis were the first to be inducted in 2006 and after a public vote on the IRB website and the deliberations of the induction panel chaired by IRB Chairman Dr Syd Millar, they are now joined by the legendary Baron Pierre de Coubertin, Wilson Whineray, Dr Danie Craven, Gareth Edwards and John Eales.

Frenchman de Coubertin founded the modern International Olympic Committee in Paris in 1894 but was also a rugby enthusiast and refereed the first ever French championship final between Racing Club and Stade Francais two years earlier.

Former All Black Whineray played 32 Tests for New Zealand between 1957 and 1965 and was captain in 30 of them. He is often cited as the greatest All Black captain of all time and his team lost just four times under his inspired leadership.

Legendary Springbok Craven made his debut for South Africa as a 21-year-old against Wales in Swansea in 1931 and was regarded the best scrum-half in the world during the decade. He won 16 caps for his country but is best remembered for his 37 years as the head of the SARFU before his death in 1993 and his efforts to end the Springboks' sporting exile on the world stage.

Wales' youngest ever captain at the age of just 20, Edwards is still regarded by many as the greatest scrum-half ever to play the game and is destined to be forever remembered for that try for the Barbarians against the All Blacks at the Arms Park in 1973. He played 53 times for his country and 10 times for the British & Irish Lions, playing a key role in the sides that clinched the 1971 series in New Zealand and the 1974 series in South Africa.

The final inductee, Eales played 86 times for the Wallabies and is one of an exclusive group of players to have won the World Cup twice. The goal-kicking second row was part of the 1991 side that beat England 12–6 at Twickenham and was captain of the Australian team that regained the Webb Ellis trophy eight years later when they beat France 35–12 in Cardiff.

Other IRB award winners were New Zealand in the Sevens Team of the Year category. The All Blacks were crowned World Seven Series champions in 2006–07 for the seventh time in the eight year history of the event while Afeleki Pelenise was named the Sevens Player of the Year.

The IRB Development Award went to Jacob Thompson for his services to rugby on the island of Jamaica over the last 30 years while the Vernon Pugh Award for Distinguished Service was given to Jose Maria Epalza of Spain. A former captain and then coach of the Spanish national team, Epalza spent nine years as the FIRA-AER representative on the IRB Executive Committee.

The IRB Referee Award for Distinguished Service was given to Dick Byres following his retirement in January 2007. Byres refereed 14 Test matches during his career and was subsequently appointed to the IRB Referee Selector panel in 1997

Australia's Sarah Corrigan, meanwhile, was named the IRB Women's Personality of the Year. Corrigan became the first female to referee at an IRB XVs tournament outside the Women's Rugby World Cup when she took charge of the IRB Under-19 World Championship match between Zimbabwe and Canada.

There were also awards for Kiwi youngster Robert Fruean, who was named the IRB's Under-19 Player of the Year and Argentinean Nicolás Pueta, who was given the Spirit of Rugby Award. Pueta plays for St. Andrew's FP in Argentina – despite missing most of his left leg – and was a worthy recipient of the award.

Frankie Deges

Nicolás Pueta's incredible achievement of playing – and captaining his side in Argentinean club rugby – with most of his leg missing was recognised as he received the Spirit of Rugby award.

WORLD CUP KITS 2007

ARGENTINA

AUSTRALIA

CANADA

ENGLAND

FIJI

FRANCE

GEORGIA

IRELAND

ITALY

JAPAN

NAMIBIA

NEW ZEALAND

PORTUGAL

ROMANIA

SAMOA

SCOTLAND

SOUTH AFRICA

TONGA

USA

WALES

FULL LIST OF IRB AWARDS WINNERS

IRB Player of the Year – Bryan Habana, South Africa
IRB Team of the Year – South Africa
IRB Coach of the Year – Jake White, South Africa
IRB Under 19 Player of the Year – Robert Fruean, New Zealand
IRB Sevens Team of the Year – New Zealand
IRB Sevens Player of the Year – Afeleke Pelenise, New Zealand
IRB Women's Personality of the Year – Sarah Corrigan

(In association with Emirates Airline)
IRB Referee Award for Distinguished Service – Dick Byres
Vernon Pugh Award for Distinguished Service – Jose Maria Epalza
IRB Development Award – Jacob Thompson
Spirit of Ruby Award – Nicolás Pueta
IRPA Try of the Year – Takudzwa Ngwenya, USA
IRPA Special Merit Award – Fabien Pelous, France
IRB Hall of Fame inductees – Baron Pierre de Coubertin, Wilson Whineary, Dr Danie Craven, Gareth Edwards, John Eales

Getty Images

IRB Player of the Year Bryan Habana.

IRB WORLD RANKINGS

ALL CHANGE AT THE TOP

By Dominic Rumbles

New Zealand's reign at the top of the IRB World Rankings finally came to end in 2007. After a record 40 months at the top of the standings, Graham Henry's side were finally overhauled by new world champions South Africa, who moved to the top of the rankings following their 15–9 victory over England in the Rugby World Cup final.

Rugby World Cup 2007 proved to be gripping throughout and the closeness of the competition was reflected in the rankings where there were some notable movers during the tournament. World Cup matches count for double in the Rankings and a team can gain a massive 1.5 times the standard amount if they win by more than 15 points.

Argentina announced their arrival as a major contender on the world stage by reaching the semi-finals for the first time and their winning run, which included notable victories over France (twice) and Ireland, saw them end the year third, their highest-ever IRB World Rankings position.

England's roller-caster campaign also saw them climb in rankings terms. Despite being overhauled by Argentina on the weekend of the final in Paris, Brian Ashton's side underlined what was an incredible recovery to the campaign by returning to the top four for the first time since February 2006.

Tournament hosts France finished the World Cup with defeat to Argentina in an entertaining Bronze Final at Parc des Princes. The defeat was France's third of the tournament and second to Argentina and proved to be costly as Bernard Laporte's last hurrah as coach saw France slip from a third to sixth.

Ireland entered the World Cup with high hopes after a year that saw them consistently positioned inside the top four after a solid RBS Six Nations campaign. However a disappointing World Cup campaign saw Eddie O'Sullivan's side fail to reach the quarter-finals and this was reflected in the rankings.

Indeed, following defeats to both Argentina and France, Ireland slipped from a high of second to finish the year in seventh.

Fiji were valiant in reaching the quarter-finals and their success on the pitch was reflected in their rankings elevation. Entering the tournament 12th in the standings, victories over Canada, Japan and Wales saw Illie Tabua's side climb inside the top ten for the first time since 2005.

Scotland and Wales retained their places inside the top 10 and Scotland's qualification for the quarter-finals resulted in elevation from 11th to eighth, highlighting the progress made under Frank Hadden, while Italy slipped to 11th after a campaign that failed to live up to the high standards set during the RBS Six Nations where they reached a peak of eighth.

Tonga, who started World Cup in 16th after an abject IRB Pacific Nations Cup campaign, climbed three places to 13th after a first victory over rivals Samoa in a decade. Georgia, Romania and Japan all made strides, while Portugal, competing in their first World Cup, finished the year in 22nd.

Away from Rugby World Cup there was much jostling for position during an action-packed year that included an entertaining FIRA-AER Championship, IRB Nations Cup, IRB Pacific Nations Cup and CAR Africa Cup.

Spain continued their progress on the European stage, moving up to 21st, while Finland moved off the bottom of the table for the first time, swapping with Bosnia and Herzagovina.

Started in 2003, the IRB World Rankings are published every week on www.irb.com and are calculated using a 'points exchange' system, in which teams take points off each other based on the match result. Whatever one side gains, the other loses.

The exchanges are based on the match result, the relative strength of the team, and the margin of victory. There is also an allowance for home advantage.

Aside from the World Cup all other international matches are treated the same to be as fair as possible to countries playing a different mix of competitive matches across the globe.

All IRB Member Unions have a rating, typically between 0 and 100. The top side in the world will usually have a rating above 90. Any match that is not a full international between the two countries does not count at all.

See www.irb.com

IRB WORLD RANKINGS 22.10.07

POSITION (Previous position)	MEMBER UNION	RATING POINTS
1(2)	SOUTH AFRICA	90.89
2(1)	NEW ZEALAND	89.63
3(6)	ARGENTINA	87.56
4(3)	ENGLAND	85.61
5(5)	AUSTRALIA	84.21
6(4)	FRANCE	80.43
7(7)	IRELAND	78.66
8(8)	SCOTLAND	76.83
9(9)	FIJI	75.82
10(10)	WALES	74.08
11(11)	ITALY	73.51
12(12)	SAMOA	71.58
13(13)	TONGA	71.50
14(14)	ROMANIA	67.61
15(15)	CANADA	66.95
16(16)	GEORGIA	66.61
17(17)	JAPAN	65.33
18(18)	RUSSIA	64.37
19(19)	USA	64.34
20(20)	URUGUAY	62.66
21(21)	SPAIN	62.32
22(22)	PORTUGAL	60.92
23(23)	KOREA	58.02
24(24)	CHILE	57.07
25(25)	NAMIBIA	56.91
26(26)	GERMANY	56.67
27(27)	MOLDOVA	54.84
28(28)	HONG KONG	54.65
29(29)	MOROCCO	54.15
30(30)	PARAGUAY	53.82
31(31)	POLAND	53.43
32(32)	BELGIUM	52.38
33(33)	BRAZIL	52.31
34(34)	CZECH REPUBLIC	51.97
35(35)	TUNISIA	51.58
36(36)	KAZAKHSTAN	50.90
37(37)	UKRAINE	50.89
38(38)	UGANDA	50.23
39(39)	SWEDEN	49.84
40(40)	MADAGASCAR	49.80
41(41)	LATVIA	49.43
42(42)	KENYA	49.29
43(43)	CHINESE TAIPEI	49.22
44(44)	IVORY COAST	49.19
45(45)	CHINA	48.74
46(46)	NETHERLANDS	48.41

47(47)	ARABIAN GULF	47.32
48(48)	CROATIA	46.28
49(49)	SRI LANKA	46.21
50(50)	COOK ISLANDS	45.87
51(51)	SWITZERLAND	45.12
52(52)	PAPUA NEW GUINEA	45.09
53(53)	SINGAPORE	44.91
54(54)	MALTA	44.89
55(55)	LITHUANIA	44.86
56(56)	DENMARK	44.64
57(57)	ZIMBABWE	44.45
58(58)	TRINIDAD & TOBAGO	43.97
59(59)	CAYMAN	43.87
60(60)	VENEZUELA	43.40
61(61)	BARBADOS	43.13
62(62)	ANDORRA	42.68
63(63)	SLOVENIA	42.42
64(64)	PERU	41.75
65(65)	BERMUDA	41.69
66(66)	COLOMBIA	41.69
67(67)	SENEGAL	41.44
68(68)	HUNGARY	41.44
69(69)	NIUE ISLANDS	40.96
70(70)	MALAYSIA	40.64
71(71)	ZAMBIA	40.64
72(72)	GUYANA	40.35
73(73)	SERBIA	40.33
74(74)	THAILAND	40.00
75(75)	ST. VINCENT & THE GRENADINES	39.30
76(76)	SOLOMON ISLANDS	39.06
77(77)	JAMAICA	38.97
78(78)	MONACO	38.81
79(79)	BOTSWANA	38.64
80(80)	LUXEMBOURG	38.40
81(81)	CAMEROON	38.26
82(82)	SWAZILAND	37.57
83(83)	ST. LUCIA	37.57
84(84)	INDIA	37.54
85(85)	AUSTRIA	36.99
86(86)	NORWAY	36.90
87(87)	GUAM	36.80
88(88)	TAHITI	36.25
89(89)	NIGERIA	36.00
90(90)	BAHAMAS	35.61
91(91)	BULGARIA	34.91
92(92)	VANUATU	34.77
93(93)	ISRAEL	32.74
94(94)	FINLAND	31.71
95(95)	BOSNIA & HERZEGOVINA	29.25

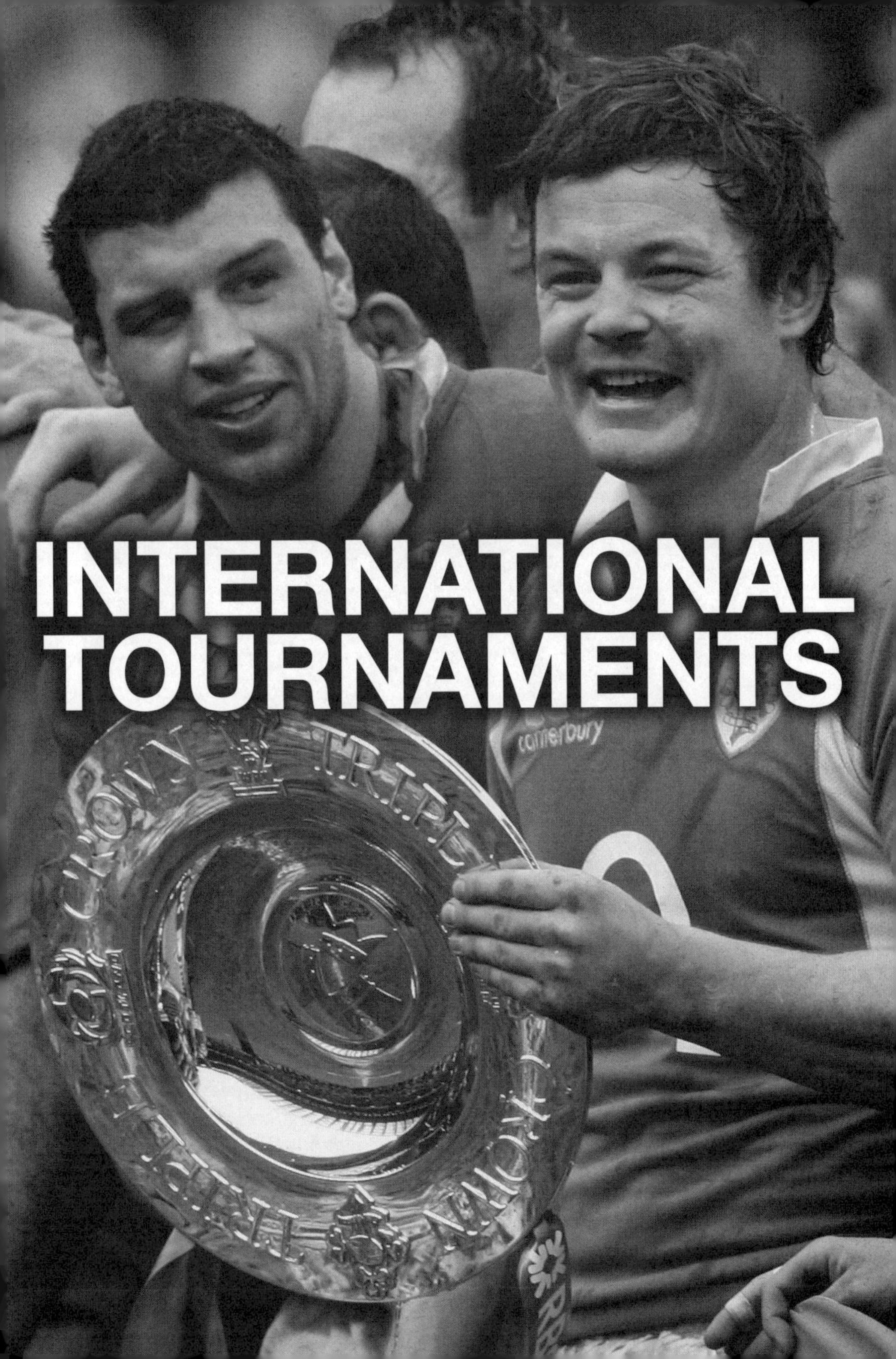

INTERNATIONAL TOURNAMENTS

FRANCE STAGE THE ULTIMATE LATE, LATE SHOW

By Will Greenwood

Alex Livesey/Getty Images

France snatched the 2007 Six Nations with a last-minute try against Scotland.

A second successive Championship triumph for France, a genuine surprise or two and equal measures of quality and infuriating inconsistency – the 2007 RBS Six Nations was a tournament that refused to become predictable even if the final standings would suggest otherwise.

Both France and Ireland's inability to claim the Grand Slam – the third successive season without a clean sweep – said it all. Here was a tournament with some excellent rugby, superb individual performances and dramatic climaxes, yet no one side was capable of stamping their absolute authority on proceedings and lifting themselves above the pack. It was a Championship that failed, albeit narrowly, to fire on all cylinders.

Of course, the final round of games were dramatic. The last-minute tries for Italy against Ireland in the Stadio Flaminio and then, hours later, for France against Scotland in the Stade de France decided the destination of the trophy and it's impossible to argue they weren't moments of pure tension for players and fans alike as the respective television match officials weighed up their decisions.

The staggered kick-off times on the final Saturday of the Championship generated a lot of debate. We all know the demands of the television companies in the modern era. It's a way of life for professional rugby but I'm definitely an advocate of all six teams playing at the same time in the final round of matches. It provides everyone with a level playing field.

I think it also shows a lack of faith in the drama the Championship supplies. Yes, what happened in Rome and then Paris was exciting but I firmly believe it would have been equally, if not more nerve-wracking if all the games started at the same time and, from a television viewer's perspective, the broadcaster cut to whichever ground when there was a score. There were three teams with a real or at least mathematical chance of winning the Championship on the final weekend and I think simultaneous kick-off times would have enhanced rather than diluted the tension.

France celebrated their third title in four years but I'm not sure whether their celebrations after beating Scotland in Paris would have been as joyous as Bernard Laporte had hoped for. To be crowned champions of the northern hemisphere just months before they host the World Cup was far from a disaster but once again Les Bleus raised almost as many questions as answers about their credentials.

The 20 minutes they produced in the first half against Ireland at Croke Park was the best period of rugby I saw throughout the whole tournament and the way France coped with the atmosphere in Dublin to snatch the game at the death spoke volumes for the character of the team. Lionel Nallet, Jerome Thion and Pascal Pape were awesome while Raphaël Ibanez lead from the front with a performance that belied the miles on his clock.

Yet a month later the same side took to the pitch at Twickenham to face an England side that was still licking its wounds after getting pounded in Dublin and they just didn't play. England did a good job of subduing the French but Laporte must, if only privately, still have been worrying which team would turn up come the World Cup.

I'm sure Ireland were delighted with a second successive Triple Crown but it's measure of the progress they've made under Eddie O'Sullivan that another Home Nations clean sweep is becoming something of an irrelevance to them. Ireland are a team reaching the peak of their powers and I think 2007 was an opportunity missed.

More than once they had the Grand Slam within their grasp and twice – at home to France and away to Italy – they shot themselves in the foot at the last. It was a season they had both France and England in Dublin and they could, perhaps should have gone through unbeaten.

There's no doubt they missed Brian O'Driscoll against the French at Croke Park but the game was there to be won and they failed to close it out. In contrast, the performance against England demonstrated what a dangerous, abrasive and effective side Ireland are capable of being.

O'Sullivan had a settled and experienced squad by now and for me Gordon D'Arcy was the man of the tournament. A few people had questioned whether he would ever recapture the form he showed when he was voted Player of the Tournament in 2004 but I think he answered all the sceptics.

For England it was a season of changes in terms of both personnel and the coaching staff. Ironically, although they began the Championship with a resounding win over Scotland and signed off with defeat in the Millennium Stadium, I'd argue England actually looked a stronger, more rounded side in March than they did at the beginning of February.

But some of the problems of recent seasons persisted. The team still seemed incapable of combating sides that played with tempo and rhythm – as Ireland did for 80 minutes and Wales for the first 20 – and Ashton must have been acutely aware England struggled when other teams put together multiple phases of play.

The good news for the coach was the emergence of new players like David Strettle, Nick Easter, Toby Flood and Shane Geraghty and if England can marry the young talent with some of the older heads, they will be heading in the right direction.

Italy's fourth place finish represented genuine progress for the Azzurri and two wins in the Championship for the first time since they joined the party must have pleased Pierre Berbizier enormously. It was certainly tremendous for Italian rugby.

In previous seasons Italy have had maybe one or two world-class players and 13 other club players making up the numbers. That ratio shifted in 2007 and

TRIVIA

The Italians won two games for the first time since they turned the Five Nations into Six in 2000. They worked hard for it, making more tackles (409) than any other side in the tournament! Rugby World Magazine's Team of the Tournament contained seven Irishmen: Girvan Dempsey; Sean Lamont, Brian O'Driscoll, Gordon D'Arcy, Jason Robinson; Ronan O'Gara, Harry Ellis; Olivier Milloud, Raphaël Ibanez, Pieter de Villiers, Donncha O'Callaghan, Paul O'Connell, Alix Popham, David Wallace and Ryan Jones.

they now boast perhaps seven genuine Test players. They are undoubtedly a side improving year on year.

I was particularly impressed with the midfield partnership of Mirco Bergamasco and Gonzalo Canale and I think they'd fancy themselves, with some justification, against any centre pairing in the world. I think Italy still have a problem at ten but if they can unearth a good fly-half, they will continue to make progress.

Wales had a disappointing season, even more so when you consider they had the same set of fixtures in 2007 and as they did in 2005 – the year they won the Grand Slam.

Beating England at the Millennium Stadium on the final weekend meant they avoided the Wooden Spoon but there were in truth relatively few other crumbs of comfort for the team.

The tone for the campaign was set by the opening day defeat to Ireland in Cardiff and speaking from experience, I know how hard it is to bounce back when you start a tournament with a loss. It saps confidence and Wales then had three successive games on the road, which was always going to be a huge ask.

The controversy of their defeat in Rome and the mix-up with the referee as to whether they had enough time for a line-out catch and drive will probably rankle with the Wales players for a while but I think they've got to hold their hands up and take their share of their blame.

It wasn't all doom and gloom though. James Hook looked like a player who's going to be wearing the red shirt with distinction for years while Ryan Jones and Alun-Wyn Jones supplied plenty of energy and drive in the pack.

After their encouraging third place finish in 2006, Scotland took a step backwards in 2007 and once again the old problem of consistency reared its ugly head. The loss of Jason White to injury exposed the chronic lack of depth in their squad and although they were competitive in both the France and Wales games, as well as giving Ireland a run for their money, the overall impression was of a side lacking a cutting edge and a little confidence.

The real body blow, however, was the defeat to Italy. Scotland committed hari-kari in the first six or so minutes when they gift-wrapped three tries for the Italians and they were unable to recover.

Simon Taylor looked back to something like his best form, while Rob Dewey and Chris Cusiter both made big contributions, but Scotland were still disappointing.

RBS SIX NATIONS 2007: FINAL TABLE

	P	W	D	L	For	Against	Pts
France	5	4	0	1	155	86	**8**
Ireland	5	4	0	1	149	84	**8**
England	5	3	0	2	119	115	**6**
Italy	5	2	0	3	94	147	**4**
Wales	5	1	0	4	86	113	**2**
Scotland	5	1	0	4	95	153	**2**

Points: Win 2; Draw 1; Defeat 0.

There were 698 points scored at an average of 46.5 a match. The Championship record (803 points at an average of 53.5 a match) was set in 2000. Ronan O'Gara was the leading individual points scorer (for the second year running) with 82, seven points shy of the Championship record Jonny Wilkinson set in 2001. Jason Robinson and Ronan O'Gara were the Championship's leading try-scorers with four each.

Stu Forster/Getty Images

Italy made a breakthrough in 2007 – with Alessandro Troncon back in the side – grabbing their first away win in the Six Nations

MATCH STATS

3 February, Stadio Flaminio, Rome

ITALY 3 (1PG) FRANCE 39 (4G 2PG 1T)

ITALY: R de Marigny; A Masi, G-J Canale, Mirco Bergamasco, D Dallan; A Scanavacca, P Griffen; S Perugini, F Ongaro, C Nieto, S Dellape, M Bortolami (*captain*), J Sole, S Parisse, Mauro Bergamasco *Substitutions:* R Pez for Scanavacca (12 mins); C Festuccia for Ongaro (48 mins); A Lo Cicero for Perugini (48 mins); M-L Castrogiovanni for Nieto (48 mins); R Mandelli for Dellape (68 mins); A Troncon for Griffen (70 mins); K Robertson for Canale (77 mins)

SCORER *Penalty Goal:* Pez

FRANCE: C Poitrenaud; C Dominici, Y Jauzion, F Fritz, C Heymans; D Skrela, P Mignoni; O Milloud, R Ibañez (*captain*), P de Villiers, L Nallet, J Thion, S Betsen, S Chabal, J Bonnaire *Substitutions:* D Szarzewski for Ibañez (57 mins); S Marconnet for Milloud (57 mins); I Harinordoquy for Bonnaire (66 mins); L Beauxis for Fritz (67 mins); P Papé for Chabal (71 mins); Milloud for De Villiers (75 mins)

SCORERS *Tries:* Chabal (2), Dominici, Heymans, Jauzion *Conversions:* Skrela (4) *Penalty Goals:* Skrela, Beauxis

REFEREE W Barnes (England)

3 February, Twickenham

ENGLAND 42 (2G 5PG 1DG 2T) SCOTLAND 20 (2G 2PG)

ENGLAND: O Morgan; O J Lewsey, M J Tindall, A Farrell, J T Robinson; J P Wilkinson, H A Ellis; P T Freshwater, G S Chuter, P J Vickery (*captain*), L P Deacon, D J Grewcock, J P R Worsley, M E Corry, M B Lund *Substitutions:* T Rees for Worsley (61 mins); L A Mears for Chuter (73 mins); J M White for Vickery (73 mins); T Flood for Wilkinson (73 mins)

SCORERS *Tries:* Robinson (2), Wilkinson, Lund *Conversions:* Wilkinson (2) *Penalty Goals:* Wilkinson (5) *Dropped Goal:* Wilkinson

SCOTLAND: H F G Southwell; S F Lamont, M P di Rollo, A R Henderson, C D Paterson (*captain*); D A Parks, C P Cusiter; G Kerr, D W H Hall, E A Murray, J L Hamilton, A D Kellock, S M Taylor, D A Callam, K D R Brown *Substitutions:* A F Jacobsen for Kerr (55 mins); A Hogg for Brown (61 mins); R E Dewey for Henderson (61 mins); S Murray for Kellock (temp 52 to 61 mins) and for Hamilton (61 mins); R W Ford for Hall (63 mins); R G M Lawson for Cusiter (66 mins); R P Lamont for Parks (68 mins); Kerr for E Murray (73 mins)

SCORERS *Tries:* Taylor, Dewey *Conversions:* Paterson (2) *Penalty Goals:* Paterson (2)

REFEREE M Jonker (South Africa)

4 February, Millennium Stadium, Cardiff

WALES 9 (3PG) IRELAND 19 (2G 1T)

WALES: K A Morgan; H N Luscombe, J P Robinson, J Hook, C D Czekaj; S M Jones (*captain*), D J Peel; G D Jenkins, T R Thomas, C L Horsman, I M Gough, A W Jones, A J Popham, R P Jones, M E Williams *Substitutions:* D J Jones for Horsman (55 mins); A Brew for Luscombe (59 mins); M Rees for T R Thomas (66 mins); R A Sidoli for Gough (temp 43 to 50 mins and 70 mins); M Phillips for Peel (72 mins); G V Thomas for R P Jones (temp 30 to 36 mins) and for Williams (72 mins)

SCORER *Penalty Goals:* S M Jones (3)

IRELAND: G T Dempsey; A Trimble, B G O'Driscoll (*captain*), G M D'Arcy, D A Hickie; R J R O'Gara, P A Stringer; M J Horan, R Best, J J Hayes, D F O'Callaghan, P J O'Connell, S H Easterby, D P Leamy, D P Wallace *Substitutions:* J Flannery for Best (64 mins); G E A Murphy for Hickie (temp 24 to 35 mins) and for O'Driscoll (74 mins)

SCORERS *Tries:* Best, O'Driscoll, O'Gara *Conversions:* O'Gara (2)

REFEREE K M Deaker (New Zealand)

10 February, Twickenham

ENGLAND 20 (5PG 1T) ITALY 7 (1G)

ENGLAND: I R Balshaw; O J Lewsey, M J Tindall, A Farrell, J T Robinson; J P Wilkinson, H A Ellis; P T Freshwater, G S Chuter, P J Vickery (*captain*), L P Deacon, D J Grewcock, N Easter, M E Corry, M B Lund *Substitutions:* M Tait for Balshaw (37 mins); T Flood for Tindall (66 mins); L A Mears for Chuter (69 mins); J M White for Freshwater (69 mins); T Palmer for Grewcock (69 mins); T Rees for Easter (75 mins)

SCORERS *Try:* Robinson *Penalty Goals:* Wilkinson (5)

ITALY: R de Marigny; K Robertson, G-J Canale, Mirco Bergamasco, D Dallan; A Scanavacca, A Troncon; A Lo Cicero, C Festuccia, M-L Castrogiovanni, S Dellape, M Bortolami (*captain*), J Sole, S Parisse, M Zaffiri *Substitutions:* R Pez for Scanavacca (temp 14 to 20 mins); M Pratichetti for Dallan (26 mins); S Perugini for Lo Cicero (57 mins); V Bernabo for Dellape (69 mins); R Mandelli for Zaffiri (74 mins)

SCORER *Try:* Scanavacca *Conversion:* Scanavacca

REFEREE N Owens (Wales)

YELLOW CARD M Bortolami (37 mins)

10 February, Murrayfield

SCOTLAND 21 (7PG) WALES 9 (3PG)

SCOTLAND: H F G Southwell; S F Lamont, M P di Rollo, R E Dewey, C D Paterson (*captain*); P J Godman, C P Cusiter; G Kerr, D W H Hall, E A Murray, J L Hamilton, S Murray, S M Taylor, D A Callam, K D R Brown *Substitutions:* N J Hines for Hamilton (48 mins); A F Jacobsen for Kerr (55 mins); A Hogg for Brown (55 mins); R W Ford for Hall (67 mins); S L Webster for Godman (69 mins); N Walker for Lamont (69 mins); R G M Lawson for Cusiter (74 mins)

SCORER *Penalty Goals:* Paterson (7)

WALES: K A Morgan; M A Jones, J P Robinson, J Hook, C D Czekaj; S M Jones (*captain*), D J Peel; D J Jones, T R Thomas, A R Jones, R A Sidoli, A W Jones, A J Popham, R P Jones, M E Williams *Substitutions:* T G L Shanklin for Hook (40 mins); I M Gough for Sidoli (52 mins); G D Jenkins for D Jones (58 mins); J Thomas for M Williams (67 mins); M Rees for M Williams (temp 58 to 66 mins) and for T R Thomas (66 mins); C Sweeney for Morgan (temp 45 to 52 mins)

SCORER *Penalty Goals:* S M Jones (3)

REFEREE A Lewis (Ireland)

YELLOW CARD T R Thomas (56 mins)

11 February, Croke Park, Dublin

IRELAND 17 (4PG 1T) FRANCE 20 (2G 2PG)

IRELAND: G T Dempsey; G E A Murphy, G M D'Arcy, S P Horgan, D A Hickie; R J R O'Gara, I J Boss; M J Horan, R Best, J J Hayes, D F O'Callaghan, P J O'Connell (*captain*), S H Easterby, D P Leamy, D P Wallace *Substitutions:* J Flannery for R Best (60 mins); A Trimble for Murphy (60 mins); N Best for Easterby (64 mins)

SCORER *Try:* O'Gara *Penalty Goals:* O'Gara (4)

FRANCE: C Poitrenaud; C Dominici, D Marty, Y Jauzion, V Clerc; D Skrela, P Mignoni; S Marconnet, R Ibañez (*captain*), P de Villiers, L Nallet, P Papé, S Betsen, S Chabal, I Harinordoquy *Substitutions:* J Thion for Papé (50 mins); J Bonnaire for Chabal (53 mins); L Beauxis for Skrela (56 mins); O Milloud for De Villiers (59 mins); S Bruno for Ibañez (74 mins); C Heymans for Poitrenaud (74 mins)

SCORERS *Tries:* Ibañez, Clerc *Conversions:* Skrela, Beauxis *Penalty Goals:* Skrela (2)

REFEREE S R Walsh (New Zealand)

24 February, Murrayfield

SCOTLAND 17 (2G 1PG) ITALY 37 (4G 3PG)

SCOTLAND: H F G Southwell; S F Lamont, M P di Rollo, R E Dewey, C D Paterson (*captain*); P J Godman, C P Cusiter; G Kerr, D W H Hall, E A Murray, N J Hines, S Murray, S M Taylor, D A Callam, K D R Brown *Substitutions:* A Hogg for Callam (49 mins); A F Jacobsen for E Murray (temp 38 to 40 mins) and for Kerr (49 mins); N Walker for Godman (58 mins); R W Ford for Hall (58 mins); R G M Lawson for Cusiter (66 mins); J L Hamilton for S Murray (73 mins); A R Henderson for Dewey (75 mins)

SCORERS *Tries:* Dewey, Paterson *Conversions:* Paterson (2) *Penalty Goal:* Paterson

ITALY: R de Marigny; K Robertson, G-J Canale, Mirco Bergamasco, A Masi; A Scanavacca, A Troncon; A Lo Cicero, C Festuccia, M-L Castrogiovanni, S Dellape, M Bortolami (*captain*), A Zanni, S Parisse, Mauro Bergamasco *Substitutions:* C Nieto for Castrogiovanni (16 mins); M Zaffiri for Masi (33 mins); F Ongaro for Festuccia (58 mins); S Perugini for Lo Cicero (58 mins); V Bernabo for Dellape (63 mins); R Pez for Scanavacca (79 mins)

SCORERS *Tries:* Scanavacca, Mauro Bergamasco, Robertson, Troncon *Conversions:* Scanavacca (4) *Penalty Goals:* Scanavacca (3)

REFEREE D M Courtney (Ireland)

YELLOW CARDS S M Taylor (19 mins); G-J Canale (78 mins)

24 February, Croke Park, Dublin

IRELAND 43 (4G 5PG) ENGLAND 13 (1G 2PG)

IRELAND: G T Dempsey; S P Horgan, B G O'Driscoll (*captain*), G M D'Arcy, D A Hickie; R J R O'Gara, P A Stringer; M J Horan, R Best, J J Hayes, D F O'Callaghan, P J O'Connell, S H Easterby, D P Leamy, D P Wallace *Substitutions:* J Flannery for R Best (62 mins); N Best for Easterby (68 mins); S J Best for Hayes (70 mins); A Trimble for O'Driscoll (72 mins); I J Boss for Stringer (76 mins); P Wallace for O'Gara (76 mins); M R O'Driscoll for Leamy (76 mins)

SCORERS *Tries:* Dempsey, D P Wallace, Horgan, Boss *Conversions:* O'Gara (3), P Wallace *Penalty Goals:* O'Gara (5)

ENGLAND: O Morgan; O J Lewsey, M J Tindall, A Farrell, D Strettle; J P Wilkinson, H A Ellis; P T Freshwater, G S Chuter, P J Vickery (*captain*), L P Deacon, D J Grewcock, J P R Worsley, M E Corry, M B Lund *Substitutions:* M Tait for Morgan (29 mins); T Rees for Lund (40 mins); J M White for Freshwater (43 mins); T Palmer for Grewcock (53 mins); L A Mears for Chuter (71 mins); S Perry for Ellis (71 mins)

SCORERS *Try:* Strettle *Conversion:* Wilkinson *Penalty Goals:* Wilkinson (2)

REFEREE J Jutge (France)

YELLOW CARD D J Grewcock (28 mins)

24 February, Stade de France, Paris

FRANCE 32 (2G 6PG) WALES 21 (3G)

FRANCE: C Poitrenaud; C Dominici, D Marty, Y Jauzion, V Clerc; D Skrela, P Mignoni; O Milloud, R Ibañez (*captain*), N Mas, L Nallet, J Thion, S Betsen, E Vermeulen, J Bonnaire *Substitutions:* S Marconnet for Mas (62 mins); I Harinordoquy for Vermeulen (67 mins); L Beauxis for Skrela (75 mins); B August for Ibañez (75 mins); G Lamboley for Nallet (75 mins)

SCORERS *Tries:* Dominici, Nallet *Conversions:* Skrela (2) *Penalty Goals:* Skrela (5), Beauxis

WALES: L M Byrne; S M Williams, T G L Shanklin, J Hook, M A Jones; S M Jones (*captain*), D J Peel; G D Jenkins, M Rees, C L Horsman, I M Gough, A W Jones, A J Popham, R P Jones, M E Williams *Substitutions:* J P Robinson for M A Jones (45 mins); D J Jones for Horsman (52 mins); M Phillips for Peel (63 mins); J Thomas for Popham (65 mins); B J Cockbain for A W Jones (temp 37 to 40 mins) and for Gough (69 mins); T R Thomas for Rees (71 mins)

SCORERS *Tries:* Popham, Shanklin, Robinson *Conversions:* S M Jones (3)

REFEREE A J Spreadbury (England)

10 March, Murrayfield

SCOTLAND 18 (6PG) IRELAND 19 (1G 4PG)

SCOTLAND: H F G Southwell; C D Paterson (*captain*), M P di Rollo, R E Dewey, S F Lamont; D A Parks, C P Cusiter; G Kerr, D W H Hall, E A Murray, N J Hines, S Murray, S M Taylor, D A Callam, K D R Brown *Substitutions:* R P Lamont for Southwell (40 mins); A Hogg for Callam (53 mins); R G M Lawson for Cusiter (57 mins); A F Jacobsen for Kerr (60 mins); R W Ford for Hall (60 mins); A R Henderson for Di Rollo (65 mins); J L Hamilton for S Murray (77 mins)

SCORER *Penalty Goals:* Paterson (6)

IRELAND: G T Dempsey; S P Horgan, B G O'Driscoll (*captain*), G M D'Arcy, D A Hickie; R J R O'Gara, P A Stringer; S J Best, R Best, J J Hayes, D F O'Callaghan, P J O'Connell, S H Easterby, D P Leamy, D P Wallace *Substitutions:* J Flannery for R Best (60 mins); N Best for Easterby (67 mins)

SCORER *Try:* O'Gara *Conversion:* O'Gara *Penalty Goals:* O'Gara (4)

REFEREE D Pearson (England)

YELLOW CARD N J Hines (41 mins)

10 March, Stadio Flaminio, Rome

ITALY 23 (2G 3PG) WALES 20 (2G 2PG)

ITALY: R de Marigny; K Robertson, G-J Canale, Mirco Bergamasco, M Pratichetti; R Pez, A Troncon; A Lo Cicero, C Festuccia, C Nieto, S Dellape, M Bortolami (*captain*), A Zanni, S Parisse, Mauro Bergamasco *Substitutions:* M Zaffiri for Canale (21 mins); S Perugini for Lo Cicero (58 mins); F Staibano for Nieto (58 mins); V Bernabo for Zanni (temp 61 to 69 mins)

SCORERS *Tries:* Mauro Bergamasco, Robertson *Conversions:* Pez (2) *Penalty Goals:* Pez (3)

WALES: K A Morgan; S M Williams, T G L Shanklin, J Hook, M A Jones; S M Jones (*captain*), D J Peel; G D Jenkins, M Rees, C L Horsman, I M Gough, A W Jones, A J Popham, R P Jones, M E Williams *Substitutions:* A R Jones for Horsman (56 mins); D J Jones for Jenkins (61 mins); J Thomas for R P Jones (70 mins); G Thomas for S M Jones (temp 28 to 40 mins and 74 mins); T R Thomas for Rees (77 mins)

SCORERS *Tries:* S M Williams, Rees *Conversions:* S M Jones, Hook *Penalty Goals:* Hook (2)

REFEREE C White (England)

11 March, Twickenham

ENGLAND 26 (2G 4PG) FRANCE 18 (6PG)

ENGLAND: O J Lewsey; D Strettle, M J Tindall, M J Catt (*captain*), J T Robinson; T Flood, H A Ellis; T A N Payne, G S Chuter, J M White, M E Corry, T Palmer, J P R Worsley, N Easter, T Rees *Substitutions:* S Geraghty for Flood (58 mins); M Tait for Strettle (73 mins); L P Deacon for Palmer (73 mins); M B Lund for Worsley (73 mins); S Perry for Catt (77 mins)

SCORERS *Tries:* Flood, Tindall *Conversions:* Flood, Geraghty *Penalty Goals:* Flood (3), Geraghty

FRANCE: C Poitrenaud; C Dominici, D Marty, Y Jauzion, V Clerc; D Skrela, D Yachvili; O Milloud, R Ibañez (*captain*), P de Villiers, L Nallet, J Thion, S Betsen, S Chabal, J Bonnaire *Substitutions:* L Beauxis for Skrela (40 mins); I Harinordoquy for Chabal (48 mins); S Bruno for Ibañez (67 mins); C Heymans for Poitrenaud (74 mins); P Mignoni for Yachvili (74 mins)

SCORERS *Penalty Goals:* Skrela (3), Yachvili (3)

REFEREE J I Kaplan (South Africa)

17 March, Stadio Flaminio, Rome

ITALY 24 (1G 2PG 2DG 1T)
IRELAND 51 (4G 1PG 4T)

ITALY: R de Marigny; K Robertson, E Galon, Mirco Bergamasco, M Pratichetti; R Pez, A Troncon; S Perugini, C Festuccia, C Nieto, S Dellape, M Bortolami (*captain*), A Zanni, S Parisse, M Zaffiri *Substitutions:* J Sole for Zaffiri (2 mins); A Scanavacca for Pez (40 mins); F Staibano for Perugini (52 mins); M Barbini for Galon (62 mins); V Bernabo for Parisse (65 mins); S Perugini for Nieto (67 mins); P Griffen for Troncon (79 mins); L Ghiraldini for Festuccia (79 mins)

SCORERS *Tries:* Bortolami, De Marigny *Conversion:* Scanavacca *Penalty Goals:* Pez (2) *Dropped Goals:* Pez (2)

IRELAND: G T Dempsey; S P Horgan, B G O'Driscoll (*captain*), G M D'Arcy, D A Hickie; R J R O'Gara, P A Stringer; M J Horan, R Best, J J Hayes, D F O'Callaghan, M R O'Driscoll, S H Easterby, D P Leamy, D P Wallace *Substitutions:* T Hogan for M O'Driscoll (53 mins); A Trimble for B O'Driscoll (59 mins); J Flannery for R Best (60 mins); S J Best for Horan (65 mins); M J Horan for S Best (79 mins)

SCORERS *Tries:* Dempsey (2), Hickie (2), Easterby, D'Arcy, Horgan, O'Gara *Conversions:* O'Gara (4) *Penalty Goal:* O'Gara

REFEREE J I Kaplan (South Africa)

17 March, Stade de France, Paris

FRANCE 46 (5G 2PG 1T) SCOTLAND 19 (2G 1T)

FRANCE: C Poitrenaud; V Clerc, D Marty, Y Jauzion, C Heymans; L Beauxis, P Mignoni; O Milloud, R Ibañez (*captain*), P de Villiers, L Nallet, J Thion, S Betsen, I Harinordoquy, J Bonnaire *Substitutions:* P Papé for Nallet (55 mins); D Traille for Poitrenaud (73 mins); E Vermeulen for Harinordoquy (77 mins); C Dominici for Clerc (77 mins)

SCORERS *Tries:* Harinordoquy, Jauzion, Marty, Heymans, Milloud, Vermeulen *Conversions:* Beauxis (5) *Penalty Goals:* Beauxis (2)

SCOTLAND: C D Paterson (*captain*); S F Lamont, R E Dewey, A R Henderson, N Walker; D A Parks, R G M Lawson; G Kerr, R W Ford, E A Murray, N J Hines, S Murray, S M Taylor, J W Beattie, A Hogg *Substitutions:* J L Hamilton for S Murray (47 mins); D A Callam for Beattie (52 mins); R P Lamont for Parks (52 mins); C P Cusiter for Lawson (61 mins); A F Jacobsen for Kerr (64 mins); D W H Hall for Ford (64 mins); M P di Rollo for Henderson (77 mins)

SCORERS *Tries:* Walker, S Lamont, E Murray *Conversions:* Paterson (2)

REFEREE C Joubert (South Africa)

YELLOW CARD S F Lamont (60 mins)

17 March, Millennium Stadium, Cardiff

WALES 27 (1G 4PG 1DG 1T)
ENGLAND 18 (1G 1PG 1DG 1T)

WALES: K A Morgan; S M Williams, T G L Shanklin, G Thomas (*captain*), M A Jones; J Hook, D J Peel; G D Jenkins, M Rees, C L Horsman, I M Gough, A W Jones, A J Popham, R P Jones, M E Williams *Substitutions:* A R Jones for Horsman (62 mins); M Phillips for Peel (68 mins); J Thomas for Popham (68 mins); D J Jones for Jenkins (69 mins); T R Thomas for Rees (72 mins)

SCORERS *Tries:* Hook, Horsman *Conversion:* Hook *Penalty Goals:* Hook (4) *Dropped Goal:* Hook

ENGLAND: M J Cueto; D Strettle, M Tait, M J Catt (*captain*), J T Robinson; T Flood, H A Ellis; T A N Payne, G S Chuter, J M White, M E Corry, T Palmer, J Haskell, J P R Worsley, T Rees *Substitutions:* M B Lund for Worsley (8 mins); S Geraghty for Catt (41 mins); L P Deacon for Palmer (57 mins); S Perry for Ellis (69 mins); L A Mears for Chuter (74 mins); S Turner for Payne (75 mins)

SCORERS *Tries:* Ellis, Robinson *Conversion:* Flood *Penalty Goal:* Flood *Dropped Goal:* Flood

REFEREE A C Rolland (Ireland)

Dave Rogers/Getty Images

Ireland missed a Grand Slam but under captain Brian O'Driscoll [above] still picked up a coveted Triple Crown

INTERNATIONAL CHAMPIONSHIP RECORDS 1883–2007

PREVIOUS WINNERS

1883 England	1884 England	1885 Not completed
1886 England & Scotland	1887 Scotland	1888 Not completed
1889 Not completed	1890 England & Scotland	1891 Scotland
1892 England	1893 Wales	1894 Ireland
1895 Scotland	1896 Ireland	1897 Not completed
1898 Not completed	1899 Ireland	1900 Wales
1901 Scotland	1902 Wales	1903 Scotland
1904 Scotland	1905 Wales	1906 Ireland & Wales
1907 Scotland	1908 Wales	1909 Wales
1910 England	1911 Wales	1912 England & Ireland
1913 England	1914 England	1920 England & Scotland & Wales
1921 England	1922 Wales	1923 England
1924 England	1925 Scotland	1926 Scotland & Ireland
1927 Scotland & Ireland	1928 England	1929 Scotland
1930 England	1931 Wales	1932 England & Ireland & Wales
1933 Scotland	1934 England	1935 Ireland
1936 Wales	1937 England	1938 Scotland
1939 England & Ireland & Wales	1947 England & Wales	1948 Ireland
1949 Ireland	1950 Wales	1951 Ireland
1952 Wales	1953 England	1954 England & Wales & France
1955 Wales & France	1956 Wales	1957 England
1958 England	1959 France	1960 England & France
1961 France	1962 France	1963 England
1964 Scotland & Wales	1965 Wales	1966 Wales
1967 France	1968 France	1969 Wales
1970 Wales & France	1971 Wales	1972 Not completed
1973 Five Nations tie	1974 Ireland	1975 Wales
1976 Wales	1977 France	1978 Wales
1979 Wales	1980 England	1981 France
1982 Ireland	1983 Ireland & France	1984 Scotland
1985 Ireland	1986 Scotland & France	1987 France
1988 Wales & France	1989 France	1990 Scotland
1991 England	1992 England	1993 France
1994 Wales	1995 England	1996 England
1997 France	1998 France	1999 Scotland
2000 England	2001 England	2002 France
2003 England	2004 France	2005 Wales
2006 France	2007 France	

England have won the title outright 25 times; Wales 23; France 16; Scotland 14; Ireland 10; Italy 0.

TRIPLE CROWN WINNERS

England (23 times) 1883, 1884, 1892, 1913, 1914, 1921, 1923, 1924, 1928, 1934, 1937, 1954, 1957, 1960, 1980, 1991, 1992, 1995, 1996, 1997, 1998, 2002, 2003.

Wales (18 times) 1893, 1900, 1902, 1905, 1908, 1909, 1911, 1950, 1952, 1965, 1969, 1971, 1976, 1977, 1978, 1979, 1988, 2005.

Scotland (10 times) 1891, 1895, 1901, 1903, 1907, 1925, 1933, 1938, 1984, 1990.

Ireland (Nine times) 1894, 1899, 1948, 1949, 1982, 1985, 2004, 2006, 2007.

GRAND SLAM WINNERS

England (12 times) 1913, 1914, 1921, 1923, 1924, 1928, 1957, 1980, 1991, 1992, 1995, 2003.

Wales (Nine times) 1908, 1909, 1911, 1950, 1952, 1971, 1976, 1978, 2005.

France (Eight times) 1968, 1977, 1981, 1987, 1997, 1998, 2002, 2004.

Scotland (Three times) 1925, 1984, 1990.

Ireland (Once) 1948.

THE SIX NATIONS CHAMPIONSHIP 2000–2007: COMPOSITE SEVEN-SEASON TABLE

	P	W	D	L	Pts
France	40	30	0	10	**60**
Ireland	40	29	0	11	**58**
England	40	27	0	13	**54**
Wales	40	15	2	23	**32**
Scotland	40	12	1	27	**25**
Italy	40	5	1	34	**11**

CHIEF RECORDS

RECORD	DETAIL		SET
Most team points in season	229 by England	in five matches	2001
Most team tries in season	29 by England	in five matches	2001
Highest team score	80 by England	80-23 v Italy	2001
Biggest team win	57 by England	80-23 v Italy	2001
Most team tries in match	12 by Scotland	v Wales	1887
Most appearances	56 for Ireland	C M H Gibson	1964 - 1979
Most points in matches	429 for England	J P Wilkinson	1998 - 2007
Most points in season	89 for England	J P Wilkinson	2001
Most points in match	35 for England	J P Wilkinson	v Italy, 2001
Most tries in matches	24 for Scotland	I S Smith	1924 - 1933
Most tries in season	8 for England	C N Lowe	1914
	8 for Scotland	I S Smith	1925
Most tries in match	5 for Scotland	G C Lindsay	v Wales, 1887
Most cons in matches	77 for England	J P Wilkinson	1998 - 2007
Most cons in season	24 for England	J P Wilkinson	2001
Most cons in match	9 for England	J P Wilkinson	v Italy, 2001
Most pens in matches	93 for Wales	N R Jenkins	1991 - 2001
Most pens in season	18 for England	S D Hodgkinson	1991
	18 for England	J P Wilkinson	2000
	18 for France	G Merceron	2002
Most pens in match	7 for England	S D Hodgkinson	v Wales, 1991
	7 for England	C R Andrew	v Scotland, 1995
	7 for England	J P Wilkinson	v France, 1999
	7 for Wales	N R Jenkins	v Italy, 2000
	7 for France	G Merceron	v Italy, 2002
	7 for Scotland	C D Paterson	v Wales, 2007
Most drops in matches	9 for France	J-P Lescarboura	1982 - 1988
	9 for England	C R Andrew	1985 - 1997
Most drops in season	5 for France	G Camberabero	1967
	5 for Italy	D Dominguez	2000
	5 for Wales	N R Jenkins	2001
	5 for England	J P Wilkinson	2003
Most drops in match	3 for France	P Albaladejo	v Ireland, 1960
	3 for France	J-P Lescarboura	v England, 1985
	3 for Italy	D Dominguez	v Scotland 2000
	3 for Wales	N R Jenkins	v Scotland 2001

Getty Images

Doug Howlett and Joe Rokocoko protect the Tri-Nations trophy (right) and Bledisloe Cup (left, with Howlett).

KIWIS MAKE IT A HAT-TRICK

By Michael Lynagh

History will probably reflect on the 2007 Tri-Nations as the tournament that was played in the shadow of an impending World Cup. People were talking about the World Cup even before the Tri-Nations kicked-off and there was a sense that the games were effectively trials for later in the year.

I couldn't disagree with that argument but I thought all three teams succeeded at playing some good stuff through the competition. It was obvious that many of the selection decisions by the coaches were made with the World Cup in mind and they experimented with their squads but there was still plenty of good rugby on display.

New Zealand, of course, made it a hat-trick of titles. I don't think many neutrals expected a different outcome at the start of the tournament and they were worthy winners in the end. Graham Henry, perhaps more than John Connolly or Jake White, took the opportunity to try out some new combinations in his starting line-up but winning the title was still vitally important for the All Blacks as the number one ranked side and he must have been satisfied with a mission accomplished.

In the process, New Zealand justified their billing as the pre-tournament favourites for the World Cup and although I didn't feel they were at their fluent best throughout, they moved through the gears smoothly enough and surely didn't lose any sleep at some occasional rustiness in their game.

The shock of the competition came in Melbourne when Australia beat the All Blacks, which was a result that woke up the rest of the rugby world. New Zealand had been building up something of an invincible reputation before the tournament and to see the Kiwis downed, as I did working on the Sky Sports coverage, was a revelation.

It's obvious where my loyalties lie as an ex-Wallaby but I genuinely thought it was a good result for the Tri-Nations and the world game. The All Blacks

Sandra Mu/Getty Images

New Zealand won a titanic final match against Australia 26–12 in Auckland to clinch the title.

were the outstanding team in the competition but it never does the game any harm to see the best side beaten. It was my highlight of the tournament.

Off the pitch, there was considerable controversy when Jake White decided to take what was effectively a shadow Springbok squad to Australia and New Zealand for the second half of the competition. I don't think there's any doubt it undermined the integrity of the Tri-Nations – and probably no coincidence that South Africa lost in Sydney and Christchurch – but I have to say I can understand his decision.

He wanted to rest the personnel he considered his key players and he was entitled to do that. The four-year cycle of having to compete in the World Cup and the Tri-Nations within months of each other tests everyone's playing resources and White decided to spread the workload.

It's easy to forget New Zealand withdrew their All Black contingent from the first half of the Super 14 earlier in the year for exactly the same reason. Graham Henry didn't want his top players exhausted by the time the World Cup came around. White felt the same and did what he felt was best for the Springbok team.

I thought the shortened format of 2007 – four games instead of six – actually tested the players' endurance more than usual. They were required to travel long distances in relatively short periods of time and that must have been hard work.

Of course, the travel integral to a Tri-Nations tournament has always been an issue and, unfortunately, one of the reasons I'm not sure Argentina should or will ever be invited to the party. It was a debate that resurfaced towards the end of the 2007 tournament but I just can't see how it could work logistically.

There's certainly no argument from me that the Pumas deserve a place in an international tournament on a regular basis. Argentina is a country with a proper rugby culture and the national team has made great strides on the pitch in recent years.

The problem is, and always will be, geography.

One of the biggest dilemmas facing the game's administrators is the amount of travel the modern calendar demands of the players and Argentina joining the Tri-Nations, or even the Six Nations, would only add to the already heavy burden.

It would be a terrible shame to keep Argentina in isolation but I think a lot more thought has to go into how to end it.

But back to the 2007 Tri-Nations and the champions New Zealand. A third successive triumph in the tournament was a great achievement. Yet again they were to be shot at but they held their nerve and while I thought the Wallabies and Springboks had managed to close the gap in comparison to recent years, the All Blacks seemed to have a bit left in the tank.

In fact, I'd have to say on the evidence of 2007 that New Zealand were capable of putting two teams out capable of claiming the title. Their strength in depth was phenomenal and Henry had the luxury of knowing his best XV and he took the chance to experiment with his impact players.

Their best performance was without doubt the win in Durban. It was a match they could have lost but they proved they could chase a game down from behind with two late tries from Richie McCaw and Joe Rokocoko.

I was amazed Dan Carter received a fair bit of criticism, especially after the Durban game. True, by his own exceptionally high standards, he was quiet but no-one can produce superhuman performances week after week after week.

It was also ominous that while Carter was slightly off colour, Aaron Mauger in the All Black midfield was sensational and saw them through. He took up the reins and proved just what a strong, rounded side New Zealand were.

Australia probably gained the most from the tournament in terms of confidence. I thought they were just going through the motions in 2006 but their win over New Zealand in Melbourne proved they could beat anyone again and there were definite signs John Connolly was making progress with the team.

They lost to South Africa in Cape Town at the start of the tournament and although a loss is a loss, I thought it was a great performance that set the tone for the rest of the campaign. Australia had virtually no ball to work with but hung in and were only beaten by a late drop goal.

The Wallaby defence looked strong in every game and the scrum – the side's Achilles Heel for the past few years – finally looked more competitive. It wasn't a weapon but it certainly wasn't the liability it has been in previous seasons.

In terms of personnel, George Gregan seemed to thrive without the extra responsibility of the captaincy and had a good tournament while Stirling Mortlock underlined his reputation as a big-match player. In the pack, Nathan Sharpe went well and was arguably one of the most consistent performers in the competition.

It wasn't a vintage Tri-Nations for South Africa and one win from four was nothing to write home about. They should have buried Australia at Newlands with the amount of possession they had throughout the game and that for me was their fundamental flaw throughout the tournament.

The problem with South Africa's game was they didn't seem to have a Plan B when their attempts to overpower the opposition didn't work. The Springboks looked bereft of ideas when the battering ram approach failed and other teams must know that they will always be in with a shout of beating them if they can weather the physical storm.

South Africa added more pace out wide and looked dangerous on the break from long range but that isn't the same as creating space. The likes of Bryan Habana are capable of going the length of the pitch given the opportunity but I would have liked to see the team carving out the chances rather than seizing on spilled ball. Waiting to pounce on the opposition's mistakes isn't a rounded game plan in itself.

The South African pack was as abrasive as ever and I thought the back row in particular was impressive, regardless of which players White picked. They continue to produce a succession of talented and physical back row forwards and Pierre Spies and Schalk Burger were both very influential in the opening games of the tournament. Victor Matfield was brilliant in the Springboks second row and had a dominant competition in the lineout.

Overall, I felt South Africa's performances revealed White had more work to do with the side but the signs of genuine progress were in evidence. I think any Springbok coach will have to wrestle with the dilemma of what style of game to play but White seemed to have taken a step or two closer to finding the answer.

Michael Lynagh is part of Sky Sports Tri-Nations commentary team

TRI NATIONS 2007: FINAL TABLE

	P	W	D	L	F	A	Bonus	Pts
New Zealand	4	3	0	1	100	59	**1**	**13**
Australia	4	2	0	2	76	80	**1**	**9**
South Africa	4	1	0	3	66	103	**1**	**5**

Points: win 4; draw 2; four or more tries, or defeat by seven or fewer points 1

16 June, Newlands, Cape Town

SOUTH AFRICA 22 (1G, 3PG, 2DG)
AUSTRALIA 19 (1G, 4PG)

SOUTH AFRICA: P C Montgomery; A K Willemse, J Fourie, J de Villiers, J-P R Pietersen; A D James, R Pienaar; G G Steenkamp, J W Smit (*captain*), B J Botha, J P Botha, V Matfield, J H Smith, P J Spies, S W P Burger *Substitutions:* G van G Botha for Smit (10 mins); D J Rossouw for Smith (53 mins); C J van der Linde for B J Botha (60 mins); F P L Steyn for Willemse (60 mins); G J Muller for J P Botha (62 mins); B J Botha back for Steenkamp (67 mins); W Olivier for Pietersen

SCORERS *Try*: Fourie *Conversion*: Montgomery *Penalty Goals*: Montgomery (3) *Dropped Goals:* Steyn (2)

AUSTRALIA: J L Huxley; L D Tuqiri, S A Mortlock (*captain*), M J Giteau, D A Mitchell; S J Larkham, G M Gregan; M J Dunning, S T Moore, G T Shepherdson, N C Sharpe, D J Vickerman, R D Elsom, W L Palu, G B Smith *Substitutions:* M D Chisholm for Elsom (57 mins); P R Waugh for Smith (57 mins); A L Freier for Moore (62 mins); A K E Baxter for Shepherdson (75 mins); S A Hoiles for Palu (79 mins); A P Ashley-Cooper for Mortlock (79 mins)

SCORERS *Try*: Giteau *Conversion*: Mortlock *Penalty Goals:* Mortlock (4)

REFEREE W Barnes (England)

YELLOW CARD P J Spies (35 mins)

23 June, ABSA Stadium, King's Park, Durban

SOUTH AFRICA 21 (1G, 3PG, 1T)
NEW ZEALAND 26 (2G, 3PG, 1DG)

SOUTH AFRICA: P C Montgomery; A K Willemse, J Fourie, J de Villiers, J-P R Pietersen; A D James, R Pienaar; J P du Randt, G van G Botha, B J Botha, J P Botha, V Matfield (*captain*), D J Rossouw, R B Skinstad, S W P Burger *Substitutions:* P J Wannenburg for Skinstad (52 mins); F P L Steyn for James (52 mins); C J van der Linde for Du Randt (53 mins); G J Muller for J P Botha (65 mins); W Olivier for Willemse (65 mins); Du Randt back for B J Botha (69 mins)

SCORERS *Tries*: Burger, James *Conversion*: Montgomery *Penalty Goals*: Montgomery (2), Pienaar

NEW ZEALAND: J M Muliaina; J T Rokocoko, I Toeava, A J D Mauger, S W Sivivatu; D W Carter, B T Kelleher; T D Woodcock, A D Oliver, C J Hayman, T V Flavell, G P Rawlinson, J Collins, R So'oialo, R H McCaw (*captain*) *Substitutions:* R A Filipo for Rawlinson (46 mins); K F Mealamu for Oliver (51 mins); C L McAlister for Mauger (66 mins); L R MacDonald for Muliaina (69 mins); P A T Weepu for Kelleher (69 mins)

SCORERS *Tries*: McCaw, Rokocoko *Conversions*: Carter (2) *Penalty Goals*: Carter (3) *Dropped Goal:* Mauger

REFEREE A C Rolland (Ireland)

YELLOW CARD P J Wannenburg (54 mins)

Alexander Joe/Getty Images

South Africa were stunned in Durban as New Zealand roared back to win 26–21.

30 June, Melbourne Cricket Ground

AUSTRALIA 20 (2G, 2PG) NEW ZEALAND 15 (1G, 1PG, 1T)

AUSTRALIA: J L Huxley; L D Tuqiri, S A Mortlock (*captain*), M J Giteau, A P Ashley-Cooper; S J Larkham, G M Gregan; M J Dunning, S T Moore, G T Shepherdson, N C Sharpe, D J Vickerman, R D Elsom, W L Palu, G B Smith *Substitutions:* S A Hoiles for Palu (40 mins); A L Freier for Moore (47 mins); S N G Staniforth for Gregan (55 mins); M D Chisholm for Elsom (70 mins); P R Waugh for Smith (70 mins); A K E Baxter for Dunning (77 mins)

SCORERS *Tries*: Ashley-Cooper, Staniforth *Conversions*: Giteau (2) *Penalty Goals:* Mortlock (2)

NEW ZEALAND: J M Muliaina; R L Gear, C L McAlister, A J D Mauger, J T Rokocoko; D W Carter, B T Kelleher; T D Woodcock, A D Oliver, C J Hayman, C R Jack, T V Flavell, J Collins, R So'oialo, R H McCaw (*captain*) *Substitutions:* R A Filipo for Flavell (45 mins); K F Mealamu for Oliver (45 mins); N S Tialata for Woodcock (45 mins); P A T Weepu for Kelleher (50 mins); M C Masoe for So'oialo (74 mins); S W Sivivatu for Rokocoko (75 mins); Woodcock back for Collins (temp 66 to 71 mins)

SCORERS *Tries*: Woodcock, Gear *Conversion*: Carter *Penalty Goal*: Carter

REFEREE M Jonker (South Africa)

YELLOW CARD C J Hayman (61 mins)

7 July, Telstra Stadium, Sydney

AUSTRALIA 25 (2G, 2PG, 1T)
SOUTH AFRICA 17 (2G, 1PG)

AUSTRALIA: J L Huxley; M A Gerrard, S A Mortlock (*captain*), M J Giteau, A P Ashley-Cooper; S J Larkham, G M Gregan; M J Dunning, A L Freier, G T Shepherdson, N C Sharpe, D J Vickerman, R D Elsom, S A Hoiles, G B Smith *Substitutions:* A K E Baxter for Shepherdson (58 mins); H J McMeniman for Elsom (60 mins); D J Lyons for Hoiles (64 mins); S P Hardman for Freiar (temp 20 to 32 mins and 47 mins); P R Waugh for Smith (71 mins); Shepherdson back for Dunning (73 mins); S N G Staniforth for Giteau (78 mins); D A Mitchell for Ashley-Cooper (78 mins)

SCORERS *Tries*: Gerrard, Hoiles, Giteau *Conversions*: Mortlock (2) *Penalty Goals:* Mortlock (2)

SOUTH AFRICA: B A Fortuin; B P Paulse, W M Murray, W Olivier, J-P R Pietersen; D J Hougaard, R Pienaar; C J van der Linde, G van G Botha, J N du Plessis, J N Ackermann, G J Muller, P J Wannenburg, R B Skinstad (*captain*), J L van Heerden *Substitutions:* P A van den Berg for Ackermann (29 mins); J Cronjé for Wannenburg (49 mins); B W du Plessis for Cronjé (temp 58 to 62 mins) and for Skinstad (62 mins); E P Andrews for J du Plessis (73 mins); M Claassens for Fortuin (73 mins); P J Grant for Hougaard (73 mins)

SCORERS *Tries*: Van Heerden, Paulse *Conversions*: Hougaard (2) *Penalty Goal*: Hougaard

REFEREE P G Honiss (New Zealand)

YELLOW CARDS G van G Botha (52 mins); G J Muller (75 mins)

14 July, Jade Stadium, Christchurch

NEW ZEALAND 33 (3G, 4PG)
SOUTH AFRICA 6 (2PG)

NEW ZEALAND: J M Muliaina; D C Howlett, I Toeava, C L McAlister, J T Rokocoko; D W Carter, P A T Weepu; T D Woodcock, K F Mealamu, C J Hayman, C R Jack, K J Robinson, R D Thorne, R So'oialo, R H McCaw (*captain*) *Substitutions:* B G Leonard for Weepu (53 mins); J Collins for Robinson (63 mins); N J Evans for Howlett (72 mins); M C Masoe for So'oialo (72 mins); A K Hore for Mealamu (72 mins); N S Tialata for Hayman (76 mins); C G Smith for Toeava (76 mins)

SCORERS *Tries*: Leonard, Evans, Carter *Conversions*: Carter (3) *Penalty Goals*: Carter (4)

SOUTH AFRICA: J-P R Pietersen; B P Paulse, W M Murray, W Olivier, J C Pretorius; D J Hougaard, R Pienaar; C J van der Linde, B W du Plessis, J N du Plessis, P A van den Berg, G J Muller (*captain*), P J Wannenburg, J Cronjé, J L van Heerden *Substitutions:* P J Grant for Hougaard (56 mins); G van G Botha for B W du Plessis (67 mins); G J J Britz for Wannenburg (67 mins); T Chavhanga for Pretprius (72 mins); H Lobberts for Van Heerden (76 mins); E P Andrews for Van der Linde (76 mins); M Claassens for Paulse (76 mins);

SCORER *Penalty Goals*: Hougaard (2)

REFEREE S J Dickinson (Australia)

YELLOW CARD P J Wannenburg (52 mins)

21 July, Eden Park, Auckland

NEW ZEALAND 26 (7PG, 1T) AUSTRALIA 12 (3PG, 1DG)

NEW ZEALAND: J M Muliaina; D C Howlett, I Toeava, C L McAlister, J T Rokocoko; D W Carter, B T Kelleher; T D Woodcock, A D Oliver, C J Hayman, C R Jack, K J Robinson, R D Thorne, R So'oialo, R H McCaw (*captain*) *Substitutions:* B G Leonard for Kelleher (48 mins); K F Mealamu for Oliver (48 mins); N J Evans for Toeava (75 mins)

SCORERS *Try*: Woodcock *Penalty Goals*: Carter (7)

AUSTRALIA: A P Ashley-Cooper; M A Gerrard, S A Mortlock (*captain*), M J Giteau, D A Mitchell; S J Larkham, G M Gregan; M J Dunning, S T Moore, G T Shepherdson, N C Sharpe, D J Vickerman, R D Elsom, S A Hoiles, G B Smith *Substitutions:* C E Latham for Mitchell (44 mins); H J McMeniman for Elsom (62 mins); P R Waugh for Hoiles (62 mins); A K E Baxter for Shepherdson (70 mins); A L Freier for Moore (73 mins); S N G Staniforth for Giteau (76 mins); M D Chisholm for Vickerman (77 mins)

SCORERS *Penalty Goals:* Mortlock (3) *Dropped Goal:* Giteau

REFEREE N Owens (Wales)

Dave Rogers/Getty Images

Dan Carter scored seven penalties in New Zealand's final victory.

TRI NATIONS RECORDS 1996–2007

PREVIOUS WINNERS

1996 New Zealand	1997 New Zealand	1998 South Africa	1999 New Zealand
2000 Australia	2001 Australia	2002 New Zealand	2003 New Zealand
2004 South Africa	2005 New Zealand	2006 New Zealand	2007 New Zealand

GRAND SLAM WINNERS

New Zealand (3 times) 1996, 1997, 2003.

South Africa (Once) 1998.

TEAM RECORD	DETAIL		SET
Most team points in season	179 by N Zealand	in six matches	2006
Most team tries in season	18 by S Africa	in four matches	1997
Highest team score	61 by S Africa	61-22 v Australia (h)	1997
Biggest team win	49 by Australia	49-0 v S Africa (h)	2006
Most team tries in match	8 by S Africa	v Australia	1997
INDIVIDUAL RECORD	**DETAIL**		**SET**
Most appearances	48 for Australia	G M Gregan	1996 to 2007
Most points in matches	328 for N Zealand	A P Mehrtens	1996 to 2004
Most points in season	99 for N Zealand	D W Carter	2006
Most points in match	29 for N Zealand	A P Mehrtens	v Australia (h) 1999
Most tries in matches	16 for N Zealand	C M Cullen	1996 to 2002
Most tries in season	7 for N Zealand	C M Cullen	2000
Most tries in match	3 for N Zealand	J T Rokocoko	v Australia (a) 2003
	3 for S Africa	M C Joubert	v N Zealand (h) 2004
	3 for N Zealand	D C Howlett	v Australia (h) 2005
Most cons in matches	34 for N Zealand	A P Mehrtens	1996 to 2004
Most cons in season	14 for N Zealand	D W Carter	2006
Most cons in match	6 for S Africa	J H de Beer	v Australia (h),1997
Most pens in matches	82 for N Zealand	A P Mehrtens	1996 to 2004
Most pens in season	21 for N Zealand	D W Carter	2006
Most pens in match	9 for N Zealand	A P Mehrtens	v Australia (h) 1999

From 1996 to 2007 inclusive, each nation played four matches in a season, except in 2006 when the nations each played six matches.

YOUNG ENGLAND STORM HOME

John Gichigi/Getty Images

The England Saxons seem pretty pleased with their win in the final.

England claimed the Churchill Cup for a third time in five years as they beat a much-fancied New Zealand Maori side at Twickenham and in the process gave beleaguered English rugby fans a timely fillip.

On the same day as a depleted England first team were being heavily mauled by the Springboks in Pretoria, a youthful Saxons side (England A team) upset the odds in London with a 17-13 victory over the Maori, the first time the England second string had beaten the Kiwis in the five-year history of the competition.

It was the first time the Churchill Cup had been staged outside Canada and America and England made the most of their home advantage in an entertaining final that was ultimately settled by a thrilling try from replacement second row Tom Croft with less than five minutes remaining on the clock.

"This has capped a fantastic three weeks for us," said Saxons coach Jim Mallinder. "We've come together as a team and proven we can play whatever style of rugby we need to win. Throughout the tournament we've been saying how important the whole squad will be and how we need all seven subs to come on a do a job.

"A good few players here must have put their hands up for selection for Brian Ashton's World Cup training squad."

England and New Zealand Maori progressed to the final from their respective groups with relative ease.

The Saxons put the USA to the sword in their group opener at Edgeley Park, running in nine unanswered tries in a 51-3 demolition of the Americans while the Maori were equally impressive against Canada at Franklin's Gardens, also crossing nine times in a 59-23 win.

England were made to work a little harder against Scotland A, the 2006 runners-up, at Twickenham. The match was tight throughout and the home side were indebted to full-back Nick Abendanon, who set up one try and scored a second to give Mallinder's team an 18-3 win that booked their place in the final. New Zealand, in contrast, had few problems in their clash with Ireland A at Exeter's Sandy Park ground, cantering to a 50-22 victory and setting up a repeat of the 2004 final.

Most neutrals predicted a Kiwi victory in the final – their first appearance at Twickenham for 81 years - but Mallinder's team had other ideas and from the first whistle signalled their intention to take the Maori on physically.

England took the lead on 17 minutes when a pass from fly-half Olly Barkley put wing Paul Sackey over but New Zealand hit back with the first of their two tries from wing Anthony Tahana.

Leading 7-5 at half-time, the Saxons went behind after the break when Tamati Ellison landed a penalty but hit back with when Tom Voyce bustled over.

New Zealand appeared to have landed the killer blow when Jason Kawau crossed on the hour and began to apply the pressure but they were unable to get back and stop Croft late on, the substitute's galloping run rounding off an ambitious Saxons break.

"We're pretty disappointed with that effort today," said Maori coach Donny Stevenson. "The boys are pretty dejected. We had some opportunities, but we didn't hang on to the ball for long enough periods to cause adequate impact.

"All the players weren't too happy with their performances, much of that can be attributed to the pressure England put on us. We didn't react that well."

Scotland and Ireland's second string sides shook off the disappointment of their group losses to England and New Zealand to reach the Plate final and produced a game brimming with drama and tension.

Scotland opened the scoring with a Calum MacRae penalty but then shot themselves in the foot to allow Ireland to establish a platform.

First, Frank Murphy charged down Rob Crystie's kick in the ninth minute to grab the game's first try and then Ireland capitalised on a loose Scotland pass that went beyond the dead-ball area and from the resulting scrum, Roger Wilson scored.

The response from Scotland, however, was immediate as Scott Lawson touched down from the restart. McRae's conversion and subsequent penalty cut Scotland's deficit to just two points and there seemed precious little to separate the two teams.

Ireland seemed to have made the contest their own with Keith Earls' 60th minute try to leave Scotland trailing 22-13 but another McRae penalty and a try from Thom Evans inside the last 10 minutes left the result hanging in the balance. But McRae was unable to add what would have been a match-winning conversion and the Irish were 22-21 winners.

"It was a good match to win against a good Scottish side," said Ireland coach Michael Bradley after his team had retained their Plate title. "In the three matches we've played, the players have been fully aware that it gives them an opportunity to show their form to [first team coaches] Eddie O'Sullivan and Niall O'Donovan."

Scotland coach Frank Hadden despite his side's narrow defeat echoed Bradley's thoughts. "The Churchill Cup gave us an opportunity to work with players we hadn't seen before," he said. "It gave us a closer look at their strengths and weaknesses.

"There was nothing much between the two teams. I think we made enough line-breaks to put more tries on the board so it was a frustrating afternoon for us."

If the Plate final was a closely-fought clash, the Shield final between Canada and the USA, which preceded it at Twickenham, was a distinctly one-sided affair.

Although the Americans opened and closed the scoring, it was Canada who ran in seven converted tries in between, including two apiece from Man of the Match Sean-Michael Stephen and captain Morgan Willams, to romp to a 52-10 win.

"It was a good win," said Williams. "For the first ten minutes they came at us and made us think twice. But we stuck to the game plan and the gaps came. I think we firmly established who is best in North America."

Canada coach Ric Suggitt was magnanimous in victory, even though it was the USA's second heaviest loss ever to their North American neighbours.

"You have to give the US credit," he said. "They have worked hard to improve. They are our cross-border rivals and we have to beat them, so it isn't hard to motivate our guys. The Americans challenge us, and we have to respond."

CHURCHILL CUP 2007 RESULTS

GROUP PHASE

18 May, Edgeley Park, Stockport	
England Saxons 51 (3G, 6T)	**USA** 3 (1PG)
19 May, Sandy Park, Exeter	
Ireland A 39 (3G, 1PG, 3T)	**Canada** 20 (2G, 2PG)
23 May, Dry Leas, Henley	
Scotland A 13 (1G, 2PG)	**USA** 9 (3PG)
25 May, Franklin's Gardens, Northampton	
New Zealand Maori 59 (7G, 2T)	**Canada** 23 (1T, 2PG, 2T)
28 May, Twickenham, London	
England Saxons 18 (1G, 2PG, 1T)	**Scotland A** 3 (1PG)
29 May, Sandy Park, Exeter	
New Zealand Maori 50 (3G, 3PG, 4T)	**Ireland A** 22 (1G, 3T)

GROUP TABLES

POOL A

	P	W	D	L	BP	Pts
England	2	2	0	0	1	9
Scotland A	2	1	0	1	0	4
USA	2	0	0	2	1	1

POOL B

	P	W	D	L	BP	Pts
NZ Maori	2	2	0	0	2	10
Ireland A	2	1	0	1	1	5
Canada	2	0	0	2	0	0

CHURCHILL CUP BOWL FINAL

2 June, Twickenham, London

USA 10 (2T) CANADA 52 (7G, 1PG)

USA: F Viljoen (captain); C Wyles, P Emerick, A Tuipulotu, S Salesi; M Valenese, K Kimball; M MacDonald, M Crick, C Osentowski, H Mexted, M Mangan, M Aylor, T Clever, L Stanfill Substitutions: B Burdette for Aylor (temp 38 to 45 mins); Burdette for Crick (57 mins); D Williams for M French for Osentowski (59 mins); T Mounga for Stanfill (61 mins)

SCORERS *Tries:* MacDonald, Salesi

CANADA: M Pyke; J Mensah-Coker, C Culpan, D Spicer, J Pritchard; R Smith, M Williams (captain); K Tkachuk, P Riordan, S Franklin, L Tait, C Yukes, S McKeen, A Kleeberger, S-M Stephen

SUBSTITUTIONS: N Dala for McKeen (53 mins); D Pletch for Tkachuk (60 mins); M Pletch for Franklin (60 mins); E Fairhurst for Williams (61 mins); J Jackson for Tait (62 mins); A Carpenter for Riordan (68 mins); D van Camp for Pritchard (75 mins)

SCORERS *Tries:* Stephen (2), Spicer, Williams (2), Kleeberger, D Pletch Conversions: Pritchard (7) Penalty Goal: Pritchard

REFEREE C Pollock (New Zealand)

YELLOW CARD Osentowski (33 mins)

RED CARD French (63 mins)

CHURCHILL CUP PLATE FINAL

2 June, Twickenham, London

IRELAND A 22 (2G, 1PG, 1T) SCOTLAND A 21 (1G, 3PG, 1T)

IRELAND A: J Murphy; P McKenzie, D Cave, S Mallon, K Earls; J Sexton, F Murphy; J Lyne, J Fogarty (captain), M Ross, R Caldwell, A Farley, J Muldoon, J O'Connor, R Wilson Substitutions: F McFadden for McKenzie (48 mins); C Kean for J Murphy (57 mins); I Keatley for Sexton (57 mins); J O'Sullivan for Muldoon (57 mins); D Fitzpatrick for Ross (58 mins); S Cronin for Fogarty (79 mins)

SCORERS *Tries:* Murphy, Wilson, Earls Conversions: Sexton, Keatley Penalty Goal: Sexton

SCOTLAND A: S Danielli; S Webster, C MacRae, G Morrison; T Evans; P Godman, R Chrystie; A Dickenson, S Lawson, C Smith, A Hall, M Rennie, A Strokosch, D Macfadyen (captain), J Beattie Substitutions: N De Luca for Danielli (14 mins); F Thomson for Lawson (40 mins); M Low for Smith (40 mins); M McMillan for Chrystie (45 mins); J Barclay for Beattie (50 mins); S Swindall for Macfadyen (75 mins)

SCORERS *Tries:* Lawson, Evans Conversion: McRae Penalty Goals: MacRae (3)

REFEREE A Small (England)

YELLOW CARD Caldwell (37 mins)

CHURCHILL CUP FINAL

2 June, Twickenham, London

ENGLAND SAXONS 17 (1G, 2T)
NEW ZEALAND MAORI 13 (1PG, 2T)

ENGLAND SAXONS: D Cipriani; P Sackey, K Sorrell, N Mordt, T Voyce; O Barkley, R Wigglesworth; N Hatley (captain), D Paice, J Brooks, R Blaze, J Evans, J Haskell, W Skinner, P Dowson Substitutions: T Mercey for Hatley (28 mins); T Croft for Blaze (53 mins); A Erinle for Mordt (53 mins); J Forster for Brooks (60 mins); J Crane for Haskell (60 mins); L Dickson for Wigglesworth (66 mins); M Thompson for Paice (66 mins)

SCORERS *Tries:* Sackey, Voyce, Croft Conversion: Barkley

NEW ZEALAND MAORI: S Paku; H Gear, J Kawau, R Tipoki (captain), A Tahana; T Ellison, C Smylie; C West, A de Malamanche, T Hoani, K Ormsby, H Triggs, A MacDonald, T Latimer, W Smith Substitutions: C Bruce for Ellison (temp 53 to 67 mins); S Walrdom for Latimer (57 mins); P Te Whare for Tahana (60 mins); L Mahoney for de Malamanche (66 mins); Ellison for Tipoki (67 mins); K Cameron for Hoani (71 mins)

SCORERS *Tries:* Tahana, Kawau Penalty Goal: Ellison

REFEREE G Clancy (Ireland)

YELLOW CARD Skinner (25 mins)

LAST GASP VICTORY FOR KIWIS

By Iain Spragg

Lee Warren/Gallo Images/Getty Images

The Sevens champions celebrate; New Zealand-style!

New Zealand dramatically reclaimed the IRB Sevens crown from old rivals Fiji on the final day of the season at Murrayfield to reaffirm their previously unchallenged dominance of the shortened game.

The Kiwis had monopolised the first six IRB titles but were finally toppled by an inspired Fiji in 2006. The uncharacteristic slip-up clearly stung the New Zealanders and, coached by Gordon Tietjens, they came storming back in 2007 to dethrone the South Sea Islanders.

They left it extremely late, however, and going into the Scotland Sevens in Edinburgh in June – the eighth and final tournament on the calendar – the All Blacks trailed the Fijians by 10 points in the standings.

The form book strongly suggested Fiji would comfortably accumulate enough points to fend off the Kiwi's charge but a shock quarter-final defeat to Wales for Waisale Serevi's side opened the door. Tietjens' team now knew they had to reach and then win the Cup final to reclaim their crown and they duly delivered by beating Samoa 34-5 in the final. New Zealand were champions once again.

"It was unbelievable really," Tietjens said after his side's dramatic victory. "Coming into the tournament, we didn't really give ourselves a chance. We looked to win the tournament but good things happened for us with Wales beating Fiji and going into the Samoa game, we knew what we had to do.

"We were disappointed last year finishing fourth but I had such a young new team and you can't go down to the shop and buy experience. Those players got that by losing those matches and now look at them holding up the series trophy."

The season had begun in Dubai in December and it was evident early on New Zealand would be an altogether tougher proposition in 2007. Comfortable winners over Canada in the Cup quarter-finals, the All Blacks faced Fiji in the last four and in a game which they would have lost in 2006, they emerged 17-12 winners.

The All Blacks faced South Africa – who overcame defending Dubai champions England in their semi-final – in the final and initially it seemed the Kiwis would coast to victory as they lead 12-0 at half-time. The Springboks had other ideas and inspired by Player of the Tournament Stefan Basson, they came storming back to score 31 unanswered points and claim the Dubai title.

"At half time I just told them to relax, keep playing the width of the pitch and believe in themselves," said South Africa coach Paul Treu. "Stefan was outstanding. He loves Sevens so much."

A week later the teams were in South Africa for the second instalment of the series and this time the Kiwis were not to be denied. It was again a New Zealand and South Africa final but two tries from Alfred Pelenise steered the Kiwis to a 24-17 win.

History was then made at the New Zealand Sevens in Wellington in February as Samoa, coached by Dicky Tafua, claimed their first ever IRB Sevens title. It was an all South Sea Island final as Samoa faced Fiji in the Westpac Stadium and although Serevi's side were clear favourites after conceding a mere seven points en route to the showdown, it was Samoa who emerged 17-14 victors courtesy of tries from Mikaele Pesamino and Ofisa Treviranus.

"The result is very important for Samoan rugby and I'm very proud," said Tafua. "It's important that we've done it for the first time and with our home based players."

The Fijians did not have to wait long for their chance to exact revenge and seven days later at the USA Sevens in San Diego, Serevi's side did just that. Facing the Samoans once again the final, Fiji cut loose, including two tries from the prolific William Ryder, and ran out 38-24 winners.

The result left Fiji and New Zealand tied on 60 points at the top of the rankings at the halfway stage of the series.

Hong Kong was the next port of call at the end of March and there was a distinct sense of déjà vu as Fiji and Samoa, winners over the All Blacks and Springboks respectively in the last four, again battled through to the final.

The Fijians had blown Samoa away in the first half in America but the boot was firmly on the other foot in Hong Kong as Pesamino scored a stunning hat-trick to steer his side to a 27-22 triumph.

The Australia Sevens in Adelaide produced yet another South Sea Island final – the fourth consecutive time the Fijians and Samoans had made it the final – and the fluctuating fortunes of the two sides was in evidence again as Serevi's side bounced back to claim a 21-7 win.

The real news in Adelaide was Kenya's stunning Cup quarter-final victory over England, their best ever result in an IRB Sevens event.

"I am lost for words," said Kenya coach Benjamin Ayimba after his team's historic 17-12 win. "England were not playing well and we knew this was the best time to beat them. I dedicate all this to what God has done for us."

Leading by 10 points, Fiji went into to the London Sevens at Twickenham – the penultimate event on the calendar – in the driving seat but it was now time for New Zealand to make their move.

The Kiwis beat Samoa to reach the final while Fiji overcame an improving Wales side to make it through but any thoughts Serevi's team had of effectively ending the All Black challenge for the overall title were quickly quashed. Afeleke Pelenise, the top try scorer at Twickenham with 11, set New Zealand on their way in London with an early score and they were comfortable 29-7 winners. Although Fiji had a 10-point cushion over the Kiwis, the destination of the 2007 title was still in doubt.

All seemed to be going according to plan for the South Sea Islanders in Scotland, however, with routine wins over Kenya, Portugal and Australia on day one at Murrayfield.

It was on the second day that the wheels came off in the quarter-final against Wales, who matched Fiji blow for blow and completed a famous 21-14 win with tries from Rhodri McAtee, Tal Selley and Wayne Evans.

New Zealand were ready to pounce. Narrow winners over South Africa in the quarter-finals and easy victors over the Welsh in the last four, the Kiwis made no mistake in the final against Samoa and a brace for both Adam Thompson and captain DJ Forbes steered them to a 34-5 victory and their seventh IRB Sevens crown in eight years.

IRB SEVENS 2006–07 RESULTS

DUBAI: 1-2 DECEMBER

1.**South Africa** (20 points), **New Zealand** (16), **Fiji** (12), **England** (12), **Samoa** (8), **France** (6), **Canada** (4), **Australia** (4), **Argentina** (2)

SOUTH AFRICA: 8-9 DECEMBER

1.**New Zealand** (20), **South Africa** (16), **Fiji** (12), **England** (12), **Wales** (8), **Tunisia** (6), **France** (4), **Samoa** (4), **Australia** (2)

NEW ZEALAND: 2-3 FEBRUARY

1.**Samoa** (20), **Fiji** (16), **New Zealand** (12), **South Africa** (12), **England** (8), **France** (6), **Canada** (4), **Kenya** (4), **Argentina** (2)

USA: 10-11 FEBRUARY

1.**Fiji** (20), **Samoa** (16), **New Zealand** (12), **France** (12), **South Africa** (8), **Scotland** (6), **England** (4), **Australia** (4), **Tonga** (2)

HONG KONG: 3-31 MARCH

1.**Samoa** (30), **Fiji** (24), **New Zealand** (18), **South Africa** (18), **Scotland** (8), **England** (8), **Australia** (8), **Tonga** (8), **Wales** (4), **Argentina** (3), **USA** (2), **Portugal** (2), **Russia** (1)

AUSTRALIA: 7-8 APRIL

1.**Fiji** (20), **Samoa** (16), **Kenya** (12), **New Zealand** (12), **Australia** (8), **South Africa** (6), **England** (4), **Scotland** (4), **Wales** (2)

ENGLAND: 26-27 MAY

1.**New Zealand** (20), **Fiji** (16), **Wales** (12), **Samoa** (12), **South Africa** (8), **Australia** (6), **Scotland** (4), **Argentina** (4), **England** (2)

SCOTLAND: 2-3 JUNE

1.**New Zealand** (20), **Samoa** (16), **Wales** (12), **Argentina** (12), **Fiji** (8), **Kenya** (6), **South Africa** (4), **Scotland** (4), **England** (2)

FINAL STANDINGS

New Zealand 130 points	**Argentina** 23
Fiji 128	**Kenya** 22
Samoa 122	**Tonga** 10
South Africa 92	**Canada** 8
England 52	**Tunisia** 6
Wales 38	**Portugal** 2
Australia 32	**USA** 2
France 28	**Russia** 1
Scotland 26	

PREVIOUS WINNERS

1999-00: New Zealand
2000-01: New Zealand
2001-02: New Zealand
2002-03: New Zealand
2003-04: New Zealand
2004-05: New Zealand
2005-06: Fiji
2006-07: New Zealand

Cameron Spencer/Getty Images

Mikaele Pesamino was in superb form in 2006–07 becoming the IRB Sevens leading try-scorer with an incredible 43 touch downs.

Ryan Pierse/Getty Images

New Zealand were the 2007 champions but Wales goalkicker Leigh Halfpenny emerged as the tournament's leading scorer.

BABY BLACKS COME OF AGE

Dave Rogers/Getty Images

Chris Smith, the New Zealand captain finally gets his hands on the IRB Under-19s trophy.

New Zealand's next generation of stars were finally crowned IRB Under-19 world champions after a resounding 31-7 victory over South Africa in Belfast.

The Baby Blacks had lost in both the 2005 and 2006 finals but made it third time lucky at Ravenhill with a scintillating display of attacking rugby that yielded five tries and destroyed the Springboks' challenge.

The young Kiwis had last won the tournament in 2004 and the side's appetite to consign their two successive final disappointments to history was evident throughout the championship as they swept all before them.

"I was on a losing side last year and know what that felt like, and it was an experience I wanted to forget," said New Zealand captain Chris Smith. "To win tonight, and also so resoundingly, was just fantastic.

"We have to give credit to South Africa because that was a hard final. That was a real brutal encounter up front. We said we had to take them on and we did."

Two tries for the young All Blacks inside the opening seven minutes set the tone and South Africa, the 2005 champions, were never able to get within touching distance.

"New Zealand are a brilliant team and if you allow them space and time they will punish you for it," conceded South Africa coach Eric Sauls.

"It is difficult to play against a team that has so much talent right across the team. They have running pace, coming hard onto the ball and you have to cover it. If you do not, you will have difficult stopping them and we did tonight."

New Zealand began the tournament with a 37-14 victory over Wales courtesy of a stunning hat-trick of tries from centre Robert Fruean in 13 devastating first-half minutes but it was their 107-6 romp over Japan in the second round of group games that signalled their intent to the other sides in the tournament.

England, who finished third in 2006, were despatched 34-13 four days later and the Kiwis went through to the play-off stages in top spot. Defending champions Australia also progressed unbeaten after victories over hosts Ireland (15-10), newly-promoted Fiji (23-12) and France (30-11) to finish second while South Africa were third. Wales, meanwhile, bounced back from their opening defeat to the Baby Blacks with wins over Samoa (33-20) and Argentina (29-0) to claim fourth place and northern hemisphere bragging rights.

The second and third place play-off between Australia and South Africa at Ravenhill saw the Springboks powerful pack lay the foundations for a hard-fought victory. The young Wallabies opened the scoring with a second minute penalty from Rowan Kellam but South Africa took control of proceedings with two tries to establish a 15-3 half-time lead.

More good work from the forwards saw the Springboks go further in the lead and despite an impressive brace of tries from 17-year-old Australian Rob Simmons, South Africa coasted to a comfortable 32-18 victory.

"The pressure from the South African pack didn't allow us any quality ball," said Australia captain Brett Gillespie. "Crucial mistakes in the first half cost us."

The first and fourth place play-off between New Zealand and Wales followed the pattern of the two side's group stage clash and although the Welsh mounted a strong second half fightback and were far from disgraced, the Baby Blacks were always in control and ran out 36-12 winners.

Wing Leigh Halfpenny, who finished as the tournament's top points scorer, landed four penalties for all of Wales points but a personal haul of 21 points from Kiwi full back Trent Renata was enough to book New Zealand's place in a fourth successive final.

"We were always going to be up against it," admitted Wales coach Justin Burnell. "Coming in as underdogs suited us and we showed what we could do in the second half. We are a team of honest players and I generally feel that we can take third spot."

The final was billed as a clash of contrasting styles between the South African's abrasive pack and the Baby Backs' mercurial backs but the game was effectively over as a contest inside seven minutes as Fruean and then Renata both went over to give the Kiwis the lead.

The Baby Blacks' seemingly inexorable charge was temporarily slowed, first by a serious ankle injury to centre Ryan Crotty who was stretchered off and then a yellow card for Fruean for an ill-advised swinging arm, but the setbacks were to merely prove brief respite for the Springboks.

The competition's top try scorer Kade Poki added New Zealand's third try before half time despite being a man down and when Renata grabbed his second score of the game after the break, the Kiwis were in danger of running away it. Substitute Jackson Willison added the fifth to make it 31-0 and although South African replacement Yaasir Hartzenberg gave the final scoreline some gloss with his side's only try of the match, New Zealand were home and dry.

"We are delighted," said New Zealand coach Kieran Crowley. "There is a lot of hard work goes into this and we are probably the lucky ones to be here on stage, there are a lot of managers and trainers back home in New Zealand who have put a lot of work into this."

In the third place play-off, Australia made it a southern hemisphere one-two-three with a dramatic 25-21 win over Wales.

In Division B of the tournament, Italy earned themselves promotion to the top table after beating Canada 22-3 in the final at Shaw's Bridge in Belfast, a repeat of the result in last year's Division B third place play-off.

The Italians reached the final unbeaten and emerged from an intensely physical encounter comfortable victors courtesy of three unanswered tries from Alberto Chiesa, Francesco Fiorani and Luca Martinelli.

"It is important for Italian rugby and the international team," said Italy coach Stefano Romagnoli. "We won a good match and gained promotion and some players were excellent. Every player has been the player of the tournament."

RESULTS
DIVISION A

ROUND ONE

South Africa 36 **Fiji** 5, **Scotland** 6 **France** 11, **New Zealand** 37 **Wales** 14, **Australia** 15 **Ireland** 10, **Argentina** 41 **Japan** 8, **Samoa** 12 **England** 20

ROUND TWO

New Zealand 107 **Japan** 6, **Argentina** 15 **England** 17, **South Africa** 8 **France** 17, **Scotland** 12 **Ireland** 13, **Samoa** 20 **Wales** 33, **Australia** 23 **Fiji** 12

ROUND THREE

Samoa 28 **Japan** 12, **Australia** 30 **France** 11, **New Zealand** 34 **England** 13, **South Africa** 31 **Ireland** 5, **Scotland** 23 **Fiji** 25, **Argentina** 0 **Wales** 29

PLAY-OFFS – PHASE ONE

10th v 11th Place Play-Off	**Fiji** 7 **Scotland** 11
9th v 12th Place Play-Off	**Ireland** 31 **Japan** 10
6th v 7th Place Play-Off	**England** 31 **Argentina** 13
5th v 8th Place Play-Off	**France** 25 **Samoa** 13
2nd v 3rd Place Play-Off	**Australia** 18 **South Africa** 32
1st v 4th Place Play-Off	**New Zealand** 36 **Wales** 12

PLAY-OFFS – PHASE TWO

11th Place Play-Off	**Fiji** 60 **Japan** 12
9th Place Play-Off	**Scotland** 0 **Ireland** 34
7th Place Play-Off	**Argentina** 12 **Samoa** 13
5th Place Play-Off	**England** 17 **France** 43

21 April, Ravenhill, Belfast

SOUTH AFRICA 7 (1G)
NEW ZEALAND 31 (3G, 2T)

SOUTH AFRICA: W Pietersen; B Botha, S Dippenaar, S Watermeyer, V Willis; F Brummer, F Hougaard; C Fourie, H Bantjes, F Kirsten, C Hess, M Muller, T Marole, J van Deventer, G van Velze (captain) Substitutions: Y Hartzenberg for van Velze (35 mins), A McDonald for S Dippenaar (40 mins), EJ Snyman for Watermeyer (60 mins), P van Vuuren for Fourie (65 mins), S Nhlapo for Marole (65 mins), W Herbst for Kirsten (65 mins), B Botha for Hess (66 mins)

SCORERS *Try*: Hartzenberg Conversion: Watermeyer

NEW ZEALAND: T Renata; Z Guildford, R Fruean, R Crotty, K Poki; D Kirkpatrick, W Ngaluafe; R Ah You, A Dixon, B Afeaki, C Smith (captain), S Whitelock, P Saili, L Braid, L Manu Substitutions: J Willison for Crotty (10 mins), P Fa'anunu for Ah You (35 mins), Q MacDonald for Dixon (46 mins), J Hardie for Braid (46 mins), S Maitland for Poki (52 mins), M Cameron for Ngaluafe (65 mins), N Barrett for Afeaki

YELLOW CARD Fruean (31 mins)

SCORERS *Try*: Fruean, Renata (2), Poki, Willison Conversions: Renata (3)

REFEREE J Jones (Wales)

IRB UNDER-19 WORLD CUP THIRD PLACE PLAY-OFF

21 April, Ravenhill, Belfast

AUSTRALIA 25 (2G, 2PG, 1T)
WALES 21 (3G)

AUSTRALIA: P McCabe; A Mafi, R Kellam, M Inman, A Barrett; B Gillespie (captain), J Ryan; A Anae, J Hanson, B Daley, R Simmons, S Wykes, B McCalman, R Maa, M Uoka Substitutions: P Betham for Inman (temp 11 to 23 mins), J Waerea-Hargreaves for Uoka (30 mins), C Harkins for Maa (60 mins)

SCORERS *Tries*: Hanson, Barrett, Mafi Conversions: Ryan (2) Penalty Goals: (2)

WALES: D Evans; J Norris, T Williams, R Williams, L Halfpenny; G Owen, R Webb; R Bevington, B Roberts, S Hobbs, N White, J Turnbull, L Phillips, N Cudd, Sam Wharburton Substitutions: J Groves for Phillips (51 mins), L Elliott for Hobbs (53 mins), J Egan for Norris (55 mins), J Griffiths for White (60 mins), H Dowden for Roberts (60 mins)

SCORERS *Tries*: T Williams, Owen, Norris Conversions: Halfpenny (3)

REFEREE P Bosch (South Africa)

DIVISION B

ROUND ONE

Tonga 36 **Uruguay** 5
Chile 29 **Cook Islands** 14
Chinese Taipei 6 **Italy** 62
Romania 0 **Georgia** 28
Zimbabwe 0 **Canada** 8
Russia 0 **USA** 6

ROUND TWO

Romania 10 **USA** 16
Russia 5 **Canada** 33
Tonga 72 **Cook Islands** 6
Chinese Taipei 5 **Uruguay** 55
Chile 13 **Italy** 32
Zimbabwe 33 **Georgia** 26

ROUND THREE

Zimbabwe 7 **USA** 22
Chile 20 **Uruguay** 30
Chinese Taipei 10 **Cook Islands** 10
Tonga 6 **Italy** 8
Romania 7 **Canada** 15
Russia 6 **Georgia** 24

PLAY-OFFS PHASE ONE

10th v 11th Place Play-Off	**Chinese Taipei** 10 **Romania** 35
9th v 12th Place Play-Off	**Cook Islands** 14 **Russia** 22
6th v 7th Place Play-Off	**Uruguay** 21 **Chile** 3
5th v 8th Place Play-Off	**Tonga** 26 **Zimbabwe** 11
2nd v 3rd Place Play-Off	**Canada** 19 **Georgia** 3
1st v 4th Place Play-Off	**Italy** 31 **USA** 6

PLAY-OFFS PHASE TWO

11th Place Play-Off	**Chinese Taipei** 29 **Cook Islands** 10
9th Place Play-Off	**Romania** 20 **Russia** 10
7th Place Play-Off	**Chile** 10 **Zimbabwe** 12
5th Place Play-Off	**Uruguay** 15 **Tonga** 24

20 April, Shaw's Bridge, Belfast, Final

CANADA 3 (1PG) ITALY 22 (2G, 1PG, 1T)

CANADA: H Jones; J Wilson-Ross, J Campbell, M Scholtz, K Buckley; N Hirayama (captain), J Mackenzie; A Tiedemann, R Hamilton, M Perizzolo, T Schwitzer, R Andrews, I Manly, K Selby, T de Goede Substitutions: B Henrikson for Scholtz (36 mins), S Manning for Buckley (36 mins), R Ward for Tiedemann (36 mins), M Mosby for Manly (56 mins), M Berry for Selby (63 mins), J McConney for Campbell (64 mins)

SCORER *Penalty Goal*: Hirayama

ITALY: F Fiorani; A Pratichetti, R Quartaroli, A Chiesa (captain), E Rotella; R Bocchino, L Martinelli; A De Marchi, G Morelli, M Ravalle, F Giusti, A Cazzola, N Simion, S Favaro, R Mernone Substitutions: G Sapuppo for Fiorani (37 mins), A Leo for N Simion (60 mins), T D'Apice for Morelli (64 mins), V Di Muro for Favaro (69 mins), E Violi for Ravalle (71 mins), L Sebastiani for De Marchi

SCORERS *Tries*: Chiesa, Fiorani, Martinelli Conversions: Bocchino (2) Penalty Goal: Bocchino

REFEREE M Stanish (New Zealand)

IRB UNDER-19 DIVISION B THIRD PLACE PLAY-OFF

20 April, Shaw's Bridge, Belfast, 3rd Place Play-Off

GEORGIA 5 (1T) USA 24 (1G, 4PG, 1T)

GEORGIA: M Tsiklauri; A Tuchashvili, G Svandize, B Tsiklauri, S Inashvili; L Khmaladze, G Rokhvadze; R Basilashvili, B Skhulukhia, G Jashitashvili, V Kolelishvili, I Mirtskhulava, V Mdzinarishvili, D Chichua (captain), V Kakovin Subsitutions: G Kalmakhelidze for Basilashvili (37 mins), R Nutsubidze for Svandize (53 mins), B Nikolaishvili for Mdzinarishvili for (62 mins), J Kikividze for Kolelishvili (65 mins)

SCORER *Try*: Skhulukhia

USA: H Roberts; A Ducoing, H Kofe, J Tracy, N Ebner; S Treacy, T Benson; K Toombs, Z Heath, S Pittman, K Erskine, S Lavalla (captain), L Murphy, A Cella, G Lambert Substitutions: T Mokate for Lavalla (temp 16 to 22 mins), E West for Murphy (42 mins), B Wynne for Heath (53 mins), N Cook for Toombs (53 mins), Mokate for Erskine (55 mins), Z Test for Benson (58 mins), R Roundy for Cella (68 mins), N Johnson for Tracy (68 mins)

SCORERS *Tries*: Kofe, Tracy Conversion: Roberts Penalty Goals: Roberts (4)

REFEREE N Paterson (Scotland)

TOP 10 INDIVIDUAL POINTS SCORERS

Leigh Halfpenny	(Wales)	**57**
German Albanell	(Uruguay)	**56**
Sione Toke	(Tonga)	**54**
Riccardo Bocchino	(Italy)	**50**
Trent Renata	(New Zealand)	**42**
Hamish Roberts	(USA)	**39**
Daniel Kirkpatrick	(New Zealand)	**37**
Stefan Watermeyer	(South Africa)	**37**
Mathieu Belie	(France)	**35**
Nathan Hirayama	(Canada)	**33**

TOP 10 TRY SCORERS

Kade Poki	(New Zealand)	**6**
Andrew Barrett	(Australia)	**5**
Alberto Chiesa	(Italy)	**5**
Bogdan Petreanu	(Romania)	**5**
Henry Speight	(Fiji)	**5**
Luke Braid	(New Zealand)	**4**
Blair Connor	(Australia)	**4**
Robert Fruean	(New Zealand)	**4**
Eoin O'Malley	(Ireland)	**4**
Lepaola Tauveli	(Tonga)	**4**

RBS WOMEN'S SIX NATIONS
A NEW DAY DAWNS
By Paul Morgan

One of English rugby's most prolific players – Sue Day – bowed out of the international game on a massive high at the end of the 2007 RBS Six Nations, leading England to their second successive Grand Slam.

Day, who has played full-back and wing for England since her debut in 1997, has scored an incredible 61 tries in her 59 Tests for the World Cup runners-up.

"It was time to go," said Day, "time to focus a little more on my club – Wasps – especially as England will now be building for the 2010 World Cup."

Accompanying Day to 'stage left' was Emily Cooke (nee Feltham) who scored the try that gave England a remarkable win in New Zealand in 2001 and prolific kicker Karen Andrew, along with England coach Geoff Richards, who was replaced by one of his assistants, Gary Street at the end of the tournament.

Day added: "We are all really sorry Geoff has resigned as he has been a great coach and has made a huge contribution to women's rugby in England."

Since joining the RFUW seven years ago, Richards had taken charge of 61 Test matches of which England have won 51. The team have also won four Six Nations Grand Slam titles and have been finalists in two Rugby World Cups. Under Richards England are also the only team to have beaten world champions New Zealand's Black Ferns.

Richards said: "I have had a wonderful time working with the RFUW and I have thoroughly enjoyed being part of this organisation which has grown considerably since I first joined."

In the 2007 Six Nations, England were far too powerful for the other five, which included a tournament debut for Italy, bringing the Women's Six Nations into line with the men, and getting the same sponsor in the shape of RBS.

Under Day they scored an incredible 183 points in their five games, conceding just 12, including a 23–0 win over Italy at Twickenham, wrapping up their second successive Grand Slam – for the first time – with a 30–0 victory away at Wales. All those 12 points conceded came in the match in France.

Retirements after the World Cup stretched the resources of the other teams, England's deep pool of talent standing them in good stead, even though they themselves lost more than a dozen players.

Wing Nolli Waterman led the try charts with eight for an England team that gained the upper hand through their pack, led by Maggie Alphonsi and Rochelle Clark.

"This side wasn't scared of losing," said Day in Rugby World Magazine, "and they're a very relaxed group, which helps when the going gets tough. In some ways we're playing a traditional English game. We try to take teams on up front and dominate them, but there's also a bit extra in the pack as they're very mobile."

Wales continued their upward curve – with three wins – after being handed the wooden spoon two years ago, but sadly they will have to continue on the path to the 2010 World Cup without prodigious lock Liza Burgess. The second rower celebrated her 21st season in international rugby, retiring after the defeat to England to continue her career as a coach.

Scotland had an awful 2007 on the pitch – finishing a very disappointing fifth – but will start 2008 in better health as women's rugby in Scotland is gearing up for a momentous season with new recruits taking up the game at both adult and youth level.

Chief among them is Donna Kennedy, the world's most-capped women's player, who will make the transition from player to coach in her new role heading up the Scottish Women's Rugby Union Academy team, a stepping stone to develop Scotland's players of the future. Kennedy became the first woman to win 100 caps, in the defeat by France, on the final day of the 2007 Championship.

The Italians who took over from Spain failed to pick up any points but they won many admirers, especially at Twickenham where their passion, commitment and tenacious defence ensured that England were shaken to their smallest score (23 points) of the Championship.

"Italy played well and tackled well and the fact they put 17 points on France a week before shows they are a good side," said England coach Richards. "They deserved to be here competing in the Six Nations and I hope they enjoyed playing at Twickenham in just their second Six Nations game. The crowd were certainly fantastic."

RBS WOMEN'S SIX NATIONS 2007

Country	P	W	D	L	For	Against	Pts
England	5	5	0	0	183	12	**10**
France	5	4	0	1	95	75	**8**
Wales	5	3	0	2	44	50	**6**
Ireland	5	2	0	3	50	73	**4**
Scotland	5	1	0	4	42	112	**2**
Italy	5	0	0	5	35	127	**0**

THE COUNTRIES

INTERNATIONAL RECORDS

RESULTS OF INTERNATIONAL MATCHES

MATCH RECORDS UP TO 31 OCTOBER 2007

Cap matches involving senior executive council member unions only. Years for International Championship matches are for the second half of the season: eg 1972 means season 1971–72. Years for matches against touring teams from the Southern Hemisphere refer to the actual year of the match.

Points-scoring was first introduced in 1886, when an International Board was formed by Scotland, Ireland and Wales. Points values varied among the countries until 1890, when England agreed to join the Board, and uniform values were adopted.

Northern Hemisphere seasons	Try	Conversions	Penalty Goal	Dropped goal	Goal from mark
1890–91	1	2	2	3	3
1891–92 to 1892–93	2	3	3	4	4
1893–94 to 1904–05	3	2	3	4	4
1905–06 to 1947–48	3	2	3	4	3
1948–49 to 1970–71	3	2	3	3	3
1971–72 to 1991–92	4	2	3	3	3*
1992–93 onwards	5	2	3	3	–

*The goal from mark ceased to exist when the free-kick clause was introduced, 1977–78.

WC indicates a fixture played during the Rugby World Cup finals. LC indicates a fixture played in the Latin Cup. TN indicates a fixture played in the Tri Nations.

ENGLAND V SCOTLAND

Played 124 England won 66, Scotland won 41, Drawn 17
Highest scores England 43–3 in 2001 and 43–22 in 2005, Scotland 33–6 in 1986
Biggest wins England 43–3 in 2001, Scotland 33–6 in 1986

1871 Raeburn Place (Edinburgh) **Scotland** 1G 1T to 1T
1872 The Oval (London) **England** 1G 1DG 2T to 1DG
1873 Glasgow **Drawn** no score
1874 The Oval **England** 1DG to 1T
1875 Raeburn Place **Drawn** no score
1876 The Oval **England** 1G 1T to 0
1877 Raeburn Place **Scotland** 1 DG to 0
1878 The Oval **Drawn** no score
1879 Raeburn Place **Drawn** Scotland 1DG England 1G
1880 Manchester **England** 2G 3T to 1G
1881 Raeburn Place **Drawn** Scotland 1G 1T England 1DG 1T
1882 Manchester **Scotland** 2T to 0
1883 Raeburn Place **England** 2T to 1T
1884 Blackheath (London) **England** 1G to 1T
1885 No Match
1886 Raeburn Place **Drawn** no score
1887 Manchester **Drawn** 1T each
1888 No Match
1889 No Match
1890 Raeburn Place **England** 1G 1T to 0
1891 Richmond (London) **Scotland** 9–3
1892 Raeburn Place **England** 5–0
1893 Leeds **Scotland** 8–0
1894 Raeburn Place **Scotland** 6–0
1895 Richmond **Scotland** 6–3
1896 Glasgow **Scotland** 11–0
1897 Manchester **England** 12–3
1898 Powderhall (Edinburgh) **Drawn** 3–3
1899 Blackheath **Scotland** 5–0
1900 Inverleith (Edinburgh) **Drawn** 0–0
1901 Blackheath **Scotland** 18–3
1902 Inverleith **England** 6–3
1903 Richmond **Scotland** 10–6
1904 Inverleith **Scotland** 6–3
1905 Richmond **Scotland** 8–0
1906 Inverleith **England** 9–3
1907 Blackheath **Scotland** 8–3
1908 Inverleith **Scotland** 16–10
1909 Richmond **Scotland** 18–8
1910 Inverleith **England** 14–5
1911 Twickenham **England** 13–8
1912 Inverleith **Scotland** 8–3
1913 Twickenham **England** 3–0
1914 Inverleith **England** 16–15
1920 Twickenham **England** 13–4
1921 Inverleith **England** 18–0
1922 Twickenham **England** 11–5
1923 Inverleith **England** 8–6
1924 Twickenham **England** 19–0
1925 Murrayfield **Scotland** 14–11
1926 Twickenham **Scotland** 17–9
1927 Murrayfield **Scotland** 21–13
1928 Twickenham **England** 6–0
1929 Murrayfield **Scotland** 12–6
1930 Twickenham **Drawn** 0–0
1931 Murrayfield **Scotland** 28–19
1932 Twickenham **England** 16–3
1933 Murrayfield **Scotland** 3–0
1934 Twickenham **England** 6–3
1935 Murrayfield **Scotland** 10–7
1936 Twickenham **England** 9–8
1937 Murrayfield **England** 6–3
1938 Twickenham **Scotland** 21–16
1939 Murrayfield **England** 9–6
1947 Twickenham **England** 24–5
1948 Murrayfield **Scotland** 6–3
1949 Twickenham **England** 19–3
1950 Murrayfield **Scotland** 13–11
1951 Twickenham **England** 5–3
1952 Murrayfield **England** 19–3
1953 Twickenham **England** 26–8
1954 Murrayfield **England** 13–3
1955 Twickenham **England** 9–6
1956 Murrayfield **England** 11–6
1957 Twickenham **England** 16–3
1958 Murrayfield **Drawn** 3–3
1959 Twickenham **Drawn** 3–3
1960 Murrayfield **England** 21–12
1961 Twickenham **England** 6–0
1962 Murrayfield **Drawn** 3–3
1963 Twickenham **England** 10–8
1964 Murrayfield **Scotland** 15–6

1965 Twickenham **Drawn** 3–3
1966 Murrayfield **Scotland** 6–3
1967 Twickenham **England** 27–14
1968 Murrayfield **England** 8–6
1969 Twickenham **England** 8–3
1970 Murrayfield **Scotland** 14–5
1971 Twickenham **Scotland** 16–15
1971 Murrayfield **Scotland** 26–6
Special centenary match
– non-championship
1972 Murrayfield **Scotland** 23–9
1973 Twickenham **England** 20–13
1974 Murrayfield **Scotland** 16–14
1975 Twickenham **England** 7–6
1976 Murrayfield **Scotland** 22–12
1977 Twickenham **England** 26–6
1978 Murrayfield **England** 15–0
1979 Twickenham **Drawn** 7–7
1980 Murrayfield **England** 30–18
1981 Twickenham **England** 23–17
1982 Murrayfield **Drawn** 9–9
1983 Twickenham **Scotland** 22–12
1984 Murrayfield **Scotland** 18–6
1985 Twickenham **England** 10–7
1986 Murrayfield **Scotland** 33–6
1987 Twickenham **England** 21–12
1988 Murrayfield **England** 9–6
1989 Twickenham **Drawn** 12–12
1990 Murrayfield **Scotland** 13–7
1991 Twickenham **England** 21–12
1991 Murrayfield WC **England** 9–6
1992 Murrayfield **England** 25–7
1993 Twickenham **England** 26–12
1994 Murrayfield **England** 15–14
1995 Twickenham **England** 24–12
1996 Murrayfield **England** 18–9
1997 Twickenham **England** 41–13
1998 Murrayfield **England** 34–20
1999 Twickenham **England** 24–21
2000 Murrayfield **Scotland** 19–13
2001 Twickenham **England** 43–3
2002 Murrayfield **England** 29–3
2003 Twickenham **England** 40–9
2004 Murrayfield **England** 35–13
2005 Twickenham **England** 43–22
2006 Murrayfield **Scotland** 18–12
2007 Twickenham **England** 42–20

ENGLAND V IRELAND

Played 120 England won 69, Ireland won 43, Drawn 8
Highest scores England 50–18 in 2000, Ireland 43–13 in 2007
Biggest wins England 46–6 in 1997, Ireland 43–13 in 2007

1875 The Oval (London) **England** 1G 1DG 1T to 0
1876 Dublin **England** 1G 1T to 0
1877 The Oval **England** 2G 2T to 0
1878 Dublin **England** 2G 1T to 0
1879 The Oval **England** 2G 1DG 2T to 0
1880 Dublin **England** 1G 1T to 1T
1881 Manchester **England** 2G 2T to 0
1882 Dublin **Drawn** 2T each
1883 Manchester **England** 1G 3T to 1T
1884 Dublin **England** 1G to 0
1885 Manchester **England** 2T to 1T
1886 Dublin **England** 1T to 0
1887 Dublin **Ireland** 2G to 0
1888 No Match
1889 No Match
1890 Blackheath (London) **England** 3T to 0
1891 Dublin **England** 9–0
1892 Manchester **England** 7–0
1893 Dublin **England** 4–0
1894 Blackheath **Ireland** 7–5
1895 Dublin **England** 6–3
1896 Leeds **Ireland** 10–4
1897 Dublin **Ireland** 13–9
1898 Richmond (London) **Ireland** 9–6
1899 Dublin **Ireland** 6–0
1900 Richmond **England** 15–4
1901 Dublin **Ireland** 10–6
1902 Leicester **England** 6–3
1903 Dublin **Ireland** 6–0

1904 Blackheath **England** 19–0
1905 Cork **Ireland** 17–3
1906 Leicester **Ireland** 16–6
1907 Dublin **Ireland** 17–9
1908 Richmond **England** 13–3
1909 Dublin **England** 11–5
1910 Twickenham **Drawn** 0–0
1911 Dublin **Ireland** 3–0
1912 Twickenham **England** 15–0
1913 Dublin **England** 15–4
1914 Twickenham **England** 17–12
1920 Dublin **England** 14–11
1921 Twickenham **England** 15–0
1922 Dublin **England** 12–3
1923 Leicester **England** 23–5
1924 Belfast **England** 14–3
1925 Twickenham **Drawn** 6–6
1926 Dublin **Ireland** 19–15
1927 Twickenham **England** 8–6
1928 Dublin **England** 7–6
1929 Twickenham **Ireland** 6–5
1930 Dublin **Ireland** 4–3
1931 Twickenham **Ireland** 6–5
1932 Dublin **England** 11–8
1933 Twickenham **England** 17–6
1934 Dublin **England** 13–3
1935 Twickenham **England** 14–3
1936 Dublin **Ireland** 6–3
1937 Twickenham **England** 9–8
1938 Dublin **England** 36–14
1939 Twickenham **Ireland** 5–0
1947 Dublin **Ireland** 22–0
1948 Twickenham **Ireland** 11–10
1949 Dublin **Ireland** 14–5
1950 Twickenham **England** 3–0
1951 Dublin **Ireland** 3–0
1952 Twickenham **England** 3–0
1953 Dublin **Drawn** 9–9
1954 Twickenham **England** 14–3
1955 Dublin **Drawn** 6–6
1956 Twickenham **England** 20–0
1957 Dublin **England** 6–0
1958 Twickenham **England** 6–0
1959 Dublin **England** 3–0
1960 Twickenham **England** 8–5
1961 Dublin **Ireland** 11–8
1962 Twickenham **England** 16–0
1963 Dublin **Drawn** 0–0
1964 Twickenham **Ireland** 18–5
1965 Dublin **Ireland** 5–0
1966 Twickenham **Drawn** 6–6
1967 Dublin **England** 8–3
1968 Twickenham **Drawn** 9–9
1969 Dublin **Ireland** 17–15
1970 Twickenham **England** 9–3
1971 Dublin **England** 9–6
1972 Twickenham **Ireland** 16–12
1973 Dublin **Ireland** 18–9
1974 Twickenham **Ireland** 26–21
1975 Dublin **Ireland** 12–9
1976 Twickenham **Ireland** 13–12
1977 Dublin **England** 4–0
1978 Twickenham **England** 15–9
1979 Dublin **Ireland** 12–7
1980 Twickenham **England** 24–9
1981 Dublin **England** 10–6
1982 Twickenham **Ireland** 16–15
1983 Dublin **Ireland** 25–15
1984 Twickenham **England** 12–9
1985 Dublin **Ireland** 13–10
1986 Twickenham **England** 25–20
1987 Dublin **Ireland** 17–0
1988 Twickenham **England** 35–3
1988 Dublin **England** 21–10
Non-championship match
1989 Dublin **England** 16–3
1990 Twickenham **England** 23–0
1991 Dublin **England** 16–7
1992 Twickenham **England** 38–9
1993 Dublin **Ireland** 17–3
1994 Twickenham **Ireland** 13–12
1995 Dublin **England** 20–8
1996 Twickenham **England** 28–15
1997 Dublin **England** 46–6
1998 Twickenham **England** 35–17
1999 Dublin **England** 27–15
2000 Twickenham **England** 50–18
2001 Dublin **Ireland** 20–14
2002 Twickenham **England** 45–11
2003 Dublin **England** 42–6
2004 Twickenham **Ireland** 19–13
2005 Dublin **Ireland** 19–13
2006 Twickenham **Ireland** 28–24
2007 Dublin **Ireland** 43–13

ENGLAND V WALES

Played 116 England won 53, Wales won 51, Drawn 12
Highest scores England 62–5 in 2007, Wales 34–21 in 1967
Biggest wins England 62–5 in 2007, Wales 25–0 in 1905

1881	Blackheath (London) **England** 7G 1DG 6T to 0
1882	No Match
1883	Swansea **England** 2G 4T to 0
1884	Leeds **England** 1G 2T to 1G
1885	Swansea **England** 1G 4T to 1G 1T
1886	Blackheath **England** 1GM 2T to 1G
1887	Llanelli **Drawn** no score
1888	No Match
1889	No Match
1890	Dewsbury **Wales** 1T to 0
1891	Newport **England** 7–3
1892	Blackheath **England** 17–0
1893	Cardiff **Wales** 12–11
1894	Birkenhead **England** 24–3
1895	Swansea **England** 14–6
1896	Blackheath **England** 25–0
1897	Newport **Wales** 11–0
1898	Blackheath **England** 14–7
1899	Swansea **Wales** 26–3
1900	Gloucester **Wales** 13–3
1901	Cardiff **Wales** 13–0
1902	Blackheath **Wales** 9–8
1903	Swansea **Wales** 21–5
1904	Leicester **Drawn** 14–14
1905	Cardiff **Wales** 25–0
1906	Richmond (London) **Wales** 16–3
1907	Swansea **Wales** 22–0
1908	Bristol **Wales** 28–18
1909	Cardiff **Wales** 8–0
1910	Twickenham **England** 11–6
1911	Swansea **Wales** 15–11
1912	Twickenham **England** 8–0
1913	Cardiff **England** 12–0
1914	Twickenham **England** 10–9
1920	Swansea **Wales** 19–5
1921	Twickenham **England** 18–3
1922	Cardiff **Wales** 28–6
1923	Twickenham **England** 7–3
1924	Swansea **England** 17–9
1925	Twickenham **England** 12–6
1926	Cardiff **Drawn** 3–3
1927	Twickenham **England** 11–9
1928	Swansea **England** 10–8
1929	Twickenham **England** 8–3
1930	Cardiff **England** 11–3
1931	Twickenham **Drawn** 11–11
1932	Swansea **Wales** 12–5
1933	Twickenham **Wales** 7–3
1934	Cardiff **England** 9–0
1935	Twickenham **Drawn** 3–3
1936	Swansea **Drawn** 0–0
1937	Twickenham **England** 4–3
1938	Cardiff **Wales** 14–8
1939	Twickenham **England** 3–0
1947	Cardiff **England** 9–6
1948	Twickenham **Drawn** 3–3
1949	Cardiff **Wales** 9–3
1950	Twickenham **Wales** 11–5
1951	Swansea **Wales** 23–5
1952	Twickenham **Wales** 8–6
1953	Cardiff **England** 8–3
1954	Twickenham **England** 9–6
1955	Cardiff **Wales** 3–0
1956	Twickenham **Wales** 8–3
1957	Cardiff **England** 3–0
1958	Twickenham **Drawn** 3–3
1959	Cardiff **Wales** 5–0
1960	Twickenham **England** 14–6
1961	Cardiff **Wales** 6–3
1962	Twickenham **Drawn** 0–0
1963	Cardiff **England** 13–6
1964	Twickenham **Drawn** 6–6
1965	Cardiff **Wales** 14–3
1966	Twickenham **Wales** 11–6
1967	Cardiff **Wales** 34–21
1968	Twickenham **Drawn** 11–11
1969	Cardiff **Wales** 30–9
1970	Twickenham **Wales** 17–13
1971	Cardiff **Wales** 22–6
1972	Twickenham **Wales** 12–3
1973	Cardiff **Wales** 25–9
1974	Twickenham **England** 16–12
1975	Cardiff **Wales** 20–4
1976	Twickenham **Wales** 21–9
1977	Cardiff **Wales** 14–9

1978 Twickenham **Wales** 9–6
1979 Cardiff **Wales** 27–3
1980 Twickenham **England** 9–8
1981 Cardiff **Wales** 21–19
1982 Twickenham **England** 17–7
1983 Cardiff **Drawn** 13–13
1984 Twickenham **Wales** 24–15
1985 Cardiff **Wales** 24–15
1986 Twickenham **England** 21–18
1987 Cardiff **Wales** 19–12
1987 Brisbane WC **Wales** 16–3
1988 Twickenham **Wales** 11–3
1989 Cardiff **Wales** 12–9
1990 Twickenham **England** 34–6
1991 Cardiff **England** 25–6
1992 Twickenham **England** 24–0
1993 Cardiff **Wales** 10–9
1994 Twickenham **England** 15–8
1995 Cardiff **England** 23–9
1996 Twickenham **England** 21–15
1997 Cardiff **England** 34–13
1998 Twickenham **England** 60–26
1999 Wembley **Wales** 32–31
2000 Twickenham **England** 46–12
2001 Cardiff **England** 44–15
2002 Twickenham **England** 50–10
2003 Cardiff **England** 26–9
2003 Cardiff **England** 43–9
Non-championship match
2003 Brisbane WC **England** 28–17
2004 Twickenham **England** 31–21
2005 Cardiff **Wales** 11–9
2006 Twickenham **England** 47–13
2007 Cardiff **Wales** 27–18
2007 Twickenham **England** 62–5

ENGLAND V FRANCE

Played 90 England won 48, France won 35, Drawn 7
Highest scores England 48–19 in 2001, France 37–12 in 1972
Biggest wins England 37–0 in 1911, France 37–12 in 1972 and 31–6 in 2006

1906 Paris **England** 35–8
1907 Richmond (London) **England** 41–13
1908 Paris **England** 19–0
1909 Leicester **England** 22–0
1910 Paris **England** 11–3
1911 Twickenham **England** 37–0
1912 Paris **England** 18–8
1913 Twickenham **England** 20–0
1914 Paris **England** 39–13
1920 Twickenham **England** 8–3
1921 Paris **England** 10–6
1922 Twickenham **Drawn** 11–11
1923 Paris **England** 12–3
1924 Twickenham **England** 19–7
1925 Paris **England** 13–11
1926 Twickenham **England** 11–0
1927 Paris **France** 3–0
1928 Twickenham **England** 18–8
1929 Paris **England** 16–6
1930 Twickenham **England** 11–5
1931 Paris **France** 14–13
1947 Twickenham **England** 6–3
1948 Paris **France** 15–0
1949 Twickenham **England** 8–3
1950 Paris **France** 6–3
1951 Twickenham **France** 11–3
1952 Paris **England** 6–3
1953 Twickenham **England** 11–0
1954 Paris **France** 11–3
1955 Twickenham **France** 16–9
1956 Paris **France** 14–9
1957 Twickenham **England** 9–5
1958 Paris **England** 14–0
1959 Twickenham **Drawn** 3–3
1960 Paris **Drawn** 3–3
1961 Twickenham **Drawn** 5–5
1962 Paris **France** 13–0
1963 Twickenham **England** 6–5
1964 Paris **England** 6–3
1965 Twickenham **England** 9–6
1966 Paris **France** 13–0
1967 Twickenham **France** 16–12
1968 Paris **France** 14–9
1969 Twickenham **England** 22–8

1970 Paris **France** 35–13
1971 Twickenham **Drawn** 14–14
1972 Paris **France** 37–12
1973 Twickenham **England** 14–6
1974 Paris **Drawn** 12–12
1975 Twickenham **France** 27–20
1976 Paris **France** 30–9
1977 Twickenham **France** 4–3
1978 Paris **France** 15–6
1979 Twickenham **England** 7–6
1980 Paris **England** 17–13
1981 Twickenham **France** 16–12
1982 Paris **England** 27–15
1983 Twickenham **France** 19–15
1984 Paris **France** 32–18
1985 Twickenham **Drawn** 9–9
1986 Paris **France** 29–10
1987 Twickenham **France** 19–15
1988 Paris **France** 10–9
1989 Twickenham **England** 11–0
1990 Paris **England** 26–7
1991 Twickenham **England** 21–19
1991 Paris WC **England** 19–10
1992 Paris **England** 31–13
1993 Twickenham **England** 16–15
1994 Paris **England** 18–14
1995 Twickenham **England** 31–10
1995 Pretoria WC **France 19–9**
1996 Paris **France** 15–12
1997 Twickenham **France** 23–20
1998 Paris **France** 24–17
1999 Twickenham **England** 21–10
2000 Paris **England** 15–9
2001 Twickenham **England** 48–19
2002 Paris **France** 20–15
2003 Twickenham **England** 25–17
2003 Marseilles **France** 17–16
2003 Twickenham **England** 45–14
Non-championship match
2003 Sydney WC **England** 24–7
2004 Paris **France** 24–21
2005 Twickenham **France** 18–17
2006 Paris **France** 31–6
2007 Twickenham **England** 26–18
2007 Twickenham **France** 21–15
2007 Marseilles **France** 22–9
2007 Paris WC **England** 14–9

ENGLAND V SOUTH AFRICA

Played 30 England won 12, South Africa won 17, Drawn 1
Highest scores England 53–3 in 2002, South Africa 58–10 in 2007
Biggest wins England 53–3 in 2002, South Africa 58–10 in 2007

1906 Crystal Palace (London) **Drawn** 3–3
1913 Twickenham **South Africa** 9–3
1932 Twickenham **South Africa** 7–0
1952 Twickenham **South Africa** 8–3
1961 Twickenham **South Africa** 5–0
1969 Twickenham **England** 11–8
1972 Johannesburg **England** 18–9
1984 *1* Port Elizabeth **South Africa** 33–15
2 Johannesburg **South Africa** 35–9
South Africa won series 2–0
1992 Twickenham **England** 33–16
1994 *1* Pretoria **England** 32–15
2 Cape Town **South Africa** 27–9
Series drawn 1–1
1995 Twickenham **South Africa** 24–14
1997 Twickenham **South Africa** 29–11
1998 Cape Town **South Africa** 18–0
1998 Twickenham **England** 13–7
1999 Paris WC **South Africa** 44–21
2000 *1* Pretoria **South Africa** 18–13
2 Bloemfontein **England** 27–22
Series drawn 1–1
2000 Twickenham **England** 25–17
2001 Twickenham **England** 29–9
2002 Twickenham **England** 53–3
2003 Perth WC **England** 25–6
2004 Twickenham **England** 32–16
2006 1 Twickenham **England** 23–21
2 Twickenham **South Africa** 25–14
Series drawn 1–1
2007 1 Bloemfontein **South Africa** 58–10
2 Pretoria **South Africa** 55–22
South Africa won series 2–0
2007 Paris WC **South Africa** 36–0
2007 Paris WC **South Africa** 15–6

ENGLAND V NEW ZEALAND

Played 29 England won 6, New Zealand won 22, Drawn 1
Highest scores England 31–28 in 2002, New Zealand 64–22 in 1998
Biggest wins England 13–0 in 1936, New Zealand 64–22 in 1998

1905 Crystal Palace (London) **New Zealand** 15–0
1925 Twickenham **New Zealand** 17–11
1936 Twickenham **England** 13–0
1954 Twickenham **New Zealand** 5–0
1963 *1* Auckland **New Zealand** 21–11
2 Christchurch **New Zealand** 9–6
New Zealand won series 2–0
1964 Twickenham **New Zealand** 14–0
1967 Twickenham **New Zealand** 23–11
1973 Twickenham **New Zealand** 9–0
1973 Auckland **England** 16–10
1978 Twickenham **New Zealand** 16–6
1979 Twickenham **New Zealand** 10–9
1983 Twickenham **England** 15–9
1985 *1* Christchurch **New Zealand** 18–13
2 Wellington **New Zealand** 42–15
New Zealand won series 2–0
1991 Twickenham WC **New Zealand** 18–12
1993 Twickenham **England** 15–9
1995 Cape Town WC **New Zealand 45–29**
1997 *1* Manchester **New Zealand** 25–8
2 Twickenham **Drawn** 26–26
New Zealand won series 1–0, with 1 draw
1998 *1* Dunedin **New Zealand** 64–22
2 Auckland **New Zealand** 40–10
New Zealand won series 2–0
1999 Twickenham WC **New Zealand** 30–16
2002 Twickenham **England** 31–28
2003 Wellington **England** 15–13
2004 1 Dunedin **New Zealand** 36–3
2 Auckland **New Zealand** 36–12
New Zealand won series 2–0
2005 Twickenham **New Zealand** 23–19
2006 Twickenham **New Zealand** 41–20

ENGLAND V AUSTRALIA

Played 35 England won 14, Australia won 20, Drawn 1
Highest scores England 32–31 in 2002, Australia 76–0 in 1998
Biggest wins England 20–3 in 1973 & 23–6 in 1976, Australia 76–0 in 1998

1909 Blackheath (London) **Australia** 9–3
1928 Twickenham **England** 18–11
1948 Twickenham **Australia** 11–0
1958 Twickenham **England** 9–6
1963 Sydney **Australia** 18–9
1967 Twickenham **Australia** 23–11
1973 Twickenham **England** 20–3
1975 *1* Sydney **Australia** 16–9
2 Brisbane **Australia** 30–21
Australia won series 2–0
1976 Twickenham **England** 23–6
1982 Twickenham **England** 15–11
1984 Twickenham **Australia** 19–3
1987 Sydney WC **Australia** 19–6
1988 *1* Brisbane **Australia** 22–16
2 Sydney **Australia** 28–8
Australia won series 2–0
1988 Twickenham **England** 28–19
1991 Sydney **Australia** 40–15
1991 Twickenham WC **Australia** 12–6
1995 Cape Town WC **England 25–22**
1997 Sydney **Australia** 25–6
1997 Twickenham **Drawn** 15–15
1998 Brisbane **Australia** 76–0
1998 Twickenham **Australia** 12–11
1999 Sydney **Australia** 22–15
2000 Twickenham **England** 22–19
2001 Twickenham **England** 21–15
2002 Twickenham **England** 32–31
2003 Melbourne **England** 25–14

2003	Sydney WC **England** 20–17 (aet)	2006	1 Sydney **Australia** 34–3
2004	Brisbane **Australia** 51–15		2 Melbourne **Australia** 43–18
2004	Twickenham **Australia** 21–19		Australia won series 2–0
2005	Twickenham **England** 26–16	2007	Marseilles WC **England** 12–10

ENGLAND V NEW ZEALAND NATIVES

Played 1 England won 1
Highest score England 7–0 in 1889, NZ Natives 0–7 in 1889
Biggest win England 7–0 in 1889, NZ Natives no win

1889	Blackheath **England** 1G 4T to 0

ENGLAND V RFU PRESIDENT'S XV

Played 1 President's XV won 1
Highest score England 11–28 in 1971, RFU President's XV 28–11 in 1971
Biggest win RFU President's XV 28–11 in 1971

1971	Twickenham **President's XV** 28–11

ENGLAND V ARGENTINA

Played 12 England won 8, Argentina won 3, Drawn 1
Highest scores England 51–0 in 1990, Argentina 33–13 in 1997
Biggest wins England 51–0 in 1990, Argentina 33–13 in 1997

1981	*1* Buenos Aires **Drawn** 19–19	1996	Twickenham **England** 20–18
	2 Buenos Aires **England** 12–6	1997	*1* Buenos Aires **England** 46–20
	England won series 1–0 with 1 draw		*2* Buenos Aires **Argentina** 33–13
1990	*1* Buenos Aires **England** 25–12		Series drawn 1–1
	2 Buenos Aires **Argentina** 15–13	2000	Twickenham **England** 19–0
	Series drawn 1–1	2002	Buenos Aires **England** 26–18
1990	Twickenham **England** 51–0	2006	Twickenham **Argentina** 25–18
1995	Durban WC **England** 24–18		

ENGLAND V ROMANIA

Played 4 England won 4
Highest scores England 134–0 in 2001, Romania 15–22 in 1985
Biggest win England 134–0 in 2001, Romania no win

1985	Twickenham **England** 22–15	1994	Twickenham **England** 54–3
1989	Bucharest **England** 58–3	2001	Twickenham **England** 134–0

ENGLAND V JAPAN

Played 1 England won 1
Highest score England 60–7 in 1987, Japan 7–60 in 1987
Biggest win England 60–7 in 1987, Japan no win

1987	Sydney WC **England** 60–7

ENGLAND V UNITED STATES

Played 5 England won 5
Highest scores England 106–8 in 1999, United States 19–48 in 2001
Biggest win England 106–8 in 1999, United States no win

1987	Sydney WC **England** 34–6	2001	San Francisco **England** 48–19
1991	Twickenham WC **England** 37–9	2007	Lens WC **England** 28–10
1999	Twickenham **England** 106–8		

ENGLAND V FIJI

Played 4 England won 4
Highest scores England 58–23 in 1989, Fiji 24–45 in 1999
Biggest win England 58–23 in 1989, Fiji no win

1988	Suva **England** 25–12	1991	Suva **England** 28–12
1989	Twickenham **England** 58–23	1999	Twickenham WC **England** 45–24

ENGLAND V ITALY

Played 13 England won 13
Highest scores England 80–23 in 2001, Italy 23–80 in 2001
Biggest win England 67–7 in 1999, Italy no win

1991	Twickenham WC **England** 36–6	2002	Rome **England** 45–9
1995	Durban WC **England 27–20**	2003	Twickenham **England** 40–5
1996	Twickenham **England** 54–21	2004	Rome **England** 50–9
1998	Huddersfield **England** 23–15	2005	Twickenham **England** 39–7
1999	Twickenham WC **England** 67–7	2006	Rome **England** 31–16
2000	Rome **England** 59–12	2007	Twickenham **England** 20–7
2001	Twickenham **England** 80–23		

ENGLAND V CANADA

Played 6 England won 6
Highest scores England 70–0 in 2004, Canada 20–59 in 2001
Biggest win England 70–0 in 2004, Canada no win

1992	Wembley **England** 26–13		*2* Burnaby **England** 59–20
1994	Twickenham **England** 60–19		England won series 2–0
1999	Twickenham **England** 36–11	2004	Twickenham **England** 70–0
2001	*1* Markham **England** 22–10		

ENGLAND V SAMOA

Played 5 England won 5
Highest scores England 44–22 in 1995 and 44–22 in 2007, Samoa 22–44 in 1995, 22–35 in 2003 and 22–44 in 2007
Biggest win England 40–3 in 2005, Samoa no win

1995	Durban WC **England** 44–22	2005	Twickenham **England** 40–3
1995	Twickenham **England** 27–9	2007	Nantes WC **England** 44–22
2003	Melbourne WC **England** 35–22		

ENGLAND V THE NETHERLANDS

Played 1 England won 1
Highest scores England 110–0 in 1998, The Netherlands 0–110 in 1998
Biggest win England 110–0 in 1998, The Netherlands no win

1998	Huddersfield **England** 110–0

ENGLAND V TONGA

Played 2 England won 2
Highest scores England 101–10 in 1999, Tonga 20–36 in 2007
Biggest win England 101–10 in 1999, Tonga no win

1999 Twickenham WC **England** 101–10	2007 Paris WC **England** 36–20

ENGLAND V GEORGIA

Played 1 England won 1
Highest scores England 84–6 in 2003, Georgia 6–84 in 2003
Biggest win England 84–6 in 2003, Georgia no win

2003 Perth WC **England** 84–6

ENGLAND V URUGUAY

Played 1 England won 1
Highest scores England 111–13 in 2003, Uruguay 13–111 in 2003
Biggest win England 111–13 in 2003, Uruguay no win

2003 Brisbane WC **England** 111–13

SCOTLAND V IRELAND

Played 121 Scotland won 62, Ireland won 53, Drawn 5, Abandoned 1
Highest scores Scotland 38–10 in 1997, Ireland 44–22 in 2000
Biggest wins Scotland 38–10 in 1997, Ireland 36–6 in 2003

1877 Belfast **Scotland** 4G 2DG 2T to 0
1878 No Match
1879 Belfast **Scotland** 1G 1DG 1T to 0
1880 Glasgow **Scotland** 1G 2DG 2T to 0
1881 Belfast **Ireland** 1DG to 1T
1882 Glasgow **Scotland** 2T to 0
1883 Belfast **Scotland** 1G 1T to 0
1884 Raeburn Place (Edinburgh) **Scotland** 2G 2T to 1T
1885 Belfast **Abandoned** Ireland 0 Scotland 1T
1885 Raeburn Place **Scotland** 1G 2T to 0
1886 Raeburn Place **Scotland** 3G 1DG 2T to 0
1887 Belfast **Scotland** 1G 1GM 2T to 0
1888 Raeburn Place **Scotland** 1G to 0
1889 Belfast **Scotland** 1DG to 0
1890 Raeburn Place **Scotland** 1DG 1T to 0
1891 Belfast **Scotland** 14–0
1892 Raeburn Place **Scotland** 2–0
1893 Belfast **Drawn** 0–0
1894 Dublin **Ireland** 5–0
1895 Raeburn Place **Scotland** 6–0
1896 Dublin **Drawn** 0–0
1897 Powderhall (Edinburgh) **Scotland** 8–3
1898 Belfast **Scotland** 8–0

1899 Inverleith (Edinburgh) **Ireland** 9–3
1900 Dublin **Drawn** 0–0
1901 Inverleith **Scotland** 9–5
1902 Belfast **Ireland** 5–0
1903 Inverleith **Scotland** 3–0
1904 Dublin **Scotland** 19–3
1905 Inverleith **Ireland** 11–5
1906 Dublin **Scotland** 13–6
1907 Inverleith **Scotland** 15–3
1908 Dublin **Ireland** 16–11
1909 Inverleith **Scotland** 9–3
1910 Belfast **Scotland** 14–0
1911 Inverleith **Ireland** 16–10
1912 Dublin **Ireland** 10–8
1913 Inverleith **Scotland** 29–14
1914 Dublin **Ireland** 6–0
1920 Inverleith **Scotland** 19–0
1921 Dublin **Ireland** 9–8
1922 Inverleith **Scotland** 6–3
1923 Dublin **Scotland** 13–3
1924 Inverleith **Scotland** 13–8
1925 Dublin **Scotland** 14–8
1926 Murrayfield **Ireland** 3–0
1927 Dublin **Ireland** 6–0
1928 Murrayfield **Ireland** 13–5
1929 Dublin **Scotland** 16–7
1930 Murrayfield **Ireland** 14–11
1931 Dublin **Ireland** 8–5
1932 Murrayfield **Ireland** 20–8
1933 Dublin **Scotland** 8–6
1934 Murrayfield **Scotland** 16–9
1935 Dublin **Ireland** 12–5
1936 Murrayfield **Ireland** 10–4
1937 Dublin **Ireland** 11–4
1938 Murrayfield **Scotland** 23–14
1939 Dublin **Ireland** 12–3
1947 Murrayfield **Ireland** 3–0
1948 Dublin **Ireland** 6–0
1949 Murrayfield **Ireland** 13–3
1950 Dublin **Ireland** 21–0
1951 Murrayfield **Ireland** 6–5
1952 Dublin **Ireland** 12–8
1953 Murrayfield **Ireland** 26–8
1954 Belfast **Ireland** 6–0
1955 Murrayfield **Scotland** 12–3
1956 Dublin **Ireland** 14–10
1957 Murrayfield **Ireland** 5–3
1958 Dublin **Ireland** 12–6
1959 Murrayfield **Ireland** 8–3
1960 Dublin **Scotland** 6–5
1961 Murrayfield **Scotland** 16–8
1962 Dublin **Scotland** 20–6
1963 Murrayfield **Scotland** 3–0
1964 Dublin **Scotland** 6–3
1965 Murrayfield **Ireland** 16–6
1966 Dublin **Scotland** 11–3
1967 Murrayfield **Ireland** 5–3
1968 Dublin **Ireland** 14–6
1969 Murrayfield **Ireland** 16–0
1970 Dublin **Ireland** 16–11
1971 Murrayfield **Ireland** 17–5
1972 No Match
1973 Murrayfield **Scotland** 19–14
1974 Dublin **Ireland** 9–6
1975 Murrayfield **Scotland** 20–13
1976 Dublin **Scotland** 15–6
1977 Murrayfield **Scotland** 21–18
1978 Dublin **Ireland** 12–9
1979 Murrayfield **Drawn** 11–11
1980 Dublin **Ireland** 22–15
1981 Murrayfield **Scotland** 10–9
1982 Dublin **Ireland** 21–12
1983 Murrayfield **Ireland** 15–13
1984 Dublin **Scotland** 32–9
1985 Murrayfield **Ireland** 18–15
1986 Dublin **Scotland** 10–9
1987 Murrayfield **Scotland** 16–12
1988 Dublin **Ireland** 22–18
1989 Murrayfield **Scotland** 37–21
1990 Dublin **Scotland** 13–10
1991 Murrayfield **Scotland** 28–25
1991 Murrayfield WC **Scotland** 24–15
1992 Dublin **Scotland** 18–10
1993 Murrayfield **Scotland** 15–3
1994 Dublin **Drawn** 6–6
1995 Murrayfield **Scotland** 26–13
1996 Dublin **Scotland** 16–10
1997 Murrayfield **Scotland** 38–10
1998 Dublin **Scotland** 17–16
1999 Murrayfield **Scotland** 30–13
2000 Dublin **Ireland** 44–22
2001 Murrayfield **Scotland** 32–10
2002 Dublin **Ireland** 43–22
2003 Murrayfield **Ireland** 36–6
2003 Murrayfield **Ireland** 29–10
2004 Dublin **Ireland** 37–16
2005 Murrayfield **Ireland** 40–13
2006 Dublin **Ireland** 15–9
2007 Murrayfield **Ireland** 19–18
2007 Murrayfield **Scotland** 31–21

SCOTLAND V WALES

Played 112 Scotland won 48, Wales won 61, Drawn 3
Highest scores Scotland 35–10 in 1924, Wales 46–22 in 2005
Biggest wins Scotland 35–10 in 1924, Wales 46–22 in 2005

1883 Raeburn Place (Edinburgh) **Scotland** 3G to 1G
1884 Newport **Scotland** 1DG 1T to 0
1885 Glasgow **Drawn** no score
1886 Cardiff **Scotland** 2G 1T to 0
1887 Raeburn Place **Scotland** 4G 8T to 0
1888 Newport **Wales** 1T to 0
1889 Raeburn Place **Scotland** 2T to 0
1890 Cardiff **Scotland** 1G 2T to 1T
1891 Raeburn Place **Scotland** 15–0
1892 Swansea **Scotland** 7–2
1893 Raeburn Place **Wales** 9–0
1894 Newport **Wales** 7–0
1895 Raeburn Place **Scotland** 5–4
1896 Cardiff **Wales** 6–0
1897 No Match
1898 No Match
1899 Inverleith (Edinburgh) **Scotland** 21–10
1900 Swansea **Wales** 12–3
1901 Inverleith **Scotland** 18–8
1902 Cardiff **Wales** 14–5
1903 Inverleith **Scotland** 6–0
1904 Swansea **Wales** 21–3
1905 Inverleith **Wales** 6–3
1906 Cardiff **Wales** 9–3
1907 Inverleith **Scotland** 6–3
1908 Swansea **Wales** 6–5
1909 Inverleith **Wales** 5–3
1910 Cardiff **Wales** 14–0
1911 Inverleith **Wales** 32–10
1912 Swansea **Wales** 21–6
1913 Inverleith **Wales** 8–0
1914 Cardiff **Wales** 24–5
1920 Inverleith **Scotland** 9–5
1921 Swansea **Scotland** 14–8
1922 Inverleith **Drawn** 9–9
1923 Cardiff **Scotland** 11–8
1924 Inverleith **Scotland** 35–10
1925 Swansea **Scotland** 24–14
1926 Murrayfield **Scotland** 8–5
1927 Cardiff **Scotland** 5–0
1928 Murrayfield **Wales** 13–0
1929 Swansea **Wales** 14–7
1930 Murrayfield **Scotland** 12–9
1931 Cardiff **Wales** 13–8
1932 Murrayfield **Wales** 6–0
1933 Swansea **Scotland** 11–3
1934 Murrayfield **Wales** 13–6
1935 Cardiff **Wales** 10–6
1936 Murrayfield **Wales** 13–3
1937 Swansea **Scotland** 13–6
1938 Murrayfield **Scotland** 8–6
1939 Cardiff **Wales** 11–3
1947 Murrayfield **Wales** 22–8
1948 Cardiff **Wales** 14–0
1949 Murrayfield **Scotland** 6–5
1950 Swansea **Wales** 12–0
1951 Murrayfield **Scotland** 19–0
1952 Cardiff **Wales** 11–0
1953 Murrayfield **Wales** 12–0
1954 Swansea **Wales** 15–3
1955 Murrayfield **Scotland** 14–8
1956 Cardiff **Wales** 9–3
1957 Murrayfield **Scotland** 9–6
1958 Cardiff **Wales** 8–3
1959 Murrayfield **Scotland** 6–5
1960 Cardiff **Wales** 8–0
1961 Murrayfield **Scotland** 3–0
1962 Cardiff **Scotland** 8–3
1963 Murrayfield **Wales** 6–0
1964 Cardiff **Wales** 11–3
1965 Murrayfield **Wales** 14–12
1966 Cardiff **Wales** 8–3
1967 Murrayfield **Scotland** 11–5
1968 Cardiff **Wales** 5–0
1969 Murrayfield **Wales** 17–3
1970 Cardiff **Wales** 18–9
1971 Murrayfield **Wales** 19–18
1972 Cardiff **Wales** 35–12
1973 Murrayfield **Scotland** 10–9
1974 Cardiff **Wales** 6–0
1975 Murrayfield **Scotland** 12–10
1976 Cardiff **Wales** 28–6
1977 Murrayfield **Wales** 18–9
1978 Cardiff **Wales** 22–14
1979 Murrayfield **Wales** 19–13

1980 Cardiff **Wales** 17–6
1981 Murrayfield **Scotland** 15–6
1982 Cardiff **Scotland** 34–18
1983 Murrayfield **Wales** 19–15
1984 Cardiff **Scotland** 15–9
1985 Murrayfield **Wales** 25–21
1986 Cardiff **Wales** 22–15
1987 Murrayfield **Scotland** 21–15
1988 Cardiff **Wales** 25–20
1989 Murrayfield **Scotland** 23–7
1990 Cardiff **Scotland** 13–9
1991 Murrayfield **Scotland** 32–12
1992 Cardiff **Wales** 15–12
1993 Murrayfield **Scotland** 20–0
1994 Cardiff **Wales** 29–6
1995 Murrayfield **Scotland** 26–13
1996 Cardiff **Scotland** 16–14
1997 Murrayfield **Wales** 34–19
1998 Wembley **Wales** 19–13
1999 Murrayfield **Scotland** 33–20
2000 Cardiff **Wales** 26–18
2001 Murrayfield **Drawn** 28–28
2002 Cardiff **Scotland** 27–22
2003 Murrayfield **Scotland** 30–22
2003 Cardiff **Wales** 23–9
2004 Cardiff **Wales** 23–10
2005 Murrayfield **Wales** 46–22
2006 Cardiff **Wales** 28–18
2007 Murrayfield **Scotland** 21–9

SCOTLAND V FRANCE

Played 80 Scotland won 34, France won 43, Drawn 3
Highest scores Scotland 36–22 in 1999, France 51–16 in 1998 and 51–9 in 2003
Biggest wins Scotland 31–3 in 1912, France 51–9 in 2003

1910 Inverleith (Edinburgh) **Scotland** 27–0
1911 Paris **France** 16–15
1912 Inverleith **Scotland** 31–3
1913 Paris **Scotland** 21–3
1914 No Match
1920 Paris **Scotland** 5–0
1921 Inverleith **France** 3–0
1922 Paris **Drawn** 3–3
1923 Inverleith **Scotland** 16–3
1924 Paris **France** 12–10
1925 Inverleith **Scotland** 25–4
1926 Paris **Scotland** 20–6
1927 Murrayfield **Scotland** 23–6
1928 Paris **Scotland** 15–6
1929 Murrayfield **Scotland** 6–3
1930 Paris **France** 7–3
1931 Murrayfield **Scotland** 6–4
1947 Paris **France** 8–3
1948 Murrayfield **Scotland** 9–8
1949 Paris **Scotland** 8–0
1950 Murrayfield **Scotland** 8–5
1951 Paris **France** 14–12
1952 Murrayfield **France** 13–11
1953 Paris **France** 11–5
1954 Murrayfield **France** 3–0
1955 Paris **France** 15–0
1956 Murrayfield **Scotland** 12–0
1957 Paris **Scotland** 6–0
1958 Murrayfield **Scotland** 11–9
1959 Paris **France** 9–0
1960 Murrayfield **France** 13–11
1961 Paris **France** 11–0
1962 Murrayfield **France** 11–3
1963 Paris **Scotland** 11–6
1964 Murrayfield **Scotland** 10–0
1965 Paris **France** 16–8
1966 Murrayfield **Drawn** 3–3
1967 Paris **Scotland** 9–8
1968 Murrayfield **France** 8–6
1969 Paris **Scotland** 6–3
1970 Murrayfield **France** 11–9
1971 Paris **France** 13–8
1972 Murrayfield **Scotland** 20–9
1973 Paris **France** 16–13
1974 Murrayfield **Scotland** 19–6
1975 Paris **France** 10–9
1976 Murrayfield **France** 13–6
1977 Paris **France** 23–3
1978 Murrayfield **France** 19–16
1979 Paris **France** 21–17

1980 Murrayfield **Scotland** 22–14
1981 Paris **France** 16–9
1982 Murrayfield **Scotland** 16–7
1983 Paris **France** 19–15
1984 Murrayfield **Scotland** 21–12
1985 Paris **France** 11–3
1986 Murrayfield **Scotland** 18–17
1987 Paris **France** 28–22
1987 Christchurch WC **Drawn** 20–20
1988 Murrayfield **Scotland** 23–12
1989 Paris **France** 19–3
1990 Murrayfield **Scotland** 21–0
1991 Paris **France** 15–9
1992 Murrayfield **Scotland** 10–6
1993 Paris **France** 11–3
1994 Murrayfield **France** 20–12
1995 Paris **Scotland** 23–21
1995 Pretoria WC **France** 22–19
1996 Murrayfield **Scotland** 19–14
1997 Paris **France** 47–20
1998 Murrayfield **France** 51–16
1999 Paris **Scotland** 36–22
2000 Murrayfield **France** 28–16
2001 Paris **France** 16–6
2002 Murrayfield **France** 22–10
2003 Paris **France** 38–3
2003 Sydney WC **France** 51–9
2004 Murrayfield **France** 31–0
2005 Paris **France** 16–9
2006 Murrayfield **Scotland** 20–16
2007 Paris **France** 46–19

SCOTLAND V SOUTH AFRICA

Played 19 Scotland won 4, South Africa won 15, Drawn 0
Highest scores Scotland 29–46 in 1999, South Africa 68–10 in 1997
Biggest wins Scotland 21–6 in 2002, South Africa 68–10 in 1997

1906 Glasgow **Scotland** 6–0
1912 Inverleith **South Africa** 16–0
1932 Murrayfield **South Africa** 6–3
1951 Murrayfield **South Africa** 44–0
1960 Port Elizabeth **South Africa** 18–10
1961 Murrayfield **South Africa** 12–5
1965 Murrayfield **Scotland** 8–5
1969 Murrayfield **Scotland** 6–3
1994 Murrayfield **South Africa** 34–10
1997 Murrayfield **South Africa** 68–10
1998 Murrayfield **South Africa** 35–10
1999 Murrayfield WC **South Africa** 46–29
2002 Murrayfield **Scotland** 21–6
2003 *1* Durban **South Africa** 29–25
2 Johannesburg **South Africa** 28–19
South Africa won series 2–0
2004 Murrayfield **South Africa** 45–10
2006 1 Durban **South Africa** 36–16
2 Port Elizabeth **South Africa** 29–15
South Africa won series 2–0
2007 Murrayfield **South Africa** 27–3

SCOTLAND V NEW ZEALAND

Played 26 Scotland won 0, New Zealand won 24, Drawn 2
Highest scores Scotland 31–62 in 1996, New Zealand 69–20 in 2000
Biggest wins Scotland no win, New Zealand 69–20 in 2000

1905 Inverleith (Edinburgh) **New Zealand** 12–7
1935 Murrayfield **New Zealand** 18–8
1954 Murrayfield **New Zealand** 3–0
1964 Murrayfield **Drawn** 0–0
1967 Murrayfield **New Zealand** 14–3
1972 Murrayfield **New Zealand** 14–9

1975	Auckland **New Zealand** 24–0	1993	Murrayfield **New Zealand** 51–15
1978	Murrayfield **New Zealand** 18–9	1995	Pretoria WC **New Zealand** 48–30
1979	Murrayfield **New Zealand** 20–6	1996	*1* Dunedin **New Zealand** 62–31
1981	*1* Dunedin **New Zealand** 11–4		*2* Auckland **New Zealand** 36–12
	2 Auckland **New Zealand** 40–15		New Zealand won series 2–0
	New Zealand won series 2–0	1999	Murrayfield WC **New Zealand** 30–18
1983	Murrayfield **Drawn** 25–25	2000	*1* Dunedin **New Zealand** 69–20
1987	Christchurch WC **New Zealand** 30–3		*2* Auckland **New Zealand** 48–14
1990	*1* Dunedin **New Zealand** 31–16		New Zealand won series 2–0
	2 Auckland **New Zealand** 21–18	2001	Murrayfield **New Zealand** 37–6
	New Zealand won series 2–0	2005	Murrayfield **New Zealand** 29–10
1991	Cardiff WC **New Zealand** 13–6	2007	Murrayfield WC **New Zealand** 40–0

SCOTLAND V AUSTRALIA

Played 25 Scotland won 7, Australia won 18, Drawn 0
Highest scores Scotland 24–15 in 1981, Australia 45–3 in 1998
Biggest wins Scotland 24–15 in 1981, Australia 45–3 in 1998

1927	Murrayfield **Scotland** 10–8		Australia won series 2–0
1947	Murrayfield **Australia** 16–7	1996	Murrayfield **Australia** 29–19
1958	Murrayfield **Scotland** 12–8	1997	Murrayfield **Australia** 37–8
1966	Murrayfield **Scotland** 11–5	1998	*1* Sydney **Australia** 45–3
1968	Murrayfield **Scotland** 9–3		*2* Brisbane **Australia** 33–11
1970	Sydney **Australia** 23–3		Australia won series 2–0
1975	Murrayfield **Scotland** 10–3	2000	Murrayfield **Australia** 30–9
1981	Murrayfield **Scotland** 24–15	2003	Brisbane WC **Australia** 33–16
1982	*1* Brisbane **Scotland** 12–7	2004	1 Melbourne **Australia** 35–15
	2 Sydney **Australia** 33–9		2 Sydney **Australia** 34–13
	Series drawn 1–1		Australia won series 2–0
1984	Murrayfield **Australia** 37–12	2004	1 Murrayfield **Australia** 31–14
1988	Murrayfield **Australia** 32–13		2 Glasgow **Australia** 31–17
1992	*1* Sydney **Australia** 27–12		Australia won series 2–0
	2 Brisbane **Australia** 37–13	2006	Murrayfield **Australia** 44–15

SCOTLAND V SRU PRESIDENT'S XV

Played 1 Scotland won 1
Highest scores Scotland 27–16 in 1972, SRU President's XV 16–27 in 1973
Biggest win Scotland 27–16 in 1973, SRU President's XV no win

1973	Murrayfield **Scotland** 27–16

SCOTLAND V ROMANIA

Played 12 Scotland won 10 Romania won 2, Drawn 0
Highest scores Scotland 60–19 in 1999, Romania 28–55 in 1987 & 28–22 in 1984
Biggest wins Scotland 48–6 in 2006 and 42–0 in 2007, Romania 28–22 in 1984 & 18–12 in 1991

1981	Murrayfield **Scotland** 12–6	1995	Murrayfield **Scotland** 49–16
1984	Bucharest **Romania** 28–22	1999	Glasgow **Scotland** 60–19
1986	Bucharest **Scotland** 33–18	2002	Murrayfield **Scotland** 37–10
1987	Dunedin WC **Scotland** 55–28	2005	Bucharest **Scotland** 39–19
1989	Murrayfield **Scotland** 32–0	2006	Murrayfield **Scotland** 48–6
1991	Bucharest **Romania** 18–12	2007	Murrayfield WC **Scotland** 42–0

SCOTLAND V ZIMBABWE

Played 2 Scotland won 2
Highest scores Scotland 60–21 in 1987, Zimbabwe 21–60 in 1987
Biggest win Scotland 60–21 in 1987 & 51–12 in 1991, Zimbabwe no win

1987	Wellington WC **Scotland** 60–21	1991	Murrayfield WC **Scotland** 51–12

SCOTLAND V FIJI

Played 4 Scotland won 3, Fiji won 1
Highest scores Scotland 38–17 in 1989, Fiji 51–26 in 1998
Biggest win Scotland 38–17 in 1989, Fiji 51–26 in 1998

1989	Murrayfield **Scotland** 38–17	2002	Murrayfield **Scotland** 36–22
1998	Suva **Fiji** 51–26	2003	Sydney WC **Scotland** 22–20

SCOTLAND V ARGENTINA

Played 7 Scotland won 1, Argentina won 6, Drawn 0
Highest scores Scotland 49–3 in 1990, Argentina 31–22 in 1999
Biggest wins Scotland 49–3 in 1990, Argentina 31–22 in 1999 and 25–16 in 2001

1990	Murrayfield **Scotland** 49–3	*2* Buenos Aires **Argentina** 19–17
1994	*1* Buenos Aires **Argentina** 16–15	Argentina won series 2–0

1999	Murrayfield **Argentina** 31–22	2005	Murrayfield **Argentina** 23–19
2001	Murrayfield **Argentina** 25–16	2007	Paris WC **Argentina** 19–13

SCOTLAND V JAPAN

Played 3 Scotland won 3
Highest scores Scotland 100–8 in 2004, Japan 11–32 in 2003
Biggest win Scotland 100–8 in 2004, Japan no win

1991	Murrayfield WC **Scotland** 47–9	2004	Perth **Scotland** 100–8
2003	Townsville WC **Scotland** 32–11		

SCOTLAND V SAMOA

Played 6 Scotland won 5, Drawn 1
Highest scores Scotland 38–3 in 2004, Samoa 20–35 in 1999
Biggest win Scotland 38–3 in 2004, Samoa no win

1991	Murrayfield WC **Scotland** 28–6	2000	Murrayfield **Scotland** 31–8
1995	Murrayfield **Drawn** 15–15	2004	Wellington (NZ) **Scotland** 38–3
1999	Murrayfield WC **Scotland** 35–20	2005	Murrayfield **Scotland** 18–11

SCOTLAND V CANADA

Played 2 Scotland won 1, Canada won 1
Highest scores Scotland 23–26 in 2002, Canada 26–23 in 2002
Biggest win Scotland 22–6 in 1995, Canada 26–23 in 2002

1995	Murrayfield **Scotland** 22–6	2002	Vancouver **Canada** 26–23

SCOTLAND V IVORY COAST

Played 1 Scotland won 1
Highest scores Scotland 89–0 in 1995, Ivory Coast 0–89 in 1995
Biggest win Scotland 89–0 in 1995, Ivory Coast no win

1995	Rustenburg WC **Scotland 89–0**

SCOTLAND V TONGA

Played 2 Scotland won 2
Highest scores Scotland 43–20 in 2001, Tonga 20–43 in 2001
Biggest win Scotland 41–5 in 1995, Tonga no win

1995 Pretoria WC **Scotland 41–5**
2001 Murrayfield **Scotland** 43–20

SCOTLAND V ITALY

Played 13 Scotland won 9, Italy won 4
Highest scores Scotland 47–15 in 2003, Italy 37–17 in 2007
Biggest wins Scotland 47–15 in 2003, Italy 37–17 in 2007

1996 Murrayfield **Scotland** 29–22
1998 Treviso **Italy** 25–21
1999 Murrayfield **Scotland** 30–12
2000 Rome **Italy** 34–20
2001 Murrayfield **Scotland** 23–19
2002 Rome **Scotland** 29–12
2003 Murrayfield **Scotland** 33–25
2003 Murrayfield **Scotland** 47–15
2004 Rome **Italy** 20–14
2005 Murrayfield **Scotland** 18–10
2006 Rome **Scotland** 13–10
2007 Murrayfield **Italy** 37–17
2007 Saint Etienne WC **Scotland** 18–16

SCOTLAND V URUGUAY

Played 1 Scotland won 1
Highest scores Scotland 43–12 in 1999, Uruguay 12–43 in 1999
Biggest win Scotland 43–12 in 1999, Uruguay no win

1999 Murrayfield WC **Scotland** 43–12

SCOTLAND V SPAIN

Played 1 Scotland won 1
Highest scores Scotland 48–0 in 1999, Spain 0–48 in 1999
Biggest win Scotland 48–0 in 1999, Spain no win

1999 Murrayfield WC **Scotland** 48–0

SCOTLAND V UNITED STATES

Played 3 Scotland won 3
Highest scores Scotland 65–23 in 2002, United States 23–65 in 2002
Biggest win Scotland 53–6 in 2000, United States no win

2000	Murrayfield **Scotland** 53–6	2003	Brisbane WC **Scotland** 39–15
2002	San Francisco **Scotland** 65–23		

SCOTLAND V PACIFIC ISLANDS

Played 1 Scotland won 1
Highest scores Scotland 34–22 in 2006, Pacific Islands 22–34 in 2006
Biggest win Scotland 34–22 in 2006, Pacific Islands no win

2006	Murrayfield **Scotland** 34–22

SCOTLAND V PORTUGAL

Played 1 Scotland won 1
Highest scores Scotland 56–10 in 2007, Portugal 10–56 in 2007
Biggest win Scotland 56–10 in 2007, Portugal no win

2007	Saint Etienne WC **Scotland** 56–10

IRELAND V WALES

Played 112 Ireland won 45, Wales won 61, Drawn 6
Highest scores Ireland 54–10 in 2002, Wales 34–9 in 1976
Biggest wins Ireland 54–10 in 2002, Wales 29–0 in 1907

1882	Dublin **Wales** 2G 2T to 0	1891	Llanelli **Wales** 6–4
1883	No Match	1892	Dublin **Ireland** 9–0
1884	Cardiff **Wales** 1DG 2T to 0	1893	Llanelli **Wales** 2–0
1885	No Match	1894	Belfast **Ireland** 3–0
1886	No Match	1895	Cardiff **Wales** 5–3
1887	Birkenhead **Wales** 1DG 1T to 3T	1896	Dublin **Ireland** 8–4
1888	Dublin **Ireland** 1G 1DG 1T to 0	1897	No Match
1889	Swansea **Ireland** 2T to 0	1898	Limerick **Wales** 11–3
1890	Dublin **Drawn** 1G each	1899	Cardiff **Ireland** 3–0

1900 Belfast **Wales** 3–0
1901 Swansea **Wales** 10–9
1902 Dublin **Wales** 15–0
1903 Cardiff **Wales** 18–0
1904 Belfast **Ireland** 14–12
1905 Swansea **Wales** 10–3
1906 Belfast **Ireland** 11–6
1907 Cardiff **Wales** 29–0
1908 Belfast **Wales** 11–5
1909 Swansea **Wales** 18–5
1910 Dublin **Wales** 19–3
1911 Cardiff **Wales** 16–0
1912 Belfast **Ireland** 12–5
1913 Swansea **Wales** 16–13
1914 Belfast **Wales** 11–3
1920 Cardiff **Wales** 28–4
1921 Belfast **Wales** 6–0
1922 Swansea **Wales** 11–5
1923 Dublin **Ireland** 5–4
1924 Cardiff **Ireland** 13–10
1925 Belfast **Ireland** 19–3
1926 Swansea **Wales** 11–8
1927 Dublin **Ireland** 19–9
1928 Cardiff **Ireland** 13–10
1929 Belfast **Drawn** 5–5
1930 Swansea **Wales** 12–7
1931 Belfast **Wales** 15–3
1932 Cardiff **Ireland** 12–10
1933 Belfast **Ireland** 10–5
1934 Swansea **Wales** 13–0
1935 Belfast **Ireland** 9–3
1936 Cardiff **Wales** 3–0
1937 Belfast **Ireland** 5–3
1938 Swansea **Wales** 11–5
1939 Belfast **Wales** 7–0
1947 Swansea **Wales** 6–0
1948 Belfast **Ireland** 6–3
1949 Swansea **Ireland** 5–0
1950 Belfast **Wales** 6–3
1951 Cardiff **Drawn** 3–3
1952 Dublin **Wales** 14–3
1953 Swansea **Wales** 5–3
1954 Dublin **Wales** 12–9
1955 Cardiff **Wales** 21–3
1956 Dublin **Ireland** 11–3
1957 Cardiff **Wales** 6–5
1958 Dublin **Wales** 9–6
1959 Cardiff **Wales** 8–6
1960 Dublin **Wales** 10–9
1961 Cardiff **Wales** 9–0
1962 Dublin **Drawn** 3–3
1963 Cardiff **Ireland** 14–6
1964 Dublin **Wales** 15–6
1965 Cardiff **Wales** 14–8
1966 Dublin **Ireland** 9–6
1967 Cardiff **Ireland** 3–0
1968 Dublin **Ireland** 9–6
1969 Cardiff **Wales** 24–11
1970 Dublin **Ireland** 14–0
1971 Cardiff **Wales** 23–9
1972 No Match
1973 Cardiff **Wales** 16–12
1974 Dublin **Drawn** 9–9
1975 Cardiff **Wales** 32–4
1976 Dublin **Wales** 34–9
1977 Cardiff **Wales** 25–9
1978 Dublin **Wales** 20–16
1978 Dublin **Wales** 20–16
1979 Cardiff **Wales** 24–21
1980 Dublin **Ireland** 21–7
1981 Cardiff **Wales** 9–8
1982 Dublin **Ireland** 20–12
1983 Cardiff **Wales** 23–9
1984 Dublin **Wales** 18–9
1985 Cardiff **Ireland** 21–9
1986 Dublin **Wales** 19–12
1987 Cardiff **Ireland** 15–11
1987 Wellington WC **Wales** 13–6
1988 Dublin **Wales** 12–9
1989 Cardiff **Ireland** 19–13
1990 Dublin **Ireland** 14–8
1991 Cardiff **Drawn** 21–21
1992 Dublin **Wales** 16–15
1993 Cardiff **Ireland** 19–14
1994 Dublin **Wales** 17–15
1995 Cardiff **Ireland** 16–12
1995 Johannesburg WC **Ireland 24–23**
1996 Dublin **Ireland** 30–17
1997 Cardiff **Ireland** 26–25
1998 Dublin **Wales** 30–21
1999 Wembley **Ireland** 29–23
2000 Dublin **Wales** 23–19
2001 Cardiff **Ireland** 36–6
2002 Dublin **Ireland** 54–10
2003 Cardiff **Ireland** 25–24
2003 Dublin **Ireland** 35–12
2004 Dublin **Ireland** 36–15
2005 Cardiff **Wales** 32–20
2006 Dublin **Ireland** 31–5
2007 Cardiff **Ireland** 19–9

IRELAND V FRANCE

Played 83 Ireland won 28, France won 50, Drawn 5
Highest scores Ireland 31–43 in 2006, France 45–10 in 1996
Biggest wins Ireland 24–0 in 1913, France 44–5 in 2002

1909 Dublin **Ireland** 19–8
1910 Paris **Ireland** 8–3
1911 Cork **Ireland** 25–5
1912 Paris **Ireland** 11–6
1913 Cork **Ireland** 24–0
1914 Paris **Ireland** 8–6
1920 Dublin **France** 15–7
1921 Paris **France** 20–10
1922 Dublin **Ireland** 8–3
1923 Paris **France** 14–8
1924 Dublin **Ireland** 6–0
1925 Paris **Ireland** 9–3
1926 Belfast **Ireland** 11–0
1927 Paris **Ireland** 8–3
1928 Belfast **Ireland** 12–8
1929 Paris **Ireland** 6–0
1930 Belfast **France** 5–0
1931 Paris **France** 3–0
1947 Dublin **France** 12–8
1948 Paris **Ireland** 13–6
1949 Dublin **France** 16–9
1950 Paris **Drawn** 3–3
1951 Dublin **Ireland** 9–8
1952 Paris **Ireland** 11–8
1953 Belfast **Ireland** 16–3
1954 Paris **France** 8–0
1955 Dublin **France** 5–3
1956 Paris **France** 14–8
1957 Dublin **Ireland** 11–6
1958 Paris **France** 11–6
1959 Dublin **Ireland** 9–5
1960 Paris **France** 23–6
1961 Dublin **France** 15–3
1962 Paris **France** 11–0
1963 Dublin **France** 24–5
1964 Paris **France** 27–6
1965 Dublin **Drawn** 3–3
1966 Paris **France** 11–6
1967 Dublin **France** 11–6
1968 Paris **France** 16–6
1969 Dublin **Ireland** 17–9
1970 Paris **France** 8–0
1971 Dublin **Drawn** 9–9
1972 Paris **Ireland** 14–9
1972 Dublin **Ireland** 24–14
Non-championship match
1973 Dublin **Ireland** 6–4
1974 Paris **France** 9–6
1975 Dublin **Ireland** 25–6
1976 Paris **France** 26–3
1977 Dublin **France** 15–6
1978 Paris **France** 10–9
1979 Dublin **Drawn** 9–9
1980 Paris **France** 19–18
1981 Dublin **France** 19–13
1982 Paris **France** 22–9
1983 Dublin **Ireland** 22–16
1984 Paris **France** 25–12
1985 Dublin **Drawn** 15–15
1986 Paris **France** 29–9
1987 Dublin **France** 19–13
1988 Paris **France** 25–6
1989 Dublin **France** 26–21
1990 Paris **France** 31–12
1991 Dublin **France** 21–13
1992 Paris **France** 44–12
1993 Dublin **France** 21–6
1994 Paris **France** 35–15
1995 Dublin **France** 25–7
1995 Durban WC **France 36–12**
1996 Paris **France** 45–10
1997 Dublin **France** 32–15
1998 Paris **France** 18–16
1999 Dublin **France** 10–9
2000 Paris **Ireland** 27–25
2001 Dublin **Ireland** 22–15
2002 Paris **France** 44–5
2003 Dublin **Ireland** 15–12
2003 Melbourne WC **France** 43–21
2004 Paris **France** 35–17
2005 Dublin **France** 26–19
2006 Paris **France** 43–31
2007 Dublin **France** 20–17
2007 Paris WC **France** 25–3

IRELAND V SOUTH AFRICA

Played 18 Ireland won 3, South Africa won 14, Drawn 1
Highest scores Ireland 32–15 in 2006, South Africa 38–0 in 1912
Biggest wins Ireland 32–15 in 2006, South Africa 38–0 in 1912

1906 Belfast **South Africa** 15–12
1912 Dublin **South Africa** 38–0
1931 Dublin **South Africa** 8–3
1951 Dublin **South Africa** 17–5
1960 Dublin **South Africa** 8–3
1961 Cape Town **South Africa** 24–8
1965 Dublin **Ireland** 9–6
1970 Dublin **Drawn** 8–8
1981 *1* Cape Town **South Africa** 23–15
2 Durban **South Africa** 12–10
South Africa won series 2–0
1998 *1* Bloemfontein **South Africa** 37–13
2 Pretoria **South Africa** 33–0
South Africa won series 2–0
1998 Dublin **South Africa** 27–13
2000 Dublin **South Africa** 28–18
2004 1 Bloemfontein **South Africa** 31–17
2 Cape Town **South Africa** 26–17
South Africa won series 2–0
2004 Dublin **Ireland** 17–12
2006 Dublin **Ireland** 32–15

IRELAND V NEW ZEALAND

Played 20 Ireland won 0, New Zealand won 19, Drawn 1
Highest scores Ireland 29–40 in 2001, New Zealand 63–15 in 1997
Biggest win Ireland no win, New Zealand 59–6 in 1992

1905 Dublin **New Zealand** 15–0
1924 Dublin **New Zealand** 6–0
1935 Dublin **New Zealand** 17–9
1954 Dublin **New Zealand** 14–3
1963 Dublin **New Zealand** 6–5
1973 Dublin **Drawn** 10–10
1974 Dublin **New Zealand** 15–6
1976 Wellington **New Zealand** 11–3
1978 Dublin **New Zealand** 10–6
1989 Dublin **New Zealand** 23–6
1992 *1* Dunedin **New Zealand** 24–21
2 Wellington **New Zealand** 59–6
New Zealand won series 2–0
1995 Johannesburg WC **New Zealand 43–19**
1997 Dublin **New Zealand** 63–15
2001 Dublin **New Zealand** 40–29
2002 *1* Dunedin **New Zealand** 15–6
2 Auckland **New Zealand** 40–8
New Zealand won series 2–0
2005 Dublin **New Zealand** 45–7
2006 1 Hamilton **New Zealand** 34–23
2 Auckland **New Zealand** 27–17
New Zealand won series 2–0

IRELAND V AUSTRALIA

Played 26 Ireland won 8, Australia won 18, Drawn 0
Highest scores Ireland 27–12 in 1979, Australia 46–10 in 1999
Biggest wins Ireland 27–12 in 1979 & 21–6 in 2006, Australia 46–10 in 1999

1927 Dublin **Australia** 5–3
1947 Dublin **Australia** 16–3
1958 Dublin **Ireland** 9–6
1967 Dublin **Ireland** 15–8
1967 Sydney **Ireland** 11–5
1968 Dublin **Ireland** 10–3
1976 Dublin **Australia** 20–10
1979 *1* Brisbane **Ireland** 27–12
2 Sydney **Ireland** 9–3
Ireland won series 2–0
1981 Dublin **Australia** 16–12
1984 Dublin **Australia** 16–9
1987 Sydney WC **Australia** 33–15
1991 Dublin WC **Australia** 19–18
1992 Dublin **Australia** 42–17
1994 *1* Brisbane **Australia** 33–13
2 Sydney **Australia** 32–18
Australia won series 2–0
1996 Dublin **Australia** 22–12
1999 *1* Brisbane **Australia** 46–10
2 Perth **Australia** 32–26
Australia won series 2–0
1999 Dublin WC **Australia** 23–3
2002 Dublin **Ireland** 18–9
2003 Perth **Australia** 45–16
2003 Melbourne WC **Australia** 17–16
2005 Dublin **Australia** 30–14
2006 Perth **Australia** 37–15
2006 Dublin **Ireland** 21–6

IRELAND V NEW ZEALAND NATIVES

Played 1 New Zealand Natives won 1
Highest scores Ireland 4–13 in 1888, Zew Zealand Natives 13–4 in 1888
Biggest win Ireland no win, New Zealand Natives 13–4 in 1888

1888 Dublin **New Zealand Natives**
4G 1T to 1G 1T

IRELAND V IRU PRESIDENT'S XV

Played 1 Drawn 1
Highest scores Ireland 18–18 in 1974, IRFU President's XV 18–18 in 1974

1974 Dublin **Drawn** 18–18

IRELAND V ROMANIA

Played 8 Ireland won 8
Highest scores Ireland 60–0 in 1986, Romania 35–53 in 1998
Biggest win Ireland 60–0 in 1986, Romania no win

1986	Dublin **Ireland** 60–0	2001	Bucharest **Ireland** 37–3
1993	Dublin **Ireland** 25–3	2002	Limerick **Ireland** 39–8
1998	Dublin **Ireland** 53–35	2003	Gosford WC **Ireland** 45–17
1999	Dublin WC **Ireland** 44–14	2005	Dublin **Ireland** 43–12

IRELAND V CANADA

Played 3 Ireland won 2 Drawn 1
Highest scores Ireland 46–19 in 1987, Canada 27–27 in 2000
Biggest win Ireland 46–19 in 1987, Canada no win

1987	Dunedin WC **Ireland** 46–19	2000	Markham **Drawn** 27–27
1997	Dublin **Ireland** 33–11		

IRELAND V TONGA

Played 2 Ireland won 2
Highest scores Ireland 40–19 in 2003, Tonga 19–40 in 2003
Biggest win Ireland 32–9 in 1987, Tonga no win

1987	Brisbane WC **Ireland** 32–9	2003	Nuku'alofa **Ireland** 40–19

IRELAND V SAMOA

Played 4 Ireland won 3, Samoa won 1, Drawn 0
Highest scores Ireland 49–22 in 1988, Samoa 40–25 in 1996
Biggest wins Ireland 49–22 in 1988 and 35–8 in 2001, Samoa 40–25 in 1996

1988	Dublin **Ireland** 49–22	2001	Dublin **Ireland** 35–8
1996	Dublin **Samoa** 40–25	2003	Apia **Ireland** 40–14

IRELAND V ITALY

Played 15 Ireland won 12, Italy won 3, Drawn 0
Highest scores Ireland 61–6 in 2003, Italy 37–29 in 1997 & 37–22 in 1997
Biggest wins Ireland 61–6 in 2003, Italy 37–22 in 1997

1988	Dublin **Ireland** 31–15	2003	Rome **Ireland** 37–13
1995	Treviso **Italy** 22–12	2003	Limerick **Ireland** 61–6
1997	Dublin **Italy** 37–29	2004	Dublin **Ireland** 19–3
1997	Bologna **Italy** 37–22	2005	Rome **Ireland** 28–17
1999	Dublin **Ireland** 39–30	2006	Dublin **Ireland** 26–16
2000	Dublin **Ireland** 60–13	2007	Rome **Ireland** 51–24
2001	Rome **Ireland** 41–22	2007	Belfast **Ireland** 23–20
2002	Dublin **Ireland** 32–17		

IRELAND V ARGENTINA

Played 10 Ireland won 5 Argentina won 5
Highest scores Ireland 32–24 in 1999, Argentina 34–23 in 2000
Biggest win Ireland 32–24 in 1999, Argentina 16–0 in 2007

1990	Dublin **Ireland** 20–18	2004	Dublin **Ireland** 21–19
1999	Dublin **Ireland** 32–24	2007	1 Santa Fé **Argentina** 22–20
1999	Lens WC **Argentina** 28–24		2 Buenos Aires **Argentina** 16–0
2000	Buenos Aires **Argentina** 34–23		Argentina won series 2–0
2002	Dublin **Ireland** 16–7	2007	Paris WC **Argentina** 30–15
2003	Adelaide WC **Ireland** 16–15		

IRELAND V NAMIBIA

Played 4 Ireland won 2, Namibia won 2
Highest scores Ireland 64–7 in 2003, Namibia 26–15 in 1991
Biggest win Ireland 64–7 in 2003, Namibia 26–15 in 1991

1991	*1* Windhoek **Namibia** 15–6	2003	Sydney WC **Ireland** 64–7
	2 Windhoek **Namibia** 26–15	2007	Bordeaux WC **Ireland** 32–17
	Namibia won series 2–0		

IRELAND V ZIMBABWE

Played 1 Ireland won 1
Highest scores Ireland 55–11 in 1991, Zimbabwe 11–55 in 1991
Biggest win Ireland 55–11 in 1991, Zimbabwe no win

1991	Dublin WC **Ireland** 55–11

IRELAND V JAPAN

Played 5 Ireland won 5
Highest scores Ireland 78–9 in 2000, Japan 28–50 in 1995
Biggest win Ireland 78–9 in 2000, Japan no win

1991	Dublin WC **Ireland** 32–16	2005	1 Osaka **Ireland** 44–12
1995	Bloemfontein WC **Ireland 50–28**		2 Tokyo **Ireland** 47–18
2000	Dublin **Ireland** 78–9		Ireland won series 2–0

IRELAND V UNITED STATES

Played 5 Ireland won 5
Highest scores Ireland 83–3 in 2000, United States 18–25 in 1996
Biggest win Ireland 83–3 in 2000, United States no win

1994	Dublin **Ireland** 26–15	2000	Manchester (NH) **Ireland** 83–3
1996	Atlanta **Ireland** 25–18	2004	Dublin **Ireland** 55–6
1999	Dublin WC **Ireland** 53–8		

IRELAND V FIJI

Played 2 Ireland won 2
Highest scores Ireland 64–17 in 2002, Fiji 17–64 in 2002
Biggest win Ireland 64–17 in 2002, Fiji no win

1995	Dublin **Ireland** 44–8	2002	Dublin **Ireland** 64–17

IRELAND V GEORGIA

Played 3 Ireland won 3
Highest scores Ireland 70–0 in 1998, Georgia 14–63 in 2002
Biggest win Ireland 70–0 in 1998, Georgia no win

1998 Dublin **Ireland** 70–0	2007 Bordeaux WC **Ireland** 14–10
2002 Dublin **Ireland** 63–14	

IRELAND V RUSSIA

Played 1 Ireland won 1
Highest scores Ireland 35–3 in 2002, Russia 3–35 in 2002
Biggest win Ireland 35–3 in 2002, Russia no win

2002 Krasnoyarsk **Ireland** 35–3

IRELAND V PACIFIC ISLANDS

Played 1 Ireland won 1
Highest scores Ireland 61–17 in 2006, Pacific Islands 17–61 in 2006
Biggest win Ireland 61–17 in 2006, Pacific Islands no win

2006 Dublin **Ireland** 61–17

WALES V FRANCE

Played 84 Wales won 42, France won 39, Drawn 3
Highest scores Wales 49–14 in 1910, France 51–0 in 1998
Biggest wins Wales 47–5 in 1909, France 51–0 in 1998

1908 Cardiff **Wales** 36–4	1921 Cardiff **Wales** 12–4
1909 Paris **Wales** 47–5	1922 Paris **Wales** 11–3
1910 Swansea **Wales** 49–14	1923 Swansea **Wales** 16–8
1911 Paris **Wales** 15–0	1924 Paris **Wales** 10–6
1912 Newport **Wales** 14–8	1925 Cardiff **Wales** 11–5
1913 Paris **Wales** 11–8	1926 Paris **Wales** 7–5
1914 Swansea **Wales** 31–0	1927 Swansea **Wales** 25–7
1920 Paris **Wales** 6–5	1928 Paris **France** 8–3

1929 Cardiff **Wales** 8–3
1930 Paris **Wales** 11–0
1931 Swansea **Wales** 35–3
1947 Paris **Wales** 3–0
1948 Swansea **France** 11–3
1949 Paris **France** 5–3
1950 Cardiff **Wales** 21–0
1951 Paris **France** 8–3
1952 Swansea **Wales** 9–5
1953 Paris **Wales** 6–3
1954 Cardiff **Wales** 19–13
1955 Paris **Wales** 16–11
1956 Cardiff **Wales** 5–3
1957 Paris **Wales** 19–13
1958 Cardiff **France** 16–6
1959 Paris **France** 11–3
1960 Cardiff **France** 16–8
1961 Paris **France** 8–6
1962 Cardiff **Wales** 3–0
1963 Paris **France** 5–3
1964 Cardiff **Drawn** 11–11
1965 Paris **France** 22–13
1966 Cardiff **Wales** 9–8
1967 Paris **France** 20–14
1968 Cardiff **France** 14–9
1969 Paris **Drawn** 8–8
1970 Cardiff **Wales** 11–6
1971 Paris **Wales** 9–5
1972 Cardiff **Wales** 20–6
1973 Paris **France** 12–3
1974 Cardiff **Drawn** 16–16
1975 Paris **Wales** 25–10
1976 Cardiff **Wales** 19–13
1977 Paris **France** 16–9
1978 Cardiff **Wales** 16–7
1979 Paris **France** 14–13
1980 Cardiff **Wales** 18–9
1981 Paris **France** 19–15
1982 Cardiff **Wales** 22–12
1983 Paris **France** 16–9
1984 Cardiff **France** 21–16
1985 Paris **France** 14–3
1986 Cardiff **France** 23–15
1987 Paris **France** 16–9
1988 Cardiff **France** 10–9
1989 Paris **France** 31–12
1990 Cardiff **France** 29–19
1991 Paris **France** 36–3
1991 Cardiff **France** 22–9
Non-championship match
1992 Cardiff **France** 12–9
1993 Paris **France** 26–10
1994 Cardiff **Wales** 24–15
1995 Paris **France** 21–9
1996 Cardiff **Wales** 16–15
1996 Cardiff **France** 40–33
Non-championship match
1997 Paris **France 27–22**
1998 Wembley **France** 51–0
1999 Paris **Wales** 34–33
1999 Cardiff **Wales** 34–23
Non-championship match
2000 Cardiff **France** 36–3
2001 Paris **Wales** 43–35
2002 Cardiff **France** 37–33
2003 Paris **France** 33–5
2004 Cardiff **France** 29–22
2005 Paris **Wales** 24–18
2006 Cardiff **France** 21–16
2007 Paris **France** 32–21
2007 Cardiff **France** 34–7

WALES V SOUTH AFRICA

Played 19 Wales won 1, South Africa won 17, Drawn 1
Highest scores Wales 36–38 in 2004, South Africa 96–13 in 1998
Biggest win Wales 29–19 in 1999, South Africa 96–13 in 1998

1906 Swansea **South Africa** 11–0
1912 Cardiff **South Africa** 3–0
1931 Swansea **South Africa** 8–3
1951 Cardiff **South Africa** 6–3
1960 Cardiff **South Africa** 3–0
1964 Durban **South Africa** 24–3

1970 Cardiff **Drawn** 6–6
1994 Cardiff **South Africa** 20–12
1995 Johannesburg **South Africa** 40–11
1996 Cardiff **South Africa** 37–20
1998 Pretoria **South Africa** 96–13
1998 Wembley **South Africa** 28–20
1999 Cardiff **Wales** 29–19
2000 Cardiff **South Africa** 23–13
2002 *1* Bloemfontein **South Africa** 34–19
2 Cape Town **South Africa** 19–8
SA won series 2–0
2004 Pretoria **South Africa** 53–18
2004 Cardiff **South Africa** 38–36
2005 Cardiff **South Africa** 33–16

WALES V NEW ZEALAND

Played 23 Wales won 3, New Zealand won 20, Drawn 0
Highest scores Wales 37–53 in 2003, New Zealand 55–3 in 2003
Biggest wins Wales 13–8 in 1953, New Zealand 55–3 in 2003

1905 Cardiff **Wales** 3–0
1924 Swansea **New Zealand** 19–0
1935 Cardiff **Wales** 13–12
1953 Cardiff **Wales** 13–8
1963 Cardiff **New Zealand** 6–0
1967 Cardiff **New Zealand** 13–6
1969 *1* Christchurch **New Zealand** 19–0
2 Auckland **New Zealand** 33–12
New Zealand won series 2–0
1972 Cardiff **New Zealand** 19–16
1978 Cardiff **New Zealand** 13–12
1980 Cardiff **New Zealand** 23–3
1987 Brisbane WC **New Zealand** 49–6
1988 *1* Christchurch **New Zealand** 52–3
2 Auckland **New Zealand** 54–9
New Zealand won series 2–0
1989 Cardiff **New Zealand** 34–9
1995 Johannesburg WC **New Zealand 34–9**
1997 Wembley **New Zealand** 42–7
2002 Cardiff **New Zealand** 43–17
2003 Hamilton **New Zealand** 55–3
2003 Sydney WC **New Zealand** 53–37
2004 Cardiff **New Zealand** 26–25
2005 Cardiff **New Zealand** 41–3
2006 Cardiff **New Zealand** 45–10

WALES V AUSTRALIA

Played 27 Wales won 9, Australia won 17, Drawn 1
Highest scores Wales 29–29 in 2006, Australia 63–6 in 1991
Biggest wins Wales 28–3 in 1975, Australia 63–6 in 1991

1908 Cardiff **Wales** 9–6
1927 Cardiff **Australia** 18–8
1947 Cardiff **Wales** 6–0
1958 Cardiff **Wales** 9–3
1966 Cardiff **Australia** 14–11
1969 Sydney **Wales** 19–16
1973 Cardiff **Wales** 24–0
1975 Cardiff **Wales** 28–3
1978 *1* Brisbane **Australia** 18–8
2 Sydney **Australia** 19–17
Australia won series 2–0
1981 Cardiff **Wales** 18–13
1984 Cardiff **Australia** 28–9
1987 Rotorua WC **Wales** 22–21
1991 Brisbane **Australia** 63–6
1991 Cardiff WC **Australia** 38–3
1992 Cardiff **Australia** 23–6
1996 *1* Brisbane **Australia** 56–25

	2 Sydney **Australia** 42–3	2005	Cardiff **Wales** 24–22
	Australia won series 2–0	2006	Cardiff **Drawn** 29–29
1996	Cardiff **Australia 28–19**	2007	1 Sydney **Australia** 29–23
1999	Cardiff WC **Australia** 24–9		2 Brisbane **Australia** 31–0
2001	Cardiff **Australia** 21–13		Australia won series 2–0
2003	Sydney **Australia** 30–10	2007	Cardiff WC **Australia** 32–20

WALES V NEW ZEALAND NATIVES

Played 1 Wales won 1
Highest scores Wales 5–0 in 1888, New Zealand Natives 0–5 in 1888
Biggest win Wales 5–0 in 1888, New Zealand Natives no win

1888	Swansea **Wales** 1G 2T to 0

WALES V NEW ZEALAND ARMY

Played 1 New Zealand Army won 1
Highest scores Wales 3–6 in 1919, New Zealand Army 6–3 in 1919
Biggest win Wales no win, New Zealand Army 6–3 in 1919

1919	Swansea **New Zealand Army** 6–3

WALES V ROMANIA

Played 8 Wales won 6, Romania won 2
Highest scores Wales 81–9 in 2001, Romania 24–6 in 1983
Biggest wins Wales 81–9 in 2001, Romania 24–6 in 1983

1983	Bucharest **Romania** 24–6	2001	Cardiff **Wales** 81–9
1988	Cardiff **Romania** 15–9	2002	Wrexham **Wales** 40–3
1994	Bucharest **Wales** 16–9	2003	Wrexham **Wales** 54–8
1997	Wrexham **Wales** 70–21	2004	Cardiff **Wales** 66–7

WALES V FIJI

Played 7 Wales won 6, Fiji won 1
Highest scores Wales 58–14 in 2002, Fiji 38–34 in 2007
Biggest win Wales 58–14 in 2002, Fiji 38–34 in 2007

1985	Cardiff **Wales** 40–3	2002	Cardiff **Wales** 58–14
1986	Suva **Wales** 22–15	2005	Cardiff **Wales** 11–10
1994	Suva **Wales** 23–8	2007	Nantes WC **Fiji** 38–34
1995	Cardiff **Wales** 19–15		

WALES V TONGA

Played 6 Wales won 6
Highest scores Wales 51–7 in 2001, Tonga 20–27 in 2003
Biggest win Wales 51–7 in 2001, Tonga no win

1986	Nuku'Alofa **Wales** 15–7	1997	Swansea **Wales** 46–12
1987	Palmerston North WC **Wales** 29–16	2001	Cardiff **Wales** 51–7
1994	Nuku'Alofa **Wales** 18–9	2003	Canberra WC **Wales** 27–20

WALES V SAMOA

Played 6 Wales won 3, Samoa won 3, Drawn 0
Highest scores Wales 50–6 in 2000, Samoa 38–31 in 1999
Biggest wins Wales 50–6 in 2000, Samoa 34–9 in 1994

1986	Apia **Wales** 32–14	1994	Moamoa **Samoa** 34–9
1988	Cardiff **Wales** 28–6	1999	Cardiff WC **Samoa** 38–31
1991	Cardiff WC **Samoa** 16–13	2000	Cardiff **Wales** 50–6

WALES V CANADA

Played 10 Wales won 9, Canada won 1, Drawn 0
Highest scores Wales 61–26 in 2006, Canada 26–24 in 1993 & 26–61 in 2006
Biggest wins Wales 60–3 in 2005, Canada 26–24 in 1993

1987	Invercargill WC **Wales** 40–9	1994	Toronto **Wales** 33–15
1993	Cardiff **Canada** 26–24	1997	Toronto **Wales** 28–25

1999	Cardiff **Wales** 33–19	2005	Toronto **Wales** 60–3
2002	Cardiff **Wales** 32–21	2006	Cardiff **Wales** 61–26
2003	Melbourne WC **Wales** 41–10	2007	Nantes WC **Wales** 42–17

WALES V UNITED STATES

Played 6 Wales won 6
Highest scores Wales 77–3 in 2005, United States 23–28 in 1997
Biggest win Wales 77–3 in 2005, United States no win

1987	Cardiff **Wales** 46–0		Wales won series 2–0
1997	Cardiff **Wales** 34–14	2000	Cardiff **Wales** 42–11
1997	*1* Wilmington **Wales** 30–20	2005	Hartford **Wales** 77–3
	2 San Francisco **Wales** 28–23		

WALES V NAMIBIA

Played 3 Wales won 3
Highest scores Wales 38–23 in 1993, Namibia 30–34 in 1990
Biggest win Wales 38–23 in 1993, Namibia no win

1990	*1* Windhoek **Wales** 18–9		Wales won series 2–0
	2 Windhoek **Wales** 34–30	1993	Windhoek **Wales** 38–23

WALES V BARBARIANS

Played 2 Wales won 1, Barbarians won 1
Highest scores Wales 31–10 in 1996, Barbarians 31–24 in 1990
Biggest wins Wales 31–10 in 1996, Barbarians 31–24 in 1990

1990	Cardiff **Barbarians** 31–24	1996	Cardiff **Wales** 31–10

WALES V ARGENTINA

Played 11 Wales won 7, Argentina won 4
Highest scores Wales 44–50 in 2004, Argentina 50–44 in 2004
Biggest win Wales 35–20 in 2004, Argentina 45–27 in 2006

1991	Cardiff WC **Wales** 16–7
1998	Llanelli **Wales** 43–30
1999	*1* Buenos Aires **Wales** 36–26
	2 Buenos Aires **Wales** 23–16
	Wales won series 2–0
1999	Cardiff WC **Wales** 23–18
2001	Cardiff **Argentina** 30–16
2004	1 Tucumán **Argentina** 50–44
	2 Buenos Aires **Wales** 35–20
	Series drawn 1–1
2006	1 Puerto Madryn **Argentina** 27–25
	2 Buenos Aires **Argentina** 45–27
	Argentina won series 2–0
2007	Cardiff **Wales** 27–20

WALES V ZIMBABWE

Played 3 Wales won 3
Highest scores Wales 49–11 in 1998, Zimbabwe 14–35 in 1993
Biggest win Wales 49–11 in 1998, Zimbabwe no win

1993	*1* Bulawayo **Wales** 35–14
	2 Harare **Wales** 42–13
	Wales won series 2–0
1998	Harare **Wales** 49–11

WALES V JAPAN

Played 7 Wales won 7
Highest scores Wales 98–0 in 2004, Japan 30–53 in 2001
Biggest win Wales 98–0 in 2004, Japan no win

1993	Cardiff **Wales** 55–5
1995	Bloemfontein WC **Wales 57–10**
1999	Cardiff WC **Wales** 64–15
2001	*1* Osaka **Wales** 64–10
	2 Tokyo **Wales** 53–30
	Wales won series 2–0
2004	Cardiff **Wales** 98–0
2007	Cardiff WC **Wales** 72–18

WALES V PORTUGAL

Played 1 Wales won 1
Highest scores Wales 102–11 in 1994, Portugal 11–102 in 1994
Biggest win Wales 102–11 in 1994, Portugal no win

1994	Lisbon **Wales** 102–11

WALES V SPAIN

Played 1 Wales won 1
Highest scores Wales 54–0 in 1994, Spain 0–54 in 1994
Bigegst win Wales 54–0 in 1994, Spain no win

1994 Madrid **Wales** 54–0

WALES V ITALY

Played 14 Wales won 11, Italy won 2, Drawn 1
Highest scores Wales 60–21 in 1999, Italy 30–22 in 2003
Biggest win Wales 60–21 in 1999, Italy 30–22 in 2003

1994 Cardiff **Wales** 29–19
1996 Cardiff **Wales** 31–26
1996 Rome **Wales** 31–22
1998 Llanelli **Wales** 23–20
1999 Treviso **Wales** 60–21
2000 Cardiff **Wales** 47–16
2001 Rome **Wales** 33–23
2002 Cardiff **Wales** 44–20
2003 Rome **Italy** 30–22
2003 Canberra WC **Wales** 27–15
2004 Cardiff **Wales** 44–10
2005 Rome **Wales** 38–8
2006 Cardiff **Drawn** 18–18
2007 Rome **Italy** 23–20

WALES V PACIFIC ISLANDS

Played 1 Wales won 1
Highest scores Wales 38–20 in 2006, Pacific Islands 20–38 in 2006
Biggest win Wales 38–20 in 2006, Pacific Islands no win

2006 Cardiff **Wales** 38–20

BRITISH/IRISH ISLES V SOUTH AFRICA

Played 43 British/Irish won 16, South Africa won 21, Drawn 6
Highest scores: British/Irish 28–9 in 1974, South Africa 35–16 in 1997
Biggest wins: British/Irish 28–9 in 1974, South Africa 34–14 in 1962

1891 *1* Port Elizabeth **British/Irish** 4–0
2 Kimberley **British/Irish** 3–0
3 Cape Town **British/Irish** 4–0
British/Irish won series 3–0
1896 *1* Port Elizabeth **British/Irish** 8–0
2 Johannesburg **British/Irish** 17–8

	3 Kimberley **British/Irish** 9–3
	4 Cape Town **South Africa** 5–0
	British/Irish won series 3–1
1903	*1* Johannesburg **Drawn** 10–10
	2 Kimberley **Drawn** 0–0
	3 Cape Town **South Africa** 8–0
	South Africa won series 1–0 with two drawn
1910	*1* Johannesburg **South Africa** 14–10
	2 Port Elizabeth **British/Irish** 8–3
	3 Cape Town **South Africa** 21–5
	South Africa won series 2–1
1924	*1* Durban **South Africa** 7–3
	2 Johannesburg **South Africa** 17–0
	3 Port Elizabeth **Drawn** 3–3
	4 Cape Town **South Africa** 16–9
	South Africa won series 3–0, with 1 draw
1938	*1* Johannesburg **South Africa** 26–12
	2 Port Elizabeth **South Africa** 19–3
	3 Cape Town **British/Irish** 21–16
	South Africa won series 2–1
1955	*1* Johannesburg **British/Irish** 23–22
	2 Cape Town **South Africa** 25–9
	3 Pretoria **British/Irish** 9–6
	4 Port Elizabeth **South Africa** 22–8
	Series drawn 2–2
1962	*1* Johannesburg **Drawn** 3–3
	2 Durban **South Africa** 3–0
	3 Cape Town **South Africa** 8–3
	4 Bloemfontein **South Africa** 34–14
	South Africa won series 3–0, with 1 draw
1968	*1* Pretoria **South Africa** 25–20
	2 Port Elizabeth **Drawn** 6–6
	3 Cape Town **South Africa** 11–6
	4 Johannesburg **South Africa** 19–6
	South Africa won series 3–0, with 1 draw
1974	*1* Cape Town **British/Irish** 12–3
	2 Pretoria **British/Irish** 28–9
	3 Port Elizabeth **British/Irish** 26–9
	4 Johannesburg **Drawn** 13–13
	British/Irish won series 3–0, with 1 draw
1980	*1* Cape Town **South Africa** 26–22
	2 Bloemfontein **South Africa** 26–19
	3 Port Elizabeth **South Africa** 12–10
	4 Pretoria **British/Irish** 17–13
	South Africa won series 3–1
1997	*1* Cape Town **British/Irish** 25–16
	2 Durban **British/Irish** 18–15
	3 Johannesburg **South Africa** 35–16
	British/Irish won series 2–1

BRITISH/IRISH ISLES V NEW ZEALAND

Played 35 British/Irish won 6, New Zealand won 27, Drawn 2
Highest scores: British/Irish 20–7 in 1993, New Zealand 48–18 in 2005
Biggest wins: British/Irish 20–7 in 1993, New Zealand 38–6 in 1983

1904	Wellington **New Zealand** 9–3
1930	*1* Dunedin **British/Irish** 6–3
	2 Christchurch **New Zealand** 13–10
	3 Auckland **New Zealand** 15–10
	4 Wellington **New Zealand** 22–8
	New Zealand won series 3–1
1950	*1* Dunedin **Drawn** 9–9
	2 Christchurch **New Zealand** 8–0
	3 Wellington **New Zealand** 6–3
	4 Auckland **New Zealand** 11–8
	New Zealand won series 3–0, with 1 draw
1959	*1* Dunedin **New Zealand** 18–17
	2 Wellington **New Zealand** 11–8
	3 Christchurch **New Zealand** 22–8
	4 Auckland **British/Irish** 9–6
	New Zealand won series 3–1
1966	*1* Dunedin **New Zealand** 20–3
	2 Wellington **New Zealand** 16–12
	3 Christchurch **New Zealand** 19–6
	4 Auckland **New Zealand** 24–11
	New Zealand won series 4–0
1971	*1* Dunedin **British/Irish** 9–3
	2 Christchurch **New Zealand** 22–12
	3 Wellington **British/Irish** 13–3

	4 Auckland **Drawn** 14–14
	British/Irish won series 2–1, with 1 draw
1977	*1* Wellington **New Zealand** 16–12
	2 Christchurch **British/Irish** 13–9
	3 Dunedin **New Zealand** 19–7
	4 Auckland **New Zealand** 10–9
	New Zealand won series 3–1
1983	*1* Christchurch **New Zealand** 16–12
	2 Wellington **New Zealand** 9–0
	3 Dunedin **New Zealand** 15–8
	4 Auckland **New Zealand** 38–6
	New Zealand won series 4–0
1993	*1* Christchurch **New Zealand** 20–18
	2 Wellington **British/Irish** 20–7
	3 Auckland **New Zealand** 30–13
	New Zealand won series 2–1
2005	1 Christchurch **New Zealand** 21–3
	2 Wellington **New Zealand** 48–18
	3 Auckland **New Zealand** 38–19
	New Zealand won series 3–0

ANGLO-WELSH V NEW ZEALAND

Played 3 New Zealand won 2, Drawn 1
Highest scores Anglo Welsh 5–32 in 1908, New Zealand 32–5 in 1908
Biggest win Anglo Welsh no win, New Zealand 29–0 in 1908

1908	*1* Dunedin **New Zealand** 32–5
	2 Wellington **Drawn** 3–3
	3 Auckland **New Zealand** 29–0
	New Zealand won series 2–0 with one drawn

BRITISH/IRISH ISLES V AUSTRALIA

Played 20 British/Irish won 15, Australia won 5, Drawn 0
Highest scores: British/Irish 31–0 in 1966, Australia 35–14 in 2001
Biggest wins: British/Irish 31–0 in 1966, Australia 35–14 in 2001

1899	*1* Sydney **Australia** 13–3
	2 Brisbane **British/Irish** 11–0
	3 Sydney **British/Irish** 11–10
	4 Sydney **British/Irish** 13–0
	British/Irish won series 3–1
1904	*1* Sydney **British/Irish** 17–0
	2 Brisbane **British/Irish** 17–3
	3 Sydney **British/Irish** 16–0
	British/Irish won series 3–0
1930	Sydney **Australia** 6–5
1950	*1* Brisbane **British/Irish** 19–6
	2 Sydney **British/Irish** 24–3
	British/Irish won series 2–0
1959	*1* Brisbane **British/Irish** 17–6
	2 Sydney **British/Irish** 24–3
	British/Irish won series 2–0
1966	*1* Sydney **British/Irish** 11–8
	2 Brisbane **British/Irish** 31–0
	British/Irish won series 2–0
1989	*1* Sydney **Australia** 30–12
	2 Brisbane **British/Irish** 19–12
	3 Sydney **British/Irish** 19–18
	British/Irish won series 2–1
2001	*1* Brisbane **British/Irish** 29–13
	2 Melbourne **Australia** 35–14
	3 Sydney **Australia** 29–23
	Australia won series 2–1

FRANCE V SOUTH AFRICA

Played 36 France won 10, South Africa won 20, Drawn 6
Highest scores France 36–26 in 2006, South Africa 52–10 in 1997
Biggest wins France 30–10 in 2002, South Africa 52–10 in 1997

1913	Bordeaux **South Africa** 38–5
1952	Paris **South Africa** 25–3
1958	*1* Cape Town **Drawn** 3–3
	2 Johannesburg **France** 9–5
	France won series 1–0, with 1 draw
1961	Paris **Drawn** 0–0
1964	Springs (SA) **France** 8–6
1967	*1* Durban **South Africa** 26–3
	2 Bloemfontein **South Africa** 16–3
	3 Johannesburg **France** 19–14
	4 Cape Town **Drawn** 6–6
	South Africa won series 2–1, with 1 draw
1968	*1* Bordeaux **South Africa** 12–9
	2 Paris **South Africa** 16–11
	South Africa won series 2–0
1971	*1* Bloemfontein **South Africa** 22–9
	2 Durban **Drawn** 8–8
	South Africa won series 1–0, with 1 draw
1974	*1* Toulouse **South Africa** 13–4
	2 Paris **South Africa** 10–8
	South Africa won series 2–0
1975	*1* Bloemfontein **South Africa** 38–25
	2 Pretoria **South Africa** 33–18
	South Africa won series 2–0
1980	Pretoria **South Africa** 37–15
1992	*1* Lyons **South Africa** 20–15
	2 Paris **France** 29–16
	Series drawn 1–1
1993	*1* Durban **Drawn** 20–20
	2 Johannesburg **France** 18–17
	France won series 1–0, with 1 draw
1995	Durban WC **South Africa 19–15**
1996	*1* Bordeaux **South Africa** 22–12
	2 Paris **South Africa** 13–12
	South Africa won series 2–0
1997	*1* Lyons **South Africa** 36–32
	2 Paris **South Africa** 52–10
	South Africa won series 2–0
2001	*1* Johannesburg **France** 32–23
	2 Durban **South Africa** 20–15
	Series drawn 1–1
2001	Paris **France** 20–10
2002	Marseilles **France** 30–10
2005	1 Durban **Drawn** 30–30
	2 Port Elizabeth **South Africa** 27–13
	South Africa won series 1–0, with 1 draw
2005	Paris **France** 26–20
2006	Cape Town **France** 36–26

FRANCE V NEW ZEALAND

Played 46 France won 11, New Zealand won 34, Drawn 1
Highest scores France 43–31 in 1999, New Zealand 61–10 in 2007
Biggest wins France 22–8 in 1994, New Zealand 61–10 in 2007

1906	Paris **New Zealand** 38–8
1925	Toulouse **New Zealand** 30–6
1954	Paris **France** 3–0
1961	*1* Auckland **New Zealand** 13–6
	2 Wellington **New Zealand** 5–3
	3 Christchurch **New Zealand** 32–3
	New Zealand won series 3–0
1964	Paris **New Zealand** 12–3
1967	Paris **New Zealand** 21–15
1968	*1* Christchurch **New Zealand** 12–9
	2 Wellington **New Zealand** 9–3
	3 Auckland **New Zealand** 19–12
	New Zealand won series 3–0
1973	Paris **France** 13–6
1977	*1* Toulouse **France** 18–13
	2 Paris **New Zealand** 15–3

Series drawn 1–1
1979 *1* Christchurch **New Zealand** 23–9
2 Auckland **France** 24–19
Series drawn 1–1
1981 *1* Toulouse **New Zealand** 13–9
2 Paris **New Zealand** 18–6
New Zealand won series 2–0
1984 *1* Christchurch **New Zealand** 10–9
2 Auckland **New Zealand** 31–18
New Zealand won series 2–0
1986 Christchurch **New Zealand** 18–9
1986 *1* Toulouse **New Zealand** 19–7
2 Nantes **France** 16–3
Series drawn 1–1
1989 *1* Christchurch **New Zealand** 25–17
2 Auckland **New Zealand** 34–20
New Zealand won series 2–0
1990 *1* Nantes **New Zealand** 24–3
2 Paris **New Zealand** 30–12
New Zealand won series 2–0
1994 *1* Christchurch **France** 22–8
2 Auckland **France** 23–20
France won series 2–0
1995 *1* Toulouse **France** 22–15
2 Paris **New Zealand** 37–12
Series drawn 1–1
1999 Wellington **New Zealand** 54–7
1999 Twickenham WC **France** 43–31
2000 *1* Paris **New Zealand** 39–26
2 Marseilles **France** 42–33
Series drawn 1–1
2001 Wellington **New Zealand** 37–12
2002 Paris **Drawn** 20–20
2003 Christchurch **New Zealand** 31–23
2003 Sydney WC **New Zealand** 40–13
2004 Paris **New Zealand** 45–6
2006 1 Lyons **New Zealand** 47–3
2 Paris **New Zealand** 23–11
New Zealand won series 2–0
2007 1 Auckland **New Zealand** 42–11
2 Wellington **New Zealand** 61–10
New Zealand won series 2–0
2007 Cardiff WC **France** 20–18

FRANCE V AUSTRALIA

Played 36 France won 16, Australia won 18, Drawn 2
Highest scores France 34–6 in 1976, Australia 48–31 in 1990
Biggest wins France 34–6 in 1976, Australia 35–12 in 1999

1928 Paris **Australia** 11–8
1948 Paris **France** 13–6
1958 Paris **France** 19–0
1961 Sydney **France** 15–8
1967 Paris **France** 20–14
1968 Sydney **Australia** 11–10
1971 *1* Toulouse **Australia** 13–11
2 Paris **France** 18–9
Series drawn 1–1
1972 *1* Sydney **Drawn** 14–14
2 Brisbane **France** 16–15
France won series 1–0, with 1 draw
1976 *1* Bordeaux **France** 18–15
2 Paris **France** 34–6
France won series 2–0
1981 *1* Brisbane **Australia** 17–15
2 Sydney **Australia** 24–14
Australia won series 2–0
1983 *1* Clermont-Ferrand **Drawn** 15–15
2 Paris **France** 15–6
France won series 1–0, with 1 draw
1986 Sydney **Australia** 27–14
1987 Sydney WC **France** 30–24
1989 *1* Strasbourg **Australia** 32–15
2 Lille **France** 25–19
Series drawn 1–1
1990 *1* Sydney **Australia** 21–9
2 Brisbane **Australia** 48–31
3 Sydney **France** 28–19
Australia won series 2–1
1993 *1* Bordeaux **France** 16–13
2 Paris **Australia** 24–3
Series drawn 1–1
1997 *1* Sydney **Australia** 29–15

	2 Brisbane **Australia** 26–19	2002	*1* Melbourne **Australia** 29–17
	Australia won series 2–0		*2* Sydney **Australia** 31–25
1998	Paris **Australia** 32–21		Australia won series 2–0
1999	Cardiff WC **Australia** 35–12	2004	Paris **France** 27–14
2000	Paris **Australia** 18–13	2005	Brisbane **Australia** 37–31
2001	Marseilles **France** 14–13	2005	Marseilles **France** 26–16

FRANCE V UNITED STATES

Played 7 France won 6, United States won 1, Drawn 0
Highest scores France 41–9 in 1991 and 41–14 in 2003, United States 31–39 in 2004
Biggest wins France 41–9 in 1991, United States 17–3 in 1924

1920	Paris **France** 14–5		*Abandoned after 43 mins
1924	Paris **United States** 17–3		France won series 2–0
1976	Chicago **France** 33–14	2003	Wollongong WC **France** 41–14
1991	*1* Denver **France** 41–9	2004	Hartford **France** 39–31
	2 Colorado Springs **France** 10–3*		

FRANCE V ROMANIA

Played 49 France won 39, Romania won 8, Drawn 2
Highest scores France 67–20 in 2000, Romania 21–33 in 1991
Biggest wins France 59–3 in 1924, Romania 15–0 in 1980

1924	Paris **France** 59–3	1974	Bucharest **Romania** 15–10
1938	Bucharest **France** 11–8	1975	Bordeaux **France** 36–12
1957	Bucharest **France** 18–15	1976	Bucharest **Romania** 15–12
1957	Bordeaux **France** 39–0	1977	Clermont-Ferrand **France** 9–6
1960	Bucharest **Romania** 11–5	1978	Bucharest **France** 9–6
1961	Bayonne **Drawn** 5–5	1979	Montauban **France** 30–12
1962	Bucharest **Romania** 3–0	1980	Bucharest **Romania** 15–0
1963	Toulouse **Drawn** 6–6	1981	Narbonne **France** 17–9
1964	Bucharest **France** 9–6	1982	Bucharest **Romania** 13–9
1965	Lyons **France** 8–3	1983	Toulouse **France** 26–15
1966	Bucharest **France** 9–3	1984	Bucharest **France** 18–3
1967	Nantes **France** 11–3	1986	Lille **France** 25–13
1968	Bucharest **Romania** 15–14	1986	Bucharest **France** 20–3
1969	Tarbes **France** 14–9	1987	Wellington WC **France** 55–12
1970	Bucharest **France** 14–3	1987	Agen **France** 49–3
1971	Béziers **France** 31–12	1988	Bucharest **France** 16–12
1972	Constanza **France** 15–6	1990	Auch **Romania** 12–6
1973	Valence **France** 7–6	1991	Bucharest **France** 33–21

1991 Béziers WC **France** 30–3
1992 Le Havre **France** 25–6
1993 Bucharest **France** 37–20
1993 Brive **France** 51–0
1995 Bucharest **France** 24–15
1995 Tucumán LC **France** **52–8**
1996 Aurillac **France** 64–12
1997 Bucharest **France** 51–20
1997 Lourdes LC **France** **39–3**
1999 Castres **France** 62–8
2000 Bucharest **France** 67–20
2003 Lens **France** 56–8
2006 Bucharest **France** 62–14

FRANCE V NEW ZEALAND MAORI

Played 1 New Zealand Maori won 1
Highest scores France 3–12 in 1926, New Zealand Maori 12–3 in 1926
Biggest win France no win, New Zealand Maori 12–3 in 1926

1926 Paris **New Zealand Maori** 12–3

FRANCE V GERMANY

Played 15 France won 13, Germany won 2, Drawn 0
Highest scores France 38–17 in 1933, Germany 17–16 in 1927 & 17–38 in 1933
Biggest wins France 34–0 in 1931, Germany 3–0 in 1938

1927 Paris **France** 30–5
1927 Frankfurt **Germany** 17–16
1928 Hanover **France** 14–3
1929 Paris **France** 24–0
1930 Berlin **France** 31–0
1931 Paris **France** 34–0
1932 Frankfurt **France** 20–4
1933 Paris **France** 38–17
1934 Hanover **France** 13–9
1935 Paris **France** 18–3
1936 *1* Berlin **France** 19–14
2 Hanover **France** 6–3
France won series 2–0
1937 Paris **France** 27–6
1938 Frankfurt **Germany** 3–0
1938 Bucharest **France** 8–5

FRANCE V ITALY

Played 28 France won 27, Italy won 1, Drawn 0
Highest scores France 60–13 in 1967, Italy 40–32 in 1997
Biggest wins France 60–13 in 1967, Italy 40–32 in 1997

1937 Paris **France** 43–5
1952 Milan **France** 17–8
1953 Lyons **France** 22–8
1954 Rome **France** 39–12

1955 Grenoble **France** 24–0	1967 Toulon **France** 60–13
1956 Padua **France** 16–3	1995 Buenos Aires LC **France 34–22**
1957 Agen **France** 38–6	1997 Grenoble **Italy** 40–32
1958 Naples **France** 11–3	1997 Auch LC **France 30–19**
1959 Nantes **France** 22–0	2000 Paris **France** 42–31
1960 Treviso **France** 26–0	2001 Rome **France** 30–19
1961 Chambéry **France** 17–0	2002 Paris **France** 33–12
1962 Brescia **France** 6–3	2003 Rome **France** 53–27
1963 Grenoble **France** 14–12	2004 Paris **France** 25–0
1964 Parma **France** 12–3	2005 Rome **France** 56–13
1965 Pau **France** 21–0	2006 Paris **France** 37–12
1966 Naples **France** 21–0	2007 Rome **France** 39–3

FRANCE V BRITISH XVS

Played 5 France won 2, British XVs won 3, Drawn 0
Highest scores France 27–29 in 1989, British XV 36–3 in 1940
Biggest wins France 21–9 in 1945, British XV 36–3 in 1940

1940 Paris **British XV** 36–3	1946 Paris **France** 10–0
1945 Paris **France** 21–9	1989 Paris **British XV** 29–27
1945 Richmond **British XV** 27–6	

FRANCE V WALES XVS

Played 2 France won 1, Wales XV won 1
Highest scores France 12–0 in 1946, Wales XV 8–0 in 1945
Biggest win France 12–0 in 1946, Wales XV 8–0 in 1945

1945 Swansea **Wales XV** 8–0	1946 Paris **France** 12–0

FRANCE V IRELAND XVS

Played 1 France won 1
Highest scores France 4–3 in 1946, Ireland XV 3–4 in 1946
Biggest win France 4–3 in 1946, Ireland XV no win

1946 Dublin **France** 4–3

FRANCE V NEW ZEALAND ARMY

Played 1 New Zealand Army won 1
Highest scores France 9–14 in 1946, New Zealand Army 14–9 in 1946
Biggest win France no win, New Zealand Army 14–9 in 1946

1946 Paris **New Zealand Army** 14–9

FRANCE V ARGENTINA

Played 41 France won 30, Argentina won 10, Drawn 1
Highest scores France 47–12 in 1995 & 47–26 in 1999, Argentina 34–10 in 2007
Biggest wins France 47–12 in 1995, Argentina 34–10 in 2007

1949	*1* Buenos Aires **France** 5–0
	2 Buenos Aires **France** 12–3
	France won series 2–0
1954	*1* Buenos Aires **France** 22–8
	2 Buenos Aires **France** 30–3
	France won series 2–0
1960	*1* Buenos Aires **France** 37–3
	2 Buenos Aires **France** 12–3
	3 Buenos Aires **France** 29–6
	France won series 3–0
1974	*1* Buenos Aires **France** 20–15
	2 Buenos Aires **France** 31–27
	France won series 2–0
1975	*1* Lyons **France** 29–6
	2 Paris **France** 36–21
	France won series 2–0
1977	*1* Buenos Aires **France** 26–3
	2 Buenos Aires **Drawn** 18–18
	France won series 1–0, with 1 draw
1982	*1* Toulouse **France** 25–12
	2 Paris **France** 13–6
	France won series 2–0
1985	*1* Buenos Aires **Argentina** 24–16
	2 Buenos Aires **France** 23–15
	Series drawn 1–1
1986	*1* Buenos Aires **Argentina** 15–13
	2 Buenos Aires **France** 22–9
	Series drawn 1–1
1988	*1* Buenos Aires **France** 18–15
	2 Buenos Aires **Argentina** 18–6
	Series drawn 1–1
1988	*1* Nantes **France** 29–9
	2 Lille **France** 28–18
	France won series 2–0
1992	*1* Buenos Aires **France** 27–12
	2 Buenos Aires **France** 33–9
	France won series 2–0
1992	Nantes **Argentina** 24–20
1995	Buenos Aires LC **France** 47–12
1996	*1* Buenos Aires **France** 34–27
	2 Buenos Aires **France** 34–15
	France won series 2–0
1997	Tarbes LC **France** 32–27
1998	*1* Buenos Aires **France** 35–18
	2 Buenos Aires **France** 37–12
	France won series 2–0
1998	Nantes **France** 34–14
1999	Dublin WC **France** 47–26
2002	Buenos Aires **Argentina** 28–27
2003	*1* Buenos Aires **Argentina** 10–6
	2 Buenos Aires **Argentina** 33–32
	Argentina won series 2–0
2004	Marseilles **Argentina** 24–14
2006	Paris **France** 27–26
2007	Paris WC **Argentina** 17–12
2007	Paris WC **Argentina** 34–10

FRANCE V CZECHOSLOVAKIA

Played 2 France won 2
Highest scores France 28–3 in 1956, Czechoslovakia 6–19 in 1968
Biggest win France 28–3 in 1956, Czechoslovakia no win

1956 Toulouse **France** 28–3	1968 Prague **France** 19–6

FRANCE V FIJI

Played 7 France won 7
Highest scores France 77–10 in 2001, Fiji 19–28 in 1999
Biggest win France 77–10 in 2001, Fiji no win

1964 Paris **France** 21–3	1999 Toulouse WC **France** 28–19
1987 Auckland WC **France** 31–16	2001 Saint Etienne **France** 77–10
1991 Grenoble WC **France** 33–9	2003 Brisbane WC **France** 61–18
1998 Suva **France** 34–9	

FRANCE V JAPAN

Played 2 France won 2
Highest scores France 51–29 in 2003, Japan 29–51 in 2003
Biggest win France 51–29 in 2003, Japan no win

1973 Bordeaux **France** 30–18	2003 Townsville WC **France** 51–29

FRANCE V ZIMBABWE

Played 1 France won 1
Highest scores France 70–12 in 1987, Zimbabwe 12–70 in 1987
Biggest win France 70–12 in 1987, Zimbabwe no win

1987 Auckland WC **France** 70–12

FRANCE V CANADA

Played 7 France won 6, Canada won 1, Drawn 0
Highest scores France 50–6 in 2005, Canada 20–33 in 1999
Biggest wins France 50–6 in 2005, Canada 18–16 in 1994

1991	Agen WC **France** 19–13	2002	Paris **France** 35–3
1994	Nepean **Canada** 18–16	2004	Toronto **France** 47–13
1994	Besançon **France** 28–9	2005	Nantes **France** 50–6
1999	Béziers WC **France** 33–20		

FRANCE V TONGA

Played 3 France won 2, Tonga won 1
Highest scores France 43–8 in 2005, Tonga 20–16 in 1999
Biggest win France 43–8 in 2005, Tonga 20–16 in 1999

1995	Pretoria WC **France** 38–10	2005	Toulouse **France** 43–8
1999	Nuku'alofa **Tonga** 20–16		

FRANCE V IVORY COAST

Played 1 France won 1
Highest scores France 54–18 in 1995, Ivory Coast 18–54 in 1995
Biggest win France 54–18 in 1995, Ivory Coast no win

1995	Rustenburg WC **France** 54–18

FRANCE V SAMOA

Played 1 France won 1
Highest scores France 39–22 in 1999, Samoa 22–39 in 1999
Biggest win France 39–22 in 1999, Samoa no win

1999	Apia **France** 39–22

FRANCE V NAMIBIA

Played 2 France won 2
Highest scores France 87–10 in 2007, Namibia 13–47 in 1999
Biggest win France 87–10 in 2007, Namibia no win

1999 Bordeaux WC **France** 47–13
2007 Toulouse WC **France** 87–10

FRANCE V GEORGIA

Played 1 France won 1
Highest scores France 64–7 in 2007, Georgia 7–64 in 2007
Biggest win France 64–7 in 2007, Georgia no win

2007 Marseilles WC **France** 64–7

SOUTH AFRICA V NEW ZEALAND

Played 72 New Zealand won 40, South Africa won 29, Drawn 3
Highest scores New Zealand 55–35 in 1997, South Africa 46–40 in 2000
Biggest wins New Zealand 52–16 in 2003, South Africa 17–0 in 1928

1921 *1* Dunedin **New Zealand** 13–5
2 Auckland **South Africa** 9–5
3 Wellington **Drawn** 0–0
Series drawn 1–1, with 1 draw

1928 *1* Durban **South Africa** 17–0
2 Johannesburg **New Zealand** 7–6
3 Port Elizabeth **South Africa** 11–6
4 Cape Town **New Zealand** 13–5
Series drawn 2–2

1937 *1* Wellington **New Zealand** 13–7
2 Christchurch **South Africa** 13–6
3 Auckland **South Africa** 17–6
South Africa won series 2–1

1949 *1* Cape Town **South Africa** 15–11
2 Johannesburg **South Africa** 12–6
3 Durban **South Africa** 9–3
4 Port Elizabeth **South Africa** 11–8
South Africa won series 4–0

1956 *1* Dunedin **New Zealand** 10–6
2 Wellington **South Africa** 8–3
3 Christchurch **New Zealand** 17–10
4 Auckland **New Zealand** 11–5
New Zealand won series 3–1

1960 *1* Johannesburg **South Africa** 13–0
2 Cape Town **New Zealand** 11–3
3 Bloemfontein **Drawn** 11–11
4 Port Elizabeth **South Africa** 8–3
South Africa won series 2–1, with 1 draw

1965 *1* Wellington **New Zealand** 6–3
2 Dunedin **New Zealand** 13–0
3 Christchurch **South Africa** 19–16
4 Auckland **New Zealand** 20–3
New Zealand won series 3–1

1970 *1* Pretoria **South Africa** 17–6
2 Cape Town **New Zealand** 9–8
3 Port Elizabeth **South Africa** 14–3
4 Johannesburg **South Africa** 20–17
South Africa won series 3–1

1976 *1* Durban **South Africa** 16–7
2 Bloemfontein **New Zealand** 15–9
3 Cape Town **South Africa** 15–10
4 Johannesburg **South Africa** 15–14

South Africa won series 3–1
1981 *1* Christchurch **New Zealand** 14–9
2 Wellington **South Africa** 24–12
3 Auckland **New Zealand** 25–22
New Zealand won series 2–1
1992 Johannesburg **New Zealand** 27–24
1994 *1* Dunedin **New Zealand** 22–14
2 Wellington **New Zealand** 13–9
3 Auckland **Drawn** 18–18
New Zealand won series 2–0, with 1 draw
1995 Johannesburg WC **South Africa** 15–12 (*aet*)
1996 Christchurch TN **New Zealand** 15–11
1996 Cape Town TN **New Zealand** 29–18
1996 *1* Durban **New Zealand** 23–19
2 Pretoria **New Zealand** 33–26
3 Johannesburg **South Africa** 32–22
New Zealand won series 2–1
1997 Johannesburg TN **New Zealand** 35–32
1997 Auckland TN **New Zealand** 55–35
1998 Wellington TN **South Africa** 13–3
1998 Durban TN **South Africa** 24–23
1999 Dunedin TN **New Zealand** 28–0
1999 Pretoria TN **New Zealand** 34–18
1999 Cardiff WC **South Africa** 22–18
2000 Christchurch TN **New Zealand** 25–12
2000 Johannesburg TN **South Africa** 46–40
2001 Cape Town TN **New Zealand** 12–3
2001 Auckland TN **New Zealand** 26–15
2002 Wellington TN **New Zealand** 41–20
2002 Durban TN **New Zealand** 30–23
2003 Pretoria TN **New Zealand** 52–16
2003 Dunedin TN **New Zealand** 19–11
2003 Melbourne WC **New Zealand** 29–9
2004 Christchurch TN **New Zealand** 23–21
2004 Johannesburg TN **South Africa** 40–26
2005 Cape Town TN **South Africa** 22–16
2005 Dunedin TN **New Zealand** 31–27
2006 Wellington TN **New Zealand** 35–17
2006 Pretoria TN **New Zealand** 45–26
2006 Rustenburg TN **South Africa** 21–20
2007 Durban TN **New Zealand** 26–21
2007 Christchurch TN **New Zealand** 33–6

SOUTH AFRICA V AUSTRALIA

Played 62 South Africa won 37, Australia won 24, Drawn 1
Highest scores South Africa 61–22 in 1997, Australia 49–0 in 2006
Biggest wins South Africa 61–22 in 1997, Australia 49–0 in 2006

1933 *1* Cape Town **South Africa** 17–3
2 Durban **Australia** 21–6
3 Johannesburg **South Africa** 12–3
4 Port Elizabeth **South Africa** 11–0
5 Bloemfontein **Australia** 15–4
South Africa won series 3–2
1937 *1* Sydney **South Africa** 9–5
2 Sydney **South Africa** 26–17
South Africa won series 2–0
1953 *1* Johannesburg **South Africa** 25–3
2 Cape Town **Australia** 18–14
3 Durban **South Africa** 18–8
4 Port Elizabeth **South Africa** 22–9
South Africa won series 3–1
1956 *1* Sydney **South Africa** 9–0
2 Brisbane **South Africa** 9–0
South Africa won series 2–0
1961 *1* Johannesburg **South Africa** 28–3
2 Port Elizabeth **South Africa** 23–11
South Africa won series 2–0
1963 *1* Pretoria **South Africa** 14–3
2 Cape Town **Australia** 9–5
3 Johannesburg **Australia** 11–9
4 Port Elizabeth **South Africa** 22–6
Series drawn 2–2
1965 *1* Sydney **Australia** 18–11
2 Brisbane **Australia** 12–8
Australia won series 2–0
1969 *1* Johannesburg **South Africa** 30–11
2 Durban **South Africa** 16–9
3 Cape Town **South Africa** 11–3
4 Bloemfontein **South Africa** 19–8
South Africa won series 4–0
1971 *1* Sydney **South Africa** 19–11

	2 Brisbane **South Africa** 14–6
	3 Sydney **South Africa** 18–6
	South Africa won series 3–0
1992	Cape Town **Australia** 26–3
1993	*1* Sydney **South Africa** 19–12
	2 Brisbane **Australia** 28–20
	3 Sydney **Australia** 19–12
	Australia won series 2–1
1995	Cape Town WC **South Africa** 27–18
1996	Sydney TN **Australia** 21–16
1996	Bloemfontein TN **South Africa** 25–19
1997	Brisbane TN **Australia** 32–20
1997	Pretoria TN **South Africa** 61–22
1998	Perth TN **South Africa** 14–13
1998	Johannesburg TN **South Africa** 29–15
1999	Brisbane TN **Australia** 32–6
1999	Cape Town TN **South Africa** 10–9
1999	Twickenham WC **Australia** 27–21
2000	Melbourne **Australia** 44–23
2000	Sydney TN **Australia** 26–6
2000	Durban TN **Australia** 19–18
2001	Pretoria TN **South Africa** 20–15
2001	Perth TN **Drawn** 14–14
2002	Brisbane TN **Australia** 38–27
2002	Johannesburg TN **South Africa** 33–31
2003	Cape Town TN **South Africa** 26–22
2003	Brisbane TN **Australia** 29–9
2004	Perth TN **Australia** 30–26
2004	Durban TN **South Africa** 23–19
2005	Sydney **Australia** 30–12
2005	Johannesburg **South Africa** 33–20
2005	Pretoria TN **South Africa** 22–16
2005	Perth TN **South Africa** 22–19
2006	Brisbane TN **Australia** 49–0
2006	Sydney TN **Australia** 20–18
2006	Johannesburg TN **South Africa** 24–16
2007	Cape Town TN **South Africa** 22–19
2007	Sydney TN **Australia** 25–17

SOUTH AFRICA V WORLD XVS

Played 3 South Africa won 3
Highest scores South Africa 45–24 in 1977, World XV 24–45 in 1977
Biggest win South Africa 45–24 in 1977, World XV no win

1977	Pretoria **South Africa** 45–24
1989	*1* Cape Town **South Africa** 20–19
	2 Johannesburg **South Africa** 22–16
	South Africa won series 2–0

SOUTH AFRICA V SOUTH AMERICA

Played 8 South Africa won 7, South America won 1, Drawn 0
Highest scores South Africa 50–18 in 1982, South America 21–12 in 1982
Biggest wins South Africa 50–18 in 1982, South America 21–12 in 1982

1980	*1* Johannesburg **South Africa** 24–9
	2 Durban **South Africa** 18–9
	South Africa won series 2–0
1980	*1* Montevideo **South Africa** 22–13
	2 Santiago **South Africa** 30–16
	South Africa won series 2–0
1982	*1* Pretoria **South Africa** 50–18
	2 Bloemfontein **South America** 21–12
	Series drawn 1–1
1984	*1* Pretoria **South Africa** 32–15
	2 Cape Town **South Africa** 22–13
	South Africa won series 2–0

SOUTH AFRICA V UNITED STATES

Played 3 South Africa won 3
Highest scores South Africa 64–10 in 2007, United States 20–43 in 2001
Biggest win South Africa 64–10 in 2007, United States no win

1981 Glenville **South Africa** 38–7
2001 Houston **South Africa** 43–20
2007 Montpellier WC **South Africa** 64–10

SOUTH AFRICA V NEW ZEALAND CAVALIERS

Played 4 South Africa won 3, New Zealand Cavaliers won 1, Drawn 0
Highest scores South Africa 33–18 in 1986, New Zealand Cavaliers 19–18 in 1986
Biggest wins South Africa 33–18 in 1986, New Zealand Cavaliers 19–18 in 1986

1986 *1* Cape Town **South Africa** 21–15
2 Durban **New Zealand Cavaliers** 19–18
3 Pretoria **South Africa** 33–18
4 Johannesburg **South Africa** 24–10
South Africa won series 3–1

SOUTH AFRICA V ARGENTINA

Played 12 South Africa won 12
Highest scores South Africa 52–23 in 1993, Argentina 33–37 in 2000
Biggest wins South Africa 39–7 in 2004, Argentina no win

1993 *1* Buenos Aires **South Africa** 29–26
2 Buenos Aires **South Africa** 52–23
South Africa won series 2–0
1994 *1* Port Elizabeth **South Africa** 42–22
2 Johannesburg **South Africa** 46–26
South Africa won series 2–0
1996 *1* Buenos Aires **South Africa** 46–15
2 Buenos Aires **South Africa** 44–21
South Africa win series 2–0
2000 Buenos Aires **South Africa** 37–33
2002 Springs **South Africa** 49–29
2003 Port Elizabeth **South Africa** 26–25
2004 Buenos Aires **South Africa** 39–7
2005 Buenos Aires **South Africa** 34–23
2007 Paris WC **South Africa** 37–13

SOUTH AFRICA V SAMOA

Played 6 South Africa won 6
Highest scores South Africa 60–8 in 1995, 60–18 in 2002 and 60–10 in 2003, Samoa 18–60 in 2002
Biggest win South Africa 60–8 in 1995 and 59–7 in 2007, Samoa no win

1995 Johannesburg **South Africa** 60–8
1995 Johannesburg WC **South Africa** 42–14
2002 Pretoria **South Africa** 60–18
2003 Brisbane WC **South Africa** 60–10
2007 Johannesburg **South Africa** 35–8
2007 Paris WC **South Africa** 59–7

SOUTH AFRICA V ROMANIA

Played 1 South Africa won 1
Highest score South Africa 21–8 in 1995, Romania 8–21 in 1995
Biggest win South Africa 21–8 in 1995, Romania no win

1995 Cape Town WC **South Africa** 21–8

SOUTH AFRICA V CANADA

Played 2 South Africa won 2
Highest scores South Africa 51–18 in 2000, Canada 18–51 in 2000
Biggest win South Africa 51–18 in 2000, Canada no win

1995 Port Elizabeth WC **South Africa** 20–0
2000 East London **South Africa** 51–18

SOUTH AFRICA V ITALY

Played 6 South Africa won 6
Highest scores South Africa 101–0 in 1999, Italy 31–62 in 1997
Biggest win South Africa 101–0 in 1999, Italy no win

1995 Rome **South Africa** 40–21
1997 Bologna **South Africa** 62–31
1999 *1* Port Elizabeth **South Africa** 74–3
2 Durban **South Africa** 101–0
South Africa won series 2–0
2001 Port Elizabeth **South Africa** 60–14
2001 Genoa **South Africa** 54–26

SOUTH AFRICA V FIJI

Played 2 South Africa won 2
Highest scores South Africa 43–18 in 1996, Fiji 20–37 in 2007
Biggest win South Africa 43–18 in 1996, Fiji no win

1996 Pretoria **South Africa** 43–18	2007 Marseilles WC **South Africa** 37–20

SOUTH AFRICA V TONGA

Played 2 South Africa won 2
Higest scores South Africa 74–10 in 1997, Tonga 25–30 in 2007
Biggest win South Africa 74–10 in 1997, Tonga no win

1997 Cape Town **South Africa** 74–10	2007 Lens WC **South Africa** 30–25

SOUTH AFRICA V SPAIN

Played 1 South Africa won 1
Highest scores South Africa 47–3 in 1999, Spain 3–47 in 1999
Biggest win South Africa 47–3 in 1999, Spain no win

1999 Murrayfield WC **South Africa** 47–3

SOUTH AFRICA V URUGUAY

Played 3 South Africa won 3
Highest scores South Africa 134–3 in 2005, Uruguay 6–72 in 2003
Biggest win South Africa 134–3 in 2005, Uruguay no win

1999 Glasgow WC **South Africa** 39–3	Perth WC **South Africa** 72–6
2003 Glasgow *WC* **South Africa** 39–3	2005 East London **South Africa** 134–3

SOUTH AFRICA V GEORGIA

Played 1 South Africa won 1
Highest scores South Africa 46–19 in 2003, Georgia 19–46 in 2003
Biggest win South Africa 46–19 in 2003, Georgia no win

2003 Sydney WC **South Africa** 46–19

SOUTH AFRICA V PACIFIC ISLANDS

Played 1 South Africa won 1
Highest scores South Africa 38–24 in 2004, Pacific Islands 24–38 in 2004
Biggest win South Africa 38–24 in 2004, Pacific Islands no win

2004 Gosford (Aus) **South Africa** 38–24

SOUTH AFRICA V NAMIBIA

Played 1 South Africa won 1
Highest scores South Africa 105–13 in 2007, Namibia 13–105 in 2007
Biggest win South Africa 105–13 in 2007, Namibia no win

2007 Cape Town **South Africa** 105–13

NEW ZEALAND V AUSTRALIA

Played 128 New Zealand won 85, Australia won 38, Drawn 5
Highest scores New Zealand 50–21 in 2003, Australia 35–39 in 2000
Biggest wins New Zealand 43–6 in 1996, Australia 28–7 in 1999

1903 Sydney **New Zealand** 22–3
1905 Dunedin **New Zealand** 14–3
1907 *1* Sydney **New Zealand** 26–6
2 Brisbane **New Zealand** 14–5
3 Sydney **Drawn** 5–5
New Zealand won series 2–0, with 1 draw
1910 *1* Sydney **New Zealand** 6–0
2 Sydney **Australia** 11–0
3 Sydney **New Zealand** 28–13
New Zealand won series 2–1
1913 *1* Wellington **New Zealand** 30–5
2 Dunedin **New Zealand** 25–13
3 Christchurch **Australia** 16–5
New Zealand won series 2–1
1914 *1* Sydney **New Zealand** 5–0
2 Brisbane **New Zealand** 17–0
3 Sydney **New Zealand** 22–7
New Zealand won series 3–0

1929 *1* Sydney **Australia** 9–8
2 Brisbane **Australia** 17–9
3 Sydney **Australia** 15–13
Australia won series 3–0

1931 Auckland **New Zealand** 20–13

1932 *1* Sydney **Australia** 22–17
2 Brisbane **New Zealand** 21–3
3 Sydney **New Zealand** 21–13
New Zealand won series 2–1

1934 *1* Sydney **Australia** 25–11
2 Sydney **Drawn** 3–3
Australia won series 1–0, with 1 draw

1936 *1* Wellington **New Zealand** 11–6
2 Dunedin **New Zealand** 38–13
New Zealand won series 2–0

1938 *1* Sydney **New Zealand** 24–9
2 Brisbane **New Zealand** 20–14
3 Sydney **New Zealand** 14–6
New Zealand won series 3–0

1946 *1* Dunedin **New Zealand** 31–8
2 Auckland **New Zealand** 14–10
New Zealand won series 2–0

1947 *1* Brisbane **New Zealand** 13–5
2 Sydney **New Zealand** 27–14
New Zealand won series 2–0

1949 *1* Wellington **Australia** 11–6
2 Auckland **Australia** 16–9
Australia won series 2–0

1951 *1* Sydney **New Zealand** 8–0
2 Sydney **New Zealand** 17–11
3 Brisbane **New Zealand** 16–6
New Zealand won series 3–0

1952 *1* Christchurch **Australia** 14–9
2 Wellington **New Zealand** 15–8
Series drawn 1–1

1955 *1* Wellington **New Zealand** 16–8
2 Dunedin **New Zealand** 8–0
3 Auckland **Australia** 8–3
New Zealand won series 2–1

1957 *1* Sydney **New Zealand** 25–11
2 Brisbane **New Zealand** 22–9
New Zealand won series 2–0

1958 *1* Wellington **New Zealand** 25–3
2 Christchurch **Australia** 6–3
3 Auckland **New Zealand** 17–8
New Zealand won series 2–1

1962 *1* Brisbane **New Zealand** 20–6
2 Sydney **New Zealand** 14–5
New Zealand won series 2–0

1962 *1* Wellington **Drawn** 9–9
2 Dunedin **New Zealand** 3–0
3 Auckland **New Zealand** 16–8
New Zealand won series 2–0, with1 draw

1964 *1* Dunedin **New Zealand** 14–9
2 Christchurch **New Zealand** 18–3
3 Wellington **Australia** 20–5
New Zealand won series 2–1

1967 Wellington **New Zealand** 29–9

1968 *1* Sydney **New Zealand** 27–11
2 Brisbane **New Zealand** 19–18
New Zealand won series 2–0

1972 *1* Wellington **New Zealand** 29–6
2 Christchurch **New Zealand** 30–17
3 Auckland **New Zealand** 38–3
New Zealand won series 3–0

1974 *1* Sydney **New Zealand** 11–6
2 Brisbane **Drawn** 16–16
3 Sydney **New Zealand** 16–6
New Zealand won series 2–0,
with 1 draw

1978 *1* Wellington **New Zealand** 13–12
2 Christchurch **New Zealand** 22–6
2 Christchurch **New Zealand** 22–6
3 Auckland **Australia** 30–16
New Zealand won series 2–1

1979 Sydney **Australia** 12–6

1980 *1* Sydney **Australia** 13–9
2 Brisbane **New Zealand** 12–9
3 Sydney **Australia** 26–10
Australia won series 2–1

1982 *1* Christchurch **New Zealand** 23–16
2 Wellington **Australia** 19–16
3 Auckland **New Zealand** 33–18
New Zealand won series 2–1

1983 Sydney **New Zealand** 18–8

1984 *1* Sydney **Australia** 16–9
2 Brisbane **New Zealand** 19–15
3 Sydney **New Zealand** 25–24
New Zealand won series 2–1

1985 Auckland **New Zealand** 10–9

1986 *1* Wellington **Australia** 13–12
2 Dunedin **New Zealand** 13–12
3 Auckland **Australia** 22–9
Australia won series 2–1

1987 Sydney **New Zealand** 30–16

1988 *1* Sydney **New Zealand** 32–7
2 Brisbane **Drawn** 19–19
3 Sydney **New Zealand** 30–9

New Zealand won series 2–0, with 1 draw
1989 Auckland **New Zealand** 24–12
1990 *1* Christchurch **New Zealand** 21–6
2 Auckland **New Zealand** 27–17
3 Wellington **Australia** 21–9
New Zealand won series 2–1
1991 *1* Sydney **Australia** 21–12
2 Auckland **New Zealand** 6–3
1991 Dublin WC **Australia** 16–6
1992 *1* Sydney **Australia** 16–15
2 Brisbane **Australia** 19–17
3 Sydney **New Zealand** 26–23
Australia won series 2–1
1993 Dunedin **New Zealand** 25–10
1994 Sydney **Australia** 20–16
1995 Auckland **New Zealand** 28–16
1995 Sydney **New Zealand** 34–23
1996 Wellington TN **New Zealand** 43–6
1996 Brisbane TN **New Zealand** 32–25
New Zealand won series 2–0
1997 Christchurch **New Zealand** 30–13
1997 Melbourne TN **New Zealand** 33–18
1997 Dunedin TN **New Zealand** 36–24
New Zealand won series 3–0
1998 Melbourne TN **Australia** 24–16
1998 Christchurch TN **Australia** 27–23
1998 Sydney Australia 19–14
Australia won series 3–0
1999 Auckland TN **New Zealand** 34–15
1999 Sydney TN **Australia** 28–7
Series drawn 1–1
2000 Sydney TN **New Zealand** 39–35
2000 Wellington TN **Australia** 24–23
Series drawn 1–1
2001 Dunedin TN **Australia** 23–15
2001 Sydney TN **Australia** 29–26
Australia won series 2–0
2002 Christchurch TN **New Zealand** 12–6
2002 Sydney TN **Australia** 16–14
Series drawn 1–1
2003 Sydney TN **New Zealand** 50–21
2003 Auckland TN **New Zealand** 21–17
New Zealand won series 2–0
2003 Sydney WC **Australia** 22–10
2004 Wellington TN **New Zealand** 16–7
2004 Sydney TN **Australia** 23–18
2005 Sydney TN **New Zealand** 30–13
2005 Auckland TN **New Zealand** 34–24
New Zealand won series 2–0
2006 Christchurch TN **New Zealand** 32–12
2006 Brisbane TN **New Zealand** 13–9
2006 Auckland TN **New Zealand** 34–27
New Zealand won series 3–0
2007 Melbourne TN **Australia** 20–15
2007 Auckland TN **New Zealand** 26–12
Series drawn 1–1

NEW ZEALAND V UNITED STATES

Played 2 New Zealand won 2
Highest scores New Zealand 51–3 in 1913, United States 6–46 in 1991
Biggest win New Zealand 51–3 in 1913, United States no win

1913 Berkeley **New Zealand** 51–3
1991 Gloucester WC **New Zealand** 46–6

NEW ZEALAND V ROMANIA

Played 2 New Zealand won 2
Highest score New Zealand 85–8 in 2007, Romania 8–85 in 2007
Biggest win New Zealand 85–8 in 2007, Romania no win

1981 Bucharest **New Zealand** 14–6	2007 Toulouse WC **New Zealand** 85–8

NEW ZEALAND V ARGENTINA

Played 13 New Zealand won 12, Drawn 1
Highest scores New Zealand 93–8 in 1997, Argentina 21–21 in 1985
Biggest win New Zealand 93–8 in 1997, Argentina no win

1985 *1* Buenos Aires **New Zealand** 33–20
2 Buenos Aires **Drawn** 21–21
New Zealand won series 1–0, with 1 draw
1987 Wellington *WC* **New Zealand** 46–15
1989 *1* Dunedin **New Zealand** 60–9
2 Wellington **New Zealand** 49–12
New Zealand won series 2–0
1991 *1* Buenos Aires **New Zealand** 28–14
2 Buenos Aires **New Zealand** 36–6
New Zealand won series 2–0
1997 *1* Wellington **New Zealand** 93–8
2 Hamilton **New Zealand** 62–10
New Zealand won series 2–0
2001 Christchurch **New Zealand** 67–19
2001 Buenos Aires **New Zealand** 24–20
2004 Hamilton **New Zealand** 41–7
2006 Buenos Aires **New Zealand** 25–19

NEW ZEALAND V ITALY

Played 9 New Zealand won 9
Highest scores New Zealand 101–3 in 1999, Italy 21–31 in 1991
Biggest win New Zealand 101–3 in 1999, Italy no win

1987 Auckland WC **New Zealand** 70–6
1991 Leicester WC **New Zealand** 31–21
1995 Bologna **New Zealand** 70–6
1999 Huddersfield WC **New Zealand** 101–3
2000 Genoa **New Zealand** 56–19
2002 Hamilton **New Zealand** 64–10
2003 Melbourne WC **New Zealand** 70–7
2004 Rome **New Zealand** 59–10
2007 Marseilles WC **New Zealand** 76–14

NEW ZEALAND V FIJI

Played 4 New Zealand won 4
Highest scores New Zealand 91–0 in 2005, Fiji 18–68 in 2002
Biggest win New Zealand 91–0 in 2005, Fiji no win

1987	Christchurch WC **New Zealand** 74–13	2002	Wellington **New Zealand** 68–18
1997	Albany **New Zealand** 71–5	2005	Albany **New Zealand** 91–0

NEW ZEALAND V CANADA

Played 4 New Zealand won 4
Highest scores New Zealand 73–7 in 1995, Canada 13–29 in 1991 & 13–64 in 2007
Biggest win New Zealand 73–7 in 1995, Canada no win

1991	Lille WC **New Zealand** 29–13	2003	Melbourne WC **New Zealand** 68–6
1995	Auckland **New Zealand** 73–7	2007	Hamilton **New Zealand** 64–13

NEW ZEALAND V WORLD XVS

Played 3 New Zealand won 2, World XV won 1, Drawn 0
Highest scores New Zealand 54–26 in 1992, World XV 28–14 in 1992
Biggest wins New Zealand 54–26 in 1992, World XV 28–14 in 1992

1992	*1* Christchurch **World XV** 28–14	*3* Auckland **New Zealand** 26–15
	2 Wellington **New Zealand** 54–26	New Zealand won series 2–1

NEW ZEALAND V SAMOA

Played 4 New Zealand won 4
Highest scores New Zealand 71–13 in 1999, Samoa 13–35 in 1993 & 13–71 in 1999
Biggest win New Zealand 71–13 in 1999, Samoa no win

1993	Auckland **New Zealand** 35–13	1999	Albany **New Zealand** 71–13
1996	Napier **New Zealand** 51–10	2001	Albany **New Zealand** 50–6

NEW ZEALAND V JAPAN

Played 1 New Zealand won 1
Highest scores New Zealand 145–17 in 1995, Japan 17–145 in 1995
Biggest win New Zealand 145–17 in 1995, Japan no win

1995 Bloemfontein WC **New Zealand** 145–17

NEW ZEALAND V TONGA

Played 3 New Zealand won 3
Highest scores New Zealand 102–0 in 2000, Tonga 9–45 in 1999
Biggest win New Zealand 102–0 in 2000, Tonga no win

1999 Bristol WC **New Zealand** 45–9
2000 Albany **New Zealand** 102–0
2003 Brisbane WC **New Zealand** 91–7

NEW ZEALAND V PACIFIC ISLANDS

Played 1 New Zealand won 1
Highest scores New Zealand 41–26 in 2004, Pacific Islands 26–41 in 2004
Biggest win New Zealand 41–26 in 2004, Pacific Islands no win

2004 Albany **New Zealand 41–26**

NEW ZEALAND V PORTUGAL

Played 1 New Zealand won 1
Highest scores New Zealand 108–13 in 2007, Portugal 13–108 in 2007
Biggest win New Zealand 108–13 in 2007, Portugal no win

2007 Lyons WC **New Zealand** 108–13

AUSTRALIA V UNITED STATES

Played 6 Australia won 6
Highest scores Australia 67–9 in 1990, United States 19–55 in 1999
Biggest win Australia 67–9 in 1990, United States no win

1912 Berkeley **Australia** 12–8
1976 Los Angeles **Australia** 24–12
1983 Sydney **Australia** 49–3
1987 Brisbane WC **Australia** 47–12
1990 Brisbane **Australia** 67–9
1999 Limerick WC **Australia** 55–19

AUSTRALIA V NEW ZEALAND XVS

Played 24 Australia won 6, New Zealand XVs won 18, Drawn 0
Highest scores Australia 26–20 in 1926, New Zealand XV 38–11 in 1923 and 38–8 in 1924
Biggest win Australia 17–0 in 1921, New Zealand XV 38–8 in 1924

1920 *1* Sydney **New Zealand XV** 26–15
2 Sydney **New Zealand XV** 14–6
3 Sydney **New Zealand XV** 24–13
New Zealand XV won series 3–0
1921 Christchurch **Australia** 17–0
1922 *1* Sydney **New Zealand XV** 26–19
2 Sydney **Australia** 14–8
3 Sydney **Australia** 8–6
Australia won series 2–1
1923 *1* Dunedin **New Zealand XV** 19–9
2 Christchurch **New Zealand XV** 34–6
3 Wellington **New Zealand XV** 38–11
New Zealand XV won series 3–0
1924 *1* Sydney **Australia** 20–16
2 Sydney **New Zealand XV** 21–5
3 Sydney **New Zealand XV** 38–8
New Zealand XV won series 2–1
1925 *1* Sydney **New Zealand XV** 26–3
2 Sydney **New Zealand XV** 4–0
3 Sydney **New Zealand XV** 11–3
New Zealand XV won series 3–0
1925 Auckland **New Zealand XV** 36–10
1926 *1* Sydney **Australia** 26–20
2 Sydney **New Zealand XV** 11–6
3 Sydney **New Zealand XV** 14–0
4 Sydney **New Zealand XV** 28–21
New Zealand XV won series 3–1
1928 *1* Wellington **New Zealand XV** 15–12
2 Dunedin **New Zealand XV** 16–14
3 Christchurch **Australia** 11–8
New Zealand XV won series 2–1

AUSTRALIA V SOUTH AFRICA XVS

Played 3 South Africa XVs won 3
Highest scores Australia 11–16 in 1921, South Africa XV 28–9 in 1921
Biggest win Australia no win, South Africa XV 28–9 in 1921

1921 *1* Sydney **South Africa XV** 25–10
2 Sydney **South Africa XV** 16–11
3 Sydney **South Africa XV** 28–9
South Africa XV won series 3–0

AUSTRALIA V NEW ZEALAND MAORIS

Played 16 Australia won 8, New Zealand Maoris won 6, Drawn 2
Highest scores Australia 31–6 in 1936, New Zealand Maoris 25–22 in 1922
Biggest wins Australia 31–6 in 1936, New Zealand Maoris 20–0 in 1946

1922 *1* Sydney **New Zealand Maoris** 25–22
2 Sydney **Australia** 28–13
3 Sydney **New Zealand Maoris** 23–22
New Zealand Maoris won series 2–1
1923 *1* Sydney **Australia** 27–23
2 Sydney **Australia** 21–16
3 Sydney **Australia** 14–12
Australia won series 3–0
1928 Wellington **New Zealand Maoris** 9–8
1931 Palmerston North **Australia** 14–3
1936 Palmerston North **Australia** 31–6
1946 Hamilton **New Zealand Maoris** 20–0
1949 *1* Sydney **New Zealand Maoris** 12–3
2 Brisbane **Drawn** 8–8
3 Sydney **Australia** 18–3
Series drawn 1–1, with 1 draw
1958 *1* Brisbane **Australia** 15–14
2 Sydney **Drawn** 3–3
3 Melbourne **New Zealand Maoris** 13–6
Series drawn 1–1, with 1 draw

AUSTRALIA V FIJI

Played 18 Australia won 15, Fiji won 2, Drawn 1
Highest scores Australia 66–20 in 1998, Fiji 28–52 in 1985
Biggest wins Australia 49–0 in 2007, Fiji 17–15 in 1952 & 18–16 in 1954

1952 *1* Sydney **Australia** 15–9
2 Sydney **Fiji** 17–15
Series drawn 1–1
1954 *1* Brisbane **Australia** 22–19
2 Sydney **Fiji** 18–16
Series drawn 1–1
1961 *1* Brisbane **Australia** 24–6
2 Sydney **Australia** 20–14
3 Melbourne **Drawn** 3–3
Australia won series 2–0, with 1 draw
1972 Suva **Australia** 21–19
1976 *1* Sydney **Australia** 22–6
2 Brisbane **Australia** 21–9
3 Sydney **Australia** 27–17
Australia won series 3–0
1980 Suva **Australia** 22–9
1984 Suva **Australia** 16–3
1985 *1* Brisbane **Australia** 52–28
2 Sydney **Australia** 31–9
Australia won series 2–0
1998 Sydney **Australia** 66–20
2007 Perth **Australia** 49–0
2007 Montpellier WC **Australia** 55–12

AUSTRALIA V TONGA

Played 4 Australia won 3, Tonga won 1, Drawn 0
Highest scores Australia 74–0 in 1998, Tonga 16–11 in 1973
Biggest wins Australia 74–0 in 1998, Tonga 16–11 in 1973

1973	*1* Sydney **Australia** 30–12	1993	Brisbane **Australia** 52–14
	2 Brisbane **Tonga** 16–11	1998	Canberra **Australia** 74–0
	Series drawn 1–1		

AUSTRALIA V JAPAN

Played 4 Australia won 4
Highest scores Australia 91–3 in 2007, Japan 25–50 in 1973
Biggest win Australia 91–3 in 2007, Japan no win

1975	*1* Sydney **Australia** 37–7	1987	Sydney WC **Australia** 42–23
	2 Brisbane **Australia** 50–25	2007	Lyons WC **Australia** 91–3
	Australia won series 2–0		

AUSTRALIA V ARGENTINA

Played 17 Australia won 12, Argentina won 4, Drawn 1
Highest scores Australia 53–7 in 1995 & 53–6 in 2000, Argentina 27–19 in 1987
Biggest wins Australia 53–6 in 2000, Argentina 18–3 in 1983

1979	*1* Buenos Aires **Argentina** 24–13	1991	Llanelli WC **Australia** 32–19
	2 Buenos Aires **Australia** 17–12	1995	*1* Brisbane **Australia** 53–7
	Series drawn 1–1		*2* Sydney **Australia** 30–13
1983	*1* Brisbane **Argentina** 18–3		Australia won series 2–0
	2 Sydney **Australia** 29–13	1997	*1* Buenos Aires **Australia** 23–15
	Series drawn 1–1		*2* Buenos Aires **Argentina** 18–16
1986	*1* Brisbane **Australia** 39–19		Series drawn 1–1
	2 Sydney **Australia** 26–0	2000	*1* Brisbane **Australia** 53–6
	Australia won series 2–0		*2* Canberra **Australia** 32–25
1987	*1* Buenos Aires **Drawn** 19–19		Australia won series 2–0
	2 Buenos Aires **Argentina** 27–19	2002	Buenos Aires **Australia** 17–6
	Argentina won series 1–0, with 1 draw	2003	Sydney WC **Australia** 24–8

AUSTRALIA V SAMOA

Played 4 Australia won 4
Highest scores Australia 74–7 in 2005, Samoa 13–25 in 1998
Biggest win Australia 73–3 in 1994, Samoa no win

1991	Pontypool WC **Australia** 9–3	1998	Brisbane **Australia** 25–13
1994	Sydney **Australia** 73–3	2005	Sydney **Australia** 74–7

AUSTRALIA V ITALY

Played 9 Australia won 9
Highest scores Australia 69–21 in 2005, Italy 21–69 in 2005
Biggest win Australia 55–6 in 1988, Italy no win

1983	Rovigo **Australia** 29–7		Australia won series 2–0
1986	Brisbane **Australia** 39–18	1996	Padua **Australia** 40–18
1988	Rome **Australia** 55–6	2002	Genoa **Australia** 34–3
1994	*1* Brisbane **Australia** 23–20	2005	Melbourne **Australia** 69–21
	2 Melbourne **Australia** 20–7	2006	Rome **Australia** 25–18

AUSTRALIA V CANADA

Played 6 Australia won 6
Highest scores Australia 74–9 in 1996, Canada 16–43 in 1993
Biggest win Australia 74–9 in 1996, Canada no win

1985	*1* Sydney **Australia** 59–3	1995	Port Elizabeth WC **Australia** 27–11
	2 Brisbane **Australia** 43–15	1996	Brisbane **Australia** 74–9
	Australia won series 2–0	2007	Bordeaux WC **Australia** 37–6
1993	Calgary **Australia** 43–16		

AUSTRALIA V KOREA

Played 1 Australia won 1
Highest scores Australia 65–18 in 1987, Korea 18–65 in 1987
Biggest win Australia 65–18 in 1987, Korea no win

1987	Brisbane **Australia** 65–18

AUSTRALIA V ROMANIA

Played 3 Australia won 3
Highest scores Australia 90–8 in 2003, Romania 9–57 in 1999
Biggest win Australia 90–8 in 2003, Romania no win

1995 Stellenbosch WC **Australia** 42–3	2003 Brisbane WC **Australia** 90–8
1999 Belfast WC **Australia** 57–9	

AUSTRALIA V SPAIN

Played 1 Australia won 1
Highest scores Australia 92–10 in 2001, Spain 10–92 in 2001
Biggest win Australia 92–10 in 2001, Spain no win

2001 Madrid **Australia** 92–10

AUSTRALIA V NAMIBIA

Played 1 Australia won 1
Highest scores Australia 142–0 in 2003, Namibia 0–142 in 2003
Biggest win Australia 142–0 in 2003, Namibia no win

2003 Adelaide WC **Australia** 142–0

AUSTRALIA V PACIFIC ISLANDS

Played 1 Australia won 1
Highest scores Australia 29–14 in 2004, Pacific Islands 14–29 in 2004
Biggest win Australia 29–14 in 2004, Pacific Islands no win

2004 Adelaide **Australia** 29–14

INTERNATIONAL WORLD RECORDS

The match and career records cover **official cap matches** *played by the dozen Executive Council Member Unions of the International Board (England, Scotland, Ireland, Wales, France, Italy, South Africa, New Zealand, Australia, Argentina, Canada and Japan) from 1871 up to 31 October 2007. Figures include Test performances for the (British/Irish Isles) Lions and (South American) Jaguars (shown in brackets). Where a world record has been set in a cap match played by another nation in membership of the IRB, this is shown as a footnote to the relevant table.*

MATCH RECORDS

MOST CONSECUTIVE TEST WINS	
17 by N Zealand	1965 SA 4, 1966 BI 1,2,3,4, 1967 A, E, W, F, S, 1968 A 1,2, F 1,2,3, 1969 W 1,2
17 by S Africa	1997 A 2, It, F 1,2, E, S, 1998 I 1,2, W 1, E 1, A 1, NZ 1,2, A 2, W 2, S, I 3

MOST CONSECUTIVE TEST WITHOUT DEFEAT			
Matches	Wins	Draws	Periods
23 by N Zealand	22	1	1987 to 1990
17 by N Zealand	15	2	1961 to 1964
17 by N Zealand	17	0	1965 to 1969
17 by S Africa	17	0	1997 to 1998

MOST POINTS IN A MATCH

BY THE TEAM

Pts.	Opponent	Venue	Year
155 by Japan	Chinese Taipei	Tokyo	2002
152 by Argentina	Paraguay	Mendoza	2002
147 by Argentina	Venezuela	Santiago	2004
145 by N Zealand	Japan	Bloemfontein	1995
144 by Argentina	Paraguay	Montevideo	2003
142 by Australia	Namibia	Adelaide	2003
134 by Japan	Chinese Taipei	Singapore	1998
134 by England	Romania	Twickenham	2001
134 by S Africa	Uruguay	East London	2005
120 by Japan	Chinese Taipei	Tainan	2002

Hong Kong scored 164 points against Singapore at Kuala Lumpur in 1994

BY A PLAYER

Pts.	Player	Opponent	Venue	Year
60 for Japan	T Kurihara	Chinese Taipei	Tainan	2002
50 for Argentina	E Morgan	Paraguay	San Pablo	1973
45 for N Zealand	S D Culhane	Japan	Bloemfontein	1995
45 for Argentina	J-M Nuñez-Piossek	Paraguay	Montevideo	2003
44 for Scotland	A G Hastings	Ivory Coast	Rustenburg	1995
44 for England	C Hodgson	Romania	Twickenham	2001
42 for Australia	M S Rogers	Namibia	Adelaide	2003
40 for Argentina	G M Jorge	Brazil	Sao Paulo	1993
40 for Japan	D Ohata	Chinese Taipei	Tokyo	2002
40 for Scotland	C D Paterson	Japan	Perth	2004
39 for Australia	M C Burke	Canada	Brisbane	1996

MOST TRIES IN A MATCH

BY THE TEAM

Tries	Opponent	Venue	Year
24 by Argentina	Paraguay	Mendoza	2002
24 by Argentina	Paraguay	Montevideo	2003
23 by Japan	Chinese Taipei	Tokyo	2002
23 by Argentina	Venezuela	Santiago	2004
22 by Australia	Namibia	Adelaide	2003
21 by N Zealand	Japan	Bloemfontein	1995
21 by S Africa	Uruguay	East London	2005
20 by Argentina	Brazil	Montevideo	1989
20 by Japan	Ch Taipei	Singapore	1998
20 by England	Romania	Twickenham	2001
19 by Argentina	Brazil	Santiago	1979
19 by Argentina	Paraguay	Asuncion	1985

Hong Kong scored 26 tries against Singapore at Kuala Lumpur in 1994

BY A PLAYER

Tries	Player	Opponent	Venue	Year
11 for Argentina	U O'Farrell	Brazil	Buenos Aires	1951
9 for Argentina	J-M Nuñez-Piossek	Paraguay	Montevideo	2003
8 for Argentina	G M Jorge	Brazil	Sao Paulo	1993
8 for Japan	D Ohata	Chinese Taipei	Tokyo	2002
6 for Argentina	E Morgan	Paraguay	San Pablo	1973
6 for Argentina	G M Jorge	Brazil	Montevideo	1989
6 for N Zealand	M C G Ellis	Japan	Bloemfontein	1995
6 for Japan	T Kurihara	Chinese Taipei	Tainan	2002
6 for S Africa	T Chavhanga	Uruguay	East London	2005
6 for Japan	D Ohata	Hong Kong	Tokyo	2005
5 for Scotland	G C Lindsay	Wales	Raeburn Place	1887
5 for England	D Lambert	France	Richmond	1907
5 for Argentina	H Goti	Brazil	Montevideo	1961
5 for Argentina	M R Jurado	Brazil	Montevideo	1971
5 for England	R Underwood	Fiji	Twickenham	1989
5 for N Zealand	J W Wilson	Fiji	Albany	1997
5 for Japan	T Masuho	Ch Taipei	Singapore	1998
5 for Argentina	P Grande	Paraguay	Asuncion	1998
5 for S Africa	C S Terblanche	Italy	Durban	1999
5 for England	O J Lewsey	Uruguay	Brisbane	2003
5 for Australia	C E Latham	Namibia	Adelaide	2003
5 for Argentina	F Higgs	Venezuela	Santiago	2004

10 tries were scored for Hong Kong by A Billington against Singapore at Kuala Lumpur in 1994

MOST CONVERSIONS IN A MATCH

BY THE TEAM

Cons	Opponent	Venue	Year
20 by N Zealand	Japan	Bloemfontein	1995
20 by Japan	Chinese Taipei	Tokyo	2002
17 by Japan	Chinese Taipei	Singapore	1998
16 by Argentina	Paraguay	Mendoza	2002
16 by Australia	Namibia	Adelaide	2003
16 by Argentina	Venezuela	Santiago	2004
15 by Argentina	Brazil	Santiago	1979
15 by England	Holland	Huddersfield	1998
15 by Japan	Chinese Taipei	Tainan	2002

BY A PLAYER

Cons	Player	Opponent	Venue	Year
20 for N Zealand	S D Culhane	Japan	Bloemfontein	1995
16 for Argentina	J-L Cilley	Paraguay	Mendoza	2002
16 for Australia	M S Rogers	Namibia	Adelaide	2003
15 for England	P J Grayson	Holland	Huddersfield	1998
15 for Japan	T Kurihara	Chinese Taipei	Tainan	2002

MOST PENALTIES IN A MATCH

BY THE TEAM

Pens	Opponent	Venue	Year
9 by Japan	Tonga	Tokyo	1999
9 by N Zealand	Australia	Auckland	1999
9 by Wales	France	Cardiff	1999
9 by N Zealand	France	Paris	2000

Portugal scored nine penalties against Georgia at Lisbon in 2000

BY A PLAYER

Pens	Player	Opponent	Venue	Year
9 for Japan	K Hirose	Tonga	Tokyo	1999
9 for N Zealand	A P Mehrtens	Australia	Auckland	1999
9 for Wales	N R Jenkins	France	Cardiff	1999
9 for N Zealand	A P Mehrtens	France	Paris	2000

Nine penalties were scored for Portugal by T Teixeira against Georgia at Lisbon in 2000

MOST DROPPED GOALS IN A MATCH

BY THE TEAM

Drops	Opponent	Venue	Year
5 by South Africa	England	Paris	1999
4 by South Africa	England	Twickenham	2006

BY A PLAYER

Drops	Player	Opponent	Venue	Year
5 for S Africa	J H de Beer	England	Paris	1999
4 for South Africa	AG Pretorius	England	Twickenham	2006

MOST CAPPED PLAYERS

Caps	Player	Career Span
139	G M Gregan (Australia)	1994 to 2007
119 (5)	J Leonard (England/Lions)	1990 to 2004
118	F Pelous (France)	1995 to 2007
111	P Sella (France)	1982 to 1995
103 (3)	Gareth Thomas (Wales/Lions)	1995 to 2007
102	S J Larkham (Australia)	1996 to 2007
101	D I Campese (Australia)	1982 to 1996
101	A Troncon (Italy)	1994 to 2007
98	R Ibañez (France)	1996 to 2007
95 (2)	C L Charvis (Wales/Lions)	1996 to 2007
94	P C Montgomery (S Africa)	1997 to 2007
93	S Blanco (France)	1980 to 1991
92	S B T Fitzpatrick (N Zealand)	1986 to 1997
92 (8)	M O Johnson (England/Lions)	1993 to 2003
92	G O Llewellyn (Wales)	1989 to 2004
91 (6)	R Underwood (England/Lions)	1984 to 1996
91 (4)	N R Jenkins (Wales/Lions)	1991 to 2002

MOST CONSECUTIVE TESTS

Tests	Player	Career span
63	S B T Fitzpatrick (N Zealand)	1986 to 1995
62	J W C Roff (Australia)	1996 to 2001
53	G O Edwards (Wales)	1967 to 1978
52	W J McBride (Ireland)	1964 to 1975
51	C M Cullen (N Zealand)	1996 to 2000

MOST TESTS AS CAPTAIN

Tests	Player	Career span
59	W D C Carling (England)	1988 to 1996
59	G M Gregan (Australia)	2001 to 2007
55	J A Eales (Australia)	1996 to 2001
51	S B T Fitzpatrick (N Zealand)	1992 to 1997
48	J W Smit (S Africa)	2003 to 2007
46 (8)	H Porta (Argentina/Jaguars)	1971 to 1990
45 (6)	M O Johnson (England/Lions)	1997 to 2003
43 (1)	B G O'Driscoll (Ireland/Lions)	2002 to 2007
42	F Pelous (France)	1997 to 2006
41	L Arbizu (Argentina)	1992 to 2002
41	R Ibañez (France)	1996 to 2007
37	M Giovanelli (Italy)	1992 to 1999
36	N C Farr-Jones (Australia)	1988 to 1992
36	G H Teichmann (S Africa)	1996 to 1999
36	K G M Wood (Ireland)	1996 to 2003

MOST POINTS IN TESTS

Points	Player	Tests	Career Span
1090 (41)	N R Jenkins (Wales/Lions)	91 (4)	1991 to 2002
1029 (47)	J P Wilkinson (England/Lions)	70 (5)	1998 to 2007
1010 (27)	D Dominguez (Italy/Argentina)	76 (2)	1989 to 2003
967	A P Mehrtens (N Zealand)	70	1995 to 2004
911	M P Lynagh (Australia)	72	1984 to 1995
878	M C Burke (Australia)	81	1993 to 2004
873	P C Montgomery (S Africa)	94	1997 to 2007
779 (0)	R J R O'Gara (Ireland/Lions)	78 (1)	2000 to 2007
733 (66)	A G Hastings (Scotland/Lions)	67 (6)	1986 to 1995

MOST TRIES IN TESTS

Tries	Player	Tests	Career Span
69	D Ohata (Japan)	58	1996 to 2007
64	D I Campese (Australia)	101	1982 to 1996
50 (1)	R Underwood (England/Lions)	91 (6)	1984 to 1996
49	D C Howlett (N Zealand)	62	2000 to 2007
46	C M Cullen (N Zealand)	58	1996 to 2002
44	J W Wilson (N Zealand)	60	1993 to 2001
43	J T Rokocoko (N Zealand)	48	2003 to 2007
41 (1)	Gareth Thomas (Wales/Lions)	103 (3)	1995 to 2007
40	C E Latham (Australia)	78	1998 to 2007
38	S Blanco (France)	93	1980 to 1991
38	J H van der Westhuizen (S Africa)	89	1993 to 2003
37	J T Lomu (N Zealand)	63	1994 to 2002
37*	J F Umaga (N Zealand)	74	1999 to 2005
35	J J Kirwan (N Zealand)	63	1984 to 1994
35 (0)	S M Williams (Wales/Lions)	52 (1)	2000 to 2007
34 (1)	I C Evans (Wales/Lions)	79 (7)	1987 to 1998

* includes a penalty try

MOST CONVERSIONS IN TESTS

Cons	Player	Tests	Career Span
169	A P Mehrtens (N Zealand)	70	1995 to 2004
150	P C Montgomery (S Africa)	94	1997 to 2007
146 (6)	J P Wilkinson (England/Lions)	70 (5)	1998 to 2007
140	M P Lynagh (Australia)	72	1984 to 1995
133 (6)	D Dominguez (Italy/Argentina)	76 (2)	1989 to 2003
131 (1)	N R Jenkins (Wales/Lions))	91 (4)	1991 to 2002
122 (0)	R J R O'Gara (Ireland/Lions)	78 (1)	2000 to 2007
122	D W Carter (N Zealand)	44	2003 to 2007
118	G J Fox (N Zealand)	46	1985 to 1993

MOST PENALTY GOALS IN TESTS

Pens	Player	Tests	Career Span
248 (13)	N R Jenkins (Wales/Lions)	91 (4)	1991 to 2002
214 (5)	D Dominguez (Italy/Argentina)	76 (2)	1989 to 2003
207 (10)	J P Wilkinson (England/Lions)	70 (5)	1998 to 2007
188	A P Mehrtens (N Zealand)	70	1995 to 2004
177	M P Lynagh (Australia)	72	1984 to 1995
174	M C Burke (Australia)	81	1993 to 2004
160 (20)	A G Hastings (Scotland/Lions)	67 (6)	1986 to 1995

MOST DROPPED GOALS IN TESTS

Drops	Player	Tests	Career Span
28 (2)	H Porta (Argentina/Jaguars)	65 (8)	1971 to 1990
27 (0)	J P Wilkinson (England/Lions)	70 (5)	1998 to 2007
23 (2)	C R Andrew (England/Lions)	76 (5)	1985 to 1997
19 (0)	D Dominguez (Italy/Argentina)	76 (2)	1989 to 2003
18	H E Botha (S Africa)	28	1980 to 1992
17	S Bettarello (Italy)	55	1979 to 1988
15	J-P Lescarboura (France)	28	1982 to 1990

ARGENTINA

ARGENTINA'S 2006–07 TEST RECORD

OPPONENTS	DATE	VENUE	RESULT
England	11 Nov	A	**Won** 25–18
Italy	18 Nov	A	**Won** 23–16
France	25 Nov	A	**Lost** 26–27
Ireland	26 May	H	**Won** 22–20
Ireland	2 June	H	**Won** 16–0
Italy	9 June	H	**Won** 24–6
Wales	18 August	A	**Lost** 20–27
France	7 September	N	**Won** 17–12 (WC)
Georgia	11 September	N	**Won** 33–3 (WC)
Namibia	22 September	N	**Won** 63–3 (WC)
Ireland	30 September	N	**Won** 30–15 (WC)
Scotland	7 October	N	**Won** 19–13 (WC)
South Africa	14 October	N	**Lost** 13–37 (WC)
France	19 October	N	**Won** 34–10 (WC)

PUMAS IN DREAMLAND

By Frankie Deges

Argentina finished third in Rugby World Cup 2007. Please allow me to write that again: Argentina finished third in Rugby World Cup 2007. Not in an arrogant way, but just to make sure I got it right. Because it feels like a dream.

Yes, the memories of September and October 2007 in France will stay with everybody in Argentina, whether heavily involved in rugby or not. Forever. And the world took notice. Not only because of the success of a team brilliantly coached and directed by now Leicester coach Marcelo Loffreda and skippered, marshalled, owned by the talismanic Agustín Pichot, but because of they way they played with their heart and soul on their sleeves.

If the first was already a hero of Argentine rugby having played for Los Pumas from 1978 to 1994 and coached the team to unimaginable heights over eight seasons (2000–2007), the second is now sitting at the top of the pantheon of sporting heroes in a country where sports takes a far more important place than in most.

They both represent what is good about Argentine rugby. Their team represented what is good about the game – "passion, soul and heart," was a repeated answer from the captain when asked about the clues to his team's success.

Arriving in France to play in the so-called "Pool of Death", they looked death in the eye and laughed as they dispatched France first, Georgia, Namibia and finally Ireland to find their way to the semi-final via a quarter-final win against Scotland. The rudder got broken that night of Stade de France against the Springboks – who of course went on to become World Champions – but they found it in them to come back to win that game that many had said players don't want to play in: the "petite final".

Argentina was desperate to win it and go home as the third best team in the world as of October 2007. And as a preview to a hard-fought yet uninspiring final, it was probably one of the best matches of the whole tournament and certainly the best of the third/fourth place play-offs in the history of the World Cup. France, hosts and one of the teams that was expected to win the tournament, lost twice against Argentina. The second was a conclusive win.

This road to the bronze medal did not start on September 7th. It actually started in December of 2003, when the "elders" in the team over Christmas roast in Paris discussed what had gone wrong in Australia earlier that year (when they crashed out of the tournament in pool play); an agreement was reached that for the next four years the focus would be on the World Cup. The resolve was evident. The coach bought into the new approach and a society was re-born slowly and steadily ensuring they made every step one that really mattered.

That is how they arrived to Twickenham in 2006 for the game that would confirm they were on the right road. The preceding year, as covered in last year's IRB Yearbook, had not been smooth sailing as the team got involved in a feud with the UAR officials over certain principles such as training structures for the players still at home.

The animosity had not ceased, but that afternoon in London, Argentina finally beat England at home. The 25–18 score was followed a week later by a 23–16 win in Rome against Italy that was harder than expected due to some unfortunate incidents – the unexpected and uninvited arrival of who was supposedly in line to replace Loffreda after 2007 to join the management – that almost led to a team walkout. Some kind of entente cordiale was agreed between the players and their Union officials that saved, probably, the World Cup campaign that was to follow.

That three-Test tour would end with a dress rehearsal of the opening game of the World Cup, as Los Pumas stayed in what would be their tournament headquarters and played against France at Stade de France.

It took them a bit more than an hour to realise that they could beat this French team. The Pumas came painstakingly close and only lost 26–27, this being the only time France would win in seven matches since France had beaten them in RWC 1999. The seeds for the success that was to come were slowly growing.

At the start of the year, with a number of players unavailable, Argentina played and beat Northampton, Leicester and a few weeks later the French Barbarians in Biarritz. One of the positive aspects of these matches was that Juan Martín Hernández finally got some match practice in national colours in his preferred number 10 jersey. A full-back for most of his international career, he never ceased to say that he wanted to play at fly-half. Yet, his own success at club level meant he, together with some other ten players were unavailable to play the summer tests because of involvement in the French finals.

Ireland came to Argentina and with a superb fly-half display from Felipe Contepomi were beaten in the first Test in Santa Fe; he would fly back to Dublin to become a doctor, having graduated with honours whilst playing professional rugby.

The second Test in Buenos Aires showed sufficient to be hopeful – a 16–0 drubbing in a game that showed the defensive qualities of an

Shaun Botterill/Getty Images

Juan Martín Hernández [right, with Felipe Contepomi] was so many people's Player of the Tournament, at the World Cup. Simply the best as Argentina's had a sensational 2007.

Argentine squad that was heading the right way. Italy was also dispatched a week later to ensure the treble.

Crucial in what would be a superb World Cup was a week spent in Pensacola, USA, in a training centre used by Olympic athletes, NFL, NHL and NBA sportsmen. It was seven days of solid fitness work that would pay off. Not in the first test of the European season as in a game in which the team seemed lost, they came within a video-ref decision of almost tying a Test against Wales at an empty Millennium Stadium. The 20–27 loss would be one of three in the whole calendar year. The biggest loss was that of centre Martín Gaitán who after the end of the game complained of chest pains and came close to dying of a heart attack. Although he has fully recovered, he will no longer be able to play professional rugby.

Arriving in Paris, via ten days in Brussels, the players were confident they could do it. French coach Bernard Laporte was helpful enough in that he made some baffling selections. Somehow, he never managed to understand Argentina and the way they play – the 17–12 victory was much celebrated by the travelling fans, but not by the team. They all acknowledged it was the start of the road and too soon to be carried away.

It was a tough ask to ask them to travel to Lyon and play Georgia four days after the opening day, but they did and took the bonus point seconds from full time. After a long break, Namibia was also duly beaten in Marseille 63–3 before the big match against Ireland at Parc des Princes.

That was one of Argentina's most accomplished performances in many seasons – they controlled the game so much that the win was seldom in doubt. There were more than 4,000 Argentine fans there to enjoy, and share, the sheer delight of Pichot & Co after the 30–15 win.

The first goal – reaching the quarter-final – was achieved, but this was a hungry team and in a much harder game than expected, probably more to do with their mental fatigue than Scotland's abilities, they managed to still win 19–13.

Playing in a semi-final was uncharted territory for Los Pumas and that showed – the players did not adhere to the proposed game plan and South Africa benefited from early Puma mistakes to win by a comfortable margin. Pichot announced his retirement that night, but after taking a couple of days off, he decided he did not want to exit that way and was there to, again, lead his team to victory at a full Parc des Princes in what might be the final game for many in his team. The 34–10 win was a fitting finale for one of the teams of the tournament.

Third place in a World Cup is a well earned price for a group of very focused players and a management unit that knew when and how to do it. There will be many fathers to this victory, but looking outside of the 45+ that were involved in the World Cup would be wrong.

It will now be crucial that the Argentine Rugby Union rises to the occasion and makes the needed provisions for what is already a huge rugby explosion in Argentina. The game has drawn new interest levels and firm and conclusive direction is needed. The players will want to exercise their new found power and unless everybody sits at the table with a clean slate then the fruits of Argentina's biggest ever rugby success might be soon lost.

It will also confirm that given the right structures and competitions, this is a rugby nation that could add a lot to any tournament it plays in it. Thus, a new home has to be found for Argentina – be it the enlarged versions of Tri or Six Nations. The International Rugby Board has been wanting to help Argentine rugby – at the crossroads it is in at the moment, Argentine rugby has to help itself. Sound decision-making, firm action and a real understanding of the new oval world is needed.

The departure of coach Loffreda means Argentina is now also capable of exporting coaches of the highest calibre. Players are respected overseas and two of them – Felipe Contepomi and Juan Martín Hernández – were amongst the Five IRB Players of the Year.

ARGENTINA INTERNATIONAL STATISTICS

MATCH RECORDS UP TO 31ST OCTOBER 2007

WINNING MARGIN

Date	Opponent	Result	Winning Margin
01/05/2002	Paraguay	152 - 0	**152**
27/04/2003	Paraguay	144 - 0	**144**
01/05/2004	Venezuela	147 - 7	**140**
02/10/1993	Brazil	114 - 3	**111**
09/10/1979	Brazil	109 - 3	**106**

MOST POINTS IN A MATCH
BY THE TEAM

Date	Opponent	Result	Pts.
01/05/2002	Paraguay	152 - 0	**152**
01/05/2004	Venezuela	147 - 7	**147**
27/04/2003	Paraguay	144 - 0	**144**
02/10/1993	Brazil	114 - 3	**114**
09/10/1979	Brazil	109 - 3	**109**

MOST TRIES IN A MATCH
BY THE TEAM

Date	Opponent	Result	Tries
01/05/2002	Paraguay	152 - 0	**24**
27/04/2003	Paraguay	144 - 0	**24**
01/05/2004	Venezuela	147 - 7	**23**
08/10/1989	Brazil	103 - 0	**20**

MOST CONVERSIONS IN A MATCH
BY THE TEAM

Date	Opponent	Result	Cons
01/05/2002	Paraguay	152 - 0	**16**
01/05/2004	Venezuela	147 - 7	**16**
09/10/1979	Brazil	109 - 3	**15**
21/09/1985	Paraguay	102 - 3	**13**
14/10/1973	Paraguay	98 - 3	**13**

MOST PENALTIES IN A MATCH
BY THE TEAM

Date	Opponent	Result	Pens
10/10/1999	Samoa	32 - 16	**8**
10/03/1995	Canada	29 - 26	**8**
17/06/2006	Wales	45 - 27	**8**

MOST DROP GOALS IN A MATCH
BY THE TEAM

Date	Opponent	Result	DGs
27/10/1979	Australia	24 - 13	**3**
02/11/1985	New Zealand	21 - 21	**3**
26/05/2001	Canada	20 - 6	**3**
21/09/1975	Uruguay	30 - 15	**3**
07/08/1971	SA Gazelles	12 - 0	**3**
30/09/2007	Ireland	30 - 15	**3**

MOST POINTS IN A MATCH
BY A PLAYER

Date	Player	Opponent	Pts.
14/10/1973	Eduardo Morgan	Paraguay	**50**
27/04/2003	José María Nuñez Piossek	Paraguay	**45**
02/10/1993	Gustavo Jorge	Brazil	**40**
24/10/1977	Martin Sansot	Brazil	**36**
13/09/1951	Uriel O'Farrell	Brazil	**33**

MOST TRIES IN A MATCH BY A PLAYER

Date	Player	Opponent	Tries
13/09/1951	Uriel O'Farrell	Brazil	**11**
27/04/2003	José María Nuñez Piossek	Paraguay	**9**
02/10/1993	Gustavo Jorge	Brazil	**8**
08/10/1989	Gustavo Jorge	Brazil	**6**
14/10/1973	Eduardo Morgan	Paraguay	**6**

MOST CONVERSIONS IN A MATCH BY A PLAYER

Date	Player	Opponent	Cons
01/05/2002	Jose Cilley	Paraguay	**16**
21/09/1985	Hugo Porta	Paraguay	**13**
14/10/1973	Eduardo Morgan	Paraguay	**13**
25/09/1975	Eduardo de Forteza	Paraguay	**11**

MOST PENALTIES IN A MATCH BY A PLAYER

Date	Player	Opponent	Pens
10/10/1999	Gonzalo Quesada	Samoa	**8**
10/03/1995	Santiago Meson	Canada	**8**
17/06/2006	Federico Todeschini	Wales	**8**

MOST DROP GOALS IN A MATCH BY A PLAYER

Date	Player	Opponent	DGs
27/10/1979	Hugo Porta	Australia	**3**
02/11/1985	Hugo Porta	New Zealand	**3**
07/08/1971	Tomas Harris-Smith	SA Gazelles	**3**
26/05/2001	Juan Fernández Miranda	Canada	**3**
30/09/2007	Juan Martín Hernández	Ireland	**3**

MOST CAPPED PLAYERS

Name	Caps
Lisandro Arbizu	**86**
Rolando Martin	**86**
Pedro Sporleder	**78**
Federico Méndez	**73**
Agustín Pichot	**71**

LEADING TRY SCORERS

Name	Tries
José María Nuñez Piossek	**29**
Diego Cuesta Silva	**28**
Gustavo Jorge	**24**
Facundo Soler	**18**
Rolando Martin	**18**

LEADING CONVERSIONS SCORERS

Name	Cons
Hugo Porta	**84**
Gonzalo Quesada	**68**
Santiago Meson	**68**
Felipe Contepomi	**55**
Juan Fernández Miranda	**41**

LEADING PENALTY SCORERS

Name	Pens
Gonzalo Quesada	**103**
Hugo Porta	**102**
Felipe Contepomi	**91**
Santiago Meson	**63**
Federico Todeschini	**51**

LEADING DROP GOAL SCORERS

Name	DGs
Hugo Porta	**26**
Lisandro Arbizu	**11**
Tomas Harris-Smith	**6**
Gonzalo Quesada	**6**
Juan Fernández Miranda	**5**

LEADING POINTS SCORERS

Name	Pts.
Hugo Porta	**593**
Gonzalo Quesada	**483**
Felipe Contepomi	**447**
Santiago Meson	**370**
Federico Todeschini	**241**

ARGENTINA INTERNATIONAL PLAYERS

UP TO 31ST OCTOBER 2007

Note: Years given for International Championship matches are for second half of season; eg 1972 means season 1971–72. Years for all other matches refer to the actual year of the match. Entries in square brackets denote matches played in RWC Finals.

Abella, A 1969 Ur, Ch
Abud, C 1975 Par, Bra, Ch (R)
Achaval, H 1948 OCC
Aguilar, J 1983 Ch, Ur
Aguirre, A 1997 Par, Ch (R)
Aguirre, ME 1990 E, S 1991 Sa
Agulla, H 2005 Sa 2006 Ur (R), E (R), It 2007 It, F, Nm, I, S, SA, F
Albacete, P 2003 Par, Ur, F, SA (R), Ur, C, A, R 2004 W, W, NZ, F, I 2005 It, It 2006 E, It, F 2007 W, F, Geo, Nm, I, S, SA, F
Albanese, DL 1995 Ur, C, E, F (R) 1996 Ur, F, SA, E 1997 NZ, Ur, R, It, F, A, A 1998 F, F, R, US, C, It, F, W (R) 1999 W, W, S, I, W, Sa, J, I, F 2000 I, A, A, SA 2001 NZ, It, W, S, NZ 2002 F, E, SA, A, It, I 2003 F, F, SA, US, C, A, Nm, I
Albina, M 2001 Ur (R), US (R) 2003 Par, Ur (R), Fj 2004 Ch, Ven, W, W (R) 2005 J (R)
Aldao, C 1961 Ch, Bra, Ur
Alexenicer, P 1997 Par, Ch (R)
Alfonso, C 1936 BI
Alfonso, H 1936 BI, BI, Ch
Allen, G 1977 Par
Allen, JG 1981 C 1985 F, F, Ur, NZ, NZ 1986 F, F, A, A 1987 Ur, Fj, It, NZ, Sp, A, A 1988 F, F, F, F 1989 Bra, Ch, Par, Ur, US
Allen, L 1951 Ur, Bra, Ch
Allen, M 1990 C, E, S 1991 NZ, Ch
Allub, A 1997 Par, Ur (R), It (R), F (R), A, A 1998 F, F, US, C, J, It, F, W 1999 W, W (R), S, I, W, Sa, J, I, F 2000 I, A, A, SA, E 2001 NZ
Alonso, M 1973 R, R, S 1977 F, F
Altberg, A 1972 SAG, SAG 1973 R, R, Par
Altube, J 1998 Par (R), Ch, Ur (R)
Alvarez, C 1958 Per, Ur, Ch 1959 JSB, JSB 1960 F
Alvarez, GM 1975 Ur, Par, Bra, Ch 1976 Ur, NZ 1977 Bra, Ur, Par, Ch
Álvarez Kairelis, R 1998 Par (R), Ch, Ur 2001 Ur, US (R), C, W, S, NZ 2002 F, E, SA, A, It, I 2003 F, SA, Fj, Ur, C (R), Nm, I 2004 F, I 2006 W, W, NZ, Ch, Ur 2007 I, It (R), W (R), F (R), Geo (R), Nm (R), I (R), S (R), SA (R), F
Amuchastegui, A 2002 Ur (R), Par, Ch (R)
Angaut, GP 1987 NZ, Ur, Ch 1990 S 1991 NZ (R), Sa
Angelillo, J-J 1987 Ur, Ch, A (R) 1988 F, F, F 1989 It, Bra, Ch, Par, Ur, US 1990 C, US, E, E 1994 US, S, S, US 1995 Par (R), Ch, R, F
Aniz, W 1960 F
Annichini, R 1983 Ch, Ur 1985 F, Ch, Par
Anthony, A 1965 OCC, Ch 1967 Ur, Ch 1968 W, W 1969 S, S, Ur, Ch 1970 I, I 1971 SAG, SAG, OCC 1972 SAG, SAG 1974 F, F
Arbizu, L 1990 I (R), S 1991 NZ, NZ, Ch, A, W, Sa 1992 F, F, Sp, Sp, R, F 1993 J, J, Bra, Ch, Par, Ur, SA, SA 1995 Ur, A, A (R), E, Sa, It, Par, Ch (R), Ur, R, It, F 1996 Ur, US, Ur, C, SA, SA, E 1997 E, E, NZ, NZ, R, It, F, A, A 1998 F, F, R, US, C, It, F, W 1999 W, W, S, I, W, Sa, J, I, F 2000 A, A, SA, E 2001 NZ, It, W, S, NZ 2002 F, A, It, I 2003 F, F, US, C 2005 It, It
Argerich, F 1979 Ur
Aristide, G 1997 E (R)
Arocena Messones, J 2005 Sa
Arriaga, E 1936 Ch, Ch
Artese, S 2004 SA
Avellaneda, M 1948 OCC, OCC 1951 Bra, Ch
Avramovic, M 2005 J, Sa 2006 Ch, Ur, E, It 2007 I
Ayerra, M 1927 GBR
Ayerza, MI 2004 SA (R) 2005 J, It, Sa 2006 W (R), W (R), Ch, Ur, E, It, F (R) 2007 I, I, Geo, F (R)
Azpiroz, M 1956 OCC 1958 Per, Ur, Ch 1959 JSB, JSB

Bach, J 1975 Par, Bra, Ch
Badano, A 1977 Bra (R), Ur, Par, Ch
Baeck, J 1983 Par
Baeck, M 1985 Ur, Ch, Par 1990 US, E, E
Baetti, DR 1980 WXV (R), Fj, Fj 1981 E, E, C 1983 WXV 1987 Ur, Par, Ch 1988 F, F 1989 It, NZ, NZ
Balfour, L 1977 Bra, Ur, Par, Ch
Barrea, C 1996 Ur, C, SA (R)
Bartolucci, O 1996 US, C, SA 1998 Ch, Ur 1999 W, W, S, I, W, Sa 2000 I, A, A, SA, E 2001 US, C 2003 Par (R), Ur
Basile, E 1983 Ch, Ur
Bavio, L 1954 F
Bazan, R 1951 Ur, Bra, Ch 1956 OCC
Beccar Varela, D 1975 F, F 1976 Ur, W, NZ 1977 F, F
Beccar Varela, G 1976 W, NZ, NZ 1977 F, F
Beccar Varela, M 1965 Rho, OCC, OCC
Beith, JW 1936 BI
Benzi, J 1965 Rho 1969 S, Ur, Ch
Bergamaschi, E 2001 US
Bernacchi, O 1954 F 1956 OCC, OCC 1958 Per, Ur, Ch
Bernardi, G 1997 Ch
Bernat, O 1932 JSB
Berro, MM 1964 Ur, Bra, Ch
Bertranou, MJS 1989 It, NZ, NZ, Ch, Par 1990 C, US, C, E, E, I, E, S 1993 SA
Bianchetti, E 1959 JSB, JSB
Blacksley, G 1971 SAG
Blades, T 1938 Ch
Bocca, G 1998 J, Par
Bofelli, C 1997 Ur (R) 1998 Par 2004 Ch, Ur, Ven (R)
Borges, L 2003 Par, Ch, Ur (R) 2004 Ch (R), Ur, Ven, W, W, NZ, F, I, SA 2005 SA, S (R) 2006 W, W, Ch, Ur 2007 W, F, Geo, I, S, SA
Bori, C 1975 F
Bosch, F 2004 Ch, SA (R) 2005 J, Sa
Bosch, MA 1991 A (R), Sa 1992 F, F
Bosch, MT 2007 It
Bossicovich, N 1995 Ur, C
Bottarini, CA 1973 Par, Ur, Bra, I 1974 F 1975 F, F 1979 Ur, Ch, Bra 1983 Ch, Par, Ur
Botting, R 1927 GBR, GBR, GBR
Bouza, L 1992 Sp (R)
Bouza, M 1966 SAG, SAG 1967 Ur, Ch
Bouza, P 1996 Ur, F, F, E 1997 E, NZ (R), NZ (R), Ur, R (R) 1998 Ur (R) 2002 Ur, Par, Ch 2003 Par, Ch, Ur (R), US, Ur, Nm, R 2004 Ch, Ur, Ven, W (R), NZ (R), SA 2005 J, It, It, SA, S, It 2006 Ch (R), Ur (R) 2007 I, I (R)
Bozzo, N 1975 Bra
Braceras, JG 1971 Bra, Par 1976 W (R), NZ 1977 F

Braddon, W 1927 GBR
Branca, EN 1976 Ur, W, NZ, NZ 1977 F, F 1980 Fj 1981 E, E, C 1983 WXV, A, A 1985 F, F, Ur, Ch, Par, NZ, NZ 1986 F, F, A, A 1987 Ur, Fj, It, NZ, Sp, A, A 1988 F, F, F, F 1989 Bra, Par, Ur 1990 E, E
Brandi, M 1997 Par, Ch 1998 Par, Ch, Ur (R)
Bridger, J 1932 JSB
Brolese, J 1998 Ch, Ur
Brouchou, E 1975 Ur, Par, Bra, Ch
Buabse, F 1991 Ur, Par, Bra 1992 Sp
Buabse, PM 1989 NZ, US 1991 Sa 1993 Bra 1995 Ur, C, A (R)
Buckley, E 1938 Ch
Bullrich, R 1991 Ur, Bra 1992 R 1993 Bra, Ch, SA (R) 1994 SA, SA
Bunader, S 1989 US 1990 C
Bush, K 1938 Ch
Bustamante, E 1927 GBR, GBR, GBR, GBR
Bustillo, F 1977 F (R), F (R), Bra, Ur, Par, Ch
Bustos, G 2003 Par, Ur (R) 2004 Ch, Ven (R)

Caffarone, E 1949 F, F 1951 Bra, Ch 1952 I, I 1954 F, F
Caldwell, M 1956 OCC
Camardon, GF 1990 E 1991 NZ, Ch, A, W, Sa 1992 F, F, Sp, R, F 1993 J, Par, Ur, SA, SA 1995 A 1996 Ur, US, Ur (R), C, SA, E 1999 W, W (R), Sa (R), J, I, F 2001 US, C, NZ, It, W, S, NZ 2002 F, E, SA, It, I
Camerlinckx, PJ 1989 Bra, Par, Ur 1990 C, US (R) 1994 S 1995 Ch 1996 Ur, F, F, US, Ur, C, SA, SA, E 1997 E, E, NZ, NZ, Ur, R, It, F, A, A 1998 R, US, C, F, W 1999 W
Cameron, A 1936 BI, BI, Ch, Ch 1938 Ch
Cameron, R 1927 GBR, GBR
Caminotti, J 1987 Ur, Par, Ch
Campo, M 1978 E, It 1979 NZ, NZ, A, A 1980 WXV, Fj 1981 E, E, C 1982 F, F, Sp 1983 WXV, A, A 1987 Ur, Fj, NZ
Canalda, A 1999 S, I, F (R) 2000 A (R) 2001 Ur (R), US (R), C (R)
Cano, R 1997 Par (R)
Capalbo, J 1975 Bra 1977 Bra, Ur, Ch
Capelletti, AE 1977 F, F 1978 E, It (R) 1979 NZ, NZ, A, A 1980 WXV, Fj, Fj 1981 E, E
Carballo, R 2006 W, Ch, Ur
Carbone, N 1969 Ur, Ch 1971 SAG 1973 I, S
Cardinali, PF 2001 US (R) 2002 Ur, Par 2004 W (R) 2007 I (R)
Carizza, M 2004 SA (R) 2005 J, SA (R), S (R), It (R) 2006 W (R), Ch, Ur 2007 It
Carlos Galvalisi, J 1983 Par, Ur
Carluccio, MA 1973 R, R, Ur, Bra (R), I 1975 F, F 1976 NZ 1977 F, F
Carmona, M 1997 Par, Ch (R)
Carossio, S 1985 NZ (R) 1987 It, NZ
Carracedo, J 1971 Ch, Bra, Par 1972 SAG, SAG 1973 R, R, Par, Ur, Bra, Ch, I, S 1975 F 1976 W, NZ, NZ 1977 F
Carreras, M 1991 NZ, NZ, Ch, A, W, Sa (R) 1992 F
Carreras, M 1987 Par
Carrique, M 1983 Par, Ur (R)
Casanegra, J 1959 JSB, JSB 1960 F, F
Casas, GF 1971 OCC (R) 1973 Par, Ch, I 1975 F, F
Cash, DM 1985 F, F, Ur, Ch, NZ, NZ 1986 F, F, A, A 1987 Ur, Fj, It, NZ, Sp, A, A 1988 F, F, F, F 1989 It, NZ, NZ, US 1990 C, US, C, E, I, E, S 1991 NZ, NZ, Ch, A, Sa 1992 F, F
Castagna, R 1977 F
Castellina, A 2004 Ch (R), Ur (R), Ven
Castro, R 1971 Ch, Bra, Par
Cato, J 1975 Ur, Par
Cazenave, R 1965 Rho, JSB, OCC, Ch 1966 SAG, SAG
Cerioni, A 1975 F 1978 E, It 1979 Ch, Bra (R)
Cernegoy, G 1938 Ch
Cespedes, H 1997 Ur (R), Ch
Chesta, M 1966 SAG, SAG 1967 Ur, Ch 1968 W, W
Chiswell, W 1949 F
Christianson, V 1954 F, F 1956 OCC
Cilley, E 1932 JSB, JSB
Cilley, J 1936 BI, Ch, Ch 1938 Ch
Cilley, JL 1994 SA 1995 Sa, It, Par (R), Ch 1996 Ur, F, F, SA, SA 1999 W (R) 2000 A 2002 Par
Clement, J 1987 Par 1989 Bra (R)
Cobelo, R 1987 Ur, Par, Ch
Comas, I 1951 Bra, Ch 1958 Per, Ch 1960 F
Conen, A 1951 Ch 1952 I, I
Conrard, J 1927 GBR, GBR
Contepomi, CA 1964 Bra, Ch
Contepomi, F 1998 Ch, Ur, F (R), W 1999 W, S (R), I (R), J (R), I (R), F (R) 2000 I (R), A, A, SA (R), E 2001 Ur, US, C, NZ, It, W, S, NZ 2002 F, E, SA, A, It, I 2003 F, F (R), SA, US, C, A, Nm (R), I 2004 W, W, F, I 2005 It, It, SA, S, It 2006 W, NZ, E, F 2007 I, W, F, Geo, Nm, I, S, SA, F
Contepomi, M 1998 US, C, It, F, W 1999 S, I, W, Sa, F (R) 2003 Ur, F, Fj, Ur, A, R 2004 Ch, Ur, Ven (R), W, W, NZ, F, I, SA 2005 SA, S 2006 It, F 2007 I, It, W (R), F, Nm, I, S, SA, F
Conti, F 1988 F
Cooke, GEF 1927 GBR
Cookson, KAM 1932 JSB
Cooper, N 1936 BI, Ch, Ch
Cooper, R 1927 GBR, GBR, GBR, GBR
Copello, J 1975 Ur, Bra
Cordeiro, C 1983 Par
Coria, J 1987 Ur, Par (R), Ch 1989 Bra
Corleto, I 1998 J, F, W 1999 I (R), J, I, F 2000 I, A, SA, E 2001 W, S, NZ 2002 F, E, SA, A, It, I 2003 F, Fj, US (R), Ur, C (R), A, I 2006 It, F 2007 W, F, Geo, Nm, I, S, SA, F
Corral, ME 1993 J, Bra, Par, Ur, SA, SA 1994 US, S, SA, SA 1995 Ur, C, A, A, E, Sa, It
Cortese, M 2005 Sa (R)
Cortopasso, F 2003 Ch, Ur
Costa Repetto, A 2005 Sa
Costante, JD 1971 OCC, OCC, Ch, Bra, Par, Ur 1976 Ur, W, NZ 1977 F
Courreges, AF 1979 Ur, Par, Bra 1982 F, F, Sp 1983 WXV, A, A 1987 Sp, A, A 1988 F
Cox, PH 1938 Ch
Creevy, A 2005 J (R), Sa 2006 Ur (R)
Cremaschi, P 1993 J, J 1995 Par, Ch, Ur, It (R)
Crexell, RH 1990 I, S 1991 Par 1992 Sp 1993 J 1995 Ur, C, A, E, Sa, It, Par, Ch (R), Ur
Criscuolo, L 1992 F, F 1993 Bra (R), SA (R) 1996 Ur, F, F
Cruz Legora, J 2002 Par, Ch (R)
Cruz Meabe, J 1997 Par
Cubelli, AG 1977 Bra, Ur, Ch 1978 E, It 1979 A, A 1980 WXV, Fj 1983 Par 1985 F, F, Ur, Par, NZ, NZ 1990 S
Cuesta Silva, D 1983 Ch, Ur 1985 F, F, Ur, Ch, NZ, NZ 1986 F, F, A, A 1987 Ur, Fj, It, Sp, A, A 1988 F, F, F, F 1989 It, NZ, NZ 1990 C, E, E, I, E, S 1991 NZ, NZ, Ch, A, W, Sa 1992 F, F, Sp, R, F 1993 J, J, Bra, Par, Ur, SA, SA 1994 US, S, S, US, SA 1995 Ur, C, E, Sa, It, Par, R, It, F
Cuesta Silva, J 1927 GBR, GBR, GBR, GBR
Cutler, M 1969 Ur 1971 Ch, Bra, Par, Ur

Da Milano, A 1964 Bra, Ch
D'Agnillo, F 1975 Ur, Bra 1977 Bra, Ur, Par, Ch
Damioli, JL 1991 Ur, Par, Bra
Dande, H 2001 Ur, C 2004 Ch, Ven
Dartiguelongue, J 1964 Bra, Ch 1968 W, W
Dassen, S 1983 Ch, Par, Ur
Davel, H 1936 BI
de Abelleyra, R 1932 JSB, JSB
de Chazal, L 2001 Ur, C 2004 SA
de Forteza, E 1975 Ur, Par, Bra, Ch
de la Arena, R 1985 Ch, Par 1992 F (R), Sp
De Pablo, JC 1948 OCC
de Robertis, G 2005 Sa 2006 Ch (R), Ur (R)
de Vedia, R 1982 F, Sp
de Vedia, T 2007 I, I
del Castillo, F 1994 US, SA (R) 1995 Ur, C, A (R) 1996 Ur (R), F 1997 Par, Ur (R) 1998 Ur
del Castillo, GJ 1991 NZ, NZ, Ch, A, W 1993 J 1994 S, S, US, SA 1995 C, A
del Chazal, L 1983 Ch, Par (R), Ur
Dell'Acqua, R 1956 OCC
Dengra, S 1982 F, Sp 1983 WXV, A, A 1986 A 1987 It, NZ, Sp, A, A 1988 F, F, F, F 1989 It, NZ, NZ
Derkheim, C 1927 GBR
Devoto, M 1975 Par, Bra 1977 Par

Devoto, PM 1982 F, F, Sp 1983 WXV
Devoto, R 1960 F
Diaz 1997 Par (R), Ch 1998 J, Par, Ch (R)
Diaz Alberdi, F 1997 Ur 1999 S (R), I (R) 2000 A, A (R)
Diez, J 1956 OCC
Dillon, R 1956 OCC
Dinisio, P 1989 NZ 1990 C, US
Dip, M 1979 Par, Bra
Dominguez, D 1989 Ch, Par
Dominguez, E 1949 F, F 1952 I, I 1954 F, F
Dorado, L 1949 F
Dumas, J 1973 R, R, Ur, Bra, S
Dumas, M 1966 SAG, SAG
Durand, MA 1997 Ch 1998 Par (R), Ch, Ur (R), It (R), F, W 2000 SA (R) 2001 Ur (R), US, C (R), It (R), NZ (R) 2002 F (R), SA (R), A (R), It (R), I (R) 2003 Ch, Ur (R), Fj (R), US, Ur, C (R), A (R), Nm, R 2004 Ch, Ur, Ven (R), W, W, NZ, F, I, SA 2005 SA, S, It 2006 W, NZ, Ch, Ur, It, F 2007 I, I, It, W (R), F (R), Geo, I (R), F

Echeverria, C 1932 JSB
Ehrman, G 1948 OCC 1949 F, F 1951 Ur, Bra, Ch 1952 I, I 1954 F, F
Elia, O 1954 F
Elliot, R 1936 BI, BI 1938 Ch
Escalante, J 1975 Ur, Par, Ch 1978 It 1979 Ur, Par, Bra
Escary, N 1927 GBR, GBR 1932 JSB, JSB
Espagnol, R 1971 SAG
Etchegaray, AM 1964 Ur, Bra, Ch 1965 Rho, JSB, Ch 1967 Ur, Ch 1968 W, W 1969 S, S 1971 SAG, OCC, OCC 1972 SAG, SAG 1973 Par, Bra, I 1974 F, F 1976 Ur, W, NZ, NZ
Etchegoyen, R 1991 Ur, Par, Bra
Ezcurra, C 1958 Per, Ur, Ch
Ezcurra, E 1990 I, E, S

Fariello, R 1973 Par, Ur, Ch, S
Farina, M 1968 W, W 1969 S, S
Farrell, D 1951 Ur
Felisari, P 1956 OCC
Fernandez, JJ 1971 SAG, Ch, Bra, Par, Ur 1972 SAG, SAG 1973 R, R, Par, Ur, Ch, I, S 1974 F, F 1975 F 1976 Ur, W, NZ, NZ 1977 F, F
Fernandez Bravo, Pablo 1993 SA, SA
Fernandez del Casal, E 1951 Ur, Bra, Ch 1952 I, I 1956 OCC, OCC
Fernandez Lobbe, CI 1996 US 1997 E (R), E 1998 F (R), F, R, US (R), Ur, C, J, It, F (R) 1999 W, W, S, I, W, Sa, J, I, F 2000 I, A, A, SA, E 2001 NZ, It, W, S, NZ 2002 F, E, SA, A, It, I 2003 F, F, SA, US, C, A, Nm (R), I 2004 W, W, NZ 2005 SA, S, It 2006 W, W, NZ, E, F 2007 It, W, F, Nm, I, S, SA
Fernandez Lobbe, JM 2004 Ur, Ven (R) 2005 S, It, Sa 2006 W, W, NZ, E, It, F 2007 I, I, It, W, F, Geo, Nm, I, S, SA, F
Fernandez Miranda, N 1994 US, S, S, US 1995 Ch, Ur (R) 1996 F (R), SA, SA, E 1997 E, E, NZ, NZ, Ur, R 1998 R (R), US, C, It (R) 1999 I, F (R) 2002 Ur, Ch, It (R) 2003 Ch, Ur, F, F, SA, US, Ur (R), Nm, R 2004 W, NZ 2005 J, It, It (R) 2006 W (R), It 2007 It, Geo, Nm (R)
Fernández Miranda, JC 1997 Ur, R, It 1998 Ur, It (R) 2000 I 2001 US, C 2002 Ur, Par (R), Ch, It (R), I (R) 2003 Par (R), Ch, Ur, Fj, US (R), Nm, R 2004 W (R), NZ, SA 2005 J (R), Sa 2006 Ch (R), Ur (R) 2007 It (R)
Ferrari, N 1992 Sp, Sp
Fessia, G 2007 I (R)
Follett, R 1948 OCC, OCC 1952 I, I 1954 F
Foster, G 1971 Ch, Bra, Par, Ur
Foster, R 1965 Rho, JSB, OCC, OCC, Ch 1966 SAG, SAG 1970 I, I 1971 SAG, SAG, OCC 1972 SAG, SAG
Franchi, P 1987 Ur, Par, Ch
Francombe, JL 1932 JSB, JSB 1936 BI, BI
Freixas, J 2003 Ch, Ur
Frigerio, R 1948 OCC, OCC 1954 F
Frigoli, J 1936 BI, BI, Ch, Ch
Fuselli, P 1998 J, Par

Gahan, E 1954 F, F
Gaitán, M 1998 Ur 2002 Par, Ch (R) 2003 Fj, US, Nm, R 2004 W 2007 It, W
Galindo, AM 2004 Ur, Ven (R)
Gallo, R 1964 Bra
Gambarini, P 2006 W (R), Ch (R), Ur (R) 2007 I, It
Garbarino, E 1992 Sp, Sp
Garcia, FL 1994 SA 1995 A, A, Par (R), Ch 1996 Ur (R), F, F 1997 NZ (R) 1998 R (R), Ur, J
Garcia, J 1998 Par (R), Ur (R) 2000 A (R)
Garcia, PT 1948 OCC
Garcia Hamilton, E 1993 Bra (R)
Garcia Hamilton, P 1998 Ch (R)
Garcia Simon, HM 1990 I 1992 F
Garcia-Orsetti, G 1992 R, F
Garreton, PA 1987 Sp, Ur, Ch, A, A 1988 F, F, F, F 1989 It, NZ, Bra, Ch, Ur, US 1990 C, E, E, I, E, S 1991 NZ, NZ, Ch, A, W, Sa 1992 F, F 1993 J, J
Garzon, P 1990 C 1991 Par, Bra
Gasso, G 1983 Ch, Par
Gauweloose, JM 1975 F, F 1976 W, NZ, NZ 1977 F, F 1981 C
Gavina, E 1956 OCC, OCC 1958 Per, Ur, Ch 1959 JSB, JSB 1960 F, F 1961 Ch, Bra, Ur
Genoud, FA 2004 Ch (R), Ur (R), Ven 2005 J, It (R)
Genoud, J 1952 I, I 1956 OCC, OCC
Gerosa, M 1987 Ur, Ch
Giannantonio, D 1996 Ur 1997 Par, Ur (R), It (R), A, A 1998 F (R), F 2000 A 2002 E (R)
Giargia, MC 1973 Par, Ur (R), Bra 1975 Par, Ch
Giles, R 1948 OCC 1949 F, F 1951 Ur 1952 I, I
Giuliano, C 1959 JSB, JSB 1960 F
Glastra, L 1948 OCC, OCC 1952 I, I
Glastra, M 1979 Ur, Ch 1981 C
Gomez, FE 1985 Ur 1987 Ur, Fj, It (R), NZ 1989 NZ (R) 1990 C, E, E
Gomez, JF 2006 It (R)
Gomez, N 1997 Par, Ch (R)
Gomez Cora, PM 2004 NZ, SA 2005 Sa 2006 E
Gonzalez, D 1988 F (R), F (R)
Gonzalez, D 1987 Par
Gonzalez, T 1975 Ur, Ch
Gonzalez Bonorino, S 2001 Ur, US, C 2002 Par (R), Ch 2003 F (R), SA (R) 2007 I, I, It (R), W (R), F (R), Geo
Gonzalez del Solar, E 1960 F 1961 Ch, Bra, Ur
Gonzalez del Solar, N 1964 Ur, Bra, Ch 1965 Rho, JSB, OCC, OCC, Ch
Goti, H 1961 Ch, Bra, Ur 1964 Ur, Bra, Ch 1965 Rho 1966 SAG
Gradin, LM 1965 OCC, OCC, Ch 1966 SAG, SAG 1969 Ch 1970 I, I 1973 R, R, Par (R), Ur, Ch, S
Grande, P 1998 Par, Ch, Ur
Grau, RD 1993 J, Bra, Ch 1995 Par, Ch 1996 F, F, US, Ur, C, SA, SA, E 1997 E, E, NZ, NZ, A, A 1998 F, It, F 1999 W, W, S, I, W, F 2000 A, SA (R), E 2001 NZ, W (R), S (R), NZ (R) 2002 F (R), E (R), SA, A (R), It 2003 F, SA, US, Ur (R), C, A, I
Gravano, L 1997 Ch 1998 Ch (R), Ur
Grigolon, B 1948 OCC 1954 F, F
Grimoldi, V 1927 GBR, GBR
Grondona, J 1990 C
Grosse, R 1952 I, I 1954 F, F
Guarrochena, P 1977 Par
Guastella, A 1956 OCC 1959 JSB, JSB 1960 F
Guidi, J 1958 Per, Ur, Ch 1959 JSB 1960 F 1961 Ch, Bra, Ur
Guiñazu, E 2003 Par, Ch, Ur 2004 Ch, Ur, Ven, W (R), W (R), SA 2005 J, It (R) 2007 I (R), It (R), F (R)

Halle, D 1989 Bra, Ch, Ur, US 1990 US
Hamilton, A 1936 BI
Handley, R 1966 SAG, SAG 1968 W, W 1969 S, S, Ur, Ch 1970 I, I 1971 SAG, SAG 1972 SAG, SAG
Hardie, G 1948 OCC
Harris-Smith, TA 1969 S, S 1971 SAG, OCC, OCC 1973 Par, Ur
Harris-smith, V 1936 BI
Hasan Jalil, O 1995 Ur 1996 Ur, C, SA, SA 1997 E (R), E (R), NZ (R), R, It, F, A (R) 1998 F (R), F, R, US, C, It (R), F, W 1999 W (R), W (R), S (R), W (R), Sa, J, I 2000 SA, E

2001 NZ, It, W, S, NZ 2002 F, E, SA (R), A, It, I 2003 US, C, A, R (R) 2004 W, W, NZ, F, I 2005 It, It, SA, S, It 2006 NZ, E, F 2007 It, Geo (R), Nm, I (R), S (R), SA (R), F
Henn, P 2004 Ch, Ur (R), Ven (R) 2005 J (R), It (R) 2007 It
Hernandez, M 1927 GBR, GBR, GBR
Hernández, JM 2003 Par, Ur, F (R), F, SA, C, A (R), Nm, R 2004 F, I, SA 2005 SA, S, It 2006 W, W, NZ, E, It, F 2007 F, Geo, I, S, SA, F
Herrera, L 1991 Ur, Par
Higgs, FA 2004 Ur (R), Ven 2005 J
Hine, D 1938 Ch
Hirsch, C 1960 F
Hirsch, C 1960 F
Hirsch, E 1954 F 1956 OCC
Hogg, R 1958 Per, Ur, Ch 1959 JSB, JSB 1961 Ch, Bra, Ur
Hogg, S 1956 OCC, OCC 1958 Per, Ur, Ch 1959 JSB, JSB
Holmberg, E 1948 OCC
Holmes, B 1949 F, F
Holmgren, E 1958 Per, Ur, Ch 1959 JSB, JSB 1960 F, F
Holmgren, G 1985 NZ, NZ
Horan, E 1956 OCC
Hughes, L 1936 Ch
Hughes, M 1954 F, F
Hughes, M 1949 F, F
Huntley Robertson, CA 1932 JSB, JSB

Iachetti, A 1975 Ur, Par 1977 Ur, Par, Ch 1978 E, It 1979 NZ, NZ, A, A 1980 WXV, Fj, Fj 1981 E, E 1982 F, F, Sp 1987 Ur, Par, A, A 1988 F, F, F, F 1989 It, NZ 1990 C, E, E
Iachetti, A 1977 Bra 1987 Ch
Iachetti, ME 1979 NZ, NZ, A, A
Iglesias, M 1973 R 1974 F, F
Illia, G 1965 Rho
Imhoff, JL 1967 Ur, Ch
Inchausti, V 1936 BI, Ch, Ch
Insua, F 1971 Ch, Bra, Par, Ur 1972 SAG, SAG 1973 R, R, Bra, Ch, I, S 1974 F, F 1976 Ur, W, NZ, NZ 1977 F, F
Iraneta, R 1974 F 1976 Ur, W, NZ
Irarrazabal, FJ 1991 Sa 1992 Sp, Sp
Irazoqui, S 1993 J, Ch, Par, Ur 1995 E (R), Sa (R), Par
Irigoyen, A 1997 Par (R)

Jacobi, C 1979 Ch, Par
Jacobs, AG 1927 GBR, GBR
Jones, AGW 1948 OCC
Jorge, GM 1989 Bra, Ch, Par (R), Ur 1990 I, E 1992 F, F, Sp, Sp, R, F 1993 J, J, Bra, Ch, Ur, SA, SA 1994 US, S, S, US
Jose Villar, J 2001 Ur, US, C 2002 Par, Ch (R)
Jurado, E 1995 A (R), A, E, Sa, It, Par, Ch, Ur, R, It, F 1996 SA, E 1997 E, E, NZ, NZ, Ur, R, It, F, A, A 1998 F, Ur, C (R), It (R) 1999 W

Karplus, E 1959 JSB, JSB 1960 F, F, F
Ker, A 1936 Ch 1938 Ch
Kossler, E 1960 F, F, F

Laborde, EH 1991 A, W, Sa
Laborde, G 1979 Ch, Bra
Lacarra, J 1989 Par, Ur
Lagarde, R 1956 OCC
Lamas, M 1998 Par, Ch
Landajo, TR 1975 Ur, Ch 1977 F, Bra, Ur, Ch 1978 E 1979 A, A 1980 WXV, Fj, Fj 1981 E, E
Lanfranco, M 1991 Ur, Par, Bra (R)
Lanusse, AR 1932 JSB
Lanusse, M 1951 Ur, Bra, Ch
Lanza, J 1985 F, Ur, Par, NZ, NZ 1986 F, F, A, A 1987 Ur, Fj, It, NZ
Lanza, P 1983 Ch, Par, Ur 1985 F (R), F, Ur, Ch, Par, NZ, NZ 1986 F, F, A, A 1987 It, NZ (R)
Lasalle, J 1964 Ur
Lavayen, J 1961 Ch, Bra, Ur
Lazcano Miranda, CG 1998 Ch 2004 Ch (R), Ur (R), Ven 2005 J (R)
le Fort, RA 1990 I, E 1991 NZ, NZ, Ch, A, W 1992 R, F 1993 J, SA, SA 1995 Ur, It

Lecot, F 2003 Par, Ur (R) 2005 J (R)
Ledesma Arocena, ME 1996 Ur, C 1997 NZ (R), NZ, Ur, R, It, F, A, A 1998 F (R), F, Ur, C (R), J, Ur, F (R), W (R) 1999 W (R), W, Sa, J, I, F 2000 SA (R) 2001 It (R), W (R), NZ (R) 2002 F (R), E (R), SA (R), A (R), It, I 2003 F, SA, Fj (R), US, C, A, Nm (R), R 2004 W (R), NZ, F, I 2005 It, It, SA, S, It 2006 W, W, NZ, Ch, Ur, E, It, F 2007 W, F, Geo, I, S, SA
Legora, J 1996 F (R), F, US (R), Ur 1997 Ch 1998 Par
Leguizamón, JM 2005 J, It, It, SA, S (R), It (R) 2006 W, NZ (R), Ch, Ur, E, It (R), F (R) 2007 I, I, It, W, F, Geo, Nm, S (R), SA (R), F (R)
Leiros, GP 1973 Bra, I
Lennon, C 1958 Per, Ur
Leonelli Morey, FJ 2001 Ur (R) 2004 Ur, Ven 2005 J, It (R), SA, S, It 2006 W (R), W 2007 I, I, It
Lerga, M 1995 Par, Ch, Ur
Lesianado 1948 OCC (R)
Lewis, I 1932 JSB
Llanes, GA 1990 I, E, S 1991 NZ, NZ, Ch, A, W 1992 F, F, Sp, R, F 1993 Bra, Ch, SA, SA 1994 US, S, S, SA, SA 1995 A, A, E, Sa, It, R, It, F 1996 SA, SA, E 1997 E, E, NZ, NZ, R, It, F 1998 F 2000 A (R)
Lobrauco, L 1996 US 1997 Ch (R) 1998 J (R), Ch, Ur
Loffreda, MH 1978 E 1979 NZ, NZ, A, A 1980 WXV, Fj, Fj 1981 E, E, C 1982 F, F, Sp 1983 WXV, A, A 1985 Ur, Ch, Par 1987 Ur, Par, Ch, A, A 1988 F, F, F, F 1989 It, NZ, Bra, Ch, Par, Ur, US 1990 C, US, E, E 1994 US, S, S, US, SA, SA
Logan, G 1936 BI, BI
Longo Elía, GM 1999 W (R), W, S, I, W, Sa, I, F 2000 I, A, A, SA, E 2001 US, NZ, It, W, S, NZ 2002 F, E, SA, A, It, I 2003 F, F, SA, Fj, C, A, I 2004 W, W, NZ, F, I 2005 It, It, SA 2006 W, W, NZ, E, It, F 2007 W, Nm (R), I, S, SA, F
Lopez Fleming, L 2004 Ur, Ven (R), W (R) 2005 Sa
Lopresti, A 1997 Par, Ch
Loures, J 1954 F
Loyola, R 1964 Ur, Ch 1965 Rho, JSB, OCC, OCC, Ch 1966 SAG, SAG 1968 W, W 1969 S, S 1970 I, I 1971 Ch, Bra, Par, Ur
Lozada, E 2006 E (R), It 2007 I, I, Geo (R), F (R)
Lucioni, F 1927 GBR
Lucke, R 1975 Ur, Par, Bra, Ch 1976 Ur 1981 C
Luna, J 1995 Par, Ch, Ur, R, It, F 1997 Par, Ch

Macadam, P 1949 F, F
Macome, AM 1990 I, E 1995 Ur, C
Madero, RM 1978 E, It 1979 NZ, NZ, A, A 1980 WXV, Fj, Fj 1981 E, E, C 1982 F, F, Sp 1983 WXV, A, A 1985 F (R), NZ (R) 1986 A (R), A 1987 Ur, It, NZ, Sp, Ur, Par, Ch, A, A 1988 F, F, F 1989 It, NZ, NZ 1990 E, E
Makin, L 1927 GBR
Mamanna, A 1991 Par 1997 Par (R)
Manuel Belgrano, J 1956 OCC
Marguery, A 1991 Ur, Bra 1993 Ch, Par
Martin, R 1938 Ch
Martin, RA 1994 US, S, S, US, SA, SA 1995 Ur, C, A, A, E, Sa, It, Ch, Ur, R, It, F 1996 Ur, F, F, Ur, C, SA, SA, E 1997 E, E, NZ, NZ, It, F, A, A 1998 F, F, R (R), US (R), Ur, J, Par, Ch, Ur, It, W (R) 1999 W, W, S, I (R), W (R), Sa, J, I, F 2000 I, A, A, SA, E 2001 Ur, US, C, NZ, It, W, S, NZ 2002 Ur, Par (R), Ch, F, E, SA, A, It, I 2003 Par (R), Ch (R), Ur, F, SA, Ur, C, A, R (R), I
Martin Aramburu, F 2004 Ch, Ven, W (R), NZ, F, I 2005 It, SA, S, It 2006 NZ 2007 Geo, F
Martin Copella, J 1989 Ch, Par
Martinez 1969 Ur, Ch 1970 I, I
Martinez, E 1971 Ch, Bra, Ur
Martinez Basante, O 1954 F
Martinez Mosquera, M 1971 Ch
Mastai, RC 1975 F 1976 Ur, W, NZ, NZ 1977 F, F (R), Bra, Ur, Par, Ch 1980 WXV
Matarazzo, R 1971 SAG, SAG (R), Par, Ur 1972 SAG, SAG 1973 R, R, Par, Ur, Ch, I, S 1974 F, F
Maurer, H 1932 JSB, JSB
Maurette, L 1948 OCC, OCC
Mazzini, C 1977 F, F

McCormick, G 1964 Bra, Ch 1965 Rho, OCC, OCC, Ch 1966 SAG, SAG
McCormick, M 1927 GBR
Memoli, A 1979 Ur, Par, Bra
Mendez, FJ 1991 Ur, Par, Bra 1992 Sp, Sp
Mendez, H 1967 Ur, Ch
Mendez, L 1958 Per, Ur, Ch 1959 JSB
Méndez, FE 1990 I, E 1991 NZ, NZ, Ch, A, W 1992 F, F, Sp, Sp, R, F 1994 S, US, SA, SA 1995 Ur, C, A, A, E, Sa, It, Par, Ch (R), Ur, R, It, F 1996 SA, SA 1997 E 1998 F, F (R), R, US, Ur (R), C, It, F, W 1999 W, W 2000 I, A, A, SA, E 2001 NZ, It, W, S, NZ 2002 Ur, Ch, F, E, SA, A 2003 F (R), F, SA (R), Fj, Ur, Nm, I 2004 Ch, Ur, W, W, NZ (R), SA
Mendy, Cl 1987 Ur, Par, Ch, A, A (R) 1988 F, F, F, F 1989 It, NZ, NZ, US 1990 C 1991 Ur, Bra
Merlo, I 1993 Bra (R), Ch
Merlo, P 1985 Ch, Par
Meson, SE 1987 Par 1989 Bra, Par, Ur, US 1990 US, C, S 1991 NZ, NZ (R), Ch, Sa (R) 1992 F, F, Sp, R, F 1993 J, Bra, Par, Ur, SA, SA 1994 US, S, S, US 1995 Ur, C, A, A 1996 US, C 1997 Ch
Miguens, BH 1983 WXV, A, A 1985 F, F, NZ, NZ 1986 F, F, A, A 1987 Sp
Miguens, E 1975 Ur, Par (R), Ch
Miguens, H 1969 S, S, Ur, Ch 1970 I, I 1971 OCC 1972 SAG, SAG 1973 R, R, Par, Ur, Bra, Ch, I, S 1975 F
Miguens, J 1982 F 1985 F, F 1986 F, F, A, A
Milano, GE 1982 F, F, Sp 1983 WXV, A, A 1985 F, F, Ur, Ch, Par, NZ, NZ 1986 F, F, A, A 1987 Ur, Fj, Sp, Ur, Ch, A, A 1988 F, F, F 1989 It, NZ, NZ
Mimesi, A 1998 J (R), Par, Ch (R)
Minguez, B 1975 Par, Bra, Ch 1979 Ur, Ch, Par 1983 WXV, A, A 1985 Ur (R), Ch
Mitchelstein, B 1936 BI
Mitchelstein, E 1956 OCC 1960 F, F
Molina, LE 1985 Ch 1987 Ur, Fj, It, NZ 1989 NZ, NZ, Bra (R), Ch, Par 1990 C, E 1991 W
Molina, M 1998 Par, Ch, Ur
Montes de Oca, G 1961 Ch, Bra, Ur
Montpelat, E 1948 OCC, OCC
Morales Oliver, G 2001 Ur, US, C (R)
Morea, C 1951 Ur, Bra, Ch
Morel, FR 1979 A, A 1980 WXV, Fj, Fj 1981 E, E, C 1982 F 1985 F, F, Ur, Par, NZ, NZ 1986 F, F, A 1987 Ur, Fj
Moreno, A 1998 Par (R), Ch (R), Ur
Morgan, D 1967 Ch 1970 I, I 1971 SAG, SAG, OCC, OCC 1972 SAG, SAG
Morgan, E 1969 S, S 1972 SAG, SAG 1973 R, R, Par, Ur, Bra, Ch, I, S 1975 F, F
Morgan, G 1977 Bra, Ur, Par, Ch 1979 Ur, Par, Bra
Morgan, M 1971 SAG, OCC, OCC
Morganti, JS 1951 Ur, Bra, Ch
Mostany, J 1987 Ur, Fj, NZ (R)
Muliero, E 1997 Ch
Muller, S 1927 GBR
Muniz, R 1975 Par, Bra, Ch

Nannini, M 2002 Ur (R), Par, Ch 2003 Par, Ch
Navajas, A 1932 JSB, JSB
Naveyra, E 1998 Ch (R)
Nazassi, G 1997 Ch
Negri, ML 1979 Ch, Bra
Neri, E 1960 F, F 1961 Ch, Bra, Ur 1964 Ur, Bra, Ch 1965 Rho, JSB, OCC 1966 SAG, SAG
Neyra, CM 1975 F, F 1976 W, NZ, NZ 1983 WXV
Nicholson, A 1979 Ur, Par, Bra
Nicola, HM 1971 SAG, OCC, OCC, Ch, Bra, Par, Ur 1975 F, F 1978 E, It (R) 1979 NZ, NZ
Noriega, EP 1991 Par 1992 Sp, Sp, R, F 1993 J, J, Ch, Par, Ur, SA, SA 1994 US, S, S, US, SA, SA 1995 Ur, C, A, A, E, Sa, It
Nuñez Piossek, JM 2001 Ur, NZ (R) 2002 Ur, Par, Ch, A 2003 Par, Ur, F, SA, Ur, C, A, R, I 2004 Ch, Ur, W, W 2005 It, It 2006 W, W (R), NZ, E, F

Ochoa, R 1956 OCC
Odriozola, M 1961 Ch, Ur
O'Farrell, J 1948 OCC 1951 Ur, Bra 1956 OCC
O'Farrell, U 1951 Ur, Bra, Ch
Ohanian, C 1998 Par, Ur
Olivera, C 1958 Per, Ur, Ch 1959 JSB, JSB
Olivieri, R 1960 F, F, F 1961 Ch, Bra, Ur
Orengo, J 1996 Ur 1997 Ur, R (R), It 1998 F, F, R, US, C (R), F, W 1999 W 2000 A, SA, E 2001 Ur, US, C, NZ, W, S, NZ 2002 F, E, SA, A, It, I 2003 F, SA, Ur, C, A, I 2004 W (R), W
Orti, C 1949 F, F
Ortiz, L 2003 Par, Ch (R), Ur (R)
Orzabal, A 1974 F, F
Ostiglia, L 1999 W (R), W (R), S, I, W, J (R), F (R) 2001 NZ (R), It, W (R), S (R) 2002 E (R), SA (R) 2003 Par, Ch (R), Ur, F, F, SA, Nm, I 2004 W, W, NZ, F, I, SA 2007 F, Nm, I, S, SA
Otaño, B 1960 F, F, F 1961 Ch, Bra, Ur 1964 Ur, Bra, Ch 1965 Rho, JSB, OCC, OCC, Ch 1966 SAG, SAG 1968 W, W 1969 S, S, Ur, Ch 1970 I, I 1971 SAG, OCC, OCC
Otaola, J 1970 I 1971 Ch, Bra, Par, Ur 1974 F, F

Pacheco, M 1938 Ch
Palma, A 1949 F, F 1952 I, I 1954 F, F
Palma, JMC 1982 F, Sp 1983 WXV, A, A
Palma, R 1985 Ch, Par
Palou, M 1996 US, Ur
Parra, M 1975 Ur, Bra, Ch
Pasalagua, A 1927 GBR, GBR
Pascual, M 1965 Rho, JSB, OCC, OCC, Ch 1966 SAG, SAG 1967 Ur, Ch 1968 W, W 1969 S, S, Ur, Ch 1970 I, I 1971 SAG, SAG, OCC, OCC
Pascuali, HR 1936 BI
Pasman, H 1936 Ch
Passaglia, R 1977 Bra, Ur, Ch 1978 E, It
Paz, G 1979 Ur, Ch, Par, Bra 1983 Ch, Par, Ur
Paz, JJ 1991 Ur, Bra
Peretti, S 1993 Bra (R), Par, SA (R)
Perez, N 1968 W
Perez, RN 1992 F, F, Sp, R, F 1993 Bra, Par, Ur, SA 1995 Ur, R, It, F 1996 US, Ur, C, SA, SA 1998 Ur 1999 I (R)
Perez Cobo, J 1979 NZ, NZ 1980 Fj 1981 E, E, C
Peri Brusa, M 1998 Ch (R)
Pesce, R 1958 Per, Ur, Ch
Petersen, TA 1978 E, It 1979 NZ, NZ, A, A 1980 Fj, Fj 1981 E, E, C 1982 F 1983 WXV, A, A 1985 F, F, Ur, Ch, Par, NZ, NZ 1986 F, F, A
Petrilli, AD 2004 SA 2005 J
Petrone, J 1949 F, F
Petti, R 1995 Par (R), Ch
Pfister, M 1994 SA, SA 1996 F 1998 R, Ur, J (R)
Phelan, S 1997 Ur, Ch (R), R (R), It (R) 1998 F (R), F, R, US, C (R), It 1999 S (R), I, W, Sa, J, I, F 2000 I, A, A, SA, E 2001 NZ, It, W, S, NZ 2002 Ur, Par, Ch, F, E, SA, A, It, I 2003 Ch, Ur, F, SA (R), Fj, C, A, R
Phillips, A 1948 OCC 1949 F, F
Piccardo, JP 1981 E (R) 1983 Ch, Par, Ur
Pichot, A 1995 A, R, It, F 1996 Ur, F, F 1997 It, F, A, A 1998 F, F, R, It, F, W 1999 W, W, S, I (R), W, Sa, J, I, F 2000 I, A, A, SA, E 2001 Ur, US, C, NZ, It, W, S, NZ 2002 F, E, SA, A, It, I 2003 Ur, C, A, R (R), I 2004 F, I, SA 2005 It, SA, S, It 2006 W, W, NZ, Ch, Ur, E, F 2007 W, F, Nm, I, S, SA, F (R)
Pimentel, G 1971 Bra
Pineo, R 1954 F
Pittinari, E 1991 Ur (R), Par, Bra
Poggi, E 1965 JSB, OCC, OCC, Ch 1966 SAG 1967 Ur 1969 Ur
Pollano, C 1927 GBR
Pont Lezica, R 1951 Ur, Bra, Ch
Porta, H 1971 Ch, Bra, Par, Ur 1972 SAG, SAG 1973 R, R, Ur, Bra, Ch, I, S 1974 F, F 1975 F, F 1976 Ur, W, NZ, NZ 1977 F, F 1978 E, It 1979 NZ, NZ, A, A 1980 WXV, Fj, Fj 1981 E, E, C 1982 F, F, Sp 1983 A, A 1985 F, F, Ur, Ch, Par, NZ, NZ 1986 F, F, A 1987 Fj, It, NZ, Sp, A, A 1990 I, E, S
Portillo, O 1995 Par, Ch (R) 1997 Par (R), Ch
Posse, J 1977 Par
Posse, S 1991 Par 1993 Bra, Ch, Ur

Promanzio, C 1995 C (R) 1996 Ur, F, F, E 1997 E (R), E, NZ, Ur (R) 1998 R (R), J (R)
Propato, U 1956 OCC
Puccio, A 1979 Ch, Par, Bra
Puigdeval, M 1964 Ur, Bra
Pulido, J 1960 F

Queirolo, JC 1964 Ur, Bra, Ch
Quesada, G 1996 US, Ur, C, SA (R), E 1997 E, E, NZ, NZ 1998 F (R), R, US, C, It 1999 W, S, I, W, Sa, J, I, F 2000 I, SA, E 2001 NZ (R), It (R), NZ (R) 2002 F (R), E, SA 2003 F, SA, Ur, C (R), Nm, R (R), I
Quetglas, E 1965 Ch
Quinones, G 2004 Ur, Ven

Raimundez, R 1959 JSB, JSB
Ramallo, C 1979 Ur, Ch, Par (R)
Ratcliff, S 1936 Ch
Rave, F 1997 Par
Reggiardo, M 1996 Ur, F, F, E 1997 E, E, NZ, NZ, R, F, A, A 1998 F, F, R, US, Ur, C, It, W 1999 W, W, S, I, W, Sa, J, I, F 2000 I, SA 2001 NZ (R), It, W, S, NZ 2002 F, E, SA, A, It (R), I 2003 F, SA, Fj (R), US (R), Ur, A (R), Nm, I
Reyes, C 1927 GBR, GBR, GBR
Ricci, M 1987 Sp
Riganti, A 1927 GBR, GBR, GBR
Righentini, MA 1989 NZ
Rios, J 1960 F, F
Rivero, G 1996 Ur, US (R), Ur (R)
Robson, F 1927 GBR
Roby, M 1992 Sp 1993 J (R)
Rocca, A 1989 US 1990 C, US, C, E 1991 Ur, Bra
Rocha, O 1974 F, F
Rodriguez, D 1998 J (R), Par, Ch, Ur
Rodriguez, D 2002 Ur, Par (R), Ch
Rodriguez, EE 1979 NZ, NZ, A, A 1980 WXV, Fj, Fj 1981 E, E, C 1983 WXV (R), A, A
Rodriguez Jurado, A 1927 GBR, GBR, GBR, GBR 1932 JSB, JSB 1936 Ch, Ch
Rodriguez Jurado, M 1971 SAG, OCC, Ch, Bra, Par, Ur
Rodriguez-Jurado, A 1965 JSB, OCC, OCC, Ch 1966 SAG, SAG 1968 W, W 1969 S, Ch 1970 I 1971 SAG 1973 R, Par, Bra, Ch, I, S 1974 F, F 1975 F, F 1976 Ur
Roldan, L 2001 Ur, C
Romagnoli, AS 2004 Ch (R), Ur, Ven
Roncero, R 1998 J 2002 Ur (R), Par, Ch (R) 2003 Fj, US (R), Nm (R), R 2004 W, W, NZ, F, I 2005 It, SA, S, It 2006 W, W, NZ 2007 W, F, Nm, I, S, SA, F
Rondinelli, S 2005 Sa (R)
Rosatti, S 1977 Par, Ch
Rospide, M 2003 Par (R), Ch, Ur
Rossi, F 1991 Ur, Par, Bra 1998 F
Rotondo, D 1997 Par, Ch
Ruiz, MA 1997 NZ (R), Ch, R, It, F, A, A 1998 F, F (R), R, US, Ur (R), C (R), J, It (R), F, W 1999 W, Sa (R), J (R), F (R) 2002 Ur (R), Par, Ch (R)

Sainz Trapaga, C 1979 Ur, Par, Bra
Salinas, A 1954 F 1956 OCC 1958 Ur, Ch 1960 F, F
Salvat, S 1987 Ur, Fj, It 1988 F (R) 1989 It, NZ 1990 C, US, C, E, E 1991 Ur, Par, Bra 1992 Sp, F 1993 Bra, Ch, Par, Ur, SA, SA 1994 SA, SA 1995 Ur, C, A, A, E, Sa, It, Par, Ch, Ur, R, It, F
Salzman, T 1936 Bl, Ch, Ch
Sambucetti, M 2001 Ur (R), US, C 2002 Ur, Ch 2003 Par, Ch, Fj 2005 It (R), Sa
Sanderson, T 1932 JSB
Sanes, D 1985 Ch, Par 1986 F, F 1987 Ur, Par, Ch 1989 Bra, Ch, Ur
Sanguinetti, EJ 1975 Ur, Par, Ch 1978 It 1979 A (R) 1982 F, F, Sp
Sanguinetti, G 1979 Ur, Ch, Par, Bra
Sansot, J 1948 OCC
Sansot, M 1975 F, F 1976 Ur, W, NZ, NZ 1977 Bra, Ch 1978 E, It 1979 NZ, NZ, A, A 1980 WXV, Fj 1983 WXV (R)
Santamarina, Jm 1991 NZ, NZ, Ch, A, W, Sa 1992 F, Sp, R, F 1993 J, J 1994 US, S, US 1995 A, A, E, Sa, It, Ur, R, It, F
Santiago, J 1948 OCC 1952 I, I
Sanz, JR 1973 Par, Ur, Bra, Ch 1974 F, F 1976 Ur 1977 F, F
Sanz, S 2003 US 2004 Ch, Ven 2005 It, Sa
Sarandon, M 1948 OCC, OCC 1949 F, F 1951 Ur, Bra, Ch 1952 I, I 1954 F
Sartori, J 1979 Ch, Par, Bra
Sauze, R 1983 Par
Scelzo, JM 1996 US, SA (R) 1997 R (R), It, F (R), A (R) 1998 F (R), US (R), Ur, C (R), Ch, F (R) 1999 I (R), Sa (R), I (R), F (R) 2000 I, A, A 2003 F, F, Fj, Ur, C (R), Nm, R, I (R) 2005 SA (R), S (R), It (R) 2006 W, W, NZ (R), Ch, Ur, E (R), It, F 2007 W, F, Nm (R), I, S, SA
Schacht, F 1989 Bra, Ch, Par, Ur, US 1990 C
Scharemberg, E 1961 Ch, Bra, Ur 1964 Ur, Bra 1965 Rho, JSB, OCC, OCC 1967 Ur, Ch
Schiavio, AM 1983 Ch, Ur 1986 A 1987 Fj (R), It, NZ
Schiavio, E 1936 Bl, Bl, Ch, Ch
Schmidt, R 1960 F, F, F 1961 Bra 1964 Ur 1965 JSB
Schmitt, G 1964 Ur, Ch
Schusterman, M 2003 Par, Fj 2004 W (R), W (R), NZ (R), F (R) 2005 It, It, SA (R), S 2006 W (R), Ch, Ur, E (R) 2007 I (R), It (R), Geo (R)
Scolni, AA 1983 Ch, Par, Ur 1985 F 1987 Sp, A 1988 F, F, F, F 1989 NZ, US 1990 C, US, E, E, I, E, S (R)
Seaton, J 1968 W, W 1969 Ur, Ch
Seaton, R 1967 Ur, Ch
Senillosa, H 2002 Ur, Par (R), Ch 2003 Par, Ch, Ur, F, SA (R), Fj, US, Nm, R 2004 Ch, Ur, Ven, W, W, NZ, F, I 2005 It, It (R) 2006 Ch (R), It (R), F (R) 2007 I, I, F (R), Geo (R), Nm, I (R), S (R), F (R)
Serra, R 1927 GBR, GBR, GBR
Serra Miras, F 2003 Ch 2005 J 2006 W (R), Ch, Ur 2007 I, It, W, Nm (R)
Serrano, C 1978 It 1980 Fj 1983 Ch, Par (R), Ur
Sharpe, R 1948 OCC
Silva, HL 1965 JSB, OCC 1967 Ur, Ch 1968 W, W 1969 S, S, Ur, Ch 1970 I, I 1971 SAG, SAG, OCC, OCC, Ur 1978 E 1979 NZ, NZ, A, A 1980 WXV
Silva, R 1998 J
Silvestre, F 1988 F 1989 Bra, Par, Ur, US 1990 C, US
Silvetti, D 1993 J
Simes, J 1989 Bra, Ch 1990 C (R), US 1993 J, J 1996 Ur, F, F, US (R), C
Simon, HG 1991 NZ, NZ, A, W, Sa
Simone, E 1996 US, SA (R), SA, E 1997 E, E, NZ, NZ, R, F, A, A 1998 F, F, US (R), Ur, C, J, It, F, W (R) 1999 W, S, I, W, Sa, J, I, F 2000 I, SA (R) 2001 Ur, US (R), It 2002 Ur, Ch
Soares-Gache, A 1978 It 1979 NZ, NZ 1981 C 1982 F, Sp 1983 WXV, A, A 1987 Sp, A, A 1988 F
Solari, T 1996 Ur, C, SA 1997 E, E, NZ, NZ (R)
Soler, F 1996 Ur, F, F, SA, SA 1997 E, E, NZ, NZ, Ur, R, It, F 1998 F, F, R, US, C, It, W 2001 Ur, US (R) 2002 Ur, Par, Ch (R)
Soler Valls, JS 1989 It (R), Bra, Par, Ur
Solveira, H 1951 Ur
Sommer, J 1927 GBR
Sorhaburu, E 1958 Per, Ur 1960 F 1961 Ch, Ur
Spain, E 1965 JSB, OCC, OCC, Ch 1967 Ur, Ch
Sporleder, PL 1990 I, E, S 1991 NZ, NZ, Ch, A, W, Sa 1992 F, F, Sp, Sp, R, F 1993 J, J, Bra (R), Ch, Par, Ur, SA, SA 1994 US, S, S, US, SA, SA 1995 A, A, E, Sa, It 1996 Ur, F, F, Ur, C, SA, SA, E 1997 E, E, NZ, NZ, Par, Ur, R, It, F, A, A 1998 F, R, US, Ur, C, Ur, It, F, W 1999 W, W, J 2002 Ur, Par, Ch, It (R), I (R) 2003 Par (R), Ch, Ur, F (R), Fj (R), US, Nm, R
Stanfield, J 1932 JSB
Stewart, A 1936 Bl
Stewart, J 1932 JSB, JSB
Stortoni, BM 1998 J, Par (R) 2001 Ur, US, C, NZ, It, NZ (R) 2002 Ur, Par, Ch 2003 F (R), Fj, US 2005 It, It, S (R), It 2007 I
Sugasti, M 1995 Par, Ch
Sutton, W 1936 Ch
Swain, C 1948 OCC 1949 F, F 1951 Ur, Bra, Ch 1952 I, I

Tagliabue, J 1936 Ch, Ch
Tahier, L 1964 Ur, Ch
Talbot, F 1936 Bl, Bl 1938 Ch
Talbot, H 1936 Bl, Bl, Ch, Ch 1938 Ch
Teran, EG 1977 Bra, Ur, Par 1979 Ch, Par, Bra
Teran, G 1988 F
Teran, MJ 1991 NZ, NZ, Ch, A, W, Sa 1992 F, Sp, R, F 1993 J, J, Ur, SA, SA 1994 US, S, S, US, SA, SA 1995 A, A, E, Sa, It, Ur, R, It, F
Tiesi, GP 2004 SA 2005 J (R), It, Sa 2006 W, W, NZ, Ch, Ur, E 2007 Geo (R), Nm, SA (R)
Todeschini, FJ 1998 R (R), Ur 2005 J, It, It, S 2006 W, W, NZ, Ch, Ur, E (R), It, F 2007 I, W, Geo (R), Nm (R)
Tolomei, A 1991 Par, Bra 1993 Bra, Ch, Par
Tompkins, N 1948 OCC 1949 F, F 1952 I, I
Topping, JA 1938 Ch
Torello, E 1983 Par 1989 Ch
Torino, F 1927 GBR, GBR
Tozer, NC 1932 JSB, JSB
Travaglini, AA 1967 Ur, Ch 1968 W 1969 S, S 1970 I, I 1971 SAG, SAG, OCC, OCC 1972 SAG, SAG 1973 R, Par, Ur, Bra, Ch, I, S 1974 F, F 1975 F, F 1976 Ur, W, NZ, NZ
Travaglini, G 1978 E, It 1979 NZ, NZ, A, A 1980 WXV, Fj, Fj 1981 E, E 1982 F, F, Sp 1983 WXV (R), A 1987 Ur, Fj, It, NZ
Travaglini, R 1996 US, Ur (R), C (R) 1997 NZ, R, F (R) 1998 Ur, C
Trucco, J 1977 Bra, Ur, Par, Ch
Turner, A 1932 JSB, JSB
Turnes, FA 1985 F, F, Ur, NZ, NZ 1986 F, F, A, A 1987 Ur, Fj, NZ, Sp, A, A 1988 F, F, F, F 1989 It, NZ, NZ 1997 Ur, F, A, A

Ugartemendia, G 1991 Ur 1993 J, Ch, Par, Ur, SA, SA 1994 US, SA, SA 1997 Ur 1998 Par 2000 E (R)
Urbano, M 1991 Ur, Bra 1995 Par, Ch, R, It, F
Ure, EM 1980 WXV, Fj, Fj 1981 E, E 1982 F, F, Sp 1983 A 1985 F, F, NZ, NZ 1986 F, F, A
Uriarte, J 1986 A 1987 Par

Valesani, E 1986 A, A
Valesani, MR 1989 It, NZ, NZ, Ch, Par, Ur, US 1990 C, US, C
Varela, GB 1979 Ur, Ch
Varela, L 1961 Ch, Bra, Ur
Varella, F 1960 F
Varone, GM 1982 F
Vazquez, C 1927 GBR, GBR, GBR
Velazquez, A 1971 Ch, Par
Ventura, R 1975 Ur, Bra, Ch 1977 Bra, Ur 1978 It 1979 Ur, Ch, Par 1983 Ch, Par, Ur
Verardo, E 1958 Ch 1959 JSB, JSB 1964 Ur, Bra, Ch 1967 Ur, Ch
Vergallo, N 2005 Sa (R) 2006 Ch (R), Ur (R) 2007 I, I
Vernet Basualdo, AV 2004 SA (R) 2005 J 2006 It (R) 2007 I, Geo (R), Nm, I (R), F
Veron, G 1997 Par
Vibart, J 1960 F
Vidou, H 1987 Par 1990 C, US, E, E 1991 NZ
Vidou, H 1960 F 1961 Bra
Viel Temperley, C 1993 Bra, Ch, Par, Ur 1994 US, S, S, US, SA, SA 1995 Ur, C, A, A, E, Sa, It, Par, Ur, R, It, F 1996 SA (R) 1997 E (R), NZ
Vila, E 1975 Ur, Par, Ch
Villen, D 1998 J, Par
Viola, M 1993 Bra
Virasoro, J 1973 R, R, Ur, Bra, Ch, S
Visca, JL 1985 Par

Walther, J 1971 OCC
Walther, M 1967 Ur, Ch 1968 W, W 1969 S, S, Ur, Ch 1970 I, I 1971 SAG, OCC, OCC 1973 Bra, Ch 1974 F, F
Werner, F 1996 US 1997 Ur
Wessek 1960 F
Wilkins, R 1936 Ch, Ch
Wittman, J 1971 SAG, SAG, OCC, OCC, Ur 1972 SAG, SAG 1973 R
Yanez, L 1965 Rho, JSB, OCC, OCC, Ch 1966 SAG, SAG 1968 W, W 1969 S, S, Ur, Ch 1970 I, I 1971 SAG, OCC (R), OCC, Ur

Yanguela, EP 1956 OCC
Yanguela, M 1987 It
Yustini, B 1954 F 1956 OCC

Zanero, R 1990 C
Zapiola, E 1998 Par (R)
Zappa, A 1927 GBR

AUSTRALIA

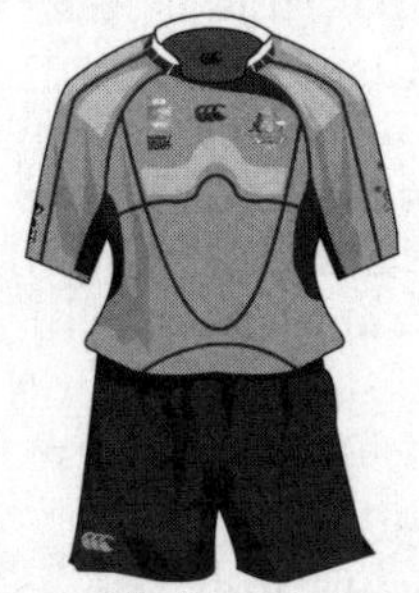

AUSTRALIA'S 2006–07 TEST RECORD

OPPONENTS	DATE	VENUE	RESULT
Wales	4 November	A	**Drew** 29–29
Italy	11 November	A	**Won** 25–18
Ireland	19 November	A	**Lost** 6–21
Scotland	25 November	A	**Won** 44–15
Wales	26 May	H	**Won** 29–23
Wales	2 June	H	**Won** 31–0
Fiji	9 June	H	**Won** 49–0
South Africa	16 June	A	**Lost** 19–22
New Zealand	30 June	H	**Won** 20–15
South Africa	7 July	H	**Won** 25–17
New Zealand	21 July	A	**Lost** 12–26
Japan	8 September	N	**Won** 91–3 (WC)
Wales	15 September	N	**Won** 32–20 (WC)
Fiji	23 September	N	**Won** 55–12 (WC)
Canada	29 September	N	**Won** 37–6 (WC)
England	6 October	N	**Lost** 10–12 (WC)

LET'S GO ROUND AGAIN

By Iain Spragg

The sense of déjà vu was palpable as Australia were once again beaten at the Rugby World Cup by England in a match that had more than one echo of the two sides' famous clash in Sydney in 2003. This time it was the quarter-final rather than the final and although the principal cast and setting was much changed from events in the Telstra Stadium four years earlier, some things had not changed.

A solitary try from Lote Tuqiri, the boot of Jonny Wilkinson and a titanic effort from the English pack all stirred memories of the previous encounter and that the result was again a narrow victory for the men in white was as painful for the Wallabies as it was unexpected.

Few had given England a prayer of beating Australia in the last eight in Marseille. John Connolly's side were the clear favourites while the defending champions had looked disjointed and ponderous in the pool stages but the Wallabies could find no answer to England's forward power in the Stade Velodrome.

They had the chance to steal victory late on but as Stirling Mortlock's penalty sailed tantalisingly wide, their fate was sealed and England could celebrate a shock 12–10 triumph.

"It was an extremely quiet dressing room and understandably so," Mortlock said after the game. "A lot of credit must go to England, the way they attacked the breakdown and didn't allow us to get into rhythm. I was disappointed a number of my kicks were extremely close. I should have kicked them, and it would have been a different game."

Australia always knew a rematch with England was on the cards. Drawn in Pool B with Japan, Wales, Fiji and Canada, the Wallabies were the undisputed front runners to win the group and if, as predicted, England came second to the Springboks in Pool B, a chance to avenge their World Cup defeat to the old enemy was imminent.

They began the campaign in explosive style. Japan were first up in Lyon and there were no signs of complacency from the Wallabies as they ran riot in the second-half to record a 91–3 win, including a hat-trick from Rocky Elsom.

"We haven't played for seven weeks so we expected to be a bit rusty in the first half but I thought we got it together in the second half," Connolly said. "We're satisfied with our performance. We went out there to play a specific way and that's what we did."

Bizarrely, the Australians were then scheduled to face Wales in Cardiff

Stu Foster/Getty Images

Australia discovered a fabulous new talent in 2007, in the shape of outside-half Berrick Barnes.

rather than in France but any hopes Gareth Jenkins' side had of capitalising on their home advantage were comprehensively quashed as the Wallabies laid down a marker at the Millennium Stadium.

It took the visitors just 15 minutes to breach the Welsh defence for the first time as young fly-half Berrick Barnes, deputising for the injured Stephen Larkham, glided through a gap to send Matt Giteau under the posts. Stirling Mortlock and Chris Latham added the second and third tries and the Wallabies were 25–3 up at half-time.

Wales rallied in front of their home crowd after the break but two tries of their own flattered to deceive and the final 32–20 scoreline barely reflected Australia's physical and tactical superiority.

"We're still warming up in this tournament," said Latham, who was named the man-of-the-match. "That was a great, spirited performance to get a victory in Cardiff. We were a bit loose at times but we stuck at it. Credit has to go to the forwards. They built the platform and were superb in defence."

Spirited performances from both Fiji in Montpellier and Canada in Bordeaux kept Australia honest in their final two pool games but both ultimately succumbed to the Wallabies' attacking prowess and Connolly side's were safely through to the knockout stages, where England lay in wait in Marseille.

The early exchanges in the Stade Velodrome were predictably fierce but Australia were the first to trouble the scorers courtesy of Mortlock's sixth-minute penalty. England hit back with two quick Wilkinson penalties midway through the half but the Wallabies eased back into the lead on 33 minutes with the only try of the game. A Mortlock break was held up just short but quick recycled ball saw Tuqiri in space on the blind side and he skipped out of Josh Lewsey's tackle to score against England as he did in Sydney in 2003. Mortlock added the two points and the Wallabies led 10–6 at the break.

The second-half, however, saw England's front five squeeze Australia ominously and it was 10–9 on 50 minutes after a third Wilkinson penalty. Ten minutes later England had their noses in front. The Wallaby scrum disintegrated, Elsom was penalised and Wilkinson made it 12–10 to the defending champions.

There was to be one last chance for Australia. Joe Worsley was blown up for hands in the ruck four minutes from time and Mortlock stepped forward to try his luck from 45 metres out but his well-struck effort drifted wide off the left upright.

It was heartbreak for the Wallabies and a particularly sad curtain call on the illustrious international careers of Larkham and George Gregan, who had both announced their retirement at the end of the tournament and finally amassed an incredible 241 caps between them.

"Stephen and George have given so much to the world of rugby," Mortlock said. "For them to bow out in a quarter-final, everyone is extremely disappointed for them."

The Australians had begun their year-long build up to the World Cup the previous November on a four-match tour of the northern hemisphere. A historic 29–29 draw with the Welsh in Cardiff – the first ever international stalemate between the two countries – kicked off proceedings and Italy were then despatched 25–18 in Rome seven days later.

Ireland at Lansdowne Road, however, were an altogether tougher nut to crack and Eddie O'Sullivan's side gave the Wallabies ample food for thought with a 21–6 win. The tour ended with a routine 44–15 victory over Scotland at Murrayfield but a modest two wins from four suggested Connolly's side had significant room for improvement.

Wales embarked on a two-Test tour Down Under in the summer and although the Wallabies won both games, the victories raised more questions than they answered, especially after the first Test in Sydney which the home side only clinched 29–23 with a last-gasp try.

"There's definitely a feeling of relief to get the win," Australian skipper Phil Waugh conceded. "There was some rustiness in the first half, some simple mistakes, and we dropped a lot of balls. Hopefully we can work on that."

The Tri-Nations would be the acid test of Australia's preparations and although two late drop goals from Francois Steyn snatched victory for the Springboks in the tournament opener in Cape Town, it was the clash with the All Blacks in Melbourne a fortnight later that reaffirmed the Wallabies as genuine World Cup contenders.

It had been three years and five games since Australia had been beaten their Antipodean neighbours and although New Zealand led 15–6 at half-time, Australia came storming back in the second half with tries from Adam Ashley-Cooper and Scott Staniforth that completed a famous 20–15 victory over the number one ranked side in the world.

"We thought we went close against the All Blacks a couple of times last year and we weren't quite good enough," Connolly said after the win at the MCG. "It was important for us to get that win tonight. We didn't play well in the first-half, we scrambled to keep ourselves in the game. You know what you've got to do to beat the All Blacks, it's just so hard to do because they're so good."

Buoyed by their victory, Connolly's side took their revenge on the South Africans in Sydney. It was the final Test appearances for Gregan and Larkham on home soil but tries from Wikus van Heerden and Breyton Paulse for the Springboks to establish a 17–0 lead put their send-off in danger. Australia rallied and second-half scores from Stephen Hoiles and Matt Giteau, plus 10 points from Mortlock's boot, earned them a 25–17 win and sent the Wallabies to the top of the Tri-Nations table.

Victory in the return match with the All Blacks at Eden Park would have handed Australia their first Tri-Nations title since 2001 but New Zealand were in no mood to surrender their crown. The home side led 12–9 at half-time but stretched away after the break with the only try of the game from Tony Woodcock and ran out 26–12 winners. Australia had to content themselves with the runners-up spot.

The World Cup now beckoned. Australia's results had been sporadic going into the competition but the victory of New Zealand and what the Wallaby coaching staff hoped was a more competitive pack suggested they had a genuine chance of reaching the final. England's front five had other ideas.

AUSTRALIA INTERNATIONAL STATISTICS

MATCH RECORDS UP TO 31ST OCTOBER 2007

MOST CONSECUTIVE TEST WINS

10 1991 Arg, WS, W, I, NZ, E, 1992 S 1,2, NZ 1,2
10 1998 NZ 3, Fj, Tg, Sm, F, E 2, 1999 I 1,2, E, SA 1
10 1999 NZ 2, R, I 3, US, W, SA 3, F, 2000 Arg 1,2,SA 1

MOST CONSECUTIVE TESTS WITHOUT DEFEAT

Matches	Wins	Draws	Periods
10	10	0	1991 to 1992
10	10	0	1998 to 1999
10	10	0	1999 to 2000

MOST POINTS IN A MATCH

BY THE TEAM

Pts.	Opponents	Venue	Year
142	Namibia	Adelaide	2003
92	Spain	Madrid	2001
91	Japan	Lyons	2007
90	Romania	Brisbane	2003
76	England	Brisbane	1998
74	Canada	Brisbane	1996
74	Tonga	Canberra	1998
74	W Samoa	Sydney	2005
73	W Samoa	Sydney	1994
69	Italy	Melbourne	2005
67	United States	Brisbane	1990

BY A PLAYER

Pts.	Player	Opponents	Venue	Year
42	M S Rogers	Namibia	Adelaide	2003
39	M C Burke	Canada	Brisbane	1996
30	E J Flatley	Romania	Brisbane	2003
29	S A Mortlock	South Africa	Melbourne	2000
28	M P Lynagh	Argentina	Brisbane	1995
27	M J Giteau	Fiji	Montpellier	2007
25	M C Burke	Scotland	Sydney	1998
25	M C Burke	France	Cardiff	1999
25	M C Burke	British/Irish Lions	Melbourne	2001
25	E J Flatley*	Ireland	Perth	2003
25	C E Latham	Namibia	Adelaide	2003
24	M P Lynagh	United States	Brisbane	1990
24	M P Lynagh	France	Brisbane	1990
24	M C Burke	New Zealand	Melbourne	1998
24	M C Burke	South Africa	Twickenham	1999

* includes a penalty try

MOST TRIES IN A MATCH

BY THE TEAM

Tries	Opponents	Venue	Year
22	Namibia	Adelaide	2003
13	South Korea	Brisbane	1987
13	Spain	Madrid	2001
13	Romania	Brisbane	2003
13	Japan	Lyons	2007
12	United States	Brisbane	1990
12	Wales	Brisbane	1991
12	Tonga	Canberra	1998
12	Samoa	Sydney	2005
11	Western Samoa	Sydney	1994
11	England	Brisbane	1998
11	Italy	Melbourne	2005

BY A PLAYER

Tries	Player	Opponents	Venue	Year
5	C E Latham	Namibia	Adelaide	2003
4	G Cornelsen	New Zealand	Auckland	1978
4	D I Campese	United States	Sydney	1983
4	J S Little	Tonga	Canberra	1998
4	C E Latham	Argentina	Brisbane	2000
4	L D Tuqiri	Italy	Melbourne	2005

MOST CONVERSIONS IN A MATCH

BY THE TEAM

Cons	Opponents	Venue	Year
16	Namibia	Adelaide	2003
12	Spain	Madrid	2001
11	Romania	Brisbane	2003
10	Japan	Lyons	2007
9	Canada	Brisbane	1996
9	Fiji	Parramatta	1998
8	Italy	Rome	1988
8	United States	Brisbane	1990
7	Canada	Sydney	1985
7	Tonga	Canberra	1998
7	Samoa	Sydney	2005
7	Italy	Melbourne	2005

BY A PLAYER

Cons	Player	Opponents	Venue	Year
16	M S Rogers	Namibia	Adelaide	2003
11	E J Flatley	Romania	Brisbane	2003
10	M C Burke	Spain	Madrid	2001
9	M C Burke	Canada	Brisbane	1996
9	J A Eales	Fiji	Parramatta	1998
8	M P Lynagh	Italy	Rome	1988
8	M P Lynagh	United States	Brisbane	1990
7	M P Lynagh	Canada	Sydney	1985
7	S A Mortlock	Japan	Lyons	2007

MOST PENALTIES IN A MATCH

BY THE TEAM

Pens	Opponents	Venue	Year
8	South Africa	Twickenham	1999
7	New Zealand	Sydney	1999
7	France	Cardiff	1999
7	Wales	Cardiff	2001
6	New Zealand	Sydney	1984
6	France	Sydney	1986
6	England	Brisbane	1988
6	Argentina	Buenos Aires	1997
6	Ireland	Perth	1999
6	France	Paris	2000
6	British/Irish Lions	Melbourne	2001
6	New Zealand	Sydney	2004

BY A PLAYER

Pens	Player	Opponents	Venue	Year
8	M C Burke	South Africa	Twickenham	1999
7	M C Burke	New Zealand	Sydney	1999
7	M C Burke	France	Cardiff	1999
7	M C Burke	Wales	Cardiff	2001
6	M P Lynagh	France	Sydney	1986
6	M P Lynagh	England	Brisbane	1988
6	D J Knox	Argentina	Buenos Aires	1997
6	M C Burke	France	Paris	2000
6	M C Burke	British/Irish Lions	Melbourne	2001

MOST DROPED GOALS IN A MATCH

BY THE TEAM

Drops	Opponents	Venue	Year
3	England	Twickenham	1967
3	Ireland	Dublin	1984
3	Fiji	Brisbane	1985

BY A PLAYER

Drops	Player	Opponent	Venue	Year
3	P F Hawthorne	England	Twickenham	1967
2	M G Ella	Ireland	Dublin	1984
2	D J Knox	Fiji	Brisbane	1985

CAREER RECORDS

MOST CAPPED PLAYERS

Caps	Player	Career Span
139	G M Gregan	1994 to 2007
102	S J Larkham	1996 to 2007
101	D I Campese	1982 to 1996
86	J A Eales	1991 to 2001
86	J W C Roff	1995 to 2004
83	G B Smith	2000 to 2007
81	M C Burke	1993 to 2004
80	T J Horan	1989 to 2000
79	D J Wilson	1992 to 2000
78	C E Latham	1998 to 2007
75	J S Little	1989 to 2000
72	M P Lynagh	1984 to 1995
72	J A Paul	1998 to 2006
67	P N Kearns	1989 to 1999
67	D J Herbert	1994 to 2002
66	P R Waugh	2000 to 2007
64	N C Sharpe	2002 to 2007
63	N C Farr Jones	1984 to 1993
63	M J Cockbain	1997 to 2003
63	S A Mortlock	2000 to 2007
60	R S T Kefu	1997 to 2003
59	S P Poidevin	1980 to 1991

MOST CONSECUTIVE TESTS

Tests	Player	Career Span
62	J W C Roff	1996 to 2001
46	P N Kearns	1989 to 1995
44	G B Smith	2003 to 2006
42	D I Campese	1990 to 1995
37	P G Johnson	1959 to 1968

MOST TESTS AS CAPTAIN

Tests	Captain	Career Span
59	G M Gregan	2001 to 2007
55	J A Eales	1996 to 2001
36	N C Farr Jones	1988 to 1992
19	A G Slack	1984 to 1987
16	J E Thornett	1962 to 1967
16	G V Davis	1969 to 1972

MOST POINTS IN TESTS

Pts	Player	Tests	Career Span
911	M P Lynagh	72	1984 to 1995
878	M C Burke	81	1993 to 2004
463	S A Mortlock	63	2000 to 2007
315	D I Campese	101	1982 to 1996
260	P E McLean	30	1974 to 1982
259	M J Giteau	51	2002 to 2007
249*	J W Roff	86	1995 to 2004
200	C E Latham	78	1998 to 2007
187*	E J Flatley	38	1997 to 2005
173	J A Eales	86	1991 to 2001

* Roff and Flatley's totals include a penalty try

MOST TRIES IN TESTS

Tries	Player	Tests	Career Span
64	D I Campese	101	1982 to 1996
40	C E Latham	78	1998 to 2007
31*	J W Roff	86	1995 to 2004
30	T J Horan	80	1989 to 2000
29	M C Burke	81	1993 to 2004
28	L D Tuqiri	58	2003 to 2007
25	S J Larkham	102	1996 to 2007
25	S A Mortlock	63	2000 to 2007
24	B N Tune	47	1996 to 2006
21	J S Little	75	1989 to 2000

* Roff's total includes a penalty try

MOST CONVERSIONS IN TESTS

Cons	Player	Tests	Career Span
140	M P Lynagh	72	1984 to 1995
104	M C Burke	81	1993 to 2004
61	S A Mortlock	63	2000 to 2007
39	M J Giteau	51	2002 to 2007
31	J A Eales	86	1991 to 2001
30	E J Flatley	38	1997 to 2005
27	P E McLean	30	1974 to 1982
27	M S Rogers	45	2002 to 2006
20	J W Roff	86	1995 to 2004
19	D J Knox	13	1985 to 1997

MOST PENALTY GOALS IN TESTS

Pens	Player	Tests	Career Span
177	M P Lynagh	72	1984 to 1995
174	M C Burke	81	1993 to 2004
72	S A Mortlock	63	2000 to 2007
62	P E McLean	30	1974 to 1982
34	J A Eales	86	1991 to 2001
34	E J Flatley	38	1997 to 2005
26	M J Giteau	51	2002 to 2007
23	M C Roebuck	23	1991 to 1993

MOST DROPPED GOALS IN TESTS

Drops	Player	Tests	Career Span
9	P F Hawthorne	21	1962 to 1967
9	M P Lynagh	72	1984 to 1995
8	M G Ella	25	1980 to 1984
4	P E McLean	30	1974 to 1982

TRI-NATIONS RECORDS

RECORD	DETAIL	HOLDER	SET
Most points in season	133	in six matches	2006
Most tries in season	14	in six matches	2006
Highest Score	49	49-0 v S Africa (h)	2006
Biggest win	49	49-0 v S Africa (h)	2006
Highest score conceded	61	22-61 v S Africa (a)	1997
Biggest defeat	39	22-61 v S Africa (a)	1997
Most points in matches	271	M C Burke	1996 to 2004
Most points in season	71	S A Mortlock	2000
Most points in match	24	M C Burke	v N Zealand (h) 1998
Most tries in matches	9	J W C Roff	1996 to 2003
Most tries in season	4	S A Mortlock	2000
Most tries in match	2	B N Tune	v S Africa (h) 1997
	2	S J Larkham	v N Zealand (a) 1997
	2	M C Burke	v N Zealand (h) 1998
	2	J W C Roff	v S Africa (h) 1999
	2	S A Mortlock	v N Zealand (h) 2000
	2	C E Latham	v S Africa (h) 2002
	2	M J Giteau	v S Africa (h) 2006
	2	L D Tuqiri	v N Zealand (a) 2006
Most cons in matches	21	S A Mortlock	2000 to 2007
Most cons in season	12	S A Mortlock	2006
Most cons in match	5	S A Mortlock	v S Africa (h) 2006
Most pens in matches	65	M C Burke	1996 to 2004
Most pens in season	14	M C Burke	2001
Most pens in match	7	M C Burke	v N Zealand (h) 1999

MISCELLANEOUS RECORDS

RECORD	HOLDER	DETAIL
Longest Test Career	G M Cooke	1932-1948
Youngest Test Cap	B W Ford	18 yrs 90 days in 1957
Oldest Test Cap	A R Miller	38 yrs 113 days in 1967

CAREER RECORDS OF AUSTRALIA INTERNATIONAL PLAYERS (UP TO 31 OCTOBER 2007)

PLAYER BACKS	DEBUT	CAPS	T	C	P	D	PTS
A P Ashley-Cooper	2005 v SA	12	4	0	0	0	20
B S Barnes	2007 v J	4	2	0	0	2	16
S J Cordingley	2000 v Arg	14	0	0	0	0	0
M A Gerrard	2005 v It	23	9	0	0	0	45
M J Giteau	2002 v E	51	20	39	26	1	259
G M Gregan	1994 v It	139	18	0	0	3	99
J L Huxley	2007 v W	9	2	3	2	0	22
D N Ioane	2007 v W	1	1	0	0	0	5
S J Larkham	1996 v W	102	25	2	0	2	135
C E Latham	1998 v F	78	40	0	0	0	200
D A Mitchell	2005 v SA	21	14	0	0	0	70
S A Mortlock	2000 v Arg	63	25	61	72	0	463
S H Norton-Knight	2007 v W	2	1	0	0	0	5
C Rathbone	2004 v S	26	8	0	0	0	40
M S Rogers	2002 v F	45	14	27	13	0	163
C B Shepherd	2006 v E	6	3	2	0	0	19
S N G Staniforth	1999 v US	12	7	0	0	0	35
L D Tuqiri	2003 v I	58	28	0	0	0	140
J J Valentine	2006 v E	4	0	0	0	0	0
FORWARDS:							
A K E Baxter	2003 v NZ	51	1	0	0	0	5
R C Blake	2006 v E	7	1	0	0	0	5
A M Campbell	2005 v F	4	0	0	0	0	0
B J Cannon	2001 v BI	42	2	0	0	0	10
M D Chisholm	2004 v S	35	5	0	0	0	25
M J Dunning	2003 v Nm	36	0	0	0	0	0
R D Elsom	2005 v Sm	32	5	0	0	0	25
A L Freier	2002 v Arg	20	2	0	0	0	10
S P Hardman	2002 v F	4	0	0	0	0	0
N J Henderson	2004 v PI	3	0	0	0	0	0
S A Hoiles	2004 v S	15	3	0	0	0	15
G S Holmes	2005 v F	13	2	0	0	0	10
J E Horwill	2007 v Fj	1	0	0	0	0	0

D J Lyons	2000 v Arg	44	4	0	0	0	20
T P McIsaac	2006 v E	8	0	0	0	0	0
H J McMeniman	2005 v Sm	12	0	0	0	0	0
S T Moore	2005 v Sm	20	1	0	0	0	5
W L Palu	2006 v E	17	1	0	0	0	5
T Polota-Nau	2005 v E	3	0	0	0	0	0
B A Robinson	2006 v SA	6	0	0	0	0	0
N C Sharpe	2002 v F	64	6	0	0	0	30
G T Shepherdson	2006 v I	18	1	0	0	0	5
G B Smith	2000 v F	83	9	0	0	0	45
D J Vickerman	2002 v F	52	0	0	0	0	0
P R Waugh	2000 v E	66	4	0	0	0	20

Cameron Shepherd/Getty Images

After an incedible Test career that brought him 139 caps George Gregan has left Australian shores to start a new life in Toulon.

AUSTRALIA INTERNATIONAL PLAYERS

UP TO 31ST OCTOBER 2007

Entries in square brackets denote matches played in RWC Finals.

Abrahams, A M F (NSW) 1967 NZ, 1968 NZ 1, 1969 W
Adams, N J (NSW) 1955 NZ 1
Adamson, R W (NSW) 1912 US
Allan, T (NSW) 1946 NZ 1, M, NZ 2, 1947 NZ 2, S, I, W, 1948 E, F, 1949 M 1,2,3, NZ 1,2
Anderson, R P (NSW) 1925 NZ 1
Anlezark, E A (NSW) 1905 NZ
Armstrong, A R (NSW) 1923 NZ 1,2
Ashley-Cooper, A P (ACT) 2005 SA4(R), 2007 W1,2,Fj,SA1(R),NZ1,SA2,NZ2, [J,Fj,C,E]
Austin, L R (NSW) 1963 E

Baker, R L (NSW) 1904 BI 1,2
Baker, W H (NSW) 1914 NZ 1,2,3
Ballesty, J P (NSW) 1968 NZ 1,2, F, I, S, 1969 W, SA 2,3,4,
Bannon, D P (NSW) 1946 M
Bardsley, E J (NSW) 1928 NZ 1,3, M (R)
Barker, H S (NSW) 1952 Fj 1,2, NZ 1,2, 1953 SA 4, 1954 Fj 1,2
Barnes, B S (Q) 2007 [J(R),W,Fj,E]
Barnett, J T (NSW) 1907 NZ 1,2,3, 1908 W, 1909 E
Barry, M J (Q) 1971 SA 3
Bartholomeusz, M A (ACT) 2002 It (R)
Barton, R F D (NSW) 1899 BI 3
Batch, P G (Q) 1975 S, W, 1976 E, Fj 1,2,3, F 1,2, 1978 W 1,2, NZ 1,2,3, 1979 Arg 2
Batterham, R P (NSW) 1967 NZ, 1970 S
Battishall, B R (NSW) 1973 E
Baxter, A J (NSW) 1949 M 1,2,3, NZ 1,2, 1951 NZ 1,2, 1952 NZ 1,2
Baxter, A K E (NSW) 2003 NZ 2(R), [Arg,R,I(R),S(R),NZ(R),E], 2004 S1,2,E1,PI,NZ1,SA1,NZ2,SA2,S3,F,S4,E2, 2005 It,F1, SA1,2,3(R),NZ1,SA4,NZ2,F2,E,I(R),W(R), 2006 E1(R),2(R), I1(R),NZ1(R),NZ3(R),SA3(R),W,It,I2,S(R), 2007 Fj, SA1(R),NZ1(R),SA2(R),NZ2(R), [J,W(R),C,E(R)]
Baxter, T J (Q) 1958 NZ 3
Beith, B McN (NSW) 1914 NZ 3, 1920 NZ 1,2,3
Bell, K R (Q) 1968 S
Bell, M D NSW) 1996 C
Bennett, W G (Q) 1931 M, 1933 SA 1,2,3,
Bermingham, J V (Q) 1934 NZ 1,2, 1937 SA 1
Berne, J E (NSW) 1975 S
Besomo, K S (NSW) 1979 I 2
Betts, T N (Q) 1951 NZ 2,3, 1954 Fj 2
Biilmann, R R (NSW) 1933 SA 1,2,3,4
Birt, R (Q) 1914 NZ 2
Black, J W (NSW) 1985 C 1,2, NZ, Fj 1
Blackwood, J G (NSW) 1922 M 1, NZ 1,2,3, 1923 M 1, NZ 1,2,3, 1924 NZ 1,2,3, 1925 NZ 1,4, 1926 NZ 1,2,3, 1927 I, W, S, 1928 E, F
Blades, A T (NSW) 1996 S, I, W 3, 1997 NZ 1(R), E 1(R), SA 1(R), NZ 3, SA 2, Arg 1,2, E 2, S, 1998 E 1, S 1,2, NZ 1, SA 1, NZ 2, SA 2, NZ 3, Fj, WS, F, E 2, 1999 I 1(R), SA 2, NZ 2, [R, I 3, W, SA 3, F]
Blades, C D (NSW) 1997 E 1
Blake, R C (Q) 2006 E1,2, NZ2,SA2,NZ3,SA3,W
Blair, M R (NSW) 1928 F, 1931 M, NZ
Bland, G V (NSW) 1928 NZ 3, M, 1932 NZ 1,2,3, 1933 SA 1,2,4,5
Blomley, J (NSW) 1949 M 1,2,3, NZ 1,2, 1950 BI 1,2
Boland, S B (Q) 1899 BI 3,4, 1903 NZ
Bond, G S G (ACT) 2001 SA 2(R), Sp (R), E (R), F, W
Bond, J H (NSW) 1920 NZ 1,2,3, 1921 NZ
Bondfield, C (NSW) 1925 NZ 2
Bonis, E T (Q) 1929 NZ 1,2,3, 1930 BI, 1931 M, NZ, 1932 NZ 1,2,3, 1933 SA 1,2,3,4,5, 1934 NZ 1,2, 1936 NZ 1,2, M, 1937 SA 1, 1938 NZ 1
Bonner, J E (NSW) 1922 NZ 1,2,3, 1923 M 1,2,3, 1924 NZ 1,2
Bosler, J M (NSW) 1953 SA 1
Bouffler, R G (NSW) 1899 BI 3
Bourke, T K (Q) 1947 NZ 2
Bowden, R (NSW) 1926 NZ 4
Bowen, S (NSW) 1993 SA 1,2,3, 1995 [R], NZ 1,2, 1996 C, NZ 1, SA 2
Bowers, A J A (NSW) 1923 M 2(R),3, NZ, 3, 1925 NZ 1,4, 1926 NZ 1, 1927 I
Bowman, T M (NSW) 1998 E 1, S 1,2, NZ 1, SA 1, NZ 2, SA 2, NZ 3, Fj, WS, F, E 2, 1999 I 1,2, SA 2, [US]
Boyce, E S (NSW) 1962 NZ 1,2, 1964 NZ 1,2,3, 1965 SA 1,2, 1966 W, S, 1967 E, I 1, F, I 2
Boyce, J S (NSW) 1962 NZ 3,4,5, 1963 E, SA 1,2,3,4, 1964 NZ 1,3, 1965 SA 1,2
Boyd, A (NSW) 1899 BI 3
Boyd, A F McC (Q) 1958 M 1
Brass, J E (NSW) 1966 BI 2, W, S, 1967 E, I 1, F, I 2, NZ, 1968 NZ 1, F, I, S
Breckenridge, J W (NSW) 1925 NZ 2(R),3, 1927 I, W, S, 1928 E, F, 1929 NZ 1,2,3, 1930 BI
Brial, M C (NSW) 1993 F 1(R), 2, 1996 W 1(R), 2, C, NZ 1, SA 1, NZ 2, SA 2, It, I, W 3, 1997 NZ 2
Bridle, O L (V) 1931 M, 1932 NZ 1,2,3, 1933 SA 3,4,5, 1934 NZ 1,2, 1936 NZ 1,2, M
Broad, E G (Q) 1949 M 1
Brockhoff, J D (NSW) 1949 M 2,3, NZ 1,2, 1950 BI 1,2, 1951 NZ 2,3
Brown, B R (Q) 1972 NZ 1,3
Brown, J V (NSW) 1956 SA 1,2, 1957 NZ 1,2, 1958 W, I, E, S, F
Brown, R C (NSW) 1975 E 1,2
Brown, S W (NSW) 1953 SA 2,3,4
Bryant, H (NSW) 1925 NZ 1,3,4
Buchan, A J (NSW) 1946 NZ 1,2, 1947 NZ 1,2, S, I, W, 1948 E, F, 1949 M 3
Buchanan, P N (NSW) 1923 M 2(R),3
Bull, D (NSW) 1928 M
Buntine, H (NSW) 1923 NZ 1(R), 1924 NZ 2
Burdon, A (NSW) 1903 NZ, 1904 BI 1,2, 1905 NZ
Burge, A B (NSW) 1907 NZ 3, 1908 W
Burge, P H (NSW) 1907 NZ 1,2,3
Burge, R (NSW) 1928 NZ 1,2,3(R), M (R)
Burke, B T (NSW) 1988 S (R)
Burke, C T (NSW) 1946 NZ 2, 1947 NZ 1,2, S, I, W, 1948 E, F, 1949 M 2,3, NZ 1,2, 1950 BI 1,2, 1951 NZ 1,2,3, 1953 SA 2,3,4, 1954 Fj 1, 1955 NZ 1,2,3, 1956 SA 1,2,
Burke, M C (NSW) 1993 SA 3(R), F 1, 1994 I 1,2, It 1,2, 1995 [C, R, E], NZ 1,2, 1996 W 1,2, C, NZ 1, SA 1, NZ 2, SA 2, It, S, I, W 3, 1997 E 1, NZ 2 , 1998 E 1, S 1,2, NZ 1, SA 1, NZ 2, SA 2, NZ 3, 1999 I 2(R), E (R), SA 1, NZ 1, SA 2, NZ 2, [R, I 3, US, W, SA 3, F], 2000 F, S, E, 2001 BI 1(R),2,3, SA 1, NZ 1, SA 2, NZ 2, Sp, E, F, W, 2002 F 1,2, NZ 1, SA 1, NZ 2, SA 2, Arg, I, E, It, 2003 SA 1, NZ 1, SA 2(R), NZ 2(R),[Arg,R,Nm(R),I], 2004 S1(R),PI(R),SA1(R),NZ2(t&R),SA2(R)
Burke, M P (NSW) 1984 E (R), I, 1985 C 1,2, NZ, Fj 1,2, 1986 It (R), F, Arg 1,2, NZ 1,2,3, 1987 SK, [US, J, I, F, W], NZ, Arg 1,2
Burnet, D R (NSW) 1972 F 1,2, NZ 1,2,3, Fj
Butler, O F (NSW) 1969 SA 1,2, 1970 S, 1971 SA 2,3, F 1,2

Calcraft, W J (NSW) 1985 C 1, 1986 It, Arg 2
Caldwell, B C (NSW) 1928 NZ 3
Cameron, A S (NSW) 1951 NZ 1,2,3, 1952 Fj 1,2, NZ 1,2, 1953 SA 1,2,3,4, 1954 Fj 1,2, 1955 NZ 1,2,3, 1956 SA 1,2, 1957 NZ 1, 1958 I

Campbell, A M (ACT) 2005 F1(R), 2006 It(R),I2(R),S
Campbell, J D (NSW) 1910 NZ 1,2,3
Campbell, W A (Q) 1984 Fj, 1986 It, F, Arg 1,2, NZ 1,2,3, 1987 SK, [E, US, J (R), I, F], NZ, 1988 E, 1989 BI 1,2,3, NZ, 1990 NZ 2,3
Campese, D I (ACT, NSW) 1982 NZ 1,2,3, 1983 US, Arg 1,2, NZ, It, F 1,2, 1984 Fj, NZ 1,2,3, E, I, W, S, 1985 Fj 1,2, 1986 It, F, Arg 1,2, NZ 1,2,3, 1987 [E, US, J, I, F, W], NZ, 1988 E 1,2, NZ 1,2,3, E, S, It, 1989 BI 1,2,3, NZ, F 1,2, 1990 F 2,3, US, NZ 1,2,3, 1991 W, E, NZ 1,2, [Arg, WS, W, I, NZ, E], 1992 S 1,2, NZ 1,2,3, SA, I, W, 1993 Tg, NZ, SA 1,2,3, C, F 1,2, 1994 I 1,2, It 1,2, WS, NZ, 1995 Arg 1,2, [SA, C, E], NZ 2(R), 1996 W 1,2, C, NZ 1, SA 1, NZ 2, SA 2, It, W3
Canniffe, W D (Q) 1907 NZ 2
Cannon, B J (NSW, WF) 2001 BI 2(R), NZ 1(R), Sp (R), F (R), W (R), 2002 F 1(R),2, SA 1(t),2(R), I (t), It (R), 2003 I (R), W (R), E (R), SA 1, NZ 1, SA 2, NZ 2, [Arg,R,I,S,NZ,E], 2004 S1,2,E1,PI,NZ1,2,SA2,S3(R),4(R), 2005 NZ1(R),SA4,NZ2,F2,E,I,W, 2006 W(R),It
Caputo, M E (ACT) 1996 W 1,2, 1997 F 1,2, NZ 1
Carberry, C M (NSW, Q) 1973 Tg 2, E, 1976 I, US, Fj 1,2,3, 1981 F 1,2, I, W, S, 1982 E
Cardy, A M (NSW) 1966 BI 1,2, W, S, 1967 E, I 1, F, 1968 NZ 1,2
Carew, P J (Q) 1899 BI 1,2,3,4
Carmichael, P (Q) 1904 BI 2, 1907 NZ 1, 1908 W, 1909 E
Carozza, P V (Q) 1990 F 1,2,3, NZ 2,3, 1992 S 1,2, NZ 1,2,3, SA, I, W, 1993 Tg, NZ
Carpenter, M G (V) 1938 NZ 1,2,
Carr, E T A (NSW) 1913 NZ 1,2,3, 1914 NZ 1,2,3
Carr, E W (NSW) 1921 SA 1,2,3, NZ (R)
Carroll, D B (NSW) 1908 W, 1912 US
Carroll, J C (NSW) 1953 SA 1
Carroll, J H (NSW) 1958 M 2,3, NZ 1,2,3, 1959 BI 1,2
Carson, J (NSW) 1899 BI 1
Carson, P J (NSW) 1979 NZ, 1980 NZ 3
Carter, D G (NSW) 1988 E 1,2, NZ 1, 1989 F 1,2
Casey, T V (NSW) 1963 SA 2,3,4, 1964 NZ 1,2,3
Catchpole, K W (NSW) 1961 Fj 1,2,3, SA 1,2, F, 1962 NZ 1,2,4, 1963 SA 2,3,4, 1964 NZ 1,2,3, 1965 SA 1,2, 1966 BI 1,2, W, S, 1967 E, I 1, F, I 2, NZ, 1968 NZ 1
Cawsey, R M (NSW) 1949 M 1, NZ 1,2
Cerutti, W H (NSW) 1928 NZ 1,2,3, M, 1929 NZ 1,2,3, 1930 BI, 1931 M, NZ, 1932 NZ 1,2,3, 1933 SA 1,2,3,4,5, 1936 M, 1937 SA 1,2
Challoner, R L (NSW) 1899 BI 2
Chambers, R (NSW) 1920 NZ 1,3
Chapman, G A (NSW) 1962 NZ 3,4,5
Chisholm, M D (ACT) 2004 S3(R), 2005 Sm,It,F1,SA1,2,3(R), NZ1(R),2,F2,E(t&R),I(R),W(R), 2006 E1(R),2,I1,NZ1,SA1(R), NZ2(R),SA2(R),NZ3(t&R),SA3(R),W(R),It,I2,S(t&R), 2007 W1, 2(R),Fj,SA1(R),NZ1(R),2(R), [W(R),Fj,C]
Clark, J G (Q) 1931 M, NZ, 1932 NZ 1,2, 1933 SA 1
Clarken, J C (NSW) 1905 NZ, 1910 NZ 1,2,3
Cleary, M A (NSW) 1961 Fj 1,2,3, SA 1,2, F
Clements, P (NSW) 1982 NZ 3
Clifford, M (NSW) 1938 NZ 3
Cobb, W G (NSW) 1899 BI 3,4
Cockbain, M J (Q) 1997 F 2(R), NZ 1, SA 1,2, 1998 E 1, S 1,2, NZ 1, SA 1, NZ 2, SA 2, NZ 3, Fj, Tg (R), WS, F, E 2, 1999 I 1,2, E, SA 1, NZ 1, SA 2, NZ 2, [US (t&R), W, SA 3, F], 2000 Arg 1,2, SA 2(t&R),3(t&R), F, S, E (R), 2001 BI 1(R),2(R),3(R), SA 1(R), NZ 1(R), SA 2(R), NZ 2(R), Sp (R), E (R), F (t+R), W, 2002 F 1(R),2(R), NZ 1(R), SA 1(R), NZ 2(R), SA 2(R), Arg, I, E, It, 2003 [Arg(R),R(R),Nm(R),I(R),S(R),NZ(R),E(R)]
Cocks, M R (NSW, Q) 1972 F 1,2, NZ 2,3, Fj, 1973 Tg 1,2, W, E, 1975 J 1
Codey, D (NSW Country, Q) 1983 Arg 1, 1984 E, W, S, 1985 C 2, NZ, 1986 F, Arg 1, 1987 [US, J, F (R), W], NZ
Cody, E W (NSW) 1913 NZ 1,2,3
Coker, T (Q, ACT) 1987 [E, US, F, W], 1991 NZ 2, [Arg, WS, NZ, E], 1992 NZ 1,2,3, W (R), 1993 Tg, NZ, 1995 Arg 2, NZ 1(R), 1997 F 1(R), 2, NZ 1, E 1, NZ 2(R), SA 1(R), NZ 3, SA 2, Arg 1,2
Colbert, R (NSW) 1952 Fj 2, NZ 1,2, 1953 SA 2,3,4
Cole, J W (NSW) 1968 NZ 1,2, F, I, S, 1969 W, SA 1,2,3,4, 1970 S, 1971 SA 1,2,3, F 1,2, 1972 NZ 1,2,3, 1973 Tg 1,2, 1974 NZ 1,2,3
Collins, P K (NSW) 1937 SA 2, 1938 NZ 2,3
Colton, A J (Q) 1899 BI 1,3
Colton, T (Q) 1904 BI 1,2
Comrie-Thomson, I R (NSW) 1926 NZ 4, 1928 NZ 1,2,3 M
Connor, D M (Q) 1958 W, I, E, S, F, M 2,3, NZ 1,2,3, 1959 BI 1,2
Connors, M R (Q) 1999 SA 1(R), NZ 1(R), SA 2(R), NZ 2, [R (R), I 3, US, W (R), SA 3(R), F(R)], 2000 Arg 1(R),2(R), SA 1, NZ 1, SA 2, NZ 2(t&R), SA 3, F (R), S (R), E (R)
Constable, R (Q) 1994 I 2(t & R)
Cook, M T (Q) 1986 F, 1987 SK, [J], 1988 E 1,2, NZ 1,2,3, E, S, It
Cooke, B P (Q) 1979 I 1
Cooke, G M (Q) 1932 NZ 1,2,3, 1933 SA 1,2,3, 1946 NZ 2, 1947 NZ 2, S, I, W, 1948 E, F
Coolican, J E (NSW) 1982 NZ 1, 1983 It, F 1,2
Cooney, R C (NSW) 1922 M 2
Cordingley, S J (Q) 2000 Arg 1(R), SA 1(R), F, S, E, 2006 E2,I1(R),NZ1(R),SA1(R),NZ2(R),SA2(R), 2007 Fj(R), [Fj(R),C]
Corfe, A C (Q) 1899 BI 2
Cornelsen, G (NSW) 1974 NZ 2,3, 1975 J 2, S, W, 1976 E, F 1,2, 1978 W 1,2, NZ 1,2,3, 1979 I 1,2, NZ, Arg 1,2, 1980 NZ 1,2,3, 1981 I, W, S, 1982 E
Cornes, J R (Q) 1972 Fj
Cornforth, R G W (NSW) 1947 NZ 1, 1950 BI 2
Cornish, P (ACT) 1990 F 2,3, NZ 1
Costello, P P S (Q) 1950 BI 2
Cottrell, N V (Q) 1949 M 1,2,3, NZ 1,2, 1950 BI 1,2, 1951 NZ 1,2,3, 1952 Fj 1,2, NZ 1,2
Cowper, D L (V) 1931 NZ, 1932 NZ 1,2,3, 1933 SA 1,2,3,4,5
Cox, B P (NSW) 1952 Fj 1,2, NZ 1,2, 1954 Fj 2, 1955 NZ 1, 1956 SA 2, 1957 NZ 1,2
Cox, M H (NSW) 1981 W, S
Cox, P A (NSW) 1979 Arg 1,2, 1980 Fj, NZ 1,2, 1981 W (R), S, 1982 S 1,2, NZ 1,2,3, 1984 Fj, NZ 1,2,3
Craig, R R (NSW) 1908 W
Crakanthorp, J S (NSW) 1923 NZ 3
Cremin, J F (NSW) 1946 NZ 1,2, 1947 NZ 1
Crittle, C P (NSW) 1962 NZ 4,5, 1963 SA 2,3,4, 1964 NZ 1,2,3, 1965 SA 1,2, 1966 BI 1,2, S, 1967 E, I
Croft, B H D (NSW) 1928 M
Croft, D N (Q) 2002 Arg (t&R), I (R), E (t&R), It (R), 2003 [Nm]
Cross, J R (NSW) 1955 NZ 1,2,3
Cross, K A (NSW) 1949 M 1, NZ 1,2, 1950 BI 1,2, 1951 NZ 2,3, 1952 NZ 1, 1953 SA 1,2,3,4, 1954 Fj 1,2, 1955 NZ 3, 1956 SA 1,2, 1957 NZ 1,2
Crossman, O C (NSW) 1923 M 1(R),2,3, 1924, NZ 1,2,3, 1925 NZ 1,3,4, 1926 NZ 1,2,3,4, 1929 NZ 2, 1930 BI
Crowe, P J (NSW) 1976 F 2, 1978 W 1,2, 1979 I 2, NZ, Arg 1
Crowley, D J (Q) 1989 BI 1,2,3, 1991 [WS], 1992 I, W, 1993 C (R), 1995 Arg 1,2, [SA, E], NZ 1, 1996 W 2(R), C, NZ 1, SA 1,2, I, W 3, 1998 E 1(R), S 1(R),2(R), NZ 1(R), SA 1, NZ 2, SA 2, NZ 3, Tg, WS, 1999 I 1,2(R), E (R), SA 1, NZ 1(R), [R (R), I 3(t&R), US, F(R)]
Curley, T G P (NSW) 1957 NZ 1,2, 1958 W, I, E, S, F, M 1, NZ 1,2,3
Curran, D J (NSW) 1980 NZ 3, 1981 F 1,2, W, 1983 Arg 1
Currie, E W (Q) 1899 BI 2
Cutler, S A G (NSW) 1982 NZ 2(R), 1984 NZ 1,2,3, E, I, W, S, 1985 C 1,2, NZ, Fj 1,2, 1986 It, F, NZ 1,2,3, 1987 SK, [E, J, I, F, W], NZ, Arg 1,2, 1988 E 1,2, NZ 1,2,3, E, S, It, 1989 BI 1,2,3, NZ, 1991 [WS]

Daly, A J (NSW) 1989 NZ, F 1,2, 1990 F 1,2,3, US, NZ 1,2,3, 1991 W, E, NZ 1,2, [Arg, W, I, NZ, E], 1992 S 1,2, NZ 1,2,3, SA, 1993 Tg, NZ, SA 1,2,3, C, F 1,2, 1994 I 1,2, It 1,2, WS, NZ, 1995 [C, R]
D'Arcy, A M (Q) 1980 Fj, NZ 3, 1981 F 1,2, I, W, S, 1982 E, S 1,2
Darveniza, P (NSW) 1969 W, SA 2,3,4
Darwin, B J (ACT) 2001 BI 1(R), SA 1(R), NZ 1(R), SA 2(R), NZ 2(t&R), Sp, E, F, W, 2002 NZ 1(R), SA 1(R), NZ 2(R), SA 2, Arg (R), I (R), E (R), It (R), 2003 I (R), W (t&R), E (R), SA 1(R), NZ 1(R), [Arg(R),R(R),Nm,I,S,NZ]
Davidson, R A L (NSW) 1952 Fj 1,2, NZ 1,2, 1953 SA 1, 1957 NZ 1,2, 1958 W, I, E, S, F, M 1
Davis, C C (NSW) 1949 NZ 1, 1951 NZ 1,2,3
Davis, E H (V) 1947 S, W, 1949 M 1,2
Davis, G V (NSW) 1963 E, SA 1,2,3,4, 1964 NZ 1,2,3, 1965 SA 1, 1966 BI 1,2, W, S, 1967 E, I 1, F, I 2, NZ, 1968 NZ 1,2, F, I, S, 1969 W, SA 1,2,3,4, 1970 S, 1971 SA 1,2,3, F 1,2, 1972 F 1,2, NZ 1,2,3

Davis, G W G (NSW) 1955 NZ 2,3
Davis, R A (NSW) 1974 NZ 1,2,3
Davis, T S R (NSW) 1920 NZ 1,2,3, 1921 SA 1,2,3, NZ, 1922 M 1,2,3, NZ 1,2,3, 1923 M 3, NZ 1,2,3, 1924 NZ 1,2, 1925 NZ 1
Davis, W (NSW) 1899 BI 1,3,4
Dawson, W L (NSW) 1946 NZ 1,2
Diett, L J (NSW) 1959 BI 1,2
Dix, W (NSW) 1907 NZ 1,2,3, 1909 E
Dixon, E J (Q) 1904 BI 3
Donald, K J (Q) 1957 NZ 1, 1958 W, I, E, S, M 2,3, 1959 BI 1,2
Dore, E (Q) 1904 BI 1
Dore, M J (Q) 1905 NZ
Dorr, R W (V) 1936 M, 1937 SA 1
Douglas, J A (V) 1962 NZ 3,4,5
Douglas, W A (NSW) 1922 NZ 3(R)
Dowse, J H (NSW) 1961 Fj 1,2, SA 1,2
Dunbar, A R (NSW) 1910 NZ 1,2,3, 1912 US
Duncan, J L (NSW) 1926 NZ 4
Dunlop, E E (V) 1932 NZ 3, 1934 NZ 1
Dunn, P K (NSW) 1958 NZ 1,2,3, 1959 BI 1,2
Dunn, V A (NSW) 1920 NZ 1,2,3, 1921 SA 1,2,3, NZ
Dunning, M J (NSW) 2003 [Nm,E(R)], 2004 S1(R),2(R),E1(R),NZ1(R),SA1(R),NZ2(t&R),SA2(R),S3(R),F(R),S4(R),E2(R), 2005 Sm,It(R),F1(t&R),SA1(R),2(R),3,NZ1(t&R),SA4(t&R),NZ2(R),F2,E,W, 2007 W1,2(R),Fj,SA1,NZ1,SA2,NZ2, [J,W,Fj,E]
Dunworth, D A (Q) 1971 F 1,2, 1972 F 1,2, 1976 Fj 2
Dwyer, L J (NSW) 1910 NZ 1,2,3, 1912 US, 1913 NZ 3, 1914 NZ 1,2,3
Dyson, F J (Q) 2000 Arg 1,2, SA 1, NZ 1, SA 2, NZ 2, SA 3, F, S, E

Eales, J A (Q) 1991 W, E, NZ 1,2, [Arg, WS, W, I, NZ, E], 1992 S 1,2, NZ 1,2,3, SA, I, 1994 I 1,2, It 1,2, WS, NZ, 1995 Arg 1,2, [SA, C, R, E], NZ 1,2, 1996 W 1,2, C, NZ 1, SA 1, NZ 2, SA 2, It, S, I, 1997 F 1,2, NZ 1, E 1, NZ 2, SA 1, Arg 1,2, E 2, S, 1998 E 1, S 1,2, NZ 1, SA 1, NZ 2, SA 2, NZ 3, Fj, Tg, WS, F, E 2, 1999 [R, I 3, W, SA 3, F], 2000 Arg 1,2, SA 1, NZ 1, SA 2, NZ 2, SA 3, F, S, E, 2001 BI 1,2,3, SA 1, NZ 1, SA 2, NZ 2
Eastes, C C (NSW) 1946 NZ 1,2, 1947 NZ 1,2, 1949 M 1,2
Edmonds, M H M (NSW) 1998 Tg, 2001 SA 1(R)
Egerton, R H (NSW) 1991 W, E, NZ 1,2, [Arg, W, I, NZ, E]
Ella, G A (NSW) 1982 NZ 1,2, 1983 F 1,2, 1988 E 2, NZ 1
Ella, G J (NSW) 1982 S 1, 1983 It, 1985 C 2(R), Fj 2
Ella, M G (NSW) 1980 NZ 1,2,3, 1981 F 2, S, 1982 E, S 1, NZ 1,2,3, 1983 US, Arg 1,2, NZ, It, F 1,2, 1984 Fj, NZ 1,2,3, E, I, W, S
Ellem, M A (NSW) 1976 Fj 3(R)
Elliott, F M (NSW) 1957 NZ 1
Elliott, R E (NSW) 1920 NZ 1, 1921 NZ, 1922 M 1,2, NZ 1(R),2,3, 1923 M 1,2,3, NZ 1,2,3
Ellis, C S (NSW) 1899 BI 1,2,3,4
Ellis, K J (NSW) 1958 NZ 1,2,3, 1959 BI 1,2
Ellwood, B J (NSW) 1958 NZ 1,2,3, 1961 Fj 2,3, SA 1, F, 1962 NZ 1,2,3,4,5, 1963 SA 1,2,3,4, 1964 NZ 3, 1965 SA 1,2, 1966 BI 1
Elsom, R D (NSW) 2005 Sm,It,F1,SA1,2,3(R),4,NZ2,F2, 2006 E1,2,I1,NZ1,SA1,NZ2,SA2,NZ3,SA3,W,It,I2,S, 2007 W1,2,SA1,NZ1,SA2,NZ2, [J,W,Fj,E]
Emanuel, D M (NSW) 1957 NZ 2, 1958 W, I, E, S, F, M 1,2,3
Emery, N A (NSW) 1947 NZ 2, S, I, W, 1948 E, F, 1949 M 2,3, NZ 1,2
Erasmus, D J (NSW) 1923 NZ 1,2
Erby, A B (NSW) 1923 M 1,2, NZ 2,3, 1925 NZ 2
Evans, L J (Q) 1903 NZ, 1904 BI 1,3
Evans, W T (Q) 1899 BI 1,2

Fahey, E J (NSW) 1912 US, 1913 NZ 1,2, 1914 NZ 3
Fairfax, R L (NSW) 1971 F 1,2, 1972 F 1,2, NZ 1, Fj, 1973 W, E
Farmer, E H (Q) 1910 NZ 1
Farquhar, C R (NSW) 1920 NZ 2
Farr-Jones, N C (NSW) 1984 E, I, W, S, 1985 C 1,2, NZ, Fj 1,2, 1986 It, F, Arg 1,2, NZ 1,2,3, 1987 SK, [E, I, F, W (R)], NZ, Arg 2, 1988 E 1,2, NZ 1,2,3, E, S, It, 1989 BI 1,2,3, NZ, F 1,2, 1990 F 1,2,3, US, NZ 1,2,3, 1991 W, E, NZ 1,2, [Arg, WS, I, NZ, E], 1992 S 1,2, NZ 1,2,3, SA, 1993 NZ, SA 1,2,3
Fava, S G (ACT, WF) 2005 E(R),I(R), 2006 NZ1(R),SA1,NZ2
Fay, G (NSW) 1971 SA 2, 1972 NZ 1,2,3, 1973 Tg 1,2, W, E, 1974 NZ 1,2,3, 1975 E 1,2, J 1, S, W, 1976 I, US, 1978 W 1,2, NZ 1,2,3, 1979 I 1
Fenwicke, P T (NSW) 1957 NZ 1, 1958 W, I, E, 1959 BI 1,2
Ferguson, R T (NSW) 1922 M 3, NZ 1, 1923 M 3, NZ 3
Fihelly, J A (Q) 1907 NZ 2
Finau, S F (NSW) 1997 NZ 3
Finegan, O D A (ACT) 1996 W 1,2, C, NZ 1, SA 1(t), S, W 3, 1997 SA 1, NZ 3, SA 2, Arg 1,2, E 2, S, 1998 E 1(R), S 1(t + R),2(t + R), NZ 1(R), SA 1(t),2(R), NZ 3(R), Fj (R), Tg, WS (t + R), F (R), E 2(R), 1999 NZ 2(R), [R, I 3(R), US, W (R), SA 3(R), F (R)], 2001 BI 1,2,3, SA 1, NZ 1, SA 2, NZ 2, Sp, E, F, W, 2002 F 1,2, NZ 1, SA 1, NZ 2, SA 2, I, 2003 SA 1(t&R), NZ 1(R), SA 2(R), NZ 2(R)
Finlay, A N (NSW) 1926 NZ 1,2,3, 1927 I, W, S, 1928 E, F, 1929 NZ 1,2,3, 1930 BI
Finley, F G (NSW) 1904 BI 3
Finnane, S C (NSW) 1975 E 1, J 1,2, 1976 E, 1978 W 1,2
Fitter, D E S (ACT) 2005 I,W
FitzSimons, P (NSW) 1989 F 1,2, 1990 F 1,2,3, US, NZ 1
Flanagan, P (Q) 1907 NZ 1,2
Flatley, E J (Q) 1997 E 2, S, 2000 S (R), 2001 BI 1(R),2(R),3, SA 1, NZ 1(R),2(R), Sp (R), F (R), W, 2002 F 1(R),2(R), NZ 1(t+R), SA 1(R), NZ 2(t), Arg (R), I (R), E, It, 2003 I, W, SA 1, NZ 1, SA 2, NZ 2, [Arg,R,I,S,NZ,E], 2004 S3(R),F(R),S4(R),E2, 2005 NZ1(R)
Flett, J A (NSW) 1990 US, NZ 2,3, 1991 [WS]
Flynn, J P (Q) 1914 NZ 1,2
Fogarty, J R (Q) 1949 M 2,3
Foley, M A (Q) 1995 [C (R), R], 1996 W 2(R), NZ 1, SA 1, NZ 2, SA 2, It, S, I, W 3, 1997 NZ 1(R), E 1, NZ 2, SA 1, NZ 3, SA 2, Arg 1,2, E 2, S, 1998 Tg (R), F (R), E 2(R), 1999 NZ 2(R), [US, W, SA 3, F], 2000 Arg 1,2, SA 1, NZ 1, SA 2, NZ 2, SA 3, F, S, E, 2001 BI 1(R),2,3, SA 1, NZ 1, SA 2, NZ 2, Sp, E, F, W
Foote, R H (NSW) 1924 NZ 2,3, 1926 NZ 2
Forbes, C F (Q) 1953 SA 2,3,4, 1954 Fj 1, 1956 SA 1,2
Ford, B (Q) 1957 NZ 2
Ford, E E (NSW) 1927 I, W, S, 1928 E, F, 1929 NZ 1,3
Ford, J A (NSW) 1925 NZ 4, 1926 NZ 1,2, 1927 I, W, S, 1928 E, 1929 NZ 1,2,3, 1930 BI
Forman, T R (NSW) 1968 I, S, 1969 W, SA 1,2,3,4
Fowles, D G (NSW) 1921 SA 1,2,3, 1922 M 2,3, 1923 M 2,3
Fox, C L (NSW) 1920 NZ 1,2,3, 1921 SA 1, NZ, 1922 M 1,2, NZ 1, 1924 NZ 1,2,3, 1925 NZ 1,2,3, 1926 NZ 1,3, 1928 F
Fox, O G (NSW) 1958 F
Francis, E (Q) 1914 NZ 1,2
Frawley, D (Q, NSW) 1986 Arg 2(R), 1987 Arg 1,2, 1988 E 1,2, NZ 1,2,3, S, It
Freedman, J E (NSW) 1962 NZ 3,4,5, 1963 SA 1
Freeman, E (NSW) 1946 NZ 1(R), M
Freier, A L (NSW) 2002 Arg (R), I, E (R), It, 2003 SA 1(R), NZ 1(t), 2005 NZ2(R), 2006 E2, 2007 W1(R),2(R),Fj,SA1(R), NZ1(R),SA2,NZ2(R), [J(R),W(R),Fj(R),C,E(R)]
Freney, M E (Q) 1972 NZ 1,2,3, 1973 Tg 1, W, E (R)
Friend, W S (NSW) 1920 NZ 3, 1921 SA 1,2,3, 1922 NZ 1,2,3, 1923 M 1,2,3
Furness, D C (NSW) 1946 M
Futter, F C (NSW) 1904 BI 3

Gardner, J M (Q) 1987 Arg 2, 1988 E 1, NZ 1, E
Gardner, W C (NSW) 1950 BI 1
Garner, R L (NSW) 1949 NZ 1,2
Gavin, K A (NSW) 1909 E
Gavin, T B (NSW) 1988 NZ 2,3, S, It (R), 1989 NZ (R), F 1,2, 1990 F 1,2,3, US, NZ 1,2,3, 1991 W, E, NZ 1, 1992 S 1,2, SA, I, W, 1993 Tg, NZ, SA 1,2,3, C, F 1,2, 1994 I 1,2, It 1,2, WS, NZ, 1995 Arg 1,2, [SA, C, R, E], NZ 1,2, 1996 NZ 2(R), SA 2, W 3
Gelling, A M (NSW) 1972 NZ 1, Fj
George, H W (NSW) 1910 NZ 1,2,3, 1912 US, 1913 NZ 1,3, 1914 NZ 1,3
George, W G (NSW) 1923 M 1,3, NZ 1,2, 1924 NZ 3, 1925 NZ 2,3, 1926 NZ 4, 1928 NZ 1,2,3, M
Gerrard, M A (ACT) 2005 It(R),SA1(R),NZ1,2,E,I,W, 2006 E1,2,I1, NZ1,SA1,NZ2,SA2,NZ3(t),SA3(R),I2,S, 2007 W1,2(R),SA2,NZ2, [J(R)]
Gibbons, E de C (NSW) 1936 NZ 1,2, M
Gibbs, P R (V) 1966 S
Giffin, D T (ACT) 1996 W 3, 1997 F 1,2, 1999 I 1,2, E, SA 1, NZ 1, SA 2, NZ 2, [R, I 3, US (R), W, SA 3, F], 2000 Arg 1,2, SA 1, NZ 1, SA 2, NZ 2, SA 3, F, S, E, 2001 BI 1,2, SA 1, NZ 2, Sp, E, F, W, 2002 Arg (R), I, E (R), It (R), 2003 I, W, E, SA 1, NZ 1, SA 2, NZ 2, [Arg,Nm(R),I,NZ(t&R),E(R)]
Gilbert, H (NSW) 1910 NZ 1,2,3

Girvan, B (ACT) 1988 E
Giteau, M J (ACT, WF) 2002 E (R), It (R), 2003 SA 2(R), NZ 2(R), [Arg(R),R(R),Nm,I(R),S(R),E(t)], 2004 S1,E1,PI,NZ1,SA1,NZ2, SA2,S3,F,S4,E2, 2005 Sm,It,F1,SA1,2,3,NZ1,SA4,F2,E(t&R), 2006 NZ1(R),SA1,NZ2,SA2,NZ3,SA3,W,It,I2,S, 2007 W1,2, SA1,NZ1,SA2,NZ2, [J,W,Fj,E]
Gordon, G C (NSW) 1929 NZ 1
Gordon, K M (NSW) 1950 BI 1,2
Gould, R G (Q) 1980 NZ 1,2,3, 1981 I, W, S, 1982 S 2, NZ 1,2,3, 1983 US, Arg 1, F 1,2, 1984 NZ 1,2,3, E, I, W, S, 1985 NZ, 1986 It, 1987 SK, [E]
Gourley, S R (NSW) 1988 S, It, 1989 BI 1,2,3
Graham, C S (Q) 1899 BI 2
Graham, R (NSW) 1973 Tg 1,2, W, E, 1974 NZ 2,3, 1975 E 2, J 1,2, S, W, 1976 I, US, Fj 1,2,3, F 1,2
Gralton, A S I (Q) 1899 BI 1,4, 1903 NZ
Grant, J C (NSW) 1988 E 1, NZ 2,3, E
Graves, R H (NSW) 1907 NZ 1(R)
Greatorex, E N (NSW) 1923 M 3, NZ 3, 1924 NZ 1,2,3, 1925 NZ 1, 1928 E, F
Gregan, G M (ACT) 1994 It 1,2, WS, NZ, 1995 Arg 1,2, [SA, C (R), R, E], 1996 W 1, C (t), SA 1, NZ 2, SA 2, It, I, W 3, 1997 F 1,2, NZ 1, E 1, NZ 2, SA 1, NZ 3, SA 2, Arg 1,2, E 2, S, 1998 E 1, S 1,2, NZ 1, SA 1, NZ 2, SA 2, NZ 3, Fj, WS, F, E 2, 1999 I 1,2, E, SA 1, NZ 1, SA 2, NZ 2, [R, I 3, W, SA 3, F], 2000 Arg 1,2, SA 1, NZ 1, SA 2, NZ 2, SA 3, 2001 BI 1,2,3, SA 1, NZ 1, SA 2, NZ 2, Sp, E, F, W, 2002 F 1,2, NZ 1, SA 1, NZ 2, SA 2, Arg, I, E, It, 2003 I, W, E, SA 1, NZ 1, SA 2, NZ 2, [Arg,R,I,S,NZ,E], 2004 S1,2,E1,PI,SA1,NZ2,SA2, S3,F,S4,E2, 2005 It,F1,SA1,2,3,NZ1,SA4,NZ2,F2,E,I,W, 2006 E1,2(R),I1,NZ1,SA1,NZ2,SA2,NZ3,SA3, 2007 W1(R),2(R),Fj, SA1,NZ1,SA2,NZ2, [J,W,Fj,C(R),E]
Gregory, S C (Q) 1968 NZ 3, F, I, S, 1969 SA 1,3, 1971 SA 1,3, F 1,2, 1972 F 1,2, 1973 Tg 1,2, W, E
Grey, G O (NSW) 1972 F 2(R), NZ 1,2,3, Fj (R)
Grey, N P (NSW) 1998 S 2(R), SA 2(R), Fj (R), Tg (R), F, E 2, 1999 I 1(R),2(R), E, SA 1, NZ 1, SA 2, NZ 2(t&R), [R (R), I 3(R), US, SA 3(R), F (R)], 2000 S (R), E (R), 2001 BI 1,2,3, SA 1, NZ 1, SA 2, NZ 2, Sp, E, F, 2003 I (R), W (R), E, [Nm,NZ(t)]
Griffin, T S (NSW) 1907 NZ 1,3, 1908 W, 1910 NZ 1,2, 1912 US
Grigg, P C (Q) 1980 NZ 3, 1982 S 2, NZ 1,2,3, 1983 Arg 2, NZ, 1984 Fj, W, S, 1985 C 1,2, NZ, Fj 1,2, 1986 Arg 1,2, NZ 1,2, 1987 SK, [E, J, I, F, W]
Grimmond, D N (NSW) 1964 NZ 2
Gudsell, K E (NSW) 1951 NZ 1,2,3
Guerassimoff, J (Q) 1963 SA 2,3,4, 1964 NZ 1,2,3, 1965 SA 2, 1966 BI 1,2, 1967 E, I, F
Gunther, W J (NSW) 1957 NZ 2

Hall, D (Q) 1980 Fj, NZ 1,2,3, 1981 F 1,2, 1982 S 1,2, NZ 1,2, 1983 US, Arg 1,2, NZ, It
Hamalainen, H A (Q) 1929 NZ 1,2,3
Hamilton, B G (NSW) 1946 M
Hammand, C A (NSW) 1908 W, 1909 E
Hammon, J D C (V) 1937 SA 2
Handy, C B (Q) 1978 NZ 3, 1979 NZ, Arg 1,2, 1980 NZ 1,2
Hanley, R G (Q) 1983 US (R), It (R), 1985 Fj 2(R)
Hardcastle, P A (NSW) 1946 NZ 1, M, NZ 2, 1947 NZ 1, 1949 M 3
Hardcastle, W R (NSW) 1899 BI 4, 1903 NZ
Harding, M A (NSW) 1983 It
Hardman, S P (Q) 2002 F 2(R), 2006 SA1(R), 2007 SA2(t&R), [C(R)]
Hardy, M D (ACT) 1997 F 1(t), 2(R), NZ 1(R), 3(R), Arg 1(R), 2(R), 1998 Tg, WS
Harrison, J B (ACT, NSW) 2001 BI 3, NZ 1, SA 2, Sp, E, F, W (R), 2002 F 1,2, NZ 1, SA 1, NZ 2, SA 2, Arg, I (R), E, It, 2003 [R(R),Nm,S,NZ,E], 2004 S1,2,E1,PI,NZ1,SA1,NZ2,SA2,S3, F,S4,E2
Harry, R L L (NSW) 1996 W 1,2, NZ 1, SA 1(t), NZ 2, It, S, 1997 F 1,2, NZ 1,2, SA 1, NZ 3, SA 2, Arg 1,2, E 2, S, 1998 E 1, S 1,2, NZ 1, Fj, 1999 SA 2, NZ 2, [R, I 3, W, SA 3, F], 2000 Arg 1,2, SA 1, NZ 1, SA 2, NZ 2, SA 3
Hartill, M N (NSW) 1986 NZ 1,2,3, 1987 SK, [J], Arg 1, 1988 NZ 1,2, E, It, 1989 BI 1(R), 2,3, F 1,2, 1995 Arg 1(R), 2(R), [C], NZ 1,2
Harvey, P B (Q) 1949 M 1,2
Harvey, R M (NSW) 1958 F, M 3
Hatherell, W I (Q) 1952 Fj 1,2
Hauser, R G (Q) 1975 J 1(R), 2, W (R), 1976 E, I, US, Fj 1,2,3, F 1,2, 1978 W 1,2, 1979 I 1,2
Hawker, M J (NSW) 1980 Fj, NZ 1,2,3, 1981 F 1,2, I, W, 1982 E, S 1,2, NZ 1,2,3, 1983 US, Arg 1,2, NZ, It, F 1,2, 1984 NZ 1,2,3, 1987 NZ
Hawthorne, P F (NSW) 1962 NZ 3,4,5, 1963 E, SA 1,2,3,4, 1964 NZ 1,2,3, 1965 SA 1,2, 1966 BI 1,2, W, 1967 E, I 1, F, I 2, NZ
Hayes, E S (Q) 1934 NZ 1,2, 1938 NZ 1,2,3
Heath, A (NSW) 1996 C, SA 1, NZ 2, SA 2, It, 1997 NZ 2, SA 1, E 2(R)
Heenan, D P (Q, ACT) 2003 W, 2006 E1
Heinrich, E L (NSW) 1961 Fj 1,2,3, SA 2, F, 1962 NZ 1,2,3, 1963 E, SA 1
Heinrich, V W (NSW) 1954 Fj 1,2
Heming, R J (NSW) 1961 Fj 2,3, SA 1,2, F, 1962 NZ 2,3,4,5, 1963 SA 2,3,4, 1964 NZ 1,2,3, 1965 SA 1,2, 1966 BI 1,2, W, 1967 F
Hemingway, W H (NSW) 1928 NZ 2,3, 1931 M, NZ, 1932 NZ 3
Henderson, N J (ACT) 2004 PI(R), 2005 Sm(R), 2006 It(R)
Henjak, M T (ACT) 2004 E1(R),NZ1(R), 2005 Sm(R),I(R)
Henry, A R (Q) 1899 BI 2
Herbert, A G (Q) 1987 SK (R), [F (R)], 1990 F 1(R), US, NZ 2,3, 1991 [WS], 1992 NZ 3(R), 1993 NZ (R), SA 2(R)
Herbert, D J (Q) 1994 I 2, It 1,2, WS (R), 1995 Arg 1,2, [SA, R], 1996 C, SA 2, It, S, I, 1997 NZ 1, 1998 E 1, S 1,2, NZ 1, SA 1, NZ 2, SA 2, Fj, Tg, WS, F, E 2, 1999 I 1,2, E, SA 1, NZ 1, SA 2, NZ 2, [R, I 3, W, SA 3, F], 2000 Arg 1,2, SA 1, NZ 1, SA 2, NZ 2, SA 3, F, S, E, 2001 BI 1,2,3, SA 1, NZ 1, SA 2, NZ 2, Sp, E, 2002 F 1,2, NZ 1, SA 1, NZ 2, SA 2, Arg, I, E, It
Herd, H V (NSW) 1931 M
Hickey, J (NSW) 1908 W, 1909 E
Hill, J (NSW) 1925 NZ 1
Hillhouse, D W (Q) 1975 S, 1976 E, Fj 1,2,3, F 1,2, 1978 W 1,2, 1983 US, Arg 1,2, NZ, It, F 1,2
Hills, E F (V) 1950 BI 1,2
Hindmarsh, J A (Q) 1904 BI 1
Hindmarsh, J C (NSW) 1975 J 2, S, W, 1976 US, Fj 1,2,3, F 1,2
Hipwell, J N B (NSW) 1968 NZ 1(R), 2, F, I, S, 1969 W, SA 1,2,3,4, 1970 S, 1971 SA 1,2, F 1,2, 1972 F 1,2, 1973 Tg 1, W, E, 1974 NZ 1,2,3, 1975 E 1,2, J 1, S, W, 1978 NZ 1,2,3, 1981 F 1,2, I, W, 1982 E
Hirschberg, W A (NSW) 1905 NZ
Hodgins, C H (NSW) 1910 NZ 1,2,3
Hodgson, A J (NSW) 1933 SA 2,3,4, 1934 NZ 1, 1936 NZ 1,2, M, 1937 SA 2, 1938 NZ 1,2,3
Hoiles, S A (NSW, ACT) 2004 S4(R),E2(R), 2006 W(R), 2007 W1(R),2(R),Fj(R),SA1(R),NZ1(R),SA2,NZ2, [J(R),W(R),Fj(R),C(R),E(R)] 2006 W(R), 2007 W1(R),2(R), Fj(R),SA1(R),NZ1(R),SA2,NZ2, [J(R),W(R),Fj(R),C(R),E(R)]
Holbeck, J C (ACT) 1997 NZ 1(R), E 1, NZ 2, SA 1, NZ 3, SA 2, 2001 BI 3(R)
Holdsworth, J W (NSW) 1921 SA 1,2,3, 1922 M 2,3, NZ 1(R)
Holmes, G S (Q) 2005 F2(R),E(t&R),I, 2006 E1,2,I1,NZ1, SA1,NZ2,SA2,NZ3, 2007 [Fj(R),C]
Holt, N C (Q) 1984 Fj
Honan, B D (Q) 1968 NZ 1(R), 2, F, I, S, 1969 SA 1,2,3,4
Honan, R E (Q) 1964 NZ 1,2
Horan, T J (Q) 1989 NZ, F 1,2, 1990 F 1, NZ 1,2,3, 1991 W, E, NZ 1,2, [Arg, WS, W, I, NZ, E], 1992 S 1,2, NZ 1,2,3, SA, I, W, 1993 Tg, NZ, SA 1,2,3, C, F 1,2, 1995 [C, R, E], NZ 1,2, 1996 W 1,2, C, NZ 1, SA 1, It, S, I, W 3, 1997 F 1,2, NZ 1, E 1, NZ 2, Arg 1,2, E 2, S, 1998 E 1, S 1,2, NZ 1, SA 1, NZ 2, SA 2, NZ 3, Fj, Tg, WS, 1999 I 1,2, E, SA 1, NZ 1, SA 2, NZ 2, [R, I 3, W, SA 3, F], 2000 Arg 1
Horodam, D J (Q) 1913 NZ 2
Horsley, G R (Q) 1954 Fj 2
Horton, P A (NSW) 1974 NZ 1,2,3, 1975 E 1,2, J 1,2, S, W, 1976 E, F 1,2, 1978 W 1,2, NZ 1,2,3, 1979 NZ, Arg 1
Horwill, J E (Q) 2007 Fj
Hoskins, J E (NSW) 1924 NZ 1,2,3
How, R A (NSW) 1967 I 2
Howard, J (Q) 1938 NZ 1,2
Howard, J L (NSW) 1970 S, 1971 SA 1, 1972 F 1(R), NZ 2, 1973 Tg 1,2, W
Howard, P W (Q, ACT) 1993 NZ, 1994 WS, NZ, 1995 NZ 1(R), 2(t), 1996 W 1,2, SA 1, NZ 2, SA 2, It, S, W 3, 1997 F 1,2, NZ 1, Arg 1,2, E 2, S
Howell, M L (NSW) 1946 NZ 1(R), 1947 NZ 1, S, I, W
Hughes, B D (NSW) 1913 NZ 2,3
Hughes, J C (NSW) 1907 NZ 1,3
Hughes, N McL (NSW) 1953 SA 1,2,3,4, 1955 NZ 1,2,3, 1956

SA 1,2, 1958 W, I, E, S, F
Humphreys, O W (NSW) 1920 NZ 3, 1921 NZ, 1922 M 1,2,3, 1925 NZ 1
Hutchinson, E E (NSW) 1937 SA 1,2
Hutchinson, F E (NSW) 1936 NZ 1,2, 1938 NZ 1,3
Huxley, J L (ACT) 2007 W1,2,Fj,SA1,NZ1,SA2, [W(R),Fj(R),C]

Ide, W P J (Q) 1938 NZ 2,3
Ioane, D N (WF) 2007 W2
Ives, W N (NSW) 1926 NZ 1,2,3,4, 1929 NZ 3

James, P M (Q) 1958 M 2,3
James, S L (NSW) 1987 SK (R), [E (R)], NZ, Arg 1,2, 1988 NZ 2(R)
Jamieson, A E (NSW) 1925 NZ 3(R)
Jaques, T (ACT) 2000 SA 1(R), NZ 1(R)
Jessep, E M (V) 1934 NZ 1,2
Johansson, L D T (Q) 2005 NZ2(R),F2(R),E(R)
Johnson, A P (NSW) 1946 NZ 1, M
Johnson, B B (NSW) 1952 Fj 1,2, NZ 1,2, 1953 SA 2,3,4, 1955 NZ 1,2
Johnson, P G (NSW) 1959 BI 1,2, 1961 Fj 1,2,3, SA 1,2, F, 1962 NZ 1,2,3,4,5, 1963 E, SA 1,2,3,4, 1964 NZ 1,2,3, 1965 SA 1,2, 1966 BI 1,2, W, S, 1967 E, I 1, F, I 2, NZ, 1968 NZ 1,2, F, I, S, 1970 S, 1971 SA 1,2, F 1,2
Johnstone, B (Q) 1993 Tg (R)
Jones, G G (Q) 1952 Fj 1,2, 1953 SA 1,2,3,4, 1954 Fj 1,2, 1955 NZ 1,2,3, 1956 SA 1
Jones, H (NSW) 1913 NZ 1,2,3
Jones, P A (NSW) 1963 E, SA 1
Jorgensen, P (NSW) 1992 S 1(R), 2(R)
Joyce, J E (NSW) 1903 NZ
Judd, H A (NSW) 1903 NZ, 1904 BI 1,2,3, 1905 NZ
Judd, P B (NSW) 1925 NZ 4, 1926 NZ 1,2,3,4, 1927 I, W, S, 1928 E, 1931 M, NZ
Junee, D K (NSW) 1989 F 1(R), 2(R), 1994 WS (R), NZ (R)

Kafer, R B (ACT) 1999 NZ 2, [R, US (R)], 2000 Arg 1(R),2, SA 1, NZ 1(t&R), SA 2(R),3(R), F, S, E
Kahl, P R (Q) 1992 W
Kanaar, A (NSW) 2005 NZ2(R)
Kassulke, N (Q) 1985 C 1,2
Kay, A R (V) 1958 NZ 2, 1959 BI 2
Kay, P (NSW) 1988 E 2
Kearney, K H (NSW) 1947 NZ 1,2, S, I, W, 1948 E, F
Kearns, P N (NSW) 1989 NZ, F 1,2, 1990 F 1,2,3, US, NZ 1,2,3, 1991 W, E, NZ 1,2, [Arg, WS, W, I, NZ, E], 1992 S 1,2, NZ 1,2,3, SA, I, W, 1993 Tg, NZ, SA 1,2,3, C, F 1,2, 1994 I 1,2, It 1,2, WS, NZ, 1995 Arg 1,2, [SA, C, E], NZ 1,2, 1998 E 1, S 1,2, NZ 1, SA 1, NZ 2, SA 2, NZ 3, Fj, WS, F, E 2, 1999 I 2(R), SA 1(R),2, NZ 2, [R, I 3]
Kefu, R S T (Q) 1997 SA 2(R), 1998 E 1, S 1,2, NZ 1, SA 1, NZ 2, SA 2, NZ 3, Fj (R), Tg, WS (R), F, E 2, 1999 I 1,2, E, SA 1, NZ 1(R), SA 2, NZ 2, [R, I 3, SA 3, F], 2000 SA 1(t&R), NZ 1(R), SA 2(R), NZ 2, SA 3(R), F, S, E, 2001 BI 1,2,3, SA 1, NZ 1, SA 2, NZ 2, Sp, E, F, W, 2002 F 1, NZ 1, SA 1, NZ 2, SA 2, Arg, I, E, It, 2003 I, W, E, SA 1, NZ 1, SA 2, NZ 2
Kefu, S (Q) 2001 W (R), 2003 I, W, E, SA 1, NZ 1(R)
Kelaher, J D (NSW) 1933 SA 1,2,3,4,5, 1934 NZ 1,2, 1936 NZ 1,2, M, 1937 SA 1,2, 1938 NZ 3
Kelaher, T P (NSW) 1992 NZ 1, I (R), 1993 NZ
Kelleher, R J (Q) 1969 SA 2,3
Keller, D H (NSW) 1947 NZ 1, S, I, W, 1948 E, F
Kelly, A J (NSW) 1899 BI 1
Kelly, R L F (NSW) 1936 NZ 1,2, M, 1937 SA 1,2, 1938 NZ 1,2
Kent, A (Q) 1912 US
Kerr, F R (V) 1938 NZ 1
King, S C (NSW) 1926 NZ 1,2,3,4(R), 1927 W, S, 1928 E, F, 1929 NZ 1,2,3, 1930 BI, 1932 NZ 1,2
Knight, M (NSW) 1978 W 1,2, NZ 1
Knight, S O (NSW) 1969 SA 2,4, 1970 S, 1971 SA 1,2,3
Knox, D J (NSW, ACT) 1985 Fj 1,2, 1990 US (R), 1994 WS, NZ, 1996 It, S, I, 1997 SA 1, NZ 3, SA 2, Arg 1,2
Kraefft, D F (NSW) 1947 NZ 2, S, I, W, 1948 E, F
Kreutzer, S D (Q) 1914 NZ 2

Lamb, J S (NSW) 1928 NZ 1,2, M
Lambie, J K (NSW) 1974 NZ 1,2,3, 1975 W
Lane, R E (NSW) 1921 SA 1
Lane, T A (Q) 1985 C 1,2, NZ
Lang, C W P (V) 1938 NZ 2,3
Langford, J F (ACT) 1997 NZ 3, SA 2, E 2, S
Larkham, S J (ACT) 1996 W 2(R), 1997 F 1,2, NZ 1,2(R), SA 1, NZ 3, SA 2, Arg 1,2, E 2, S, 1998 E 1, S 1,2, NZ 1, SA 1, NZ 2, SA 2, NZ 3, Fj, Tg (t), WS, F, E 2, 1999 [I 3, US, W, SA 3, F], 2000 Arg 1,2, SA 1, NZ 1, SA 2, NZ 2, SA 3, 2001 BI 1,2, NZ 1, SA 2, NZ 2, Sp, E, F, W, 2002 F 1,2, NZ 1, SA 1, NZ 2, SA 2, Arg, I, E, 2003 SA 1(R), NZ 1, SA 2, NZ 2,[Arg,R,I,S,NZ,E], 2004S1,2,E1,PI,NZ1,SA1,NZ2,SA2,S3,F,S4, 2005 Sm(R),It,F1,SA1,2,3, 2006 E1,2,I1,NZ1,SA1,NZ2, SA2,NZ3,SA3,W,It,I2,S, 2007 W2,Fj,SA1,NZ1,SA2,NZ2, [J]
Larkin, E R (NSW) 1903 NZ
Larkin, K K (Q) 1958 M 2,3
Latham, C E (Q) 1998 F, E 2, 1999 I 1,2, E, [US], 2000 Arg 1,2, SA 1, NZ 1, SA 2, NZ 2, SA 3, F, S, E, 2001 BI 1,2(R), SA 1(R), NZ 1(R), SA 2, NZ 2, Sp, E, F, W (R), 2002 F 1,2, NZ 1, SA 1, NZ 2, SA 2, 2003 I, W, E, NZ 1(R), SA 2, NZ 2,[Nm], 2004 S1(R),2(R),E1(R),PI(t&R),NZ1,SA1,NZ2,SA2,S3,F,S4,E2, 2005 Sm,F1,SA2,3,F2,E,I,W, 2006 E1,2,I1,NZ1,SA1,NZ2, SA2,NZ3,SA3,W,It,I2,S, 2007 NZ2(R), [J,W,Fj,C,E]
Latimer, N B (NSW) 1957 NZ 2
Lawton, R (Q) 1988 E 1, NZ 2(R), 3, S
Lawton, T (NSW, Q) 1920 NZ 1,2, 1925 NZ 4, 1927 I, W, S, 1928 E, F, 1929 NZ 1,2,3, 1930 BI, 1932 NZ 1,2
Lawton, T A (Q) 1983 F 1(R), 2, 1984 Fj, NZ 1,2,3, E, I, W, S, 1985 C 1,2, NZ, Fj 1, 1986 It, F, Arg 1,2, NZ 1,2,3, 1987 SK, [E, US, I, F, W], NZ, Arg 1,2, 1988 E 1,2, NZ 1,2,3, E, S, It, 1989 BI 1,2,3
Laycock, W M B (NSW) 1925 NZ 2,3,4, 1926 NZ 2
Leeds, A J (NSW) 1986 NZ 3, 1987 [US, W], NZ, Arg 1,2, 1988 E 1,2, NZ 1,2,3, E, S, It
Lenehan, J K (NSW) 1958 W, E, S, F, M 1,2,3, 1959 BI 1,2, 1961 SA 1,2, F, 1962 NZ 2,3,4,5, 1965 SA 1,2, 1966 W, S, 1967 E, I 1, F, I 2
L'Estrange, R D (Q) 1971 F 1,2, 1972 NZ 1,2,3, 1973 Tg 1,2, W, E, 1974 NZ 1,2,3, 1975 S, W, 1976 I, US
Lewis, L S (Q) 1934 NZ 1,2, 1936 NZ 2, 1938 NZ 1
Lidbury, S (NSW) 1987 Arg 1, 1988 E 2
Lillicrap, C P (Q) 1985 Fj 2, 1987 [US, I, F, W], 1989 BI 1, 1991 [WS]
Lindsay, R T G (Q) 1932 NZ 3
Lisle, R J (NSW) 1961 Fj 1,2,3, SA 1
Little, J S (Q, NSW) 1989 F 1,2, 1990 F 1,2,3, US, 1991 W, E, NZ 1,2, [Arg, W, I, NZ, E], 1992 NZ 1,2,3, SA, I, W, 1993 Tg, NZ, SA 1,2,3, C, F 1,2, 1994 WS, NZ, 1995 Arg 1,2, [SA, C, E], NZ 1,2, 1996 It (R), I, W 3, 1997 F 1,2, E 1, NZ 2, SA 1, NZ 3, SA 2, 1998 E 1(R), S 2(R), NZ 2, SA 2(R), NZ 3, Fj, Tg, WS, F, E 2, 1999 I 1(R),2, SA 2(R), NZ 2, [R, I 3(t&R), US, W (R), SA 3(t&R), F (R)], 2000 Arg 1(R),2(R), SA 1(R), NZ 1, SA 2, NZ 2, SA 3
Livermore, A E (Q) 1946 NZ 1, M
Loane, M E (Q) 1973 Tg 1,2, 1974 NZ 1, 1975 E 1,2, J 1, 1976 E, I, Fj 1,2,3, F 1,2, 1978 W 1,2, 1979 I 1,2, NZ, Arg 1,2, 1981 F 1,2, I, W, S, 1982 E, S 1,2
Logan, D L (NSW) 1958 M 1
Loudon, D B (NSW) 1921 NZ, 1922 M 1,2,3
Loudon, R B (NSW) 1923 NZ 1(R), 2,3, 1928 NZ 1,2,3, M, 1929 NZ 2, 1933 SA 2,3,4,5, 1934 NZ 2
Love, E W (NSW) 1932 NZ 1,2,3
Lowth, D R (NSW) 1958 NZ 1
Lucas, B C (Q) 1905 NZ
Lucas, P W (NSW) 1982 NZ 1,2,3
Lutge, D (NSW) 1903 NZ, 1904 BI 1,2,3
Lynagh, M P (Q) 1984 Fj, E, I, W, S, 1985 C 1,2, NZ, 1986 It, F, Arg 1,2, NZ 1,2,3, 1987 [E, US, J, I, F, W], Arg 1,2, 1988 E 1,2, NZ 1,3(R), E, S, It, 1989 BI 1,2,3, NZ, F 1,2, 1990 F 1,2,3, US, NZ 1,2,3, 1991 W, E, NZ 1,2, [Arg, WS, W, I, NZ, E], 1992 S 1,2, NZ 1,2,3, SA, I, 1993 Tg, C, F 1,2, 1994 I 1,2, It 1, 1995 Arg 1,2, [SA, C, E]
Lyons, D J (NSW) 2000 Arg 1(t&R),2(R), 2001 BI 1(R), SA 1(R), 2002 F 1(R),2, NZ 1(R), SA 1(R), NZ 2(R), SA 2(t+R), 2003 I, W, E, SA 1, [Arg,R,Nm,I,S,NZ,E], 2004 S1,2,E1,PI,NZ1, SA1,NZ2,SA2,S3(R),F(R),S4,E2, 2005 Sm,It,F1,SA1,2,NZ1, SA4, 2006 S, 2007 Fj,SA2(R), [C]

McArthur, M (NSW) 1909 E
McBain, M I (Q) 1983 It, F 1, 1985 Fj 2, 1986 It (R), 1987 [J], 1988 E 2(R), 1989 BI 1(R)
MacBride, J W T (NSW) 1946 NZ 1, M, NZ 2, 1947 NZ 1,2, S, I, W, 1948 E, F
McCabe, A J M (NSW) 1909 E

McCall, R J (Q) 1989 F 1,2, 1990 F 1,2,3, US, NZ 1,2,3, 1991 W, E, NZ 1,2, [Arg, W, I, NZ, E], 1992 S 1,2, NZ 1,2,3, SA, I, W, 1993 Tg, NZ, SA 1,2,3, C, F 1,2, 1994 It 2, 1995 Arg 1,2, [SA, R, E]
McCarthy, F J C (Q) 1950 BI 1
McCowan, R H (Q) 1899 BI 1,2,4
McCue, P A (NSW) 1907 NZ 1,3, 1908 W, 1909 E
McDermott, L C (Q) 1962 NZ 1,2
McDonald, B S (NSW) 1969 SA 4, 1970 S
McDonald, J C (Q) 1938 NZ 2,3
Macdougall, D G (NSW) 1961 Fj 1, SA 1
Macdougall, S G (NSW, ACT) 1971 SA 3, 1973 E, 1974 NZ 1,2,3, 1975 E 1,2, 1976 E
McGhie, G H (Q) 1929 NZ 2,3, 1930 BI
McGill, A N (NSW) 1968 NZ 1,2, F, 1969 W, SA 1,2,3,4, 1970 S, 1971 SA 1,2,3, F 1,2, 1972 F 1,2, NZ 1,2,3, 1973 Tg 1,2
McIntyre, A J (Q) 1982 NZ 1,2,3, 1983 F 1,2, 1984 Fj, NZ 1,2,3, E, I, W, S, 1985 C 1,2, NZ, Fj 1,2, 1986 It, F, Arg 1,2, 1987 [E, US, I, F, W], NZ, Arg 2, 1988 E 1,2, NZ 1,2,3, E, S, It, 1989 NZ
McIsaac, T P (WF) 2006 E1,I1,NZ1,2(R),SA2,3(R),W,I2
McKay, G R (NSW) 1920 NZ 2, 1921 SA 2,3, 1922 M 1,2,3
MacKay, L J (NSW) 2005 NZ2(R)
McKenzie, E J A (NSW, ACT) 1990 F 1,2,3, US, NZ 1,2,3, 1991 W, E, NZ 1,2, [Arg, W, I, NZ, E], 1992 S 1,2, NZ 1,2,3, SA, I, W, 1993 Tg, NZ, SA 1,2,3, C, F 1,2, 1994 I 1,2, It 1,2, WS, NZ, 1995 Arg 1,2, [SA, C (R), R, E], NZ 2, 1996 W 1,2, 1997 F 1,2, NZ 1, E 1
McKid, W A (NSW) 1976 E, Fj 1, 1978 NZ 2,3, 1979 I 1,2
McKinnon, A (Q) 1904 BI 2
McKivat, C H (NSW) 1907 NZ 1,3, 1908 W, 1909 E
McLaren, S D (NSW) 1926 NZ 4
McLaughlin, R E M (NSW) 1936 NZ 1,2
McLean, A D (Q) 1933 SA 1,2,3,4,5, 1934 NZ 1,2, 1936 NZ 1,2, M
McLean, J D (Q) 1904 BI 2,3, 1905 NZ
McLean, J J (Q) 1971 SA 2,3, F 1,2, 1972 F 1,2, NZ 1,2,3, Fj, 1973 W, E, 1974 NZ 1
McLean, P E (Q) 1974 NZ 1,2,3, 1975 J 1,2, S, W, 1976 E, I, Fj 1,2,3, F 1,2, 1978 W 1,2, NZ 2, 1979 I 1,2, NZ, Arg 1,2, 1980 Fj, 1981 F 1,2, I, W, S, 1982 E, S 2
McLean, P W (Q) 1978 NZ 1,2,3, 1979 I 1,2, NZ, Arg 1,2, 1980 Fj (R), NZ 3, 1981 I, W, S, 1982 E, S 1,2
McLean, R A (NSW) 1971 SA 1,2,3, F 1,2
McLean, W M (Q) 1946 NZ 1, M, NZ 2, 1947 NZ 1,2
McMahon, M J (Q) 1913 NZ 1
McMaster, R E (Q) 1946 NZ 1, M, NZ 2, 1947 NZ 1,2, I, W
McMeniman, H J (Q) 2005 Sm(R),It(R),F2(R),E,I,W, 2007 SA2(R),NZ2(R), [J(R),Fj(R),C,E(t&R)]
MacMillan, D I (Q) 1950 BI 1,2
McMullen, K V (NSW) 1962 NZ 3,5, 1963 E, SA 1
McShane, J M S (NSW) 1937 SA 1,2
Mackay, G (NSW) 1926 NZ 4
Mackney, W A R (NSW) 1933 SA 1,5, 1934 NZ 1,2
Magrath, E (NSW) 1961 Fj 1, SA 2, F
Maguire, D J (Q) 1989 BI 1,2,3
Malcolm, S J (NSW) 1927 S, 1928 E, F, NZ 1,2, M, 1929 NZ 1,2,3, 1930 BI, 1931 NZ, 1932 NZ 1,2,3, 1933 SA 4,5, 1934 NZ 1,2
Malone, J H (NSW) 1936 NZ 1,2, M, 1937 SA 2
Malouf, B P (NSW) 1982 NZ 1
Mandible, E F (NSW) 1907 NZ 2,3, 1908 W
Manning, J (NSW) 1904 BI 2
Manning, R C S (Q) 1967 NZ
Mansfield, B W (NSW) 1975 J 2
Manu, D T (NSW) 1995 [R (t)], NZ 1,2, 1996 W 1,2(R), SA 1, NZ 2, It, S, I, 1997 F 1, NZ 1(t), E 1, NZ 2, SA 1
Marks, H (NSW) 1899 BI 1,2
Marks, R J P (Q) 1962 NZ 4,5, 1963 E, SA 2,3,4, 1964 NZ 1,2,3, 1965 SA 1,2, 1966 W, S, 1967 E, I 1, F, I 2
Marrott, R (NSW) 1920 NZ 1,3
Marrott, W J (NSW) 1922 NZ 2,3, 1923 M 1,2,3, NZ 1,2
Marshall, J S (NSW) 1949 M 1
Martin, G J (Q) 1989 BI 1,2,3, NZ, F 1,2, 1990 F 1,3(R), NZ 1
Martin, M C (NSW) 1980 Fj, NZ 1,2, 1981 F 1,2, W (R)
Massey-Westropp, M (NSW) 1914 NZ 3
Mathers, M J (NSW) 1980 Fj, NZ 2(R)
Maund, J W (NSW) 1903 NZ
Mayne, A V (NSW) 1920 NZ 1,2,3, 1922 M 1
Meadows, J E C (V, Q) 1974 NZ 1, 1975 S, W, 1976 I, US, Fj 1,3, F 1,2, 1978 NZ 1,2,3, 1979 I 1,2, 1981 I, S, 1982 E, NZ 2,3, 1983 US, Arg 2, NZ
Meadows, R W (NSW) 1958 M 1,2,3, NZ 1,2,3
Meagher, F W (NSW) 1923 NZ 3, 1924 NZ 3, 1925 NZ 4, 1926 NZ 1,2,3, 1927 I, W
Meibusch, J H (Q) 1904 BI 3
Meibusch, L S (Q) 1912 US
Melrose, T C (NSW) 1978 NZ 3, 1979 I 1,2, NZ, Arg 1,2
Merrick, S (NSW) 1995 NZ 1,2
Messenger, H H (NSW) 1907 NZ 2,3
Middleton, S A (NSW) 1909 E, 1910 NZ 1,2,3
Miller, A R (NSW) 1952 Fj 1,2, NZ 1,2, 1953 SA 1,2,3,4, 1954 Fj 1,2, 1955 NZ 1,2,3, 1956 SA 1,2, 1957 NZ 1,2, 1958 W, E, S, F, M 1,2,3, 1959 BI 1,2, 1961 Fj 1,2,3, SA 2, F, 1962 NZ 1,2, 1966 BI 1,2, W, S, 1967 I 1, F, I 2, NZ
Miller, J M (NSW) 1962 NZ 1, 1963 E, SA 1, 1966 W, S, 1967 E
Miller, J S (Q) 1986 NZ 2,3, 1987 SK, [US, I, F], NZ, Arg 1,2, 1988 E 1,2, NZ 2,3, E, S, It, 1989 BI 1,2,3, NZ, 1990 F 1,3, 1991 W, [WS, W, I]
Miller, S W J (NSW) 1899 BI 3
Mingey, N (NSW) 1920 NZ 3, 1921 SA 1,2,3, 1923 M 1, NZ 1,2
Mitchell, D A (Q, WF) 2005 SA1(R),2(R),3(R),NZ1,SA4, NZ2,F2(R),E,I,W, 2007 W1,2,Fj,SA1,2(R),NZ2, [J(R),W,Fj,C,E(R)]
Monaghan, L E (NSW) 1973 E, 1974 NZ 1,2,3, 1975 E 1,2, S, W, 1976 E, I, US, F 1, 1978 W 1,2, NZ 1, 1979 I 1,2
Monti, C I A (Q) 1938 NZ 2
Moon, B J (Q) 1978 NZ 2,3, 1979 I 1,2, NZ, Arg 1,2, 1980 Fj, NZ 1,2,3, 1981 F 1,2, I, W, S, 1982 E, S 1,2, 1983 US, Arg 1,2, NZ, It, F 1,2, 1984 Fj, NZ 1,2,3, E, 1986 It, F, Arg 1,2
Mooney, T P (Q) 1954 Fj 1,2
Moore, R C (ACT, NSW) 1999 [US], 2001 BI 2,3, SA 1, NZ 1, SA 2, NZ 2, Sp (R), E (R), F (R), W (R), 2002 F 1(R),2(R), SA 2(R)
Moore, S T (Q) 2005 Sm(R),It(R),F1(R),SA2(R),3(R),F2(t&R), 2006 It(t),I2(R),S, 2007 W1,2,Fj(R),SA1,NZ1,2, [J,W,Fj,E]
Moran, H M (NSW) 1908 W
Morgan, G (Q) 1992 NZ 1(R), 3(R), W, 1993 Tg, NZ, SA 1,2,3, C, F 1,2, 1994 I 1,2, It 1, WS, NZ, 1996 W 1,2, C, NZ 1, SA 1, NZ 2, 1997 E 1, NZ 2
Morrissey, C V (NSW) 1925 NZ 2,3,4, 1926 NZ 2,3
Morrissey, W (Q) 1914 NZ 2
Mortlock, S A (ACT) 2000 Arg 1,2, SA 1, NZ 1, SA 2, NZ 2, SA 3, F, S, E, 2002 F 1,2, NZ 1, SA 1, NZ 2, SA 2, Arg, I, E, It, 2003 [R(R),Nm,S,NZ,E], 2004 S2,E1,PI,NZ1,SA1,NZ2,SA2, S3,F,S4, 2005 Sm,It,F1,SA2,3(R),NZ1, 2006 E1,2,I1, NZ1,SA1,NZ2,SA2,NZ3,SA3,It,I2,S, 2007 W1,2,Fj(R),SA1, NZ1,SA2,NZ2, [J,W,E]
Morton, A R (NSW) 1957 NZ 1,2, 1958 F, M 1,2,3, NZ 1,2,3, 1959 BI 1,2
Mossop, R P (NSW) 1949 NZ 1,2, 1950 BI 1,2, 1951 NZ 1
Moutray, I E (NSW) 1963 SA 2
Mulligan, P J (NSW) 1925 NZ 1(R)
Munsie, A (NSW) 1928 NZ 2
Murdoch, A R (NSW) 1993 F 1, 1996 W 1
Murphy, P J (Q) 1910 NZ 1,2,3, 1913 NZ 1,2,3, 1914 NZ 1,2,3
Murphy, W (Q) 1912 US

Nasser, B P (Q) 1989 F 1,2, 1990 F 1,2,3, US, NZ 2, 1991 [WS]
Newman, E W (NSW) 1922 NZ 1
Nicholson, F C (Q) 1904 BI 3
Nicholson, F V (Q) 1903 NZ, 1904 BI 1
Niuqila, A S (NSW) 1988 S, It, 1989 BI 1
Noriega, E P (ACT, NSW) 1998 F, E 2, 1999 I 1,2, E, SA 1, NZ 1, SA 2(R), NZ 2(R), 2002 F 1,2, NZ 1, SA 1, NZ 2, Arg, I, E, It, 2003 I, W, E, SA 1, NZ 1, SA 2
Norton-Knight, S H (NSW) 2007 W1,Fj(R)
Nothling, O E (NSW) 1921 SA 1,2,3, NZ, 1922 M 1,2,3, NZ 1,2,3, 1923 M 1,2,3, NZ 1,2,3, 1924 NZ 1,2,3
Nucifora, D V (Q) 1991 [Arg (R)], 1993 C (R)

O'Brien, F W H (NSW) 1937 SA 2, 1938 NZ 3
O'Connor, J A (NSW) 1928 NZ 1,2,3, M
O'Connor, M (ACT) 1994 I 1
O'Connor, M D (ACT, Q) 1979 Arg 1,2, 1980 Fj, NZ 1,2,3, 1981 F 1,2, I, 1982 E, S 1,2
O'Donnell, C (NSW) 1913 NZ 1,2
O'Donnell, I C (NSW) 1899 BI 3,4
O'Donnell, J B (NSW) 1928 NZ 1,3, M
O'Donnell, J M (NSW) 1899 BI 4
O'Gorman, J F (NSW) 1961 Fj 1, SA 1,2, F, 1962 NZ 2, 1963 E, SA 1,2,3,4, 1965 SA 1,2, 1966 W, S, 1967 E, I 1, F, I 2
O'Neill, D J (Q) 1964 NZ 1,2

O'Neill, J M (Q) 1952 NZ 1,2, 1956 SA 1,2
Ofahengaue, V (NSW) 1990 NZ 1,2,3, 1991 W, E, NZ 1,2, [Arg, W, I, NZ, E], 1992 S 1,2, SA, I, W, 1994 WS, NZ, 1995 Arg 1,2(R), [SA, C, E], NZ 1,2, 1997 Arg 1(t + R), 2(R), E 2, S, 1998 E 1(R), S 1(R),2(R), NZ 1(R), SA 1(R), NZ 2(R), SA 2(R), NZ 3(R), Fj, WS, F (R)
Ormiston, I W L (NSW) 1920 NZ 1,2,3
Osborne, D H (V) 1975 E 1,2, J 1
Outterside, R (NSW) 1959 BI 1,2
Oxenham, A McE (Q) 1904 BI 2, 1907 NZ 2
Oxlade, A M (Q) 1904 BI 2,3, 1905 NZ, 1907 NZ 2
Oxlade, B D (Q) 1938 NZ 1,2,3

Palfreyman, J R L (NSW) 1929 NZ 1, 1930 BI, 1931 NZ, 1932 NZ 3
Palu, W L (NSW) 2006 E2(t&R),I1(R),SA2,NZ3,SA3,W,It,I2,S(R), 2007 W1,2,SA1,NZ1, [J,W,Fj,E]
Panoho, G M (Q) 1998 SA 2(R), NZ 3(R), Fj (R), Tg, WS (R), 1999 I 2, E, SA 1(R), NZ 1, 2000 Arg 1(R),2(R), SA 1(R), NZ 1(R), SA 2(R),3(R), F (R), S (R), E (R), 2001 BI 1, 2003 SA 2(R), NZ 2
Papworth, B (NSW) 1985 Fj 1,2, 1986 It, Arg 1,2, NZ 1,2,3, 1987 [E, US, J (R), I, F], NZ, Arg 1,2
Parker, A J (Q) 1983 Arg 1(R), 2, NZ
Parkinson, C E (Q) 1907 NZ 2
Pashley, J J (NSW) 1954 Fj 1,2, 1958 M 1,2,3
Paul, J A (ACT) 1998 S 1(R), NZ 1(R), SA 1(t), Fj (R), Tg, 1999 I 1,2, E, SA 1, NZ 1, [R (R), I 3(R), W (t), F (R)], 2000 Arg 1(R),2(R), SA 1(R), NZ 1(R), SA 2(R), NZ 2(R), SA 3(R), F (R), S (R), E (R), 2001 BI 1, 2002 F 1, NZ 1, SA 1, NZ 2, SA 2, Arg, E, 2003 I, W, E, SA 2(t&R), NZ2(R),[Arg(R),R(R),Nm, I(R),S(R),NZ(R),E(R)], 2004 S1(R),2(R),E1(R),PI(R),NZ1(t&R), SA1,NZ2(R),SA2(R),S3,F,S4,E2, 2005 Sm,It,F1,SA1,2,3, NZ1,2006 E1(R),2(R),I1(R),NZ1(R),SA1,NZ2,SA2(R),NZ3,SA3
Pauling, T P (NSW) 1936 NZ 1, 1937 SA 1
Payne, S J (NSW) 1996 W 2, C, NZ 1, S, 1997 F 1(t), NZ 2(R), Arg 2(t)
Pearse, G K (NSW) 1975 W (R), 1976 I, US, Fj 1,2,3, 1978 NZ 1,2,3
Penman, A P (NSW) 1905 NZ
Perrin, P D (Q) 1962 NZ 1
Perrin, T D (NSW) 1931 M, NZ
Phelps, R (NSW) 1955 NZ 2,3, 1956 SA 1,2, 1957 NZ 1,2, 1958 W, I, E, S, F, M 1, NZ 1,2,3, 1961 Fj 1,2,3, SA 1,2, F, 1962 NZ 1,2
Phipps, J A (NSW) 1953 SA 1,2,3,4, 1954 Fj 1,2, 1955 NZ 1,2,3, 1956 SA 1,2
Phipps, W J (NSW) 1928 NZ 2
Piggott, H R (NSW) 1922 M 3(R)
Pilecki, S J (Q) 1978 W 1,2, NZ 1,2, 1979 I 1,2, NZ, Arg 1,2, 1980 Fj, NZ 1,2, 1982 S 1,2, 1983 US, Arg 1,2, NZ
Pini, M (Q) 1994 I 1, It 2, WS, NZ, 1995 Arg 1,2, [SA, R (t)]
Piper, B J C (NSW) 1946 NZ 1, M, NZ 2, 1947 NZ 1, S, I, W, 1948 E, F, 1949 M, 1,2,3
Poidevin, S P (NSW) 1980 Fj, NZ 1,2,3, 1981 F 1,2, I, W, S, 1982 E, NZ 1,2,3, 1983 US, Arg 1,2, NZ, It, F 1,2, 1984 Fj, NZ 1,2,3, E, I, W, S, 1985 C 1,2, NZ, Fj 1,2, 1986 It, F, Arg 1,2, NZ 1,2,3, 1987 SK, [E, J, I, F, W], Arg 1, 1988 NZ 1,2,3, 1989 NZ, 1991 E, NZ 1,2, [Arg, W, I, NZ, E]
Polota-Nau, T (NSW) 2005 E(R),I(R), 2006 S(R)
Pope, A M (Q) 1968 NZ 2(R)
Potter, R T (Q) 1961 Fj 2
Potts, J M (NSW) 1957 NZ 1,2, 1958 W, I, 1959 BI 1
Prentice, C W (NSW) 1914 NZ 3
Prentice, W S (NSW) 1908 W, 1909 E, 1910 NZ 1,2,3, 1912 US
Price, R A (NSW) 1974 NZ 1,2,3, 1975 E 1,2, J 1,2, 1976 US
Primmer, C J (Q) 1951 NZ 1,3
Proctor, I J (NSW)) 1967 NZ
Prosser, R B (NSW) 1967 E, I 1,2, NZ, 1968 NZ 1,2, F, I, S, 1969 W, SA 1,2,3,4, 1971 SA 1,2,3, F 1,2, 1972 F 1,2, NZ 1,2,3, Fj
Pugh, G H (NSW) 1912 US
Purcell, M P (Q) 1966 W, S, 1967 I 2
Purkis, E M (NSW) 1958 S, M 1
Pym, J E (NSW) 1923 M 1

Rainbow, A E (NSW) 1925 NZ 1
Ramalli, C (NSW) 1938 NZ 2,3
Ramsay, K M (NSW) 1936 M, 1937 SA 1, 1938 NZ 1,3
Rankin, R (NSW) 1936 NZ 1,2, M, 1937 SA 1,2, 1938 NZ 1,2
Rathbone, C (ACT) 2004 S1,2(R),E1,PI,NZ1,SA1,NZ2,SA2, S3,F,S4, 2005 Sm,NZ1(R),SA4,NZ2, 2006E1(R),2(R),I1(R), SA1(R),NZ2(R),SA2(R),NZ3,SA3,W,It,I2
Rathie, D S (Q) 1972 F 1,2
Raymond, R L (NSW) 1920 NZ 1,2, 1921 SA 2,3, NZ, 1922 M 1,2,3, NZ 1,2,3, 1923 M 1,2
Redwood, C (Q) 1903 NZ, 1904 BI 1,2,3
Reid, E J (NSW) 1925 NZ 2,3,4
Reid, T W (NSW) 1961 Fj 1,2,3, SA 1, 1962 NZ 1
Reilly, N P (Q) 1968 NZ 1,2, F, I, S, 1969 W, SA 1,2,3,4
Reynolds, L J (NSW) 1910 NZ 2(R), 3
Reynolds, R J (NSW) 1984 Fj, NZ 1,2,3, 1985 Fj 1,2, 1986 Arg 1,2, NZ 1, 1987 [J]
Richards, E W (Q) 1904 BI 1,3, 1905 NZ, 1907 NZ 1(R), 2
Richards, G (NSW) 1978 NZ 2(R), 3, 1981 F 1
Richards, T J (Q) 1908 W, 1909 E, 1912 US
Richards, V S (NSW) 1936 NZ 1,2(R), M, 1937 SA 1, 1938 NZ 1
Richardson, G C (Q) 1971 SA 1,2,3, 1972 NZ 2,3, Fj, 1973 Tg 1,2, W
Rigney, W A (NSW) 1925 NZ 2,4, 1926 NZ 4
Riley, S A (NSW) 1903 NZ
Ritchie, E V (NSW) 1924 NZ 1,3, 1925 NZ 2,3
Roberts, B T (NSW) 1956 SA 2
Roberts, H F (Q) 1961 Fj 1,3, SA 2, F
Robertson, I J (NSW) 1975 J 1,2
Robinson, B A (NSW) 2006 SA3,I2(R),S, 2007 W1(R),2,Fj(R)
Robinson, B J (ACT) 1996 It (R), S (R), I (R), 1997 F 1,2, NZ 1, E 1, NZ 2, SA 1(R), NZ 3(R), SA 2(R), Arg 1,2, E 2, S, 1998 Tg
Roche, C (Q) 1982 S 1,2, NZ 1,2,3, 1983 US, Arg 1,2, NZ, It, F 1,2, 1984 Fj, NZ 1,2,3, I
Rodriguez, E E (NSW) 1984 Fj, NZ 1,2,3, E, I, W, S, 1985 C 1,2, NZ, Fj 1, 1986 It, F, Arg 1,2, NZ 1,2,3, 1987 SK, [E, J, W (R)], NZ, Arg 1,2
Roe, J A (Q) 2003 [Nm(R)], 2004 E1(R),SA1(R),NZ2(R), SA2(t&R),S3,F, 2005 Sm(R),It(R),F1(R),SA1(R),3,NZ1, SA4(t&R),NZ2(R),F2(R),E,I,W
Roebuck, M C (NSW) 1991 W, E, NZ 1,2, [Arg, WS, W, I, NZ, E], 1992 S 1,2, NZ 2,3, SA, I, W, 1993 Tg, SA 1,2,3, C, F 2
Roff, J W (ACT) 1995 [C, R], NZ 1,2, 1996 W 1,2, NZ 1, SA 1, NZ 2, SA 2(R), S, I, W 3, 1997 F 1,2, NZ 1, E 1, NZ 2, SA 1, NZ 3, SA 2, Arg 1,2, E 2, S, 1998 E 1, S 1,2, NZ 1, SA 1, NZ 2, SA 2, NZ 3, Fj, Tg, WS, F, E 2, 1999 I 1,2, E, SA 1, NZ 1, SA 2, NZ 2(R), [R (R), I 3, US (R), W, SA 3, F], 2000 Arg 1,2, SA 1, NZ 1, SA 2, NZ 2, SA 3, F, S, E, 2001 BI 1,2,3, SA 1, NZ 1, SA 2, NZ 2, Sp, E, F, W, 2003 I, W, E, SA 1, [Arg,R,I,S(R),NZ(t&R),E(R)], 2004 S1,2,E1,PI
Rogers, M S (NSW) 2002 F 1(R),2(R), NZ 1(R), SA 1(R), NZ 2(R), SA 2(t&R), Arg, 2003 E (R), SA 1, NZ 1, SA 2, NZ 2, [Arg,R,Nm,I,S,NZ,E],2004S3(R),F(R),S4(R),E2(R), 2005 Sm(R),It,F1(R),SA1,4,NZ2,F2,E,I,W, 2006 E1,2,I1,NZ1,SA1(R),NZ2(R),SA2(R),NZ3(R),W,It,I2(R),S(R)
Rose, H A (NSW), 1967 I 2, NZ, 1968 NZ 1,2, F, I, S, 1969 W, SA 1,2,3,4, 1970 S
Rosenblum, M E (NSW) 1928 NZ 1,2,3, M
Rosenblum, R G (NSW) 1969 SA 1,3, 1970 S
Rosewell, J S H (NSW) 1907 NZ 1,3
Ross, A W (NSW) 1925 NZ 1,2,3, 1926 NZ 1,2,3, 1927 I, W, S, 1928 E, F, 1929 NZ 1, 1930 BI, 1931 M, NZ, 1932 NZ 2,3, 1933 SA 5, 1934 NZ 1,2
Ross, W S (Q) 1979 I 1,2, Arg 2, 1980 Fj, NZ 1,2,3, 1982 S 1,2, 1983 US, Arg 1,2, NZ
Rothwell, P R (NSW) 1951 NZ 1,2,3, 1952 Fj 1
Row, F L (NSW) 1899 BI 1,3,4
Row, N E (NSW) 1907 NZ 1,3, 1909 E, 1910 NZ 1,2,3
Rowles, P G (NSW) 1972 Fj, 1973 E
Roxburgh, J R (NSW) 1968 NZ 1,2, F, 1969 W, SA 1,2,3,4, 1970 S
Ruebner, G (NSW) 1966 BI 1,2
Russell, C J (NSW) 1907 NZ 1,2,3, 1908 W, 1909 E
Ryan, J R (NSW) 1975 J 2, 1976 I, US, Fj 1,2,3
Ryan, K J (Q) 1958 E, M 1, NZ 1,2,3
Ryan, P F (NSW) 1963 E, SA 1, 1966 BI 1,2
Rylance, M H (NSW) 1926 NZ 4(R)

Sailor, W J (Q) 2002 F 1,2, Arg (R), I, E, It, 2003 I, W, E, SA 1, NZ 1, SA 2, NZ 2, [Arg,R,I,S,NZ,E], 2004 S1,2,NZ1(R), 2(R),SA2(R),S3(R),F(R),S4(R),E2, 2005 Sm,It,F1,SA1,2,3,F2, I(R),W(R)
Samo, R U (ACT) 2004 S1,2,E1,PI,NZ1,S4(R)
Sampson, J H (NSW) 1899 BI 4
Sayle, J L (NSW) 1967 NZ

Schulte, B G (Q) 1946 NZ 1, M
Scott, P R I (NSW) 1962 NZ 1,2
Scott-Young, S J (Q) 1990 F 2,3(R), US, NZ 3, 1992 NZ 1,2,3
Shambrook, G G (Q) 1976 Fj 2,3
Sharpe, N C (Q, WF) 2002 F 1,2, NZ 1, SA 1, NZ 2, SA 2, 2003 I, W, E, SA 1(R), NZ 1(R), SA 2(R), NZ 2(R),[Arg,R,Nm,I,S,NZ,E], 2004 S1,2,E1,PI,NZ1,SA1,NZ2,SA2, 2005 Sm,It,F1,SA1,2,3, NZ1,SA4,NZ2,F2,E,I,W, 2006 E1,2,I1,NZ1,SA1,NZ2,SA2, NZ3,SA3,W,It,I2,S, 2007 W1,2,SA1,NZ1,SA2,NZ2, [J,W,C,E]
Shaw, A A (Q) 1973 W, E, 1975 E 1,2, J 2, S, W, 1976 E, I, US, Fj 1,2,3, F 1,2, 1978 W 1,2, NZ 1,2,3, 1979 I 1,2, NZ, Arg 1,2, 1980 Fj, NZ 1,2,3, 1981 F 1,2, I, W, S, 1982 S 1,2
Shaw, C (NSW) 1925 NZ 2,3,4(R)
Shaw, G A (NSW) 1969 W, SA 1(R), 1970 S, 1971 SA 1,2,3, F 1,2, 1973 W, E, 1974 NZ 1,2,3, 1975 E 1,2, J 1,2, W, 1976 E, I, US, Fj 1,2,3, F 1,2, 1979 NZ
Sheehan, B R (ACT) 2006 SA3(R)
Sheehan, W B J (NSW) 1921 SA 1,2,3, 1922 NZ 1,2,3, 1923 M 1,2, NZ 1,2,3, 1924 NZ 1,2, 1926 NZ 1,2,3, 1927 W, S
Shehadie, N M (NSW) 1947 NZ 2, 1948 E, F, 1949 M 1,2,3, NZ 1,2, 1950 BI 1,2, 1951 NZ 1,2,3, 1952 Fj 1,2, NZ 2, 1953 SA 1,2,3,4, 1954 Fj 1,2, 1955 NZ 1,2,3, 1956 SA 1,2, 1957 NZ 2, 1958 W, I
Sheil, A G R (Q) 1956 SA 1
Shepherd, C B (WF) 2006 E1(R),2(R),I1(R),SA3,W, 2007 [C]
Shepherd, D J (V) 1964 NZ 3, 1965 SA 1,2, 1966 BI 1,2
Shepherdson, G T (ACT) 2006 I1,NZ1,SA1,NZ2(R),SA2(R),It,I2,S, 2007 W1,2,SA1,NZ1,SA2,NZ2, [J(R),W,Fj,E]
Shute, J L (NSW) 1920 NZ 3, 1922 M 2,3
Simpson, R J (NSW) 1913 NZ 2
Skinner, A J (NSW) 1969 W, SA 4, 1970 S
Slack, A G (Q) 1978 W 1,2, NZ 1,2, 1979 NZ, Arg 1,2, 1980 Fj, 1981 I, W, S, 1982 E, S 1, NZ 3, 1983 US, Arg 1,2 NZ, It, 1984 Fj, NZ 1,2,3, E, I, W, S, 1986 It, F, NZ 1,2,3, 1987 SK, [E, US, J, I, F, W]
Slater, S H (NSW) 1910 NZ 3
Slattery, P J (Q) 1990 US (R), 1991 W (R), E (R), [WS (R), W, I (R)], 1992 I, W, 1993 Tg, C, F 1,2, 1994 I 1,2, It 1(R), 1995 [C, R (R)]
Smairl, A M (NSW) 1928 NZ 1,2,3
Smith, B A (Q) 1987 SK, [US, J, I (R), W], Arg 1
Smith, D P (Q) 1993 SA 1,2,3, C, F 2, 1994 I 1,2, It 1,2, WS, NZ, 1995 Arg 1,2, [SA, R, E], NZ 1,2, 1998 SA 1(R), NZ 3(R), Fj
Smith, F B (NSW) 1905 NZ, 1907 NZ 1,2,3
Smith, G B (ACT) 2000 F, S, E, 2001 BI 1,2,3, SA 1, NZ 1, SA 2, NZ 2, Sp, E, F (R), W (R), 2002 F 1,2, NZ 1, SA 1, NZ 2, SA 2, Arg, I, E, It, 2003 I, NZ 1, SA 2, NZ 2, [Arg,R,Nm,I,S,NZ,E], 2004 S1,2(R),E1(t&R),PI(R),NZ1(R),SA1,NZ2,SA2,S3,F,S4,E2, 2005 Sm,It,F1,SA1,2,3,NZ1,SA4(R),NZ2,F2,E,I,W, 2006 E1,2,I1,NZ1,SA1,NZ2,SA2,NZ3(t),SA3(R),It,I2(R),S, 2007 W1(R),2,Fj(R),SA1,NZ1,SA2,NZ2, [J,W,C,E]
Smith, L M (NSW) 1905 NZ
Smith, N C (NSW) 1922 NZ 2,3, 1923 NZ 1, 1924 NZ 1,3(R), 1925 NZ 2,3
Smith, P V (NSW) 1967 NZ, 1968 NZ 1,2, F, I, S, 1969 W, SA 1
Smith, R A (NSW) 1971 SA 1,2, 1972 F 1,2, NZ 1,2(R), 3, Fj, 1975 E 1,2, J 1,2, S, W, 1976 E, I, US, Fj 1,2,3, F 1,2
Smith, T S (NSW) 1921 SA 1,2,3, NZ, 1922 M 2,3, NZ 1,2,3, 1925 NZ 1,3,4
Snell, H W (NSW) 1925 NZ 2,3, 1928 NZ 3
Solomon, H J (NSW) 1949 M 3, NZ 2, 1950 BI 1,2, 1951 NZ 1,2, 1952 Fj 1,2, NZ 1,2, 1953 SA 1,2,3, 1955 NZ 1
Spooner, N R (Q) 1999 I 1,2
Spragg, S A (NSW) 1899 BI 1,2,3,4
Staniforth, S N G (NSW,WF) 1999 [US], 2002 I, It, 2006 SA3(R),I2(R),S, 2007 Fj,NZ1(R),SA2(R),NZ2(R), [W(R),Fj(R)]
Stanley, R G (NSW) 1921 NZ, 1922 M 1,2,3, NZ 1,2,3, 1923 M 2,3, NZ 1,2,3, 1924 NZ 1,3
Stapleton, E T (NSW) 1951 NZ 1,2,3, 1952 Fj 1,2, NZ 1,2, 1953 SA 1,2,3,4, 1954 Fj 1, 1955 NZ 1,2,3, 1958 NZ 1
Steggall, J C (Q) 1931 M, NZ, 1932 NZ 1,2,3, 1933 SA 1,2,3,4,5
Stegman, T R (NSW) 1973 Tg 1,2
Stephens, O G (NSW) 1973 Tg 1,2, W, 1974 NZ 2,3
Stewart, A A (NSW) 1979 NZ, Arg 1,2
Stiles, N B (Q) 2001 BI 1,2,3, SA 1, NZ 1, SA 2, NZ 2, Sp, E, F, W, 2002 I
Stone, A H (NSW) 1937 SA 2, 1938 NZ 2,3
Stone, C G (NSW) 1938 NZ 1
Stone, J M (NSW) 1946 M, NZ 2
Storey, G P (NSW) 1926 NZ 4, 1927 I, W, S, 1928 E, F, 1929 NZ 3(R), 1930 BI
Storey, K P (NSW) 1936 NZ 2
Storey, N J D (NSW) 1962 NZ 1
Strachan, D J (NSW) 1955 NZ 2,3
Strauss, C P (NSW) 1999 I 1(R),2(R), E (R), SA 1(R), NZ 1, SA 2(R), NZ 2(R), [R (R), I 3(R), US, W]
Street, N O (NSW) 1899 BI 2
Streeter, S F (NSW) 1978 NZ 1
Stuart, R (NSW) 1910 NZ 2,3
Stumbles, B D (NSW) 1972 NZ 1(R), 2,3, Fj
Sturtridge, G S (V) 1929 NZ 2, 1932 NZ 1,2,3, 1933 SA 1,2,3,4,5
Sullivan, P D (NSW) 1971 SA 1,2,3, F 1,2, 1972 F 1,2, NZ 1,2, Fj, 1973 Tg 1,2, W
Summons, A J (NSW) 1958 W, I, E, S, M 2, NZ 1,2,3, 1959 BI 1,2
Suttor, D C (NSW) 1913 NZ 1,2,3
Swannell, B I (NSW) 1905 NZ
Sweeney, T L (Q) 1953 SA 1

Taafe, B S (NSW) 1969 SA 1, 1972 F 1,2
Tabua, I (Q) 1993 SA 2,3, C, F 1, 1994 I 1,2, It 1,2, 1995 [C, R]
Tancred, A J (NSW) 1927 I, W, S
Tancred, H E (NSW) 1923 M 1,2
Tancred, J L (NSW) 1926 NZ 3,4, 1928 F
Tanner, W H (Q) 1899 BI 1,2
Tarleton, K (NSW) 1925 NZ 2,3
Tasker, W G (NSW) 1913 NZ 1,2,3, 1914 NZ 1,2,3
Tate, M J (NSW) 1951 NZ 3, 1952 Fj 1,2, NZ 1,2, 1953 SA 1, 1954 Fj 1,2
Taylor, D A (Q) 1968 NZ 1,2, F, I, S
Taylor, H C (NSW) 1923 NZ 1,2,3, 1924 NZ 4
Taylor, J I (NSW) 1971 SA 1, 1972 F 1,2, Fj
Taylor, J M (NSW) 1922 M 1,2
Teitzel, R G (Q) 1966 W, S, 1967 E, I 1, F, I 2, NZ
Telford, D G (NSW) 1926 NZ 3(R)
Thompson, C E (NSW) 1922 M 1, 1923 M 1,2, NZ 1, 1924 NZ 2,3
Thompson, E G (Q) 1929 NZ 1,2,3, 1930 BI
Thompson, F (NSW) 1913 NZ 1,2,3, 1914 NZ 1,2,3
Thompson, J (Q) 1914 NZ 1
Thompson, P D (Q) 1950 BI 1
Thompson, R J (WA) 1971 SA 3, F 2(R), 1972 Fj
Thorn, A M (NSW) 1921 SA 1,2,3, NZ, 1922 M 1,3
Thorn, E J (NSW) 1922 NZ 1,2,3, 1923 NZ 1,2,3, 1924 NZ 1,2,3, 1925 NZ 1,2, 1926 NZ 1,2,3,4
Thornett, J E (NSW) 1955 NZ 1,2,3, 1956 SA 1,2, 1958 W, I, S, F, M 2,3, NZ 2,3, 1959 BI 1,2, 1961 Fj 2,3, SA 1,2, F, 1962 NZ 2,3,4,5, 1963 E, SA 1,2,3,4, 1964 NZ 1,2,3, 1965 SA 1,2, 1966 BI 1,2, 1967 F
Thornett, R N (NSW) 1961 Fj 1,2,3, SA 1,2, F, 1962 NZ 1,2,3,4,5
Thorpe, A C (NSW) 1929 NZ 1(R)
Timbury, F R V (Q) 1910 NZ 1,2,
Tindall, E N (NSW) 1973 Tg 2
Toby, A E (NSW) 1925 NZ 1,4
Tolhurst, H A (NSW) 1931 M, NZ
Tombs, R C (NSW) 1992 S 1,2, 1994 I 2, It 1, 1996 NZ 2
Tonkin, A E J (NSW) 1947 S, I, W, 1948 E, F, 1950 BI 2
Tooth, R M (NSW) 1951 NZ 1,2,3, 1954 Fj 1,2, 1955 NZ 1,2,3, 1957 NZ 1,2
Towers, C H T (NSW) 1926 NZ 1,3(R),4, 1927 I, 1928 E, F, NZ 1,2,3, M, 1929 NZ 1,3, 1930 BI, 1931 M, NZ, 1934 NZ 1,2, 1937 SA 1,2
Trivett, R K (Q) 1966 BI 1,2
Tune, B N (Q) 1996 W 2, C, NZ 1, SA 1, NZ 2, SA 2, 1997 F 1,2, NZ 1, E 1, NZ 2, SA 1, NZ 3, SA 2, Arg, 1,2, E 2, S, 1998 E 1, S 1,2, NZ 1, SA 1,2, NZ 3, 1999 I 1, E, SA 1, NZ 1, SA 2, NZ 2, [R, I 3, W, SA 3, F], 2000 SA 2(R), NZ 2(t&R), SA 3(R), 2001 F (R), W, 2002 NZ 1, SA 1, NZ 2, SA 2, Arg, 2006 NZ1(R)
Tuqiri, L D (NSW) 2003 I (R), W (R), E (R), SA 1(R), NZ 1, SA 2, NZ 2, [Arg(R),R(R),Nm,I(R),S,NZ,E], 2004 S1,2,E1,PI,NZ1,SA1, NZ2,SA2,S3,F,S4,E2, 2005 It,F1,SA1,2,3,NZ1,SA4,NZ2, F2,E,I,W, 2006 E1,2,I1,NZ1,SA1,NZ2,SA2,NZ3,W,It,I2,S, 2007 Fj,SA1,NZ1, [J,W,Fj,C,E]
Turinui, M P (NSW) 2003 I, W, E, 2003 [Nm(R)], 2004 S1(R),2,E2, 2005 Sm,It(R),F1(R),SA1,2(t&R),3,NZ1,SA4,NZ2,F2,E,I,W
Turnbull, A (V) 1961 Fj 3
Turnbull, R V (NSW) 1968 I
Tuynman, S N (NSW) 1983 F 1,2, 1984 E, I, W, S, 1985 C 1,2, NZ, Fj 1,2, 1986 It, F, Arg 1,2, NZ 1,2,3, 1987 SK, [E, US, J,

I, W], NZ, Arg 1(R), 2, 1988 E, It, 1989 Bl 1,2,3, NZ, 1990 NZ 1

Tweedale, E (NSW) 1946 NZ 1,2, 1947 NZ 2, S, I, 1948 E, F, 1949 M 1,2,3

Valentine, J J (Q) 2006 E1(R),W(R),I2(R),S(R)

Vaughan, D (NSW) 1983 US, Arg 1, It, F 1,2

Vaughan, G N (V) 1958 E, S, F, M 1,2,3

Verge, A (NSW) 1904 Bl 1,2

Vickerman, D J (ACT, NSW) 2002 F 2(R), Arg, E, It, 2003 I (R), W (R), E (R), SA 1, NZ 1, SA 2, NZ 2, [Arg(R),R,I(R),S(R)], 2004 S1(t&R),2(R),E1(R),PI(R),NZ1(R),SA1(R),NZ2(R),SA2(R),S3,F,S4, E2, 2005 SA2(R),3,NZ1,SA4, 2006 E1,2,I1,NZ1,SA1,NZ2, SA2,NZ3,SA3,W, 2007 W1(R),2,Fj,SA1,NZ1,SA2,NZ2, [J,W,Fj,E]

Walden, R J (NSW) 1934 NZ 2, 1936 NZ 1,2, M

Walker, A K (NSW) 1947 NZ 1, 1948 E, F, 1950 Bl 1,2

Walker, A M (ACT) 2000 NZ 1(R), 2001 Bl 1,2,3, SA 1, NZ 1,2(R)

Walker, A S B (NSW) 1912 US, 1920 NZ 1,2, 1921 SA 1,2,3, NZ, 1922 M 1,3, NZ 1,2,3, 1923 M 2,3, 1924 NZ 1,2

Walker, L F (NSW) 1988 NZ 2,3, S, It, 1989 Bl 1,2,3, NZ

Walker, L R (NSW) 1982 NZ 2,3

Wallace, A C (NSW) 1921 NZ, 1926 NZ 3,4, 1927 I, W, S, 1928 E, F

Wallace, T M (NSW) 1994 It 1(R), 2

Wallach, C (NSW) 1913 NZ 1,3, 1914 NZ 1,2,3

Walsh, J J (NSW) 1953 SA 1,2,3,4

Walsh, P B (NSW) 1904 Bl 1,2,3

Walsham, K P (NSW) 1962 NZ 3, 1963 E

Ward, P G (NSW) 1899 Bl 1,2,3,4

Ward, T (Q) 1899 Bl 2

Watson, G W (Q) 1907 NZ 1

Watson, W T (NSW) 1912 US, 1913 NZ 1,2,3, 1914 NZ 1, 1920 NZ 1,2,3

Waugh, P R (NSW) 2000 E (R), 2001 NZ 1(R), SA 2(R), NZ 2(R), Sp (R), E (R), F, W, 2003 I (R), W, E, SA 1, NZ 1, SA 2, NZ2, [Arg,R,I,S,NZ,E], 2004 S1(R),2,E1,PI,NZ1,SA1,NZ2,SA2, S3,F,S4,E2,2005 SA1(R),2(R),3,NZ1(R),SA4,NZ2,F2,E,I,W, 2006 E1(R),2(R),I1(R),NZ1(R),SA1(R),NZ2(R),SA2(R),NZ3,SA3,W,I2,S(R), 2007 W1,2(R),Fj,SA1(R),NZ1(R),SA2(R),NZ2(R) , [W(R),Fj, C(R),E(R)]

Waugh, W W (NSW, ACT) 1993 SA 1, 1995 [C], NZ 1,2, 1996 S, I, 1997 Arg 1,2

Weatherstone, L J (ACT) 1975 E 1,2, J 1,2, S (R), 1976 E, I

Webb, W (NSW) 1899 Bl 3,4

Welborn J P (NSW) 1996 SA 2, It, 1998 Tg, 1999 E, SA 1, NZ 1

Wells, B G (NSW) 1958 M 1

Westfield, R E (NSW) 1928 NZ 1,2,3, M, 1929 NZ 2,3

Whitaker, C J (NSW) 1998 SA 2(R), Fj (R), Tg, 1999 NZ 2(R), [R (R), US, F (R)], 2000 S (R), 2001 Sp (R), W (R), 2002 Arg (R), It (R), 2003 I (R), W (R), SA 2(R),[Arg(R),Nm,S(R)], 2004 PI(R),NZ1, 2005 Sm,It(R),F1(R),SA1(R),2(R),NZ1(t&R),SA4(R), NZ2(R),F2(R),E(R),W(R)

White, C J B (NSW) 1899 Bl 1, 1903 NZ, 1904 Bl 1

White, J M (NSW) 1904 Bl 3

White, J P L (NSW) 1958 NZ 1,2,3, 1961 Fj 1,2,3, SA 1,2, F, 1962 NZ 1,2,3,4,5, 1963 E, SA 1,2,3,4, 1964 NZ 1,2,3, 1965 SA 1,2

White, M C (Q) 1931 M, NZ 1932 NZ 1,2, 1933 SA 1,2,3,4,5

White, S W (NSW) 1956 SA 1,2, 1958 I, E, S, M 2,3

White, W G S (Q) 1933 SA 1,2,3,4,5, 1934 NZ 1,2, 1936 NZ 1,2, M

White, W J (NSW) 1928 NZ 1, M, 1932 NZ 1

Wickham, S M (NSW) 1903 NZ, 1904 Bl 1,2,3, 1905 NZ

Williams, D (Q) 1913 NZ 3, 1914 NZ 1,2,3

Williams, I M (NSW) 1987 Arg 1,2, 1988 E 1,2, NZ 1,2,3, 1989 Bl 2,3, NZ, F 1,2, 1990 F 1,2,3, US, NZ 1

Williams, J L (NSW) 1963 SA 1,3,4

Williams, R W (ACT) 1999 I 1(t&R),2(t&R), E (R), [US], 2000 Arg 1,2, SA 1, NZ 1, SA 2, NZ 2, SA 3, F (R), S (R), E

Williams, S A (NSW) 1980 Fj, NZ 1,2, 1981 F 1,2, 1982 E, NZ 1,2,3, 1983 US, Arg 1(R), 2, NZ, It, F 1,2, 1984 NZ 1,2,3, E, I, W, S, 1985 C 1,2, NZ, Fj 1,2

Wilson, B J (NSW) 1949 NZ 1,2

Wilson, C R (Q) 1957 NZ 1, 1958 NZ 1,2,3

Wilson, D J (Q) 1992 S 1,2, NZ 1,2,3, SA, I, W, 1993 Tg, NZ, SA 1,2,3, C, F 1,2, 1994 I 1,2, It 1,2, WS, NZ, 1995 Arg 1,2, [SA, R, E], 1996 W 1,2, C, NZ 1, SA 1, NZ 2, SA 2, It, S, I, W 3, 1997 F 1,2, NZ 1, E 1(t + R), NZ 2(R), SA 1, NZ 3, SA 2, E 2(R), S (R), 1998 E 1, S 1,2, NZ 1, SA 1, NZ 2, SA 2, NZ 3, Fj, WS, F, E 2, 1999 I 1,2, E, SA 1, NZ 1, SA 2, NZ 2, [R, I 3, W, SA 3, F], 2000 Arg 1,2, SA 1, NZ 1, SA 2, NZ 2, SA 3

Wilson, V W (Q) 1937 SA 1,2, 1938 NZ 1,2,3

Windon, C J (NSW) 1946 NZ 1,2, 1947 NZ 1, S, I, W, 1948 E, F, 1949 M 1,2,3, NZ 1,2, 1951 NZ 1,2,3, 1952 Fj 1,2, NZ 1,2

Windon, K S (NSW) 1937 SA 1,2, 1946 M

Windsor, J C (Q) 1947 NZ 2

Winning, K C (Q) 1951 NZ 1

Wogan, L W (NSW) 1913 NZ 1,2,3, 1914 NZ 1,2,3, 1920 NZ 1,2,3, 1921 SA 1,2,3, NZ, 1922 M 3, NZ 1,2,3, 1923 M 1,2, 1924 NZ 1,2,3

Wood, F (NSW) 1907 NZ 1,2,3, 1910 NZ 1,2,3, 1913 NZ 1,2,3, 1914 NZ 1,2,3

Wood, R N (Q) 1972 Fj

Woods, H F (NSW) 1925 NZ 4, 1926 NZ 1,2,3, 1927 I, W, S, 1928 E

Wright, K J (NSW) 1975 E 1,2, J 1, 1976 US, F 1,2, 1978 NZ 1,2,3

Wyld, G (NSW) 1920 NZ 2

Yanz, K (NSW) 1958 F

Young, W K (ACT, NSW) 2000 F, S, E, 2002 F 1,2, NZ 1, SA 1, NZ 2, SA 2, Arg, E, It, 2003 I, W, E, SA 1, NZ 1, SA 2, NZ 2, [Arg,R,I,S,NZ,E], 2004 S1,2,E1,PI,NZ1,SA1,NZ2,SA2,S3, F,S4,E2, 2005 Sm,It,F1,SA1,2,3,NZ1,SA4,NZ2

CANADA

CANADA'S 2006–07 TEST RECORD

OPPONENTS	DATE	VENUE	RESULT
Wales	17 Nov	A	**Lost** 26–61
Italy	25 Nov	A	**Lost** 6–41
Ireland	19 May	N	**Lost** 20–39
USA	2 June	N	**Won** 52–10
New Zealand	16 June	A	**Lost** 13–64
Portugal	18 Aug	H	**Won** 42–12
Wales	9 Sept	N	**Lost** 17–42 (WC)
Fiji	16 Sept	N	**Lost** 16–29 (WC)
Japan	25 Sept	N	**Drew** 12–12 (WC)
Australia	29 Sept	N	**Lost** 6–37 (WC)

FRUSTRATING TIMES FOR CANUCKS

By Ian Kennedy

Canada had hoped to be part of the 'minnow's revolution' at the 2007 Rugby World Cup in September in France and their coach Ric Suggitt had stated well before going to France that Canada hoped to: " . . . win three games and a quarter-final spot." Instead Fiji, against whom Canada had been within a whisker of defeating, went on to win the Pool B quarter-final spot Canada had so much coveted leaving the Canucks to finish bottom of Pool B recording their worst ever finish at six World Cups.

It all could have been so much different. All of Canada's hopes and aspirations for a successful 2007 season evaporated in the space of five minutes at the end of two games at the World Cup

Canada appeared to be on track to fulfill its goal in its first World Cup game against Wales, in Nantes on 9 September when, at the 55-minute mark, it led 17–9 after scoring unanswered tries through flanker Jamie Cudmore, centre Craig Culpan and captain, scrum-half Morgan Williams.

After Williams' score, Welsh coach Gareth Jenkins injected his World Cup captain Gareth Thomas and outside-half Stephen Jones, and the two orchestrated a Welsh comeback to win, 42–17. One down and three to go.

In their next encounter against Fiji on September 16th in Cardiff, Canada appeared to be in command in the early going, using its driving maul to effect and denying the fleet-footed Fijian backs the ball, but handling errors and failure to follow its successful early game plan, saw Fiji leading 15–6 at half-time. Following a severe tongue-lashing from coach Ric Suggitt at the interval, Canada began to play the kind of rugby it had played in the first half against Wales the week before.

Outside-half Ryan Smith scored under the posts and James Pritchard converted as Canada continued to contain the Fijians in their own 22 by attacking at close quarters. First lock Mike James appeared to score, then full-back Mike Pyke went over in the corner and touched down only to be denied by the Television Match Official.

At 72 minutes Pritchard hit a penalty putting Canada within a goal of winning the game and the team rallied to the challenge. Its forwards won a line-out near the Fiji line at 79 minutes and drove for the in-goal. Time after time Fiji thwarted Canada's efforts to gain the try it needed. Then, with the ball right under the posts, a Canadian spilled the ball as he lunged for the line and Fijian full-back Kamali Ratuvou picked it up and ran to the other end to score. Heartbreak for Canada and a 29–16 win for Fiji. Two down and two to go.

In its next match against Japan, also winless and looking for its first World Cup win since its only one, over Zimbabwe 52–8 in Belfast in 1991, Canada enjoyed a territorial edge for most of the match but a staunch Japanese defense kept the score close at 12–5 despite second-half tries by hooker Pat Riordan, and wing DTH van der Merwe, the latter converted by James Pritchard. With the game winding down and television monitors showing 81 minutes and 30 seconds, Canada cleared to touch, thinking the game won. Referee Jonathan Kaplan, the sole arbiter of time, allowed play to continue until, after a frenzied final few minutes, Japanese substitute centre Koji Taira scored, and Shotaro Onishi kicked the conversion: a 12–12 draw. Three down and one to go.

Canada faced world second-ranked, Australia, four days later at the same Chaban Delmas stadium in Bordeaux, and in a steady downpour, defended like men possessed, holding the Wallabies to a creditable 37–6 score-line. Canada seemed to be able to play better against teams ranked higher than it, but couldn't win games it was expected to win.

Canada's 2007 season began in November 2006 when, after thumping the USA 56–7 in its Rugby World Cup Qualifying match in August 2006, it flew overseas to take on Wales in Cardiff in the first of its two November test matches. Squeezed between visits by the Pacific Islands and New Zealand, in a brilliant piece of marketing by the Welsh Rugby Union, it enticed 74,050 people to show up on Friday November 17 to watch Canada and Wales square off. It was the largest crowd to ever watch any Canadian team play any sport.

Without professionals Stade Francais lock Mike James, Clermont-Auvergne flanker Jamie Cudmore and prop Rod Snow, Canada struggled to contain the more powerful Welsh forwards. The score, however, demonstrated the reality of professionalism over amateurism as Wales ran out 62–26 winners.

The next weekend in Fontanafredda against the powerful Italian pack, the biggest in the Six Nations, Canada found difficulty coping and only two penalties by outside-half Ander Monro prevented the whitewash in a 41–6 defeat.

With Canada's top 22 domestically-based players living and training in Victoria and heavily involved in their IRB funded Tier ll High Performance Programs, the test of their improvements in strength, speed and fitness came in May's Churchill Cup, held for the first time in England.

In their first game, Canada faced Ireland 'A' at Sandy Park, Exeter and came back from a 17–6 deficit at half-time, to take a 20–17 lead early in the second on tries by centre Craig Culpan and wing Dean Van Camp, both converted by Pritchard, who had accounted for Canada's two penalties in the first half. Ireland 'A', however, managed two late tries to win 32–20.

A week later, the New Zealand Maori defeated Canada 59–23. The sheer skill and pace of the Maori saw them run in nine tries to Canada's three with Canada's tries going to flanker Adam Kleeberger, wing Mike Pyke, and substitute No.8 Aaron Carpenter, with Pritchard adding two penalties and a conversion. Late in the game nineteen year-old Nathan Hirayama came off the bench to win his first 'A' cap and become the youngest player ever to play for Canada. As the son of former Canada outside-half Gary Hirayama, the two become the first father-son combination to play for Canada.

By finishing last in its Pool, Canada faced the USA at Twickenham on June 2 to play for fifth or sixth spot, in the Bowl Final. Following on from its thrashing of the Americans in Newfoundland the previous August, Canada continued to show its North American rugby supremacy by besting the USA 52–10. Canada scored seven tries with two each to Man of the Match No 8 Sean-Michael Stephen and captain Morgan Williams, and singles by centre David Spicer, flanker Adam Kleeberger and prop Dan Pletch. James Pritchard accounted for 17 points in a perfect day, hitting a penalty and all seven conversions.

On a cross-Canada tour prior to flying to France for the RWC, Canada played Portugal in Ottawa on August 18th and with wing DTH van der Merwe leading the way with two tries, defeated the totally amateur Los Lobos 42–12. Fullback Mike Pyke, prop Jon Thiel, centre David Spicer and wing Justin Mensah-Coker added single tries with Pritchard converting three.

Following the RWC Canada must look back on its 2–8–1 overall season record and contemplate what lies ahead. Will the IRB continue to support it in its quest to have its relatively young team improve, given that three of its great servants of the game its World Cup captain Morgan Williams, its inspirational lock Mike James and prop Rod Snow retired following the Australia game?

On the home front Canada's Women's program won both games 18–5 and 46–7 against the USA in Blaine, Minnesota in August 2007. In Rugby Canada Super League action, in its third time to the championship in as many years the Saskatchewan Prairie Fire finally won the MCTier Cup defeating the Niagara Thunder 28–12. In the inaugural eight-team National Women's League British Columbia defeated Ontario 22–15 to take the title.

CANADA INTERNATIONAL RECORDS

UP TO 31ST OCTOBER 2007

WINNING MARGIN

Date	Opponent	Result	Winning Margin
24/06/2006	Barbados	69–3	**66**
14/10/1999	Namibia	72–11	**61**
12/08/2006	USA	56–7	**49**
06/07/1996	Hong Kong	57–9	**48**

MOST POINTS IN A MATCH

BY THE TEAM

Date	Opponent	Result	Pts.
14/10/1999	Namibia	72–11	**72**
24/06/2006	Barbados	69–3	**69**
15/07/2000	Japan	62–18	**62**
06/07/1996	Hong Kong	57–9	**57**
12/08/2006	USA	56–7	**56**

MOST TRIES IN A MATCH

BY THE TEAM

Date	Opponent	Result	Tries
24/06/2006	Barbados	69–3	**11**
14/10/1999	Namibia	72–11	**9**
11/05/1991	Japan	49–26	**8**
15/07/2000	Japan	62–18	**8**

MOST CONVERSIONS IN A MATCH

BY THE TEAM

Date	Opponent	Result	Cons
14/10/1999	Namibia	72–11	**9**
15/07/2000	Japan	62–18	**8**
24/06/2006	Barbados	69–3	**7**
02/06/2007	USA	52–10	**7**
11/05/1991	Japan	49–26	**7**

MOST PENALTIES IN A MATCH

BY THE TEAM

Date	Opponent	Result	Pens
25/05/1991	Scotland	24–19	**8**
22/08/1998	Argentina	28–54	**7**

MOST DROP GOALS IN A MATCH

BY THE TEAM

Date	Opponent	Result	DGs
08/11/1986	USA	27–16	**2**
04/07/2001	Fiji	23–52	**2**
08/06/1980	USA	16–0	**2**
24/05/1997	Hong Kong	35–27	**2**

MOST POINTS IN A MATCH

BY A PLAYER

Date	Player	Opponent	Pts.
12/08/2006	James Pritchard	USA	**36**
24/06/2006	James Pritchard	Barbados	**29**
14/10/1999	Gareth Rees	Namibia	**27**
13/07/1996	Bobby Ross	Japan	**26**
25/05/1991	Mark Wyatt	Scotland	**24**

MOST TRIES IN A MATCH

BY A PLAYER

Date	Player	Opponent	Tries
15/07/2000	Kyle Nichols	Japan	**4**
24/06/2006	James Pritchard	Barbados	**3**
12/08/2006	James Pritchard	USA	**3**
10/05/1987	Steve Gray	USA	**3**

MOST CONVERSIONS IN A MATCH

BY A PLAYER

Date	Player	Opponent	Cons
14/10/1999	Gareth Rees	Namibia	9
15/07/2000	Jared Barker	Japan	8
24/06/2006	James Pritchard	Barbados	7
02/06/2007	James Pritchard	USA	7
11/05/1991	Mark Wyatt	Japan	7

MOST PENALTIES IN A MATCH

BY A PLAYER

Date	Player	Opponent	Pens
25/05/1991	Mark Wyatt	Scotland	8
22/08/1998	Gareth Rees	Argentina	7

MOST DROP GOALS IN A MATCH

BY A PLAYER

Date	Player	Opponent	DGs
04/07/2001	Bobby Ross	Fiji	2
24/05/1997	Bobby Ross	Hong Kong	2

MOST CAPPED PLAYERS

Name	Caps
Al Charron	76
Winston Stanley	66
Scott Stewart	64
Rod Snow	62
Bobby Ross	58

LEADING TRY SCORERS

Name	Tries
Winston Stanley	24
Morgan Williams	13
Pat Palmer	10
Kyle Nichols	10
John Graf	9
Al Charron	9

LEADING CONVERSIONS SCORERS

Name	Cons
Bobby Ross	52
Gareth Rees	51
James Pritchard	39
Jared Barker	24
Mark Wyatt	24

LEADING PENALTY SCORERS

Name	Pens
Gareth Rees	110
Bobby Ross	84
Mark Wyatt	64
Jared Barker	55
James Pritchard	29

LEADING DROP GOAL SCORERS

Name	DGs
Bobby Ross	10
Gareth Rees	9
Mark Wyatt	5

LEADING POINTS SCORERS

Name	Pts.
Gareth Rees	491
Bob Ross	424
Mark Wyatt	263
Jared Barker	226
James Pritchard	205

CANADIAN INTERNATIONAL PLAYERS
UP TO 31ST OCTOBER 2007

Note: Years given for International Championship matches are for second half of season; eg 1972 means season 1971–72. Years for all other matches refer to the actual year of the match. Entries in square brackets denote matches played in RWC Finals.

Abrams, AD 2003 *US* (R), *NZ*, *Tg* (R) 2004 *US*, *J*, *E*, *US*, *F*, *It* (R), *E* 2005 *US* (R), *J*, *W*, *E*, *US*, *Ar*, *F*, *R* (R) 2006 *S* (R), *E*, *US* (R), *It* (R)
Alder, MJ 1976 *Bb*
Aldous, P 1971 *W*
Arthurs, AS 1988 *US*
Ashton, M 1971 *W*
Asselin, F 1999 *Fj* (R) 2000 *Tg*, *US*, *SA* 2001 *Ur*, *Ar*, *Fj* 2002 *S*, *US*, *US*, *Ur*, *Ur*, *Ch*, *W*, *F*
Atkinson, O 2005 *J*, *Ar* (R) 2006 *E* (R), *US* (R), *It*
Ault, S 2006 *W* (R), *It* (R)

Bain, JC 1932 *J*
Banks, RG 1999 *J*, *Fj* (R), *Sa*, *US*, *Tg*, *W* (R), *E*, *F* (R), *Nm* (R) 2000 *US*, *SA*, *I*, *J*, *It* 2001 *US*, *Ur* (R), *Ar*, *E*, *Fj*, *J* (R) 2002 *S*, *US*, *US*, *Ur*, *Ch*, *Ur*, *Ch*, *W*, *F* 2003 *E*, *US*, *M*, *M*, *Ur*, *NZ*, *It*
Barber, S 1973 *W* 1976 *Bb*
Barbieri, M 2006 *E*, *US* (R)
Barker, B 1966 *BI* 1971 *W*
Barker, J 2000 *Tg*, *J*, *It* 2002 *S*, *US*, *US*, *Ur*, *Ch*, *Ur*, *Ch* (R), *W* 2003 *US*, *NZ*, *It* 2004 *US*, *J*, *F*, *It*
Bauer, T 1977 *US*, *E* 1978 *US*, *F* 1979 *US*
Baugh, D 1998 *J*, *HK*, *US*, *HK* (R), *J* (R), *Ur*, *Ar* (R) 1999 *J*, *Fj*, *Sa*, *US*, *Tg*, *W*, *E*, *F*, *Fj*, *Nm* 2000 *US*, *SA*, *I* (R), *It* 2001 *E*, *E* 2002 *S*, *US*, *Ur*, *Ch*
Bianco, A 1966 *BI*
Bibby, AJ 1979 *US*, *F* 1980 *W*, *US*, *NZ* 1981 *US*, *Ar*
Bice, R 1996 *US*, *A* 1997 *US* (R), *J*, *HK*, *US*, *W* (R), *I* 1998 *US*, *US* (R), *HK*, *J*, *Ur*, *US* (R), *Ar* 1999 *J* (R), *Fj*, *Sa*, *US*, *Tg*, *W*, *F* (R)
Bickerton, P 2004 *US*, *J*
Biddle, D 2006 *Sa* (R), *E*, *Bar* (R) 2007 *M*, *W*, *Fj*, *A*
Billingsley, JM 1974 *Tg* 1977 *US* 1978 *F* 1979 *US* (R) 1980 *W* 1983 *US* (R), *It*, *It* 1984 *US*
Bjarneson, WG 1962 *Bb*
Blackwell, TJH 1973 *W*
Bonenberg, B 1983 *US*, *It*, *It*
Boone, J 1932 *J*, *J*
Bourne, T 1967 *E*
Breen, B 1986 *US* (R) 1987 *W* 1990 *US* 1991 *J*, *S*, *US*, *R* 1993 *E*, *US*
Breen, R 1983 *E* 1987 *US*
Brewer, R 1967 *E*
Brown, STT 1989 *I*, *US*
Browne, N 1973 *W* 1974 *Tg*
Bryan, S 1996 *Ur*, *US*, *Ar* 1997 *HK*, *J*, *US*, *W* 1998 *HK*, *J*, *US*, *Ar* 1999 *Fj* (R), *Sa*, *US*, *Tg*, *W*, *E*, *F*, *Fj*, *Nm* (R)
Burak, M 2004 *US* (R), *J* (R), *E* (R), *US*, *F* (R), *It*, *E* 2005 *E* (R), *US*, *Ar*, *F* (R), *R* 2006 *US*, *Bar*, *W* 2007 *IrA*, *M*, *NZ*, *Pt* (R), *W* (R), *Fj*, *J*, *A* (R)
Burford, C 1970 *Fj*
Burgess, D 1962 *Bb*, *W23*
Burleigh, D 2001 *Ur*, *Ar* (R), *E* (R), *E*
Burnham, JB 1966 *BI* 1967 *E* 1970 *Fj* 1971 *W*
Buydens, H 2006 *E* (R) *Bar*

Cameron, GE 1932 *J*
Cannon, JWD 2001 *US*, *Ar*, *E*, *E*, *Fj*, *J* 2002 *S*, *US*, *Ur*, *Ch*, *Ur*, *Ch*, *W*, *F* 2003 *E*, *M*, *M*, *Ur*, *US*, *Ar*, *NZ*, *It* 2004 *US*, *F*, *It*, *E* (R) 2005 *W*, *E*, *US*, *F*
Card, R 1996 *US*, *A* (R), *Ur*, *US*, *Ar* 1997 *US* (R), *J* (R), *HK*
Cardinal, ME 1986 *US* (R) 1987 *US*, *Tg*, *I*, *US* 1991 *S* 1993 *A* (R) 1994 *US*, *F*, *E*, *F* (R) 1995 *S*, *Fj* (R), *NZ*, *R*, *SA* 1996 *US*, *US*, *HK*, *J*, *A*, *HK*, *J* 1997 *US*, *US*, *W* (R), *I* 1998 *US*, *HK* (R) 1999 *Fj*, *US*, *W*, *E* (R), *Fj* (R), *Nm*
Carlson, LAG 2002 *Ur* (R), *W* (R) 2003 *E* (R)
Carpenter, A 2005 *US*, *J* (R), *E*, *US*, *Ar*, *F*, *R* 2006 *S*, *E* (R), *US* (R), *W* (R), *It* 2007 *IrA* (R), *M* (R), *US* (R), *NZ* (R), *Pt* (R), *W* (R), *Fj* (R), *J*, *A* (R)
Carr, NS 1985 *A*, *A*
Carson, DJ 1980 *W*, *US*, *NZ* 1981 *US*, *Ar* 1982 *J*, *E*, *US* 1983 *It*, *It*
Carson, SFB 1977 *E* (R)
Chambers, MP 1962 *Bb*, *W23* 1966 *BI*
Charron, AJ 1990 *Ar*, *US*, *Ar* 1991 *J*, *S*, *Fj*, *F*, *NZ* 1992 *US* 1993 *E*, *E*, *US*, *A*, *W* 1994 *US*, *F*, *W* 1995 *Fj*, *NZ*, *R*, *A*, *SA*, *US* 1996 *US*, *US*, *A*, *HK*, *J*, *Ur*, *US*, *Ar* 1997 *US*, *J*, *HK*, *HK*, *J*, *US*, *W*, *I* 1998 *US*, *HK*, *J*, *Ur*, *US*, *Ar* 1999 *Fj*, *Sa*, *US*, *Tg*, *W*, *E*, *F*, *Fj*, *Nm* 2000 *Tg*, *US*, *SA*, *Sa*, *Fj*, *J*, *It* 2001 *Ur*, *Ar*, *E*, *E* 2002 *S*, *US*, *US*, *Ur*, *Ch*, *Ur*, *Ch*, *F* 2003 *W*, *It*, *Tg*
Chung, L 1978 *F* (R)
Clapinson, N 1995 *US* (R) 1996 *US*
Clark, RM 1962 *Bb*
Clarke, D 1996 *A*
Clarkin, ME 1985 *A*, *A*
Collins, B 2004 *US* (R), *J* (R)
Collins, W 1977 *US*, *E*
Cooke, GG 2000 *Tg*, *US* 2001 *Fj*, *J* (R) 2003 *E*, *US*, *M*, *M*, *Ur*, *US* (R), *Ar* (R), *W* (R), *NZ*, *Tg* 2004 *E*, *US*, *It*, *E* (R) 2005 *US*, *J* (R), *W*, *Ar*, *F*, *R* 2006 *US* (R)
Cooper, I 1993 *W* (R)
Cordle, JA 1998 *HK* (R), *J* 1999 *J*, *Fj*, *Sa* (R) 2001 *J*
Cox, GER 1932 *J*
Creagh, S 1988 *US*
Cudmore, J 2002 *US* (R), *Ch*, *W* (R), *F* (R) 2003 *E*, *US*, *W* (R), *NZ*, *It*, *Tg* 2004 *US*, *F*, *It*, *E* 2005 *W*, *F* 2006 *US* 2007 *Pt*, *W*, *Fj*
Culpan, C 2006 *E* (R) 2007 *IrA*, *M*, *US*, *NZ*, *Pt*, *W*, *Fj*, *J*
Cummings, TJ 1966 *BI* 1973 *W*
Cvitak, Z 1983 *E*

Dala, N 2007 *IrA*, *US* (R)
Dandy, MJW 1977 *E*, *E*
Danskin, M 2001 *J* (R) 2004 *E*, *F* (R)
Daypuck, D 2004 *E* (R), *F* (R), *It* (R), *E* 2005 *US*, *J*, *W*, *E*, *Ar*, *F*, *R* (R) 2006 *S*, *US* (R), *US* (R), *W*, *It* 2007 *IrA* (R), *M*, *A*
de Goede, H 1976 *Bb* 1977 *US*, *E*, *E* 1978 *US* 1979 *US*, *F* 1980 *W*, *US*, *NZ* 1981 *US* 1982 *J*, *J*, *E*, *US* 1984 *US* 1985 *US* 1986 *J*, *US* 1987 *US*, *Tg*, *I*, *W*
de Goede, HW 1974 *Tg*
Deacy, F 1973 *W*
Delaney, J 1983 *E*
Densmore, P 2005 *E* (R)
Devlin, JD 1985 *US* 1986 *US*
di Girolamo, M 2001 *Ur*, *Ar* (R) 2002 *US*, *Ur* (R), *Ch*, *Ur*, *W* (R), *F* (R) 2003 *US*, *M* (R), *M*, *Ur*, *W*, *NZ*, *It*, *Tg* 2004 *E*, *US*, *F*, *It*, *E*
Dixon, GA 2000 *US* (R), *SA* (R), *I*, *Sa*, *Fj*, *J*, *It* (R) 2001 *US*, *Ar*, *E*, *E*
Docherty, D 1973 *W*
Donaldson, WJ 1978 *F* 1979 *US*, *F* 1980 *W*, *US*, *NZ* 1981 *US* 1982 *E*, *US* 1983 *US*, *It*, *It* 1984 *US*

Douglas, A 1974 *Tg*
Douglas, JT 2003 *M* (R), *M, Ur, US* (R), *Ar, NZ, It* 2004 *US, F* (R)
du Temple, A 1932 *J, J*
Dukelow, G 1980 *W, US, NZ* 1981 *US* 1982 *J, J, E, US* 1983 *US, It, It, E* 1984 *US* 1990 *US*
Dunkley, PJ 1998 *J, HK, US, HK, J, US, Ar* (R) 1999 *J, Fj* (R), *Sa, US* (R), *Tg, E, F, Fj, Nm* (R) 2000 *Tg, SA, I, Sa, Fj* 2001 *US, Ar, E, Fj, J* (R) 2002 *S, US, US, Ur, Ch, W, F* 2003 *M* (R), *M, Ur, Ar* 2005 *W* (R)
Dunning, C 2005 *E* (R), *US, Ar* (R), *F* (R), *R* (R)

Ebl, B 1995 *NZ* 1998 *J, HK*
Eburne, DC 1977 *US, E, E*
Eckardt, MA 1974 *Tg* 1977 *US, E, E* 1978 *US*
Edwards, IJ 1967 *E*
Ellwand, G 1973 *W*
Ennis, GD 1986 *J, US* 1987 *US, Tg* (R), *I, W* 1988 *US* 1989 *I, US* 1990 *Ar, US, Ar* (R) 1991 *J, S, US, Fj, R, F, NZ* 1993 *E, E* 1994 *US, W* (R) 1995 *Fj, NZ, R, A* (R), *SA* 1998 *J, HK, US, US*
Evans, EA 1986 *US* 1987 *US, Tg, I, US* 1989 *I, US* 1990 *Ar, Ar* 1991 *J, S, US, Fj, R, F, NZ* 1992 *US, E* 1993 *E, E* 1994 *US, F, W, E, F* 1995 *S, Ur, Ar, Fj, NZ, R, A, SA* 1996 *J, HK, J* 1997 *US, J, HK, J, US, W, I* (R) 1998 *J, HK, US* (R), *US, US, Ar*
Exner, I 2005 *E* (R), *US* (R)

Fairhurst, EG 2001 *US, Ar* 2002 *US* (R), *Ur* (R), *Ch* (R), *Ur, Ch, W* (R), *F* (R) 2003 *E* (R), *M* (R), *M* (R), *US, NZ, Tg* (R) 2004 *US, J, E* (R), *US, F* (R), *It, E* 2005 *US* (R), *W* (R), *E* (R), *US, F* 2006 *S, E, US* (R), *Bar* (R), *US* (R), *W, It* 2007 *IrA* (R), *M, US* (R), *NZ* (R), *Pt, W* (R), *A* (R)
Fauth, SC 2000 *Tg, US, SA, I, Sa, Fj, J, It* 2001 *US, Ar, E, E, Fj, J* 2002 *S, US, US, Ur, Ch, Ch, W, F* 2003 *US, M, Ur* (R), *US, Ar, NZ, Tg*
Felix, M 1985 *A, A* 1996 *Ur, US*
Fleck, P 2004 *US* (R), *J, It* (R), *E* 2005 *US, W* (R)
Fleming, I 1976 *Bb*
Forbes, AC 1932 *J, J*
Forster, F 1983 *US, It, It*
Foster, AE 1970 *Fj* 1976 *Bb* 1977 *US, E, E*
Fowler, C 1988 *US* 1990 *US*
Fraine, TE 1967 *E*
Frame, RP 1986 *J* 1987 *US, Tg, I, W, US*
Franklin, S 2007 *IrA, M, US, NZ, J* (R)
Fraser, G 1983 *E*
Frize, P 1962 *Bb, W23*
Fumano, GW 1967 *E* 1970 *Fj*
Fyffe, QA 2003 *E, US, NZ, It, Tg* 2004 *US, J, E, US, F, It* 2005 *US, J, W, Ar*

Gainer, F 2004 *US, J, E* (R), *US* (R), *F, It* (R), *E* 2005 *J, W* (R), *E, US, F* (R), *R* (R) 2006 *W, It*
Godziek, A 1982 *J, E, US* 1983 *US, It, It, E* 1984 *US*
Gonis, G 1977 *US, E, E,* 1978 *US*
Gordon, I 1991 *S* (R) 1992 *US, E* 1993 *US, A, W* 1994 *F, W, E, F* 1995 *S, R, SA, US* 1996 *US, HK, J, A, HK* 1997 *US* (R), *J, HK* (R) 1998 *J, HK, US* (R), *J* (R), *US, Ar* (R)
Graf, JD 1989 *I, US* 1990 *Ar* 1991 *S, R* 1992 *US, E* 1993 *E, E, US, A* 1994 *US, F, W, E, F* 1995 *S, Ur, Ar, Fj, NZ, R, A, SA, US* 1996 *US, HK, J, A, HK, J* 1997 *US, J, HK, HK, US, W, I* 1998 *J, HK, US, US* (R), *HK, J, Ur, US, Ar* 1999 *J, Fj, Sa, US, Tg, F* (R), *Nm* (R)
Granleese, W 1962 *W23*
Grant, G 1977 *E* (R), *E* 1978 *US* 1979 *US, F* 1980 *W*
Grant, I 1983 US, It, It, E
Grantham, PR 1962 *Bb, W23* 1966 *BI*
Gray, SD 1984 *US* 1987 *US, W, US* 1989 *I* 1990 *Ar, US, Ar* 1991 *J, S, Fj, F, NZ* 1992 *US, E* 1993 *E, E, US, A, W* 1994 *US, F, W, E* (R), *F* 1995 *S, Ar, Fj, NZ, R, A, SA, US* 1996 *US, US, HK, J, A, HK, J, US, Ar* 1997 *US, J, HK, J, US* (R)
Greig, GR 1973 *W*
Greig, J 1977 *US, E*
Grieg, JR 1978 *US* 1979 *US, F* 1980 *W, US, NZ* 1981 *Ar*
Grout, J 1995 *Ur*
Gudmundseth, G 1973 *W*

Hadley, N 1987 *US* 1989 *I, US* 1990 *Ar* 1991 *S, US, Fj, R, F, NZ* 1992 *US, E* 1993 *E* 1994 *E, F*
Haley, J 1996 *Ur*
Hall, J 1996 *US* (R) 1997 *HK* (R) 1998 *J, HK, J* (R), *US, Ar*
Handson, WT 1985 *A, A, US* 1986 *J, US* 1987 *US, Tg, I, W*
Hawthorn, JP 1982 *J, J, E* 1983 *US, It, It*
Healy, A 1996 *HK, J, HK, J, Ur, US, Ar* 1997 *US, HK, HK, I* (R) 1998 *HK, J, Ur* 1999 *J*
Heaman, AR 1988 *US*
Henderson, B 2005 *J, F, R*
Hendry, S 1996 *Ur, US, Ar*
Henrikson, G 1971 *W*
Hillier, L 1973 *W*
Hindson, RE 1973 *W* 1974 *Tg,* 1976 *Bb* 1977 *US, E, E* 1978 *US, F* 1979 *US, F* 1980 *W, US, NZ* 1981 *US, Ar* 1982 *J, J, E, US* 1983 *US, It, It* 1984 *US* 1985 *A, A, US* 1986 *J* 1987 *US, I, W* 1990 *Ar*
Hirayama, G 1977 *E, E* 1978 *US* 1979 *US, F* 1980 *W, US, NZ* 1981 *US* 1982 *J, E, US*
Hirayama, N 2007 *M* (R)
Holmes, M 1987 *US*
Howlett, P 1974 *Tg*
Hunnings, BM 1932 *J, J*
Hunt, E 1966 *BI* 1967 *E*
Hunter, S 2005 *R*
Hutchinson, J 1993 *E* (R), *A, W* 1995 *S* (R), *Ar, Fj* (R), *A, SA* (R), *US* 1996 *US, US, HK, J, A, HK, J, Ur, US, Ar* 1997 *US, J, HK, HK, J, US, W, I* 1998 *J, HK, US, US, HK, J, Ur* (R), *US, Ar* 1999 *J, Fj, Sa, US, Tg, W, E* (R), *F, Fj* (R), *Nm* 2000 *US, Sa, Fj, J*
Hyde-Lay, I 1986 *J* 1987 *US* 1988 *US*

Irvine, M 2000 *Tg* (R), *SA* (R), *I, Sa, Fj, J* (R) 2001 *US, Ar*

Jackart, DC 1991 *J, S, US, Fj, R, F* 1992 *US, E* 1993 *E, E, US, A, W* 1994 *US, F, W, E, F* 1995 *S, Ar, Fj*
Jackson, J 2003 *Ur, US, Ar, W, It* (R), *Tg* 2004 *E, US* (R), *It* (R), *E* 2005 *W* (R), *US, Ar, R* 2006 *S* 2007 *IrA, M* (R), *US* (R), *NZ* (R), *J* (R)
Jackson, RO 1970 *Fj* 1971 *W*
James, MB 1994 *US, F, W, E, F* 1995 *S, Ur, Ar, Fj, NZ, R, A, US* 1996 *US, US, HK, J, A, HK, J* 1997 *J, US, W, I* 1998 *US, US, Ur, US, Ar* 1999 *Sa, W, E, F, Fj, Nm* 2000 *It* 2002 *S, US, US, Ur, Ch, W, F* 2003 *M, M, Ur, US, Ar, W, Tg* 2005 *F* 2006 *US* 2007 *Pt, W, Fj, J, A*
Jennings, G 1981 *Ar* 1983 *US, It, It, E*
Johnson, O 1970 *Fj*
Johnston, G 1978 *F*
Johnstone, RR 2001 *Ur, Fj, J* 2002 *Ch, Ur, Ch* 2003 *E*
Jones, C 1983 *E* 1987 *US* (R)
Jones, EL 1982 *J* 1983 *US*

Kariya, TK 1967 *E* 1970 *Fj* 1971 *W*
Kennedy, A 1985 *A* (R), *A* (R)
Kennedy, I 1993 *A, W*
Kettleson, ED 1985 *US*
King, MMG 2002 *US* (R), *Ur* (R) 2003 *M, US, Ar* (R), *NZ* 2005 *US, J, W, E, US, Ar*
Kingham, A 1974 *Tg*
Kleeberger, A 2005 *F* (R), *R* (R) 2006 *S* (R), *E, US, Bar, It* (R) 2007 *IrA* (R), *M, US, NZ* (R), *Pt, J*
Knaggs, ERP 2000 *Tg, US* (R), *SA* (R), *I, Sa* (R), *Fj* (R), *J* (R) 2001 *US, Ur, Ar, E, E* (R), *Fj, J* 2002 *S* (R) 2003 *E, Ur, Ar* (R), *NZ*
Knauer, JD 1992 *E* 1993 *E, E, US, W*
Kokan, MJ 1984 *US* 1985 *US*
Kyle, P 1984 *US* (R)

La Carte, A 2004 *US* (R), *J* (R)
Langley, M 2004 *E* 2005 *Ar*
Lawson, MJ 2002 *US* (R), *Ur* (R), *Ch* (R), *Ur, Ch, F* (R) 2003 *E, US, M, M* (R), *Ur* (R), *US, Ar* (R), *W, It, Tg* 2004 *F* (R), *It, E* (R) 2005 *US, J, F* (R), *R* 2006 *US* (R), *W*
le Blanc, P 1994 *F* (R) 1995 *Ur, Fj* (R), *NZ*
le Fevre, CE 1976 *Bb*
Lecky, J 1962 *Bb, W23*
Lecky, JL 1982 *J, US* 1983 *US, It, It* 1984 *US* 1985 *A, US* 1986 *J, US* 1987 *I, W, US* 1991 *J, S, Fj, R*
Legh, GB 1973 *W* 1974 *Tg* 1976 *Bb*

Leroy, LSF 1932 *J*
Lorenz, J 1966 *Bl* 1970 *Fj* 1971 *W*
Lougheed, DC 1990 *Ar* 1991 *J, US* 1992 *US, E* 1993 *E, E, US* 1994 *F, W, E, F* 1995 *Fj, NZ, R, A, SA* 1996 *A, HK* 1997 *J, W, I* 1998 *US, Ar* 1999 *US, Tg, W, E, F, Fj, Nm* 2003 *W, It*
Loveday, J 1993 *E, E, US, A* 1996 *HK, J* 1998 *J* (R), *Ur* (R) 1999 *Sa* (R), *US* (R)
Luke, B 2004 *US* (R), *J* (R)
Luke, M 1974 *Tg* 1976 *Bb* 1977 *US, E, E* 1978 *US, F* 1979 *US, F* 1980 *W, US, NZ* 1981 *US* 1982 *J, US*
Lytton, S 1995 *Ur, Ar, US* 1996 *US, HK, J, J* (R), *US, Ar*

MacDonald, G 1970 *Fj*
MacDonald, GDT 1998 *HK* (R)
MacKay, I 1993 *A, W* (R)
MacKinnon, GI 1985 *US* 1986 *J* 1988 *US* 1989 *I, US* 1990 *Ar, Ar* 1991 *J, S, Fj, R, F, NZ* 1992 *US, E* 1993 *E* 1994 *US, F, W, E, F* 1995 *S, Ur, Ar, Fj, NZ, A, SA*
MacKinnon, S 1992 *US* 1995 *Ur, Ar, Fj* (R)
MacLachlan, C 1981 *Ar* 1982 *J, E*
Maclean, P 1983 *US, It, It, E*
Macmillan, I 1981 *Ar* 1982 *J, J, E, US*
Major, B 2001 *Fj* (R), *J*
Major, D 1999 *E* (R), *Fj* (R), *Nm* (R) 2000 *Tg* (R), *US, SA* (R), *I* (R), *Fj* (R) 2001 *Ur, E* (R), *E* (R)
Marshall, A 1997 *J* 1998 *Ur*
Mason, P 1974 *Tg*
McCarthy, B 1996 *US* (R), *Ar* 1998 *J* (R), *HK* (R), *J* (R)
McDonald, J 1974 *Tg*
McDonald, RN 1966 *Bl* 1967 *E* 1970 *Fj*
McGann, AG 1985 *A, A*
McGeein, R 1973 *W* (R)
McInnes, RI 1979 *F* 1980 *NZ* 1981 *US, Ar* 1982 *J, J, E, US* 1983 *US, It, It* 1984 *US* 1985 *US*
McKee, R 1962 *Bb, W23*
McKee, B 1966 *Bl* 1970 *Fj*
McKeen, S 2004 *US, J, E* (R), *US, F, It, E* 2005 *US, J, W, E, F, R* 2006 *S, US, US, W, It* 2007 *IrA, US, NZ*
McKellar, JR 1985 *A, A* 1986 *J* 1987 *W*
McKenna, JH 1967 *E*
McKenzie, C 1992 *US, E* 1993 *E, US, A, W* 1994 *US, F, W, E, F* 1995 *S, Ur, Ar, Fj, NZ, R, SA* 1996 *US, HK, J, J* 1997 *J, HK, I* (R)
McTavish, SG 1970 *Fj* 1971 *W* 1976 *Bb* 1977 *US, E, E* 1978 *US, F* 1979 *US, F* 1980 *W, US* 1981 *US, Ar* 1982 *J, J, E, US* 1985 *US* 1987 *US, Tg, I*
McWhinney, R 2005 *F* (R), *R*
Mensah-Coker, J 2006 *S, E, US, Bar, US, W* (R), *It* 2007 *US, NZ, Pt* (R), *J* (R), *A*
Michaluk, C 1995 *SA* (R) 1996 *US* (R), *J* (R) 1997 *US* (R), *HK*
Milau, N 2000 *US, J* (R)
Milne, DRW 1966 *Bl* 1967 *E*
Mitchell, AB 1932 *J, J*
Monaghan, P 1982 *J*
Monro, A 2006 *E, US, Bar, US, W* (R), *It* 2007 *M, W, A*
Moonlight, D 2003 *E* 2004 *E, E* 2005 *US*
Moore, DL 1962 *Bb, W23*
Morgan, K 1997 *HK, HK, J, W*
Moroney, VJP 1962 *Bb*
Mosychuk, B 1996 *Ur* 1997 *J* (R)
Moyes, J 1981 *Ar* 1982 *J, J, E, US*
Murphy, PT 2000 *Tg, US* (R), *SA, I, Sa, Fj, J* (R) 2001 *Fj, J* 2002 *S, US* (R), *US, Ur* (R), *Ch* (R), *W, F* 2003 *US, M, M* (R) 2004 *F*
Murray, WA 1932 *J*
Myhre, K 1970 *Fj*

Newton, J 1962 *W23*
Niblo, GN 1932 *J, J*
Nichols, K 1996 *Ur* 1998 *J, HK, US, US, Ur* 1999 *J, Fj, Sa, US, Tg* (R), *Fj, Nm* 2000 *Tg, US, SA, I, Sa, Fj, J, It* 2001 *Ur, E* (R), *Fj, J* (R) 2002 *S* (R)
Nikas, D 1995 *Ur*

O'Leary, S 2004 *US, J, E, E* (R) 2005 *J* (R)

Pacey, S 2005 *W* (R)
Pack, C 2006 *S, US*
Pagano, J 1997 *I* 1998 *J, HK, US, HK, J, US* 1999 *J, Fj, Nm*
Pahl, DV 1971 *W*
Palmer, P 1983 *E* 1984 *US* 1985 *A* 1986 *J, US* 1987 *Tg, I, W* 1988 *US* 1990 *Ar, US* 1991 *J, US, Fj, R, F* 1992 *US*
Parfrey, K 2005 *J* (R)
Pasutto, A 2004 *US, J* (R)
Peace, K 1978 *F* 1979 *US, F* 1980 *W, US*
Penaluna, J 1996 *Ur* (R)
Penney, DN 1995 *US* 1996 *US, A* (R), *US, Ar* 1997 *HK* (R) 1999 *E* (R)
Phelan, JM 1980 *NZ* 1981 *Ar* 1982 *J, J* 1985 *A, A*
Phinney, M 2006 *S* (R), *E*
Pinkham, EC 1932 *J*
Plater, C 2003 *E* (R)
Pletch, D 2004 *US* (R), *J, E* (R), *It* (R), *E* (R) 2005 *US* (R), *J, W* (R), *E* 2006 *S, E* (R), *US, Bar, US* (R), *W* (R), *It* 2007 *IrA, M* (R), *US* (R), *NZ* (R), *Pt* (R), *W* (R), *Fj* (R), *J* (R), *A* (R)
Pletch, M 2005 *Ar* (R) 2006 *S, E, US* (R), *Bar* (R), *W* (R), *It* (R) 2007 *IrA* (R), *M* (R), *US* (R), *NZ* (R), *Pt* (R), *W* (R), *J* (R), *A* (R)
Pritchard, J 2003 *M, M, Ur, US, Ar, W, Tg* (R) 2006 *S, US, Bar, US, W* 2007 *IrA, M, US, NZ, Pt, W, Fj, J, A*
Puil, G 1962 *Bb, W23*
Pyke, M 2004 *US, J, US, It* 2005 *US, F, R* 2006 *S, E, US, Bar, US, W, It* 2007 *IrA, M, US, NZ, Pt, W, Fj, J, A*

Quigley, DLJ 1976 *Bb* 1979 *F*

Radu, RE 1985 *A* 1986 *US* 1987 *US, Tg, I, US* 1988 *US* 1989 *I, US* 1990 *Ar* (R), *Ar* 1991 *US*
Ramsey, D 2005 *US*
Rees, GL 1986 *US* 1987 *US, Tg, I, W, US* 1989 *I, US* 1990 *Ar, Ar* 1991 *J, S, US, Fj, R, F, NZ* 1992 *US, E* 1993 *E, E, US, W* 1994 *US, F, W, E, F* 1995 *S, Fj, NZ, R, A, SA* 1996 *HK, J* 1997 *US, J, HK, J, US, W, I* 1998 *US, US, Ur* (R), *US, Ar* 1999 *Sa, Tg, W, E, F, Fj, Nm*
Reid, J 2003 *M* (R), *US, Ar, NZ, Tg* (R)
Relph, G 1974 *Tg*
Richmond, S 2004 *E, US, F, It, E* 2005 *US, W, E, US*
Riordan, PD 2003 *E* (R) 2004 *US* (R), *J* (R), *E* (R), *US* (R) 2006 *S, E* (R), *US, Bar, US, W* (R), *It* 2007 *IrA, M, US, NZ, Pt, W, Fj, J, A*
Robertsen, JR 1985 *A, A, US* 1986 *US* 1987 *Tg, US* 1989 *I, US* 1990 *Ar, US, Ar* 1991 *Fj, F*
Robertson, C 1997 *HK* (R) 1998 *US, US, HK, J, Ur* 2001 *Ur*
Robinson, AK 1998 *HK* (R)
Robinson, G 1966 *Bl*
Robson, R 1998 *HK* (R), *US* (R) 1999 *J* (R), *Tg* (R)
Rodgers, S 2005 *US* (R)
Ross, RP 1989 *I, US* (R) 1990 *US* 1995 *Ar* (R), *NZ* 1996 *US, US* (R), *HK, J, A, HK, J, Ur, US, Ar* 1997 *US* (R), *J* (R), *HK, HK, J, US, W* 1998 *J, HK, US, US* (R), *HK, J, Ur, US* (R) 1999 *J, Fj, Sa* (R), *US, W* (R), *E* (R), *F* (R), *Nm* (R) 2001 *Ur, E, E, Fj, J* 2002 *S* (R), *US* (R), *US* (R), *Ur* (R), *Ch* (R), *Ur* (R), *Ch, F* 2003 *E, US, M, Ur, Ar, W, Tg*
Rowland, JG 1932 *J, J*
Rowlands, G 1995 *Ar, NZ* (R), *A, US* 1996 *US, US*
Russell, RJ 1979 *US* 1983 *E* 1985 *A, A* (R)
Ryan, JB 1966 *Bl* 1967 *E*

Saundry, IH 1932 *J, J*
Schiefler, MD 1981 *US, Ar* 1982 *J, E, US* 1983 *US* 1984 *US*
Schielfer, MD 1980 *US, NZ*
Schmid, M 1996 *Ur, US, Ar* 1997 *US, J, US, W, I* 1998 *US, HK, J, Ur, Ar* 1999 *Sa* (R), *US* (R), *W* (R), *E* (R), *F* (R), *Fj, Nm* (R) 2001 *US, Ur, E* (R), *E* (R)
Scott, T 1976 *Bb*
Selkirk, S 1932 *J*
Shaw, JD 1978 *F*
Shergold, CJ 1980 *US* (R), *NZ* 1981 *US*
Shick, DM 1970 *Fj* 1971 *W*
Sinnott, DC 1979 *F* 1981 *US, Ar*
Skillings, FG 1932 *J, J*
Slater, DM 1971 *W*
Smith, C 1995 *Ur, US* 1996 *HK, J, Ur, US, Ar* 1997 *US* 1998 *J, HK, US, HK, Ur* 1999 *J, Fj, Sa, US, Tg, W, E, F*
Smith, RJ 2003 *E* (R), *M* (R), *M, Ur* (R), *US* (R), *Ar* (R), *W* (R), *NZ* (R), *Tg* (R) 2004 *US, J, E, US, F, It* (R), *E* 2005 *US, J, W, E, US* (R), *Ar, F, R* 2006 *S, Bar, US, W, It* 2007 *IrA, M* (R), *US, NZ, Pt, W* (R), *Fj, J*
Smythe, C 1997 *J, HK*

Snow, RGA 1995 *Ar, NZ* (R), *R, A, SA, US* 1996 *HK, J, A, HK, J* 1997 *US, HK, J, W, I* 1998 *US, US, US, Ar* 1999 *J, Fj, Sa, US, W, E, F, Fj, Nm* 2000 *I, J, It* 2001 *US, Ar, E, E, Fj, J* 2002 *S, US, US, Ur, Ch, Ur, Ch, W, F* 2003 *Ur, US* (R), *Ar, W, NZ* (R), *It, Tg* 2006 *US, Bar, US* 2007 *Pt, W, Fj, J, A* (R)
Spicer, D 2004 *E* (R) 2005 *R* 2006 *S* (R), *E, US, Bar, US, W* 2007 *IrA, US, NZ, Pt, W, Fj, J*
Spiers, DA 1988 *US* 1989 *I, US* 1991 *Fj, NZ*
Spofford, WE 1981 *Ar*
Stanley, W 1994 *US, F* 1995 *S, Ur, Ar, R, A, SA, US* 1996 *US, US, A, HK, J* 1997 *US, J, HK, HK, US, W, I* 1998 *US, US, HK, Ur, US, Ar* 1999 *J, Fj, Sa, US* (R), *Tg, W, E, F, Fj, Nm* 2000 *Tg, US, SA, I, Sa, Fj, J, It* 2001 *E, E* 2002 *S, US, US, Ur, Ch, Ur, Ch, W, F* 2003 *E, US, M, M, Ur, US, Ar, W, It, Tg*
Stanton, AI 1971 *W* 1973 *W* 1974 *Tg*
Stapleton, E 1978 *US, F*
Steen, D 1966 *BI*
Stephen, SM 2005 *E* (R), *US* (R) 2006 *S, E, US, Bar, US, W* 2007 *US, NZ, Pt, W, Fj, A*
Stewart, C 1991 *S, US, Fj, R, F, NZ* 1994 *E, F* 1995 *S, Fj, NZ* (R), *R, A, SA*
Stewart, DS 1989 *US* 1990 *Ar* (R) 1991 *US, Fj, R, F* (R), *NZ* 1992 *E* 1993 *E, E, US, A, W* 1994 *US, F, W, E, F* 1995 *S, Fj, NZ, R, A, SA, US* 1996 *US, US, A, HK, J, Ur, US, Ar* 1997 *US, J, HK, HK, J, US, W, I* 1998 *US, J, Ur, Ar* 1999 *Sa, US, Tg, W, E, F, Fj, Nm* 2000 *US, SA, I, Sa, Fj, It* 2001 *US, Ur, Ar, E, E*
Stewart, R 2005 *R*
Stoikos, B 2001 *Ur*
Stover, G 1962 *Bb*
Strang, R 1983 *E*
Strubin, C 2004 *E*
Stuart, IC 1984 *US* 1985 *A, A* 1986 *J* 1987 *US* (R), *Tg, I, W, US* 1988 *US* 1989 *US* 1990 *Ar, US, Ar* 1992 *E* 1993 *A, W* 1994 *US, F, W, E*
Stubbs, JD 1962 *Bb, W23*
Sturrock, FJ 1971 *W*
Suter, CW 1932 *J*
Svoboda, KF 1985 *A, A, US* 1986 *J, US* 1987 *W* 1990 *Ar, US, Ar* 1991 *J, US, R, F* 1992 *US, E* 1993 *E, E, US* 1994 *F* (R), *W, F* 1995 *Fj, A, US*
Szabo, P 1989 *I, US* 1990 *Ar, US, Ar* 1991 *NZ* 1993 *US* (R), *A, W*

Tait, JN 1997 *US, J, HK, HK, J, US, W, I* 1998 *US, Ur* (R), *Ar* 1999 *J, Fj, Sa* (R), *US, Tg, W, E, F, Fj, Nm* 2000 *Tg, US, SA, I, Sa, Fj, J, It* 2001 *US, Ur* (R), *Ar, E, E* 2002 *US, W, F*
Tait, L 2005 *US, J, W, E* 2006 *S, E, US, Bar, US, W, It* 2007 *M, US, NZ, Pt, W, Fj* (R), *A*
Taylor, WG 1978 *F* 1979 *US, F* 1980 *W, US, NZ* 1981 *US, Ar* 1983 *US* (R), *It* (R)
Thiel, J 1998 *HK, J, Ur* (R) 1999 *J, Fj* (R), *Sa* (R), *US* (R), *Tg, W* (R), *E, F, Fj, Nm* 2000 *SA, I, Sa, Fj, J* 2001 *US, Ar, E, E* 2002 *S, US, US, Ur, Ch, Ur, W, F* 2003 *Ur* (R), *US, Ar, W, It* 2004 *F* (R) 2007 *Pt, W, Fj, J, A*
Thompson, S 2001 *Fj* (R), *J*
Thomson, W 1970 *Fj*
Tkachuk, K 2000 *Tg, US* (R), *SA, Sa, Fj, It* 2001 *Fj* (R), *J* (R) 2002 *Ch* (R), *Ur* (R), *Ch* (R), *W* (R), *F* (R) 2003 *E, US, M, M, Ur* (R), *US, Ar* (R), *W* (R), *NZ, It* (R), *Tg* (R) 2004 *E, US, F, It, E* 2005 *US, J* (R), *W, Ar, F, R* 2006 *US, W, It* (R) 2007 *IrA* (R), *M, US, NZ*
Toews, H 1997 *HK* (R) 1998 *J, HK, HK* (R), *Ur* 1999 *Tg* (R) 2000 *US, Sa* (R), *J, It* 2001 *Fj* (R), *J*
Toews, R 1993 *W* 1994 *US, F, W, E* 1995 *S, Ur, Ar, Fj* 1996 *US, HK, J, A* (R) 1997 *US, I*
Tomlinson, J 1996 *A* (R) 2001 *Ur*
Trenkel, N 2007 *A* (R)
Tucker, DM 1985 *A, A, US* 1986 *US* 1987 *US, W* (R)
Tyler, A 2005 *Ar*
Tynan, A 1995 *Ur, Ar, US* 1997 *J* (R)
Tynan, CJ 1987 *US* 1988 *US* 1990 *Ar, US, Ar* 1991 *J, US, Fj, F, NZ* 1992 *US* 1993 *E, E, US, W* 1995 *NZ* (R) 1996 *US, J* 1997 *HK, J* 1998 *US*

Ure, DN 1962 *Bb, W23*

Vaesen, PC 1985 *US* 1986 *J* 1987 *US, Tg, US*
van Camp, D 2005 *J, R* (R) 2006 *It* (R) 2007 *IrA, M, US* (R), *NZ* (R)
van den Brink, R 1986 *US* 1987 *Tg* 1988 *US* 1991 *J, US, R, F* (R), *NZ*
van der Merwe, D 2006 *Bar* (R), *It* (R) 2007 *Pt, W, Fj, J, A*
Van Eeuwen, D 1978 *F* (R) 1979 *US*
van Staveren, A 2000 *Tg, Sa* (R), *Fj* (R) 2002 *US* (R), *US, Ur* (R), *Ch* (R), *Ur, Ch, W, F* (R) 2003 *E, US, M, M, Ur* (R), *US, W, NZ* (R), *Tg*
Verstraten, J 2000 *US* (R), *SA* (R), *Fj* (R), *J*
Vivian, J 1983 *E* 1984 *US*

Walt, KC 1976 *Bb* 1977 *US, E, E* 1978 *US, F*
Ward, JM 1962 *W23*
Webb, M 2004 *US, J, US* (R), *F, It* 2005 *US, J, W, E, US, Ar, F* 2006 *US* (R), *W, It* 2007 *M, J* (R), *A* (R)
Weingart, M 2004 *J* (R) 2005 *J, E, US, F* (R), *R* (R) 2007 *Pt* (R)
Wessels, GJM 1962 *W23*
Wharton, WR 1932 *J, J*
Whitley, K 1995 *S*
Whittaker, C 1993 *US* (R), *A* 1995 *Ur* 1996 *A* 1997 *J* (R) 1998 *J, HK, US* (R), *US* (R), *HK, J, US, Ar* (R) 1999 *J* (R), *Fj, US* (R)
Whitty, LW 1967 *E*
Whyte, DW 1974 *Tg* 1977 *US, E, E*
Wickland, RR 1966 *BI* 1967 *E*
Wiley, JP 1977 *US, E, E* 1978 *US, F* 1979 *US* 1980 *W, US, NZ* 1981 *US*
Wilke, K 1971 *W* 1973 *W* 1976 *Bb* 1978 *US*
Wilkinson, K 1976 *Bb* 1978 *F* 1979 *F*
Williams, BN 1962 *W23*
Williams, J 2001 *US, Ur, Ar, Fj, J*
Williams, M 1999 *Tg* (R), *W, E, F, Fj, Nm* 2000 *Tg, SA, I, Sa, Fj, J, It* 2001 *E, E, Fj, J* 2002 *S, US, US, Ur, Ch, W, F* 2003 *E, US, M, M, Ur, US* (R), *Ar, W, It, Tg* 2004 *E, US, F* 2005 *W, Ar, F, R* 2006 *E, US, Bar, US, W, It* 2007 *IrA, M* (R), *US, NZ, W, Fj, J, A*
Williams, M 1992 *E* 1993 *A, W*
Williams, MH 1978 *US, F* 1980 *US*, 1982 *J*
Wilson, PG 1932 *J, J*
Wilson, RS 1962 *Bb*
Wirachowski, K 1992 *E* (R) 1993 *US* 1996 *US, HK, Ur, US, Ar* 1997 *US* (R), *HK* 2000 *It* (R) 2001 *Ur* (R), *E* (R), *Fj* (R), *J* 2002 *S* (R), *Ch* 2003 *E* (R), *US* (R), *M* (R)
Wish, T 2004 *US, J*
Witkowski, K 2005 *E, Ar* 2006 *E* (R)
Witkowski, N 1998 *US* (R), *J* (R) 2000 *Tg, US, SA, I, Sa, Fj, J, It* 2001 *US, E, E* 2002 *S, US, US, Ur, Ch, Ur, Ch, W, F* 2003 *E, US, M, M* (R), *Ur, Ar, W, NZ* (R), *Tg* 2005 *E* (R), *US* 2006 *E*
Woller, AH 1967 *E*
Wood, S 1977 *E* (R)
Woods, TA 1984 *US* 1986 *J, US* 1987 *US, Tg, I, W* 1988 *US* 1989 *I, US* 1990 *Ar, US* 1991 *S, F, NZ* 1996 *US, US* 1997 *US, J*
Wyatt, MA 1982 *J, J, E, US* 1983 *US, It, It, E* 1985 *A, A, US* 1986 *J, US* 1987 *Tg, I, W, US* 1988 *US* 1989 *I, US* 1990 *Ar, US, Ar* 1991 *J, S, US, R, F, NZ*
Wyndham, H 1973 *W*

Yeganegi, JJ 1996 *US* (R) 1998 *J* (R)
Yukes, C 2001 *Ur* (R), *Fj, J* 2002 *S* (R), *US* (R), *Ur, Ur* 2003 *E* (R), *US, M, M, US, Ar, W, NZ* (R), *It, Tg* (R) 2004 *US, J, E, US, F, It, E* 2005 *W, E, US* 2006 *Bar, US* (R) 2007 *IrA, US, NZ, Pt* (R), *W* (R), *Fj* (R), *J, A*

ENGLAND

ENGLAND'S 2006–07 TEST RECORD

OPPONENTS	DATE	VENUE	RESULT
New Zealand	5 November	H	**Lost** 20–41
Argentina	11 November	H	**Lost** 18–25
South Africa	18 November	H	**Won** 23–21
South Africa	25 November	H	**Lost** 14–25
Scotland	3 February	H	**Won** 42–20
Italy	10 February	A	**Won** 20–7
Ireland	24 February	A	**Lost** 13–43
France	11 March	H	**Won** 26–18
Wales	17 March	A	**Lost** 18–27
South Africa	26 May	A	**Lost** 10–58
South Africa	2 June	A	**Lost** 22–55
Wales	4 August	H	**Won** 62–5
France	11 August	H	**Lost** 15–21
France	18 August	A	**Lost** 9–22
USA	8 September	N	**Won** 28–10 (WC)
South Africa	14 September	N	**Lost** 0–36 (WC)
Samoa	22 September	N	**Won** 44–22 (WC)
Tonga	28 September	N	**Won** 36–20 (WC)
Australia	6 October	N	**Won** 12–10 (WC)
France	13 October	N	**Won** 14–9 (WC)
South Africa	20 October	N	**Lost** 6–15 (WC)

GLORY BOYS DEFY THE ODDS

By Iain Spragg

Dave Rogers/Getty Images

There was a lot for England captain Phil Vickery to be happy about at the World Cup.

"**They did fantastically well** getting into the final but in days to come, they'll reflect on what they've done and be really proud," England coach Brian Ashton said after his side's 15–6 defeat to South Africa in the final of the Rugby World Cup. "I don't think anyone outside the squad gave them a cat in hell's chance of doing anything at all."

The fact England pushed the Springboks so close in the final in Paris was not a surprise – the fact they made it to the Stade de France at all to defend their title was. Ashton's side had been written off before the tournament had even started and after their 36–0 mauling by the South Africans in the group stages, the sceptics were confidently predicting an early flight home for the 2003 champions.

But England were made of sterner stuff and although they fell at the final hurdle against the Springboks, it was a valiant attempt to become the first side to mount a successful defence of the World Cup.

The final itself was an epic if not expansive encounter. England shaded the territory and possession over the 80 minutes but were punished by Percy Montgomery's boot and trailed 9–3 at half-time.

The second-half started explosively when Mark Cueto thought he had scored in the corner only for the TMO to adjudge his boot had brushed the line before he grounded the ball and although Jonny Wilkinson landed his second penalty for an earlier infringement, England's big chance had gone. Montgomery landed his fourth penalty minutes later and when youngster Francois Steyn kicked a three-pointer from half-way, the writing was on the wall.

"South Africa deserve to win, they've been fantastic all tournament so big respect to them," Wilkinson conceded. "It's well due and it's their moment. But it's disappointing. We gave it everything. At times we got close enough and we never really felt we were going to lose. We had a lot of ground to catch up in this tournament and the guys all took the responsibility and I was proud of them all. It has been a hell of a journey."

England's first tentative, timid steps at the World Cup did little to suggest Ashton's side had the self-belief, let alone playing resources, to make any significant impression on the tournament. In fact, the defending champions were so thoroughly abject in their opening two Pool A games that there were serious doubts whether they would even make the knockout stages.

Their opener against the USA in Lens should have been the ideal warm-up for the sterner tests ahead. The Americans were expected to offer little more than token resistance at the Stade Felix Bollaert but England stuttered in every facet of their game in the face of an impassioned Eagles performance and their eventual 28–10 victory – with one solitary try in the second-half – did nothing to dispel the pre-tournament fears that the side had no chance of defending their title.

"We've made a winning start but it was less than a satisfactory performance," Ashton conceded after the game. "I am disappointed with the display but we need to put that behind us. We have six days before we play South Africa."

If the English were hoping facing the powerful Springboks in Paris six days later would galvanise the team, they were sorely mistaken. South Africa dominated a one-sided game from start to finish and Ashton's side failed to trouble the scorers.

First-half tries from Juan Smith and JP Pietersen set the ominous tone and after the break, Pietersen's second score completed a 36–0 rout. England's misery was compounded when Jason Robinson, the only player

Cameron Spencer/Getty Images

Mark Cueto's 'try' is disallowed in the final, and with that decision went England's hopes.

to emerge with any credit, limped off with a hamstring injury and the men in white crashed to their first defeat in the World Cup since their 1999 reverse to the Springboks in the French capital. It was a body blow to the English challenge and with the big-hitting Samoans and then Tonga lying in wait for the wounded champions, the vultures were circling.

The good news was that Ashton was able to welcome Wilkinson back for the Samoa clash in Nantes. The Newcastle fly-half had recovered from his ankle injury and he was one of seven changes to the starting XV who took to the pitch at the Stade de la Beaujoire hoping to get the campaign back on track before it was fatally derailed.

The green shoots of recovery were not exactly bursting through in England's performance but it was undoubtedly a better display against a fiercely-committed Samoan team and two tries apiece from Paul Sackey and stand-in captain Martin Corry, both either side of the break, were enough to steer the side to a 44–22 victory.

"We want to congratulate England," said Samoa coach and legendary All Black flanker Michael Jones. "They've made a statement that they're on their way back. England hang tough and that's a sign of a good team."

Victory set up a winner-takes-all clash with Tonga in the final group game at the famous old Parc des Princes. England were showing signs of improvement but defeat would still condemn the team to an ignominious and decidedly early exit from the tournament.

The final 36–20 scoreline in Paris suggested a nerve-inducing 80 minutes and although the Tongans did lead 10–8 after 20 minutes, England stepped up their game and three further tries to add to Sackey's opener ensured the reigning world champions progressed safely to the quarter-finals.

In a repeat of the dramatic 2003 final, England faced Australia in Marseille. The Wallabies played down all talk of revenge before the game but the sense of payback hung in the air as the two teams stepped out in the south of France. The English were becoming accustomed to their billing as underdogs while the Australians emanated self-belief.

The opening 20 minutes were agonisingly tense as Stirling Mortlock and Wilkinson traded penalties but England's forward power got its first tangible reward when the Australian front row were penalised for collapsing the scrum and Wilkinson's second penalty made it 6–3.

The lead lasted 10 minutes. The Australian mounted a multi-phased onslaught on England's defences and the line finally gave way in the corner as Lote Tuqiri beat Josh Lewsey's tackle and scored, as he had done in the 2003 final. Mortlock added the two points and the Wallabies had a 10–6 cushion.

After the break, however, England's pack were becoming increasingly influential as the Australian scrum creaked alarmingly and Wilkinson's third penalty after 51 minutes made it a one-point game. Ten minutes later the champions had their noses in front as the Wallaby scrum disintegrated and Rocky Elsom was penalised for offside. Wilkinson duly obliged once again with the boot and it was 12–10 to Ashton's team.

There were still 20 minutes to play. The Australians had just one significant chance to rescue themselves but Mortlock's 45 metre penalty attempt from the touchline sailed wide and against the odds England were through to the semi-finals. In a tournament replete with upsets, it was still a stunning result.

France in the last four was England's reward – a rerun of their encounter four years earlier – but this time Les Bleus had home advantage on their side, an expectant Stade de France crowd behind them and a stunning victory over the All Blacks under their belt.

The game began in explosive fashion as Josh Lewsey crashed over the line after just 78 seconds after a horrendous misjudgement by full-back Damien Traille and although Wilkinson was wayward with his touchline conversion attempt, England were ahead.

Three penalties from Lionel Beauxis dragged France back into the

Shaun Botterill/Getty Images

This Jonny Wilkinson drop goal sent England through against France.

game but England squeezed the life out of the home side in the second-half and Wilkinson rediscovered his range with two penalties to establish a slender 11–9 lead. The crowd knew the next score would probably settle matters and, perhaps predictably, it was Wilkinson who provided it with a trademark drop goal. England had once again broken French hearts and despite their desperate travails earlier in the competition, they were through to a second successive World Cup final against all the odds. A day later, South Africa ended Argentina's brave challenge in the second semi-final and the stage was set for the second instalment of England against the Springboks.

England, however, could not have begun their World Cup build-up in less convincing fashion. The four Autumn internationals in the bosom of Twickenham saw the side well beaten by New Zealand, lose for the first time to Argentina at home – a record seventh straight Test defeat – and although they narrowly won the first of their two games against South Africa, the Springboks claimed the second to complete a miserable pre-Christmas programme.

The debacle cost Andy Robinson his job as head coach and Brian Ashton was promoted from attack coach as his replacement. The change initially seemed to transform England's fortunes with successive wins over Scotland and Italy in the Six Nations but a demoralising 43–13 mauling by the Irish at Croke Park saw the storm clouds gathering once again. France were beaten at Twickenham to restore some confidence but defeat to Wales in Cardiff in their final game was ample evidence of the team's continuing frailties.

The two-Test summer tour of South Africa was the last thing Ashton needed and he was forced to name a shadow squad that were like lambs to the slaughter. The first Test in Bloemfontein produced a 58–10 hammering and although the second game in Pretoria a week later saw England provide more stubborn resistance, the final 55–22 scoreline was hardly a step in the right direction.

Ashton's pre-World Cup woes were briefly alleviated with a record 62–5 warm-up win over Wales at Twickenham but it was the French who brought England back down to earth in the next two games with back-to-back wins that suggested England's reign as world champions was about to come to an abrupt and imminent end. That the side made it all the way through to the final was as surprising as it was dramatic.

ENGLAND INTERNATIONAL STATISTICS

MATCH RECORDS UP TO 31ST OCTOBER 2007

MOST CONSECUTIVE TEST WINS

14	2002 W,It,Arg,NZ,A,SA,	2003 F1,W1,It,S,I, NZ,A,W2
11	2000 SA 2,A,Arg,SA3,	2001 W,It,S,F,C1,2, US
10	1882 W, 1883 I,S,	1884 W,I,S, 1885 W,I, 1886 W,I
10	1994 R,C,	1995 I,F,W,S, Arg, It, WS, A
10	2003 F,Gg,SA,Sm,U,W,F,A,	2004 It,S

MOST CONSECUTIVE TESTS WITHOUT DEFEAT

Matches	Wins	Draws	Periods
14	14	0	2002 to 2003
12	10	2	1882 to 1887
11	10	1	1922 to 1924
11	11	0	2000 to 2001

MOST POINTS IN A MATCH

BY THE TEAM

Pts.	Opponents	Venue	Year
134	Romania	Twickenham	2001
111	Uruguay	Brisbane	2003
110	Netherlands	Huddersfield	1998
106	U S A	Twickenham	1999
101	Tonga	Twickenham	1999
84	Georgia	Perth	2003
80	Italy	Twickenham	2001

BY A PLAYER

Pts.	Player	Opponents	Venue	Year
44	C Hodgson	Romania	Twickenham	2001
36	P J Grayson	Tonga	Twickenham	1999
35	J P Wilkinson	Italy	Twickenham	2001
32	J P Wilkinson	Italy	Twickenham	1999
30	C R Andrew	Canada	Twickenham	1994
30	P J Grayson	Netherlands	Huddersfield	1998
30	J P Wilkinson	Wales	Twickenham	2002
29	D J H Walder	Canada	Burnaby	2001
27	C R Andrew	South Africa	Pretoria	1994
27	J P Wilkinson	South Africa	Bloemfontein	2000
27	C C Hodgson	South Africa	Twickenham	2004
27	J P Wilkinson	Scotland	Twickenham	2007
26	J P Wilkinson	United States	Twickenham	1999

MOST TRIES IN A MATCH

BY THE TEAM

Tries	Opponents	Venue	Year
20	Romania	Twickenham	2001
17	Uruguay	Brisbane	2003
16	Netherlands	Huddersfield	1998
16	United States	Twickenham	1999
13	Wales	Blackheath	1881
13	Tonga	Twickenham	1999
12	Georgia	Perth	2003
12	Canada	Twickenham	2004
10	Japan	Sydney	1987
10	Fiji	Twickenham	1989
10	Italy	Twickenham	2001

BY A PLAYER

Tries	Player	Opponents	Venue	Year
5	D Lambert	France	Richmond	1907
5	R Underwood	Fiji	Twickenham	1989
5	O J Lewsey	Uruguay	Brisbane	2003
4	G W Burton	Wales	Blackheath	1881
4	A Hudson	France	Paris	1906
4	R W Poulton	France	Paris	1914
4	C Oti	Romania	Bucharest	1989
4	J C Guscott	Netherlands	Huddersfield	1998
4	N A Back	Netherlands	Huddersfield	1998
4	J C Guscott	United States	Twickenham	1999
4	J Robinson	Romania	Twickenham	2001
4	N Easter	Wales	Twickenham	2007

MOST CONVERSIONS IN A MATCH

BY THE TEAM

Cons	Opponents	Venue	Year
15	Netherlands	Huddersfield	1998
14	Romania	Twickenham	2001
13	United States	Twickenham	1999
13	Uruguay	Brisbane	2003
12	Tonga	Twickenham	1999
9	Italy	Twickenham	2001
9	Georgia	Perth	2003
8	Romania	Bucharest	1989
7	Wales	Blackheath	1881
7	Japan	Sydney	1987
7	Argentina	Twickenham	1990
7	Wales	Twickenham	1998
7	Wales	Twickenham	2007

BY A PLAYER

Cons	Player	Opponents	Venue	Year
15	P J Grayson	Netherlands	Huddersfield	1998
14	C Hodgson	Romania	Twickenham	2001
13	J P Wilkinson	United States	Twickenham	1999
12	P J Grayson	Tonga	Twickenham	1999
11	P J Grayson	Uruguay	Brisbane	2003
9	J P Wilkinson	Italy	Twickenham	2001
8	S D Hodgkinson	Romania	Bucharest	1989
7	J M Webb	Japan	Sydney	1987
7	S D Hodgkinson	Argentina	Twickenham	1990
7	P J Grayson	Wales	Twickenham	1998
7	J P Wilkinson	Wales	Twickenham	2007

MOST PENALTIES IN A MATCH

BY THE TEAM

Pens	Opponents	Venue	Year
8	South Africa	Bloemfontein	2000
7	Wales	Cardiff	1991
7	Scotland	Twickenham	1995
7	France	Twickenham	1999
7	Fiji	Twickenham	1999
7	South Africa	Paris	1999
7	South Africa	Twickenham	2001
6	Wales	Twickenham	1986
6	Canada	Twickenham	1994
6	Argentina	Durban	1995
6	Scotland	Murrayfield	1996
6	Ireland	Twickenham	1996
6	South Africa	Twickenham	2000
6	Australia	Twickenham	2002
6	Wales	Brisbane	2003

BY A PLAYER

Pens	Player	Opponents	Venue	Year
8	J P Wilkinson	South Africa	Bloemfontein	2000
7	S D Hodgkinson	Wales	Cardiff	1991
7	C R Andrew	Scotland	Twickenham	1995
7	J P Wilkinson	France	Twickenham	1999
7	J P Wilkinson	Fiji	Twickenham	1999
7	J P Wilkinson	South Africa	Twickenham	2001
6	C R Andrew	Wales	Twickenham	1986
6	C R Andrew	Canada	Twickenham	1994
6	C R Andrew	Argentina	Durban	1995
6	P J Grayson	Scotland	Murrayfield	1996
6	P J Grayson	Ireland	Twickenham	1996
6	P J Grayson	South Africa	Paris	1999
6	J P Wilkinson	South Africa	Twickenham	2000
6	J P Wilkinson	Australia	Twickenham	2002
6	J P Wilkinson	Wales	Brisbane	2003

MOST DROPPED GOALS IN A MATCH

BY THE TEAM

Drops	Opponents	Venue	Year
3	France	Sydney	2003
2	Ireland	Twickenham	1970
2	France	Paris	1978
2	France	Paris	1980
2	Romania	Twickenham	1985
2	Fiji	Suva	1991
2	Argentina	Durban	1995
2	France	Paris	1996
2	Australia	Twickenham	2001
2	Wales	Cardiff	2003
2	Ireland	Dublin	2003
3	South Africa	Perth	2003
2	Samoa	Nantes	2007
2	Tonga	Paris	2007

BY A PLAYER

Drops	Player	Opponents	Venue	Year
3	J P Wilkinson	France	Sydney	2003
2	R Hiller	Ireland	Twickenham	1970
2	A G B Old	France	Paris	1978
2	J P Horton	France	Paris	1980
2	C R Andrew	Romania	Twickenham	1985
2	C R Andrew	Fiji	Suva	1991
2	C R Andrew	Argentina	Durban	1995
2	P J Grayson	France	Paris	1996
2	J P Wilkinson	Australia	Twickenham	2001
2	J P Wilkinson	Wales	Cardiff	2003
2	J P Wilkinson	Ireland	Dublin	2003
2	J P Wilkinson	South Africa	Perth	2003
2	J P Wilkinson	Samoa	Nantes	2007
2	J P Wilkinson	Tonga	Paris	2007

CAREER RECORDS

MOST CAPPED PLAYERS

Caps	Player	Career Span
114	J Leonard	1990 to 2004
85	R Underwood	1984 to 1996
85	L B N Dallaglio	1995 to 2007
84	M O Johnson	1993 to 2003
77	M J S Dawson	1995 to 2006
75	M J Catt	1994 to 2007
72	W D C Carling	1988 to 1997
71	C R Andrew	1985 to 1997
71	R A Hill	1997 to 2004
69	D J Grewcock	1997 to 2007
66	N A Back	1994 to 2003
65	J C Guscott	1989 to 1999
65	J P Wilkinson	1998 to 2007
65	J P R Worsley	1999 to 2007
64	B C Moore	1987 to 1995
64	M E Corry	1997 to 2007
60	P J Vickery	1998 to 2007
58	P J Winterbottom	1982 to 1993
57	B C Cohen	2000 to 2006
55	W A Dooley	1985 to 1993
55	W J H Greenwood	1997 to 2004
55	O J Lewsey	1998 to 2007
54	G C Rowntree	1995 to 2006
53	M J Tindall	2000 to 2007
53	B J Kay	2001 to 2007
52	L W Moody	2001 to 2007
51	A S Healey	1997 to 2003
51	K P P Bracken	1993 to 2003
51	J T Robinson	2001 to 2007

MOST CONSECUTIVE TESTS

Tests	Player	Span
44	W D C Carling	1989 to 1995
40	J Leonard	1990 to 1995
36	J V Pullin	1968 to 1975
33	W B Beaumont	1975 to 1982
30	R Underwood	1992 to 1996

MOST TESTS AS CAPTAIN

Tests	Player	Span
59	W D C Carling	1988 to 1996
39	M O Johnson	1998 to 2003
22	L B N Dallaglio	1997 to 2004
21	W B Beaumont	1978 to 1982
17	M E Corry	2005 to 2007
13	W W Wakefield	1924 to 1926
13	N M Hall	1949 to 1955
13	E Evans	1956 to 1958
13	R E G Jeeps	1960 to 1962
13	J V Pullin	1972 to 1975

MOST POINTS IN TESTS

Points	Player	Tests	Career
982	J P Wilkinson	65	1998 to 2007
400	P J Grayson	32	1995 to 2004
396	C R Andrew	71	1985 to 1997
296	J M Webb	33	1987 to 1993
259	C C Hodgson	29	2001 to 2006
240	W H Hare	25	1974 to 1984
210	R Underwood	85	1984 to 1996

MOST TRIES IN TESTS

Tries	Player	Tests	Career
49	R Underwood	85	1984 to 1996
31	W J H Greenwood	55	1997 to 2004
31	B C Cohen	57	2000 to 2006
30	J C Guscott	65	1989 to 1999
28	J T Robinson	51	2001 to 2007
24	D D Luger	38	1998 to 2003
22	O J Lewsey	55	1998 to 2007
18	C N Lowe	25	1913 to 1923
17	L B N Dallaglio	85	1995 to 2007
16	N A Back	66	1994 to 2003
16	M J S Dawson	77	1995 to 2006
15	A S Healey	51	1997 to 2003
13	T Underwood	27	1992 to 1998
13	M J Tindall	53	2000 to 2007
13	M J Cueto	24	2004 to 2007
13	I R Balshaw	30	2000 to 2007

MOST CONVERSIONS IN TESTS

Cons	Player	Tests	Career
140	J P Wilkinson	65	1998 to 2007
78	P J Grayson	32	1995 to 2004
44	C C Hodgson	29	2001 to 2006
41	J M Webb	33	1987 to 1993
35	S D Hodgkinson	14	1989 to 1991
33	C R Andrew	71	1985 to 1997
17	L Stokes	12	1875 to 1881

MOST DROPPED GOALS IN TESTS

Drops	Player	Tests	Career
27	J P Wilkinson	65	1998 to 2007
21	C R Andrew	71	1985 to 1997
6	P J Grayson	32	1995 to 2004
4	J P Horton	13	1978 to 1984
4	L Cusworth	12	1979 to 1988

MOST PENALTY GOALS IN TESTS

Pens	Player	Tests	Career
197	J P Wilkinson	65	1998 to 2007
86	C R Andrew	71	1985 to 1997
72	P J Grayson	32	1995 to 2004
67	W H Hare	25	1974 to 1984
66	J M Webb	33	1987 to 1993
44	C C Hodgson	29	2001 to 2006
43	S D Hodgkinson	14	1989 to 1991

INTERNATIONAL CHAMPIONSHIP RECORDS

RECORD	DETAIL		SET
Most points in season	229	in five matches	2001
Most tries in season	29	in five matches	2001
Highest Score	80	80–23 v Italy	2001
Biggest win	57	80–23 v Italy	2001
Highest score conceded	43	13–43 v Ireland	2007
Biggest defeat	30	13–43 v Ireland	2007
Most appearances	54	J Leonard	1991–2004
Most points in matches	429	J P Wilkinson	1998–2007
Most points in season	89	J P Wilkinson	2001
Most points in match	35	J P Wilkinson	v Italy, 2001
Most tries in matches	18	C N Lowe	1913–1923
	18	R Underwood	1984–1996
Most tries in season	8	C N Lowe	1914
Most tries in match	4	R W Poulton	v France, 1914
Most cons in matches	77	J P Wilkinson	1998–2007
Most cons in season	24	J P Wilkinson	2001
Most cons in match	9	J P Wilkinson	v Italy, 2001
Most pens in matches	78	J P Wilkinson	1998–2007
Most pens in season	18	S D Hodgkinson	1991
	18	J P Wilkinson	2000
Most pens in match	7	S D Hodgkinson	v Wales, 1991
	7	C R Andrew	v Scotland, 1995
	7	J P Wilkinson	v France, 1999
Most drops in matches	9	C R Andrew	1985–1997
Most drops in season	5	J P Wilkinson	2003
Most drops in match	2	R Hiller	v Ireland, 1970
	2	A G B Old	v France, 1978
	2	J P Horton	v France, 1980
	2	P J Grayson	v France, 1996
	2	J P Wilkinson	v Wales, 2003
	2	J P Wilkinson	v Ireland, 2003

MISCELLANEOUS RECORDS

RECORD	HOLDER	DETAIL
Longest Test Career	J Leonard	1990 to 2004
Youngest Test Cap	H C C Laird	18 yrs 134 days in 1927
Oldest Test Cap	F Gilbert	38 yrs 362 days in 1923

CAREER RECORDS OF ENGLAND INTERNATIONAL PLAYERS (PLAYERS CAPPED SINCE THE START OF RWC 2003 UP TO 31 OCTOBER 2007)

PLAYER BACKS	DEBUT	CAPS	T	C	P	D	PTS
N Abendanon	2007 v SA	2	0	0	0	0	0
A Allen	2006 v NZ	2	0	0	0	0	0
I R Balshaw	2000 v I	30	13	0	0	0	65
O J Barkley	2001 v US	21	2	6	16	0	70
M Brown	2007 v SA	2	0	0	0	0	0
M J Catt	1994 v W	75	7	16	22	3	142
B C Cohen	2000 v I	57	31	0	0	0	155
M J Cueto	2004 v C	24	13	0	0	0	65
H A Ellis	2004 v SA	18	3	0	0	0	15
A Farrell	2007 v S	8	1	0	0	0	5
T Flood	2006 v Arg	12	1	2	5	1	27
S Geraghty	2007 v F	2	0	1	1	0	5
A J Goode	2005 v It	9	0	7	10	1	47
A C T Gomarsall	1996 v It	33	6	2	0	1	37
D Hipkiss	2007 v W	6	0	0	0	0	0
C C Hodgson	2001 v R	29	6	44	44	3	259
O J Lewsey	1998 v NZ	55	22	0	0	0	110
O Morgan	2007 v S	2	0	0	0	0	0
J D Noon	2001 v C	27	6	0	0	0	30
S Perry	2006 v NZ	14	2	0	0	0	10
P C Richards	2006 v A	12	0	0	0	0	0
J T Robinson	2001 v It	51	28	0	0	0	140
P H Sackey	2006 v NZ	10	5	0	0	0	25
D G R Scarbrough	2003 v W	2	1	0	0	0	5
J D Simpson-Daniel	2002 v NZ	10	3	0	0	0	15
D Strettle	2007 v I	4	1	0	0	0	5
M Tait	2005 v W	19	2	0	0	0	10
M J Tindall	2000 v I	53	13	2	0	0	69
J P Wilkinson	1998 v I	65	6	140	197	27	982

FORWARDS

S W Borthwick	2001 v F	32	2	0	0	0	10
A Brown	2006 v A	3	0	0	0	0	0
M I Cairns	2007 v SA	1	0	0	0	0	0
G S Chuter	2006 v A	19	1	0	0	0	5
M E Corry	1997 v Arg	64	6	0	0	0	30
D E Crompton	2007 v SA	1	0	0	0	0	0
L B N Dallaglio	1995 v SA	85	17	0	0	0	85
L P Deacon	2005 v Sm	8	0	0	0	0	0
N Easter	2007 v It	12	4	0	0	0	20
P T Freshwater	2005 v Sm	10	0	0	0	0	0
D J Grewcock	1997 v Arg	69	2	0	0	0	10
J Haskell	2007 v W	2	0	0	0	0	0
A R Hazell	2004 v C	7	1	0	0	0	5
C M Jones	2004 v It	12	1	0	0	0	5
B J Kay	2001 v C	53	2	0	0	0	10
M B Lund	2006 v A	10	1	0	0	0	5
L A Mears	2005 v Sm	18	0	0	0	0	0
L W Moody	2001 v C	52	9	0	0	0	45
T Palmer	2001 v US	8	0	0	0	0	0
T A N Payne	2004 v A	5	0	0	0	0	0
T Rees	2007 v S	8	1	0	0	0	5
M P Regan	1995 v SA	43	3	0	0	0	15
P H Sanderson	1998 v NZ	16	1	0	0	0	5
D Schofield	2007 v SA	2	0	0	0	0	0
S D Shaw	1996 v It	43	2	0	0	0	10
A J Sheridan	2004 v C	20	0	0	0	0	0
B Skirving	2007 v SA	1	0	0	0	0	0
M J H Stevens	2004 v NZ	21	0	0	0	0	0
A J Titterrell	2004 v NZ	5	0	0	0	0	0
S C Turner	2007 v W	3	0	0	0	0	0
P J Vickery	1998 v W	60	2	0	0	0	10
J M White	2000 v SA	44	0	0	0	0	0
R A Winters	2007 v SA	2	0	0	0	0	0
J P R Worsley	1999 v Tg	65	9	0	0	0	45
K P Yates	1997 v Arg	4	0	0	0	0	0

ENGLAND INTERNATIONAL PLAYERS (UP TO 31 OCTOBER 2007)

Note: Years given for International Championship matches are for second half of season; eg 1972 means season 1971-72. Years for all other matches refer to the actual year of the match. Entries in square brackets denote matches played in RWC Finals.

Aarvold, C D (Cambridge U, W Hartlepool, Headingley, Blackheath) 1928 A, W, I, F, S, 1929 W, I, F, 1931 W, S, F, 1932 SA, W, I, S, 1933 W
Abbott, S R (Wasps, Harlequins) 2003 W2, F3, [Sm, U, W(R)], 2004 NZ1(t&R), 2, 2006 I, A2(R)
Abendanon, N (Bath) 2007 SA2(R),F2
Ackford, P J (Harlequins) 1988 A, 1989 S, I, F, W, R, Fj, 1990 I, F, W, S, Arg 3, 1991 W, S, I, F, A, [NZ, It, F, S, A]
Adams, A A (London Hospital) 1910 F
Adams, F R (Richmond) 1875 I, S, 1876 S, 1877 I, 1878 S, 1879 S, I
Adebayo, A A (Bath) 1996, It, 1997 Arg 1,2, A 2, NZ 1, 1998 S
Adey, G J (Leicester) 1976 I, F
Adkins, S J (Coventry) 1950 I, F, S, 1953 W, I, F, S
Agar, A E (Harlequins) 1952 SA, W, S, I, F, 1953 W, I
Alcock, A (Guy's Hospital) 1906 SA
Alderson, F H R (Hartlepool R) 1891 W, I, S, 1892 W, S, 1893 W
Alexander, H (Richmond) 1900 I, S, 1901 W, I, S, 1902 W, I
Alexander, W (Northern) 1927 F
Allen, A (Gloucester) 2006 NZ,Arg
Allison, D F (Coventry) 1956 W, I, S, F, 1957 W, 1958 W, S
Allport, A (Blackheath) 1892 W, 1893 I, 1894 W, I, S
Anderson, S (Rockcliff) 1899 I
Anderson, W F (Orrell) 1973 NZ 1
Anderton, C (Manchester FW) 1889 M
Andrew, C R (Cambridge U, Nottingham, Wasps, Toulouse, Newcastle) 1985 R, F, S, I, W, 1986 W, S, I, F, 1987 I, F, W, [J (R), US], 1988 S, I 1,2, A 1,2, Fj, A, 1989 S, I, F, W, R, Fj, 1990 I, F, W, S, Arg 3, 1991 W, S, I, F, Fj, A, [NZ, It, US, F, S, A], 1992 S, I, F, W, C, SA, 1993 F, W, NZ, 1994 S, I, F, W, SA 1,2, R, C, 1995 I, F, W, S, [Arg, It, A, NZ, F], 1997 W (R)
Appleford, G (London Irish) 2002 Arg
Archer, G S (Bristol, Army, Newcastle) 1996 S, I, 1997 A 2, NZ 1, SA, NZ 2, 1998 F, W, S, I, A 1, NZ 1, H, It, 1999 Tg, Fj, 2000 I, F, W, It, S
Archer, H (Bridgwater A) 1909 W, F, I
Armstrong, R (Northern) 1925 W
Arthur, T G (Wasps) 1966 W, I
Ashby, R C (Wasps) 1966 I, F, 1967 A
Ashcroft, A (Waterloo) 1956 W, I, S, F, 1957 W, I, F, S, 1958 W, A, I, F, S, 1959 I, F, S
Ashcroft, A H (Birkenhead Park) 1909 A
Ashford, W (Richmond) 1897 W, I, 1898 S, W
Ashworth, A (Oldham) 1892 I
Askew, J G (Cambridge U) 1930 W, I, F
Aslett, A R (Richmond) 1926 W, I, F, S, 1929 S, F
Assinder, E W (O Edwardians) 1909 A, W
Aston, R L (Blackheath) 1890 S, I
Auty, J R (Headingley) 1935 S

Back, N A (Leicester) 1994 S, I, 1995 [Arg (t), It, WS], 1997 NZ 1(R), SA, NZ 2, 1998 F, W, S, I, H, It, A 2, SA 2, 1999 S, I, F, W, A, US, C, [It, NZ, Fj, SA], 2000 I, F, W, It, S, SA 1,2, A, Arg, SA 3, 2001 W, It, S, F, I, A, R, SA, 2002 S, I, F, W, It, NZ (t + R), A, SA, 2003 F 1, W 1, S, I, NZ, A, F 3, [Gg, SA, Sm, W, F, A]
Bailey, M D (Cambridge U, Wasps) 1984 SA 1,2, 1987 [US], 1989 Fj, 1990 I, F, S (R)
Bainbridge, S (Gosforth, Fylde) 1982 F, W, 1983 F, W, S, I, NZ, 1984 S, I, F, W, 1985 NZ 1,2, 1987 F, W, S, [J, US]
Baker, D G S (OMTs) 1955 W, I, F, S
Baker, E M (Moseley) 1895 W, I, S, 1896 W, I, S, 1897 W
Baker, H C (Clifton) 1887 W
Balshaw, I R (Bath, Leeds, Gloucester) 2000 I (R), F (R), It (R), S (R), A (R), Arg, SA 3(R), 2001 W, It, S, F, I, 2002 S (R), I (R), 2003 F2,3, [Sm, U, A(R)], 2004 It, S, I, 2005 It, S, 2006 A1, 2, NZ,Arg, 2007 It,SA1
Bance, J F (Bedford) 1954 S
Barkley, O J (Bath) 2001 US (R), 2004 It(R), I(t), W, F, NZ2(R), A1(R), 2005 W(R), F, I, It, S, A(R), Sm(R), 2006 A1, 2(R), 2007 F2,3(R), [US,Sm,Tg]
Barley, B (Wakefield) 1984 I, F, W, A, 1988 A 1,2, Fj
Barnes, S (Bristol, Bath) 1984 A, 1985 R (R), NZ 1,2, 1986 S (R), F (R), 1987 I (R), 1988 Fj, 1993 S, I
Barr, R J (Leicester) 1932 SA, W, I
Barrett, E I M (Lennox) 1903 S
Barrington, T J M (Bristol) 1931 W, I
Barrington-Ward, L E (Edinburgh U) 1910 W, I, F, S
Barron, J H (Bingley) 1896 S, 1897 W, I
Bartlett, J T (Waterloo) 1951 W
Bartlett, R M (Harlequins) 1957 W, I, F, S, 1958 I, F, S
Barton, J (Coventry) 1967 I, F, W, 1972 F
Batchelor, T B (Oxford U) 1907 F
Bates, S M (Wasps) 1989 R
Bateson, A H (Otley) 1930 W, I, F, S
Bateson, H D (Liverpool) 1879 I
Batson, T (Blackheath) 1872 S, 1874 S, 1875 I
Batten, J M (Cambridge U) 1874 S
Baume, J L (Northern) 1950 S
Baxendell, J J N (Sale) 1998 NZ 2, SA 1
Baxter, J (Birkenhead Park) 1900 W, I, S
Bayfield, M C (Northampton) 1991 Fj, A, 1992 S, I, F, W, C, SA, 1993 F, W, S, I, 1994 S, I, SA 1,2, R, C, 1995 I, F, W, S, [Arg, It, A, NZ, F], SA, WS, 1996 F, W
Bazley, R C (Waterloo) 1952 I, F, 1953 W, I, F, S, 1955 W, I, F, S
Beal, N D (Northampton) 1996 Arg, 1997 A 1, 1998 NZ 1,2, SA 1, H (R), SA 2, 1999 S, F (R), A (t), C (R), [It (R), Tg (R), Fj, SA]
Beaumont, W B (Fylde) 1975 I, A 1(R),2, 1976 A, W, S, I, F, 1977 S, I, F, W, 1978 F, W, S, I, NZ, 1979 S, I, F, W, NZ, 1980 I, F, W, S, 1981 W, S, I, F, Arg 1,2, 1982 A, S
Bedford, H (Morley) 1889 M, 1890 S, I
Bedford, L L (Headingley) 1931 W, I
Beer, I D S (Harlequins) 1955 F, S
Beese, M C (Liverpool) 1972 W, I, F
Beim, T D (Sale) 1998 NZ 1(R),2
Bell, D S C (Bath) 2005 It(R), S
Bell, F J (Northern) 1900 W
Bell, H (New Brighton) 1884 I
Bell, J L (Darlington) 1878 I
Bell, P J (Blackheath) 1968 W, I, F, S
Bell, R W (Northern) 1900 W, I, S
Bendon, G J (Wasps) 1959 W, I, F, S
Bennett, N O (St Mary's Hospital, Waterloo) 1947 W, S, F, 1948 A, W, I, S
Bennett, W N (Bedford, London Welsh) 1975 S, A1, 1976 S (R), 1979 S, I, F, W

Bennetts, B B (Penzance) 1909 A, W
Bentley, J (Sale, Newcastle) 1988 I 2, A 1, 1997 A 1, SA
Bentley, J E (Gipsies) 1871 S, 1872 S
Benton, S (Gloucester) 1998 A 1
Berridge, M J (Northampton) 1949 W, I
Berry, H (Gloucester) 1910 W, I, F, S
Berry, J (Tyldesley) 1891 W, I, S
Berry, J T W (Leicester) 1939 W, I, S
Beswick, E (Swinton) 1882 I, S
Biggs, J M (UCH) 1878 S, 1879 I
Birkett, J G G (Harlequins) 1906 S, F, SA, 1907 F, W, S, 1908 F, W,I , S, 1910 W, I, S, 1911 W, F, I , S, 1912 W, I , S, F
Birkett L (Clapham R) 1875 S, 1877 I, S
Birkett, R H (Clapham R) 1871 S, 1875 S, 1876 S, 1877 I
Bishop, C C (Blackheath) 1927 F
Black, B H (Blackheath) 1930 W, I, F, S, 1931 W, I, S, F, 1932 S, 1933 W
Blacklock, J H (Aspatria) 1898 I, 1899 I
Blakeway, P J (Gloucester) 1980 I, F, W, S, 1981 W, S, I, F, 1982 I, F, W, 1984 I, F, W, SA 1, 1985 R, F, S, I
Blakiston, A F (Northampton) 1920 S, 1921 W, I, S, F, 1922 W, 1923 S, F, 1924 W, I, F, S, 1925 NZ, W, I, S, F
Blatherwick, T (Manchester) 1878 I
Body, J A (Gipsies) 1872 S, 1873 S
Bolton, C A (United Services) 1909 F
Bolton, R (Harlequins) 1933 W, 1936 S, 1937 S, 1938 W, I
Bolton, W N (Blackheath) 1882 I, S, 1883 W, I, S, 1884 W, I, S, 1885 I, 1887 I, S
Bonaventura, M S (Blackheath) 1931 W
Bond, A M (Sale) 1978 NZ, 1979 S, I, NZ, 1980 I, 1982 I
Bonham-Carter, E (Oxford U) 1891 S
Bonsor, F (Bradford) 1886 W, I, S, 1887 W, S, 1889 M
Boobbyer, B (Rosslyn Park) 1950 W, I, F, S, 1951 W, F, 1952 S, I, F
Booth, L A (Headingley) 1933 W, I, S, 1934 S, 1935 W, I, S
Borthwick, S W (Bath) 2001 F, C 1,2(R), US, R, 2003 A(t), W 2(t), F 2, 2004 I, F(R), NZ1(R), 2, A1, C, SA, A2, 2005 W(R), It(R), S(R), A, NZ, Sm, 2006 W, It, S, F, I, 2007 W2,F3, [SA1(t&R),Sm(R),Tg]
Botting, I J (Oxford U) 1950 W, I
Boughton, H J (Gloucester) 1935 W, I, S
Boyle, C W (Oxford U) 1873 S
Boyle, S B (Gloucester) 1983 W, S, I
Boylen, F (Hartlepool R) 1908 F, W, I, S
Bracken, K P P (Bristol, Saracens) 1993 NZ, 1994 S, I, C, 1995 I, F, W, S, [It, WS (t)], SA, 1996 It (R), 1997 Arg 1,2, A 2, NZ 1,2, 1998 F, W, 1999 S(R), I, F, A, 2000 SA 1,2, A, 2001 It (R), S (R), F (R), C 1,2, US, I (R), A, R (R), SA, 2002 S, I, F, W, It, 2003 W 1, It(R), I(t), NZ, A, F3, [SA, U(R), W(R), F(t&R)]
Bradby, M S (United Services) 1922 I, F
Bradley, R (W Hartlepool) 1903 W
Bradshaw, H (Bramley) 1892 S, 1893 W, I, S, 1894 W, I, S
Brain, S E (Coventry) 1984 SA 2, A (R), 1985 R, F, S, I, W, NZ 1,2, 1986 W, S, I, F
Braithwaite, J (Leicester) 1905 NZ
Braithwaite-Exley, B (Headingley) 1949 W
Brettargh, A T (Liverpool OB) 1900 W, 1903 I, S, 1904 W, I, S, 1905 I, S
Brewer, J (Gipsies) 1876 I
Briggs, A (Bradford) 1892 W, I, S
Brinn, A (Gloucester) 1972 W, I, S
Broadley, T (Bingley) 1893 W, S, 1894 W, I, S, 1896 S
Bromet, W E (Richmond) 1891 W, I, 1892 W, I, S, 1893 W, I, S, 1895 W, I, S, 1896 I
Brook, P W P (Harlequins) 1930 S, 1931 F, 1936 S
Brooke, T J (Richmond) 1968 F, S
Brooks, F G (Bedford) 1906 SA
Brooks, M J (Oxford U) 1874 S
Brophy, T J (Liverpool) 1964 I, F, S, 1965 W, I, 1966 W, I, F
Brough, J W (Silloth) 1925 NZ, W
Brougham, H (Harlequins) 1912 W, I, S, F
Brown A (Gloucester) 2006 A1, 2007 SA1,2
Brown, A A (Exeter) 1938 S
Brown, L G (Oxford U, Blackheath) 1911 W, F, I, S, 1913 SA, W, F, I, S, 1914 W, I, S, F, 1921 W, I, S, F, 1922 W
Brown, M (Harlequins) 2007 SA1,2
Brown S P (Richmond) 1998 A 1, SA 1
Brown, T W (Bristol) 1928 S, 1929 W, I, S, F, 1932 S, 1933 W, I, S
Brunton, J (N Durham) 1914 W, I, S
Brutton, E B (Cambridge U) 1886 S
Bryden, C C (Clapham R) 1876 I, 1877 S
Bryden, H A (Clapham R) 1874 S
Buckingham, R A (Leicester) 1927 F
Bucknall, A L (Richmond) 1969 SA, 1970 I, W, S, F, 1971 W, I, F, S (2[1C])
Buckton, J R D (Saracens) 1988 A (R), 1990 Arg 1,2
Budd, A (Blackheath) 1878 I, 1879 S, I, 1881 W, S
Budworth, R T D (Blackheath) 1890 W, 1891 W, S
Bull, A G (Northampton) 1914 W
Bullough, E (Wigan) 1892 W, I, S
Bulpitt, M P (Blackheath) 1970 S
Bulteel, A J (Manchester) 1876 I
Bunting, W L (Moseley) 1897 I, S, 1898 I, S, W, 1899 S, 1900 S, 1901 I, S
Burland, D W (Bristol) 1931 W, I, F, 1932 I, S, 1933 W, I, S
Burns, B H (Blackheath) 1871 S
Burton, G W (Blackheath) 1879 S, I, 1880 S, 1881 I, W, S
Burton, H C (Richmond) 1926 W
Burton, M A (Gloucester) 1972 W, I, F, S, SA, 1974 F, W, 1975 S, A 1,2, 1976 A, W, S, I, F, 1978 F, W
Bush, J A (Clifton) 1872 S, 1873 S, 1875 S, 1876 I, S
Butcher, C J S (Harlequins) 1984 SA 1,2, A
Butcher, W V (Streatham) 1903 S, 1904 W, I, S, 1905 W, I, S
Butler, A G (Harlequins) 1937 W, I
Butler, P E (Gloucester) 1975 A 1, 1976 F
Butterfield, J (Northampton) 1953 F, S, 1954 W, NZ, I, S, F, 1955 W, I, F, S, 1956 W, I, S, F, 1957 W, I, F, S, 1958 W, A, I, F, S, 1959 W, I, F, S
Byrne, F A (Moseley) 1897 W
Byrne, J F (Moseley) 1894 W, I, S, 1895 I, S, 1896 I, 1897 W, I, S, 1898 I, S, W, 1899 I

Cain, J J (Waterloo) 1950 W
Cairns, M I (Saracens) 2007 SA1(R)
Callard, J E B (Bath) 1993 NZ, 1994 S, I, 1995 [WS], SA
Campbell, D A (Cambridge U) 1937 W, I
Candler, P L (St Bart's Hospital) 1935 W, 1936 NZ, W, I, S, 1937 W, I, S, 1938 W, S
Cannell, L B (Oxford U, St Mary's Hospital) 1948 F, 1949 W, I, F, S, 1950 W, I, F, S, 1952 SA, W, 1953 W, I, F, 1956 I, S, F, 1957 W, I
Caplan, D W N (Headingley) 1978 S, I
Cardus, R M (Roundhay) 1979 F, W
Carey, G M (Blackheath) 1895 W, I, S, 1896 W, I
Carleton, J (Orrell) 1979 NZ, 1980 I, F, W, S, 1981 W, S, I, F, Arg 1,2, 1982 A, S, I, F, W, 1983 F, W, S, I, NZ, 1984 S, I, F, W, A
Carling, W D C (Durham U, Harlequins) 1988 F, W, S, I 1,2, A2, Fj, A, 1989 S, I, F, W, Fj, 1990 I, F, W, S, Arg 1,2,3, 1991 W, S, I, F, Fj, A, [NZ, It, US, F, S, A], 1992 S, I, F, W, C, SA, 1993 F, W, S, I, NZ, 1994 S, I, F, W, SA 1,2, R, C, 1995 I, F, W, S, [Arg, WS, A, NZ, F], SA, WS, 1996 F, W, S, I, It, Arg, 1997 S, I, F, W
Carpenter, A D (Gloucester) 1932 SA
Carr, R S L (Manchester) 1939 W, I, S
Cartwright, V H (Nottingham) 1903 W, I, S, 1904 W, S, 1905 W, I, S, NZ, 1906 W, I, S, F, SA
Catcheside, H C (Percy Park) 1924 W, I, F, S, 1926 W, I, 1927 I, S
Catt, M J (Bath, London Irish) 1994 W (R), C (R), 1995 I, F, W, S, [Arg, It, WS, A, NZ, F], SA, WS, 1996 F, W, S, I, It, Arg, 1997 W, Arg 1, A 1,2, NZ 1, SA, 1998 F, W (R), I, A 2(R), SA 2, 1999 S, F, W, A, C (R), [Tg (R), Fj, SA (R)], 2000 I, F, W, It, S, SA 1,2, A, Arg, 2001 W, It, S, F, I, A, R (R), SA, 2003 [Sm(R), U, W(R), F, A(R)], 2004 W(R), F(R), NZ1, A1, 2006 A1, 2, 2007 F1,W1,F2, [US,SA1,A,F,SA2]
Cattell, R H B (Blackheath) 1895 W, I, S, 1896 W, I, S, 1900 W
Cave, J W (Richmond) 1889 M
Cave, W T C (Blackheath) 1905 W
Challis, R (Bristol) 1957 I, F, S
Chambers, E L (Bedford) 1908 F, 1910 W, I

Chantrill, B S (Bristol) 1924 W, I, F, S
Chapman, C E (Cambridge U) 1884 W
Chapman D E (Richmond) 1998 A 1(R)
Chapman, F E (Hartlepool) 1910 W, I, F, S, 1912 W, 1914 W, I
Cheesman, W I (OMTs) 1913 SA, W, F, I
Cheston, E C (Richmond) 1873 S, 1874 S, 1875 I, S, 1876 S
Chilcott, G J (Bath) 1984 A, 1986 I, F, 1987 F (R), W, [J, US, W (R)], 1988 I 2(R), Fj, 1989 I (R), F, W, R
Christophers, P (Bristol) 2002 Arg, SA, 2003 W 1 (R)
Christopherson, P (Blackheath) 1891 W, S
Chuter, G S (Leicester) 2006 A1(R), 2, NZ, Arg, SA1,2(R), 2007 S,It,I,F1,W1,2(R), [US(R),SA1(R),Sm,Tg,A(R),F(R),SA2(R)]
Clark, C W H (Liverpool) 1876 I
Clarke, A J (Coventry) 1935 W, I, S, 1936 NZ, W, I
Clarke, B B (Bath, Richmond) 1992 SA, 1993 F, W, S, I, NZ, 1994 S, F, W, SA 1,2, R, C, 1995 I, F, W, S, [Arg, It, A, NZ, F], SA, WS, 1996 F, W, S, I, Arg (R), 1997 W, Arg 1,2, A 1(R), 1998 A 1(t),NZ 1,2, SA 1, H, It, 1999 A (R)
Clarke, S J S (Cambridge U, Blackheath) 1963 W, I, F, S, NZ 1,2, A, 1964 NZ, W, I, 1965 I, F, S
Clayton, J H (Liverpool) 1871 S
Clements, J W (O Cranleighans) 1959 I, F, S
Cleveland, C R (Blackheath) 1887 W, S
Clibborn, W G (Richmond) 1886 W, I, S, 1887 W, I, S
Clough, F J (Cambridge U, Orrell) 1986 I, F, 1987 [J (R), US]
Coates, C H (Yorkshire W) 1880 S, 1881 S, 1882 S
Coates, V H M (Bath) 1913 SA, W, F, I, S
Cobby, W (Hull) 1900 W
Cockerham, A (Bradford Olicana) 1900 W
Cockerill, R (Leicester) 1997 Arg 1(R),2, A 2(t+R), NZ 1, SA, NZ 2, 1998 W, S, I, A 1, NZ 1,2, SA 1, H, It, A 2, SA 2, 1999 S, I, F, W, A, C (R), [It, NZ, Tg (R), Fj (R)]
Codling, A (Harlequins) 2002 Arg
Cohen, B C (Northampton) 2000 I, F, W, It, S, SA 2, Arg, SA 3, 2001 W, It, S, F, R, 2002 S, I, F, W, It, NZ, A, SA, 2003 F 1, W 1, S, I, NZ, A, F2, 3, [Gg, SA, Sm, W, F, A], 2004 It, S, I, W, F, NZ1, 2, A1,C(R), A2(R), 2005 F(R), A, NZ, 2006 W, It, S, F, I, NZ, Arg, SA1, 2
Colclough, M J (Angoulême, Wasps, Swansea) 1978 S, I, 1979 NZ, 1980 F, W, S, 1981 W, S, I, F, 1982 A, S, I, F, W, 1983 F, NZ, 1984 S, I, F, W, 1986 W, S, I, F
Coley, E (Northampton) 1929 F, 1932 W
Collins, P J (Camborne) 1952 S, I, F
Collins, W E (O Cheltonians) 1874 S, 1875 I, S, 1876 I, S
Considine, S G U (Bath) 1925 F
Conway, G S (Cambridge U, Rugby, Manchester) 1920 F, I, S, 1921 F, 1922 W, I, F, S, 1923 W, I, S, F, 1924 W, I, F, S, 1925 NZ, 1927 W
Cook, J G (Bedford) 1937 S
Cook, P W (Richmond) 1965 I, F
Cooke, D A (Harlequins) 1976 W, S, I, F
Cooke, D H (Harlequins) 1981 W, S, I, F, 1984 I, 1985 R, F, S, I, W, NZ 1,2
Cooke, P (Richmond) 1939 W, I
Coop, T (Leigh) 1892 S
Cooper, J G (Moseley) 1909 A, W
Cooper, M J (Moseley) 1973 F, S, NZ 2(R), 1975 F, W, 1976 A, W, 1977 S, I, F, W
Coopper, S F (Blackheath) 1900 W, 1902 W, I, 1905 W, I, S, 1907 W
Corbett, L J (Bristol) 1921 F, 1923 W, I, 1924 W, I, F, S, 1925 NZ, W, I, S, F, 1927 W, I, S, F
Corless, B J (Coventry, Moseley) 1976 A, I (R), 1977 S, I, F, W, 1978 F, W, S, I
Corry, M E (Bristol, Leicester) 1997 Arg 1,2, 1998 H, It, SA 2(t), 1999 F(R), A, C (t), [It (R), NZ (t+R), SA (R)], 2000 I (R), F (R), W (R), It (R), S (R), Arg (R), SA 3(t), 2001 W (R), It (R), F (t), C 1, I, 2002 F (t+R), W (t), 2003 W 2, F 2,3, [U], 2004 A1(R), C, SA, A2, 2005 F, I, It, S, A, NZ, Sm, 2006 W, It, S, F, I, NZ,Arg, SA1,2, 2007 S,It,I,F1,W1,2, F2(R),3, [US(R),SA1,Sm,Tg,A,F,SA2]
Cotton, F E (Loughborough Colls, Coventry, Sale) 1971 S (2[1C]), P, 1973 W, I, F, S, NZ 2, A, 1974 S, I, 1975 I, F, W, 1976 A, W, S, I, F, 1977 S, I, F, W, 1978 S, I, 1979 NZ, 1980 I, F, W, S, 1981 W
Coulman, M J (Moseley) 1967 A, I, F, S, W, 1968 W, I, F, S
Coulson, T J (Coventry) 1927 W, 1928 A, W
Court, E D (Blackheath) 1885 W
Coverdale, H (Blackheath) 1910 F, 1912 I, F, 1920 W
Cove-Smith, R (OMTs) 1921 S, F, 1922 I, F, S, 1923 W, I, S, F, 1924 W, I, S, F, 1925 NZ, W, I, S, F, 1927 W, I, S, F, 1928 A, W, I, F, S, 1929 W, I
Cowling, R J (Leicester) 1977 S, I, F, W, 1978 F, NZ, 1979 S, I
Cowman, A R (Loughborough Colls, Coventry) 1971 S (2[1C]), P, 1973 W, I
Cox, N S (Sunderland) 1901 S
Cranmer, P (Richmond, Moseley) 1934 W, I, S, 1935 W, I, S, 1936 NZ, W, I, S, 1937 W, I, S, 1938 W, I, S
Creed, R N (Coventry) 1971 P
Cridlan, A G (Blackheath) 1935 W, I, S
Crompton, C A (Blackheath) 1871 S
Crompton, D E (Bristol) 2007 SA1(R)
Crosse, C W (Oxford U) 1874 S, 1875 I
Cueto, M J (Sale) 2004 C, SA, A2, 2005 W, F, I, It, S, A, NZ, Sm, 2006 W, It, S, F, I, SA1,2, 2007 W1,F3, [US,Sm,Tg,SA2]
Cumberlege, B S (Blackheath) 1920 W, I, S, 1921 W, I, S, F, 1922 W
Cumming, D C (Blackheath) 1925 S, F
Cunliffe, F L (RMA) 1874 S
Currey, F I (Marlborough N) 1872 S
Currie, J D (Oxford U, Harlequins, Bristol) 1956 W, I, S, F, 1957 W, I, F, S, 1958 W, A, I, F, S, 1959 W, I, F, S, 1960 W, I, F, S, 1961 SA, 1962 W, I, F
Cusani, D A (Orrell) 1987 I
Cusworth, L (Leicester) 1979 NZ, 1982 F, W, 1983 F, W, NZ, 1984 S, I, F, W, 1988 F, W

D'Aguilar, F B G (Royal Engineers) 1872 S
Dallaglio, L B N (Wasps) 1995 SA (R), WS, 1996 F, W, S, I, It, Arg, 1997 S, I, F, A 1,2, NZ 1, SA, NZ 2, 1998 F, W, S, I, A 2, SA 2, 1999 S, I, F, W, US, C, [It, NZ, Tg, Fj, SA], 2000 I, F, W, It, S, SA 1,2, A, Arg, SA 3, 2001 W, It, S, F, 2002 It (R), NZ, A (t), SA(R), 2003 F 1 (R), W 1, It, S, I, NZ, A, [Gg, SA, Sm, U, W, F, A], 2004 It, S, I, W, F, NZ1, 2, A1,2006 W(t&R), It(R), S(R), F(R), 2007 W2(R),F2,3(R),[US,Tg(R),A(R),F(R),SA2(R)]
Dalton, T J (Coventry) 1969 S(R)
Danby, T (Harlequins) 1949 W
Daniell, J (Richmond) 1899 W, 1900 I, S, 1902 I, S, 1904 I, S
Darby, A J L (Birkenhead Park) 1899 I
Davenport, A (Ravenscourt Park) 1871 S
Davey, J (Redruth) 1908 S, 1909 W
Davey, R F (Teignmouth) 1931 W
Davidson, Jas (Aspatria) 1897 S, 1898 S, W, 1899 I, S
Davidson, Jos (Aspatria) 1899 W, S
Davies, G H (Cambridge U, Coventry, Wasps) 1981 S, I, F, Arg 1,2, 1982 A, S, I, 1983 F, W, S, 1984 S, SA 1,2, 1985 R (R), NZ 1,2, 1986 W, S, I, F
Davies, P H (Sale) 1927 I
Davies, V G (Harlequins) 1922 W, 1925 NZ
Davies, W J A (United Services, RN) 1913 SA, W, F, I, S, 1914 I, S, F, 1920 F, I, S, 1921 W, I, S, F, 1922 I, F, S, 1923 W, I, S, F
Davies, W P C (Harlequins) 1953 S, 1954 NZ, I, 1955 W, I, F, S, 1956 W, 1957 F, S, 1958 W
Davis, A M (Torquay Ath, Harlequins) 1963 W, I, S, NZ 1,2, 1964 NZ, W, I, F, S, 1966 W, 1967 A, 1969 SA, 1970 I, W, S
Dawe, R G R (Bath) 1987 I, F, W, [US], 1995 [WS]
Dawson, E F (RIEC) 1878 I
Dawson, M J S (Northampton, Wasps) 1995 WS, 1996 F, W, S, I, 1997 A 1, SA, NZ 2(R), 1998 W (R), S, I, NZ 1,2, SA 1, H, It, A 2, SA 2, 1999 S, F(R), W, A(R), US, C, [It, NZ, Tg, Fj (R), SA], 2000 I, F, W, It, S, A (R), Arg, SA 3, 2001 W, It, S, F, I, 2002 W (R), It (R), NZ, A, SA, 2003 It, S, I, A(R), F3(R), [Gg, Sm, W, F, A], 2004It(R), S(R), I, W, F, NZ1, 2(R), A1(R), 2005 W, F(R), I(R), It(R), S(R), A, NZ, 2006 W(R), It(R), S(t&R), F, I(R)
Day, H L V (Leicester) 1920 W, 1922 W, F, 1926 S
Deacon, L P (Leicester) 2005 Sm, 2006 A1, 2(R), 2007 S,It,I,F1(R),W1(R)
Dean, G J (Harlequins) 1931 I
Dee, J M (Hartlepool R) 1962 S, 1963 NZ 1

Devitt, Sir T G (Blackheath) 1926 I, F, 1928 A, W
Dewhurst, J H (Richmond) 1887 W, I, S, 1890 W
De Glanville, P R (Bath) 1992 SA (R), 1993 W (R), NZ, 1994 S, I, F, W, SA 1,2, C (R), 1995 [Arg (R), It, WS], SA (R), 1996 W (R), I (R), It, 1997 S, I, F, W, Arg 1,2, A 1,2, NZ 1,2, 1998 W (R), S (R), I (R), A 2, SA 2, 1999 A (R), US, [It, NZ, Fj (R), SA]
De Winton, R F C (Marlborough N) 1893 W
Dibble, R (Bridgwater A) 1906 S, F, SA, 1908 F, W, I, S, 1909 A, W, F, I, S, 1910 S, 1911 W, F, S, 1912 W, I, S
Dicks, J (Northampton) 1934 W, I, S, 1935 W, I, S, 1936 S, 1937 I
Dillon, E W (Blackheath) 1904 W, I, S, 1905 W
Dingle, A J (Hartlepool R) 1913 I, 1914 S, F
Diprose, A J (Saracens) 1997 Arg 1,2, A 2, NZ 1, 1998 W (R), S (R), I, A 1, NZ 2, SA 1
Dixon, P J (Harlequins, Gosforth) 1971 P, 1972 W, I, F, S, 1973 I, F, S, 1974 S, I, F, W, 1975 I, 1976 F, 1977 S, I, F, W, 1978 F, S, I, NZ
Dobbs, G E B (Devonport A) 1906 W, I
Doble, S A (Moseley) 1972 SA, 1973 NZ 1, W
Dobson, D D (Newton Abbot) 1902 W, I, S, 1903 W, I, S
Dobson, T H (Bradford) 1895 S
Dodge, P W (Leicester) 1978 W, S, I, NZ, 1979 S, I, F, W, 1980 W, S, 1981 W, S, I, F, Arg 1,2, 1982 A, S, F, W, 1983 F, W, S, I, NZ, 1985 R, F, S, I, W, NZ 1,2
Donnelly, M P (Oxford U) 1947 I
Dooley, W A (Preston Grasshoppers, Fylde) 1985 R, F, S, I, W, NZ 2(R), 1986 W, S, I, F, 1987 F, W, [A, US, W], 1988 F, W, S, I 1,2, A 1,2, Fj, A, 1989 S, I, F, W, R, Fj, 1990 I, F, W, S, Arg 1,2,3, 1991 W, S, I, F, [NZ, US, F, S, A], 1992 S, I, F, W, C, SA, 1993 W, S, I
Dovey, B A (Rosslyn Park) 1963 W, I
Down, P J (Bristol) 1909 A
Dowson, A O (Moseley) 1899 S
Drake-Lee, N J (Cambridge U, Leicester) 1963 W, I, F, S, 1964 NZ, W, I, 1965 W
Duckett, H (Bradford) 1893 I, S
Duckham, D J (Coventry) 1969 I, F, S, W, SA, 1970 I, W, S, F, 1971 W, I, F, S (2[1C]), P, 1972 W, I, F, S, 1973 NZ 1, W, I, F, S, NZ 2, A, 1974 S, I, F, W, 1975 I, F, W, 1976 A, W, S
Dudgeon, H W (Richmond) 1897 S, 1898 I, S, W, 1899 W, I, S
Dugdale, J M (Ravenscourt Park) 1871 S
Dun, A F (Wasps) 1984 W
Duncan, R F H (Guy's Hospital) 1922 I, F, S
Duncombe, N (Harlequins) 2002 S (R), I (R)
Dunkley, P E (Harlequins) 1931 I, S, 1936 NZ, W, I, S
Duthie, J (W Hartlepool) 1903 W
Dyson, J W (Huddersfield) 1890 S, 1892 S, 1893 I, S

Easter, N (Harlequins) 2007 It, F1, SA1, 2, W2, F3, [SA1, Sm, Tg, A, F, SA2]
Ebdon, P J (Wellington) 1897 W, I
Eddison, J H (Headingley) 1912 W, I, S, F
Edgar, C S (Birkenhead Park) 1901 S
Edwards, R (Newport) 1921 W, I, S, F, 1922 W, F, 1923 W, 1924 W, F, S, 1925 NZ
Egerton, D W (Bath) 1988 I 2, A 1, Fj (R), A, 1989 Fj, 1990 I, Arg 2(R)
Elliot, C H (Sunderland) 1886 W
Elliot, E W (Sunderland) 1901 W, I, S, 1904 W
Elliot, W (United Services, RN) 1932 I, S, 1933 W, I, S, 1934 W, I
Elliott, A E (St Thomas's Hospital) 1894 S
Ellis, H A (Leicester) 2004 SA(R), A2(R), 2005 W(R), F, I, It, S, Sm, 2006 W, It, S, F(R), I, 2007 S,It,I,F1,W1
Ellis, J (Wakefield) 1939 S
Ellis, S S (Queen's House) 1880 I
Emmott, C (Bradford) 1892 W
Enthoven, H J (Richmond) 1878 I
Estcourt, N S D (Blackheath) 1955 S
Evans, B J (Leicester) 1988 A 2, Fj
Evans, E (Sale) 1948 A, 1950 W, 1951 I, F, S, 1952 SA, W, S, I, F, 1953 I, F, S, 1954 W, NZ, I, F, 1956 W, I, S, F, 1957 W, I, F, S, 1958 W, A, I, F, S
Evans, G W (Coventry) 1972 S, 1973 W (R), F, S, NZ 2, 1974 S, I, F, W
Evans, N L (RNEC) 1932 W, I, S, 1933 W, I
Evanson, A M (Richmond) 1883 W, I, S, 1884 S
Evanson, W A D (Richmond) 1875 S, 1877 S, 1878 S, 1879 S, I
Evershed, F (Blackheath) 1889 M, 1890 W, S, I, 1892 W, I, S, 1893 W, I, S
Eyres, W C T (Richmond) 1927 I

Fagan, A R St L (Richmond) 1887 I
Fairbrother, K E (Coventry) 1969 I, F, S, W, SA, 1970 I, W, S, F, 1971 W, I, F
Faithfull, C K T (Harlequins) 1924 I, 1926 F, S
Fallas, H (Wakefield T) 1884 I
Farrell, A (Saracens) 2007 S,It,I,W2,F3, [US(R),SA1,Tg(R)]
Fegan, J H C (Blackheath) 1895 W, I, S
Fernandes, C W L (Leeds) 1881 I, W, S
Fidler, J H (Gloucester) 1981 Arg 1,2, 1984 SA 1,2
Fidler, R J (Gloucester) 1998 NZ 2, SA 1
Field, E (Middlesex W) 1893 W, I
Fielding, K J (Moseley, Loughborough Colls) 1969 I, F, S, SA, 1970 I, F, 1972 W, I, F, S
Finch, R T (Cambridge U) 1880 S
Finlan, J F (Moseley) 1967 I, F, S, W, NZ, 1968 W, I, 1969 I, F, S, W, 1970 F, 1973 NZ 1
Finlinson, H W (Blackheath) 1895 W, I, S
Finney, S (RIE Coll) 1872 S, 1873 S
Firth, F (Halifax) 1894 W, I, S
Flatman, D L (Saracens) 2000 SA 1(t),2(t+R), A (t), Arg (t+R), 2001 F (t), C 2(t+R), US (t+R), 2002 Arg
Fletcher, N C (OMTs) 1901 W, I, S, 1903 S
Fletcher, T (Seaton) 1897 W
Fletcher, W R B (Marlborough N) 1873 S, 1875 S
Flood, T (Newcastle) 2006 Arg(R),SA2(R), 2007 S(R), It(R), F1, W1, SA1, 2,W2(t), [A(R), F(R),SA2(R)]
Fookes, E F (Sowerby Bridge) 1896 W, I, S, 1897 W, I, S, 1898 I, W, 1899 I, S
Ford, P J (Gloucester) 1964 W, I, F, S
Forrest, J W (United Services, RN) 1930 W, I, F, S, 1931 W, I, S, F, 1934 I, S
Forrest, R (Wellington) 1899 W, 1900 S, 1902 I, S, 1903 I, S
Forrester, J (Gloucester) 2005 W(t), Sm(t&R)
Foulds, R T (Waterloo) 1929 W, I
Fowler, F D (Manchester) 1878 S, 1879 S
Fowler, H (Oxford U) 1878 S, 1881 W, S
Fowler, R H (Leeds) 1877 I
Fox, F H (Wellington) 1890 W, S
Francis, T E S (Cambridge U) 1926 W, I, F, S
Frankcom, G P (Cambridge U, Bedford) 1965 W, I, F, S
Fraser, E C (Blackheath) 1875 I
Fraser, G (Richmond) 1902 W, I, S, 1903 W, I
Freakes, H D (Oxford U) 1938 W, 1939 W, I
Freeman, H (Marlborough N) 1872 S, 1873 S, 1874 S
French, R J (St Helens) 1961 W, I, F, S
Freshwater, P T (Perpignan) 2005 v Sm(R), 2006 S(t&R), I(R),Arg, 2007 S,It,I,F3, [SA1(R),Sm(R)]
Fry, H A (Liverpool) 1934 W, I, S
Fry, T W (Queen's House) 1880 I, S, 1881 W
Fuller, H G (Cambridge U) 1882 I, S, 1883 W, I, S, 1884 W

Gadney, B C (Leicester, Headingley) 1932 I, S, 1933 I, S, 1934 W, I, S, 1935 S, 1936 NZ, W, I, S, 1937 S, 1938 W
Gamlin, H T (Blackheath) 1899 W, S, 1900 W, I, S, 1901 S, 1902 W, I, S, 1903 W, I, S, 1904 W, I, S
Gardner, E R (Devonport Services) 1921 W, I, S, 1922 W, I, F, 1923 W, I, S, F
Gardner, H P (Richmond) 1878 I
Garforth, D J (Leicester) 1997 W (R), Arg 1,2, A 1, NZ 1, SA, NZ 2, 1998 F, W (R), S, I, H, It, A 2, SA 2, 1999 S, I, F, W, A, C (R), [It (R), NZ (R), Fj], 2000 It
Garnett, H W T (Bradford) 1877 S
Gavins, M N (Leicester) 1961 W
Gay, D J (Bath) 1968 W, I, F, S
Gent, D R (Gloucester) 1905 NZ, 1906 W, I, 1910 W, I
Genth, J S M (Manchester) 1874 S, 1875 S
George, J T (Falmouth) 1947 S, F, 1949 I

Geraghty, S (London Irish) 2007 F1(R),W1(R)
Gerrard, R A (Bath) 1932 SA, W, I, S, 1933 W, I, S, 1934 W, I, S, 1936 NZ, W, I, S
Gibbs, G A (Bristol) 1947 F, 1948 I
Gibbs, J C (Harlequins) 1925 NZ, W, 1926 F, 1927 W, I, S, F
Gibbs, N (Harlequins) 1954 S, F
Giblin, L F (Blackheath) 1896 W, I, 1897 S
Gibson, A S (Manchester) 1871 S
Gibson, C O P (Northern) 1901 W
Gibson, G R (Northern) 1899 W, 1901 S
Gibson, T A (Northern) 1905 W, S
Gilbert, F G (Devonport Services) 1923 W, I
Gilbert, R (Devonport A) 1908 W, I, S
Giles, J L (Coventry) 1935 W, I, 1937 W, I, 1938 I, S
Gittings, W J (Coventry) 1967 NZ
Glover, P B (Bath) 1967 A, 1971 F, P
Godfray, R E (Richmond) 1905 NZ
Godwin, H O (Coventry) 1959 F, S, 1963 S, NZ 1,2, A, 1964 NZ, I, F, S, 1967 NZ
Gomarsall, A C T (Wasps, Bedford, Gloucester, Harlequins) 1996 It, Arg, 1997 S, I, F, Arg 2(R) 2000 It (R), 2002 Arg, SA(R), 2003 F 1, W 1(R),2, F2(R), [Gg(R), U], 2004 It, S, NZ1(R), 2, A1, C, SA, A2, 2007 SA1,2,F2(R),3(R), [SA1(R),Sm,Tg,A,F,SA2]
Goode, A J (Leicester) 2005 It(R), S(R), 2006 W(R), F(R), I, A1(R), 2, SA1(R),2
Gordon-Smith, G W (Blackheath) 1900 W, I, S
Gotley, A L H (Oxford U) 1910 F, S, 1911 W, F, I, S
Graham, D (Aspatria) 1901 W
Graham, H J (Wimbledon H) 1875 I, S, 1876 I, S
Graham, J D G (Wimbledon H) 1876 I
Gray, A (Otley) 1947 W, I, S
Grayson, P J (Northampton) 1995 WS, 1996 F, W, S, I, 1997 S, I, F, A 2(t), SA (R), NZ 2, 1998 F, W, S, I, H, It, A 2, 1999 I, [NZ (R), Tg, Fj (R), SA], 2003 S(R), I(t), F2, 3(R), [Gg(R), U], 2004 It, S, I
Green, J (Skipton) 1905 I, 1906 S, F, SA, 1907 F, W, I, S
Green, J F (West Kent) 1871 S
Green, W R (Wasps) 1997 A 2, 1998 NZ 1(t+R), 1999 US (R), 2003 W 2(R)
Greening, P B T (Gloucester, Wasps) 1996 It (R), 1997 W (R), Arg 1 1998 NZ 1(R),2(R), 1999 A (R), US, C, [It (R), NZ (R), Tg, Fj, SA], 2000 I, F, W, It, S, SA 1,2, A, SA 3, 2001 F, I
Greenstock, N J J (Wasps) 1997 Arg 1,2, A 1, SA
Greenwell, J H (Rockcliff) 1893 W, I
Greenwood, J E (Cambridge U, Leicester) 1912 F, 1913 SA, W, F, I, S, 1914 W, S, F, 1920 W, F, I, S
Greenwood, J R H (Waterloo) 1966 I, F, S, 1967 A, 1969 I
Greenwood, W J H (Leicester, Harlequins) 1997 A 2, NZ 1, SA, NZ 2, 1998 F, W, S, I, H, It, 1999 C, [It, Tg, Fj, SA], 2000 Arg (R), SA 3, 2001 W, It, S, F, I, A, R, SA, 2002 S, I, F, W, It, NZ, A, SA, 2003 F 1, W 1, It, S, I, NZ, A, F3, [Gg, SA, U(R), W, F, A], 2004 It, S, I, W, F, C(R), SA(R), A2(R)
Greg, W (Manchester) 1876 I, S
Gregory, G G (Bristol) 1931 I, S, F, 1932 SA, W, I, S, 1933 W, I, S, 1934 W, I, S
Gregory, J A (Blackheath) 1949 W
Grewcock, D J (Coventry, Saracens, Bath) 1997 Arg 2, SA, 1998 W (R), S (R), I (R), A 1, NZ 1, SA 2(R), 1999 S (R), A (R), US, C, [It, NZ, Tg (R), SA], 2000 SA 1,2, A, Arg, SA 3, 2001 W, It, S, I, A, R (R), SA, 2002 S (R), I (R), F (R), W, It, NZ, SA (R), 2003 F 1 (R), W 1 (R), It, S (R), I (t), W 2, F 2, [U], 2004 It, S, W, F, NZ1, 2(R), C, SA, A2, 2005 W, F, I, It, S, A, NZ, 2006 W, It, S, F, I(R),NZ, Arg, 2007 S, It, I
Grylls, W M (Redruth) 1905 I
Guest, R H (Waterloo) 1939 W, I, S, 1947 W, I, S, F, 1948 A, W, I, S, 1949 F, S
Guillemard, A G (West Kent) 1871 S, 1872 S
Gummer, C H A (Plymouth A) 1929 F
Gunner, C R (Marlborough N) 1876 I
Gurdon, C (Richmond) 1880 I, S, 1881 I, W, S, 1882 I, S, 1883 S, 1884 W, S, 1885 I, 1886 W, I, S
Gurdon, E T (Richmond) 1878 S, 1879 I, 1880 S, 1881 I, W, S, 1882 S, 1883 W, I, S, 1884 W, I, S, 1885 W, I, 1886 S
Guscott, J C (Bath) 1989 R, Fj, 1990 I, F, W, S, Arg 3, 1991 W, S, I, F, Fj, A, [NZ, It, F, S, A], 1992 S, I, F, W, C, SA, 1993 F, W, S, I, 1994 R, C, 1995 I, F, W, S, [Arg, It, A, NZ, F], SA, WS, 1996 F, W, S, I, Arg, 1997 I (R), W (R), 1998 F, W, S, I, H, It, A 2, SA 2, 1999 S, I, F, A, US, C, [It (R), NZ, Tg]

Haag, M (Bath) 1997 Arg 1,2
Haigh, L (Manchester) 1910 W, I, S, 1911 W, F, I, S
Hale, P M (Moseley) 1969 SA, 1970 I, W
Hall, C (Gloucester) 1901 I, S
Hall, J (N Durham) 1894 W, I, S
Hall, J P (Bath) 1984 S (R), I, F, SA 1,2, A, 1985 R, F, S, I, W, NZ 1,2, 1986 W, S, 1987 I, F, W, S, 1990 Arg 3, 1994 S
Hall, N M (Richmond) 1947 W, I, S, F, 1949 W, I, 1952 SA, W, S, I, F, 1953 W, I, F, S, 1955 W, I
Halliday, S J (Bath, Harlequins) 1986 W, S, 1987 S, 1988 S, I 1,2, A 1, A, 1989 S, I, F, W, R, Fj (R), 1990 W, S, 1991 [US, S, A], 1992 S, I, F, W
Hamersley, A St G (Marlborough N) 1871 S, 1872 S, 1873 S, 1874 S
Hamilton-Hill, E A (Harlequins) 1936 NZ, W, I
Hamilton-Wickes, R H (Cambridge U) 1924 I, 1925 NZ, W, I, S, F, 1926 W, I, S, 1927 W
Hammett, E D G (Newport) 1920 W, F, S, 1921 W, I, S, F, 1922 W
Hammond, C E L (Harlequins) 1905 S, NZ, 1906 W, I, S, F, 1908 W, I
Hancock, A W (Northampton) 1965 F, S, 1966 F
Hancock, G E (Birkenhead Park) 1939 W, I, S
Hancock, J H (Newport) 1955 W, I
Hancock, P F (Blackheath) 1886 W, I, 1890 W
Hancock, P S (Richmond) 1904 W, I, S
Handford, F G (Manchester) 1909 W, F, I, S
Hands, R H M (Blackheath) 1910 F, S
Hanley, J (Plymouth A) 1927 W, S, F, 1928 W, I, F, S
Hanley, S M (Sale) 1999 W
Hannaford, R C (Bristol) 1971 W, I, F
Hanvey, R J (Aspatria) 1926 W, I, F, S
Harding, E H (Devonport Services) 1931 I
Harding, R M (Bristol) 1985 R, F, S, 1987 S, [A, J, W], 1988 I 1(R),2, A 1,2, Fj
Harding, V S J (Saracens) 1961 F, S, 1962 W, I, F, S
Hardwick, P F (Percy Park) 1902 I, S, 1903 W, I, S, 1904 W, I, S
Hardwick, R J K (Coventry) 1996 It (R)
Hardy, E M P (Blackheath) 1951 I, F, S
Hare, W H (Nottingham, Leicester) 1974 W, 1978 F, NZ, 1979 NZ, 1980 I, F, W, S, 1981 W, S, Arg 1,2, 1982 F, W, 1983 F, W, S, I, NZ, 1984 S, I, F, W, SA 1,2
Harper, C H (Exeter) 1899 W
Harriman, A T (Harlequins) 1988 A
Harris, S W (Blackheath) 1920 I, S
Harris, T W (Northampton) 1929 S, 1932 I
Harrison, A C (Hartlepool R) 1931 I, S
Harrison, A L (United Services, RN) 1914 I, F
Harrison, G (Hull) 1877 I, S, 1879 S, I, 1880 S, 1885 W, I
Harrison, H C (United Services, RN) 1909 S, 1914 I, S, F
Harrison, M E (Wakefield) 1985 NZ 1,2, 1986 S, I, F, 1987 I, F, W, S, [A, J, US, W], 1988 F, W
Hartley, B C (Blackheath) 1901 S, 1902 S
Haskell, J (Wasps) 2007 W1,F2
Haslett, L W (Birkenhead Park) 1926 I, F
Hastings, G W D (Gloucester) 1955 W, I, F, S, 1957 W, I, F, S, 1958 W, A, I, F, S
Havelock, H (Hartlepool R) 1908 F, W, I
Hawcridge, J J (Bradford) 1885 W, I
Hayward, L W (Cheltenham) 1910 I
Hazell, A R (Gloucester) 2004 C, SA(t&R), 2005 W, F(t), It(R), S(R), 2007 SA1
Hazell, D St G (Leicester) 1955 W, I, F, S
Healey, A S (Leicester) 1997 I (R), W, A 1(R),2(R), NZ 1(R), SA (R), NZ 2, 1998 F, W, S, I, A 1, NZ 1,2, H, It, A 2, SA 2(R), 1999 US, C, [It, NZ, Tg, Fj, SA (R)], 2000 I, F, W, It, S, SA 1,2, A, SA 3(R), 2001 W (R), It, S, F, I (R), A, R, SA, 2002 S, I, F, W, It (R), NZ (R), A (R), SA(R), 2003 F2
Hearn, R D (Bedford) 1966 F, S, 1967 I, F, S, W
Heath, A H (Oxford U) 1876 S
Heaton, J (Waterloo) 1935 W, I, S, 1939 W, I, S, 1947 I, S, F
Henderson, A P (Edinburgh Wands) 1947 W, I, S, F, 1948 I, S, F, 1949 W, I

Henderson, R S F (Blackheath) 1883 W, S, 1884 W, S, 1885 W
Heppell, W G (Devonport A) 1903 I
Herbert, A J (Wasps) 1958 F, S, 1959 W, I, F, S
Hesford, R (Bristol) 1981 S (R), 1982 A, S, F (R), 1983 F (R), 1985 R, F, S, I, W
Heslop, N J (Orrell) 1990 Arg 1,2,3, 1991 W, S, I, F, [US, F], 1992 W (R)
Hetherington, J G G (Northampton) 1958 A, I, 1959 W, I, F, S
Hewitt, E N (Coventry) 1951 W, I, F
Hewitt, W W (Queen's House) 1881 I, W, S, 1882 I
Hickson, J L (Bradford) 1887 W, I, S, 1890 W, S, I
Higgins, R (Liverpool) 1954 W, NZ, I, S, 1955 W, I, F, S, 1957 W, I, F, S, 1959 W
Hignell, A J (Cambridge U, Bristol) 1975 A 2, 1976 A, W, S, I, 1977 S, I, F, W, 1978 W, 1979 S, I, F, W
Hill, B A (Blackheath) 1903 I, S, 1904 W, I, 1905 W, NZ, 1906 SA, 1907 F, W
Hill, R A (Saracens) 1997 S, I, F, W, A 1,2, NZ 1, SA, NZ 2, 1998 F, W, H (R), It (R), A 2, SA 2, 1999 S, I, F, W, A, US, C, [It, NZ, Tg, Fj (R), SA], 2000 I, F, W, It, S, SA 1,2, A, Arg, SA 3, 2001 W, It, S, F, I, A, SA, 2002 S, I, F, W, It, NZ, A, SA, 2003 F 1, W 1, It, S, I, NZ, A, F 3, [Gg, F, A], 2004 It, S, I, W, F, NZ1, 2, A1
Hill, R J (Bath) 1984 SA 1,2, 1985 I (R), NZ 2(R), 1986 F (R), 1987 I, F, W, [US], 1989 Fj, 1990 I, F, W, S, Arg 1,2,3, 1991 W, S, I, F, Fj, A, [NZ, It, US, F, S, A]
Hillard, R J (Oxford U) 1925 NZ
Hiller, R (Harlequins) 1968 W, I, F, S, 1969 I, F, S, W, SA, 1970 I, W, S, 1971 I, F, S (2[1C]), P, 1972 W, I
Hind, A E (Leicester) 1905 NZ, 1906 W
Hind, G R (Blackheath) 1910 S, 1911 I
Hipkiss, D (Leicester) 2007 W2,F3, [Sm(R),Tg(R),F(R),SA2(R)]
Hobbs, R F A (Blackheath) 1899 S, 1903 W
Hobbs, R G S (Richmond) 1932 SA, W, I, S
Hodges, H A (Nottingham) 1906 W, I
Hodgkinson, S D (Nottingham) 1989 R, Fj, 1990 I, F, W, S, Arg 1,2,3, 1991 W, S, I, F, [US]
Hodgson, C C (Sale) 2001 R, 2002 S (R), I (R), It (R), Arg, 2003 F 1, W 1, It (R), 2004 NZ1, 2, A1, C, SA, A2, 2005 W, F, I, It, S, A, NZ, Sm, 2006 W, It, S, F,NZ, Arg, SA1
Hodgson, J McD (Northern) 1932 SA, W, I, S, 1934 W, I, 1936 I
Hodgson, S A M (Durham City) 1960 W, I, F, S, 1961 SA, W, 1962 W, I, F, S, 1964 W
Hofmeyr, M B (Oxford U) 1950 W, F, S
Hogarth, T B (Hartlepool R) 1906 F
Holford, G (Gloucester) 1920 W, F
Holland, D (Devonport A) 1912 W, I, S
Holliday, T E (Aspatria) 1923 S, F, 1925 I, S, F, 1926 F, S
Holmes, C B (Manchester) 1947 S, 1948 I, F
Holmes, E (Manningham) 1890 S, I
Holmes, W A (Nuneaton) 1950 W, I, F, S, 1951 W, I, F, S, 1952 SA, S, I, F, 1953 W, I, F, S
Holmes, W B (Cambridge U) 1949 W, I, F, S
Hook, W G (Gloucester) 1951 S, 1952 SA, W
Hooper, C A (Middlesex W) 1894 W, I, S
Hopley, D P (Wasps) 1995 [WS (R)], SA, WS
Hopley, F J V (Blackheath) 1907 F, W, 1908 I
Horak, M J (London Irish) 2002 Arg
Hordern, P C (Gloucester) 1931 I, S, F, 1934 W
Horley, C H (Swinton) 1885 I
Hornby, A N (Manchester) 1877 I, S, 1878 S, I, 1880 I, 1881 I, S, 1882 I, S
Horrocks-Taylor, J P (Cambridge U, Leicester, Middlesbrough) 1958 W, A, 1961 S, 1962 S, 1963 NZ 1,2, A, 1964 NZ, W
Horsfall, E L (Harlequins) 1949 W
Horton, A L (Blackheath) 1965 W, I, F, S, 1966 F, S, 1967 NZ
Horton, J P (Bath) 1978 W, S, I, NZ, 1980 I, F, W, S, 1981 W, 1983 S, I, 1984 SA 1,2
Horton, N E (Moseley, Toulouse) 1969 I, F, S, W, 1971 I, F, S, 1974 S, 1975 W, 1977 S, I, F, W, 1978 F, W, 1979 S, I, F, W, 1980 I
Hosen, R W (Bristol, Northampton) 1963 NZ 1,2, A, 1964 F, S, 1967 A, I, F, S, W
Hosking, G R d'A (Devonport Services) 1949 W, I, F, S, 1950 W
Houghton, S (Runcorn) 1892 I, 1896 W
Howard, P D (O Millhillians) 1930 W, I, F, S, 1931 W, I, S, F
Hubbard, G C (Blackheath) 1892 W, I
Hubbard, J C (Harlequins) 1930 S
Hudson, A (Gloucester) 1906 W, I, F, 1908 F, W, I, S, 1910 F
Hughes, G E (Barrow) 1896 S
Hull, P A (Bristol, RAF) 1994 SA 1,2, R, C
Hulme, F C (Birkenhead Park) 1903 W, I, 1905 W, I
Hunt, J T (Manchester) 1882 I, S, 1884 W
Hunt, R (Manchester) 1880 I, 1881 W, S, 1882 I
Hunt, W H (Manchester) 1876 S, 1877 I, S, 1878 I
Hunter, I (Northampton) 1992 C, 1993 F, W, 1994 F, W, 1995 [WS, F]
Huntsman, R P (Headingley) 1985 NZ 1,2
Hurst, A C B (Wasps) 1962 S
Huskisson, T F (OMTs) 1937 W, I, S, 1938 W, I, 1939 W, I, S
Hutchinson, F (Headingley) 1909 F, I, S
Hutchinson, J E (Durham City) 1906 I
Hutchinson, W C (RIE Coll) 1876 S, 1877 I
Hutchinson, W H H (Hull) 1875 I, 1876 I
Huth, H (Huddersfield) 1879 S
Hyde, J P (Northampton) 1950 F, S
Hynes, W B (United Services, RN) 1912 F

Ibbitson, E D (Headingley) 1909 W, F, I, S
Imrie, H M (Durham City) 1906 NZ, 1907 I
Inglis, R E (Blackheath) 1886 W, I, S
Irvin, S H (Devonport A) 1905 W
Isherwood, F W (Ravenscourt Park) 1872 S

Jackett, E J (Leicester, Falmouth) 1905 NZ, 1906 W, I, S, F, SA, 1907 W, I, S, 1909 W, F, I, S
Jackson, A H (Blackheath) 1878 I, 1880 I
Jackson, B S (Broughton Park) 1970 S (R), F
Jackson, P B (Coventry) 1956 W, I, F, 1957 W, I, F, S, 1958 W, A, F, S, 1959 W, I, F, S, 1961 S, 1963 W, I, F, S
Jackson, W J (Halifax) 1894 S
Jacob, F (Cambridge U) 1897 W, I, S, 1898 I, S, W, 1899 W, I
Jacob, H P (Blackheath) 1924 W, I, F, S, 1930 F
Jacob, P G (Blackheath) 1898 I
Jacobs, C R (Northampton) 1956 W, I, S, F, 1957 W, I, F, S, 1958 W, A, I, F, S, 1960 W, I, F, S, 1961 SA, W, I, F, S, 1963 NZ 1,2, A, 1964 W, I, F, S
Jago, R A (Devonport A) 1906 W, I, SA, 1907 W, I
Janion, J P A G (Bedford) 1971 W, I, F, S (2[1C]), P, 1972 W, S, SA, 1973 A, 1975 A 1,2
Jarman, J W (Bristol) 1900 W
Jeavons, N C (Moseley) 1981 S, I, F, Arg 1,2, 1982 A, S, I, F, W, 1983 F, W, S, I
Jeeps, R E G (Northampton) 1956 W, 1957 W, I, F, S, 1958 W, A, I, F, S, 1959 I, 1960 W, I, F, S, 1961 SA, W, I, F, S, 1962 W, I, F, S
Jeffery, G L (Blackheath) 1886 W, I, S, 1887 W, I, S
Jennins, C R (Waterloo) 1967 A, I, F
Jewitt, J (Hartlepool R) 1902 W
Johns, W A (Gloucester) 1909 W, F, I, S, 1910 W, I, F
Johnson, M O (Leicester) 1993 F, NZ, 1994 S, I, F, W, R, C, 1995 I, F, W, S, [Arg, It, WS, A, NZ, F], SA, WS, 1996 F, W, S, I, It, Arg, 1997 S, I, F, W, A 2, NZ 1,2, 1998 F, W, S, I, H, It, A 2, SA 2, 1999 S, I, F, W, A, US, C, [It, NZ, Tg, Fj, SA], 2000 SA 1,2, A, Arg, SA 3, 2001 W, It, S, F, SA, 2002 S, I, F, It (t+R), NZ, A, SA, 2003 F 1, W 1, S, I, NZ, A, F 3, [Gg, SA, Sm, U(R),W, F, A]
Johnston, B (Saracens) 2002 Arg, NZ (R)
Johnston, W R (Bristol) 1910 W, I, S, 1912 W, I, S, F, 1913 SA, W, F, I, S, 1914 W, I, S, F
Jones, C M (Sale) 2004 It(R), S, I(R), W, NZ1, 2005 W, 2006 A1(R), 2, SA1(R),2, 2007 SA1, 2(R)
Jones, F P (New Brighton) 1893 S
Jones, H A (Barnstaple) 1950 W, I, F
Jorden, A M (Cambridge U, Blackheath, Bedford) 1970 F, 1973 I, F, S, 1974 F, 1975 W, S
Jowett, D (Heckmondwike) 1889 M, 1890 S, I, 1891 W, I, S
Judd, P E (Coventry) 1962 W, I, F, S, 1963 S, NZ 1,2, A, 1964 NZ, 1965 I, F, S, 1966 W, I, F, S, 1967 A, I, F, S, W, NZ

Kay, B J (Leicester) 2001 C 1,2, A, R, SA (t+R), 2002 S, I, F,

W, It, Arg, NZ (R), A, SA, 2003 F 1, W 1, It, S, I, NZ, A, F 3, [Gg, SA, Sm, W, F, A], 2004 It, S, I, W, F, C(R), SA(R), 2005 W, F, I, It, S, 2006 A2, NZ, Arg, SA1,2(R), 2007 F2, [US,SA1,Sm,Tg,A,F, SA2]
Kayll, H E (Sunderland) 1878 S
Keeling, J H (Guy's Hospital) 1948 A, W
Keen, B W (Newcastle U) 1968 W, I, F, S
Keeton, G H (Leicester) 1904 W, I, S
Kelly, G A (Bedford) 1947 W, I, S, 1948 W
Kelly, T S (London Devonians) 1906 W, I, S, F, SA, 1907 F, W, I, S, 1908 F, I, S
Kemble, A T (Liverpool) 1885 W, I, 1887 I
Kemp, D T (Blackheath) 1935 W
Kemp, T A (Richmond) 1937 W, I, 1939 S, 1948 A, W
Kendall, P D (Birkenhead Park) 1901 S, 1902 W, 1903 S
Kendall-Carpenter, J MacG K (Oxford U, Bath) 1949 I, F, S, 1950 W, I, F, S, 1951 I, F, S, 1952 SA, W, S, I, F, 1953 W, I, F, S, 1954 W, NZ, I, F
Kendrew, D A (Leicester) 1930 W, I, 1933 I, S, 1934 S, 1935 W, I, 1936 NZ, W, I
Kennedy, R D (Camborne S of M) 1949 I, F, S
Kent, C P (Rosslyn Park) 1977 S, I, F, W, 1978 F (R)
Kent, T (Salford) 1891 W, I, S, 1892 W, I, S
Kershaw, C A (United Services, RN) 1920 W, F, I, S, 1921 W, I, S, F, 1922 W, I, F, S, 1923 W, I, S, F
Kewley, E (Liverpool) 1874 S, 1875 S, 1876 I, S, 1877 I, S, 1878 S
Kewney, A L (Leicester) 1906 W, I, S, F, 1909 A, W, F, I, S, 1911 W, F, I, S, 1912 I, S, 1913 SA
Key, A (O Cranleighans) 1930 I, 1933 W
Keyworth, M (Swansea) 1976 A, W, S, I
Kilner, B (Wakefield T) 1880 I
Kindersley, R S (Exeter) 1883 W, 1884 S, 1885 W
King, A D (Wasps) 1997 Arg 2(R), 1998 SA 2(R), 2000 It (R), 2001 C 2(R), 2003 W2
King, I (Harrogate) 1954 W, NZ, I
King, J A (Headingley) 1911 W, F, I, S, 1912 W, I, S, 1913 SA, W, F, I, S
King, Q E M A (Army) 1921 S
Kingston, P (Gloucester) 1975 A 1,2, 1979 I, F, W
Kitching, A E (Blackheath) 1913 I
Kittermaster, H J (Harlequins) 1925 NZ, W, I, 1926 W, I, F, S
Knight, F (Plymouth) 1909 A
Knight, P M (Bristol) 1972 F, S, SA
Knowles, E (Millom) 1896 S, 1897 S
Knowles, T C (Birkenhead Park) 1931 S
Krige, J A (Guy's Hospital) 1920 W

Labuschagne, N A (Harlequins, Guy's Hospital) 1953 W, 1955 W, I, F, S
Lagden, R O (Richmond) 1911 S
Laird, H C C (Harlequins) 1927 W, I, S, 1928 A, W, I, F, S, 1929 W, I
Lambert, D (Harlequins) 1907 F, 1908 F, W, S, 1911 W, F, I
Lampkowski, M S (Headingley) 1976 A, W, S, I
Lapage, W N (United Services, RN) 1908 F, W, I, S
Larter, P J (Northampton, RAF) 1967 A, NZ, 1968 W, I, F, S, 1969 I, F, S, W, SA, 1970 I, W, F, S, 1971 W, I, F, S (2[1C]), P, 1972 SA, 1973 NZ 1, W
Law, A F (Richmond) 1877 S
Law, D E (Birkenhead Park) 1927 I
Lawrence, Hon H A (Richmond) 1873 S, 1874 S, 1875 I, S
Lawrie, P W (Leicester) 1910 S, 1911 S
Lawson, R G (Workington) 1925 I
Lawson, T M (Workington) 1928 A, W
Leadbetter, M M (Broughton Park) 1970 F
Leadbetter, V H (Edinburgh Wands) 1954 S, F
Leake, W R M (Harlequins) 1891 W, I, S
Leather, G (Liverpool) 1907 I
Lee, F H (Marlborough N) 1876 S, 1877 I
Lee, H (Blackheath) 1907 F
Le Fleming, J (Blackheath) 1887 W
Leonard, J (Saracens, Harlequins) 1990 Arg 1,2,3, 1991 W, S, I, F, Fj, A, [NZ, It, US, F, S, A], 1992 S, I, F, W, C, SA, 1993 F, W, S, I, NZ, 1994 S, I, F, W, SA 1,2, R, C, 1995 I, F, W, S, [Arg, It, A, NZ, F], SA, WS, 1996 F, W, S, I, It, Arg, 1997 S, I, F, W, A 2, NZ 1, SA, NZ 2, 1998 F, W, S, I, H, It, A 2 SA 2, 1999 S, I, F, W, A, C (R), [It, NZ, Fj, SA], 2000 I, F, W, It, S, SA 1,2, A, Arg, SA 3, 2001 W, It, S, F, I, R, 2002 S (R), I (R), F (R), It (R), A, SA, 2003 F 1, S, I, NZ, W 2, F 2(t+R), 3(R), [Gg(t&R), SA(R), Sm, U, W, F(t&R), A(R)], 2004 It(R)
Leslie-Jones, F A (Richmond) 1895 W, I
Lewis, A O (Bath) 1952 SA, W, S, I, F, 1953 W, I, F, S, 1954 F
Lewsey, O J (Wasps) 1998 NZ 1,2, SA 1, 2001 C 1,2, US, 2003 It, S, I, NZ, A, F2, 3(t+R), [Gg, SA, U, F, A], 2004 It, S, I, W, F, NZ1, 2, A1, C, SA, A2, 2005 W, F, I, It, S, A, NZ, Sm, 2006 W, S, F,Arg(R), SA1,2, 2007 S,It,I,F1,2,3, [US,SA1,Sm,Tg,A,F]
Leyland, R (Waterloo) 1935 W, I, S
Linnett, M S (Moseley) 1989 Fj
Lipman, M R (Bath) 2004 NZ2(R), A1(R), 2006 A2
Livesay, R O'H (Blackheath) 1898 W, 1899 W
Lloyd, L D (Leicester) 2000 SA 1(R),2(R), 2001 C 1,2, US
Lloyd, R H (Harlequins) 1967 NZ, 1968 W, I, F, S
Locke, H M (Birkenhead Park) 1923 S, F, 1924 W, F, S, 1925 W, I, S, F, 1927 W, I, S
Lockwood, R E (Heckmondwike) 1887 W, I, S, 1889 M, 1891 W, I, S, 1892 W, I, S, 1893 W, I, 1894 W, I
Login, S H M (RN Coll) 1876 I
Lohden, F C (Blackheath) 1893 W
Long, A E (Bath) 1997 A 2, 2001 US (R)
Longland, R J (Northampton) 1932 S, 1933 W, S, 1934 W, I, S, 1935 W, I, S, 1936 NZ, W, I, S, 1937 W, I, S, 1938 W, I, S
Lowe, C N (Cambridge U, Blackheath) 1913 SA, W, F, I, S, 1914 W, I, S, F, 1920 W, F, I, S, 1921 W, I, S, F, 1922 W, I, F, S, 1923 W, I, S, F
Lowrie, F (Wakefield T) 1889 M, 1890 W
Lowry, W M (Birkenhead Park) 1920 F
Lozowski, R A P (Wasps) 1984 A
Luddington, W G E (Devonport Services) 1923 W, I, S, F, 1924 W, I, F, S, 1925 W, I, S, F, 1926 W
Luger, D D (Harlequins, Saracens) 1998 H, It, SA 2, 1999 S, I, F, W, A, US, C, [It, NZ, Tg, Fj, SA], 2000 SA 1, A, Arg, SA 3, 2001 W, I, A, R, SA, 2002 F (R), W, It, 2003 F 1, W 1, It, S (R), I (R), NZ(R), W 2, [Gg(R), SA(R), U, W]
Lund, M B (Sale) 2006 A1, 2(R), NZ(R), Arg(t&R), 2007 S, It, I, F1(R),W1(R), SA2
Luscombe, F (Gipsies) 1872 S, 1873 S, 1875 I, S, 1876 I, S
Luscombe, J H (Gipsies) 1871 S
Luxmoore, A F C C (Richmond) 1900 S, 1901 W
Luya, H F (Waterloo, Headingley) 1948 W, I, S, F, 1949 W
Lyon, A (Liverpool) 1871 S
Lyon, G H d'O (United Services, RN) 1908 S, 1909 A

McCanlis, M A (Gloucester) 1931 W, I
McCarthy, N (Gloucester) 1999 I (t), US (R), 2000 It (R)
McFadyean, C W (Moseley) 1966 I, F, S, 1967 A, I, F, S, W, NZ, 1968 W, I
MacIlwaine, A H (United Services, Hull & E Riding) 1912 W, I, S, F, 1920 I
Mackie, O G (Wakefield T, Cambridge U) 1897 S, 1898 I
Mackinlay, J E H (St George's Hospital) 1872 S, 1873 S, 1875 I
MacLaren, W (Manchester) 1871 S
MacLennan, R R F (OMTs) 1925 I, S, F
McLeod, N F (RIE Coll) 1879 S, I
Madge, R J P (Exeter) 1948 A, W, I, S
Malir, F W S (Otley) 1930 W, I, S
Mallett, J A (Bath) 1995 [WS (R)]
Mallinder, J (Sale) 1997 Arg 1,2
Mangles, R H (Richmond) 1897 W, I
Manley, D C (Exeter) 1963 W, I, F, S
Mann, W E (United Services, Army) 1911 W, F, I
Mantell, N D (Rosslyn Park) 1975 A 1
Mapletoft, M S (Gloucester) 1997 Arg 2
Markendale, E T (Manchester R) 1880 I
Marques, R W D (Cambridge U, Harlequins) 1956 W, I, S, F, 1957 W, I, F, S, 1958 W, A, I, F, S, 1959 W, I, F, S, 1960 W, I, F, S, 1961 SA, W
Marquis, J C (Birkenhead Park) 1900 I, S
Marriott, C J B (Blackheath) 1884 W, I, S, 1886 W, I, S, 1887 I

Marriott, E E (Manchester) 1876 I
Marriott, V R (Harlequins) 1963 NZ 1,2, A, 1964 NZ
Marsden, G H (Morley) 1900 W, I, S
Marsh, H (RIE Coll) 1873 S
Marsh, J (Swinton) 1892 I
Marshall, H (Blackheath) 1893 W
Marshall, M W (Blackheath) 1873 S, 1874 S, 1875 I, S, 1876 I, S, 1877 I, S, 1878 S, I
Marshall, R M (Oxford U) 1938 I, S, 1939 W, I, S
Martin, C R (Bath) 1985 F, S, I, W
Martin, N O (Harlequins) 1972 F (R)
Martindale, S A (Kendal) 1929 F
Massey, E J (Leicester) 1925 W, I, S
Mather, B-J (Sale) 1999 W
Mathias, J L (Bristol) 1905 W, I, S, NZ
Matters, J C (RNE Coll) 1899 S
Matthews, J R C (Harlequins) 1949 F, S, 1950 I, F, S, 1952 SA, W, S, I, F
Maud, P (Blackheath) 1893 W, I
Maxwell, A W (New Brighton, Headingley) 1975 A 1, 1976 A, W, S, I, F, 1978 F
Maxwell-Hyslop, J E (Oxford U) 1922 I, F, S
Maynard, A F (Cambridge U) 1914 W, I, S
Mears, L A (Bath) 2005 Sm(R), 2006 W(R), It(R), F(R), I, A1, 2(R), NZ(R), Arg(R), SA1(R),2, 2007 S(R), It(R), I(R), W1(R), F2(R), 3(R), [Tg(R)]
Meikle, G W C (Waterloo) 1934 W, I, S
Meikle, S S C (Waterloo) 1929 S
Mellish, F W (Blackheath) 1920 W, F, I, S, 1921 W, I
Melville, N D (Wasps) 1984 A, 1985 I, W, NZ 1,2, 1986 W, S, I, F, 1988 F, W, S, I 1
Merriam, L P B (Blackheath) 1920 W, F
Michell, A T (Oxford U) 1875 I, S, 1876 I
Middleton, B B (Birkenhead Park) 1882 I, 1883 I
Middleton, J A (Richmond) 1922 S
Miles, J H (Leicester) 1903 W
Millett, H (Richmond) 1920 F
Mills, F W (Marlborough N) 1872 S, 1873 S
Mills, S G F (Gloucester) 1981 Arg 1,2, 1983 W, 1984 SA 1, A
Mills, W A (Devonport A) 1906 W, I, S, F, SA, 1907 F, W, I, S, 1908 F, W
Milman, D L K (Bedford) 1937 W, 1938 W, I, S
Milton, C H (Camborne S of M) 1906 I
Milton, J G (Camborne S of M) 1904 W, I, S, 1905 S, 1907 I
Milton, W H (Marlborough N) 1874 S, 1875 I
Mitchell, F (Blackheath) 1895 W, I, S, 1896 W, I, S
Mitchell, W G (Richmond) 1890 W, S, I, 1891 W, I, S, 1893 S
Mobbs, E R (Northampton) 1909 A, W, F, I, S, 1910 I, F
Moberley, W O (Ravenscourt Park) 1872 S
Moody, L W (Leicester) 2001 C 1,2, US, I (R), R, SA (R), 2002 I (R), W, It, Arg, NZ, A, SA, 2003 F 1, W 2, F 2, 3(R), [Gg(R), SA, Sm(R), U, W, F(R), A(R)], 2004 C, SA, A2, 2005 F, I, It, S, A, NZ, Sm, 2006 W, It, S, F, I, A1, NZ, Arg, SA1(R),2(R),W2(R), 2007 [US(R),SA1(R),Sm(R),Tg,A,F,SA2]
Moore, B C (Nottingham, Harlequins) 1987 S, [A, J, W], 1988 F, W, S, I 1,2, A 1, 2, Fj, A, 1989 S, I, F, W, R, Fj, 1990 I, F, W, S, Arg 1,2, 1991 W, S, I, F, Fj, A, [NZ, It, F, S, A], 1992 S, I, F, W, SA, 1993 F, W, S, I, NZ, 1994 S, I, F, W, SA 1,2, R, C, 1995 I, F, W, S, [Arg, It, WS (R), A, NZ, F]
Moore, E J (Blackheath) 1883 I, S
Moore, N J N H (Bristol) 1904 W, I, S
Moore, P B C (Blackheath) 1951 W
Moore, W K T (Leicester) 1947 W, I, 1949 F, S, 1950 I, F, S
Mordell, R J (Rosslyn Park) 1978 W
Morfitt, S (W Hartlepool) 1894 W, I, S, 1896 W, I, S
Morgan, J R (Hawick) 1920 W
Morgan, O (Gloucester) 2007 S,I
Morgan, W G D (Medicals, Newcastle) 1960 W, I, F, S, 1961 SA, W, I, F, S
Morley, A J (Bristol) 1972 SA, 1973 NZ 1, W, I, 1975 S, A 1,2
Morris, A D W (United Services, RN) 1909 A, W, F
Morris, C D (Liverpool St Helens, Orrell) 1988 A, 1989 S, I, F, W, 1992 S, I, F, W, C, SA, 1993 F, W, S, I, 1994 F, W, SA 1,2, R, 1995 S (t), [Arg, WS, A, NZ, F]
Morris, R (Northampton) 2003 W 1, It
Morrison, P H (Cambridge U) 1890 W, S, I, 1891 I
Morse, S (Marlborough N) 1873 S, 1874 S, 1875 S

Mortimer, W (Marlborough N) 1899 W
Morton, H J S (Blackheath) 1909 I, S, 1910 W, I
Moss, F (Broughton) 1885 W, I, 1886 W
Mullins, A R (Harlequins) 1989 Fj
Mycock, J (Sale) 1947 W, I, S, F, 1948 A
Myers, E (Bradford) 1920 I, S, 1921 W, I, 1922 W, I, F, S, 1923 W, I, S, F, 1924 W, I, F, S, 1925 S, F
Myers, H (Keighley) 1898 I

Nanson, W M B (Carlisle) 1907 F, W
Nash, E H (Richmond) 1875 I
Neale, B A (Rosslyn Park) 1951 I, F, S
Neale, M E (Blackheath) 1912 F
Neame, S (O Cheltonians) 1879 S, I, 1880 I, S
Neary, A (Broughton Park) 1971 W, I, F, S (2[1C]), P, 1972 W, I, F, S, SA, 1973 NZ 1, W, I, F, S, NZ 2, A, 1974 S, I, F, W, 1975 I, F, W, S, A 1, 1976 A, W, S, I, F, 1977 I, 1978 F (R), 1979 S, I, F, W, NZ, 1980 I, F, W, S
Nelmes, B G (Cardiff) 1975 A 1,2, 1978 W, S, I, NZ
Newbold, C J (Blackheath) 1904 W, I, S, 1905 W, I, S
Newman, S C (Oxford U) 1947 F, 1948 A, W
Newton, A W (Blackheath) 1907 S
Newton, P A (Blackheath) 1882 S
Newton-Thompson, J O (Oxford U) 1947 S, F
Nichol, W (Brighouse R) 1892 W, S
Nicholas, P L (Exeter) 1902 W
Nicholson, B E (Harlequins) 1938 W, I
Nicholson, E S (Leicester) 1935 W, I, S, 1936 NZ, W
Nicholson, E T (Birkenhead Park) 1900 W, I
Nicholson, T (Rockcliff) 1893 I
Ninnes, B F (Coventry) 1971 W
Noon, J D (Newcastle) 2001 C 1,2, US, 2003 W 2, F 2(t+R), 2005 W, F, I, It, S, A, NZ, 2006 W, It, S, F, I, 2006 A1(R), 2, NZ, Arg, SA1,2, 2007 SA2, F2, [US, SA1]
Norman, D J (Leicester) 1932 SA, W
North, E H G (Blackheath) 1891 W, I, S
Northmore, S (Millom) 1897 I
Novak, M J (Harlequins) 1970 W, S, F
Novis, A L (Blackheath) 1929 S, F, 1930 W, I, F, 1933 I, S

Oakeley, F E (United Services, RN) 1913 S, 1914 I, S, F
Oakes, R F (Hartlepool R) 1897 W, I, S, 1898 I, S, W, 1899 W, S
Oakley, L F L (Bedford) 1951 W
Obolensky, A (Oxford U) 1936 NZ, W, I, S
Ojomoh, S O (Bath, Gloucester) 1994 I, F, SA 1(R),2, R, 1995 S (R), [Arg, WS, A (t), F], 1996 F, 1998 NZ 1
Old, A G B (Middlesbrough, Leicester, Sheffield) 1972 W, I, F, S, SA, 1973 NZ 2, A, 1974 S, I, F, W, 1975 I, A 2, 1976 S, I, 1978 F
Oldham, W L (Coventry) 1908 S, 1909 A
Olver, C J (Northampton) 1990 Arg 3, 1991 [US], 1992 C
O'Neill, A (Teignmouth, Torquay A) 1901 W, I, S
Openshaw, W E (Manchester) 1879 I
Orwin, J (Gloucester, RAF, Bedford) 1985 R, F, S, I, W, NZ 1,2, 1988 F, W, S, I 1,2, A 1,2
Osborne, R R (Manchester) 1871 S
Osborne, S H (Oxford U) 1905 S
Oti, C (Cambridge U, Nottingham, Wasps) 1988 S, I 1, 1989 S, I, F, W, R, 1990 Arg 1,2, 1991 Fj, A, [NZ, It]
Oughtred, B (Hartlepool R) 1901 S, 1902 W, I, S, 1903 W, I
Owen, J E (Coventry) 1963 W, I, F, S, A, 1964 NZ, 1965 W, I, F, S, 1966 I, F, S, 1967 NZ
Owen-Smith, H G O (St Mary's Hospital) 1934 W, I, S, 1936 NZ, W, I, S, 1937 W, I, S

Page, J J (Bedford, Northampton) 1971 W, I, F, S, 1975 S
Pallant, J N (Notts) 1967 I, F, S
Palmer, A C (London Hospital) 1909 I, S
Palmer, F H (Richmond) 1905 W
Palmer, G V (Richmond) 1928 I, F, S
Palmer, J A (Bath) 1984 SA 1,2, 1986 I (R)
Palmer, T (Leeds, Wasps) 2001 US (R), 2006 Arg(R), SA1,2, 2007 It(R), I(R), F1, W1
Pargetter, T A (Coventry) 1962 S, 1963 F, NZ 1
Parker, G W (Gloucester) 1938 I, S
Parker, Hon S (Liverpool) 1874 S, 1875 S

Parsons, E I (RAF) 1939 S
Parsons, M J (Northampton) 1968 W, I, F, S
Patterson, W M (Sale) 1961 SA, S
Pattisson, R M (Blackheath) 1883 I, S
Paul, H R (Gloucester) 2002 F(R), 2004 It(t&R), S(R), C, SA, A2
Paul, J E (RIE Coll) 1875 S
Payne, A T (Bristol) 1935 I, S
Payne, C M (Harlequins) 1964 I, F, S, 1965 I, F, S, 1966 W, I, F, S
Payne, J H (Broughton) 1882 S, 1883 W, I, S, 1884 I, 1885 W, I
Payne, T A N (Wasps) 2004 A1, 2006 A1(R), 2(R), 2007 F1, W1
Pearce, G S (Northampton) 1979 S, I, F, W, 1981 Arg 1,2, 1982 A, S, 1983 F, W, S, I, NZ, 1984 S, SA 2, A, 1985 R, F, S, I, W, NZ 1,2, 1986 W, S, I, F, 1987 I, F, W, S, [A, US, W], 1988 Fj, 1991 [US]
Pears, D (Harlequins) 1990 Arg 1,2, 1992 F (R), 1994 F
Pearson, A W (Blackheath) 1875 I, S, 1876 I, S, 1877 S, 1878 S, I
Peart, T G A H (Hartlepool R) 1964 F, S
Pease, F E (Hartlepool R) 1887 I
Penny, S H (Leicester) 1909 A
Penny, W J (United Hospitals) 1878 I, 1879 S, I
Percival, L J (Rugby) 1891 I, 1892 I, 1893 S
Periton, H G (Waterloo) 1925 W, 1926 W, I, F, S, 1927 W, I, S, F, 1928 A, I, F, S, 1929 W, I, S, F, 1930 W, I, F, S
Perrott, E S (O Cheltonians) 1875 I
Perry, D G (Bedford) 1963 F, S, NZ 1,2, A 1964 NZ, W, I, 1965 W, I, F, S, 1966 W, I, F
Perry, M B (Bath) 1997 A 2, NZ 1, SA, NZ 2, 1998 W, S, I, A 1, NZ 1,2, SA 1, H, It, A 2, 1999 I, F, W, A US, C, [It, NZ, Tg, Fj, SA], 2000 I, F, W, It, S, SA 1,2, A, SA 3, 2001 W (R), F (R)
Perry, S (Bristol) 2006 NZ,Arg,SA1(R),2(R), 2007 I(R), F1(R), W1(R), SA1(R),2(R),W2, F2,3, [US,SA1]
Perry, S V (Cambridge U, Waterloo) 1947 W, I, 1948 A, W, I, S, F
Peters, J (Plymouth) 1906 S, F, 1907 I, S, 1908 W
Phillips, C (Birkenhead Park) 1880 S, 1881 I, S
Phillips, M S (Fylde) 1958 A, I, F, S, 1959 W, I, F, S, 1960 W, I, F, S, 1961 W, 1963 W, I, F, S, NZ 1,2, A, 1964 NZ, W, I, F, S
Pickering, A S (Harrogate) 1907 I
Pickering, R D A (Bradford) 1967 I, F, S, W, 1968 F, S
Pickles, R C W (Bristol) 1922 I, F
Pierce, R (Liverpool) 1898 I, 1903 S
Pilkington, W N (Cambridge U) 1898 S
Pillman, C H (Blackheath) 1910 W, I, F, S, 1911 W, F, I, S, 1912 W, F, 1913 SA, W, F, I, S, 1914 W, I, S
Pillman, R L (Blackheath) 1914 F
Pinch, J (Lancaster) 1896 W, I, 1897 S
Pinching, W W (Guy's Hospital) 1872 S
Pitman, I J (Oxford U) 1922 S
Plummer, K C (Bristol) 1969 W, 1976 S, I, F
Pool-Jones, R J (Stade Francais) 1998 A 1
Poole, F O (Oxford U) 1895 W, I, S
Poole, R W (Hartlepool R) 1896 S
Pope, E B (Blackheath) 1931 W, S, F
Portus, G V (Blackheath) 1908 F, I
Potter, S (Leicester) 1998 A 1(t)
Poulton, R W (later Poulton Palmer) (Oxford U, Harlequins, Liverpool) 1909 F, I, S, 1910 W, 1911 S, 1912 W, I, S, 1913 SA, W, F, I, S, 1914 W, I, S, F
Powell, D L (Northampton) 1966 W, I, 1969 I, F, S, W, 1971 W, I, F, S (2[1C])
Pratten, W E (Blackheath) 1927 S, F
Preece, I (Coventry) 1948 I, S, F, 1949 F, S, 1950 W, I, F, S, 1951 W, I, F
Preece, P S (Coventry) 1972 SA, 1973 NZ 1, W, I, F, S, NZ 2, 1975 I, F, W, A 2, 1976 W (R)
Preedy, M (Gloucester) 1984 SA 1
Prentice, F D (Leicester) 1928 I, F, S
Prescott, R E (Harlequins) 1937 W, I, 1938 I, 1939 W, I, S
Preston, N J (Richmond) 1979 NZ, 1980 I, F
Price, H L (Harlequins) 1922 I, S, 1923 W, I
Price, J (Coventry) 1961 I
Price, P L A (RIE Coll) 1877 I, S, 1878 S
Price, T W (Cheltenham) 1948 S, F, 1949 W, I, F, S
Probyn, J A (Wasps, Askeans) 1988 F, W, S, I 1,2, A 1, 2, A, 1989 S, I, R (R), 1990 I, F, W, S, Arg 1,2,3, 1991 W, S, I, F, Fj, A, [NZ, It, F, S, A], 1992 S, I, F, W, 1993 F, W, S, I
Prout, D H (Northampton) 1968 W, I
Pullin, J V (Bristol) 1966 W, 1968 W, I, F, S, 1969 I, F, S, W, SA, 1970 I, W, S, F, 1971 W, I, F, S (2[1C]), P, 1972 W, I, F, S, SA, 1973 NZ 1, W, I, F, S, NZ 2, A, 1974 S, I, F, W, 1975 I, W (R), S, A 1,2, 1976 F
Purdy, S J (Rugby) 1962 S
Pyke, J (St Helens Recreation) 1892 W
Pym, J A (Blackheath) 1912 W, I, S, F

Quinn, J P (New Brighton) 1954 W, NZ, I, S, F

Rafter, M (Bristol) 1977 S, F, W, 1978 F, W, S, I, NZ, 1979 S, I, F, W, NZ, 1980 W(R), 1981 W, Arg 1,2
Ralston, C W (Richmond) 1971 S (C), P, 1972 W, I, F, S, SA, 1973 NZ 1, W, I, F, S, NZ 2, A, 1974 S, I, F, W, 1975 I, F, W, S
Ramsden, H E (Bingley) 1898 S, W
Ranson, J M (Rosslyn Park) 1963 NZ 1,2, A, 1964 W, I, F, S
Raphael, J E (OMTs) 1902 W, I, S, 1905 W, S, NZ, 1906 W, S, F
Ravenscroft, J (Birkenhead Park) 1881 I
Ravenscroft, S C W (Saracens) 1998 A 1, NZ 2(R)
Rawlinson, W C W (Blackheath) 1876 S
Redfern, S (Leicester) 1984 I (R)
Redman, N C (Bath) 1984 A, 1986 S (R), 1987 I, S, [A, J, W], 1988 Fj, 1990 Arg 1,2, 1991 Fj, [It, US], 1993 NZ, 1994 F, W, SA 1,2, 1997 Arg 1, A 1
Redmond, G F (Cambridge U) 1970 F
Redwood, B W (Bristol) 1968 W, I
Rees, D L (Sale) 1997 A 2, NZ 1, SA, NZ 2, 1998 F, W, SA 2(R), 1999 S, I, F, A
Rees, G W (Nottingham) 1984 SA 2(R), A, 1986 I, F, 1987 F, W, S, [A, J, US, W], 1988 S (R), I 1,2, A 1,2, Fj, 1989 W (R), R (R), Fj (R), 1990 Arg 3(R), 1991 Fj, [US]
Rees, T (Wasps) 2007 S(R), It(R), I(R), F1, W1, F3, [US, SA1]
Reeve, J S R (Harlequins) 1929 F, 1930 W, I, F, S, 1931 W, I, S
Regan, M (Liverpool) 1953 W, I, F, S, 1954 W, NZ, I, S, F, 1956 I, S, F
Regan, M P (Bristol, Bath, Leeds) 1995 SA, WS, 1996 F, W, S, I, It, Arg, 1997 S, I, F, W, A 1, NZ 2(R), 1998 F, 2000 SA 1(t), A(R), Arg, SA 3(t), 2001 It(R), S(R), C 2(R), R, 2003 F 1(t), It(R), W 2, [Gg(R), Sm], 2004 It(R), I(R), NZ1(R), 2, A1, 2007 SA1,2,W2, F2,3, [US,SA1,A,F,SA2]
Rendall, P A G (Wasps, Askeans) 1984 W, SA 2, 1986 W, S, 1987 I, F, S, [A, J, W], 1988 F, W, S, I 1,2, A 1,2, A, 1989 S, I, F, W, R, 1990 I, F, W, S, 1991 [It (R)]
Rew, H (Blackheath) 1929 S, F, 1930 F, S, 1931 W, S, F, 1934 W, I, S
Reynolds, F J (O Cranleighans) 1937 S, 1938 I, S
Reynolds, S (Richmond) 1900 W, I, S, 1901 I
Rhodes, J (Castleford) 1896 W, I, S
Richards, D (Leicester) 1986 I, F, 1987 S, [A, J, US, W], 1988 F, W, S, I 1, A 1,2, Fj, A, 1989 S, I, F, W, R, 1990 Arg 3, 1991 W, S, I, F, Fj, A, [NZ, It, US], 1992 S (R), F, W, C, 1993 NZ, 1994 W, SA 1, C, 1995 I, F, W, S, [WS, A, NZ], 1996 F (t), S, I
Richards, E E (Plymouth A) 1929 S, F
Richards, J (Bradford) 1891 W, I, S
Richards, P C (Gloucester, London Irish) 2006 A1, 2,NZ(R), Arg(R), SA1,2, 2007 [US(R),SA1(R),Tg(R),A(t),F(R),SA2(R)]
Richards, S B (Richmond) 1965 W, I, F, S, 1967 A, I, F, S, W
Richardson, J V (Birkenhead Park) 1928 A, W, I, F, S
Richardson, W R (Manchester) 1881 I
Rickards, C H (Gipsies) 1873 S
Rimmer, G (Waterloo) 1949 W, I, 1950 W, 1951 W, I, F, 1952 SA, W, 1954 W, NZ, I, S
Rimmer, L I (Bath) 1961 SA, W, I, F, S
Ripley, A G (Rosslyn Park) 1972 W, I, F, S, SA, 1973 NZ 1, W, I, F, S, NZ 2, A, 1974 S, I, F, W, 1975 I, F, S, A 1,2, 1976 A, W, S
Risman, A B W (Loughborough Coll) 1959 W, I, F, S, 1961 SA, W, I, F

Ritson, J A S (Northern) 1910 F, S, 1912 F, 1913 SA, W, F, I, S
Rittson-Thomas, G C (Oxford U) 1951 W, I, F
Robbins, G L (Coventry) 1986 W, S
Robbins, P G D (Oxford U, Moseley, Coventry) 1956 W, I, S, F, 1957 W, I, F, S, 1958 W, A, I, S, 1960 W, I, F, S, 1961 SA, W, 1962 S
Roberts, A D (Northern) 1911 W, F, I, S, 1912 I, S, F, 1914 I
Roberts, E W (RNE Coll) 1901 W, I, 1905 NZ, 1906 W, I, 1907 S
Roberts, G D (Harlequins) 1907 S, 1908 F, W
Roberts, J (Sale) 1960 W, I, F, S, 1961 SA, W, I, F, S, 1962 W, I, F, S, 1963 W, I, F, S, 1964 NZ
Roberts, R S (Coventry) 1932 I
Roberts, S (Swinton) 1887 W, I
Roberts, V G (Penryn, Harlequins) 1947 F, 1949 W, I, F, S, 1950 I, F, S, 1951 W, I, F, S, 1956 W, I, S, F
Robertshaw, A R (Bradford) 1886 W, I, S, 1887 W, S
Robinson, A (Blackheath) 1889 M, 1890 W, S, I
Robinson, E T (Coventry) 1954 S, 1961 I, F, S
Robinson, G C (Percy Park) 1897 I, S, 1898 I, 1899 W, 1900 I, S, 1901 I, S
Robinson, J T (Sale) 2001 It (R), S (R), F (R), I, A, R, SA, 2002 S, I, F, It, NZ, A, SA, 2003 F 1, W 1, S, I, NZ, A, F 3, [Gg, SA, Sm, U(R), W, F, A], 2004 It, S, I, W, F, C, SA, A2, 2005 W, F, I, 2007 S,It,F1,W1,SA1,W2,F3, [US,SA1,A,F,SA2]
Robinson, J J (Headingley) 1893 S, 1902 W, I, S
Robinson, R A (Bath) 1988 A 2, Fj, A, 1989 S, I, F, W, 1995 SA
Robson, A (Northern) 1924 W, I, F, S, 1926 W
Robson, M (Oxford U) 1930 W, I, F, S
Rodber, T A K (Army, Northampton) 1992 S, I, 1993 NZ, 1994 I, F, W, SA 1,2, R, C, 1995 I, F, W, S, [Arg, It, WS (R), A, NZ, F], SA, WS, 1996 W, S (R), I (t), It, Arg, 1997 S, I, F, W, A 1, 1998 H (R), It (R), A 2, SA 2, 1999 S, I, F, W, A, US (R), [NZ (R), Fj (R)]
Rogers, D P (Bedford) 1961 I, F, S, 1962 W, I, F, 1963 W, I, F, S, NZ 1,2, A, 1964 NZ, W, I, F, S, 1965 W, I, F, S, 1966 W, I, F, S, 1967 A, S, W, NZ, 1969 I, F, S, W
Rogers, J H (Moseley) 1890 W, S, I, 1891 S
Rogers, W L Y (Blackheath) 1905 W, I
Rollitt, D M (Bristol) 1967 I, F, S, W, 1969 I, F, S, W, 1975 S, A 1,2
Roncoroni, A D S (West Herts, Richmond) 1933 W, I, S
Rose, W M H (Cambridge U, Coventry, Harlequins) 1981 I, F, 1982 A, S, I, 1987 I, F, W, S, [A]
Rossborough, P A (Coventry) 1971 W, 1973 NZ 2, A, 1974 S, I, 1975 I, F
Rosser, D W A (Wasps) 1965 W, I, F, S, 1966 W
Rotherham, Alan (Richmond) 1883 W, S, 1884 W, S, 1885 W, I, 1886 W, I, S, 1887 W, I, S
Rotherham, Arthur (Richmond) 1898 S, W, 1899 W, I, S
Roughley, D (Liverpool) 1973 A, 1974 S, I
Rowell, R E (Leicester) 1964 W, 1965 W
Rowley, A J (Coventry) 1932 SA
Rowley, H C (Manchester) 1879 S, I, 1880 I, S, 1881 I, W, S, 1882 I, S
Rowntree, G (Leicester) 1995 S (t), [It, WS], WS, 1996 F, W, S, I, It, Arg, 1997 S, I, F, W, A 1, 1998 A 1, NZ 1, 2, SA 1, H (R), It (R), 1999 US, C, [It (R), Tg, Fj (R)], 2001 C 1,2, US, I(R), A, R, SA, 2002 S, I, F, W, It, 2003 F 1(R), W 1, It, S, I, NZ, F 2, 2004 C, SA, A2, 2005 W, F, I, It, 2006 A1, 2
Royds, P M R (Blackheath) 1898 S, W, 1899 W
Royle, A V (Broughton R) 1889 M
Rudd, E L (Liverpool) 1965 W, I, S, 1966 W, I, S
Russell, R F (Leicester) 1905 NZ
Rutherford, D (Percy Park, Gloucester) 1960 W, I, F, S, 1961 SA, 1965 W, I, F, S, 1966 W, I, F, S, 1967 NZ
Ryalls, H J (New Brighton) 1885 W, I
Ryan, D (Wasps, Newcastle) 1990 Arg 1,2, 1992 C, 1998 S
Ryan, P H (Richmond) 1955 W, I

Sackey, P H (Wasps) 2006 NZ,Arg, 2007 F2,3(R), [SA1, Sm, Tg, A, F, SA2]
Sadler, E H (Army) 1933 I, S
Sagar, J W (Cambridge U) 1901 W, I
Salmon, J L B (Harlequins) 1985 NZ 1,2, 1986 W, S, 1987 I, F, W, S, [A, J, US, W]
Sample, C H (Cambridge U) 1884 I, 1885 I, 1886 S
Sampson, P C (Wasps) 1998 SA 1, 2001 C 1,2
Sanders, D L (Harlequins) 1954 W, NZ, I, S, F, 1956 W, I, S, F
Sanders, F W (Plymouth A) 1923 I, S, F
Sanderson, A (Sale) 2001 R (R), 2002 Arg, 2003 It(t + R), W 2(R), F 2
Sanderson, P H (Sale, Harlequins, Worcester) 1998 NZ 1,2, SA 1, 2001 C 1(R),2(R), US(t+R), 2005 A, NZ, Sm, 2006 A1, 2, NZ, Arg, SA1,2, 2007 SA1(R)
Sandford, J R P (Marlborough N) 1906 I
Sangwin, R D (Hull and E Riding) 1964 NZ, W
Sargent, G A F (Gloucester) 1981 I (R)
Savage, K F (Northampton) 1966 W, I, F, S, 1967 A, I, F, S, W, NZ, 1968 W, F, S
Sawyer, C M (Broughton) 1880 S, 1881 I
Saxby, L E (Gloucester) 1932 SA, W
Scarbrough, D G R (Leeds, Saracens) 2003 W 2, 2007 SA2
Schofield, D (Sale) 2007 SA1,2(R)
Schofield, J W (Manchester) 1880 I
Scholfield, J A (Preston Grasshoppers) 1911 W
Schwarz, R O (Richmond) 1899 S, 1901 W, I
Scorfield, E S (Percy Park) 1910 F
Scott, C T (Blackheath) 1900 W, I, 1901 W, I
Scott, E K (St Mary's Hospital, Redruth) 1947 W, 1948 A, W, I, S
Scott, F S (Bristol) 1907 W
Scott, H (Manchester) 1955 F
Scott, J P (Rosslyn Park, Cardiff) 1978 F, W, S, I, NZ, 1979 S (R), I, F, W, NZ, 1980 I, F, W, S, 1981 W, S, I, F, Arg 1,2, 1982 I, F, W, 1983 F, W, S, I, NZ, 1984 S, I, F, W, SA 1,2
Scott, J S M (Oxford U) 1958 F
Scott, M T (Cambridge U) 1887 I, 1890 S, I
Scott, W M (Cambridge U) 1889 M
Seddon, R L (Broughton R) 1887 W, I, S
Sellar, K A (United Services, RN) 1927 W, I, S, 1928 A, W, I, F
Sever, H S (Sale) 1936 NZ, W, I, S, 1937 W, I, S, 1938 W, I, S
Shackleton, I R (Cambridge U) 1969 SA, 1970 I, W, S
Sharp, R A W (Oxford U, Wasps, Redruth) 1960 W, I, F, S, 1961 I, F, 1962 W, I, F, 1963 W, I, F, S, 1967 A
Shaw, C H (Moseley) 1906 S, SA, 1907 F, W, I, S
Shaw, F (Cleckheaton) 1898 I
Shaw, J F (RNE Coll) 1898 S, W
Shaw, S D (Bristol, Wasps) 1996 It, Arg, 1997 S, I, F, W, A 1, SA (R), 2000 I, F, W, It, S, SA 1(R),2(R), 2001 C 1(R), 2, US, I, 2003 It (R), W 2, F 2(R), 3(R), 2004 It(t&R), S(R), NZ1, 2, A1, 2005 Sm(R), 2006 W(R), It(R), S(R), F(R), I, 2007 W2,F2,3, [US, SA1,Sm,A,F,SA2]
Sheasby, C M A (Wasps) 1996 It, Arg, 1997 W (R), Arg 1(R),2(R), SA (R), NZ 2(t)
Sheppard, A (Bristol) 1981 W (R), 1985 W
Sheridan, A J (Sale) 2004 C(R), 2005 A, NZ, Sm, 2006 W, It, S, F(R), I, NZ, SA1, 2007 W2, F2, [US, SA1, Sm, Tg, A, F, SA2]
Sherrard, C W (Blackheath) 1871 S, 1872 S
Sherriff, G A (Saracens) 1966 S, 1967 A, NZ
Shewring, H E (Bristol) 1905 I, NZ, 1906 W, S, F, SA, 1907 F, W, I, S
Shooter, J H (Morley) 1899 I, S, 1900 I, S
Shuttleworth, D W (Headingley) 1951 S, 1953 S
Sibree, H J H (Harlequins) 1908 F, 1909 I, S
Silk, N (Harlequins) 1965 W, I, F, S
Simms, K G (Cambridge U, Liverpool, Wasps) 1985 R, F, S, I, W, 1986 I, F, 1987 I, F, W, [A, J, W], 1988 F, W
Simpson, C P (Harlequins) 1965 W
Simpson, P D (Bath) 1983 NZ, 1984 S, 1987 I
Simpson, T (Rockcliff) 1902 S, 1903 W, I, S, 1904 I, S, 1905 I, S, 1906 S, SA, 1909 F
Simpson-Daniel, J D (Gloucester) 2002 NZ, A, 2003 W 1(t + R), It, W 2, 2004 I(R), NZ1, 2005 Sm, 2006 It(R), 2007 SA1(R)
Sims, D (Gloucester) 1998 NZ 1(R),2, SA 1
Skinner, M G (Harlequins) 1988 F, W, S, I 1,2, 1989 Fj, 1990 I, F, W, S, Arg 1,2, 1991 Fj (R), [US, F, S, A], 1992 S, I, F, W
Skirving, B (Saracens) 2007 SA2
Sladen, G M (United Services, RN) 1929 W, I, S
Sleightholme, J M (Bath) 1996 F, W, S, I, It, Arg, 1997 S, I, F, W, Arg 1,2

Slemen, M A C (Liverpool) 1976 I, F, 1977 S, I, F, W, 1978 F, W, S, I, NZ, 1979 S, I, F, W, NZ, 1980 I, F, W, S, 1981 W, S, I, F, 1982 A, S, I, F, W, 1983 NZ, 1984 S
Slocock, L A N (Liverpool) 1907 F, W, I, S, 1908 F, W, I, S
Slow, C F (Leicester) 1934 S
Small, H D (Oxford U) 1950 W, I, F, S
Smallwood, A M (Leicester) 1920 F, I, 1921 W, I, S, F, 1922 I, S, 1923 W, I, S, F, 1925 I, S
Smart, C E (Newport) 1979 F, W, NZ, 1981 S, I, F, Arg 1,2, 1982 A, S, I, F, W, 1983 F, W, S, I
Smart, S E J (Gloucester) 1913 SA, W, F, I, S, 1914 W, I, S, F, 1920 W, I, S
Smeddle, R W (Cambridge U) 1929 W, I, S, 1931 F
Smith, C C (Gloucester) 1901 W
Smith, D F (Richmond) 1910 W, I
Smith, J V (Cambridge U, Rosslyn Park) 1950 W, I, F, S
Smith, K (Roundhay) 1974 F, W, 1975 W, S
Smith, M J K (Oxford U) 1956 W
Smith, O J (Leicester) 2003 It (R), W 2(R), F 2, 2005 It(R), S(R)
Smith, S J (Sale) 1973 I, F, S, A, 1974 I, F, 1975 W (R), 1976 F, 1977 F (R), 1979 NZ, 1980 I, F, W, S, 1981 W, S, I, F, Arg 1,2, 1982 A, S, I, F, W, 1983 F, W, S
Smith, S R (Richmond) 1959 W, F, S, 1964 F, S
Smith, S T (Wasps) 1985 R, F, S, I, W, NZ 1,2, 1986 W, S
Smith, T H (Northampton) 1951 W
Soane, F (Bath) 1893 S, 1894 W, I, S
Sobey, W H (O Millhillians) 1930 W, F, S, 1932 SA, W
Solomon, B (Redruth) 1910 W
Sparks, R H W (Plymouth A) 1928 I, F, S, 1929 W, I, S, 1931 I, S, F
Speed, H (Castleford) 1894 W, I, S, 1896 S
Spence, F W (Birkenhead Park) 1890 I
Spencer, J (Harlequins) 1966 W
Spencer, J S (Cambridge U, Headingley) 1969 I, F, S, W, SA, 1970 I, W, S, F, 1971 W, I, S (2[1C]), P
Spong, R S (O Millhillians) 1929 F, 1930 W, I, F, S, 1931 F, 1932 SA, W
Spooner, R H (Liverpool) 1903 W
Springman, H H (Liverpool) 1879 S, 1887 S
Spurling, A (Blackheath) 1882 I
Spurling, N (Blackheath) 1886 I, S, 1887 W
Squires, P J (Harrogate) 1973 F, S, NZ 2, A, 1974 S, I, F, W, 1975 I, F, W, S, A 1,2, 1976 A, W, 1977 S, I, F, W, 1978 F, W, S, I, NZ, 1979 S, I, F, W
Stafford R C (Bedford) 1912 W, I, S, F
Stafford, W F H (RE) 1874 S
Stanbury, E (Plymouth A) 1926 W, I, S, 1927 W, I, S, F, 1928 A, W, I, F, S, 1929 W, I, S, F
Standing, G (Blackheath) 1883 W, I
Stanger-Leathes, C F (Northern) 1905 I
Stark, K J (O Alleynians) 1927 W, I, S, F, 1928 A, W, I, F, S
Starks, A (Castleford) 1896 W, I
Starmer-Smith, N C (Harlequins) 1969 SA, 1970 I, W, S, F, 1971 S (C), P
Start, S P (United Services, RN) 1907 S
Steeds, J H (Saracens) 1949 F, S, 1950 I, F, S
Steele-Bodger, M R (Cambridge U) 1947 W, I, S, F, 1948 A, W, I, S, F
Steinthal, F E (Ilkley) 1913 W, F
Stephenson, M (Newcastle) 2001 C 1,2, US
Stevens, C B (Penzance-Newlyn, Harlequins) 1969 SA, 1970 I, W, S, 1971 P, 1972 W, I, F, S, SA, 1973 NZ 1, W, I, F, S, NZ 2, A, 1974 S, I, F, W, 1975 I, F, W, S
Stevens, M J H (Bath) 2004 NZ1(R), 2(t), 2005 I, It, S, NZ(R), Sm, 2006 W, It, F, 2007 SA2, W2(R), F2, 3(R), [US(R), SA1, Sm, Tg, A(R), F(R), SA2(R)]
Still, E R (Oxford U, Ravenscourt P) 1873 S
Stimpson, T R G (Newcastle, Leicester) 1996 It, 1997 S, I, F, W, A 1, NZ 2(t+R), 1998 A 1, NZ 1,2(R), SA 1(R), 1999 US (R), C (R), 2000 SA 1, 2001 C 1(t),2(R), 2002 W (R), Arg, SA (R)
Stirling, R V (Leicester, RAF, Wasps) 1951 W, I, F, S, 1952 SA, W, S, I, F, 1953 W, I, F, S, 1954 W, NZ, I, S, F
Stoddart, A E (Blackheath) 1885 W, I, 1886 W, I, S, 1889 M, 1890 W, I, 1893 W, S
Stoddart, W B (Liverpool) 1897 W, I, S
Stokes, F (Blackheath) 1871 S, 1872 S, 1873 S
Stokes, L (Blackheath) 1875 I, 1876 S, 1877 I, S, 1878 S, 1879 S, I, 1880 I, S, 1881 I, W, S
Stone, F le S (Blackheath) 1914 F
Stoop, A D (Harlequins) 1905 S, 1906 S, F, SA, 1907 F, W, 1910 W, I, S, 1911 W, F, I, S, 1912 W, S
Stoop, F M (Harlequins) 1910 S, 1911 F, I, 1913 SA
Stout, F M (Richmond) 1897 W, I, 1898 I, S, W, 1899 I, S, 1903 S, 1904 W, I, S, 1905 W, I, S
Stout, P W (Richmond) 1898 S, W, 1899 W, I, S
Strettle, D (Harlequins) 2007 I,F1,W1,2
Stringer, N C (Wasps) 1982 A (R), 1983 NZ (R), 1984 SA 1(R), A, 1985 R
Strong, E L (Oxford U) 1884 W, I, S
Sturnham B (Saracens) 1998 A 1, NZ 1(t),2(t)
Summerscales, G E (Durham City) 1905 NZ
Sutcliffe, J W (Heckmondwike) 1889 M
Swarbrick, D W (Oxford U) 1947 W, I, F, 1948 A, W, 1949 I
Swayne, D H (Oxford U) 1931 W
Swayne, J W R (Bridgwater) 1929 W
Swift, A H (Swansea) 1981 Arg 1,2, 1983 F, W, S, 1984 SA 2
Syddall, J P (Waterloo) 1982 I, 1984 A
Sykes, A R V (Blackheath) 1914 F
Sykes, F D (Northampton) 1955 F, S, 1963 NZ 2, A
Sykes, P W (Wasps) 1948 F, 1952 S, I, F, 1953 W, I, F
Syrett, R E (Wasps) 1958 W, A, I, F, 1960 W, I, F, S, 1962 W, I, F

Tait, M (Newcastle) 2005 W, 2006 A1, 2,SA1,2,2007 It(R), I(R), F1(R), W1, SA1, 2,W2, [US(R),SA1(R),Sm,Tg,A,F,SA2]
Tallent, J A (Cambridge U, Blackheath) 1931 S, F, 1932 SA, W, 1935 I
Tanner, C C (Cambridge U, Gloucester) 1930 S, 1932 SA, W, I, S
Tarr, F N (Leicester) 1909 A, W, F, 1913 S
Tatham, W M (Oxford U) 1882 S, 1883 W, I, S, 1884 W, I, S
Taylor, A S (Blackheath) 1883 W, I, 1886 W, I
Taylor, E W (Rockcliff) 1892 I, 1893 I, 1894 W, I, S, 1895 W, I, S, 1896 W, I, 1897 W, I, S, 1899 I
Taylor, F (Leicester) 1920 F, I
Taylor, F M (Leicester) 1914 W
Taylor, H H (Blackheath) 1879 S, 1880 S, 1881 I, W, 1882 S
Taylor, J T (W Hartlepool) 1897 I, 1899 I, 1900 I, 1901 W, I, 1902 W, I, S, 1903 W, I, 1905 S
Taylor, P J (Northampton) 1955 W, I, 1962 W, I, F, S
Taylor, R B (Northampton) 1966 W, 1967 I, F, S, W, NZ, 1969 F, S, W, SA, 1970 I, W, S, F, 1971 S (2[1C])
Taylor, W J (Blackheath) 1928 A, W, I, F, S
Teague, M C (Gloucester, Moseley) 1985 F (R), NZ 1, 2, 1989 S, I, F, W, R, 1990 F, W, S, 1991 W, S, I, F, Fj, A, [NZ, It, F, S, A], 1992 SA, 1993 F, W, S, I
Teden, D E (Richmond) 1939 W, I, S
Teggin, A (Broughton R) 1884 I, 1885 W, 1886 I, S, 1887 I, S
Tetley, T S (Bradford) 1876 S
Thomas, C (Barnstaple) 1895 W, I, S, 1899 I
Thompson, P H (Headingley, Waterloo) 1956 W, I, S, F, 1957 W, I, F, S, 1958 W, A, I, F, S, 1959 W, I, F, S
Thompson, S G (Northampton) 2002 S, I, F, W, It, Arg, NZ, A, SA, 2003 F 1, W 1, It, S, I, NZ, A, F 2(R), 3, [Gg, SA, Sm(R), W, F, A], 2004 It, S, I, W, F, NZ1, A1(R), C, SA, A2, 2005 W, F, I, It, S, A, NZ, Sm, 2006 W, It, S, F, I(R)
Thomson, G T (Halifax) 1878 S, 1882 I, S, 1883 W, I, S, 1884 I, S, 1885 I
Thomson, W B (Blackheath) 1892 W, 1895 W, I, S
Thorne, J D (Bristol) 1963 W, I, F
Tindall, M J (Bath, Gloucester) 2000 I, F, W, It, S, SA 1,2, A Arg, SA 3, 2001 W (R), R, SA (R), 2002 S, I, F, W, It, NZ, A, SA, 2003 It, S, I, NZ, A, F 2, [Gg, SA, Sm, W, F(R), A], 2004 W, F, NZ1, 2, A1, C, SA, A2, 2005 A, NZ, Sm, 2006 W, It, S, F, I(t&R), 2007 S,It,I,F1
Tindall, V R (Liverpool U) 1951 W, I, F, S
Titterrell, A J (Sale) 2004 NZ2(R), C(R), 2005 It(R), S(R), 2007 SA2(R)
Tobin, F (Liverpool) 1871 S
Todd, A F (Blackheath) 1900 I, S
Todd, R (Manchester) 1877 S
Toft, H B (Waterloo) 1936 S, 1937 W, I, S, 1938 W, I, S, 1939 W, I, S

Toothill, J T (Bradford) 1890 S, I, 1891 W, I, 1892 W, I, S, 1893 W, I, S, 1894 W, I
Tosswill, L R (Exeter) 1902 W, I, S
Touzel, C J C (Liverpool) 1877 I, S
Towell, A C (Bedford) 1948 F, 1951 S
Travers, B H (Harlequins) 1947 W, I, 1948 A, W, 1949 F, S
Treadwell, W T (Wasps) 1966 I, F, S
Trick, D M (Bath) 1983 I, 1984 SA 1
Tristram, H B (Oxford U) 1883 S, 1884 W, S, 1885 W, 1887 S
Troop, C L (Aldershot S) 1933 I, S
Tucker, J S (Bristol) 1922 W, 1925 NZ, W, I, S, F, 1926 W, I, F, S, 1927 W, I, S, F, 1928 A, W, I, F, S, 1929 W, I, F, 1930 W, I, F, S, 1931 W
Tucker, W E (Blackheath) 1894 W, I, 1895 W, I, S
Tucker, W E (Blackheath) 1926 I, 1930 W, I
Turner, D P (Richmond) 1871 S, 1872 S, 1873 S, 1874 S, 1875 I, S
Turner, E B (St George's Hospital) 1876 I, 1877 I, 1878 I
Turner, G R (St George's Hospital) 1876 S
Turner, H J C (Manchester) 1871 S
Turner, M F (Blackheath) 1948 S, F
Turner, S C (Sale) 2007 W1(R), SA1,2(R)
Turquand-Young, D (Richmond) 1928 A, W, 1929 I, S, F
Twynam, H T (Richmond) 1879 I, 1880 I, 1881 W, 1882<j> I, 1883 I, 1884 W, I, S

Ubogu, V E (Bath) 1992 C, SA, 1993 NZ, 1994 S, I, F, W, SA 1,2, R, C, 1995 I, F, W, S, [Arg, WS, A, NZ, F], SA, 1999 F (R), W (R), A (R)
Underwood, A M (Exeter) 1962 W, I, F, S, 1964 I
Underwood, R (Leicester, RAF) 1984 I, F, W, A, 1985 R, F, S, I, W, 1986 W, I, F, 1987 I, F, W, S, [A, J, W], 1988 F, W, S, I 1,2, A 1,2, Fj, A, 1989 S, I, F, W, R, Fj, 1990 I, F, W, S, Arg 3, 1991 W, S, I, F, Fj, A, [NZ, It, US, F, S, A], 1992 S, I, F, W, SA, 1993 F, W, S, I, NZ, 1994 S, I, F, W, SA 1,2, R, C, 1995 I, F, W, S, [Arg, It, WS, A, NZ, F], SA, WS, 1996 F, W, S, I
Underwood, T (Leicester, Newcastle) 1992 C, SA, 1993 S, I, NZ, 1994 S, I, W, SA 1,2, R, C, 1995 I, F, W, S, [Arg, It, A, NZ], 1996 Arg, 1997 S, I, F, W, 1998 A 2, SA 2
Unwin, E J (Rosslyn Park, Army) 1937 S, 1938 W, I, S
Unwin, G T (Blackheath) 1898 S
Uren, R (Waterloo) 1948 I, S, F, 1950 I
Uttley, R M (Gosforth) 1973 I, F, S, NZ 2, A, 1974 I, F, W, 1975 F, W, S, A 1,2, 1977 S, I, F, W, 1978 NZ 1979 S, 1980 I, F, W, S

Valentine J (Swinton) 1890 W, 1896 W, I, S
Vanderspar, C H R (Richmond) 1873 S
Van Gisbergen, M C (Wasps) 2005 A(t)
Van Ryneveld, C B (Oxford U) 1949 W, I, F, S
Varley, H (Liversedge) 1892 S
Varndell, T W (Leicester) 2005 Sm(R), 2006 A1, 2
Vassall, H (Blackheath) 1881 W, S, 1882 I, S, 1883 W
Vassall, H H (Blackheath) 1908 I
Vaughan, D B (Headingley) 1948 A, W, I, S, 1949 I, F, S, 1950 W
Vaughan-Jones, A (Army) 1932 I, S, 1933 W
Verelst, C L (Liverpool) 1876 I, 1878 I
Vernon, G F (Blackheath) 1878 S, I, 1880 I, S, 1881 I
Vickery, G (Aberavon) 1905 I
Vickery, P J (Gloucester, Wasps) 1998 W, A 1, NZ 1,2, SA 1, 1999 US, C, [It, NZ, Tg, SA], 2000 I, F, W, S, A, Arg (R), SA 3(R), 2001 W, It, S, A, SA, 2002 I, F, Arg, NZ, A, SA, 2003 NZ(R), A, [Gg, SA, Sm(R), U, W, F, A], 2004 It, S, I, W, F, 2005 W(R), F, A, NZ, 2006 SA1(R),2, 2007 S, It, I, W2, F2(R),3, [US, Tg(R), A, F, SA2]
Vivyan, E J (Devonport A) 1901 W, 1904 W, I, S
Voyce, A T (Gloucester) 1920 I, S, 1921 W, I, S, F, 1922 W, I, F, S, 1923 W, I, S, F, 1924 W, I, F, S, 1925 NZ, W, I, S, F, 1926 W, I, F, S
Voyce, T M D (Bath, Wasps) 2001 US (R), 2004 NZ2, A1, 2005 Sm, 2006 W(R), It, F(R), I, A1
Vyvyan, H D (Saracens) 2004 C(R)

Wackett, J A S (Rosslyn Park) 1959 W, I
Wade, C G (Richmond) 1883 W, I, S, 1884 W, S, 1885 W, 1886 W, I
Wade, M R (Cambridge U) 1962 W, I, F
Wakefield, W W (Harlequins) 1920 W, F, I, S, 1921 W, I, S, F, 1922 W, I, F, S, 1923 W, I, S, F, 1924 W, I, F, S, 1925 NZ, W, I, S, F, 1926 W, I, F, S, 1927 S, F
Walder, D J H (Newcastle) 2001 C 1,2, US, 2003 W 2(R)
Walker, G A (Blackheath) 1939 W, I
Walker, H W (Coventry) 1947 W, I, S, F, 1948 A, W, I, S, F
Walker, R (Manchester) 1874 S, 1875 I, 1876 S, 1879 S, 1880 S
Wallens, J N S (Waterloo) 1927 F
Walshe, N P J (Bath) 2006 A1(R), 2(R)
Walton, E J (Castleford) 1901 W, I, 1902 I, S
Walton, W (Castleford) 1894 S
Ward, G (Leicester) 1913 W, F, S, 1914 W, I, S
Ward, H (Bradford) 1895 W
Ward, J I (Richmond) 1881 I, 1882 I
Ward, J W (Castleford) 1896 W, I, S
Wardlow, C S (Northampton) 1969 SA (R), 1971 W, I, F, S (2[1C])
Warfield, P J (Rosslyn Park, Durham U) 1973 NZ 1, W, I, 1975 I, F, S
Warr, A L (Oxford U) 1934 W, I
Waters, F H H (Wasps) 2001 US, 2004 NZ2(R), A1(R)
Watkins, J A (Gloucester) 1972 SA, 1973 NZ 1, W, NZ 2, A, 1975 F, W
Watkins, J K (United Services, RN) 1939 W, I, S
Watson, F B (United Services, RN) 1908 S, 1909 S
Watson, J H D (Blackheath) 1914 W, S, F
Watt, D E J (Bristol) 1967 I, F, S, W
Webb, C S H (Devonport Services, RN) 1932 SA, W, I, S, 1933 W, I, S, 1935 S, 1936 NZ, W, I, S
Webb, J M (Bristol, Bath) 1987 [A (R), J, US, W], 1988 F, W, S, I 1,2, A 1,2, A, 1989 S, I, F, W, 1991 Fj, A, [NZ, It, F, S, A], 1992 S, I, F, W, C, SA, 1993 F, W, S, I
Webb, J W G (Northampton) 1926 F, S, 1929 S
Webb, R E (Coventry) 1967 S, W, NZ, 1968 I, F, S, 1969 I, F, S, W, 1972 I, F
Webb, St L H (Bedford) 1959 W, I, F, S
Webster, J G (Moseley) 1972 W, I, SA, 1973 NZ 1, W, NZ 2, 1974 S, W, 1975 I, F, W
Wedge, T G (St Ives) 1907 F, 1909 W
Weighill, R H G (RAF, Harlequins) 1947 S, F, 1948 S, F
Wells, C M (Cambridge U, Harlequins) 1893 S, 1894 W, S, 1896 S, 1897 W, S
West, B R (Loughborough Colls, Northampton) 1968 W, I, F, S, 1969 SA, 1970 I, W, S
West, D E (Leicester) 1998 F (R), S (R), 2000 Arg (R), 2001 W, It, S, F (t), C 1,2, US, I (R), A, SA, 2002 F (R), W (R), It (R), 2003 W 2(R), F 2,3(t+R), [U, F(R)]
West, R (Gloucester) 1995 [WS]
Weston, H T F (Northampton) 1901 S
Weston, L E (W of Scotland) 1972 F, S
Weston, M P (Richmond, Durham City) 1960 W, I, F, S, 1961 SA, W, I, F, S, 1962 W, I, F, 1963 W, I, F, S, NZ 1,2, A, 1964 NZ, W, I, F, S, 1965 F, S, 1966 S, 1968 F, S
Weston, W H (Northampton) 1933 I, S, 1934 I, S, 1935 W, I, S, 1936 NZ, W, S, 1937 W, I, S, 1938 W, I, S
Wheatley, A A (Coventry) 1937 W, I, S, 1938 W, S
Wheatley, H F (Coventry) 1936 I, 1937 S, 1938 W, S, 1939 W, I, S
Wheeler, P J (Leicester) 1975 F, W, 1976 A, W, S, I, 1977 S, I, F, W, 1978 F, W, S, I, NZ, 1979 S, I, F, W, NZ, 1980 I, F, W, S, 1981 W, S, I, F, 1982 A, S, I, F, W, 1983 F, S, I, NZ, 1984 S, I, F, W
White, C (Gosforth) 1983 NZ, 1984 S, I, F
White, D F (Northampton) 1947 W, I, S, 1948 I, F, 1951 S, 1952 SA, W, S, I, F, 1953 W, I, S
White, J M (Saracens, Bristol, Leicester) 2000 SA 1,2, Arg, SA 3, 2001 F, C 1,2, US, I, R (R), 2002 S, W, It, 2003 F 1(R), W 2, F 2,3, [Sm, U(R)], 2004 W(R), F(R), NZ1,2, A1,C, SA, A2, 2005 W, 2006 W(R), It(R), S, F, I, A1,2, NZ, Arg, SA1,2, 2007 S(R), It(R), I(R), F1, W1
White-Cooper, S (Harlequins) 2001 C 2, US
Whiteley, E C P (O Alleynians) 1931 S, F
Whiteley, W (Bramley) 1896 W
Whitely, H (Northern) 1929 W
Wightman, B J (Moseley, Coventry) 1959 W, 1963 W, I, NZ 2, A

ENGLAND

Wigglesworth, H J (Thornes) 1884 I
Wilkins, D T (United Services, RN, Roundhay) 1951 W, I, F, S, 1952 SA, W, S, I, F, 1953 W, I, F, S
Wilkinson, E (Bradford) 1886 W, I, S, 1887 W, S
Wilkinson, H (Halifax) 1929 W, I, S, 1930 F
Wilkinson, H J (Halifax) 1889 M
Wilkinson, J P (Newcastle) 1998 I (R), A 1, NZ 1, 1999 S, I, F, W, A, US, C, [It, NZ, Fj, SA (R)], 2000 I, F, W, It, S, SA 2, A, Arg, SA 3, 2001 W, It, S, F, I, A, SA, 2002 S, I, F, W, It, NZ, A, SA, 2003 F 1, W 1, It, S, I, NZ, A, F 3, [Gg, SA, Sm, W, F, A], 2007 S,It,I, SA1, 2, W2, F2(R), F3, [Sm,Tg,A,F,SA2]
Wilkinson, P (Law Club) 1872 S
Wilkinson, R M (Bedford) 1975 A 2, 1976 A, W, S, I, F
Willcocks, T J (Plymouth) 1902 W
Willcox, J G (Oxford U, Harlequins) 1961 I, F, S, 1962 W, I, F, S, 1963 W, I, F, S, 1964 NZ, W, I, F, S
William-Powlett, P B R W (United Services, RN) 1922 S
Williams, C G (Gloucester, RAF) 1976 F
Williams, C S (Manchester) 1910 F
Williams, J E (O Millhillians, Sale) 1954 F, 1955 W, I, F, S, 1956 I, S, F, 1965 W
Williams, J M (Penzance-Newlyn) 1951 I, S
Williams, P N (Orrell) 1987 S, [A, J, W]
Williams, S G (Devonport A) 1902 W, I, S, 1903 I, S, 1907 I, S
Williams, S H (Newport) 1911 W, F, I, S
Williamson, R H (Oxford U) 1908 W, I, S, 1909 A, F
Wilson, A J (Camborne S of M) 1909 I
Wilson, C E (Blackheath) 1898 I
Wilson, C P (Cambridge U, Marlborough N) 1881 W
Wilson, D S (Met Police, Harlequins) 1953 F, 1954 W, NZ, I, S, F, 1955 F, S
Wilson, G S (Tyldesley) 1929 W, I
Wilson, K J (Gloucester) 1963 F
Wilson, R P (Liverpool OB) 1891 W, I, S
Wilson, W C (Richmond) 1907 I, S
Winn, C E (Rosslyn Park) 1952 SA, W, S, I, F, 1954 W, S, F
Winterbottom, P J (Headingley, Harlequins) 1982 A, S, I, F, W, 1983 F, W, S, I, NZ, 1984 S, F, W, SA 1,2, 1986 W, S, I, F, 1987 I, F, W, [A, J, US, W], 1988 F, W, S, 1989 R, Fj, 1990 I, F, W, S, Arg 1,2,3, 1991 W, S, I, F, A, [NZ, It, F, S, A], 1992 S, I, F, W, C, SA, 1993 F, W, S, I
Winters, R A (Bristol) 2007 SA1(R),2
Wintle, T C (Northampton) 1966 S, 1969 I, F, S, W
Wodehouse, N A (United Services, RN) 1910 F, 1911 W, F, I, S, 1912 W, I, S, F, 1913 SA, W, F, I, S
Wood, A (Halifax) 1884 I
Wood, A E (Gloucester, Cheltenham) 1908 F, W, I
Wood, G W (Leicester) 1914 W
Wood, M B, (Wasps) 2001 C 2(R), US (R)
Wood, R (Liversedge) 1894 I
Wood, R D (Liverpool OB) 1901 I, 1903 W, I
Woodgate, E E (Paignton) 1952 W
Woodhead, E (Huddersfield) 1880 I
Woodman, T J, (Gloucester) 1999 US (R), 2000 I (R), It (R), 2001 W (R), It (R), 2002 NZ, 2003 S (R), I(t + R), A, F 3, [Gg, SA, W(R), F, A], 2004 It, S, I, W, F, NZ1, 2
Woodruff, C G (Harlequins) 1951 W, I, F, S
Woods, S M J (Cambridge U, Wellington) 1890 W, S, I, 1891 W, I, S, 1892 I, S, 1893 W, I, 1895 W, I, S
Woods, T (Bridgwater) 1908 S
Woods, T (United Services, RN) 1920 S, 1921 W, I, S, F
Woodward, C R (Leicester) 1980 I (R), F, W, S, 1981 W, S, I, F, Arg 1,2, 1982 A, S, I, F, W, 1983 I, NZ, 1984 S, I, F, W
Woodward, J E (Wasps) 1952 SA, W, S, 1953 W, I, F, S, 1954 W, NZ, I, S, F, 1955 W, I, 1956 S
Wooldridge, C S (Oxford U, Blackheath) 1883 W, I, S, 1884 W, I, S, 1885 I
Wordsworth, A J (Cambridge U) 1975 A 1(R)
Worsley, J P R (Wasps) 1999 [Tg, Fj], 2000 It (R), S (R), SA 1(R),2(R), 2001 It (R), S (R), F (R), C 1,2, US, A, R, SA, 2002 S, I, F, W (t+R), Arg, 2003 W 1(R), It, S(R), I(t), NZ(R), A(R), W 2, [SA(t), Sm, U], 2004 It, I, W(R), F, NZ1(R), 2, A1, SA, A2, 2005 W, F, I, It, S, 2006 W, It, S, F, I, A1(R), 2, SA1,2, 2007 S, I, F1,W1,2, F2,3(R), [US, Sm, A(R), F(R), SA2(R)]
Worsley, M A (London Irish, Harlequins) 2003 It(R), 2004 A1(R), 2005 S(R)
Worton, J R B (Harlequins, Army) 1926 W, 1927 W
Wrench, D F B (Harlequins) 1964 F, S
Wright, C C G (Cambridge U, Blackheath) 1909 I, S
Wright, F T (Edinburgh Acady, Manchester) 1881 S
Wright, I D (Northampton) 1971 W, I, F, S (R)
Wright. J C (Met Police) 1934 W
Wright, J F (Bradford) 1890 W
Wright, T P (Blackheath) 1960 W, I, F, S, 1961 SA, W, I, F, S, 1962 W, I, F, S
Wright, W H G (Plymouth) 1920 W, F
Wyatt, D M (Bedford) 1976 S (R)

Yarranton, P G (RAF, Wasps) 1954 W, NZ, I, 1955 F, S
Yates, K P (Bath, Saracens) 1997 Arg 1,2, 2007 SA1,2
Yiend, W (Hartlepool R, Gloucester) 1889 M, 1892 W, I, S, 1893 I, S
Young, A T (Cambridge U, Blackheath, Army) 1924 W, I, F, S, 1925 NZ, F, 1926 I, F, S, 1927 I, S, F, 1928 A, W, I, F, S, 1929 I
Young, J R C (Oxford U, Harlequins) 1958 I, 1960 W, I, F, S, 1961 SA, W, I, F
Young, M (Gosforth) 1977 S, I, F, W, 1978 F, W, S, I, NZ, 1979 S
Young, P D (Dublin Wands) 1954 W, NZ, I, S, F, 1955 W, I, F, S
Youngs, N G (Leicester) 1983 I, NZ, 1984 S, I, F, W

THE TIGERS SHOW THEIR CLAWS

John Gichigi/Getty Images

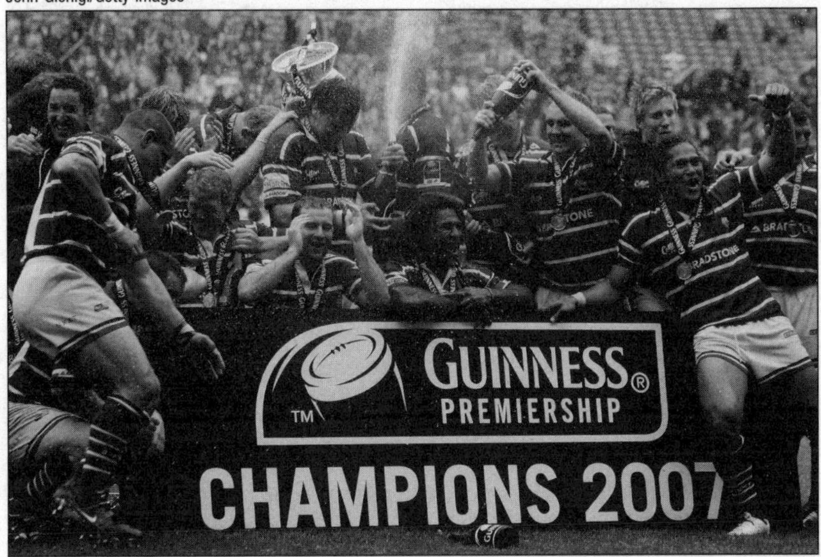

Leicester are finally crowned English champions, again.

Leicester were crowned English league champions for the seventh time in the club's silverware-strewn history after adding the Guinness Premiership title to the EDF Energy Cup they clinched less than a month earlier.

The Tigers, coached by Pat Howard in his last season at the helm at Welford Road, had completed the first phase of what could have been a unique trophy treble by beating the Ospreys in the Anglo-Welsh final at Twickenham and made it two out of three at the same venue in May when they comprehensively demolished the challenge of Gloucester.

As so often since the introduction of the play-off system to the English top-flight in 2002, Leicester did not finish top of the final league table – that dubious honour belonged to the Cherry and Whites – but The Tigers made a mockery of pre-match predictions of an epic encounter with a seven-try burst to spectacularly derail Gloucester.

Their eventual 44–16 triumph ensured the league trophy would be heading back to the East Midlands for the first time in five years and with the club's eagerly-anticipated Heineken Cup final showdown with Wasps just eight days away, Leicester were on the verge of making history.

"It is great to turn out for the big days," said Howard after his side had completed the domestic double and banished the memories of two successive Premiership final defeats in 2005 and 2006 behind them. "We have been guilty of not doing that before. It was a very good performance, there were some lovely tries, and to repeat that next week will be a massive challenge now.

"Defensively we worked hard, some of our clinical finishing was pretty good, we took our opportunities. I don't think we are a 40-point better side than Gloucester. I think the best two teams made the final and we just played better today."

The disappointment for Gloucester, who had pipped Leicester to top spot courtesy of their superior points difference, was palpable. "Today we just couldn't do it, there's no hiding from that," admitted coach Dean Ryan. "The whole game is about mismatch and if you've got that across the field, in reality it was so far across the team it was difficult."

There were few signs as the campaign began in early September that the Tigers would reach the final to face Ryan's team.

Gloucester began in confident style winning seven of their eight opening games but it was initially Bristol and Wasps, rather than Leicester, who mounted the most concerted challenge to the Cherry and Whites.

Coached by Richard Hill, Bristol had finished second bottom the previous season but from the start of the new campaign looked a very different proposition and in their opening nine games lost just once – a surprise 26–21 reverse at Newcastle.

Perennial challengers Wasps also started well with four wins from their first five and the race for the all-important top four places was on.

It was, however, an altogether contrasting story for the defending champions Sale. Five wins from their opening eight victories suggested the Sharks would be genuine contenders once again but they were then rocked by a crippling series of injuries that were to completely devastate their title challenge.

Club captain Jason White and England duo Andy Sheridan and Charlie Hodgson were all sidelined and the Sharks were deprived of the services of the influential trio for the rest of the season.

"This is a terrible blow," said Sharks director of rugby Philippe Saint-Andre in November. "Their loss is a blow to our aspirations to retain

Getty Images

Bristol – with scrum-half Shaun Perry in great form – were the surprise package of 2006–07.

our title, and also to our chances in the EDF Energy and Heineken Cup competitions."

The New Year saw Gloucester, Bristol, Wasps and Leicester, who had by now recovered from their uncharacteristically sluggish start, jockey for position but they were now joined by Saracens, coached by Alan Gaffney, who were hoping to reach the play-offs for the first time since their introduction.

Sarries had opened up with three losses from their first six matches but began to gain ground after morale-boosting home wins over Leicester (22–16), Gloucester (24–22) and Bristol (36–5).

None of the quintet, however, were able to string together a significant run of victories and pull away and the end of the regular season loomed. In hindsight, Gloucester could have claimed top spot outright if they had managed to beat old rivals Bath at the Recreation Ground for the first time since the inception of English league rugby but were held to a 21–21 draw.

Before the final round of games in April, Gloucester, Leicester and Bristol were already guaranteed play-off rugby and it was left to London rivals Saracens and Wasps to fight it out for fourth place. In the end, Wasps went down 40–26 at Leicester while Sarries were beaten 22 at Worcester and it was Gaffney's side who progressed.

At the other end of the table, the Warriors' victory preserved their top-flight status and condemned Northampton – 27–22 winners over

London Irish – to only the club's second relegation from the Premiership.

"Ultimately you get what you deserve and we deserved what we got," said Saints head coach Paul Grayson. "We should never have been in this position in the first place. The players haven't produced and we take responsibility for that collectively."

The first semi-final saw Leicester entertain Bristol at Welford Road in a game, which saw the Tigers display, all their trademark forward control and ultimately take the honours 26–14. Tries from Harry Ellis and Geordan Murphy sealed the victory and Leicester were safely through to their third consecutive Premiership final.

Saracens made the journey to Kingsholm for the second semi but any hopes the Londoners had of pulling off a major surprise were clinically crushed by Gloucester.

The visitors only trailed 14–3 at the break but second-half tries from Luke Narraway, Mark Foster, Anthony Allen, Andy Hazell and Christian Califano, plus 15 points from the boot of Willie Walker, steered the Cheery and Whites to a thumping 50–9 win.

With the momentum behind them, many predicted Gloucester would give Leicester more than a run for their money at Twickenham but the omens darkened for Ryan's side on the morning of the final when they lost influential captain Marco Bortolami, who failed a late fitness test on a knee injury.

Their luck didn't improve in the match itself when Bortolami's replacement as skipper – Peter Buxton – was taken off after just 15 minutes with a hand injury and the Tigers smelled blood.

Leicester scrum-half Frank Murphy crossed for the first try and it was a score that effectively breached the Cherry and White dam. Man-of-the-match Alesana Tuilagi and Martin Corry crossed before the break to give the Tigers a platform and it became a rout in the second 40 minutes with scores from Andy Goode, Shane Jennings and a second from Tuilagi as Leicester cantered to a 44–16 victory.

"It showed we are dangerous when we have the ball," said Corry. "The important thing was the ball retention. Things went our way, especially the way we finished the first half. We take a huge amount of satisfaction from that."

Elsewhere in England, Leeds bounced back from the disappointment of Premiership relegation to claim the National One title ahead of second-placed Earth Titans and make a quick return to the top table.

The club, who will be known as Leeds Carnegie for the 2007–08 season, lost 25 first-team players after relegation and promoted Stuart Lancaster from academy manager to director of rugby but made light of the wholesale changes to be crowned champions. Wing Richard

Welding was top try scorer with 17 while full-back Leigh Hinton topped the division's scoring charts with 300 points to his name.

In National Two, Esher claimed only the third league title in the club's history to win promotion. Inspired by a club record 398 points from full-back Neil Hallett, Esher lost just twice in 26 league fixtures and finished an impressive 19 points clear of second-placed of Launceston.

Blaydon won their fourth promotion in 12 years to claim the National Three North title while Southend, captained by Ben Green, were National Three South champions.

The 2006–07 season also saw the 118-year-old County Championship renamed the Bill Beaumont Cup in honour of the former England and British & Irish Lions captain.

"The competition has changed," admitted Beaumont, who played in the tournament for Lancashire between 1972 and 1982. "If my association with the competition can give it an extra lift, then I'll be delighted. It's still got a great deal to offer."

The RFU also decided to use the rebranded tournament to test three new laws – known as the Experimental Law Variations (ELVs) – designed to encourage a more open style of rugby. Pulling a maul down became legal, tackled players had to play the ball immediately while all line outs resulting from kicks inside the 22 would be taken in line with where the kicker made contact.

The law changes, however, did not help Beaumont's former county as Lancashire were beaten 27–6 in the Twickenham final in May by Devon – a reverse of the 2006 final result. It was Devon's third triumph in four seasons.

GUINNESS PREMIERSHIP 2006–07 RESULTS

2 September, 2006: **London Irish** 20 **Harlequins** 19, **Gloucester** 24 **Bath** 19, **Worcester** 11 **Bristol** 41, **Saracens** 19 **Wasps** 21. 3 September, 2006: **Northampton** 25 **Newcastle** 23, **Leicester** 35 **Sale** 23. 8 September, 2006: **Wasps** 23 **London Irish** 17, **Newcastle** 20 **Worcester** 19. 9 September, 2006: **Sale** 32 **Northampton** 20, **Bath** 43 **Leicester** 25, **Harlequins** 21 **Gloucester** 28. 10 September, 2006: **Bristol** 13 **Saracens** 13. 15 September, 2006: **Worcester** 13 **Sale** 25. 16 September, 2006: **Northampton** 33 **Bath** 18. **London Irish** 11 **Bristol** 23, **Leicester** 27 **Gloucester** 27. 17 September, 2006: **Saracens** 44 **Newcastle** 20, **Wasps** 42 **Harlequins** 23. 22 September, 2006: **Sale** 34 **Saracens** 26, **Newcastle** 21 **London Irish** 26. 23 September, 2006: **Bath** 17 **Worcester** 11, **Gloucester** 28 **Northampton** 7, **Harlequins** 15 **Leicester** 21. 24 September, 2006: **Bristol** 26 **Wasps** 21. 13 October, 2006: **Worcester** 24 **Gloucester** 33. 14 October, 2006: **Northampton** 10 **Leicester** 15. 15 October, 2006: **Wasps** 35 **Newcastle** 15, **Bristol** 33 **Harlequins** 20, **London Irish** 14 **Sale** 31, **Saracens** 55 **Bath** 23. 3 November, 2006: **Sale** 18 **Wasps** 12, **Newcastle** 26 **Bristol** 21. 4 November, 2006: **Leicester** 40 **Worcester** 21, **Harlequins** 34 **Northampton** 19, **Gloucester** 21 **Saracens** 12, **Bath** 17 **London Irish** 21. 10 November, 2006: **Newcastle** 3 **Harlequins** 14, **London Irish** 11 **Gloucester** 22, **Bristol** 15 **Sale** 9. 11 November, 2006: **Worcester** 18 **Northampton** 23. 12 November, 2006: **Wasps** 47 **Bath** 18, **Saracens** 22 **Leicester** 16. 17 November, 2006: **Harlequins** 20 **Worcester** 6, **Sale** 18 **Newcastle** 26. 18 November, 2006: **Northampton** 13 **Saracens** 35, **Leicester** 26 **London Irish** 18, **Gloucester** 27 **Wasps** 21, **Bath** 12 **Bristol** 19. 24 November, 2006: **Sale** 17 **Harlequins** 12, **Bristol** 14 **Gloucester** 12. 25 November, 2006: **Bath** 20 **Newcastle** 14. 26 November, 2006: **Wasps** 13 **Leicester** 19, **Saracens** 17 **Worcester** 20, **London Irish** 40 **Northampton** 5. 22 December, 2006: **Worcester** 14 **London Irish** 16, **Northampton** 8 **Wasps** 6, **Leicester** 43 **Bristol** 15, **Harlequins** 16 **Saracens** 20, **Bath** 18 **Sale** 16. 26 December, 2006: **Wasps** 33 **Gloucester** 12, **Newcastle** 40 **Sale** 25, **London Irish** 26 **Leicester** 25. 27 December, 2006: **Worcester** 20 **Harlequins** 27, **Saracens** 38 **Northampton** 15, **Bristol** 16 **Bath** 6. 1 January, 2007: **Sale** 6 **Bristol** 10, **Northampton** 9 **Worcester** 10, **Leicester** 28 **Saracens** 15, **Harlequins** 42 **Newcastle** 15, **Gloucester** 15 **London Irish** 3, **Bath** 30 **Wasps** 19. 6 January, 2007: **Sale** 20 **Gloucester** 19, **Harlequins** 9 **Bath** 3. 7 January, 2007: **Newcastle** 31 **Leicester** 29, **Wasps** 19 **Worcester** 14. 26 January, 2007: **Worcester** 3 **Wasps** 3. 27 January, 2007: **Northampton** 8 **Bristol** 14, **Leicester** 39 **Newcastle** 5, **Gloucester** 44 **Sale** 24, **Bath** 31 **Harlequins** 23. 28 January, 2007: **Saracens** 19 **London Irish** 8. 17 February, 2007: **Worcester** 6 **Leicester** 13, **Northampton** 15 **Harlequins** 28, **London Irish** 15 **Bath** 7. 18 February, 2007: **Bristol** 22 **Newcastle** 21, **Saracens** 24 **Gloucester** 22, **Wasps** 26 **Sale** 18. 23 February, 2007: **Newcastle** 37 **Wasps** 11, **Sale** 9 **London Irish** 14. 24 February, 2007: **Leicester** 9 **Northampton** 10, **Harlequins** 15 **Bristol** 8, **Gloucester** 33 **Worcester** 19, **Bath** 20 **Saracens** 20. 3 March, 2007: **Worcester** 21 **Bath** 15, **Northampton** 5 **Gloucester** 7, **London Irish** 38 **Newcastle** 12, **Leicester** 27 **Harlequins** 22. 4 March, 2007: **Saracens** 22 **Sale** 9, **Wasps** 28 **Bristol** 0. 9 March, 2007: **Sale** 12 **Worcester** 18, **Newcastle** 20 **Saracens** 14. 10 March, 2007: **Harlequins** 16 **Wasps** 23, **Bristol** 7 **London Irish** 12, **Bath** 22 **Northampton** 17. 11 March, 2007: **Gloucester** 28 **Leicester** 24. 16 March, 2007: **Worcester** 23 **Newcastle** 21. 17 March, 2007: **Northampton** 18 **Sale** 18, **Leicester** 29 **Bath** 25, **Gloucester** 34 **Harlequins** 25. 18 March, 2007: **Saracens** 36 **Bristol** 5, **London Irish** 16 **Wasps** 3. 23 March, 2007: **London Irish** 7 **Saracens** 22. 24 March, 2007: **Gloucester** 24 **Newcastle** 18. 25 March, 2007: **Bristol** 31 **Northampton** 19. 6 April, 2007: **Sale** 25 **Leicester** 26. 7 April, 2007: **Harlequins** 34 **London Irish** 17, **Bristol** 22 **Worcester** 17, **Bath** 21 **Gloucester** 21. 8 April, 2007: **Wasps** 27 **Saracens** 26, **Newcastle** 16 **Northampton** 7. 13 April, 2007: **Newcastle** 19 **Gloucester** 12, **Sale** 25 **Bath** 23. 15 April, 2007: **Wasps** 35 **Northampton** 29, **Saracens** 33 **Harlequins** 19, **London Irish** 26 **Worcester** 16. 24 April, 2007: **Bristol** 30 **Leicester** 13. 28 April, 2007: **Worcester** 22 **Saracens** 7, **Northampton** 27 **London Irish** 22, **Newcastle** 12 **Bath** 20, **Leicester** 40 **Wasps** 26, **Harlequins** 49 **Sale** 0, **Gloucester** 35 **Bristol** 13.

THE 2006–07 FINAL TABLE

	P	W	D	L	For	A	BP	Pts
Gloucester	22	15	2	5	531	404	7	71
Leicester	22	14	1	7	569	456	14	71
Bristol	22	14	1	7	398	394	6	64
Saracens	22	12	2	8	539	399	11	63
Wasps	22	12	1	9	504	431	11	61
London Irish	22	12	0	10	398	407	5	53
Harlequins	22	10	0	12	503	438	11	51
Bath	22	8	2	12	428	492	9	45
Newcastle	22	9	0	13	435	528	8	44
Sale	22	8	1	13	414	500	8	42
Worcester	22	6	1	15	346	459	8	34
Northampton	22	6	1	15	342	499	7	33

PREVIOUS ENGLISH CHAMPIONS

1987/1988: Leicester
1988/1989: Bath
1989/1990: Wasps
1990/1991: Bath
1991/1992: Bath
1992/1993: Bath
1993/1994: Bath
1994/1995: Leicester
1995/1996: Bath
1996/1997: Wasps
1997/1998: Newcastle
1998/1999: Leicester
1999/2000: Leicester
2000/2001: Leicester
2001/2002: Leicester
2002/2003: Wasps
2003/2004: Wasps
2004/2005: Wasps
2005/2006: Sale
2006/2007: Leicester

2006–07 PLAY-OFFS

5 May, Welford Road, Leicester

LEICESTER 26 (2G, 4PG) BRISTOL 14 (3PG, 1T)

LEICESTER: G Murphy; S Rabeni, D Hipkiss, S Vesty, T Varndell; A Goode, H Ellis; M Ayerza, G Chuter, A Moreno, L Deacon, L Cullen, L Moody, S Jennings, M Corry (captain) Substitutions: A Tuilagi for Varndell (40 mins); J White for Moreno (47 mins); O Smith for Vesty (58 mins); F Murphy for Ellis (67 mins); B Kay for Cullen (67 mins); J Buckland for Chuter (80 mins)

SCORERS *Tries:* Ellis, G Murphy *Conversions*: Goode (2) *Penalty Goals*: Goode (4)

BRISTOL: L Arscott; L Robinson, N Brew, S Cox, D Lemi; D Gray, S Perry; D Hilton, M Regan, D Crompton, S Hohneck, G Llewellyn (captain), N Budgett, J El Abd, A To'oala Substitutions: M Sambucetti for Llewellyn (63 mins); C Morgan for Brew (63 mins); D Hill for Gray (63 mins); S Linklater for Regan (70 mins); A Clarke for Hilton (71 mins); G Nicholls for Budgett (80 mins); G Lewis for To'oala (80 mins)

SCORERS *Try:* Cox *Penalty Goals*: Gray (3)

REFEREE C White (Gloucestershire).

YELLOW CARDS Tuilagi (74 mins), El Abd (80 mins)

5 May, Kingsholm, Gloucester

GLOUCESTER 50 (6G, 1PG, 1T) SARACENS 9 (3PG)

GLOUCESTER: W Walker; I Balshaw, J Simpson-Daniel, A Allen, M Foster; R Lamb, P Richards; N Wood, O Azam, C Nieto, M Bortolami (captain), A Brown, P Buxton, A Hazell, L Narraway Substitutions: M Davies for Azam (50 mins); R Lawson for Richards (56 mins); C Califano for Wood (63 mins); J Goodridge for Walker (67 mins); W James for Bortolami (69 mins); A Eustace for Hazell (74 mins); J Adams for Allen (77 mins)

SCORERS *Tries:* Penalty try, Richards, Narraway, Allen, Foster, Hazell, Califano *Conversions*: Walker (6) *Penalty Goal*: Walker

SARACENS: T Castaignede; D Scarbrough, K Sorrell, A Farrell, K Ratuvou; G Jackson, N de Kock; N Lloyd, S Byrne (M Cairns 77), C Visagie, I Fullarton, S Raiwalui (captain), P Gustard, R Hill, B Skirving Substitutions: C Johnson for Visagie (36 mins); K Chesney for Gustard (50 mins); R Penney for Castaignede (58 mins); D Seymour for Hill (62 mins); A Powell for Farrell (67 mins); M Rauluni for de Kock (70 mins); Visagie for Lloyd (70 mins); M Cairns for Byrne (77 mins)

SCORERS *Penalty Goals:* Jackson (3)

REFEREE W Barnes (London)

YELLOW CARD Ratuvou (42 mins)

FINAL

12 May, Twickenham, London

GLOUCESTER 16 (1G, 3PG)
LEICESTER 44 (3G, 1PG, 4T)

GLOUCESTER: W Walker; M Foster, J Simpson-Daniel, A Allen, I Balshaw; R Lamb; P Richards; N Wood, O Azam, C Nieto, W James, A Brown, P Buxton (captain), A Hazell, L Narraway Substitutions: J Boer for Buxton (17 mins); M Davies for Azam (47 mins); R Lawson for Richards (52 mins); C Califano for Wood (54 mins); A Eustace for James (83 mins)

SCORERS *Try:* Lamb *Conversion*: Walker *Penalty Goals*: Walker (3)

LEICESTER: G Murphy; S Rabeni, D Hipkiss, O Smith, A Tuilagi; A Goode, F Murphy; M Ayerza, G Chuter, J White, L Deacon, B Kay, L Moody, S Jennings, M Corry (captain) Substitutions: L Cullen for L Deacon (55mins); S Vesty for Smith (57 mins); T Varndell for Rabeni (63 mins); B Youngs for F Murphy (69 mins); A Moreno for White (69 mins); B Deacon for Jennings (72 mins); J Buckland for Chuter (73 mins)

SCORERS *Tries:* F Murphy, A Tuilagi (2), Corry, Goode, Jennings, Moody *Conversions*: Goode (3) *Penalty Goal*: Goode

REFEREE D Pearson (Northumberland)

Clive Rose/Getty Images

Leicester's Alesana Tuilagi destroyed Gloucester in the final.

OTHER MAJOR DOMESTIC WINNERS

NATIONAL ONE
Leeds
NATIONAL TWO
Esher
NATIONAL THREE NORTH
Blaydon
NATIONAL THREE SOUTH
Southend
NORTH ONE
Caldy
SOUTH WEST ONE
Mounts Bay
MIDLANDS ONE
Luton
LONDON ONE
London Scottish

FIJI

FIJI'S 2006–07 TEST RECORD

OPPONENTS	DATE	VENUE	RESULT
Samoa	19 May	A	**Lost** 3–8
Japan	26 May	H	**Won** 30–15
Australia	9 June	A	**Lost** 0–49
Tonga	16 June	H	**Lost** 15–21
Japan	12 Sept	N	**Won** 35–31 (WC)
Canada	16 Sept	N	**Won** 29–16 (WC)
Australia	23 Sept	N	**Lost** 12–55 (WC)
Wales	29 Sept	N	**Won** 38–34 (WC)
South Africa	7 Oct	N	**Lost** 20–37 (WC)

FIJI'S TURNING POINT

By Jeremy Duxbury

Fiji's helter-skelter rugby year came to an emotional close in Marseille in early October when soon-to-be world champions South Africa fought off the brave resistance from the Pacific Islanders and closed out their quarter-final match 37–20 in a rather professional manner.

Some 20 minutes earlier, Fiji had pulled level 20–20 by scoring two converted tries in a two-minute span without the Springboks even touching the ball; and all this with star centre Seru Rabeni in the sin-bin.

Moments later, prop forward Jone Railomo dived for the try line only to be stopped inches short, and Rabeni, following up, knocked on.

Still, buoyed by the crowd of 56,000 urging them forward, Fiji pressed in search of what would have been an extraordinary victory. With the Boks on the back foot, another free-flowing move saw Ifereimi Rawaqa force his way over in the left corner only for the big lock's own hand to get between the ball and the grass, thus having the effort disallowed by the TV match official.

South Africa regrouped, stepped up a notch, and showed why they were the best team at the tournament with two late tries snuffing out Fiji's improbable dream of a semi-final berth.

And while the Boks went on to win the Webb Ellis Cup with what could be argued were less-scary matches against Argentina and England, Fiji were left to soak up the adoration from the Marseille crowd during a lap of honour that concluded with the players sitting in a line and clapping to show respect to Fiji's Ambassador to the European Union, Ratu Tui Cavuilati, and his fellow dignitaries up in the VIP stand.

Cavuilati, a high chief, is also a former Test wing and scored a memorable try against the All Blacks in Suva back in 1974.

In the changing room, Fiji half-back and captain, Moses Rauluni, fought back the tears to tell his men how proud he was: "You're the bravest team I have ever played with," he said, before announcing that he was ending his Test career.

Forwards coach, the Reverend Joji Rinakama, then said a prayer in Fijian just as he had done on a daily basis for the previous three months. Even the good reverend's voice quivered as he thanked the Lord and his players for the magnificent performance.

Rauluni, who had played with so much heart throughout the campaign, later mulled things over and decided that perhaps he would return in 2009 after a year off to spend time with his family.

At 32, Rauluni is probably playing the best rugby of his career, and his outstanding leadership qualities may well see him persuaded to stick around until the 2011 World Cup.

And who's to say fly-half hero Nicky Little, now with 641 Test points to his credit, won't be his midfield partner?

The Padova pivot also enjoyed a terrific World Cup and played a vital role in the all-important 38–34 Pool B win over Wales in what many pundits described as the most exciting rugby match they'd ever seen.

Little, 31, had a couple of years in the wilderness but returned this year to claim the No.10 jersey in emphatic fashion. His painful knee injury on the stroke of full-time against Wales saw an outpouring of get-well-soon messages on Fiji's blog sites and faxes to the team hotel including one from the country's president, Ratu Josefa Iloilo, no less.

The *Fiji Times* newspaper ran a full double-page spread of messages for Little, and so moved were the people of Fiji by his contribution that "Nicky Little for PM" became another favourite shout.

No.8 Sisa Koyamaibole, with 39 Test caps dating back to 2000, was one of the more seasoned players in the squad. "This is the best Fiji team I've played with," he concurred. "There's a tremendous spirit and feeling of togetherness amongst the players, and it comes from the coach's belief in us."

It appears that 2007 may be a turning point in Fiji rugby. In January, the Fiji Rugby Union shuffled highly paid Kiwi coach Wayne Pivac out the door, and turned to the local nous of Ilivasi Tabua to guide the team.

Tabua, a former Test flanker for Australia and Fiji, did what none of his ex-pat predecessors had managed – win three matches at a World Cup and reach the quarter-finals.

The Human Skewer, as was his nickname in his playing days, was ably assisted by Rev. Rinakama in the forwards and Iosefo Bele in the backs, with valuable technical help coming from Greg Mumm of the NSW Waratahs academy.

The Pacific Nations Cup in May and June had seen a disjointed Fiji side stumble through to just one win from five matches, owing partly to the number of overseas professionals still involved in the French Championship.

But Fiji's last match saw a swing to the good with a 14–14 draw against Australia A, a team of would-be Wallabies that had put 80 points on Pivac's side a year earlier.

Fiji's difficulty with overseas players being unavailable in time meant that nine of the 30-man World Cup squad had not played in the Pacific Nations Cup. This also implied, however, that Fiji's eventual squad for France 2007 would be a mite stronger than the PNC team.

And so it turned out.

In Fiji's opening match against Japan, the lead changed hands seven times. Fiji looked to have sealed the match before a 78th-minute converted try from Japan's Luke Thompson put his team within striking distance at 31–35.

In four and a half minutes of frantic time added-on, Japan kept the ball alive and pummelled the Fiji line with everything they had as the Toulouse crowd cheered them on wildly. But the Fiji defence held firm.

"In other years," skipper Rauluni pointed out, "Fiji might have crumbled under such pressure. I think that's the difference with this team – they're fit and have the will to survive."

A mere four days later, Fiji found themselves in Cardiff facing Canada.

"It's not an ideal schedule," Tabua explained before the kick-off, "but we're not complaining. We've known about it for ages and prepared for it accordingly."

In yet another edge-of-your-seat battle, Fiji hung on desperately under their own posts with a six-point lead that looked like it wasn't going to be enough as the burly Canadian pack picked and drove forward with ease.

With a mere two seconds left on the clock, replacement fullback Norman Ligairi put in a heavy tackle that dislodged the ball just metres from the line. Young prop Graham Dewes snapped it up, popped a pass to flanker Netani Talei who flicked it out to man-of-the-match Kameli Ratuvou who sprinted 80 metres to the Canadian end for a bonus point try to seal the match 29–16. Amazing stuff.

For the trip to Montpellier to face the Wallabies, Fiji gave their younger players a run to keep their best fresh for Wales the following week.

Even so, Fiji managed two nice tries against Australia – one to stocky wing Isoa Neivua and the other to flanker Aca Ratuva after a brilliant run from Rauluni. The Aussies won 55–12, but it didn't matter too much; Fiji went to Nantes for their date with destiny and played out of their skins to defeat Wales for the first time in their history.

Lock Kele Leawere picked up his third try in as many games, as did athletic flanker Akapusi Qera. Wing Vilimoni Delasau also showed he was back to his best with a stunning try down the right, and Dewes scored his first try for his side with two minutes left on the clock to give Fiji the win after an intercept try from Martyn Williams moments earlier had temporarily disturbed Fiji's dream.

The scenes of jubilation at the end of this match were mirrored all over Fiji in the early hours of Sunday morning as tens of thousands of rugby-mad Fijians stayed up all night to watch the spectacle. The celebrations lasted right the way through to the quarter-finals and beyond.

"I hope this victory has helped unite our often-divided country," coach Tabua said afterwards. "Rugby is a tool that can do so much for our nation. We all worked so hard to get to this point and knowing what it means to the fans back home makes all the sacrifices worthwhile."

After the loss to the Springboks, he also made reference to Fiji's limited opportunities to play Tests against the Tier 1 teams: "If we could play South Africa every year, then in four or fives years' time, I think we'd beat them."

Western giants Nadi regained provincial supremacy in September by seeing off Naitasiri 22–8 in an enthralling Sanyo Cup Final.

Nadi, who had gone unbeaten through the 11 rounds of pool play, weren't able to add the Sullivan-Farebrother Trophy to their cabinet a few weeks later when surprise package Tailevu hung on to win 13–8. As the crowds grew steadily each week, a last-minute try from Jim Patrick also gave Tailevu a stunning 25–22 win over Suva to add to their victories over Nadroga and Naitasiri in this winner-stays-on event.

Earlier in the year, Rev Joji Rinakama's Stallions won a terrific Colonial Cup Final, 14–12 over the Crusaders in front of a 10,000-strong Churchill Park crowd.

FIJI INTERNATIONAL RECORDS

WINNING MARGIN

Date	Opponent	Result	Winning Margin
10/09/1983	Niue Island	120–4	**116**
21/08/1969	Solomon Islands	113–13	**100**
08/09/1983	Solomon Islands	86–0	**86**
30/08/1979	Papua New Guinea	86–0	**86**
23/08/1969	Papua New Guinea	88–3	**85**

MOST POINTS IN A MATCH BY THE TEAM

Date	Opponent	Result	Pts.
10/09/1983	Niue Island	120–4	**120**
21/08/1969	Solomon Islands	113–13	**113**
23/08/1969	Papua New Guinea	88–3	**88**
08/09/1983	Solomon Islands	86–0	**86**
30/08/1979	Papua New Guinea	86–0	**86**

MOST TRIES IN A MATCH BY THE TEAM

Date	Opponent	Result	Tries
21/08/1969	Solomon Islands	113–13	**25**
10/09/1983	Niue Island	120–4	**21**
18/08/1969	Papua New Guinea	79–0	**19**
30/08/1979	Papua New Guinea	86–0	**18**
08/09/1983	Solomon Islands	86–0	**16**

MOST CONVERSIONS IN A MATCH BY THE TEAM

Date	Opponent	Result	Cons
21/08/1969	Solomon Islands	113–13	**19**
10/09/1983	Niue Island	120–4	**18**

MOST PENALTIES IN A MATCH BY THE TEAM

Date	Opponent	Result	Pens
08/07/2001	Samoa	28–17	**7**

MOST DROP GOALS IN A MATCH BY THE TEAM

Date	Opponent	Result	DGs
02/07/1994	Samoa	20–13	**3**
12/10/1991	Romania	15–17	**3**

MOST POINTS IN A MATCH BY A PLAYER

Date	Player	Opponent	Pts.
10/09/1983	Severo Koroduadua	Niue Island	**36**
07/10/1989	Waisale Serevi	Belgium	**26**
28/08/1999	Nicky Little	Italy	**25**

MOST TRIES IN A MATCH BY A PLAYER

Date	Player	Opponent	Tries
30/08/1979	Tevita Makutu	Papua New Guinea	**6**
18/08/1969	George Sailosi	Papua New Guinea	**5**

MOST CONVERSIONS IN A MATCH BY A PLAYER

Date	Player	Opponent	Cons
10/09/1983	Severo Koroduadua	Niue Island	**18**
21/08/1969	Semesa Sikivou	Solomon Islands	**12**
07/10/1989	Waisale Serevi	Belgium	**11**

MOST PENALTIES IN A MATCH BY A PLAYER

Date	Player	Opponent	Pens
08/07/2001	Nicky Little	Samoa	**7**
26/05/2000	Nicky Little	Tonga	**6**
25/05/2001	Nicky Little	Tonga	**6**
05/10/1996	Nicky Little	Hong Kong	**6**
08/07/1967	Inoke Tabualevu	Tonga	**6**

MOST DROP GOALS IN A MATCH BY A PLAYER

Date	Player	Opponent	Pens
02/07/1994	Opeti Turuva	Samoa	**3**
12/10/1991	Tomasi Rabaka	Romania	**2**

MOST CAPPED PLAYERS

Name	Caps
Nicky Little	**63**
Jacob Rauluni	**50**
Joeli Veitayaki	**49**
Emori Katalau	**47**

LEADING TRY SCORERS

Name	Tries
Senivalati Laulau	**20**
Norman Ligairi	**16**
Viliame Satala	**16**
Fero Lasagavibau	**16**

LEADING CONVERSIONS SCORERS

Name	Cons
Nicky Little	**113**
Waisale Serevi	**51**
Severo Koroduadua	**43**
Seremaia Baikeinuku	**20**

LEADING PENALTY SCORERS

Name	Pens
Nicky Little	**133**
Severo Koroduadua	**37**
Waisale Serevi	**27**
Seremaia Baikeinuku	**18**

LEADING DROP GOAL SCORERS

Name	DGs
Opeti Turuva	**5**
Severo Koroduadua	**5**
Waisale Serevi	**3**

LEADING POINTS SCORERS

Name	Pts.
Nicky Little	**641**
Waisale Serevi	**239**
Severo Koroduadua	**212**
Seremaia Baikeinuku	**117**

FRANCE

FRANCE'S 2006–07 TEST RECORD

OPPONENTS	DATE	VENUE	RESULT
New Zealand	11 November	H	**Lost** 3–47
New Zealand	18 November	H	**Lost** 11–23
Argentina	25 November	H	**Won** 27–26
Italy	3 February	A	**Won** 39–3
Ireland	11 February	A	**Won** 20–17
Wales	24 February	H	**Won** 32–21
England	11 March	A	**Lost** 18–26
Scotland	17 March	H	**Won** 46–19
New Zealand	2 June	A	**Lost** 11–42
New Zealand	9 June	A	**Lost** 10–61
England	11 August	A	**Won** 21–15
England	18 August	H	**Won** 22–9
Wales	26 August	A	**Won** 34–7
Argentina	7 September	N	**Lost** 12–17 (WC)
Namibia	16 September	N	**Won** 87–10 (WC)
Ireland	21 September	N	**Won** 25–3 (WC)
Georgia	30 September	N	**Won** 64–7 (WC)
New Zealand	6 October	N	**Won** 20–18 (WC)
England	13 October	N	**Lost** 9–14 (WC)
Argentina	19 October	N	**Lost** 10–34 (WC)

ONCE AGAIN THE BRIDESMAIDS

By Iain Spragg

"**We are a great** rugby nation and the players can hold their heads up high," insisted Bernard Laporte after his side were stopped in their tracks by England in their Rugby World Cup semi-final in Paris. "It stops tonight but I don't think it was a bad World Cup by us."

It certainly wasn't a good tournament for Les Bleus. For so long the bridesmaids of the World Cup, France once again suffered the heart-break of losing in the last four to the English and if their 24–7 defeat in Sydney in 2003 was painful, their 14–9 reverse four years later in the Stade de France was simply agonising. Twenty years after its inception, France's name remains conspicuous by its absence on the Webb Ellis trophy.

It was not, of course, the first time France had come close to lifting the cup. Beaten finalists in both 1987 and 1999 and three time semi-finalists, the French have become accustomed to disappointment but 2007 was undoubtedly the bitterest pill of all to swallow. A famous victory over New Zealand in the quarter-final had only heightened the national belief it could finally be their year, only for England to shatter the dream in front of their own fans in Paris.

"It is difficult to find the words to express my disappointment," France captain Raphael Ibanez said. "We thought this would be the match, but it was difficult in the end and the result did not go in our favour. We will need a few days to digest this. But this is sport – it goes one way or the other. England deserved to win and they took their chances when it mattered."

The tournament began for the hosts in Paris against Argentina but if the South Americans were simply supposed to roll over, no-one had told Marcelo Loffreda's side. The Pumas were clearly intent on stating their case for inclusion in an international tournament on a regular basis while France froze in front of 80,000 supporters and produced an error-strewn performance that belied their billing as one of the tournament favourites.

Argentina scored the only try of the match through full-back Ignacio Corleto in the first-half and although David Skrela contributed with four penalties, 12 points from the boot Felipe Contepomi kept the Pumas in front and an inspired defensive performance from the visitors earned them a shock 17–12 victory.

"When you begin a World Cup and it is imperative to win the match and you lose, you can say only one thing that the sky has fallen in on your head," Laporte said after the game. "We won't let our heads drop. France will still play a key role in this World Cup."

With nine days respite before their next game, France at least had time to regroup and when they emerged for their clash with Namibia in Toulouse, they seemed to have conquered their nerves. The African minnows offered little resistance to the hosts and Vincent Clerc helped himself to a hat-trick as France ran in 13 tries in an 87–10 romp. The French were back on track.

Ireland were the next opponents and Laporte was keenly aware that defeat would signal the end of the tournament for his side. The stakes could not have been higher but if France had been uncharacteristically nervous in the opener against Argentina, they were close to their destructive best against the Irish in Paris.

The home side were always in control of proceedings in the Stade de France and four first-half penalties from scrum-half Jean-Baptiste Elissalde kept the scoreboard ticking over while Ireland could only respond with a solitary Ronan O'Gara drop goal. Another Elissalde penalty stretched the lead before France delivered the knockout blow with a Clerc try on the hour. The wing added a second before full-time and France emerged convincing 25–3 winners.

"A win is a win. It was a big effort from the boys," Ibanez said. "Of course, we don't know if it is enough to finish top of the pool but if we carry on like that with such passion and team spirit, everything is possible. We were pretty good under pressure, which wasn't the case 15 days ago against Argentina, but we still have another game to finish."

Georgia were duly despatched 64–7 in the final group game in Marseille but Argentina's victory over Ireland confirmed the Pumas as group winners and France would have to travel to Cardiff to face the All Blacks in the last eight.

The French had not beaten the All Blacks for seven years but they were in inspired form in the Millennium Stadium and refused to be intimidated by the New Zealanders even after going 13–3 down by half-time. They were on terms by the 53rd minute with a try from Thierry Dusautoir and although the Kiwis edged back in front with a score from Rodney So'oialo, Les Bleus came back once more, rode their luck with a forward pass that wasn't spotted by the referee and crossed through Yannick Jauzion to make it 18–18. Elissalde's successful conversion made it 20–18 to Laporte's men and although New Zealand threw everything at them in the final 10 minutes, France clung on for a 20–18 victory that reminded everyone of their famous semi-final victory against the odds over the All Blacks in 1999.

But just as the French failed to follow up that performance eight years earlier in the final against Australia, they once again fluffed their lines against England in the semi-final.

The home side could not have endured a worst start. Andy Gomarsall's early box kick bounced unpredictably, full-back Damien Traille was caught in two minds and Josh Lewsey made the most of the indecision to collect the loose ball and crash over. England had scored with only 78 seconds on the clock and although an unusually profligate Jonny Wilkinson missed the conversion, the score set the tone for the rest of the match.

Three penalties from young fly-half Lionel Beauxis saw France claw their way back into the match but they were to be their only scores. Two Wilkinson penalties gave England a precarious two point lead but time was running out and when the English fly-half landed a 78th minute drop goal, France were dead and buried. "England did exactly what they had to do," a dejected Ibanez conceded. "We didn't have the tempo. We worked really hard after a bad start to the tournament. We believed in ourselves. We thought we could do it, be world champions. In the end, we couldn't."

The dreaded Bronze Final clash with Argentina merely added insult to injury. The French crowd were desperate to witness their side sign off with a victory brimming with Gallic flair but the Pumas were once again destined to spoil the party.

The much-maligned play-off game had failed to capture the imagination in previous tournaments but Argentina still had a point to prove on the world stage and treated the game like a final and destroyed Les Bleus at the Parc des Princes. France conceded five tries in a 34–10 defeat and the World Cup for the hosts ended in ignominy.

France's season had begun inauspiciously. New Zealand arrived for a two Test series in November and their 47–3 mauling of Laporte's team in Lyon in the first game did not bode well. The second match in Paris was closer but the All Blacks emerged 23–11 victors and France's narrow 27–26 victory over Argentina seven days later did little to dispel the consensus that Les Bleus had much work to do if they were to mount a credible World Cup bid.

Their defence of their Six Nations crown was, however, more encouraging. Italy were no match for them in the tournament opener but their last-gasp won over the Irish at Croke Park the following week instilled a greater sense of self-belief and a comfortable win over Wales in Paris kept their hopes of the Grand Slam alive.

To achieve it they had to beat England at Twickenham but they found the men in white in stubborn mood and despite leading 12–9 at half-time, France succumbed to a second-half English revival and were beaten 26–18. It was England's first win over their cross Channel rivals since the 2003 World Cup.

"Maybe it was the pressure of the result because the players were thinking about the Grand Slam," said Laporte. "I think the pressure got to the French. We were not ambitious enough."

Victory over Scotland in their final game secured a 17th title for France but the disappointment after their Twickenham ambush persisted and there were renewed questions about Les Bleus' big match mentality.

In the summer, Laporte took an understrength squad to New Zealand for a two-Test series but the French second string were no match for the All Blacks. The first Test in Auckland ended in a chastening 42–11 defeat and their 61–10 reverse in Wellington a week later completed a miserable tour with few redeeming features for France.

The team was at least back to winning ways in August with warm-up victories over the English and Wales but as the World Cup approached, there were no clear signs what kind of French side would grace the tournament. In the end, it was one, which again failed to lift the Webb Ellis Cup.

Stade Francais ended Biarritz's two-year reign as champions of France, claiming the club's 13th Top 14 title – and their third in only five years – after coming from behind in the final to beat Clermont.

The powerful Parisians suffered the bitter disappointment of going out of the Heineken Cup to Leicester at the quarter-final stage in April but salvaged their season against Clermont, the European Challenge Cup winners, with late tries from Argentine scrum-half Agustin Pichot and Fijian forward Radike Samo in a 23–18 victory.

FRANCE INTERNATIONAL STATISTICS

MATCH RECORDS UP TO 31ST OCTOBER 2007

MOST CONSECUTIVE TEST WINS

10 1931 E,G, 1932 G, 1933 G, 1934 G, 1935 G, 1936 G1,2, 1937 G,It
8 1998 E, S, I, W, Arg 1,2, Fj, Arg 3
8 2001 SA 3 A, Fj 2002 It, W, E, S,I
8 2004 I, It, W, S, E, US, C, A

MOST CONSECUTIVE TESTS WITHOUT DEFEAT

Matches	Wins	Draws	Period
10	10	0	1931 to 1938
10	8	2	1958 to 1959
10	9	1	1986 to 1987

MOST POINTS IN A MATCH

BY THE TEAM

Pts.	Opponents	Venue	Year
87	Namibia	Toulouse	2007
77	Fiji	Saint Etienne	2001
70	Zimbabwe	Auckland	1987
67	Romania	Bucharest	2000
64	Romania	Aurillac	1996
64	Georgia	Marseilles	2007
62	Romania	Castres	1999
62	Romania	Bucharest	2006
61	Fiji	Brisbane	2003
60	Italy	Toulon	1967
59	Romania	Paris	1924
56	Romania	Lens	2003
56	Italy	Rome	2005

BY A PLAYER

Pts.	Player	Opponents	Venue	Year
30	D Camberabero	Zimbabwe	Auckland	1987
28	C Lamaison	New Zealand	Twickenham	1999
28	F Michalak	Scotland	Sydney	2003
27	J-B Elissalde	Namibia	Toulouse	2007
27	G Camberabero	Italy	Toulon	1967
27	C Lamaison	New Zealand	Marseilles	2000
27	G Merceron	South Africa	Johannesburg	2001
26	T Lacroix	Ireland	Durban	1995
26	F Michalak	Fiji	Brisbane	2003
25	J-P Romeu	United States	Chicago	1976
25	P Berot	Romania	Agen	1987
25	T Lacroix	Tonga	Pretoria	1995

MOST TRIES IN A MATCH

BY THE TEAM

Tries	Opponents	Venue	Year
13	Romania	Paris	1924
13	Zimbabwe	Auckland	1987
13	Namibia	Toulouse	2007
12	Fiji	Saint Etienne	2001
11	Italy	Toulon	1967
10	Romania	Aurillac	1996
10	Romania	Bucharest	2000

BY A PLAYER

Tries	Player	Opponents	Venue	Year
4	A Jauréguy	Romania	Paris	1924
4	M Celhay	Italy	Paris	1937

MOST CONVERSIONS IN A MATCH

BY THE TEAM

Cons	Opponents	Venue	Year
11	Namibia	Toulouse	2007
9	Italy	Toulon	1967
9	Zimbabwe	Auckland	1987
8	Romania	Wellington	1987
8	Romania	Lens	2003

BY A PLAYER

Cons	Player	Opponents	Venue	Year
11	J-B Elissalde	Namibia	Toulouse	2007
9	G Camberabero	Italy	Toulon	1967
9	D Camberabero	Zimbabwe	Auckland	1987
8	G Laporte	Romania	Wellington	1987

MOST PENALTIES IN A MATCH

BY THE TEAM

Pens	Opponents	Venue	Year
8	Ireland	Durban	1995
7	Wales	Paris	2001
7	Italy	Paris	2002
6	Argentina	Buenos Aires	1977
6	Scotland	Paris	1997
6	Italy	Auch	1997
6	Ireland	Paris	2000
6	South Africa	Johannesburg	2001
6	Argentina	Buenos Aires	2003
6	Fiji	Brisbane	2003
6	England	Twickenham	2005
6	Wales	Paris	2007
6	England	Twickenham	2007

BY A PLAYER

Pens	Player	Opponents	Venue	Year
8	T Lacroix	Ireland	Durban	1995
7	G Merceron	Italy	Paris	2002
6	J-M Aguirre	Argentina	Buenos Aires	1977
6	C Lamaison	Scotland	Paris	1997
6	C Lamaison	Italy	Auch	1997
6	G Merceron	Ireland	Paris	2000
6	G Merceron	South Africa	Johannesburg	2001
6	D Yachvili	England	Twickenham	2005
6	F Michalak	Fiji	Brisbane	2003

MOST DROPPED GOALS IN A MATCH

BY THE TEAM

Drops	Opponents	Venue	Year
3	Ireland	Paris	1960
3	England	Twickenham	1985
3	New Zealand	Christchurch	1986
3	Australia	Sydney	1990
3	Scotland	Paris	1991
3	New Zealand	Christchurch	1994

BY A PLAYER

Drops	Player	Opponents	Venue	Year
3	P Albaladejo	Ireland	Paris	1960
3	J-P Lescarboura	England	Twickenham	1985
3	J-P Lescarboura	New Zealand	Christchurch	1986
3	D Camberabero	Australia	Sydney	1990

CAREER RECORDS

MOST CAPPED PLAYERS

Caps	Player	Career Span
118	F Pelous	1995 to 2007
111	P Sella	1982 to 1995
98	R Ibañez	1996 to 2007
93	S Blanco	1980 to 1991
89	O Magne	1997 to 2007
78	A Benazzi	1990 to 2001
71	J-L Sadourny	1991 to 2001
71	O Brouzet	1994 to 2003
71	C Califano	1994 to 2007
71	S Marconnet	1998 to 2007
69	R Bertranne	1971 to 1981
69	P Saint-André	1990 to 1997
69	P de Villiers	1999 to 2007
67	C Dominici	1998 to 2007
64	F Galthié	1991 to 2003
63	M Crauste	1957 to 1966
63	B Dauga	1964 to 1972
63	S Betsen	1997 to 2007

MOST CONSECUTIVE TESTS

Tests	Player	Career Span
46	R Bertranne	1973 to 1979
45	P Sella	1982 to 1987
44	M Crauste	1960 to 1966
35	B Dauga	1964 to 1968

MOST TESTS AS CAPTAIN

Tests	Captain	Career Span
42	F Pelous	1997 to 2006
41	R Ibanez	1998 to 2007
34	J-P Rives	1978 to 1984
34	P Saint-André	1994 to 1997
25	D Dubroca	1986 to 1988
25	F Galthié	1999 to 2003
24	G Basquet	1948 to 1952
22	M Crauste	1961 to 1966

MOST POINTS IN TESTS

Pts	Player	Tests	Career
380	C Lamaison	37	1996 to 2001
367	T Lacroix	43	1989 to 1997
354	D Camberabero	36	1982 to 1993
267	G Merceron	32	1999 to 2003
265	J-P Romeu	34	1972 to 1977
247	T Castaignède	54	1995 to 2007
246	F Michalak		2001 to 2007
233	S Blanco	93	1980 to 1991
234	D Yachvili	33	2002 to 2007
200	J-P Lescarboura	28	1982 to 1990

MOST TRIES IN TESTS

Tries	Player	Tests	Career
38	S Blanco	93	1980 to 1991
33	P Saint-André	69	1990 to 1997
30	P Sella	111	1982 to 1995
26	E Ntamack	46	1994 to 2000
26	P Bernat Salles	41	1992 to 2001
25	C Dominici	67	1998 to 2007
23	C Darrouy	40	1957 to 1967

MOST CONVERSIONS IN TESTS

Cons	Player	Tests	Career
59	C Lamaison	37	1996 to 2001
48	D Camberabero	36	1982 to 1993
45	M Vannier	43	1953 to 1961
42	T Castaignède	54	1995 to 2007
36	R Dourthe	31	1995 to 2001
36	G Merceron	32	1999 to 2003
36	F Michalak	50	2001 to 2007
35	J-B Elissalde	30	2000 to 2007
34	D Yachvili	33	2002 to 2007
32	T Lacroix	43	1989 to 1997
29	P Villepreux	34	1967 to 1972

MOST PENALTY GOALS IN TESTS

Pens	Player	Tests	Career
89	T Lacroix	43	1989 to 1997
78	C Lamaison	37	1996 to 2001
59	D Camberabero	36	1982 to 1993
57	G Merceron	32	1999 to 2003
56	J-P Romeu	34	1972 to 1977
50	D Yachvili	33	2002 to 2007
38	F Michalak	50	2001 to 2007
35	J-B Elissalde	30	2000 to 2007
33	P Villepreux	34	1967 to 1972
33	P Bérot	19	1986 to 1989

MOST DROPPED GOALS IN TESTS

Drops	Player	Tests	Career
15	J-P Lescarboura	28	1982 to 1990
12	P Albaladejo	30	1954 to 1964
11	G Camberabero	14	1961 to 1968
11	D Camberabero	36	1982 to 1993
9	J-P Romeu	34	1972 to 1977

INTERNATIONAL CHAMPIONSHIP RECORDS

RECORD	DETAIL		SET
Most points in season	156	in five matches	2002
Most tries in season	18	in four matches	1998
	18	in five matches	2006
Highest Score	56	56–13 v Italy	2005
Biggest win	51	51–0 v Wales	1998
Highest score conceded	49	14–49 v Wales	1910
Biggest defeat	37	0–37 v England	1911
Most appearances	50	P Sella	1983–1995
Most points in matches	164	D Yachvili	2003–2007
Most points in season	80	G Merceron	2002
Most points in match	24	S Viars	v Ireland, 1992
	24	C Lamaison	v Scotland, 1997
	24	J-B Elissalde	v Wales, 2004
Most tries in matches	14	S Blanco	1981–1991
	14	P Sella	1983–1995
Most tries in season	5	P Estève	1983
	5	E Bonneval	1987
	5	E Ntamack	1999
	5	P Bernat Salles	2001
Most tries in match	3	M Crauste	v England, 1962
	3	C Darrouy	v Ireland, 1963
	3	E Bonneval	v Scotland, 1987
	3	D Venditti	v Ireland, 1997
	3	E Ntamack	v Wales, 1999
Most cons in matches	23	C Lamaison	1997–2001
	23	D Yachvili	2003–2007
Most cons in season	9	C Lamaison	1998
	9	G Merceron	2002
	9	D Yachvili	2003
Most cons in match	6	D Yachvili	v Italy, 2003
Most pens in matches	36	D Yachvili	2003–2007
Most pens in season	18	G Merceron	2002
Most pens in match	7	G Merceron	v Italy, 2002
Most drops in matches	9	J-P Lescarboura	1982–1988
Most drops in season	5	G Camberabero	1967
Most drops in match	3	P Albaladejo	v Ireland, 1960
	3	J-P Lescarboura	v England, 1985

MISCELLANEOUS RECORDS

RECORD	HOLDER	DETAIL
Longest Test Career	F Haget	1974 to 1987
	C Califano	1994 to 2007
Youngest Test Cap	C Dourthe	18 yrs 7 days in 1966
Oldest Test Cap	A Roques	37 yrs 329 days in 1963

CAREER RECORDS OF FRANCE INTERNATIONAL PLAYERS (PLAYERS CAPPED SINCE THE START OF RWC 2003 UP TO 31 OCTOBER 2007)

PLAYER BACKS	DEBUT	CAPS	T	C	P	D	PTS
L Beauxis	2007 v It	12	1	16	14	0	79
B Boyet	2006 v I	3	0	1	3	0	11
T Castaignède	1995 v R	54	17	42	21	5	247
V Clerc	2002 v SA	28	15	0	0	0	75
J-F Coux	2007 v NZ	2	1	0	0	0	5
C Dominici	1998 v E	67	25	0	0	0	125
N Durand	2007 v NZ	2	0	0	0	0	0
P Elhorga	2001 v NZ	18	3	0	0	0	15
J-B Elissalde	2000 v S	30	4	35	35	0	195
M Forest	2007 v NZ	2	0	0	0	0	0
F Fritz	2005 v SA	13	3	0	0	2	21
J-P Grandclaude	2005 v E	3	0	0	0	0	0
C Heymans	2000 v It	37	10	0	0	0	50
Y Jauzion	2001 v SA	50	16	0	0	1	83
J Laharrague	2005 v W	12	4	0	0	0	20
N Laharrague	2007 v NZ	2	0	0	0	0	0
D Marty	2005 v It	19	8	0	0	0	40
L Mazars	2007 v NZ	1	0	0	0	0	0
F Michalak	2001 v SA	50	9	36	38	5	246
A Mignardi	2007 v NZ	2	0	0	0	0	0
P Mignoni	1997 v R	28	6	0	0	0	30
C Poitrenaud	2001 v SA	32	6	0	0	0	30
A Rougerie	2001 v SA	51	20	0	0	0	100
D Skrela	2001 v NZ	11	0	7	21	0	77
B Thiéry	2007 v NZ	2	0	0	0	0	0
D Traille	2001 v SA	58	12	7	10	1	107
L Valbon	2004 v US	5	1	0	0	0	5
D Yachvili	2002 v C	33	2	34	50	2	234

FORWARDS							
B August	2007 v W	1	0	0	0	0	0
S Betsen	1997 v It	63	9	0	0	0	45
J Bonnaire	2004 v S	37	6	0	0	0	30
S Bruno	2002 v W	24	4	0	0	0	20
C Califano	1994 v NZ	71	6	0	0	0	30
S Chabal	2000 v S	37	5	0	0	0	25
D Chouly	2007 v NZ	2	0	0	0	0	0
P de Villiers	1999 v W	69	2	0	0	0	10
T Dusautoir	2006 v R	10	3	0	0	0	15
I Harinordoquy	2002 v W	46	10	0	0	0	50
R Ibañez	1996 v W	98	8	0	0	0	40
L Jacquet	2006 v NZ	2	0	0	0	0	0
G Lamboley	2005 v S	13	1	0	0	0	5
G Le Corvec	2007 v NZ	1	0	0	0	0	0
O Magne	1997 v W	89	14	0	0	0	70
S Marconnet	1998 v Arg	71	3	0	0	0	15
R Martin	2002 v E	21	3	0	0	0	15
N Mas	2003 v NZ	14	0	0	0	0	0
O Milloud	2000 v R	50	1	0	0	0	5
F Montanella	2007 v NZ	1	0	0	0	0	0
L Nallet	2000 v R	32	5	0	0	0	25
Y Nyanga	2004 v US	25	4	0	0	0	20
O Olibeau	2007 v NZ	2	0	0	0	0	0
F Ouedraogo	2007 v NZ	1	0	0	0	0	0
P Papé	2004 v I	19	2	0	0	0	10
F Pelous	1995 v R	118	8	0	0	0	40
J Pierre	2007 v NZ	2	0	0	0	0	0
J-B Poux	2001 v Fj	20	3	0	0	0	15
O Sourgens	2007 v NZ	1	0	0	0	0	0
D Szarzewski	2004 v C	22	3	0	0	0	15
J Thion	2003 v Arg	42	1	0	0	0	5
E Vermeulen	2001 v SA	8	1	0	0	0	5

FRENCH INTERNATIONAL PLAYERS (UP TO 31 OCTOBER 2007)

Note: Years given for International Championship matches are for second half of season; eg 1972 means season 1971-72. Years for all other matches refer to the actual year of the match. Entries in square brackets denote matches played in RWC Finals.

Abadie, A (Pau) 1964 I
Abadie, A (Graulhet) 1965 R, 1967 SA 1,3,4, NZ, 1968 S, I
Abadie, L (Tarbes) 1963 R
Accoceberry, G (Bègles) 1994 NZ 1,2, C 2, 1995 W, E, S, I, R 1, [Iv, S], It, 1996 I, W 1, R, Arg 1, W 2(R), SA 2, 1997 S, It 1
Aguerre, R (Biarritz O) 1979 S
Aguilar, D (Pau) 1937 G
Aguirre, J-M (Bagnères) 1971 A 2, 1972 S, 1973 W, I, J, R, 1974 I, W, Arg 2, R, SA 1, 1976 W (R), E, US, A 2, R, 1977 W, E, S, I, Arg 1,2, NZ 1,2, R, 1978 E, S, I, W, R, 1979 I, W, E, S, NZ 1,2, R, 1980 W, I
Ainciart, E (Bayonne) 1933 G, 1934 G, 1935 G, 1937 G, It, 1938 G 1
Albaladejo, P (Dax) 1954 E, It, 1960 W, I, It, R, 1961 S, SA, E, W, I, NZ 1,2, A, 1962 S, E, W, I, 1963 S, I, E, W, It, 1964 S, NZ, W, It, I, SA, Fj
Albouy, A (Castres) 2002 It (R)
Alvarez, A-J (Tyrosse) 1945 B2, 1946 B, I, K, W, 1947 S, I, W, E, 1948 I, A, S, W, E, 1949 I, E, W, 1951 S, E, W
Amand, H (SF) 1906 NZ
Ambert, A (Toulouse) 1930 S, I, E, G, W
Amestoy, J-B (Mont-de-Marsan) 1964 NZ, E
André, G (RCF) 1913 SA, E, W, I, 1914 I, W, E
Andrieu, M (Nîmes) 1986 Arg 2, NZ 1, R 2, NZ 2, 1987 [R, Z], R, 1988 E, S, I, W, Arg 1,2,3,4, R, 1989 I, W, E, S, NZ 2, B, A 2, 1990 W, E, I (R)
Anduran, J (SCUF) 1910 W
Aqua, J-L (Toulon) 1999 R, Tg, NZ 1(R)
Araou, R (Narbonne) 1924 R
Arcalis, R (Brive) 1950 S, I, 1951 I, E, W
Arino, M (Agen) 1962 R
Aristouy, P (Pau) 1948 S, 1949 Arg 2, 1950 S, I, E, W
Arlettaz, P (Perpignan) 1995 R 2
Armary, L (Lourdes) 1987 [R], R, 1988 S, I, W, Arg 3,4, R, 1989 W, S, A 1,2, 1990 W, E, S, I, A 1,2,3, NZ 1, 1991 W 2, 1992 S, I, R, Arg 1,2, SA 1,2, Arg, 1993 E, S, I, W, SA 1,2, R 2, A 1,2, 1994 I, W, NZ 1(t),2(t), 1995 I, R 1 [Tg, I, SA]
Arnal, J-M (RCF) 1914 I, W
Arnaudet, M (Lourdes) 1964 I, 1967 It, W
Arotca, R (Bayonne) 1938 R
Arrieta, J (SF) 1953 E, W
Arthapignet, P (see Harislur-Arthapignet)
Artiguste, E (Castres) 1999 WS
Astre, R (Béziers) 1971 R, 1972 I 1, 1973 E (R), 1975 E, S, I, SA 1,2, Arg 2, 1976 A 2, R
Attoub, D (Castres) 2006 R
Aucagne, D (Pau) 1997 W (R), S, It 1, R 1(R), A 1, R 2(R), SA 2(R), 1998 S (R), W (R), Arg 2(R), Fj (R), Arg 3, A, 1999 W 1(R), S (R)
Audebert, A (Montferrand) 2000 R, 2002 W (R)
Aué, J-M (Castres) 1998 W (R)
Augé, J (Dax) 1929 S, W
Augras-Fabre, L (Agen) 1931 I, S, W
August, B (Biarritz) 2007 W1(R)
Auradou, D (SF) 1999 E (R), S (R), WS (R), Tg, NZ 1, W 2(R), [Arg (R)], 2000 A (R), NZ 1,2, 2001 S, I, It, W, E (R), SA 1,2, NZ (R), SA 3, A, Fj, 2002 It, E, I (R), C (R), 2003 S (R), It (R), W (R), Arg, 1,2, NZ (R), R (R), E 2(R),3, [J(R),US,NZ] , 2004 I(R), It(R),S(R),E(R)
Averous, J-L (La Voulte) 1975 S, I, SA 1,2, 1976 I, W, E, US, A 1,2, R, 1977 W, E, S, I, Arg 1, R, 1978 E, S, I, 1979 NZ 1,2, 1980 E, S, 1981 A 2
Avril, D (Biarritz) 2005 A1
Azam, O (Montferrand, Gloucester) 1995 R 2, Arg (R), 2000 A (R), NZ 2(R), 2001 SA 2(R), NZ, 2002 E (R), I (R), Arg (R), A 1
Azarete, J-L (Dax, St Jean-de-Luz) 1969 W, R, 1970 S, I, W, R, 1971 S, I, E, SA 1,2, A 1, 1972 E, W, I 2, A 1, R, 1973 NZ, W, I, R, 1974 I, R, SA 1,2, 1975 W

Baby, B (Toulouse) 2005 I,SA2(R),A1
Bacqué, N (Pau) 1997 R 2
Bader, E (Primevères) 1926 M, 1927 I, S
Badin, C (Chalon) 1973 W, I, 1975 Arg 1
Baillette, M (Perpignan) 1925 I, NZ, S, 1926 W, M, 1927 I, W, G 2, 1929 G, 1930 S, I, E, G, 1931 I, S, E, 1932 G
Baladie, G (Agen) 1945 B 1,2, W, 1946 B, I, K
Ballarin, J (Tarbes) 1924 E, 1925 NZ, S
Baquey, J (Toulouse) 1921 I
Barbazanges, A (Roanne) 1932 G, 1933 G
Barrau, M (Beaumont, Toulouse) 1971 S, E, W, 1972 E, W, A 1,2, 1973 S, NZ, E, I, J, R, 1974 I, S
Barrau, M (Agen) 2004 US,C(R),NZ(R)
Barrère, P (Toulon) 1929 G, 1931 W
Barrière, R (Béziers) 1960 R
Barthe, E (SBUC) 1925 W, E
Barthe, J (Lourdes) 1954 Arg 1,2, 1955 S, 1956 I, W, It, E, Cz, 1957 S, I, E, W, R 1,2, 1958 S, E, A, W, It, I, SA 1,2, 1959 S, E, It, W
Basauri, R (Albi) 1954 Arg 1
Bascou, P (Bayonne) 1914 E
Basquet, G (Agen) 1945 W, 1946 B, I, K, W, 1947 S, I, W, E, 1948 I, A, S, W, E, 1949 S, I, E, W, Arg 1, 1950 S, I, E, W, 1951 S, I, E, W, 1952 S, I, SA, W, E, It
Bastiat, J-P (Dax) 1969 R, 1970 S, I, W, 1971 S, I, SA 2, 1972 S, A 1, 1973 E, 1974 Arg 1,2, SA 2, 1975 W, Arg 1,2, R, 1976 S, I, W, E, A 1,2, R, 1977 W, E, S, I, 1978 E, S, I, W
Baudry, N (Montferrand) 1949 S, I, W, Arg 1,2
Baulon, R (Vienne, Bayonne) 1954 S, NZ, W, E, It, 1955 I, E, W, It, 1956 S, I, W, It, E, Cz, 1957 S, I, It
Baux, J-P (Lannemezan) 1968 NZ 1,2, SA 1,2
Bavozet, J (Lyon) 1911 S, E, W
Bayard, J (Toulouse) 1923 S, W, E, 1924 W, R, US
Bayardon, J (Chalon) 1964 S, NZ, E
Beaurin-Gressier, C (SF) 1907 E, 1908 E
Beauxis, L (SF) 2007 It(R),I(R),W1(R),E1(R),S,W2, [Nm(R),I(R),Gg,NZ,E,Arg 2(R)]
Bégu, J (Dax) 1982 Arg 2(R), 1984 E, S
Béguerie, C (Agen) 1979 NZ 1
Beguet, L (RCF) 1922 I, 1923 S, W, E, I, 1924 S, I, E, R, US
Behoteguy, A (Bayonne, Cognac) 1923 E, 1924 S, I, E, W, R, US, 1926 E, 1927 E, G 1,2, 1928 A, I, E, G, W, 1929 S, W, E
Behoteguy, H (RCF, Cognac) 1923 W, 1928 A, I, E, G, W
Belascain, C (Bayonne) 1977 R, 1978 E, S, I, W, R, 1979 I, W, E, S, 1982 W, E, S, I, 1983 E, S, I, W
Belletante, G (Nantes) 1951 I, E, W
Belot, F (Toulouse) 2000 I (R)
Benazzi, A (Agen) 1990 A 1,2,3, NZ 1,2, 1991 E, US 1(R),2, [R, Fj, C], 1992 SA 1(R),2, Arg, 1993 E, S, I, W, A 1,2,

1994 I, W, E, S, C 1, NZ 1,2, C 2, 1995 W, E, S, I, [Tg, Iv, S, I, SA, E], NZ 1,2, 1996 E, S, I, W 1, Arg 1,2, W 2, SA 1,2, 1997 I, W, E, S, R 1, A 1,2, It 2, R 2(R), Arg, SA 1,2, 1999 R, WS, W 2, [C, Nm (R), Fj, Arg, NZ 2, A], 2000 W, E, I, It (R), R, 2001 S (R), I (t&R), E

Bénésis, R (Narbonne) 1969 W, R, 1970 S, I, W, E, R, 1971 S, I, E, W, A 2, R, 1972 S, I 1, E, W, I 2, A 1, R, 1973 NZ, E, W, I, J, R, 1974 I, W, E, S Benetière, J (Roanne) 1954 It, Arg 1

Benetton, P (Agen) 1989 B, 1990 NZ 2, 1991 US 2, 1992 Arg 1,2(R), SA 1(R),2, Arg, 1993 E, S, I, W, SA 1,2, R 2, A 1,2, 1994 I, W, E, S, C 1, NZ 1,2, C 2, 1995 W, E, S, I, [Tg, Iv (R), S], It, R 2(R), Arg, NZ 1,2, 1996 Arg 1,2, W 2, SA 1,2, 1997 I, It 1,2(R), R 2, Arg, SA 1,2 1998 E, S (R), I (R), W (R), Arg 1(R),2(R), Fj (R), 1999 I, W 1, S (R)

Benezech, L (RCF) 1994 E, S, C 1, NZ 1,2, C 2, 1995 W, E, [Iv, S, E], R 2, Arg, NZ 1,2

Berbizier, P (Lourdes, Agen) 1981 S, I, W, E, NZ 1,2, 1982 I, R, 1983 S, I, 1984 S (R), NZ 1,2, 1985 Arg 1,2, 1986 S, I, W, E, R 1, Arg 1, A, NZ 1, R 2, NZ 2,3, 1987 W, E, S, I, [S, R, Fj, A, NZ], R, 1988 E, S, I, W, Arg 1,2, 1989 I, W, E, S, NZ 1,2, B, A 1, 1990 W, E, 1991 S, I, W 1, E

Berejnoi, J-C (Tulle) 1963 R, 1964 S, W, It, I, SA, Fj, R, 1965 S, I, E, W, It, R, 1966 S, I, E, W, It, R, 1967 S, A, E, It, W, I, R

Berges, B (Toulouse) 1926 I

Berges-Cau, R (Lourdes) 1976 E (R)

Bergese, F (Bayonne) 1936 G 2, 1937 G, It, 1938 G 1, R, G 2

Bergougnan, Y (Toulouse) 1945 B 1, W, 1946 B, I, K, W, 1947 S, I, W, E, 1948 S, W, E, 1949 S, E, Arg 1,2

Bernard, R (Bergerac) 1951 S, I, E, W

Bernat-Salles, P (Pau, Bègles-Bordeaux, Biarritz) 1992 Arg, 1993 R 1, SA 1,2, R 2, A 1,2, 1994 I, 1995 E, S, 1996 E (R), 1997 R 1, A 1,2, 1998 E, S, I, W, Arg 1,2, Fj, Arg 3(R), A 1999 I, W 1, R, Tg, [Nm, Fj, Arg, NZ 2, A], 2000 I, It, NZ 1(R),2, 2001 S, I, It, W, E

Bernon, J (Lourdes) 1922 I, 1923 S

Bérot, J-L (Toulouse) 1968 NZ 3, A, 1969 S, I, 1970 E, R, 1971 S, I, E, W, SA 1,2, A 1,2, R, 1972 S, I 1, E, W, A 1, 1974 I

Bérot, P (Agen) 1986 R 2, NZ 2,3, 1987 W, E, S, I, R, 1988 E, S, I, Arg 1,2,3,4, R, 1989 S, NZ 1,2

Bertrand, P (Bourg) 1951 I, E, W, 1953 S, I, E, W, It

Bertranne, R (Bagnères) 1971 E, W, SA 2, A 1,2, 1972 S, I 1, 1973 NZ, E, J, R, 1974 I, W, E, S, Arg 1,2, R, SA 1,2, 1975 W, E, S, I, SA 1,2, Arg 1,2, R, 1976 S, I, W, E, US, A 1,2, R, 1977 W, E, S, I, Arg 1,2, NZ 1,2, R, 1978 E, S, I, W, R, 1979 I, W, E, S, R, 1980 W, E, S, I, SA, R, 1981 S, I, W, E, R, NZ 1,2

Berty, D (Toulouse) 1990 NZ 2, 1992 R (R), 1993 R 2, 1995 NZ 1(R), 1996 W 2(R), SA 1

Besset, E (Grenoble) 1924 S

Besset, L (SCUF) 1914 W, E

Besson, M (CASG) 1924 I, 1925 I, E, 1926 S, W, 1927 I

Besson, P (Brive) 1963 S, I, E, 1965 R, 1968 SA 1

Betsen, S (Biarritz) 1997 It 1(R), 2000 W (R), E (R), A (R), NZ 1(R),2(R), 2001 S (R), I (R), It (R), W (R), SA 3(R), A, Fj, 2002 It, W, E, S, I, Arg, A 1,2, SA, NZ, C, 2003 E 1, S, I, It, W, R, E 2, [Fj,J,S,I,E], 2004 I,It,W,S,E,A,Arg,NZ, 2005 E,W,I,It, 2006 SA, NZ2(R),Arg(R), 2007 It,I,W1,E1,S,E2,W2, [Arg 1,I,Gg,NZ,E]

Bianchi, J (Toulon) 1986 Arg 1

Bichindaritz, J (Biarritz O) 1954 It, Arg 1,2

Bidabé, P (Biarritz) 2004 C, 2006 R

Bidart, L (La Rochelle) 1953 W

Biemouret, P (Agen) 1969 E, W, 1970 I, W, E, 1971 W, SA 1,2, A 1, 1972 E, W, I 2, A 2, R, 1973 S, NZ, E, W, I

Biénès, R (Cognac) 1950 S, I, E, W, 1951 S, I, E, W, 1952 S, I, SA, W, E, It, 1953 S, I, E, 1954 S, I, NZ, W, E, Arg 1,2, 1956 S, I, W, It, E

Bigot, C (Quillan) 1930 S, E, 1931 I, S

Bilbao, L (St Jean-de-Luz) 1978 I, 1979 I

Billac, E (Bayonne) 1920 S, E, W, I, US, 1921 S, W, 1922 W, 1923 E

Billière, M (Toulouse) 1968 NZ 3

Bioussa, A (Toulouse) 1924 W, US, 1925 I, NZ, S, E, 1926 S, I, E, 1928 E, G, W, 1929 I, S, W, E, 1930 S, I, E, G, W

Bioussa, C (Toulouse) 1913 W, I, 1914 I

Biraben, M (Dax) 1920 W, I, US, 1921 S, W, E, I, 1922 S, E, I

Blain, A (Carcassonne) 1934 G

Blanco, S (Biarritz O) 1980 SA, R, 1981 S, W, E, A 1,2, R, NZ 1,2, 1982 W, E, S, I, R, Arg 1,2, 1983 E, S, I, W, 1984 I, W, E, S, NZ 1,2, R, 1985 E, S, I, W, Arg 1,2, 1986 S, I, W, E, R 1, Arg 2, A, NZ 1, R 2, NZ 2,3, 1987 W, E, S, I, [S, R, Fj, A, NZ], R, 1988 E, S, I, W, Arg 1,2,3,4, R, 1989 I, W, E, S, NZ 1,2, B, A 1, 1990 E, S, I, R, A 1,2,3, NZ 1,2, 1991 S, I, W 1, E, R, US 1,2, W 2, [R, Fj, C, E]

Blond, J (SF) 1935 G, 1936 G 2, 1937 G, 1938 G 1, R, G 2

Blond, X (RCF) 1990 A 3, 1991 S, I, W 1, E, 1994 NZ 2(R)

Boffelli, V (Aurillac) 1971 A 2, R, 1972 S, I 1, 1973 J, R, 1974 I, W, E, S, Arg 1,2, R, SA 1,2, 1975 W, S, I

Bonal, J-M (Toulouse) 1968 E, W, Cz, NZ 2,3, SA 1,2, R, 1969 S, I, E, R, 1970 W, E

Bonamy, R (SB) 1928 A, I

Bondouy, P (Narbonne, Toulouse) 1997 S (R), It 1, A 2(R), R 2, 2000 R (R)

Bonetti, S (Biarritz) 2001 It, W, NZ (R)

Boniface, A (Mont-de-Marsan) 1954 I, NZ, W, E, It, Arg 1,2, 1955 S, I, 1956 S, I, W, It, Cz, 1957 S, I, W, R 2, 1958 S, E, 1959 E, 1961 NZ 1,3, A, R, 1962 E, W, I, It, R, 1963 S, I, E, W, It, R, 1964 S, NZ, E, W, It, 1965 W, It, R, 1966 S, I, E, W

Boniface, G (Mont-de-Marsan) 1960 W, I, It, R, Arg 1,2,3, 1961 S, SA, E, W, It, I, NZ 1,2,3, R, 1962 R, 1963 S, I, E, W, It, R, 1964 S, 1965 S, I, E, W, It, R, 1966 S, I, E, W

Bonnaire, J (Bourgoin) 2004 S(t&R),A(R),NZ(R), 2005 S, E, W, I, It, SA1,2,A1,C,Tg,SA3, 2006 S, I, It(R), E(R), W, R, SA(R), NZ1, 2, Arg, 2007 It,I(R),W1,E1,S,E2,3(R), [Arg1(R), Nm,I,Gg,NZ,E]

Bonnes, E (Narbonne) 1924 W, R, US

Bonneval, E (Toulouse) 1984 NZ 2(R), 1985 W, Arg 1, 1986 W, E, R 1, Arg 1,2, A, R 2, NZ 2,3, 1987 W, E, S, I, [Z], 1988 E

Bonnus, F (Toulon) 1950 S, I, E, W

Bonnus, M (Toulon) 1937 It, 1938 G 1, R, G 2, 1940 B

Bontemps, D (La Rochelle) 1968 SA 2

Borchard, G (RCF) 1908 E, 1909 E, W, I, 1911 I

Borde, F (RCF) 1920 I, US, 1921 S, W, E, 1922 S, W, 1923 S, I, 1924 E, 1925 I, 1926 E

Bordenave, L (Toulon) 1948 A, S, W, E, 1949 S

Bory, D (Montferrand) 2000 I, It, A, NZ 1, 2001 S, I, SA 1,2,3, A, Fj, 2002 It, E, S, I, C, 2003 [US,NZ]

Boubée, J (Tarbes) 1921 S, E, I, 1922 E, W, 1923 E, I, 1925 NZ, S

Boudreaux, R (SCUF) 1910 W, S

Bouet, D (Dax) 1989 NZ 1,2, B, A 2, 1990 A 3

Bouguyon, G (Grenoble) 1961 SA, E, W, It, I, NZ 1,2,3, A

Bouic, G (Agen) 1996 SA 1

Bouilhou, J (Toulouse) 2001 NZ, 2003 Arg 1

Boujet, C (Grenoble) 1968 NZ 2, A (R), SA 1

Bouquet, J (Bourgoin, Vienne) 1954 S, 1955 E, 1956 S, I, W, It, E, Cz, 1957 S, E, W, R 2, 1958 S, E, 1959 S, It, W, I, 1960 S, E, W, I, R, 1961 S, SA, E, W, It, I, R, 1962 S, E, W, I

Bourdeu, J R (Lourdes) 1952 S, I, SA, W, E, It, 1953 S, I, E

Bourgarel, R (Toulouse) 1969 R, 1970 S, I, E, R, 1971 W, SA 1,2, 1973 S

Bourguignon, G (Narbonne) 1988 Arg 3, 1989 I, E, B, A 1, 1990 R

Bousquet, A (Béziers) 1921 E, I, 1924 R

Bousquet, R (Albi) 1926 M, 1927 I, S, W, E, G 1, 1929 W, E, 1930 W

Bousses, G (Bourgoin) 2006 S(R)

Boyau, M (SBUC) 1912 I, S, W, E, 1913 W, I

Boyer, P (Toulon) 1935 G

Boyet, B (Bourgoin) 2006 I(R), 2007 NZ1,2

Branca, G (SF) 1928 S, 1929 I, S

Branlat, A (RCF) 1906 NZ, E, 1908 W

Brejassou, R (Tarbes) 1952 S, I, SA, W, E, 1953 W, E, 1954 S, I, NZ, 1955 S, I, E, W, It

Brethes, R (St Sever) 1960 Arg 2

Bringeon, A (Biarritz O) 1925 W

Brouzet, O (Grenoble, Bègles, Northampton, Montferrand) 1994 S, NZ 2(R), 1995 E, S, I, R 1, [Tg, Iv, E (t)], It, Arg (R), 1996 W 1(R), 1997 R 1, A 1,2, It 2, Arg, SA 1,2, 1998 E, S, I, W, Arg 1,2, Fj, Arg 3, A, 1999 I, W 1, E, S, R, [C (R), Nm, Fj (R), Arg, NZ 2(R), A (R)], 2000 W, E, S, I, It, A, NZ 1(R),2(R), 2001 SA 1,2, NZ, 2002 W, E, S, I, Arg, A

1(R),2, SA, NZ, C, 2003 E 1, S, I, It, W, E 3, [Fj(R),J,S(R),US,I(R)]
Bru, Y (Toulouse) 2001 A (R), Fj (R), 2002 It, 2003 Arg 2, NZ, R, E 2,3(R), [J,S(R),US, I(t&R),NZ], 2004 I(R),It(R),W(R),S(R),E(R)
Brun, G (Vienne) 1950 E, W, 1951 S, E, W, 1952 S, I, SA, W, E, It, 1953 E, W, It
Bruneau, M (SBUC) 1910 W, E, 1913 SA, E
Brunet, Y (Perpignan) 1975 SA 1, 1977 Arg 1
Bruno, S (Béziers, Sale) 2002 W (R), 2004 A(R),NZ(t&R), 2005 S(R),E,W,I,It,SA1,2(R), A1(R),2(R),C,SA3(R), 2006 S(R), I(R), 2007 I(R),E1(R),NZ1,2,E3(R),W2(R), [Gg,Arg 2(t&R)]
Brusque, N (Pau, Biarritz) 1997 R 2(R), 2002 W, E, S, I, Arg, A 2, SA, NZ, C, 2003 E 2, [Fj,S,I,E,NZ(R)], 2004 I,It,W,S,E,A,Arg, 2005 SA1(R),2,A1, 2006 S
Buchet, E (Nice) 1980 R, 1982 E, R (R), Arg 1,2
Buisson, H (see Empereur-Buisson)
Buonomo, Y (Béziers) 1971 A 2, R, 1972 I 1
Burgun, M (RCF) 1909 I, 1910 W, S, I, 1911 S, E, 1912 I, S, 1913 S, E, 1914 E
Bustaffa, D (Carcassonne) 1977 Arg 1,2, NZ 1,2, 1978 W, R, 1980 W, E, S, SA, R
Buzy, C-E (Lourdes) 1946 K, W, 1947 S, I, W, E, 1948 I, A, S, W, E, 1949 S, I, E, W, Arg 1,2

Cabanier, J-M (Montauban) 1963 R, 1964 S, Fj, 1965 S, I, W, It, R, 1966 S, I, E, W, It, R, 1967 S, A, E, It, W, I, SA 1,3, NZ, R, 1968 S, I
Cabannes, L (RCF, Harlequins) 1990 NZ 2(R), 1991 S, I, W 1, E, US 2, W 2, [R, Fj, C, E], 1992 W, E, S, I, R, Arg 2, SA 1,2, 1993 E, S, I, W, R 1, SA 1,2, 1994 E, S, C 1, NZ 1,2, 1995 W, E, S, R 1, [Tg (R), Iv, S, I, SA, E], 1996 E, S, I, W 1, 1997 It 2, Arg, SA 1,2
Cabrol, H (Béziers) 1972 A 1(R),2, 1973 J, 1974 SA 2
Cadenat, J (SCUF) 1910 S, E, 1911 W, I, 1912 W, E, 1913 I
Cadieu, J-M (Toulouse) 1991 R, US 1, [R, Fj, C, E], 1992 W, I, R, Arg 1,2, SA 1
Cahuc, F (St Girons) 1922 S
Califano, C (Toulouse, Saracens, Gloucester) 1994 NZ 1,2, C 2, 1995 W, E, S, I, [Iv, S, I, SA, E], It, Arg, NZ 1,2, 1996 E, S, I, W 1, R, Arg 1,2, SA 1,2, 1997 I, W, E, A 1,2, It 2, R 2(R), Arg, SA 1,2, 1998 E, S, I, W, 1999 I, W 1, E (R), S, WS, Tg (R), NZ 1, W 2, [C, Nm, Fj], 2000 W, E, S, I, It, R, A, NZ 1,2(R), 2001 S (R), I (R), It, W, SA 1(R),2(R), NZ, 2003 E 1, S (R), I (R), 2007 NZ1,2
Cals, R (RCF) 1938 G 1
Calvo, G (Lourdes) 1961 NZ 1,3
Camberabero, D (La Voulte, Béziers) 1982 R, Arg 1,2, 1983 E, W, 1987 [R (R), Z, Fj (R), A, NZ], 1988 I, 1989 B, A 1, 1990 W, S, I, R, A 1,2,3, NZ 1,2, 1991 S, I, W 1, E, R, US 1,2, W 2, [R, Fj, C], 1993 E, S, I
Camberabero, G (La Voulte) 1961 NZ 3, 1962 R, 1964 R, 1967 A, E, It, W, I, SA 1,3,4, 1968 S, E, W
Camberabero, L (La Voulte) 1964 R, 1965 S, I, 1966 E, W, 1967 A, E, It, W, I, 1968 S, E, W
Cambré, T (Oloron) 1920 E, W, I, US
Camel, A (Toulouse) 1928 S, A, I, E, G, W, 1929 W, E, G, 1930 S, I, E, G, W, 1935 G
Camel, M (Toulouse) 1929 S, W, E
Camicas, F (Tarbes) 1927 G 2, 1928 S, I, E, G, W, 1929 I, S, W, E
Camo, E (Villeneuve) 1931 I, S, W, E, G, 1932 G
Campaes, A (Lourdes) 1965 W, 1967 NZ, 1968 S, I, E, W, Cz, NZ 1,2, A, 1969 S, W, 1972 R, 1973 NZ
Campan, O (Agen) 1993 SA 1(R),2(R), R 2(R), 1996 I, W 1, R
Candelon, J (Narbonne) 2005 SA1,A1(R)
Cantoni, J (Béziers) 1970 W, R, 1971 S, I, E, W, SA 1,2, R, 1972 S, I 1, 1973 S, NZ, W, I, 1975 W (R)
Capdouze, J (Pau) 1964 SA, Fj, R, 1965 S, I, E
Capendeguy, J-M (Bègles) 1967 NZ, R
Capitani, P (Toulon) 1954 Arg 1,2
Capmau, J-L (Toulouse) 1914 E
Carabignac, G (Agen) 1951 S, I, 1952 SA, W, E, 1953 S, I
Carbonne, J (Perpignan) 1927 W
Carbonneau, P (Toulouse, Brive, Pau) 1995 R 2, Arg, NZ 1,2, 1996 E, S, R (R), Arg 2, W 2, SA 1, 1997 I (R), W, E, S (R), R 1(R), A 1,2, 1998 E, S, I, W, Arg 1,2, Fj, Arg 3, A, 1999 I, W 1, E, S, 2000 NZ 2(R), 2001 I
Carminati, A (Béziers, Brive) 1986 R 2, NZ 2, 1987 [R, Z], 1988 I, W, Arg 1,2, 1989 I, W, S, NZ 1(R),2, A 2, 1990 S, 1995 It, R 2, Arg, NZ 1,2
Caron, L (Lyon O, Castres) 1947 E, 1948 I, A, W, E, 1949 S, I, E, W, Arg 1
Carpentier, M (Lourdes) 1980 E, SA, R, 1981 S, I, A 1, 1982 E, S
Carrère, C (Toulon) 1966 R, 1967 S, A, E, W, I, SA 1,3,4, NZ, R, 1968 S, I, E, W, Cz, NZ 3, A, R, 1969 S, I, 1970 S, I, W, E, 1971 E, W
Carrère, J (Vichy, Toulon) 1956 S, 1957 E, W, R 2, 1958 S, SA 1,2, 1959 I
Carrère, R (Mont-de-Marsan) 1953 E, It
Casadei, D (Brive) 1997 S, R 1, SA 2(R)
Casaux, L (Tarbes) 1959 I, It, 1962 S
Cassagne, P (Pau) 1957 It
Cassayet-Armagnac, A (Tarbes, Narbonne) 1920 S, E, W, US, 1921 W, E, I, 1922 S, E, W, 1923 S, W, E, I, 1924 S, E, W, R, US, 1925 I, NZ, S, W, 1926 S, I, E, W, M, 1927 I, S, W
Cassiède, M (Dax) 1961 NZ 3, A, R
Castaignède, S (Mont-de-Marsan) 1999 W 2, [C (R), Nm (R), Fj, Arg (R), NZ 2(R), A (R)]
Castaignède, T (Toulouse, Castres, Saracens) 1995 R 2, Arg, NZ 1,2, 1996 E, S, I, W 1, Arg 1,2, 1997 I, A 1,2, It 2, 1998 E, S, I, W, Arg 1,2, Fj, 1999 I, W 1, E, S, R, WS, Tg (R), NZ 1, W 2, [C], 2000 W, E, S, It, 2002 SA, NZ, C, 2003 E 1(R), S (R), It, W, Arg 1, 2005 A2(R),C,Tg,SA3, 2006 It,E,W,R,SA(R), 2007 NZ1,2
Castel, R (Toulouse, Béziers) 1996 I, W 1, W 2, SA 1(R),2, 1997 I (R), W, E (R), S (R), A 1(R), 1998 Arg 3(R), A (R), 1999 W 1(R), E, S
Castets, J (Toulon) 1923 W, E, I
Caujolle, J (Tarbes) 1909 E, 1913 SA, E, 1914 W, E
Caunègre, R (SB) 1938 R, G 2
Caussade, A (Lourdes) 1978 R, 1979 I, W, E, NZ 1,2, R, 1980 W, E, S, 1981 S (R), I
Caussarieu, G (Pau) 1929 I
Cayrefourcq, E (Tarbes) 1921 E
Cazalbou, J (Toulouse) 1997 It 2(R), R 2, Arg, SA 2(R)
Cazals, P (Mont-de-Marsan) 1961 NZ 1, A, R
Cazenave, A (Pau) 1927 E, G 1, 1928 S, A, G
Cazenave, F (RCF) 1950 E, 1952 S, 1954 I, NZ, W, E
Cecillon, M (Bourgoin) 1988 I, W, Arg 2,3,4, R, 1989 I, E, NZ 1,2, A 1, 1991 S, I, E (R), R, US 1, W 2, [E], 1992 W, E, S, I, R, Arg 1,2, SA 1,2, 1993 E, S, I, W, R 1, SA 1,2, R 2, A 1,2, 1994 I, W, NZ 1(R), 1995 I, R 1, [Tg, S (R), I, SA] Celaya, M (Biarritz O, SBUC) 1953 E, W, It, 1954 I, E, It, Arg 1,2, 1955 S, I, E, W, It, 1956 S, I, W, It, E, Cz 1957 S, I, E, W, R 2, 1958 S, E, A, W, It, 1959 S, E, 1960 S, E, W, I, R, Arg 1,2,3, 1961 S, SA, E, W, It, I, NZ 1,2,3, A, R
Celhay, M (Bayonne) 1935 G, 1936 G 1, 1937 G, It, 1938 G 1, 1940 B
Cermeno, F (Perpignan) 2000 R
Cessieux, N (Lyon) 1906 NZ
Cester, E (TOEC, Valence) 1966 S, I, E, 1967 W, 1968 S, I, E, W, Cz, NZ 1,3, A, SA 1,2, R, 1969 S, I, E, W, 1970 S, I, W, E, 1971 A 1, 1972 R, 1973 S, NZ, W, I, J, R, 1974 I, W, E, S
Chabal, S (Bourgoin, Sale) 2000 S, 2001 SA 1,2, NZ (R), Fj (R), 2002 Arg (R), A 2, SA (R), NZ (t), C (R), 2003 E 1(R), S (R), I (R), Arg 2, NZ (R), E 2(R),3, [J(R),US,NZ], 2005 S,E,A2(R),Tg, 2007 It,I,E1,NZ1,2,E2(R),W2, [Arg 1(R),Nm,I,NZ(R),E(R),Arg 2(R)]
Chaban-Delmas, J (CASG) 1945 B 2
Chabowski, H (Nice, Bourgoin) 1985 Arg 2, 1986 R 2, NZ 2, 1989 B (R)
Chadebech, P (Brive) 1982 R, Arg 1,2, 1986 S, I
Champ, E (Toulon) 1985 Arg 1,2, 1986 I, W, E, R 1, Arg 1,2, A, NZ 1, R 2, NZ 2,3, 1987 W, E, S, I, [S, R, Fj, A, NZ], R, 1988 E, S, Arg 1,3,4, R, 1989 W, S, A 1,2, 1990 W, E, NZ 1, 1991 R, US 1, [R, Fj, C, E]
Chapuy, L (SF) 1926 S
Charpentier, G (SF) 1911 E, 1912 W, E
Charton, P (Montferrand) 1940 B
Charvet, D (Toulouse) 1986 W, E, R 1, Arg 1, A, NZ 1,3, 1987 W, E, S, I, [S, R, Z, Fj, A, NZ], R, 1989 E (R), 1990 W, E, 1991 S, I
Chassagne, J (Montferrand) 1938 G 1
Chatau, A (Bayonne) 1913 SA

THE COUNTRIES

Chaud, E (Toulon) 1932 G, 1934 G, 1935 G
Chazalet, A (Bourgoin) 1999 Tg
Chenevay, C (Grenoble) 1968 SA 1
Chevallier, B (Montferrand) 1952 S, I, SA, W, E, It, 1953 E, W, It, 1954 S, I, NZ, W, Arg 1, 1955 S, I, E, W, It, 1956 S, I, W, It, E, Cz, 1957 S
Chiberry, J (Chambéry) 1955 It
Chilo, A (RCF) 1920 S, W, 1925 I, NZ
Cholley, G (Castres) 1975 E, S, I, SA 1,2, Arg 1,2, R, 1976 S, I, W, E, A 1,2, R, 1977 W, E, S, I, Arg 1,2, NZ 1,2, R, 1978 E, S, I, W, R, 1979 I, S
Chouly, D (Brive) 2007 NZ1(R),2
Choy J (Narbonne) 1930 S, I, E, G, W, 1931 I, 1933 G, 1934 G, 1935 G, 1936 G 2
Cigagna, A (Toulouse) 1995 [E]
Cimarosti, J (Castres) 1976 US (R)
Cistacq, J-C (Agen) 2000 R (R)
Clady, A (Lezignan) 1929 G, 1931 I, S, E, G
Clarac, H (St Girons) 1938 G 1
Claudel, R (Lyon) 1932 G, 1934 G
Clauzel, F (Béziers) 1924 E, W, 1925 W
Clavé, J (Agen) 1936 G 2, 1938 R, G 2
Claverie, H (Lourdes) 1954 NZ, W
Cléda, T (Pau) 1998 E (R), S (R), I (R), W (R), Arg 1(R), Fj (R), Arg 3(R), 1999 I (R), S
Clément, G (RCF) 1931 W
Clément, J (RCF) 1921 S, W, E, 1922 S, E, W, I, 1923 S, W, I
Clemente, M (Oloron) 1978 R, 1980 S, I
Clerc, V (Toulouse) 2002 SA, NZ, C, 2003 E 1, S, I, It (R), W (R), Arg 2, NZ, 2004 I,It, W, 2005 SA2,Tg, 2006 SA, 2007 I,W1,E1,S,E2,W2, [Nm,I,Gg(R),NZ,E,Arg 2(R)]
Cluchague, L (Biarritz O) 1924 S, 1925 E
Coderc, J (Chalon) 1932 G, 1933 G, 1934 G, 1935 G, 1936 G 1
Codorniou, D (Narbonne) 1979 NZ 1,2, R, 1980 W, E, S, I, 1981 S, W, E, A 2, 1983 E, S, I, W, A 1,2, R, 1984 I, W, E, S, NZ 1,2, R, 1985 E, S, I, W, Arg 1,2
Coeurveille, C (Agen) 1992 Arg 1(R),2
Cognet, L (Montferrand) 1932 G, 1936 G 1,2, 1937 G, It
Collazo, P (Bègles) 2000 R
Colombier, J (St Junien) 1952 SA, W, E
Colomine, G (Narbonne) 1979 NZ 1
Comba, F (SF) 1998 Arg 1,2, Fj, Arg 3, 1999 I, W 1, E, S, 2000 A, NZ 1,2, 2001 S, I
Combe, J (SF) 1910 S, E, I, 1911 S
Combes, G (Fumel) 1945 B 2
Communeau, M (SF) 1906 NZ, E, 1907 E, 1908 E, W, 1909 E, W, I, 1910 S, E, I, 1911 S, E, I, 1912 I, S, W, E, 1913 SA, E, W
Condom, J (Boucau, Biarritz O) 1982 R, 1983 E, S, I, W, A 1,2, R, 1984 I, W, E, S, NZ 1,2, R, 1985 E, S, I, W, Arg 1,2, 1986 S, I, W, E, R 1, Arg 1,2, NZ 1, R 2, NZ 2,3, 1987 W, E, S, I, [S, R, Z, A, NZ], R, 1988 E, S, W, Arg 1,2,3,4, R, 1989 I, W, E, S, NZ 1,2, A 1, 1990 I, R, A 2,3(R)
Conilh de Beyssac, J-J (SBUC) 1912 I, S, 1914 I, W, E
Constant, G (Perpignan) 1920 W
Coscolla, G (Béziers) 1921 S, W
Costantino, J (Montferrand) 1973 R
Costes, A (Montferrand) 1994 C 2, 1995 R 1, [Iv], 1997 It 1, 1999 WS, Tg (R), NZ 1, [Nm (R), Fj (R), Arg (R), NZ 2(R), A (t&R)], 2000 S (R), I
Costes, F (Montferrand) 1979 E, S, NZ 1,2, R, 1980 W, I
Couffignal, H (Colomiers) 1993 R 1
Coulon, E (Grenoble) 1928 S
Courtiols, M (Bègles) 1991 R, US 1, W 2
Coux, J-F (Bourgoin) 2007 NZ1,2
Couzinet, D (Biarritz) 2004 US,C(R)
Crabos, R (RCF) 1920 S, E, W, I, US, 1921 S, W, E, I, 1922 S, E, W, I, 1923 S, I, 1924 S, I
Crampagne, J (Bègles) 1967 SA 4
Crancee, R (Lourdes) 1960 Arg 3, 1961 S
Crauste, M (RCF, Lourdes) 1957 R 1,2, 1958 S, E, A, W, It, I, 1959 E, It, W, I, 1960 S, E, W, I, It, R, Arg 1,3, 1961 S, SA, E, W, It, I, NZ 1,2,3, A, R, 1962 S, E, W, I, It, R, 1963 S, I, E, W, It, R, 1964 S, NZ, E, W, It, I, SA, Fj, R, 1965 S, I, E, W, It, R, 1966 S, I, E, W, It
Cremaschi, M (Lourdes) 1980 R, 1981 R, NZ 1,2, 1982 W, S, 1983 A 1,2, R, 1984 I, W
Crenca, J-J (Agen) 1996 SA 2(R), 1999 R, Tg, WS (R), NZ 1(R), 2001 SA 1,2, NZ (R), SA 3, A, Fj, 2002 It, W, E, S, I, Arg, A 2, SA, NZ, C, 2003 E 1, S, I, It, W, R, E 2, [Fj, J(t&R),S,I,E,NZ(R)], 2004 I(R),It(R),W(R),S(R),E(R)
Crichton, W H (Le Havre) 1906 NZ, E
Cristina, J (Montferrand) 1979 R
Cussac, P (Biarritz O) 1934 G
Cutzach, A (Quillan) 1929 G

Daguerre, F (Biarritz O) 1936 G 1
Daguerre, J (CASG) 1933 G
Dal Maso, M (Mont-de-Marsan, Agen, Colomiers) 1988 R (R), 1990 NZ 2, 1996 SA 1(R),2, 1997 I, W, E, S, It 1, R 1(R), A 1,2, It 2, Arg, SA 1,2, 1998 W (R), Arg 1(t), Fj (R), 1999 R (R), WS (R), Tg, NZ 1(R), W 2(R), [Nm (R), Fj (R), Arg (R), A (R)], 2000 W, E, S, I, It
Danion, J (Toulon) 1924 I
Danos, P (Toulon, Béziers) 1954 Arg 1,2, 1957 R 2, 1958 S, E, W, It, I, SA 1,2, 1959 S, E, It, W, I, 1960 S, E
Dantiacq, D (Pau) 1997 R 1
Darbos, P (Dax) 1969 R
Darracq, R (Dax) 1957 It
Darrieussecq, A (Biarritz O) 1973 E
Darrieussecq, J (Mont-de-Marsan) 1953 It
Darrouy, C (Mont-de-Marsan) 1957 I, E, W, It, R 1, 1959 E, 1961 R, 1963 S, I, E, W, It, 1964 NZ, E, W, It, I, SA, Fj, R, 1965 S, I, E, It, R, 1966 S, I, E, W, It, R, 1967 S, A, E, It, W, I, SA 1,2,4
Daudé, J (Bourgoin) 2000 S
Daudignon, G (SF) 1928 S
Dauga, B (Mont-de-Marsan) 1964 S, NZ, E, W, It, I, SA, Fj, R, 1965 S, I, E, W, It, R, 1966 S, I, E, W, It, R, 1967 S, A, E, It, W, I, SA 1,2,3,4, NZ, R, 1968 S, I, NZ 1,2,3, A, SA 1,2, R, 1969 S, I, E, R, 1970 S, I, W, E, R, 1971 S, I, E, W, SA 1,2, A 1,2, R, 1972 S, I 1, W
Dauger, J (Bayonne) 1945 B 1,2, 1953 S
Daulouede, P (Tyrosse) 1937 G, It, 1938 G 1, 1940 B
Debaty, V (Perpignan) 2006 R(R)
De Besombes, S (Perpignan) 1998 Arg 1(R), Fj (R)
Decamps, P (RCF) 1911 S
Dedet, J (SF) 1910 S, E, I, 1911 W, I, 1912 S, 1913 E, I
Dedeyn, P (RCF) 1906 NZ
Dedieu, P (Béziers) 1963 E, It, 1964 W, It, I, SA, Fj, R, 1965 S, I, E, W
De Gregorio, J (Grenoble) 1960 S, E, W, I, It, R, Arg 1,2, 1961 S, SA, E, W, It, I, 1962 S, E, W, 1963 S, W, It, 1964 NZ, E
Dehez, J-L (Agen) 1967 SA 2, 1969 R
De Jouvencel, E (SF) 1909 W, I
De Laborderie, M (RCF) 1921 I, 1922 I, 1925 W, E
Delage, C (Agen) 1983 S, I
De Malherbe, H (CASG) 1932 G, 1933 G
De Malmann, R (RCF) 1908 E, W, 1909 E, W, I, 1910 E, I
De Muizon, J J (SF) 1910 I
Delaigue, G (Toulon) 1973 J, R
Delaigue, Y (Toulon, Toulouse, Castres) 1994 S, NZ 2(R), C 2, 1995 I, R 1, [Tg, Iv], It, R 2(R), 1997 It 1, 2003 Arg 1,2, 2005 S,E,W,I,It,A2(R),Tg,SA3(R)
Delmotte, G (Toulon) 1999 R, Tg
Delque, A (Toulouse) 1937 It, 1938 G 1, R, G 2
De Rougemont, M (Toulon) 1995 E (t), R 1(t), [Iv], NZ 1,2, 1996 I (R), Arg 1,2, W 2, SA 1, 1997 E (R), S (R), It 1
Desbrosse, C (Toulouse) 1999 [Nm (R)], 2000 I
Descamps, P (SB) 1927 G 2
Desclaux, F (RCF) 1949 Arg 1,2, 1953 It
Desclaux, J (Perpignan) 1934 G, 1935 G, 1936 G 1,2, 1937 G, It, 1938 G 1, R, G 2, 1945 B 1
Deslandes, C (RCF) 1990 A 1, NZ 2, 1991 W 1, 1992 R, Arg 1,2
Desnoyer, L (Brive) 1974 R
Destarac, L (Tarbes) 1926 S, I, E, W, M, 1927 W, E, G 1,2
Desvouges, R (SF) 1914 W
Detrez, P-E (Nîmes) 1983 A 2(R), 1986 Arg 1(R),2, A (R), NZ1
Devergie, T (Nîmes) 1988 R, 1989 NZ 1,2, B, A 2, 1990 W, E, S, I, R, A 1,2,3, 1991 US 2, W 2, 1992 R (R), Arg 2(R)
De Villiers, P (SF) 1999 W 2, [Arg (R), NZ 2(R), A (R)], 2000 W (R), E (R), S (R), I (R), It (R), NZ 1(R),2, 2001 S, I, It, W, E, SA 1,2, NZ (R), SA 3, A, Fj, 2002 It, W, E, I, SA, NZ, C, 2003 Arg 1,2, NZ (R), 2004 I, It, W, S, E, US, C, NZ, 2005 S,I(R),It(R),SA1(R),2, A1(R),2,C,Tg(R),SA3,

2006 S, I, It, E, W, SA, NZ1, 2, Arg, 2007 It,I,E1,S,W2, [Arg 1,Nm,I, NZ,E]
Deygas, M (Vienne) 1937 It
Deylaud, C (Toulouse) 1992 R, Arg 1,2, SA 1, 1994 C 1, NZ 1,2, 1995 W, E, S, [Iv (R), S, I, SA], It, Arg
Dintrans, P (Tarbes) 1979 NZ 1,2, R, 1980 E, S, I, SA, R, 1981 S, I, W, E, A 1,2, R, NZ 1,2, 1982 W, E, S, I, R, Arg 1,2, 1983 E, W, A 1,2, R, 1984 I, W, E, S, NZ 1,2, R, 1985 E, S, I, W, Arg 1,2, 1987 [R], 1988 Arg 1,2,3, 1989 W, E, S, 1990 R
Dispagne, S (Toulouse) 1996 I (R), W 1
Dizabo, P (Tyrosse) 1948 A, S, E, 1949 S, I, E, W, Arg 2, 1950 S, I, 1960 Arg 1,2,3
Domec, A (Carcassonne) 1929 W
Domec, H (Lourdes) 1953 W, It, 1954 S, I, NZ, W, E, It, 1955 S, I, E, W, 1956 I, W, It, 1958 E, A, W, It, I
Domenech, A (Vichy, Brive) 1954 W, E, It, 1955 S, I, E, W, 1956 S, I, W, It, E, Cz, 1957 S, I, E, W, It, R 1,2, 1958 S, E, It, 1959 It, 1960 S, E, W, I, It, R, Arg 1,2,3, 1961 S, SA, E, W, It, I, NZ 1,2,3, A, R, 1962 S, E, W, I, It, R, 1963 W, It
Domercq, J (Bayonne) 1912 I, S
Dominici, C (SF) 1998 E, S, Arg 1,2, 1999 E, S, WS, NZ 1, W 2, [C, Fj, Arg, NZ 2, A], 2000 W, E, S, R, 2001 I (R), It, W, E, SA 1,2, NZ, Fj, 2003 Arg 1, R, E 2,3, [Fj,J,S,I,E], 2004 I,It,W,S,E,A(R),NZ(R), 2005 S,E,W,I,It, 2006 S, I, It, E, W, NZ1, 2(R), Arg, 2007 It,I, W1,E1,S(R),E3,W2(R), [Arg 1,Gg,NZ(R),E(R),Arg 2]
Dorot, J (RCF) 1935 G
Dospital, P (Bayonne) 1977 R, 1980 I, 1981 S, I, W, E, 1982 I, R, Arg 1,2, 1983 E, S, I, W, 1984 E, S, NZ 1,2, R, 1985 E, S, I, W, Arg 1
Dourthe, C (Dax) 1966 R, 1967 S, A, E, W, I, SA 1,2,3, NZ, 1968 W, NZ 3, SA 1,2, 1969 W, 1971 SA 2(R), R, 1972 I 1,2, A 1,2, R, 1973 S, NZ, E, 1974 I, Arg 1,2, SA 1,2, 1975 W, E, S
Dourthe, M (Dax) 2000 NZ 2(t)
Dourthe, R (Dax, SF, Béziers) 1995 R 2, Arg, NZ 1,2, 1996 E, R, 1996 Arg 1,2, W 2, SA 1,2, 1997 W, A 1, 1999 I, W 1,2, [C, Nm, Fj, Arg, NZ 2, A], 2000 W, E, It, R, A, NZ 1,2, 2001 S, I
Doussau, E (Angoulême) 1938 R
Droitecourt, M (Montferrand) 1972 R, 1973 NZ (R), E, 1974 E, S, Arg 1, SA 2, 1975 SA 1,2, Arg 1,2, R, 1976 S, I, W, A 1, 1977 Arg 2
Dubertrand, A (Montferrand) 1971 A 1,2, R, 1972 I 2, 1974 I, W, E, SA 2, 1975 Arg 1,2, R, 1976 S, US
Dubois, D (Bègles) 1971 S
Dubroca, D (Agen) 1979 NZ 2, 1981 NZ 2(R), 1982 E, S, 1984 W, E, S, 1985 Arg 2, 1986 S, I, W, E, R 1, Arg 2, A, NZ 1, R 2, NZ 2,3, 1987 W, E, S, I, [S, Z, Fj, A, NZ], R, 1988 E, S, I, W
Duché, A (Limoges) 1929 G
Duclos, A (Lourdes) 1931 S
Ducousso, J (Tarbes) 1925 S, W, E
Dufau, G (RCF) 1948 I, A, 1949 I, W, 1950 S, E, W, 1951 S, I, E, W, 1952 SA, W, 1953 S, I, E, W, 1954 S, I, NZ, W, E, It, 1955 S, I, E, W, It, 1956 S, I, W, It, 1957 S, I, E, W, It, R 1
Dufau, J (Biarritz) 1912 I, S, W, E
Duffaut, Y (Agen) 1954 Arg 1,2
Duffour, R (Tarbes) 1911 W
Dufourcq, J (SBUC) 1906 NZ, E, 1907 E, 1908 W
Duhard, Y (Bagnères) 1980 E
Duhau, J (SF) 1928 I,1930 I, G, 1931 I, S, W, 1933 G
Dulaurens, C (Toulouse) 1926 I, 1928 S, 1929 W
Duluc, A (Béziers) 1934 G
Du Manoir, Y le P (RCF) 1925 I, NZ, S, W, E, 1926 S, 1927 I, S
Dupont, C (Lourdes) 1923 S, W, I, 1924 S, I, W, R, US, 1925 S, 1927 E, G 1,2, 1928 A, G, W, 1929 I
Dupont, J-L (Agen) 1983 S
Dupont, L (RCF) 1934 G, 1935 G, 1936 G 1,2, 1938 R, G 2
Dupouy, A (SB) 1924 W, R
Duprat, B (Bayonne) 1966 E, W, It, R, 1967 S, A, E, SA 2,3, 1968 S, I, 1972 E, W, I 2, A 1
Dupré, P (RCF) 1909 W
Dupuy, J (Tarbes) 1956 S, I, W, It, E, Cz, 1957 S, I, E, W, It, R 2, 1958 S, E, SA 1,2, 1959 S, E, It, W, I, 1960 W, I, It, Arg 1,3, 1961 S, SA, E, NZ 2, R, 1962 S, E, W, I, It, 1963 W, It, R, 1964 S
Durand, N (Perpignan) 2007 NZ1,2
Dusautoir, T (Biarritz, Toulouse) 2006 R,SA,NZ1, 2007 E3,W2(R), [Nm,I,NZ,E,Arg 2]
Du Souich, C J (see Judas du Souich)
Dutin, B (Mont-de-Marsan) 1968 NZ 2, A, SA 2, R
Dutour, F X (Toulouse) 1911 E, I, 1912 S, W, E, 1913 S
Dutrain, H (Toulouse) 1945 W, 1946 B, I, 1947 E, 1949 I, E, W, Arg 1
Dutrey, J (Lourdes) 1940 B
Duval, R (SF) 1908 E, W, 1909 E, 1911 E, W, I

Echavé, L (Agen) 1961 S
Elhorga, P (Agen) 2001 NZ, 2002 A 1,2, 2003 Arg 2, NZ (R), R, [Fj(R),US,I(R),NZ], 2004 I(R),It(R),S,E, 2005 S,E, 2006 NZ2,Arg
Elissalde, E (Bayonne) 1936 G 2, 1940 B
Elissalde, J-B (La Rochelle, Toulouse) 2000 S (R), R (R), 2003 It (R), W (R), 2004 I,It, W,A,Arg, 2005 SA1,2(R),A1,2,SA3, 2006 S,I,It,W(R),NZ1(R),2, 2007 E2(R),3,W2(R), [Arg 1(R),Nm,I,Gg(R),NZ,E,Arg 2]
Elissalde, J-P (La Rochelle) 1980 SA, R, 1981 A 1,2, R
Empereur-Buisson, H (Béziers) 1931 E, G
Erbani, D (Agen) 1981 A 1,2, NZ 1,2, 1982 Arg 1,2, 1983 S (R), I, W, A 1,2, R, 1984 W, E, R, 1985 E, W (R), Arg 2, 1986 S, I, W, E, R 1, Arg 2, NZ 1,2(R),3, 1987 W, E, S, I, [S, R, Fj, A, NZ], 1988 E, S, 1989 I (R), W, E, S, NZ 1, A 2, 1990 W, E
Escaffre, P (Narbonne) 1933 G, 1934 G
Escommier, M (Montelimar) 1955 It
Esponda, J-M (RCF) 1967 SA 1,2, R, 1968 NZ 1,2, SA 2, R, 1969 S, I (R), E
Estève, A (Béziers) 1971 SA 1, 1972 I 1, E, W, I 2, A 2, R, 1973 S, NZ, E, I, 1974 I, W, E, S, R, SA 1,2, 1975 W, E
Estève, P (Narbonne, Lavelanet) 1982 R, Arg 1,2, 1983 E, S, I, W, A 1,2, R, 1984 I, W, E, S, NZ 1,2, R, 1985 E, S, I, W, 1986 S, I, 1987 [S, Z]
Etcheberry, J (Rochefort, Cognac) 1923 W, I, 1924 S, I, E, W, R, US, 1926 S, I, E, M, 1927 I, S, W, G 2
Etchenique, J-M (Biarritz O) 1974 R, SA 1, 1975 E, Arg 2
Etchepare, A (Bayonne) 1922 I
Etcheverry, M (Pau) 1971 S, I
Eutrope, A (SCUF) 1913 I

Fabre, E (Toulouse) 1937 It, 1938 G 1,2
Fabre, J (Toulouse) 1963 S, I, E, W, It, 1964 S, NZ, E
Fabre, L (Lezignan) 1930 G
Fabre, M (Béziers) 1981 A 1, R, NZ 1,2, 1982 I, R
Failliot, P (RCF) 1911 S, W, I, 1912 I, S, E, 1913 E, W
Fargues, G (Dax) 1923 I
Fauré, F (Tarbes) 1914 I, W, E
Fauvel, J-P (Tulle) 1980 R
Favre, M (Lyon) 1913 E, W
Ferrand, L (Chalon) 1940 B
Ferrien, R (Tarbes) 1950 S, I, E, W
Finat, R (CASG) 1932 G, 1933 G
Fite, R (Brive) 1963 W, It
Forest, M (Bourgoin) 2007 NZ1(R),2(R)
Forestier, J (SCUF) 1912 W
Forgues, F (Bayonne) 1911 S, E, W, 1912 I, W, E, 1913 S, SA, W, 1914 I, E
Fort, J (Agen) 1967 It, W, I, SA 1,2,3,4
Fourcade, G (BEC) 1909 E, W
Foures, H (Toulouse) 1951 S, I, E, W
Fournet, F (Montferrand) 1950 W
Fouroux, J (La Voulte) 1972 I 2, R, 1974 W, E, Arg 1,2, R, SA 1,2, 1975 W, Arg 1, R, 1976 S, I, W, E, US, A 1, 1977 W, E, S, I, Arg 1,2, NZ 1,2, R
Francquenelle, A (Vaugirard) 1911 S, 1913 W, I
Fritz, F (Toulouse) 2005 SA1,A2,SA3, 2006 S,I,It,E,W,SA,NZ1,2,Arg, 2007 It
Froment, R (Castres) 2004 US(R)
Furcade, R (Perpignan) 1952 S

Gabernet, S (Toulouse) 1980 E, S, 1981 S, I, W, E, A 1,2, R, NZ 1,2, 1982 I, 1983 A 2, R
Gachassin, J (Lourdes) 1961 S, I, 1963 R, 1964 S, NZ, E,

W, It, I, SA, Fj, R, 1965 S, I, E, W, It, R, 1966 S, I, E, W, 1967 S, A, It, W, I, NZ, 1968 I, E, 1969 S, I
Galasso, A (Toulon, Montferrand) 2000 R (R), 2001 E (R)
Galau, H (Toulouse) 1924 S, I, E, W, US
Galia, J (Quillan) 1927 E, G 1,2, 1928 S, A, I, E, W, 1929 I, E, G, 1930 S, I, E, G, W, 1931 S, W, E, G
Gallart, P (Béziers) 1990 R, A 1,2(R),3, 1992 S, I, R, Arg 1,2, SA 1,2, Arg, 1994 I, W, E, 1995 I (t), R 1, [Tg]
Gallion, J (Toulon) 1978 E, S, I, W, 1979 I, W, E, S, NZ 2, R, 1980 W, E, S, I, 1983 A 1,2, R, 1984 I, W, E, S, R, 1985 E, S, I, W, 1986 Arg 2 Galthié, F (Colomiers, SF) 1991 R, US 1, [R, Fj, C, E], 1992 W, E, S, R, Arg, 1994 I, W, E, 1995 [SA, E], 1996 W 1(R), 1997 I, It 2, SA 1,2, 1998 W (R), Fj (R), 1999 R, WS (R), Tg, NZ 1(R), [Fj (R), Arg, NZ 2, A], 2000 W, E, A, NZ 1,2, 2001 S, It, W, E, SA 1,2, NZ, SA 3, A, Fj, 2002 E, S, I, SA, NZ, C, 2003 E 1, S, Arg 1,2, NZ, R, E 2, [Fj,J,S,I,E]
Galy, J (Perpignan) 1953 W
Garbajosa, X (Toulouse) 1998 I, W, Arg 2(R), Fj, 1999 W 1(R), E, S, WS, NZ 1, W 2, [C, Nm (R), Fj (R), Arg, NZ 2, A], 2000 A, NZ 1,2, 2001 S, I, E, 2002 It (R), W, SA (R), C (R), 2003 E 1, S, I, It, W, E 3
Garuet-Lempirou, J-P (Lourdes) 1983 A 1,2, R, 1984 I, NZ 1,2, R, 1985 E, S, I, W, Arg 1, 1986 S, I, W, E, R 1, Arg 1, NZ 1, R 2, NZ 2,3, 1987 W, E, S, I, [S, R, Fj, A, NZ], 1988 E, S, Arg 1,2, R, 1989 E (R), S, NZ 1,2, 1990 W, E
Gasc, J (Graulhet) 1977 NZ 2
Gasparotto, G (Montferrand) 1976 A 2, R
Gauby, G (Perpignan) 1956 Cz
Gaudermen, P (RCF) 1906 E
Gayraud, W (Toulouse) 1920 I
Gelez, F (Agen) 2001 SA 3, 2002 I (R), A 1, SA, NZ, C (R), 2003 S, I
Geneste, R (BEC) 1945 B 1, 1949 Arg 2
Genet, J-P (RCF) 1992 S, I, R
Gensane, R (Béziers) 1962 S, E, W, I, It, R, 1963 S
Gerald, G (RCF) 1927 E, G 2, 1928 S, 1929 I, S, W, E, G, 1930 S, I, E, G, W, 1931 I, S, E, G
Gérard, D (Bègles) 1999 Tg
Gerintes, G (CASG) 1924 R, 1925 I, 1926 W
Geschwind, P (RCF) 1936 G 1,2
Giacardy, M (SBUC) 1907 E
Gimbert, P (Bègles) 1991 R, US 1, 1992 W, E
Giordani, P (Dax) 1999 E, S
Glas, S (Bourgoin) 1996 S (t), I (R), W 1, R, Arg 2(R), W 2, SA 1,2, 1997 I, W, E, S, It 2(R), R 2, Arg, SA 1,2, 1998 E, S, I, W, Arg 1,2, Fj, Arg 3, A, 1999 W 2, [C,Nm, Arg (R), NZ 2(R), A (t&R)], 2000 I, 2001 E, SA 1,2, NZ
Gomès, A (SF) 1998 Arg 1,2, Fj, Arg 3, A, 1999 I (R)
Gommes, J (RCF) 1909 I
Gonnet, C-A (Albi) 1921 E, I, 1922 E, W, 1924 S, E, 1926 S, I, E, W, M, 1927 I, S, W, E, G 1
Gonzalez, J-M (Bayonne) 1992 Arg 1,2, SA 1,2, Arg, 1993 R 1, SA 1,2, R 2, A 1,2, 1994 I, W, E, S, C 1, NZ 1,2, C 2, 1995 W, E, S, I, R 1, [Tg, S, I, SA, E], It, Arg, 1996 E, S, I, W 1
Got, R (Perpignan) 1920 I, US, 1921 S, W, 1922 S, E, W, I, 1924 I, E, W, R, US
Gourdon, J-F (RCF, Bagnères) 1974 S, Arg 1,2, R, SA 1,2, 1975 W, E, S, I, R, 1976 S, I, W, E, 1978 E, S, 1979 W, E, S, R, 1980 I
Gourragne, J-F (Béziers) 1990 NZ 2, 1991 W 1
Goutta, B (Perpignan) 2004 C
Goyard, A (Lyon U) 1936 G 1,2, 1937 G, It, 1938 G 1, R, G 2
Graciet, R (SBUC) 1926 I, W, 1927 S, G 1, 1929 E, 1930 W
Grandclaude, J-P (Perpignan) 2005 E(R),W(R), 2007 NZ1
Graou, S (Auch, Colomiers) 1992 Arg (R), 1993 SA 1,2, R 2, A 2(R), 1995 R 2, Arg (t), NZ 2(R)
Gratton, J (Agen) 1984 NZ 2, R, 1985 E, S, I, W, Arg 1,2, 1986 S, NZ 1
Graule, V (Arl Perpignan) 1926 I, E, W, 1927 S, W, 1931 G
Greffe, M (Grenoble) 1968 W, Cz, NZ 1,2, SA 1
Griffard, J (Lyon U) 1932 G, 1933 G, 1934 G
Gruarin, A (Toulon) 1964 W, It, I, SA, Fj, R, 1965 S, I, E, W, It, 1966 S, I, E, W, It, R, 1967 S, A, E, It, W, I, NZ, 1968 S, I
Guelorget, P (RCF) 1931 E, G
Guichemerre, A (Dax) 1920 E, 1921 E, I, 1923 S
Guilbert, A (Toulon) 1975 E, S, I, SA 1,2, 1976 A 1, 1977 Arg 1,2, NZ 1,2, R, 1979 I, W, E
Guillemin, P (RCF) 1908 E, W, 1909 E, I, 1910 W, S, E, I, 1911 S, E, W
Guilleux, P (Agen) 1952 SA, It
Guiral, M (Agen) 1931 G, 1932 G, 1933 G
Guiraud, H (Nîmes) 1996 R

Haget, A (PUC) 1953 E, 1954 I, NZ, E, Arg 2, 1955 E, W, It, 1957 I, E, It, R 1, 1958 It, SA 2
Haget, F (Agen, Biarritz O) 1974 Arg 1,2, 1975 SA 2, Arg 1,2, R, 1976 S, 1978 S, I, W, R, 1979 I, W, E, S, NZ 1,2, R, 1980 W, S, I, 1984 S, NZ 1,2, R, 1985 E, S, I, 1986 S, I, W, E, R 1, Arg 1, A, NZ 1, 1987 S, I, [R, Fj]
Haget, H (CASG) 1928 S, 1930 G
Halet, R (Strasbourg) 1925 NZ, S, W
Hall, S (Béziers) 2002 It, W
Harinordoquy, I (Pau, Biarritz)) 2002 W, E, S, I, A 1,2, SA, NZ, C, 2003 E 1, S, I, It, W, Arg 1(R),2, NZ, R, E 2,3(R), [Fj,S,I,E], 2004 I,It,W,E,A,Arg,NZ, 2005 W(R),2006 R(R), SA, 2007 It(R), I, W1(R),E1(R),S,E3,W2, [Arg 1, Nm(R), NZ(R), E(R), Arg 2]
Harislur-Arthapignet, P (Tarbes) 1988 Arg 4(R)
Harize, D (Cahors, Toulouse) 1975 SA 1,2, 1976 A 1,2, R, 1977 W, E, S, I
Hauc, J (Toulon) 1928 E, G, 1929 I, S, G
Hauser, M (Lourdes) 1969 E
Hedembaigt, M (Bayonne) 1913 S, SA, 1914 W
Hericé, D (Bègles) 1950 I
Herrero, A (Toulon) 1963 R, 1964 NZ, E, W, It, I, SA, Fj, R, 1965 S, I, E, W, 1966 W, It, R, 1967 S, A, E, It, I, R
Herrero, B (Nice) 1983 I, 1986 Arg 1
Heyer, F (Montferrand) 1990 A 2
Heymans, C (Agen, Toulouse) 2000 It (R) R, 2002 A 2(R), SA, NZ, 2004 W(R),US, C(R),A,Arg,NZ, 2005 I, It, SA1, 2, A1, 2, C, SA3, 2006 S,I,W(R),R,SA,NZ2,Arg, 2007 It, I(R), E1(R), S, E3, W2, [Arg 1,Nm,I,NZ,E]
Hiquet, J-C (Agen) 1964 E
Hoche, M (PUC) 1957 I, E, W, It, R 1
Hondagné-Monge, M (Tarbes) 1988 Arg 2(R)
Hontas, P (Biarritz) 1990 S, I, R, 1991 R, 1992 Arg, 1993 E, S, I, W
Hortoland, J-P (Béziers) 1971 A 2
Houblain, H (SCUF) 1909 E, 1910 W
Houdet, R (SF) 1927 S, W, G 1, 1928 G, W, 1929 I, S, E, 1930 S, E
Hourdebaigt, A (SBUC) 1909 I, 1910 W, S, E, I
Hubert, A (ASF) 1906 E, 1907 E, 1908 E, W, 1909 E, W, I
Hueber, A (Lourdes, Toulon) 1990 A 3, NZ 1, 1991 US 2, 1992 I, Arg 1,2, SA 1,2, 1993 E, S, I, W, R 1, SA 1,2, R 2, A 1,2, 1995 [Tg, S (R), I], 2000 It, R
Hutin, R (CASG) 1927 I, S, W
Hyardet, A (Castres) 1995 It, Arg (R)

Ibañez, R (Dax, Perpignan, Castres, Saracens, Wasps) 1996 W 1(R), 1997 It 1(R), R 1, It 2(R), R 2, SA 2(R), 1998 E, S, I, W, Arg 1,2, Fj, Arg 3, A, 1999 I, W 1, E, S, R, WS, Tg (R), NZ 1, W 2, [C, Nm, Fj, Arg, NZ 2, A], 2000 W (R), E (R), S (R), I (R), It (R), R, 2001 S, I, It, W, E, SA 1,2, NZ (R), SA 3, A, Fj, 2002 It (R), W, E, S, I, Arg, A 1(R),2, SA, NZ, C, 2003 E 1, S, I, It, W, R (R), E 2(R),3, [Fj,J(R),S,I,E,NZ(R)], 2005 C(R),Tg, 2006 I, It, E, W, R, SA(R),NZ1(R),2,Arg, 2007 It,I,W1,E1,S,NZ1(R),2(R),E2,3, [Arg 1, Nm(R),I,NZ,E,Arg 2]
Icard, J (SF) 1909 E, W
Iguiniz, E (Bayonne) 1914 E
Ihingoué, D (BEC) 1912 I, S
Imbernon, J-F (Perpignan) 1976 I, W, E, US, A 1, 1977 W, E, S, I, Arg 1,2, NZ 1,2, 1978 E, R, 1979 I, 1981 S, I, W, E, 1982 I, 1983 I, W
Iraçabal, J (Bayonne) 1968 NZ 1,2, SA 1, 1969 S, I, W, R, 1970 S, I, W, E, R, 1971 W, SA 1,2, A 1, 1972 E, W, I 2, A 2, R, 1973 S, NZ, E, W, I, J, 1974 I, W, E, S, Arg 1,2, SA 2(R)
Isaac, H (RCF) 1907 E, 1908 E
Ithurra, E (Biarritz O) 1936 G 1,2, 1937 G

Jacquet, L (Clermont-Auvergne) 2006 NZ2(R),Arg
Janeczek, T (Tarbes) 1982 Arg 1,2, 1990 R
Janik, K (Toulouse) 1987 R
Jarasse, A (Brive) 1945 B 1
Jardel, J (SB) 1928 I, E
Jaureguy, A (RCF, Toulouse, SF) 1920 S, E, W, I, US, 1922

S, W, 1923 S, W, E, I, 1924 S, W, R, US, 1925 I, NZ, 1926 S, E, W, M, 1927 I, E, 1928 S, A, E, G, W, 1929 I, S, E
Jaureguy, P (Toulouse) 1913 S, SA, W, I
Jauzion, Y (Colomiers, Toulouse) 2001 SA 1,2, NZ, 2002 A 1(R),2(R), 2003 Arg 2, NZ, R, E 2,3, [Fj,S,I,E], 2004 I,It,W,S,E,A,Arg,NZ(t), 2005 W,I,It,SA1,2,A1,2,C,Tg(R),SA3, 2006 R,SA,NZ1,2,Arg, 2007 It,I,W1,E1,S,E3,W2, [Arg 1,Nm(R),I(R),Gg,NZ,E]
Jeangrand, M-H (Tarbes) 1921 I
Jeanjean, N (Toulouse) 2001 SA 1,2, NZ, SA 3(R), A (R), Fj (R), 2002 It, Arg, A 1
Jeanjean, P (Toulon) 1948 I
Jérôme, G (SF) 1906 NZ, E
Joinel, J-L (Brive) 1977 NZ 1, 1978 R, 1979 I, W, E, S, NZ 1,2, R, 1980 W, E, S, I, SA, 1981 S, I, W, E, R, NZ 1,2, 1982 E, S, I, R, 1983 E, S, I, W, A 1,2, R, 1984 I, W, E, S, NZ 1,2, 1985 S, I, W, Arg 1, 1986 S, I, W, E, R 1, Arg 1,2, A, 1987 [Z]
Jol, M (Biarritz O) 1947 S, I, W, E, 1949 S, I, E, W, Arg 1,2
Jordana, J-L (Pau, Toulouse) 1996 R (R), Arg 1(t),2, W 2, 1997 I (t), W, S (R)
Judas du Souich, C (SCUF) 1911 W, I
Juillet, C (Montferrand, SF) 1995 R 2, Arg, 1999 E, S, WS, NZ 1, [C, Fj, Arg, NZ 2, A], 2000 A, NZ 1,2, 2001 S, I, It, W
Junquas, L (Tyrosse) 1945 B 1,2, W, 1946 B, I, K, W, 1947 S, I, W, E, 1948 S, W

Kaczorowski, D (Le Creusot) 1974 I (R)
Kaempf, A (St Jean-de-Luz) 1946 B

Labadie, P (Bayonne) 1952 S, I, SA, W, E, It, 1953 S, I, It, 1954 S, I, NZ, W, E, Arg 2, 1955 S, I, E, W, 1956 I, 1957 I
Labarthete, R (Pau) 1952 S
Labazuy, A (Lourdes) 1952 I, 1954 S, W, 1956 E, 1958 A, W, I, 1959 S, E, It, W
Labit, C (Toulouse) 1999 S, R (R), WS (R), Tg, 2000 R (R), 2002 Arg, A 1(R), 2003 Arg 1,2, NZ (R), R (R), E 3, [Fj(R),J,US,E(R),NZ]
Laborde, C (RCF) 1962 It, R, 1963 R, 1964 SA, 1965 E
Labrousse, T (Brive) 1996 R, SA 1
Lacans, P (Béziers) 1980 SA, 1981 W, E, A 2, R, 1982 W
Lacassagne, H (SBUC) 1906 NZ, 1907 E
Lacaussade, R (Bègles) 1948 A, S
Lacaze, C (Lourdes, Angoulême) 1961 NZ 2,3, A, R, 1962 E, W, I, It, 1963 W, R, 1964 S, NZ, E, 1965 It, R, 1966 S, I, E, W, It, R, 1967 S, E, SA 1,3,4, R, 1968 S, E, W, Cz, NZ 1, 1969 E
Lacaze, H (Périgueux) 1928 I, G, W, 1929 I, W
Lacaze, P (Lourdes) 1958 SA 1,2, 1959 S, E, It, W, I
Lacazedieu, C (Dax) 1923 W, I, 1928 A, I, 1929 S
Lacombe, B (Agen) 1989 B, 1990 A 2
Lacome, M (Pau) 1960 Arg 2
Lacoste, R (Tarbes) 1914 I, W, E
Lacrampe, F (Béziers) 1949 Arg 2
Lacroix, P (Mont-de-Marsan, Agen) 1958 A, 1960 W, I, It, R, Arg 1,2,3, 1961 S, SA, E, W, I, NZ 1,2,3, A, R, 1962 S, E, W, I, R, 1963 S, I, E, W
Lacroix, T (Dax, Harlequins) 1989 A 1(R),2, 1991 W 1(R),2(R), [R, C (R), E], 1992 SA 2, 1993 E, S, I, W, SA 1,2, R 2, A 1,2, 1994 I, W, E, S, C 1, NZ 1,2, C 2, 1995 W, E, S, R 1, [Tg, Iv, S, I, SA, E], 1996 E, S, I, 1997 It 2, R 2, Arg, SA 1,2
Lafarge, Y (Montferrand) 1978 R, 1979 NZ 1, 1981 I (R)
Laffitte, R (SCUF) 1910 W, S
Laffont, H (Narbonne) 1926 W
Lafond, A (Bayonne) 1922 E
Lafond, J-B (RCF) 1983 A 1, 1985 Arg 1,2 1986 S, I, W, E, R 1, 1987 I (R), 1988 W, 1989 I, W, E, 1990 W, A 3(R), NZ 2, 1991 S, I, W 1, E, R, US 1, W 2, [R (R), Fj, C, E], 1992 W, E, S, I (R), SA 2, 1993 E, S, I, W Lagisquet, P (Bayonne) 1983 A 1,2, R, 1984 I, W, NZ 1,2, 1986 R 1(R), Arg 1,2, A, NZ 1, 1987 [S, R, Fj, A, NZ], R, 1988 S, I, W, Arg 1,2,3,4, R, 1989 I, W, E, S, NZ 1,2, B, A 1,2, 1990 W, E, S, I, A 1,2,3, 1991 S, I, US 2, [R]
Lagrange, J-C (RCF) 1966 It
Laharrague, J (Brive, Perpignan, Sale) 2005 W,I,It,SA1,A1,2,C(R),Tg, 2006 R(R),SA, NZ1, 2007 NZ2
Laharrague, N (Perpignan) 2007 NZ1(R),2(R)
Lalande, M (RCF) 1923 S, W, I
Lalanne, F (Mont-de-Marsan) 2000 R
Lamaison, C (Brive, Agen) 1996 SA 1(R),2, 1997 W, E, S, R 1, A 2, It 2, R 2, Arg, SA 1,2, 1998 E, S, I, W, Arg 3(R), A, 1999 R, WS (R), Tg, NZ 1(R), W 2(R), [C (R), Nm, Fj, Arg, NZ 2, A], 2000 W, A, NZ 1,2, 2001 S, I, It, W (R)
Lamboley, G (Toulouse) 2005 S(R),E(R),W(R),I(R),It(R),SA1(R),2(R),A1,2(R),C(R),Tg, SA3(R), 2007 W1(R)
Landreau, F (SF) 2000 A, NZ 1,2, 2001 E (R) Lane, G (RCF) 1906 NZ, E, 1907 E, 1908 E, W, 1909 E, W, I, 1910 W, E, 1911 S, W, 1912 I, W, E, 1913 S
Langlade, J-C (Hyères) 1990 R, A 1, NZ 1
Laperne, D (Dax) 1997 R 1(R)
Laporte, G (Graulhet) 1981 I, W, E, R, NZ 1,2, 1986 S, I, W, E, R 1, Arg 1, A (R), 1987 [R, Z (R), Fj]
Larreguy, P (Bayonne) 1954 It
Larribau, J (Périgueux) 1912 I, S, W, E, 1913 S, 1914 I, E
Larrieu, J (Tarbes) 1920 I, US, 1921 W, 1923 S, W, E, I
Larrieux, M (SBUC) 1927 G 2
Larrue, H (Carmaux) 1960 W, I, It, R, Arg 1,2,3
Lasaosa, P (Dax) 1950 I, 1952 S, I, E, It, 1955 It
Lascubé, G (Agen) 1991 S, I, W 1, E, US 2, W 2, [R, Fj, C, E], 1992 W, E
Lassegue, J-B (Toulouse) 1946 W, 1947 S, I, W, 1948 W, 1949 I, E, W, Arg 1
Lasserre, F (René) (Bayonne, Cognac, Grenoble) 1914 I, 1920 S, 1921 S, W, I, 1922 S, E, W, I, 1923 W, E, 1924 S, I, R, US
Lasserre, J-C (Dax) 1963 It, 1964 S, NZ, E, W, It, I, Fj, 1965 W, It, R, 1966 R, 1967 S
Lasserre, M (Agen) 1967 SA 2,3, 1968 E, W, Cz, NZ 3, A, SA 1,2, 1969 S, I, E, 1970 E, 1971 E, W
Laterrade, G (Tarbes) 1910 E, I, 1911 S, E, I
Laudouar, J (Soustons, SBUC) 1961 NZ 1,2, R, 1962 I, R
Lauga, P (Vichy) 1950 S, I, E, W
Laurent, A (Biarritz O) 1925 NZ, S, W, E, 1926 W
Laurent, J (Bayonne) 1920 S, E, W
Laurent, M (Auch) 1932 G, 1933 G, 1934 G, 1935 G, 1936 G 1
Laussucq, C (SF) 1999 S (R), 2000 W (R), S, I
Lavail, G (Perpignan) 1937 G, 1940 B
Lavaud, R (Carcassonne) 1914 I, W
Lavergne, P (Limoges) 1950 S
Lavigne, B (Agen) 1984 R, 1985 E
Lavigne, J (Dax) 1920 E, W
Lazies, H (Auch) 1954 Arg 2, 1955 It, 1956 E, 1957 S
Le Bourhis, R (La Rochelle) 1961 R
Lecointre, M (Nantes) 1952 It
Le Corvec, G (Perpignan) 2007 NZ1
Le Droff, J (Auch) 1963 It, R, 1964 S, NZ, E, 1970 E, R, 1971 S, I
Lefevre, R (Brive) 1961 NZ 2
Leflamand, L (Bourgoin) 1996 SA 2, 1997 W, E, S, It 2, Arg, SA 1,2(R)
Lefort, J-B (Biarritz O) 1938 G 1
Le Goff, R (Métro) 1938 R, G 2
Legrain, M (SF) 1909 I, 1910 I, 1911 S, E, W, I, 1913 S, SA, E, I, 1914 I, W
Lemeur, Y (RCF) 1993 R 1
Lenient, J-J (Vichy) 1967 R
Lepatey, J (Mazamet) 1954 It, 1955 S, I, E, W
Lepatey, L (Mazamet) 1924 S, I, E
Lescarboura, J-P (Dax) 1982 W, E, S, I, 1983 A 1,2, R, 1984 I, W, E, S, NZ 1,2, R, 1985 E, S, I, W, Arg 1,2, 1986 Arg 2, A, NZ 1, R 2, NZ 2, 1988 S, W, 1990 R
Lesieur, E (SF) 1906 E, 1908 E, W, 1909 E, W, I, 1910 S, E, I, 1911 E, I, 1912 W
Leuvielle, M (SBUC) 1908 W, 1913 S, SA, E, W, 1914 W, E
Levasseur, R (SF) 1925 W, E
Levée, H (RCF) 1906 NZ
Lewis, E W (Le Havre) 1906 E
Lhermet, J-M (Montferrand) 1990 S, I, 1993 R 1
Libaros, G (Tarbes) 1936 G 1, 1940 B
Liebenberg, B (SF) 2003 R (R), E 2(R),3, [US,I(R),NZ(R)], 2004 I(R),US,C,NZ, 2005 S,E
Lièvremont, M (Perpignan, SF) 1995 It, R 2, Arg (R), NZ 2(R), 1996 R, Arg 1(R), SA 2(R), 1997 R 1, A 2(R), 1998 E

(R), S, I, W, Arg 1,2, Fj, Arg 3, A, 1999 W 2, [C, Nm, Fj, Arg, NZ 2, A]
Lièvremont, T (Perpignan, SF, Biarritz) 1996 W 2(R), 1998 E, S, I, W, Arg 1,2, Fj, Arg 3, A, 1999 I, W 1, E, W 2, [Nm], 2000 W (R), E (R), S (R), I, It, 2001 E (R), 2004 I(R), It(R),W,S,US,C, 2005 A2,C,Tg(t&R),SA3(R), 2006 S(R),It,E,W
Lira, M (La Voulte) 1962 R, 1963 I, E, W, It, R, 1964 W, It, I, SA, 1965 S, I, R
Llari, R (Carcassonne) 1926 S
Lobies, J (RCF) 1921 S, W, E
Lombard, F (Narbonne) 1934 G, 1937 It
Lombard, T (SF) 1998 Arg 3, A, 1999 I, W 1, S (R), 2000 W, E, S, A, NZ 1, 2001 It, W
Lombarteix, R (Montferrand) 1938 R, G 2
Londios, J (Montauban) 1967 SA 3
Loppy, L (Toulon) 1993 R 2
Lorieux, A (Grenoble, Aix) 1981 A 1, R, NZ 1,2, 1982 W, 1983 A 2, R, 1984 I, W, E, 1985 Arg 1,2(R), 1986 R 2, NZ 2,3, 1987 W, E, [S, Z, Fj, A, NZ], 1988 S, I, W, Arg 1,2,4, 1989 W, A 2
Loury, A (RCF) 1927 E, G 1,2, 1928 S, A, I
Loustau, L (Perpignan) 2004 C
Loustau, M (Dax) 1923 E
Lubin-Lebrère, M-F (Toulouse) 1914 I, W, E, 1920 S, E, W, I, US, 1921 S, 1922 S, E, W, 1924 W, US, 1925 I
Lubrano, A (Béziers) 1972 A 2, 1973 S
Lux, J-P (Tyrosse, Dax) 1967 E, It, W, I, SA 1,2,4, R, 1968 I, E, Cz, NZ 3, A, SA 1,2, 1969 S, I, E, 1970 S, I, W, E, R, 1971 S, I, E, W, A 1,2, 1972 S, I 1, E, W, I 2, A 1,2, R, 1973 S, NZ, E, 1974 I, W, E, S, Arg 1,2, 1975 W

Macabiau, A (Perpignan) 1994 S, C 1
Maclos, P (SF) 1906 E, 1907 E
Magne, O (Dax, Brive, Montferrand, Clermont-Auvergne, London Irish) 1997 W (R), E, S, R 1(R), A 1,2, It 2(R), R 2, Arg (R), 1998 E, S, I, W, Arg 1,2, Fj, Arg 3, A, 1999 I, R, WS, NZ 1, W 2, [C, Nm, Fj, Arg, NZ 2, A], 2000 W, E, S, It, R, A, NZ 1,2, 2001 S, I, It, W, E, SA 1,2, NZ, SA 3, A, Fj, 2002 It, E, S, I, Arg, A 1,2(R), SA, NZ, C, 2003 E 1, S, I, It, W, R, E 2,3(R), [Fj,J,S,I,E,NZ(R)], 2004 I, It, W(R), S, E, A, Arg,NZ, 2005 SA1,2(R),A1, 2006 I,It,E,W(R), 2007 NZ1,2
Magnanou, C (RCF) 1923 E, 1925 W, E, 1926 S, 1929 S, W, 1930 S, I, E, W
Magnol, L (Toulouse) 1928 S, 1929 S, W, E
Magois, H (La Rochelle) 1968 SA 1,2, R
Majerus, R (SF) 1928 W, 1929 I, S, 1930 S, I, E, G, W
Malbet, J-C (Agen) 1967 SA 2,4
Maleig, A (Oloron) 1979 W, E, NZ 2, 1980 W, E, SA, R
Mallier, L (Brive) 1999 R, W 2(R), [C (R)], 2000 I (R), It
Malquier, Y (Narbonne) 1979 S
Manterola, T (Lourdes) 1955 It, 1957 R 1
Mantoulan, C (Pau) 1959 I
Marcet, J (Albi) 1925 I, NZ, S, W, E, 1926 I, E
Marchal, J-F (Lourdes) 1979 S, R, 1980 W, S, I
Marconnet, S (SF) 1998 Arg 3, A, 1999 I (R), W 1(R), E, S (R), R, Tg, 2000 A, NZ 1,2, 2001 S, I, It (R), W (R), E, 2002 S (R), Arg (R), A 1,2, SA (R), C (R), 2003 E 1(R), S, I, It, W, Arg 1(t+R),2, NZ, R, E 2,3(t+R), [S,US(R),I,E,NZ], 2004 I, It, W,S,E,A,Arg,NZ, 2005 S, E, W, I, It, SA1, 2, A1(R), 2(R), C,Tg,SA3(R), 2006 S, I(R), It(R), E, W, R, SA, NZ1, 2(R), Arg(R), 2007 It(R),I,W1(R)
Marchand, R (Poitiers) 1920 S, W
Marfaing, M (Toulouse) 1992 R, Arg 1
Marlu, J (Montferrand, Biarritz)) 1998 Fj (R), 2002 S (R), I (R), 2005 E
Marocco, P (Montferrand) 1968 S, I, W, E, R 1, Arg 1,2, A, 1988 Arg 4, 1989 I, 1990 E (R), NZ 1(R), 1991 S, I, W 1, E, US 2, [R, Fj, C, E]
Marot, A (Brive) 1969 R, 1970 S, I, W, 1971 SA 1, 1972 I 2, 1976 A 1
Marquesuzaa, A (RCF) 1958 It, SA 1,2, 1959 S, E, It, W, 1960 S, E, Arg 1
Marracq, H (Pau) 1961 R
Marsh, T (Montferrand) 2001 SA 3, A, Fj, 2002 It, W, E, S, I, Arg, A 1,2, 2003 [Fj,J,S,I, E,NZ], 2004 C,A,Arg,NZ
Martin, C (Lyon) 1909 I, 1910 W, S
Martin, H (SBUC) 1907 E, 1908 W
Martin, J-L (Béziers) 1971 A 2, R, 1972 S, I 1
Martin, L (Pau) 1948 I, A, S, W, E, 1950 S
Martin, R (SF) 2002 E (t+R), S (R), I (R), 2005 SA1(t&R),2,A1,2,C,SA3, 2006 S,I(t&R), R, SA(R), NZ1(R), 2, Arg, 2007 E2,W2, [Arg 1,Gg(R),Arg 2(R)]
Martine, R (Lourdes) 1952 S, I, It, 1953 It, 1954 S, I, NZ, W, E, It, Arg 2, 1955 S, I, W, 1958 A, W, It, I, SA 1,2, 1960 S, E, Arg 3, 1961 S, It
Martinez, A (Narbonne) 2002 A 1, 2004 C
Martinez, G (Toulouse) 1982 W, E, S, Arg 1,2, 1983 E, W
Marty, D (Perpignan) 2005 It,C,Tg, 2006 I, It(R), R(R), NZ1(R), Arg(R), 2007 I,W1,E1,S, E2, [Nm,I,Gg,NZ,E,Arg 2]
Mas, F (Béziers) 1962 R, 1963 S, I, E, W
Mas, N (Perpignan) 2003 NZ, 2005 E,W,I,It, 2007 W1,NZ1,2(R),E2(R),3(R),W2, [Nm(R),Gg(R),Arg 2]
Maso, J (Perpignan, Narbonne) 1966 It, R, 1967 S, R, 1968 S, W, Cz, NZ 1,2,3, A, R, 1969 S, I, W, 1971 SA 1,2, R, 1972 E, W, A 2, 1973 W, I, J, R
Massare, J (PUC) 1945 B 1,2, W, 1946 B, I, W
Massé, A (SBUC) 1908 W, 1909 E, W, 1910 W, S, E, I
Masse, H (Grenoble) 1937 G
Matheu-Cambas, J (Agen) 1945 W, 1946 B, I, K, W, 1947 S, I, W, E, 1948 I, A, S, W, E, 1949 S, I, E, W, Arg 1,2, 1950 E, W, 1951 S, I
Matiu, L (Biarritz) 2000 W, E
Mauduy, G (Périgueux) 1957 It, R 1,2, 1958 S, E, 1961 W, It
Mauran, J (Castres) 1952 SA, W, E, It, 1953 I, E
Mauriat, P (Lyon) 1907 E, 1908 E, W, 1909 W, I, 1910 W, S, E, I, 1911 S, E, W, I, 1912 I, S, 1913 S, SA, W, I
Maurin, G (ASF) 1906 E
Maury, A (Toulouse) 1925 I, NZ, S, W, E, 1926 S, I, E
Mayssonnié, A (Toulouse) 1908 E, W, 1910 W
Mazars, L (Narbonne) 2007 NZ2
Mazas, L (Colomiers, Biarritz) 1992 Arg, 1996 SA 1
Melville, E (Toulon) 1990 I (R), A 1,2,3, NZ 1, 1991 US 2
Menrath, R (SCUF) 1910 W
Menthiller, Y (Romans) 1964 W, It, SA, R, 1965 E
Merceron, G (Montferrand) 1999 R (R), Tg, 2000 S, I, R, 2001 S (R), W, E, SA 1,2, NZ (R), Fj, 2002 It, W, E, S, I, Arg, A 2, C, 2003 E 1, It (R), W (R), NZ (t+R), R (R), E 3, [Fj(R),J(R),S(R),US,E(R),NZ]
Meret, F (Tarbes) 1940 B
Mericq, S (Agen) 1959 I, 1960 S, E, W, 1961 I
Merle, O (Grenoble, Montferrand) 1993 SA 1,2, R 2, A 1,2, 1994 I, W, E, S, C 1, NZ 1,2, C 2, 1995 W, I, R 1, [Tg, S, I, SA, E], It, R 2, Arg, NZ 1,2, 1996 E, S, R, Arg 1,2, W 2, SA 2, 1997 I, W, E, S, It 1, R 1, A 1,2, It 2, R 2, SA 1(R),2
Merquey, J (Toulon)1950 S, I, E, W
Mesnel, F (RCF) 1986 NZ 2(R),3, 1987 W, E, S, I, [S, Z, Fj, A, NZ], R, 1988 E, Arg 1,2,3,4, R, 1989 I, W, E, S, NZ 1, A 1,2, 1990 E, S, I, A 2,3, NZ 1,2, 1991 S, I, W 1, E, R, US 1,2, W 2, [R, Fj, C, E], 1992 W, E, S, I, SA 1,2, 1993 E (R), W, 1995 I, R 1, [Iv, E]
Mesny, P (RCF, Grenoble) 1979 NZ 1,2, 1980 SA, R, 1981 I, W (R), A 1,2, R, NZ 1,2, 1982 I, Arg 1,2
Meyer, G-S (Périgueux) 1960 S, E, It, R, Arg 2
Meynard, J (Cognac) 1954 Arg 1, 1956 Cz
Mias, L (Mazamet) 1951 S, I, E, W, 1952 I, SA, W, E, It, 1953 S, I, W, It, 1954 S, I, NZ, W, 1957 R 2, 1958 S, E, A, W, I, SA 1,2, 1959 S, It, W, I Michalak, F (Toulouse) 2001 SA 3(R), A, Fj (R), 2002 It, A 1,2, 2003 It, W, Arg 2(R), NZ, R, E 2, [Fj,J,S,I,E,NZ(R)], 2004 I,W,S,E,A,Arg,NZ, 2005 S(R),E(R),W(R),I(R), It(R), SA1, 2, A1,2,C,Tg(R),SA3, 2006 S,I,It,E,W, 2007 E2(R),3, [Arg1(t&R),Nm,I, NZ(R), E(R), Arg 2]
Mignardi, A (Agen) 2007 NZ1,2
Mignoni, P (Béziers, Clermont-Auvergne)) 1997 R 2(R), Arg (t), 1999 R (R), WS, NZ 1, W 2(R), [C, Nm], 2002 W, E (R), I (R), Arg, A 2(R), 2005 S,It(R),C(R), 2006 R, 2007 It, I,W1,E1(R),S,E2,3(R),W2, [Arg 1,Gg,Arg 2(R)]
Milhères, C (Biarritz) 2001 E
Milliand, P (Grenoble) 1936 G 2, 1937 G, It
Millo-Chlusky, R (Toulouse) 2005 SA1
Milloud, O (Bourgoin) 2000 R (R), 2001 NZ, 2002 W (R), E (R), 2003 It (R), W (R), Arg 1, R (R), E 2(t+R),3, [J, S(R), US,I(R),E(R)], 2004 US,C(R),A,Arg,NZ(R), 2005 S(R), E(R), W(R), SA1,2(R),A1,2,C(R),Tg,SA3,2006 S(R), I, It, E(R), W(R), NZ1(R), 2,Arg, 2007 It,I(R),W1,E1,S,E2,3, [Arg 1,I, Gg,NZ,E]
Minjat, R (Lyon) 1945 B 1
Miorin, H (Toulouse) 1996 R, SA 1, 1997 I, W, E, S, It 1, 2000 It (R), R (R)

Mir, J-H (Lourdes) 1967 R, 1968 I
Mir, J-P (Lourdes) 1967 A
Modin, R (Brive) 1987 [Z]
Moga, A-M-A (Bègles) 1945 B 1,2, W, 1946 B, I, K, W, 1947 S, I, W, E, 1948 I, A, S, W, E, 1949 S, I, E, W, Arg 1,2
Mola, U (Dax, Castres) 1997 S (R), 1999 R (R), WS, Tg (R), NZ 1, W 2, [C, Nm, Fj, Arg (R), NZ 2(R), A (R)]
Mommejat, B (Cahors, Albi) 1958 It, I, SA 1,2, 1959 S, E, It, W, I, 1960 S, E, I, R, 1962 S, E, W, I, It, R, 1963 S, I, W
Moncla, F (RCF, Pau) 1956 Cz, 1957 I, E, W, It, R 1, 1958 SA 1,2, 1959 S, E, It, W, I, 1960 S, E, W, I, It, R, Arg 1,2,3, 1961 S, SA, E, W, It, I, NZ 1,2,3
Moni, C (Nice, SF) 1996 R, 2000 A, NZ 1,2, 2001 S, I, It, W
Monié, R (Perpignan) 1956 Cz, 1957 E
Monier, R (SBUC) 1911 I, 1912 S
Monniot, M (RCF) 1912 W, E
Montade, A (Perpignan) 1925 I, NZ, S, W, 1926 W
Montanella, F (Auch) 2007 NZ1(R)
Montlaur, P (Agen) 1992 E (R), 1994 S (R)
Moraitis, B (Toulon) 1969 E, W
Morel, A (Grenoble) 1954 Arg 2
Morere, J (Toulouse) 1927 E, G 1, 1928 S, A
Moscato, V (Bègles) 1991 R, US 1, 1992 W, E
Mougeot, C (Bègles) 1992 W, E, Arg
Mouniq, P (Toulouse) 1911 S, E, W, I,1912 I, E, 1913 S, SA, E
Moure, H (SCUF) 1908 E
Moureu, P (Béziers) 1920 I, US, 1921 W, E, I, 1922 S, W, I, 1923 S, W, E, I, 1924 S, I, E, W, 1925 E
Mournet, A (Bagnères) 1981 A 1(R)
Mouronval, F (SF) 1909 I
Muhr, A H (RCF) 1906 NZ, E, 1907 E
Murillo, G (Dijon) 1954 It, Arg 1

Nallet, L (Bourgoin, Castres) 2000 R, 2001 E, SA 1(R),2(R), NZ, SA 3(R), A (R), Fj (R), 2003 NZ, 2005 A2(R), C, Tg(R),SA3, 2006 I(R),It(R),E(R),W(R),R,SA(R),NZ1(R),2,Arg, 2007 It,I,W1,E1,S,E3(R), [Nm,I(R),Gg,Arg 2]
Namur, R (Toulon) 1931 E, G
Noble, J-C (La Voulte) 1968 E, W, Cz, NZ 3, A, R
Normand, A (Toulouse) 1957 R 1
Novès, G (Toulouse) 1977 NZ 1,2, R, 1978 W, R, 1979 I, W
Ntamack, E (Toulouse) 1994 W, C 1, NZ 1,2, C 2, 1995 W, I, R 1, [Tg, S, I, SA, E], It, R 2, Arg, NZ 1,2, 1996 E, S, I, W 1, R (R), Arg 1,2, W 2, 1997 I, 1998 Arg 3, 1999 I, W 1, E, S, WS, NZ 1, W 2(R), [C (R), Nm, Fj, Arg, NZ 2, A], 2000 W, E, S, I, It
Ntamack F (Colomiers) 2001 SA 3
Nyanga, Y (Béziers, Toulouse) 2004 US,C, 2005 S(R),E(R),W,I,It,SA1,2,A1(R),2, C(t&R),Tg,SA3, 2006 S,I,It,E,W, 2007 E2(R),3, [Nm,I(R),Gg,Arg 2]

Olibeau, O (Perpignan) 2007 NZ1(R),2(R)
Olive, D (Montferrand) 1951 I, 1952 I
Ondarts, P (Biarritz O) 1986 NZ 3, 1987 W, E, S, I, [S, Z, Fj, A, NZ], R, 1988 E, I, W, Arg 1,2,3,4, R, 1989 I, W, E, NZ 1,2, A 2, 1990 W, E, S, I, R (R), NZ 1,2, 1991 S, I, W 1, E, US 2, W 2, [R, Fj, C, E]
Orso, J-C (Nice, Toulon) 1982 Arg 1,2, 1983 E, S, A 1, 1984 E (R), S, NZ 1, 1985 I (R), W, 1988 I
Othats, J (Dax) 1960 Arg 2,3
Ouedraogo, F (Montpellier) 2007 NZ2(R)
Ougier, S (Toulouse) 1992 R, Arg 1, 1993 E (R), 1997 It 1

Paco, A (Béziers) 1974 Arg 1,2, R, SA 1,2, 1975 W, E, Arg 1,2, R, 1976 S, I, W, E, US, A 1,2, R, 1977 W, E, S, I, NZ 1,2, R, 1978 E, S, I, W, R, 1979 I, W, E, S, 1980 W
Palat, J (Perpignan) 1938 G 2
Palmié, M (Béziers) 1975 SA 1,2, Arg 1,2, R, 1976 S, I, W, E, US, 1977 W, E, S, I, Arg 1,2, NZ 1,2, R, 1978 E, S, I, W
Paoli, R (see Simonpaoli)
Paparemborde, R (Pau) 1975 SA 1,2, Arg 1,2, R, 1976 S, I, W, E, US, A 1,2, R, 1977 W, E, S, I, Arg 1, NZ 1,2, 1978 E, S, I, W, R, 1979 I, W, E, S, NZ 1,2, R, 1980 W, E, S, SA, R, 1981 S, I, W, E, A 1,2, R, NZ 1,2, 1982 W, I, R, Arg 1,2 1983 E, S, I, W
Papé, P (Bourgoin, Castres) 2004 I,It,W,S,E,C,NZ(R), 2005 I(R),It(R),SA1,2,A1, 2006 NZ1,2, 2007 It(R),I,S(R),NZ1,2
Pardo, L (Hendaye) 1924 I, E
Pardo, L (Bayonne) 1980 SA, R, 1981 S, I, W, E, A 1, 1982 W, E, S, 1983 A 1(R), 1985 S, I, Arg 2
Pargade, J-H (Lyon U) 1953 It
Paries, L (Biarritz O) 1968 SA 2, R, 1970 S, I, W, 1975 E, S, I
Pascalin, P (Mont-de-Marsan) 1950 I, E, W, 1951 S, I, E, W
Pascarel, J-R (TOEC) 1912 W, E, 1913 S, SA, E, I
Pascot, J (Perpignan) 1922 S, E, I, 1923 S, 1926 I, 1927 G 2
Paul, R (Montferrand) 1940 B
Pauthe, G (Graulhet) 1956 E
Pebeyre, E-J (Fumel, Brive) 1945 W, 1946 I, K, W, 1947 S, I, W, E
Pebeyre, M (Vichy, Montferrand) 1970 E, R, 1971 I, SA 1,2, A 1, 1973 W
Péclier, A (Bourgoin) 2004 US,C
Pecune, J (Tarbes) 1974 W, E, S, 1975 Arg 1,2, R, 1976 I, W, E, US
Pedeutour, P (Begles) 1980 I
Pellissier, L (RCF) 1928 A, I, E, G, W
Pelous, F (Dax, Toulouse) 1995 R 2, Arg, NZ 1,2, 1996 E, S, I, R (R), Arg 1,2, W 2, SA 1,2, 1997 I, W, E, S, It 1, R 1, A 1,2, It 2, R 2, Arg, SA 1,2(R), 1998 E, S, I, W, Arg 1,2, Fj, Arg 3, A, 1999 I, W 1, E, R (R), WS, Tg (R), NZ 1, W 2, [C, Nm, Fj, NZ 2, A], 2000 W, E, S, I, It, A, NZ 1,2, 2001 S, I, It, W, E, 2002 It (R), W (R), E (R), S, I, Arg, A 1,2, SA, NZ, C, 2003 E 1, S, I, It, W, R, E 2,3(R), [Fj,J,S,I,E,NZ(R)], 2004 I,It,W,S,E,US,C, A,Arg,NZ, 2005 S,E,W,I,It,A2, 2006 S,I,It,E,W,R,SA,NZ1, 2007 E2,3,W2(R), [Arg1, Nm(R),Gg(R),NZ,E]
Penaud, A (Brive, Toulouse) 1992 W, E, S, I, R, Arg 1,2, SA 1,2, Arg, 1993 R 1, SA 1,2, R 2, A 1,2, 1994 I, W, E, 1995 NZ 1,2, 1996 S, R, Arg 1,2, W 2, 1997 I, E, R 1, A 2, 2000 W (R), It
Périé, M (Toulon) 1996 E, S, I (R)
Peron, P (RCF) 1975 SA 1,2
Perrier, P (Bayonne) 1982 W, E, S, I (R)
Pesteil, J-P (Béziers) 1975 SA 1, 1976 A 2, R
Petit, C (Lorrain) 1931 W
Peyrelade, H (Tarbes) 1940 B
Peyrelongue, J (Biarritz) 2004 It,S(R),C(R),A(R),Arg(R),NZ
Peyroutou, G (Périgueux) 1911 S, E
Phliponeau, J-F (Montferrand) 1973 W, I
Piazza, A (Montauban) 1968 NZ 1, A
Picard, T (Montferrand) 1985 Arg 2, 1986 R 1(R), Arg 2
Pierre, J (Bourgoin) 2007 NZ1,2
Pierrot, G (Pau) 1914 I, W, E
Pilon, J (Périgueux) 1949 E, 1950 E
Piqué, J (Pau) 1961 NZ 2,3, A, 1962 S, It, 1964 NZ, E, W, It, I, SA, Fj, R, 1965 S, I, E, W, It
Piquemal, M (Tarbes) 1927 I, S, 1929 I, G, 1930 S, I, E, G, W
Piquiral, E (RCF) 1924 S, I, E, W, R, US, 1925 E, 1926 S, I, E, W, M, 1927 I, S, W, E, G 1,2, 1928 E
Piteu, R (Pau) 1921 S, W, E, I, 1922 S, E, W, I, 1923 E, 1924 E, 1925 I, NZ, W, E, 1926 E
Plantefol, A (RCF) 1967 SA 2,3,4, NZ, R, 1968 E, W, Cz, NZ 2, 1969 E, W
Plantey, S (RCF) 1961 A, 1962 It
Podevin, G (SF) 1913 W, I
Poeydebasque, F (Bayonne) 1914 I, W
Poirier, A (SCUF) 1907 E
Poitrenaud, C (Toulouse) 2001 SA 3, A, Fj, 2003 E 1, S, I, It, W, Arg 1, NZ, E 3, [J,US, E(R),NZ], 2004 E(R), US, C, Arg(R), NZ, 2006 R, 2007 It,I,W1,E1,S,E2,3, [Nm,I,Gg,Arg 2]
Pomathios, M (Agen, Lyon U, Bourg) 1948 I, A, S, W, E, 1949 S, I, E, W, Arg 1,2, 1950 S, I, W, 1951 S, I, E, W, 1952 W, E, 1953 S, I, W, 1954 S
Pons, P (Toulouse) 1920 S, E, W, 1921 S, W, 1922 S
Porcu, C (Agen) 2002 Arg (R), A 1,2(R)
Porra, M (Lyon) 1931 I
Porthault, A (RCF) 1951 S, E, W, 1952 I, 1953 S, I, It
Portolan, C (Toulouse) 1986 A, 1989 I, E
Potel, A (Begles) 1932 G
Poux, J-B (Narbonne, Toulouse) 2001 Fj (R), 2002 S, I (R), Arg, A 1(R),2(R), 2003 E 3, [Fj,J,US,NZ], 2007 E2,3,W2(R), [Nm,I(R),Gg,NZ(R),E(R),Arg 2] Prat, J (Lourdes) 1945 B 1,2, W, 1946 B, I, K, W, 1947 S, I, W, E, 1948 I, A, S, W, E, 1949 S, I, E, W, Arg 1,2, 1950 S, I, E, W, 1951 S, E, W, 1952 S, I, SA, W, E, It, 1953 S, I, E, W, It, 1954 S, I, NZ, W, E, It, 1955 S, I, E, W, It

Prat, M (Lourdes) 1951 I, 1952 S, I, SA, W, E, 1953 S, I, E, 1954 I, NZ, W, E, It, 1955 S, I, E, W, It, 1956 I, W, It, Cz, 1957 S, I, W, It, R 1, 1958 A, W, I
Prevost, A (Albi) 1926 M, 1927 I, S, W
Prin-Clary, J (Cavaillon, Brive) 1945 B 1,2, W, 1946 B, I, K, W, 1947 S, I, W
Privat, T (Béziers, Clermont-Auvergne) 2001 SA 3, A, Fj, 2002 It, W, S (R), SA (R), 2003 [NZ], 2005 SA2,A1(R)
Puech, L (Toulouse) 1920 S, E, I, 1921 E, I
Puget, M (Toulouse) 1961 It, 1966 S, I, It, 1967 SA 1,3,4, NZ, 1968 Cz, NZ 1,2, SA 1,2, R, 1969 E, R, 1970 W
Puig, A (Perpignan) 1926 S, E
Pujol, A (SOE Toulouse) 1906 NZ
Pujolle, M (Nice) 1989 B, A 1, 1990 S, I, R, A 1,2, NZ 2

Quaglio, A (Mazamet) 1957 R 2, 1958 S, E, A, W, I, SA 1,2, 1959 S, E, It, W, I
Quilis, A (Narbonne) 1967 SA 1,4, NZ, 1970 R, 1971 I

Rabadan, P (SF) 2004 US(R),C(R)
Ramis, R (Perpignan) 1922 E, I, 1923 W
Rancoule, H (Lourdes, Toulon, Tarbes) 1955 E, W, It, 1958 A, W, It, I, SA 1, 1959 S, It, W, 1960 I, It, R, Arg 1,2, 1961 SA, E, W, It, NZ 1,2, 1962 S, E, W, I, It
Rapin, A (SBUC) 1938 R
Raymond, F (Toulouse) 1925 S, 1927 W, 1928 I
Raynal, F (Perpignan) 1935 G, 1936 G 1,2, 1937 G, It
Raynaud, F (Carcassonne) 1933 G
Raynaud, M (Narbonne) 1999 W 1, E (R)
Razat, J-P (Agen) 1962 R, 1963 S, I, R
Rebujent, R (RCF) 1963 E
Revailler, D (Graulhet) 1981 S, I, W, E, A 1,2, R, NZ 1,2, 1982 W, S, I, R, Arg 1
Revillon, J (RCF) 1926 I, E, 1927 S
Ribère, E (Perpignan, Quillan) 1924 I, 1925, I, NZ, S, 1926 S, I, W, M, 1927 I, S, W, E, G 1,2, 1928 S, A, I, E, G, W, 1929 I, E, G, 1930 S, I, E, W, 1931 I, S, W, E, G, 1932 G, 1933 G
Rives, J-P (Toulouse, RCF) 1975 E, S, I, Arg 1,2, R, 1976 S, I, W, E, US, A 1,2, R, 1977 W, E, S, I, Arg 1,2, R, 1978 E, S, I, W, R, 1979 I, W, E, S, NZ 1,2, R, 1980 W, E, S, I, SA, 1981 S, I, W, E, A 2, 1982 W, E, S, I, R, 1983 E, S, I, W, A 1,2, R, 1984 I, W, E, S
Rochon, A (Montferrand) 1936 G 1
Rodrigo, M (Mauléon) 1931 I, W
Rodriguez, L (Mont-de-Marsan, Montferrand, Dax) 1981 A 1,2, R, NZ 1,2, 1982 W, E, S, I, R, 1983 E, S, 1984 I, NZ 1,2, R, 1985 E, S, I, W, 1986 Arg 1, A, R 2, NZ 2,3, 1987 W, E, S, I, [S, Z, Fj, A, NZ], R, 1988 E, S, I, W, Arg 1,2,3,4, R, 1989 I, E, S, NZ 1,2, B, A 1, 1990 W, E, S, I, NZ 1
Rogé, L (Béziers) 1952 It, 1953 E, W, It, 1954 S, Arg 1,2, 1955 S, I, 1956 W, It, E, 1957 S, 1960 S, E
Rollet, J (Bayonne) 1960 Arg 3, 1961 NZ 3, A, 1962 It, 1963 I
Romero, H (Montauban) 1962 S, E, W, I, It, R, 1963 E
Romeu, J-P (Montferrand) 1972 R, 1973 S, NZ, E, W, I, R, 1974 W, E, S, Arg 1,2, R, SA 1,2(R), 1975 W, SA 2, Arg 1,2, R, 1976 S, I, W, E, US, 1977 W, E, S, I, Arg 1,2, NZ 1,2, R
Roques, A (Cahors) 1958 A, W, It, I, SA 1,2, 1959 S, E, W, I, 1960 S, E, W, I, It, Arg 1,2,3, 1961 S, SA, E, W, It, I, 1962 S, E, W, I, It, 1963 S
Roques, J-C (Brive) 1966 S, I, It, R
Rossignol, J-C (Brive) 1972 A 2
Rouan, J (Narbonne) 1953 S, I
Roucaries, G (Perpignan) 1956 S
Rouffia, L (Narbonne) 1945 B 2, W, 1946 W, 1948 I
Rougerie, A (Montferrand, Clermont-Auvergne) 2001 SA 3, A, Fj (R), 2002 It, W, E, S, I, Arg, A 1,2, 2003 E 1, S, I, It, W, Arg 1,2, NZ, R, E 2,3(R), [Fj,J,S,I,E], 2004 US,C,A, Arg,NZ, 2005 S,W,A2,C,Tg,SA3, 2006 I,It,E,W,NZ1,2, 2007 E2,W2, [Arg1,Nm(R),I(R), Gg,Arg 2]
Rougerie, J (Montferrand) 1973 J
Rougé-Thomas, P (Toulouse) 1989 NZ 1,2
Roujas, F (Tarbes) 1910 I
Roumat, O (Dax) 1989 NZ 2(R), B, 1990 W, E, S, I, R, A 1,2,3, NZ 1,2, 1991 S, I, W 1, E, R, US 1, W 2, [R, Fj, C, E], 1992 W (R), E (R), S, I, SA 1,2, Arg, 1993 E, S, I, W, R 1, SA 1,2, R 2, A 1,2, 1994 I, W, E, C 1, NZ 1,2, C 2, 1995 W, E, S, [Iv, S, I, SA, E], 1996 E, S, I, W 1, Arg 1,2
Rousie, M (Villeneuve) 1931 S, G, 1932 G, 1933 G
Rousset, G (Béziers) 1975 SA 1, 1976 US
Rué, J-B (Agen) 2002 SA (R), C (R), 2003 E 1(R), S (R), It (R), W (R), Arg 1,2(R)
Ruiz, A (Tarbes) 1968 SA 2, R
Rupert, J-J (Tyrosse) 1963 R, 1964 S, Fj, 1965 E, W, It, 1966 S, I, E, W, It, 1967 It, R, 1968 S

Sadourny, J-L (Colomiers) 1991 W 2(R), [C (R)], 1992 E (R), S, I, Arg 1(R),2, SA 1,2, 1993 R 1, SA 1,2, R 2, A 1,2, 1994 I, W, E, S, C 1, NZ 1,2, C 2, 1995 W, E, S, I, R 1, [Tg, S, I, SA, E], It, R 2, Arg, NZ 1,2, 1996 E, S, I, W 1, Arg 1,2, W 2, SA 1,2, 1997 I, W, E, S, It 1, R 1, A 1,2, It 2, R 2, Arg, SA 1,2, 1998 E, S, I, W, 1999 R, Tg, NZ 1(R), 2000 NZ 2, 2001 It, W, E
Sagot, P (SF) 1906 NZ, 1908 E, 1909 W
Sahuc, A (Métro) 1945 B 1,2
Sahuc, F (Toulouse) 1936 G 2
Saint-André, P (Montferrand, Gloucester) 1990 R, A 3, NZ 1,2, 1991 I (R), W 1, E, US 1,2, W 2, [R, Fj, C, E], 1992 W, E, S, I, R, Arg 1,2, SA 1,2, 1993 E, S, I, W, SA 1,2, A 1,2, 1994 I, W, E, S, C 1, NZ 1,2, C 2, 1995 W, E, S, I, R 1, [Tg, Iv, S, I, SA, E], It, R 2, Arg, NZ 1,2, 1996 E, S, I, W 1, R, Arg 1,2, W 2, 1997 It 1,2, R 2, Arg, SA 1,2
Saisset, O (Béziers) 1971 R, 1972 S, I 1, A 1,2, 1973 S, NZ, E, W, I, J, R, 1974 I, Arg 2, SA 1,2, 1975 W
Salas, P (Narbonne) 1979 NZ 1,2, R, 1980 W, E, 1981 A 1, 1982 Arg 2
Salinié, R (Perpignan) 1923 E
Sallefranque, M (Dax) 1981 A 2, 1982 W, E, S
Salut, J (TOEC) 1966 R, 1967 S, 1968 I, E, Cz, NZ 1, 1969 I
Samatan, R (Agen) 1930 S, I, E, G, W, 1931 I, S, W, E, G
Sanac, A (Perpignan) 1952 It, 1953 S, I, 1954 E, 1956 Cz, 1957 S, I, E, W, It
Sangalli, F (Narbonne) 1975 I, SA 1,2, 1976 S, A 1,2, R, 1977 W, E, S, I, Arg 1,2, NZ 1,2
Sanz, H (Narbonne) 1988 Arg 3,4, R, 1989 A 2, 1990 S, I, R, A 1,2, NZ 2, 1991 W 2
Sappa, M (Nice) 1973 J, R, 1977 R
Sarrade, R (Pau) 1929 I
Sarraméa, O (Castres) 1999 R, WS (R), Tg, NZ 1
Saux, J-P (Pau) 1960 W, It, Arg 1,2, 1961 SA, E, W, It, I, NZ 1,2,3, A, 1962 S, E, W, I, It, 1963 S, I, E, It
Savitsky, M (La Voulte) 1969 R
Savy, M (Montferrand) 1931 I, S, W, E, 1936 G 1
Sayrou, J (Perpignan) 1926 W, M, 1928 E, G, W, 1929 S, W, E, G
Scohy, R (BEC) 1931 S, W, E, G
Sébedio, J (Tarbes) 1913 S, E, 1914 I, 1920 S, I, US, 1922 S, E, 1923 S
Seguier, N (Béziers) 1973 J, R
Seigne, L (Agen, Merignac) 1989 B, A 1, 1990 NZ 1, 1993 E, S, I, W, R 1, A 1,2, 1994 S, C 1, 1995 E (R), S
Sella, P (Agen) 1982 R, Arg 1,2, 1983 E, S, I, W, A 1,2, R, 1984 I, W, E, S, NZ 1,2, R, 1985 E, S, I, W, Arg 1,2, 1986 S, I, W, E, R 1, Arg 1,2, A, NZ 1, R 2, NZ 2,3, 1987 W, E, S, I, [S, R, Z (R), Fj, A, NZ], 1988 E, S, I, W, Arg 1,2,3,4, R, 1989 I, W, E, S, NZ 1,2, B, A 1,2, 1990 W, E, S, I, A 1,2,3, 1991 W 1, E, R, US 1,2, W 2, [Fj, C, E], 1992 W, E, S, I, Arg, 1993 E, S, I, W, R 1, SA 1,2, R 2, A 1,2, 1994 I, W, E, S, C 1, NZ 1,2, C 2, 1995 W, E, S, I, [Tg, S, I, SA, E]
Semmartin, J (SCUF) 1913 W, I
Senal, G (Béziers) 1974 Arg 1,2, R, SA 1,2, 1975 W
Sentilles, J (Tarbes) 1912 W, E, 1913 S, SA
Serin, L (Béziers) 1928 E, 1929 W, E, G, 1930 S, I, E, G, W, 1931 I, W, E
Serre, P (Perpignan) 1920 S, E
Serrière, P (RCF) 1986 A, 1987 R, 1988 E
Servat, W (Toulouse) 2004 I,It,W,S,E,US,C,A,Arg,NZ 2005 S,E(R),W(R),It(R),SA1(R), 2
Servole, L (Toulon) 1931 I, S, W, E, G, 1934 G, 1935 G
Sicart, N (Perpignan) 1922 I
Sillières, J (Tarbes) 1968 R, 1970 S, I, 1971 S, I, E, 1972 E, W
Siman, M (Montferrand) 1948 E, 1949 S, 1950 S, I, E, W
Simon, S (Bègles) 1991 R, US 1
Simonpaoli, R (SF) 1911 I, 1912 I, S
Sitjar, M (Agen) 1964 W, It, I, R, 1965 It, R, 1967 A, E, It, W, I, SA 1,2

Skrela, D (Colomiers, SF) 2001 NZ, 2007 It,I,W1,E1,2,3(R),W2, [Arg 1,Gg(R),Arg 2]
Skrela, J-C (Toulouse) 1971 SA 2, A 1,2, 1972 I 1(R), E, W, I 2, A 1, 1973 W, J, R, 1974 W, E, S, Arg 1, R, 1975 W (R), E, S, I, SA 1,2, Arg 1,2, R, 1976 S, I, W, E, US, A 1,2, R, 1977 W, E, S, I, Arg 1,2, NZ 1,2, R, 1978 E, S, I, W
Soler, M (Quillan) 1929 G
Soro, R (Lourdes, Romans) 1945 B 1,2, W, 1946 B, I, K, 1947 S, I, W, E, 1948 I, A, S, W, E, 1949 S, I, E, W, Arg 1,2
Sorondo, L-M (Montauban) 1946 K, 1947 S, I, W, E, 1948 I
Soulette, C (Béziers, Toulouse) 1997 R 2, 1998 S (R), I (R), W (R), Arg 1,2, Fj, 1999 W 2(R), [C (R), Nm (R), Arg, NZ 2, A]
Soulié, E (CASG) 1920 E, I, US, 1921 S, E, I, 1922 E, W, I
Sourgens, J (Bègles) 1926 M
Sourgens, O (Bourgoin) 2007 NZ2
Souverbie, J-M (Bègles) 2000 R
Spanghero, C (Narbonne) 1971 E, W, SA 1,2, A 1,2, R, 1972 S, E, W, I 2, A 1,2, 1974 I, W, E, S, R, SA 1, 1975 E, S, I
Spanghero, W (Narbonne) 1964 SA, Fj, R, 1965 S, I, E, W, It, R, 1966 S, I, E, W, It, R, 1967 S, A, E, SA 1,2,3,4, NZ, 1968 S, I, E, W, NZ 1,2,3, A, SA 1,2, R, 1969 S, I, W, 1970 R, 1971 E, W, SA 1, 1972 E, I 2, A 1,2, R, 1973 S, NZ, E, W, I
Stener, G (PUC) 1956 S, I, E, 1958 SA 1,2
Struxiano, P (Toulouse) 1913 W, I, 1920 S, E, W, I, US
Sutra, G (Narbonne) 1967 SA 2, 1969 W, 1970 S, I
Swierczinski, C (Bègles) 1969 E, 1977 Arg 2
Szarzewski, D (Béziers, SF) 2004 C(R), 2005 I(R),A1,2, SA3, 2006 S,E(R),W(t&R), R(R),SA,NZ1,2(R),Arg(R), 2007 It(R),E2(R),W2,[Arg1(R),Nm,I(R),Gg(R),NZ(R),E(R)]

Tabacco, P (SF) 2001 SA 1,2, NZ, SA 3, A, Fj, 2003 It (R), W (R), Arg 1, NZ, E 2(R),3, [S(R),US,I(R),NZ], 2004 US, 2005 S
Tachdjian, M (RCF) 1991 S, I, E
Taffary, M (RCF) 1975 W, E, S, I
Taillantou, J (Pau) 1930 I, G, W
Tarricq, P (Lourdes) 1958 A, W, It, I
Tavernier, H (Toulouse) 1913 I
Techoueyres, W (SBUC) 1994 E, S, 1995 [Iv]
Terreau, M-M (Bourg) 1945 W, 1946 B, I, K, W, 1947 S, I, W, E, 1948 I, A, W, E, 1949 S, Arg 1,2, 1951 S
Theuriet, A (SCUF) 1909 E, W, 1910 S, 1911 W, 1913 E
Thevenot, M (SCUF) 1910 W, E, I
Thierry, R (RCF) 1920 S, E, W, US
Thiers, P (Montferrand) 1936 G 1,2, 1937 G, It, 1938 G 1,2, 1940 B, 1945 B, 1,2
Thiéry, B (Bayonne) 2007 NZ1,2(R)
Thion, J (Perpignan, Biarritz) 2003 Arg 1,2, NZ, R, E 2, [Fj,S,I,E], 2004 A,Arg,NZ 2005 S,E,W,I,It,A2,C,Tg,SA3, 2006 S,I,It,E,W,R(R),SA, 2007 It,I(R),W1,E1,S,E2,3,W2, [Arg 1,I,Gg,NZ,E,Arg 2]
Tignol, P (Toulouse) 1953 S, I
Tilh, H (Nantes) 1912 W, E, 1913 S, SA, E, W
Tolot, J-L (Agen) 1987 [Z]
Tordo, J-F (Nice) 1991 US 1(R), 1992 W, E, S, I, R, Arg 1,2, SA 1, Arg, 1993 E, S, I, W, R 1
Torossian, F (Pau) 1997 R 1
Torreilles, S (Perpignan) 1956 S
Tournaire, F (Narbonne, Toulouse) 1995 It, 1996 I, W 1, R, Arg 1,2(R), W 2, SA 1,2, 1997 I, E, S, It 1, R 1, A 1,2, It 2, R 2, Arg, SA 1,2, 1998 E, S, I, W, Arg 1,2, Fj, Arg 3, A, 1999 I, W 1, E, S, R (R), WS, NZ 1, [C, Nm, Fj, Arg, NZ 2, A], 2000 W, E, S, I, It, A (R)
Tourte, R (St Girons) 1940 B
Traille, D (Pau, Biarritz) 2001 SA 3, A, Fj, 2002 It, W, E, S, I, Arg, A 1,2, SA, NZ, C, 2003 E 1, S, I, It, W, Arg, 1,2, NZ, R, E 2, [Fj(R),J,S(R),US,NZ], 2004 I,It,W,S,E, 2005 S,E,W,It(R),SA1(R),2,A1(R), 2006 It,E,W,R,SA,NZ1,2,Arg, 2007 S(R),E2,3,W2(R), [Arg 1,Nm,I,NZ,E]
Trillo, J (Bègles) 1967 SA 3,4, NZ, R, 1968 S, I, NZ 1,2,3, A, 1969 I, E, W, R, 1970 E, R, 1971 S, I, SA 1,2, A 1,2, 1972 S, A 1,2, R, 1973 S, E
Triviaux, R (Cognac) 1931 E, G
Tucco-Chala, M (PUC) 1940 B

Ugartemendia, J-L (St Jean-de-Luz) 1975 S, I

Vaills, G (Perpignan) 1928 A, 1929 G
Valbon, L (Brive) 2004 US, 2005 S(R), 2006 S,E(R), 2007 NZ1(R)
Vallot, C (SCUF) 1912 S
Van Heerden, A (Tarbes) 1992 E, S
Vannier, M (RCF, Chalon) 1953 W, 1954 S, I, Arg 1,2, 1955 S, I, E, W, It, 1956 S, I, W, It, E, 1957 S, I, E, W, It, R 1,2, 1958 S, E, A, W, It, I, 1960 S, E, W, I, It, R, Arg 1,3, 1961 SA, E, W, It, I, NZ 1, A
Vaquer, F (Perpignan) 1921 S, W, 1922 W
Vaquerin, A (Béziers) 1971 R, 1972 S, I 1, A 1, 1973 S, 1974 W, E, S, Arg 1,2, R, SA 1,2, 1975 W, E, S, I, 1976 US, A 1(R),2, R, 1977 Arg 2, 1979 W, E, 1980 S, I
Vareilles, C (SF) 1907 E, 1908 E, W, 1910 S, E
Varenne, F (RCF) 1952 S
Varvier, T (RCF) 1906 E, 1909 E, W, 1911 E, W, 1912 I
Vassal, G (Carcassonne) 1938 R, G 2
Vaysse, J (Albi) 1924 US, 1926 M
Vellat, E (Grenoble) 1927 I, E, G 1,2, 1928 A
Venditti, D (Bourgoin, Brive) 1996 R, SA 1(R),2, 1997 I, W, E, S, R 1, A 1, SA 2, 2000 W (R), E, S, It (R)
Vergé, L (Bègles) 1993 R 1(R)
Verger, A (SF) 1927 W, E, G 1, 1928 I, E, G, W
Verges, S-A (SF) 1906 NZ, E, 1907 E
Vermeulen, E (Brive, Montferrand, Clermont-Auvergne) 2001 SA 1(R),2(R), 2003 NZ, 2006 NZ1,2,Arg, 2007 W1,S(R)
Viard, G (Narbonne) 1969 W, 1970 S, R, 1971 S, I
Viars, S (Brive) 1992 W, E, I, R, Arg 1,2, SA 1,2(R), Arg, 1993 R 1, 1994 C 1(R), NZ 1(t), 1995 E (R), [Iv], 1997 R 1(R), A 1(R),2
Vigerie, M (Agen) 1931 W
Vigier, R (Montferrand) 1956 S, W, It, E, Cz, 1957 S, E, W, It, R 1,2, 1958 S, E, A, W, It, I, SA 1,2, 1959 S, E, It, W, I
Vigneau, A (Bayonne) 1935 G
Vignes, C (RCF) 1957 R 1,2, 1958 S, E
Vila, E (Tarbes) 1926 M
Vilagra, J (Vienne) 1945 B 2
Villepreux, P (Toulouse) 1967 It, I, SA 2, NZ, 1968 I, Cz, NZ 1,2,3, A, 1969 S, I, E, W, R, 1970 S, I, W, E, R, 1971 S, I, E, W, A 1,2, R, 1972 S, I 1, E, W, I 2, A 1,2
Viviès, B (Agen) 1978 E, S, I, W, 1980 SA, R, 1981 S, A 1, 1983 A 1(R)
Volot, M (SF) 1945 W, 1946 B, I, K, W

Weller, S (Grenoble) 1989 A 1,2, 1990 A 1, NZ 1
Wolf, J-P (Béziers) 1980 SA, R, 1981 A 2, 1982 E

Yachvili, D (Biarritz) 2002 C (R), 2003 S (R), I, It, W, R (R), E 3, [US,NZ], 2004 I(R), It(R),W(R),S,E, 2005 S(R),E,W,I,It,SA1(R),2,C,Tg, 2006 S(R),I(R),It(R),E,W,SA, NZ1, 2(R),Arg, 2007 E1
Yachvili, M (Tulle, Brive) 1968 E, W, Cz, NZ 3, A, R, 1969 S, I, R, 1971 E, SA 1,2 A 1, 1972 R, 1975 SA 2

Zago, F (Montauban) 1963 I, E

GEORGIA

GEORGIA'S 2006–07 TEST RECORD

OPPONENTS	DATE	VENUE	RESULT
Portgual	11 Nov	H	**Won** 17–3
Portugal	25 Nov	A	**Draw** 11–11
Romania	3 Feb	A	**Won** 20–17
Spain	17 Mar	A	**Lost** 17–31
Russia	24 Mar	H	**Won** 31–12
Czech Republic	7 April	H	**Won** 98–3
Namibia	5 June	N	**Won** 26–18
Emerging Springboks	10 June	N	**Lost** 7–24
Italy A	16 June	N	**Won** 22–20
Argentina	11 Sept	N	**Lost** 3–33 (WC)
Ireland	15 Sept	N	**Lost** 10–14 (WC)
Namibia	26 Sept	N	**Won** 30–0 (WC)
France	30 Sept	N	**Lost** 7–64 (WC)

MOVING TO THE NEXT LEVEL

By Frankie Deges

Warren Little/Getty Images

Georgia were ecstatic with their first win at the World Cup finals, against Namibia.

The story of Georgia in the Rugby World Cup was one that captured the imagination of so many back at home that it meant a huge rush of interest. The biggest coming from the national government, based in Tbilisi, who has found in the game the values that they want pursued by its society.

National president Mikheil Saakashvili said during the World Cup that he was considering building new stadiums in the near future and the full backing of his government should ensure there is sustained growth of the oval game. He also pledged to finance a top-flight competition in recognition of the exposure the IRB Rugby World Cup has given Georgia.

The newest of rugby nations in this World Cup, Georgia only took up the game in the late 1950s and whilst it did not have to fight for survival – the contact part of rugby is something that appeals to the beefy Georgians who have wrestling as one of their biggest sports – it did not grow during the Soviet regime due to the fact it was not an Olympic sport. When independence from the old Soviet regime came in the early

1990s, they began playing as a nation and became an IRB Member Union.

The IRB has earmarked Georgia as a team that can potentially become a big player in the world scene. After a big review – technical, high performance, governance and commercial set-up – it was clear that it was a nation that could make that extra step given assistance and resources.

Their RWC 2007 campaign saw them earn their first ever finals win when they beat Namibia, but they made it very hard for an Argentina team that was on its way to their best ever RWC, came painstakingly close to beating Ireland, got that first win against Namibia and ended with a loss against a France XV needing to win and win good to ensure passage to the quarter-finals.

What was clear that in four years since their previous World Cup, the Georgian Lelos had made sufficient improvement to be considered a happy surprise in a tournament in which the form book confounded the best of critics.

Prior to reaching the tournament, they had a busy 2006–2007, playing nine matches in the build-up to France 2007, including a series win against Portugal in November 2006 that clinched their place in the World Cup. The home game in Tbilisi was won 17–3 whilst the return tie, in Lisbon, ended in a draw 11–11. After that they beat Romania in Bucharest, a city to which they returned later in 2007 to play in the IRB Nations Cup in which they played with great credit, beating future RWC rivals Namibia and Italy A, with a loss to the Emerging Springboks in between.

As the World Cup approached, the intensity of the Lelos preparation grew, with camps in France ensuring the squad was ready for the tournament. France and Georgia have a common link in that most of the best talent to come out of the Eastern European country finds its way to France to further advance in their rugby careers – the strength of the Euro when taken back to Georgia means that many play in the lower divisions of French rugby. As positive as it has been for, roughly, the best 100 Georgian players (a round figure that explains how many actually leave their country to pursue the rugby dream) and the Lelos, the home club scene is deprived of its stars.

There is a lot of pride in wearing the national colours and in representing the nation, and it all came out soon enough in their opening match.

With a squad that had only two home-based players – the other twenty-eight based in France – it all started for them in a nice evening in Lyon against Argentina.

Whilst many believed that Georgia would be an easy win for the South Americans, it was far from that. With their huge bulk and strength, the Lelos took them up front and ensured that everybody knew they were in the tournament to leave a mark. Their huge forwards made an instant impression

Described in some reports as a "piranha team", the Georgians were strong in the forwards and had the able boot of fly-half Merab Kvirikashvili to thank for solid ground advantage for long periods. Needless to say, most of the 40,240 spectators at the Stade Gerland cheered for the red-shirted Georgians which made them even bigger, stronger and actually better.

In the end, in spite of the huge efforts of influential captain Illia Zedginidze, the 33–3 win was a proof of the gap countries such as Georgia still have to reduce with Tier One nations. With 15 survivors of the previous World Cup, the experience would come through later in the tournament.

It didn't take long for that to happen. In a magnificent performance, the Georgians almost completed the most remarkable upset of probably the history of the game. Ireland, who had a dismal tournament, had to work very hard to beat Georgia 14–10. A moral victory of sorts, as the Georgians would have deserved to win the game had they managed to keep the composure in key moments. If anything, the match according to captain Zedginidze was "very inspiring". Unfortunately, the likeable Georgian captain suffered a broken rotula (kneecap) during the match against Ireland, but it is very important that he remains an integral part of the future of the game in his country, in whichever capacity he so decides.

Relaxed, as the lock wanted his team to be and playing for the injured skipper, the Georgians were extremely hungry against Namibia and the prize was a win; solid, conclusive, beyond any doubt. The 30–0 win not only became the first in the country RWC history but one that confirmed their coming of age.

They were stronger in every facet of the game in cold, wet and windy conditions. In the end, they were hungrier than the Namibians and their fans appreciated what they saw – typical Georgian forward play that set up the platform for a good first win. Not only for their capacity to score points but their ability to keep their opponents with a score-less sheet.

Three of everything – three tries, three goals and three penalties for coach Makhaz Cheisvili's team. He said: "This match was not just a victory it was of great importance to us. Everyone really invested in this game, to attain this goal.

"We had this need, this drive that we had to win tonight and we managed to do so."

The focus got somehow lost in the ensuing days as they travelled to Marseille where a French team full of intent awaited, as they needed a win with bonus-point to clinch their place in the quarter finals (which was far from certain when the match kicked-off).

Georgia scored a deserved try in the 70th when replacement forward Zviad Maisuradze barged over 10 minutes from time. Fly half Malkhaz Urjukashvili kicked the conversion, the only points in the 64–7 loss.

The IRB has already been assisting the Georgians and in the near past a new gymnasium was put in place with seminars on how to use the strength and conditioning programmes that were given to the Georgian by the IRB staff.

This gym, to be used by the national teams and the High Performance units, will be and incentive for the more than 3,000 player in the two main rugby centres, Tbilisi and Kutaisi. As well as this, their analysis systems have been put in place by the IRB in the country in what has been a significant investment in the game in the country.

Not every club has access to pitches, which is hampering the growth of the game, but if the promised governmental support arrives, a game with a strong support – when the Lelos played at home against Russia recently, they got some 60,000 spectators – and hard working people ready to give their blood for the cause, Georgia will continue to rise.

As retired captain Zedginidze said: "In the next five years we have to do much more for the internal competition in Georgia. I hope that rugby will become the number one sport in Georgia. Now everybody plays football and for our national team we have to choose 30 people out of less than 500 senior players. If you look at our younger players, we have some very good 11, 12 and 13 year-olds. They're as good as the French or English boys. In the future we will pay more attention to developing that age group so that we can become as strong as the French, English or any of the top sides. That's our objective."

GEORGIA INTERNATIONAL PLAYERS
UP TO 31ST OCTOBER 2007

Compiled By Hugh Copping

Abashidze, V 1998 *It* (R), *Ukr*, *I* 1999 *Tg* (R), *Tg* 2000 *It* (R), *Mor*, *Sp* 2001 *H*, *Pt* (R), *Rus*, *Sp*, *R* 2006 *J* (R)
Abdaladze, N 1997 *Cro*, *De*
Abuseridze, I 2000 *It*, *Pt*, *Mor*, *Sp*, *H*, *R* 2001 *H*, *Pt*, *Rus*, *Sp*, *R* 2002 *Pt*, *Rus*, *Sp* (R), *R* (R), *I*, *Rus* 2003 *Pt*, *Rus*, *CZR*, *R*, *It*, *E*, *Sa*, *SA* (R) 2004 *Rus* 2005 *Pt*, *Ukr*, *R* 2006 *Rus*, *R*, *Pt*, *Ukr*, *J*, *R*, *Sp* (R), *Pt* (R), *Pt* 2007 *R*, *Rus*, *CZR*, *Nm*, *ESp* (R), *ItA*, *Ar*, *I* (R), *Nm*, *F*
Akhvlediani, V 2007 *CZR* (R)
Alania, K 1993 *Lux* 1994 *Swi* 1996 *CZR*, *CZR*, *Rus* 1997 *Pt* (R), *Pol*, *Cro*, *De* 1998 *It* 2001 *H*, *Pt*, *Sp* (R), *F*, *SA* 2002 *H*, *Pt* (R), *Rus* (R), *Sp*, *R*, *I*, *Rus* 2003 *Rus* (R) 2004 *Pt*, *Sp*
Andghuladze, N 1997 *Pol* (R) 2000 *It*, *Pt* (R), *Mor*, *Sp*, *H*, *R* 2004 *Sp* (R), *Rus*, *CZR* (R), *R*
Ashvetia, D 1998 *Ukr* (R) 2005 *Pt* (R) 2006 *R* 2007 *Sp*

Babunashvili, G 1992 *Ukr*, *Ukr*, *Lat* 1993 *Rus*, *Pol*, *Lux* 1996 *CZR*
Bakuradze, Z 1989 *Z* 1990 *Z* 1991 *Ukr*, *Ukr* 1993 *Rus* (R), *Pol* (R)
Baramidze, D 2000 *H* (R)
Barkalaia, O 2002 *I* (R) 2004 *Sp*, *Rus*, *CZR*, *R*, *Ur*, *Ch*, *Rus* (R) 2005 *Pt* (R), *Ukr*, *R*, *CZR*, *Ch* 2006 *Rus*, *R*, *Pt* (R), *Ukr*, *J* (R), *Bb*, *R*, *Sp* 2007 *Nm*, *ItA*, *I*, *F*
Belkania, R 2004 *Sp* (R) 2005 *Ch* 2007 *Sp*, *Rus* (R)
Beriashvili, G 1993 *Rus*, *Pol* 1995 *Ger* (R)
Besselia, M 1991 *Ukr* 1993 *Rus*, *Pol* 1996 *Rus* 1997 *Pt*
Bolgashvili, D 2000 *It*, *Pt* (R), *H* (R), *R* (R) 2001 *H*, *Pt*, *Rus*, *Sp*, *R*, *F*, *SA* 2002 *H*, *Pt*, *Rus*, *I* 2003 *Pt* (R), *Sp*, *Rus* (R), *CZR* (R), *R* (R), *E* (R), *Sa* (R), *SA* 2004 *Rus*, *Ur*, *Ch*, *Rus* (R) 2005 *CZR* (R) 2007 *Sp*
Buguianishvili, G 1996 *CZR*, *Rus* (R) 1997 *Pol* 1998 *It*, *Rus* (R), *I*, *R* 2000 *Sp* (R), *H* (R), *R* (R) 2001 *H* (R), *F* (R), *SA* 2002 *Rus*

Chavleishvili, D 1990 *Z* (R), *Z* 1992 *Ukr*, *Ukr*, *Lat* 1993 *Pol*, *Lux*
Cheishvili, M 1989 *Z* 1990 *Z*, *Z* 1995 *H*
Chikava, I 1993 *Pol*, *Lux* 1994 *Swi* 1995 *Bul*, *Mol*, *H* 1996 *CZR*, *CZR* 1997 *Pol* (R) 1998 *I*
Chikvaidze, R 2004 *Ur*, *Ch* (R)
Chikvinidze, L 1994 *Swi* 1995 *Bul*, *Mol*, *Ger*, *H* 1996 *CZR*, *Rus* (R)
Chkhaidze, G 2002 *H*, *R* (R), *I*, *Rus* (R) 2003 *Pt*, *CZR* (R), *It*, *E*, *SA*, *Ur* 2004 *CZR*, *R* 2006 *Pt* (R), *Ukr* 2007 *R*, *Rus*, *CZR*, *Nm*, *ESp*, *ItA*, *Ar*, *I*, *Nm*, *F*
Chkhenkeli, S 1997 *Pol* (R)
Chkhikvadze, I 2005 *Ch* (R) 2007 *Sp* (R)
Chkonia, I 2007 *ESp*, *ItA*

Dadunashvili, D 2003 *It* (R), *E* (R), *SA*, *Ur* 2004 *Sp*, *Rus*, *CZR*, *R* 2005 *Ch* 2007 *Sp* (R), *Rus*, *CZR*, *Nm*, *ItA* (R)
Datunashvili, L 2004 *Sp* (R) 2005 *Pt* (R), *Ukr* (R), *R* (R), *CZR* (R) 2006 *Rus* (R), *R*, *Pt* (R), *Ukr*, *J*, *Bb*, *CZR* (R), *Pt* (R), *Pt* (R) 2007 *R*, *Rus*, *Nm*, *ESp*, *ItA* (R), *I* (R), *Nm*, *F* (R)
Didebulidze, V 1991 *Ukr* 1994 *Kaz* 1995 *Bul*, *Mol* 1996 *CZR* 1997 *De* (R) 1999 *Tg* (R) 2000 *H* (R) 2001 *H*, *Pt*, *Rus*, *Sp*, *R*, *F*, *SA* 2002 *H*, *Pt*, *Rus* (R), *Sp*, *R*, *I*, *Rus* 2003 *Pt*, *Sp*, *Rus*, *CZR* (R), *R* (R), *It*, *E*, *Sa* (R), *SA* 2004 *Rus* 2005 *Pt* 2006 *R* (R), *R* (R) 2007 *R* (R), *Sp*, *Rus* (R), *CZR*, *Nm*, *ESp* (R), *ItA*, *Ar* (R), *Nm* (R), *F*

Dzagnidze, E 1992 *Ukr*, *Ukr*, *Lat* 1993 *Rus*, *Pol* 1995 *Bul*, *Mol*, *Ger*, *H* 1998 *I*
Dzagnidze, N 1989 *Z* 1990 *Z*, *Z* 1991 *Ukr* 1992 *Ukr*, *Ukr*, *Lat* 1993 *Rus*, *Pol* 1994 *Swi* 1995 *Ger*, *H*
Dzneladze, D 1992 *Ukr* (R), *Lat* (R) 1993 *Lux* 1994 *Kaz*
Dzotsenidze, P 1995 *Ger*, *H* 1997 *Pt*, *Pol*

Elizbarashvili, G 2002 *Rus* (R) 2003 *Sp* (R) 2004 *Ch* 2005 *CZR* 2006 *Pt* (R), *Ukr*, *J*, *Bb* (R), *CZR*, *Sp* (R), *Pt* (R) 2007 *R* (R), *Sp*, *Rus* (R), *I*, *F* (R)
Eloshvili, O 2002 *H* (R) 2003 *SA* 2006 *Bb*, *CZR* (R) 2007 *Sp*, *CZR* (R), *Nm*, *ESp*, *ItA*, *I* (R), *F* (R)
Essakia, S 1999 *Tg* (R), *Tg* (R) 2000 *It*, *Mor*, *Sp*, *H* 2004 *CZR* (R), *R*

Gagnidze, M 1991 *Ukr*, *Ukr*
Gasviani, D 2004 *Sp*, *Rus* (R) 2005 *CZR* (R), *Ch* (R) 2006 *Ukr* (R), *J* (R) 2007 *Rus* (R), *CZR*
Ghibradze, A 1992 *Ukr*, *Ukr*, *Lat* 1994 *Swi* 1995 *Bul*, *Mol*, *Ger* 1996 *CZR*
Ghudushauri, D 1989 *Z* 1991 *Ukr*, *Ukr*
Ghvaberidze, L 2004 *Pt*
Gigauri, R 2006 *Ukr* (R), *J* (R), *Bb*, *CZR*, *Sp*, *Pt*, *Pt* 2007 *R*, *Nm*, *ESp*, *ItA* (R), *Ar* (R), *Nm* (R), *F*
Giorgadze, A 1996 *CZR* (R) 1998 *It*, *Ukr*, *Rus*, *R* 1999 *Tg*, *Tg* 2000 *It*, *Pt*, *Mor*, *H*, *R* 2001 *H* (R), *Pt* (R), *Rus*, *Sp*, *R*, *F*, *SA* 2002 *H* (R), *Pt*, *Rus*, *Sp*, *R*, *I*, *Rus* 2003 *Pt*, *Sp*, *Rus*, *R*, *It*, *E*, *Sa*, *SA* (R), *Ur* (R) 2005 *Pt*, *Ukr*, *R*, *CZR* 2006 *Rus*, *R*, *Pt*, *Bb*, *CZR*, *Sp*, *Pt* 2007 *R*, *Ar*, *I* (R), *Nm*, *F*
Giorgadze, I 2001 *F* (R), *SA* (R) 2003 *Pt*, *Sp*, *Rus*, *R*, *It*, *E*, *Sa*, *Ur* 2004 *Rus* 2005 *Pt*, *R*, *CZR* 2006 *Rus*, *R*, *Pt*, *Bb*, *CZR*, *R*, *Sp*, *Pt*, *Pt* 2007 *R*, *Sp*, *Rus*, *CZR*, *Ar*, *Nm*, *F*
Gorgodze, M 2003 *Sp* (R), *Rus* (R) 2004 *Pt*, *Sp*, *Rus* (R), *CZR*, *R*, *Ur*, *Ch*, *Rus* (R) 2005 *Pt* (R), *Ukr*, *R*, *CZR*, *Ch* 2006 *Rus*, *Pt*, *Bb*, *CZR*, *R*, *Sp*, *Pt*, *Pt* 2007 *Ar*, *I*, *Nm*
Gueguchadze, E 1990 *Z*, *Z*
Gugava, L 2004 *Sp*, *Rus* (R), *CZR*, *Ur*, *Ch*, *Rus* (R) 2005 *Pt* (R), *Ukr* 2006 *Bb* (R), *CZR*
Guiorkhelidze, I 1998 *R* 1999 *Tg* (R), *Tg* (R)
Guiunashvili, G 1989 *Z* 1990 *Z* 1991 *Ukr*, *Ukr* 1992 *Ukr*, *Ukr*, *Lat* 1993 *Rus*, *Pol* (R), *Lux* 1994 *Swi* 1996 *Rus* 1997 *Pt* (R)
Guiunashvili, K 1990 *Z*, *Z* (R) 1991 *Ukr*, *Ukr* 1992 *Ukr*, *Ukr*, *Lat*
Gujaraidze, S 2003 *SA*, *Ur*
Gundishvili, I 2002 *I* (R) 2003 *Pt* (R), *Sp* (R), *Rus*, *CZR*
Gurgenidze, D 2007 *Sp* (R), *ItA* (R)
Gusharashvili, A 1998 *Ukr*

Iobidze, D 1993 *Rus* (R), *Pol*
Iovadze, E 1993 *Lux* 1994 *Kaz* 1995 *Bul*, *Mol*, *Ger* (R), *H* (R) 2001 *Sp* (R), *F*, *SA* 2002 *H* (R), *Rus* (R), *Sp* (R), *R*, *I* (R)
Issakadze, A 1989 *Z*
Iurini, N 1991 *Ukr* (R) 1994 *Swi* (R) 1995 *Ger*, *H* 1996 *CZR*, *CZR*, *Rus* 1997 *Pt*, *Pol*, *Cro*, *De* 1998 *Ukr*, *Rus* 2000 *It* (R), *Sp* (R), *H*, *R* (R)

Janelidze, S 1991 *Ukr* (R), *Ukr* 1993 *Rus* 1994 *Kaz* 1995 *Ger* 1997 *Pt* (R) 1998 *Ukr* (R), *I*, *R* (R) 1999 *Tg* 2000 *R* (R)
Japarashvili, R 1992 *Ukr*, *Ukr*, *Lat* 1993 *Pol*, *Lux* (R) 1996 *CZR* 1997 *Pt* (R)

Javelidze, L 1997 *Cro* (R) 1998 *I* 2001 *H* (R), *R* (R), *F* (R), *SA* (R) 2002 *H* (R), *R* (R) 2004 *R* (R) 2005 *Ukr* (R) 2007 *Sp* (R)
Jgenti, G 2007 *Nm* (R), *ESp* (R), *ItA* (R)
Jghenti, D 2004 *CZR* (R), *R* (R)
Jhamutashvili, D 2005 *Ch*
Jhghenti, G 2004 *Ur* (R) 2005 *Ch* 2007 *Sp* (R), *CZR* (R)
Jimsheladze, P 1995 *Bul*, *Mol*, *H* (R) 1996 *CZR*, *CZR*, *Rus* 1997 *De* 1998 *It*, *Ukr*, *Rus*, *I* (R), *R* 1999 *Tg*, *Tg* 2000 *Pt*, *Mor*, *Sp*, *H*, *R* 2001 *H*, *Pt*, *Rus*, *Sp*, *R*, *F*, *SA* 2002 *H*, *Pt*, *Rus*, *Sp*, *I*, *Rus* 2003 *Pt*, *Sp*, *Rus*, *CZR*, *R*, *It*, *E*, *Sa*, *SA*, *Ur* 2004 *Rus* 2005 *R* 2006 *Rus*, *R*, *Pt*, *Ukr*, *J*, *Bb*, *CZR*, *Pt*, *Pt* 2007 *R*, *Rus*, *CZR*, *Ar*
Jintcharadze, K 1993 *Rus*, *Pol* (R) 2000 *It* (R), *Mor* (R)

Kacharava, D 2006 *Ukr* (R), *J*, *R*, *Sp* (R), *Pt* (R) 2007 *R* (R), *Sp*, *Rus* (R), *CZR* (R), *Nm*, *ESp*, *ItA*, *I*, *Nm*
Kacharava, G 2005 *Ukr* (R) 2006 *J* (R), *Bb* (R), *CZR* (R), *R* (R) 2007 *Sp* (R)
Kakhiani, G 1995 *Bul*, *Mol*
Katsadze, V 1997 *Pol* 1998 *It*, *Ukr*, *Rus* (R), *I*, *R* (R) 1999 *Tg*, *Tg* 2000 *Pt*, *Mor*, *Sp*, *H*, *R* 2001 *H*, *Pt*, *Rus*, *Sp*, *R* 2002 *Pt*, *Rus*, *Sp*, *R*, *I* (R), *Rus* 2003 *Pt*, *Sp*, *CZR*, *R*, *E*, *Sa*, *SA*, *Ur* (R) 2004 *Sp* 2005 *Ukr*
Kavtarashvili, A 1994 *Swi* 1995 *Bul*, *Mol*, *Ger* (R) 1996 *CZR*, *Rus* 1997 *Pt*, *Cro*, *De* 1998 *It*, *Rus*, *I*, *R* 1999 *Tg*, *Tg* (R) 2000 *It*, *H*, *R* 2001 *H* (R) 2003 *SA*, *Ur*
Kerauli, I 1991 *Ukr*, *Ukr* 1992 *Ukr* (R), *Ukr*
Khachirashvili, L 2005 *Ukr* (R)
Khakhaleishili, T 1994 *Kaz*
Khamashuridze, B 1998 *It*, *Ukr*, *Rus*, *I* (R), *R* 1999 *Tg*, *Tg* 2000 *It*, *Pt*, *Sp*, *H*, *R* 2001 *Pt*, *Rus*, *Sp*, *R*, *F*, *SA* 2002 *H*, *Pt*, *Rus*, *Sp*, *R*, *I*, *Rus* 2003 *Pt*, *CZR*, *R* (R), *It*, *E*, *Sa* (R), *SA* (R), *Ur* (R) 2004 *Pt*, *Rus*, *Rus* 2005 *Pt*, *Ukr*, *Ch* 2006 *Rus*, *R*, *Pt*, *R*, *Sp*, *Pt*, *Pt* 2007 *Rus*, *CZR*, *ESp* (R), *Ar*, *Nm* (R), *F*
Khamashuridze, B 1989 *Z*
Kharshiladze, M 1991 *Ukr*
Khekhelashvili, B 1999 *Tg*, *Tg* 2000 *It*, *Pt*, *Mor*, *Sp* (R), *H* (R), *R* 2001 *H* (R), *Pt* (R), *R* (R), *F*, *SA* (R) 2002 *H* (R), *Pt*, *Rus*, *Sp*, *R*, *I* 2003 *Sp*, *Rus*, *CZR*, *R*, *E* (R), *Sa* 2004 *Sp* (R)
Khinchagashvili, D 2003 *Sp* (R), *CZR* (R) 2004 *Pt*, *Sp*, *Rus* (R) 2006 *Bb* (R), *CZR* (R), *Sp* (R), *Pt*, *Pt* 2007 *R*, *Rus*, *Nm*, *ESp*, *ItA*, *Ar*, *I* (R), *Nm* (R)
Khonelidze, G 2003 *SA*
Khuade, N 1989 *Z* 1990 *Z*, *Z* 1991 *Ukr* (R), *Ukr* 1993 *Rus*, *Pol*, *Lux* 1994 *Swi* (R) 1995 *Ger*
Khutsishvili, Z 1993 *Lux* 1994 *Kaz*, *Swi* 1995 *Bul* (R) 1996 *CZR* (R) 1997 *Pol* 1998 *Rus* (R)
Khvedelidze, A 1989 *Z* 1990 *Z*, *Z* 1991 *Ukr*, *Ukr* 1992 *Ukr*, *Ukr*, *Lat* 1993 *Rus*, *Pol*
Kiknadze, D 2004 *Rus* 2005 *Pt*, *Ukr* (R)
Kobakhidze, A 1997 *Cro* (R) 1998 *I*
Kobakhidze, K 1995 *Ger* (R), *H* 1996 *Rus* (R) 1997 *Pt* 1998 *It* (R), *Ukr*, *Rus*, *I*, *R* 1999 *Tg* (R) 2000 *It*
Koberidze, Z 2004 *Ur*
Kopaleishvili, A 2004 *Ur* (R)
Kopaliani, A 2003 *It*, *SA*, *Ur* 2004 *Pt* 2005 *Ukr* (R), *R* (R) 2006 *Rus* (R), *R* (R), *Ukr*, *J*, *Bb*, *CZR* (R), *R* (R), *Sp* (R), *Pt* (R) 2007 *R* (R), *Sp*, *Rus*, *CZR*, *Ar* (R), *I*, *Nm* (R), *F* (R)
Kuparadze, E 2007 *ESp*
Kutarashvili, G 2004 *Pt* (R), *Sp* (R), *CZR* (R), *R* 2005 *Ch* 2006 *Rus* (R), *R* (R), *Pt* (R), *Ukr*, *J*, *R* (R)
Kvinikhidze, B 2002 *R* (R) 2004 *Pt*, *Sp*, *CZR*, *R* 2005 *Ch*
Kvirikashvili, M 2003 *Pt* (R), *Sp*, *CZR* (R), *E* (R), *Sa* (R), *SA* (R), *Ur* (R) 2004 *Rus* (R), *CZR*, *R*, *Ch* 2005 *CZR* (R), *Ch* (R) 2007 *R*, *Sp*, *Rus*, *CZR*, *Nm*, *ESp*, *ItA*, *Ar*, *I*, *Nm*, *F*

Labadze, G 1996 *CZR*, *Rus* 1997 *Pt*, *Pol*, *Cro*, *De* 1998 *It* (R), *Ukr*, *Rus*, *I*, *R* 1999 *Tg*, *Tg* 2000 *It*, *Pt*, *Sp*, *H*, *R* 2001 *H*, *Pt*, *Rus*, *Sp*, *F*, *SA* 2002 *Pt*, *Rus*, *Sp*, *R*, *Rus* 2003 *Rus*, *CZR*, *R*, *It* (R), *E*, *Sa* 2004 *Rus* 2005 *R* 2006 *Rus*, *R*, *Pt*, *J*, *R*, *Pt*, *Pt* 2007 *Rus*, *Ar*, *Nm*
Lezhava, I 1991 *Ukr* (R), *Ukr* 1992 *Ukr* (R) 1995 *Bul* (R)
Lezhava, Z 1991 *Ukr* (R) 1995 *Ger* 1996 *CZR* (R), *CZR*, *Rus* 1997 *Pt*, *Cro*, *De* (R) 1998 *It*, *Rus*, *R* 1999 *Tg* (R)
Liluashvili, B 1989 *Z* 1990 *Z*, *Z*
Liluashvili, L 1997 *Pt*
Liparteliani, O 1989 *Z* 1990 *Z*, *Z*
Liparteliani, S 1991 *Ukr* 1994 *Kaz*, *Swi* 1996 *CZR*
Liparteliani, Z 1994 *Kaz* (R), *Swi* 1995 *Bul*, *Mol*, *Ger*, *H*
Lossaberidze, M 1989 *Z*

Machitidze, K 1989 *Z* (R) 1993 *Rus* 1995 *Bul*, *Mol*, *Ger*, *H* 1996 *CZR*, *CZR* (R), *Rus* 1997 *Pt*, *Pol*, *Cro*, *De* 1998 *It*, *Ukr*, *Rus*, *R* 1999 *Tg* (R)
Machkhaneli, I 2002 *H*, *R* (R) 2003 *It*, *E* (R), *Sa* (R), *SA*, *Ur* 2004 *Pt*, *Ur*, *Ch* (R), *Rus* 2005 *Pt*, *Ukr*, *R*, *CZR*, *Ch* 2006 *Rus*, *R*, *Pt*, *Bb*, *CZR*, *R*, *Pt* 2007 *R*, *Ar*, *I* (R), *Nm*
Magrakvelidze, M 1998 *Ukr* (R) 2000 *Mor* (R) 2001 *F* (R) 2002 *Pt* (R), *Sp* (R), *R* 2004 *Rus* 2005 *Pt*, *R* 2006 *Bb*, *CZR*, *Pt* (R), *Pt* (R) 2007 *R* (R), *CZR* (R), *Nm*, *ESp* (R), *ItA*, *I*, *F*
Maisuradze, I 1997 *Cro* (R) 1998 *It* (R), *Ukr* (R) 1999 *Tg*, *Tg* 2004 *Rus*, *R* 2005 *CZR* 2006 *Bb*, *CZR*, *R*, *Pt* (R), *Pt* (R) 2007 *R*, *Sp*, *Rus* (R), *CZR*, *ESp*, *ItA* (R), *I*, *F*
Maisuradze, Z 2004 *Pt*, *Sp*, *CZR*, *Ur*, *Ch* (R), *Rus* 2005 *Ukr* (R), *R* 2006 *Rus* (R), *R* (R), *Pt*, *Ukr*, *J*, *Bb* (R), *CZR* (R), *Sp* 2007 *Nm* (R), *ESp* (R), *ItA*, *Ar* (R), *I* (R), *F* (R)
Margvelashvili, K 2003 *It*, *E*, *Sa* (R), *SA*
Marjanishvili, M 1990 *Z*, *Z* 1992 *Ukr*, *Ukr*, *Lat* 1993 *Rus*, *Pol*, *Lux*
Matchutadze, A 1993 *Lux* 1994 *Kaz* 1995 *Bul* (R), *Mol* 1997 *Pt* (R), *Pol*, *Cro*, *De*
Matiashvili, Z 2003 *Sp* 2005 *Ch* (R)
Mgueladze, L 1992 *Ukr* (R), *Ukr* (R)
Mgueladze, N 1995 *Bul*, *Mol*, *H* 1997 *Pol* (R)
Modebadze, I 2003 *SA*, *Ur* 2004 *Sp*
Modebadze, S 1994 *Kaz* 1995 *Mol* (R) 1996 *CZR*, *CZR*, *Rus* 1997 *Pt*, *Pol*, *Cro*, *De* 1998 *It*, *Ukr*, *Rus* 1999 *Tg* 2000 *It*, *Pt* (R) 2001 *Sp* (R), *F* (R), *SA* (R) 2002 *H*, *Pt* (R), *Rus* (R), *Sp*, *R*
Mtchedlishvili, A 2004 *Ur*, *Ch*
Mtchedlishvili, S 2000 *It* (R) 2007 *Sp*
Mtchedlishvili, Z 1995 *Mol* (R) 1996 *CZR* 1997 *Cro*, *De* 1998 *It*, *Ukr*, *Rus*, *I* (R), *R* 1999 *Tg*, *Tg* 2000 *Pt*, *Mor*, *Sp*, *H*, *R* 2001 *Rus* (R), *Sp* (R), *R* (R), *F*, *SA* 2002 *H* (R), *Pt*, *Rus* (R), *I* (R), *Rus* 2003 *Pt*, *Sp* (R), *Rus* (R), *CZR*, *R*, *It*, *E*, *Sa*, *Ur* 2004 *Pt* (R), *Rus* 2005 *Pt* 2006 *J* 2007 *Rus*, *CZR*, *Nm* (R), *ESp*, *ItA*, *F*
Mtiulishvili, M 1991 *Ukr* (R) 1994 *Kaz* (R) 1996 *CZR*, *CZR*, *Rus* 1997 *Pt*, *Pol*, *Cro*, *De* 1998 *It*, *Ukr*, *Rus*, *R* 2001 *H*, *Pt*, *Rus*, *Sp*, *R* 2002 *H*, *Pt*, *Rus* (R), *Sp*, *R*, *I* (R) 2003 *Rus* (R), *CZR*, *R* (R) 2004 *Rus*, *CZR*, *R* (R)

Nadiradze, V 1994 *Kaz*, *Swi* 1995 *H* 1996 *Rus* 1997 *Pt*, *De* 1998 *I*, *R* (R) 1999 *Tg* 2000 *Pt*, *Mor*, *Sp*, *H*, *R* 2001 *H*, *Pt*, *Rus*, *Sp*, *R*, *F*, *SA* 2002 *H*, *Pt*, *Rus*, *Sp*, *R*, *I*, *Rus* 2003 *Rus*, *CZR*, *R*, *It* (R), *E* (R), *Sa*
Natchqebia, A 1990 *Z*, *Z*
Natriashvili, I 2006 *Ukr* (R), *J* (R) 2007 *ItA* (R)
Natroshvili, N 1992 *Ukr*, *Ukr* (R), *Lat*
Nemsadze, G 2005 *Ch* 2006 *Ukr* (R) 2007 *Sp* (R)
Nikolaenko, I 1999 *Tg* (R), *Tg* (R) 2000 *It* (R), *Mor* (R), *Sp* (R), *H* (R), *R* (R) 2001 *R* (R), *F* (R) 2003 *Pt* (R), *Sp*, *E* (R), *Sa*, *SA* (R), *Ur* (R)
Ninidze, I 2004 *Ur*, *Ch* (R)

Oboladze, D 1993 *Rus*, *Pol*, *Lux* 1994 *Swi* 1995 *Bul*, *Mol*, *Ger*, *H* 1996 *CZR*, *CZR*, *Rus* 1997 *Pt*, *Pol* 1998 *It*, *Ukr* (R)
Odisharia, T 1989 *Z* (R) 1994 *Kaz* (R)

Papashvili, S 2001 *SA* (R) 2004 *CZR* (R), *R* (R) 2006 *Bb* (R), *CZR* (R) 2007 *Sp*
Partsikanashvili, S 1994 *Kaz* 1996 *CZR*, *Rus* (R) 1997 *Pol* 1999 *Tg*, *Tg* 2000 *It*, *Pt*, *Mor*
Peradze, G 1991 *Ukr*
Peradze, Z 1997 *Pol* 1998 *Rus* (R)
Pinchukovi, D 2004 *CZR* (R)
Pirpilashvili, L 2004 *Rus* (R), *CZR*, *R*, *Ur*, *Ch* 2005 *Ukr*, *R* (R), *CZR* (R)
Pirtskhalava, G 1989 *Z* (R) 1995 *Ger* 1996 *CZR*, *Rus* (R) 1997 *Pt* (R), *Pol*
Pkhakadze, T 1989 *Z* 1990 *Z*, *Z* 1993 *Rus*, *Pol*, *Lux* 1994 *Kaz* 1996 *CZR*

Rapava-Ruskini, G 1990 *Z* 1992 *Ukr*, *Lat* 1994 *Kaz* (R) 1996 *Rus* 1997 *Pt*, *Cro*, *De* 1998 *It*, *Ukr*, *Rus*, *R* 1999 *Tg*
Ratianidze, T 2000 *It* (R) 2001 *H* (R), *Pt* (R), *Sp* (R), *R* (R), *SA* (R) 2002 *Pt* (R), *Rus*, *Sp* (R), *R* (R), *I* (R), *Rus* (R) 2003 *Pt*, *Sp* (R), *Rus*, *CZR*, *R*
Rekhviashvili, Z 1995 *H* (R) 1997 *Pt*, *Pol* (R)

Sakandelidze, S 1996 *CZR* (R) 1998 *Ukr* (R)
Samkharadze, B 2004 *Pt*, *Sp* (R), *Rus*, *CZR* (R), *R* (R), *Ur*, *Ch* (R) 2005 *CZR*, *Ch* 2006 *Rus* (R), *R* (R), *Pt* (R), *Ukr* (R), *Bb*, *CZR*, *R* (R), *Sp*, *Pt*, *Pt* (R) 2007 *R* (R), *Sp*, *Rus* (R), *CZR* (R), *Nm* (R), *ESp*, *Ar* (R), *I*, *Nm* (R), *F* (R)
Sanadze, A 2004 *Ch*
Saneblidze, P 1994 *Kaz*
Sanikidze, G 2004 *Ur* (R), *Ch*
Sardanashvili, B 2004 *Ch*
Satseradze, V 1989 *Z* 1990 *Z* 1991 *Ukr* 1992 *Ukr* (R), *Ukr*, *Lat* (R)
Shanidze, E 1994 *Swi*
Shkinin, G 2004 *CZR*, *R*, *Ch* 2005 *Ch* 2006 *Rus* (R), *R* (R), *Ukr*, *J*, *R* (R), *Sp*, *Pt*, *Pt* (R) 2007 *R*, *Sp*, *Rus*, *CZR*, *Nm*, *ESp*, *ItA*, *Ar* (R), *I*, *Nm*
Shvanguiradze, B 1990 *Z*, *Z* 1992 *Ukr*, *Ukr*, *Lat* 1993 *Rus*, *Pol*, *Lux*
Shvelidze, G 1998 *I*, *R* (R) 1999 *Tg*, *Tg* 2000 *It*, *Pt*, *Sp*, *H*, *R* 2001 *H*, *Pt*, *Sp* (R), *F*, *SA* 2002 *H*, *Rus*, *I*, *Rus* 2003 *Pt*, *Sp*, *Rus*, *CZR*, *R*, *It* (R), *E*, *Sa*, *Ur* 2004 *Rus* 2005 *Pt*, *CZR* 2006 *Rus*, *R*, *Pt*, *R*, *Sp*, *Pt*, *Pt* 2007 *Ar* (R), *I*, *Nm*, *F* (R)
Sikharulidze , I 1994 *Kaz*
Sokhadze, T 2005 *CZR* (R) 2006 *Rus* (R), *R* (R), *Pt*, *Ukr*, *J*, *Pt*, *Pt*
Sujashvili, M 2004 *Pt* (R), *Rus* 2005 *Pt* (R), *Ukr*, *R* (R), *CZR* (R) 2006 *Pt* (R), *Ukr*, *J*, *Bb* (R), *CZR*
Sultanishvili, S 1998 *Ukr* (R)
Sutiashvili, S 2005 *Ch* (R) 2006 *Ukr* (R) 2007 *CZR* (R), *Nm*, *ESp* (R)
Svanidze, P 1992 *Ukr*

Tavadze, T 1991 *Ukr*, *Ukr*
Tchavtchavadze, N 1998 *It* (R), *Ukr* (R) 2004 *CZR*, *R* (R), *Ur*, *Ch*
Tepnadze, B 1995 *H* (R) 1996 *CZR* 1997 *Cro* 1998 *I*, *R* (R) 1999 *Tg* (R)
Tqabladze, P 1993 *Lux* 1995 *Bul* (R)
Tsabadze, L 1994 *Kaz*, *Swi* 1995 *Bul*, *Ger*, *H* 1996 *CZR* (R), *Rus* 1997 *Cro*, *De* 1998 *It*, *Rus*, *I* (R), *R* 1999 *Tg*, *Tg* 2000 *Pt*, *Mor*, *Sp*, *R* 2001 *H*, *Pt*, *Rus*, *Sp*, *R*, *F*, *SA* 2002 *H*, *Pt*, *Rus*, *Sp*, *R*, *I*, *Rus*
Tsiklauri, G 2003 *SA*, *Ur* (R)
Tskhvediani, D 1998 *Ukr* (R)
Tskitishvili, V 1994 *Swi* 1995 *Bul*, *Mol*
Turdzeladze, T 1989 *Z* 1990 *Z*, *Z* 1991 *Ukr* 1995 *Ger*, *H*

Uchava, K 2002 *Sp* (R) 2004 *Sp*
Udesiani, B 2001 *Sp* (R), *F* (R) 2002 *H* (R) 2004 *Pt*, *Sp*, *CZR*, *R*, *Rus* 2005 *Pt*, *Ukr*, *R*, *CZR*, *Ch* 2006 *Rus*, *R*, *Ukr*, *J*, *Bb*, *CZR*, *R*, *Sp*, *Pt*, *Pt* 2007 *R*, *Rus*, *CZR*, *Ar*, *Nm* (R)
Urjukashvili, M 1997 *Cro*, *De* 1998 *Ukr*, *Rus*, *R* 1999 *Tg*, *Tg* 2000 *It*, *Pt*, *Mor*, *Sp* 2001 *Pt* (R), *Rus*, *Sp*, *R*, *F*, *SA* 2002 *H*, *Pt*, *Sp*, *R*, *I*, *Rus* 2003 *Pt*, *Sp*, *Rus*, *R*, *It*, *E*, *Sa*, *Ur* 2004 *Pt*, *Rus*, *Ur*, *Ch*, *Rus* 2005 *Pt*, *R*, *CZR* 2006 *Rus*, *R*, *Pt*, *Ukr*, *J*, *R*, *Sp* 2007 *Rus*, *CZR*, *Nm* (R), *ESp*, *ItA*, *Ar*, *I*, *Nm*, *F*
Urushadze, R 1997 *Pol* 2002 *R* (R) 2004 *Pt*, *Rus* (R), *Rus* 2005 *Pt*, *Ukr*, *R* (R), *CZR*, *Ch* 2006 *Rus*, *R*, *Pt*, *Bb*, *CZR*, *R* (R), *Sp*, *Pt*, *Pt* 2007 *Nm*, *ESp*, *ItA*, *I*, *Nm*, *F* (R)

Valishvili, Z 2004 *Ch*
Vartaniani, D 1991 *Ukr*, *Ukr* 1992 *Ukr*, *Ukr*, *Lat* 1997 *Pol* (R) 2000 *Sp* (R), *H*, *R*
Vashadze, L 1991 *Ukr* 1992 *Ukr*, *Ukr* (R), *Lat*
Yachvili, G 2001 *H*, *Pt*, *R* 2003 *Pt*, *Sp*, *Rus*, *CZR*, *R*, *It*, *E*, *Sa*, *Ur*

Zedginidze, I 1998 *I* 2000 *It*, *Pt*, *Mor*, *Sp*, *H*, *R* 2001 *H*, *Pt*, *Rus*, *Sp*, *R* 2002 *H*, *Rus*, *Sp*, *I*, *Rus* 2003 *Pt*, *Sp*, *Rus*, *CZR*, *R*, *It*, *Sa*, *SA* (R), *Ur* 2004 *Pt*, *Sp*, *Rus*, *CZR*, *R*, *Rus* 2005 *Pt*, *Ukr*, *R*, *CZR* 2006 *Rus*, *R*, *Pt*, *Ukr*, *CZR*, *R*, *Sp*, *Pt*, *Pt* 2007 *R*, *Ar*, *I*
Zibzibadze, T 2000 *It* (R), *Pt*, *Mor*, *Sp* 2001 *H*, *Pt*, *Rus*, *Sp*, *R*, *F*, *SA* 2002 *H*, *Pt*, *Rus*, *Sp*, *R*, *I*, *Rus* 2003 *Pt*, *Sp*, *Rus*, *CZR*, *R*, *It*, *E*, *Sa*, *Ur* 2004 *Pt*, *Sp*, *Rus*, *CZR*, *R*, *Rus* 2005 *Pt*, *Ukr*, *R*, *CZR*
Zirakashvili, D 2004 *Ur*, *Ch* (R), *Rus* 2005 *Ukr*, *R*, *CZR* 2006 *Rus*, *R*, *Pt*, *R*, *Sp*, *Pt* 2007 *R*, *Ar*, *Nm*, *F*

GEORGIAN INTERNATIONAL RECORDS

WINNING MARGIN

Date	Opponent	Result	Winning Margin
07/04/2007	Czech Republic	98–3	**95**
03/02/2002	Netherlands	88–0	**88**
26/02/2005	Ukraine	65–0	**65**
12/06/2005	Czech Republic	75–10	**65**

MOST POINTS IN A MATCH BY THE TEAM

Date	Opponent	Result	Pts.
07/04/2007	Czech Republic	98–3	**98**
03/02/2002	Netherlands	88–0	**88**
12/06/2005	Czech Republic	75–10	**75**
23/03/1995	Bulgaria	70–8	**70**

MOST TRIES IN A MATCH BY THE TEAM

Date	Opponent	Result	Tries
07/04/2007	Czech Republic	98–3	**16**
03/02/2002	Netherlands	88–0	**14**
23/03/1995	Bulgaria	70–8	**11**
26/02/2005	Ukraine	65–0	**11**
12/06/2005	Czech Republic	75–10	**11**

MOST CONVERSIONS IN A MATCH BY THE TEAM

Date	Opponent	Result	Cons
103/02/2002	Netherlands	88–0	**9**
07/04/2007	Czech Republic	98–3	**9**
12/06/2005	Czech Republic	75–10	**7**
23/03/1995	Bulgaria	70–8	**6**

MOST PENALTIES IN A MATCH BY THE TEAM

Date	Opponent	Result	Pens
08/03/2003	Russia	23–17	**6**

MOST DROP GOALS IN A MATCH BY THE TEAM

Date	Opponent	Result	DGs
20/10/1996	Russia	29–20	**2**
21/11/1991	Ukraine	19–15	**2**
15/07/1992	Ukraine	15–0	**2**
04/06/1994	Switzerland	22–21	**2**

MOST POINTS IN A MATCH BY A PLAYER

Date	Player	Opponent	Pts.
08/03/2003	Pavle Jimsheladze	Russia	**23**
07/04/2007	Merab Kvirikashvili	Czech Republic	**23**
12/06/2005	Malkhaz Urjukashvili	Czech Republic	**20**
28/10/2006	Malkhaz Urjukashvili	Spain	**19**
06/04/2002	Malkhaz Urjukashvili	Romania	**18**
03/02/2002	Pavle Jimsheladze	Netherlands	**18**

MOST TRIES IN A MATCH BY A PLAYER

Date	Player	Opponent	Tries
23/03/1995	Pavle Jimsheladze	Bulgaria	**3**
23/03/1995	Archil Kavtarashvili	Bulgaria	**3**
12/06/2005	Mamuka Gorgodze	Czech Republic	**3**
07/04/2007	David Dadunashvili	Czech Republic	**3**
07/04/2007	Malkhaz Urjukashvili	Czech Republic	**3**

MOST CONVERSIONS IN A MATCH BY A PLAYER

Date	Player	Opponent	Cons
03/02/2002	Pavle Jimsheladze	Netherlands	**9**
07/04/2007	Merab Kvirikashvili	Czech Republic	**9**
12/06/2005	Malkhaz Urjukashvili	Czech Republic	**7**
23/03/1995	Kakha Machitidze	Bulgaria	**6**

MOST PENALTIES IN A MATCH BY A PLAYER

Date	Player	Opponent	Pens
08/03/2003	Pavle Jimsheladze	Russia	6
03/03/2002	Pavle Jimsheladze	Russia	4
06/09/2003	Pavle Jimsheladze	Italy	4
12/10/1997	Shota Modebadze	Croatia	4
20/05/1998	Malkhaz Urjukashvili	Russia	4
13/10/2002	Malkhaz Urjukashvili	Russia	4
12/09/1989	Nugzar Dzagnidze	Zimbabwe	4

MOST DROP GOALS IN A MATCH BY A PLAYER

Date	Player	Opponent	DGs
15/07/1992	Davit Chavleishvili	Ukraine	2

MOST CAPPED PLAYERS

Player	Caps
Pavle Jimsheladze	57
Malkhaz Urjukashvili	55
Besiki Khamashuridze	52
Akvsenti Giorgadze	51

LEADING TRY SCORERS

Player	Tries
Malkhaz Urjukashvili	15
Ilia Zedginidze	13
Tedo Zibzibadze	11
Akvsenti Giorgadze	11
Besiki Khamashuridze	11

LEADING CONVERSIONS SCORERS

Player	Cons
Pavle Jimsheladze	61
Malkhaz Urjukashvili	40
Merab Kvirikashvili	20
Nugzar Dzagnidze	9

LEADING PENALTY SCORERS

Player	Pens
Pavle Jimsheladze	48
Malkhaz Urjukashvili	37
Nugzar Dzagnidze	22
Merab Kvirikashvili	14

LEADING DROP GOAL SCORERS

Player	DGs
Kakha Machitidze	4
Nugzar Dzagnidze	3
Pavle Jimsheladze	3

LEADING POINTS SCORERS

Player	Pts.
Pavle Jimsheladze	320
Malkhaz Urjukashvili	269
Nugzar Dzagnidze	105
Merab Kvirikashvili	95

IRELAND

IRELAND'S 2006–07 TEST RECORD

OPPONENTS	DATE	VENUE	RESULT
South Africa	11 November	H	**Won** 32–15
Australia	19 November	H	**Won** 21–6
Pacific Islands	26 November	H	**Won** 61–17
Wales	4 February	A	**Won** 19–9
France	11 February	H	**Lost** 17–20
England	24 February	H	**Won** 43–13
Scotland	10 March	A	**Won** 19–18
Italy	17 March	A	**Won** 51–24
Argentina	26 May	A	**Lost** 20–22
Argentina	2 June	A	**Lost** 0–16
Scotland	11 August	A	**Lost** 21–31
Italy	24 August	H	**Won** 23–20
Namibia	9 September	N	**Won** 32–17 (WC)
Georgia	15 September	N	**Won** 14–10 (WC)
France	21 September	N	**Lost** 3–25 (WC)
Argentina	30 September	N	**Lost** 15–30 (WC)

ROLLERCOASTER RIDE

By Iain Spragg

Dave Rogers/Getty Images

Oh the agony! Ireland underachieved at the World Cup.

High expectations and Irish rugby have not always been natural bed fellows and so it was to prove as their World Cup campaign began unconvincingly, got steadily worse and climaxed with a 30–15 defeat to Argentina in Paris that condemned Eddie O'Sullivan's much-vaunted side to a premature return home.

It was first time the men in green had failed to reach the knockout stages in World Cup history and with some serious – and neutral – observers predicting a possible march to the semi-finals before the tournament began, O'Sullivan will probably be wondering exactly what went so disastrously wrong for years to come.

True, the Irish were plunged into Pool D, the ominously termed 'group of death' with both the rapidly-improving Pumas and hosts France, but quite how they made such a spectacular mess of their bid to reach the last eight was mystifying. Ireland simply fell to pieces at the World Cup after a 12-month build-up that had promised so much.

That Ireland went into what was to be their final game of the tournament needing to beat Argentina by eight points and score four tries in the process to garner the required bonus points was not a situation all of their own making, but their abject performances against Namibia, Georgia and France and their ultimate failure to raise the tempo against the Pumas was. O'Sullivan and his side went out of the World Cup with barely a whimper.

"We needed to score four tries and gave it our best shot but we did not get enough field position to make it happen," the coach said in the post-match post mortem. "I feel sorry for the players. They played their guts out but it was not to be and that is how it goes. It has been a tough World Cup for us. I have no complaints really."

Ireland could not have asked for a more gentle opener at the tournament. Faced with the minnows of Namibia in Bordeaux, they were expected to stroll to victory but the deluge of points failed to materialise after a disjointed performance and they stuttered to a 32–17 win. The Irish camp dismissed the game as a loosener but the doubts really began to surface after they had played Georgia.

The Georgians were abrasive opponents but Ireland laboured badly and limped to an unconvincing 14–10 victory. The Irish even had to weather a late onslaught from Georgia and could have lost the game. "We're going to need a considerably better performance against the French," captain Brian O'Driscoll conceded. "We're still in the competition but it's looking likely that we're going to need to win our last two games. We knew we were going to have to pull out big performances to come out of this group and nothing's changed."

It wasn't, however, win-or-bust against Les Bleus. Argentina had shocked the French in Paris in the opening match of the tournament which meant Ireland, although in a desperate need for a morale-boosting victory, could lose but then beat the Pumas and progress to the quarter-finals.

The Irish had pushed France close at the Stade de France in the Six Nations in February but never got within striking distance in the same stadium when it mattered. Five penalties from the boot of Jean-Baptiste Elissalde and two tries from Vincent Clerc destroyed Ireland's challenge and a solitary drop goal from Ronan O'Gara was their only consolation in a 25–3 defeat.

Everything now rested on the Argentina game. The Pumas had beaten Ireland on successive weekends in the summer in South America and their victory over France had shown they were a force to be reckoned with.

Irish fans made the old Parc des Princes in the French capital their own for the match but their team was unable to produce the necessary fireworks on the pitch. The pressure to score four tries in victory seemed to stifle the players and except for a few minutes late in the first half, Ireland trailed throughout.

Wing Lucas Borges scored the game's first try to give the Pumas a platform and although a converted O'Driscoll try on 32 minutes put Ireland 10–8 up, it was to prove a brief advantage. Wing Horacio Agulla

Jeff J Mitchell/Getty Images

In the Six Nations Brian O'Driscoll (centre) led his side to another Triple Crown.

scored Argentina's second in the second-half and although Geordan Murphy replied in kind to give the massed Ireland supporters hope, Felipe Contepomi's boot kept O'Sullivan's side at arm's length and the Pumas were 30–15 winners. The World Cup dream was over.

"We're out of the tournament and everything's relative now," said centre Gordon D'Arcy. "We played better, but we didn't play well enough. You don't become a bad team overnight. You don't become bad individuals in the space of a few months. We came into pre-season fresh and we came to the World Cup as one of the pre-tournament favourites. But we just didn't deliver."

It was a sad end to a 12-month build-up that had initially promised so much. The 2006–07 season began in Dublin with the visit of South Africa. Ireland were looking for a second successive win over the powerful Springboks and first-half tries from Andrew Trimble, David Wallace and Marcus Horan laid the platform for an inspired performance at Lansdowne Road and a 32–15 triumph. A week later Australia came calling on the back of a four-match winning streak against their hosts but Ireland once again showed they were a side firmly on the up and scores from Denis Hickie and Geordan Murphy steered them to a 21–6 victory. O'Sullivan's side had recorded a hugely impressive double over southern hemisphere opposition and went into the Six Nations with high hopes of adding a 2007 Grand Slam to their only other previous clean sweep back in 1948.

Their bid began with a scrappy 19–9 win over the Welsh in Cardiff but the chance of the Grand Slam was wrenched from their grasp by the French at Croke Park seven days later. There was little to separate the two best teams in the tournament and although O'Gara scored a try and kicked four penalties in the game, a late try from Vincent Clerc stole it for the visitors and France emerged 20–17 winners.

"The boys all put their bodies on the line for 80 minutes and when the win is snatched away from you at the death it is as cruel as you can get," O'Sullivan said in the aftermath of the last-minute drama. "We got ourselves back into the game before half-time and played really well in the second half but the ball broke their way and that's how it goes. Everyone gave it everything they had and I have no complaints about effort."

To their credit, Ireland dusted themselves off quickly and although they only sneaked past Scotland by a single point at Murrayfield, they recorded big wins over England (43–13) at Croke Park and Italy (51–24) in Rome to suggest they were still very much a force to be reckoned with.

The signs of frailty that were to haunt them at the World Cup began to manifest themselves in Argentina in the summer. O'Sullivan left his big name players at home to rest as Ireland looked for their first ever win on Argentinean soil and although they were only denied by a late Felipe Contepomi drop goal in the first Test in Santa Fe, defeat was still a worrying sign.

The second Test in Buenos Aries wasn't even close. Ireland's performance was strewn with errors and Argentina completed a 16–0 win to wrap up the series 2–0.

"After two weeks with two Tests, I am much clearer on the squad that will go to the World Cup," O'Sullivan said. "We are a little disappointed because we did not win one Test but the point of this tour was to select some players for the World Cup, so I knew coming here with that strategy there was a risk we would lose the Tests. We are also wiser on Argentina now. The more we play the more we learn."

No-one was pressing the panic button but two successive defeats to their Pool D opponents was far from ideal. Ireland had fielded a second-string side and the players were keen to stress the World Cup encounter would be a different proposition altogether. "They will be very different teams," said Neil Best, "because there are a lot of players missing." Hindsight was to prove the Ulster prop off the mark.

Ireland completed their preparations in August with a 31–21 defeat to Scotland in Edinburgh and a 23–20 win over the Azzurri in the Italian capital and embarked for France.

After their headline-grabbing performances against the Springboks and Wallabies and a Six Nations campaign that had impressed without bringing home the ultimate prize, the reality was the Irish were beginning to stutter. Three defeats in their final four games going into the tournament told its own story and ultimately O'Sullivan and his players were unable to turn things around during the competition itself.

IRELAND INTERNATIONAL STATISTICS

MATCH RECORDS UP TO 31ST OCTOBER 2007

MOST CONSECUTIVE TEST WINS

10	2002 R,Ru,Gg,A,Fj,Arg,	2003 S1,It1,F,W1
8	2003 Tg, Sm,W2 ,It2, S2,	R ,Nm, Arg
6	1968 S,W,A,	1969 F,E,S
6	2004 SA,US,Arg,	2005 It,S,E

MOST CONSECUTIVE TEST WITHOUT DEFEAT

Matches	Wins	Draws	Period
10	10	0	2002 to 2003
8	8	0	2003
7	6	1	1968 to 1969
6	6	0	2004 to 2005

MOST POINTS IN A MATCH

BY THE TEAM

Pts.	Opponents	Venue	Year
83	United States	Manchester (NH)	2000
78	Japan	Dublin	2000
70	Georgia	Dublin	1998
64	Fiji	Dublin	2002
64	Namibia	Sydney	2003
63	Georgia	Dublin	2002
61	Italy	Limerick	2003
61	Pacific Islands	Dublin	2006
60	Romania	Dublin	1986
60	Italy	Dublin	2000
55	Zimbabwe	Dublin	1991
55	United States	Dublin	2004
54	Wales	Dublin	2002
53	Romania	Dublin	1998
53	United States	Dublin	1999
51	Italy	Rome	2007
50	Japan	Bloemfontein	1995

BY A PLAYER

Pts.	Player	Opponents	Venue	Year
32	R J R O'Gara	Samoa	Apia	2003
30	R J R O'Gara	Italy	Dublin	2000
26	D G Humphreys	Scotland	Murrayfield	2003
26	D G Humphreys	Italy	Limerick	2003
26	P Wallace	Pacific Islands	Dublin	2006
24	P A Burke	Italy	Dublin	1997
24	D G Humphreys	Argentina	Lens	1999
23	R P Keyes	Zimbabwe	Dublin	1991
23	R J R O'Gara	Japan	Dublin	2000
22	D G Humphreys	Wales	Dublin	2002
21	S O Campbell	Scotland	Dublin	1982
21	S O Campbell	England	Dublin	1983
21	R J R O'Gara	Italy	Rome	2001
21	R J R O'Gara	Argentina	Dublin	2004
21	R J R O'Gara	England	Dublin	2007
20	M J Kiernan	Romania	Dublin	1986
20	E P Elwood	Romania	Dublin	1993
20	S J P Mason	Samoa	Dublin	1996
20	E P Elwood	Georgia	Dublin	1998
20	K G M Wood	United States	Dublin	1999
20	D A Hickie	Italy	Limerick	2003
20	D G Humphreys	United States	Dublin	2004

MOST TRIES IN A MATCH

BY THE TEAM

Tries	Opponents	Venue	Year
13	United States	Manchester (NH)	2000
11	Japan	Dublin	2000
10	Romania	Dublin	1986
10	Georgia	Dublin	1998
10	Namibia	Sydney	2003
9	Fiji	Dublin	2003
8	Western Samoa	Dublin	1988
8	Zimbabwe	Dublin	1991
8	Georgia	Dublin	2002
8	Italy	Limerick	2003
8	Pacific Islands	Dublin	2006
8	Italy	Rome	2007
7	Japan	Bloemfontein	1995
7	Romania	Dublin	1998
7	United States	Dublin	1999
7	United States	Dublin	2004
7	Japan	Tokyo	2005

BY A PLAYER

Tries	Player	Opponents	Venue	Year
4	B F Robinson	Zimbabwe	Dublin	1991
4	K G M Wood	United States	Dublin	1999
4	D A Hickie	Italy	Limerick	2003
3	R Montgomery	Wales	Birkenhead	1887
3	J P Quinn	France	Cork	1913
3	E O'D Davy	Scotland	Murrayfield	1930
3	S J Byrne	Scotland	Murrayfield	1953
3	K D Crossan	Romania	Dublin	1986
3	B J Mullin	Tonga	Brisbane	1987
3	M R Mostyn	Argentina	Dublin	1999
3	B G O'Driscoll	France	Paris	2000
3	M J Mullins	United States	Manchester (NH)	2000
3	D A Hickie	Japan	Dublin	2000
3	R A J Henderson	Italy	Rome	2001
3	B G O'Driscoll	Scotland	Dublin	2002
3	K M Maggs	Fiji	Dublin	2002

MOST CONVERSIONS IN A MATCH

BY THE TEAM

Cons	Opponents	Venue	Year
10	Georgia	Dublin	1998
10	Japan	Dublin	2000
9	United States	Manchester (NH)	2000
7	Romania	Dublin	1986
7	Georgia	Dublin	2002
7	Namibia	Sydney	2003
7	United States	Dublin	2004
6	Japan	Bloemfontein	1995
6	Romania	Dublin	1998
6	United States	Dublin	1999
6	Italy	Dublin	2000
6	Italy	Limerick	2003
6	Japan	Tokyo	2005
6	Pacific Islands	Dublin	2006

BY A PLAYER

Cons	Player	Opponents	Venue	Year
10	E P Elwood	Georgia	Dublin	1998
10	R J R O'Gara	Japan	Dublin	2000
8	R J R O'Gara	United States	Manchester (NH)	2000
7	M J Kiernan	Romania	Dublin	1986
7	R J R O'Gara	Namibia	Sydney	2003
7	D G Humphreys	United States	Dublin	2004
6	P A Burke	Japan	Bloemfontein	1995
6	R J R O'Gara	Italy	Dublin	2000
6	D G Humphreys	Italy	Limerick	2003
6	D G Humphreys	Japan	Tokyo	2005
6	P Wallace	Pacific Islands	Dublin	2006
5	M J Kiernan	Canada	Dunedin	1987
5	E P Elwood	Romania	Dublin	1999
5	R J R O'Gara	Georgia	Dublin	2002
5	D G Humphreys	Fiji	Dublin	2002
5	D G Humphreys	Romania	Dublin	2005

MOST PENALTIES IN A MATCH

BY THE TEAM

Pens	Opponents	Venue	Year
8	Italy	Dublin	1997
7	Argentina	Lens	1999
6	Scotland	Dublin	1982
6	Romania	Dublin	1993
6	United States	Atlanta	1996
6	Western Samoa	Dublin	1996
6	Italy	Dublin	2000
6	Wales	Dublin	2002
6	Australia	Dublin	2002
6	Samoa	Apia	2003
6	Japan	Osaka	2005

BY A PLAYER

Pens	Player	Opponents	Venue	Year
8	P A Burke	Italy	Dublin	1997
7	D G Humphreys	Argentina	Lens	1999
6	S O Campbell	Scotland	Dublin	1982
6	E P Elwood	Romania	Dublin	1993
6	S J P Mason	Western Samoa	Dublin	1996
6	R J R O'Gara	Italy	Dublin	2000
6	D G Humphreys	Wales	Dublin	2002
6	R J R O'Gara	Australia	Dublin	2002

MOST DROPPED GOALS IN A MATCH

BY THE TEAM

Drops	Opponents	Venue	Year
2	Australia	Dublin	1967
2	France	Dublin	1975
2	Australia	Sydney	1979
2	England	Dublin	1981
2	Canada	Dunedin	1987
2	England	Dublin	1993
2	Wales	Wembley	1999
2	New Zealand	Dublin	2001
2	Argentina	Dublin	2004
2	England	Dublin	2005

BY A PLAYER

Drops	Player	Opponents	Venue	Year
2	C M H Gibson	Australia	Dublin	1967
2	W M McCombe	France	Dublin	1975
2	S O Campbell	Australia	Sydney	1979
2	E P Elwood	England	Dublin	1993
2	D G Humphreys	Wales	Wembley	1999
2	D G Humphreys	New Zealand	Dublin	2001
2	R J R O'Gara	Argentina	Dublin	2004
2	R J R O'Gara	England	Dublin	2005

MOST CAPPED PLAYERS

Caps	Player	Career Span
89	M E O'Kelly	1997 to 2007
79	B G O'Driscoll	1999 to 2007
79	P A Stringer	2000 to 2007
79	J J Hayes	2000 to 2007
78	G T Dempsey	1998 to 2007
77	R J R O'Gara	2000 to 2007
72	D G Humphreys	1996 to 2005
70	K M Maggs	1997 to 2005
69	C M H Gibson	1964 to 1979
63	W J McBride	1962 to 1975
62	A G Foley	1995 to 2005
62	D A Hickie	1997 to 2007
62	S H Easterby	2000 to 2007
61	J F Slattery	1970 to 1984
59	P S Johns	1990 to 2000
58	P A Orr	1976 to 1987
58	K G M Wood	1994 to 2003
58	S P Horgan	2000 to 2007
55	B J Mullin	1984 to 1995
54	T J Kiernan	1960 to 1973
54	P M Clohessy	1993 to 2002
52	D G Lenihan	1981 to 1992
52	G E A Murphy	2000 to 2007
51	M I Keane	1974 to 1984
51	M J Horan	2000 to 2007

MOST CONSECUTIVE TESTS

Tests	Player	Span
52	W J McBride	1964 to 1975
49	P A Orr	1976 to 1986
43	D G Lenihan	1981 to 1989
39	M I Keane	1974 to 1981
38	P A Stringer	2003 to 2007
37	G V Stephenson	1920 to 1929

MOST TESTS AS CAPTAIN

Tests	Captain	Span
42	B G O'Driscoll	2002 to 2007
36	K G M Wood	1996 to 2003
24	T J Kiernan	1963 to 1973
19	C F Fitzgerald	1982 to 1986
17	J F Slattery	1979 to 1981
17	D G Lenihan	1986 to 1990

MOST POINTS IN TESTS

Pts	Player	Tests	Career
779	R J R O'Gara	77	2000 to 2007
565*	D G Humphreys	72	1996 to 2005
308	M J Kiernan	43	1982 to 1991
296	E P Elwood	35	1993 to 1999
217	S O Campbell	22	1976 to 1984
167	B G O'Driscoll	79	1999 to 2007
158	T J Kiernan	54	1960 to 1973
145	D A Hickie	62	1997 to 2007
113	A J P Ward	19	1978 to 1987

* Humphreys's total includes a penalty try against Scotland in 1999

MOST TRIES IN TESTS

Tries	Player	Tests	Career
31	B G O'Driscoll	79	1999 to 2007
29	D A Hickie	62	1997 to 2007
20	S P Horgan	58	2000 to 2007
18	G T Dempsey	78	1998 to 2007
18	G E A Murphy	52	2000 to 2007
17	B J Mullin	55	1984 to 1995
15	K G M Wood	58	1994 to 2003
15	K M Maggs	70	1997 to 2005
14	G V Stephenson	42	1920 to 1930
14	R J R O'Gara	77	2000 to 2007
12	K D Crossan	41	1982 to 1992
11	A T A Duggan	25	1963 to 1972
11	S P Geoghegan	37	1991 to 1996

MOST CONVERSIONS IN TESTS

Cons	Player	Tests	Career
122	R J R O'Gara	77	2000 to 2007
88	D G Humphreys	72	1996 to 2005
43*	E P Elwood	35	1993 to 1999
40	M J Kiernan	43	1982 to 1991
26	T J Kiernan	54	1960 to 1973
16	R A Lloyd	19	1910 to 1920
15	S O Campbell	22	1976 to 1984

MOST PENALTY GOALS IN TESTS

Pens	Player	Tests	Career
144	R J R O'Gara	77	2000 to 2007
110	D G Humphreys	72	1996 to 2005
68	E P Elwood	35	1993 to 1999
62	M J Kiernan	43	1982 to 1991
54	S O Campbell	22	1976 to 1984
31	T J Kiernan	54	1960 to 1973
29	A J P Ward	19	1978 to 1987

MOST DROPPED GOALS IN TESTS

Drops	Player	Tests	Career
11	R J R O'Gara	77	2000 to 2007
8	D G Humphreys	72	1996 to 2005
7	R A Lloyd	19	1910 to 1920
7	S O Campbell	22	1976 to 1984
6	C M H Gibson	69	1964 to 1979
6	B J McGann	25	1969 to 1976
6	M J Kiernan	43	1982 to 1991

INTERNATIONAL CHAMPIONSHIP RECORDS

RECORD	DETAIL		SET
Most points in season	168	in five matches	2000
Most tries in season	17	in five matches	2000
	17	in five matches	2004
	17	in five matches	2007
Highest Score	60	60-13 v Italy	2000
Biggest win	47	60-13 v Italy	2000
Highest score conceded	50	18-50 v England	2000
Biggest defeat	40	6-46 v England	1997
Most appearances	56	C M H Gibson	1964 - 1979
Most points in matches	395	R J R O'Gara	2000 - 2007
Most points in season	82	R J R O'Gara	2007
Most points in match	30	R J R O'Gara	v Italy, 2000
Most tries in matches	17	B G O'Driscoll	2000 - 2007
Most tries in season	5	J E Arigho	1928
	5	B G O'Driscoll	2000
Most tries in match	3	R Montgomery`	v Wales, 1887
	3	J P Quinn	v France, 1913
	3	E O'D Davy	v Scotland, 1930
	3	S J Byrne	v Scotland, 1953
	3	B G O'Driscoll	v France, 2000
	3	R A J Henderson	v Italy, 2001
	3	B G O'Driscoll	v Scotland, 2002
Most cons in matches	55	R J R O'Gara	2000 - 2007
Most cons in season	11	R J R O'Gara	2000
	11	R J R O'Gara	2004
Most cons in match	6	R J R O'Gara	v Italy, 2000
Most pens in matches	77	R J R O'Gara	2000 - 2007
Most pens in season	17	R J R O'Gara	2006
Most pens in match	6	S O Campbell	v Scotland, 1982
	6	R J R O'Gara	v Italy, 2000
	6	D G Humphreys	v Wales, 2002
Most drops in matches	7	R A Lloyd	1910 – 1920
Most drops in season	2	on several	Occasions
Most drops in match	2	W M McCombe	v France, 1975
	2	E P Elwood	v England, 1993
	2	D G Humphreys	v Wales, 1999
	2	R J R O'Gara	v England, 2005

MISCELLANEOUS RECORDS

RECORD	HOLDER	DETAIL
Longest Test Career	A J F O'Reilly	1955 to 1970
	C M H Gibson	1964 to 1979
Youngest Test Cap	F S Hewitt	17 yrs 157 days in 1924
Oldest Test Cap	C M H Gibson	36 yrs 195 days in 1979

CAREER RECORDS OF IRELAND INTERNATIONAL PLAYERS (PLAYERS CAPPED SINCE THE START OF RWC 2003 UP TO 31 OCTOBER 2007)

PLAYER BACKS	DEBUT	CAPS	T	C	P	D	PTS
I J Boss	2006 v NZ	12	2	0	0	0	10
T J Bowe	2004 v US	10	3	0	0	0	15
B B Carney	2007 v Arg	4	1	0	0	0	5
G M D'Arcy	1999 v R	36	4	0	0	0	20
G T Dempsey	1998 v Gg	78	18	0	0	0	90
G W Duffy	2004 v SA	8	3	0	1	0	18
L Fitzgerald	2006 v PI	2	0	0	0	0	0
D A Hickie	1997 v W	62	29	0	0	0	145
S P Horgan	2000 v S	58	20	0	0	0	100
R D J Kearney	2007 v Arg	1	0	0	0	0	0
K P Lewis	2005 v J	3	0	0	0	0	0
B J Murphy	2007 v Arg	2	0	0	0	0	0
G E A Murphy	2000 v US	52	18	1	1	1	98
B G O'Driscoll	1999 v A	79	31	0	0	4	167
R J R O'Gara	2000 v S	77	14	122	144	11	779
T G O'Leary	2007 v Arg	1	0	0	0	0	0
E G Reddan	2006 F	5	0	0	0	0	0
J W Staunton	2001 v Sm	5	1	2	4	0	21
P A Stringer	2000 v S	79	6	0	0	0	30
A D Trimble	2005 v A	19	8	0	0	0	40
P W Wallace	2006 v SA	6	1	10	6	0	43

FORWARDS							
N A Best	2005 v NZ	18	2	0	0	0	10
R Best	2005 v NZ	17	3	0	0	0	15
S J Best	2003 v Tg	23	1	0	0	0	5
T D Buckley	2007 v Arg	2	0	0	0	0	0
L F M Cullen	2002 v NZ	19	0	0	0	0	0
S H Easterby	2000 v S	62	8	0	0	0	40
S Ferris	2006 v PI	4	0	0	0	0	0
J P Flannery	2005 v R	21	3	0	0	0	15
K D Gleeson	2002 v W	27	4	0	0	0	20
J J Hayes	2000 v S	79	2	0	0	0	10
J P R Heaslip	2006 v PI	3	0	0	0	0	0
T Hogan	2005 v J	4	0	0	0	0	0
M J Horan	2000 v US	51	5	0	0	0	25
B J Jackman	2005 v J	4	0	0	0	0	0
S Jennings	2007 v Arg	1	0	0	0	0	0
D P Leamy	2004 v US	27	1	0	0	0	5
D P O'Callaghan	2003 v W	40	1	0	0	0	5
P J O'Connell	2002 v W	49	6	0	0	0	30
M R O'Driscoll	2001 v R	11	0	0	0	0	0
M E O'Kelly	1997 v NZ	89	8	0	0	0	40
A N Quinlan	1999 v R	25	5	0	0	0	25
F J Sheahan	2000 v US	29	5	0	0	0	25
D P Wallace	2000 v Arg	41	7	0	0	0	35
B G Young	2006 v NZ	8	0	0	0	0	0

Shaun Botterill/Getty Images

Mal O'Kelly ended the season as Ireland's most-capped player, after 89 Tests.

IRELAND INTERNATIONAL PLAYERS

UP TO 31ST OCTOBER 2007

Note: Years given for International Championship matches are for second half of season; eg 1972 means season 1971–72. Years for all other matches refer to the actual year of the match. Entries in square brackets denote matches played in RWC Finals.

Abraham, M (Bective Rangers) 1912 E, S, W, SA, 1914 W
Adams, C (Old Wesley), 1908 E, 1909 E, F, 1910 F, 1911 E, S, W, F, 1912 S, W, SA, 1913 W, F, 1914 F, E, S
Agar, R D (Malone) 1947 F, E, S, W, 1948 F, 1949 S, W, 1950 F, E, W
Agnew, P J (CIYMS) 1974 F (R), 1976 A
Ahearne, T (Queen's Coll, Cork) 1899 E
Aherne, L F P (Dolphin, Lansdowne) 1988 E 2, WS, It, 1989 F, W, E, S, NZ, 1990 E, S, F, W (R), 1992 E, S, F, A
Alexander, R (NIFC, Police Union) 1936 E, S, W, 1937 E, S, W, 1938 E, S, 1939 E, S, W
Allen, C E (Derry, Liverpool) 1900 E, S, W, 1901 E, S, W, 1903 S, W, 1904 E, S, W, 1905 E, S, W, NZ, 1906 E, S, W, SA, 1907 S, W
Allen, G G (Derry, Liverpool) 1896 E, S, W, 1897 E, S, 1898 E, S, 1899 E, W
Allen, T C (NIFC) 1885 E, S 1
Allen, W S (Wanderers) 1875 E
Allison, J B (Edinburgh U) 1899 E, S, 1900 E, S, W, 1901 E, S, W, 1902 E, S, W, 1903 S
Anderson, F E (Queen's U, Belfast, NIFC) 1953 F, E, S, W, 1954 NZ, F, E, S, W, 1955 F, E, S, W
Anderson, H J (Old Wesley) 1903 E, S, 1906 E, S
Anderson, W A (Dungannon) 1984 A, 1985 S, F, W, E, 1986 F, S, R, 1987 E, S, F, W, [W, C, Tg, A], 1988 S, F, W, E 1,2, 1989 F, W, E, NZ, 1990 E, S
Andrews, G (NIFC) 1875 E, 1876 E
Andrews, H W (NIFC) 1888 M, 1889 S, W
Archer, A M (Dublin U, NIFC) 1879 S
Arigho, J E (Lansdowne) 1928 F, E, W, 1929 F, E, S, W, 1930 F, E, S, W, 1931 F, E, S, W, SA
Armstrong, W K (NIFC) 1960 SA, 1961 E
Arnott, D T (Lansdowne) 1876 E
Ash, W H (NIFC) 1875 E, 1876 E, 1877 S
Aston, H R (Dublin U) 1908 E, W
Atkins, A P (Bective Rangers) 1924 F
Atkinson, J M (NIFC) 1927 F, A
Atkinson, J R (Dublin U) 1882 W, S

Bagot, J C (Dublin U, Lansdowne) 1879 S, E, 1880 E, S, 1881 S
Bailey, A H (UC Dublin, Lansdowne) 1934 W, 1935 E, S, W, NZ, 1936 E, S, W, 1937 E, S, W, 1938 E, S
Bailey, N (Northampton) 1952 E
Bardon, M E (Bohemians) 1934 E
Barlow, M (Wanderers) 1875 E
Barnes, R J (Dublin U, Armagh) 1933 W
Barr, A (Methodist Coll, Belfast) 1898 W, 1899 S, 1901 E, S
Barry, N J (Garryowen) 1991 Nm 2(R)
Beamish, C E St J (RAF, Leicester) 1933 W, S, 1934 S, W, 1935 E, S, W, NZ, 1936 E, S, W, 1938 W
Beamish, G R (RAF, Leicester) 1925 E, S, W, 1928 F, E, S, W, 1929 F, E, S, W, 1930 F, S, W, 1931 F, E, S, W, SA, 1932 E, S, W, 1933 E, W, S
Beatty, W J (NIFC, Richmond) 1910 F, 1912 F, W
Becker, V A (Lansdowne) 1974 F, W
Beckett, G G P (Dublin U) 1908 E, S, W
Bell, J C (Ballymena, Northampton, Dungannon) 1994 A 1,2, US, 1995 S, It, [NZ, W, F], Fj, 1996 US, S, F, W, E, WS, A, 1997 It 1, F, W, E, S, 1998 Gg, R, SA 3, 1999 F, W, S It (R), A 2, [US (R), A 3(R), R], 2001 R (R), 2003 Tg, Sm, It 2(R)
Bell, R J (NIFC) 1875 E, 1876 E
Bell, W E (Belfast Collegians) 1953 F, E, S, W
Bennett, F (Belfast Collegians) 1913 S
Bent, G C (Dublin U) 1882 W, E
Berkery, P J (Lansdowne) 1954 W, 1955 W, 1956 S, W, 1957 F, E, S, W, 1958 A, E, S
Bermingham, J J C (Blackrock Coll) 1921 E, S, W, F
Best, N A (Ulster) 2005 NZ(R),R, 2006 NZ1,2,A1,SA,A2, 2007 F(R),E(R),S1(R),Arg1,2(R),S2,It2, [Nm(R),Gg(R),F(R),Arg(t&R]
Best, R (Ulster) 2005 NZ(R),A(t), 2006 W(R),A1(R),SA,A2,PI(R), 2007 W,F,E,S1,It1,S2(R),It2, [Nm,Gg,Arg(R)]
Best, S J (Belfast Harlequins, Ulster) 2003 Tg (R), W 2, S 2(R), 2003 [Nm(R)], 2004 W(R),US(R), 2005 J1,2,NZ(R),R, 2006 F(R), W(R),PI(R), 2007 E(R),S1,It1(R),Arg1,2,S2,It2(R), [Nm(R),Gg(R),F(R)]
Bishop, J P (London Irish) 1998 SA, 1,2, Gg, R, SA 3, 1999 F, W, E, S, It, A 1,2, Arg 1, [US, A 3, Arg 2], 2000 E, Arg, C, 2002 NZ 1,2, Fj, Arg, 2003 W 1, E
Blackham, J C (Queen's Coll, Cork) 1909 S, W, F, 1910 E, S, W
Blake-Knox, S E F (NIFC) 1976 E, S, 1977 F (R)
Blayney, J J (Wanderers) 1950 S
Bond, A T W (Derry) 1894 S, W
Bornemann, W W (Wanderers) 1960 E, S, W, SA
Boss, I J (Ulster) 2006 NZ2(R),A1(R),SA(R),A2,PI(R), 2007 F,E(R),Arg1,S2,It2(R), [Gg(R),Arg(R)]
Bowe, T J (Ulster) 2004 US, 2005 J1,2,NZ,A,R, 2006 It,F, 2007 Arg1,S2
Bowen, D St J (Cork Const) 1977 W, E, S
Boyd, C A (Dublin U) 1900 S, 1901 S, W
Boyle, C V (Dublin U) 1935 NZ, 1936 E, S, W, 1937 E, S, W, 1938 W, 1939 W
Brabazon, H M (Dublin U) 1884 E, 1885 S 1, 1886 E
Bradley, M J (Dolphin) 1920 W, F, 1922 E, S, W, F, 1923 E, S, W, F, 1925 F, S, W, 1926 F, E, S, W, 1927 F, W
Bradley, M T (Cork Constitution) 1984 A, 1985 S, F, W, E, 1986 F, W, E, S, R, 1987 E, S, F, W, [W, C, Tg, A], 1988 S, F, W, E 1, 1990 W, 1992 NZ 1,2, 1993 S, F, W, E, R, 1994 F, W, E, S, A 1,2, US, 1995 S, F, [NZ]
Bradshaw, G (Belfast Collegians) 1903 W
Bradshaw, R M (Wanderers) 1885 E, S 1,2
Brady, A M (UC Dublin, Malone) 1966 S, 1968 E, S, W
Brady, J A (Wanderers) 1976 E, S
Brady, J R (CIYMS) 1951 S, W, 1953 F, E, S, W, 1954 W, 1956 W, 1957 F, E, S, W
Bramwell, T (NIFC) 1928 F
Brand, T N (NIFC) 1924 NZ
Brennan, J I (CIYMS) 1957 S, W
Brennan, T (St Mary's Coll, Barnhall) 1998 SA 1(R),2(R), 1999 F (R), S (R), It, A 2, Arg 1, [US, A 3], 2000 E (R), 2001 W (R), E (R), Sm (R)
Bresnihan, F P K (UC Dublin, Lansdowne, London Irish) 1966 E, W, 1967 A 1, E, S, W, F, 1968 F, E, S, W, A, 1969 F, E, S, W, 1970 SA, F, E, S, W, 1971 F, E, S, W
Brett, J T (Monkstown) 1914 W
Bristow, J R (NIFC) 1879 E
Brophy, N H (Blackrock Coll, UC Dublin, London Irish) 1957 F, E, 1959 E, S, W, F, 1960 F, SA, 1961 S, W, 1962 E, S, W, 1963 E, W, 1967 E, S, W, F, A 2

Brown, E L (Instonians) 1958 F
Brown, G S (Monkstown, United Services) 1912 S, W, SA
Brown, H (Windsor) 1877 E
Brown, T (Windsor) 1877 E, S
Brown, W H (Dublin U) 1899 E
Brown, W J (Malone) 1970 SA, F, S, W
Brown, W S (Dublin U) 1893 S, W, 1894 E, S, W
Browne, A W (Dublin U) 1951 SA
Browne, D (Blackrock Coll) 1920 F
Browne, H C (United Services and RN) 1929 E, S, W
Browne, W F (United Services and Army) 1925 E, S, W, 1926 S, W, 1927 F, E, S, W, A, 1928 E, S
Browning, D R (Wanderers) 1881 E, S
Bruce, S A M (NIFC) 1883 E, S, 1884 E
Brunker, A A (Lansdowne) 1895 E, W
Bryant, C H (Cardiff) 1920 E, S
Buchanan, A McM (Dublin U) 1926 E, S, W, 1927 S, W, A
Buchanan, J W B (Dublin U) 1882 S, 1884 E, S
Buckley, J H (Sunday's Well) 1973 E, S
Buckley, T D (Munster) 2007 Arg1(R),2(R)
Bulger, L Q (Lansdowne) 1896 E, S, W, 1897 E, S, 1898 E, S, W
Bulger, M J (Dublin U) 1888 M
Burges, J H (Rosslyn Park) 1950 F, E
Burgess, R B (Dublin U) 1912 SA
Burke, P A (Cork Constitution, Bristol, Harlequins) 1995 E, S, W (R), It, [J], Fj, 1996 US (R), A, 1997 It 1, S (R), 2001 R (R), 2003 S 1(R), Sm (R)
Burkitt, J C S (Queen's Coll, Cork) 1881 E
Burns, I J (Wanderers) 1980 E (R)
Butler, L G (Blackrock Coll) 1960 W
Butler, N (Bective Rangers) 1920 E
Byers, R M (NIFC) 1928 S, W, 1929 E, S, W
Byrne, E (St Mary's Coll) 2001 It (R), F (R), S (R), W (R), E (R), Sm, NZ (R), 2003 A (R), Sm (R)
Byrne, E M J (Blackrock Coll) 1977 S, F, 1978 F, W, E, NZ
Byrne, J S (Blackrock Coll, Leinster, Saracens) 2001 R (R), 2002 W (R), E (R), S (R), It, NZ 2(R), R, Ru (R), Gg, A, Arg, 2003 S 1, It 1, F, W 1, E, A, Tg, Sm, W 2(R), It 2, S2(R), [R(R),Nm(R)], 2004 F,W,E,It,S,SA1,2,3,Arg, 2005 It,S,E,F,W,NZ,A,R
Byrne, N F (UC Dublin) 1962 F
Byrne, S J (UC Dublin, Lansdowne) 1953 S, W, 1955 F
Byron, W G (NIFC) 1896 E, S, W, 1897 E, S, 1898 E, S, W, 1899 E, S, W

Caddell, E D (Dublin U, Wanderers) 1904 S, 1905 E, S, W, NZ, 1906 E, S, W, SA, 1907 E, S, 1908 S, W
Cagney, S J (London Irish) 1925 W, 1926 F, E, S, W, 1927 F, 1928 E, S, W, 1929 F, E, S, W
Callan, C P (Lansdowne) 1947 F, E, S, W, 1948 F, E, S, W, 1949 F, E
Cameron, E D (Bective Rangers) 1891 S, W
Campbell, C E (Old Wesley) 1970 SA
Campbell, E F (Monkstown) 1899 S, W, 1900 E, W
Campbell, K P (Ulster) 2005 J1(R),2(R),R
Campbell, S B B (Derry) 1911 E, S, W, F, 1912 F, E, S, W, SA, 1913 E, S, F
Campbell, S O (Old Belvedere) 1976 A, 1979 A 1,2, 1980 E, S, F, W, 1981 F, W, E, S, SA 1, 1982 W, E, S, F, 1983 S, F, W, E, 1984 F, W
Canniffe, D M (Lansdowne) 1976 W, E
Cantrell, J L (UC Dublin, Blackrock Coll) 1976 A, F, W, E, S, 1981 S, SA 1,2, A
Carey, R W (Dungannon) 1992 NZ 1,2
Carney, B B (Munster) 2007 Arg1,2,S2,It2(R)
Carpendale, M J (Monkstown) 1886 S, 1887 W, 1888 W, S
Carr, N J (Ards) 1985 S, F, W, E, 1986 W, E, S, R, 1987 E, S, W
Carroll, C (Bective Rangers) 1930 F
Carroll, R (Lansdowne) 1947 F, 1950 S, W
Casement, B N (Dublin U) 1875 E, 1876 E, 1879 E
Casement, F (Dublin U) 1906 E, S, W
Casey, J C (Young Munster) 1930 S, 1932 E
Casey, P J (UC Dublin, Lansdowne) 1963 F, E, S, W, NZ, 1964 E, S, W, F, 1965 F, E, S
Casey, R E (Blackrock Coll) 1999 [A 3(t), Arg 2(R)], 2000 E, US (R), C (R)
Chambers, J (Dublin U) 1886 E, S, 1887 E, S, W
Chambers, R R (Instonians) 1951 F, E, S, W, 1952 F, W
Clancy, T P J (Lansdowne) 1988 W, E 1,2, WS, It, 1989 F, W, E, S
Clarke, A T H (Northampton, Dungannon) 1995 Fj (R), 1996 W, E, WS, 1997 F (R), It 2(R), 1998 Gg (R), R
Clarke, C P (Terenure Coll) 1993 F, W, E, 1998 W, E
Clarke, D J (Dolphin) 1991 W, Nm 1,2, [J, A], 1992 NZ 2(R)
Clarke, J A B (Bective Rangers) 1922 S, W, F, 1923 F, 1924 E, S, W
Clegg, R J (Bangor) 1973 F, 1975 E, S, F, W
Clifford, J T (Young Munster) 1949 F, E, S, W, 1950 F, E, S, W, 1951 F, E, SA, 1952 F, S, W
Clinch, A D (Dublin U, Wanderers) 1892 S, 1893 W, 1895 E, S, W, 1896 E, S, W, 1897 E, S
Clinch, J D (Wanderers, Dublin U) 1923 W, 1924 F, E, S, W, NZ, 1925 F, E, S, 1926 E, S, W, 1927 F, 1928 F, E, S, W, 1929 F, E, S, W, 1930 F, E, S, W, 1931 F, E, S, W, SA
Clohessy, P M (Young Munster) 1993 F, W, E, 1994 F, W, E, S, A 1,2, US, 1995 E, S, F, W, 1996 S, F, 1997 It 2, 1998 F (R), W (R), SA 2(R), Gg, R, SA 3, 1999 F, W, E, S, It, A 1,2 Arg 1, [US, A 3(R)], 2000 E, S, It, F, W, Arg, J, SA, 2001 It, F, R, S, W, E, Sm (R), NZ, 2002 W, E, S, It, F
Clune, J J (Blackrock Coll) 1912 SA, 1913 W, F, 1914 F, E, W
Coffey, J J (Lansdowne) 1900 E, 1901 W, 1902 E, S, W, 1903 E, S, W, 1905 E, S, W, NZ, 1906 E, S, W, SA, 1907 E, 1908 W, 1910 F
Cogan, W St J (Queen's Coll, Cork) 1907 E, S
Collier, S R (Queen's Coll, Belfast) 1883 S
Collins, P C (Lansdowne, London Irish) 1987 [C], 1990 S (R)
Collis, W R F (KCH, Harlequins) 1924 F, W, NZ, 1925 F, E, S, 1926 F
Collis, W S (Wanderers) 1884 W
Collopy, G (Bective Rangers) 1891 S, 1892 S
Collopy, R (Bective Rangers) 1923 E, S, W, F, 1924 F, E, S, W, NZ, 1925 F, E, S, W
Collopy, W P (Bective Rangers) 1914 F, E, S, W, 1921 E, S, W, F, 1922 E, S, W, F, 1923 S, W, F, 1924 F, E, S, W
Combe, A (NIFC) 1875 E
Condon, H C (London Irish) 1984 S (R)
Cook, H G (Lansdowne) 1884 W
Coote, P B (RAF, Leicester) 1933 S
Corcoran, J C (London Irish) 1947 A, 1948 F
Corken, T S (Belfast Collegians) 1937 E, S, W
Corkery, D S (Cork Constitution, Bristol) 1994 A 1,2, US, 1995 E, [NZ, J, W, F], Fj, 1996 US, S, F, W, E, WS, A, 1997 It 1, F, W, E, S, 1998 S, F, W, E, 1999 A 1(R),2(R)
Corley, H H (Dublin U, Wanderers) 1902 E, S, W, 1903 E, S, W, 1904 E, S
Cormac, H S T (Clontarf) 1921 E, S, W
Corrigan, R (Greystones, Lansdowne, Leinster) 1997 C (R), It 2, 1998 S, F, W, E, SA 3(R), 1999 A 1(R),2(R), [Arg 2], 2002 NZ 1,2, R, Ru, Gg, A, Fj (R), Arg, 2003 S 1, It 1, A, Tg, Sm, W 2, It 2, S 2, [R,Arg,A,F], 2004 F,W,E,It,S,SA1,2,3,Arg, 2005 It,S,E,F,W,J1(R),2(R), 2006 F
Costello, P (Bective Rangers) 1960 F
Costello, R A (Garryowen) 1993 S
Costello, V C P (St Mary's Coll, London Irish) 1996 US, F, W, E. WS (R), 1997 C, It 2(R), 1998 S (R), F, W, E, SA 1,2, Gg, R, SA 3, 1999 F, W (R), E, S (R), It, A 1, 2002 R (R), A, Arg, 2003 S 1, It 1, F, E, A, It 2, S 2, [R,Arg,F], 2004 F(R),W(R),It(R), S(R)
Cotton, J (Wanderers) 1889 W
Coulter, H H (Queen's U, Belfast) 1920 E, S, W
Courtney, A W (UC Dublin) 1920 S, W, F, 1921 E, S, W, F
Cox, H L (Dublin U) 1875 E, 1876 E, 1877 E, S
Craig, R G (Queen's U, Belfast) 1938 S, W
Crawford, E C (Dublin U) 1885 E, S 1
Crawford, W E (Lansdowne) 1920 E, S, W, F, 1921 E, S, W, F, 1922 E, S, 1923 E, S, W, F, 1924 F, E, W, NZ, 1925 F, E, S, W, 1926 F, E, S, W, 1927 F, E, S, W
Crean, T J (Wanderers) 1894 E, S, W, 1895 E, S, W, 1896 E, S, W
Crichton, R Y (Dublin U) 1920 E, S, W, F, 1921 F, 1922 E, 1923 W, F, 1924 F, E, S, W, NZ, 1925 E, S
Croker, E W D (Limerick) 1878 E
Cromey, G E (Queen's U, Belfast) 1937 E, S, W, 1938 E, S, W, 1939 E, S, W
Cronin, B M (Garryowen) 1995 S, 1997 S
Cronyn, A P (Dublin U, Lansdowne) 1875 E, 1876 E, 1880 S

Crossan, K D (Instonians) 1982 S, 1984 F, W, E, S, 1985 S, F, W, E, 1986 E, S, R, 1987 E, S, F, W, [W, C, Tg, A], 1988 S, F, W, E 1, WS, It, 1989 W, S, NZ, 1990 E, S, F, W, Arg, 1991 E, S, Nm 2 [Z, J, S], 1992 W
Crotty, D J (Garryowen) 1996 A, 1997 It 1, F, W, 2000 C
Crowe, J F (UC Dublin) 1974 NZ
Crowe, L (Old Belvedere) 1950 E, S, W
Crowe, M P (Lansdowne) 1929 W, 1930 E, S, W, 1931 F, S, W, SA, 1932 S, W, 1933 W, S, 1934 E
Crowe, P M (Blackrock Coll) 1935 E, 1938 E
Cullen, L F M (Blackrock Coll, Leinster, Leicester) 2002 NZ 2(R), R (R), Ru (R), Gg (R), A (R), Fj, Arg (R), 2003 S 1(R), It 1(R), F (R), W 1, Tg, Sm, It 2, 2004 US(R), 2005 J1,2,R, 2007 Arg2
Cullen, T J (UC Dublin) 1949 F
Cullen, W J (Monkstown and Manchester) 1920 E
Culliton, M G (Wanderers) 1959 E, S, W, F, 1960 E, S, W, F, SA, 1961 E, S, W, F, 1962 S, F, 1964 E, S, W, F
Cummins, W E A (Queen's Coll, Cork) 1879 S, 1881 E, 1882 E
Cunningham, D McC (NIFC) 1923 E, S, W, 1925 F, E, W
Cunningham, M J (UC Cork) 1955 F, E, S, W, 1956 F, S, W
Cunningham, V J G (St Mary's Coll) 1988 E 2, It, 1990 Arg (R), 1991 Nm 1,2, [Z, J(R)], 1992 NZ 1,2, A, 1993 S, F, W, E, R, 1994 F
Cunningham, W A (Lansdowne) 1920 W, 1921 E, S, W, F, 1922 E, 1923 S, W
Cuppaidge, J L (Dublin U) 1879 E, 1880 E, S
Currell, J (NIFC) 1877 S
Curtis, A B (Oxford U) 1950 F, E, S
Curtis, D M (London Irish) 1991 W, E, S, Nm 1,2, [Z, J, S, A], 1992 W, E, S (R), F
Cuscaden, W A (Dublin U, Bray) 1876 E
Cussen, D J (Dublin U) 1921 E, S, W, F, 1922 E, 1923 E, S, W, F, 1926 F, E, S, W, 1927 F, E

Daly, J C (London Irish) 1947 F, E, S, W, 1948 E, S, W
Daly, M J (Harlequins) 1938 E
Danaher, P P A (Lansdowne, Garryowen) 1988 S, F, W, WS, It, 1989 F, NZ (R), 1990 F, 1992 S, F, NZ 1, A, 1993 S, F, W, E, R, 1994 F, W, E, S, A 1,2, US, 1995 E, S, F, W
D'Arcy, G M (Lansdowne, Leinster) 1999 [R (R)], 2002 Fj (R), 2003 Tg (R), Sm (R), W 2(R), 2004 F,W,E,It,S,SA1, 2005 It,NZ,A,R, 2006 It,F,W,S,E,NZ1,2,A1,SA,A2,PI(R), 2007 W,F,E,S1,It1,2, [Nm,Gg,F,Arg]
Dargan, M J (Old Belvedere) 1952 S, W
Davidson, C T (NIFC) 1921 F
Davidson, I G (NIFC) 1899 E, 1900 S, W, 1901 E, S, W, 1902 E, S, W
Davidson, J C (Dungannon) 1969 F, E, S, W, 1973 NZ, 1976 NZ
Davidson, J W (Dungannon, London Irish, Castres) 1995 Fj, 1996 S, F, W, E, WS, A, 1997 It 1, F, W, E, S, 1998 Gg (R), R (R), SA 3(R), 1999 F, W, E, S, It, A 1,2(R), Arg 1, [US,R (R), Arg 2], 2000 S (R), W (R), US, C, 2001 It (R), S
Davies, F E (Lansdowne) 1892 S, W, 1893 E, S, W
Davis, J L (Monkstown) 1898 E, S
Davis, W J N (Edinburgh U, Bessbrook) 1890 S, W, E, 1891 E, S, W, 1892 E, S, 1895 S
Davison, W (Belfast Academy) 1887 W
Davy, E O'D (UC Dublin, Lansdowne) 1925 W, 1926 F, E, S, W, 1927 F, E, S, W, A, 1928 F, E, S, W, 1929 F, E, S, W, 1930 F, E, S, W, 1931 F, E, S, W, SA, 1932 E, S, W, 1933 E, W, S, 1934 E
Dawson, A R (Wanderers) 1958 A, E, S, W, F, 1959 E, S, W, F, 1960 F, SA, 1961 E, S, W, F, SA, 1962 S, F, W, 1963 F, E, S, W, NZ, 1964 E, S, F
Dawson, K (London Irish) 1997 NZ, C, 1998 S, 1999 [R, Arg 2], 2000 E, S, It, F, W, J, SA, 2001 R, S, W (R), E (R), Sm, 2002 Fj, 2003 Tg, It 2(R), S 2(R)
Dean, P M (St Mary's Coll) 1981 SA 1,2, A, 1982 W, E, S, F, 1984 A, 1985 S, F, W, E, 1986 F, W, R, 1987 E, S, F, W, [W, A], 1988 S, F, W, E 1,2, WS, It, 1989 F, W, E, S
Deane, E C (Monkstown) 1909 E
Deering, M J (Bective Rangers) 1929 W
Deering, S J (Bective Rangers) 1935 E, S, W, NZ, 1936 E, S, W, 1937 E, S
Deering, S M (Garryowen, St Mary's Coll) 1974 W, 1976 F, W, E, S, 1977 W, E, 1978 NZ
de Lacy, H (Harlequins) 1948 E, S
Delany, M G (Bective Rangers) 1895 W
Dempsey, G T (Terenure Coll, Leinster) 1998 Gg (R). SA 3, 1999 F, E, S, It, A 2, 2000 E (R), S, It, F, W, SA, 2001 It, F, S, W, E, NZ, 2002 W, E, S, It, F, NZ 1,2, R, Ru, Gg, A, Arg, 2003 S 1, E (R), A, Sm, W 2(R), It 2, S 2(R),[R,Nm,Arg,A,F], 2004 F,W, E,It,S,SA1,2,3,US(R),Arg, 2005 It(R),S,E,F,W,J1, 2,NZ(R),R(R), 2006 E(R),NZ1(R),2(t&R),A1,SA,A2(R),PI, 2007 W,F,E,S1,It1,2, [Nm,Gg,F]
Dennison, S P (Garryowen) 1973 F, 1975 E, S
Dick, C J (Ballymena) 1961 W, F, SA, 1962 W, 1963 F, E, S, W
Dick, J S (Queen's U, Belfast) 1962 E
Dick, J S (Queen's U, Cork) 1887 E, S, W
Dickson, J A N (Dublin U) 1920 E, W, F
Doherty, A E (Old Wesley) 1974 P (R)
Doherty, W D (Guy's Hospital) 1920 E, S, W, 1921 E, S, W, F
Donaldson, J A (Belfast Collegians) 1958 A, E, S, W
Donovan, T M (Queen's Coll, Cork) 1889 S
Dooley, J F (Galwegians) 1959 E, S, W
Doran, B R W (Lansdowne) 1900 S, W, 1901 E, S, W, 1902 E, S, W
Doran, E F (Lansdowne) 1890 S, W
Doran, G P (Lansdowne) 1899 S, W, 1900 E, S, 1902 S, W, 1903 W, 1904 E
Douglas, A C (Instonians) 1923 F, 1924 E, S, 1927 A, 1928 S
Downing, A J (Dublin U) 1882 W
Dowse, J C A (Monkstown) 1914 F, S, W
Doyle, J A P (Greystones) 1984 E, S
Doyle, J T (Bective Rangers) 1935 W
Doyle, M G (Blackrock Coll, UC Dublin, Cambridge U, Edinburgh Wands) 1965 F, E, S, W, SA, 1966 F, E, S, W, 1967 A 1, E, S, W, F, A 2, 1968 F, E, S, W, A
Doyle, T J (Wanderers) 1968 E, S, W
Duffy, G W (Harlequins, Connacht) 2004 SA 2(R), 2005 S(R),J1,2, 2007 Arg1,2,S2, [Arg(R)]
Duggan, A T A (Lansdowne) 1963 NZ, 1964 F, 1966 W, 1967 A 1, S, W, A 2, 1968 F, E, S, W, 1969 F, E, S, W, 1970 SA, F, E, S, W, 1971 F, E, S, W, 1972 F 2
Duggan, W (UC Cork) 1920 S, W
Duggan, W P (Blackrock Coll) 1975 E, S, F, W, 1976 A, F, W, S, NZ, 1977 W, E, S, F, 1978 S, F, W, E, NZ, 1979 E, S, A 1,2, 1980 E, 1981 F, W, E, S, SA 1,2, A, 1982 W, E, S, 1983 S, F, W, E, 1984 F, W, E, S
Duignan, P (Galwegians) 1998 Gg, R
Duncan, W R (Malone) 1984 W, E
Dunlea, F J (Lansdowne) 1989 W, E, S
Dunlop, R (Dublin U) 1889 W, 1890 S, W, E, 1891 E, S, W, 1892 E, S, 1893 W, 1894 W
Dunn, P E F (Bective Rangers) 1923 S
Dunn, T B (NIFC) 1935 NZ
Dunne, M J (Lansdowne) 1929 F, E, S, 1930 F, E, S, W, 1932 E, S, W, 1933 E, W, S, 1934 E, S, W
Dwyer, P J (UC Dublin) 1962 W, 1963 F, NZ, 1964 S, W

Easterby, S H (Llanelli Scarlets) 2000 S, It, F, W, Arg, US, C, 2001 S, Sm (R), 2002 W, E (R), S (R), It, F, NZ 1,2, R, Ru, Gg, 2003 Tg, Sm, It 2, S 2(t+R), [Nm,Arg,A,F], 2004 F,W,E,It,S,SA1,2,3,US,Arg, 2005 It,S,E,F,W,NZ,A, 2006 It,F,W,S,E,SA(R),A2(R),PI, 2007 W,F,E,S1,It1,2, [Nm,Gg, F,Arg]
Easterby, W G (Ebbw Vale, Ballynahinch, Llanelli, Leinster) 2000 US, C (R), 2001 R (R), S, W (R), Sm (R), 2002 W (R), S (R), R (R), Ru (R), Gg (R), Fj, 2003 S 1(R), It 1(R), Tg, Sm, W 2(R), It 2, S 2(R), [R(R),Nm(R),F(R)], 2004 W(R),It(R),S(R),SA2(R),US, 2005 S(R)
Edwards, H G (Dublin U) 1877 E, 1878 E
Edwards, R W (Malone) 1904 W
Edwards, T (Lansdowne) 1888 M, 1890 S, W, E, 1892 W, 1893 E
Edwards, W V (Malone) 1912 F, E
Egan, J D (Bective Rangers) 1922 S
Egan, J T (Cork Constitution) 1931 F, E, SA
Egan, M S (Garryowen) 1893 E, 1895 S
Ekin, W (Queen's Coll, Belfast) 1888 W, S
Elliott, W R J (Bangor) 1979 S
Elwood, E P (Lansdowne, Galwegians) 1993 W, E, R, 1994 F, W, E, S, A 1,2, 1995 F, W, [NZ, W, F], 1996 US, S, 1997 F, W, E, NZ, C, It 2(R), 1998 F, W, E, SA 1,2, Gg, R, SA 3, 1999 It, Arg 1(R), [US (R), A 3(R), R]

English, M A F (Lansdowne, Limerick Bohemians) 1958 W, F, 1959 E, S, F, 1960 E, S, 1961 S, W, F, 1962 F, W, 1963 E, S, W, NZ
Ennis, F N G (Wanderers) 1979 A 1(R)
Ensor, A H (Wanderers) 1973 W, F, 1974 F, W, E, S, P, NZ, 1975 E, S, F, W, 1976 A, F, W, E, NZ, 1977 E, 1978 S, F, W, E
Entrican, J C (Queen's U, Belfast) 1931 S
Erskine, D J (Sale) 1997 NZ (R), C, It 2

Fagan, G L (Kingstown School) 1878 E
Fagan, W B C (Wanderers) 1956 F, E, S
Farrell, J L (Bective Rangers) 1926 F, E, S, W, 1927 F, E, S, W, A, 1928 F, E, S, W, 1929 F, E, S, W, 1930 F, E, S, W, 1931 F, E, S, W, SA, 1932 E, S, W
Feddis, N (Lansdowne) 1956 E
Feighery, C F P (Lansdowne) 1972 F 1, E, F 2
Feighery, T A O (St Mary's Coll) 1977 W, E
Ferris, H H (Queen's Coll, Belfast) 1901 W
Ferris, J H (Queen's Coll, Belfast) 1900 E, S, W
Ferris, S (Ulster) 2006 PI, 2007 Arg1(R),2,S2
Field, M J (Malone) 1994 E, S, A 1(R), 1995 F (R), W (t), It (R), [NZ(t + R), J], Fj, 1996 F (R), W, E, A (R), 1997 F, W, E, S
Finlay, J E (Queen's Coll, Belfast) 1913 E, S, W, 1920 E, S, W
Finlay, W (NIFC) 1876 E, 1877 E, S, 1878 E, 1879 S, E, 1880 S, 1882 S
Finn, M C (UC Cork, Cork Constitution) 1979 E, 1982 W, E, S, F, 1983 S, F, W, E, 1984 E, S, A, 1986 F, W
Finn, R G A (UC Dublin) 1977 F
Fitzgerald, C C (Glasgow U, Dungannon) 1902 E, 1903 E, S
Fitzgerald, C F (St Mary's Coll) 1979 A 1,2, 1980 E, S, F, W, 1982 W, E, S, F, 1983 S, F, W, E, 1984 F, W, A, 1985 S, F, W, E, 1986 F, W, E, S
Fitzgerald, D C (Lansdowne, De La Salle Palmerston) 1984 E, S, 1986 W, E, S, R, 1987 E, S, F, W, [W, C, A], 1988 S, F, W, E 1, 1989 NZ (R), 1990 E, S, F, W, Arg, 1991 F, W, E, S, Nm 1,2, [Z, S, A], 1992 W, S (R)
Fitzgerald, J (Wanderers) 1884 W
Fitzgerald, J J (Young Munster) 1988 S, F, 1990 S, F, W, 1991 F, W, E, S, [J], 1994 A 1,2
Fitzgerald, L (Leinster) 2006 PI, 2007 Arg2(R)
Fitzgibbon, M J J (Shannon) 1992 W, E, S, F, NZ 1,2
Fitzpatrick, J M (Dungannon) 1998 SA 1,2 Gg (R), R (R), SA 3, 1999 F (R), W (R), E (R), It, Arg 1(R), [US (R), A 3, R, Arg 2(t&R)], 2000 S (R), It (R), Arg (R), US, C, SA (t&R), 2001 R (R), 2003 W 1(R), E (R), Tg, W 2(R), It 2(R)
Fitzpatrick, M P (Wanderers) 1978 S, 1980 S, F, W, 1981 F, W, E, S, A, 1985 F (R)
Flannery, J P (Munster) 2005 R(R), 2006 It,F,W,S,E,NZ1,2,A1, 2007 W(R),F(R),E(R),S1(R),It1(R),Arg1,S2,It2(R), [Nm(R),Gg(R), F,Arg]
Flavin, P (Blackrock Coll) 1997 F (R), S
Fletcher, W W (Kingstown) 1882 W, S, 1883 E
Flood, R S (Dublin U) 1925 W
Flynn, M K (Wanderers) 1959 F, 1960 F, 1962 E, S, F, W, 1964 E, S, W, F, 1965 F, E, S, W, SA, 1966 F, E, S, 1972 F 1, E, F 2, 1973 NZ
Fogarty, T (Garryowen) 1891 W
Foley, A G (Shannon, Munster) 1995 E, S, F, W, It, [J(t + R)], 1996 A, 1997 It 1, E (R), 2000 E, S, It, F, W, Arg, C, J, SA, 2001 It, F, R, S, W, E, Sm, NZ, 2002 W, E, S, It, F, NZ 1,2, R, Ru, Gg, A, Fj, Arg, 2003 S 1, It 1, F, W 1, E, W 2, [R,A], 2004 F,W,E,It,S,SA1,2,3,US(R),Arg, 2005 It,S,E,F,W
Foley, B O (Shannon) 1976 F, E, 1977 W (R), 1980 F, W, 1981 F, E, S, SA 1,2, A
Forbes, R E (Malone) 1907 E
Forrest, A J (Wanderers) 1880 E, S, 1881 E, S, 1882 W, E, 1883 E, 1885 S 2
Forrest, E G (Wanderers) 1888 M, 1889 S, W, 1890 S, E, 1891 E, 1893 S, W, 1894 E, S, W, 1895 W, 1897 E, S
Forrest, H (Wanderers) 1893 S, W
Fortune, J J (Clontarf) 1963 NZ, 1964 E
Foster, A R (Derry) 1910 E, S, F, 1911 E, S, W, F, 1912 F, E, S, W, 1914 E, S, W, 1921 E, S, W
Francis, N P J (Blackrock Coll, London Irish, Old Belvedere) 1987 [Tg, A], 1988 WS, It, 1989 S, 1990 E, F, W, 1991 E, S, Nm 1,2, [Z, J, S, A], 1992 W, E, S, 1993 F, R, 1994 F, W, E, S, A 1,2, US, 1995 E, [NZ, J, W, F], Fj, 1996 US, S
Franks, J G (Dublin U) 1898 E, S, W
Frazer, E F (Bective Rangers) 1891 S, 1892 S
Freer, A E (Lansdowne) 1901 E, S, W
Fulcher, G M (Cork Constitution, London Irish) 1994 A 2, US, 1995 E (R), S, F, W, It, [NZ, W, F], Fj, 1996 US, S, F, W, E, A, 1997 It 1, W (R), 1998 SA 1(R)
Fulton, J (NIFC) 1895 S, W, 1896 E, 1897 E, 1898 W, 1899 E, 1900 W, 1901 E, 1902 E, S, W, 1903 E, S, W, 1904 E, S
Furlong, J N (UC Galway) 1992 NZ 1,2

Gaffikin, W (Windsor) 1875 E
Gage, J H (Queen's U, Belfast) 1926 S, W, 1927 S, W
Galbraith, E (Dublin U) 1875 E
Galbraith, H T (Belfast Acad) 1890 W
Galbraith, R (Dublin U) 1875 E, 1876 E, 1877 E
Galwey, M J (Shannon) 1991 F, W, Nm 2(R), [J], 1992 E, S, F, NZ 1,2, A, 1993 F, W, E, R, 1994 F, W, E, S, A 1, US (R), 1995 E, 1996 WS, 1998 F (R), 1999 W (R), 2000 E (R), S, It, F, W, Arg, C, 2001 It, F, R, W, E, Sm, NZ, 2002 W, E, S
Ganly, J B (Monkstown) 1927 F, E, S, W, A, 1928 F, E, S, W, 1929 F, S, 1930 F
Gardiner, F (NIFC) 1900 E, S, 1901 E, W, 1902 E, S, W, 1903 E, W, 1904 E, S, W, 1906 E, S, W, 1907 S, W, 1908 S, W, 1909 E, S, F
Gardiner, J B (NIFC) 1923 E, S, W, F, 1924 F, E, S, W, NZ, 1925 F, E, S, W
Gardiner, S (Belfast Albion) 1893 E, S
Gardiner, W (NIFC) 1892 E, S, 1893 E, S, W, 1894 E, S, W, 1895 E, S, W, 1896 E, S, W, 1897 E, S, 1898 W
Garry, M G (Bective Rangers) 1909 E, S, W, F, 1911 E, S, W
Gaston, J T (Dublin U) 1954 NZ, F, E, S, W, 1955 W 1956 F, E
Gavin, T J (Moseley, London Irish) 1949 F, E
Geoghegan, S P (London Irish, Bath) 1991 F, W, E, S, Nm 1, [Z, S, A], 1992 E, S, F, A, 1993 S, F, W, E, R, 1994 F, W, E, S, A 1,2, US, 1995 E, S, F, W, [NZ, J, W, F], Fj, 1996 US, S, W, E
Gibson, C M H (Cambridge U, NIFC) 1964 E, S, W, F, 1965 F, E, S, W, SA, 1966 F, E, S, W, 1967 A 1, E, S, W, F, A 2, 1968 E, S, W, A, 1969 E, S, W, 1970 SA, F, E, S, W, 1971 F, E, S, W, 1972 F 1, E, F 2, 1973 NZ, E, S, W, F, 1974 F, W, E, S, P, 1975 E, S, F, W, 1976 A, F, W, E, S, NZ, 1977 W, E, S, F, 1978 F, W, E, NZ, 1979 S, A 1,2
Gibson, M E (Lansdowne, London Irish) 1979 F, W, E, S, 1981 W (R), 1986 R, 1988 S, F, W, E 2
Gifford, H P (Wanderers) 1890 S
Gillespie, J C (Dublin U) 1922 W, F
Gilpin, F G (Queen's U, Belfast) 1962 E, S, F
Glass, D C (Belfast Collegians) 1958 F, 1960 W, 1961 W, SA
Gleeson, K D (St Mary's Coll, Leinster) 2002 W (R), F (R), NZ 1,2, R, Ru, Gg, A, Arg, 2003 S 1, It 1, F, W 1, E, A, W 2, [R,A,F], 2004 F,W,E,It, 2006 NZ1(R),A1(R), 2007 Arg1,S2(R)
Glennon, B T (Lansdowne) 1993 F (R)
Glennon, J J (Skerries) 1980 E, S, 1987 E, S, F, [W (R)]
Godfrey, R P (UC Dublin) 1954 S, W
Goodall, K G (City of Derry, Newcastle U) 1967 A 1, E, S, W, F, A 2, 1968 F, E, S, W, A, 1969 F, E, S, 1970 SA, F, E, S, W
Gordon, A (Dublin U) 1884 S
Gordon, T G (NIFC) 1877 E, S, 1878 E
Gotto, R P C (NIFC) 1906 SA
Goulding, W J (Cork) 1879 S
Grace, T O (UC Dublin, St Mary's Coll) 1972 F 1, E, 1973 NZ, E, S, W, 1974 E, S, P, NZ, 1975 E, S, F, W, 1976 A, F, W, E, S, NZ, 1977 W, E, S, F, 1978 S
Graham, R I (Dublin U) 1911 F
Grant, E L (CIYMS) 1971 F, E, S, W
Grant, P J (Bective Rangers) 1894 S, W
Graves, C R A (Wanderers) 1934 E, S, W, 1935 E, S, W, NZ, 1936 E, S, W, 1937 E, S, 1938 E, S, W
Gray, R D (Old Wesley) 1923 E, S, 1925 F, 1926 F
Greene, E H (Dublin U, Kingstown) 1882 W, 1884 W, 1885 E, S 2, 1886 E
Greer, R (Kingstown) 1876 E
Greeves, T J (NIFC) 1907 E, S, W, 1909 W, F
Gregg, R J (Queen's U, Belfast) 1953 F, E, S, W, 1954 F, E, S
Griffin, C S (London Irish) 1951 F, E
Griffin, J L (Wanderers) 1949 S, W
Griffiths, W (Limerick) 1878 E
Grimshaw, C (Queen's U, Belfast) 1969 E (R)
Guerin, B N (Galwegians) 1956 S

Gwynn, A P (Dublin U) 1895 W
Gwynn, L H (Dublin U) 1893 S, 1894 E, S, W, 1897 S, 1898 E, S

Hakin, R F (CIYMS) 1976 W, S, NZ, 1977 W, E, F
Hall, R O N (Dublin U) 1884 W
Hall, W H (Instonians) 1923 E, S, W, F, 1924 F, S
Hallaran, C F G T (Royal Navy) 1921 E, S, W, 1922 E, S, W, 1923 E, F, 1924 F, E, S, W, 1925 F, 1926 F, E
Halpin, G F (Wanderers, London Irish) 1990 E, 1991 [J], 1992 E, S, F, 1993 R, 1994 F (R), 1995 It, [NZ, W, F]
Halpin, T (Garryowen) 1909 S, W, F, 1910 E, S, W, 1911 E, S, W, F, 1912 F, E, S
Halvey, E O (Shannon) 1995 F, W, It, [J, W (t), F (R)], 1997 NZ, C (R)
Hamilton, A J (Lansdowne) 1884 W
Hamilton, G F (NIFC) 1991 F, W, E, S, Nm 2, [Z, J, S, A], 1992 A
Hamilton, R L (NIFC) 1926 F
Hamilton, R W (Wanderers) 1893 W
Hamilton, W J (Dublin U) 1877 E
Hamlet, G T (Old Wesley) 1902 E, S, W, 1903 E, S, W, 1904 S, W, 1905 E, S, W, NZ, 1906 SA, 1907 E, S, W, 1908 E, S, W, 1909 E, S, W, F, 1910 E, S, F, 1911 E, S, W, F
Hanrahan, C J (Dolphin) 1926 S, W, 1927 E, S, W, A, 1928 F, E, S, 1929 F, E, S, W, 1930 F, E, S, W, 1931 F, 1932 S, W
Harbison, H T (Bective Rangers) 1984 W (R), E, S, 1986 R, 1987 E, S, F, W
Hardy, G G (Bective Rangers) 1962 S
Harman, G R A (Dublin U) 1899 E, W
Harper, J (Instonians) 1947 F, E, S
Harpur, T G (Dublin U) 1908 E, S, W
Harrison, T (Cork) 1879 S, 1880 S, 1881 E
Harvey, F M W (Wanderers) 1907 W, 1911 F
Harvey, G A D (Wanderers) 1903 E, S, 1904 W, 1905 E, S
Harvey, T A (Dublin U) 1900 W, 1901 S, W, 1902 E, S, W, 1903 E, W
Haycock, P P (Terenure Coll) 1989 E
Hayes, J J (Shannon, Munster) 2000 S, It, F, W, Arg, C, J, SA, 2001 It, F, R, S, W, E, Sm, NZ, 2002 W, E, S, It, F, NZ 1,2, R, Ru, Gg, A, Fj, Arg, 2003 S 1, It 1, F, W 1, E, [R(R),Nm,Arg,A,F], 2004 F,W,E,It,S,SA1,2,3,US,Arg, 2005 It,S,E,F,W,NZ,A,R(R), 2006 It,F,W,S,E,NZ1,2,A1,SA,A2,PI, 2007 W,F,E,S1,It1,S2(R),It2, [Nm,Gg,F,Arg]
Headon, T A (UC Dublin) 1939 S, W
Healey, P (Limerick) 1901 E, S, W, 1902 E, S, W, 1903 E, S, W, 1904 S
Heaslip, J P R (Leinster) 2006 PI, 2007 Arg1,S2
Heffernan, M R (Cork Constitution) 1911 E, S, W, F
Hemphill, R (Dublin U) 1912 F, E, S, W
Henderson, N J (Queen's U, Belfast, NIFC) 1949 S, W, 1950 F, 1951 F, E, S, W, SA, 1952 F, S, W, E, 1953 F, E, S, W, 1954 NZ, F, E, S, W, 1955 F, E, S, W, 1956 S, W, 1957 F, E, S, W, 1958 A, E, S, W, F, 1959 E, S, W, F
Henderson R A J (London Irish, Wasps, Young Munster) 1996 WS, 1997 NZ, C, 1998 F, W, SA 1(R),2(R), 1999 F (R), E, S (R), It, 2000 S (R), It (R), F, W, Arg, US, J (R), SA, 2001 It, F, 2002 W (R), E (R), F, R (R), Ru (t), Gg (R), 2003 It 1(R),2
Henebrey, G J (Garryowen) 1906 E, S, W, SA, 1909 W, F
Heron, A G (Queen's Coll, Belfast) 1901 E
Heron, J (NIFC) 1877 S, 1879 E
Heron, W T (NIFC) 1880 E, S
Herrick, R W (Dublin U) 1886 S
Heuston, F S (Kingstown) 1882 W, 1883 E, S
Hewitt, D (Queen's U, Belfast, Instonians) 1958 A, E, S, F, 1959 S, W, F, 1960 E, S, W, F, 1961 E, S, W, F, 1962 S, F, 1965 W
Hewitt, F S (Instonians) 1924 W, NZ, 1925 F, E, S, 1926 E, 1927 E, S, W
Hewitt, J A (NIFC) 1981 SA 1(R),2(R)
Hewitt, T R (Queen's U, Belfast) 1924 W, NZ, 1925 F, E, S, 1926 F, E, S, W
Hewitt, V A (Instonians) 1935 S, W, NZ, 1936 E, S, W
Hewitt, W J (Instonians) 1954 E, 1956 S, 1959 W, 1961 SA
Hewson, F T (Wanderers) 1875 E
Hickie, D A (St Mary's Coll, Leinster) 1997 W, E, S, NZ, C, It 2, 1998 S, F, W, E, SA 1,2, 2000 S, It, F, W, J, SA, 2001 F, R, S, W, E, NZ, 2002 W, E, S, It, F, R, Ru, Gg, A, 2003 S 1, It 1, F, W 1, E, It 2, S 2, [R,Nm,Arg,A], 2004 SA3,Arg, 2005 It,S,E,F,W, 2006 A2,PI, 2007 W,F,E,S1,It1,2, [Nm,Gg,Arg]
Hickie, D J (St Mary's Coll) 1971 F, E, S, W, 1972 F 1, E
Higgins, J A D (Civil Service) 1947 S, W, A, 1948 F, S, W
Higgins, W W (NIFC) 1884 E, S
Hillary, M F (UC Dublin) 1952 E
Hingerty, D J (UC Dublin) 1947 F, E, S, W
Hinton, W P (Old Wesley) 1907 W, 1908 E, S, W, 1909 E, S, 1910 E, S, W, F, 1911 E, S, W, 1912 F, E, W
Hipwell, M L (Terenure Coll) 1962 E, S, 1968 F, A, 1969 F (R), S (R), W, 1971 F, E, S, W, 1972 F 2
Hobbs, T H M (Dublin U) 1884 S, 1885 E
Hobson, E W (Dublin U) 1876 E
Hogan, N A (Terenure Coll, London Irish) 1995 E, W, [J, W, F], 1996 F, W, E, WS, 1997 F, W, E, It 2
Hogan, P (Garryowen) 1992 F
Hogan, T (Munster, Leinster) 2005 J1(R),2(R), 2007 It1(R),Arg1
Hogg, W (Dublin U) 1885 S 2
Holland, J J (Wanderers) 1981 SA 1,2, 1986 W
Holmes, G W (Dublin U) 1912 SA, 1913 E, S
Holmes, L J (Lisburn) 1889 S, W
Hooks, K J (Queen's U, Belfast, Ards, Bangor) 1981 S, 1989 NZ, 1990 F, W, Arg, 1991 F
Horan, A K (Blackheath) 1920 E, W
Horan, M J (Shannon, Munster) 2000 US (R), 2002 Fj, Arg (R), 2003 S 1(R), It 1(R), F, W 1, E, A, Sm, It 2, S 2, [R,Nm,Arg(t&R),A(R),F(R)], 2004 It(R),S(R),SA1(R),2(t&R),3(R), US, 2005 It(R),S(R),E(R),F(R),W(R),J1,2,NZ,A,R, 2006 It,W,S,E,NZ1,2,A1,SA,A2(R), 2007 W,F,E,It1,2, [Nm,Gg,F,Arg]
Horgan, A P (Cork Const, Munster) 2003 Sm, W 2, S 2, 2004 F(R), 2005 J1,2,NZ
Horgan, S P (Lansdowne, Leinster) 2000 S, It, W, Arg, C, J, SA (R), 2001 It, S, W, E, NZ, 2002 S, It, F, A, Fj, Arg, 2003 S 1, [R,Nm,Arg,A,F], 2004 F,W,E,It,S,SA1,2,3,US,Arg, 2005 It,S,E,NZ,A,R, 2006 It,F,W,S,E,NZ1,2,A1,SA,A2,PI, 2007 F,E,S1,It1, [Gg,F,Arg]
Houston, K J (Oxford U, London Irish) 1961 SA, 1964 S, W, 1965 F, E, SA
Howe, T G (Dungannon, Ballymena, Ulster) 2000 US, J, SA, 2001 It, F, R, Sm, 2002 It (R), 2003 Tg, W 2, 2004 F,W,E,SA2
Hughes, R W (NIFC) 1878 E, 1880 E, S, 1881 S, 1882 E, S, 1883 E, S, 1884 E, S, 1885 E, 1886 E
Humphreys, D G (London Irish, Dungannon, Ulster) 1996 F, W, E, WS, 1997 E (R), S, It 2, 1998 S, E (R), SA 2(t + R), R (R), 1999 F, W, E, S, A 1,2, Arg 1, [US, A 3, Arg 2], 2000 E, S (R), F (t&R), W (R), Arg, US (R), C, J (R), SA (R), 2001 It (R), R, S (R), W, E, NZ, 2002 W, E, S, It, F, NZ 1(R),2(R), R (t+R), Ru (R), Gg (R), Fj, 2003 S 1, It 1, F, W 1, E, A, W 2, It 2, S 2(R), [R,Arg,A(R),F(R)], 2004W(R),It(R),S(R),SA2(R),US, 2005 S(R),W(R),J1,2,NZ(R),A(R),R
Hunt, E W F de Vere (Army, Rosslyn Park) 1930 F, 1932 E, S, W, 1933 E
Hunter, D V (Dublin U) 1885 S 2
Hunter, L (Civil Service) 1968 W, A
Hunter, W R (CIYMS) 1962 E, S, W, F, 1963 F, E, S, 1966 F, E, S
Hurley, H D (Old Wesley, Moseley) 1995 Fj (t), 1996 WS
Hutton, S A (Malone) 1967 S, W, F, A 2

Ireland J (Windsor) 1876 E, 1877 E
Irvine, H A S (Collegians) 1901 S
Irwin, D G (Queen's U, Belfast, Instonians) 1980 F, W, 1981 F, W, E, S, SA 1,2, A, 1982 W, 1983 S, F, W, E, 1984 F, W, 1987 [Tg, A (R)], 1989 F, W, E, S, NZ, 1990 E, S
Irwin, J W S (NIFC) 1938 E, S, 1939 E, S, W
Irwin, S T (Queen's Coll, Belfast) 1900 E, S, W, 1901 E, W, 1902 E, S, W, 1903 S

Jack, H W (UC Cork) 1914 S, W, 1921 W
Jackman, B J (Leinster) 2005 J1(R),2(R), 2007 Arg1(R),2(R)
Jackson, A R V (Wanderers) 1911 E, S, W, F, 1913 W, F, 1914 F, E, S, W
Jackson, F (NIFC) 1923 E
Jackson, H W (Dublin U) 1877 E
Jameson, J S (Lansdowne) 1888 M, 1889 S, W, 1891 W, 1892 E, W, 1893 S
Jeffares, E W (Wanderers) 1913 E, S
Jennings, S (Leicester) 2007 Arg2
Johns, P S (Dublin U, Dungannon, Saracens) 1990 Arg, 1992 NZ 1,2, A, 1993 S, F, W, E, R, 1994 F, W, E, S, A 1,2, US, 1995 E, S, W, It, [NZ, J, W, F], Fj, 1996 US, S, F, WS, 1997

It 1(R), F, W, E, S, NZ, C, It 2, 1998 S, F, W, E, SA 1,2, Gg, R, SA 3, 1999 F, W, E, S, It, A 1,2, Arg 1, [US, A 3, R], 2000 F (R), J
Johnston, J (Belfast Acad) 1881 S, 1882 S, 1884 S, 1885 S 1,2, 1886 E, 1887 E, S, W
Johnston, M (Dublin U) 1880 E, S, 1881 E, S, 1882 E, 1884 E, S, 1886 E
Johnston, R (Wanderers) 1893 E, W
Johnston, R W (Dublin U) 1890 S, W, E
Johnston, T J (Queen's Coll, Belfast) 1892 E, S, W, 1893 E, S, 1895 E
Johnstone, W E (Dublin U) 1884 W
Johnstone-Smyth, T R (Lansdowne) 1882 E

Kavanagh, J R (UC Dublin, Wanderers) 1953 F, E, S, W, 1954 NZ, S, W, 1955 F, E, 1956 E, S, W, 1957 F, E, S, W, 1958 A, E, S, W, 1959 E, S, W, F, 1960 E, S, W, F, SA, 1961 E, S, W, F, SA, 1962 F
Kavanagh, P J (UC Dublin, Wanderers) 1952 E, 1955 W
Keane, K P (Garryowen) 1998 E (R)
Keane, M I (Lansdowne) 1974 F, W, E, S, P, NZ, 1975 E, S, F, W, 1976 A, F, W, E, S, NZ, 1977 W, E, S, F, 1978 S, F, W, E, NZ, 1979 F, W, E, S, A 1,2, 1980 E, S, F, W, 1981 F, W, E, S, 1982 W, E, S, F, 1983 S, F, W, E, 1984 F, W, E, S
Kearney, R D J (Leinster) 2007 Arg2
Kearney, R K (Wanderers) 1982 F, 1984 A, 1986 F, W
Keeffe, E (Sunday's Well) 1947 F, E, S, W, A, 1948 F
Kelly, H C (NIFC) 1877 E, S, 1878 E, 1879 S, 1880 E, S
Kelly, J C (UC Dublin) 1962 F, W, 1963 F, E, S, W, NZ, 1964 E, S, W, F
Kelly, J P (Cork Constitution) 2002 It, NZ 1,2, R, Ru, Gg, A (R), 2003 It 1, F, A, Tg, Sm, It 2, [R(R),Nm(R),A(R),F]
Kelly, S (Lansdowne) 1954 S, W, 1955 S, 1960 W, F
Kelly, W (Wanderers) 1884 S
Kennedy, A G (Belfast Collegians) 1956 F
Kennedy, A P (London Irish) 1986 W, E
Kennedy, F (Wanderers) 1880 E, 1881 E, 1882 W
Kennedy, F A (Wanderers) 1904 E, W
Kennedy, H (Bradford) 1938 S, W
Kennedy, J M (Wanderers) 1882 W, 1884 W
Kennedy, K W (Queen's U, Belfast, London Irish) 1965 F, E, S, W, SA, 1966 F, E, W, 1967 A 1, E, S, W, F, A 2, 1968 F, A, 1969 F, E, S, W, 1970 SA, F, E, S, W, 1971 F, E, S, W, 1972 F 1, E, F 2, 1973 NZ, E, S, W, F, 1974 F, W, E, S, P, NZ, 1975 F, W
Kennedy, T J (St Mary's Coll) 1978 NZ, 1979 F, W, E (R), A 1,2, 1980 E, S, F, W, 1981 SA 1,2, A
Kenny, P (Wanderers) 1992 NZ 2(R)
Keogh, F S (Bective Rangers) 1964 W, F
Keon, J J (Limerick) 1879 E
Keyes, R P (Cork Constitution) 1986 E, 1991 [Z, J, S, A], 1992 W, E, S
Kidd, F W (Dublin U, Lansdowne) 1877 E, S, 1878 E
Kiely, M D (Lansdowne) 1962 W, 1963 F, E, S, W
Kiernan, M J (Dolphin, Lansdowne) 1982 W (R), E, S, F, 1983 S, F, W, E, 1984 E, S, A, 1985 S, F, W, E, 1986 F, W, E, S, R, 1987 E, S, F, W, [W, C, A], 1988 S, F, W, E 1,2, WS, 1989 F, W, E, S, 1990 E, S, F, W, Arg, 1991 F
Kiernan, T J (UC Cork, Cork Const) 1960 E, S, W, F, SA, 1961 E, S, W, F, SA, 1962 E, W, 1963 F, S, W, NZ, 1964 E, S, 1965 F, E, S, W, SA, 1966 F, E, S, W, 1967 A 1, E, S, W, F, A 2, 1968 F, E, S, W, A, 1969 F, E, S, W, 1970 SA, F, E, S, W, 1971 F, 1972 F 1, E, F 2, 1973 NZ, E, S
Killeen, G V (Garryowen) 1912 E, S, W, 1913 E, S, W, F, 1914 E, S, W
King, H (Dublin U) 1883 E, S
Kingston, T J (Dolphin) 1987 [W, Tg, A], 1988 S, F, W, E 1, 1990 F, W, 1991 [J], 1993 F, W, E, R, 1994 F, W, E, S, 1995 F, W, It, [NZ, J (R), W, F], Fj, 1996 US, S, F
Knox, J H (Dublin U, Lansdowne) 1904 W, 1905 E, S, W, NZ, 1906 E, S, W, 1907 W, 1908 S
Kyle, J W (Queen's U, Belfast, NIFC) 1947 F, E, S, W, A, 1948 F, E, S, W, 1949 F, E, S, W, 1950 F, E, S, W, 1951 F, E, S, W, SA, 1952 F, S, W, E, 1953 F, E, S, W, 1954 NZ, F, 1955 F, E, W, 1956 F, E, S, W, 1957 F, E, S, W, 1958 A, E, S

Lambert, N H (Lansdowne) 1934 S, W
Lamont, R A (Instonians) 1965 F, E, SA, 1966 F, E, S, W, 1970 SA, F, E, S, W
Landers, M F (Cork Const) 1904 W, 1905 E, S, W, NZ
Lane, D (UC Cork) 1934 S, W, 1935 E, S
Lane, M F (UC Cork) 1947 W, 1949 F, E, S, W, 1950 F, E, S, W, 1951 F, S, W, SA, 1952 F, S, 1953 F, E
Lane, P (Old Crescent) 1964 W
Langan, D J (Clontarf) 1934 W
Langbroek, J A (Blackrock Coll) 1987 [Tg]
Lavery, P (London Irish) 1974 W, 1976 W
Lawlor, P J (Clontarf) 1951 S, SA, 1952 F, S, W, E, 1953 F, 1954 NZ, E, S, 1956 F, E
Lawlor, P J (Bective Rangers) 1935 E, S, W, 1937 E, S, W
Lawlor, P J (Bective Rangers) 1990 Arg, 1992 A, 1993 S
Leahy, K T (Wanderers) 1992 NZ 1
Leahy, M W (UC Cork) 1964 W
Leamy, D P (Munster) 2004 US, 2005 It,J2,NZ,A,R, 2006 It,F,W,S,E,NZ1,2,A1,SA,A2,PI(R), 2007 W,F,E,S1,It1,2, [Nm,Gg,F,Arg]
Lee, S (NIFC) 1891 E, S, W, 1892 E, S, W, 1893 E, S, W, 1894 E, S, W, 1895 E, W, 1896 E, S, W, 1897 E, 1898 E
Le Fanu, V C (Cambridge U, Lansdowne) 1886 E, S, 1887 E, W, 1888 S, 1889 W, 1890 E, 1891 E, 1892 E, S, W
Lenihan, D G (UC Cork, Cork Const) 1981 A, 1982 W, E, S, F, 1983 S, F, W, E, 1984 F, W, E, S, A, 1985 S, F, W, E, 1986 F, W, E, S, R, 1987 E, S, F, W, [W, C, Tg, A], 1988 S, F, W, E 1,2, WS, It, 1989 F, W, E, S, NZ, 1990 S, F, W, Arg, 1991 Nm 2, [Z, S, A], 1992 W
L'Estrange, L P F (Dublin U) 1962 E
Levis, F H (Wanderers) 1884 E
Lewis, K P (Leinster) 2005 J2(R), 2007 Arg1,2(R)
Lightfoot, E J (Lansdowne) 1931 F, E, S, W, SA, 1932 E, S, W, 1933 E, W, S
Lindsay, H (Dublin U, Armagh) 1893 E, S, W, 1894 E, S, W, 1895 E, 1896 E, S, W, 1898 E, S, W
Little, T J (Bective Rangers) 1898 W, 1899 S, W, 1900 S, W, 1901 E, S
Lloyd, R A (Dublin U, Liverpool) 1910 E, S, 1911 E, S, W, F, 1912 F, E, S, W, SA, 1913 E, S, W, F, 1914 F, E, 1920 E, F
Longwell, G W (Ballymena) 2000 J (R), SA, 2001 F (R), R, S (R), Sm, NZ (R), 2002 W (R), E (R), S (R), It, F, NZ 1,2, R, Ru, Gg, A, Arg, 2003 S 1, It 1, F, E, A, It 2, 2004 It(R)
Lydon, C T J (Galwegians) 1956 S
Lyle, R K (Dublin U) 1910 W, F
Lyle, T R (Dublin U) 1885 E, S 1,2, 1886 E, 1887 E, S
Lynch, J F (St Mary's Coll) 1971 F, E, S, W, 1972 F 1, E, F 2, 1973 NZ, E, S, W, 1974 F, W, E, S, P, NZ
Lynch, L (Lansdowne) 1956 S
Lytle, J H (NIFC) 1894 E, S, W, 1895 W, 1896 E, S, W, 1897 E, S, 1898 E, S, 1899 S
Lytle, J N (NIFC) 1888 M, 1889 W, 1890 E, 1891 E, S, 1894 E, S, W
Lyttle, V J (Collegians, Bedford) 1938 E, 1939 E, S

McAleese, D R (Ballymena) 1992 F
McAllan, G H (Dungannon) 1896 S, W
Macauley, J (Limerick) 1887 E, S
McBride, W D (Malone) 1988 W, E 1, WS, It, 1989 S, 1990 F, W, Arg, 1993 S, F, W, E, R, 1994 W, E, S, A 1(R), 1995 S, F, [NZ, W, F], Fj (R), 1996 W, E, WS, A, 1997 It 1(R), F, W, E, S
McBride, W J (Ballymena) 1962 E, S, F, W, 1963 F, E, S, W, NZ, 1964 E, S, F, 1965 F, E, S, W, SA, 1966 F, E, S, W, 1967 A 1, E, S, W, F, A 2, 1968 F, E, S, W, A, 1969 F, E, S, W, 1970 SA, F, E, S, W, 1971 F, E, S, W, 1972 F 1, E, F 2, 1973 NZ, E, S, W, F, 1974 F, W, E, S, P, NZ, 1975 E, S, F, W
McCahill, S A (Sunday's Well) 1995 Fj (t)
McCall, B W (London Irish) 1985 F (R), 1986 E, S
McCall, M C (Bangor, Dungannon, London Irish) 1992 NZ 1(R),2, 1994 W, 1996 E (R), A, 1997 It 1, NZ, C, It 2, 1998 S, E, SA 1,2
McCallan, B (Ballymena) 1960 E, S
McCarten, R J (London Irish) 1961 E, W, F
McCarthy, E A (Kingstown) 1882 W
McCarthy, J S (Dolphin) 1948 F, E, S, W, 1949 F, E, S, W, 1950 W, 1951 F, E, S, W, SA, 1952 F, S, W, E, 1953 F, E, S, 1954 NZ, F, E, S, W, 1955 F, E
McCarthy, P D (Cork Const) 1992 NZ 1,2, A, 1993 S, R (R)
MacCarthy, St G (Dublin U) 1882 W
McCarthy, T (Cork) 1898 W
McClelland, T A (Queen's U, Belfast) 1921 E, S, W, F, 1922 E, W, F, 1923 E, S, W, F, 1924 F, E, S, W, NZ

McClenahan, R O (Instonians) 1923 E, S, W
McClinton, A N (NIFC) 1910 W, F
McCombe, W McM (Dublin U, Bangor) 1968 F, 1975 E, S, F, W
McConnell, A A (Collegians) 1947 A, 1948 F, E, S, W, 1949 F, E
McConnell, G (Derry, Edinburgh U) 1912 F, E, 1913 W, F
McConnell, J W (Lansdowne) 1913 S
McCormac, F M (Wanderers) 1909 W, 1910 W, F
McCormick, W J (Wanderers) 1930 E
McCoull, H C (Belfast Albion) 1895 E, S, W, 1899 E
McCourt, D (Queen's U, Belfast) 1947 A
McCoy, J J (Dungannon, Bangor, Ballymena) 1984 W, A, 1985 S, F, W, E, 1986 F, 1987 [Tg], 1988 E 2, WS, It, 1989 F, W, E, S, NZ
McCracken, H (NIFC) 1954 W
McCullen, A (Lansdowne) 2003 Sm
McCullough, M T (Ulster) 2005 J1,2,NZ(R),A(R)
McDermott, S J (London Irish) 1955 S, W
Macdonald, J A (Methodist Coll, Belfast) 1875 E, 1876 E, 1877 S, 1878 E, 1879 S, 1880 E, 1881 S, 1882 E, S, 1883 E, S, 1884 E, S
McDonald, J P (Malone) 1987 [C], 1990 E (R), S, Arg
McDonnell, A C (Dublin U) 1889 W, 1890 S, W, 1891 E
McDowell, J C (Instonians) 1924 F, NZ
McFarland, B A T (Derry) 1920 S, W, F, 1922 W
McGann, B J (Lansdowne) 1969 F, E, S, W, 1970 SA, F, E, S, W, 1971 F, E, S, W, 1972 F 1, E, F 2, 1973 NZ, E, S, W, 1976 F, W, E, S, NZ
McGowan, A N (Blackrock Coll) 1994 US
McGown, T M W (NIFC) 1899 E, S, 1901 S
McGrath, D G (UC Dublin, Cork Const) 1984 S, 1987 [W, C, Tg, A]
McGrath, N F (Oxford U, London Irish) 1934 W
McGrath, P J (UC Cork) 1965 E, S, W, SA, 1966 F, E, S, W, 1967 A 1, A 2
McGrath, R J M (Wanderers) 1977 W, E, F (R), 1981 SA 1,2, A, 1982 W, E, S, F, 1983 S, F, W, E, 1984 F, W
McGrath, T (Garryowen) 1956 W, 1958 F, 1960 E, S, W, F, 1961 SA
McGuinness, C D (St Mary's Coll) 1997 NZ, C, 1998 F, W, E, SA 1,2, Gg, R (R), SA 3, 1999 F, W, E, S
McGuire, E P (UC Galway) 1963 E, S, W, NZ, 1964 E, S, W, F
MacHale, S (Lansdowne) 1965 F, E, S, W, SA, 1966 F, E, S, W, 1967 S, W, F
McHugh, M (St Mary's Coll) 2003 Tg
McIldowie, G (Malone) 1906 SA, 1910 E, S, W
McIlrath, J A (Ballymena) 1976 A, F, NZ, 1977 W, E
McIlwaine, E H (NIFC) 1895 S, W
McIlwaine, E N (NIFC) 1875 E, 1876 E
McIlwaine, J E (NIFC) 1897 E, S, 1898 E, S, W, 1899 E, W
McIntosh, L M (Dublin U) 1884 S
MacIvor, C V (Dublin U) 1912 F, E, S, W, 1913 E, S, F
McIvor, S C (Garryowen) 1996 A, 1997 It 1, S (R)
McKay, J W (Queen's U, Belfast) 1947 F, E, S, W, A, 1948 F, E, S, W, 1949 F, E, S, W, 1950 F, E, S, W, 1951 F, E, S, W, SA, 1952 F
McKee, W D (NIFC) 1947 A, 1948 F, E, S, W, 1949 F, E, S, W, 1950 F, E, 1951 SA
McKeen, A J W (Lansdowne) 1999 [R (R)]
McKelvey, J M (Queen's U, Belfast) 1956 F, E
McKenna, P (St Mary's Coll) 2000 Arg
McKibbin, A R (Instonians, London Irish) 1977 W, E, S, 1978 S, F, W, E, NZ, 1979 F, W, E, S, 1980 E, S
McKibbin, C H (Instonians) 1976 S (R)
McKibbin, D (Instonians) 1950 F, E, S, W, 1951 F, E, S, W
McKibbin, H R (Queen's U, Belfast) 1938 W, 1939 E, S, W
McKinney, S A (Dungannon) 1972 F 1, E, F 2, 1973 W, F, 1974 F, E, S, P, NZ, 1975 E, S, 1976 A, F, W, E, S, NZ, 1977 W, E, S, 1978 S (R), F, W, E
McLaughlin, J H (Derry) 1887 E, S, 1888 W, S
McLean, R E (Dublin U) 1881 S, 1882 W, E, S, 1883 E, S, 1884 E, S, 1885 E, S 1
Maclear, B (Cork County, Monkstown) 1905 E, S, W, NZ, 1906 E, S, W, SA, 1907 E, S, W
McLennan, A C (Wanderers) 1977 F, 1978 S, F, W, E, NZ, 1979 F, W, E, S, 1980 E, F, 1981 F, W, E, S, SA 1,2
McLoughlin, F M (Northern) 1976 A
McLoughlin, G A J (Shannon) 1979 F, W, E, S, A 1,2, 1980 E, 1981 SA 1,2, 1982 W, E, S, F, 1983 S, F, W, E, 1984 F
McLoughlin, R J (UC Dublin, Blackrock Coll, Gosforth) 1962 E, S, F, 1963 E, S, W, NZ, 1964 E, S, 1965 F, E, S, W, SA, 1966 F, E, S, W, 1971 F, E, S, W, 1972 F 1, E, F 2, 1973 NZ, E, S, W, F, 1974 F, W, E, S, P, NZ, 1975 E, S, F, W
McMahon, L B (Blackrock Coll, UC Dublin) 1931 E, SA, 1933 E, 1934 E, 1936 E, S, W, 1937 E, S, W, 1938 E, S
McMaster, A W (Ballymena) 1972 F 1, E, F 2, 1973 NZ, E, S, W, F, 1974 F, E, S, P, 1975 F, W, 1976 A, F, W, NZ
McMordie, J (Queen's Coll, Belfast) 1886 S
McMorrow, A (Garryowen) 1951 W
McMullen, A R (Cork) 1881 E, S
McNamara, V (UC Cork) 1914 E, S, W
McNaughton, P P (Greystones) 1978 S, F, W, E, 1979 F, W, E, S, A 1,2, 1980 E, S, F, W, 1981 F
MacNeill, H P (Dublin U, Oxford U, Blackrock Coll, London Irish) 1981 F, W, E, S, A, 1982 W, E, S, F, 1983 S, F, W, E, 1984 F, W, E, A, 1985 S, F, W, E, 1986 F, W, E, S, R, 1987 E, S, F, W, [W, C, Tg, A], 1988 S (R), E 1,2
McQuilkin, K P (Bective Rangers, Lansdowne) 1996 US, S, F, 1997 F (t & R), S
MacSweeney, D A (Blackrock Coll) 1955 S
McVicker, H (Army, Richmond) 1927 E, S, W, A, 1928 F
McVicker, J (Collegians) 1924 F, E, S, W, NZ, 1925 F, E, S, W, 1926 F, E, S, W, 1927 F, E, S, W, A, 1928 W, 1930 F
McVicker, S (Queen's U, Belfast) 1922 E, S, W, F
McWeeney, J P J (St Mary's Coll) 1997 NZ
Madden, M N (Sunday's Well) 1955 E, S, W
Magee, J T (Bective Rangers) 1895 E, S
Magee, A M (Louis) (Bective Rangers, London Irish) 1895 E, S, W, 1896 E, S, W, 1897 E, S, 1898 E, S, W, 1899 E, S, W, 1900 E, S, W, 1901 E, S, W, 1902 E, S, W, 1903 E, S, W, 1904 W
Maggs, K M (Bristol, Bath, Ulster) 1997 NZ (R), C, It 2, 1998 S, F, W, E, SA 1,2, Gg, R (R), SA 3, 1999 F, W, E, S, It, A 1,2, Arg 1, [US, A 3, Arg 2], 2000 E, F, Arg, US (R), C, 2001 It (R), F (R), R, S (R), W, E, Sm, NZ, 2002 W, E, S, R, Ru, Gg, A, Fj, Arg, 2003 S 1, It 1, F, W 1, E, A, W 2, S 2, [R,Nm,Arg,A,F], 2004 F,W(R),E(R),It(R),S(R),SA1(R),2,US, 2005 S,F,W,J1
Maginiss, R M (Dublin U) 1875 E, 1876 E
Magrath, R M (Cork Constitution) 1909 S
Maguire, J F (Cork) 1884 S
Mahoney, J (Dolphin) 1923 E
Malcolmson, G L (RAF, NIFC) 1935 NZ, 1936 E, S, W, 1937 E, S, W
Malone, N G (Oxford U, Leicester) 1993 S, F, 1994 US (R)
Mannion, N P (Corinthians, Lansdowne, Wanderers) 1988 WS, It, 1989 F, W, E, S, NZ, 1990 E, S, F, W, Arg, 1991 Nm 1(R),2, [J], 1993 S
Marshall, B D E (Queen's U, Belfast) 1963 E
Mason, S J P (Orrell, Richmond) 1996 W, E, WS
Massey-Westropp, R H (Limerick, Monkstown) 1886 E
Matier, R N (NIFC) 1878 E, 1879 S
Matthews, P M (Ards, Wanderers) 1984 A, 1985 S, F, W, E, 1986 R, 1987 E, S, F, W, [W, Tg, A], 1988 S, F, W, E 1,2, WS, It, 1989 F, W, E, S, NZ, 1990 E, S, 1991 F, W, E, S, Nm 1 [Z, S, A], 1992 W, E, S
Mattsson, J (Wanderers) 1948 E
Mayne, R B (Queen's U, Belfast) 1937 W, 1938 E, W, 1939 E, S, W
Mayne, R H (Belfast Academy) 1888 W, S
Mayne, T (NIFC) 1921 E, S, F
Mays, K M A (UC Dublin) 1973 NZ, E, S, W
Meares, A W D (Dublin U) 1899 S, W, 1900 E, W
Megaw, J (Richmond, Instonians) 1934 W, 1938 E
Millar, A (Kingstown) 1880 E, S, 1883 E
Millar, H J (Monkstown) 1904 W, 1905 E, S, W
Millar, S (Ballymena) 1958 F, 1959 E, S, W, F, 1960 E, S, W, F, SA, 1961 E, S, W, F, SA, 1962 E, S, F, 1963 F, E, S, W, 1964 F, 1968 F, E, S, W, A, 1969 F, E, S, W, 1970 SA, F, E, S, W
Millar, W H J (Queen's U, Belfast) 1951 E, S, W, 1952 S, W
Miller, E R P (Leicester, Terenure Coll, Leinster) 1997 It 1, F, W, E, NZ, It 2, 1998 S, W (R), Gg, R, 1999 F, W, E (R), S, Arg 1(R), [US (R), A 3(t&R), Arg 2(R)], 2000 US, C (R), SA, 2001 R, W, E, Sm, NZ, 2002 E, S, It (R), Fj (R), 2003 W 1(t+R), Tg, Sm, It 2, S 2, [Nm,Arg(R),A(t&R),F(R)], 2004 SA3(R),US,Arg(R), 2005 It(R),S(R),F(R),W(R),J1(R),2
Miller, F H (Wanderers) 1886 S
Milliken, R A (Bangor) 1973 E, S, W, F, 1974 F, W, E, S, P, NZ, 1975 E, S, F, W

Millin, T J (Dublin U) 1925 W
Minch, J B (Bective Rangers) 1912 SA, 1913 E, S, 1914 E, S
Moffat, J (Belfast Academy) 1888 W, S, M, 1889 S, 1890 S, W, 1891 S
Moffatt, J E (Old Wesley) 1904 S, 1905 E, S, W
Moffett, J W (Ballymena) 1961 E, S
Molloy, M G (UC Galway, London Irish) 1966 F, E, 1967 A 1, E, S, W, F, A 2, 1968 F, E, S, W, A, 1969 F, E, S, W, 1970 F, E, S, W, 1971 F, E, S, W, 1973 F, 1976 A
Moloney, J J (St Mary's Coll) 1972 F 1, E, F 2, 1973 NZ, E, S, W, F, 1974 F, W, E, S, P, NZ, 1975 E, S, F, W, 1976 S, 1978 S, F, W, E, 1979 A 1,2, 1980 S, W
Moloney, L A (Garryowen) 1976 W (R), S, 1978 S (R), NZ
Molony, J U (UC Dublin) 1950 S
Monteith, J D E (Queen's U, Belfast) 1947 E, S, W
Montgomery, A (NIFC) 1895 S
Montgomery, F P (Queen's U, Belfast) 1914 E, S, W
Montgomery, R (Cambridge U) 1887 E, S, W, 1891 E, 1892 W
Moore, C M (Dublin U) 1887 S, 1888 W, S
Moore, D F (Wanderers) 1883 E, S, 1884 E, W
Moore, F W (Wanderers) 1884 W, 1885 E, S 2, 1886 S
Moore, H (Windsor) 1876 E, 1877 S
Moore, H (Queen's U, Belfast) 1910 S, 1911 W, F, 1912 F, E, S, W, SA
Moore, T A P (Highfield) 1967 A 2, 1973 NZ, E, S, W, F, 1974 F, W, E, S, P, NZ
Moore, W D (Queen's Coll, Belfast) 1878 E
Moran, F G (Clontarf) 1936 E, 1937 E, S, W, 1938 S, W, 1939 E, S, W
Morell, H B (Dublin U) 1881 E, S, 1882 W, E
Morgan, G J (Clontarf) 1934 E, S, W, 1935 E, S, W, NZ, 1936 E, S, W, 1937 E, S, W, 1938 E, S, W, 1939 E, S, W
Moriarty, C C H (Monkstown) 1899 W
Moroney, J C M (Garryowen) 1968 W, A, 1969 F, E, S, W
Moroney, R J M (Lansdowne) 1984 F, W, 1985 F
Moroney, T A (UC Dublin) 1964 W, 1967 A 1, E
Morphy, E McG (Dublin U) 1908 E
Morris, D P (Bective Rangers) 1931 W, 1932 E, 1935 E, S, W, NZ
Morrow, J W R (Queen's Coll, Belfast) 1882 S, 1883 E, S, 1884 E, W, 1885 S 1,2, 1886 E, S, 1888 S
Morrow, R D (Bangor) 1986 F, E, S
Mortell, M (Bective Rangers, Dolphin) 1953 F, E, S, W, 1954 NZ, F, E, S, W
Morton, W A (Dublin U) 1888 S
Mostyn, M R (Galwegians) 1999 A 1, Arg 1, [US, A 3, R, Arg 2]
Moyers, L W (Dublin U) 1884 W
Moylett, M M F (Shannon) 1988 E 1
Mulcahy, W A (UC Dublin, Bective Rangers, Bohemians) 1958 A, E, S, W, F, 1959 E, S, W, F, 1960 E, S, W, SA, 1961 E, S, W, SA, 1962 E, S, F, W, 1963 F, E, S, W, NZ, 1964 E, S, W, F, 1965 F, E, S, W, SA
Mullan, B (Clontarf) 1947 F, E, S, W, 1948 F, E, S, W
Mullane, J P (Limerick Bohemians) 1928 W, 1929 F
Mullen, K D (Old Belvedere) 1947 F, E, S, W, A, 1948 F, E, S, W, 1949 F, E, S, W, 1950 F, E, S, W, 1951 F, E, S, W, SA, 1952 F, S, W
Mulligan, A A (Wanderers) 1956 F, E, 1957 F, E, S, W, 1958 A, E, S, F, 1959 E, S, W, F, 1960 E, S, W, F, SA, 1961 W, F, SA
Mullin, B J (Dublin U, Oxford U, Blackrock Coll, London Irish) 1984 A, 1985 S, W, E, 1986 F, W, E, S, R, 1987 E, S, F, W, [W, C, Tg, A], 1988 S, F, W, E 1,2, WS, It, 1989 F, W, E, S, NZ, 1990 E, S, W, Arg, 1991 F, W, E, S, Nm 1,2, [J, S, A], 1992 W, E, S, 1994 US, 1995 E, S, F, W, It, [NZ, J, W, F]
Mullins, M J (Young Munster, Old Crescent) 1999 Arg 1(R), [R], 2000 E, S, It, Arg (t&R), US, C, 2001 It, R, W (R), E (R), Sm (R), NZ (R), 2003 Tg, Sm
Murphy, B J (Munster) 2007 Arg1(R),2
Murphy, C J (Lansdowne) 1939 E, S, W, 1947 F, E
Murphy, G E A (Leicester) 2000 US, C (R), J, 2001 R, S, Sm, 2002 W, E, NZ 1,2, Fj, 2003 S 1(R), It 1, F, W 1, E, A, W 2, It 2(R), S 2, 2004 It,S,SA1,3,US,Arg, 2005 It,S,E,F,W,NZ,A,R, 2006 It,F,W,S,E,NZ1,2,A1(R),SA(R),A2, 2007 W(t&R),F,Arg1(t&R), 2,S2,It2, [Nm(R),Arg]
Murphy, J G M W (London Irish) 1951 SA, 1952 S, W, E, 1954 NZ, 1958 W
Murphy, J J (Greystones) 1981 SA 1, 1982 W (R), 1984 S
Murphy, J N (Greystones) 1992 A
Murphy, K J (Cork Constitution) 1990 E, S, F, W, Arg, 1991 F, W (R), S (R), 1992 S, F, NZ 2(R)
Murphy, N A A (Cork Constitution) 1958 A, E, S, W, F, 1959 E, S, W, F, 1960 E, S, W, F, SA, 1961 E, S, W, 1962 E, 1963 NZ, 1964 E, S, W, F, 1965 F, E, S, W, SA, 1966 F, E, S, W, 1967 A 1, E, S, W, F, 1969 F, E, S, W
Murphy, N F (Cork Constitution) 1930 E, W, 1931 F, E, S, W, SA, 1932 E, S, W, 1933 E
Murphy-O'Connor, J (Bective Rangers) 1954 E
Murray, H W (Dublin U) 1877 S, 1878 E, 1879 E
Murray, J B (UC Dublin) 1963 F
Murray, P F (Wanderers) 1927 F, 1929 F, E, S, 1930 F, E, S, W, 1931 F, E, S, W, SA, 1932 E, S, W, 1933 E, W, S
Murtagh, C W (Portadown) 1977 S
Myles, J (Dublin U) 1875 E

Nash, L C (Queen's Coll, Cork) 1889 S, 1890 W, E, 1891 E, S, W
Neely, M R (Collegians) 1947 F, E, S, W
Neill, H J (NIFC) 1885 E, S 1,2, 1886 S, 1887 E, S, W, 1888 W, S
Neill, J McF (Instonians) 1926 F
Nelson, J E (Malone) 1947 A, 1948 E, S, W, 1949 F, E, S, W, 1950 F, E, S, W, 1951 F, E, W, 1954 F
Nelson, R (Queen's Coll, Belfast) 1882 E, S, 1883 S, 1886 S
Nesdale, R P (Newcastle) 1997 W, E, S, NZ (R), C, 1998 F (R), W (R), Gg, SA 3(R), 1999 It, A 2(R), [US (R), R]
Nesdale, T J (Garryowen) 1961 F
Neville, W C (Dublin U) 1879 S, E
Nicholson, P C (Dublin U) 1900 E, S, W
Norton, G W (Bective Rangers) 1949 F, E, S, W, 1950 F, E, S, W, 1951 F, E, S
Notley, J R (Wanderers) 1952 F, S
Nowlan, K W (St Mary's Coll) 1997 NZ, C, It 2

O'Brien, B (Derry) 1893 S, W
O'Brien, B A P (Shannon) 1968 F, E, S
O'Brien, D J (London Irish, Cardiff, Old Belvedere) 1948 E, S, W, 1949 F, E, S, W, 1950 F, E, S, W, 1951 F, E, S, W, SA, 1952 F, S, W, E
O'Brien, K A (Broughton Park) 1980 E, 1981 SA 1(R),2
O'Brien-Butler, P E (Monkstown) 1897 S, 1898 E, S, 1899 S, W, 1900 E
O'Callaghan, C T (Carlow) 1910 W, F, 1911 E, S, W, F, 1912 F
O'Callaghan, D P (Cork Const, Munster) 2003 W 1(R), Tg (R), Sm (R), W 2(R), It 2(R), [R(R),A(t&R)], 2004 F(t&R),W,It,S(t&R), SA2(R),US, 2005 It(R),S(R),W(R),NZ,A,R, 2006 It(R),F(R),W, S(R),E(R),NZ1,2,A1,SA,A2,PI(R), 2007 W,F,E,S1,It1,2, [Nm,Gg, F,Arg]
O'Callaghan, M P (Sunday's Well) 1962 W, 1964 E, F
O'Callaghan, P (Dolphin) 1967 A 1, E, A 2, 1968 F, E, S, W, 1969 F, E, S, W, 1970 SA, F, E, S, W, 1976 F, W, E, S, NZ
O'Connell, K D (Sunday's Well) 1994 F, E (t)
O'Connell, P (Bective Rangers) 1913 W, F, 1914 F, E, S, W
O'Connell, P J (Young Munster, Munster) 2002 W, It (R), F (R), NZ 1, 2003 E (R), A (R), Tg, Sm, W 2, S 2, [R(R),A(t&R)], 2004 F(t&R),W,It,S(t&R),SA1(R),US, 2005 It(R),S(R),W(R),NZ,A,R, 2006 It(R),F(R),W,S(R),E(R),NZ1,2,A1,SA,A2,PI, 2007 W,F,E, S1,2,It2, [Nm,Gg,F,Arg]
O'Connell, W J (Lansdowne) 1955 F
O'Connor, H S (Dublin U) 1957 F, E, S, W
O'Connor, J (Garryowen) 1895 S
O'Connor, J H (Bective Rangers) 1888 M, 1890 S, W, E, 1891 E, S, 1892 E, W, 1893 E, S, 1894 E, S, W, 1895 E, 1896 E, S, W
O'Connor, J H (Wasps) 2004 SA3,Arg, 2005 S,E,F,W,J1,NZ,A,R, 2006 W(R),E(t&R)
O'Connor, J J (Garryowen) 1909 F
O'Connor, J J (UC Cork) 1933 S, 1934 E, S, W, 1935 E, S, W, NZ, 1936 S, W, 1938 S
O'Connor, P J (Lansdowne) 1887 W
O'Cuinneagain, D (Sale, Ballymena) 1998 SA 1,2, Gg (R), R (R), SA 3, 1999 F, W, E, S, It, A 1,2, Arg 1, [US, A 3, R, Arg 2], 2000 E, It (R)
Odbert, R V M (RAF) 1928 F
O'Donnell, R C (St Mary's Coll) 1979 A 1,2, 1980 S, F, W

O'Donoghue, P J (Bective Rangers) 1955 F, E, S, W, 1956 W, 1957 F, E, 1958 A, E, S, W
O'Driscoll, B G (Blackrock Coll, Leinster) 1999 A 1,2, Arg 1, [US, A 3, R (R), Arg 2], 2000 E, S, It, F, W, J, SA, 2001 F, S, W, E, Sm, NZ, 2002 W, E, S, It, F, NZ 1,2, R, Ru, Gg, A, Fj, Arg, 2003 S 1, It 1, F, W 1, E, W 2, It 2, S 2, [R,Nm,Arg,A,F], 2004 W,E,It,S,SA1,2,3,US,Arg, 2005 It,E,F,W, 2006 It,F,W,S,E,NZ1,2,A1,SA,A2,PI, 2007 W,E,S1,It1,S2, [Nm,Gg, F,Arg]
O'Driscoll, B J (Manchester) 1971 F (R), E, S, W
O'Driscoll, J B (London Irish, Manchester) 1978 S, 1979 A 1,2, 1980 E, S, F, W, 1981 F, W, E, S, SA 1,2, A, 1982 W, E, S, F, 1983 S, F, W, E, 1984 F, W, E, S
O'Driscoll, M R (Cork Const, Munster) 2001 R (R), 2002 Fj (R), 2005 R(R), 2006 W(R),NZ1(R),2(R),A1(R), 2007 E(R),It1, Arg1(t&R),2
O'Flanagan, K P (London Irish) 1947 A
O'Flanagan, M (Lansdowne) 1948 S
O'Gara, R J R (Cork Const, Munster) 2000 S, It, F, W, Arg (R), US, C (R), J, SA, 2001 It, F, S, W (R), E (R), Sm, 2002 W (R), E (R), S (R), It (t), F (R), NZ 1,2, R, Ru, Gg, A, Arg, 2003 W 1(R), E (R), A (t+R), Tg, Sm, S 2, [R(R),Nm,Arg(R),A,F], 2004 F,W,E,It,S,SA1,2,3,Arg, 2005 It,S,E,F,W,NZ,A,R(R), 2006 It,F,W,S,E,NZ1,2,A1,SA,A2,PI(R), 2007 W,F,E,S1,It1,S2(R),It2, [Nm,Gg,F,Arg]
O'Grady, D (Sale) 1997 It 2
O'Hanlon, B (Dolphin) 1947 E, S, W, 1948 F, E, S, W, 1949 F, E, S, W, 1950 F
O'Hara, P T J (Sunday's Well, Cork Const) 1988 WS (R), 1989 F, W, E, NZ, 1990 E, S, F, W, 1991 Nm 1, [J], 1993 F, W, E, 1994 US
O'Kelly, M E (London Irish, St Mary's Coll, Leinster) 1997 NZ, C, It 2, 1998 S, F, W, E, SA 1,2, Gg, R, SA 3, 1999 A 1(R),2, Arg 1(R), [US (R), A 3, R, Arg 2], 2000 E, S, It, F, W, Arg, US, J, SA, 2001 It, F, S, W, E, NZ, 2002 E, S, It, F, NZ 1(R),2, R, Ru, Gg, A, Fj, Arg, 2003 S 1, It 1, F, W 1, E, A, W 2, S 2, [R,Nm,Arg,A,F], 2004 F,W(R),E,It,S,SA1,2,3,Arg, 2005 It,S,E,F,W,NZ,A, 2006 It,F,W,S,E,SA(R),A2(R),PI, 2007 Arg1,2(R),S2,It2(R), [F(R),Arg(R)]
O'Leary, A (Cork Constitution) 1952 S, W, E
O'Leary, T G (Munster) 2007 Arg1(R)
O'Loughlin, D B (UC Cork) 1938 E, S, W, 1939 E, S, W
O'Mahony, D W (UC Dublin, Moseley, Bedford) 1995 It, [F], 1997 It 2, 1998 R
O'Mahony, David (Cork Constitution) 1995 It
O'Meara, B T (Cork Constitution) 1997 E (R), S, NZ (R), 1998 S, 1999 [US (R), R (R)], 2001 It (R), 2003 Sm (R), It 2(R)
O'Meara, J A (UC Cork, Dolphin) 1951 F, E, S, W, SA, 1952 F, S, W, E, 1953 F, E, S, W, 1954 NZ, F, E, S, 1955 F, E, 1956 S, W, 1958 W
O'Neill, H O'H (Queen's U, Belfast, UC Cork) 1930 E, S, W, 1933 E, S, W
O'Neill, J B (Queen's U, Belfast) 1920 S
O'Neill, W A (UC Dublin, Wanderers) 1952 E, 1953 F, E, S, W, 1954 NZ
O'Reilly, A J F (Old Belvedere, Leicester) 1955 F, E, S, W, 1956 F, E, S, W, 1957 F, E, S, W, 1958 A, E, S, W, F, 1959 E, S, W, F, 1960 E, 1961 E, F, SA, 1963 F, S, W, 1970 E
Orr, P A (Old Wesley) 1976 F, W, E, S, NZ, 1977 W, E, S, F, 1978 S, F, W, E, NZ, 1979 F, W, E, S, A 1,2, 1980 E, S, F, W, 1981 F, W, E, S, SA 1,2, A, 1982 W, E, S, F, 1983 S, F, W, E, 1984 F, W, E, S, A, 1985 S, F, W, E, 1986 F, S, R, 1987 E, S, F, W, [W, C, A]
O'Shea, C M P (Lansdowne, London Irish) 1993 R, 1994 F, W, E, S, A 1,2, US, 1995 E, S, [J, W, F], 1997 It 1, F, S (R), 1998 S, F, SA 1,2, Gg, R, SA 3, 1999 F, W, E, S, It, A 1, Arg 1, [US, A 3, R, Arg 2], 2000 E
O'Sullivan, A C (Dublin U) 1882 S
O'Sullivan, J M (Limerick) 1884 S, 1887 S
O'Sullivan, P J A (Galwegians) 1957 F, E, S, W, 1959 E, S, W, F, 1960 SA, 1961 E, S, 1962 F, W, 1963 F, NZ
O'Sullivan, W (Queen's Coll, Cork) 1895 S
Owens, R H (Dublin U) 1922 E, S

Parfrey, P (UC Cork) 1974 NZ
Parke, J C (Monkstown) 1903 W, 1904 E, S, W, 1905 W, NZ, 1906 E, S, W, SA, 1907 E, S, W, 1908 E, S, W, 1909 E, S, W, F
Parr, J S (Wanderers) 1914 F, E, S, W
Patterson, C S (Instonians) 1978 NZ, 1979 F, W, E, S, A 1,2, 1980 E, S, F, W
Patterson, R d'A (Wanderers) 1912 F, S, W, SA, 1913 E, S, W, F
Payne, C T (NIFC) 1926 E, 1927 F, E, S, A, 1928 F, E, S, W, 1929 F, E, W, 1930 F, E, S, W
Pedlow, A C (CIYMS) 1953 W, 1954 NZ, F, E, 1955 F, E, S, W, 1956 F, E, S, W, 1957 F, E, S, W, 1958 A, E, S, W, F, 1959 E, 1960 E, S, W, F, SA, 1961 S, 1962 W, 1963 F
Pedlow, J (Bessbrook) 1882 S, 1884 W
Pedlow, R (Bessbrook) 1891 W
Pedlow, T B (Queen's Coll, Belfast) 1889 S, W
Peel, T (Limerick) 1892 E, S, W
Peirce, W (Cork) 1881 E
Phipps, G C (Army) 1950 E, W, 1952 F, W, E
Pike, T O (Lansdowne) 1927 E, S, W, A, 1928 F, E, S, W
Pike, V J (Lansdowne) 1931 E, S, W, SA, 1932 E, S, W, 1933 E, W, S, 1934 E, S, W
Pike, W W (Kingstown) 1879 E, 1881 E, S, 1882 E, 1883 S
Pinion, G (Belfast Collegians) 1909 E, S, W, F
Piper, O J S (Cork Constitution) 1909 E, S, W, F, 1910 E, S, W, F
Polden, S E (Clontarf) 1913 W, F, 1914 F, 1920 F
Popham, I (Cork Constitution) 1922 S, W, F, 1923 F
Popplewell, N J (Greystones, Wasps, Newcastle) 1989 NZ, 1990 Arg, 1991 Nm 1,2, [Z, S, A], 1992 W, E, S, F, NZ 1,2, A, 1993 S, F, W, E, R, 1994 F, W, E, S, US, 1995 E, S, F, W, It, [NZ, J, W, F], Fj, 1996 US, S, F, W, E, A, 1997 It 1, F, W, E, NZ, C, 1998 S (t), F (R)
Potterton, H N (Wanderers) 1920 W
Pratt, R H (Dublin U) 1933 E, W, S, 1934 E, S
Price, A H (Dublin U) 1920 S, F
Pringle, J C (NIFC) 1902 S, W
Purcell, N M (Lansdowne) 1921 E, S, W, F
Purdon, H (NIFC) 1879 S, E, 1880 E, 1881 E, S
Purdon, W B (Queen's Coll, Belfast) 1906 E, S, W
Purser, F C (Dublin U) 1898 E, S, W

Quinlan, A N (Shannon, Munster) 1999 [R (R)], 2001 It, F, 2002 NZ 2(R), Ru (R), Gg (R), A (R), Fj, Arg (R), 2003 S 1(R), It 1(R), F (R), W 1, E (R), A, W 2, [R(R),Nm,Arg], 2004 SA1(R),2(R), 2005 J1,2(t&R), 2007 Arg2,S2(t&R)
Quinlan, D P (Northampton) 2005 J1(R),2
Quinlan, S V J (Blackrock Coll) 1956 F, E, W, 1958 W
Quinn, B T (Old Belvedere) 1947 F
Quinn, F P (Old Belvedere) 1981 F, W, E
Quinn, J P (Dublin U) 1910 E, S, 1911 E, S, W, F, 1912 E, S, W, 1913 E, W, F, 1914 F, E, S
Quinn, K (Old Belvedere) 1947 F, A, 1953 F, E, S
Quinn, M A M (Lansdowne) 1973 F, 1974 F, W, E, S, P, NZ, 1977 S, F, 1981 SA 2
Quirke, J M T (Blackrock Coll) 1962 E, S, 1968 S

Rainey, P I (Ballymena) 1989 NZ
Rambaut, D F (Dublin U) 1887 E, S, W, 1888 W
Rea, H H (Edinburgh U) 1967 A 1, 1969 F
Read, H M (Dublin U) 1910 E, S, 1911 E, S, W, F, 1912 F, E, S, W, SA, 1913 E, S
Reardon, J V (Cork Constitution) 1934 E, S
Reddan, E G (Wasps) 2006 F(R), 2007 Arg2,S2(R), [F,Arg]
Reid, C (NIFC) 1899 S, W, 1900 E, 1903 W
Reid, J L (Richmond) 1934 S, W
Reid, P J (Garryowen) 1947 A, 1948 F, E, W
Reid, T E (Garryowen) 1953 E, S, W, 1954 NZ, F, 1955 E, S, 1956 F, E, 1957 F, E, S, W
Reidy, C J (London Irish) 1937 W
Reidy, G F (Dolphin, Lansdowne) 1953 W, 1954 F, E, S, W
Richey, H A (Dublin U) 1889 W, 1890 S
Ridgeway, E C (Wanderers) 1932 S, W, 1935 E, S, W
Rigney, B J (Greystones) 1991 F, W, E, S, Nm 1, 1992 F, NZ 1(R),2
Ringland, T M (Queen's U, Belfast, Ballymena) 1981 A, 1982 W, E, F, 1983 S, F, W, E, 1984 F, W, E, S, A, 1985 S, F, W, E, 1986 F, W, E, S, R, 1987 E, S, F, W, [W, C, Tg, A], 1988 S, F, W, E 1
Riordan, W F (Cork Constitution) 1910 E
Ritchie, J S (London Irish) 1956 F, E
Robb, C G (Queen's Coll, Belfast) 1904 E, S, W, 1905 NZ, 1906 S

Robbie, J C (Dublin U, Greystones) 1976 A, F, NZ, 1977 S, F, 1981 F, W, E, S
Robinson, B F (Ballymena, London Irish) 1991 F, W, E, S, Nm 1,2, [Z, S, A], 1992 W, E, S, F, NZ 1,2, A, 1993 W, E, R, 1994 F, W, E, S, A 1,2
Robinson, T T H (Wanderers) 1904 E, S, 1905 E, S, W, NZ, 1906 SA, 1907 E, S, W
Roche, J (Wanderers) 1890 S, W, E, 1891 E, S, W, 1892 W
Roche, R E (UC Galway) 1955 E, S, 1957 S, W
Roche, W J (UC Cork) 1920 E, S, F
Roddy, P J (Bective Rangers) 1920 S, F
Roe, R (Lansdowne) 1952 E, 1953 F, E, S, W, 1954 F, E, S, W, 1955 F, E, S, W, 1956 F, E, S, W, 1957 F, E, S, W
Rolland, A C (Blackrock Coll) 1990 Arg, 1994 US (R), 1995 It (R)
Rooke, C V (Dublin U) 1891 E, W, 1892 E, S, W, 1893 E, S, W, 1894 E, S, W, 1895 E, S, W, 1896 E, S, W, 1897 E, S
Ross, D J (Belfast Academy) 1884 E, 1885 S 1,2, 1886 E, S
Ross, G R P (CIYMS) 1955 W
Ross, J F (NIFC) 1886 S
Ross, J P (Lansdowne) 1885 E, S 1,2, 1886 E, S
Ross, N G (Malone) 1927 F, E
Ross, W McC (Queen's U, Belfast) 1932 E, S, W, 1933 E, W, S, 1934 E, S, 1935 NZ
Russell, J (UC Cork) 1931 F, E, S, W, SA, 1933 E, W, S, 1934 E, S, W, 1935 E, S, W, 1936 E, S, W, 1937 E, S
Russell, P (Instonians) 1990 E, 1992 NZ 1,2, A
Rutherford, W G (Tipperary) 1884 E, S, 1885 E, S 1, 1886 E, 1888 W
Ryan, E (Dolphin) 1937 W, 1938 E, S
Ryan, J (Rockwell Coll) 1897 E, 1898 E, S, W, 1899 E, S, W, 1900 S, W, 1901 E, S, W, 1902 E, 1904 E
Ryan, J G (UC Dublin) 1939 E, S, W
Ryan, M (Rockwell Coll) 1897 E, S, 1898 E, S, W, 1899 E, S, W, 1900 E, S, W, 1901 E, S, W, 1903 E, 1904 E, S

Saunders, R (London Irish) 1991 F, W, E, S, Nm 1,2, [Z, J, S, A], 1992 W, 1994 F (t)
Saverimutto, C (Sale) 1995 Fj, 1996 US, S
Sayers, H J M (Lansdowne) 1935 E, S, W, 1936 E, S, W, 1938 W, 1939 E, S, W
Scally, C J (U C Dublin) 1998 Gg (R), R, 1999 S (R), It
Schute, F (Wanderers) 1878 E, 1879 E
Schute, F G (Dublin U) 1912 SA, 1913 E, S
Scott, D (Malone) 1961 F, SA, 1962 S
Scott, R D (Queen's U, Belfast) 1967 E, F, 1968 F, E, S
Scovell, R H (Kingstown) 1883 E, 1884 E
Scriven, G (Dublin U) 1879 S, E, 1880 E, S, 1881 E, 1882 S, 1883 E, S
Sealy, J (Dublin U) 1896 E, S, W, 1897 S, 1899 E, S, W, 1900 E, S
Sexton, J F (Dublin U, Lansdowne) 1988 E 2, WS, It, 1989 F
Sexton, W J (Garryowen) 1984 A, 1988 S, E 2
Shanahan, T (Lansdowne) 1885 E, S 1,2, 1886 E, 1888 S, W
Shaw, G M (Windsor) 1877 S
Sheahan, F J (Cork Const, Munster) 2000 US (R), 2001 It (R), R, W (R), Sm, 2002 W, E, S, Gg (R), A (t+R), Fj, 2003 S 1(R), It 1(R), 2004 F(R),W(R),It(R),S(R),SA1(R),US, 2005 It(R),S(R),W(R),J1,2, 2006 SA(R),A2(R),PI, 2007 Arg2, [F(t&R)]
Sheehan, M D (London Irish) 1932 E
Sherry, B F (Terenure Coll) 1967 A 1, E, S, A 2, 1968 F, E
Sherry, M J A (Lansdowne) 1975 F, W
Shields, P M (Ballymena) 2003 Sm (R), It 2(R)
Siggins, J A E (Belfast Collegians) 1931 F, E, S, W, SA, 1932 E, S, W, 1933 E, W, S, 1934 E, S, W, 1935 E, S, W, NZ, 1936 E, S, W, 1937 E, S, W
Slattery, J F (UC Dublin, Blackrock Coll) 1970 SA, F, E, S, W, 1971 F, E, S, W, 1972 F 1, E, F 2, 1973 NZ, E, S, W, F, 1974 F, W, E, S, P, NZ, 1975 E, S, F, W, 1976 A, 1977 S, F, 1978 S, F, W, E, NZ, 1979 F, W, E, S, A 1,2, 1980 E, S, F, W, 1981 F, W, E, S, SA 1,2, A, 1982 W, E, S, F, 1983 S, F, W, E, 1984 F
Smartt, F N B (Dublin U) 1908 E, S, 1909 E
Smith, B A (Oxford U, Leicester) 1989 NZ, 1990 S, F, W, Arg, 1991 F, W, E, S
Smith, J H (London Irish) 1951 F, E, S, W, SA, 1952 F, S, W, E, 1954 NZ, W, F
Smith, R E (Lansdowne) 1892 E
Smith, S J (Ballymena) 1988 E 2, WS, It, 1989 F, W, E, S, NZ, 1990 E, 1991 F, W, E, S, Nm 1,2, [Z, S, A], 1992 W, E, S, F, NZ 1,2, 1993 S
Smithwick, F F S (Monkstown) 1898 S, W
Smyth, J T (Queen's U, Belfast) 1920 F
Smyth, P J (Belfast Collegians) 1911 E, S, F
Smyth, R S (Dublin U) 1903 E, S, 1904 E
Smyth, T (Malone, Newport) 1908 E, S, W, 1909 E, S, W, 1910 E, S, W, F, 1911 E, S, W, 1912 E
Smyth, W S (Belfast Collegians) 1910 W, F, 1920 E
Solomons, B A H (Dublin U) 1908 E, S, W, 1909 E, S, W, F, 1910 E, S, W
Spain, A W (UC Dublin) 1924 NZ
Sparrow, W (Dublin U) 1893 W, 1894 E
Spillane, B J (Bohemians) 1985 S, F, W, E, 1986 F, W, E, 1987 F, W, [W, C, A (R)], 1989 E (R)
Spring, D E (Dublin U) 1978 S, NZ, 1979 S, 1980 S, F, W, 1981 W
Spring, R M (Lansdowne) 1979 F, W, E
Spunner, H F (Wanderers) 1881 E, S, 1884 W
Stack, C R R (Dublin U) 1889 S
Stack, G H (Dublin U) 1875 E
Staples, J E (London Irish, Harlequins) 1991 W, E, S, Nm 1,2, [Z, J, S, A], 1992 W, E, NZ 1,2, A, 1995 F, W, It, [NZ], Fj, 1996 US, S, F, A, 1997 W, E, S
Staunton, J W (Garryowen, Wasps) 2001 Sm, 2005 J1(R),2(R), 2006 A1(R), 2007 Arg2
Steele, H W (Ballymena) 1976 E, 1977 F, 1978 F, W, E, 1979 F, W, E, A 1,2
Stephenson, G V (Queen's U, Belfast, London Hosp) 1920 F, 1921 E, S, W, F, 1922 E, S, W, F, 1923 E, S, W, F, 1924 F, E, S, W, NZ, 1925 F, E, S, W, 1926 F, E, S, W, 1927 F, E, S, W, A, 1928 F, E, S, W, 1929 F, E, W, 1930 F, E, S, W
Stephenson, H W V (United Services) 1922 S, W, F, 1924 F, E, S, W, NZ, 1925 F, E, S, W, 1927 A, 1928 E
Stevenson, J (Dungannon) 1888 M, 1889 S
Stevenson, J B (Instonians) 1958 A, E, S, W, F
Stevenson, R (Dungannon) 1887 E, S, W, 1888 M, 1889 S, W, 1890 S, W, E, 1891 W, 1892 W, 1893 E, S, W
Stevenson, T H (Belfast Acad) 1895 E, W, 1896 E, S, W, 1897 E, S
Stewart, A L (NIFC) 1913 W, F, 1914 F
Stewart, W J (Queen's U, Belfast, NIFC) 1922 F, 1924 S, 1928 F, E, S, W, 1929 F, E, S, W
Stoker, E W (Wanderers) 1888 W, S
Stoker, F O (Wanderers) 1886 S, 1888 W, M, 1889 S, 1891 W
Stokes, O S (Cork Bankers) 1882 E, 1884 E
Stokes, P (Garryowen) 1913 E, S, 1914 F, 1920 E, S, W, F, 1921 E, S, F, 1922 W, F
Stokes, R D (Queen's Coll, Cork) 1891 S, W
Strathdee, E (Queen's U, Belfast) 1947 E, S, W, A, 1948 W, F, 1949 E, S, W
Stringer, P A (Shannon, Munster) 2000 S, It, F, W, Arg, C, J, SA, 2001 It, F, R, S (R), W, E, Sm, NZ, 2002 W, E, S, It, F, NZ 1,2, R, Ru, Gg, A, Arg, 2003 S 1, It 1, F, W 1, E, A, W 2, S 2, [R,Nm,Arg,A,F], 2004 F,W,E,It,S,SA1,2,3,US(R),Arg, 2005 It,S,E,F,W,J1,2,NZ,A,R(R), 2006 It,F,W,S,E,NZ1,2, A1,SA,A2(R),PI, 2007 W,E,S1,It1,2, [Nm,Gg]
Stuart, C P (Clontarf) 1912 SA
Stuart, I M B (Dublin U) 1924 E, S
Sugars, H S (Dublin U) 1905 NZ, 1906 SA, 1907 S
Sugden, M (Wanderers) 1925 F, E, S, W, 1926 F, E, S, W, 1927 E, S, W, A, 1928 F, E, S, W, 1929 F, E, S, W, 1930 F, E, S, W, 1931 F, E, S, W
Sullivan, D B (UC Dublin) 1922 E, S, W, F
Sweeney, J A (Blackrock Coll) 1907 E, S, W
Symes, G R (Monkstown) 1895 E
Synge, J S (Lansdowne) 1929 S

Taggart, T (Dublin U) 1887 W
Taylor, A S (Queen's Coll, Belfast) 1910 E, S, W, 1912 F
Taylor, D R (Queen's Coll, Belfast) 1903 E
Taylor, J (Belfast Collegians) 1914 E, S, W
Taylor, J W (NIFC) 1879 S, 1880 E, S, 1881 S, 1882 E, S, 1883 E, S
Tector, W R (Wanderers) 1955 F, E, S
Tedford, A (Malone) 1902 E, S, W, 1903 E, S, W, 1904 E, S, W, 1905 E, S, W, NZ, 1906 E, S, W, SA, 1907 E, S, W, 1908 E, S, W
Teehan, C (UC Cork) 1939 E, S, W

Thompson, C (Belfast Collegians) 1907 E, S, 1908 E, S, W, 1909 E, S, W, F, 1910 E, S, W, F
Thompson, J A (Queen's Coll, Belfast) 1885 S 1,2
Thompson, J K S (Dublin U) 1921 W, 1922 E, S, F, 1923 E, S, W, F
Thompson, R G (Lansdowne) 1882 W
Thompson, R H (Instonians) 1951 SA, 1952 F, 1954 NZ, F, E, S, W, 1955 F, S, W, 1956 W
Thornhill, T (Wanderers) 1892 E, S, W, 1893 E
Thrift, H (Dublin U) 1904 W, 1905 E, S, W, NZ, 1906 E, W, SA, 1907 E, S, W, 1908 E, S, W, 1909 E, S, W, F
Tierney, D (UC Cork) 1938 S, W, 1939 E
Tierney, T A (Garryowen) 1999 A 1,2, Arg 1, [US, A 3, R, Arg 2], 2000 E
Tillie, C R (Dublin U) 1887 E, S, 1888 W, S
Todd, A W P (Dublin U) 1913 W, F, 1914 F
Topping, J A (Ballymena) 1996 WS, A, 1997 It 1, F, E, 1999 [R], 2000 US, 2003 A
Torrens, J D (Bohemians) 1938 W, 1939 E, S, W
Trimble, A D (Ulster) 2005 A,R, 2006 F(R),W,S,E,NZ1,2,A1,SA, 2007 W,F(R),E(R),It1(R),Arg1,S2(R),It2, [Nm,F]
Tucker, C C (Shannon) 1979 F, W, 1980 F (R)
Tuke, B B (Bective Rangers) 1890 E, 1891 E, S, 1892 E, 1894 E, S, W, 1895 E, S
Turley, N (Blackrock Coll) 1962 E
Tweed, D A (Ballymena) 1995 F, W, It, [J]
Tydings, J J (Young Munster) 1968 A
Tyrrell, W (Queen's U, Belfast) 1910 F, 1913 E, S, W, F, 1914 F, E, S, W

Uprichard, R J H (Harlequins, RAF) 1950 S, W

Waide, S L (Oxford U, NIFC) 1932 E, S, W, 1933 E, W
Waites, J (Bective Rangers) 1886 S, 1888 M, 1889 W, 1890 S, W, E, 1891 E
Waldron, O C (Oxford U, London Irish) 1966 S, W, 1968 A
Walker, S (Instonians) 1934 E, S, 1935 E, S, W, NZ, 1936 E, S, W, 1937 E, S, W, 1938 E, S, W
Walkington, D B (NIFC) 1887 E, W, 1888 W, 1890 W, E, 1891 E, S, W
Walkington, R B (NIFC) 1875 E, 1876 E, 1877 E, S, 1878 E, 1879 S, 1880 E, S, 1882 E, S
Wall, H (Dolphin) 1965 S, W
Wallace, D P (Garryowen, Munster) 2000 Arg, US, 2001 It, F, R (R), S (R), W, E, NZ, 2002 W, E, S, It, F, 2003 Tg (R), Sm (R), W 2(t+R), S 2, 2004 S,SA1,2, 2005 J2, 2006 It,F,W,S,E,NZ1,2,A1,SA,A2, 2007 W,F,E,S1,It1, [Nm,Gg,F,Arg]
Wallace, Jas (Wanderers) 1904 E, S
Wallace, Jos (Wanderers) 1903 S, W, 1904 E, S, W, 1905 E, S, W, NZ, 1906 W
Wallace, P S (Blackrock Coll, Saracens) 1995 [J], Fj, 1996 US, W, E, WS, A, 1997 It 1, F, W, E, S, NZ, C, 1998 S, F, W, E, SA 1,2, Gg, R, 1999 F, W, E, S, It (R), 1999 A 1,2, Arg 1, [US, A 3, R, Arg 2], 2000 E, US, C (R), 2002 W (R), E (R), S (R), It (R), F (R), NZ 2(R), Ru (R), Gg (R)
Wallace, P W (Ulster) 2006 SA(R),PI, 2007 E(R),Arg1,S2, [Nm(R)]
Wallace, R M (Garryowen, Saracens) 1991 Nm 1(R), 1992 W, E, S, F, A, 1993 S, F, W, E, R, 1994 F, W, E, S, 1995 W, It, [NZ, J, W], Fj, 1996 US, S, F, WS, 1998 S, F, W, E
Wallace, T H (Cardiff) 1920 E, S, W
Wallis, A K (Wanderers) 1892 E, S, W, 1893 E, W
Wallis, C O'N (Old Cranleighans, Wanderers) 1935 NZ
Wallis, T G (Wanderers) 1921 F, 1922 E, S, W, F
Wallis, W A (Wanderers) 1880 S, 1881 E, S, 1882 W, 1883 S
Walmsley, G (Bective Rangers) 1894 E
Walpole, A (Dublin U) 1888 S, M
Walsh, E J (Lansdowne) 1887 E, S, W, 1892 E, S, W, 1893 E
Walsh, H D (Dublin U) 1875 E, 1876 E
Walsh, J C (UC Cork, Sunday's Well) 1960 S, SA, 1961 E, S, F, SA, 1963 E, S, W, NZ, 1964 E, S, W, F, 1965 F, S, W, SA, 1966 F, S, W, 1967 E, S, W, F, A 2
Ward, A J (Ballynahinch) 1998 F, W, E, SA 1,2, Gg, R, SA 3, 1999 W, E, S, It (R), A 1,2, Arg 1, [US, A 3, R, Arg 2], 2000 F (R), W (t&R), Arg (R), US (R), C, J, SA (R), 2001 It (R), F (R)
Ward, A J P (Garryowen, St Mary's Coll, Greystones) 1978 S, F, W, E, NZ, 1979 F, W, E, S, 1981 W, E, S, A, 1983 E (R), 1984 E, S, 1986 S, 1987 [C, Tg]
Warren, J P (Kingstown) 1883 E
Warren, R G (Lansdowne) 1884 W, 1885 E, S 1,2, 1886 E, 1887 E, S, W, 1888 W, S, M, 1889 S, W, 1890 S, W, E
Watson, R (Wanderers) 1912 SA
Wells, H G (Bective Rangers) 1891 S, W, 1894 E, S
Westby, A J (Dublin U) 1876 E
Wheeler, G H (Queen's Coll, Belfast) 1884 S, 1885 E
Wheeler, J R (Queen's U, Belfast) 1922 E, S, W, F, 1924 E
Whelan, P C (Garryowen) 1975 E, S, 1976 NZ, 1977 W, E, S, F, 1978 S, F, W, E, NZ, 1979 F, W, E, S, 1981 F, W, E
White, M (Queen's Coll, Cork) 1906 E, S, W, SA, 1907 E, W
Whitestone, A M (Dublin U) 1877 E, 1879 S, E, 1880 E, 1883 S
Whittle, D (Bangor) 1988 F
Wilkinson, C R (Malone) 1993 S
Wilkinson, R W (Wanderers) 1947 A
Williamson, F W (Dolphin) 1930 E, S, W
Willis, W J (Lansdowne) 1879 E
Wilson, F (CIYMS) 1977 W, E, S
Wilson, H G (Glasgow U, Malone) 1905 E, S, W, NZ, 1906 E, S, W, SA, 1907 E, S, W, 1908 E, S, W, 1909 E, S, W, 1910 W
Wilson, R G (Ulster) 2005 J1
Wilson, W H (Bray) 1877 E, S
Withers, H H C (Army, Blackheath) 1931 F, E, S, W, SA
Wolfe, E J (Armagh) 1882 E
Wood, G H (Dublin U) 1913 W, 1914 F
Wood, B G M (Garryowen) 1954 E, S, 1956 F, E, S, W, 1957 F, E, S, W, 1958 A, E, S, W, F, 1959 E, S, W, F, 1960 E, S, W, F, SA, 1961 E, S, W, F, SA
Wood, K G M (Garryowen, Harlequins) 1994 A 1,2, US, 1995 E, S, [J], 1996 A, 1997 It 1, F, 1997 NZ, It 2, 1998 S, F, W, E, SA 1,2, R (R), SA 3, 1999 F, W, E, S, It (R), A 1,2, Arg 1, [US, A 3, R (R), Arg 2], 2000 E, S, It, F, W, Arg, US, C, J, SA, 2001 It, F, S, W, E, NZ, 2002 F, NZ 1,2, Ru, 2003 W 2, S 2, [R,Nm,Arg,A,F]
Woods, D C (Bessbrook) 1888 M, 1889 S
Woods, N K P J (Blackrock Coll, London Irish) 1994 A 1,2, 1995 E, F, 1996 F, W, E, 1999 W
Wright, R A (Monkstown) 1912 S

Yeates, R A (Dublin U) 1889 S, W
Young, B G (Ulster) 2006 NZ2(R),A1(R),SA(R),A2,PI, 2007 Arg1,2,S2
Young, G (UC Cork) 1913 E
Young, R M (Collegians) 1965 F, E, S, W, SA, 1966 F, E, S, W, 1967 W, F, 1968 W, A, 1969 F, E, S, W, 1970 SA, F, E, S, W, 1971 F, E, S, W

IRELAND: DOMESTIC 2006–07

CHANGING OF THE GUARD

Garryowen finally wrested Shannon's seemingly vice-like grip from the AIB Division One title and in the process completed the club's first ever domestic league and cup double.

Shannon had enjoyed a three-year reign as Division One champions but the 2006–07 campaign saw Garryowen put the disappointment of the previous year behind them to clinch championship honours for the first time in 13 years, just three weeks after they had triumphed in the AIB Cup final against Belfast Harlequins.

The 2005–06 season had seen Garryowen top the table with just one defeat in 15 only to be knocked out in the play-off semi-final by The Parishmen but they made no mistake this time around in not one but two showpiece finals.

The manner of their league triumph, however, was certainly dramatic as Garryowen held their nerve to see off the challenge of the form team Cork Constitution in the final at Musgrave Park and emerge 16–15 victors.

"For the last three or four months, these guys have dogged out results and never given up," said Garryowen coach Paul Cunningham. "The defence in the last 30 seconds was outstanding. Con played really good rugby all day, Denis Hurley at full-back was a beautiful performer, but at the end we wanted it so much not having won it since 1994."

The league campaign began in mid October and it soon became evident the race for the four play-off places would boil down to a battle between Cork, Garryowen, Bohemians, Shannon and Clontarf. One of the quintet would not make the knockout stages.

All five sides enjoyed mixed fortunes initially, with Clontarf suffering an opening day 20–10 defeat to Cork at Temple Hill while the third weekend of games saw both Cork and Garryowen suffer their first reverses of the season to Dungannon and St. Mary's College respectively. The following week Bohemians and Shannon surrendered their unbeaten records after losses to Lansdowne (15–14) and Garryowen (19–11) and it was difficult to separate the five clubs.

That remained the situation until the New Year when Cork began to assert their authority and their main rivals were to start to falter. Con's 12–11 victory over Garryowen in early January was the first win of eight in succession, while the defeat sparked a mini collapse for Paul Cunningham's side and they were to lose two more games on the bounce before returning to wining ways. Clontarf, Bohemians and Shannon were also unable to mount a serious challenge and it was little surprise that Cork were clear at the top at the conclusion of the regular season in April.

Clontarf snatched second place but Garryowen, Bohemians and Shannon all finished on 48 points and it was the defending champions who were denied a place in the play-offs courtesy of their inferior points difference.

The first of the play-off semi-finals saw Garryowen tackle Clontarf at Castle Avenue. Two tries from Derek Keane seemingly put 'Tarf in control of proceedings but Garryowen hit back with scores from Paul Neville, Damien Varley and Gerry Hurley to win 28–15, book their place in the final and end Phil Werahiko's six-year reign as Clontarf coach with a defeat.

The second semi between Cork and Bohemians at Temple Hill was a real thriller with the visitors so nearly upsetting the form book until Con wing Cronan Healy crossed in the 78th minute to snatch a 21–18 win for the home side.

The final a week later at Musgrave Park was to prove just as dramatic.

Both sides displayed nerves in the opening exchanges but Garryowen fly-half Eoghan Hickey landed two first-half penalties to establish a 6–0 lead after 30 minutes. Wing Richie Lane hit back for Brian Walsh's team with three points before they scored their the first try of the game as centre Tom Gleeson went over under the posts in first-half injury time.

Full-back Denis Hurley added a second, unconverted try for Con after the break to stretch the lead but Garryowen snatched victory from the jaws of defeat seven minutes from time when hooker Damien Varley crashed over for the decisive score and a famous 16–15 victory.

The first instalment of Garryowen's domestic double came in April when the side faced Belfast Harlequins in the AIB Cup final in Dublin. Quins had struggled in the league all season but booked their place at Dubarry Park with a surprise 32–28 semi-final win over Shannon while Garryowen overcame Clonakilty with relative ease in their last four clash.

Any hopes Quins had of springing another upset in the final itself were quickly dashed however as Garryowen ran in two tries from wing Ciaran O'Boyle and then prop Eugene McGovern in the first nine minutes to effectively end the game as a genuine contest.

Two penalties from Hickey established a 20-point advantage before the break and although Quins finally crossed in the 70th minute of the second half through centre Paul McKenzie, Garryowen never looked in danger of being overhauled.

"The All-Ireland League in 1994, when I was on the bench and Keith Wood was hooker, was the last national title we'd won," said Cunningham. "This is just massive for the club and the players. It means an awful lot."

With both the Munster Senior and Junior cups already safely sitting in the Garryowen trophy cabinet, the 2006–7 season was quickly becoming one of the best in the club's history and Quins coach Alan Solomons was happy to acknowledge that the Dooradoyle club were worthy winners.

"Garryowen were the better side on the day," Solomons said after the final. "I thought they played very well. Of the sides we have played against, that was, I think, the best performance.

"They got a jump on us. The first try, I thought, we gifted to them, and then we had a great opportunity on a two-on-one. Not that it would have been a fair reflection, but if we had turned 13–7, it might have been a different ball game."

AIB DIVISION ONE 2006–07

14 October, 2006: **Ballymena** 11 **Shannon** 22, **Buccaneers** 20 **Blackrock College** 30, **Cork Constitution** 20 **Clontarf** 10, **Dolphin** 24 **UCD** 17, **Dungannon** 23 **Garryowen** 29, **Galwegians** 29 **Belfast Harlequins** 8, **Lansdowne** 34 **St. Mary's College** 18, **U.L. Bohemian** 43 **Terenure College** 8. 21 October, 2006: **Blackrock College** 24 **Cork Constitution** 25, **Clontarf** 19 **Lansdowne** 10, **Garryowen** 12 **Ballymena** 10, **Shannon** 34 **Buccaneers** 6, **St. Mary's College** 22 **Galwegians** 16, **Terenure College** 23 **Dungannon** 12, **UCD** 3 **U.L. Bohemian** 39. 28 October, 2006: **Ballymena** 16 **Buccaneers** 18, **Belfast Harlequins** 18 **Terenure College** 23, **Dungannon** 22 **Cork Constitution** 18, **Galwegians** 14 **Shannon** 15, **St. Mary's College** 12 **Garryowen** 8, **UCD** 20 **Lansdowne** 20. 29 October, 2006: **Dolphin** 24 **Blackrock College** 3, **U.L. Bohemian** 10 **Clontarf** 3. 4 November, 2006: **Ballymena** 25 **Galwegians** 14, **Blackrock College** 31 **Terenure College** 19, **Buccaneers** 12 **St. Mary's College** 12, **Clontarf** 27 **UCD** 6, **Cork Constitution** 25 **Belfast Harlequins** 3, **Dungannon** 30 **Dolphin** 12, **Lansdowne** 15 **U.L. Bohemian** 14, **Shannon** 11 **Garryowen** 19. 18 November, 2006: **Belfast Harlequins** 3 **Dolphin** 13, **Shannon** 16 **St. Mary's College** 3. 2 December, 2006: **Blackrock College** 32 **Galwegians** 47, **Buccaneers** 19 **Dungannon** 14, **Dolphin** 9 **Clontarf** 18, **Garryowen** 17 **Belfast Harlequins** 0, **Lansdowne** 20 **Ballymena** 13, **Terenure College** 22 **UCD** 28, **U.L. Bohemian** 8 **Cork Constitution** 11. 9 December, 2006: **Ballymena** 19 **Dolphin** 12, **Belfast Harlequins** 16 **Clontarf** 27, **Galwegians** 18 **Buccaneers** 18, **Garryowen** 16 **Lansdowne** 15, **St. Mary's College** 13 **Cork Constitution** 24, **Terenure College** 13 **Shannon** 27, **U.L. Bohemian** 21 **Dungannon** 22, **UCD** 21 **Blackrock College** 29. 16 December, 2006: **Ballymena** 29 **Terenure College** 10, **Buccaneers** 8 **Garryowen** 6, **Clontarf** 26 **Blackrock College** 22, **Dungannon** 29 **UCD** 24, **Lansdowne** 17 **Galwegians** 16, **U.L. Bohemian** 15 **Belfast Harlequins** 9. 17 December, 2006: **Cork Constitution** 17 **Shannon** 17, **Dolphin** 19 **St. Mary's College** 13. 6 January, 2007: **Belfast Harlequins** 6 **Dungannon** 23, **Blackrock College** 20 **Lansdowne** 24, **Galwegians** 45 **Dolphin** 15, **Garryowen** 11 **Cork Constitution** 12, **Shannon** 16 **Clontarf** 17, **St. Mary's College** 10 **U.L. Bohemian** 24, **Terenure College** 18 **Buccaneers** 8, **UCD** 10 **Ballymena** 40. 20 January, 2007: **Belfast Harlequins** 19 **Shannon** 17, **Dungannon** 15 **Ballymena** 8, **Galwegians** 8 **Clontarf** 8, **Lansdowne** 3 **Terenure College** 7, **St. Mary's College** 38 **Blackrock College** 10, **UCD** 20 **Garryowen** 13. 21 January, 2007: **Dolphin** 18 **Cork Constitution** 27, **U.L. Bohemian** 19 **Buccaneers** 17. 27 January, 2007: **Ballymena** 22 **U.L. Bohemian** 29, **Blackrock College** 36 **Belfast Harlequins** 43, **Buccaneers** 12 **Dolphin** 27, **Clontarf** 22 **St. Mary's College** 23, **Cork Constitution** 19 **Galwegians** 15, **Dungannon** 20 **Lansdowne** 8, **Shannon** 31 **UCD** 15, **Terenure College** 23 **Garryowen** 13. 17 February, 2007: **Belfast Harlequins** 19 **St. Mary's College** 3, **Blackrock College** 41 **Ballymena** 24, **Clontarf** 20 **Buccaneers** 3, **Cork Constitution** 28 **Lansdowne** 20, **Galwegians** 24 **UCD** 31, **Garryowen** 18 **U.L. Bohemian** 5, **Shannon** 31 **Dungannon** 0, **Terenure College** 22 **Dolphin** 16. 3 March, 2007: **Ballymena** 6 **Clontarf** 36, **Buccaneers** 16 **Cork Constitution** 29, **Dolphin** 14 **Garryowen** 34, **Dungannon** 24 **Blackrock**

College 26, **Galwegians** 13 **Terenure College** 25, **Lansdowne** 8 **Belfast Harlequins** 5, **St. Mary's College** 27 **UCD** 20, **U.L. Bohemian** 15 **Shannon** 6. 24 March, 2007: **Belfast Harlequins** 14 **Buccaneers** 12, **Dolphin** 12 Bohemian 19, **Galwegians** 14 **Dungannon** 10, **Garryowen** 39 **Blackrock College** 5, **Shannon** 26 **Lansdowne** 17, **St. Mary's College** 15 **Ballymena** 13, **Terenure College** 27 **Clontarf** 39, **UCD** 21 **Cork Constitution** 28. 7 April, 2007: **Ballymena** 12 **Belfast Harlequins** 20, **Blackrock College** 15 **Shannon** 26, **Buccaneers** 16 **UCD** 37, **Clontarf** 10 **Garryowen** 12, **Cork Constitution** 62 **Terenure College** 12, **Dungannon** 17 **St. Mary's College** 17, **Lansdowne** 23 **Dolphin** 17, **U.L. Bohemian** 29 **Galwegians** 7. 21 April, 2007: **Blackrock College** 24 **U.L. Bohemian** 16, **Clontarf** 43 **Dungannon** 0, **Cork Constitution** 24 **Ballymena** 17, **Garryowen** 50 **Galwegians** 7, **Lansdowne** 12 **Buccaneers** 24, **Shannon** 22 **Dolphin** 19, **UCD** 6 **Belfast Harlequins** 3, **Terenure College** 15 **St. Mary's College** 11.

FINAL TABLE

	P	W	D	L	For	A	BP	Pts
Cork Constitution	15	13	1	1	369	227	6	60
Clontarf	15	10	1	4	325	188	9	51
Garryowen	15	10	0	5	297	175	8	48
UL Bohemians	15	10	0	5	306	187	8	48
Shannon	15	10	1	4	317	200	6	48
Dungannon	15	7	1	7	261	299	7	37
Blackrock College	15	6	0	9	348	416	13	37
Terenure College	15	8	0	7	267	353	4	36
Lansdowne	15	7	1	7	246	263	3	33
St Mary's College	15	6	2	7	237	269	4	32
Galwegians	15	4	2	9	287	324	8	28
UCD	15	5	1	9	279	372	5	27
Ballymena	15	4	0	11	265	298	10	26
Dolphin	15	5	0	10	251	307	6	26
Belfast Harlequins	15	5	0	10	186	266	5	25
Buccaneers	15	4	2	9	209	306	2	22

Play-Off Semis: Cork Constitution 21 **U.L. Bohemian** 18 **Garryowen** 28 **Clontarf** 15

Play-Off Final: **Cork Constitution** 15 **Garryowen** 16

AIB Division Two: Winners – Old Belvedere

AIB Division Three: Winners – Bruff

AIB CUP 2006–07 RESULTS

QUARTER-FINALS

3 February, 2007

Belfast Harlequins 22 **Galwegians** 19

Garryowen 13 **St Mary's College** 13

Terenure College 22 **Clonakilty** 31

UCD 24 **Shannon** 34

SEMI-FINALS

31 March, 2007

Belfast Harlequins 32 **Shannon** 28

Garryowen 32 **Clonakilty** 13

FINAL

14 April, Dubarry Park, Dublin

GARRYOWEN 20 (2G, 2PG)
BELFAST HARLEQUINS 7 (1G)

GARRYOWEN: C Kilroy; A O'Loughlin, K Hartigan, C Doyle, Ciaran O'Boyle; E Hickey, G Hurley; R Brosnan, D Varley, E McGovern, M Melbourne, E Mackey, P Neville (captain), A Kavanagh, P Malone Substitutes: J Staunton for McGovern (20 mins); N Melbourne for Staunton (temp 52 to 59 mins); D Sheehan for Mackey (62 mins); C O'Boyle for O'Loughlin (62 mins); F Quaglia for Doyle (77 mins); A Kingsley for Hickey (77 mins)

SCORERS *Tries*: O'Boyle, McGovern Conversions: Hickey (2) Penalty Goals: Eoghan Hickey (2)

BELFAST HARLEQUINS: M Kettyle; J Lowe, P McKenzie, K Pyper, G McLaughlin; N O'Connor, P Marshall; N Conlon, S Philpott, J Andress; G Rourke, L Stevenson; A Ward, C Atkinson (captain), A Gillespie Substitutes: R Blake-Knox for O'Connor (20 mins), S Ray for McLaughlin (50 mins), D Johnston for Gillespie (50 mins)

SCORERS *Try*: McKenzie Conversion: Pyper

REFEREE: A Rolland (IRFU)

ITALY

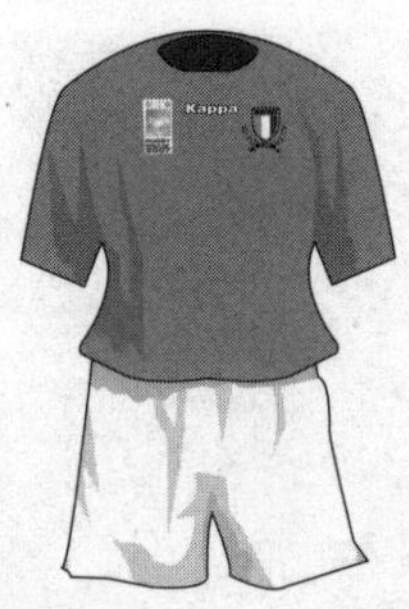

ITALY'S 2006–07 TEST RECORD

OPPONENTS	DATE	VENUE	RESULT
Portugal	7 Oct	H	**Won** 83–0
Russia	14 Oct	A	**Won** 67–7
Australia	11 Nov	H	**Lost** 18–25
Argentina	18 Nov	H	**Lost** 16–23
Canada	25 Nov	H	**Won** 41–6
France	3 Feb	H	**Lost** 3–39
England	10 Feb	A	**Lost** 7–20
Scotland	24 Feb	A	**Won** 37–17
Wales	10 Mar	H	**Won** 23–20
Ireland	17 Mar	H	**Lost** 24–51
Uruguay	2 June	A	**Won** 29–5
Argentina	9 June	A	**Lost** 6–24
Japan	18 Aug	H	**Won** 36–12
Ireland	24 Aug	A	**Lost** 20–23
New Zealand	8 Sept	N	**Lost** 14–76 (WC)
Romania	12 Sept	N	**Won** 24–18 (WC)
Portugal	19 Sept	N	**Won** 31–5 (WC)
Scotland	29 Sept	N	**Lost** 16–18 (WC)

ECSTASY THEN AGONY

By Gianluca Barca

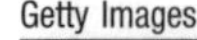

Getty Images

Italy had their best Six Nations championship since joining in 2000.

Italy's best international season ever ended on a sour note in Saint Etienne when a late penalty by full-back David Bortolussi just fell short of the uprights, costing them victory against Scotland, 16–18, and the World Cup quarter-finals.

The Azzurri had never gone beyond the pool stages in the tournament and this year looked like their best chance yet.

They had beaten Scotland in Murrayfield, in the Six Nations in February, and were set for a repeat performance in France. With the top spot in Pool C already booked by the All Blacks, and Romania and Portugal the other two contenders, the Scotland vs Italy clash had long been seen as the runner-up decider.

It was a sad, drizzly night for Italy and the record 15,000 supporters who had travelled to cheer them on in France: the final whistle not only put paid to their Rugby World Cup glory, but also saw veteran Alessandro Troncon (101 caps) leave the field for the last time and coach Pierre Berbizier, as announced, part ways with the squad.

"I thought we were stronger, but they were the better team on the night," said Berbizier in his farewell comment. The difference lay in the boot of Chris Paterson who kicked an impeccable six out of six for Scotland while Italy's David Bortolussi could only add a below par three out of six to Troncon's converted try. To their dismay the Azzurri saw history repeating itself: four years earlier, in the 2003 World Cup in Australia, they had found themselves wanting in exactly the same way, going out to Wales who they had beaten in that season's Six Nations, in Rome.

At the 2007 Rugby World Cup, however, expectations were much higher in Italy. After a record-breaking two wins in the Six Nations including their first ever away victory, in Scotland, rugby fever started to grip the nation.

The 2006–2007 international season got off to a promising start in October for Frenchman Pierre Berbizier's squad. They picked up their pass to France with two convincing victories over Portugal (83–0, in L'Aquila) and Russia (67–7, in Moscow) in the World Cup qualifiers. But in November they seemed to be back to their role as the perennial underachievers when they lost to Australia (18–25) and to Argentina (16–23) in Rome, before sweeping aside Canada, 41–6.

The two defeats left supporters unhappy about the squad's ability to rise to the occasion and "carpe diem". Especially as the Pumas had faced Italy resting a good part of the squad that had seen off England in Twickenham the week before. Berbizier, though, had other ideas.

"Maybe a loss today means we will be able to win tomorrow," he said. "A year and a half ago we lost to the Wallabies in Melbourne 69–21. This time it was 25–18. We proved we are narrowing the gap and are definitely in with a real chance now."

People saw that chance being in the Six Nations opener, two months later, against France, in Rome. A little verbal skirmish between Frenchmen Pierre Berbizier and Bernard Laporte in the build-up to the match added an extra edge to the game. But the match turned out to be a no show for Italy who were outplayed, 39–3, by the French.

England was looming the next week and fear was growing in the camp that they were set for a whitewash in Twickenham. Spirit and character were needed and the idea that the squad was lacking charisma and leadership began to creep in, despite the captaincy of Gloucester skipper Marco Bortolami. It was to be a doubt that would niggle Italy for the rest of the season. For the England clash Berbizier decided to hand the number nine jersey to veteran scrum half Alessandro Troncon, 33, who had spent a couple of seasons in the international wilderness and had started on the bench in the match with France.

Against England, the scrum-half was the hero of the day. He mastered his forwards in his characteristic way to limit the damage to a 7–20 defeat.

Troncon was named man of the match and fly-half Andrea Scanavacca scored and converted his team's only try of the day. Scanavacca was to be another controversial name in Italy's season.

Then came Murrayfield and those mad opening seven minutes which caught Scotland napping. The early onslaught gave Italy three tries and left Scotland 0–21 down wondering what had hit them. First, with not even a minute on the clock, Mauro Bergamasco charged down a kick by fly-half Phil Godman and scored near the posts.

Seconds after, Andrea Scanavacca intercepted a long pass in midfield and sprinted his way to Italy's second try.

A repeat interception by winger Kaine Robertson took the tally to three. It took Scotland 30 minutes to recover composure and just when tries by Rob Dewey and Chris Paterson seemed to put them back in the match, it was a formidable effort by the Azzurri forwards that opened the way for Troncon to sneak over and seal the match, 37–22.

Troncon was once more voted man of the match and Scanavacca celebrated the day with a personal score of 22 points. It was Italy's first ever Six Nations away win.

A football mad country, went crazy for rugby. Leading sports daily, La Gazzetta dello Sport, put the story on the front page and overnight rugby fever took hold.

Two weeks later things reached a head when the Azzurri beat Wales in Rome in a dramatic finale, 23–20, which saw Wales' misunderstanding with referee Chris White, about time-keeping, cost them a probable draw.

With everyone celebrating the win nobody questioned Ramiro Pez's surprise selection over Scanavacca at fly-half.

Italy's heavy defeat against Ireland, 24–51, in the last game of the tournament did nothing to change the buoyant mood of the country.

Crowds of supporters gathered in mass in Rome's Piazza del Popolo to cheer the squad and to celebrate the new heroes.

Expectations for the World Cup began to mount.

At the top of his popularity among the Italians, however, Berbizier announced he wouldn't be staying on after France 2007. A move many thought to be badly timed.

Then he took a second string side on tour to South America, where Italy beat Uruguay, 29–5, and lost to Argentina, 24–6, in two unimpressive performances.

On his return, the coach named the 40-man squad to train for the World Cup. It was not without its surprises: Andrea Scanavacca, one of the heroes of Murrayfield and new top scorer in the league, with more then 3,000 points, was left out.

The number ten jersey was up for grabs between Argentinean born Ramiro Pez and South African Roland De Marigny. Into the squad also came utility back Aussie born Chris Burton, from French Fourth Division club Orleans.

The choice raised a few eyebrows, which Bortolussi's poor kicking in the World Cup decider against Scotland didn't help to lower.

Warm up games with Japan (36–12) and Ireland (a narrow and controversial loss 20–23, at Ravenhill) seemed to show that things were bubbling nicely. Maybe too nicely.

Debate about playing a second team in the World Cup opening game, in Marseille, against New Zealand, was put to an end when Berbizier announced the squad which was the best Italy could offer.

The bold decision turned against them. After choosing not to face the haka the Azzuri were taken apart by the All Blacks, 76–14.

"It's difficult to talk about a game which we failed to play," a disappointed coach said after the match. "We simply weren't there".

Two scrappy victories against Romania and Portugal, however, showed something was amiss inside the squad. Had expectations been too high, both for Berbizier, wanting to impress his home country, and a squad which wasn't strong enough to bear the pressure of new found fame?

Had Italy's last penalty kick gone over, then the story might have been a very different one.

On the domestic scene, the continual stream of foreign imports into the clubs didn't help build a strong base either.

In the Premiership there were more than 150 players from abroad out of a total of 300.

Not surprising then that the national squad was a mixed bunch which included Kiwis, South Africans, Argentineans and even a Fijian. On the other hand the exodus of Italy's top players to France and England did nothing to boost the national championship that Benetton Treviso won for the fourth time in five years.

This time however the Super 10 Final, between Benetton and Italian Cup winners Viadana, was a tighter affair.

A last-minute try by Treviso lock Marco Wentzel tied the game at the end of the second half. In extra time, another try by Treviso, scored by Massimiliano Perziano, secured them victory, 28–24.

Three days after the defeat against Scotland, the Italian Federation named former Springbok Nick Mallett as the national squad's new coach. But that will be another story.

ITALY INTERNATIONAL PLAYERS

UP TO 31ST OCTOBER 2007

Compiled by Hugh Copping

Abbiati, E 1968 *WGe* 1970 *R* 1971 *Mor, F* 1972 *Pt, Sp, Sp, Yug* 1973 *Pt, ETv* 1974 *Leo*
Agosti, A 1933 *Cze* (R)
Aguero, M 2005 *Tg* (R), *Ar* (R), *Fj* 2006 *Fj* (R) 2007 *Ur* (R), *Ar* (R), *I* (R), *Pt* (R)
Agujari, A 1967 *Pt*
Aio, E 1974 *WGe*
Aiolfi, G 1952 *Sp, Ger, F* 1953 *F* 1955 *Ger, F*
Alacevich, A 1939 *R* (R)
Albonico, A 1934 *R* 1935 *F* 1936 *Ger, R* 1937 *Ger, R, Bel, Ger, F* 1938 *Ger*
Aldorvandi, N 1994 *Sp, CZR, H*
Alfonsetti, M 1994 *F*
Allevi, E 1929 *Sp* 1933 *Cze* (R)
Aloisio, I 1933 *Cze, Cze* 1934 *Cat, R* 1935 *Cat* 1936 *Ger, R*
Altigeri, A 1973 *Rho, WTv, Bor, NEC, Nat, Leo, FS, Tva, Cze, Yug, A* 1974 *Pt, WGe* 1975 *F, E, Pol, H, Sp* 1976 *F, R, J* 1978 *Ar, USS, Sp* 1979 *F, Pol, R*
Altissimi, T 1929 *Sp*
Ambron, V 1962 *Ger, R* 1963 *F* 1964 *Ger, F* 1965 *F, Cze* 1966 *F, Ger, R* 1967 *Pt, R* 1968 *Pt, WGe, Yug* 1969 *Bul, Sp, Bel* 1970 *Mad, Mad, R* 1971 *Mor* 1972 *Sp, Sp*
Ambrosio, R 1987 *NZ, USS, Sp* 1988 *F, R, A, I* 1989 *R, Sp, Ar, Z* (R), *USS*
Ancillotti, B 1978 *Sp* 1979 *F, Pol, R*
Andina, E 1952 *F* 1955 *F*
Angelozzi, C 1979 *E, Mor* 1980 *Coo*
Angioli, A 1960 *Ger, F* 1961 *Ger, F* 1962 *F, Ger, R* 1963 *F*
Angrisiani, A 1979 *Mor, F, Pol, USS, Mor* 1980 *Coo* 1984 *Tun*
Annibal, S 1980 *Fj, Coo, Pol, Sp* 1981 *F, WGe* 1982 *R, E, WGe* 1983 *F, USS, Sp, Mor, F, A* 1984 *F* 1985 *F, Z, Z* (R) 1986 *Tun, F, Pt* 1990 *F*
Antoni, JM 2001 *Nm* (R), *SA*
Appiani, C 1976 *Sp* (R) 1977 *Mor, Pol, Sp* 1978 *USS*
Appiani, S 1985 *R* 1986 *Pt* (R) 1988 *A* (R) 1989 *F*
Arancio, O 1993 *Rus* (R) 1994 *CZR, H, A, A, R, W, F* 1995 *S, I, Sa, E, Ar, F, R* (R), *NZ* (R), *SA* 1996 *W, Pt, W, A, E, S* 1997 *I, I* (R) 1998 *S* (R), *Ar, E* (R) 1999 *F, W* (R), *I, SA* (R), *E, NZ* (R)
Armellin, D 1965 *Cze* 1966 *Ger* 1968 *Pt, WGe, Yug* 1969 *Bul, Sp, Bel, F*
Arrigoni, A 1949 *Cze*
Artuso, G 1977 *Pol, R* 1978 *Sp* 1979 *F, E, NZ, Mor* 1980 *F, R, JAB* 1981 *F* 1982 *F, E, Mor* 1983 *F, R, USS, C* (R), *C* 1984 *USS* 1985 *R, E, USS, R* 1986 *Tun, F, Tun* 1987 *Pt, F, R, NZ*
Augeri, E 1962 *F, Ger, R* 1963 *F*
Autore, A 1961 *Ger, F* 1962 *F* 1964 *Ger* 1966 *Ger* 1968 *Pt, WGe, Yug* 1969 *Bul, Sp, Bel, F*
Avigo, L 1959 *F* 1962 *F, Ger, R* 1963 *F* 1964 *Ger, F* 1965 *F, Cze* 1966 *Ger, R*
Aymonod, R 1933 *Cze* 1934 *Cat, R* 1935 *F* (R)
Azzali, A 1981 *WGe* 1982 *F, R, WGe* 1983 *F, R, USS, Sp, Mor, F* (R) 1984 *F, Mor, R* 1985 *R, E, Sp*
Babbo, S 1996 *Pt*
Balducci, A 1929 *Sp* (R)
Baraldi, F 1973 *Cze, Yug* 1974 *Mid, Sus, Oxo* (R) 1975 *E, Pol, H, Sp* 1976 *F, R, A* 1977 *F, Mor, Cze*
Baraldi, R 1971 *R*
Barattin, A 1996 *A* (R), *E* (R)
Barba, S 1985 *R* (R), *E* 1986 *E, A* 1987 *Pt, F, R, Ar, Fj* 1988 *R, USS, A* 1990 *F, Pol, Sp, H, R, USS* 1991 *F, R, Nm, Nm, US, E, USS* 1992 *Sp, F, R, R, S* 1993 *Sp, F, Cro, Mor, Sp*
Barbieri, RJ 2006 *J* (R), *Fj* (R), *Pt* 2007 *Ur, Ar, I*
Barbini, G 1978 *USS* (R)
Barbini, M 2002 *NZ* (R), *Sp, Ar, A* 2003 *I, NZ* 2004 *F, I, R* (R), *J, NZ, US* (R) 2005 *W* (R), *E* 2007 *I* (R)
Barbini, N 1953 *Ger, R* 1954 *Sp, F* 1955 *Ger, F, Sp, Cze* 1956 *Ger* 1957 *Ger* 1958 *R* 1960 *Ger, F*
Bargelli, F 1979 *E, Sp, Mor, F, Pol, USS, NZ, Mor* 1980 *F, R, Fj, Sp* 1981 *F, R*
Barilari, S 1948 *Cze* 1953 *Ger, R*
Baroni, M 1999 *F, W* (R), *I, SA* (R), *SA* (R) 2000 *C*
Barzaghi, V 1929 *Sp* 1930 *Sp* 1933 *Cze*
Basei, JL 1979 *E, Sp, Mor* (R), *F, Pol, USS, NZ, Mor* 1980 *F, R, Fj, JAB, Coo, USS* 1981 *R*
Battagion, A 1948 *F, Cze*
Battaglini, F 1948 *F*
Battaglini, M 1940 *R, Ger* 1951 *Sp* 1953 *F, R*
Becca, A 1937 *R* 1938 *Ger* 1939 *R* 1940 *Ger*
Bellinazzo, E 1958 *R* 1959 *F* 1960 *Ger, F* 1961 *Ger, F* 1962 *F, Ger* 1964 *Ger, F* 1966 *F, Ger, R* 1967 *F*
Benatti, A 2001 *Fj* (R), *SA* (R), *Sa* 2002 *W* (R) 2003 *NZ* (R)
Bentivoglio, C 1977 *Pol*
Beretta, D 1993 *S*
Bergamasco, A 1973 *Bor, Tva* 1977 *Pol* 1978 *USS*
Bergamasco, M 1998 *H, E* 1999 *SA, E* 2000 *S, W, I, E, F, C* 2001 *I, E, F, S, W, Fj, SA, Sa* 2002 *F, S, W, I, E, NZ* (R), *Sp* (R), *R* (R), *A* 2003 *W, I, S* (R), *I, Geo* (R), *NZ, W* (R) 2004 *J, C, NZ* 2005 *I, W, Ar, A, Ar* (R), *Fj* 2006 *I, E, F, J, Fj, Pt, Rus, A, Ar, C* 2007 *F, S, W, J, NZ, R, Pt, S*
Bergamasco, M 2002 *F* (R), *S, W, Ar, A* 2003 *W* (R), *I* (R), *E, F, S, S, Geo, NZ, C* 2004 *E* (R), *F, S* (R), *I* (R), *W* (R) 2005 *I, W, S, Tg, Ar, Fj* 2006 *I, E, F, W, S, J, Fj, Pt, Rus, A, Ar, C* 2007 *F, E, S, W, I, J, I, NZ, R, S*
Bernabo, L 1970 *Mad, Mad, R* 1972 *Sp, Sp*
Bernabò, V 2004 *US* 2005 *Tg* (R), *Fj* (R) 2007 *E* (R), *S* (R), *W* (R), *I* (R), *Ur, Ar, J* (R), *I, NZ* (R), *R* (R)
Berni, F 1985 *R, Sp, Z, Z* 1986 *E, A* 1987 *R, NZ* 1988 *A* 1989 *F*
Bertoli 1967 *R*
Bertolotto, V 1936 *Ger, R* 1937 *Ger, R* 1942 *R* 1948 *F*
Bettarello, O 1958 *F* 1959 *F* 1961 *Ger*
Bettarello, R 1953 *Ger, R*
Bettarello, S 1979 *Pol, E, Sp, F, NZ, Mor* 1980 *F, R, Fj, JAB, Coo, Pol, USS, Sp* 1981 *F, R, USS, WGe* 1982 *F, R, E, WGe, Mor* 1983 *F, R, USS, C, Sp, Mor, F, A* 1984 *F, Mor, R, Tun, USS* 1985 *F, R, E, Sp, Z, USS, R* 1986 *Tun, F, Pt, E, A* (R), *Tun, USS* 1987 *R, USS, Sp* 1988 *USS, A*
Bettella, L 1969 *Sp, Bel, F*
Bevilacqua, R 1937 *Bel, Ger, F* 1938 *Ger* 1939 *Ger, R* 1940 *R, Ger* 1942 *R*
Bezzi, C 2003 *W, I, E, F, S, I, NZ, W* (R) 2004 *US* 2005 *Ar, A*
Biadene, G 1958 *R* 1959 *F*
Bigi, G 1930 *Sp* 1933 *Cze*
Bimbati, M 1989 *Z*
Birtig, M 1998 *H* (R) 1999 *F*
Blessano, F 1975 *F, R, Pol, H, Sp* 1976 *F, R, J* 1977 *F, Mor, Pol, R, Cze, R, Sp* 1978 *F, Ar, Sp* 1979 *F, Pol, R*
Boccaletto, L 1969 *Bul, Bel, F* 1970 *Cze, Mad, Mad, R* (R) 1971 *F, R* 1972 *Pt, Sp, Sp* 1975 *E* (R)
Boccazzi, S 1985 *Z* (R) 1988 *USS*

Bocconelli, M 1967 *R*
Bollesan, M 1963 *F* 1964 *F* 1965 *F* 1966 *F*, *Ger* 1967 *F*, *Pt* 1968 *Pt*, *WGe*, *Yug* 1969 *Bul*, *Sp*, *Bel*, *F* 1970 *Cze*, *Mad*, *Mad*, *R* 1971 *Mor*, *F*, *R* 1972 *Pt*, *Pt*, *Sp*, *Sp*, *Yug* 1973 *Pt*, *Rho*, *WTv*, *Bor*, *NEC*, *Nat*, *ETv*, *Leo*, *FS*, *Tva*, *Yug*, *A* 1974 *Pt*, *Mid*, *Sus*, *Oxo*, *WGe*, *Leo* 1975 *F*, *Sp*, *Cze*
Bona, A 1972 *Sp*, *Yug* 1973 *Rho*, *WTv*, *Bor*, *NEC*, *Nat*, *ETv*, *Leo*, *FS*, *Tva*, *Cze*, *Yug*, *A* 1974 *Pt*, *WGe*, *Leo* 1975 *F*, *Sp*, *R*, *Cze*, *E*, *Pol*, *H*, *Sp* 1976 *F*, *R*, *J*, *A*, *Sp* 1977 *F*, *Mor* 1978 *Ar*, *USS*, *Sp* 1979 *F*, *Sp*, *Mor*, *F*, *Pol*, *USS*, *NZ*, *Mor* 1980 *F*, *R*, *Fj*, *JAB*, *Pol*, *Sp* 1981 *F*
Bonaiti, L 1979 *R* 1980 *Pol*
Bonati, G 1939 *Ger*, *R* (R)
Bonetti, S 1972 *Yug* 1973 *Rho*, *WTv*, *Bor*, *NEC*, *Nat*, *ETv*, *Leo*, *FS*, *Tva* 1974 *Pt*, *Mid*, *Sus*, *Oxo*, *Leo* 1975 *F*, *Sp*, *R*, *Cze*, *E*, *Pol*, *H*, *Sp* 1976 *R*, *J*, *A*, *Sp* 1977 *F*, *Mor*, *R*, *Sp* 1978 *F* 1979 *F* 1980 *USS*
Bonfante, S 1936 *Ger*, *R*
Bonino, G 1949 *F*
Bonomi, M 1988 *F*, *R* 1990 *Sp*, *H*, *R*, *USS* 1991 *F*, *R*, *Nm*, *Nm*, *E* (R), *NZ*, *USS* 1992 *R* (R), *R* 1993 *Cro*, *Mor*, *Sp*, *F*, *S* 1994 *Sp* (R), *R*, *H*, *A*, *A*, *W* 1995 *S*, *I*, *Sa*, *F*, *Ar*, *R*, *NZ* 1996 *W* (R)
Bordon, S 1990 *R*, *USS* 1991 *Nm*, *USS* (R) 1992 *F*, *R* 1993 *Sp*, *F*, *Pt*, *Rus*, *F* 1994 *R*, *A* (R), *A*, *R*, *W*, *F* 1995 *I* (R), *E*, *Ar*, *F*, *Ar*, *NZ*, *SA* 1996 *W*, *A*, *E* 1997 *I*, *F*
Borsetto, L 1977 *Pol*
Borsetto, V 1948 *F*, *Cze*
Bortolami, M 2001 *Nm*, *SA* (R), *Fj*, *SA* (R), *Sa* 2002 *F*, *S*, *W*, *I*, *E*, *NZ*, *Sp*, *R*, *Ar*, *A* 2003 *W*, *I*, *E* (R), *S*, *Geo*, *Tg*, *C* 2004 *E*, *F*, *S*, *I*, *W*, *R*, *J*, *C*, *NZ* 2005 *I*, *W*, *S*, *E*, *F*, *Ar*, *Ar*, *A*, *Tg*, *Ar*, *Fj* 2006 *I*, *E*, *F*, *W*, *S*, *J*, *Fj* (R), *Pt*, *Rus*, *A*, *Ar*, *C* 2007 *F*, *E*, *S*, *W*, *I*, *J*, *I*, *NZ*, *R*, *Pt*
Bortolini, G 1933 *Cze* 1934 *Cat*
Bortolussi, D 2006 *J*, *Fj*, *Pt*, *Rus*, *Ar*, *C* 2007 *Ur* (R), *Ar*, *J*, *I*, *NZ*, *R*, *Pt*, *S*
Boscaino, L 1967 *Pt*
Bossi, L 1940 *R*, *Ger*
Bottacchiara, A 1991 *NZ*, *USS* 1992 *Sp*, *F*, *R*, *R*
Bottacin, G 1956 *Cze*
Bottonelli, O 1929 *Sp* 1934 *R* 1935 *Cat*, *F* 1937 *Ger* 1939 *Ger*
Bove, L 1948 *Cze* 1949 *F*, *Cze*
Bracaglia, O 1939 *R*
Braga, M 1958 *R*
Bricchi, L 1929 *Sp* 1930 *Sp* 1933 *Cze* (R)
Brighetti, L 1934 *Cat*
Brunelli, A 1969 *Bel* 1970 *Mad* 1971 *F* (R)
Brunello, M 1988 *I* 1989 *F* 1990 *F*, *Sp*, *H*, *R*, *USS* 1993 *Pt*
Brusin, S 1957 *Ger*
Burton, CS 2007 *Ur*, *Ar*
Busson, G 1957 *Ger* 1958 *R* 1959 *F* 1960 *Ger*, *F* 1961 *Ger*, *F* 1962 *F*, *Ger* 1963 *F*
Caccia-Dominioni, F 1935 *F* (R) 1937 *Ger*
Caione, C 1995 *R* (R) 1996 *Pt* 1997 *F* (R), *R* (R) 1998 *Rus*, *Ar*, *H*, *E* 1999 *F*, *S* (R), *SA* (R), *Ur*, *Sp*, *Fj*, *Tg*, *NZ* 2000 *Sa*, *Fj*, *C*, *R*, *NZ* 2001 *I*, *E*, *S* (R), *Fj*
Caligiuri, R 1969 *F* (R) 1973 *Pt*, *Rho*, *WTv*, *NEC*, *Nat*, *ETv*, *Leo* (R), *FS*, *Tva* 1975 *E*, *Pol*, *H*, *Sp* 1976 *F*, *R*, *J*, *A*, *Sp* 1978 *F*, *Ar*, *USS*, *Sp* 1979 *F*, *Pol*, *R*
Caluzzi, A 1970 *R* 1971 *Mor*, *F* 1972 *Pt*, *Pt*, *Sp*, *Sp* 1973 *Pt* 1974 *Oxo*, *WGe*, *Leo*
Camiscioni, P 1975 *E* 1976 *R* (R), *J*, *A*, *Sp* 1977 *F* 1978 *F*
Campagna, M 1933 *Cze* 1934 *Cat* 1936 *Ger*, *R* 1937 *Ger*, *R*, *Bel* 1938 *Ger*
Canale, G-J 2003 *S* (R), *Geo*, *NZ* (R), *Tg*, *C*, *W* 2004 *S*, *I*, *W*, *R*, *J*, *C* 2005 *I*, *Ar*, *Ar*, *A*, *Tg*, *Ar*, *Fj* 2006 *I*, *E*, *F*, *W*, *S*, *A*, *Ar*, *C* (R) 2007 *F*, *E*, *S*, *W*, *J*, *I*, *R*, *Pt*, *S*
Canavosio, PL 2005 *A* (R), *Tg* (R), *Fj* (R) 2006 *I*, *E*, *F*, *W*, *S*, *Fj*, *Pt* (R), *Rus* (R), *A*, *Ar* 2007 *Ar*, *J* (R), *I* (R), *Pt*
Cantoni, C 1956 *Ger*, *F*, *Cze* 1957 *Ger*
Capitani, L 1989 *F*, *R*, *Sp*, *Ar*, *Z*, *USS*
Capuzzoni, M 1993 *Cro* 1995 *I* (R)
Caranci, A 1989 *R* (R)
Carli, M 1955 *Sp*, *Cze*
Carloni, C 1935 *F*
Carpente, D 2004 *R* (R), *J* (R)
Carraro, T 1937 *R* (R)
Casagrande, T 1977 *R* (R)
Cassellato, U 1990 *Sp* 1992 *R* (R), *S* 1993 *Sp*, *F*, *Pt*, *Cro*, *Mor*, *F* (R), *S*
Cassina, R 1992 *R* (R), *S* (R)
Castellani, A 1994 *CZR* 1995 *Ar* (R), *R* 1996 *W* (R), *S* 1997 *Ar* (R), *R*, *I* 1998 *S*, *W*, *Rus*, *H*, *E* (R) 1999 *F* (R), *W* (R), *Ur* (R), *Sp*, *Fj*, *Tg*, *NZ*
Castrogiovanni, LM 2002 *NZ* (R), *Sp*, *R*, *Ar* (R), *A* 2003 *I* (R), *E* (R), *F* (R), *S* (R), *I*, *Geo*, *NZ* (R), *Tg*, *C*, *W* 2004 *E*, *F*, *S*, *I*, *W*, *J* 2005 *I*, *W*, *S*, *E* (R), *F* (R), *Ar* (R), *A*, *Ar* (R), *Fj* 2006 *I* (R), *E* (R), *F* (R), *W* (R), *S*, *Pt*, *Rus*, *A*, *Ar*, *C* (R) 2007 *F* (R), *E*, *S*, *J*, *I*, *NZ*, *R*, *Pt*, *S*
Catotti, L 1979 *Pol*, *E*
Cazzini, A 1933 *Cze*, *Cze* 1934 *Cat*, *R* 1935 *Cat*, *F* 1936 *Ger*, *R* 1937 *Ger*, *R*, *Bel*, *Ger*, *F* 1939 *R* 1942 *R*
Cecchetto, G 1955 *F*
Cecchetto-Milani, A 1952 *Sp*, *Ger*, *F*
Cecchin, G 1970 *Cze*, *R* 1971 *F*, *R* 1972 *Pt*
Ceccotti, G 1972 *Pt*, *Sp*
Centinari, A 1930 *Sp* (R)
Centinari, R 1935 *F* 1936 *Ger*, *R* 1937 *Bel*, *F* 1939 *Ger*
Cepolino, A 1999 *Ur* (R), *Sp*, *Fj*, *Tg*, *NZ*
Cesani, L 1929 *Sp* 1930 *Sp* 1935 *Cat*, *F*
Ceselin, F 1989 *F* (R), *R*
Checchinato, C 1990 *Sp* 1991 *Nm*, *Nm*, *US*, *NZ*, *USS* 1992 *Sp*, *F*, *R*, *S* 1993 *Pt*, *Cro* (R), *Sp*, *F*, *Rus*, *F*, *S* 1994 *Sp*, *R*, *CZR*, *A*, *A*, *R*, *W*, *F* 1995 *Sa*, *F*, *Ar*, *R*, *NZ* 1996 *W*, *E* 1997 *I* (R), *F*, *Ar*, *R*, *SA*, *I* 1998 *Rus*, *Ar*, *H*, *E* 1999 *F*, *S*, *SA*, *SA*, *Ur*, *Fj*, *E* (R), *Tg*, *NZ* 2000 *S*, *W*, *I*, *E*, *F*, *Sa*, *Fj* 2001 *I*, *E*, *F*, *S*, *W*, *Nm*, *SA*, *Ur*, *Ar*, *Fj*, *SA*, *Sa* 2002 *F*, *S*, *W*, *Sp* (R), *R* (R) 2003 *Geo* (R), *NZ*, *Tg* (R), *C* (R), *W* 2004 *E* (R), *F* (R), *I*
Chechinato, G 1973 *Cze*, *Yug*, *A* 1974 *WGe*, *Leo*
Cherubini, G 1949 *Cze* 1951 *Sp*
Ciccio, T 1992 *R* 1993 *Sp*, *F*, *Mor*, *F*
Cicognani, E 1940 *Ger*
Cinelli, R 1968 *Pt* 1969 *Sp*
Cinti, G 1973 *Rho*, *WTv*, *ETv*
Cioni, F 1967 *Pt*, *R* 1968 *Pt* 1969 *Bul*, *Sp*, *Bel* 1970 *Cze*, *Mad*, *Mad*, *R*
Clerici, L 1939 *Ger*
Colella, A 1983 *R*, *USS*, *C*, *C*, *Sp*, *Mor*, *F*, *A*, *USS* 1984 *R*, *Tun*, *USS* 1985 *F*, *R*, *E*, *Sp*, *Z*, *Z*, *USS*, *R* 1986 *Tun*, *F*, *Pt*, *E*, *A*, *Tun*, *USS* 1987 *Pt*, *F*, *Ar*, *Fj*, *USS*, *Sp* 1988 *F*, *R*, *USS* 1989 *R*, *Sp*, *Ar* 1990 *Pol*, *R*
Collodo, O 1977 *Pol*, *Cze*, *R*, *Sp* 1978 *F* 1986 *Pt*, *E*, *A*, *USS* 1987 *Pt*, *F*, *R*, *NZ*, *Ar*, *Fj*
Colombini, S 1971 *R*
Colombo, F 1933 *Cze*
Colussi, G 1957 *F* 1958 *F* 1964 *Ger*, *F* 1965 *F*, *Cze* 1968 *Pt*
Colusso, C 1982 *F*
Comin, A 1955 *Ger*, *F*, *Sp*, *F*, *Cze* 1956 *F*, *Cze* 1958 *F*
Conforto, U 1965 *Cze* 1966 *Ger*, *R* 1967 *F*, *R* 1968 *Pt*, *WGe*, *Yug* 1969 *Bul*, *Sp*, *Bel*, *F* 1970 *Cze* 1971 *Mor*, *F* 1972 *Yug* 1973 *Pt*
Coppio, F 1993 *F* (R), *Pt*, *Cro*, *Mor*, *Sp*
Cornella, L 1999 *Sp*
Corvo, R 1985 *F* (R), *Sp*, *Z*
Cossara, U 1971 *Mor*, *F*, *R* 1972 *Pt*, *Sp* 1973 *Pt*, *Rho*, *NEC*, *Nat*, *Leo*, *FS*, *Tva*, *Cze* 1975 *F*, *Sp*, *R*, *Cze*, *E*, *Pol*, *H* 1976 *F*, *J*, *A* (R) 1977 *Pol*
Costa, A 1940 *R*, *Ger* 1942 *R*
Costanzo, S 2004 *R*, *C* (R), *NZ* (R), *US* (R)
Cottafava, E 1973 *Pt*
Cova, R 1937 *Bel*, *Ger*, *F* 1938 *Ger* 1939 *Ger*, *R* 1942 *R*
Covi, C 1988 *F*, *R*, *USS*, *A*, *I* 1989 *F*, *R*, *Sp*, *Ar*, *Z*, *USS* 1990 *F*, *Pol* (R), *R* 1991 *F*, *R*, *Nm*, *Nm* 1996 *E*
Crepaz, F 1972 *Pt*
Crescenzo, M 1984 *R* (R)
Crespi, U 1933 *Cze*, *Cze* 1934 *Cat*, *R* 1935 *Cat* 1937 *Ger*
Cristofoletto, W 1992 *R* 1993 *Mor*, *Sp*, *F* (R) 1996 *Pt* (R), *A*, *E*, *S* 1997 *I*, *F*, *F*, *Ar*, *SA* (R), *I* (R) 1998 *S*, *W*, *Rus*, *Ar*, *E* 1999 *F*, *S*, *W*, *I*, *SA*, *SA*, *Sp*, *Fj* (R), *E*, *NZ* (R) 2000 *E*, *F*
Croci, G 1990 *Sp*, *H*, *R*, *USS* 1991 *F*, *R*, *Nm*, *US*, *E*, *NZ*, *USS* 1992 *Sp*, *F* 1993 *S* 1996 *S* 1997 *I*, *F*, *F*, *Ar*, *R*, *SA*, *I* 1998 *S*, *W*

Crotti, R 1993 *S* 1995 *SA* (R)
Cuccharelli, L 1966 *R* 1967 *R*
Cucchiella, G 1973 *A* (R) 1974 *Sus* 1979 *Sp, F, Pol, USS, NZ, Mor* 1980 *F, R, Fj, JAB, Coo* 1985 *USS, R* 1986 *Tun, F, Pt, E* 1987 *Pt, F, Fj*
Cuttitta, M 1990 *Pol, R, Sp, H, R, USS* 1991 *F, Nm, Nm, US, E, NZ, USS* 1992 *Sp, F, R, R, S* 1993 *Sp, F, Pt, Cro, Mor, Sp, F, Rus, F, S* 1994 *Sp, R, CZR* (R), *H, A, A, W, F* 1995 *S, I, Sa, E, Ar, F, Ar, R, NZ, SA* 1996 *W, Pt, W, E, S* 1997 *I, F, F, Ar, SA, I* 1998 *W, Rus, Ar* (R), *H, E* 1999 *F, S, W* 2000 *S, W, I, E* (R)
Cuttitta, M 1987 *Pt, F, R, NZ, Ar, Fj, USS, Sp* 1988 *F, R* 1989 *Z, USS* 1990 *Pol, R* 1991 *F, R, Nm, US, E, NZ, USS* 1992 *Sp, F, R, R, S* 1993 *Sp, F, Mor, Sp, F, F* 1994 *Sp, R, H, A, A, F* 1995 *S, I, Sa* 1996 *S* 1997 *I, F, F, Ar, R, SA, I* 1998 *S, W, Rus, Ar* 1999 *F*
Dagnini, G 1949 *F*
Dal Maso, D 2000 *Sa* (R), *Fj* 2001 *I, E* (R) 2004 *J, C, NZ, US* 2005 *I* (R), *W* (R), *S, E, F, A*
Dal Sie, M 1993 *Pt* 1994 *R, W* (R), *F* 1995 *F, Ar* 1996 *A*
D'Alberton, A 1966 *F, Ger, R* 1967 *F, R*
Daldoss, D 1979 *Pol, R, E, Sp, Mor*
D'Alessio, C 1937 *R, Bel, F* 1938 *Ger* 1939 *Ger*
Dallan, D 1999 *F, S, W* 2000 *S, W, I, E, F* (R), *C, R, NZ* 2001 *I, E, F, W, Fj, SA, Sa* 2002 *F, S, I, E, NZ, Sp, R* 2003 *W, I, E, F, S, Tg, C, W* 2004 *E, F, S, I, W, C* 2006 *J* 2007 *F, E*
Dallan, M 1997 *Ar, R, I* 1998 *Ar* (R), *H, E* 1999 *SA, SA* (R) 2000 *S, Sa, C* 2001 *F, S* 2003 *Tg, C* 2004 *E, F* (R), *S*
Danieli, A 1955 *Ger, F, Sp, F, Cze*
D'Anna, V 1993 *Rus*
Dari, P 1951 *Sp* (R) 1952 *Sp, Ger, F* 1953 *Ger, R* 1954 *Sp, F*
De Angelis, G 1934 *Cat, R* 1935 *Cat, F* 1937 *R*
De Anna, E 1972 *Yug* 1973 *Cze, A* 1975 *F, Sp, R, Cze, E, Pol, H, Sp* 1976 *F, R* 1978 *Ar, USS, Sp* 1979 *F, R, Sp, Mor, F, USS, NZ* 1980 *F, R, Fj, JAB*
De Bernardo, R 1980 *USS, Sp* 1981 *F, R, USS, WGe* 1982 *R, E* 1983 *R, USS, C, C, Sp, Mor, F, A, USS* 1984 *F, USS* 1985 *R, E* 1988 *I* 1989 *Ar, Z*
De Biase, CF 1987 *Sp* 1988 *F, A*
De Carli, G 1996 *W* (R) 1997 *R* 1998 *S, Rus* (R), *Ar, H* (R), *E* 1999 *F, I, SA, SA, Ur, Fj* (R) 2000 *S* (R), *Sa* (R), *Fj* 2001 *I* (R), *E* (R), *W* (R), *SA* (R), *Ur, Fj* (R), *SA* (R), *Sa* 2002 *F* (R), *S, W, I, E* 2003 *W, I, E*
de Jager, B 2006 *J*
De Joanni, L 1983 *C* (R), *Mor, F, A* (R), *USS* 1984 *R, Tun, USS* 1985 *F, R, E, Sp* (R), *Z* 1986 *A, Tun* 1989 *F, R, Sp, Ar, Z* 1990 *R*
De Marchis, R 1935 *F*
De Marco, H 1993 *Pt*
de Marigny, JR 2004 *E* (R), *F, S, I, W, US* 2005 *I, W, S* 2007 *F, E, S, W, I, Ur, J* (R), *I, NZ, Pt*
de Rossi, A 1999 *Ur* (R), *Sp* (R), *E* (R) 2000 *I, E, F, Sa, C* (R), *R* (R), *NZ* (R) 2001 *SA, Ur* (R), *Ar* (R) 2002 *I* (R), *E* (R), *NZ, Sp, R* 2003 *W, I, E, F, S, I, Geo, Tg, C, W* 2004 *E, F, S, I, W, R*
De Rossi, C 1994 *Sp, H* (R), *R* (R)
De Santis, L 1952 *Sp*
De Stefani, M 1989 *Z*
De Vecchi, C 1948 *F*
Degli Antoni, G 1963 *F* 1965 *F* 1966 *F, Ger, R* 1967 *F*
Del Bono, G 1951 *Sp*
Del Bono, M 1960 *Ger, F* 1961 *Ger, F* 1962 *F, Ger, R* 1963 *F* 1964 *Ger, F*
Del Fava, CA 2004 *W, R, J* 2005 *I* (R), *W* (R), *S* (R), *E, F* (R), *Tg, Ar, Fj* 2006 *I* (R), *E* (R), *F, W* (R), *S* (R), *J* (R), *Fj, Pt* (R) 2007 *Ur, Ar, Pt, S*
Della Valle, C 1968 *WGe, Yug* 1969 *F* 1970 *Mad, Mad* 1971 *F*
Dellapè, S 2002 *F, S, I* (R), *E* (R), *NZ* (R), *Sp, Ar* 2003 *F* (R), *S* (R), *S, Geo, Tg, C, W* 2004 *E, F, S, I* (R), *W, C, NZ* 2005 *I, W, S, E* (R), *F, Ar* 2006 *I, E, W, S, J, Fj, Pt, Rus, A, Ar, C* 2007 *F, E, S, W, I, J, NZ, R, S*
Delli Ficorilli, G 1969 *F*
Di Bello, A 1930 *Sp* 1933 *Cze, Cze* 1934 *Cat*
Di Carlo, F 1975 *Sp, R, Cze, Sp* (R) 1976 *F* (R), *Sp* 1977 *Pol, R, Pol* 1978 *Ar, USS*
Di Cola, B 1973 *A*
Di Cola, G 1972 *Sp* (R), *Sp* 1973 *A*
Di Maura, F 1971 *Mor*
Di Zitti, A 1958 *R* 1960 *Ger* 1961 *Ger, F* 1962 *F, Ger, R* 1964 *Ger, F* 1965 *F, Cze* 1966 *F, Ger, R* 1967 *F, Pt, R* 1969 *Bul, Sp, Bel* 1972 *Pt, Sp*
Dolfato, R 1985 *F* 1986 *A* 1987 *Pt, Fj, USS, Sp* 1988 *F, R, USS*
Dominguez, D 1991 *F, R, Nm, Nm* (R), *US, E, NZ, USS* 1992 *Sp, F, R, S* 1993 *Sp, F, Rus, F, S* 1994 *R, H, R, W* 1995 *S, I, Sa, E, Ar, SA* 1996 *W, Pt, W, A, E, S* 1997 *I, F, F, Ar, R, SA, I* 1998 *S, W, Rus, Ar, H, E* 1999 *F, S, W, I, Ur, Sp, Fj, E, Tg, NZ* 2000 *S, W, I, E, F* 2001 *F, S, W, Fj, SA, Sa* 2002 *F, S, I, E, Ar* 2003 *W, I*
Donadona, D 1929 *Sp* 1930 *Sp*
Dora, G 1929 *Sp*
D'Orazio, R 1969 *Bul*
Dotti IV, M 1939 *R* 1940 *R, Ger*
Dotto, F 1971 *Mor, F* (R) 1972 *Pt, Pt, Sp*
Dotto, P 1993 *Sp* (R), *Cro* 1994 *Sp, R*
Faccioli, U 1948 *F*
Falancia, A 1975 *E, Pol*
Faliva, G 1999 *SA* (R) 2002 *NZ, Ar, A* (R)
Faltiba, G 1993 *Pt* (R)
Fanton, G 1979 *Pol* (R)
Farina, P 1987 *F, NZ, Fj*
Farinelli, P 1940 *R* 1949 *F, Cze* 1951 *Sp* 1952 *Sp*
Fattori, T 1936 *Ger, R* 1937 *R, Ger, F* 1938 *Ger* 1939 *Ger, R* 1940 *R, Ger*
Fava, E 1948 *F, Cze*
Favaretto, P 1951 *Sp*
Favaro, R 1988 *F, USS, A, I* 1989 *F, R, Sp, Ar, Z, USS* 1990 *F, Pol, R, H, R, USS* 1991 *F, R, Nm, Nm, US, E, NZ, USS* 1992 *Sp, F, R* 1993 *Sp, F, Cro, Sp, F* 1994 *CZR* (R), *A, A, R, W, F* 1995 *S, I, Sa* 1996 *Pt*
Favretto, G 1948 *Cze* 1949 *Cze*
Fedrigo, A 1972 *Yug* 1973 *Pt, Rho, WTv, Bor, NEC, Nat, ETv, Leo, FS, Cze, Yug, A* 1974 *Pt, Mid, Sus, Oxo, WGe, Leo* 1975 *F, Sp, R, Cze, E, Pol, H, Sp* 1976 *F, J, A, Sp* 1977 *F, Pol, R, Cze, R, Sp* 1978 *F, Ar* 1979 *Pol, R*
Fedrigo, P 1973 *Pt*
Ferracin, P 1975 *R, Cze, E, Pol, H, Sp* 1976 *F* 1977 *Mor, Pol* 1978 *USS*
Festuccia, C 2003 *W, I, E, F, S, S, I* (R), *Geo* (R), *NZ, Tg* (R), *C* (R), *W* (R) 2004 *E* (R), *F* (R), *S* (R), *I* (R) 2005 *F* (R), *Ar* (R), *Ar, A, Tg, Ar* 2006 *E* (R), *F* (R), *W, S* (R), *Pt* (R), *Rus* (R), *A, Ar, C* (R) 2007 *F* (R), *E, S, W, I, Ur, Ar* (R), *J, NZ* (R), *R, S*
Figari, G 1940 *R, Ger* 1942 *R* (R)
Filizzola, EG 1993 *Pt, Mor, Sp, F, Rus, F, S* 1994 *Sp, CZR, A* 1995 *R* (R), *NZ* (R)
Finocchi, M 1968 *Yug* (R) 1969 *F* (R) 1970 *Cze, Mad, Mad, R* 1971 *Mor, R*
Fornari, G 1952 *Sp, Ger, F* 1953 *F, Ger, R* 1954 *Sp, F* 1955 *Ger, F, Sp, F, Cze* 1956 *Ger, F, Cze*
Francescato, B 1977 *Cze, R, Sp* 1978 *F, Sp* (R) 1979 *F* 1981 *R*
Francescato, I 1990 *R, USS* 1991 *F, R, US, E, NZ, USS* 1992 *R, S* 1993 *Mor, F* 1994 *Sp, H, R, W, F* 1995 *S, I, Sa, E, Ar, F, Ar, R, NZ, SA* 1996 *W, Pt, W, A, E, S* 1997 *F, F, Ar, R, SA*
Francescato, N 1972 *Yug* 1973 *Rho, WTv, Bor, NEC, Nat, ETv, Leo* 1974 *Pt* 1976 *J, A, Sp* 1977 *F, Mor, Pol, R, R, Sp* 1978 *F, Ar, USS, Sp* 1979 *F, R, E, Sp, Mor, F, Pol, USS, NZ* 1980 *F, R, Fj, JAB, Coo, Pol, USS, Sp* 1981 *F, R* 1982 *Mor*
Francescato, R 1976 *Sp* 1978 *Ar, USS* 1979 *Sp, F, Pol, USS, NZ, Mor* 1980 *F, R, Fj, JAB, Coo, Pol, USS, Sp* 1981 *F, R* 1982 *WGe* 1983 *F, R, USS, C, C, Sp, Mor, F, A* 1984 *Mor, R, Tun* 1985 *F, Sp, Z, USS* 1986 *Tun, F*
Franceschini, G 1975 *H, Sp* 1976 *F, J* 1977 *F, Pol, Pol, Cze, R, Sp*
Francese, A 1939 *R* 1940 *R*
Francesio, J 2000 *W* (R), *I, Sa* (R) 2001 *Ur*
Frati, F 2000 *C, NZ* (R) 2001 *I* (R), *S*
Frelich, F 1955 *Cze* 1957 *F, Ger* 1958 *F, R*
Fumei, M 1984 *F*

Fusco, A 1982 *E* (R) 1985 *R* 1986 *Tun, F, Tun* (R)
Fusco, E 1960 *Ger, F* 1961 *F* 1962 *F, Ger, R* 1963 *F* 1964 *Ger, F* 1965 *F* 1966 *F*
Gabanella, R 1951 *Sp* 1952 *Sp*
Gabrielli, P 1948 *Cze* 1949 *F, Cze* 1951 *Sp* 1954 *F*
Gaetaniello, F 1975 *H* (R) 1976 *R, A, Sp* (R) 1977 *F, Pol, R, Pol, R, Sp* 1978 *Sp* 1979 *Pol, R, E, Sp, Mor, F, Pol, USS, NZ, Mor* 1980 *Fj, JAB, Sp* 1981 *F, R, USS, WGe* 1982 *F, R, E, WGe, Mor* 1983 *F, R, USS, C, C, Sp*
Gaetaniello, F 1980 *Sp* (R) 1982 *E* 1984 *USS* 1985 *R, Sp, Z* (R), *Z, USS, R* 1986 *Pt, E, A, Tun, USS* 1987 *Pt, F, NZ, Ar, Fj, USS, Sp* 1988 *F* 1990 *F, R, Sp, H* 1991 *Nm, US, E, NZ*
Galante, A 2007 *Ur* (R), *Ar*
Galeazzo, A 1985 *Sp* 1987 *Pt, R, Ar, USS*
Galletto, M 1972 *Pt, Sp, Yug*
Galon, E 2001 *I* (R) 2005 *Tg, Ar, Fj* 2006 *W, S* (R), *Rus* (R) 2007 *I, Ur* (R), *Ar* (R), *I* (R), *NZ* (R), *R* (R), *S* (R)
Ganzerla, R 1973 *Bor, NEC*
Gardin, M 1981 *USS, WGe* 1982 *Mor* 1983 *F, R* 1984 *Mor, R, USS* 1985 *E, USS, R* 1986 *Tun, F, Pt, Tun, USS* 1987 *Pt, F, R, NZ, Ar, Fj, USS, Sp* 1988 *R*
Gardner, JM 1992 *R, S* 1993 *Rus, F* 1994 *Sp, R, H, F* 1995 *S* (R), *I, Sa, E, Ar* 1996 *W* 1997 *I, F, SA, I* 1998 *S, W*
Gargiullo, P 1973 *FS* (R) 1974 *Mid, Sus, Oxo*
Garguillo, F 1972 *Yug*
Garguilo, F 1967 *F, Pt* 1968 *Yug* 1974 *Sus*
Garozzo, S 2001 *Ur, Ar* 2002 *Ar*
Gatto, M 1967 *Pt, R*
Gattoni, G 1933 *Cze, Cze*
Gerardo, A 1968 *Yug* 1969 *Sp* 1970 *Cze, Mad* 1971 *R* 1972 *Sp*
Geremia, F 1980 *JAB, Pol*
Geremia, G 1956 *Cze*
Gerosa, E 1952 *Sp, Ger, F* 1953 *F, Ger, R* 1954 *Sp*
Gerosa, M 1994 *CZR, A, A, R, W* 1995 *E, Ar*
Ghezzi, C 1938 *Ger* 1939 *Ger, R* 1940 *R, Ger*
Ghini, A 1981 *USS* (R), *WGe* 1982 *F, R, E, Mor* 1983 *F, R, C, Mor, F, A, USS* 1984 *F, Mor, R, USS* 1985 *F, R, E, Z, Z, USS* 1987 *Fj* 1988 *R, USS* (R)
Ghiraldini, L 2006 *J* (R), *Fj* (R) 2007 *I* (R), *J* (R), *Pt*
Ghizzoni, S 1977 *F, Mor* (R), *Pol, R, Pol, Cze, R, Sp* 1978 *F, Ar, USS* 1979 *F, Pol, Sp, Mor, F, Pol* 1980 *R, Fj, JAB, Coo, Pol, USS, Sp* 1981 *F* 1982 *F, R, E, WGe, Mor* 1983 *F, USS, C, C, Sp, Mor, F, A, USS* 1984 *F, Mor, R, Tun, USS* 1985 *F, R, E, Z, Z, USS, R* 1986 *F, E, A, Tun, USS* 1987 *Pt, F, R, NZ*
Giacheri, M 1992 *R* 1993 *Sp, F, Pt, Rus, F, S* 1994 *Sp, R, CZR* (R), *H, A, A, F* 1995 *S, I, E, Ar, F, Ar, R, NZ, SA* 1996 *W* 1999 *S, W, I, Ur, Fj, E, Tg, NZ* 2001 *Nm* (R), *SA, Ur, Ar, SA* 2002 *F* (R), *S* (R), *W, I, E, NZ, A* (R) 2003 *E, F, S, I*
Giani, G 1966 *Ger, R* 1967 *F, Pt, R*
Gini, G 1968 *Pt, WGe, Yug* 1969 *Bul, Sp, Bel, F* 1970 *Cze, Mad, Mad, R* 1971 *Mor, F* 1972 *Pt, Pt* 1974 *Mid, Oxo*
Giorgio, G 1968 *Pt, WGe*
Giovanelli, M 1989 *Z* (R), *USS* 1990 *Pol, Sp, H, R, USS* 1991 *F, R, Nm, E, NZ, USS* 1992 *Sp, F, S* 1993 *Sp, F, Pt, Cro, Mor* (R), *Sp, F* 1994 *R, CZR, H, A, A* 1995 *F* (R), *Ar, R, NZ, SA* 1996 *A, E, S* 1997 *F, F, Ar, R, SA, I* 1998 *S, W, Rus, Ar, H, E* 1999 *S, W, I, SA, SA, Ur, Sp* (R), *Fj, E, Tg, NZ* 2000 *S*
Giugovaz, E 1965 *Cze* 1966 *F*
Giuliani, R 1951 *Sp*
Gorni, M 1939 *R* 1940 *R, Ger*
Goti, M 1990 *H*
Grasselli, G 1952 *Ger*
Grespan, G 1989 *F, Sp, USS* 1990 *F, R* (R) 1991 *R, NZ* (R), *USS* 1992 *R, S* 1993 *Sp, F, Cro, Sp, F* (R), *Rus* (R) 1994 *Sp, CZR, R, W*
Griffen, PR 2004 *E, F, S, I, W, R* (R), *J, C, NZ, US* 2005 *W* (R), *S* (R), *F* (R), *Ar, Ar, A, Tg, Ar, Fj* 2006 *I, E, F, W, S, J, Fj, Rus, A, Ar, C* 2007 *F, I* (R), *Ur, Ar* (R), *I* (R), *NZ* (R), *R, Pt* (R)
Gritti, A 1996 *Pt* 2000 *S, W, I, E, F, Sa, Fj, C, R, NZ* 2001 *E, F, S, W*
Guidi, G 1996 *Pt, E* (R) 1997 *F* (R), *Ar* (R), *R*
Innocenti, M 1981 *WGe* 1982 *F, R, E, WGe, Mor* 1983 *F, USS* (R), *C, C, Mor, F, A, USS* 1984 *F, Mor, Tun, USS* 1985 *F, R, E, Sp, USS, R* 1986 *Tun, F, Pt, E, A, Tun, USS* 1987 *Pt, F, R, NZ, Ar, Fj, USS, Sp* 1988 *F, R, A*
Intoppa, G 2004 *R* (R), *J* (R), *C* (R), *NZ* (R) 2005 *I* (R), *W* (R), *E* (R)
Jannone, C 1981 *USS* 1982 *F, R*
Lanfranchi, S 1949 *F, Cze* 1953 *F, Ger, R* 1954 *Sp, F* 1955 *F* 1956 *Ger, Cze* 1957 *F* 1958 *F* 1959 *F* 1960 *F* 1961 *F* 1962 *F, Ger, R* 1963 *F* 1964 *Ger, F*
Lanzi, G 1998 *Ar* (R), *H* (R), *E* (R) 1999 *Sp* 2000 *S* (R), *W, I* (R) 2001 *I* (R)
Lari, G 1972 *Yug* (R) 1973 *Yug, A* 1974 *Pt, Mid, Sus, Oxo, Leo*
Lazzarini, E 1970 *Cze* 1971 *Mor, F, R* 1972 *Pt, Pt, Sp, Sp* 1973 *Pt, Rho, WTv, Bor, NEC, Leo, FS, Tva, Cze, Yug, A* 1974 *Pt, Mid, Sus, Oxo, WGe*
Levorato, U 1956 *Ger, F* 1957 *F* 1958 *F, R* 1959 *F* 1961 *Ger, F* 1962 *F, Ger, R* 1963 *F* 1964 *Ger, F* 1965 *F*
Lijoi, A 1977 *Pol, R* (R) 1978 *Sp* 1979 *R* (R), *Mor*
Limone, G 1979 *E, Mor, USS* (R), *Mor* 1980 *JAB, Sp* 1981 *USS, WGe* 1982 *E* (R) 1983 *USS*
Lo Cicero, A 2000 *E, F, Sa, Fj, C, R, NZ* 2001 *I, E, F, S, W, Fj, SA, Sa* (R) 2002 *F, S* (R), *W* (R), *Sp, R, A* 2003 *F, S, S, I, Geo, Tg, C, W* 2004 *E, F, S, I, W, R, J, C, NZ, US* 2005 *I, W, S, E, F, Ar, Ar, A, Tg, Ar* 2006 *E* (R), *F* (R), *W* (R), *S* (R), *J, Fj, Pt* (R), *Rus* (R), *A, Ar, C* 2007 *F* (R), *E, S, W, Ur, Ar, J, NZ* (R), *R, Pt, S* (R)
Loranzi, C 1973 *Nat* (R), *ETv, Leo* (R), *FS* (R), *Tva* (R)
Lorigiola, F 1979 *Sp, F, Pol, USS, NZ, Mor* 1980 *F, R, Fj, JAB, Pol, USS, Sp* 1981 *F, R, USS* 1982 *WGe* 1983 *R* (R), *USS, C, Sp* 1984 *Tun* 1985 *Sp* 1986 *Pt, E, A, Tun, USS* 1987 *Pt, F, R, NZ, Ar* 1988 *F*
Luchini, G 1973 *Rho, Nat*
Luise, L 1955 *Ger, F, Sp, F, Cze* 1956 *Ger, F, Cze* 1957 *Ger* 1958 *F*
Luise III, R 1959 *F* 1960 *Ger, F* 1961 *Ger, F* 1962 *F, Ger, R* 1965 *F, Cze* 1966 *F* 1971 *R* 1972 *Pt, Sp, Sp* (R)
Lupini, T 1987 *R, NZ, Ar, Fj, USS, Sp* 1988 *F, R, USS, A* 1989 *R*
Maestri, O 1935 *Cat, F* 1937 *Ger* (R)
Maffioli, R 1933 *Cze, Cze* 1934 *Cat, R* 1935 *Cat* 1936 *Ger, R* 1937 *Ger, R, Bel, Ger*
Maini, R 1948 *F, Cze*
Malosti, G 1953 *F* 1954 *Sp* 1955 *F* 1956 *Ger, F* 1957 *F* 1958 *F*
Mancini, G 1952 *Ger, F* 1953 *F, Ger, R* 1954 *Sp, F* 1955 *Cze* 1956 *Ger, F, Cze* 1957 *F*
Mandelli, R 2004 *I* (R), *W* (R), *R* (R), *J* (R), *US* (R) 2007 *F* (R), *E* (R), *Ur* (R), *Ar*
Mannato, A 2004 *US* (R) 2005 *Ar, A*
Manni, E 1976 *J* (R), *A, Sp* 1977 *Mor*
Manteri, L 1996 *W, A, E, S* (R)
Marcato, A 2006 *J* (R), *Pt* (R)
Marchetto, M 1972 *Yug* 1973 *Pt, Cze, Yug* 1974 *Pt, Mid, Sus, WGe, Leo* 1975 *F, Sp, R, Cze, E, Pol, H, Sp* 1976 *F, R, J, A, Sp* 1977 *F, Mor, Pol, R, Cze* (R), *R, Sp* 1978 *F, USS* (R), *Sp* 1979 *F, Pol* (R), *R, E, Pol* (R), *USS, NZ, Mor* 1980 *F, Coo* 1981 *USS*
Marescalchi, A 1933 *Cze* 1935 *F* (R) 1937 *R*
Mariani, P 1976 *R, A, Sp* 1977 *F, Pol* 1978 *F* (R), *Ar, USS, Sp* 1979 *F, Pol, R, Sp, F, Pol, USS, NZ, Mor* 1980 *F, R, Fj, JAB*
Marini, P 1949 *F, Cze* 1951 *Sp* 1953 *F, Ger, R* 1955 *Ger*
Martin, L 1997 *F* (R), *R* (R) 1998 *S, W, Rus, H, E* 1999 *F, S, W, I, SA, SA, Ur, Sp* (R), *Fj, E* 2000 *S, W, I, E, F, Sa, Fj, C, R, NZ* 2001 *I, E, S, W* (R), *SA, Ar, Fj* (R), *SA, Sa* 2002 *F, S* (R)
Martinenghi, F 1952 *Sp, Ger*
Martinez-Frugoni, R 2002 *NZ, Sp* (R), *R* (R) 2003 *W, I, E, F, S, S* (R), *NZ*
Martini, G 1965 *F* 1967 *F* 1968 *Pt*
Martini, R 1959 *F* 1960 *Ger, F* 1961 *Ger, F* 1964 *Ger, F* 1965 *F* 1968 *WGe, Yug*
Masci, P 1948 *Cze* 1949 *F, Cze* 1952 *Sp, Ger, F* 1953 *F* 1954 *Sp* 1955 *F*
Mascioletti, M 1977 *Mor, Pol* 1978 *Ar, USS, Sp* 1979 *Pol, E, Sp, Mor, F, Pol, USS, NZ, Mor* 1980 *F, R, Fj* 1981 *WGe*

1982 *F, R, WGe* 1983 *F, R, USS, C, C, Sp, Mor, F, A, USS* 1984 *F, Mor, Tun* 1985 *F, R, Z, Z, USS, R* 1986 *Tun, F, Pt, E, Tun, USS* 1987 *NZ, Ar, Fj* 1989 *Sp, Ar, Z, USS* 1990 *Pol*
Masi, A 1999 *Sp* 2003 *E* (R), *F* (R), *S, S, I* (R), *NZ, Tg* (R), *C* (R), *W* 2004 *E, I* (R), *W, R, J, C* 2005 *I, W, S, E, F, Ar, Ar, A* 2006 *J, Fj, Pt, Rus* 2007 *F, S, J* (R), *NZ, R* (R), *Pt, S*
Mastrodomenico, L 2000 *Sa* (R), *C* (R), *NZ* (R) 2001 *Nm, Ar* (R)
Matacchini, I 1948 *F, Cze* 1949 *F, Cze* 1954 *Sp* 1955 *Ger, F, Sp, F*
Mattarolo, L 1973 *Bor, Nat, ETv, Leo, FS, Tva, Cze*
Mattei, M 1967 *R*
Mattei, R 1978 *F, USS*
Mazzantini, F 1965 *Cze* 1966 *F* 1967 *F*
Mazzantini, M 2000 *S* (R) 2001 *S* (R), *W* 2002 *E* (R), *NZ* 2003 *E* (R), *F* (R), *Geo, NZ, C* (R)
Mazzariol, F 1995 *F, Ar* (R), *R, NZ* 1996 *Pt* (R) 1997 *F* (R), *R* (R), *SA* (R) 1998 *Ar, H* (R) 1999 *F* (R), *SA, SA, Sp* (R), *E* (R), *NZ* (R) 2000 *Fj* (R), *C* 2001 *Nm, SA, Ur, Ar, Fj* (R), *SA* (R) 2002 *W* (R), *NZ, Sp* 2003 *S* (R), *I, NZ, C* (R), *W* (R) 2004 *R*
Mazzi, G 1998 *H* (R) 1999 *SA, SA, Ur* (R), *Sp* (R)
Mazzucato, N 1995 *SA* 1996 *Pt, S* 1997 *I* (R) 1999 *Sp, E* (R), *Tg* (R), *NZ* (R) 2000 *F, Sa, Fj, R* 2001 *Nm, SA, Ur, Ar* 2002 *W, I, E, NZ, Sp, R, Ar, A* 2003 *E, F, S, I, NZ, Tg, W* 2004 *E, F* (R), *S, I, W, R, J* (R)
Mazzucchelli, I 1965 *F, Cze* 1966 *F, Ger, R* 1967 *F* 1968 *Pt, WGe* 1969 *Bul, F* 1971 *F* 1972 *Pt, Sp* 1974 *WGe* 1975 *F, R, Cze, Pol* 1976 *F, R*
Menapace, P 1996 *Pt* (R)
Michelon, E 1969 *Bel, F* 1970 *Cze, Mad, Mad, R* (R) 1971 *R*
Miele, A 1968 *Yug* 1970 *Mad* (R) 1971 *R* 1972 *Pt, Sp*
Milano, GE 1990 *USS* (R)
Mioni, A 1955 *Ger, F, F* 1957 *F*
Modonesi, A 1929 *Sp*
Modonesi, L 1966 *Ger, R* 1967 *F, Pt, R* 1968 *Pt, WGe* 1970 *Cze, Mad, Mad, R* 1971 *F* 1974 *Leo* 1975 *F, Sp, R, Cze*
Molari, N 1957 *F* 1958 *R*
Molinari, F 1973 *NEC*
Molinari, G 1948 *F*
Monfeli, P 1970 *R* 1971 *Mor, F* 1972 *Pt* 1976 *J, A, Sp* 1977 *F, R, Cze, R, Sp* 1978 *F*
Morelli, G 1988 *I* 1989 *F, R*
Morelli, G 1976 *F* (R) 1982 *F, R, Mor* 1983 *R, C, Sp, A, USS* 1984 *Mor, R, USS* 1985 *R, E, Z, Z, USS, R* 1986 *Tun, F, E, A, Tun, USS* 1987 *F, NZ*
Morelli, G 1981 *WGe* 1982 *R, E, Mor* 1983 *USS* (R) 1984 *F*
Moreno, A 1999 *Tg, NZ* 2002 *F* (R), *S* (R)
Moretti, A 1997 *R* (R) 1998 *Rus* (R) 1999 *Ur* (R), *Sp, Tg* (R), *NZ* 2002 *E* (R), *NZ, Sp, R, Ar, A* (R) 2005 *Ar*
Moretti, U 1933 *Cze* (R) 1934 *R* 1935 *Cat* 1937 *R, Ger, F* 1942 *R*
Morimondi, A 1930 *Sp* 1933 *Cze* 1934 *Cat* 1935 *Cat*
Moscardi, A 1993 *Pt* 1995 *R* (R) 1996 *S* (R) 1998 *Ar, H, E* 1999 *F, S, W, I, SA, SA, Ur, Fj, E, Tg, NZ* (R) 2000 *S, W, I, E, F, Sa, Fj, C, R, NZ* 2001 *I, E, F, S, W, Nm, SA, Ur, Ar, Fj, SA, Sa* 2002 *F, S, W, I, E*
Muraro, A 2000 *C, R, NZ* 2001 *I, E, Nm, SA, Ur* (R), *Ar, Fj, SA, Sa* 2002 *F*
Nathan, E 1930 *Sp*
Navarini, G 1957 *Ger* 1958 *R*
Nicolosi, M 1982 *R*
Nieto, C 2002 *E* 2005 *Ar, Ar, A* (R), *Tg, Ar, Fj* (R) 2006 *I, E, F, W, J, Fj, A* (R), *Ar* (R), *C* 2007 *F, S* (R), *W, I, Ar*
Nisti, A 1929 *Sp* (R) 1930 *Sp*
Nitoglia, L 2004 *C, NZ, US* 2005 *I, W, S, E, F, Ar, Tg, Ar, Fj* 2006 *I, E, F, W, S*
Ongaro, F 2000 *C* 2001 *Nm* (R), *SA, Ur* (R), *Ar* (R) 2002 *Ar* (R), *A* 2003 *E* (R), *F* (R), *S* (R), *I, Geo, NZ* (R), *Tg, C, W* 2004 *E, F, S, I, W, R, J, C, NZ, US* 2005 *I, W, S, E, F, Tg* (R), *Ar* (R), *Fj* 2006 *I, E, F, W* (R), *S, J, Fj, Pt, Rus, Ar* (R), *C* 2007 *F, S* (R), *Ur* (R), *Ar, I, NZ, S* (R)
Orlandi, C 1992 *S* 1993 *Sp, F, Mor, F, Rus, F, S* 1994 *Sp, CZR, H, A, A, R, W* 1995 *S, I, Sa, E, Ar, F, Ar, R, NZ, SA* 1996 *W, Pt, W, A, E, S* 1997 *I, F, F, Ar, R, SA, I* 1998 *S, W* 2000 *W* (R), *F* (R)
Orlando, S 2004 *E* (R), *S* (R), *W* (R), *C* (R), *NZ* (R), *US* 2005 *E* (R), *F* (R), *Ar* (R), *A* (R) 2006 *J* 2007 *Ur* (R), *Ar* (R), *Pt* (R)
Orquera, L 2004 *C* (R), *NZ* (R), *US* 2005 *I, W, S, E, F, Ar, Tg* (R)
Osti, A 1981 *F, R, USS* 1982 *E, Mor* 1983 *R, C, A, USS* 1984 *R, USS* 1985 *F* 1986 *Tun* 1988 *R*
Pace, S 2001 *SA* (R), *Sa* 2005 *Fj*
Pace, S 1977 *Mor* 1984 *R, Tun*
Pacifici, P 1969 *Bul, Sp, F* 1970 *Cze, Mad, Mad, R* 1971 *Mor, F*
Paciucci, R 1937 *R, Ger, F*
Paganelli, F 1972 *Sp* (R)
Palmer, S 2002 *Ar, A* (R) 2003 *I* (R), *E* (R), *F* (R), *S* (R), *S, NZ, C* (R), *W* (R) 2004 *I, R* (R)
Paoletti, P 1972 *Pt, Sp, Yug* 1973 *Pt, Rho, WTv, Bor, NEC, Nat, ETv, Leo, FS, Tva* 1974 *Mid, Oxo, WGe, Leo* 1975 *F, Sp* 1976 *R*
Paoletti, T 2000 *S, W, I, E, F, Sa, C* (R), *R* (R), *NZ* (R) 2001 *F, Nm* (R), *Ur* (R), *Ar* (R), *Fj* (R), *SA* (R)
Paolin, G 1929 *Sp*
Parisse, S 2002 *NZ, Sp, R, Ar* (R), *A* 2003 *S* (R), *I, Geo, NZ* (R), *Tg, C, W* 2004 *E, F, S* 2005 *I, W, S, E, F, Ar, Ar, A, Tg, Ar, Fj* 2006 *I, E, F, W, S, Fj, Pt, Rus, A, Ar, C* 2007 *F, E, S, W, I, J, I, NZ, R, Pt, S*
Parmiggiani, E 1942 *R* 1948 *Cze*
Paseli, P 1929 *Sp* 1930 *Sp* 1933 *Cze*
Passarotto, E 1975 *Sp* (R)
Patrizio, E 2007 *Ur*
Pavanello, A 2007 *Ar* (R)
Pavanello, E 2002 *R, Ar* (R), *A* 2004 *R, J, C* (R), *NZ* (R), *US* 2005 *Ar* (R), *A* (R)
Pavesi, P 1977 *Pol* 1979 *Mor* 1980 *USS*
Pavin, M 1980 *USS* 1986 *F* (R), *Pt, E, A, Tun, USS* 1987 *Ar*
Pedrazzi, R 2001 *Nm, Ar* (R) 2002 *F, S, W* 2005 *S* (R), *E, F* (R)
Pedroni, P 1989 *Z, USS* 1990 *F, Pol, R* 1991 *F, R* (R), *Nm* 1993 *Rus, F* 1994 *Sp, R, CZR, H* 1995 *I, Sa, E, Ar, F, Ar, R, NZ, SA* 1996 *W, W*
Peens, G 2002 *W, I, E, NZ, Sp, R, Ar* (R), *A* (R) 2003 *E* (R), *F* (R), *S* (R), *S, I, Geo* (R), *NZ* 2004 *NZ* (R) 2005 *E, F, Ar, Ar, A* 2006 *Pt* (R), *A*
Pelliccione, L 1983 *Sp, Mor, F*
Pelliccione, L 1977 *Pol*
Percudani, M 1952 *F* 1954 *F* 1955 *Ger, Sp, F, Cze* 1956 *Cze* 1957 *F* 1958 *R*
Perrini, F 1955 *Sp, F, Cze* 1956 *Ger, F, Cze* 1957 *F* 1958 *F* 1959 *F* 1962 *R* 1963 *F*
Perrone, F 1951 *Sp*
Persico, AR 2000 *S* (R), *W* (R), *E* (R), *F* (R), *Sa, Fj* 2001 *F, S, W, Nm, SA* (R), *Ur, Ar, Fj, SA, Sa* (R) 2002 *F* (R), *S* (R), *W, I, E, NZ, Sp, R, Ar, A* 2003 *W, I, E, F, S, I* (R), *Geo, Tg, C, W* 2004 *E, F, S, I, W, R, J* (R), *C, NZ* 2005 *I, W, S, E, F, Ar, Ar, Tg, Ar* 2006 *I* (R), *E* (R)
Pertile, J 1994 *R* 1995 *Ar* 1996 *W* (R), *A, E, S* 1997 *I, F, SA* 1998 *Rus* 1999 *S, W, I, SA, SA*
Perugini, S 2000 *I* (R), *F* (R), *Sa* (R), *Fj* (R) 2001 *S* (R), *W* (R), *Nm, SA, Ur, Ar* 2002 *W, I* (R) 2003 *W* (R), *S, Geo* (R), *NZ, Tg* (R), *W* (R) 2004 *E* (R), *F* (R), *I* (R), *W* (R), *C, NZ, US* 2005 *I* (R), *W* (R), *S* (R), *E, F* 2006 *I, E, F, W, S, Pt, Rus* 2007 *F, E* (R), *S* (R), *W* (R), *I, J* (R), *I, NZ* (R), *Pt* (R), *S* (R)
Perziano, L 1993 *Pt*
Perziano, M 2000 *NZ* 2001 *F, S, W, Nm, SA, Ur, Ar, Fj, SA*
Pesce, V 1988 *I* 1989 *R* (R)
Pescetto, P 1956 *Ger, Cze* 1957 *F*
Petralia, G 1984 *F*
Pez, R 2000 *Sa, Fj, C* (R), *R, NZ* 2001 *I* 2002 *S* (R), *W, E* (R), *A* 2003 *I* (R), *E, F, S, S, Geo* 2005 *Ar, A, Tg, Ar, Fj* 2006 *I, E, F, W, S, J, Fj, Pt, Rus, A, Ar* 2007 *F* (R), *E* (R), *S* (R), *W, I, J, R, S*
Phillips, M 2002 *F, S, W* (R), *I, E* 2003 *W, I, E, F, S, S, I* (R), *NZ, W* (R)
Pianna, G 1934 *R* 1935 *Cat, F* 1936 *Ger, R* 1938 *Ger*
Piazza, A 1990 *USS*
Piccini, F 1963 *F* 1964 *Ger* 1966 *F*
Picone, S 2004 *I* (R), *W* (R) 2005 *F* 2006 *E* (R), *F* (R), *S* (R), *J* (R), *Pt, Rus* (R), *Ar* (R), *C* (R)
Pietroscanti, F 1987 *USS, Sp* 1988 *A, I* 1989 *F, R, Sp, Ar,*

Z, *USS* 1990 *F*, *Pol*, *R*, *H* 1991 *Nm*, *Nm* 1992 *Sp*, *F*, *R* 1993 *Sp* (R), *Mor* (R), *Sp*, *F*, *Rus*, *F*
Pignotti, F 1968 *WGe*, *Yug* 1969 *Bul*, *Sp*, *Bel*
Pilat, C 1997 *I* 1998 *S*, *W* 2000 *E*, *Sa* 2001 *I*, *W* (R)
Pini, MJ 1998 *H*, *E* 1999 *F*, *Ur*, *Fj*, *E*, *Tg*, *NZ* 2000 *S*, *W*, *I*, *F*
Piovan, M 1973 *Pt* 1974 *Pt*, *Mid*, *Sus* (R), *Oxo* 1976 *A* 1977 *F*, *Mor*, *R* 1979 *F* (R)
Piovan, R 1996 *Pt* (R) 1997 *R* 2000 *R*, *NZ*
Piovene, M 1995 *NZ* (R)
Piras, E 1971 *R* (R)
Pisaneschi, M 1948 *Cze* (R) 1949 *Cze* 1953 *F*, *Ger*, *R* 1954 *Sp*, *F* 1955 *Ger*, *F*, *Sp*, *F*, *Cze*
Pitorri, F 1948 *Cze* 1949 *F*
Pitorri, M 1973 *NEC* (R)
Pivetta, G 1979 *R* (R), *E*, *Mor* 1980 *Coo*, *USS* 1981 *R*, *USS*, *WGe* 1982 *F*, *R*, *WGe*, *Mor* 1983 *F*, *USS* (R), *C*, *Sp*, *Mor* (R), *F* (R), *USS* 1984 *F*, *Mor*, *R*, *Tun* 1985 *F*, *R* (R), *Sp*, *Z*, *Z* 1986 *Pt* 1987 *Sp* 1989 *R*, *Sp* 1990 *F*, *Pol* (R), *R*, *Sp*, *R*, *USS* 1991 *F*, *R*, *Nm*, *Nm*, *US*, *E*, *NZ*, *USS* 1992 *Sp*, *F*, *R*, *R* 1993 *Cro*, *Mor* (R), *Sp*
Platania, M 1994 *F* 1995 *F* (R), *R* 1996 *Pt*
Ponchia, I 1955 *F*, *Sp*, *F*, *Cze* 1956 *F* 1957 *Ger* 1958 *F*
Ponzi, E 1973 *Cze*, *A* 1974 *WGe* 1975 *F*, *Sp*, *R*, *Cze*, *E*, *Pol*, *H*, *Sp* 1976 *F*, *R*, *J*, *A*, *Sp* 1977 *F*, *Mor*, *Pol*, *R*
Porcellato, G 1989 *R*
Porzio, G 1970 *Cze*, *Mad*, *Mad*
Possamai, C 1970 *Cze*, *Mad*, *Mad*
Pozzebon, W 2001 *I* (R), *E*, *F*, *S*, *W*, *Nm*, *SA*, *Ur*, *Ar*, *Fj*, *SA*, *Sa* 2002 *NZ* (R), *Sp* (R) 2004 *R*, *J*, *C* (R), *NZ*, *US* 2005 *W*, *E* (R) 2006 *C*
Pratichetti, C 1988 *R* 1990 *Pol*
Pratichetti, M 2004 *NZ* 2007 *E* (R), *W*, *I*, *Ur*, *Ar*, *I*, *Pt*
Preo, G 1999 *I* 2000 *I* (R), *E* (R), *Sa* (R), *Fj*, *R* (R), *NZ* (R)
Presutti, P 1974 *Mid*, *Sus*, *Oxo* 1977 *Pol*, *Cze*, *R*, *Sp* 1978 *F*
Properzi-Curti, FP 1990 *Pol*, *Sp*, *H*, *R* 1991 *F*, *Nm*, *Nm*, *US*, *E*, *NZ* 1992 *Sp*, *F*, *R* 1993 *Cro* (R), *Mor*, *F*, *Rus*, *F*, *S* 1994 *Sp* (R), *R*, *H*, *A*, *A* 1995 *S*, *I*, *Sa*, *E*, *Ar*, *NZ*, *SA* 1996 *W*, *Pt*, *W*, *A*, *E* 1997 *I*, *F*, *F*, *Ar*, *SA* 1998 *Ar* 1999 *S*, *W*, *I*, *SA*, *SA*, *Ur*, *E*, *Tg* (R), *NZ* (R) 2001 *F* (R), *S*, *W*
Prosperini, C 1966 *R* 1967 *F*, *Pt*, *R*
Pucciarello, F 1999 *Sp*, *Fj*, *E* 2002 *S*, *W* (R), *I* (R), *E* (R), *Ar*
Puglisi, G 1971 *F* 1972 *Yug* 1973 *Cze*
Pulli, M 1968 *Pt* 1972 *Pt*, *Pt*
Puppo, A 1972 *Pt* (R), *Pt*, *Sp*, *Sp* 1973 *Pt*, *Rho*, *WTv*, *Bor*, *NEC*, *Nat*, *ETv*, *Leo*, *FS*, *Tva* 1974 *Mid*, *Sus*, *Oxo*, *WGe*, *Leo* 1977 *R*
Quaglio, I 1970 *R* 1971 *R* 1972 *Pt*, *Sp* 1973 *WTv*, *Bor*, *NEC*, *Nat*, *Leo*, *FS*, *Tva* 1975 *H*, *Sp* 1976 *F*, *R*
Quaglio, M 1984 *Tun* (R) 1988 *F*, *R*
Queirolo, JM 2000 *Sa*, *Fj* 2001 *E*, *F* (R), *Fj* (R) 2002 *NZ* (R), *Sp* (R), *A* 2003 *Geo* (R)
Quintavala, P 1958 *R*
Raffo, C 1929 *Sp* 1930 *Sp* 1933 *Cze*, *Cze* 1937 *R*, *Bel*
Raineri, G 1998 *H* (R) 2000 *Fj*, *R*, *NZ* 2001 *I*, *E*, *S* (R), *W*, *Nm*, *SA* (R), *Ur*, *Ar* 2002 *W* (R), *I*, *E*, *NZ* 2003 *W*, *I*, *E*, *F*, *S*, *Geo*
Raisi, G 1956 *Ger*, *F* 1957 *F*, *Ger* 1960 *Ger* 1964 *Ger*, *F*
Rampazzo, R 1996 *W* (R) 1999 *I* (R)
Ravazzolo, M 1993 *Cro*, *Sp*, *F*, *F* (R), *S* 1994 *Sp* (R), *R* (R), *CZR*, *H* 1995 *S*, *I*, *Sa*, *F* (R), *Ar*, *NZ* 1996 *W*, *Pt*, *W*, *A* 1997 *F*, *Ar*, *R*, *SA* (R)
Re Garbagnati, A 1936 *Ger*, *R* 1937 *Ger*, *Bel*, *Ger*, *F* 1938 *Ger* 1939 *Ger*, *R* 1940 *R*, *Ger* 1942 *R*
Reale, P 1987 *USS*, *Sp* 1988 *USS*, *A*, *I* 1989 *Z* 1992 *S*
Riccardi, G 1955 *Ger*, *F*, *Sp*, *F*, *Cze* 1956 *F*, *Cze*
Ricci, G 1967 *Pt* 1969 *Bul*, *Sp*, *Bel*, *F*
Ricciarelli, G 1962 *Ger*
Riccioni, L 1951 *Sp* 1952 *Sp*, *Ger*, *F* 1953 *F*, *Ger* 1954 *F*
Rigo, S 1992 *S* 1993 *Sp*, *F*, *Pt*
Rinaldo, A 1977 *Mor*, *Pol*, *R*, *Cze*
Rista, W 1968 *Yug* (R) 1969 *Bul*, *Sp*, *Bel*, *F*
Rivaro, M 2000 *S* (R), *W*, *I* (R) 2001 *E* (R)
Rizzo, M 2005 *A* (R)
Rizzoli, G 1935 *F* (R) 1936 *Ger*, *R*
Robazza, C 1978 *Ar*, *Sp* 1979 *F*, *Pol*, *R*, *E*, *Sp*, *F*, *Pol*, *USS*, *NZ*, *Mor* 1980 *F*, *R*, *Fj*, *JAB*, *Coo*, *Pol*, *Sp* 1981 *F*, *R*, *USS*, *WGe* 1982 *E*, *WGe* 1983 *F*, *USS*, *C*, *Mor*, *F* 1984 *F*, *Tun* 1985 *F*
Robertson, KP 2004 *R*, *J*, *C*, *NZ*, *US* 2005 *I* (R), *W* (R), *S* (R), *F*, *Ar*, *Ar*, *A* 2006 *Pt*, *Rus* 2007 *F* (R), *E*, *S*, *W*, *I*, *Ur*, *Ar*, *J*, *I*, *NZ*, *R*, *S*
Rocca, A 1973 *WTv* (R), *Bor*, *NEC* (R) 1977 *R*
Romagnoli, G 1965 *F*, *Cze* 1967 *Pt*, *R*
Romagnoli, S 1982 *Mor* 1984 *R*, *Tun*, *USS* 1985 *F*, *Z*, *Z* 1986 *Tun* (R), *Pt*, *A*, *Tun*, *USS* 1987 *Pt*, *F*, *Fj*
Romano, G 1942 *R*
Romano, P 1942 *R*
Roselli, F 1995 *F*, *R* 1996 *W* 1998 *Rus*, *Ar*, *H*, *E* 1999 *F* (R), *S*, *W*, *I*, *SA*, *SA*, *Ur*, *Fj*, *Tg*
Rosi, P 1948 *F*, *Cze* 1949 *F*, *Cze* 1951 *Sp* 1952 *Ger*, *F* 1953 *F*, *Ger*, *R* 1954 *Sp*, *F*
Rossi, G 1981 *USS*, *WGe* (R) 1982 *E*, *WGe*, *Mor* 1983 *F*, *R*, *USS*, *C*, *C*, *Mor*, *F*, *A*, *USS* 1984 *Mor* 1985 *F* (R), *R*, *E*, *Sp*, *Z*, *USS*, *R* 1986 *Tun*, *F*, *E*, *A*, *Tun*, *USS* 1987 *R*, *NZ*, *Ar*, *USS*, *Sp* 1988 *USS*, *A*, *I* 1989 *F*, *R*, *Sp*, *Ar*, *Z*, *USS* 1990 *F*, *R* 1991 *R*
Rossi, N 1973 *Yug* 1974 *Pt*, *Mid*, *Sus*, *Oxo*, *WGe*, *Leo* 1975 *Sp*, *Cze*, *E*, *H* (R) 1976 *J*, *A*, *Sp* 1977 *Cze* 1980 *USS*
Rossi, Z 1959 *F* 1961 *Ger*, *F* 1962 *F*, *Ger*, *R*
Rossini, E 1948 *F*, *Cze* 1949 *F*, *Cze* 1951 *Sp* 1952 *Ger*
Rovelli, B 1960 *Ger*, *F* 1961 *Ger*, *F*
Russo, A 1986 *E*
Sacca, D 2003 *I*
Saetti, R 1988 *USS* (R), *I* 1989 *F*, *R*, *Sp*, *Ar*, *Z*, *USS* 1990 *F* (R), *Sp*, *H*, *R*, *USS* 1991 *R*, *Nm*, *Nm* (R), *US*, *E* 1992 *R*
Saetti, R 1957 *Ger* 1958 *F*, *R* 1959 *F* 1960 *F* 1961 *Ger*, *F* 1964 *Ger*, *F*
Sagramora, A 1970 *Mad*, *Mad* 1971 *R*
Saibene, E 1957 *F*, *Ger*
Salmasco, C 1965 *F* 1967 *F*
Salsi, L 1971 *Mor* 1972 *Pt*, *Sp*, *Yug* 1973 *Pt*, *Rho*, *WTv*, *Nat*, *ETv*, *Leo*, *FS*, *Tva*, *Cze*, *Yug*, *A* 1974 *Pt*, *Oxo*, *WGe*, *Leo* 1975 *Sp*, *R*, *Sp* 1977 *R*, *Pol*, *Cze*, *R*, *Sp* 1978 *F*
Salvadego, F 1985 *Z*
Salvan, R 1973 *Yug* 1974 *Pt*
Salvati, L 1987 *USS* 1988 *USS*, *I*
Santofadre, R 1952 *Sp*, *Ger*, *F* 1954 *Sp*, *F*
Sartorato, F 1956 *Ger*, *F* 1957 *F*
Savi, M 2004 *R* (R), *J* (R) 2005 *E* (R)
Saviozzi, S 1998 *Rus*, *H* (R) 1999 *W* (R), *I*, *SA*, *SA*, *Ur*, *Fj* (R), *Tg*, *NZ* 2000 *C* (R), *NZ* (R) 2002 *NZ* (R), *Sp* (R)
Scaglia, D 1994 *R*, *W* 1995 *S* 1996 *W*, *A* 1999 *W*
Scalzotto, E 1974 *Mid*, *Sus*, *Oxo*
Scanavacca, A 1999 *Ur* (R) 2001 *E* 2002 *Sp* (R), *R* 2004 *US* (R) 2006 *Ar* (R), *C* 2007 *F*, *E*, *S*, *I* (R)
Sciacol, R 1965 *Cze*
Scodavolpe, I 1954 *Sp*
Screnci, F 1977 *Cze*, *R*, *Sp* 1978 *F* 1979 *Pol*, *R*, *E* 1982 *F* 1984 *Mor*
Selvaggio, A 1973 *Rho*, *WTv*, *ETv*, *Leo*, *FS*, *Tva*
Sepe, M 2006 *J* (R), *Fj*
Sesenna, D 1992 *R* 1993 *Cro*, *Mor*, *F* (R) 1994 *R* (R)
Sessa, G 1930 *Sp*
Sessi, G 1942 *R* (R)
Sgorbati, E 1968 *WGe*, *Yug*
Sgorbati, E 1933 *Cze* 1934 *Cat*, *R* 1935 *Cat*, *F* 1936 *Ger* 1937 *Ger* 1938 *Ger* 1939 *Ger* 1940 *R*, *Ger* 1942 *R*
Sgorlon, A 1993 *Pt* (R), *Mor*, *Sp* (R), *F*, *Rus*, *F*, *S* 1994 *CZR*, *R*, *W* 1995 *S*, *E*, *Ar*, *F*, *Ar*, *R*, *NZ*, *SA* 1996 *W*, *Pt*, *W*, *A*, *E* (R), *S* 1997 *I*, *F*, *F*, *Ar*, *R*, *SA*, *I* 1998 *S*, *W*, *Rus* 1999 *F* (R), *S*, *W*
Sguario, P 1958 *R* 1959 *F* 1960 *Ger*, *F* 1961 *Ger* 1962 *R*
Silini, M 1955 *Ger*, *Sp*, *F*, *Cze* 1956 *Cze* 1957 *Ger* 1958 *F* 1959 *F*
Silvestri, S 1954 *F*
Silvestri, U 1967 *Pt*, *R* 1968 *Pt*, *WGe*
Silvestri, U 1949 *F*, *Cze*
Simonelli, L 1956 *Ger*, *F*, *Cze* 1958 *F* 1960 *Ger*, *F*
Sinitich, F 1980 *Fj* (R), *Coo*, *Pol*, *Sp* 1981 *R* 1983 *USS* (R)
Sole, JW 2005 *Ar*, *Tg*, *Ar* 2006 *I*, *E*, *F*, *W*, *S*, *J*, *Fj*, *Rus*, *A* (R), *Ar* (R), *C* 2007 *F*, *E*, *I* (R), *Ur*, *Ar*, *J*, *I* (R), *R*, *S*
Soro, F 1965 *Cze* 1966 *F*, *Ger*, *R*

Spagnoli, A 1973 *Rho* (R)
Speziali, E 1965 *Cze*
Spragg, W 2006 *C*
Staibano, F 2006 *J* (R), *Fj* (R) 2007 *W* (R), *I* (R), *Ur*, *Ar* (R)
Stanojevic, MP 2006 *Pt*, *Rus*, *A*, *Ar*, *C* 2007 *J*, *NZ*
Stenta, U 1937 *Bel*, *Ger*, *F* 1938 *Ger* 1939 *Ger*, *R* 1940 *R*, *Ger* 1942 *R*
Stievano, P 1948 *F* 1952 *F* 1953 *F*, *Ger*, *R* 1954 *Sp*, *F* 1955 *Ger*
Stocco, S 1998 *H* 1999 *S* (R), *I* (R) 2000 *Fj* (R)
Stoica, CA 1997 *I*, *F*, *SA*, *I* 1998 *S*, *W*, *Rus*, *Ar*, *H*, *E* 1999 *S*, *W*, *SA*, *SA*, *Ur*, *Sp*, *Fj*, *E*, *Tg*, *NZ* 2000 *S*, *W*, *I*, *E*, *F*, *Sa*, *Fj*, *C*, *R*, *NZ* 2001 *I*, *E*, *F*, *S*, *W*, *Fj*, *SA*, *Sa* 2002 *F*, *S*, *W*, *I*, *E*, *Sp*, *R*, *Ar*, *A* 2003 *W*, *I*, *S*, *I*, *Geo*, *Tg*, *C*, *W* 2004 *E*, *F*, *S*, *I*, *W*, *US* 2005 *S*, *Tg*, *Ar* 2006 *I*, *E*, *F*, *W* (R), *S* 2007 *Ur*, *Ar*
Tagliabue, L 1930 *Sp* (R) 1933 *Cze*, *Cze* 1934 *Cat*, *R* 1935 *F* 1937 *Ger*
Tartaglini, S 1948 *Cze* 1949 *F*, *Cze* 1951 *Sp* 1952 *Sp*, *Ger*, *F* 1953 *F*
Tassin, A 1973 *A*
Taveggia, A 1954 *F* 1955 *Ger*, *F*, *Sp*, *F* 1956 *Ger*, *F*, *Cze* 1957 *F*, *Ger* 1958 *F*, *R* 1959 *F* 1960 *Ger*, *F* 1967 *Pt*
Tebaldi, D 1985 *Z*, *Z* 1987 *R*, *Ar*, *Fj*, *USS*, *Sp* 1988 *F*, *A* (R), *I* 1989 *F* 1990 *F*, *Pol*, *R* 1991 *Nm* (R)
Tedeschi 1948 *F*
Testoni, G 1937 *Bel* 1938 *Ger* 1942 *R*
Tinari, C 1980 *JAB* (R), *Coo*, *Pol*, *USS*, *Sp* 1981 *USS*, *WGe* 1982 *F*, *WGe* 1983 *R*, *USS*, *C*, *C*, *Sp*, *Mor* (R), *A*, *USS* 1984 *Mor*, *R*
Tommasi, M 1990 *Pol* (R) 1992 *R* (R), *S* (R) 1993 *Pt*, *Cro*, *Sp*, *F* (R)
Torresan, C 1980 *F*, *R*, *Fj* (R), *Coo*, *Pol*, *USS* 1981 *R* (R), *USS* 1982 *R* (R), *Mor* (R) 1983 *C*, *F*, *A*, *USS* 1984 *F*, *Mor*, *Tun*, *USS* 1985 *Z*, *Z*, *USS*
Tozzi, F 1933 *Cze* (R)
Travagli, P 2004 *C* (R), *NZ* (R)
Travini, L 1999 *SA* (R), *Ur* (R), *Sp*, *Fj* 2000 *I* (R)
Trebbi, F 1933 *Cze* (R), *Cze*
Trentin, F 1979 *Mor*, *F* (R), *Pol*, *USS* 1981 *R* (R)
Trevisiol, M 1988 *F*, *USS*, *A*, *I* 1989 *F*, *Ar*, *USS* 1994 *R*
Trippiteli, M 1979 *Pol* 1980 *Pol*, *Sp* 1981 *F*, *R* 1982 *F*, *E*, *WGe* 1984 *Tun*
Troiani, L 1985 *R* 1986 *Tun*, *F*, *Pt*, *A*, *USS* 1987 *Pt*, *F* 1988 *R*, *USS*, *A*, *I* 1989 *Sp*, *Ar*, *Z*, *USS* 1990 *F*, *Pol*, *R*, *Sp*, *H*, *R*, *USS* 1991 *F*, *R*, *Nm*, *Nm*, *US*, *E* 1992 *Sp*, *F*, *R*, *R*, *S* 1993 *Sp*, *F*, *Cro*, *Rus*, *F* 1994 *Sp*, *CZR*, *A*, *A*, *F* 1995 *S*, *E*, *Ar*
Troncon, A 1994 *Sp* (R), *R*, *CZR*, *H* (R), *A*, *A*, *R*, *W*, *F* 1995 *S*, *I*, *Sa*, *E*, *Ar*, *F*, *Ar*, *R*, *NZ*, *SA* 1996 *W*, *W*, *A*, *E*, *S* 1997 *I*, *F*, *F*, *Ar*, *SA*, *I* 1998 *S*, *W*, *Rus*, *Ar*, *H*, *E* 1999 *F*, *S*, *W*, *I*, *Ur*, *Sp*, *Fj*, *E*, *Tg*, *NZ* 2000 *S*, *W*, *I*, *E*, *F*, *R*, *NZ* 2001 *I*, *F*, *Nm*, *SA*, *Ur*, *Ar*, *Fj*, *SA*, *Sa* 2002 *F*, *S*, *W*, *I*, *E*, *Sp*, *R*, *Ar*, *A* (R) 2003 *W*, *I*, *E*, *F*, *S*, *S*, *I*, *Geo*, *NZ* (R), *Tg*, *C*, *W* 2004 *R*, *J* (R) 2005 *I*, *W*, *S*, *E*, *F* 2007 *F* (R), *E*, *S*, *W*, *I*, *J*, *I*, *NZ*, *R* (R), *Pt*, *S*
Troncon, G 1962 *F*, *Ger*, *R* 1963 *F* 1964 *Ger*, *F* 1965 *Cze* 1966 *F*, *R* 1967 *F* 1968 *Yug* 1972 *Pt* (R)
Turcato, L 1952 *Sp*, *Ger*, *F* 1953 *Ger*, *R*
Turcato, M 1949 *F* 1951 *Sp*
Vaccari, P 1991 *Nm*, *Nm*, *US*, *E*, *NZ*, *USS* 1992 *Sp*, *F*, *R*, *R*, *S* 1993 *Mor*, *Sp* (R), *F*, *Rus*, *F*, *S* 1994 *Sp*, *R*, *CZR*, *H*, *A*, *A*, *R*, *W*, *F* 1995 *I*, *Sa*, *E*, *Ar*, *F*, *Ar*, *R*, *NZ*, *SA* 1996 *W*, *W*, *E*, *S* 1997 *I*, *F*, *F*, *Ar*, *R*, *SA*, *I* 1998 *S*, *W*, *Ar* 1999 *Ur*, *Sp*, *E*, *Tg*, *NZ* 2001 *Fj* 2002 *F*, *S*, *Ar*, *A* 2003 *W*, *I*, *E*, *F*, *S*
Vagnetti, V 1939 *R* (R) 1940 *R*
Valier, F 1968 *Yug* 1969 *F* 1970 *Cze*, *R* 1971 *Mor*, *R* 1972 *Pt*
Valtorta, L 1957 *Ger* 1958 *F*
Vene, O 1966 *F*
Venturi, E 1983 *C* 1985 *E*, *Sp* 1986 *Tun*, *Pt* 1988 *USS*, *A* 1989 *F*, *R*, *Sp*, *Ar*, *USS* 1990 *F*, *Pol*, *R*, *Sp*, *H*, *R*, *USS* 1991 *F*, *R*, *NZ*, *USS* 1992 *Sp*, *F* (R), *R* (R) 1993 *Sp*, *F*
Vezzani, P 1973 *Yug* 1975 *F*, *Sp*, *R*, *Cze*, *E*, *Pol*, *H*, *Sp* 1976 *F*
Vialetto, F 1972 *Yug*
Viccariotto, V 1948 *F*
Vigliano, S 1937 *R* (R), *Bel*, *Ger*, *F* 1939 *R* 1942 *R*
Villagra, L 2000 *Sa* (R), *Fj* (R)
Vinci I, E 1929 *Sp* (R)
Vinci II, P 1929 *Sp* 1930 *Sp* 1933 *Cze*
Vinci III, F 1929 *Sp* 1930 *Sp* 1934 *Cat*, *R* 1935 *Cat*, *F* 1936 *Ger*, *R* 1937 *Ger*, *R*, *Ger*, *F* 1939 *Ger*, *R* 1940 *Ger*
Vinci IV, P 1929 *Sp* 1930 *Sp* 1933 *Cze*, *Cze* 1934 *Cat*, *R* 1935 *Cat*, *F* 1937 *Ger*, *Bel*, *Ger*, *F* 1939 *Ger*
Visentin, A 1970 *R* 1972 *Pt*, *Sp* (R) 1973 *Rho* (R), *WTv*, *Bor*, *NEC*, *Nat*, *ETv*, *Leo*, *FS*, *Tva*, *Cze*, *Yug*, *A* 1974 *Pt*, *Leo* 1975 *F*, *Sp*, *R*, *Cze* 1976 *R* 1978 *Ar*
Visentin, G 1935 *Cat*, *F* 1936 *R* 1937 *Ger*, *Bel*, *Ger*, *F* 1938 *Ger* 1939 *Ger*
Visentin, T 1996 *W*
Visser, W 1999 *I* (R), *SA*, *SA* 2000 *S*, *W*, *I*, *F* (R), *C*, *R*, *NZ* 2001 *I*, *E*, *F*, *S*, *W*, *Nm*, *SA*, *Ur*, *Ar*, *Fj* (R), *SA*, *Sa*
Vitadello, F 1985 *Sp* 1987 *Pt* (R)
Vitelli, C 1973 *Cze*, *Yug* 1974 *Pt*, *Sus*
Vittorini, I 1969 *Sp* (R)
Vosawai, RMS 2007 *J* (R), *I* (R), *NZ* (R), *R* (R), *Pt*
Wakarua, RS 2003 *Tg*, *C*, *W* 2004 *E*, *F*, *S* (R), *W* (R), *J*, *C*, *NZ* 2005 *Fj* (R)
Williams, F 1995 *SA*
Zaffiri, M 2000 *Fj* (R), *R*, *NZ* 2001 *W* (R) 2003 *S* 2005 *Tg* (R), *Fj* (R) 2006 *W*, *S*, *C* (R) 2007 *E*, *S* (R), *W* (R), *I*
Zanatta, R 1954 *Sp*, *F*
Zanchi, G 1953 *Ger*, *R* 1955 *Sp*, *Cze* 1957 *Ger*
Zanella, A 1977 *Mor*
Zanella, M 1976 *J*, *Sp* 1977 *R*, *Pol*, *Cze* 1978 *Ar* (R) 1980 *Pol*, *USS*
Zanetti, E 1942 *R*
Zani, F 1960 *Ger*, *F* 1961 *Ger*, *F* 1962 *F*, *R* 1963 *F* 1964 *F* 1965 *F* 1966 *Ger*, *R*
Zani, G 1934 *R*
Zanni, A 2005 *Tg* (R), *Ar* (R), *Fj* 2006 *F* (R), *W* (R), *S* (R), *Pt* (R), *Rus* (R), *A*, *Ar*, *C* (R) 2007 *S*, *W*, *I*, *Ur*, *I*, *NZ*
Zanoletti, C 2001 *Sa* (R) 2002 *E* (R), *NZ*, *R*, *Ar* (R), *A* (R) 2005 *A* (R)
Zanon, G 1981 *F*, *R*, *USS*, *WGe* 1982 *R*, *E*, *WGe*, *Mor* 1983 *F*, *R*, *USS*, *C*, *C*, *Sp*, *Mor*, *F*, *A*, *USS* 1984 *F*, *Mor*, *R*, *USS* 1985 *F*, *R*, *E*, *Sp*, *Z*, *Z*, *USS* 1986 *USS* 1987 *R*, *Ar*, *USS* (R) 1989 *Sp*, *Ar* 1990 *F*, *Pol*, *R*, *Sp*, *H*, *R*, *USS* 1991 *Nm* (R), *US*, *E*
Zingarelli, M 1973 *A*
Zisti, N 1999 *E*, *NZ* 2000 *E*, *F*
Zoffoli, G 1936 *Ger*, *R* 1937 *Ger*, *R*, *Ger* 1938 *Ger* 1939 *R*
Zorzi, S 1985 *R* 1986 *Tun*, *F* 1988 *F* (R), *R* (R), *USS* 1992 *R*
Zucchelo, A 1956 *Ger*, *F*
Zucchi, C 1952 *Sp* 1953 *F*
Zuin, L 1977 *Cze* 1978 *Ar*, *USS*, *Sp* 1979 *F*, *Pol*, *R*

ITALY INTERNATIONAL RECORDS

UP TO 31ST OCTOBER 2007

WINNING MARGIN

Date	Opponent	Result	Winning Margin
18/05/1994	Czech Republic	104–8	**96**
07/10/2006	Portugal	83–0	**83**
17/06/1993	Croatia	76–11	**65**
19/06/1993	Morocco	70–9	**61**
02/03/1996	Portugal	64–3	**61**

MOST POINTS IN A MATCH
BY THE TEAM

Date	Opponent	Result	Pts.
18/05/1994	Czech Republic	104–8	**104**
07/10/2006	Portugal	83–0	**83**
17/06/1993	Croatia	76–11	**76**
19/06/1993	Morocco	70–9	**70**

MOST TRIES IN A MATCH
BY THE TEAM

Date	Opponent	Result	Tries
18/05/1994	Czech Republic	104–8	**16**
07/10/2006	Portugal	83–0	**13**
18/11/1998	Netherlands	67–7	**11**
17/06/1993	Croatia	76–11	**11**

MOST CONVERSIONS IN A MATCH
BY THE TEAM

Date	Opponent	Result	Cons
18/05/1994	Czech Republic	104–8	**12**
19/06/1993	Morocco	70–9	**10**
17/06/1993	Croatia	76–11	**9**
07/10/2006	Portugal	83–0	**9**

MOST PENALTIES IN A MATCH
BY THE TEAM

Date	Opponent	Result	Pens
01/10/1994	Romania	24–6	**8**
10/11/2001	Fiji	66–10	**7**

MOST DROP GOALS IN A MATCH
BY THE TEAM

Date	Opponent	Result	DGs
07/10/1990	Romania	29–21	**3**
05/02/2000	Scotland	34–20	**3**
11/07/1973	Transvaal	24–28	**3**

MOST POINTS IN A MATCH
BY A PLAYER

Date	Player	Opponent	Pts.
10/11/2001	Diego Dominguez	Fiji	**29**
05/02/2000	Diego Dominguez	Scotland	**29**
01/07/1983	Stefano Bettarello	Canada	**29**

MOST TRIES IN A MATCH
BY A PLAYER

Date	Player	Opponent	Tries
19/06/1993	Ivan Francescato	Morocco	**4**
10/10/1937	Renzo Cova	Belgium	**4**

MOST CONVERSIONS IN A MATCH
BY A PLAYER

Date	Player	Opponent	Cons
18/05/1994	Luigi Troiani	Czech Republic	**12**
19/06/1993	Gabriel Filizzola	Morocco	**10**
17/06/1993	Luigi Troiani	Croatia	**9**

MOST PENALTIES IN A MATCH
BY A PLAYER

Date	Player	Opponent	Pens
01/10/1994	Diego Dominguez	Romania	**8**
10/11/2001	Diego Dominguez	Fiji	**7**

MOST DROP GOALS IN A MATCH
BY A PLAYER

Date	Player	Opponent	DGs
05/02/2000	Diego Dominguez	Scotland	**3**
11/07/1973	Rocco Caligiuri	Transvaal	**3**

MOST CAPPED PLAYERS

Player	Caps
Alessandro Troncon	101
Carlo Checchinato	83
Diego Dominguez	74
Cristian Stoica	71
Andrea Lo Cicero	71

LEADING PENALTY SCORERS

Player	Pens
Diego Dominguez	209
Stefano Bettarello	106
Luigi Troiani	57
Ramiro Pez	52
Ennio Ponzi	31

LEADING TRY SCORERS

Player	Tries
Marcello Cuttitta	25
Paolo Vaccari	22
Manrico Marchetto	21
Carlo Checchinato	21
Alessandro Troncon	19

LEADING DROP GOAL SCORERS

Player	DGs
Diego Dominguez	19
Stefano Bettarello	15
Ramiro Pez	6
Massimo Bonomi	5
Oscar Collodo	5

LEADING CONVERSIONS SCORERS

Player	Cons
Diego Dominguez	127
Luigi Troiani	57
Stefano Bettarello	46
David Bortolussi	34
Ramiro Pez	33

LEADING POINT SCORERS

Player	Pts.
Diego Dominguez	983
Stefano Bettarello	483
Luigi Troiani	294
Ramiro Pez	260
David Bortolussi	133
Ennio Ponzi	133

JAPAN

JAPAN'S 2006–07 TEST RECORD

OPPONENTS	DATE	VENUE	RESULT
Hong Kong	18 November	A	**Won** 52–3
South Korea	25 November	N	**Won** 54–0
South Korea	22 April	H	**Won** 82–0
Hong Kong	29 April	H	**Won** 73–3
Fiji	26 May	A	**Lost** 15–30
Tonga	2 June	A	**Won** 20–17
Australia A	9 June	A	**Lost** 10–71
Samoa	16 June	H	**Lost** 3–13
Junior All Blacks	24 June	H	**Lost** 3–51
Italy	19 August	A	**Lost** 12–36
Portugal	25 August	N	**Won** 15–13
Australia	8 September	N	**Lost** 3–91 (WC)
Fiji	12 September	N	**Lost** 31–35 (WC)
Wales	20 September	N	**Lost** 18–72 (WC)
Canada	25 September	N	**Drew** 12–12 (WC)

FINISHING ON A HIGH NOTE

By Rich Freeman

"**Bitter sweet," was Japan** coach John Kirwan's description of the 12–12 draw with Canada that rounded off the Brave Blossoms' Rugby World Cup 2007 campaign. And it was probably the best way to describe Japan's year on the international front. Kirwan had come on board in the wake of the mess left behind by Jean-Pierre Elissalde. Officially just an advisor when Japan comfortably beat Hong Kong and South Korea to earn a spot in the World Cup, Kirwan took office on 1 January, giving him just eight months to prepare for rugby's flagship tournament.

Ironically, one of the first things Kirwan said following the 91–3 loss to Australia that opened the Brave Blossoms' World Cup campaign was that Japan should not be playing their traditional Asian rivals.

"If we want to get better, we need to be playing the All Blacks and Wallabies, not Hong Kong and South Korea," he said.

Besides his experience of having played and coached in Japan with the NEC club, Kirwan was also taken on board because he shared the Japan Rugby Football Union's vision of coming away from France with two wins. That they came so close, says much for Kirwan, his coaching team and the players.

Japan's build up to the World Cup included a further two games against Hong Korea and South Korea, before taking on the Classic All Blacks. In the first of two games against the Kiwis, Kosuke Endo gave fans in Osaka an idea of things to come, when he scored a sensational try that began on Japan's own try line – beating Jonah Lomu for pace and easily brushing aside Carlos Spencer's attempt at a tackle.

Four months later, Endo repeated the trick against Wales, and then scored a superb individual try from 45 meters out against Canada.

At the World Cup Japan also suffered from the loss of world record try-scorer, Daisuke Ohata, who had ruptured an Achilles in a Top League game in January. He recovered but at a pre-World Cup training camp Ohata ruptured his other Achilles and fly-half Eji Ando was also ruled out of the tournament.

With 20-year-old Kosei Ono, the only other flyhalf in the squad, Kirwan was forced to move Bryce Robins into the key position. Hooker Mitsugu Yamamoto was forced out of the World Cup just before the team arrived in Toulouse and Japan's injury run continued following their opening game.

True to his word Kirwan had picked his second-string team against Australia and it was no surprise they went down 91–3.

Things weren't looking good, but Japan responded in the best possible manner.

They may have been beaten 35–31 by Fiji, but their never-say-die attitude had the crowd in Toulouse on their feet well after the final whistle.

Wales in Cardiff was always going to be tricky and so it proved.

Japan may have scored one of the tries of the tournament through Endo, but they also committed far too many errors and in the end the Welsh ran away with the game 72–18.

And so to Bordeaux. Canada are Japan's oldest international rivals and the two teams have generally been evenly matched.

With the Canadian pack looking at using its brute force and the Japanese hoping to use their quick feet, the game was always going to be one of contrasting styles.

Endo reinforced his reputation with a wonderful individual try following a steal at a line out on the halfway line, as Japan went into the break 5–0 up.

Solid forward play and some quick thinking from Canada captain Morgan Williams saw Canada edge ahead 12–5, and with 80 minutes on the clock, most thought the game over.

But referee Jonathan Kaplan allowed four more minutes and Japan made the most of it with Koji Taira crossing in the 84th minute.

It was all down to Shotaro Onishi.

The Yamaha Jubilo centre had initially been ruled out of the game with a rib injury but he showed great composure to slot over the kick from out wide and bring the sides level.

It wasn't quite the win Kirwan had hoped for but bearing in mind the injuries and the limited time the 42-year-old had been in charge, it wasn't a bad effort. The Japanese media certainly thought so, with calls for JK (as he is known) to be given an extension to his contract or in one case asking the JRFU to give the New Zealander the job for life.

On the domestic front, Toshiba Brave Lupus gave coach Masahiro Kunda the ideal leaving present, winning both the Microsoft Cup and the All Japan Championships.

The format of the domestic competition had changed with playoffs (the Microsoft Cup) determining the Top League champion.

Toshiba had finished the season on top of the table and were up against local rival Suntory Sungoliath in the final.

It seemed Toshiba's stranglehold on the domestic silverware was about to be broken, until Luatangi Samurai Vatuvei crossed in the fourth minute of injury time. Hiroki Yoshida added the conversion as Toshiba won 14–13. Three weeks later Kunda's men beat Toyota Verblitz 19–10 to claim the All-Japan Championship.

The thrilling finish to last year's domestic competitions and the improved performance from the national team have many thinking Japan rugby is finally about to fulfill its potential.

JAPAN INTERNATIONAL RECORDS

UP TO 31ST OCTOBER 2007

WINNING MARGIN

Date	Opponent	Result	Winning Margin
06/07/2002	Chinese Taipei	155–3	**152**
27/10/1998	Chinese Taipei	134–6	**128**
21/07/2002	Chinese Taipei	120–3	**117**
08/05/2005	Hong Kong	91–3	**88**
15/06/2003	Korea	86–3	**83**

MOST POINTS IN A MATCH

BY THE TEAM

Date	Opponent	Result	Pts.
06/07/2002	Chinese Taipei	155–3	**155**
27/10/1998	Chinese Taipei	134–6	**134**
21/07/2002	Chinese Taipei	120–3	**120**
08/05/2005	Hong Kong	91–3	**91**
16/06/2002	Korea	90–24	**90**

MOST TRIES IN A MATCH

BY THE TEAM

Date	Opponent	Result	Tries
06/07/2002	Chinese Taipei	155–3	**23**
27/10/1998	Chinese Taipei	134–6	**20**
21/07/2002	Chinese Taipei	120–3	**18**

MOST CONVERSIONS IN A MATCH

BY THE TEAM

Date	Opponent	Result	Cons
06/07/2002	Chinese Taipei	155–3	**20**
27/10/1998	Chinese Taipei	134–6	**17**
21/07/2002	Chinese Taipei	120–3	**15**

MOST PENALTIES IN A MATCH

BY THE TEAM

Date	Opponent	Result	Pens
08/05/1999	Tonga	44–17	**9**
08/04/1990	Tonga	28–16	**6**

MOST DROP GOALS IN A MATCH

BY THE TEAM

Date	Opponent	Result	DGs
15/09/1998	Argentina	44–29	**2**

MOST POINTS IN A MATCH

BY A PLAYER

Date	Player	Opponent	Pts.
21/07/2002	Toru Kurihara	Chinese Taipei	**60**
06/07/2002	Daisuke Ohata	Chinese Taipei	**40**
16/06/2002	Toru Kurihara	Korea	**35**
08/05/1999	Keiji Hirose	Tonga	**34**
08/05/2005	Keiji Hirose	Hong Kong	**31**

MOST TRIES IN A MATCH

BY A PLAYER

Date	Player	Opponent	Tries
06/07/2002	Daisuke Ohata	Chinese Taipei	**8**
21/07/2002	Toru Kurihara	Chinese Taipei	**6**
08/05/2005	Daisuke Ohata	Hong Kong	**6**
27/10/1998	Terunori Masuho	Chinese Taipei	**5**

MOST CONVERSIONS IN A MATCH

BY A PLAYER

Date	Player	Opponent	Cons
21/07/2002	Toru Kurihara	Chinese Taipei	15
06/07/2002	Andy Miller	Chinese Taipei	12
16/06/2002	Toru Kurihara	Korea	11
08/05/2005	Keiji Hirose	Hong Kong	11

MOST PENALTIES IN A MATCH

BY A PLAYER

Date	Player	Opponent	Pens
08/05/1999	Keiji Hirose	Tonga	9
08/04/1990	Takahiro Hosokawa	Tonga	6

MOST DROP GOALS IN A MATCH

BY A PLAYER

Date	Player	Opponent	DGs
15/09/1998	Kensuke Iwabuchi	Argentina	2

MOST CAPPED PLAYERS

Name	Caps
Yukio Motoki	79
Takeomi Ito	62
Daisuke Ohata	58
Masahiro Kunda	48
Terunori Masuho	47

LEADING TRY SCORERS

Name	Tries
Daisuke Ohata	69
Terunori Masuho	28
Hirotoki Onozawa	24
Toru Kurihara	20
Yoshihito Yoshida	17

LEADING CONVERSIONS SCORERS

Name	Cons
Keiji Hirose	77
Toru Kurihara	71
Andy Miller	17
Shotaro Onishi	17
Takahiro Hosokawa	14

LEADING PENALTY SCORERS

Name	Pens
Keiji Hirose	76
Toru Kurihara	35
Takahiro Hosokawa	24
Wataru Ikeda	12
Kyohei Morita	12

LEADING DROP GOAL SCORERS

Name	DGs
Kyohei Morita	5
Yuji Matsuo	2
Katsuhiro Matsuo	2
Keiji Hirose	2
Kensuke Iwabuchi	2

LEADING POINTS SCORERS

Name	Pts.
Keiji Hirose	413
Toru Kurihara	347
Daisuke Ohata	345
Terunori Masuho	142
Hirotoki Onozawa	120

Shaun Botterill/Getty Images

Shotaro Onishi's ice cool nerves, with a last-minute conversion against Canada, gave Japan their first draw at the Rugby World Cup Finals, and coach John Kirwan (left) celebrates.

NAMIBIA

NAMIBIA'S 2006–07 TEST RECORD

OPPONENTS	DATE	VENUE	RESULT
Morocco	28 October	H	**Won** 25–7
Morocco	11 November	A	**Won** 27–8
Zambia	26 May	H	**Won** 83–10
Georgia	5 June	N	**Lost** 18–26
Argentina A	10 June	N	**Lost** 13–47
Romania	16 June	N	**Lost** 16–28
Uganda	23 June	A	**Lost** 19–20
South Africa	15 August	A	**Lost** 13–105
Ireland	9 September	N	**Lost** 17–32 (WC)
France	16 September	N	**Lost** 10–87 (WC)
Argentina	22 September	N	**Lost** 3–63 (WC)
Georgia	26 September	N	**Lost** 0–30 (WC)

DRAMA ON AND OFF THE FIELD

By Helge Schutz

A brilliant performance against Ireland at Rugby World Cup 2007 was the highlight for Namibia in a year, which saw the union begin to make headway on the international stage.

Long gone were the days – just four years ago – when they were losing 142–0 at the World Cup to Australia. In 2007 they were a completely different – far more competitive – team.

The 32–17 defeat in Bordeaux to the Irish may well have been recorded as a loss in the record books, but for the newly installed Namibian head coach Hakkies Husselman the performance and the result against one of the tournament's favoured sides, was a personal triumph for all associated with Namibian rugby.

Prior to the tournament few outside of the Namibian camp could have thought that such a performance was possible. After all Namibian rugby was in the throws of a transitional period after the departure of stalwart coach Johan Venter and the acrimonious withdrawal from the squad of influential Sharks hooker Skipper Badenhorst just days before kick-off in Paris.

Yet the Namibians showed that they are made of stern stuff. Experienced campaigners such as the evergreen and ever impressive Kees Lensing, Marius Visser, Hugo Horn, Heino Senekal and the impressive young back row star Jacques Burger pulled the squad along, while Hussleman, a veteran RWC campaigner himself, proved to be a valuable asset as head coach.

The first signs of improvement came during the IRB's Nations Cup tournament, held this year in Bucharest.

Following Venter's departure in May, only weeks before the team's scheduled departure for Romania, the team had little time to gel. Venter had been dismissed after the NRU accused the coach of causing embarrassment after a promotional celebration that involved the arrival in Namibia of the Webb Ellis Cup.

Thirty-four year old Hussleman, Venter's assistant, was thrown into the fore and immediately made an impression, guiding his side to a 83–10 victory against Zambia in the Africa Cup. The team set off for Romania with renewed enthusiasm.

Despite losing all three matches on what was a rebuilding tour, the Namibians made vast improvements in all areas of their game, while garnering much-needed experience of what to expect at Rugby World Cup 2007 later in the year.

"There is a great atmosphere in the team," commented Husselman after the tournament. "We are using every minute to improve with Rugby World Cup in mind."

Hussleman's preparations were also given a boost when the IRB, as part of its US$50 million strategic investment programme, announced additional assistance to three RWC countries; debutants Portugal, Georgia and Namibia.

For Namibia the help was significant, renewing ties with South African rugby and providing access to much-needed expertise in key areas such as the set piece, defence and kicking.

Not only did the union have access to the world class facilities at the South African Institute of Sport, but the teams also had access to Springboks coach Jake White and former South Africa coach Nick Mallett.

The programme, which was well received, culminated in a match against the Springboks. Again, although 100 points were leaked, against the world champions elect, the experience was significant.

So it was an optimistic Namibian squad that set off for France. Hussleman had targeted one win and of course the encounter against Georgia would provide the most realistic opportunity of achieving that goal.

The brilliant performance against Ireland in Bordeaux raised hopes further while winning the hearts of rugby fans all over the world with what was a pretty gutsy display.

No one had given Namibia a chance against one of the favourites for the Rugby World Cup, but Namibia rose to the occasion with a memorable and inspired performance.

Ireland had taken a 20–3 lead at half-time and when they scored a penalty try shortly after the break to go 27–3 up, it looked like Namibia were in for a hiding.

But the Namibians dug deep and put their bodies on the line in a courageous display that won over the support of the fans.

Midway through the second half, wing Ryan Witbooi cut through Ireland's defence with a great break, and although he was tackled a few metres from the line, he managed to offload to flanker Jacques Nieuwenhuis, who crashed over for a try.

The crowd was up on its feet and cheering for Namibia, as fly-half Emile Wessels added the conversion, but there was more to come. Barely three minutes later centre Piet van Zyl chased a kick ahead to score Namibia's second try and when Wessels added the conversion Namibia were just 27–17 behind.

But Ireland had the final say when they got a try that should not have been allowed, as television replays showed that the ball had not been dotted down cleanly.

When the final whistle finally went Namibia received a standing ovation, while Ryan Witbooi won the Man of the Match award.

Captain Lensing who has played for Leeds in England's top flight thought the performance was so good that it could lead to some of his team mates getting offers that could lead to them leaving the amateur game behind them.

"If we keep playing like that I would not be surprised if some guys got offers to play professional in Europe. The guys showed a lot of commitment, especially our amateur players," he said.

After that inspired performance, the rest of the World Cup was a bit of an anti-climax for Namibia but they managed to play well enough to make that 142–0 defeat four years ago, a distant memory.

A week later they took on the hosts, France in Toulouse, but any hopes of another giant-killing act were dispelled when No 8 Jacques Nieuwenhuis was red-carded for a high tackle on French lock Sebastian Chabal after only 18 minutes, ending the game as a contest.

With brilliant running rugby, France launched attack after attack and eventually ran in 13 tries to score an emphatic 87–10 victory.

Namibia's points came via a drop goal by Emile Wessels and an intercept try in the final minute by winger Bradley Langenhoven, which was converted by TC Losper.

"We played with 14 guys and I don't think any other team would have played at the level we played at. I don't think a team of 14 guys could have played a team (France) at this level," said Husselman, clearly delighted with the pride and passion his side showed.

Argentina overpowered Namibia 63–3 in their third with a great performance built on forward dominance and slick backline attacks.

Namibia were competitive for the first quarter of the match and even took the lead when fly-half Morne Schreuder landed a penalty in the sixth minute. But once Argentina scored their opening try in the 24th minute, they took control of the game and went on to run in nine tries in a comprehensive victory.

Namibia were hoping to register their first World Cup victory in their final match against Georgia on September 26, but it was not to be as the powerful Georgians won the match 30–0.

In a hard, physical battle, Georgia gained the upper hand amongst the forwards, gradually wearing down Namibia with their driving mauls.

Their backs also made better use of their possession, running with conviction, while their fly-half Merab Kvirikashvili put Namibia under pressure with well-judged kicks into open space.

Namibia's forwards battled their hearts out but could not break down Georgia's tight defence. Namibia's backs, by contrast, ran aimlessly, made unnecessary knock-ons and kicked away far too much possession.

It was a disappointing end to the World Cup, but Namibian coach Hakkies Husselmann remained positive.

"We had talks with the IRB. If Namibia could get more money for development and help, we can go further . . . We have the players, we just need assistance. We are waiting for the IRB to be in contact with us," he said.

"Everyone played their heart out. At the end it wasn't enough, but we will be back."

Lensing added: "It was a great World Cup and I'm honoured to be the captain of the Namibian side. Although we didn't reach our goals it was an honour to represent Namibia.

"(Just) playing against the best teams in the world like Argentina, France and Ireland was a personal highlight for me. For the team, (the highlight was) the first three games and the opportunity to play against the big guys and to show what potential we have."

Namibia's Confederation of African Rugby Cup campaign was affected by Venter's departure, leaving Hussleman to pick up the pieces in his first appointment against Zambia.

He made a successful debut as Namibia thrashed Zambia 83–10 after leading 33–0 at half-time, and a few days later the national squad left for Bucharest, Romania to participate in the IRB Nations Cup tournament for emerging rugby nations.

Here, Namibia found the going much tougher, as they lost all four their matches, finishing last amongst the six competing nations.

On June 5, Namibia lost 26–18 to Georgia, who clinched victory through their heavy pack and their speedy wings. Namibia's tries were scored by prop Marius Visser and a fine individual try by fly-half Justinus van der Westhuizen.

On June 10 Namibia put up a much better performance against Argentina A, before losing 47–13.

Namibia's cause was however not helped when two players – Jacques Burger and Wolfie Duvenhage were sin-binned in quick succession – and Argentina ran in 22 points during their absence.

Namibia's only try scorer was flanker Jacques Nieuwenhuis, while TC Losper added a conversion and two penalties.

On June 16, Namibia put in a brave and committed display, but eventually lost 28–16 to Romania in their final match.

Flanker Tinus du Plessis scored Namibia's only try, while fly-half TC Losper added three penalties and a conversion.

A week later, on June 23, Namibia suffered a shock 20–19 defeat to Uganda in a Confederation of African Rugby Cup match in Kampala.

Namibia took an early 12–0 lead, but allowed Uganda to come back into the match as the home side went ahead 14–12 at the break.

Namibia regained the lead in the second half, but Uganda fought back to snatch a historic first victory against Namibia.

Namibia's points came via two tries by flanker Jacques Nieuwenhuis and one by prop Jane du Toit and two conversions by Losper.

Namibia's final World Cup squad of 30 players was announced on July 12, with the only surprises being the selection of flyhalves Morne Schreuder and Emile Wessels, who were both not in the original list of 50 players. Both were veterans from the 2003 World Cup, and although they missed the national trials, their experience was deemed to be too important and they were recalled to the national squad.

On July 21, Namibia beat a South African Amateur team 42–34 after leading 13–10 at half time.

Namibia secured the victory with a display of exciting running rugby, while wing Ryan Witbooi was the pick of the players, scoring two tries.

A week later, however, Namibia gave a poor performance, going down 32–20 to South African Universities in Windhoek.

Namibia's forwards put in a great effort but their good work was undone by a bungling backline that knocked the ball on on countless occasions.

Jacques Nieuwenhuis and Ryan Witbooi scored Namibia's tries while TC Losper added two conversions and two penalties.

Namibia took on the Springboks in their final warm up match for the World Cup at Newlands in Cape Town on August 15.

The Springboks were just too powerful and slick for a game Namibia, who hardly got any possession and had to defend for most of the match.

With backs and forwards combining brilliantly, the Springboks ran in a total of 15 tries to notch up a 105–13 victory, after leading 44–7 at half time.

Namibia's points came via an intercept try by Bradley Langenhoven and a conversion and two penalties by Emile Wessels.

Reho Falcon dominated the Namibian club rugby scene, winning both legs of the National Premier league as well as the MTC Club Championships.

On March 3 they beat Western Suburbs 6–3 in the MTC Club Championships final.

The MTC Premier League was contested by six clubs from Windhoek and Rehoboth, and was divided into two legs.

Clubs were allowed to make use of their World Cup players during the first leg, but not in the second after the final World Cup squad was announced.

Reho Falcon again proved their superiority when they beat Western Suburbs 18–9 in the first final on August 4.

Falcons beat Wanderers 34–26 in an ill-tempered second leg final on September 22.

In a fiery match, three Wanderers players and one from Reho Falcons received red cards, while the referee dished out a further four yellow cards – all against Wanderers players.

NAMIBIA INTERNATIONAL RECORDS

UP TO 31ST OCTOBER 2007

WINNING MARGIN

Date	Opponent	Result	Winning Margin
15/06/2002	Madagascar	112–0	**112**
21/04/1990	Portugal	86–9	**77**
27/05/2006	Kenya	82–12	**70**
26/05/2007	Zambia	80–10	**70**

MOST POINTS IN A MATCH

BY THE TEAM

Date	Opponent	Result	Pts.
15/06/2002	Madagascar	112–0	**112**
21/04/1990	Portugal	86–9	**86**
31/08/2003	Uganda	82–13	**82**
27/05/2006	Kenya	82–12	**82**

MOST TRIES IN A MATCH

BY THE TEAM

Date	Opponent	Result	Tries
15/06/2002	Madagascar	112–0	**18**
21/04/1990	Portugal	86–9	**16**
17/10/1999	Germany	79–13	**13**

MOST CONVERSIONS IN A MATCH

BY THE TEAM

Date	Opponent	Result	Cons
15/06/2002	Madagascar	112–0	**11**
21/04/1990	Portugal	86–9	**11**
31/08/2003	Uganda	82–13	**11**
27/05/2006	Kenya	82–12	**11**

MOST PENALTIES IN A MATCH

BY THE TEAM

Date	Opponent	Result	Pens
22/06/1991	Italy	33–19	**5**
23/01/1998	Portugal	36–19	**5**
30/06/1990	France A	20–25	**5**

MOST DROP GOALS IN A MATCH

BY THE TEAM

1 on 7 Occasions

MOST POINTS IN A MATCH

BY A PLAYER

Date	Player	Opponent	Pts.
06/07/1993	Jaco Coetzee	Kenya	**35**
26/05/2007	Justinus van der Westhuizen	Zambia	**33**
21/04/1990	Moolman Olivier	Portugal	**26**
15/06/2002	Riaan van Wyk	Madagascar	**25**
21/04/1990	Gerhard Mans	Portugal	**24**

MOST TRIES IN A MATCH

BY A PLAYER

Date	Player	Opponent	Tries
21/04/1990	Gerhard Mans	Portugal	**6**
15/06/2002	Riaan van Wyk	Madagascar	**5**
16/05/1992	Eden Meyer	Zimbabwe	**4**
16/08/2003	Melrick Africa	Kenya	**4**

MOST CONVERSIONS IN A MATCH

BY A PLAYER

Date	Player	Opponent	Cons
21/04/1990	Moolman Olivier	Portugal	11
27/05/2006	Morne Schreuder	Kenya	11
26/05/2007	Justinus van der Westhuizen	Zambia	9
31/08/2003	Rudi van Vuuren	Uganda	8
04/07/1993	Jaco Coetzee	Arabian Gulf	8

MOST PENALTIES IN A MATCH

BY A PLAYER

Date	Player	Opponent	Pens
22/06/1991	Jaco Coetzee	Italy	5
23/01/1998	Rudi van Vuuren	Portugal	5
30/06/1990	Shaun McCulley	France A	5

MOST DROP GOALS IN A MATCH

BY A PLAYER

1 on 7 Occasions

MOST CAPPED PLAYERS

Name	Caps
Herman Lindvelt	32
Jaco Coetzee	28
Casper Derks	28

LEADING TRY SCORERS

Name	Tries
Gerhard Mans	27
Eden Meyer	21
Melrick Africa	12

LEADING CONVERSIONS SCORERS

Name	Cons
Jaco Coetzee	84
Morne Schreuder	36
Rudi van Vuuren	26
Emile Wessels	13

LEADING PENALTY SCORERS

Name	Pens
Jaco Coetzee	46
Morne Schreuder	18
Rudi van Vuuren	14
Lean van Dyk	11

LEADING DROP GOAL SCORERS

Name	DGs
Jaco Coetzee	3

LEADING POINTS SCORERS

Name	Pts.
Jaco Coetzee	344
Morne Schreuder	146
Gerhard Mans	118
Rudi van Vuuren	109
Eden Meyer	98

NEW ZEALAND

NEW ZEALAND'S 2006–07 TEST RECORD

OPPONENTS	DATE	VENUE	RESULT
England	5 November	A	**Won** 41–20
France	11 November	A	**Won** 47–3
France	18 November	A	**Won** 23–11
Wales	25 November	A	**Won** 45–10
France	2 June	H	**Won** 42–11
France	9 June	H	**Won** 61–10
Canada	16 June	H	**Won** 64–13
South Africa	23 June	A	**Won** 26–21
Australia	30 June	A	**Lost** 15–20
South Africa	14 July	H	**Won** 33–6
Australia	21 July	H	**Won** 26–12
Italy	8 September	N	**Won** 76–14 (WC)
Portugal	15 September	N	**Won** 108–13 (WC)
Scotland	24 September	N	**Won** 40–0 (WC)
Romania	29 September	N	**Won** 85–8 (WC)
France	6 October	N	**Lost** 20–18 (WC)

MASTER PLAN HITS THE BUFFERS

By Iain Spragg

Phil Walter/Getty Images

The defeated All Blacks got a sympathetic response on their return to New Zealand.

New Zealand's agonising wait to reclaim the Webb Ellis Cup will be prolonged until 2011 at the earliest after the All Blacks yet again contrived to defy the form book and crash out of the Rugby World Cup to France.

The Kiwis host the tournament in four years time but whether the mental scars of their shock quarter-final defeat to France have healed by then remains to be seen.

It was the first time the All Blacks have failed to reach the last four and the memories of their inaugural triumph in 1987 are becoming increasingly sepia-tinted by the year.

New Zealand were the hottest favourites in the history of the competition but it was France again who proved their nemesis – as they had done in their famous 1999 semi-final clash – and the Kiwis' 20–18 defeat in Cardiff was as heartbreaking as it was unexpected for a nation so desperate to be crowned world champions for a second time.

The fallout from defeat at the Millennium Stadium was swift. Henry's four-year master plan to reassert All Black dominance – which had yielded 38 wins in 43 Tests since 2003 – lay in tatters and the soul searching and recrimination began.

"They were the right strategies coming into this World Cup," Henry said defiantly after the defeat. "Everybody agreed they were the right strategies within the group and we worked extremely hard on those strategies and they have been successful in our test match record over a long period of time.

"I feel comfortable that I've done everything I can to try to ensure that we have done the best we can as an All Blacks side, so that's for other people to judge really."

There were certainly no signs of any chinks in the All Black armour at the start of the tournament. They made their bow against the Italians in Marseille but any thoughts the abrasive Azzurri might stretch the Kiwis were dispelled after just 60 seconds when captain Richie McCaw strolled over for the first of their 11 tries. Doug Howlett helped himself to a hat-trick and New Zealand were 76–14 winners.

World Cup debutantes Portugal were never going to be more than sacrificial lambs on the All Black altar in Lyon and so it proved as Henry's side moved effortlessly through the gears in a 108–13 romp which revealed little about their readiness for the latter stages of the competition.

Their third Pool C game against Scotland was supposed to be the sterner examination they needed but Scotland coach Frank Hadden, mindful of his team's make-or-break clash with Italy a week later, decided to rest most of his first-choice line-up and effectively fielded his second team at Murrayfield. The match was not a classic and although New Zealand coasted to a 40–0 victory in Edinburgh, the performance was far from faultless and the first questions about the Blacks' position as tournament favourites were raised.

"We blew a few tries through errors so that was a little disappointing and we will address that," Henry conceded after the game. "It was highly contested in the tackle area, a very physical game, the most physical we have had and that will be a valuable lesson for us. We scrummed the best we have in the tournament. Defensively we were good and offensively we scored six tries."

Romania were the final opponents in the group stages and once again the Kiwis crossed in the first minute of the match through Sitiveni Sivivatu. Twelve more tries followed in Toulouse and the All Blacks were safely through to the quarter-finals.

The form book had suggested they would face Argentina in the last eight but the Pumas' surprise victory over France in Paris had changed all that and it was Les Bleus who now stood in their way at the Millennium Stadium.

France opted to face down the Blacks' haka in Cardiff but it was the Kiwis who drew first blood with a Dan Carter penalty and they extended their advantage when Luke McAlister dived over after breaking through the French midfield. Carter's second penalty on the half hour made it 13–0 and New Zealand appeared to be coasting to victory. Fly-half Lionel Beauxis landed a penalty with the final kick of the first-half to get France on the scoreboard but there were still no signs of the drama that was to unfold after the break.

The defining moment of the match came on 46 minutes. Beauxis chipped through, Yannick Jauzion gave chase but collided with McAlister and referee Wayne Barnes decided the New Zealander had to go to the sin bin. Replays suggested it was a harsh decision but Beauxis landed the subsequent penalty and France were clawing their way back into the game.

New Zealand suddenly looked vulnerable and France capitalised on their numerical advantage with a try from flanker Thierry Dusatoir, which Beauxis converted, and it was all square at 13–13. Minutes later Carter limped off but the All Blacks were back in front on 62 minutes when Rodney So'oialo wriggled over from close range although McAlister crucially spurned the extra two points.

The stage was set for a grandstand finish and it was the French who provided it. Damien Traille broke the defensive line and although his offload to replacement Frederic Michalak looked forward, play continued and Yannick Jauzion was on hand to finish off the move. Jean-Baptiste Elissalde landed the conversion and Les Bleus were 20–18 in front.

New Zealand had 10 minutes to redeem themselves but France had the momentum and they repelled the inevitable onslaught and when Elissalde kicked to touch to confirm another famous victory, the look on the All Black faces said it all.

"I'm lost for words," McCaw as he forlornly surveyed the wreckage. "With France, we always knew they could come back in the second half. We lost our composure but I thought we could get it back. I can't explain it. We believed we had what it takes. It's a day you try to forget."

It will be even harder to forget when they look back on their impressive run to the World Cup, which suggested the Kiwis' name was already etched on the trophy. The autumn internationals saw England, France and Wales all convincingly put in their place and the French provided little more resistance in the summer when they travelled to New Zealand for a two-Test series.

The French squad bore no resemblance to the one that would shock the Blacks in Cardiff because of a fixture clash with the final two weeks of the Top 14 programme and Henry's side had little trouble despatching the weakened visitors in Auckland.

"When sides are coming to this side of the world that are not as strong as they should be, that's not good for the game," Henry said after his side's 42–11 victory. "We're holding up our end of the bargain, we're showing a lot of integrity there. We're putting the international game first but it's not a good situation at the moment."

The second Test in Wellington was just as one-sided as the All Blacks ran in nine tries to condemn France to a record 61–10 loss and set a new world record of 23 straight home wins. Les Bleus may have been a second string side but New Zealand looked in irresistible form.

A truncated Tri-Nations campaign would stretch them further but neither Australia nor South Africa could ultimately stop the Kiwis claiming their eighth title and third in succession.

The tournament began with a hard-fought win over the Springboks in Durban. South Africa led 21–12 with quarter of an hour to go and seemed to be heading for victory but late tries from Richie McCaw and Joe Rokocoko sealed an impressive comeback and New Zealand emerged 26–21 victors.

Australia then lay in wait in Melbourne but the Kiwis appeared in control at half-time with tries from Tony Woodcock and Rico Gear and a 15–6 advantage. But the Wallabies had other ideas and when Carl Hayman was yellow-carded on the hour they came storming back with scores from Adam Ashley-Cooper and Scott Staniforth to grab a 20–15 triumph and their first win over their old rivals since 2004.

"Obviously we're disappointed in the result," Henry said after the game. "But it could be a good thing in a couple of respects. It will make us re-think what we're doing. Hopefully it will be character building and motivational for us."

New Zealand bounced back against a depleted Springbok XV in Christchurch and although it was a far from fluid performance, Henry's side were never in trouble in a 33–6 win and they welcomed the Wallabies a week later for the decider at Eden Park.

Four Carter penalties gave the home side a platform in the rain in Auckland and when Tony Woodcock crashed over for the game's only try on the hour, New Zealand were out of sight and they wrapped up the match 26–12 to claim the Tri-Nations title and Bledisloe Cup.

The All Blacks had reaffirmed their status as the number one side in the game and headed to the World Cup confident they were ready to end their tortuous 20 year wait to lift the Webb Ellis Cup once again. France, however, failed to read the script.

Sandra Mu/Getty Images

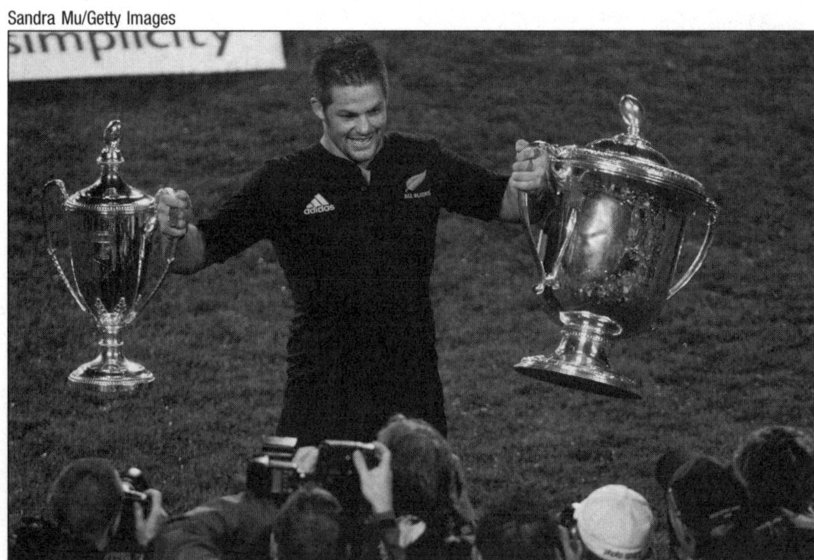

At least New Zealand captain Richie McCaw emerged from 2007 with the Tri-Nations tournament trophy and Bledisloe Cup trophies . . . scant consolation for the World Cup though.

NEW ZEALAND INTERNATIONAL STATISTICS

MATCH RECORDS UP TO 31ST OCTOBER 2007

MOST CONSECUTIVE TEST WINS

17 1965 SA 4, 1966 BI 1,2,3,4, 1967 A,E,W,F,S, 1968 A 1,2, F 1,2,3, 1969 W 1,2

15 2005 A 1, SA 2, A 2, W,I E,S, 2006 I 1,2, Arg, A 1, SA 1, A 2, 3, SA 2

12 1988 A 3, 1989 F 1,2, Arg 1,2, A,W,I, 1990 S 1,2 A 1,2

MOST CONSECUTIVE TESTS WITHOUT DEFEAT

Matches	Wins	Draws	Periods
23	22	1	1987 to 1990
17	17	0	1965 to 1969
17	15	2	1961 to 1964
15	15	0	2005 to 2006

MOST POINTS IN A MATCH

BY THE TEAM

Pts.	Opponent	Venue	Year
145	Japan	Bloemfontein	1995
108	Portugal	Lyon	2007
102	Tonga	Albany	2000
101	Italy	Huddersfield	1999
93	Argentina	Wellington	1997
91	Tonga	Brisbane	2003
91	Fiji	Albany	2005
85	Romania	Toulouse	2007
76	Italy	Marseille	2007
74	Fiji	Christchurch	1987
73	Canada	Auckland	1995
71	Fiji	Albany	1997
71	Samoa	Albany	1999

BY A PLAYER

Pts.	Player	Opponent	Venue	Year
45	S D Culhane	Japan	Bloemfontein	1995
36	T E Brown	Italy	Huddersfield	1999
33	C J Spencer	Argentina	Wellington	1997
33	A P Mehrtens	Ireland	Dublin	1997
33	D W Carter	British/Irish	Wellington	2005
33	N J Evans	Portugal	Lyons	2007
32	T E Brown	Tonga	Albany	2000
30	M C G Ellis	Japan	Bloemfontein	1995
30	T E Brown	Samoa	Albany	2001
29	A P Mehrtens	Australia	Auckland	1999
29	A P Mehrtens	France	Paris	2000
29	L R MacDonald	Tonga	Brisbane	2003
29	D W Carter	Canada	Hamilton	2007

MOST TRIES IN A MATCH

BY THE TEAM

Tries	Opponent	Venue	Year
21	Japan	Bloemfontein	1995
16	Portugal	Lyon	2007
15	Tonga	Albany	2000
15	Fiji	Albany	2005
14	Argentina	Wellington	1997
14	Italy	Huddersfield	1999
13	U S A	Berkeley	1913
13	Tonga	Brisbane	2003
13	Romania	Toulouse	2007
12	Italy	Auckland	1987
12	Fiji	Christchurch	1987

BY A PLAYER

Tries	Player	Opponent	Venue	Year
6	M C G Ellis	Japan	Bloemfontein	1995
5	J W Wilson	Fiji	Albany	1997
4	D McGregor	England	Crystal Palace	1905
4	C I Green	Fiji	Christchurch	1987
4	J A Gallagher	Fiji	Christchurch	1987
4	J J Kirwan	Wales	Christchurch	1988
4	J T Lomu	England	Cape Town	1995
4	C M Cullen	Scotland	Dunedin	1996
4	J W Wilson	Samoa	Albany	1999
4	J M Muliaina	Canada	Melbourne	2003
4	S W Sivivatu	Fiji	Albany	2005

MOST CONVERSIONS IN A MATCH

BY THE TEAM

Cons	Opponent	Venue	Year
20	Japan	Bloemfontein	1995
14	Portugal	Lyon	2007
13	Tonga	Brisbane	2003
12	Tonga	Albany	2000
11	Italy	Huddersfield	1999
10	Fiji	Christchurch	1987
10	Argentina	Wellington	1997
10	Romania	Toulouse	2007
9	Canada	Melbourne	2003
9	Italy	Marseille	2007
8	Italy	Auckland	1987
8	Wales	Auckland	1988
8	Fiji	Albany	1997
8	Italy	Hamilton	2003
8	Fiji	Albany	2005

BY A PLAYER

Cons	Player	Opponent	Venue	Year
20	S D Culhane	Japan	Bloemfontein	1995
14	N J Evans	Portugal	Lyons	2007
12	T E Brown	Tonga	Albany	2000
12	L R MacDonald	Tonga	Brisbane	2003
11	T E Brown	Italy	Huddersfield	1999
10	G J Fox	Fiji	Christchurch	1987
10	C J Spencer	Argentina	Wellington	1997
9	D W Carter	Canada	Melbourne	2003
8	G J Fox	Italy	Auckland	1987
8	G J Fox	Wales	Auckland	1988
8	A P Mehrtens	Italy	Hamilton	2002

MOST DROPED GOALS IN A MATCH

BY THE TEAM

Drops	Opponent	Venue	Year
3	France	Christchurch	1986

BY A PLAYER

Drops	Player	Opponent	Venue	Year
2	O D Bruce	Ireland	Dublin	1978
2	F M Botica	France	Christchurch	1986
2	A P Mehrtens	Australia	Auckland	1995

MOST PENALTIES IN A MATCH

BY THE TEAM

Pens	Opponent	Venue	Year
9	Australia	Auckland	1999
9	France	Paris	2000
7	Western Samoa	Auckland	1993
7	South Africa	Pretoria	1999
7	South Africa	Wellington	2006
7	Australia	Auckland	2007
6	British/Irish Lions	Dunedin	1959
6	England	Christchurch	1985
6	Argentina	Wellington	1987
6	Scotland	Christchurch	1987
6	France	Paris	1990
6	South Africa	Auckland	1994
6	Australia	Brisbane	1996
6	Ireland	Dublin	1997
6	South Africa	Cardiff	1999
6	Scotland	Murrayfield	2001
6	South Africa	Christchurch	2004
6	Australia	Sydney	2004

BY A PLAYER

Pens	Player	Opponent	Venue	Year
9	A P Mehrtens	Australia	Auckland	1999
9	A P Mehrtens	France	Paris	2000
7	G J Fox	Western Samoa	Auckland	1993
7	A P Mehrtens	South Africa	Pretoria	1999
7	D W Carter	South Africa	Wellington	2006
7	D W Carter	Australia	Auckland	2007
6	D B Clarke	British/Irish Lions	Dunedin	1959
6	K J Crowley	England	Christchurch	1985
6	G J Fox	Argentina	Wellington	1987
6	G J Fox	Scotland	Christchurch	1987
6	G J Fox	France	Paris	1990
6	S P Howarth	South Africa	Auckland	1994
6	A P Mehrtens	Australia	Brisbane	1996
6	A P Mehrtens	Ireland	Dublin	1997
6	A P Mehrtens	South Africa	Cardiff	1999
6	A P Mehrtens	Scotland	Murrayfield	2001

MOST CAPPED PLAYERS

Caps	Player	Career Span
92	S B T Fitzpatrick	1986 to 1997
81	J W Marshall	1995 to 2005
79	I D Jones	1990 to 1999
74	J F Umaga	1997 to 2005
70	A P Mehrtens	1995 to 2004
67	C R Jack	2001 to 2007
63	J J Kirwan	1984 to 1994
63	J T Lomu	1994 to 2002
62	R M Brooke	1992 to 1999
62	D C Howlett	2000 to 2007
60	C W Dowd	1993 to 2001
60	J W Wilson	1993 to 2001
59	R H McCaw	2001 to 2007
59	A D Oliver	1997 to 2007
58	G W Whetton	1981 to 1991
58	Z V Brooke	1987 to 1997
58	C M Cullen	1996 to 2002
57	B T Kelleher	1999 to 2007
57	G M Somerville	2000 to 2007
56	O M Brown	1992 to 1998
55	C E Meads	1957 to 1971
55	F E Bunce	1992 to 1997
55	M N Jones	1987 to 1998
55	J M Muliaina	2003 to 2007
54	J A Kronfeld	1995 to 2000

MOST CONSECUTIVE TESTS

Tests	Player	Career span
63	S B T Fitzpatrick	1986 to 1995
51	C M Cullen	1996 to 2000
49	R M Brooke	1995 to 1999
41	J W Wilson	1996 to 1999
40	G W Whetton	1986 to 1991

MOST TESTS AS CAPTAIN

Tests	Player	Career span
51	S B T Fitzpatrick	1992 to 1997
30	W J Whineray	1958 to 1965
23	R H McCaw	2004 to 2007
22	T C Randell	1998 to 2002
22	R D Thorne	2002 to 2003
21	J F Umaga	2004 to 2005
19	G N K Mourie	1977 to 1982
18	B J Lochore	1966 to 1970
17	A G Dalton	1981 to 1985

MOST POINTS IN TESTS

Points	Player	Tests	Career
967	A P Mehrtens	70	1995 to 2004
676	D W Carter	44	2003 to 2007
645	G J Fox	46	1985 to 1993
291	C J Spencer	35	1997 to 2004
245	D C Howlett	62	2000 to 2007
236	C M Cullen	58	1996 to 2002
234	J W Wilson	60	1993 to 2001
215	J T Rokocoko	48	2003 to 2007
207	D B Clarke	31	1956 to 1964
201	A R Hewson	19	1981 to 1984
185	J T Lomu	63	1994 to 2002
185	J F Umaga	74	1997 to 2005

MOST TRIES IN TESTS

Tries	Player	Tests	Career
49	D C Howlett	62	2000 to 2007
46	C M Cullen	58	1996 to 2002
44	J W Wilson	60	1993 to 2001
43	J T Rokocoko	48	2003 to 2007
37	J T Lomu	63	1994 to 2002
37*	J F Umaga	74	1999 to 2005
35	J J Kirwan	63	1984 to 1994
24	J W Marshall	81	1995 to 2005
21	D W Carter	44	2003 to 2007
21	S W Sivivatu	21	2005 to 2007
20	F E Bunce	55	1992 to 1997
19	S S Wilson	34	1977 to 1983
19*	T J Wright	30	1986 to 1991

* Umaga and Wright's hauls each include a penalty try

MOST CONVERSIONS IN TESTS

Cons	Player	Tests	Career
169	A P Mehrtens	70	1995 to 2004
122	D W Carter	44	2003 to 2007
118	G J Fox	46	1985 to 1993
49	C J Spencer	35	1997 to 2004
43	T E Brown	18	1999 to 2001
33	D B Clarke	31	1956 to 1964
32	S D Culhane	6	1995 to 1996

MOST PENALTY GOALS IN TESTS

Penalties	Player	Tests	Career
188	A P Mehrtens	70	1995 to 2004
128	G J Fox	46	1985 to 1993
108	D W Carter	44	2003 to 2007
43	A R Hewson	19	1981 to 1984
41	C J Spencer	35	1997 to 2004
38	D B Clarke	31	1956 to 1964
24	W F McCormick	16	1965 to 1971

MOST DROPPED GOALS IN TESTS

Drops	Player	Tests	Career
10	A P Mehrtens	70	1995 to 2004
7	G J Fox	46	1985 to 1993
5	D B Clarke	31	1956 to 1964
5	M A Herewini	10	1962 to 1967
5	O D Bruce	14	1976 to 1978

TRI NATIONS RECORDS

RECORD	DETAIL	HOLDER	SET
Most points in season	179	in six matches	2006
Most tries in season	17	in four matches	1997
	17	in four matches	2003
	17	in six matches	2006
Highest Score	55	55-35 v S Africa (h)	1997
Biggest win	37	43-6 v Australia (h)	1996
Highest score conceded	46	40-46 v S Africa (a)	2000
Biggest defeat	21	7-28 v Australia (a)	1999
Most points in matches	328	A P Mehrtens	1996 to 2004
Most points in season	99	D W Carter	2006
Most points in match	29	A P Mehrtens	v Australia (h) 1999
Most tries in matches	16	C M Cullen	1996 to 2002
Most tries in season	7	C M Cullen	2000
Most tries in match	3	J T Rokococo	v Australia (a) 2003
	3	D C Howlett	v Australia (h) 2005
Most cons in matches	34	A P Mehrtens	1996 to 2004
Most cons in season	14	D W Carter	2006
Most cons in match	4	C J Spencer	(v S Africa h) 1997
	4	A P Mehrtens	v Australia (a) 2000
	4	A P Mehrtens	v S Africa (a) 2000
	4	C J Spencer	v S Africa (a) 2003
	4	D W Carter	v S Africa (a) 2006
Most pens in matches	82	A P Mehrtens	1996 to 2004
Most pens in season	21	D W Carter	2006
Most pens in match	9	A P Mehrtens	v Australia (h) 1999

MISCELLANEOUS RECORDS

RECORD	HOLDER	DETAIL
Longest Test Career	E Hughes/C E Meads	1907-21/1957-71
Youngest Test Cap	J T Lomu	19 yrs 45 days in 1994
Oldest Test Cap	E Hughes	40 yrs 123 days in 1921

CAREER RECORDS OF NEW ZEALAND INTERNATIONAL PLAYERS (PLAYERS CAPPED SINCE THE START OF RWC 2003 UP TO 31 OCTOBER 2007)

PLAYER BACKS	DEBUT	CAPS	T	C	P	D	PTS
D W Carter	2003 v W	44	21	122	108	1	676
A M Ellis	2006 v E	4	1	0	0	0	5
N J Evans	2004 v E	16	5	30	6	0	103
R L Gear	2004 v PI	19	11	0	0	0	55
D C Howlett	2000 v Tg	62	49	0	0	0	245
B T Kelleher	1999 v WS	57	8	0	0	0	40
B G Leonard	2007 v F	9	2	0	0	0	10
C L McAlister	2005 v BI	22	7	23	13	0	120
L R MacDonald	2000 v S	51	15*	25	7	0	146
A J D Mauger	2001 v I	45	13	8	1	2	90
J M Muliaina	2003 v E	55	16	0	0	0	80
M A Nonu	2003 v E	18	3	0	0	0	15
J T Rokocoko	2003 v E	48	43	0	0	0	215
S W Sivivatu	2005 v Fj	21	21	0	0	0	105
C G Smith	2004 v It	12	6	0	0	0	30
I Toeava	2005 v S	15	5	0	0	0	25
P A T Weepu	2004 v W	20	3	1	1	0	20

FORWARDS							
I F Afoa	2005 v I	3	0	0	0	0	0
J Collins	2001 v Arg	48	5	0	0	0	25
C D Dermody	2006 v I	3	1	0	0	0	5
J J Eaton	2005 v I	10	1	0	0	0	5
R A Filipo	2007 v C	3	0	0	0	0	0
T V Flavell	2000 v Tg	22	6	0	0	0	30
C J Hayman	2001 v Sm	45	2	0	0	0	10
A K Hore	2002 v E	25	3	0	0	0	15
C R Jack	2001 v Arg	67	5	0	0	0	25
S T Lauaki	2005 v Fj	11	1	0	0	0	5
R H McCaw	2001 v I	59	13	0	0	0	65
M C Masoe	2005 v W	20	3	0	0	0	15
K F Mealamu	2002 v W	50	8	0	0	0	40
A D Oliver	1997 v Fj	59	3	0	0	0	15
G P Rawlinson	2006 v I	4	0	0	0	0	0
K J Robinson	2002 v E	12	0	0	0	0	0
J A C Ryan	2005 v Fj	9	0	0	0	0	0
J E Schwalger	2007 v C	1	1	0	0	0	5
G M Somerville	2000 v Tg	57	1	0	0	0	5
R So'oialo	2002 v W	41	6	0	0	0	30
R D Thorne	1999 v SA	50	5	0	0	0	25
N S Tialata	2005 v W	21	1	0	0	0	5
A J Williams	2002 v E	46	6	0	0	0	30
T D Woodcock	2002 v W	37	2	0	0	0	10

NB MacDonald's figures include a penalty try awarded against South Africa in 2001.

Stu Foster/Getty Images

New Zealand lost serveral of their most experienced players after the World Cup, including their most-capped current player, Chris Jack, who moved to Saracens.

NEW ZEALAND INTERNATIONAL PLAYERS

UP TO 31ST OCTOBER 2007

Entries in square brackets denote matches played in RWC Finals.

Abbott, H L (Taranaki) 1906 F
Afoa, I F (Auckland) 2005 I,S, 2006 E(R)
Aitken, G G (Wellington) 1921 SA 1,2
Alatini, P F (Otago) 1999 F 1(R), [It, SA 3(R)], 2000 Tg, S 1, A 1, SA 1, A 2, SA 2, It, 2001 Sm, Arg 1, F, SA 1, A 1, SA 2, A 2
Allen, F R (Auckland) 1946 A 1,2, 1947 A 1,2, 1949 SA 1,2
Allen, M R (Taranaki, Manawatu) 1993 WS (t), 1996 S 2 (t), 1997 Arg 1(R),2(R), SA 2(R), A 3(R), E 2, W (R)
Allen, N H (Counties) 1980 A 3, W
Alley, G T (Canterbury) 1928 SA 1,2,3
Anderson, A (Canterbury) 1983 S, E, 1984 A 1,2,3, 1987 [Fj]
Anderson, B L (Wairarapa-Bush) 1986 A 1
Anesi, S R (Waikato) 2005 Fj(R)
Archer, W R (Otago, Southland) 1955 A 1,2, 1956 SA 1,3
Argus, W G (Canterbury) 1946 A 1,2, 1947 A 1,2
Arnold, D A (Canterbury) 1963 I, W, 1964 E, F
Arnold, K D (Waikato) 1947 A 1,2
Ashby, D L (Southland) 1958 A 2
Asher, A A (Auckland) 1903 A
Ashworth, B G (Auckland) 1978 A 1,2
Ashworth, J C (Canterbury, Hawke's Bay) 1978 A 1,2,3, 1980 A 1,2,3, 1981 SA 1,2,3, 1982 A 1,2, 1983 BI 1,2,3,4, A, 1984 F 1,2, A 1,2,3, 1985 E 1,2, A
Atiga, B A C (Auckland) 2003 [Tg(R)]
Atkinson, H (West Coast) 1913 A 1
Avery, H E (Wellington) 1910 A 1,2,3

Bachop, G T M (Canterbury) 1989 W, I, 1990 S 1,2, A 1,2,3, F 1,2, 1991 Arg 1,2, A 1,2, [E, US, C, A, S], 1992 Wld 1, 1994 SA 1,2,3, A, 1995 C, [I, W, S, E, SA], A 1,2
Bachop, S J (Otago) 1994 F 2, SA 1,2,3, A
Badeley, C E O (Auckland) 1921 SA 1,2
Baird, J A S (Otago) 1913 A 2
Ball, N (Wellington) 1931 A, 1932 A 2,3, 1935 W, 1936 E
Barrett, J (Auckland) 1913 A 2,3
Barry, E F (Wellington) 1934 A 2
Barry, L J (North Harbour) 1995 F 2
Bates, S P (Waikato) 2004 It(R)
Batty, G B (Wellington, Bay of Plenty) 1972 W, S, 1973 E 1, I, F, E 2, 1974 A 1,3, I, 1975 S, 1976 SA 1,2,3,4, 1977 BI 1
Batty, W (Auckland) 1930 BI 1,3,4, 1931 A
Beatty, G E (Taranaki) 1950 BI 1
Bell, R H (Otago) 1951 A 3, 1952 A 1,2
Bellis, E A (Wanganui) 1921 SA 1,2,3
Bennet, R (Otago) 1905 A
Berghan, T (Otago) 1938 A 1,2,3
Berry, M J (Wairarapa-Bush) 1986 A 3(R)
Berryman, N R (Northland) 1998 SA 2(R)
Bevan, V D (Wellington) 1949 A 1,2, 1950 BI 1,2,3,4
Birtwistle, W M (Canterbury) 1965 SA 1,2,3,4, 1967 E, W, S
Black, J E (Canterbury) 1977 F 1, 1979 A, 1980 A 3
Black, N W (Auckland) 1949 SA 3
Black, R S (Otago) 1914 A 1
Blackadder, T J (Canterbury) 1998 E 1(R),2, 2000 Tg, S 1,2, A 1, SA 1, A 2, SA 2, F 1,2, It
Blair, B A (Canterbury) 2001 S (R), Arg 2, 2002 E, W
Blake, A W (Wairarapa) 1949 A 1
Blowers, A F (Auckland) 1996 SA 2(R),4(R), 1997 I, E 1(R), W (R), 1999 F 1(R), SA 1, A 1(R), SA 2, A 2(R), [It]
Boggs, E G (Auckland) 1946 A 2, 1949 SA 1
Bond, J G (Canterbury) 1949 A 2
Booth, E E (Otago) 1906 F, 1907 A 1,3
Boroevich, K G (Wellington) 1986 F 1, A 1, F 3(R)
Botica, F M (North Harbour) 1986 F 1, A 1,2,3, F 2,3, 1989 Arg 1(R)
Bowden, N J G (Taranaki) 1952 A 2
Bowers, R G (Wellington) 1954 I, F
Bowman, A W (Hawke's Bay) 1938 A 1,2,3
Braid, D J (Auckland) 2002 W, 2003 [C(R),Tg]
Braid, G J (Bay of Plenty) 1983 S, E
Bremner, S G (Auckland, Canterbury) 1952 A 2, 1956 SA 2
Brewer, M R (Otago, Canterbury) 1986 F 1, A 1,2,3, F 2,3, 1988 A 1, 1989 A, W, I, 1990 S 1,2, A 1,2,3, F 1,2, 1992 I 2, A 1, 1994 F 1,2, SA 1,2,3, A, 1995 C, [I, W, E, SA], A 1,2
Briscoe, K C (Taranaki) 1959 BI 2, 1960 SA 1,2,3,4, 1963 I, W, 1964 E, S
Brooke, R M (Auckland) 1992 I 2, A 1,2,3, SA, 1993 BI 1,2,3, A, WS, 1994 SA 2,3, 1995 C, [J, S, E, SA], A 1,2, It, F 1,2, 1996 WS, S 1,2, A 1, SA 1, A 2, SA 2,3,4,5, 1997 Fj, Arg 1,2, A 1, SA 1, A 2, SA 2, A 3, I, E 1, W, E 2, 1998 E 1,2, A 1, SA 1, A 2, SA 2, A 3, 1999 WS, F 1, SA 1, A 1, SA 2, A 2, [Tg, E, It (R), S, F 2]
Brooke, Z V (Auckland) 1987 [Arg], 1989 Arg 2(R), 1990 A 1,2,3, F 1(R), 1991 Arg 2, A 1,2, [E, It, C, A, S], 1992 A 2,3, SA, 1993 BI 1,2,3(R), WS (R), S, E, 1994 F 2, SA 1,2,3, A, 1995 [J, S, E, SA], A 1,2, It, F 1,2, 1996 WS, S 1,2, A 1, SA 1, A 2, SA 2,3,4,5, 1997 Arg 1,2, A 1, SA 1, A 2, SA 2, A 3, I, E 1, W, E 2
Brooke-Cowden, M (Auckland) 1986 F 1, A 1, 1987 [W]
Broomhall, S R (Canterbury) 2002 SA 1(R),2(R), E, F
Brown, C (Taranaki) 1913 A 2,3
Brown, O M (Auckland) 1992 I 2, A 1,2,3, SA, 1993 BI 1,2,3, A, S, E, 1994 F 1,2, SA 1,2,3, A, 1995 C, [I, W, S, E, SA], A 1,2, It, F 1,2, 1996 WS, S 1,2, A 1, SA 1, A 2, SA 2,3,4,5, 1997 Fj, Arg 1,2, A 1, SA 1, A 2, SA 2, A 3, I, E 1, W, E 2, 1998 E 1,2, A 1, SA 1, A 2, SA 2
Brown, R H (Taranaki) 1955 A 3, 1956 SA 1,2,3,4, 1957 A 1,2, 1958 A 1,2,3, 1959 BI 1,3, 1961 F 1,2,3, 1962 A 1
Brown, T E (Otago) 1999 WS, F 1(R), SA 1(R), A 1(R),2(R), [E (R), It, S (R)], 2000 Tg, S 2(R), A 1(R), SA 1(R), A 2(R), 2001 Sm, Arg 1(R), F, SA 1, A 1
Brownlie, C J (Hawke's Bay) 1924 W, 1925 E, F
Brownlie, M J (Hawke's Bay) 1924 I, W, 1925 E, F, 1928 SA 1,2,3,4
Bruce, J A (Auckland) 1914 A 1,2
Bruce, O D (Canterbury) 1976 SA 1,2,4, 1977 BI 2,3,4, F 1,2, 1978 A 1,2, I, W, E, S
Bryers, R F (King Country) 1949 A 1
Budd, T A (Southland) 1946 A 2, 1949 A 2
Bullock-Douglas, G A H (Wanganui) 1932 A 1,2,3, 1934 A 1,2
Bunce, F E (North Harbour) 1992 Wld 1,2,3, I 1,2, A 1,2,3, SA, 1993 BI 1,2,3, A, WS, S, E, 1994 F 1,2, SA 1,2,3, A, 1995 C, [I, W, S, E, SA], A 1,2, It, F 1,2, 1996 WS, S 1,2, A1, SA 1, A 2, SA 2,3,4,5, 1997 Fj, Arg 1,2, A 1, SA 1, A 2, SA 2, A 3, I, E 1, W, E 2
Burgess, G A J (Auckland) 1981 SA 2
Burgess, G F (Southland) 1905 A
Burgess, R E (Manawatu) 1971 BI 1,2,3, 1972 A 3, W, 1973 I, F
Burke, P S (Taranaki) 1955 A 1, 1957 A 1,2

Burns, P J (Canterbury) 1908 AW 2, 1910 A 1,2,3, 1913 A 3
Bush, R G (Otago) 1931 A
Bush, W K (Canterbury) 1974 A 1,2, 1975 S, 1976 I, SA, 2,4, 1977 BI 2,3,4(R), 1978 I, W, 1979 A
Buxton, J B (Canterbury) 1955 A 3, 1956 SA 1

Cain, M J (Taranaki) 1913 US, 1914 A 1,2,3
Callesen, J A (Manawatu) 1974 A 1,2,3, 1975 S
Cameron, D (Taranaki) 1908 AW 1,2,3
Cameron, L M (Manawatu) 1980 A 3, 1981 SA 1(R),2,3, R
Carleton, S R (Canterbury) 1928 SA 1,2,3, 1929 A 1,2,3
Carrington, K R (Auckland) 1971 BI 1,3,4
Carter, D W (Canterbury) 2003 W, F, A 1(R),[It,C,Tg,SA(R),F(R)], 2004 E1,2,PI,A1,SA1,A2,It,W,F, 2005 Fj,BI1,2,SA1,A1,W,E, 2006 Arg,A1,SA1,A2,3,SA2,3,E,F1,2,W, 2007 F1,C,SA1,A1, SA2,A2, [It,S,F]
Carter, M P (Auckland) 1991 A 2, [It, A], 1997 Fj (R), A 1(R), 1998 E 2(R), A 2
Casey, S T (Otago) 1905 S, I, E, W, 1907 A 1,2,3, 1908 AW 1
Cashmore, A R (Auckland) 1996 S 2(R), 1997 A 2(R)
Catley, E H (Waikato) 1946 A 1, 1947 A 1,2, 1949 SA 1,2,3,4
Caughey, T H C (Auckland) 1932 A 1,3, 1934 A 1,2, 1935 S, I, 1936 E, A 1, 1937 SA 3
Caulton, R W (Wellington) 1959 BI 2,3,4, 1960 SA 1,4, 1961 F 2, 1963 E 1,2, I, W, 1964 E, S, F, A 1,2,3
Cherrington, N P (North Auckland) 1950 BI 1
Christian, D L (Auckland) 1949 SA 4
Clamp, M (Wellington) 1984 A 2,3
Clark, D W (Otago) 1964 A 1,2
Clark, W H (Wellington) 1953 W, 1954 I, E, S, 1955 A 1,2, 1956 SA 2,3,4
Clarke, A H (Auckland) 1958 A 3, 1959 BI 4, 1960 SA 1
Clarke, D B (Waikato) 1956 SA 3,4, 1957 A 1,2, 1958 A 1,3, 1959 BI 1,2,3,4, 1960 SA 1,2,3,4, 1961 F 1,2,3, 1962 A 1,2,3,4,5, 1963 E 1,2, I, W, 1964 E, S, F, A 2,3
Clarke, E (Auckland) 1992 Wld 2,3, I 1,2, 1993 BI 1,2, S (R), E, 1998 SA 2, A 3
Clarke, I J (Waikato) 1953 W, 1955 A 1,2,3, 1956 SA 1,2,3,4, 1957 A 1,2, 1958 A 1,3, 1959 BI 1,2, 1960 SA 2,4, 1961 F 1,2,3, 1962 A 1,2,3, 1963 E 1,2
Clarke, R L (Taranaki) 1932 A 2,3
Cobden, D G (Canterbury) 1937 SA 1
Cockerill, M S (Taranaki) 1951 A 1,2,3
Cockroft, E A P (South Canterbury) 1913 A 3, 1914 A 2,3
Codlin, B W (Counties) 1980 A 1,2,3
Collins, A H (Taranaki) 1932 A 2,3, 1934 A 1
Collins, J (Wellington) 2001 Arg 1, 2003 E (R), W, F, SA 1, A 1, SA 2, A 2,[It,W,SA,A,F], 2004 E2(R),Arg,PI(R),A1(R),SA1,It,F, 2005 Fj,BI1,2,3,SA1,A1,SA2,W,E, 2006 Arg,A1,2,3,SA2(R),3, F1,2,W, 2007 F2,C,SA1,A1,SA2(R),A2, [It,Pt,R,F]
Collins, J L (Poverty Bay) 1964 A 1, 1965 SA 1,4
Colman, J T H (Taranaki) 1907 A 1,2, 1908 AW 1,3
Connor, D M (Auckland) 1961 F 1,2,3, 1962 A 1,2,3,4,5, 1963 E 1,2, 1964 A 2,3
Conway, R J (Otago, Bay of Plenty) 1959 BI 2,3,4, 1960 SA 1,3,4, 1965 SA 1,2,3,4
Cooke, A E (Auckland, Wellington) 1924 I, W, 1925 E, F, 1930 BI 1,2,3,4
Cooke, R J (Canterbury) 1903 A
Cooksley, M S B (Counties, Waikato) 1992 Wld 1, 1993 BI 2,3(R), A, 1994 F 1,2, SA 1,2, A, 2001 A 1(R), SA 2(t&R)
Cooper, G J L (Auckland, Otago) 1986 F 1, A 1,2, 1992 Wld 1,2,3, I 1
Cooper, M J A (Waikato) 1992 I 2, SA (R), 1993 BI 1(R),3(t), WS (t), S, 1994 F 1,2
Corner, M M N (Auckland) 1930 BI 2,3,4, 1931 A, 1934 A 1, 1936 E
Cossey, R R (Counties) 1958 A 1
Cottrell, A I (Canterbury) 1929 A 1,2,3, 1930 BI 1,2,3,4, 1931 A, 1932 A 1,2,3
Cottrell, W D (Canterbury) 1968 A 1,2, F 2,3, 1970 SA 1, 1971 BI 1,2,3,4
Couch, M B R (Wairarapa) 1947 A 1, 1949 A 1,2
Coughlan, T D (South Canterbury) 1958 A 1
Cowan, Q J (Southland) 2004 It(R), 2005 W(R),I(R),S(R), 2006 I1(R),SA1(R),A2(R),SA2(R),3
Creighton, J N (Canterbury) 1962 A 4
Cribb, R T (North Harbour) 2000 S 1,2, A 1, SA 1, A 2, SA 2, F 1,2, It, 2001 Sm, F, SA 1, A 1, SA 2, A 2
Crichton, S (Wellington) 1983 S, E
Cross, T (Canterbury) 1904 BI, 1905 A
Crowley, K J (Taranaki) 1985 E 1,2, A, Arg 1,2, 1986 A 3, F 2,3, 1987 [Arg], 1990 S 1,2, A 1,2,3, F 1,2, 1991 Arg 1,2, [A]
Crowley, P J B (Auckland) 1949 SA 3,4, 1950 BI 1,2,3,4
Culhane, S D (Southland) 1995 [J], It, F 1,2, 1996 SA 3,4
Cullen C M (Manawatu, Central Vikings, Wellington) 1996 WS, S 1,2, A 1, SA 1, A 2, SA 2,3,4,5, 1997 Fj, Arg 1,2, A 1, SA 1, A 2, SA 2, A 3, I, E 1, W, E 2, 1998 E 1,2, A 1, SA 1, A 2, SA 2, A 3, 1999 WS, F 1, SA 1, A 1, SA 2, A 2, [Tg, E, It (R), S, F 2, SA 3], 2000 Tg, S 1,2, A 1, SA 1, A 2, SA 2, F 1,2, It, 2001 A 2(R), 2002 It, Fj, A 1, SA 1, A 2, F
Cummings, W (Canterbury) 1913 A 2,3
Cundy, R T (Wairarapa) 1929 A 2(R)
Cunningham, G R (Auckland) 1979 A, S, E, 1980 A 1,2
Cunningham, W (Auckland) 1905 S, I, 1906 F, 1907 A 1,2,3, 1908 AW 1,2,3
Cupples, L F (Bay of Plenty) 1924 I, W
Currie, C J (Canterbury) 1978 I, W
Cuthill, J E (Otago) 1913 A 1, US

Dalley, W C (Canterbury) 1924 I, 1928 SA 1,2,3,4
Dalton, A G (Counties) 1977 F 2, 1978 A 1,2,3, I, W, E, S, 1979 F 1,2, S, 1981 S 1,2, SA 1,2,3, R, F 1,2, 1982 A 1,2,3, 1983 BI 1,2,3,4, A, 1984 F 1,2, A 1,2,3, 1985 E 1,2, A
Dalton, D (Hawke's Bay) 1935 I, W, 1936 A 1,2, 1937 SA 1,2,3, 1938 A 1,2
Dalton, R A (Wellington) 1947 A 1,2
Dalzell, G N (Canterbury) 1953 W, 1954 I, E, S, F
Davie, M G (Canterbury) 1983 E (R)
Davies, W A (Auckland, Otago) 1960 SA 4, 1962 A 4,5
Davis, K (Auckland) 1952 A 2, 1953 W, 1954 I, E, S, F, 1955 A 2, 1958 A 1,2,3
Davis, L J (Canterbury) 1976 I, 1977 BI 3,4
Davis, W L (Hawke's Bay) 1967 A, E, W, F, S, 1968 A 1,2, F 1, 1969 W 1,2, 1970 SA 2
Deans, I B (Canterbury) 1988 W 1,2, A 1,2,3, 1989 F 1,2, Arg 1,2, A
Deans, R G (Canterbury) 1905 S, I, E, W, 1908 AW 3
Deans, R M (Canterbury) 1983 S, E, 1984 A 1(R),2,3
Delamore, G W (Wellington) 1949 SA 4
Dermody, C (Southland) 2006 I1,2,E(R)
Devine, S J (Auckland) 2002 E, W 2003 E (R), W, F, SA 1, A 1(R), [C,SA(R),F]
Dewar, H (Taranaki) 1913 A 1, US
Diack, E S (Otago) 1959 BI 2
Dick, J (Auckland) 1937 SA 1,2, 1938 A 3
Dick, M J (Auckland) 1963 I, W, 1964 E, S, F, 1965 SA 3, 1966 BI 4, 1967 A, E, W, F, 1969 W 1,2, 1970 SA 1,4
Dixon, M J (Canterbury) 1954 I, E, S, F, 1956 SA 1,2,3,4, 1957 A 1,2
Dobson, R L (Auckland) 1949 A 1
Dodd, E H (Wellington) 1905 A
Donald, A J (Wanganui) 1983 S, E, 1984 F 1,2, A 1,2,3
Donald, J G (Wairarapa) 1921 SA 1,2
Donald, Q (Wairarapa) 1924 I, W, 1925 E, F
Donaldson, M W (Manawatu) 1977 F 1,2, 1978 A 1,2,3, I, E, S, 1979 F 1,2, A, S (R), 1981 SA 3(R)
Dougan, J P (Wellington) 1972 A 1, 1973 E 2
Dowd, C W (Auckland) 1993 BI 1,2,3, A, WS, S, E, 1994 SA 1(R), 1995 C, [I, W, J, E, SA], A 1,2, It, F 1,2, 1996 WS, S 1,2, A 1, SA 1, A 2, SA 2,3,4,5, 1997 Fj, Arg 1,2, A 1, SA 1, A 2, SA 2, A 3, I, E 1, W, 1998 E 1,2, A 1, SA 1, A 2,3(R), 1999 SA 2(R), A 2(R), [Tg (R), E, It, S, F 2, SA 3], 2000 Tg, S 1(R),2(R), A 1(R), SA 1(R), A 2(R)
Dowd, G W (North Harbour) 1992 I 1(R)
Downing, A J (Auckland) 1913 A 1, US, 1914 A 1,2,3
Drake, J A (Auckland) 1986 F 2,3, 1987 [Fj, Arg, S, W, F], A
Duff, R H (Canterbury) 1951 A 1,2,3, 1952 A 1,2, 1955 A 2,3, 1956 SA 1,2,3,4
Duggan, R J L (Waikato) 1999 [It (R)]
Duncan, J (Otago) 1903 A

Duncan, M G (Hawke's Bay) 1971 BI 3(R),4
Duncan, W D (Otago) 1921 SA 1,2,3
Dunn, E J (North Auckland) 1979 S, 1981 S 1
Dunn, I T W (North Auckland) 1983 BI 1,4, A
Dunn, J M (Auckland) 1946 A 1

Earl, A T (Canterbury) 1986 F 1, A 1, F 3(R), 1987 [Arg], 1989 W, I, 1991 Arg 1(R),2, A 1, [E (R), US, S], 1992 A 2,3(R)
Eastgate, B P (Canterbury) 1952 A 1,2, 1954 S
Eaton, J J (Taranaki) 2005 I,E(t),S(R), 2006 Arg,A1,2(R),3, SA3(R),F1(R),2(R)
Elliott, K G (Wellington) 1946 A 1,2
Ellis, A M (Canterbury) 2006 E(R),F2(R), 2007 [Pt(R),R]
Ellis, M C G (Otago) 1993 S, E, 1995 C, [I (R), W, J, S, SA (R)]
Elsom, A E G (Canterbury) 1952 A 1,2, 1953 W, 1955 A 1,2,3
Elvidge, R R (Otago) 1946 A 1,2, 1949 SA 1,2,3,4, 1950 BI 1,2,3
Erceg, C P (Auckland) 1951 A 1,2,3, 1952 A 1
Evans, D A (Hawke's Bay) 1910 A 2
Evans, N J (North Harbour, Otago) 2004 E1(R),2,Arg,PI(R), 2005 I,S, 2006 F2(R),W(R), 2007 F1(R),2,SA2(R),A2(R), [Pt,S(R),R,F(R)]
Eveleigh, K A (Manawatu) 1976 SA 2,4, 1977 BI 1,2

Fanning, A H N (Canterbury) 1913 A 3
Fanning, B J (Canterbury) 1903 A, 1904 BI
Farrell, C P (Auckland) 1977 BI 1,2
Fawcett, C L (Auckland) 1976 SA 2,3
Fea, W R (Otago) 1921 SA 3
Feek, G E (Canterbury) 1999 WS (R), A 1(R), SA 2, [E (t), It], 2000 F 1,2, It, 2001 I, S
Filipo, R A (Wellington) 2007 C,SA1(R),A1(R)
Finlay, B E L (Manawatu) 1959 BI 1
Finlay, J (Manawatu) 1946 A 1
Finlayson, I (North Auckland) 1928 SA 1,2,3,4, 1930 BI 1,2
Fitzgerald, J T (Wellington) 1952 A 1
Fitzpatrick, B B J (Wellington) 1953 W, 1954 I, F
Fitzpatrick, S B T (Auckland) 1986 F 1, A 1, F 2,3, 1987 [It, Fj, Arg, S, W, F], A, 1988 W 1,2, A 1,2,3, 1989 F 1,2, Arg 1,2, A, W, I, 1990 S 1,2, A 1,2,3, F 1,2, 1991 Arg 1,2, A 1,2, [E, US, It, C, A, S], 1992 Wld 1,2,3, I 1,2, A 1,2,3, SA, 1993 BI 1,2,3, A, WS, S, E, 1994 F 1,2, SA 1,2,3, A, 1995 C, [I, W, S, E, SA], A 1,2, It, F 1,2, 1996 WS, S 1,2, A 1, SA 1, A 2, SA 2,3,4,5, 1997 Fj, Arg 1,2, A 1, SA 1, A 2, SA 2, A 3, W (R)
Flavell, T V (North Harbour, Auckland) 2000 Tg, S 1(R), A 1(R), SA 1,2(t), F 1(R),2(R), It, 2001 Sm, Arg 1, F, SA 1, A 1, SA 2, A 2, 2006 I1(R),2, 2007 F1(R),2(R),C,SA1,A1
Fleming, J K (Wellington) 1979 S, E, 1980 A 1,2,3
Fletcher, C J C (North Auckland) 1921 SA 3
Flynn, C R (Canterbury) 2003 [C(R),Tg], 2004 It(R)
Fogarty, R (Taranaki) 1921 SA 1,3
Ford, B R (Marlborough) 1977 BI 3,4, 1978 I, 1979 E
Forster, S T (Otago) 1993 S, E, 1994 F 1,2, 1995 It, F 1
Fox, G J (Auckland) 1985 Arg 1, 1987 [It, Fj, Arg, S, W, F], A, 1988 W 1,2, A 1,2,3, 1989 F 1,2, Arg 1,2, A, W, I, 1990 S 1,2, A 1,2,3, F 1,2, 1991 Arg 1,2, A 1,2, [E, It, C, A], 1992 Wld 1,2(R), A 1,2,3, SA, 1993 BI 1,2,3, A, WS
Francis, A R H (Auckland) 1905 A, 1907 A 1,2,3, 1908 AW 1,2,3, 1910 A 1,2,3
Francis, W C (Wellington) 1913 A 2,3, 1914 A 1,2,3
Fraser, B G (Wellington) 1979 S, E, 1980 A 3, W, 1981 S 1,2, SA 1,2,3, R, F 1,2, 1982 A 1,2,3, 1983 BI 1,2,3,4, A, S, E, 1984 A 1
Frazer, H F (Hawke's Bay) 1946 A 1,2, 1947 A 1,2, 1949 SA 2
Fryer, F C (Canterbury) 1907 A 1,2,3, 1908 AW 2
Fuller, W B (Canterbury) 1910 A 1,2
Furlong, B D M (Hawke's Bay) 1970 SA 4

Gallagher, J A (Wellington) 1987 [It, Fj, S, W, F], A, 1988 W 1,2, A 1,2,3, 1989 F 1,2, Arg 1,2, A, W, I
Gallaher, D (Auckland) 1903 A, 1904 BI, 1905 S, E, W, 1906 F
Gard, P C (North Otago) 1971 BI 4
Gardiner, A J (Taranaki) 1974 A 3
Gear, R L (North Harbour, Nelson Bays, Tasman) 2004 PI,It, 2005 BI1(R),2,3,SA1,A1,SA2,W,S, 2006 Arg,A1,2,SA2,3(R), E,W, 2007 C(R),A1
Geddes, J H (Southland) 1929 A 1
Geddes, W McK (Auckland) 1913 A 2
Gemmell, B McL (Auckland) 1974 A 1,2
George, V L (Southland) 1938 A 1,2,3
Gibbes, J B (Waikato) 2004 E1,2,Arg(R),PI,A1,2,SA2, 2005 BI2(R)
Gibson, D P E (Canterbury) 1999 WS, F 1, SA 1, A 1, SA 2, A 2, [Tg (R), E (R), It, S (R), F 2(R)], 2000 F 1,2, 2002 It, I 1(R),2(R), Fj, A 2(R), SA 2(R)
Gilbert, G D M (West Coast) 1935 S, I, W, 1936 E
Gillespie, C T (Wellington) 1913 A 2
Gillespie, W D (Otago) 1958 A 3
Gillett, G A (Canterbury, Auckland) 1905 S, I, E, W, 1907 A 2,3, 1908 AW 1,3
Gillies, C C (Otago) 1936 A 2
Gilray, C M (Otago) 1905 A
Glasgow, F T (Taranaki, Southland) 1905 S, I, E, W, 1906 F, 1908 AW 3
Glenn, W S (Taranaki) 1904 BI, 1906 F
Goddard, M P (South Canterbury) 1946 A 2, 1947 A 1,2, 1949 SA 3,4
Going, S M (North Auckland) 1967 A, F, 1968 F 3, 1969 W 1,2, 1970 SA 1(R),4, 1971 BI 1,2,3,4, 1972 A 1,2,3, W, S, 1973 E 1, I, F, E 2, 1974 I, 1975 S, 1976 I (R), SA 1,2,3,4, 1977 BI 1,2
Gordon, S B (Waikato) 1993 S, E
Graham, D J (Canterbury) 1958 A 1,2, 1960 SA 2,3, 1961 F 1,2,3, 1962 A 1,2,3,4,5, 1963 E 1,2, I, W, 1964 E, S, F, A 1,2,3
Graham, J B (Otago) 1913 US, 1914 A 1,3
Graham, W G (Otago) 1979 F 1(R)
Grant, L A (South Canterbury) 1947 A 1,2, 1949 SA 1,2
Gray, G D (Canterbury) 1908 AW 2, 1913 A 1, US
Gray, K F (Wellington) 1963 I, W, 1964 E, S, F, A 1,2,3, 1965 SA 1,2,3,4, 1966 BI 1,2,3,4, 1967 W, F, S, 1968 A 1, F 2,3, 1969 W 1,2
Gray, W N (Bay of Plenty) 1955 A 2,3, 1956 SA 1,2,3,4
Green, C I (Canterbury) 1983 S (R), E, 1984 A 1,2,3, 1985 E 1,2, A, Arg 1,2, 1986 A 2,3, F 2,3, 1987 [It, Fj, S, W, F], A
Grenside, B A (Hawke's Bay) 1928 SA 1,2,3,4, 1929 A 2,3
Griffiths, J L (Wellington) 1934 A 2, 1935 S, I, W, 1936 A 1,2, 1938 A 3
Guy, R A (North Auckland) 1971 BI 1,2,3,4

Haden, A M (Auckland) 1977 BI 1,2,3,4, F 1,2, 1978 A 1,2,3, I, W, E, S, 1979 F 1,2, A, S, E, 1980 A 1,2,3, W, 1981 S 2, SA 1,2,3, R, F 1,2, 1982 A 1,2,3, 1983 BI 1,2,3,4, A, 1984 F 1,2, 1985 Arg 1,2
Hadley, S (Auckland) 1928 SA 1,2,3,4
Hadley, W E (Auckland) 1934 A 1,2, 1935 S, I, W, 1936 E, A 1,2
Haig, J S (Otago) 1946 A 1,2
Haig, L S (Otago) 1950 BI 2,3,4, 1951 A 1,2,3, 1953 W, 1954 E, S
Hales, D A (Canterbury) 1972 A 1,2,3, W
Hamilton, D C (Southland) 1908 AW 2
Hamilton, S E (Canterbury) 2006 Arg,SA1
Hammett, M G (Canterbury) 1999 F 1(R), SA 2(R), [It, S (R), SA 3], 2000 Tg, S 1(R),2(t&R), A 1(R), SA 1(R), A 2(R), SA 2(R), F 2(R), It (R), 2001 Arg 1(t), 2002 It (R), I 1,2, A 1, SA 1,2(R), 2003 SA 1(R), A 1(R), SA 2, [It(R),C,W(R),SA(R),F(R)]
Hammond, I A (Marlborough) 1952 A 2
Harper, E T (Canterbury) 1904 BI, 1906 F
Harding, S (Otago) 2002 Fj
Harris, P C (Manawatu) 1976 SA 3
Hart, A H (Taranaki) 1924 I
Hart, G F (Canterbury) 1930 BI 1,2,3,4, 1931 A, 1934 A 1, 1935 S, I, W, 1936 A 1,2
Harvey, B A (Wairarapa-Bush) 1986 F 1
Harvey, I H (Wairarapa) 1928 SA 4
Harvey, L R (Otago) 1949 SA 1,2,3,4, 1950 BI 1,2,3,4
Harvey, P (Canterbury) 1904 BI
Hasell, E W (Canterbury) 1913 A 2,3
Hayman, C J (Otago) 2001 Sm (R), Arg 1, F (R), A 1(R), SA

2(R), A 2(R), 2002 F (t), W, 2004 E1,2,PI,A1,2,SA2,It,W(R),F, 2005 BI1,SA1,A1,SA2,A2,W,E, 2006 I1,2,A1,SA1,A2,3, SA3,E,F1,2,W, 2007 F1,2,SA1,A1,SA2,A2, [It,Pt(R),S,F]
Hayward, H O (Auckland) 1908 AW 3
Hazlett, E J (Southland) 1966 BI 1,2,3,4, 1967 A, E
Hazlett, W E (Southland) 1928 SA 1,2,3,4, 1930 BI 1,2,3,4
Heeps, T R (Wellington) 1962 A 1,2,3,4,5
Heke, W R (North Auckland) 1929 A 1,2,3
Hemi, R C (Waikato) 1953 W, 1954 I, E, S, F, 1955 A 1,2,3, 1956 SA 1,3,4, 1957 A 1,2, 1959 BI 1,3,4
Henderson, P (Wanganui) 1949 SA 1,2,3,4, 1950 BI 2,3,4
Henderson, P W (Otago) 1991 Arg 1, [C], 1992 Wld 1,2,3, I 1, 1995 [J]
Herewini, M A (Auckland) 1962 A 5, 1963 I, 1964 S, F, 1965 SA 4, 1966 BI 1,2,3,4, 1967 A
Hewett, D N (Canterbury) 2001 I (R), S (R), Arg 2, 2002 It (R), I 1,2, A 1, SA 1, A 2, SA 2, 2003 E, F, SA 1, A 1, SA 2, A 2, [It,Tg(R),W,SA,A,F]
Hewett, J A (Auckland) 1991 [It]
Hewitt, N J (Southland) 1995 [I (t), J], 1996 A 1(R), 1997 SA 1(R), I, E 1, W, E 2, 1998 E 2(t + R)
Hewson, A R (Wellington) 1981 S 1,2, SA 1,2,3, R, F 1,2, 1982 A 1,2,3, 1983 BI 1,2,3,4, A, 1984 F 1,2, A 1
Higginson, G (Canterbury, Hawke's Bay) 1980 W, 1981 S 1, SA 1, 1982 A 1,2, 1983 A
Hill, D W (Waikato) 2006 I2(R)
Hill, S F (Canterbury) 1955 A 3, 1956 SA 1,3,4, 1957 A 1,2, 1958 A 3, 1959 BI 1,2,3,4
Hines, G R (Waikato) 1980 A 3
Hobbs, M J B (Canterbury) 1983 BI 1,2,3,4, A, S, E, 1984 F 1,2, A 1,2,3, 1985 E 1,2, A, Arg 1,2, 1986 A 2,3, F 2,3
Hoeft, C H (Otago) 1998 E 2(t + R), A 2(R), SA 2, A 3, 1999 WS, F 1, SA 1, A 1,2, [Tg,E, S, F 2, SA 3(R)], 2000 S 1,2, A 1, SA 1, A 2, SA 2, 2001 Sm, Arg 1, F, SA 1, A 1, SA 2, A 2, 2003 W, [C,F(R)]
Holah, M R (Waikato) 2001 Sm, Arg 1(t&R), F (R), SA 1(R), A 1(R), SA 2(R), A 2(R), 2002 It, I 2(R), A 2(t), E, F, W (R), 2003 W, F (R), A 1(R), SA 2, [It(R),C,Tg(R),W(R),SA(t&R),A(R), F(t&R)], 2004 E1(R),2,Arg(R),PI,A1,SA1,A2,SA2, 2005 BI3(R),A1(R), 2006 I1,SA3(t)
Holder, E C (Buller) 1934 A 2
Hook, L S (Auckland) 1929 A 1,2,3
Hooper, J A (Canterbury) 1937 SA 1,2,3
Hopkinson, A E (Canterbury) 1967 S, 1968 A 2, F 1,2,3, 1969 W 2, 1970 SA 1,2,3
Hore, A K (Taranaki) 2002 E, F, 2004 E1(t),2(R),Arg,A1(t), 2005 W(R),I(R),S(R), 2006 I2(R),Arg(R),A1(R),SA1(R),A2(R),SA3,E(R),F2(R),W(R), 2007 F1(R),C,SA2(R), [Pt,S(R),R(R),F(R)]
Hore, J (Otago) 1930 BI 2,3,4, 1932 A 1,2,3, 1934 A 1,2, 1935 S, 1936 E
Horsley, R H (Wellington) 1960 SA 2,3,4
Hotop, J (Canterbury) 1952 A 1,2, 1955 A 3
Howarth, S P (Auckland) 1994 SA 1,2,3, A
Howlett, D C (Auckland) 2000 Tg (R), F 1,2, It, 2001 Sm, Arg 1(R), F (R), SA 1, A 1,2, I, S, Arg 2, 2002 It, I 1,2(R), Fj, A 1, SA 1, A 2, SA 2, E, F, W, 2003 E, W, F, SA 1, A 1, SA 2, A 2, [It,C(R),Tg,W,SA,A,F], 2004 E1,A1,SA1,A2,SA2,W,F, 2005 Fj,BI1,A2,I,E, 2006 I1,2,SA1,A3,SA3, 2007 F2(R),C,SA2,A2, [It,S,R(R)]
Hughes, A M (Auckland) 1949 A 1,2, 1950 BI 1,2,3,4
Hughes, E (Southland, Wellington) 1907 A 1,2,3, 1908 AW 1, 1921 SA 1,2
Hunter, B A (Otago) 1971 BI 1,2,3
Hunter, J (Taranaki) 1905 S, I, E, W, 1906 F, 1907 A 1,2,3, 1908 AW 1,2,3
Hurst, I A (Canterbury) 1973 I, F, E 2, 1974 A 1,2

Ieremia, A (Wellington) 1994 SA 1,2,3, 1995 [J], 1996 SA 2(R),5(R), 1997 A 1(R), SA 1(R), A 2, SA 2, A 3, I, E 1, 1999 WS, F 1, SA 1, A 1, SA 2, A 2, [Tg, E, S, F 2, SA 3], 2000 Tg, S 1,2, A 1,2, SA 2
Ifwersen, K D (Auckland) 1921 SA 3
Innes, C R (Auckland) 1989 W, I, 1990 A 1,2,3, F 1,2, 1991 Arg 1,2, A 1,2, [E, US, It, C, A, S]
Innes, G D (Canterbury) 1932 A 2
Irvine, I B (North Auckland) 1952 A 1
Irvine, J G (Otago) 1914 A 1,2,3
Irvine, W R (Hawke's Bay, Wairarapa) 1924 I, W, 1925 E, F, 1930 BI 1
Irwin, M W (Otago) 1955 A 1,2, 1956 SA 1, 1958 A 2, 1959 BI 3,4, 1960 SA 1

Jack, C R (Canterbury, Tasman) 2001 Arg 1(R), SA 1(R),2, A 2, I, S, Arg 2, 2002 I 1,2, A 1, SA 1, A 2, SA 2, 2003 E, W, F, SA 1, A 1, SA 2(R), A 2, [It,C,SA,A,F], 2004 E1,2,Arg,PI,A1,SA1,A2,SA2,It,W,F, 2005 Fj(R),BI1,2,3,SA1, A1,SA2,A2,W,E,S, 2006 I1,2,A1,SA1,A2,3,SA2(R),3,E,F2, 2007 F1,2,A1,SA2,A2, [It,Pt,S(R),R(R),F(R)]
Jackson, E S (Hawke's Bay) 1936 A 1,2, 1937 SA 1,2,3, 1938 A 3
Jaffray, J L (Otago, South Canterbury) 1972 A 2, 1975 S, 1976 I, SA 1, 1977 BI 2, 1979 F 1,2
Jarden, R A (Wellington) 1951 A 1,2, 1952 A 1,2, 1953 W, 1954 I, E, S, F, 1955 A 1,2,3, 1956 SA 1,2,3,4
Jefferd, A C R (East Coast) 1981 S 1,2, SA 1
Jessep, E M (Wellington) 1931 A, 1932 A 1
Johnson, L M (Wellington) 1928 SA 1,2,3,4
Johnston, W (Otago) 1907 A 1,2,3
Johnstone, B R (Auckland) 1976 SA 2, 1977 BI 1,2, F 1,2, 1978 I, W, E, S, 1979 F 1,2, S, E
Johnstone, C R (Canterbury) 2005 Fj(R),BI2(R),3(R)
Johnstone, P (Otago) 1949 SA 2,4, 1950 BI 1,2,3,4, 1951 A 1,2,3
Jones, I D (North Auckland, North Harbour) 1990 S 1,2, A 1,2,3, F 1,2, 1991 Arg 1,2, A 1,2, [E, US, It, C, A, S], 1992 Wld 1,2,3, I 1,2, A 1,2,3, SA, 1993 BI 1,2(R),3, WS, S, E, 1994 F 1,2, SA 1,3, A, 1995 C, [I, W, S, E, SA], A 1,2, It, F 1,2, 1996 WS, S 1,2, A 1, SA 1, A 2, SA 2,3,4,5, 1997 Fj, Arg 1,2, A 1, SA 1, A 2, SA 2, A 3, I, E 1, W, E 2, 1998 E 1,2, A 1, SA 1, A 2,3(R), 1999 F 1(R), [It, S (R)]
Jones, M G (North Auckland) 1973 E 2
Jones, M N (Auckland) 1987 [It, Fj, S, F], A, 1988 W 1,2, A 2,3, 1989 F 1,2, Arg 1,2, 1990 F 1,2, 1991 Arg 1,2, A 1,2, [E, US, S], 1992 Wld 1,3, I 2, A 1,3, SA, 1993 BI 1,2,3, A, WS, 1994 SA 3(R), A, 1995 A 1(R),2, It, F 1,2, 1996 WS, S 1,2, A 1, SA 1, A 2, SA 2,3,4,5, 1997 Fj, 1998 E 1, A 1, SA 1, A 2
Jones, P F H (North Auckland) 1954 E, S, 1955 A 1,2, 1956 SA 3,4, 1958 A 1,2,3, 1959 BI 1, 1960 SA 1
Joseph, H T (Canterbury) 1971 BI 2,3
Joseph, J W (Otago) 1992 Wld 2,3(R), I 1, A 1(R),3, SA, 1993 BI 1,2,3, A, WS, S, E, 1994 SA 2(t), 1995 C, [I, W, J (R), S, SA (R)]

Kaino, J (Auckland) 2006 I1(R),2
Karam, J F (Wellington, Horowhenua) 1972 W, S, 1973 E 1, I, F, 1974 A 1,2,3, I, 1975 S
Katene, T (Wellington) 1955 A 2
Kearney, J C (Otago) 1947 A 2, 1949 SA 1,2,3
Kelleher, B T (Otago, Waikato) 1999 WS (R), SA 1(R), A 2(R), [Tg (R), E (R), It, F 2], 2000 S 1, A 1(R),2(R), It (R), 2001 Sm, F (R), A 1(R), SA 2, A 2, I, S, 2002 It, I 2(R), Fj, SA 1(R),2(R), 2003 F (R), [A(R)], 2004 Arg,PI(R),SA1(R),2(R),It, W(R),F, 2005 Fj,BI1(R),2,3,SA1,W,E, 2006 I1,2,A1,2,3, SA3(R),E,F1(R),2,W, 2007 F2,C,SA1,A1,2, [It,S,F]
Kelly, J W (Auckland) 1949 A 1,2
Kember, G F (Wellington) 1970 SA 4
Ketels, R C (Counties) 1980 W, 1981 S 1,2, R, F 1
Kiernan, H A D (Auckland) 1903 A
Kilby, F D (Wellington) 1932 A 1,2,3, 1934 A 2
Killeen, B A (Auckland) 1936 A 1
King, R M (Waikato) 2002 W
King, R R (West Coast) 1934 A 2, 1935 S, I, W, 1936 E, A 1,2, 1937 SA 1,2,3, 1938 A 1,2,3
Kingstone, C N (Taranaki) 1921 SA 1,2,3
Kirk, D E (Auckland) 1985 E 1,2, A, Arg 1, 1986 F 1, A 1,2,3, F 2,3, 1987 [It, Fj, Arg, S, W, F], A
Kirkpatrick, I A (Canterbury, Poverty Bay) 1967 F, 1968 A 1(R),2, F 1,2,3, 1969 W 1,2, 1970 SA 1,2,3,4, 1971 BI 1,2,3,4, 1972 A 1,2,3, W, S, 1973 E 1, I, F, E 2, 1974 A 1,2,3, I 1975 S, 1976 I, SA 1,2,3,4, 1977 BI 1,2,3,4
Kirton, E W (Otago) 1967 E, W, F, S, 1968 A 1,2, F 1,2,3, 1969 W 1,2, 1970 SA 2,3

Kirwan, J J (Auckland) 1984 F 1,2, 1985 E 1,2, A, Arg 1,2, 1986 F 1, A 1,2,3, F 2,3, 1987 [It, Fj, Arg, S, W, F], A, 1988 W 1,2, A 1,2,3, 1989 F 1,2, Arg 1,2, A, 1990 S 1,2, A 1,2,3, F 1,2, 1991 Arg 2, A 1,2, [E, It, C, A, S], 1992 Wld 1,2(R),3, I 1,2, A 1,2,3, SA, 1993 BI 2,3, A, WS, 1994 F 1,2, SA 1,2,3
Kivell, A L (Taranaki) 1929 A 2,3
Knight, A (Auckland) 1934 A 1
Knight, G A (Manawatu) 1977 F 1,2, 1978 A 1,2,3, E, S, 1979 F 1,2, A, 1980 A 1,2,3, W, 1981 S 1,2, SA 1,3, 1982 A 1,2,3, 1983 BI 1,2,3,4, A, 1984 F 1,2, A 1,2,3, 1985 E 1,2, A, 1986 A 2,3
Knight, L G (Poverty Bay) 1977 BI 1,2,3,4, F 1,2
Koteka, T T (Waikato) 1981 F 2, 1982 A 3
Kreft, A J (Otago) 1968 A 2
Kronfeld, J A (Otago) 1995 C, [I, W, S, E, SA], A 1,2(R) 1996 WS, S 1,2, A 1, SA 1, A 2, SA 2,3,4,5, 1997 Fj, Arg 1,2, A 1, SA 1, A 2, SA 2, A 3, I (R), E 1, W, E 2, 1998 E 1,2, A 1, SA 1,2 A 3, 1999 WS, F 1, SA 1, A 1, SA 2, A 2, [Tg, E, S, F 2, SA 3], 2000 Tg, S 1(R),2, A 1(R), SA 1, A 2, SA 2

Laidlaw, C R (Otago, Canterbury) 1964 F, A 1, 1965 SA 1,2,3,4, 1966 BI 1,2,3,4, 1967 E, W, S, 1968 A 1,2, F 1,2, 1970 SA 1,2,3
Laidlaw, K F (Southland) 1960 SA 2,3,4
Lambert, K K (Manawatu) 1972 S (R), 1973 E 1, I, F, E 2, 1974 I, 1976 SA 1,3,4, 1977 BI 1,4
Lambourn, A (Wellington) 1934 A 1,2, 1935 S, I, W, 1936 E, 1937 SA 1,2,3, 1938 A 3
Larsen, B P (North Harbour) 1992 Wld 2,3, I 1, 1994 F 1,2, SA 1,2,3, A (t), 1995 [I, W, J, E(R)], It, F 1, 1996 S 2(t), SA 4(R)
Lauaki, S T (Waikato) 2005 Fj(R),BI1(R),2(R),3,A2,I,S, 2007 [It(R),Pt,S(R),R]
Laulala, C D E (Canterbury) 2004 W, 2006 I2
Le Lievre, J M (Canterbury) 1962 A 4
Lee, D D (Otago) 2002 E (R), F
Lendrum, R N (Counties) 1973 E 2
Leonard, B G (Waikato) 2007 F1(R),2(R),SA2(R),A2(R), [It(R),Pt,S(R),R(R),F(R)]
Leslie, A R (Wellington) 1974 A 1,2,3, I, 1975 S, 1976 I, SA 1,2,3,4
Leys, E T (Wellington) 1929 A 3
Lilburne, H T (Canterbury, Wellington) 1928 SA 3,4, 1929 A 1,2,3, 1930 BI 1,4, 1931 A, 1932 A 1, 1934 A 2
Lindsay, D F (Otago) 1928 SA 1,2,3
Lineen, T R (Auckland) 1957 A 1,2, 1958 A 1,2,3, 1959 BI 1,2,3,4, 1960 SA 1,2,3
Lister, T N (South Canterbury) 1968 A 1,2, F 1, 1969 W 1,2, 1970 SA 1,4, 1971 BI 4
Little, P F (Auckland) 1961 F 2,3, 1962 A 2,3,5, 1963 I, W, 1964 E, S, F
Little, W K (North Harbour) 1990 S 1,2, A 1,2,3, F 1,2, 1991 Arg 1,2, A 1, [It, S], 1992 Wld 1,2,3, I 1,2, A 1,2,3, SA, 1993 BI 1, WS (R), 1994 SA 2(R), A, 1995 C, [I, W, S, E, SA], A 1,2, It, F 1,2, 1996 S 2, A 1, SA 1, A 2, SA 2,3,4,5, 1997 W, E 2, 1998 E 1, A 1, SA 1, A 2
Loader, C J (Wellington) 1954 I, E, S, F
Lochore, B J (Wairarapa) 1964 E, S, 1965 SA 1,2,3,4, 1966 BI 1,2,3,4, 1967 A, E, W, F, S, 1968 A 1, F 2,3, 1969 W 1,2, 1970 SA 1,2,3,4, 1971 BI 3
Loe, R W (Waikato, Canterbury) 1987 [It, Arg], 1988 W 1,2, A 1,2,3, 1989 F 1,2, Arg 1,2, A, W, I, 1990 S 1,2, A 1,2,3, F 1,2, 1991 Arg 1,2, A 1,2, [E, It, C, A, S], 1992 Wld 1,2,3, I 1, A 1,2,3, SA, 1994 F 1,2, SA 1,2,3, A, 1995 [J, S, SA (R)], A 2(t), F 2(R)
Lomu, J T (Counties Manukau, Wellington) 1994 F 1,2, 1995 [I, W, S, E, SA], A 1,2, It, F 1,2, 1996 WS, S 1, A 1, SA 1, A 2, 1997 E 1, W, E 2, 1998 E 1,2, A 1(R), SA 1, A 2, SA 2, A 3, 1999 WS (R), SA 1(R), A 1(R), SA 2(R), A 2(R), [Tg, E, It, S, F 2, SA 3], 2000 Tg, S 1,2, A 1, SA 1, A 2, SA 2, F 1, 2001 Arg 1, F, SA 1, A 1, SA 2, A 2, I, S, Arg 2, 2002 It (R), I 1(R),2, Fj, SA 1(R), E, F, W
Long, A J (Auckland) 1903 A
Loveridge, D S (Taranaki) 1978 W, 1979 S, E, 1980 A 1,2,3, W, 1981 S 1,2, SA 1,2,3, R, F 1,2, 1982 A 1,2,3, 1983 BI 1,2,3,4, A, 1985 Arg 2
Lowen, K R (Waikato) 2002 E
Lucas, F W (Auckland) 1924 I, 1925 F, 1928 SA 4, 1930 BI 1,2,3,4
Lunn, W A (Otago) 1949 A 1,2
Lynch, T W (South Canterbury) 1913 A 1, 1914 A 1,2,3
Lynch, T W (Canterbury) 1951 A 1,2,3

McAlister, C L (North Harbour) 2005 BI3,SA1(R),A1(R), SA2(R),A2(R), 2006 I1,2,SA1(R),A3,SA2,F1,W, 2007 F2,C,SA1(R),A1,SA2,A2, [It,S,R,F]
McAtamney, F S (Otago) 1956 SA 2
McCahill, B J (Auckland) 1987 [Arg, S (R), W (R)], 1989 Arg 1(R),2(R), 1991 A 2, [E, US, C, A]
McCaw, R H (Canterbury) 2001 I, S, Arg 2, 2002 I 1,2, A 1, SA 1, A 2, SA 2, 2003 E, F, SA 1, A 1,2, [It,C(R),Tg(R), W,SA,A,F], 2004 E1,Arg,It,W,F, 2005 Fj,BI1,2,SA1,A1, SA2,A2,W(R),I,S, 2006 I1,2,A1,SA1,A2,3,SA2,3,E,F1,2,W, 2007 F1,2,C(R),SA1,A1,SA2,A2, [It,S,R(R),F]
McCaw, W A (Southland) 1951 A 1,2,3, 1953 W, 1954 F
McCool, M J (Wairarapa-Bush) 1979 A
McCormick, W F (Canterbury) 1965 SA 4, 1967 E, W, F, S, 1968 A 1,2, F 1,2,3, 1969 W 1,2, 1970 SA 1,2,3, 1971 BI 1
McCullough, J F (Taranaki) 1959 BI 2,3,4
McDonald, A (Otago) 1905 S, I, E, W, 1907 A 1, 1908 AW 1, 1913 A 1, US
Macdonald, A J (Auckland) 2005 W(R),S
Macdonald, H H (Canterbury, North Auckland) 1972 W, S, 1973 E 1, I, F, E 2, 1974 I, 1975 S, 1976 I, SA 1,2,3
MacDonald, L R (Canterbury) 2000 S 1(R),2(R), SA 1(t),2(R), 2001 Sm, Arg 1, F, SA 1(R), A 1(R), SA 2, A 2, I, S, 2002 I 1,2, Fj (R), A 2(R), SA 2, 2003 A 2(R),[It(R),C,Tg,W,SA,A,F], 2005 BI1,2(R),SA1,2,A2,W(R),I,E(R),S(R), 2006 Arg,A1, SA1,A2,3(R),SA2,F1,2, 2007 F1,2,C(R),SA1(R), [It,Pt(R),S,F]
McDonnell, J M (Otago) 2002 It, I 1(R),2(R), Fj, SA 1(R), A 2(R), E, F
McDowell, S C (Auckland, Bay of Plenty) 1985 Arg 1,2, 1986 A 2,3, F 2,3, 1987 [It, Fj, S, W, F], A, 1988 W 1,2, A 1,2,3, 1989 F 1,2, Arg 1,2, A, W, I, 1990 S 1,2, A 1,2,3, F 1,2, 1991 Arg 1,2, A 1,2, [E, US, It, C, A, S], 1992 Wld 1,2,3, I 1,2
McEldowney, J T (Taranaki) 1977 BI 3,4
MacEwan, I N (Wellington) 1956 SA 2, 1957 A 1,2, 1958 A 1,2,3, 1959 BI 1,2,3, 1960 SA 1,2,3,4, 1961 F 1,2,3, 1962 A 1,2,3,4
McGrattan, B (Wellington) 1983 S, E, 1985 Arg 1,2, 1986 F 1, A 1
McGregor, A J (Auckland) 1913 A 1, US
McGregor, D (Canterbury, Southland) 1903 A, 1904 BI, 1905 E, W
McGregor, N P (Canterbury) 1924 W, 1925 E
McGregor, R W (Auckland) 1903 A, 1904 BI
McHugh, M J (Auckland) 1946 A 1,2, 1949 SA 3
McIntosh, D N (Wellington) 1956 SA 1,2, 1957 A 1,2
McKay, D W (Auckland) 1961 F 1,2,3, 1963 E 1,2
McKechnie, B J (Southland) 1977 F 1,2, 1978 A 2(R),3, W (R), E, S, 1979 A, 1981 SA 1(R), F 1
McKellar, G F (Wellington) 1910 A 1,2,3
McKenzie, R J (Wellington) 1913 A 1, US, 1914 A 2,3
McKenzie, R McC (Manawatu) 1934 A 1, 1935 S, 1936 A 1, 1937 SA 1,2,3, 1938 A 1,2,3
McLachlan, J S (Auckland) 1974 A 2
McLaren, H C (Waikato) 1952 A 1
McLean, A L (Bay of Plenty) 1921 SA 2,3
McLean, H F (Wellington, Auckland) 1930 BI 3,4, 1932 A 1,2,3, 1934 A 1, 1935 I, W, 1936 E
McLean, J K (King Country, Auckland) 1947 A 1, 1949 A 2
McLeod, B E (Counties) 1964 A 1,2,3, 1965 SA 1,2,3,4, 1966 BI 1,2,3,4, 1967 E, W, F, S, 1968 A 1,2, F 1,2,3, 1969 W 1,2, 1970 SA 1,2
McLeod, S J (Waikato) 1996 WS, S 1, 1997 Fj (R), Arg 2(t + R), I (R), E 1(R), W (t), E 2(R), 1998 A 1, SA 1(R)
McMinn, A F (Wairarapa, Manawatu) 1903 A, 1905 A
McMinn, F A (Manawatu) 1904 BI
McMullen, R F (Auckland) 1957 A 1,2, 1958 A 1,2,3, 1959 BI 1,2,3, 1960 SA 2,3,4
McNab, J R (Otago) 1949 SA 1,2,3, 1950 BI 1,2,3
McNaughton, A M (Bay of Plenty) 1971 BI 1,2,3

McNeece, J (Southland) 1913 A 2,3, 1914 A 1,2,3
McPhail, B E (Canterbury) 1959 BI 1,4
Macpherson, D G (Otago) 1905 A
MacPherson, G L (Otago) 1986 F 1
MacRae, I R (Hawke's Bay) 1966 BI 1,2,3,4, 1967 A, E, W, F, S, 1968 F 1,2, 1969 W 1,2, 1970 SA 1,2,3,4
McRae, J A (Southland) 1946 A 1(R),2
McWilliams, R G (Auckland) 1928 SA 2,3,4, 1929 A 1,2,3, 1930 BI 1,2,3,4
Mackrell, W H C (Auckland) 1906 F
Macky, J V (Auckland) 1913 A 2
Maguire, J R (Auckland) 1910 A 1,2,3
Mahoney, A (Bush) 1935 S, I, W, 1936 E
Mains, L W (Otago) 1971 BI 2,3,4, 1976 I
Major, J (Taranaki) 1967 A
Maka, I (Otago) 1998 E 2(R), A 1(R), SA 1(R),2
Maling, T S (Otago) 2002 It, I 2(R), Fj, A 1, SA 1, A 2, SA 2, 2004 Arg,A1,SA1,2
Manchester, J E (Canterbury) 1932 A 1,2,3, 1934 A 1,2, 1935 S, I, W, 1936 E
Mannix, S J (Wellington) 1994 F 1
Marshall, J W (Southland, Canterbury) 1995 F 2, 1996 WS, S 1,2, A 1, SA 1, A 2, SA 2,3,4,5, 1997 Fj, Arg 1,2, A 1, SA 1, A 2, SA 2, A 3, I, E 1, W, E 2, 1998 A 1, SA 1, A 2, SA 2, A 3, 1999 WS, F 1, SA 1, A 1, SA 2, A 2, [Tg, E, S, F 2(R), SA 3], 2000 Tg, S 2, A 1, SA 1, A 2, SA 2, F 1,2, It, 2001 Arg 1, F, SA 1, A 1,2(R), 2002 I 1,2, Fj (R), A 1, SA 1, A 2, SA 2, 2003 E, SA 1(R), A 1, SA 2, A 2, [It,Tg,W,SA,A], 2004 E1,2,PI,A1,SA1,A2,SA2, 2005 Fj(R),BI1,2(R),3(R)
Masoe, M C (Taranaki, Wellington) 2005 W,E, 2006Arg, A1(R),SA1(R),A2(R),3(R),SA2,E,F2(R), 2007 F1,2(R),C,A1(R), SA2(R), [It(R),Pt,S,R,F(R)]
Mason, D F (Wellington) 1947 A 2(R)
Masters, R R (Canterbury) 1924 I, W, 1925 E, F
Mataira, H K (Hawke's Bay) 1934 A 2
Matheson, J D (Otago) 1972 A 1,2,3, W, S
Mauger, A J D (Canterbury) 2001 I, S, Arg 2, 2002 It (R), I 1,2, Fj, A 1, SA 1, A 2, SA 2, 2003 SA 1, A 1, SA 2, A 2, [W,SA,A,F], 2004 SA2(R),It(R),W,F(R), 2005 Fj,BI1,2,SA1 ,A1,SA2,A2,I,E, 2006 I1,2,A1,2,SA3,E, 2007 F1,C,SA1,A1, [It(R),Pt,R]
Max, D S (Nelson) 1931 A, 1934 A 1,2
Maxwell, N M C (Canterbury) 1999 WS, F 1, SA 1, A 1, SA 2, A 2, [Tg, E, S, F 2, SA 3], 2000 S 1,2, A 1, SA 1(R), A 2, SA 2, F 1,2, It (R), 2001 Sm, Arg 1, F, SA 1, A 1, SA 2, A2, I, S, Arg 2, 2002 It, I 1,2, Fj, 2004 It,F
Mayerhofler, M A (Canterbury) 1998 E 1,2, SA 1, A 2, SA 2, A 3
Meads, C E (King Country) 1957 A 1,2, 1958 A 1,2,3, 1959 BI 2,3,4, 1960 SA 1,2,3,4, 1961 F 1,2,3, 1962 A 1,2,3,5, 1963 E 1,2, I, W, 1964 E, S, F, A 1,2,3, 1965 SA 1,2,3,4, 1966 BI 1,2,3,4, 1967 A, E, W, F, S, 1968 A 1,2, F 1,2,3, 1969 W 1,2, 1970 SA 3,4, 1971 BI 1,2,3,4
Meads, S T (King Country) 1961 F 1, 1962 A 4,5, 1963 I, 1964 A 1,2,3, 1965 SA 1,2,3,4, 1966 BI 1,2,3,4
Mealamu, K F (Auckland) 2002 W, 2003 E (R), W, F (R), SA 1, A 1, SA 2(R), A 2,[It,W,SA,A,F], 2004 E1,2,PI,A1,SA1, A2,SA2,W,F(R), 2005 Fj(R),BI1,2,3,SA1,A1,SA2,A2,I,E, 2006 I1,2,A1,2,3,SA2(R),E,F1(R),2, 2007 F1,2(R),SA1(R),A1(R), SA2,A2(R), [It,Pt(R),R]
Meates, K F (Canterbury) 1952 A 1,2
Meates, W A (Otago) 1949 SA 2,3,4, 1950 BI 1,2,3,4
Meeuws, K J (Otago, Auckland) 1998 A 3, 1999 WS, F 1, SA 1, A 1, SA 2, A 2, [Tg, It (R), S (R), F 2(R), SA 3], 2000 Tg (R), S 2, A 1, SA 1, A 2, SA 2, 2001 Arg 2, 2002 It, Fj, E, F, W (R), 2003 W, F (R), SA 1(R), A 1(R), SA 2, [It(R),C,Tg,W(R),SA(R),A(R)],2004 E1,2,PI,A1,SA1,A2,SA2
Mehrtens, A P (Canterbury) 1995 C, [I, W, S, E, SA], A 1,2, 1996 WS, S 1,2, A 1, SA 1, A 2, SA 2,5, 1997 Fj, SA 2(R), I, E 1, W, E 2, 1998 E 1,2, A 1, SA 1(R), A 2, SA 2, A 3, 1999 F 1, SA 1, A 1, SA 2, A 2, [Tg, E, S, F 2, SA 3], 2000 S 1,2, A 1, SA 1, A 2, SA 2, F 1,2, It (R), 2001 Arg 1, A 1(R), SA 2, A 2, I, S, Arg 2, 2002 It, I 1,2, Fj (R), A 1, SA 1, A 2, SA 2, E (R), F, W, 2004 E2(R),Arg,A2(R),SA2
Metcalfe, T C (Southland) 1931 A, 1932 A 1
Mexted, G G (Wellington) 1950 BI 4
Mexted, M G (Wellington) 1979 S, E, 1980 A 1,2,3, W, 1981 S 1,2, SA 1,2,3, R, F 1,2, 1982 A 1,2,3, 1983 BI 1,2,3,4, A, S, E, 1984 F 1,2, A 1,2,3, 1985 E 1,2, A, Arg 1,2
Mika, B M (Auckland) 2002 E (R), F, W (R)
Mika, D G (Auckland) 1999 WS, F 1, SA 1(R), A 1,2, [It, SA 3(R)]
Mill, J J (Hawke's Bay, Wairarapa) 1924 W, 1925 E, F, 1930 BI 1
Milliken, H M (Canterbury) 1938 A 1,2,3
Milner, H P (Wanganui) 1970 SA 3
Mitchell, N A (Southland, Otago) 1935 S, I, W, 1936 E, A 2, 1937 SA 3, 1938 A 1,2
Mitchell, T W (Canterbury) 1976 SA 4(R)
Mitchell, W J (Canterbury) 1910 A 2,3
Mitchinson, F E (Wellington) 1907 A 1,2,3, 1908 AW 1,2,3, 1910 A 1,2,3, 1913 A 1(R), US
Moffitt, J E (Wellington) 1921 SA 1,2,3
Moore, G J T (Otago) 1949 A 1
Moreton, R C (Canterbury) 1962 A 3,4, 1964 A 1,2,3, 1965 SA 2,3
Morgan, J E (North Auckland) 1974 A 3, I, 1976 SA 2,3,4
Morris, T J (Nelson Bays) 1972 A 1,2,3
Morrison, T C (South Canterbury) 1938 A 1,2,3
Morrison, T G (Otago) 1973 E 2(R)
Morrissey, P J (Canterbury) 1962 A 3,4,5
Mourie, G N K (Taranaki) 1977 BI 3,4, F 1,2, 1978 I, W, E, S, 1979 F 1,2, A, S, E, 1980 W, 1981 S 1,2, F 1,2, 1982 A 1,2,3
Muliaina, J M (Auckland, Waikato) 2003 E (R), W, F, SA 1, A 1, SA 2, A 2, [It,C,Tg,W,SA,A,F], 2004 E1,2,Arg,PI,A1, SA1,A2,SA2,It,W,F, 2005 Fj,BI1(R),2,3,SA1,A1,SA2,A2,W,E, 2006 I1,2,A1,SA1,A2,3,SA2,3,E,F1(R),2,W, 2007 C,SA1,A1, SA2,A2, [It,Pt,F]
Muller, B L (Taranaki) 1967 A, E, W, F, 1968 A 1, F 1, 1969 W 1, 1970 SA 1,2,4, 1971 BI 1,2,3,4
Mumm, W J (Buller) 1949 A 1
Murdoch, K (Otago) 1970 SA 4, 1972 A 3, W
Murdoch, P H (Auckland) 1964 A 2,3, 1965 SA 1,2,3
Murray, H V (Canterbury) 1913 A 1, US, 1914 A 2,3
Murray, P C (Wanganui) 1908 AW 2
Myers, R G (Waikato) 1978 A 3
Mynott, H J (Taranaki) 1905 I, W, 1906 F, 1907 A 1,2,3, 1910 A 1,3

Nathan, W J (Auckland) 1962 A 1,2,3,4,5, 1963 E 1,2, W, 1964 F, 1966 BI 1,2,3,4, 1967 A
Nelson, K A (Otago) 1962 A 4,5
Nepia, G (Hawke's Bay, East Coast) 1924 I, W, 1925 E, F, 1929 A 1, 1930 BI 1,2,3,4
Nesbit, S R (Auckland) 1960 SA 2,3
Newby, C A (North Harbour) 2004 E2(t),SA2(R), 2006 I2(R)
Newton, F (Canterbury) 1905 E, W, 1906 F
Nicholls, H E (Wellington) 1921 SA 1
Nicholls, M F (Wellington) 1921 SA 1,2,3, 1924 I, W, 1925 E, F, 1928 SA 4, 1930 BI 2,3
Nicholson, G W (Auckland) 1903 A, 1904 BI, 1907 A 2,3
Nonu, M A (Wellington) 2003 E, [It(R),C,Tg(R)], 2004 It(R),W(R),F(R), 2005 BI2(R),W(R),I,S(R), 2006 I1,E,F1(R), 2,W(R), 2007 F1(R),2(R)
Norton, R W (Canterbury) 1971 BI 1,2,3,4, 1972 A 1,2,3, W, S, 1973 E 1, I, F, E 2, 1974 A 1,2,3, I, 1975 S, 1976 I, SA 1,2,3,4, 1977 BI 1,2,3,4

O'Brien, J G (Auckland) 1914 A 1
O'Callaghan, M W (Manawatu) 1968 F 1,2,3
O'Callaghan, T R (Wellington) 1949 A 2
O'Donnell, D H (Wellington) 1949 A 2
O'Halloran, J D (Wellington) 2000 It (R)
Old, G H (Manawatu) 1981 SA 3, R (R), 1982 A 1(R)
O'Leary, M J (Auckland) 1910 A 1,3, 1913 A 2,3
Oliver, A D (Otago) 1997 Fj (t), 1998 E 1,2, A 1, SA 1, A 2, SA 2, A 3, 1999 WS, F 1, SA 1, A 1, SA 2, A 2, [Tg, E, S, F 2, SA 3(R)], 2000 Tg (R), S 1,2, A 1, SA 1, A 2, SA 2, F 1,2, It, 2001 Sm, Arg 1, F, SA 1, A 1, SA 2, A 2, I, S, Arg 2, 2003 E, F, 2004 It,F, 2005 W,S, 2006 Arg,SA1,2,3(R),F1,W, 2007 F2,SA1,A1,2, [It(R),Pt(R),S,F]
Oliver, C J (Canterbury) 1929 A 1,2, 1934 A 1, 1935 S, I, W, 1936 E

Oliver, D J (Wellington) 1930 BI 1,2
Oliver, D O (Otago) 1954 I, F
Oliver, F J (Southland, Otago, Manawatu) 1976 SA 4, 1977 BI 1,2,3,4, F 1,2, 1978 A 1,2,3, I, W, E, S, 1979 F 1,2, 1981 SA 2
Orr, R W (Otago) 1949 A 1
Osborne, G M (North Harbour) 1995 C, [I, W, J, E, SA], A 1,2, F 1(R),2, 1996 SA 2,3,4,5, 1997 Arg 1(R), A 2,3, I, 1999 [It]
Osborne, W M (Wanganui) 1975 S, 1976 SA 2(R),4(R), 1977 BI 1,2,3,4, F 1(R),2, 1978 I, W, E, S, 1980 W, 1982 A 1,3
O'Sullivan, J M (Taranaki) 1905 S, I, E, W, 1907 A 3
O'Sullivan, T P A (Taranaki) 1960 SA 1, 1961 F 1, 1962 A 1,2

Page, J R (Wellington) 1931 A, 1932 A 1,2,3, 1934 A 1,2
Palmer, B P (Auckland) 1929 A 2, 1932 A 2,3
Parker, J H (Canterbury) 1924 I, W, 1925 E
Parkhill, A A (Otago) 1937 SA 1,2,3, 1938 A 1,2,3
Parkinson, R M (Poverty Bay) 1972 A 1,2,3, W, S, 1973 E 1,2
Paterson, A M (Otago) 1908 AW 2,3, 1910 A 1,2,3
Paton, H (Otago) 1910 A 1,3
Pene, A R B (Otago) 1992 Wld 1(R),2,3, I 1,2, A 1,2(R), 1993 BI 3, A, WS, S, E, 1994 F 1,2(R), SA 1(R)
Phillips, W J (King Country) 1937 SA 2, 1938 A 1,2
Philpott, S (Canterbury) 1991 [It (R), S (R)]
Pickering, E A R (Waikato) 1958 A 2, 1959 BI 1,4
Pierce, M J (Wellington) 1985 E 1,2, A, Arg 1, 1986 A 2,3, F 2,3, 1987 [It, Arg, S, W, F], A, 1988 W 1,2, A 1,2,3, 1989 F 1,2, Arg 1,2, A, W, I
Pokere, S T (Southland, Auckland) 1981 SA 3, 1982 A 1,2,3, 1983 BI 1,2,3,4, A, S, E, 1984 F 1,2, A 2,3, 1985 E 1,2, A
Pollock, H R (Wellington) 1932 A 1,2,3, 1936 A 1,2
Porter, C G (Wellington) 1925 F, 1929 A 2,3, 1930 BI 1,2,3,4
Preston, J P (Canterbury, Wellington) 1991 [US, S], 1992 SA (R), 1993 BI 2,3, A, WS, 1996 SA 4(R), 1997 I (R), E 1(R)
Procter, A C (Otago) 1932 A 1
Purdue, C A (Southland) 1905 A
Purdue, E (Southland) 1905 A
Purdue, G B (Southland) 1931 A, 1932 A 1,2,3
Purvis, G H (Waikato) 1991 [US], 1993 WS
Purvis, N A (Otago) 1976 I

Quaid, C E (Otago) 1938 A 1,2

Ralph, C S (Auckland, Canterbury) 1998 E 2, 2002 It, I 1,2, A 1, SA 1, A 2, SA 2, 2003 E, A 1(R), [C,Tg,SA(R),F(t&R)]
Ranby, R M (Waikato) 2001 Sm (R)
Randell, T C (Otago) 1997 Fj, Arg 1,2, A 1, SA 1, A 2, SA 2, A 3, I, E 1, W, E 2, 1998 E 1,2, A 1, SA 1, A 2, SA 2, A 3, 1999 WS, F 1, SA 1, A 1, SA 2, A 2, [Tg, E, It, S, F 2, SA 3], 2000 Tg, S 1,2(R), A 1, SA 1, A 2, SA 2, F 2(R), It (R), 2001 Arg 1, F, SA 1, A 1, SA 2, A 2, 2002 It, Fj, E, F, W
Rangi, R E (Auckland) 1964 A 2,3, 1965 SA 1,2,3,4, 1966 BI 1,2,3,4
Rankin, J G (Canterbury) 1936 A 1,2, 1937 SA 2
Rawlinson, G P (North Harbour) 2006 I1,2(R),SA2, 2007 SA1
Reedy, W J (Wellington) 1908 AW 2,3
Reid, A R (Waikato) 1952 A 1, 1956 SA 3,4, 1957 A 1,2
Reid, H R (Bay of Plenty) 1980 A 1,2, W, 1983 S, E, 1985 Arg 1,2, 1986 A 2,3
Reid, K H (Wairarapa) 1929 A 1,3
Reid, S T (Hawke's Bay) 1935 S, I, W, 1936 E, A 1,2, 1937 SA 1,2,3
Reihana, B T (Waikato) 2000 F 2, It
Reside, W B (Wairarapa) 1929 A 1
Rhind, P K (Canterbury) 1946 A 1,2
Richardson, J (Otago, Southland) 1921 SA 1,2,3, 1924 I, W, 1925 E, F
Rickit, H (Waikato) 1981 S 1,2
Riechelmann, C C (Auckland) 1997 Fj (R), Arg 1(R), A 1(R), SA 2(t), I (R), E 2(t)
Ridland, A J (Southland) 1910 A 1,2,3
Roberts, E J (Wellington) 1914 A 1,2,3, 1921 SA 2,3
Roberts, F (Wellington) 1905 S, I, E, W, 1907 A 1,2,3, 1908 AW 1,3, 1910 A 1,2,3
Roberts, R W (Taranaki) 1913 A 1, US, 1914 A 1,2,3
Robertson, B J (Counties) 1972 A 1,3, S, 1973 E 1, I, F, 1974 A 1,2,3, I, 1976 I, SA 1,2,3,4, 1977 BI 1,3,4, F 1,2, 1978 A 1,2,3, W, E, S, 1979 F 1,2, A, 1980 A 2,3, W, 1981 S 1,2
Robertson, D J (Otago) 1974 A 1,2,3, I, 1975 S, 1976 I, SA 1,3,4, 1977 BI 1
Robertson, S M (Canterbury) 1998 A 2(R), SA 2(R), A 3(R), 1999 [It (R)], 2000 Tg (R), S 1,2(R), A 1, SA 1(R),2(R), F 1,2, It, 2001 I, S, Arg 2, 2002 I 1,2, Fj (R), A 1, SA 1, A 2, SA 2
Robilliard, A C C (Canterbury) 1928 SA 1,2,3,4
Robinson, C E (Southland) 1951 A 1,2,3, 1952 A 1,2
Robinson, K J (Waikato) 2002 E, F (R), W, 2004 E1,2,PI, 2006 E,W, 2007 SA2,A2, [R,F]
Robinson, M D (North Harbour) 1998 E 1(R), 2001 S (R), Arg 2
Robinson, M P (Canterbury) 2000 S 2, SA 1, 2002 It, I 2, A 1, SA 1, E (t&R), F, W (R)
Rokocoko, J T (Auckland) 2003 E, W, F, SA 1, A 1, SA 2, A 2, [It,W,SA,A,F], 2004 E1,2,Arg,PI,A1,SA1,A2,SA2,It,W,F, 2005 SA1(R),A1,SA2,A2,W,E(R),S, 2006 I1,2,A1,2,3,SA3,E,F1,2, 2007 F1,2,SA1,A1,SA2,A2, [Pt,R,F]
Rollerson, D L (Manawatu) 1980 W, 1981 S 2, SA 1,2,3, R, F 1(R),2
Roper, R A (Taranaki) 1949 A 2, 1950 BI 1,2,3,4
Rowley, H C B (Wanganui) 1949 A 2
Rush, E J (North Harbour) 1995 [W (R), J], It, F 1,2, 1996 S 1(R),2, A 1(t), SA 1(R)
Rush, X J (Auckland) 1998 A 3, 2004 E1,2,PI,A1,SA1,A2,SA2
Rutledge, L M (Southland) 1978 A 1,2,3, I, W, E, S, 1979 F 1,2, A, 1980 A 1,2,3
Ryan, J (Wellington) 1910 A 2, 1914 A 1,2,3
Ryan, J A C (Otago) 2005 Fj,BI3(R),A1(R),SA2(R),A2(R),W,S, 2006 F1,W(R)

Sadler, B S (Wellington) 1935 S, I, W, 1936 A 1,2
Salmon, J L B (Wellington) 1981 R, F 1,2(R)
Savage, L T (Canterbury) 1949 SA 1,2,4
Saxton, C K (South Canterbury) 1938 A 1,2,3
Schuler, K J (Manawatu, North Harbour) 1990 A 2(R), 1992 A 2, 1995 [I (R), J]
Schuster, N J (Wellington) 1988 A 1,2,3, 1989 F 1,2, Arg 1,2, A, W, I
Schwalger, J E (Wellington) 2007 C
Scott, R W H (Auckland) 1946 A 1,2, 1947 A 1,2, 1949 SA 1,2,3,4, 1950 BI 1,2,3,4, 1953 W, 1954 I, E, S, F
Scown, A I (Taranaki) 1972 A 1,2,3, W (R), S
Scrimshaw, G (Canterbury) 1928 SA 1
Seear, G A (Otago) 1977 F 1,2, 1978 A 1,2,3, I, W, E, S, 1979 F 1,2, A
Seeling, C E (Auckland) 1904 BI, 1905 S, I, E, W, 1906 F, 1907 A 1,2, 1908 AW 1,2,3
Sellars, G M V (Auckland) 1913 A 1, US
Senio, K (Bay of Plenty) 2005 A2(R)
Shaw, M W (Manawatu, Hawke's Bay) 1980 A 1,2,3(R), W, 1981 S 1,2, SA 1,2, R, F 1,2, 1982 A 1,2,3, 1983 BI 1,2,3,4, A, S, E, 1984 F 1,2, A 1, 1985 E 1,2, A, Arg 1,2, 1986 A 3
Shelford, F N K (Bay of Plenty) 1981 SA 3, R, 1984 A 2,3
Shelford, W T (North Harbour) 1986 F 2,3, 1987 [It, Fj, S, W, F], A, 1988 W 1,2, A 1,2,3, 1989 F 1,2, Arg 1,2, A, W, I, 1990 S 1,2
Siddells, S K (Wellington) 1921 SA 3
Simon, H J (Otago) 1937 SA 1,2,3
Simpson, J G (Auckland) 1947 A 1,2, 1949 SA 1,2,3,4, 1950 BI 1,2,3
Simpson, V L J (Canterbury) 1985 Arg 1,2
Sims, G S (Otago) 1972 A 2
Sivivatu, S W (Waikato) 2005 Fj,BI1,2,3,I,E, 2006 SA2,3,E(R),F1,2,W, 2007 F1,2,C,SA1,A1(R), [It,S,R,F]
Skeen, J R (Auckland) 1952 A 2
Skinner, K L (Otago, Counties) 1949 SA 1,2,3,4, 1950 BI 1,2,3,4, 1951 A 1,2,3, 1952 A 1,2, 1953 W, 1954 I, E, S, F, 1956 SA 3,4
Skudder, G R (Waikato) 1969 W 2
Slater, G L (Taranaki) 2000 F 1(R),2(R), It (R)
Sloane, P H (North Auckland) 1979 E

Smith, A E (Taranaki) 1969 W 1,2, 1970 SA 1
Smith, B W (Waikato) 1984 F 1,2, A 1
Smith, C G (Wellington) 2004 It,F, 2005 Fj(R),BI3,W,S, 2006 F1,W, 2007 SA2(R), [Pt,S,R(R)]
Smith, G W (Auckland) 1905 S, I
Smith, I S T (Otago, North Otago) 1964 A 1,2,3, 1965 SA 1,2,4, 1966 BI 1,2,3
Smith, J B (North Auckland) 1946 A 1, 1947 A 2, 1949 A 1,2
Smith, R M (Canterbury) 1955 A 1
Smith, W E (Nelson) 1905 A
Smith, W R (Canterbury) 1980 A 1, 1982 A 1,2,3, 1983 BI 2,3, S, E, 1984 F 1,2, A 1,2,3, 1985 E 1,2, A, Arg 2
Snow, E M (Nelson) 1929 A 1,2,3
Solomon, F (Auckland) 1931 A, 1932 A 2,3
Somerville, G M (Canterbury) 2000 Tg, S 1, SA 2(R), F 1,2, It, 2001 Sm, Arg 1(R), F, SA 1, A 1, SA 2, A 2, I, S, Arg 2(t+R), 2002 I 1,2, A 1, SA 1, A 2, SA 2, 2003 E, F, SA 1, A 1, SA 2(R), A 2, [It,Tg,W,SA,A,F], 2004 Arg,SA1,A2(R), SA2(R),It(R),W,F(R), 2005 Fj,BI1(R)2,3,SA1(R),A1(R),SA2(R), A2(R), 2006 Arg,A1(R),SA1(R),A2(R),3(R),SA2, 2007 [Pt,R]
Sonntag, W T C (Otago) 1929 A 1,2,3
So'oialo, R (Wellington) 2002 W, 2003 E, SA 1(R), [It(R),C,Tg,W(t)], 2004 W,F, 2005 Fj,BI1,2,3,SA1,A1,SA2, A2,W,I(R),E, 2006 I1,2,A1,SA1,A2,3,SA3,E(R),F1,2,W, 2007 F1(R),2,SA1,A1,SA2,A2, [It,Pt(R),S,F]
Speight, M W (Waikato) 1986 A 1
Spencer, C J (Auckland) 1997 Arg 1,2, A 1, SA 1, A 2, SA 2, A 3, E 2(R), 1998 E 2(R), A 1(R), SA 1, A 3(R), 2000 F 1(t&R), It, 2002 E, 2003 E, W, F, SA 1, A 1, SA 2, A 2, [It,C,Tg,W,SA,A,F], 2004 E1,2,PI,A1,SA1,A2
Spencer, J C (Wellington) 1905 A, 1907 A 1(R)
Spiers, J E (Counties) 1979 S, E, 1981 R, F 1,2
Spillane, A P (South Canterbury) 1913 A 2,3
Stanley, J T (Auckland) 1986 F 1, A 1,2,3, F 2,3, 1987 [It, Fj, Arg, S, W, F], A, 1988 W 1,2, A 1,2,3, 1989 F 1,2, Arg 1,2, A, W, I, 1990 S 1,2
Stead, J W (Southland) 1904 BI, 1905 S, I, E, 1906 F, 1908 AW 1,3
Steel, A G (Canterbury) 1966 BI 1,2,3,4, 1967 A, F, S, 1968 A 1,2
Steel, J (West Coast) 1921 SA 1,2,3, 1924 W, 1925 E, F
Steele, L B (Wellington) 1951 A 1,2,3
Steere, E R G (Hawke's Bay) 1930 BI 1,2,3,4, 1931 A, 1932 A 1
Steinmetz, P C (Wellington) 2002 W (R)
Stensness, L (Auckland) 1993 BI 3, A, WS, 1997 Fj, Arg 1,2, A 1, SA 1
Stephens, O G (Wellington) 1968 F 3
Stevens, I N (Wellington) 1972 S, 1973 E 1, 1974 A 3
Stewart, A J (Canterbury, South Canterbury) 1963 E 1,2, I, W, 1964 E, S, F, A 3
Stewart, J D (Auckland) 1913 A 2,3
Stewart, K W (Southland) 1973 E 2, 1974 A 1,2,3, I, 1975 S, 1976 I, SA 1,3, 1979 S, E, 1981 SA 1,2
Stewart, R T (South Canterbury, Canterbury) 1928 SA 1,2,3,4, 1930 BI 2
Stohr, L B (Taranaki) 1910 A 1,2,3
Stone, A M (Waikato, Bay of Plenty) 1981 F 1,2, 1983 BI 3(R), 1984 A 3, 1986 F 1, A 1,3, F 2,3
Storey, P W (South Canterbury) 1921 SA 1,2
Strachan, A D (Auckland, North Harbour) 1992 Wld 2,3, I 1,2, A 1,2,3, SA, 1993 BI 1, 1995 [J, SA (t)]
Strahan, S C (Manawatu) 1967 A, E, W, F, S, 1968 A 1,2, F 1,2,3, 1970 SA 1,2,3, 1972 A 1,2,3, 1973 E 2
Strang, W A (South Canterbury) 1928 SA 1,2, 1930 BI 3,4, 1931 A
Stringfellow, J C (Wairarapa) 1929 A 1(R),3
Stuart, K C (Canterbury) 1955 A 1
Stuart, R C (Canterbury) 1949 A 1,2, 1953 W, 1954 I, E, S, F
Stuart, R L (Hawke's Bay) 1977 F 1(R)
Sullivan, J L (Taranaki) 1937 SA 1,2,3, 1938 A 1,2,3
Sutherland, A R (Marlborough) 1970 SA 2,4, 1971 BI 1, 1972 A 1,2,3, W, 1973 E 1, I, F
Svenson, K S (Wellington) 1924 I, W, 1925 E, F
Swain, J P (Hawke's Bay) 1928 SA 1,2,3,4

Tanner, J M (Auckland) 1950 BI 4, 1951 A 1,2,3, 1953 W
Tanner, K J (Canterbury) 1974 A 1,2,3, I, 1975 S, 1976 I, SA 1
Taumoepeau, S (Auckland) 2004 It, 2005 I(R),S
Taylor, G L (Northland) 1996 SA 5(R)
Taylor, H M (Canterbury) 1913 A 1, US, 1914 A 1,2,3
Taylor, J M (Otago) 1937 SA 1,2,3, 1938 A 1,2,3
Taylor, M B (Waikato) 1979 F 1,2, A, S, E, 1980 A 1,2
Taylor, N M (Bay of Plenty, Hawke's Bay) 1977 BI 2,4(R), F 1,2, 1978 A 1,2,3, I, 1982 A 2
Taylor, R (Taranaki) 1913 A 2,3
Taylor, W T (Canterbury) 1983 BI 1,2,3,4, A, S, 1984 F 1,2, A 1,2, 1985 E 1,2, A, Arg 1,2, 1986 A 2, 1987 [It, Fj, S, W, F], A, 1988 W 1,2
Tetzlaff, P L (Auckland) 1947 A 1,2
Thimbleby, N W (Hawke's Bay) 1970 SA 3
Thomas, B T (Auckland, Wellington) 1962 A 5, 1964 A 1,2,3
Thomson, H D (Wellington) 1908 AW 1
Thorn, B C (Conterbury) 2003 W (R), F (R), SA 1(R), A 1(R), SA 2,[It,C,Tg,W,SA(R),A(R),F(R)]
Thorne, G S (Auckland) 1968 A 1,2, F 1,2,3, 1969 W 1, 1970 SA 1,2,3,4
Thorne, R D (Canterbury) 1999 SA 2(R), [Tg, E, S, F 2, SA 3], 2000 Tg, S 2, A 2(R), F 1,2, 2001 Sm, Arg 1, F, SA 1, A 1, I, S, Arg 2, 2002 It, I 1,2, Fj, A 1, SA 1, A2, SA 2, 2003 E, W, F, SA 1, A 1, SA 2, A 2, [It,C,Tg,W,SA,A,F], 2006 SA1,2,E,W(R), 2007 F1,C,SA2, [S,R]
Thornton, N H (Auckland) 1947 A 1,2, 1949 SA 1
Tialata, N S (Wellington) 2005 W,E(t),S(R), 2006 I1(R),2(R), Arg(R),SA1,2,3(R),F1(R),2(R),W, 2007 F1(R),2(R),C,A1(R),SA2(R), [It(t&R),Pt,S(R),R]
Tiatia, F I (Wellington) 2000 Tg (R), It
Tilyard, J T (Wellington) 1913 A 3
Timu, J K R (Otago) 1991 Arg 1, A 1,2, [E, US, C, A], 1992 Wld 2, I 2, A 1,2,3, SA, 1993 BI 1,2,3, A, WS, S, E, 1994 F 1,2, SA 1,2,3, A
Tindill, E W T (Wellington) 1936 E
Toeava, I (Auckland) 2005 S, 2006 Arg,A1(t&R),A3,SA2(R), 2007 F1,2,SA1,2,A2, [It(R),Pt,S(R),R,F(R)]
Tonu'u, O F J (Auckland) 1997 Fj (R), A 3(R), 1998 E 1,2, SA 1(R)
Townsend, L J (Otago) 1955 A 1,3
Tremain, K R (Canterbury, Hawke's Bay) 1959 BI 2,3,4, 1960 SA 1,2,3,4, 1961 F 2,3 1962 A 1,2,3, 1963 E 1,2, I, W, 1964 E, S, F, A 1,2,3, 1965 SA 1,2,3,4, 1966 BI 1,2,3,4, 1967 A, E, W, S, 1968 A 1, F 1,2,3
Trevathan, D (Otago) 1937 SA 1,2,3
Tuck, J M (Waikato) 1929 A 1,2,3
Tuiali'i, M M (Auckland) 2004 Arg,A2(R),SA2(R),It,W, 2005 I,E(R),S(R), 2006 Arg
Tuigamala, V L (Auckland) 1991 [US, It, C, S], 1992 Wld 1,2,3, I 1, A 1,2,3, SA, 1993 BI 1,2,3, A, WS, S, E
Tuitupou, S (Auckland) 2004 E1(R),2(R),Arg,SA1(R),A2(R),SA2, 2006 Arg,SA1,2(R)
Turner, R S (North Harbour) 1992 Wld 1,2(R)
Turtill, H S (Canterbury) 1905 A
Twigden, T M (Auckland) 1980 A 2,3
Tyler, G A (Auckland) 1903 A, 1904 BI, 1905 S, I, E, W, 1906 F

Udy, D K (Wairarapa) 1903 A
Umaga, J F (Wellington) 1997 Fj, Arg 1,2, A 1, SA 1,2, 1999 WS, F 1, SA 1, A 1, SA 2, A 2, [Tg, E, S, F 2, SA 3], 2000 Tg, S 1,2, A 1, SA 1, A 2, SA 2, F 1,2, It, 2001 Sm, Arg 1, F, SA 1, A 1, SA 2, A 2, I, S, Arg 2, 2002 I 1, Fj, SA 1(R), A 2, SA 2, E, F, W, 2003 E, W, F, SA 1, A 1, SA 2, A 2, [It], 2004 E1,2,Arg,PI,A1,SA1,A2,SA2,It,F, 2005 Fj,BI1,2,3,SA1,A1,SA2,A2,W,E,S
Urbahn, R J (Taranaki) 1959 BI 1,3,4
Urlich, R A (Auckland) 1970 SA 3,4
Uttley, I N (Wellington) 1963 E 1,2

Vidiri, J (Counties Manukau) 1998 E 2(R), A 1
Vincent, P B (Canterbury) 1956 SA 1,2
Vodanovich, I M H (Wellington) 1955 A 1,2,3

Wallace, W J (Wellington) 1903 A, 1904 BI, 1905 S, I, E, W, 1906 F, 1907 A 1,2,3, 1908 AW 2

Waller, D A G (Wellington) 2001 Arg 2(t)
Walsh, P T (Counties) 1955 A 1,2,3, 1956 SA 1,2,4, 1957 A 1,2, 1958 A 1,2,3, 1959 BI 1, 1963 E 2
Ward, R H (Southland) 1936 A 2, 1937 SA 1,3
Waterman, A C (North Auckland) 1929 A 1,2
Watkins, E L (Wellington) 1905 A
Watt, B A (Canterbury) 1962 A 1,4, 1963 E 1,2, W, 1964 E, S, A 1
Watt, J M (Otago) 1936 A 1,2
Watt, J R (Wellington) 1958 A 2, 1960 SA 1,2,3,4, 1961 F 1,3, 1962 A 1,2
Watts, M G (Taranaki) 1979 F 1,2, 1980 A 1,2,3(R)
Webb, D S (North Auckland) 1959 BI 2
Weepu, P A T (Wellington) 2004 W, 2005 SA1(R),A1,SA2, A2,I,E(R),S, 2006 Arg,A1(R),SA1,A3(R),SA2,F1,W(R), 2007 F1,C(R),SA1(R),A1(R),SA2
Wells, J (Wellington) 1936 A 1,2
West, A H (Taranaki) 1921 SA 2,3
Whetton, A J (Auckland) 1984 A 1(R),3(R), 1985 A (R), Arg 1(R), 1986 A 2, 1987 [It, Fj, Arg, S, W, F], A, 1988 W 1,2, A 1,2,3, 1989 F 1,2, Arg 1,2, A, 1990 S 1,2, A 1,2,3, F 1,2, 1991 Arg 1, [E, US, It, C, A]
Whetton, G W (Auckland) 1981 SA 3, R, F 1,2, 1982 A 3, 1983 BI 1,2,3,4, 1984 F 1,2, A 1,2,3, 1985 E 1,2, A, Arg 2, 1986 A 2,3, F 2,3, 1987 [It, Fj, Arg, S, W, F], A, 1988 W 1,2, A 1,2,3, 1989 F 1,2, Arg 1,2, A, W, I, 1990 S 1,2, A 1,2,3, F 1,2, 1991 Arg 1,2, A 1,2, [E, US, It, C, A, S]
Whineray, W J (Canterbury, Waikato, Auckland) 1957 A 1,2, 1958 A 1,2,3, 1959 BI 1,2,3,4, 1960 SA 1,2,3,4, 1961 F 1,2,3, 1962 A 1,2,3,4,5, 1963 E 1,2, I, W, 1964 E, S, F, 1965 SA 1,2,3,4
White, A (Southland) 1921 SA 1, 1924 I, 1925 E, F
White, H L (Auckland) 1954 I, E, F, 1955 A 3
White, R A (Poverty Bay) 1949 A 1,2, 1950 BI 1,2,3,4, 1951 A 1,2,3, 1952 A 1,2, 1953 W, 1954 I, E, S, F, 1955 A 1,2,3, 1956 SA 1,2,3,4
White, R M (Wellington) 1946 A 1,2, 1947 A 1,2
Whiting, G J (King Country) 1972 A 1,2, S, 1973 E 1, I, F
Whiting, P J (Auckland) 1971 BI 1,2,4, 1972 A 1,2,3, W, S, 1973 E 1, I, F, 1974 A 1,2,3, I, 1976 I, SA 1,2,3,4
Williams, A J (Auckland) 2002 E, F, W, 2003 E, W, F, SA 1, A 1, SA 2, A 2, [Tg,W,SA,A,F], 2004 SA1(R),A2,It(R),W,F(R), 2005 Fj,BI1,2,3,SA1,A1,SA2,A2,I,E, 2006 Arg,A1(R),SA1,A2, 3(R),SA2,3,F1,2,W, 2007 F1,2, [It,Pt,S,F]
Williams, B G (Auckland) 1970 SA 1,2,3,4, 1971 BI 1,2,4, 1972 A 1,2,3, W, S, 1973 E 1, I, F, E 2, 1974 A 1,2,3, I, 1975 S, 1976 I, SA 1,2,3,4, 1977 BI 1,2,3,4, F 1, 1978 A 1,2,3, I (R), W, E, S
Williams, G C (Wellington) 1967 E, W, F, S, 1968 A 2
Williams, P (Otago) 1913 A 1
Williment, M (Wellington) 1964 A 1, 1965 SA 1,2,3, 1966 BI 1,2,3,4, 1967 A
Willis, R K (Waikato) 1998 SA 2, A 3, 1999 SA 1(R), A 1(R), SA 2(R), A 2(R), [Tg (R), E (R), It, F 2(R), SA 3], 2002 SA 1(R)
Willis, T E (Otago) 2002 It, Fj, SA 2(R), A 2, SA 2
Willocks, C (Otago) 1946 A 1,2, 1949 SA 1,3,4
Wilson, B W (Otago) 1977 BI 3,4, 1978 A 1,2,3, 1979 F 1,2, A
Wilson, D D (Canterbury) 1954 E, S
Wilson, H W (Otago) 1949 A 1, 1950 BI 4, 1951 A 1,2,3
Wilson, J W (Otago) 1993 S, E, 1994 A, 1995 C, [I, J, S, E, SA], A 1,2, It, F 1, 1996 WS, S 1,2, A 1, SA 1, A 2, SA 2,3,4,5, 1997 Fj, Arg 1,2, A 1, SA 1, A 2, SA 2, A 3, I, E 1, W, E 2, 1998 E 1,2, A 1, SA 1, A 2, SA 2, A 3, 1999 WS, F 1, SA 1, A 1, SA 2, A 2, [Tg, E, It, S, F 2, SA 3], 2001 Sm, Arg 1, F, SA 1, A 1, SA 2
Wilson, N A (Wellington) 1908 AW 1,2, 1910 A 1,2,3, 1913 A 2,3, 1914 A 1,2,3
Wilson, N L (Otago) 1951 A 1,2,3
Wilson, R G (Canterbury) 1979 S, E
Wilson, S S (Wellington) 1977 F 1,2, 1978 A 1,2,3, I, W, E, S, 1979 F 1,2, A, S, E, 1980 A 1, W, 1981 S 1,2, SA 1,2,3, R, F 1,2, 1982 A 1,2,3, 1983 BI 1,2,3,4, A, S, E
Witcombe, D J C (Auckland) 2005 Fj,BI1(R),2(R),SA1(R), A1(R)
Wolfe, T N (Wellington, Taranaki) 1961 F 1,2,3, 1962 A 2,3, 1963 E 1
Wood, M E (Canterbury, Auckland) 1903 A, 1904 BI
Woodcock, T D (North Harbour) 2002 W, 2004 E1(t&R),2(t&R),Arg,W,F, 2005 Fj,BI1,2,3,SA1,A1,SA2,A2, W(R),I,E, 2006 Arg,A1,2,3,SA2(R),3,E,F1,2,W(R), 2007 F1,2,SA1,A1,SA2,A2, [It,Pt(R),S,F]
Woodman, F A (North Auckland) 1981 SA 1,2, F 2
Wrigley, E (Wairarapa) 1905 A
Wright, T J (Auckland) 1986 F 1, A 1, 1987 [Arg], 1988 W 1,2, A 1,2,3, 1989 F 1,2, Arg 1,2, A, W, I, 1990 S 1,2, A 1,2,3, F 1,2, 1991 Arg 1,2, A 1,2, [E, US, It, S]
Wylie, J T (Auckland) 1913 A 1, US
Wyllie, A J (Canterbury) 1970 SA 2,3, 1971 BI 2,3,4, 1972 W, S, 1973 E 1, I, F, E 2

Yates, V M (North Auckland) 1961 F 1,2,3
Young, D (Canterbury) 1956 SA 2, 1958 A 1,2,3, 1960 SA 1,2,3,4, 1961 F 1,2,3, 1962 A 1,2,3,5, 1963 E 1,2, I, W, 1964 E, S, F

NEW ZEALAND: DOMESTIC RUGBY

LAM LEADS AUCKLAND BACK

Auckland recaptured the Air New Zealand Cup title – in 2007 – which they had surrendered a year earlier and in the process emulated Gary Whetton's famous 1990 side that had won the domestic championship without suffering a single defeat.

Pat Lam's all-conquering team won all 10 of their league clashes – also claiming the Ranfurly Shield from Canterbury in week ten of the competition – and disposed of Taranaki and then Hawke's Bay in the knockout stages en route to the final and a showdown with Wellington at Eden Park.

The Lions were the runners-up the previous season and it was heartbreak again for Wellington in the final as Auckland edged a pulsating encounter 23–14 to claim a 16th domestic title and their fourth cup in six years.

Victory, however, marked the end of an era for Auckland. The final was the last game in the famous blue and white for 12 of Lam's side, with six players heading overseas, two to rival provinces and four into retirement but Lam refused to let the imminent exodus spoil the celebrations.

"We'll be in a bit of a rebuild next season but after what these young guys have already done it's going to be exciting times in the next couple of years," Lam said. "We plan for this, we knew these guys were going. These guys have done a fantastic job in our leadership group, they've incorporated everyone into the team and these guys have passed all the traditions on. In the last few weeks we've had the next tier of guys attend the leadership meeting just to get a taste so they can pick it up after they go."

Defeat was a bitter pill to swallow for Wellington after losing to Waikato in the 2006 final but coach Aussie McLean was determined to accentuate the positives after his side had been beaten at a wet and windy Eden Park.

"I'm proud of our guys, we stuck at it the whole way," he said. "We just weren't good enough. There were a lot of key moments in the match, we made a couple of errors in the first half and gifted them a couple of easy tries. But I'm really proud of our forwards, I think there's the basis of a really strong Wellington team going forward. When you have a

World Cup year, one positive is a number of guys are able to grow. The guys get the continuous footy they don't get when the stars are here."

The revamped Air New Zealand Cup campaign began in late July and although Auckland kicked off with a solid 39–5 win over Counties Manukau courtesy of a hat-trick from All Black wing Doug Howlett, it was Wellington who laid down the most convincing opening marker with a 68–7 demolition of Otago. McLean's side ran in nine tries in the rout at the Westpac Stadium and the domestic season began with a bang.

Week Two saw the Lions travel to Napier to face Hawke's Bay and the two title hopefuls produced a titanic clash at McLean Park which was scoreless at half-time. The decisive moment of the match came in the 69th minute when the home side drove from a lineout 10 metres out and No 8 George Naoupu crashed over. It was the only try of the game and Hawke's Bay clung on for a tense 8–6 win.

The biggest clash of the season to date came in Week Four when Canterbury faced Wellington at the AMI Stadium. The home side were unbeaten in three and although the outcome was still in doubt until the final 10 minutes, Canterbury scored twice late on to clinch a 41–23 victory with Stephen Brett the star of the show with his 26 point haul.

"This team is setting its own standards and they're starting to set some quite lofty ones," said Canterbury coach Rob Penney. "We stepped forward tonight because Wellington is obviously a legitimate first-class contender. We were prepared for a good battle and we got it. Some areas we still need to refine but 41 points is not bad against a side like that."

Auckland were pushed close in Week Five but eventually saw off Taranaki 22–13 at Eden Park and as the league progressed, Lam's side headed a quartet of Auckland, Canterbury, Wellington and Hawke's bay at the top of the table.

Week Ten would decide the quarter-final line-ups and all eyes were on Auckland's trip to Canterbury. The visitors were yet to be beaten and with the Ranfurly Shield up for grabs, the stakes could not have been higher.

The game was Auckland skipper Sam Tuitupou's 50th appearance for the province but it was his forwards who laid the platform for victory and two tries from full-back Brent Ward helped secure a 26–15 win. The result was the fifth time Auckland had relieved the red and blacks of the Ranfurly Shield and secured Lam's side home advantage in the play-offs.

The first quarter-final saw Wellington despatch Southland 45–3 without incident and Canterbury were similarly untroubled during their 44–6 win over Otago. Auckland made it 11 domestic victories in succession with a 30–10 triumph over Taranaki but the pick of the quarter-finals was

Hawke's Bay's clash with Waikato in Napier, which the Magpies edged 38–31 in an engrossing encounter.

The first semi-final pitted Canterbury against Wellington in Christchurch and it was the visitors who made early inroads with two tries from Tane Tuipulotu to establish an early advantage and seemingly leave the Cantabs with no hope.

The second-half however saw Canterbury stage a spirited fightback and late tries from Johny Leo'o and Campbell Johnstone meant Wellington had a nervous last seven minutes before the referee finally blew and they were confirmed as 26–21 victors.

"It was very disappointing to lose, especially because we didn't play a lot of rugby in that first 50 minutes," conceded Penney. "But you could only be proud of how the guys kept going until the end. Facing a 20-point scoreline like we were, a lot of teams would have capitulated. We didn't and instead fought to the end, which said a lot for the guts and the character within the group."

Auckland's last-four clash with Hawke's Bay was in contrast an altogether more one-sided affair as Lam's team maintained their dominant form and ran out comfortable 38–3 winners. Progress to the semi-finals was a fairytale story for the unfancied Magpies but the astute tactical kicking of Isa Nacewa and five well-taken tries ensured there was no upset at Eden Park.

"Right front the start we knew we were up against it," admitted Bay coach Peter Russell. "They put our back three under enormous pressure and seemed to come away with points almost at will."

The stage was set for the final seven days later and although Lam welcomed back All Blacks Keven Mealamu and Isaia Toeava after New Zealand's shock World Cup defeat to France, the Auckland coach resisted the temptation to change a winning formula and named the same starting XV to face Wellington.

The match was played in atrocious conditions and Lions fly-half Jimmy Gopperth opened the scoring for the visitors in the fifth minute with a well-taken penalty. Lock Jay Williams hit back for Auckland with the first try of the match and the home side stamped their mark on proceedings when Nacewa crossed for a second try and a 14–3 lead.

Wellington were now forced to play catch-up rugby. Second row Jeremy Thrush cut the deficit with a try for McLean's side after a stunning counter attack early in the second-half but there were to be no further five-point scores for either side as the driving rain made handling a lottery.

Nacewa and Gopperth traded penalties and although Auckland were forced to play 10 of the final 15 minutes with 14 men after Troy Flavell was sin binned for handling in a ruck, Lam's team clung for a 23–14 win.

"I'm very pleased with the efforts," said Lam after the final whistle. "It was a true final. It was a game that we had to really grind out. I just feel proud of the guys because of what they've put in place. We've looked at every part of our game and even when we were beating teams quite comfortably, the guys would front up on areas that could improve and they've put a lot of work in."

Skipper Sam Tuitupou and full-back Brent Ward were among the dozen players making their last appearances for Auckland and the latter admitted it was difficult to say goodbye to the champion province.

"Most of us guys have played together for a long time," Ward said at Eden Park. "We've got fantastic friendships between the guys and it's pretty emotional to leave. Winning the Shield and going out on a high by winning this Air New Zealand Cup is a fantastic way to go out and we'll treasure the memories for a very long time."

AIR NEW ZEALAND CUP 2007 RESULTS

26 July: **Manawatu** 15 **Waikato** 41

27 July: **Wellington** 68 **Otago** 7, **Taranaki** 29 **Tasman** 17

28 July: **Northland** 27 **North Harbour** 27, **Auckland** 39 **Counties Manukau** 5, **Canterbury** 34 **Bay of Plenty** 3

29 July: **Southland** 13 **Hawke's Bay** 41

2 August: **Tasman** 33 **Manawatu** 10

3 August: **Bay of Plenty** 3 **Auckland** 41, **Otago** 23 **Northland** 20

4 August: **Hawke's Bay** 8 **Wellington** 6, **Waikato** 22 **Southland** 11, **North Harbour** 19 **Taranaki** 13

5 August: **Counties Manukau** 13 **Canterbury** 52

9 August: **Bay of Plenty** 17 **Northland** 24

10 August: **Counties Manukau** 13 **North Harbour** 13, **Tasman** 23 **Hawke's Bay** 17

11 August: **Wellington** 37 **Manawatu** 7, **Auckland** 47 **Waikato** 26, **Otago** 7 **Canterbury** 27

12 August: **Taranaki** 20 **Southland** 25

16 August: **Northland** 9 **Tasman** 3

17 August: **Waikato** 30 **Counties Manukau** 8, **Hawke's Bay** 35 **North Harbour** 25

18 August: **Southland** 19 **Auckland** 44, **Taranaki** 15 **Otago** 18, **Canterbury** 41 **Wellington** 23

19 August: **Manawatu** 30 **Bay of Plenty** 18

23 August: **Counties Manukau** 14 **Hawke's Bay** 38

24 August: **Southland** 24 **Northland** 16, **Auckland** 22 **Taranaki** 13

25 August: **Bay of Plenty** 25 **Otago** 29, **Wellington** 38 **Tasman** 25, **North Harbour** 7 **Waikato** 52

26 August: **Canterbury** 64 **Manawatu** 10

30 August: **Hawke's Bay** 11 **Auckland** 38

31 August: **Counties Manukau** 18 **Wellington** 33, **Otago** 20 **Southland** 26

1 September: **Tasman** 26 **Bay of Plenty** 33, **Northland** 20 **Taranaki** 22, **Waikato** 20 **Canterbury** 33

2 September: **North Harbour** 34 **Manawatu** 16

6 September: **Southland** 47 **Counties Manukau** 10

7 September: **Canterbury** 44 **Hawke's Bay** 6, **Taranaki** 36 **Bay of Plenty** 19

8 September: **Tasman** 23 **Waikato** 25, **Northland** 25 **Auckland** 33, **Wellington** 39 **North Harbour** 14

9 September: **Manawatu** 25 **Otago** 25

13 September: **Taranaki** 13 **Canterbury** 20

14 September: **Waikato** 27 **Wellington** 41, **Hawke's Bay** 35 **Northland** 29

15 September: **Manawatu** 31 **Counties Manukau** 18, **Auckland** 49 **Tasman** 7, **Otago** 31 **North Harbour** 22

16 September: **Bay of Plenty** 0 **Southland** 19

20 September: **Wellington** 53 **Taranaki** 12

21 September: **Tasman** 14 **Canterbury** 21, **Auckland** 32 **Otago** 21

22 September: **Southland** 30 **Manawatu** 11, **Hawke's Bay** 30 **Waikato** 26, **North Harbour** 42 **Bay of Plenty** 24

23 September: **Northland** 20 **Counties Manukau** 10

27 September: **Otago** 32 **Tasman** 13

28 September: **North Harbour** 19 **Southland** 17, **Bay of Plenty** 13 **Wellington** 16

29 September: **Waikato** 20 **Northland** 16, **Manawatu** 3 **Hawke's Bay** 31, **Canterbury** 15 **Auckland** 26

30 September: **Counties Manukau** 21 **Taranaki** 45

FINAL TABLE

	P	W	D	L	F	A	BP1	BP2	PTS
Auckland	10	10	0	0	371	145	8	0	48
Canterbury	10	9	0	1	351	135	6	0	42
Wellington	10	8	0	2	354	172	6	1	39
Hawke's Bay	10	7	0	3	252	221	5	1	34
Waikato	10	6	0	4	289	231	3	1	28
Southland	10	6	0	4	231	203	1	1	26
Otago	10	5	1	4	213	273	1	1	24
Taranaki	10	4	0	6	218	234	3	4	23
North Harbour	10	4	2	4	222	267	2	0	22
Northland	10	3	1	6	206	214	1	4	19
Tasman	10	2	0	8	184	263	0	4	12
Manawatu	10	2	1	7	158	331	1	0	11
Bay of Plenty	10	1	0	9	155	297	2	3	9
Counties	10	0	1	9	130	348	0	0	2

QUARTER FINALS

5 October: **Wellington** 45 **Southland** 3

6 October: **Canterbury** 44 **Otago** 6, **Auckland** 30 **Taranaki** 10

7 October: **Hawke's Bay** 38 **Waikato** 31

SEMI FINALS

6 October, Jade Stadium, Christchurch

CANTERBURY 21 (1G, 3PG, 1T) WELLINGTON 26 (2G, 4PG)

CANTERBURY: S Hamilton; R Gear, C Laulala, T Bateman, P Williams; S Brett, K Senio; B Franks, C Flynn (captain), C Johnstone, M Paterson, K O'Neill, K Read, J Leo'o, N Manu

SUBSTITUTES: M Tuu'u, M Smith, I Ross, H Hopgood, T Keats, H Gard, S Yates

SCORERS *Tries:* Leo'o, Johnstone *Conversion:* Brett Penalty *Goals:* Brett (3)

WELLINGTON: C Jane; M Nonu, T Tu'ipulotu, T Ellison (captain), S Paku; J Gopperth, P Weepu; J Ellison, L Mahoney, J Schwalger, J Thrush, B Upton, A Naikatini, T Harding, T Waldrom

SUBSTITUTES: D Coles, A Perenise, F Levave, A Tulou, A Mathewson, D Kirkpatrick, H Gear

SCORERS *Tries:* Tuipulotu (2) *Conversions:* Gopperth (2) *Penalty Goals:* Gopperth (4)

REFEREE K Brown (New Zealand)

YELLOW CARD: Paterson (55 mins)

7 October, Eden Park, Auckland

AUCKLAND 38 (5G, 1PG)
HAWKE'S BAY 3 (1PG)

AUCKLAND: B Ward; D Smith, B Atiga, S Tuitupou (captain), B Stanley; I Nacewa, T Moa; S Taumoepeau, T McCartney, J Afoa, K Haiu, J Williams, J Kaino, D Braid, B Mika

SUBSTITUTES: C Heard, N White, T Flavell, A Macdonald, G Hart, L Munro, C Mahony

SCORERS *Tries:* Taumoepeau, Smith, Tuitupou, Flavell, Munro *Conversions:* Nacewa (5) *Penalty Goal:* Nacewa

HAWKE'S BAY: I Dagg; B Batger, J Shoemark, S Giddens, Z Guildford; M Berquist, C Eaton; F Taumalolo, H Elliott, T Fairbrother, M Egan, B Evans, M Johnson (captain), K Lowe, G Webb

SUBSTITUTES: J Muir, C Pera, W Crutchley, G Naoupu, C Shepherd, A Clarke, J Wilson

SCORERS *Penalty Goal:* Berquist

REFEREE V Munro (New Zealand)

FINAL

20 October, Eden Park, Auckland

AUCKLAND 23 (2G, 3PG)
WELLINGTON 14 (3PG, 1T)

AUCKLAND: B Ward; D Smith, I Toeava, S Tuitupou (captain), B Stanley; I Nacewa, T Moa: S Taumoepeau, T McCartney, J Afoa, K Haiu, J Williams, J Kaino, D Braid, B Mika

SUBSTITUTES: K Mealamu, N White, T Flavell, A Macdonald, G Hart, L Munro

SCORERS *Tries:* Williams, Nacewa *Conversions:* Nacewa (2) *Penalty Goals:* Nacewa (3)

WELLINGTON: C Jane; H Gear, T Tu'ipulotu, M Nonu, S Paku, J Gopperth, P Weepu (captain): J Ellison, L Mahoney, J Schwalger, J Thrush, B Upton, A Naikatini, T Harding, T Waldrom

SUBSTITUTES: D Coles, A Perenise, F Levave, R So'oialo, A Tulou, A Mathewson, C Smith

SCORERS *Try:* Thrush *Penalty Goals:* Gopperth (3)

REFEREE C Pollock (New Zealand)

PORTUGAL

PORTUGAL'S 2006–07 TEST RECORD

OPPONENTS	DATE	VENUE	RESULT
Georgia	11 Nov	A	**Lost** 3-17
Georgia	25 Nov	H	**Draw** 11-11
Morocco	20 Jan	A	**Won** 10-5
Morocco	27 Jan	H	**Won** 16-15
Spain	3 Feb	H	**Won** 21-18
Uruguay	10 Mar	H	**Won** 12-5
Uruguay	24 Mar	A	**Lost** 12-18
Russia	12 May	A	**Lost** 13-21
Czech Republic	19 May	A	**Won** 23-3
Canada	18 Aug	A	**Lost** 12-42
Japan	25 Aug	N	**Lost** 13–15
Scotland	9 Sept	N	**Lost** 10-56 (WC)
New Zealand	15 Sept	N	**Lost** 13-108 (WC)
Italy	19 Sept	N	**Lost** 5-31 (WC)
Romania	25 Sept	N	**Lost** 10-14 (WC)

A PLACE IN THE SUN

By Frankie Deges

One of the indelible highlights of Portugal's RWC 2007 campaign will have been all that was associated with the match they played in Lyon against New Zealand. Recognised as the biggest ever game in the history of Portuguese rugby, a history that goes back some 100 years, it was the one they had been dreaming of ever since the players in the squad started playing rugby. Yet, it was one that could have been the worst in their lives.

Even with no real hope of winning the game and acknowledging that it would be a damage limitation job, Portugal did not hesitate to put their bodies on the line, fight for every ball in what would be a losing battle and remain positive throughout the game.

They could have tried to kill the ball, slow everything and wait for the seconds and minutes on the clock to pass with the least possible rugby activity. They didn't and tried to match their heroes in black, and where they couldn't they still tried.

It all started with the Haka. As lock Gonçalo Uva aptly described it: "We will not have a second chance of standing so close to one so why not face it and enjoy it." From pitch-side it looked as if the Portuguese players were about to clap their heroes.

Going into the game, the team had set a few goals that did not involve winning the war, but making sure some of the battles were won. The way the players spoke at the end of the match showed that, clearly, most goals had been achieved. The one they failed, but only narrowly, was to keep the score under 100; at the final whistle it was 108–13.

Fly-half Gonçalo Malheiro kicked an impressive drop goal that got more cheers from the crowd than the tries the All Blacks had already scored, and when in the second half replacement hooker Rui Cordeiro crashed for the try, it brought the house down.

Whilst the battered but proud Lobos' were in the changing room after the game, and with the crowds not wanting to leave the comfortable Stade Gerland in glorious weather, the non-playing members of both teams returned to the field to exercise. A round ball was produced by the All Blacks and, shyly, the Portuguese asked if Mr R. McCaw, D. Carter and others would care for a game of soccer. With maybe some 5,000 fans still in the stands, the Portuguese and Kiwis then played a game of touch.

To round what was already a superb day in which the spirit of the game was reinforced, Graham Henry led his troops into the Portuguese changing room to share a cold beer with the RWC debutants. Cameras were produced and all the Portuguese took home photos with their peers in black.

What Portugal, the only in 20 nations that had never before played in World Cup finals, brought to this tournament was that sense of joy of being invited. They made sure this was to be the best possible experience and for that performing on the field was crucial.

Their long year that would include 13 internationals became glorious when they beat Uruguay in a home and away series to advance to Rugby World Cup. With one win each, it came down to a one-point difference that put Os Lobos in France 2007. That was the start of the new rugby revolution in the country.

In that respect, no stone was left unturned in their World Cup preparation and to ensure the people would know and understand what was rugby, until then a little known sport in the country.

With the much-needed assistance of the national government and the IRB, players were put on stringent training and given preparation matches and technical support. All this was led by the likeable Tomaz Morais, a coach of superb passion for the game and deep knowledge.

Unfortunately, at the start of the tournament Morais was caught in a problematic situation. His newborn daughter had complications, which meant that for the first couple of weeks he came and went to Portugal and was not able to give all the passion he has for team, country and sport. Fortunately, at the time of writing, the baby was recovering and in fact it was a much more relieved coach that led the team for the two final matches.

The way Portugal qualified to this Rugby World Cup had many thinking that they would struggle to mix it with the big boys. Scotland did not find it easy in St. Etienne, even with the Portuguese showing debutante nerves. They did manage to pose some questions to the Scots who would be in the quarter-finals – with three early tries by the winners it was always an uphill battle for Os Lobos.

But they still managed to score a try and a neat try it was. After a long period of possession it was finally winger Pedro Carvalho that crossed for his country's first ever World Cup finals try. A casualty of this match was fiery flanker Juan Severino Somoza, who would be suspended for three weeks after a head butt two seconds before the final whistle.

Having survived the All Blacks' and on a high, they went to play against an Italian side that found out that Portugal were not only enjoying their Rugby World Cup but getting better with every game.

Their 5–31 loss to the Italians again confirmed they were on the right road and when their lock David Penalva scored a try in the 33rd minute, the Parc des Princes celebrated in unison. Throughout the tournament, Portugal had great support, but the big Portuguese community came out in full force to Paris, the biggest community outside of Portugal. Denying a Six Nations team, that in the qualifying process had put 80 points on them, their bonus point for try-scoring was a victory in itself.

The last game of the tournament took them to Toulouse to play Romania, a team that has historically had the upper hand on the Portuguese. Their hunger and desperation to leave with a win brought them very close of their goal – to win the last game.

Two Romanian tries in the last half hour finished them off, but by then it was a team that was working on passion as the toll of four hard games in two weeks put them on the verge of exhaustion. They also missed the leadership of Vasco Uva, one of the stars of the tournament. In losing 10–14, they at least managed to leave with a bonus point and scored a try in each one of their games.

Os Lobos returned to Portugal as heroes after their World Cup matches were seen by one in every five Portuguese, their best rating had more than two million glued to television.

"People that before did not know that in rugby you pass the ball backwards was speaking about the game and the numbers are already rising even if the season has not started," said Morais upon returning to Lisbon. "It is now a question of how we handle this growth in numbers. In this sense it has also been a victory for the IRB as they have been trying to get the numbers in my country to grow and with us playing in the RWC that was achieved overnight."

It was a proud moment for all of the country to finally play in the biggest of rugby showdowns, the passion with which they sang their national anthem, "A Portuguesa" was soon compared with the lip-singing of their soccer counterparts in the 2006 FIFA World Cup.

"They recognise us for the way we played the game and get stopped on the street," added outside centre Miguel Portela, a lawyer by trade. "When we qualified for World Cup, judges would want to talk about the game. Now it has grown even bigger."

Soccer has even bowed to the team and the oval cousin – right after the tournament, Os Lobos were invited to a Benfica v Sporting tie, the biggest in the country; when they took the field during the half time break it was amidst a thunderous reception.

Children are now coming to the game in droves, something the Federaçao Portuguesa de Rugby will need to address to ensure they are looked after. The honeymoon might take some more time but it is the structures that will ensure that the growth is sustained and well supported.

When the local season starts, and Agronomía defends their first ever title won by beating Direito 15–8, the impetus of the game will be huge. Direito, five times champions in the last eight years have nine players from the RWC squad which will bring back to the local scene not only experience but fitness levels like never seen before.

Already organised is a Test against Romania, the re-match of the last World Cup game. Sponsors, media and public have already given the thumbs up to this team and it will be played in a big soccer stadium, with home crowds surpassing any wild dream of a year ago. That is what the World Cup can do to a so-called "minnow."

The next two years will be crucial in ensuring that Portugal manages to follow-up on the great deeds of a committed group of players and officials, spearheaded by Morais and his captain Uva, but with the great support of Daniel Hourcade and Adam Leach on the technical side. If anything, the country has awoken to rugby and is loving what it sees.

PORTUGAL INTERNATIONAL RECORDS

WINNING MARGIN

Date	Opponent	Result	Winning Margin
23/11/1996	Netherlands	55–11	**44**
30/05/1998	Andorra	53–11	**42**
28/02/1981	Switzerland	39–0	**39**
13/05/2006	Ukraine	52–14	**38**
08/04/1984	Denmark	40–3	**37**

MOST CONVERSIONS IN A MATCH BY THE TEAM

Date	Opponent	Result	Cons
13/05/2006	Ukraine	52–14	**6**
28/02/1981	Switzerland	39–0	**4**
08/04/1984	Denmark	40–3	**4**
30/05/1998	Andorra	53–11	**4**
10/06/2004	Barbarians	34–66	**4**

MOST POINTS IN A MATCH BY THE TEAM

Date	Opponent	Result	Pts.
23/11/1996	Netherlands	55–11	**55**
30/05/1998	Andorra	53–11	**53**
13/05/2006	Ukraine	52–14	**52**
15/05/1981	Denmark	45–16	**45**
08/03/2003	Czech Republic	43–10	**43**

MOST PENALTIES IN A MATCH BY THE TEAM

Date	Opponent	Result	Pens
06/02/2000	Georgia	30–32	**9**
23/03/2003	Spain	35–16	**7**
29/03/2003	Russia	25–14	**6**
16/02/2003	Georgia	34–30	**5**
04/03/2001	Spain	15–31	**5**

MOST TRIES IN A MATCH BY THE TEAM

Date	Opponent	Result	Tries
30/05/1998	Andorra	53–11	**9**
15/05/1981	Denmark	45–16	**9**
13/05/2006	Ukraine	52–14	**8**
28/02/1981	Switzerland	39–0	**7**

MOST DROP GOALS IN A MATCH BY THE TEAM

Date	Opponent	Result	DGs
17/03/1985	Morocco	12–6	**2**

MOST POINTS IN A MATCH BY A PLAYER

Date	Player	Opponent	Pts.
06/02/2000	Thierry Teixeira	Georgia	30
23/03/2003	Gonçalo Malheiro	Spain	25
08/03/2003	Gonçalo Malheiro	Czech Republic	24
10/06/2004	Gonçalo Malheiro	Barbarians	21

MOST TRIES IN A MATCH BY A PLAYER

Date	Player	Opponent	Tries
21/03/2004	Nuno Garváo	Spain	3
10/06/2004	Gonçalo Malheiro	Barbarians	3

MOST CONVERSIONS IN A MATCH BY A PLAYER

Date	Player	Opponent	Cons
30/05/1998	Nuno Mourao	Andorra	4
08/04/1984	Joao Queimado	Denmark	4
13/05/2006	João Diogo Mota	Ukraine	4

MOST PENALTIES IN A MATCH BY A PLAYER

Date	Player	Opponent	Pens
06/02/2000	Thierry Teixeira	Georgia	9
23/03/2003	Gonçalo Malheiro	Spain	7
29/03/2003	Gonçalo Malheiro	Russia	6
16/02/2003	Gonçalo Malheiro	Georgia	5
04/03/2001	Franck Cather	Spain	5

MOST DROP GOALS IN A MATCH BY A PLAYER

Date	Player	Opponent	DGs
17/03/1985	Joao Queimado	Morocco	2

MOST CAPPED PLAYERS

Name	Caps
Joaquim Ferreira	84
Luis Pissarra	71
Marcello Dias	57
Miguel Portela de Morais	56
Diogo Mateus	53

LEADING TRY SCORERS

Name	Tries
Diogo Mateus	13
Nuno Durão	13
António Aguilar	12
Nuno Garváo	10
Carlos Moita	8

LEADING CONVERSIONS SCORERS

Name	Cons
Gonçalo Malheiro	20
Duarte Cardoso Pinto	14
Joao Queimado	14
Nuno Mourao	11
Pedro Leal	11

LEADING PENALTY SCORERS

Name	Pens
Gonçalo Malheiro	51
Joao Queimado	39
Duarte Cardoso Pinto	21
José Maria Vilar Gomes	18
Thierry Teixeira	14

LEADING DROP GOAL SCORERS

Name	DGs
Joao Queimado	10
Luís Lynce de Faria	2
Gonçalo Malheiro	2

LEADING POINTS SCORERS

Name	Pts.
Gonçalo Malheiro	234
Joao Queimado	198
Duarte Cardoso Pinto	101
Rohan Hoffman	72
José Maria Vilar Gomes	69

PORTUGAL INTERNATIONAL PLAYERS

UP TO 31ST OCTOBER 2007

Note: Years given for International Championship matches are for second half of season; eg 1972 means season 1971–72. Years for all other matches refer to the actual year of the match. Entries in square brackets denote matches played in RWC Finals.

Acosta, ED 2006 *Rus, Ur*
Águas, A 1984 *H, Bel, De* 1985 *Mor, Cze, Pol, Z* 1986 *R, R* 1987 *Z, Z, Tun, Bel* 1988 *Ger*
Aguiar, D 1970 *H, Mor, Sp* 1981 *Swi, De* (R), *Swe* 1982 *Mor, Sp*
Aguiar, R 2005 *Ur* (R) 2006 *Ukr* (R), *CZR* (R)
Aguilar, A 1999 *H, Ur, Ur* 2000 *Geo, Sp, SA23* 2001 *R, H, Rus* 2002 *R, Geo, Sp, H, Rus, Pol, Sp* 2003 *Geo, Sp* (R) 2004 *Geo, R, CZR, Sp, Rus, Bb* 2005 *Rus, R, Ch, Ur, Fj* 2006 *Rus, Geo, R, Ukr, CZR, Rus, Ur, It, Rus, Geo, Geo* 2007 *C, NZ, It, R*
Albergaria, E 1935 *Sp*
Albergaria, JM 1981 *Swi*
Albuquerque, M 1987 *USS* 1988 *Yug*
Almeida, AV 1983 *Sp, H, Pol, Swe* 1984 *Sp, H, Bel, De* 1985 *Mor, Cze, Pol, Z* 1986 *R, F, It, Tun, R* 1987 *It, Bel* 1988 *H, Ger, Yug* 1989 *H, Bel, Yug, Ger, Cze, H* 1990 *Bel, Tun, Sp* 1991 *Nm*
Almeida, J 1954 *Sp*
Almeida, PM 1974 *Ger*
Alpuim, G 1998 *US, And* (R) 2006 *CZR* (R)
Álvares, FP 1954 *Sp*
Amaral, AF 1965 *Sp* 1969 *Sp*
Amaral, SF 1997 *Geo, Sp* 1998 *Nm, Ger, US, CZR, Mor, Sp, And, S, Sp* 1999 *H, Ur, Ur* 2000 *Geo* (R), *Sp, R, Mor, H*
Andrade, A 1970 *H, Mor* 1972 *It*
Andrade, AR 1994 *Bel, Ger, Mor, Tun, W, Sp* 1995 *Mor* 1997 *Geo, Sp*
Andrade, LR 2002 *Sp* (R) 2003 *Rus* (R) 2004 *Geo, R, CZR, Sp, Rus, Bb, Ch* (R), *Ur* (R), *Ukr* (R) 2005 *Geo, CZR, Rus* (R) 2006 *Ukr* (R), *CZR* (R) 2007 *CZR*
Antunes, T 1970 *Sp*
Araújo, FX 1935 *Sp* 1936 *Sp*
Ascenção, M 1999 *Ur*
Augusto, JC 1970 *Sp* 1972 *It, It* (R)
Ávila, GB 1973 *It, Yug, Swi, Pol, Pol*
Avilez, AM 1936 *Sp*
Azevedo, S 1997 *Sp* 1998 *Nm, Ger, US, CZR, Mor, Sp, And*
Baptista, J 1998 *US, And* (R) 2002 *R* (R)
Baptista, M 1993 *It, Bel* 1994 *Bel, Ger, Mor, Tun, W, Sp*
Barata, R 1998 *Nm* (R), *Ger* (R)
Barbosa, M 1996 *Sp, H, Tun* 1998 *S, Sp* 1999 *H, Ur, Ur* 2000 *Geo, Sp, R, Mor, H* 2001 *H, Rus* (R)
Barceló, J 1936 *Sp*
Bastos, R 1935 *Sp*
Begonha, R 1966 *Sp, Bel*
Belo, FL 1986 *R* 1987 *It, F, Z, Z* 1988 *H, Ger, Yug*
Belo, J 1954 *Sp*
Belo, JFL 1985 *Mor, Cze, Pol* 1986 *F, It, Tun, USS, R* 1987 *It, F, Z, Z, Tun, USS* 1988 *H, Ger, Yug* 1989 *H, Bel, Yug, Ger, Cze, H* 1990 *Sp*
Benedito, R 2000 *SA23* 2001 *Geo* (R), *Sp* (R)
Bento, J 1997 *Geo, Sp* 1998 *Nm*
Bergh, H 2003 *R* (R), *CZR, Sp, Rus*
Bessa, JP 1969 *Sp* (R), *Mor* (R) 1972 *It, It* 1974 *It*
Borges, A 1966 *Sp, Bel*
Borges, F 1989 *H* 1991 *Tun, Mor, Nm* 1992 *And, Mor, Tun* 1993 *It, Tun, Swi*
Borges, O 1979 *Swi* 1981 *Swi, De, Swe*
Borges, R 1997 *Geo, Sp*
Braga, F 1995 *Mor, Sp*
Branco, A 1968 *Sp, Bel, Mor, It* 1970 *Sp* 1974 *Ger*
Branco, E 2000 *Mor, H* 2001 *R* 2002 *Geo, Sp, H, Rus*
Branco, E 1935 *Sp* 1936 *Sp*
Branco, MA 1965 *Sp* 1970 *H, Sp*
Branco, MdePC 1965 *Sp* 1966 *Sp, Bel* 1967 *Sp, F, R* 1968 *Sp, Bel, Mor, It* 1969 *Sp, Mor* 1970 *H, Mor*
Bravo, GVB 1954 *Sp*
Brito, JS 1973 *It, Yug, Swi, Pol, Pol* 1974 *It, Ger*
Briz, L 1973 *Yug, Pol, Pol*
Bruxelas, C 1936 *Sp*
Cabral, P 2006 *Ur* 2007 *Sp, Rus* (R), *CZR* (R), *C, S* (R), *It*
Cabrita, P 1966 *Sp, Bel*
Caldas, L 1954 *Sp*
Calheiros, F 1935 *Sp*
Canha, J 1999 *Ur* (R), *Ur*
Carapuço, A 1987 *It* (R)
Cardoso, F 1999 *H, Ur, Ur* (R)
Cardoso, M 2000 *Geo, Sp, R, Mor, H* 2001 *R, Geo, Sp, H, Rus*
Carqueijeiro, AM 1965 *Sp*
Cartucho, A 1970 *Sp*
Carvalho, J 1998 *Sp* (R), *Sp* 1999 *H* 2000 *Geo, Sp, R* (R)
Carvalho, P 2004 *Ch, Ur, Ukr* 2005 *Geo, CZR, Rus, Fj* (R) 2006 *Ukr, CZR, Rus* (R), *Ur, It, Rus, Geo, Geo* 2007 *Mor, Mor, Sp, Ur, Ur, CZR, C, S, NZ, R*
Carvoeira, R 1990 *Mor, Nm* 1991 *And, Nm*
Castro, C 2000 *Sp, R, Mor, H, SA23* 2001 *R* (R), *Sp* (R), *Rus* (R)
Castro, PM 1995 *Sp, CZR, Ger* 1996 *It, Bel, Pol, R, Tun* 1997 *Geo, Sp* 1998 *Ger, CZR* (R), *Sp* (R), *And, S, Sp* 2002 *Geo* (R) 2006 *Geo* (R)
Cather, F 2001 *Sp, H, Rus*
Catulo, J 1993 *R* 1996 *It, Bel, Pol*
Cayola, V 1935 *Sp*
Chança, J 1990 *Mor, Nm* 1992 *Tun* (R)
Chança, R 1998 *Nm, Ger, US, CZR* 2002 *R*
Chaves, LM 1965 *Sp* 1966 *Sp, Bel* 1967 *It, F, R* 1969 *Sp* 1970 *Sp* (R)
Claro, L 1981 *Swi* (R)
Cláudio, A 1997 *Geo* (R), *Sp* 1998 *Sp* (R), *And* (R)
Coelho, A 1935 *Sp*
Conceicao, B 2006 *Rus* (R), *Geo* (R), *R* (R)
Consciência, P 1979 *Swi*
Cordeiro, R 2002 *R, Geo, Sp, H, Rus, Pol, Sp* 2003 *Geo, R, CZR, Sp, Rus* 2004 *Geo, R, CZR, Sp, Rus, Bb, Ch* (R), *Ur* (R), *Ukr* 2005 *Rus* (R), *R, Fj* 2006 *Rus, Geo, R, CZR, Rus* (R), *Ur, It* (R), *Rus, Geo, Geo* (R) 2007 *Mor, Mor, Sp, Ur* (R), *CZR, S, NZ* (R), *It, R*
Correia 1990 *Mor, Nm, Bel, Tun* 1993 *It, Swi, Sp*
Correia, E 1998 *US, Mor*
Correia, H 1935 *Sp* 1936 *Sp*
Correia, J 1999 *Ur*
Correia, J 2003 *CZR* (R), *Sp* (R) 2004 *Bb* (R), *Ch, Ur, Ukr* 2005 *Geo, CZR, Rus, R, Ch, Ur, Fj* 2006 *Rus, R, Ukr, Rus, It, Rus, Geo, Geo* 2007 *Mor, Mor, Sp, Ur, Ur, C* (R), *S* (R), *NZ, It, R* (R)
Costa, AP 1967 *Sp* 1968 *Bel, It* 1969 *Sp, Mor* 1970 *H, Mor*
Costa, JP 1996 *It, Bel, Pol, R*
Costa, LC 1979 *Swi* 1981 *Bel* 1982 *Mor* (R), *Sp, Tun, Pol* (R)
Costa, LP 1969 *Sp, Mor* 1970 *H, Mor*
Costa, MF 1973 *Yug* 1981 *Swi, De, Swe* 1982 *Mor, Sp, H, Pol* 1983 *Sp* 1984 *Sp, H, Bel, De*

Costa, MMd 1987 *Bel*
Costa, P 2000 *R, H*
Costa, RB 1969 *Sp, Mor*
Costa, T 1998 *Nm*
Couceiro, V 2004 *Sp* (R)
Coutinho, D 2000 *SA23* 2001 *H, Rus* 2002 *Sp* (R), *Pol, Sp* 2004 *Bb* (R) 2005 *Geo* (R), *CZR, Ur* (R), *Fj* 2006 *Rus, Geo, R, Ukr, CZR, Rus, Ur, It, Rus, Geo, Geo* 2007 *Mor* (R), *Sp* (R), *Ur* (R), *Rus, CZR, C, S* (R), *NZ, R*
Coutinho, P 1986 *USS*
Cruz, C 1935 *Sp* 1936 *Sp*
Cunha, A 1990 *Nm* (R), *Tun, Sp* 1991 *Nm* 1992 *And, Mor, Tun* 1993 *R, It, Tun, Bel, Swi, Sp* 1994 *Mor, W* (R), *Sp* 1995 *Mor, Sp, CZR, Ger* 1996 *It, Pol, R, Sp, H, Tun* 2000 *SA23* 2001 *Geo* (R), *H* (R) 2002 *R* (R), *Geo, Sp, H, Rus, Pol, Sp* (R) 2003 *Geo* (R), *R* (R), *CZR, Sp, Rus* 2004 *Geo, R, CZR, Sp, Rus, Bb, Ch, Ur* (R), *Ukr* 2005 *Geo, CZR* (R)
Cunha, J 1969 *Mor*
Cunha, S 1992 *And, Mor, Tun* 1993 *R, It, Tun, Bel, Swi, Sp* 1994 *Bel*
Cunha, S 2004 *R* (R), *Ch* (R), *Ukr* (R) 2005 *Geo* (R), *CZR* (R), *Ch* (R), *Ur* (R) 2006 *Rus* (R)
Curvelo, P 1989 *Bel, Yug, Ger*

Dias, M 1996 *Sp, H, Tun* 1997 *Geo, Sp* 1998 *Nm, Ger, US, CZR, Mor, Sp, And, Sp* 1999 *Ur* 2002 *R, Geo, Sp, H, Rus, Pol, Sp* 2003 *Geo, R, CZR, Sp, Rus* 2004 *Geo, R, CZR, Sp, Rus, Bb, Ch, Ur, Ukr* 2005 *Geo, CZR, Rus, R, Ch* (R), *Ur, Fj* 2006 *Rus, Geo, R, Ukr* (R), *CZR* (R), *Ur, It, Rus, Geo, Geo* 2007 *Mor, Mor, Ur, Ur, NZ*
Dias, V 1968 *Bel, Mor, It*
Domingos, P 1994 *Bel, Ger, Mor, Tun, W, Sp*
Dores, A 1979 *Swi* 1981 *Swi, Bel, De*
D'Orey Branco, R 2007 *Rus* (R), *CZR* (R)
Duarte, G 2006 *Geo* (R) 2007 *Mor* (R), *Sp* (R), *Rus* (R), *CZR* (R)
Duarte, J 1999 *Ur* (R)
Duarte, J 1936 *Sp*
Duque, AG 1972 *It* 1973 *It, Yug, Pol, Pol* 1974 *It* 1981 *De, Swe* (R) 1982 *Mor, Sp, Tun, Pol*
Durão, N 1983 *Sp* 1984 *H, Bel, De* 1985 *Mor, Cze, Pol, Z* 1986 *R, F, It, Tun, USS, R* 1987 *It, F, Z, Z, Tun, USS, Bel* 1988 *H, Ger, Yug* 1989 *H, Bel, Yug, Ger, Cze, H* 1990 *Sp* 1991 *And, Tun, Mor* 1992 *And, Mor, Tun* 1994 *Bel, Ger* 1995 *Mor, Sp, CZR, Ger* 1996 *It*
Durão, R 1986 *R, F* (R), *R* (R) 1987 *Z, Z, Tun, Bel* 1988 *H, Ger, Yug*
Durão, V 1989 *H* 1990 *Mor, Nm, Bel, Tun* 1991 *And, Mor, Nm* 1992 *And, Mor, Tun* 1995 *Mor, Sp, CZR, Ger* 1996 *It, Bel, Pol, R, Sp, H, Tun*

Eiró, P 1979 *Swi* (R) 1981 *Swi, Bel, De, Swe* 1982 *Mor, Tun, H, Pol*
Escarduça, R 1998 *And* (R)
Esteves, A 1995 *Mor, Sp*
Esteves, A 2006 *Rus* (R), *It* (R) 2007 *Mor* (R)
Esteves, F 1995 *Ger*

Fachada, O 1987 *It, Z, Z* (R), *USS*
Faria, DL 1979 *Swi* 1981 *Bel*
Faria, G 2001 *Geo* (R) 2002 *Pol* (R), *Sp*
Faria, J 1967 *Sp, It* 1968 *Sp, Bel, It*
Faria, LL 1966 *Sp, Bel* 1967 *Sp, It, F, R* 1968 *Sp, Bel, Mor, It*
Faria, NL 1968 *Sp, Bel, Mor, It* 1970 *Sp* 1972 *It, It* 1973 *It, Yug, Swi, Pol, Pol* 1974 *It, Ger*
Faria, PL 1966 *Sp, Bel* 1967 *Sp, It, F, R* 1970 *H, Mor, Sp* 1973 *It, Yug* (R), *Swi, Pol, Pol*
Faria, VL 1981 *De, Swe* 1982 *Mor, Sp, Tun, H*
Fernandes, A 1973 *Swi*
Fernandes, AC 1970 *H, Mor, Sp* 1972 *It, It* 1973 *Swi* 1974 *Ger*
Fernandes, JC 1972 *It, It* 1974 *It* 1979 *Swi* 1981 *Swi, Bel, De, Swe* 1982 *Mor, Sp, Tun, H, Pol*
Fernandes, PN 1993 *R, Tun, Bel* 1994 *Mor, Tun, W, Sp* 1996 *Sp, H*
Fernandes, R 1991 *Mor, Nm*
Ferreira, A 2005 *Rus* (R), *R, Ur* (R), *Fj* (R)
Ferreira, AB 1982 *Sp, Tun, H, Pol* 1983 *Sp, H, Pol* 1984 *Sp, H, Bel, De* 1985 *Mor, Cze, Pol, Z* 1986 *R, F, It, Tun, USS* 1987 *Z, Z, Tun, USS, Bel* 1988 *H, Ger, Yug* 1989 *H, Bel, Yug, Ger, Cze, H*
Ferreira, CD 1979 *Swi* (R) 1981 *Swi, Bel*
Ferreira, CN 1965 *Sp* 1966 *Sp, Bel* 1967 *Sp, It, F, R* 1968 *Sp, Mor, It* 1969 *Sp, Mor* 1970 *H* (R), *Mor, Sp* 1972 *It* (R) 1973 *It, Yug, Swi, Pol, Pol*
Ferreira, J 1993 *R, It* (R), *Tun, Swi* 1995 *Mor, Sp, CZR, Ger* 1996 *It, Bel, Pol, R, Sp, H, Tun* 1997 *Geo, Sp* 1998 *Nm, Ger, US, CZR, Mor, Sp, And, S, Sp* 1999 *H, Ur, Ur* 2000 *Geo, Sp, R, Mor, H* 2001 *R, Geo, Sp, H* (R), *Rus* (R) 2002 *H, Pol* 2003 *Geo, R, CZR, Sp, Rus* 2004 *Geo, R, CZR, Sp, Rus, Bb, Ch, Ur, Ukr* 2005 *Geo, CZR, Rus, R, Ch, Ur, Fj* 2006 *Rus* (R), *Geo, R, Ukr, CZR, Rus, Ur, It, Rus, Geo, Geo* 2007 *Mor, Mor, Sp, Ur, Ur, Rus, CZR, C, S, NZ* (R), *R*
Ferreira, PB 1983 *H, Pol, Swe* 1984 *Sp, Bel, De* 1985 *Mor, Cze, Pol, Z* 1986 *R, F, It, Tun, USS, R* 1987 *Bel* 1989 *H*
Ferreira, S 1991 *Tun, Mor, Nm* 1994 *Bel, Ger, Mor, Tun, W, Sp* 1995 *CZR, Ger* 1996 *Sp, H, Tun* 1997 *Geo* (R), *Sp* 1998 *Nm, Ger* (R) 2000 *SA23*
Figueiredo, DAA 2007 *Ur* (R), *Rus* (R), *CZR* (R), *It* (R)
Fonseca, P 1996 *Bel* 1998 *Nm* (R) 2000 *SA23* 2001 *R* (R), *Geo* (R), *H, Rus* 2002 *R, Geo, Sp, H, Rus, Pol, Sp* (R) 2003 *Geo, R, CZR, Sp, Rus* 2004 *CZR, Sp, Rus, Bb* 2005 *Ch, Ur, Fj* (R)
Fontes, F 2003 *Geo, R, CZR* (R)
Foro, G 2007 *Rus, CZR* (R), *It* (R)
Fragateima, F 2007 *CZR* (R)
Franco, JS 1974 *Ger*
Franco, SM 1983 *Pol, Swe*
Frazão, NCR 1974 *Ger*
Freitas, A 1992 *Tun* 1993 *R*

Gaio, RM 1982 *Pol* 1983 *Sp, Swe*
Galvão, E 1996 *It, Bel*
Gama, D 2006 *Rus* (R), *Geo* (R), *R* 2007 *Mor, Mor, Ur, Ur, Rus* (R), *CZR* (R), *It* (R)
Gameiro, F 1954 *Sp*
Garcia, FR 1983 *H, Pol, Swe* 1984 *H* (R), *Bel* (R) 1985 *Cze* (R), *Pol, Z* 1986 *R, F* 1987 *It, Z, Z, USS*
Garcia, M 1936 *Sp*
Garváo, N 2001 *R, H, Rus* 2002 *R, Geo, Sp, H, Rus, Pol, Sp* 2003 *R* (R), *CZR, Sp, Rus* 2004 *CZR, Sp, Bb* (R) 2005 *CZR* (R)
Gaspar, JR 1967 *Sp, F, R*
Girão, T 2006 *Geo* (R), *R* (R), *It* (R) 2007 *NZ* (R), *It, R*
Goes, F 2000 *SA23*
Gomes, JMV 1989 *Cze, H* 1990 *Mor, Nm, Bel, Tun, Sp* 1991 *And, Tun, Mor, Nm* 1992 *And, Mor, Tun* 1993 *R, Tun, Bel, Swi* 1994 *Bel, Ger, Mor, Tun, W* 1995 *Mor, Sp, CZR, Ger* 1996 *It, Bel, Sp* 1998 *S* 2000 *SA23*
Gomes, NMV 1996 *It, Bel, Pol, R, H*
Gomes, R 1998 *S* (R), *Sp* (R) 1999 *Ur*
Goncalves, V 2005 *Ch* (R)
Gonçalves, G 1983 *Sp, H, Pol, Swe*
Gonçalves, G 1935 *Sp*
Gonçalves, P 2000 *SA23* 2001 *R, Geo, Sp* 2002 *R, Geo, Sp, H, Rus, Pol, Sp* 2003 *Geo, R, CZR* (R), *Sp* (R)
Grenho, F 2001 *R* (R), *Geo* (R), *Rus* 2004 *Geo, R, CZR, Ukr* 2005 *Ch* (R), *Ur, Fj* (R) 2006 *Rus, Geo, R* (R)
Grenho, F 1979 *Swi*
Guedes, FN 1969 *Sp, Mor* 1972 *It, It*
Guedes, JFN 1967 *It, F, R* 1968 *Sp, Bel, Mor, It* 1969 *Mor* 1972 *It*

Heitor, R 2001 *Geo* (R), *Sp* (R), *H* (R), *Rus* 2005 *Ch* (R)
Herédia, J 1991 *And, Tun, Mor, Nm* 1992 *And, Mor, Tun* 1993 *It, Tun, Bel, Swi, Sp* 1994 *Bel*
Hoffman, PR 1996 *It, Pol, Sp, H, Tun* 1997 *Geo, Sp* 1998 *Nm, Ger, US, CZR, Sp, S, Sp* 1999 *H, Ur, Ur* 2000 *Geo, R, SA23* 2002 *R, Geo, Sp, H, Rus, Pol, Sp*

Jalles, A 1983 *H, Pol* (R) 1986 *R* (R) 1987 *Z* (R), *Tun* 1988 *Yug*
Jesus, F 1968 *Mor*
Jónatas, H 1989 *Cze, H*
Jonet, J 1990 *Mor, Nm, Bel, Tun, Sp* 1991 *And, Tun, Mor, Nm* 1992 *And, Mor, Tun* 1993 *R, It, Swi, Sp* 1994 *Bel, Ger* 1995 *Mor, Sp, CZR, Ger*

King, T 1998 *Sp, And* 2001 *R* (R), *Geo, Sp, H, Rus* (R)

Lamas, L 1998 *S* 2000 *R, Mor, H* 2001 *Geo, Sp*
Laureano, J 1989 *Bel, Yug, Ger* 1990 *Mor, Nm, Bel, Sp*
Leal, P 2005 *CZR* (R), *R, Ch, Ur, Fj* 2006 *Rus, R, Rus, Ur, It, Rus, Geo* (R), *Geo* 2007 *Mor, Mor, Ur, Ur, Rus, CZR, C, S, NZ, R*

Leal, PR 1973 *Swi*, *Pol*, *Pol*
Leitão, AL 1982 *Sp* (R), *Tun* (R), *H*, *Pol* 1983 *Sp*, *H*, *Pol*, *Swe* 1984 *Sp*, *De*
Leite, O 1970 *Sp* 1972 *It*
Lencastre, J 1999 *Ur* (R)
Lencastre, P 1967 *Sp*, *It*, *F*, *R*
Lima, A 1995 *Mor*, *Sp*, *CZR*, *Ger* 1996 *It*, *R*, *H*, *Tun* 1997
Lima, F *Sp* 2000 *SA23* 2001 *R* (R)
Lima, JA 2002 *Pol*, *Sp* (R) 2003 *R*, *CZR* (R), *Sp* (R) 2004 *R* (R)
Lima, MS 1979 *Swi* 1981 *Bel*, *Swe* 1982 *Tun*
Lince, FR 1954 *Sp*
Lino, L 1968 *Bel*, *Mor* 1969 *Sp*, *Mor*
Lopes, AC 1987 *It*, *Z*, *Z*
Lopes, JM 1954 *Sp*
Lourenço, A 2007 *Ur*, *Ur*, *Rus*, *NZ*, *It* (R)
Lourenço, AdS 2000 *Geo* (R), *Sp*, *R*, *Mor*, *H* 2001 *Geo*, *Sp*, *H*, *Rus*
Lucena, F 1969 *Sp*, *Mor* 1970 *H*, *Mor*
Luìs, L 1986 *F*, *It* 1987 *It*, *F*, *Z*, *Z*, *USS* 1988 *H*, *Ger*, *Yug* 1989 *Bel*, *Yug*, *Ger*, *Cze*, *H* 1990 *Mor*, *Nm*, *Tun*, *Sp* 1991 *And*, *Tun*, *Mor*, *Nm* 1993 *It*, *Tun*, *Bel*, *Swi*, *Sp*
Luz, S 1987 *Z*, *Z*

Macedo, E 1988 *H* 1989 *H*, *Bel*, *Cze*, *H* 1990 *Mor*, *Nm*, *Bel*, *Tun*, *Sp* 1991 *And*, *Tun*, *Nm* 1992 *And*, *Mor*, *Tun* 1993 *R*, *It*, *Tun*, *Bel*, *Swi*, *Sp* 1994 *Mor*, *W* (R), *Sp*
Macieira, H 1979 *Swi* 1981 *Swi*, *Bel*, *Swe* 1982 *Mor*, *Tun*
Magalhães, JP 1981 *Bel*, *De*, *Swe*
Magalhães, VP 1936 *Sp*
Maia, MG 1981 *Bel*, *De*, *Swe* (R)
Maleitas, E 1979 *Swi* 1983 *Sp*
Malheiro, G 1998 *Mor* 1999 *H*, *Ur* 2000 *SA23* 2001 *R*, *Geo*, *Sp* (R), *H*, *Rus* (R) 2003 *Geo*, *R*, *CZR*, *Sp*, *Rus* 2004 *Geo*, *R*, *CZR*, *Sp*, *Rus*, *Bb*, *Ch*, *Ur* 2005 *Geo*, *CZR*, *Rus* 2006 *Ukr* (R), *CZR*, *Rus*, *Geo*, *Geo* 2007 *Mor* (R), *Ur* (R), *Ur* (R), *Rus* (R), *NZ*, *R* (R)
Malo, P 1986 *R*, *It*, *Tun*, *USS*
Marques, A 1996 *Bel*, *R*
Marques, JD 1996 *Pol*, *Sp*, *H*, *Tun*
Marques, MS 1936 *Sp*
Marques, P 1998 *Ger*, *US*, *CZR*, *Mor*, *Sp*, *And*, *S*
Martins, MB 1954 *Sp*
Martins, R 1967 *Sp*, *It*, *F*, *R* 1968 *Sp*, *Bel*, *Mor*, *It* 1970 *Sp* 1972 *It*, *It* 1973 *It*, *Yug*, *Swi*, *Pol*, *Pol* 1974 *It*, *Ger* 1981 *Swi*, *De*, *Swe*
Mateus, D 2003 *Geo*, *R*, *CZR*, *Sp*, *Rus* 2004 *Geo*, *R*, *CZR* (R), *Rus*, *Bb*, *Ch*, *Ur* 2006 *Rus*, *It* (R) 2007 *Mor* (R), *Ur*, *Rus*, *S*, *It*
Mateus, D 2000 *Geo*, *Sp*, *R*, *Mor* 2001 *R*, *Geo*, *Sp*, *H* (R), *Rus* 2002 *Pol* (R), *Sp* 2003 *Geo*, *R*, *CZR*, *Sp*, *Rus* 2004 *Geo*, *R*, *CZR*, *Sp*, *Rus*, *Bb*, *Ch*, *Ur*, *Ukr* 2005 *Geo*, *CZR*, *Rus*, *R*, *Ch*, *Ur*, *Fj* 2006 *Rus*, *Geo*, *R*, *Ukr*, *CZR*, *Rus*, *Ur*, *It*, *Rus*, *Geo*, *Geo* 2007 *Mor*, *Mor*, *Sp*, *Ur*, *Rus*, *CZR*, *C*, *S*, *NZ*, *It*
Mauricio, M 1990 *Sp* (R)
Mayer, T 1965 *Sp* 1966 *Sp*, *Bel* 1967 *It*, *F*, *R* 1970 *H*, *Mor* 1972 *It* (R)
Megre, D 1974 *Ger* 1979 *Swi* 1981 *Swi*, *Bel*, *De*, *Swe* 1982 *Mor*, *Sp*, *Tun*, *H*, *Pol* 1983 *Sp*, *H*, *Pol*, *Swe* 1984 *Sp*, *H*, *Bel*, *De* 1985 *Mor*, *Cze*, *Pol*, *Z* 1986 *R*, *F*, *It*, *Tun*, *USS*, *R* 1987 *It*, *F*, *Z*, *Z*, *Tun*, *USS*, *Bel* 1989 *H*, *Bel*, *Yug*, *Ger*
Megre, J 1979 *Swi*
Meira, A 1936 *Sp*
Melo, JA 1974 *It*
Melo, M 1998 *Nm* (R), *US*, *S* 1999 *H*, *Ur*, *Ur* 2000 *Geo* (R), *Sp*, *R* 2001 *R*, *H*, *Rus* 2002 *R* (R), *H* (R)
Metelo, J 1968 *Bel*, *Mor*, *It*
Minhoto, A 1972 *It* 1973 *It*, *Yug*, *Swi* (R), *Pol*
Mira, F 2007 *Sp*
Miranda, J 1965 *Sp* 1966 *Sp*, *Bel* 1967 *Sp*, *It*, *F*, *R* 1968 *Sp*
Moita, A 1986 *R*, *R* 1987 *F*, *Z* 1989 *Bel*, *Cze*, *H*
Moita, C 1974 *It* 1979 *Swi* 1981 *Swi*, *Bel*, *De*, *Swe* 1982 *Mor*, *Sp*, *Tun*, *H*, *Pol* 1983 *Sp*, *H*, *Pol*, *Swe* 1984 *Sp* 1985 *Cze*, *Z*
Monteiro, A 1982 *Sp*
Monteiro, B 1965 *Sp* 1966 *Sp*, *Bel* 1967 *Sp*, *It*, *F*, *R* 1968 *Sp*
Morais, E 1982 *Sp*, *Tun* 1986 *It*, *Tun*, *USS* 1987 *It*, *F*, *Z*
Morais, L 1984 *Sp*, *H*, *Bel*, *De* 1986 *F* (R), *It*, *R* 1987 *F*, *Z*, *Tun*, *Bel* 1988 *H* 1989 *H*, *Bel*, *Yug*, *Ger*, *Cze*, *H*
Morais, N 1985 *Mor*, *Cze*, *Pol*, *Z* 1986 *R*, *F*, *Tun*, *USS* 1987 *It*, *Z*, *Z*, *USS* 1988 *H*, *Ger*, *Yug* 1995 *Mor*, *Sp*, *CZR*, *Ger*
Morais, T 1991 *Tun*, *Mor*, *Nm* 1992 *And*, *Mor*, *Tun* 1993 *R*, *It*, *Tun*, *Bel*, *Swi*, *Sp* 1994 *Mor*, *Tun*, *W*, *Sp* 1995 *Mor*, *Sp*, *CZR*, *Ger*
Morgado, A 1935 *Sp* (R)
Mota, B 2000 *SA23* 2004 *Geo* (R), *R* (R), *Ukr* (R) 2005 *Rus* (R) 2006 *Geo* (R)
Mota, JD 1998 *S* (R), *Sp* 1999 *H*, *Ur* (R) 2000 *Sp*, *R*, *Mor*, *H*, *SA23* 2001 *Sp* 2004 *Ch*, *Ur* 2006 *Geo* (R), *R* (R), *Ukr* (R), *CZR*
Moura , M 1997 *Geo* 1998 *Nm* 1999 *H*, *Ur* 2002 *Sp* (R) 2004 *Ch*, *Ur*, *Ukr* (R) 2005 *Geo*, *CZR*
Mourao, N 1993 *R*, *It*, *Tun*, *Bel*, *Swi*, *Sp* 1994 *Bel*, *Ger*, *Mor*, *Tun*, *W*, *Sp* 1995 *CZR*, *Ger* 1996 *It*, *Bel*, *Pol*, *R*, *Sp*, *H*, *Tun* 1997 *Geo*, *Sp* 1998 *Nm*, *Ger*, *US*, *CZR*, *Mor*, *Sp*, *And*, *S*, *Sp* (R) 1999 *H*, *Ur*, *Ur* 2000 *Sp*
Muré, JM 2007 *C*, *S* (R), *It* (R), *R* (R)
Murinello, P 2003 *Rus* (R) 2004 *Geo*, *R*, *CZR*, *Sp*, *Rus*, *Bb*, *Ch* (R), *Ur* (R), *Ukr* (R) 2005 *Geo*, *CZR* 2006 *Ukr*, *CZR*, *Rus* (R), *It*, *Rus*, *Geo*, *Geo* 2007 *Mor*, *Mor* (R), *Ur* (R), *Ur* (R), *C* (R), *S* (R), *NZ*, *It* (R), *R* (R)
Murinello, P 1993 *R*, *It*, *Tun*, *Bel*, *Swi*, *Sp* 1994 *Bel*, *Ger*, *Mor*, *Tun*, *W*, *Sp* 1995 *Mor*, *Sp*, *CZR*, *Ger* 1996 *It*, *Bel*, *R*, *Sp*, *H*, *Tun* 2000 *Mor*, *H*

Neto, A 1968 *Sp* 1969 *Sp*, *Mor* 1970 *Sp* 1972 *It*, *It* 1973 *Yug* (R), *Swi* (R), *Pol* (R), *Pol* 1974 *It*, *Ger*
Neto, G 1997 *Sp* 1998 *US*, *Mor*
Neto, N 1995 *Mor* (R)
Neves, M 2002 *R* (R), *H* (R)
Neves, R 2002 *R*
Neves, VP 1986 *R*, *R*
Norton, J 1935 *Sp*
Nunes, AC 1954 *Sp*
Nunes, FP 2000 *Geo*, *Sp*, *R*, *Mor*, *H*, *SA23* 2001 *R*, *Sp*, *H* (R) 2002 *R*, *Geo*, *Sp*, *H*, *Rus*, *Pol*, *Sp* 2003 *Geo*, *R*, *CZR*, *Sp*, *Rus* 2004 *Ch*, *Ur* 2005 *Ch*
Nunes, M 1982 *Tun*, *H*, *Pol*
Nunes, R 1998 *Nm*, *Ger*, *US*, *CZR*, *And*, *Sp* 1999 *H* 2002 *R* (R), *H* (R)

Oliveira, LF 1974 *It* (R) 1981 *Swe* 1982 *Mor*, *Sp*, *Tun*, *H*, *Pol* 1983 *Sp*, *H*, *Pol*, *Swe*

Paisana, M 1981 *De* 1982 *Mor*, *Sp*, *Tun*, *H*, *Pol*
Paixao, JM 1974 *It*
Palha, S 2006 *Geo* (R) 2007 *Rus* (R), *R* (R)
Pardal, CV 1965 *Sp* 1967 *It* 1969 *Sp*, *Mor* (R)
Pardal, M 1989 *Yug*, *Ger*
Peças, A 1994 *Ger*, *Mor*, *Tun*, *W*, *Sp*
Pegado, C 1972 *It*
Penalva, D 2002 *Sp* (R), *H* (R) 2004 *Sp* (R), *Ur* 2005 *Rus*, *R*, *Ch*, *Ur*, *Fj* (R) 2006 *Rus*, *Geo*, *R*, *Ukr*, *CZR*, *Rus*, *Geo* (R) 2007 *Ur* (R), *Ur* (R), *Rus*, *C* (R), *S*, *NZ* (R), *It*, *R*
Pereira, J 1965 *Sp* 1966 *Sp*, *Bel* 1967 *Sp*, *R* 1970 *H*, *Mor*, *Sp* 1974 *Ger* 1981 *De* 1982 *Pol* (R) 1983 *Sp*, *H*, *Pol*, *Swe* 1984 *Sp*
Pereira, JC 1984 *H*, *Bel*, *De* 1986 *R* (R), *USS* (R) 1987 *F*, *Z*, *Z* (R), *Tun* 1989 *Cze*, *H* 1990 *Mor*, *Nm*, *Bel*, *Tun*
Pereira, JC 1969 *Mor* 1970 *H* 1972 *It* (R)
Pereira, MC 1965 *Sp* 1966 *Sp* 1967 *Sp*, *R* 1968 *Bel*, *Mor*, *It* 1969 *Sp*
Pereira, MM 2006 *Ukr* (R), *CZR* (R), *Rus* (R), *It* (R)
Pereira, RC 1987 *Bel* 1988 *H* 1989 *H* 1991 *And*, *Tun* 1992 *And*, *Mor*, *Tun* 1993 *R*, *It*, *Tun*, *Bel* 1994 *Bel*, *Ger*, *Mor*, *Tun*, *W*, *Sp* 1995 *Mor*, *Sp*
Pereira, VS 1973 *It*, *Yug*, *Swi* (R), *Pol*, *Pol* 1974 *Ger*
Picão, P 1994 *Ger*, *Mor*, *Tun*, *W*, *Sp*
Pimentel, PS 1973 *It* (R), *Yug*, *Swi* (R), *Pol*, *Pol*
Pinto, A 1998 *US*, *Mor*, *And* 1999 *H*, *Ur*, *Ur*
Pinto, AC 1970 *Mor* 1972 *It*, *It* 1973 *It*, *Yug*, *Swi*, *Pol*, *Pol* 1974 *It*, *Ger*
Pinto, AF 1998 *And* (R) 2000 *SA23* 2001 *Sp*, *H*
Pinto, BM 1979 *Swi* 1981 *Swi*, *Bel*, *De*, *Swe* 1982 *Mor*, *Sp*, *Tun*, *H*, *Pol* 1983 *Sp*, *H*, *Pol*, *Swe* 1984 *Sp*, *H* 1985 *Mor*, *Cze*, *Pol*, *Z* 1986 *R*, *F*, *It*, *Tun*, *USS*, *R* 1987 *It*, *F*, *Z*, *Z*, *Tun*, *USS*, *Bel* 1988 *H*, *Ger*, *Yug* 1989 *H*, *Bel*, *Yug*, *Ger*, *Cze*, *H*
Pinto, CR 1972 *It*, *It* 1973 *It*
Pinto, DC 2003 *CZR* (R), *Rus* 2004 *Sp* (R), *Bb* (R), *Ch* (R), *Ur* (R) 2005 *Rus* (R), *R*, *Ch*, *Ur* (R), *Fj* 2006 *Geo*, *R*, *Ukr*, *CZR* (R), *Rus*, *Rus* (R), *Geo* (R), *Geo* (R) 2007 *Mor*, *Mor*, *Sp*, *Ur*, *Ur*, *Rus*, *CZR*, *C* (R), *S*, *NZ* (R), *It*, *R*
Pinto, EA 1969 *Mor* 1981 *Swi*, *Bel*, *Swe* 1982 *H*
Pinto, J 2001 *H* (R), *Rus* 2002 *R* (R) 2004 *Sp* (R), *Bb* (R), *Ch* (R), *Ur* (R), *Ukr* (R) 2005 *Rus* (R), *R*, *Ch*, *Ur*, *Fj* 2006 *Rus*, *Geo*, *R*, *Ukr*, *CZR*, *Rus*, *Ur*, *It*, *Rus*, *Geo*, *Geo* 2007 *Mor* (R), *Sp* (R), *Ur* (R), *C* (R), *S*, *NZ* (R), *It*, *R*

Pinto, JM 1982 *Mor, Sp* (R), *H, Pol* 1983 *H, Pol, Swe* 1984 *Sp, H, Bel, De* 1985 *Mor, Cze, Pol, Z* 1986 *R, F, USS* (R), *R* 1987 *Tun, USS, Bel* 1988 *H, Ger, Yug* 1989 *H, Bel, Yug, Ger, Cze, H*
Pires, F 1982 *Mor, H, Pol* 1983 *Sp, H, Pol, Swe* 1984 *Sp, H, Bel, De* 1985 *Mor, Cze, Pol, Z* 1986 *R, F, It, Tun, USS*
Pires, JC 1990 *Mor, Nm, Bel, Tun* 1991 *And, Tun, Mor, Nm* 1993 *R, Tun, Bel, Swi, Sp* 1994 *Bel, Ger, Mor, Tun, W, Sp* 1996 *Pol* 1997 *Geo, Sp* 1998 *Nm*
Pissarra, L 1996 *It, Bel, Pol, R, H, Tun* 1997 *Geo, Sp* 1998 *Nm, Ger, Sp, And, Sp* 1999 *H, Ur, Ur* (R) 2000 *Geo, Sp, R* (R), *Mor, H, SA23* 2001 *R, Geo* 2002 *R, Geo, Sp, H, Rus, Pol, Sp* 2003 *Geo, R, CZR, Sp, Rus* 2004 *Geo, R, CZR, Sp, Rus, Bb, Ch, Ur, Ukr* 2005 *Geo, CZR, Rus, Ur* (R), *Fj* (R) 2006 *Rus* (R), *Geo, R* (R), *Ukr* (R), *CZR* (R), *Rus* (R), *Rus* (R), *Geo* (R), *Geo* (R) 2007 *Mor, Mor, Sp, Ur, Ur, Rus, CZR, C, S* (R), *NZ, It* (R), *R* (R)
Portela de Morais, M 1996 *R, H, Tun* 1997 *Geo, Sp* 1998 *US, CZR, Mor, Sp, S, Sp* 1999 *H, Ur* 2000 *Geo, Sp, Mor, H, SA23* 2002 *R, Geo, Sp, H, Rus, Pol, Sp* 2004 *Sp, Rus, Bb, Ukr* 2005 *Geo, CZR, Rus, R, Ch, Ur, Fj* 2006 *Rus, Geo, R, Ukr, Rus, It, Rus, Geo, Geo* 2007 *Mor, Mor, Sp, Ur, Ur, Rus, CZR, C* (R), *S* (R), *NZ, R*

Quadrio, A 1966 *Sp, Bel* 1967 *It, F*
Queimado, JF 1984 *Sp, H, Bel, De* 1985 *Mor, Cze, Pol, Z* 1986 *F, It, Tun, USS, R* 1987 *It, F, Z, Z, Tun, USS, Bel* 1989 *H, Bel, Cze, H* 1990 *Mor, Nm, Bel, Tun, Sp* 1991 *And, Tun, Mor, Nm* 1992 *And, Mor, Tun* 1993 *R, It, Tun, Bel, Swi, Sp* 1994 *Bel, Ger, Mor, Tun, W, Sp*

Rafachinho, JA 1973 *It* 1974 *It, Ger*
Ramos, JG 1967 *Sp* 1968 *Sp, Bel, Mor, It* 1969 *Sp, Mor* 1970 *H, Mor, Sp* 1972 *It, It* 1973 *It, Yug, Swi, Pol, Pol* 1974 *It*
Rankine, T 2000 *Geo, Sp, R* (R), *Mor, H*
Raws, D 1936 *Sp*
Reis, CC 1965 *Sp* 1966 *Sp, Bel* 1967 *Sp* 1968 *Sp*
Reis, CJ 1984 *H, Bel* 1985 *Mor, Cze, Pol, Z* 1986 *Tun, USS, R* 1987 *Tun, USS, Bel* 1988 *Yug* 1989 *H, Bel, Yug, Ger*
Reis, LN 1983 *Sp, H, Pol, Swe* 1984 *Sp, H, Bel, De* 1985 *Mor*
Reis, P 1981 *Swi*
Ribeiro, JC 1973 *Yug, Pol*
Ribeiro, MS 1998 *Nm, Ger, US, CZR, Mor, Sp, And, S, Sp* 1999 *H, Ur, Ur* 2000 *Geo, Sp, R* (R), *H, SA23* 2001 *R* (R), *Geo, Sp* (R)
Rocha, E 1973 *Swi, Pol*
Rocha, F 1998 *Nm* (R), *Ger* (R), *US, CZR, Mor, S* 1999 *H, Ur* (R), *Ur*
Rocha, O 1954 *Sp*
Rocheta, J 1990 *Mor, Nm, Bel, Tun, Sp* 1991 *And, Tun, Nm* 1992 *And, Mor, Tun* 1993 *R, Tun, Bel, Swi, Sp*
Rodrigues, JL 1982 *Mor* 1984 *Sp, H, Bel, De* 1985 *Mor, Cze, Pol, Z* 1986 *R, F, It, Tun, USS, R* 1987 *It, F, Z, Z, Tun, USS, Bel* (R) 1988 *H, Ger, Yug* 1989 *H, Bel, Yug, Ger, Cze, H* 1990 *Mor, Nm, Bel, Tun, Sp* 1991 *And, Tun, Mor, Nm* 1996 *It, Bel*
Rodrigues, P 1990 *Nm* (R), *Bel, Sp* 1991 *And, Tun, Mor, Nm* 1993 *R, Swi*
Rogério, M 1990 *Bel, Tun, Sp* 1991 *And, Tun, Mor, Nm* 1992 *And, Mor, Tun* 1993 *It, Tun, Bel, Sp* 1994 *Bel, Ger, Mor, Tun, W, Sp* 1995 *Mor, Sp, CZR, Ger* 1996 *It, Bel, Pol, R, Sp, H, Tun* 1998 *Ger, US, CZR, Mor, Sp* 2000 *Mor*
Roque, JB 1954 *Sp*
Rosa, LV 1954 *Sp*
Rosado, J 1990 *Nm*
Roxo, LF 1981 *Bel* (R) 1982 *Mor* (R), *Sp*
Rozendo, JM 1936 *Sp*

Sá, N 1998 *Sp* 1999 *Ur, Ur*
Saldanha, F 1998 *Mor, Sp, S* 1999 *Ur, Ur* 2001 *Geo*
Salgado, M 1968 *Sp, Bel, Mor, It* 1970 *Mor*
Sampaio, JM 1987 *F* 1988 *H, Ger*
Santos, F 1936 *Sp*
Santos, M 1973 *It, Yug, Swi, Pol, Pol* 1974 *It*
Santos, P 2004 *Geo, R, CZR* (R) 2005 *CZR* (R)
Saraiva, M 1979 *Swi*
Sarmento, A 2004 *R* (R), *Bb* (R)
Segurado, J 2005 *Ch* (R)
Sequeira, F 1974 *Ger*
Sequeira, JC 2001 *H* (R), *Rus* (R) 2002 *R, Geo* (R), *Sp* (R), *H* (R), *Pol* (R), *Sp* 2004 *R* (R), *CZR* (R), *Sp* (R), *Rus* (R) 2005 *Geo* (R)
Sequeira, L 1997 *Geo* (R), *Sp*
Sequeira, R 1988 *H, Ger*
Silva, A 1996 *Sp, H, Tun* 1997 *Geo, Sp* 1998 *Nm* (R), *S*
Silva, A 1936 *Sp*
Silva, D 1993 *Tun*
Silva, F 1935 *Sp*
Silva, JG 1972 *It, It*
Silva, JN 1967 *It, F, R* 1968 *Sp, Bel, Mor, It*
Silva, M 2000 *R*
Silva, P 1992 *And, Mor, Tun* (R) 1996 *It, Bel, Pol, R, Sp, H, Tun* 1997 *Geo, Sp* 1998 *Nm, Ger, US, CZR, Mor, Sp, And, S* 1999 *H, Ur, Ur* 2000 *H* 2002 *R* (R), *Geo* (R), *H* (R), *Pol* (R), *Sp* 2003 *CZR* (R), *Sp* (R)
Silva, V 2000 *Geo, Sp, R, Mor, H* 2001 *R, Geo, Sp, H, Rus*
Silvestre, A 1969 *Sp, Mor* 1970 *H, Mor* 1972 *It* 1973 *It, Swi, Pol, Pol* (R) 1974 *It*
Simıes, AC 1995 *Ger* 1996 *Bel, R, Tun* 2000 *SA23* 2001 *R*
Soares, C 1987 *Bel* 1988 *H, Ger, Yug* 1989 *H, Bel, Yug, Ger*
Soares, M 1954 *Sp*
Somoza, JS 2006 *Rus* (R), *Geo* (R), *Geo* (R) 2007 *Mor, Mor, Sp, Ur, Ur, Rus, CZR, C, S*
Sousa, F 2000 *Geo, Sp* 2001 *R, Geo, Sp, H, Rus* 2002 *R, Geo, Sp, H, Rus* 2003 *Geo, R, CZR, Sp, Rus* 2004 *Geo, R, CZR, Sp, Rus, Bb, Ukr* 2005 *Geo, CZR, Rus, R, Ch, Ur, Fj* 2006 *Ukr, CZR, Rus, Ur, It, Geo, Geo* (R) 2007 *CZR, C, S, It, R*
Sousa, O 1986 *R, F, It, Tun, USS* 1987 *It*
Sousa, V 1979 *Swi* (R) 1987 *F* 1988 *H*
Spachuck, RC 2005 *Geo* (R), *CZR* (R), *Rus, R* (R) 2006 *Rus, Geo, R* (R), *Ukr, CZR, Rus, It, Rus* (R), *Geo* (R), *Geo* 2007 *Rus, CZR, C, S, NZ, It, R*

Taful, N 2006 *Ur* (R), *It* (R)
Tavares, AH 1970 *H*
Teixeira, J 1935 *Sp*
Teixeira, T 1998 *Sp* 1999 *H, Ur* 2000 *Geo, Sp, R, Mor, H*
Telles, A 1988 *Yug*
Thomáz, LF 1991 *Mor* 1996 *Pol*
Thomáz, NF 1990 *Mor, Nm, Bel, Tun, Sp* 1991 *Tun, Mor, Nm* 1993 *Swi, Sp*
Tiago, J 1995 *CZR, Ger*
Tomé, M 2002 *R, Geo, Sp, H, Rus, Pol, Sp* 2003 *Geo, R, CZR, Sp* 2004 *Ch, Ur, Ukr* 2005 *Geo, CZR*
Trindade, AN 1969 *Sp* (R) 1973 *It* (R), *Swi* (R)

Uva, G 2004 *Bb* (R), *Ukr* 2005 *Geo* (R), *CZR* (R), *Rus, R, Ch, Ur, Fj* 2006 *Rus, Geo, R, Ukr, CZR, Rus, Ur, It, Rus, Geo, Geo* 2007 *Mor, Mor, Sp, Ur, Ur, Rus, C, S, NZ, It, R*
Uva, JS 2000 *SA23* 2001 *R, Geo, Sp* 2003 *Geo, R, CZR, Sp, Rus* 2004 *Geo* (R), *R* (R), *CZR* (R), *Rus* (R), *Ch, Ur, Ukr* 2005 *Rus, R* (R), *Ch, Ur, Fj* 2006 *It* (R), *Rus* (R), *Geo* (R) 2007 *Mor* (R), *Mor, Sp, Ur, Ur, CZR, C, S, NZ* (R), *It, R*
Uva, VS 2003 *Geo* (R), *R* (R), *Sp* (R) 2004 *Geo, R, CZR, Sp, Rus, Bb, Ch, Ur, Ukr* 2005 *Geo, CZR, Rus, R, Ch, Ur, Fj* 2006 *Rus, Geo, R, Ukr, CZR, Rus, Ur, It, Rus, Geo, Geo* 2007 *Mor, Mor, Sp, Ur, Ur, Rus, CZR, C, S, NZ, It*

Valente, AO 1954 *Sp*
Vareiro, G 2002 *R, Geo, Sp, Rus*
Varela, JP 1997 *Geo, Sp* 1998 *Ger, US, CZR, Mor, Sp, And, S* 1999 *Ur* (R) 2000 *H*
Vargas, JM 2006 *Rus* (R), *Ur*
Vasconcelos, JM 1965 *Sp* 1966 *Bel* 1967 *It, F* 1970 *Mor* (R)
Vaz, CR 1981 *Bel* 1987 *F, Z, Tun, USS*
Vaz, L 1935 *Sp* 1936 *Sp*
Vicente, D 1965 *Sp*
Vieira, ÁM 1936 *Sp*
Vieira, P 1998 *Nm* (R), *Sp, And* 1999 *H, Ur* (R) 2000 *Sp, R, Mor, H* 2001 *Geo, Sp, H, Rus* 2003 *CZR* (R), *Sp* (R), *Rus* (R) 2007 *Mor* (R), *Mor* (R), *Sp*
Vieira, R 1997 *Geo, Sp*
Vilela, JC 1973 *Swi*

ROMANIA

ROMANIA'S 2006–07 TEST RECORD

OPPONENTS	DATE	VENUE	RESULT
Georgia	3 Feb	H	**Lost** 17–20
Spain	10 March	H	**Won** 50–14
Czech Rep	17 March	A	**Won** 46–13
Namibia	16 June	H	**Won** 28–16
Italy	12 Sept	N	**Lost** 18–24 (WC)
Scotland	18 Sept	N	**Lost** 0–42 (WC)
Portugal	25 Sept	N	**Won** 14–10 (WC)
New Zealand	29 Sept	N	**Lost** 8–85 (WC)

THE OAKS CONTINUE TO GROW

By Radu Constantin

Getty Images

Romania celebrate their hard-fought,14–10, win over Portugal at the 2007 Rubgy World Cup.

Romanian Rugby had great ambitions for the 2007 Rugby World Cup. Their objective was two victories in the pool stage and a final position in the first 12 teams of the world, thereby giving them an automatic right to play in the 2011 tournament, in New Zealand.

Romania has participated at every World Cup finals but has only ever achieved single victories in the pool stages.

With a mixture of players coming from the French championship and also from Romanian domestic competition, the manager Robert Antonin started to prepare the World Cup participation with three matches in the European Nations Cup (Second Division of the Six Nations).

Antonin made a far from perfect start as Romania lost by 20–17 at home to Georgia. This was the first home defeat against the Lelos since 2001. A big number of handling mistakes and lost opportunities showed the weak points of the team.

The Oaks took some pride back one month later when they defeated Spain (50–14) in Bucuresti and Czech Republic (46–13) in Ricany.

Part of the IRB's High Performance programme, Romania hosted – in Bucuresti – the new IRB Nations Cup, a competition for the Tier 2 nations and for the second representatives of a handful of Tier 1 teams.

The competition was a perfect way to prepare for Romania's World Cup campaign. Without some of the key players, like captain Sorin Socol who was injured, Romeo Gontineac or Alexandru Manta, who were on duty with their French clubs, Romania received a rugby lesson from the Emerging Springboks who won the game by 61–7 at the brand new National Rugby Stadium "Arcul de Triumf" in Bucuresti.

The second game was against Italy A when the Oaks forced a 19–8 victory, with big hopes to repeat the success three months later with Italy for their first 2007 World Cup. And Romania finished in style the IRB Nations Cup with a 28–16 win against Namibia. With two victories and one loss, the Oaks finished the tournament in fourth place.

After a short holiday, Robert Antonin called his troops again to continue the preparation. Three sessions in the capital city Bucuresti were staged and then the programme went on with a physical stage in the French Pyrenees at La Mongie, for some altitude training.

The team remained in France but moved to Agen waiting for the big challenge, Rugby World Cup. With their objective to win two matches, the Oaks were clearly targetting the games against Italy and Portugal, the matches against New Zealand and Scotland – at Murrayfield – were probably out of reach.

"Every day we are thinking about the game with the Italians." says Sorin Socol, the captain. "We beat them in 2004 but they have progressed a lot since then. If we repeat the performance, that will be great."

Hard training, video sessions, analysis, mental preparation, all these were in the Romanians daily program while waiting the game with Italy. The team was accommodated in Agen and was preparing at the Armandie Stadium, a well-known place for the Socol who played until last season at Agen and Cezar Popescu who is still member of this club.

Romania received two big blows before the clash with Italy, powerful prop Petru Balan – one of their most experienced players – and winger Ioan Teodorescu picked up knee injuries and both were forced out of the World Cup, just few days before the match.

Paulica Ion, the former Steaua Bucuresti player, now a new recruit at Bath in England, was called in replacing Balan, while Catalin Dascalu from Steaua replaced Teodorescu.

The clash against Italy was staged in Marseille and went against the Romanians, although they were far from disgraced by the result, losing just 24–18 to a side that had recently beaten Scotland in the RBS Six Nations.

Romania in fact fought their way back into the game and tries from Alexandru Manta and Marius Tincu put them 12–10 ahead, but the boot of Ramiro Pez and a penalty try will force Romania into a long route to the 2011 World Cup.

Italy coach Pierre Berbizier said: "We won but not without hardship and Romania knew how to make it difficult for us."

"We are, of course, disappointed, because we trusted in our chance, we thought we can win this game" said Romania coach Antonin. "But I can say we should take the positive things from here, as the team played well in the second half."

The team returned to their base camp in Agen preparing the next game against Scotland. "The home ground will be a huge advantage for them" said Socol. "We know them well since last year when we played at Murrayfield. They are very strong and quick. We need to defense very well to stop them."

The squad flew to Edinburgh on 17th September, one day before the game and had the captain's run on the same day. The staff named the same starting XV.

The match was the most disappointing performance of the Romanian team but the quick turnaround certainly didn't help them. The Scots dominated in all the game areas, while the Oaks had no chance to play in the attack phase. Six tries conceded by Romania was a disappointing tally, and a record – against Scotland – defeat for Romania.

"It was not the way we need to play into the international scene. We need to perform better in order to win at least one game, with Portugal," said Romania coach.

It was clear the objective set by Romania, with two victories in the pool stage, was not to be achievable, as a win against the All Blacks was impossible.

Another blow was the injury of Ionut Tofan, a biceps rupture which forced him to leave the team. A young player, Stefan Ciuntu, with no international experience, was brought in from Romania.

The second day after the big defeat the team returned to Agen. "It is forbidden to loose against Portugal." said Antonin. "A defeat with Portugal means the disaster. We have to focus on the next game. The World Cup is not finished yet. The minimum that we can do here is a win with Portugal."

The players had a meeting only between them and promised each other they will try to produce something different in the next game.

The staff announced seven changes for the match. The most important were hooker Marius Tincu, second row Sorin Socol, back row Florin Corodeanu and scrum-half Lucian Sirbu who was put on the bench. "They are not punished," said Antonin. "We need them to go into the field in the second half with their power and lucidity."

Antonin's changes and the clear the air meeting held by the players worked its own magic as they indeed scored their first win of the World Cup, beating Portugal, 14–10.

The Romanians came from behind to snatch their win although it won't stop them having to qualify for the next World Cup.

Marius Tincu barged over with 16 minutes left and after Portugal went back in front with a penalty Romania sealed the win through Socol's close-range try late on.

"It was a very important victory for us because it's our first victory at this World Cup," said Romania prop Bogdan Balan.

"I want to congratulate the Romanian team because we believed in ourselves. And also Portugal, because they played very well."

Romania ended the World Cup on the wrong end of a 85–8 defeat to the world's number one, New Zealand.

The match was played again in Toulouse, the first try coming after only 37 seconds, the only saving grace being that they kept the All Blacks below the 100-point mark! The Oaks were also happy to score a try through Marius Tincu.

The New Zealand game not only marked the end of the World Cup for the Class of 2007 but also for coaching duo Robert Antonin and Daniel Santamans. In three years since they took the Romanian team, the Oaks had 36 matches with 21 victories and 15 defeats (eight of these defeat against the big rugby nations).

Romania will now hope that the IRB decide to include 20, rather than the proposed 16, teams at the next World Cup, or they may miss out on their first World Cup finals.

"I hope the International Rugby Board will maintain 20 teams at the World Cup, because this is the only way the minnows can progress, playing against the major nations. Romania will never progress if they play only in the European Nations Cup. They need to have an international exposure each year with hard matches in the rugby calendar." concluded Robert Antonin the Romanian participation at the biggest rugby event.

On the Romanian domestic scene, there are 12 clubs in the First League, called Divizia Nationala, in which the old rivals, Bucuresti clubs Steaua (the Army club) and Dinamo (the Police club), chased each other in the regular season.

There were four meetings between two teams before the finals and each took two victories. Dominating the whole championship, Steaua and Dinamo met again in the final and Dinamo won by 16–9.

With five Romanian players coming from France and Italy for good lucrative contracts, Dinamo Bucuresti proved to be the strongest club in the 2006–2007 season. In the Romanian Cup, Dinamo lost in the semi-finals and the two clubs who met in the Cup final were Steaua and Remin Baia Mare, with the Bucuresti team winning by 14–13.

ROMANIA INTERNATIONAL PLAYERS
UP TO 31ST OCTOBER 2007

Compiled by Hugh Copping

Achim, A 1974 *Pol* 1976 *Pol, Mor* (R)
Aldea, M 1979 *USS, W, Pol, F* 1980 *It* (R), *USS, I, F* 1981 *It, Sp, USS, S, NZ, F* 1982 *WGe, It, USS, Z, Z, F* 1983 *Mor, WGe, It, USS, Pol, W, USS, F* 1984 *It, S, F* 1985 *E, USS*
Alexandrescu, C 1934 *It*
Alexandru, D 1974 *Pol* 1975 *Sp, JAB* 1976 *Sp, USS, Bul, Pol, F, Mor* 1977 *Sp, It, F, Pol, F* 1978 *Cze, Sp* 1979 *It, Sp, USS, W, F* (R) 1980 *It, I, Pol, F* 1981 *Sp, USS, S, NZ, F* 1982 *Z* (R) 1983 *It, USS, Pol, W* 1984 *It, S, F, Sp* 1985 *E* 1987 *It, USS, Z, S, USS, F* 1988 *USS*
Anastasiade, N 1927 *Cze* 1934 *It* (R)
Anastasiade, V 1939 *It*
Andrei, I 2003 *W* (R), *I* (R), *Ar* (R), *Nm* (R) 2004 *CZR, Pt, Sp* (R), *Rus* (R), *Geo, It* (R), *W* (R), *J* (R), *CZR* (R) 2005 *Rus* (R), *US* (R), *S, Pt* (R) 2006 *CZR* (R)
Andriesi, I 1937 *It, H, Ger* 1938 *F, Ger* 1939 *It* 1940 *It*
Apjoc, E 1996 *Bel* 2000 *It* (R) 2001 *Pt* (R)
Armasel, D 1924 *F, US*
Atanasiu, A 1970 *It, F* 1971 *It, Mor, F* 1972 *Mor, Cze, WGe* 1973 *Sp, Mor, Ar, Ar, WGe* (R) 1974 *Pol*
Bacioiu, I 1976 *USS, Bul, Pol, F, Mor*
Baciu, N 1964 *Cze, EGe* 1967 *It, F* 1968 *Cze, Cze, F* (R) 1969 *Pol* (R), *WGe, F* 1970 *It* 1971 *It, Mor, F* 1972 *Mor, Cze* (R), *WGe* (R) 1973 *Ar* (R), *Ar* (R) 1974 *Cze, EGe*
Balan, B 2003 *Pt* (R), *Sp, Geo* (R) 2004 *W* (R) 2005 *Rus* (R), *Ukr* (R), *J* (R), *US* (R), *S* (R), *Pt* (R) 2006 *Geo* (R), *Pt* (R), *Ukr, Rus* (R), *F, Geo, Sp* (R), *S* 2007 *Sp* (R), *ESp* (R), *ItA, Nm* (R), *It, S, Pt* (R), *NZ*
Balan, D 1983 *F* (R)
Balan, PV 1998 *H* (R), *Pol* (R), *Ukr* (R), *Ar, Geo* (R), *I* (R) 1999 *F* (R), *S, A, US, I* 2000 *Mor, H, Pt, Sp, Geo, F* (R), *It* 2001 *Pt, Sp, H* (R), *Rus, Geo* (R), *I, E* 2002 *Pt* (R), *Sp, H, Rus, Geo, Sp, S* 2003 *CZR, F, W, I, Nm* 2004 *It, W, J, CZR* 2005 *Geo, C, I* 2006 *Geo, Pt, F, Geo, Sp, S* 2007 *Geo*
Balcan, L 1963 *Bul, EGe, Cze* (R)
Balmus, F 2000 *Mor* (R), *H, Pt* (R)
Bals, S 1927 *F, Ger, Cze*
Baltaretu, G 1965 *WGe, F*
Barascu, C 1957 *F*
Baraulea, M 2004 *CZR, Pt, Geo* (R)
Barbu, A 1958 *WGe, It* 1959 *EGe, Pol, Cze, EGe* 1960 *F*
Bargaunas, S 1971 *It, Mor* (R) 1972 *F* (R) 1974 *Cze* 1975 *It*
Barsan, S 1934 *It* 1936 *F, It* 1937 *It, H, F, Ger* 1938 *F, Ger* 1939 *It* 1940 *It* 1942 *It*
Beches, E 1979 *It, Sp, USS* 1982 *WGe, It* 1983 *Pol* (R)
Bejan, M 2001 *I, W* 2002 *Pt* 2003 *Geo* (R), *CZR* 2004 *It* (R)
Beju, C 1936 *F, It, Ger*
Bentia, G 1919 *US, F* 1924 *F, US*
Bezarau, V 1995 *Ar, F, It*
Bezuscu, R 1985 *It* 1987 *F*
Blagescu, M 1952 *EGe, EGe* 1953 *It* 1955 *Cze* 1957 *F, Cze, Bel, F*
Blasek, G 1937 *It, H, F, Ger* 1940 *It* 1942 *It*
Bogheanu, A 1980 *Mor*
Boldor, D 1988 *It, Sp, US, USS, USS, W* 1989 *It, E, Sp, Z*
Boroi, A 1975 *Sp*
Bors, P 1975 *JAB* 1976 *Sp* 1977 *It* 1980 *It, USS, I, Pol, F* 1981 *It, Sp, USS, S, NZ, F* 1982 *WGe* 1983 *Mor, WGe, It* (R), *USS* 1984 *It*
Bozian, D 1997 *Bel* 1998 *H, Pol, Ukr* (R)
Brabateanu, V 1919 *US, F*
Braga, M 1970 *It, F*
Branescu, C 1994 *It, E* 1997 *F*
Bratulescu, I 1927 *Ger, Cze*
Brezoianu, G 1996 *Bel* 1997 *F* 1998 *H, Pol, Ukr, Ar, Geo, I* 1999 *F, S, A, US, I* 2000 *H, Pt, Sp, Geo, F, It* 2001 *Sp, Rus, Geo, I, W, E* 2002 *Pt, Sp, H, Rus, Geo, I, It, Sp, W, S* 2003 *Pt, Sp, Rus, Geo, CZR, F, W, I, A, Ar, Nm* 2005 *Rus, Ukr, J, US, S, Pt, C, I* 2006 *CZR, Pt* (R), *Ukr* (R), *Rus, F* (R), *Geo, Sp, S* 2007 *Geo, Sp, CZR, ESp, ItA, Nm, It, S, NZ*
Brici, V 1991 *NZ* (R) 1992 *USS, F, It* 1993 *Tun, F, Sp, I* 1994 *Sp, Ger, Rus, It, W, It, E* 1995 *F, S, J, J* (R), *SA, A* 1996 *Pt, F* 1997 *F*
Brinza, TE 1990 *It, USS* (R) 1991 *C* (R) 1992 *It, Ar* 1993 *Pt, Tun, F, F, I* 1994 *Sp, Ger, It* (R), *W, It* (R), *E* 1995 *F, S, J, J, SA, A* 1996 *Pt, F, Pol* 1997 *F, W, Ar, F, It* 1998 *Ukr* 1999 *A, US, I* 2000 *H, Geo* 2002 *H* (R)
Bucan, I 1976 *Bul* (R) 1977 *Sp* 1978 *Cze* 1979 *F* 1980 *It, USS, I, Pol, F* 1981 *It, Sp, USS, S, NZ, F* 1982 *WGe, It, USS, Z, Z, F* 1983 *Mor, WGe, It, USS, Pol, W, USS, F* 1984 *It, S, F, Sp* 1985 *E, Tun, USS, USS, It* 1986 *Pt, S, F* (R), *Pt* 1987 *It, USS, Z, S, USS, F*
Bucos, M 1972 *Mor, Cze, WGe* (R) 1973 *Sp* 1975 *JAB, Pol, F* 1976 *H, It, Sp, USS, Bul, Pol, F, Mor* 1977 *Sp, It, F, Pol, It, F* 1978 *Pol, F* 1979 *W* 1980 *It, Mor*
Buda, P 1953 *It* 1955 *Cze* 1957 *F, Cze*
Budica, C 1974 *Cze* (R), *EGe* (R), *Cze* (R)
Burcea, S 2006 *F* 2007 *ESp* (R), *ItA, Nm*
Burghelea, M 1974 *Cze* (R), *EGe, F* 1975 *It*
Burlescu, S 1936 *F, It, Ger* 1938 *F, Ger* 1939 *It*
Butugan, M 2003 *Pt* (R)
Calafeteanu, VN 2004 *J* 2005 *Ukr* (R) 2006 *CZR, Pt* (R), *Ukr* (R), *F* (R), *Sp* (R), *S* 2007 *Geo* (R), *Sp, CZR, ESp, ItA, Nm, It* (R), *S* (R), *Pt, NZ* (R)
Caligari, A 1951 *EGe* 1953 *It*
Caliman, S 1958 *EGe* 1960 *Pol, EGe, Cze*
Calistrat, P 1940 *It* 1942 *It*
Camenita, Ion 1939 *It*
Caplescu, CF 2007 *Sp* (R), *CZR* (R)
Capmare, C 1983 *Pol* 1984 *It*
Capusan, N 1960 *F* 1961 *Pol, Cze, EGe, F* 1962 *Cze, EGe, Pol*
Capusan, R *It* 1963 *Bul, EGe, Cze*
Caracostea, G 1919 *US, F*
Caragea, G 1980 *I, Pol, F* 1981 *It, Sp, USS, S, NZ* (R), *F* 1982 *WGe, It, USS, Z, Z, F* 1983 *Mor, WGe, It, USS, Pol, W, F* 1984 *F, Sp* 1985 *E, Tun* 1986 *S, F, Tun, Tun, Pt, F, I* 1988 *It, Sp, US, USS* 1989 *E*
Carp, C 1989 *Z, Sa, USS*
Carpo, D 2007 *ItA* (R)
Celea, G 1963 *EGe*
Chiriac, D 1999 *S, A* (R), *I* (R) 2001 *H*
Chiriac, G 1996 *Bel* (R) 2001 *Pt, Rus* 2002 *Sp, H, Rus* (R), *Geo, I, Sp* (R), *W* (R), *S* 2003 *Sp, Rus* (R), *Geo, F, W, I, A, Ar, Nm*
Chiriac, R 1952 *EGe* 1955 *Cze* 1957 *F, Bel, F* 1958 *Sp, WGe* 1960 *F* 1961 *Pol, EGe, Cze, EGe, F* 1962 *Cze, EGe, Pol, It, F* 1963 *Bul, EGe, Cze, F* 1964 *Cze, EGe* (R), *WGe, F*
Chiricencu, M 1980 *It, Pol*

Chirila, S 1989 *Sp*, *S* 1990 *F*, *H*, *Sp*, *It*, *USS* 1991 *It*
Chirita, V 1999 *S* (R)
Cilinca, G 1993 *Pt*
Cioarec, N 1974 *Pol* (R) 1976 *It* 1979 *Pol* (R)
Ciobanel, P 1961 *Pol*, *EGe*, *Cze*, *EGe*, *F* 1962 *Cze*, *EGe*, *Pol*, *It*, *F* 1963 *F* 1964 *Cze*, *EGe*, *WGe*, *F* 1965 *WGe*, *F* 1966 *Cze*, *It*, *F* 1967 *F* 1968 *Cze*, *Cze*, *F* 1969 *Pol*, *WGe*, *Cze*, *F* 1970 *F* 1971 *F*
Ciobanu, I 1952 *EGe* (R)
Ciobanu, M 1949 *Cze* 1951 *EGe*
Cioca, R 1994 *Sp*, *Ger*, *Rus*, *It*, *It*, *E* 1995 *S*, *J* 1996 *Bel* (R)
Ciofu, I 2000 *It* 2003 *Pt*
Ciolacu, ML 1998 *Ukr* (R), *Ar* (R), *Geo* (R), *I* (R) 1999 *F* 2001 *Sp*, *H*, *Rus*, *Geo*, *W* (R), *E* (R)
Ciorascu, S 1988 *US*, *USS*, *USS*, *F*, *W* 1989 *It*, *E*, *Sp*, *Z*, *Sa*, *USS*, *S* 1990 *It*, *F*, *H*, *Sp*, *USS* 1991 *It*, *NZ*, *S*, *F*, *C*, *Fj* 1992 *Sp*, *It*, *It*, *Ar* 1994 *Ger*, *Rus*, *It*, *W* 1995 *F*, *S*, *J*, *C*, *SA*, *A* 1996 *F* 1997 *F*, *It* 1999 *F*
Ciornei, M 1972 *WGe*, *F* 1973 *Ar*, *Ar*, *WGe*, *F* 1974 *Mor*, *Pol*, *EGe*, *F*, *Cze* 1975 *It*, *Sp*
Ciuntu, SE 2007 *NZ*
Cocor, C 1940 *It* (R) 1949 *Cze*
Codea, M 1998 *Ukr* (R) 2001 *E* (R)
Codoi, L 1980 *I*, *Pol* 1984 *F* 1985 *Tun* (R), *USS*
Cojocariu, C 1990 *It*, *F*, *H*, *Sp*, *It*, *USS* 1991 *It*, *NZ*, *F*, *S*, *F*, *C*, *Fj* 1992 *Sp*, *It*, *USS*, *F*, *Ar* 1993 *Pt*, *F*, *F*, *I* (R) 1994 *Sp*, *Ger* (R), *Rus*, *It*, *W*, *It*, *E* 1995 *F*, *S*, *J*, *J*, *C*, *SA*, *A*, *Ar*, *F*, *It* 1996 *F*
Colceriu, L 1991 *S*, *Fj* 1992 *Sp*, *It*, *It* 1993 *I* 1994 *Sp*, *Ger*, *Rus*, *It*, *W*, *It* 1995 *F*, *J* (R), *J*, *C*, *SA*, *A* 1997 *F*, *W*, *Bel*, *Ar*, *F*, *It* 1998 *Pol*, *Ukr*
Coliba, D 1987 *USS*, *F*
Coltuneac, M 2002 *Sp* (R), *W* (R), *S* (R)
Coman, T 1984 *Sp* 1986 *F*, *Tun*, *Tun*, *I* (R) 1988 *Sp* (R), *US*, *USS*, *USS* (R) 1989 *It* (R) 1992 *F*
Constantin, C 2001 *Pt* (R) 2002 *Geo* (R), *W* (R)
Constantin, F 1972 *Mor*, *Cze*, *WGe* 1973 *Ar* (R), *Ar*, *WGe* (R) 1980 *Mor* (R) 1982 *It* (R)
Constantin, I 1971 *Mor* 1972 *WGe* 1973 *Ar*, *Ar*, *WGe*, *F* 1974 *Mor*, *Pol*, *Sp* (R), *F*, *Cze* 1975 *It*, *Sp*, *JAB*, *Pol*, *F* 1976 *H*, *It*, *Sp*, *USS*, *Bul*, *Pol* 1977 *It*, *F* 1978 *Pol*, *F* 1979 *It*, *Sp*, *USS*, *W*, *Pol*, *F* 1980 *It*, *USS*, *I*, *Pol*, *F* 1981 *It*, *Sp*, *USS*, *S*, *NZ*, *F* 1982 *WGe* (R), *It*, *USS*, *Z*, *Z* 1983 *WGe*, *USS* 1985 *It*
Constantin, L 1983 *USS*, *F* (R) 1984 *It*, *S*, *F*, *Sp* 1985 *E*, *It*, *Tun* (R), *USS*, *USS*, *It* 1986 *Pt*, *S*, *F*, *Tun*, *Tun*, *Pt*, *F*, *I* 1987 *It*, *USS*, *Z*, *F*, *S*, *USS*, *F* 1991 *It* (R), *NZ* (R), *F*
Constantin, LT 1985 *USS*
Constantin, S 1980 *Mor* 1982 *Z*, *Z* 1983 *Pol*, *W*, *USS*, *F* 1984 *S*, *F* (R) 1985 *USS* 1986 *Pt*, *S*, *F*, *Tun* 1987 *It*, *Z*, *S*
Constantin, T 1992 *USS*, *F*, *It* 1993 *Pt* (R), *F*, *Sp* 1996 *Pt* 1997 *It* 1999 *F*, *US*, *I* 2000 *Pt*, *Sp*, *Geo*, *F* 2002 *Rus*, *Geo*
Constantin, T 1985 *USS*
Copil, N 1985 *USS*, *It* 1986 *S* (R)
Coravu, D 1968 *F*
Cordos, N 1958 *EGe* 1961 *EGe* 1963 *Bul*, *Cze* 1964 *Cze* (R), *EGe* (R)
Cornel, V 1977 *F* 1978 *Cze*, *Sp*
Corneliu, G 1980 *Mor*, *USS* (R) 1982 *WGe*, *It*, *Z*, *Z* 1986 *Tun*, *Pt*, *F* 1993 *I* 1994 *W* (R)
Corneliu, G 1976 *USS*, *Bul* 1977 *F* (R) 1979 *It* 1981 *S* 1982 *Z*
Corneliu, M 1979 *USS*
Corodeanu, F 1997 *F*, *W* 1998 *H* (R), *Pol*, *Ar*, *Geo* 1999 *F*, *S*, *A* (R), *US* (R), *I* (R) 2000 *H*, *Sp*, *Geo*, *F*, *It* 2001 *Pt*, *Sp*, *H*, *Rus*, *Geo*, *I*, *E* 2002 *Pt*, *Sp*, *Rus*, *Geo*, *It*, *Sp*, *W*, *S* 2003 *Sp* 2005 *Geo*, *J*, *US*, *S*, *Pt*, *C*, *I* 2006 *Geo*, *CZR*, *Pt*, *Geo*, *Sp*, *S* 2007 *Geo*, *ESp*, *ItA*, *Nm*, *It*, *S*, *Pt*, *NZ*
Costea, L 1994 *E* 1995 *S*, *J*, *J*, *Ar*, *F* 1997 *F*
Coter, L 1957 *F*, *Cze* 1959 *EGe*, *Pol*, *Cze* 1960 *F*
Covaci, F 1936 *Ger* 1937 *H*, *F*, *Ger* 1940 *It* 1942 *It*
Cratunescu, C 1919 *US*, *F*
Crissoveloni, N 1936 *F*, *It* 1937 *H*, *F*, *Ger* 1938 *F*, *Ger*
Cristea, S 1973 *Mor*
Cristoloveanu, C 1952 *EGe*
Crivat, G 1938 *F*, *Ger*
Csoma, V 1983 *WGe* (R)
Curea, D 2005 *Rus* (R), *Ukr*, *J*, *US*, *S*, *Pt*
Daiciulescu, V 1966 *Cze*, *F* 1967 *It*, *Pol* 1968 *F* 1969 *Pol*
Damian, A 1934 *It* 1936 *F*, *It*, *Ger* 1937 *It* 1938 *F*, *Ger* 1939 *It* 1949 *Cze*
Daraban, G 1969 *Cze* 1972 *Mor*, *Cze*, *WGe*, *F* 1973 *Sp*, *Mor*, *Ar*, *Ar* 1974 *Cze*, *EGe*, *F*, *Cze* 1975 *It*, *Sp*, *JAB*, *Pol*, *F* 1976 *H*, *It*, *Sp*, *USS*, *Bul*, *Pol*, *F*, *Mor* 1977 *Sp*, *It*, *F* 1978 *Cze*, *Sp*, *Pol*, *F* 1982 *F* 1983 *Mor* (R), *WGe* (R), *It*, *USS*, *W*
Dascalu, CR 2006 *Ukr*, *F*, *Geo*, *Sp*, *S* 2007 *Sp*, *CZR*, *ESp*, *NZ* (R)
David, V 1984 *Sp* (R) 1986 *Pt*, *S*, *F*, *Tun* 1987 *USS* (R), *Z*, *F* 1992 *USS* (R)
Demci, S 1998 *Ar* (R) 2001 *H*, *Rus* (R), *Geo*, *I* (R), *W*
Demian, R 1959 *EGe* 1960 *F* 1961 *Pol*, *EGe*, *Cze*, *EGe*, *F* 1962 *Cze*, *Pol*, *It*, *F* 1963 *Bul*, *EGe*, *Cze*, *F* 1964 *WGe*, *F* 1965 *WGe*, *F* 1966 *Cze*, *It*, *F* 1967 *It*, *Pt*, *Pol*, *WGe*, *F* 1968 *Cze*, *F* 1969 *Pol*, *WGe*, *F* 1971 *It*, *Mor*
Denischi, E 1949 *Cze* 1952 *EGe*, *EGe*
Diaconu, I 1942 *It*
Diamandi-Telu, C 1938 *Ger* 1939 *It*
Dima, D 1999 *A* (R), *US* (R), *I* (R) 2000 *H*, *Pt*, *Geo*, *F*, *It* 2001 *Sp*, *H* (R), *Rus*, *Geo*, *W*, *E* 2002 *Pt*, *Sp*, *Rus*, *W* (R), *S* 2004 *CZR* (R), *Pt*, *Sp*, *Rus*, *Geo* (R)
Dimofte, TI 2004 *It* (R), *W* (R), *CZR* 2005 *C*, *I* 2006 *Geo*, *CZR*, *Pt*, *Ukr*, *Rus*, *F*, *Geo*, *Sp*, *S* 2007 *ESp* (R), *ItA*, *Nm*, *It*, *S*, *Pt*, *NZ*
Dinescu, C 1934 *It* 1936 *F*, *It*, *Ger* 1937 *It*, *H*, *F*, *Ger* 1938 *F*, *Ger* 1940 *It* 1942 *It*
Dinu, C 1965 *WGe*, *F* 1966 *Cze*, *It*, *F* 1967 *It*, *Pt*, *Pol*, *WGe* 1968 *F* 1969 *Pol*, *WGe*, *Cze*, *F* 1970 *It*, *F* 1971 *Mor*, *F* 1972 *Mor*, *Cze*, *WGe*, *F* 1973 *Sp*, *Mor*, *Ar*, *Ar*, *WGe*, *F* 1974 *Mor*, *Pol*, *Sp*, *Cze*, *F*, *Cze* 1975 *It*, *Sp* 1976 *H*, *It*, *Sp*, *Pol*, *F*, *Mor* 1977 *Sp*, *It*, *F*, *Pol*, *It*, *F* 1978 *Sp*, *Pol*, *F* 1979 *Sp*, *USS*, *W*, *Pol* 1980 *I*, *Pol*, *F* 1981 *It*, *Sp*, *USS*, *NZ*, *F* 1982 *F* 1983 *Mor*, *WGe*, *It*, *USS*
Dinu, F 2000 *Mor* (R), *H* (R)
Dinu, G 1990 *It*, *F*, *H*, *Sp*, *It*, *USS* 1991 *It*, *S*, *F*, *C*, *Fj* 1992 *Sp*, *It*, *USS*, *F*, *It* 1993 *F*
Dinu, G 1975 *Pol* 1979 *It*, *Sp* 1983 *Pol*, *USS*
Dobre, F 2001 *E* 2004 *W* (R), *CZR*
Dobre, I 1951 *EGe* 1952 *EGe* 1953 *It* 1955 *Cze* 1957 *Cze*, *Bel*, *F* 1958 *Sp*
Doja, I 1986 *Tun*, *Pt*, *F*, *I* 1988 *F*, *W* 1989 *Sp*, *Z*, *Sa*, *S* 1990 *It* 1991 *It*, *NZ*, *F*, *C* 1992 *Sp*
Doja, V 1997 *Bel* 1998 *Pol* (R), *Geo* (R), *I*
Domocos, A 1989 *Z*, *Sa*, *USS*
Dorutiu, I 1957 *Cze*, *Bel*, *F* 1958 *Sp*, *WGe*
Draghici, A 1919 *US*
Dragnea, C 1995 *F* 1996 *Pol* (R) 1997 *F* (R), *Bel*, *Ar*, *F*, *It* 1998 *H*, *Pol* (R) 1999 *F* (R) 2000 *F* (R)
Dragnea, I 1985 *Tun*
Dragnea, S 2002 *S* (R)
Dragomir, M 1996 *Bel* 1997 *Bel* 1998 *H*, *Pol*, *Ukr*, *Geo*, *I* 2001 *I* (R), *W*, *E* (R)
Dragomir, M 2001 *H* (R), *Geo* (R) 2002 *I*
Dragomir, V 1964 *Cze*, *EGe* 1966 *It* 1967 *Pol*, *WGe*
Dragomirescu, G 1919 *F*
Dragomirescu-Rahtopol, G 1963 *Bul* (R), *EGe*, *Cze*, *F* 1964 *Cze*, *EGe*, *WGe*, *F* 1965 *WGe*, *F* 1966 *Cze* 1967 *It*, *Pt*, *Pol*, *WGe*, *F* 1968 *Cze*, *Cze*, *F* 1969 *Pol*, *Cze*, *F* 1970 *It*, *F* 1971 *It*, *Mor* 1972 *Mor*, *Cze*, *WGe*, *F* 1973 *WGe*, *F*
Dragos, N 1995 *Ar* (R), *It* (R) 1997 *F*, *Ar*, *F*, *It* 1998 *H*, *Pol*, *Ukr*, *Ar*, *Geo*, *I* 1999 *F*, *S* 2000 *Sp*, *Geo* (R), *F*
Draguceanu, CS 1994 *Sp*, *Ger*, *Rus*, *It*, *W* (R), *It*, *E* (R) 1995 *S* (R), *J*, *Ar*, *F*, *It* (R) 1996 *Bel* 1997 *W*, *Bel*, *Ar*, *F*, *It* 1998 *H*, *Pol*, *Ukr*, *Ar*, *Geo*, *I* 1999 *S*, *A*, *US*, *I* 2000 *Mor*, *H*, *Pt*, *Sp*, *Geo*, *F*, *It*
Dragulescu, C 1969 *Cze* 1970 *F* 1971 *It* 1972 *Cze*
Drobota, G 1960 *Pol*, *Cze* 1961 *EGe*, *EGe*, *F* 1962 *Cze*, *EGe*, *Pol*, *F* 1964 *Cze*, *EGe*, *F*
Dumbrava, D 2002 *W* 2003 *Sp* (R), *Rus* (R), *Geo*, *CZR*, *F*, *W*, *I*, *A*, *Nm* 2004 *CZR*, *Pt*, *Sp*, *Rus*, *Geo*, *It*, *J* (R), *CZR* (R) 2005 *Rus*, *Geo*, *Ukr*, *J*, *US*, *S*, *Pt*, *C* (R) 2006 *Geo* (R), *Pt*, *Rus* (R) 2007 *Sp*, *CZR*, *Pt*

Dumitras, H 1984 *It* (R) 1985 *E* (R), *It*, *USS* (R) 1986 *Pt*, *F*, *I* 1987 *It*, *USS*, *Z*, *S*, *USS*, *F* 1988 *It*, *Sp*, *US*, *USS*, *USS*, *F*, *W* 1989 *It*, *E*, *Z*, *Sa*, *USS*, *S* 1990 *It*, *F*, *H*, *Sp*, *USS* 1991 *It*, *NZ*, *F*, *S*, *F*, *C*, *Fj* 1992 *Sp*, *USS*, *F*, *Ar* 1993 *Pt*, *Tun*, *F*, *Sp*, *F*, *I*

Dumitras, I 2002 *H* (R) 2006 *Geo*, *CZR*, *Ukr*, *Rus*, *F* (R) 2007 *Geo* (R), *Sp*, *CZR*, *ESp*, *ItA*, *Nm*, *It*, *S*, *Pt*, *NZ*

Dumitrescu, E 1953 *It* 1958 *Sp*, *WGe*

Dumitrescu, G 1988 *It*, *Sp*, *F*, *W* 1989 *It*, *E*, *Sp*, *Z*, *Sa*, *USS*, *S* 1990 *It*, *F*, *H*, *Sp*, *It*, *USS* 1991 *It*, *NZ*, *F* 1997 *It* (R)

Dumitrescu, L 1997 *Bel* (R), *Ar* (R) 2001 *W* (R)

Dumitriu, G 1937 *H*, *F*, *Ger*

Dumitru, G 1973 *Sp*, *Mor*, *Ar*, *Ar*, *WGe*, *F* 1974 *Mor*, *Sp*, *Cze*, *EGe*, *F* 1975 *JAB*, *Pol*, *F* 1976 *H*, *It*, *Sp* 1977 *Sp*, *Pol*, *F* 1978 *Cze*, *Sp*, *Pol*, *F* 1979 *It*, *Sp*, *USS*, *W*, *Pol*, *F* 1980 *It*, *Mor*, *USS*, *I*, *Pol*, *F* 1981 *It*, *Sp*, *USS*, *S*, *NZ*, *F* 1982 *WGe*, *It*, *USS*, *Z*, *Z*, *F* 1983 *Mor*, *WGe*, *It*, *USS*, *Pol*, *USS*, *F* 1984 *It*, *S*, *F* 1985 *E*, *It*, *Tun*, *USS* 1986 *F*, *I* 1987 *USS*, *F*, *S* (R), *USS*, *F*

Dumitru, M 1990 *F*, *H*, *Sp*, *It*, *USS* 1991 *NZ*, *F*, *F*, *C* 1992 *F* 1993 *F*, *Sp* (R), *F*

Dumitru, M 1998 *Ar* (R) 1999 *F* 2000 *Mor*, *H*, *Pt*, *Sp*, *Geo*, *F* 2002 *H* (R) 2003 *Sp*

Dumitru, M 2002 *Pt*, *Sp* (R), *H*, *I*

Dumitru, S 2004 *It* (R) 2005 *Rus* (R), *Ukr* (R), *US*, *S* (R), *Pt*

Durbac, R 1968 *Cze* 1969 *WGe*, *Cze* 1970 *It*, *F* 1971 *It*, *Mor*, *F* 1972 *WGe*, *F* 1973 *Ar* (R), *Ar*, *WGe*, *F* 1974 *Mor*, *Pol*, *Sp*, *Cze*, *EGe*, *F*, *Cze* 1975 *It*, *Sp*, *JAB*, *Pol*, *F*

Duta, A 1973 *Ar*

Eckert, R 1927 *F*, *Ger*, *Cze*

Enache, I 1977 *It*

Ezaru, M 2000 *Pt*, *Geo* (R), *F* (R)

Falcusanu, V 1974 *Sp*, *Cze*

Fantaneanu, G 1934 *It* 1936 *F*, *It*, *Ger* 1937 *It*, *H*, *F*, *Ger*

Fercu, C 2005 *C*, *I* 2006 *Geo*, *CZR*, *Pt*, *Ukr*, *Rus*, *F*, *Geo*, *Sp* 2007 *Geo*, *Sp*, *CZR*, *ESp*, *ItA*, *Nm*, *It*, *S*, *Pt*

Florea, C 1937 *It*, *F*, *Ger*

Florea, G 1981 *S*, *NZ*, *F* 1982 *WGe*, *It*, *USS*, *Z*, *Z* 1984 *Sp* 1985 *USS* 1986 *Pt*, *F*

Florea, S 2000 *It* 2001 *Sp* (R), *Geo* (R), *I*, *E* (R) 2002 *It*, *Sp*, *W* 2003 *Sp* (R), *Rus* (R), *Geo*, *CZR*, *A*, *Ar*, *Nm* (R) 2007 *Sp*, *CZR*, *S* (R), *NZ* (R)

Florescu, I 1957 *F*, *Cze*

Florescu, M 1995 *F*

Florescu, P 1967 *It*, *Pt*, *Pol*, *WGe*, *F* 1968 *Cze*, *Cze*, *F* 1969 *Pol*, *WGe*, *Cze*, *F* 1971 *Mor* 1973 *Sp*, *Mor*, *Ar*, *Ar* (R) 1974 *Cze*, *EGe*, *F*

Florian, P 1927 *F* 1934 *It*

Florian, T 1927 *F*, *Ger*

Flutur, V 1994 *Ger* (R) 1995 *J* (R), *J*, *C* (R), *SA*, *A*, *Ar*, *F* (R), *It* 1996 *Bel*, *Pol* 1997 *F*

Foca, M 1992 *It*, *USS*, *It*, *Ar* (R) 1993 *Pt*, *Tun* (R), *F*

Fugigi, C 1964 *Cze* (R) 1969 *Cze* (R) 1972 *Mor*, *Cze*, *WGe*, *F* 1973 *Sp*, *Ar*, *Ar* (R), *WGe*, *F* 1974 *Mor*, *Sp*, *Cze*, *EGe* 1975 *It*, *Sp*, *JAB*

Fugigi, C 1992 *Ar*

Fugigi, R 1995 *It* 1996 *Pt*, *F*, *Pol* 1998 *Ukr*, *Ar*, *I* 1999 *S*, *I* (R)

Fuicu, S 1976 *H* 1980 *USS*, *I*, *Pol*, *F* 1981 *It*, *Sp*, *USS*, *S*, *NZ*, *F* 1982 *Z*, *Z*, *F* 1983 *Mor*, *WGe*, *It*, *USS*, *W* 1984 *It*

Fulina, N 1988 *F*, *W* 1989 *It*, *E*, *Sp*, *Sa* (R), *USS* 1990 *It*, *F*, *H*, *Sp*, *USS* 1991 *NZ*, *C*, *Fj* 1992 *It*, *It* 1993 *Pt*, *F*, *Sp*, *F*, *I* 1994 *Sp*, *Ger*, *Rus*, *It*, *W*, *It*

Gal, C 2005 *I* (R) 2006 *Geo*, *CZR*, *Pt*, *S* (R) 2007 *Geo* (R), *CZR* (R), *ESp* (R), *ItA*, *Nm*, *It*, *S*, *NZ*

Galan, S 1985 *It* (R), *It*

Garlesteanu, I 1924 *F*, *US* 1927 *F*, *Cze*

Gealapu, A 1994 *It*, *E* 1995 *F*, *S*, *J*, *J*, *C*, *SA*, *A*, *Ar*, *F*, *It* 1996 *Pt*, *F*, *Pol*

Gheara, C 2004 *CZR*, *Sp*, *Rus* (R), *Geo*

Gheorghe, C 1992 *It* 1993 *Tun*, *F* (R), *Sp* (R) 1994 *Sp* (R), *Ger*, *Rus*, *E* (R)

Gherasim, D 1959 *Cze*

Ghiata, V 1951 *EGe*

Ghica, S 1937 *H*, *F* 1942 *It*

Ghioc, V 2000 *It* 2001 *Pt*, *Sp*, *Rus*, *Geo*, *I*, *W*, *E* 2002 *Pt*, *Sp* (R), *H*, *W*, *S* 2003 *CZR*, *Ar* (R) 2004 *It*, *W*, *CZR* (R) 2005 *Ukr*, *J* (R), *S* (R)

Ghiondea, N 1949 *Cze* 1951 *EGe*

Ghiuzelea, D 1951 *EGe* 1952 *EGe*, *EGe* 1953 *It* 1955 *Cze* 1957 *Cze*

Girbu, A 1992 *Ar* (R) 1993 *Tun* (R), *Sp*, *F* (R), *I* 1994 *Sp* 1995 *Ar*, *F* (R), *It* 1996 *Pt*, *F* (R), *Pol* 1997 *F*, *Ar*, *F*, *It* 1998 *H*, *Pol*, *Geo*, *I*

Giucal, M 1985 *It*, *Tun*, *USS*, *It* 1986 *Pt*, *F*, *Tun*

Giugiuc, A 1963 *Bul* (R), *EGe* (R), *Cze* (R) 1964 *Cze* (R), *EGe* 1966 *Cze*

Giuglea, V 1986 *S*, *Tun* (R)

Glavan, I 1942 *It*

Gontineac, RS 1995 *F*, *S*, *J*, *J*, *C*, *SA*, *A* 1996 *Pt*, *F*, *Pol* 1997 *F*, *W*, *Ar*, *F*, *It* 1998 *H*, *Pol*, *Ukr*, *Ar*, *Geo*, *I* 1999 *F*, *S*, *A*, *US*, *I* 2000 *H*, *Sp*, *Geo*, *F* 2001 *Rus*, *Geo* 2002 *Pt*, *Sp*, *Rus*, *Geo*, *I*, *It*, *Sp*, *W*, *S* 2003 *Pt*, *Sp*, *Geo*, *CZR*, *F*, *W*, *I*, *A*, *Ar*, *Nm* 2004 *CZR*, *Pt*, *Rus*, *Geo*, *It*, *W*, *J*, *CZR* 2005 *Geo*, *C* 2006 *Geo*, *Pt*, *Ukr*, *Rus*, *F*, *Geo*, *Sp*, *S* 2007 *Geo*, *Sp*, *It*, *S*, *Pt*, *NZ*

Graur, G 1958 *It* 1959 *EGe*, *Pol*, *Cze*, *EGe* 1960 *Pol*, *EGe*, *Cze* 1961 *EGe* 1962 *EGe*, *It*

Grigore, E 1982 *WGe* 1984 *Sp* 1985 *E*, *Tun* 1987 *It*, *USS*, *Z*, *F* (R), *S*

Grigorescu, V 1936 *F*, *It*, *Ger* 1939 *It*

Guramare, M 1982 *WGe* (R), *It* 1983 *Mor*, *WGe* 1988 *Sp* (R)

Guranescu, A 1991 *S*, *F* 1992 *USS* (R), *It* (R) 1993 *Pt*, *Tun*, *I* 1994 *Ger*, *Rus*, *It*, *W*, *E* (R) 1995 *SA*, *A*, *Ar* (R), *F*, *It*

Guranescu, S 1997 *W*, *Bel*, *Ar* (R) 2001 *Sp*, *H* (R), *Rus* (R), *I* (R)

Hariton, A 1973 *Mor* (R), *Ar*, *Ar* 1978 *Cze*, *Sp* (R)

Hell, T 1958 *EGe*

Hildan, CN 1998 *H*, *Pol*, *Geo* 1999 *S* (R)

Hodorca, L 1984 *It* 1985 *Tun* 1986 *Pt*, *S*, *F*, *Tun*, *Tun*, *I* 1987 *It*, *Z* (R) 1988 *F*

Holban, M 1980 *Mor* 1982 *F* 1985 *It*, *USS* 1986 *Pt* (R), *I* (R)

Hussar, J 1919 *US*

Iacob, D 1996 *Bel* 2001 *Pt* (R), *Sp*, *H*, *Geo*, *W*

Iacob, ML 1997 *W*, *Bel* (R), *Ar* (R), *F* (R), *It* (R) 1999 *S* (R)

Ianusevici, P 1974 *Pol*, *Cze*, *EGe*, *Cze* 1975 *It* (R) 1976 *USS*, *Bul*, *Pol*, *F*, *Mor* 1977 *Sp*, *Pol*, *It*, *F* 1978 *F*

Iconomu, I 1919 *US*, *F*

Iconomu, M 1919 *US*, *F*

Ifrim, N 1937 *F*, *Ger*

Ignat, G 1986 *Pt*, *S*, *F*, *Tun* 1988 *It*, *Sp*, *US*, *USS*, *USS*, *F*, *W* 1989 *It*, *E*, *Sp*, *S* 1990 *It*, *F*, *H*, *Sp* 1991 *It*, *NZ* 1992 *Sp* (R), *It*, *USS*, *F*

Ilca, V 1987 *F*

Ilie, I 1952 *EGe*, *EGe* 1953 *It* 1955 *Cze* (R) 1957 *F*, *Cze*, *Bel*, *F* 1958 *It* 1959 *EGe*

Iliescu, M 1961 *EGe* 1963 *Bul*, *EGe*, *Cze*, *F* 1965 *WGe*, *F* 1967 *WGe* (R)

Ioan, T 1937 *H*, *F* (R), *Ger*

Ioan, V 1927 *Ger*, *Cze* 1937 *It*

Ion, F 1991 *S* 1992 *Sp* 1993 *F*

Ion, G 1984 *Sp* 1986 *F* (R), *I* 1988 *USS*, *F*, *W* 1989 *It*, *E*, *Sp* (R), *Sa* (R), *USS*, *S* 1990 *It*, *F*, *H*, *Sp*, *It*, *USS* 1991 *It*, *NZ*, *F*, *S*, *F*, *C*, *Fj* 1992 *Sp*, *It*, *USS*, *F*, *Ar* 1993 *Pt*, *F*, *Sp*, *F* 1994 *Sp*, *It*, *W*, *It*

Ion, P 2003 *Ar* (R) 2004 *It* (R) 2005 *Rus* (R), *Ukr*, *J* (R), *US* (R), *S* (R) 2006 *Geo* (R), *CZR* (R), *Pt*, *Ukr* (R), *Rus*, *F* (R), *Geo* (R), *S* (R) 2007 *Geo* (R), *Sp* (R), *CZR* (R), *ESp*, *ItA* (R), *Pt* (R), *NZ* (R)

Ion, V 1980 *Mor*, *USS* 1982 *Z*, *Z*, *F* 1983 *Mor*, *It*, *USS*, *W*, *USS*, *F* 1984 *S* 1985 *It* (R) 1987 *It*, *USS*, *Z* (R), *F*, *S*

Ionescu, A 1958 *EGe*, *It* 1959 *EGe*, *Pol*, *Cze* 1960 *Pol*, *EGe*, *Cze* 1961 *Pol*, *Cze*, *EGe*, *F* 1962 *EGe*, *It*, *F* 1963 *F* 1964 *Cze*, *EGe*, *F* 1965 *WGe* (R) 1966 *Cze*, *It*, *F*

Ionescu, D 1949 *Cze* 1951 *EGe* 1952 *EGe*, *EGe* 1953 *It* 1955 *Cze* 1957 *F*, *Cze*, *F* 1958 *Sp*, *It*

Ionescu, G 1934 *It* 1936 *F*, *It*, *Ger* 1937 *It*, *F* 1938 *F*, *Ger* 1940 *It* 1942 *It*

Ionescu, G 1949 *Cze*

Ionescu, M 1972 *Mor* 1976 *USS*, *Bul*, *Pol*, *F* 1977 *It*, *F*, *Pol*, *It*, *F* 1978 *Cze*, *Sp*, *Pol*, *F* 1979 *It*, *Sp*, *USS*, *W*, *Pol*, *F* 1980 *I* (R) 1981 *NZ* 1983 *USS* (R)

Ionescu, R 1968 *Cze*, *Cze* 1971 *F*
Ionescu, S 1936 *It*, *Ger* 1937 *It*
Ionescu, V 1993 *Tun* (R), *F* (R) 1994 *Rus* (R) 1998 *Ukr*
Ionescu, V 1992 *It*
Ionita, F 1974 *Sp* 1978 *Pol*, *F*
Iordachescu, P 1957 *F*, *Cze*, *Bel*, *F* 1958 *Sp*, *WGe*, *EGe*, *It* 1959 *EGe*, *Pol*, *Cze*, *EGe* 1960 *Pol*, *EGe*, *Cze* 1961 *EGe* 1963 *F* 1964 *Cze*, *EGe*, *WGe* 1965 *WGe*, *F* 1966 *Cze*
Iordan, M 1980 *Mor*
Iordanescu, P 1949 *Cze*
Iorgulescu, V 1967 *WGe* (R) 1968 *Cze*, *F* 1969 *Pol*, *WGe*, *Cze* 1970 *It*, *F* 1971 *F* 1973 *Ar*, *Ar*
Irimescu, V 1960 *F* 1961 *Pol*, *Cze*, *EGe*, *F* 1962 *Cze*, *EGe*, *Pol*, *It*, *F* 1963 *F* 1964 *F* 1965 *WGe*, *F* 1966 *Cze*, *It*, *F* 1967 *It*, *Pt*, *Pol*, *WGe*, *F* 1968 *Cze*, *Cze*, *F* 1969 *Pol*, *WGe*, *Cze*, *F* 1970 *It*, *F* 1971 *F*
Irimia, I 1936 *F*, *It*, *Ger* 1937 *It*, *H*, *Ger* 1938 *F*, *Ger* 1939 *It* 1940 *It*
Irisescu, G 1993 *Sp* (R)
Iulian, A 2003 *CZR* (R)
Ivanciuc, I 1991 *Fj* (R) 1994 *E* 1995 *J*, *C* (R), *SA*, *A*
Jipescu, I 1927 *F*
Kramer, C 1955 *Cze* 1958 *Sp*, *WGe*, *It* 1960 *Pol* (R), *EGe*, *Cze*
Krantz, T 1940 *It* 1942 *It*
Kurtzbauer, C 1939 *It*
Lapusneanu, C 1934 *It*
Leonte, G 1984 *S*, *F* 1985 *E*, *It*, *USS* 1987 *It*, *USS*, *Z*, *S*, *USS*, *F* 1988 *It*, *Sp*, *US*, *USS*, *USS*, *F*, *W* 1989 *It*, *E*, *Sp*, *Z*, *Sa*, *USS*, *S* 1990 *It*, *F*, *H*, *Sp*, *It* 1991 *It*, *NZ*, *F*, *S*, *F*, *C* 1992 *USS*, *F*, *It*, *Ar* 1993 *Tun*, *F*, *Sp*, *F*, *I* 1994 *Sp*, *Ger*, *Rus*, *It*, *W*, *It* 1995 *F*, *S*, *J*, *J*, *C*, *SA*, *A*
Leuciuc, M 1987 *F* (R)
Luca, T 1995 *Ar*, *F*, *It* 1996 *F*
Lucaci, V 1996 *Bel*
Lungu, A 1980 *It*, *USS* 1981 *It*, *Sp*, *USS*, *S*, *NZ*, *F* 1982 *WGe*, *It*, *USS*, *Z*, *Z*, *F* 1983 *Mor*, *WGe*, *It*, *USS*, *Pol*, *W*, *USS*, *F* 1984 *It*, *S*, *F*, *Sp* 1985 *E*, *It*, *Tun*, *USS*, *USS*, *It* 1986 *Pt*, *S*, *F*, *Tun*, *Tun*, *Pt*, *F*, *I* 1987 *It*, *USS*, *Z*, *F*, *S*, *USS*, *F* 1988 *It*, *Sp*, *US*, *USS*, *USS*, *F*, *W* 1989 *It*, *E*, *Sp*, *Z*, *Sa*, *USS*, *S* 1990 *It*, *F*, *It* 1991 *It*, *NZ*, *F*, *S*, *F*, *C*, *Fj* 1992 *Sp*, *It*, *USS*, *F*, *Ar* 1995 *A* (R)
Lungu, R 2002 *Pt*, *H* (R), *It* (R), *Sp* (R), *W* (R) 2003 *Pt* (R)
Lupu, A 2006 *S* (R)
Lupu, C 1998 *Pol* (R), *I* (R) 1999 *F* (R) 2000 *Mor*, *It* 2001 *Pt*, *H* (R), *Rus* (R), *W* 2002 *H*, *Rus* (R)
Luric, S 1951 *EGe* 1952 *EGe*, *EGe* 1953 *It* 1955 *Cze*
Luscal, V 1958 *Sp*, *WGe*, *EGe*
Macaneata, F 1983 *USS*
Macovei, M 2006 *Ukr* (R), *Rus* (R) 2007 *Geo*
Maftei, V 1995 *Ar*, *F*, *It* 1996 *Bel* 1997 *W*, *F* 1998 *Ar* (R) 2001 *Pt*, *Sp*, *H*, *Geo*, *I* 2002 *Pt*, *Sp*, *Rus*, *Geo*, *I*, *It*, *Sp*, *S* 2003 *Pt*, *Geo*, *CZR*, *F*, *W*, *I*, *A*, *Ar*, *Nm* 2004 *Pt*, *Sp*, *Rus*, *Geo*, *W*, *J*, *CZR* 2005 *Rus*, *Geo*, *Ukr*, *C*, *I* 2006 *CZR* (R)
Malancu, G 1976 *H*, *It*, *USS*, *Bul*
Man, A 1988 *US*, *USS*, *USS*
Manoileanu, D 1949 *Cze*
Manole, G 1959 *Pol* 1960 *Pol*, *EGe*, *Cze*
Manta, A 1996 *Bel* 1997 *F* (R) 1998 *Ar*, *Geo*, *I* 2000 *F* 2001 *Pt*, *Sp*, *Rus*, *Geo* 2002 *Sp* (R), *H*, *Rus*, *I*, *It*, *Sp* 2003 *Pt*, *Rus* 2005 *C*, *I* 2006 *Geo*, *CZR*, *Pt*, *Geo* 2007 *It*, *S*, *NZ*
Manu, H 1919 *US*, *F* 1927 *F*, *Ger*
Marascu, N 1919 *F* 1924 *F*, *US* 1927 *F*, *Cze*
Marasescu, A 1927 *F*, *Ger* 1936 *It*, *Ger*
Marculescu, E 1936 *F*, *It*, *Ger* 1937 *It* 1939 *It* (R) 1940 *It*
Marghescu, A 1980 *Pol* (R) 1981 *It* 1983 *W*, *USS*, *F* 1984 *S*, *F*, *Sp* 1985 *E*
Marica, I 1972 *WGe*, *F* 1973 *Sp*, *Mor*, *WGe*, *F* 1974 *Mor*, *Sp*, *Cze*, *EGe*, *F*, *Cze* 1975 *It*, *Sp*
Marin, A 1978 *Cze*, *Sp*, *Pol* 1979 *F* 1980 *Pol* 1982 *USS* 1983 *Pol* 1984 *Sp* 1985 *USS*, *It* 1986 *Pt* 1987 *USS*, *Z*
Marin, N 1991 *Fj* 1992 *Sp* (R), *It* 1993 *F* (R), *I* (R) 1995 *Ar*, *F*, *It*
Marinache, A 1949 *Cze* 1951 *EGe* 1952 *EGe*, *EGe* 1955 *Cze* 1957 *F*, *Bel*, *F* 1960 *F* 1961 *Pol*, *EGe*, *Cze*, *EGe*, *F* 1962 *Cze*, *Pol*
Marinescu, V 1967 *Pt*, *WGe* 1968 *Cze* 1969 *Cze* (R), *F*
Marioara, F 1994 *E* (R) 1996 *Pol* (R) 1998 *Geo* (R), *I*
Mateescu, A 1959 *EGe*, *Pol*, *Cze*, *EGe* 1960 *Pol*, *EGe*, *Cze* 1962 *EGe*, *Pol* 1963 *Bul* (R), *EGe*, *Cze* (R) 1964 *Cze*, *EGe* 1965 *WGe*, *F* 1966 *F* 1970 *It*, *F* 1973 *Sp* (R), *WGe*, *F* 1974 *Mor*, *Pol*, *Sp*
Mateiescu, A 1934 *It* 1936 *F*, *Ger*
Mavrodin, R 1998 *Geo*, *I* 1999 *F*, *A* (R), *US*, *I* 2000 *H*, *Pt*, *Sp*, *Geo*, *F*, *It* 2002 *Pt*, *Sp*, *H*, *I*, *It* (R), *Sp* (R), *W* 2003 *I*, *A*, *Ar*, *Nm* 2004 *Pt*, *Sp* (R), *Rus*, *Geo*, *W* (R), *J*, *CZR* 2005 *Rus*, *J*, *US*, *S*, *Pt* 2006 *Ukr*, *Rus*, *F* (R), *Geo*, *Sp*, *S* (R) 2007 *Geo* (R), *ESp* (R), *ItA* (R), *Nm* (R), *It* (R), *S* (R), *Pt*, *NZ* (R)
Mazilu, G 1958 *Sp*, *WGe* 1959 *EGe*, *Pol*, *Cze*
Mehedinti, S 1951 *EGe* 1953 *It*
Melinte, G 1958 *EGe*, *It*
Mergisescu, P 1960 *Pol*, *EGe*, *Cze*
Mersoiu, C 2000 *Mor*, *Pt* 2001 *I* 2002 *S* (R) 2003 *Pt* (R), *Sp* (R), *Geo*, *CZR*, *F*, *W* 2004 *CZR*, *Pt*, *Sp*, *Rus* (R), *It*, *W*, *J*, *CZR* 2005 *Rus*, *Geo*, *Ukr*, *I* (R) 2006 *CZR* (R), *Pt* (R), *Geo* (R), *Sp* (R) 2007 *Geo*, *Sp*, *CZR*
Miclescu, A 1971 *Mor* (R)
Mihailescu, S 1919 *F* 1924 *F*, *US* 1927 *F*
Mihalache, D 1973 *Mor*
Mihalascu, V 1967 *Pol*, *WGe*
Mitocaru, A 1992 *Ar* 1993 *Pt*, *Sp*, *F*
Mitu, P 1996 *Bel* (R), *Pol* 1997 *W* (R), *Bel*, *Ar*, *It* 1998 *H* (R), *Pol*, *Ukr*, *Ar*, *Geo*, *I* 1999 *F*, *S*, *A*, *US*, *I* 2000 *H*, *Pt*, *Sp*, *Geo*, *It* 2001 *Pt*, *Sp*, *H*, *Rus* 2002 *Pt*, *Sp*, *H* (R), *Rus*, *Geo*, *Sp* (R), *W*, *S* 2003 *Geo* 2005 *I* 2006 *Geo*
Miu, M 2003 *Pt*, *Sp* (R)
Mladin, V 1955 *Cze* (R) 1957 *Bel*, *F* 1958 *Sp*, *WGe*, *It* 1959 *EGe* (R) 1960 *F*
Mocanu, S 1996 *Bel* 1998 *H* (R), *Pol* (R), *Ukr* (R) 2000 *Mor*, *Pt* (R)
Moldoveanu, T 1937 *F*, *Ger* 1938 *F*, *Ger* 1939 *It* 1940 *It*
Morariu, F 1976 *H*, *USS*, *Bul*, *Pol*, *F*, *Mor* 1977 *Sp*, *It*, *F*, *Pol*, *It*, *F* 1978 *Cze*, *Sp*, *Pol*, *F* 1979 *It*, *Sp*, *USS*, *W*, *Pol*, *F* 1980 *It*, *I*, *Pol*, *F* 1981 *USS* (R), *NZ* 1982 *USS*, *Z*, *Z*, *F* 1983 *Mor*, *WGe*, *It*, *USS*, *Pol*, *W*, *F* 1984 *It*, *S*, *F*, *Sp* 1985 *E*, *It*, *Tun*, *USS*, *USS*, *It* 1986 *Pt*, *S*, *F*, *Tun* 1987 *It*, *USS*, *Z*, *S*, *USS*, *F* 1988 *It*, *Sp*, *US*, *USS*, *USS*, *F*, *W* 1989 *It*, *E*, *Sp*, *Z*
Morariu, O 1984 *Sp* 1985 *Tun*
Morariu, V 1952 *EGe*, *EGe* 1953 *It* 1955 *Cze* 1957 *F*, *Cze*, *Bel*, *F* 1959 *EGe* 1960 *F* 1961 *Pol*, *Cze*, *EGe*, *F* 1962 *Cze*, *EGe*, *Pol*, *It*, *F* 1963 *F* 1964 *WGe*, *F*
Moscu, C 1934 *It* 1937 *It*
Mot, M 1980 *Mor* 1982 *It*, *USS*, *Z* 1985 *It*, *It* 1986 *F*, *Tun* 1988 *US*, *USS*
Motoc, M 1988 *US* (R) 1989 *S*
Motrescu, P 1973 *Mor*, *Ar*, *Ar* 1974 *Mor*, *Pol*, *Sp*, *Cze* 1975 *JAB*, *Pol*, *F* 1976 *H*, *It*, *Sp*, *Bul* (R), *Pol* (R), *F*, *Mor* 1977 *Sp*, *It*, *F*, *Pol*, *It*, *F* 1978 *Cze*, *Sp*, *Pol*, *F* 1979 *It*, *Sp*, *USS*, *W*, *Pol* 1980 *It*, *Mor*
Munteanu, B 2000 *It*
Munteanu, IC 1940 *It* (R) 1942 *It*
Munteanu, M 1973 *WGe*, *F* 1974 *Mor*, *Sp*, *Cze*, *EGe*, *F*, *Cze* 1975 *It*, *Sp*, *JAB*, *Pol*, *F* 1976 *H*, *It*, *Sp*, *Pol*, *Mor* 1978 *Pol*, *F* 1979 *It*, *Sp*, *W*, *Pol* 1980 *It*, *I*, *Pol*, *F* 1981 *It*, *Sp*, *USS*, *S*, *NZ*, *F* 1982 *F* 1983 *Mor*, *WGe*, *It*, *USS*, *Pol*, *W*, *USS*, *F* 1984 *It*, *S*, *F* 1985 *USS* 1986 *S*, *Tun*, *Pt*, *F* 1988 *It*, *Sp*
Munteanu, T 2003 *CZR* (R) 2004 *CZR* (R)
Musat, D 1974 *Sp*, *Cze*, *EGe*, *Cze* 1975 *It*, *JAB*, *Pol*, *F* 1976 *Mor* 1980 *Mor*
Nache, M 1980 *Mor*
Nagel, M 1958 *EGe* 1960 *Pol*, *EGe*, *Cze*
Nanu, R 1952 *EGe*, *EGe* 1953 *It* 1955 *Cze* (R) 1957 *F*, *Bel*, *F*
Nastase, V 1985 *Tun*, *USS* 1986 *Tun*, *Pt*, *F*, *I*
Neaga, D 1988 *It*, *Sp*, *USS*, *F*, *W* 1989 *It*, *E*, *Sp*, *Z*, *Sa*, *USS*, *S* 1990 *It*, *F*, *H*, *Sp*, *USS* 1991 *It*, *F*, *S*, *F*, *C*, *Fj* 1993 *Tun*, *F*, *Sp*, *I* 1994 *Sp*, *Ger*, *Rus*, *It*, *W*, *It*, *E* 1995 *F*, *S*, *J*, *J* (R), *C* 1996 *Pt*, *F*

Neagu, I 1972 *Mor, Cze*
Necula, E 1987 *It, F*
Nedelcovici, P 1924 *F*
Nedelcu, C 1964 *Cze, EGe*
Nedelcu, M 1993 *Pt, Tun, F* 1994 *Sp* (R), *It* (R) 1995 *Ar, F, It*
Nedelcu, V 1996 *Pol* (R) 1997 *F, W, Ar, F* (R) 1998 *H, Pol, Ukr, Ar* 2000 *H* (R) 2001 *I, W, E* 2002 *Rus* (R), *Geo* (R)
Negreci, I 1994 *E* 1995 *F, J, C, SA, A, Ar, F* (R), *It*
Nemes, I 1924 *F, US* 1927 *Ger, Cze*
Nere, N 2006 *CZR* (R) 2007 *CZR* (R)
Nica, G 1964 *Cze, EGe, WGe* 1966 *It, F* 1967 *Pol, F* 1969 *Pol, WGe, Cze, F* 1970 *It, F* 1971 *It, Mor, F* 1972 *Mor, Cze, WGe, F* 1973 *Sp, Mor, Ar, Ar, WGe, F* 1974 *Mor, Pol, Sp, Cze, EGe, F, Cze* 1975 *It, Sp, JAB, Pol, F* 1976 *H, It, Sp, USS, Bul, Pol, F, Mor* 1977 *Sp, It, F, Pol, It, F* 1978 *Pol, F*
Nichitean, N 1990 *It, Sp* (R), *It, USS* 1991 *It, F, F, C, Fj* 1992 *USS, It, Ar* 1993 *Pt* (R), *Tun, F, Sp* 1994 *Sp, Ger, Rus, It, W, It* 1995 *F, S, J* (R), *J, C* 1997 *F*
Nicola, G 1927 *F, Ger, Cze*
Nicolae, C 2003 *Pt, Rus* 2006 *Sp* (R) 2007 *ItA* (R), *Nm, Pt*
Nicolae, M 2003 *I* (R), *A*
Nicolau, N 1940 *It*
Nicolescu, M 1969 *Pol* (R), *WGe, Cze, F* 1971 *It, Mor, F* 1972 *Mor, Cze, WGe, F* 1973 *Sp, Mor, Ar, Ar, WGe, F* 1974 *Mor, Cze* (R), *EGe, F, Cze* 1975 *It, Sp, Pol* (R), *F*
Niculescu, P 1958 *It* 1959 *EGe, Cze*
Niculescu, V 1938 *F, Ger*
Nistor, F 1986 *Tun*
Nistor, V 1959 *EGe, Pol, EGe*
Oblomenco, M 1967 *It, Pt, WGe, F*
Olarasu, G 2000 *Mor, H* (R)
Olarasu, M 2000 *Mor*
Onutu, V 1967 *It, Pt, Pol, WGe, F* 1968 *Cze* 1969 *F* 1971 *It, Mor*
Oprea, N 2000 *It* 2001 *Pt, Sp* (R), *H, Rus, Geo, I, W, E*
Opris, F 1986 *F, Tun, Tun, Pt* (R), *F, I* 1987 *F*
Oprisor, G 2004 *W* (R), *J, CZR* (R) 2005 *Rus* (R), *Ukr* (R), *J* (R), *US, S* (R), *Pt*
Oroian, T 1988 *F* (R), *W* (R) 1989 *It, E* (R), *Sp, Z, USS* 1990 *Sp, It* 1993 *Pt* (R), *Tun, F* (R), *Sp, I* 1994 *Sp, Ger, Rus, It, W, It, E* 1995 *F, S, J, J, C*
Ortelecan, M 1972 *Mor, Cze, WGe, F* 1974 *Pol* 1976 *It, Sp, USS, Bul, F* 1977 *Sp, It, F, Pol, It, F* 1978 *Cze, Sp* 1979 *F* 1980 *USS*
Palosanu, A 1952 *EGe, EGe* 1955 *Cze* 1957 *F, Cze*
Pana, E 1937 *F* (R), *Ger*
Paraschiv, M 1975 *Sp, JAB, Pol, F* 1976 *H, It, Sp, USS, Bul, F, Mor* 1977 *Sp, It, Pol, F* 1978 *Cze, Sp, Pol, F* 1979 *It, Sp, W* 1980 *It, I, F* 1981 *It, USS, S, NZ, F* 1982 *WGe, It, USS, Z, Z, F* 1983 *Mor, WGe, It, USS, Pol, W, USS* (R), *F* 1984 *It, S, F* 1985 *E, It, Tun, USS, USS, It* 1986 *Pt, S, Tun* (R) 1987 *It, USS, Z, F, S, USS, F*
Parcalabescu, G 1940 *It* 1942 *It* 1949 *Cze* 1951 *EGe* 1952 *EGe, EGe* 1953 *It* 1955 *Cze* 1957 *Cze, Bel, F* 1958 *It* 1959 *EGe, Pol, Cze* 1960 *Pol, EGe, Cze*
Pasache, G 2001 *E* (R)
Pascu, V 1983 *It* (R), *Pol, W, USS, F* 1984 *It* 1985 *USS* 1986 *Pt, S, F, Tun, I* 1987 *F* 1988 *It* (R)
Patrichi, C 1993 *Pt* (R), *Tun*
Pavlovici, A 1972 *Mor* (R), *Cze*
Penciu, A 1955 *Cze* 1957 *F, Cze, Bel, F* 1958 *Sp, WGe, EGe, It* 1959 *EGe, Pol, Cze, EGe* 1960 *F* 1961 *Pol, EGe, Cze, EGe, F* 1962 *Cze, EGe, Pol, It, F* 1963 *Bul, Cze, F* 1964 *WGe, F* 1965 *WGe, F* 1966 *It, F* 1967 *F*
Peter, I 1973 *Sp, Mor*
Petrache, AA 1998 *H* (R), *Pol* (R) 1999 *F, S, A, US, I* 2000 *Mor, H, Pt, Sp, Geo, F* 2001 *W, E* 2002 *Pt, Sp, H, Rus, I, It, Sp, W, S* 2003 *Pt, Sp, Rus* 2004 *It, W, J, CZR*
Petre, C 2001 *E* 2002 *Pt, Sp, H, Rus, Geo, I, It, Sp, W, S* 2003 *Pt, Rus, Geo, CZR, F, W, I, A, Ar, Nm* 2004 *CZR, Pt, Sp, Rus, Geo* (R), *It, W, J, CZR* 2005 *Rus, Geo, Ukr, J, US, S, Pt, C, I* 2006 *Geo, CZR, Pt, Ukr, Rus, F, Geo, Sp, S* 2007 *Geo, Sp, CZR, ESp, ItA, Nm, It, S, Pt, NZ*
Petrichei, A 2002 *I* (R), *S* 2003 *Sp, Rus* (R), *Geo* (R), *CZR, F* (R), *W* (R), *I, Ar* (R), *Nm* 2004 *Pt* (R), *Sp, Rus, Geo* 2007 *ESp* (R), *Nm* (R)
Petrisor, P 1985 *It* 1987 *USS* (R)
Peuciulescu, H 1927 *F*
Picoiu, M 2001 *Pt, H* 2002 *Pt* (R), *Sp, H, Rus, I* (R), *It* (R), *Sp* (R), *W*
Pinghert, C 1996 *Bel* (R)
Pintea, I 1974 *Pol* 1976 *Pol, F, Mor* 1977 *Sp, It, F, Pol, It, F* 1979 *It, Sp, USS, W, Pol, F* 1980 *It, USS*
Piti, D 1987 *USS, F* 1988 *It, Sp, US* 1991 *S*
Pllotschi, A 1985 *It, Tun* 1987 *S*
Plumea 1927 *Ger*
Podarescu, S 1979 *Pol, F* 1980 *USS* 1982 *WGe, It, USS, F* 1983 *Mor, WGe, USS, F* 1984 *It* (R) 1985 *E, It*
Podea, C 2001 *Geo* (R), *I* (R) 2002 *I* (R), *It* (R), *Sp, W* (R) 2003 *Pt* (R), *Sp, Rus, F* (R), *A* (R)
Polizu, R 1919 *US*
Pop, A 1970 *It* 1971 *It, Mor* 1972 *Mor* (R), *Cze, F* (R) 1973 *WGe, F* 1974 *Mor, Pol, Sp, EGe, F, Cze* 1975 *It, Sp, JAB, Pol, F*
Popa, D 1993 *Tun, F, Sp*
Popa, D 1994 *Ger* (R)
Popa, I 1934 *It* 1936 *F, It, Ger* 1937 *H, F* 1938 *F, Ger* 1939 *It* 1940 *It* 1942 *It*
Popa, M 1962 *EGe*
Popa, N 1952 *EGe* (R)
Poparlan, V 2007 *Nm* (R)
Popean, A 1999 *S* (R) 2001 *Pt, H*
Popescu, C 1997 *Bel* (R) 2003 *CZR* (R), *F* (R), *W* (R), *I* (R), *A* (R), *Ar* (R), *Nm* (R) 2004 *CZR* (R), *Pt, Sp* (R), *Rus* (R), *Geo* (R), *J* (R), *CZR* (R) 2005 *Rus, S, Pt* (R), *C* (R) 2006 *CZR, Ukr* (R), *Rus, F* (R), *Geo* (R), *Sp* (R), *S* (R) 2007 *Geo* (R), *Sp, CZR, ESp* (R), *ItA, Nm, It* (R), *Pt*
Popescu, C 1986 *Tun, Pt, F*
Popescu, I 1958 *EGe*
Popescu, I 2001 *Pt, Sp, H, Rus, Geo*
Popescu-Colibasi, C 1934 *It*
Popisteanu, V 1996 *Pt, F, Pol*
Popovici, F 1973 *Sp, Mor*
Postolache, N 1972 *WGe* (R), *F* 1973 *Sp, Mor, WGe, F* 1974 *Mor, Pol, Sp, EGe* (R), *F, Cze* 1975 *It, Sp, Pol, F* 1976 *H, It*
Preda, C 1961 *Pol, Cze* 1962 *EGe, F* 1963 *Bul, EGe, Cze, F* 1964 *Cze, EGe, WGe, F*
Racean, NF 1988 *USS, USS, F, W* 1989 *It, E, Z, Sa, USS* (R) 1990 *H, Sp, It, USS* 1991 *NZ, F, F, C, Fj* 1992 *Sp, It, USS, F, It, Ar* 1993 *Pt, Tun, F, Sp* 1994 *Ger* (R), *Rus, It, W* 1995 *F, S, J, J, C, SA, A*
Radoi, M 1995 *F* 1996 *Pt, Pol* (R) 1997 *F, W, Bel, Ar, F, It* 1998 *H, Pol, Ukr*
Radoi, P 1980 *Mor*
Radu, T 1991 *NZ*
Raducanu, C 1985 *It* 1987 *It* (R), *USS, Z, F, S* 1989 *It* (R), *E* (R), *Sp, Z* (R)
Radulescu, A 1980 *USS, Pol* (R) 1981 *It, Sp, USS, S, F* 1982 *WGe, It, USS, Z* (R), *Z* (R) 1983 *Pol, W, USS, F* 1984 *It, S, F, Sp* 1985 *E, USS* 1988 *It, Sp, US, USS, USS, F, W* 1989 *It, E, Sa, USS* 1990 *It, F, H, Sp* (R), *It* (R), *USS*
Radulescu, T 1958 *Sp, WGe* 1959 *EGe, Pol, Cze, EGe* 1963 *Bul, EGe, Cze* 1964 *F* 1965 *WGe, F* 1966 *Cze*
Rascanu, D 1972 *WGe, F*
Rascanu, G 1966 *It, F* 1967 *It, Pt, Pol, WGe, F* 1968 *Cze, Cze, F* 1969 *Pol, WGe, Cze, F* 1970 *It, F* 1971 *It, Mor, F* 1972 *Mor, Cze, WGe, F* 1974 *Sp*
Ratiu, C 2003 *CZR* (R) 2005 *J, US, S, Pt, C* (R), *I* (R) 2006 *CZR* (R), *Pt* (R), *Ukr, Rus, F, Geo* (R), *Sp, S* 2007 *Sp, CZR, ESp, It* (R), *S* (R), *Pt, NZ* (R)
Ratiu, I 1992 *It* (R)
Rentea, S 2000 *Mor*
Roman, I 1976 *Bul* (R)
Rosu, C 1993 *I*
Rotaru, I 1995 *J, C, Ar, It* (R) 1996 *Pt, F* (R), *Pol* 1997 *W, Bel, Ar, F*
Rotaru, L 1999 *F* (R), *A, I* (R)
Rusu, M 1959 *EGe* 1960 *F* 1961 *Pol, Cze* 1962 *Cze, EGe, Pol, It, F* 1963 *Bul, EGe, Cze, F* 1964 *WGe, F* 1965 *WGe, F* 1966 *Cze, It, F* 1967 *It, Pt, Pol*
Rusu, V 1960 *Pol, EGe, Cze* 1961 *EGe, F* 1962 *Cze, EGe,*

Pol, It, F 1964 *Cze* (R), *EGe* (R), *WGe* (R), *F* 1965 *WGe* (R) 1966 *It, F* 1967 *WGe* 1968 *Cze*
Sadoveanu, I 1939 *It* 1942 *It*
Salageanu, AA 1995 *Ar* (R), *F, It* 1996 *Pt, F, Pol* 1997 *W, Bel, F* (R)
Samuil, V 2000 *It* (R) 2001 *Pt, E* 2002 *Pt* (R), *Sp* (R), *Geo*
Sasu, C 1989 *Z* 1991 *It, NZ, F, S, F, C, Fj* 1993 *I*
Sauan, C 1999 *S, A, US, I* 2000 *It* (R) 2002 *Geo, I, It, Sp* 2003 *Pt, Rus, Geo, CZR, F, W, I, A, Ar* (R), *Nm* (R) 2004 *CZR, Pt, Sp, Rus, Geo, It, W, J, CZR* 2005 *Rus, Geo, Ukr* (R), *J, US* (R), *S, Pt* 2006 *Rus* 2007 *Geo*
Sava, G 1989 *Z* (R), *S* 1990 *H, Sp, It, USS* 1991 *It, F, S, F, C* (R) 1992 *Sp*
Sava, I 1959 *EGe, Pol, Cze, EGe* 1960 *F* 1961 *Pol, EGe, Cze, EGe, F* 1962 *Cze, Pol, It, F*
Scarlat, C 1976 *H, Sp* 1977 *F* 1978 *Cze, Sp* 1979 *It* (R), *Sp, USS, W, Pol, F* 1980 *It, USS* 1982 *USS*
Schmettau, R 1919 *US, F*
Sebe, V 1960 *Pol, EGe, Cze*
Seceleanu, I 1992 *It, USS, F, It, Ar* 1993 *Pt, Tun, F, Sp, F*
Seceleanu, S 1986 *Pt, F, I* 1990 *It*
Septar, E 1996 *Bel, Pol* 1997 *W* 1998 *Pol* (R), *Ukr, I* (R) 1999 *F, S, A, US, I* 2000 *It*
Serban, B 1989 *Sa, USS, S* 1990 *It* 1992 *It, USS*
Serban, C 1964 *Cze, EGe, WGe* 1967 *Pol* (R) 1968 *Cze* (R), *F* 1969 *Pol, WGe, Cze, F* 1970 *It, F* 1971 *It, Mor, F* 1972 *F* 1973 *WGe, F* 1974 *Mor*
Serbu, M 1967 *It*
Sfetescu, E 1924 *F, US* 1927 *Cze*
Sfetescu, E 1934 *It* 1936 *F, Ger* 1937 *It*
Sfetescu, G 1927 *F, Ger*
Sfetescu, M 1924 *F, US* 1927 *Ger, Cze*
Sfetescu, N 1927 *F, Ger, Cze*
Simion, G 1998 *H*
Simion, G 1919 *US*
Simion, I 1976 *H, It, Sp* 1979 *Pol, F* 1980 *F*
Sirbu, L 1996 *Pt* (R) 2000 *Mor, H, Pt, Geo, F* 2001 *H* (R), *Rus* (R), *Geo, I, W, E* 2002 *Pt* (R), *Sp* (R), *H, Rus* (R), *I, It, S* (R) 2003 *Pt, Sp* (R), *CZR, F, W, I, A, Ar, Nm* 2004 *Pt* (R), *Sp, Rus, Geo, It, W, CZR* 2005 *Rus, Geo, Ukr, J, US, S* (R), *Pt, C* 2006 *Geo* (R), *Pt, Ukr, Rus, F, Geo, Sp* 2007 *Geo, ItA* (R), *It, S, Pt* (R), *NZ*
Slobozeanu, M 1936 *F* 1937 *H, F, Ger* 1938 *F, Ger*
Slusariuc, OS 1993 *Tun* (R) 1995 *J* (R), *J* (R), *C* 1996 *Pt* (R), *F* 1997 *Bel, Ar, F* 1998 *H* (R), *Ar, Geo* (R), *I* (R) 1999 *F* (R), *S* (R), *A*
Soare, S 2001 *I* (R), *W* (R) 2002 *Geo*
Soare, S 1924 *F, US*
Socaciu, M 2000 *It* (R) 2001 *I, W, E* 2002 *It* (R), *W* (R), *S* (R) 2003 *Pt, Sp, Rus, Geo* (R), *CZR* (R), *F, W, I, A* (R), *Nm* 2004 *CZR, Pt* (R), *Sp, Rus, Geo, It, W, J, CZR* 2005 *Rus, Geo, Ukr, J, US, Pt, C* (R), *I* (R) 2006 *CZR*
Socol, S 2001 *Sp, H, Rus, Geo* 2002 *Pt, It* (R), *Sp* (R), *W* 2003 *Sp, Rus, Geo, F, W, I, A, Ar, Nm* 2004 *CZR, Pt, Sp, Rus, Geo* 2005 *Rus, Geo, Ukr, C, I* 2006 *Geo, CZR, Pt, Ukr, Rus, F, Geo, Sp, S* 2007 *Geo, Sp, CZR, It, S, Pt* (R), *NZ*
Soculescu, N 1949 *Cze* 1951 *EGe* 1952 *EGe, EGe* 1953 *It* 1955 *Cze*
Soculescu, N 1927 *Ger*
Soculescu, V 1927 *Cze*
Solomie, GL 1992 *Sp, F, It, Ar* 1993 *Pt, Tun, F, Sp, F, I* 1994 *Sp, Ger, W, It, E* 1995 *F, S, J, J, C, SA, A, Ar, F, It* 1996 *Pt, F, Pol* 1997 *F, W, Bel, Ar, F, It* 1998 *H, Pol, Ukr, Ar, Geo, I* 1999 *S* (R), *A, US, I* 2000 *Sp, F, It* 2001 *Sp, H, Rus*
Stan, C 1990 *H* (R), *USS* 1991 *It* (R), *F* (R), *S, F, C, Fj* 1992 *Sp, It, It* (R), *Ar* (R) 1996 *Pt* (R), *Bel, F* (R), *Pol* 1997 *F* (R), *W* (R), *Bel* 1998 *Ar, Geo* 1999 *F, S, A, US, I*
Stanca, A 1996 *Pt, Pol*
Stanca, R 1997 *F* (R) 2003 *Sp* (R), *Rus* (R)
Stanciu, A 1958 *EGe, It*
Stanciu, G 1958 *EGe, It* (R)
Stanescu, C 1957 *Bel* 1958 *WGe* 1959 *EGe* 1960 *F* 1961 *Pol, EGe, Cze* 1962 *Cze, It, F* 1963 *Bul, EGe, Cze, F* 1964 *WGe, F* 1966 *Cze, It*
Stefan, C 1951 *EGe* 1952 *EGe*
Stoian, E 1927 *Cze*
Stoica, E 1973 *Ar, Ar* 1974 *Cze* 1975 *Sp* (R), *Pol, F* 1976 *Sp, USS, Bul, F, Mor* 1977 *Sp, It, F, Pol, It, F* 1978 *Cze, Sp, Pol, F* 1979 *It, Sp, USS, W, Pol, F* 1980 *It, USS, I, Pol, F* 1981 *It, Sp, USS, S, NZ, F* 1982 *WGe, It, USS, Z, Z, F*
Stoica, G 1963 *Bul, Cze* (R) 1964 *WGe* 1966 *It, F* 1967 *Pt, F* 1968 *Cze, Cze, F* 1969 *Pol*
Stroe, I 1986 *Pt*
Suciu, E 1976 *Bul* (R), *Pol* 1977 *It* (R), *F, It* 1979 *USS, Pol, F* 1981 *Sp*
Suciu, M 1968 *F* 1969 *Pol, WGe, Cze* 1970 *It, F* 1971 *It, Mor, F* 1972 *Mor, F*
Sugar, O 1983 *It* 1989 *Z* (R), *Sa, USS, S* 1991 *NZ, F*
Suiogan, K 1996 *Bel*
Talaba, D 1996 *Bel* 1997 *F* (R), *It*
Tanase, C 1938 *F, Ger* 1939 *It* 1940 *It*
Tanasescu, A 1919 *F* 1924 *F, US*
Tanoviceanu, N 1937 *It, H, F* 1939 *It*
Tarabega, I 1934 *It* 1936 *It*
Tata, V 1971 *F* 1973 *Ar* (R), *Ar*
Tatu, CF 2003 *Ar* (R) 2004 *CZR, Pt, Sp* (R), *Rus* (R), *Geo, It, W* 2005 *Ukr, J*
Tatucu, I 1973 *Sp, Mor* 1974 *Cze, F*
Teleasa, D 1971 *It* 1973 *Sp, Ar* (R), *Ar* (R)
Tenescu, D 1951 *EGe*
Teodorescu, I 2001 *I, W, E* 2002 *Pt, Sp, S* 2003 *Pt* (R), *Sp, Rus, W* (R), *I* (R), *A* (R), *Ar, Nm* 2004 *CZR, Pt, Sp, Rus, Geo* (R), *W, J, CZR* 2005 *Rus, Geo, Ukr, J, US, S, Pt, C, I* 2006 *Geo, CZR, Pt, Ukr, F, Geo* (R), *S* 2007 *ESp, ItA*
Teodorescu, I 1958 *Sp, WGe, EGe, It* 1960 *Pol, EGe, Cze* 1963 *Bul, EGe, Cze* 1965 *WGe, F*
Teofilovici, A 1957 *F, Cze, Bel, F* 1958 *Sp, WGe* 1959 *EGe* 1960 *F* 1961 *Pol, EGe, Cze, EGe, F* 1962 *Cze, Pol, It, F* 1963 *Bul, EGe, Cze, F* 1964 *WGe*
Tepurica, O 1985 *USS* (R)
Tibuleac, M 1957 *Bel, F* 1959 *Pol, Cze* 1966 *Cze* 1967 *It, Pt, Pol* (R), *WGe* (R) 1968 *Cze, Cze*
Ticlean, G 1919 *F*
Tigora, M 2004 *CZR* (R)
Tinca, A 1987 *USS, F*
Tincu, VM 2002 *Pt* (R), *Sp, H, Rus, Geo, I, It, Sp, S* 2003 *Pt, Sp, Rus, Geo, F, W* 2004 *Sp* 2005 *Geo, Ukr, C, I* 2006 *Geo, CZR, F, S* 2007 *Geo, Sp, CZR, ESp, ItA, Nm, It* (R), *S, Pt* (R), *NZ*
Toader, M 1982 *WGe* 1984 *Sp* 1985 *E, It, Tun, USS* 1986 *S, F, Tun, Tun, Pt, F, I* 1987 *It, USS, Z, F, S, USS, F* 1988 *F, W* 1989 *It, E, Sp, Sa, USS, S* 1990 *It, F, It* (R)
Toderasc, P 2000 *It* (R) 2001 *Pt* (R), *Rus* (R), *Geo* (R), *W* (R), *E* (R) 2002 *H* (R), *Rus* (R), *Geo* (R), *I* (R), *It, Sp* (R), *W, S* (R) 2003 *Sp* (R), *Rus, Geo, CZR, F* (R), *W* (R), *I* (R), *A, Ar, Nm* (R) 2004 *CZR, Pt* (R), *Sp* (R), *Rus* (R), *Geo, It* (R), *J* (R), *CZR* (R) 2005 *J, US, S, Pt, C, I* 2006 *Geo, Pt, Ukr, Sp* 2007 *Geo, ESp, ItA* (R), *Nm, It, S*
Tofan, IR 1997 *Bel, Ar, F, It* 1998 *H, Ar* 1999 *I* (R) 2000 *Mor* (R), *Sp* (R), *Geo* 2001 *Pt, Sp* (R), *H, Geo* (R), *I, W, E* 2002 *Pt* (R), *Sp, H, Rus, Geo, I, It, Sp, W, S* 2003 *Pt, Sp, Rus, Geo, CZR* (R), *F, W, I, A, Ar, Nm* 2004 *Sp* (R), *Geo* (R), *It, W, J* 2005 *Rus, Geo, Ukr* (R), *J* (R), *US, I* 2006 *Geo* (R), *CZR* (R), *Pt* (R), *Geo* (R), *Sp* (R), *S* (R) 2007 *Geo, ESp, ItA* (R), *Nm* (R), *S* (R)
Tofan, S 1985 *USS, It* 1986 *Tun, Pt, F, I* 1987 *It, USS, Z, F, S, USS, F* 1988 *It, Sp, US, USS* 1991 *NZ* (R) 1992 *Ar* 1993 *Pt* 1994 *It* (R), *E*
Tonita, O 2000 *Mor, H, Pt, Sp, F* (R) 2001 *Pt, Sp, H, Rus, Geo, I* 2002 *Sp* (R), *It, Sp, W* 2003 *Rus, Geo, F, W, I, A, Ar, Nm* 2004 *Sp, Rus, Geo, It* 2005 *Rus, Pt, C, I* 2006 *Geo, Pt, Geo, Sp, S* 2007 *Sp, CZR, It, S, Pt, NZ*
Traian 1942 *It*
Tranca, N 1992 *Sp*
Tudor, B 2003 *CZR, A* (R)
Tudor, F 1924 *F, US*
Tudor, M 1924 *F, US*
Tudori, AM 2003 *F* (R), *W* (R), *I* (R), *A* (R), *Ar, Nm* (R) 2004 *Sp* (R), *Rus, Geo, W, J, CZR* 2005 *Rus, Geo, Ukr, J, US, S, Pt* (R) 2006 *Geo* (R), *CZR, Ukr, Rus, F* 2007 *Sp* (R), *CZR* (R), *ESp, ItA, Nm, It* (R), *S* (R), *Pt*

Tudosa, D 1999 *S* (R) 2002 *Geo* (R), *I* (R), *It* (R) 2003 *Pt*, *W* (R)
Tudose, T 1977 *It* 1978 *Cze*, *Sp*, *Pol*, *F* 1979 *It*, *Sp*, *USS* 1980 *USS*
Tufa, V 1985 *USS* 1986 *Pt*, *S* (R) 1990 *It* (R) 1991 *F* (R) 1995 *F* (R), *S*, *J*, *J* (R), *SA* (R), *A* (R) 1996 *Pt* (R), *F*, *Pol*
Tunaru, D 1985 *It*
Turlea, V 1974 *Sp* (R) 1975 *JAB*, *Pol*, *F* 1977 *Pol*
Turut, C 1937 *H* 1938 *F*
Tutuianu, I 1960 *Pol*, *EGe* 1963 *Bul* (R), *EGe* (R), *Cze* 1964 *Cze*, *EGe*, *WGe* (R) 1965 *WGe*, *F* 1966 *Cze*, *It*, *F* 1967 *Pt*, *Pol*, *WGe*, *F* 1968 *Cze*, *Cze*, *F* 1969 *Pol*, *WGe*, *Cze*, *F* 1970 *It*, *F* 1971 *F*
Tutunea, G 1992 *Sp* (R)
Ungur, M 1996 *Bel*
Ungureanu, V 1979 *It*
Urdea, V 1979 *F* (R)
Ursache, V 2004 *It* (R), *W* (R), *CZR* 2005 *S*, *C* (R) 2006 *Geo* (R), *Ukr*, *Rus*, *F* (R), *S* (R) 2007 *Geo* (R), *Sp* (R), *CZR* (R), *ESp*, *ItA*, *Nm*, *Pt* (R), *NZ* (R)
Vacioiu, R 1977 *It*, *F*, *It*
Valeriu, E 1949 *Cze* (R) 1952 *EGe* (R)
Vardala, M 1924 *F*, *US*
Vardela, N 1927 *F*, *Ger*
Varga, G 1976 *It*, *USS*, *Bul*, *Pol*, *F*, *Mor* 1977 *Sp*, *It*, *F*, *Pol* 1978 *Sp*
Varta, N 1958 *EGe*
Varzaru, G 1980 *Mor*, *I*, *Pol*, *F* 1981 *It*, *Sp*, *USS*, *F* (R) 1983 *Mor*, *WGe*, *It*, *USS*, *F* 1984 *S*, *F* 1985 *Tun*, *USS* 1986 *F* 1988 *It*, *Sp*, *US*, *USS*, *USS*
Vasluianu, Z 1989 *Sp*, *Z*, *Sa*
Veluda, P 1967 *It*, *Pt*, *Pol*, *WGe*, *F* 1968 *Cze*, *Cze*
Veluda, R 1949 *Cze* 1952 *EGe* 1967 *Pol* (R)
Veres, N 1986 *Tun*, *Pt* 1987 *F*, *USS*, *F* 1988 *It*, *Sp*, *USS*
Vidrascu, M 1919 *US*, *F*
Vidrascu, P 1919 *US* 1924 *F*, *US* 1927 *Cze*
Vioreanu, M 1994 *E* 1998 *H*, *Pol*, *Ukr*, *Ar*, *Geo*, *I* 1999 *F*, *S*, *A*, *US*, *I* 2000 *Mor*, *Pt*, *Sp*, *Geo*, *F* 2001 *Geo* (R) 2002 *Rus*, *Geo*, *I*, *It*, *Sp* 2003 *Sp*, *Rus*, *F* (R), *I* (R), *A* (R), *Ar*, *Nm* (R)
Visan, A 1949 *Cze*
Vlad, D 2005 *US* (R), *S*, *C* (R), *I* (R) 2006 *Rus* (R) 2007 *Sp* (R), *CZR*, *It* (R)
Vlad, G 1991 *C* (R), *Fj* 1992 *Sp*, *It* (R), *USS*, *F*, *It*, *Ar* 1993 *Pt*, *F*, *I* 1994 *Sp*, *Ger*, *Rus*, *It*, *W*, *It*, *E* 1995 *F*, *C*, *SA*, *A*, *Ar*, *It* 1996 *Pt*, *F* 1997 *W*, *Ar*, *F*, *It* 1998 *Ar* (R)
Vlad, V 1980 *Mor* (R)
Vlaicu, FA 2006 *Ukr* (R), *F*, *Geo*, *Sp*, *S* 2007 *Geo*, *Sp* (R), *CZR* (R), *ESp* (R), *ItA* (R), *Nm* (R), *S* (R), *NZ* (R)
Vlasceanu, C 2000 *Mor*, *Pt* (R), *Sp* (R), *Geo* (R), *F* (R)
Voicu, B 2003 *CZR* (R) 2004 *CZR*, *Pt*, *Sp*, *Rus*, *It*, *J* 2005 *J*, *Pt* (R)
Voicu, M 1979 *Pol* (R)
Voicu, M 2002 *Pt* (R)
Voicu, V 1951 *EGe* 1952 *EGe* (R), *EGe* 1953 *It* 1955 *Cze*
Voinov, R 1985 *It* 1986 *Pt*, *S*, *F* (R), *Tun*
Volvoreanu, P 1924 *US*
Vraca, G 1919 *US*, *F*
Vusec, M 1959 *EGe*, *Pol*, *Cze*, *EGe* 1960 *F* 1961 *Pol*, *EGe*, *Cze*, *EGe*, *F* 1962 *Cze*, *EGe*, *Pol*, *It*, *F* 1963 *Bul*, *EGe*, *Cze*, *F* 1964 *WGe*, *F* 1965 *WGe*, *F* 1966 *It*, *F* 1967 *It*, *Pt*, *Pol*, *WGe*, *F* 1968 *Cze*, *Cze*, *F* 1969 *Pol*, *WGe*, *F*
Vusec, RL 1998 *Geo*, *I* 1999 *F*, *S*, *A*, *US*, *I* 2000 *Mor*, *H*, *Pt*, *Sp*, *F* 2002 *H*, *Rus* (R), *I* (R)
Wirth, F 1934 *It*
Zafiescu, I 1979 *W*, *Pol*, *F*
Zafiescu, M 1980 *Mor* 1986 *I*
Zamfir, D 1949 *Cze*
Zebega, B 2004 *CZR*, *Pt* (R), *Rus* (R), *Geo* (R), *It*, *W*, *CZR* (R) 2005 *Rus* (R), *Ukr* (R), *US* (R), *S* (R) 2006 *Ukr* (R), *Sp* (R)
Zlatoianu, D 1958 *Sp*, *WGe*, *EGe*, *It* 1959 *EGe* 1960 *Pol*, *EGe*, *Cze* 1961 *EGe*, *EGe*, *F* 1964 *Cze*, *EGe* 1966 *Cze*

Getty Images

Romania battled hard to keep their position in world rugby in 2007.

ROMANIAN INTERNATIONAL STATISTICS

BIGGEST WINNING MARGIN

Date	Opponent	Result	Winning Margin
21/09/1976	Bulgaria	100–0	**100**
19/03/2005	Ukraine	97–0	**97**
13/04/1996	Portugal	92–0	**92**
17/11/1976	Morocco	89–0	**89**

MOST POINTS IN A MATCH

BY THE TEAM

Date	Opponent	Result	Points
21/09/1976	Bulgaria	100–0	**100**
19/03/2005	Ukraine	97–0	**97**
13/04/1996	Portugal	92–0	**92**
17/11/1976	Morocco	89–0	**89**

BY A PLAYER

Date	Name	Opponent	Points
05/10/2002	Ionut Tofan	Spain	**30**
13/04/1996	Virgil Popisteanu	Portugal	**27**
04/02/2001	Petre Mitu	Portugal	**27**
13/04/1996	Ionel Rotaru	Portugal	**25**

MOST TRIES IN A MATCH

BY THE TEAM

Date	Opponent	Result	Tries
17/11/1976	Morocco	89–0	**17**
21/10/1951	East Germany	64–26	**16**
19/03/2005	Ukraine	97–0	**15**
16/04/1978	Spain	74–3	**14**

BY A PLAYER

Date	Name	Opponent	Tries
30/04/1972	Gheorghe Rascanu	Morocco	**5**
18/10/1986	Cornel Popescu	Portugal	**5**
13/04/1996	Ionel Rotaru	Portugal	**5**

MOST CONVERSIONS IN A MATCH

BY THE TEAM

Date	Opponent	Result	Cons
13/04/1996	Portugal	92–0	**12**
19/03/2005	Ukraine	97–0	**11**
04/10/1997	Belgium	83–13	**10**

BY A PLAYER

Date	Name	Opponent	Cons
13/04/1996	Virgil Popisteanu	Portugal	**12**
04/10/1997	Serban Guranescu	Belgium	**10**
19/03/2005	Dan Dumbrava	Ukraine	**8**

MOST PENALTIES IN A MATCH

BY THE TEAM

Date	Opponent	Result	Pens
14/05/1994	Italy	26–12	**6**
04/02/2001	Portugal	47–0	**6**

BY A PLAYER

Date	Name	Opponent	Pens
14/05/1994	Neculai Nichitean	Italy	**6**
04/02/2001	Petre Mitu	Portugal	**6**

MOST DROP GOALS IN A MATCH

BY THE TEAM

Date	Opponent	Result	DGs
29/10/1967	West Germany	27–5	**4**
14/11/1965	West Germany	9–8	**3**
17/10/1976	Poland	38–8	**3**
03/10/1990	Spain	19–6	**3**

BY A PLAYER

Date	Name	Opponent	DGs
29/10/1967	Valeriu Irimescu	West Germany	**3**
17/10/1976	Dumitru Alexandru	Poland	**3**

MOST CAPPED PLAYERS

Name	Caps
Adrian Lungu	77
Romeo Gontineac	75
Gabriel Brezoianu	71
Florica Morariu	70

LEADING PENALTY SCORERS

Name	Pens
Neculai Nichitean	54
Ionut Tofan	46
Petre Mitu	46
Gelu Ignat	39

LEADING TRY SCORERS

Name	Tries
Petre Motrescu	33
Gabriel Brezoianu	28
Florica Morariu	26
Mihai Vusec	22

LEADING DROP GOAL SCORERS

Name	DGs
Dumitru Alexandru	13
Neculai Nichitean	10
Valeriu Irimescu	10
Gelu Ignat	7

LEADING CONVERSIONS SCORERS

Name	Cons
Ionut Tofan	51
Petre Mitu	49
Dan Dumbrava	36
Ion Constantin	34

LEADING POINTS SCORERS

Name	Points
Ionut Tofan	315
Petre Mitu	296
Neculai Nichitean	246
Dumitru Alexandru	240
Ion Constantin	222

THE IRB/EMIRATES AIRLINE RUGBY PHOTOGRAPH OF THE YEAR 2007

After Morgan Treacy's triumph last year it was time to find the heir to his throne with the game's biggest photography competition, open to amateur and professional photographers alike, drawing a much bigger entry than 12 months before.

More than 100 entries were submitted from nine different countries. Each panellist was asked to select their top 10 images best depicting the 'Spirit of Rugby' theme and points were awarded (10pts for 1st and 1pt for 10th). From this a top 10 was selected and then whittled down to a final six. From the final six, the top three were selected and following a period of deliberation the winner was confirmed.

The Judging Panel was: Paul Morgan - Editor of Rugby World Magazine, Greg Thomas - Head of Communications, IRB, Lynda Glennon - Graphic Designer, IRB, Richard Prescott - Director of Communications, RFU, Barry Newcombe - Sports Journalist's Association and Jed Smith - Curator, Museum of Rugby.

The prize for the winner is a trophy plus a trip for two to the Emirates Airline Dubai Sevens, courtesy of Emirates Airline.

For details on how to enter the 2008 competition, see the back page of this picture section.

THE RUNNERS-UP: IN NO PARTICULAR ORDER

◄ Gulp of Glory
(Chas Williamson, CW Sport)
London Wasps and France captain Raphael Ibanez takes a moment to savour the sweet taste of victory after his club's victory in the Heineken Cup final in June.

Retirement ►
(Paul Thomas)
Jason Robinson is held aloft by Sale Sharks team mates Juan Lobbe and Sebastien Chabal after playing his final match for the club in May before retiring from the domestic scene.

Rough and Tumble ▲
(Denis Minihane)
Ireland's Denis Leamy manages to hold onto the ball as he and Scottish scrum half Chris Cusiter take a tumble at Murrayfield where Ireland defeated Scotland to win the Triple Crown.

cAfee
Proven Security
BETESH
FOX
ukfast
SHARKS
cAfee
Proven Security

The Elation of Defeat (Alain Grosclaude)

Montpellier players celebrate in the dressing room, even though they've just lost! Despite defeat away to Perpignan, Montpellier had held onto their place in the Top 14 by picking up a defensive bonus point on the final day of the French season.

Concentration (Hans Willink)
(*The Mail on Sunday*, UK)
All Blacks coach Graham Henry watches on as his side go through their final preparations ahead of the November 2006 test against France at the Stade de France.

AND THE WINNER IS...

‘Commitment’ Andrew Orchard

Commitment
(Andrew Orchard)
Wales fly half Rachel Poolman shields herself from the pouring December rain during her side’s 31-7 victory over Italy at Glamorgan Wanderers RFC in December 2006.

“It started raining halfway through the first half. It was torrential, absolutely pouring with hailstones and everything and it was pretty cold too. I remember desperately trying to keep all my equipment covered up. The game was being played under floodlights at Glamorgan Wanderers’ ground near Cardiff, which can be a bit dark, so when it started raining I knew there would be a chance of getting something a bit different. I think the rain was at its worst when I took this shot. In the background the girls are preparing for a scrum and Rachel just turned her back for a few seconds, I think she’s trying to shield herself from the rain.To be honest she looks like she wants to be somewhere else, and that’s pretty much how I felt at the time too!”
Andrew Orchard

TAKEN ON: Canon Eos 1D Mk II, with Canon 300m 2.8 lens.

THE IRB/EMIRATES AIRLINE RUGBY PHOTOGRAPH OF THE YEAR 2008

The IRB/Emirates Airline Rugby Photograph of the Year competition is open to all photographers, professional or amateur, and the subject matter can be from any level of the game – from mini-rugby to the Rugby World Cup Final.

To request an entry form for next year's competition, send an e-mail to:

dominic.rumbles@irb.com

Or write to:
IRB/Emirates Airline Rugby Photograph of the Year Competition
c/o Dominic Rumbles
IRB
Huguenot House
35-38 St Stephen's Green
Dublin 2, Ireland

www.irb.com

SAMOA

SAMOA'S 2006–07 TEST RECORD

OPPONENTS	DATE	VENUE	RESULT
Fiji	19 May	H	**Won** 8–3
Junior All Blacks	26 May	H	**Lost** 10–21
Australia A	2 June	A	**Lost** 15–27
South Africa	9 June	A	**Lost** 8–35
Japan	16 June	A	**Won** 13–3
Tonga	23 June	H	**Won** 50–3
South Africa	9 Sept	N	**Lost** 7–59 (WC)
Tonga	16 Sept	N	**Lost** 15–19 (WC)
England	22 Sept	N	**Lost** 22–44 (WC)
USA	26 Sept	N	**Won** 25–21 (WC)

TURNING A NEW PAGE

By Frankie Deges

It was sad to see Michael Jones, certainly one of the game's finest players and an ambassador, coming to the end of a happy 17-year association with Manu Samoa without the success he has so much craved for the country of his origins. Also, another fine servant of the game, Brian Lima, ended his 17-season association with his country's national team in what was Samoa's worst ever Rugby World Cup campaign.

The one-cap Samoan and 55 times capped All Black, Jones and Lima, the only player to have played in five Rugby World Cup finals, deserved more from their final curtain call. It wasn't to be for a Samoan side that failed to capture the imagination of the world as it had done in previous tournaments.

Debutants in RWC in 1991, they went on to advance to the quarter-finals in their first two tournaments. In 1991 they were the new boys, but by 1995 they were amongst the elite of the game. Unlucky in 1999, they had to fight in a hard pool in 2003 with no prizes for coming third.

A similar situation was to occur four years later – in 2007 – when they were pooled with defending champions England, the South African Springboks, Tonga and USA. One thing Samoa had the world accustomed to was to see them defying the odds and at times punching over their weight. This time it was not to happen – in 2007 – for a variety of reasons.

With a squad captained by the experienced Semo Sititi and with able lieutenants in Lima, the Tuilagi brothers and a number of players in some of the best clubs in various countries, the spark never became a fire. Injuries also were a problem for a team that failed to get into second gear for most of Rugby World Cup 2007.

It was sad as for a few years, more so since the International Rugby Board started investing money in the Pacific Islands and Samoa particularly, the Samoans have been doing their homework and in silence worked hard.

Former Test prop, captain and one of the real characters of world rugby, Peter Fatialofa, a forwards' coach in France 2007, explained that "we used to just lift coconuts and banana trees, now we've got dieticians, weights, everything.

"The players look after their bodies now. In my day as a player we never used to have bodies like these guys – they're cut. We had muscle, but no definition."

He added: "Because of the High Performance Unit (set up by the IRB in the last 18 months) and professionalism, players going overseas are learning things and bringing the information back.

"Once we go fully professional, once we get a big company to sponsor us, we'll have 15 Michael Jones' so look out." This is a process that will not become an overnight success, but one that with time, funding, and effort – which is what the IRB is doing – will provide the world with yet another competitive nation.

Starting with South Africa their campaign in France, a team that had already beaten them earlier in the year, was never going to be easy.

No-one was expecting the Springboks to be so good on the day, winning by a convincing 59–7, Bryan Habana setting the benchmark for wingers with four tries in a match in which the winners scored eight tries, with a personal contribution from Percy Montgomery of 29 points.

The Samoan points came through Gavin Williams, son of former Samoan mentor and All Black great Brian Williams.

It was brutal rugby for the first 40 minutes as the Samoans ensured the Springboks felt their presence, yet did not manage to close them down. Securing enough first-phase ball was a problem for the Pacific Islanders who were to see their game plan disintegrate in the final 40 minutes. Whilst the physicality was not a problem for Samoa, it was all the rest that mattered.

Taking the field in the second half, Lima officially became the first man to play in five World Cups, but it wasn't something to remember; going into a tackle he hit his head and was helped groggily from the field, only a few minutes after coming on.

With a week to lick the wounds, the Samoans faced the Tongans in Montpellier and what had, in previous years, been an almost certain win for Manu Samoa. This game turned into a nightmare.

Tonga, with far less time to recover from their first match at the tournament, showed the passion and hunger that at times was missing from Samoa.

With a player sent-off and finishing the game with 13 defenders, the Tongans managed to beat Samoa 19–15 in a bruising encounter.

Never before in 20 years of RWC had there been a direct Pacific Islands clash and the first one was exciting because of the way both teams played.

Tonga would score the only try with the Samoans unable to capitalise on their two-man advantage in the final five minutes.

The result was a massive reversal of when the teams last met in June at Apia, when the Samoans romped to a 50–3 triumph, and the first Samoan loss in nine encounters.

Michael Jones was straightforward in his assessment: "We are better than how we played in that second half. We didn't have the mental toughness to push through in that last 5–10 minutes when they were down.

"We just needed to keep our composure but at the end of the day we were beaten by a team who were hungrier, and it hurts to say that."

If they were to have any hopes of advancing to the quarter-finals, Samoa had to beat England in the third match – and hope Tonga did not earn a bonus point elsewhere. They failed, losing 22–44 a match they had targeted from the start of the World Cup campaign as one they would love to win.

In 2003 it took England all of their ability to beat them by 35–22 in Melbourne. This time it would be different, the English never in doubt of their win.

In their third game of the tournament, the Samoans could not master the set-pieces where the winners were far more superior. Instability in the scrum and lack of nous in the lineouts was to prove too dear for them.

With dirty ball, the more than dangerous backs were unable to show their magic and were sitting ducks for the England defence. Rhythm and cohesion were absent in Lens.

This match would also be the last in a Samoan jersey for Brian Lima. The much-travelled Samoan was to be suspended after being cited for a dangerous tackle on England's Jonny Wilkinson.

The three-week suspension was a sad end for someone who not only played in five World Cups, but represented Samoa in countless Sevens tournaments and had never been sent off or even cited.

His frustration echoed that of a team that was already having its worst tournament since its first World Cup, 16 years earlier.

The Samoans still had to beat the USA Eagles to return home with some of their ancient pride restored, but even that won't prevent them having to qualify for the 2011 event.

A win is always a win and the 25–21 was celebrated but it was not as clear as Jones and his team would have wanted.

Samoa was unable to use a large number of players – up to ten – because of injury or suspension, and had to reorganise sufficiently to beat a team made mostly of amateurs.

At one stage, Manu Samoa was leading 22–3 yet lost the compass to the game and had to, again, work hard until the final minute when the Eagles, who never gave up, eventually were beaten by the clock as much as the Samoans. The wet weather did not contribute but was a problem for both teams.

"We've spent more time in valleys than in the mountain-tops," said Michael Jones of the tournament campaign.

"We are obviously disappointed that we couldn't get to the levels we set ourselves – because we firmly believe we were capable of them. We have under-achieved. The expectation of our people was for us to do better – and I take that on my shoulders as coach."

"We need to take time to analyse why we didn't fulfil the potential," he added, concluding that "the team showed glimpses but weren't capable of doing when it mattered, for 80 minutes."

So, for Samoans the time to address a few issues has arrived. The game is advancing at fast pace and the assistance of the International Rugby Board will ensure they keep up with these changes.

There are few countries that have more naturally gifted players than Samoa, Fiji or Tonga.

The Pacific Islands teams will certainly benefit from the exposure and competition that is being provided by the successful new tournament for the region, The IRB Pacific Nations Cup. The number of matches played by Manu Samoa will allow them to develop the next generation that will certainly ensure the history written by players such as Fatialofa and Anitelea Aiolupo, former captain Pat Lam and Brian Lima to name but a very few in a proud list is kept very much alive.

Whilst Samoa needs the world, the world also needs Samoa. The domestic competition can't grow bigger than where it is now and probably a domestic professional tournament is not viable for a variety or reasons, but as long as the many stars produced in the shores of the island, are happy to return to play for their country, then the team will continue to grow.

From the original World Cup squad only three players were still playing at home, the balance coming from clubs in New Zealand, England, Scotland, Japan and France. Eighteen of the players were born in Samoa, the rest all in New Zealand. On the other hand, six in the All Black squad were born in Samoa.

In the domestic front, Samoa continued to make excellent progress in 2007. Like Tonga, KPMG undertook a review of the Union's financial and administrative structures and again one of the key recommendations was the need to employ a Finance Manager, which, the IRB agreed to part fund.

At the High Performance Unit, based at the temporary facility at the University of the South Pacific, all but eight of the LTC Scholarship athletes have represented Samoa at the International levels either in the IRB 7's, Under 19 World Championships or Manu Samoa team.

All scholarship athletes are required to undertake career and education programmes including English language lessons and computer courses in addition to their rugby training. Fourteen players progressed from the Pacific Rugby Cup to represent Samoa in 2007 – ten of which were scholarship athletes.

SAMOA INTERNATIONAL RECORDS

UP TO 31ST OCTOBER 2007

WINNING MARGIN

Date	Opponent	Result	Winning Margin
08/04/1990	Korea	74–7	**67**
10/06/2000	Japan	68–9	**59**
29/06/1997	Tonga	62–13	**49**
15/10/2003	Uruguay	60–13	**47**
23/06/2007	Tonga	50–3	**47**

MOST POINTS IN A MATCH

BY THE TEAM

Date	Opponent	Result	Pts.
08/04/1990	Korea	74–7	**74**
10/06/2000	Japan	68–9	**68**
29/06/1997	Tonga	62–13	**62**
15/10/2003	Uruguay	60–13	**60**
30/09/1989	West Germany	55–9	**55**

MOST TRIES IN A MATCH

BY THE TEAM

Date	Opponent	Result	Tries
08/04/1990	Korea	74–7	**13**
29/06/1997	Tonga	62–13	**10**
10/06/2000	Japan	68–9	**10**
30/09/1989	West Germany	55–9	**10**
15/10/2003	Uruguay	60–13	**10**

MOST CONVERSIONS IN A MATCH

BY THE TEAM

Date	Opponent	Result	Cons
08/04/1990	Korea	74–7	**8**

MOST PENALTIES IN A MATCH

BY THE TEAM

Date	Opponent	Result	Pens
29/05/2004	Tonga	24–14	**8**

MOST DROP GOALS IN A MATCH

BY THE TEAM

1 on 9 Occasions

MOST POINTS IN A MATCH

BY A PLAYER

Date	Player	Opponent	Pts.
29/05/2004	Roger Warren	Tonga	**24**
03/10/1999	Silao Leaega	Japan	**23**
08/04/1990	Andy Aiolupo	Korea	**23**
08/07/2000	Toa Samania	Italy	**23**
04/06/1994	Darren Kellet	Tonga	**22**

MOST TRIES IN A MATCH

BY A PLAYER

Date	Player	Opponent	Tries
28/05/1991	Tupo Fa'amasino	Tonga	**4**
10/06/2000	Elvis Seveali'I	Japan	**4**
02/07/2005	Alesana Tuilagi	Tonga	**4**

MOST CONVERSIONS IN A MATCH

BY A PLAYER

Date	Player	Opponent	Cons
08/04/1990	Andy Aiolupo	Korea	**8**
10/06/2000	Tanner Vili	Japan	**6**
04/07/2001	Earl Va'a	Japan	**6**

MOST PENALTIES IN A MATCH

BY A PLAYER

Date	Player	Opponent	Pens
29/05/2004	Roger Warren	Tonga	**8**

MOST DROP GOALS IN A MATCH

BY A PLAYER

1 on 9 Occasions

MOST CAPPED PLAYERS

Name	Caps
Brian Lima	65
To'o Vaega	60
Semo Sititi	52
Opeta Palepoi	42
Steve So'oialo	38

LEADING TRY SCORERS

Name	Tries
Brian Lima	31
Afato So'oialo	15
To'o Vaega	15
Rolagi Koko	12
Semo Sititi	12

LEADING CONVERSIONS SCORERS

Name	Cons
Andy Aiolupo	35
Earl Va'a	33
Silao Leaega	26
Tanner Vili	21
Darren Kellett	17

LEADING PENALTY SCORERS

Name	Pens
Darren Kellett	35
Earl Va'a	31
Silao Leaega	31
Roger Warren	29
Andy Aiolupo	24

LEADING DROP GOAL SCORERS

Name	DGs
Darren Kellett	2
Roger Warren	2
Steve Bachop	2

LEADING POINTS SCORERS

Name	Pts.
Earl Va'a	184
Andy Aiolupo	172
Silao Leaega	160
Darren Kellett	155
Brian Lima	150

Shaun Botterill/Getty Images

Brian Lima set a World Cup record in 2007, becoming the first man to play in five different Finals.

SCOTLAND

SCOTLAND'S 2006–07 TEST RECORD

OPPONENTS	DATE	VENUE	RESULT
Romania	11 Nov	H	**Won** 48–6
Pacific Islands	18 Nov	H	**Won** 34–22
Australia	25 Nov	H	**Lost** 15–44
England	3 Feb	A	**Lost** 20–42
Wales	10 Feb	H	**Won** 21–9
Italy	24 Feb	H	**Lost** 17–37
Ireland	10 Mar	H	**Lost** 18–19
France	17 Mar	A	**Lost** 19–46
Ireland	11 Aug	H	**Won** 31–21
South Africa	25 Aug	H	**Lost** 3–27
Portugal	9 Sept	N	**Won** 56–10 (WC)
Romania	18 Sept	N	**Won** 42–0 (WC)
New Zealand	23 Sept	N	**Lost** 0–40 (WC)
Italy	29 Sept	N	**Won** 18–16 (WC)
Argentina	7 Oct	N	**Lost** 13–19 (WC)

PAR FOR THE COURSE

By Iain Spragg

When the final whistle blew on Scotland's quarter-final clash with Argentina at the Stade de France, it was difficult to gauge the mood in the Scottish camp. There was, of course, the predictable disappointment in the wake a 19–13 defeat to the Pumas but there was also a sense of sangfroid in Paris despite the side's World Cup exit.

The tournament could, in truth, have gone a lot worse for coach Frank Hadden's players. True, victory over Argentina would have taken Scotland through to their first semi-final in 16 years but equally they could have suffered the ignominy of failing to reach the quarter-finals for the first time in their history had they not beaten Italy the previous week in the group stages.

"I'm very confident our young side will learn from this," Hadden said after the Pumas survived his team's second-half comeback in the French capital. "Some of these youngsters have matured in a very short space of time. I believe in the next two or three Six Nations, we'll be a serious threat."

Scotland always knew progress to the knockout stages from Pool C was far from a foregone conclusion. In 25 previous attempts, they had never managed to beat New Zealand and if, as predicted, the All Blacks prolonged the record, qualification would rest on the clash with Italy in St Etienne. The Azzurri had thumped Hadden's side 37–17 at Murrayfield in the Six Nations earlier in the year and a repeat performance would condemn Scotland to an early flight home.

Their tournament began against minnows Portugal at the Stade Geoffroy-Guichard. It was the ideal opener for Hadden and his players and they were comfortable throughout as they ran in eight tries, including two from Rory Lamont, in a 56–10 victory that eased them gently into the competition.

"We've prepared extremely well and have got the first hurdle out of the way," Hadden said. "It wasn't a tremendous performance but it was our first game and we wanted to start with a win. Tremendous credit to the Portuguese, it was obviously a cup final for them. They never gave up and were incredibly tenacious throughout."

Romania provided a marginally sterner test of Scottish resolve in their next game in Edinburgh but again they looked confident and compact and eventually ran out 42–0 winners.

It was now time to face the might of tournament favourites New

Richard Heathcote/Getty Images

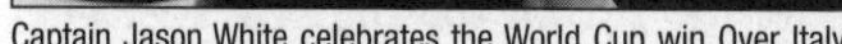

Captain Jason White celebrates the World Cup win Over Italy.

Zealand but with Italy lurking in the wings, Hadden showed his hand and decided to rest 13 of the team who had faced Romania. The coach had unashamedly decided to accept defeat before a ball had been kicked and Scotland would tackle the Kiwis with a second string side.

Mercifully, any fears that his reserves would be decimated by the All Blacks at Murrayfield failed to be realised. New Zealand seemed to be unnerved by Scotland's explicit pre-match declaration of surrender and although they ran in six unanswered tries, neither side really got out of second gear and the match limped uneventfully towards a 40–0 win for the Kiwis.

"Let's look forward," Hadden argued after the final whistle. "We've got a tremendous opportunity to do something really special in this competition. The huge advantage we've got is that instead of taking four or five days to recover, we can train tomorrow.

"It gives us five days of quality build-up to the match which is going to ultimately decide how well we do in this competition. We will be judged on whether we qualify for the quarter-finals."

The stage was set for the winner-takes-all rendezvous with Italy and Hadden recalled the 13 he had rested for the All Blacks game. Scotland were at full strength and a sixth successive appearance in the quarter-finals beckoned.

Unsurprisingly, it was a bruising encounter in St Etienne with chances at a premium and Scotland were hugely indebted to the unerring boot of Chris Paterson who kicked all his side's points in a tense 18–16 victory. Veteran scrum-half Alessandro Troncon scored the only try of the match but Paterson's six successful penalties from six attempts was the difference between the two sides and Scotland were through to the last eight.

"It was a gritty performance," Paterson conceded. "There was a lot of pressure but we wanted to win for ourselves and the fans and we are not finished yet. We cut short holidays, some of the lads cut short honeymoons to prepare for the World Cup and it was all for tonight . . . and we did it."

The sense of relief was clear but with Argentina awaiting them, there was also the dawning realisation they could emulate the 1991 side that had reached the semi-final stage. The Pumas had already beaten France and Ireland to progress but after defeats in the last eight to New Zealand in 1995 and 1999 and Australia four years later, Scotland knew this was their best chance for more than a decade.

The game in Paris was a war of attrition from the first whistle. Dan Parks drew first blood for Scotland with an early penalty, Felipe Contepomi replied with six points with the boot and Argentina stretched further ahead when Parks' clearance was charged down and Gonzalo Longo was first to the loose ball to score.

Scotland were now desperate to put more width on their game and although substitute scrum-half Chris Cusiter provided the finish to a flowing attack, they left it too little, too late and the Pumas clung on for the win that sent them into the semi-finals for the first time.

"I think we are capable of a lot more," prop Euan Murray insisted after the defeat. "We didn't play to our potential but we are a relatively young squad. We've got relatively low experience in terms of numbers of caps. We just need to keep going in the right direction."

The 2006–07 season began for the Scots in modest fashion with the visit of Romania and the Pacific Islands to Murrayfield and the men in blue had little trouble dispatching either team.

Australia, in contrast, were an altogether different proposition. An early try in Edinburgh from wing Simon Webster gave the home side fleeting hope but the Wallabies eased through the gears, scored five tries and ran out convincing winners 44–15. Scotland had come up against one of the game's heavyweights and had been found wanting.

The Six Nations was to offer precious little respite. England at Twickenham was a daunting way to start the tournament and their task was made the more arduous with the return of Jonny Wilkinson to the English side. The fly-half duly helped himself to 27 points in a full house and Hadden's side were demolished 42–20.

Faith was partially restored seven days later when Wales were beaten 21–9 at Murrayfield courtesy of Paterson's seven penalties but the celebrations were to be short-lived. A fortnight later Italy were in Edinburgh and the Azzurri's 37–17 win was unquestionably the lowest point for Hadden and his troops as they built-up towards the World Cup.

Scotland simply imploded in the first six minutes against the Italians and three self-inflicted mistakes – including a charge-down of fly-half Phil Godman's kick just 18 seconds after kick-off – gifted the visitors three quick-fire tries and a barely comprehensible 21 point lead. Hadden's side fought back but the damage had been done and Italy had their historic first win at Murrayfield.

"We wanted a fast-tempo start and to get the ball moving around and excite the crowd," a chastened Hadden said. "But the charge-down was a bitter blow and after the two interception tries the players were shell-shocked. When things don't go for you it is a measure of how deep you are prepared to dig. I'd like to think we've learned a lot today and it will be a measure of this side as to how well they bounce back against Ireland in two weeks. It's a watershed moment and it's absolutely vital that they respond appropriately."

The team did respond against the Irish but still found themselves on the wrong end of a 19–18 scoreline and they were simply blown away by the French in Paris at the end of the tournament. One Six Nations win from five was not the kind of form Hadden had hoped to take into the World Cup.

The World Cup now beckoned and in terms of both their results and performances, Scotland seemed no better or worse off than they had been 12 months earlier. Their eventual progress to the quarter-finals – mirroring exactly what they had achieved in the five previous tournaments – maintained the status quo.

SCOTLAND INTERNATIONAL STATISTICS

MATCH RECORDS UP TO 31ST OCTOBER 2007

MOST CONSECUTIVE TEST WINS

6 1925 *F,W,I,E*, 1926 *F,W*
6 1989 *Fj*, *R*, 1990 I,F,W,E

MOST CONSECUTIVE TESTS WITHOUT DEFEAT

Matches	Wins	Draws	Periods
9	6*	3	1885 to 1887
6	6	0	1925 to 1926
6	6	0	1989 to 1990
6	4	2	1877 to 1880
6	5	1	1983 to 1984

* includes an abandoned match

MOST POINTS IN A MATCH

BY THE TEAM

Pts.	Opponents	Venue	Year
100	Japan	Perth	2004
89	Ivory Coast	Rustenburg	1995
65	United States	San Francisco	2002
60	Zimbabwe	Wellington	1987
60	Romania	Hampden Park	1999
56	Portugal	Saint Etienne	2007
55	Romania	Dunedin	1987
53	United States	Murrayfield	2000
51	Zimbabwe	Murrayfield	1991
49	Argentina	Murrayfield	1990
49	Romania	Murrayfield	1995

BY A PLAYER

Pts.	Player	Opponents	Venue	Year
44	A G Hastings	Ivory Coast	Rustenburg	1995
40	C D Paterson	Japan	Perth	2004
33	G P J Townsend	United States	Murrayfield	2000
31	A G Hastings	Tonga	Pretoria	1995
27	A G Hastings	Romania	Dunedin	1987
26	K M Logan	Romania	Hampden Park	1999
24	B J Laney	Italy	Rome	2002
23	G Ross	Tonga	Murrayfield	2001
21	A G Hastings	England	Murrayfield	1986
21	A G Hastings	Romania	Bucharest	1986
21	C D Paterson	Wales	Murrayfield	2007

MOST TRIES IN A MATCH

BY THE TEAM

Tries	Opponents	Venue	Year
15	Japan	Perth	2004
13	Ivory Coast	Rustenburg	1995
12	Wales	Raeburn Place	1887
11	Zimbabwe	Wellington	1987
10	United States	San Francisco	2002
9	Romania	Dunedin	1987
9	Argentina	Murrayfield	1990

BY A PLAYER

Tries	Player	Opponents	Venue	Year
5	G C Lindsay	Wales	Raeburn Place	1887
4	W A Stewart	Ireland	Inverleith	1913
4	I S Smith	France	Inverleith	1925
4	I S Smith	Wales	Swansea	1925
4	A G Hastings	Ivory Coast	Rustenburg	1995

MOST CONVERSIONS IN A MATCH

BY THE TEAM

Cons	Opponents	Venue	Year
11	Japan	Perth	2004
9	Ivory Coast	Rustenburg	1995
8	Zimbabwe	Wellington	1987
8	Romania	Dunedin	1987
8	Portugal	Saint Etienne	2007

BY A PLAYER

Cons	Player	Opponents	Venue	Year
11	C D Paterson	Japan	Perth	2004
9	A G Hastings	Ivory Coast	Rustenburg	1995
8	A G Hastings	Zimbabwe	Wellington	1987
8	A G Hastings	Romania	Dunedin	1987

MOST PENALTIES IN A MATCH

BY THE TEAM

Penalties	Opponents	Venue	Year
8	Tonga	Pretoria	1995
7	Wales	Murrayfield	2007
6	France	Murrayfield	1986
6	Italy	Murrayfield	2005
6	Ireland	Murrayfield	2007
6	Italy	Saint Etienne	2007

BY A PLAYER

Pens	Player	Opponents	Venue	Year
8	A G Hastings	Tonga	Pretoria	1995
7	C D Paterson	Wales	Murrayfield	2007
6	A G Hastings	France	Murrayfield	1986
6	C D Paterson	Italy	Murrayfield	2005
6	C D Paterson	Ireland	Murrayfield	2007
6	C D Paterson	Italy	Saint Etienne	2007

MOST DROPPED GOALS IN A MATCH

BY THE TEAM

Drops	Opponents	Venue	Year
3	Ireland	Murrayfield	1973
2	on several	occasions	

BY A PLAYER

Drops	Player	Opponents	Venue	Year
2	R C MacKenzie	Ireland	Belfast	1877
2	N J Finlay	Ireland	Glasgow	1880
2	B M Simmers	Wales	Murrayfield	1965
2	D W Morgan	Ireland	Murrayfield	1973
2	B M Gossman	France	Parc des Princes	1983
2	J Y Rutherford	New Zealand	Murrayfield	1983
2	J Y Rutherford	Wales	Murrayfield	1985
2	J Y Rutherford	Ireland	Murrayfield	1987
2	C M Chalmers	England	Twickenham	1995

CAREER RECORDS

MOST CAPPED PLAYERS

Caps	Player	Career Span
87	S Murray	1997 to 2007
82	G P J Townsend	1993 to 2003
81	C D Paterson	1999 to 2007
75	G C Bulloch	1997 to 2005
71	S B Grimes	1997 to 2005
70	K M Logan	1992 to 2003
65	S Hastings	1986 to 1997
63	J P R White	2000 to 2007
61	A G Hastings	1986 to 1995
61	G W Weir	1990 to 2000
61	T J Smith	1997 to 2005
60	C M Chalmers	1989 to 1999
60	B W Redpath	1993 to 2003
58	S M Taylor	2000 to 2007
52	J M Renwick	1972 to 1984
52	C T Deans	1978 to 1987
52	A G Stanger	1989 to 1998
52	A P Burnell	1989 to 1999
51	A R Irvine	1972 to 1982
51	G Armstrong	1988 to 1999

MOST TESTS AS CAPTAIN

Tests	Captain	Span
25	D M B Sole	1989 to 1992
21	B W Redpath	1998 to 2003
20	A G Hastings	1993 to 1995
19	J McLauchlan	1973 to 1979
17	J P R White	2005 to 2007
16	R I Wainwright	1995 to 1998
15	M C Morrison	1899 to 1904
15	A R Smith	1957 to 1962
15	A R Irvine	1980 to 1982

MOST CONSECUTIVE TESTS

Tests	Player	Span
49	A B Carmichael	1967 to 1978
40	H F McLeod	1954 to 1962
37	J M Bannerman	1921 to 1929
35	A G Stanger	1989 to 1994

MOST POINTS IN TESTS

Points	Player	Tests	Career
667	A G Hastings	61	1986 to 1995
614	C D Paterson	81	1999 to 2007
273	A R Irvine	51	1972 to 1982
220	K M Logan	70	1992 to 2003
210	P W Dods	23	1983 to 1991
166	C M Chalmers	60	1989 to 1999
164	G P J Townsend	82	1993 to 2003
141	B J Laney	20	2001 to 2004
123	D W Hodge	26	1997 to 2002
106	A G Stanger	52	1989 to 1998

MOST TRIES IN TESTS

Tries	Player	Tests	Career
24	I S Smith	32	1924 to 1933
24	A G Stanger	52	1989 to 1998
22	C D Paterson	81	1999 to 2007
17	A G Hastings	61	1986 to 1995
17	A V Tait	27	1987 to 1999
17	G P J Townsend	82	1993 to 2003
15	I Tukalo	37	1985 to 1992
13	K M Logan	70	1992 to 2003
12	A R Smith	33	1955 to 1962

MOST PENALTY GOALS IN TESTS

Penalties	Player	Tests	Career
140	A G Hastings	61	1986 to 1995
114	C D Paterson	81	1999 to 2007
61	A R Irvine	51	1972 to 1982
50	P W Dods	23	1983 to 1991
32	C M Chalmers	60	1989 to 1999
29	K M Logan	70	1992 to 2003
29	B J Laney	20	2001 to 2004
21	M Dods	8	1994 to 1996
21	R J S Shepherd	20	1995 to 1998

MOST CONVERSIONS IN TESTS

Cons	Player	Tests	Career
86	A G Hastings	61	1986 to 1995
78	C D Paterson	81	1999 to 2007
34	K M Logan	70	1992 to 2003
26	P W Dods	23	1983 to 1991
25	A R Irvine	51	1972 to 1982
19	D Drysdale	26	1923 to 1929
17	B J Laney	20	2001 to 2004
15	D W Hodge	26	1997 to 2002
14	F H Turner	15	1911 to 1914
14	R J S Shepherd	20	1995 to 1998

MOST DROPPED GOALS IN TESTS

Drops	Player	Tests	Career
12	J Y Rutherford	42	1979 to 1987
9	C M Chalmers	60	1989 to 1999
7	I R McGeechan	32	1972 to 1979
7	G P J Townsend	82	1993 to 2003
6	D W Morgan	21	1973 to 1978
5	H Waddell	15	1924 to 1930

Getty Images

Gavin Hastings still heads Scotland's scoring charts, with Chris Paterson hot on his heels.

INTERNATIONAL CHAMPIONSHIP RECORDS

RECORD	DETAIL	HOLDER	SET
Most points in season	120	in four matches	1999
Most tries in season	17	in four matches	1925
Highest Score	38	38-10 v Ireland	1997
Biggest win	28	31-3 v France	1912
	28	38-10 v Ireland	1997
Highest score conceded	51	16-51 v France	1998
Biggest defeat	40	3-43 v England	2001
Most appearances	43	G P J Townsend	1993 – 2003
Most points in matches	288	A G Hastings	1986 – 1995
Most points in season	65	C D Paterson	2007
Most points in match	24	B J Laney	v Italy, 2002
Most tries in matches	24	I S Smith	1924 – 1933
Most tries in season	8	I S Smith	1925
Most tries in match	5	G C Lindsay	v Wales, 1887
Most cons in matches	25	C D Paterson	2000 – 2007
Most cons in season	11	K M Logan	1999
Most cons in match	5	F H Turner	v France, 1912
	5	J W Allan	v England, 1931
	5	R J S Shepherd	v Ireland, 1997
Most pens in matches	77	A G Hastings	1986 – 1995
Most pens in season	16	C D Paterson	2007
Most pens in match	7	C D Paterson	v Wales, 2007
Most drops in matches	8	J Y Rutherford	1979 – 1987
	8	C M Chalmers	1989 – 1998
Most drops in season	3	J Y Rutherford	1987
Most drops in match	2	on several	occasions

MISCELLANEOUS RECORDS

RECORD	HOLDER	DETAIL
Longest Test Career	W C W Murdoch	1935 to 1948
Youngest Test Cap	N J Finlay	17 yrs 36 days in 1875*
Oldest Test Cap	J McLauchlan	37 yrs 210 days in 1979

* C Reid, also 17 yrs 36 days on debut in 1881, was a day *older* than Finlay, having lived through an extra leap-year day.

CAREER RECORDS OF SCOTLAND INTERNATIONAL PLAYERS (PLAYERS CAPPED SINCE THE START OF RWC 2003 UP TO 31 OCTOBER 2007)

PLAYER	DEBUT	CAPS	T	C	P	D	PTS
BACKS							
M R L Blair	2002 v C	43	4	0	0	0	20
C P Cusiter	2004 v W	36	3	0	0	0	15
R E Dewey	2006 v R	13	4	0	0	0	20
M P di Rollo	2002 v US	21	2	0	0	1	13
P J Godman	2005 v R	8	1	5	1	0	18
A R Henderson	2001 v I	49	8	0	0	0	40
R P Lamont	2005 v W	14	5	0	0	0	25
S F Lamont	2004 v Sm	35	7	0	0	0	35
R G.M.Lawson	2006 v A	9	0	0	0	0	0
D A Parks	2004 v W	37	4	8	8	3	69
C D Paterson	1999 v Sp	81	22	78	114	2	614
H F G Southwell	2004 v Sm	36	8	0	0	0	40
N Walker	2002 v R	10	2	0	0	0	10
S L Webster	2003 v I	29	7	0	0	0	35
FORWARDS							
J A Barclay	2007 v NZ	1	0	0	0	0	0
J W Beattie	2006 v R	3	1	0	0	0	5
K D R Brown	2005 v R	19	3	0	0	0	15
D A Callam	2006 v R	10	1	0	0	0	5
A Dickinson	2007 v NZ	1	0	0	0	0	0
R W Ford	2004 v A	16	1	0	0	0	5
D W H Hall	2003 v W	19	1	0	0	0	5
J L Hamilton	2006 v R	13	0	0	0	0	0
N J Hines	2000 v NZ	48	1	0	0	0	5
A Hogg	2004 v W	39	9	0	0	0	45
A F Jacobsen	2002 v C	24	0	0	0	0	0
A D Kellock	2004 v A	14	0	0	0	0	0
G Kerr	2003 v I	47	1	0	0	0	5
S Lawson	2005 v R	15	2	0	0	0	10
S J MacLeod	2004 v A	14	0	0	0	0	0
E A Murray	2005 v R	15	2	0	0	0	10
S Murray	1997 v A	87	3	0	0	0	15

C J Smith	2002 v C	23	0	0	0	0	0
A K Strokosch	2006 v A	1	0	0	0	0	0
S M Taylor	2000 v US	58	6	0	0	0	30
F M A Thomson	2007 v I	3	0	0	0	0	0
J P R White	2000 v E	63	4	0	0	0	20

Richard Heathcote/Getty Images

Scott Murray has passed Gregor Townsend's previous record and is now Scotland's most-capped player.

SCOTLAND INTERNATIONAL PLAYERS
UP TO 31ST OCTOBER 2007

Note: Years given for International Championship matches are for second half of season; eg 1972 means season 1971–72. Years for all other matches refer to the actual year of the match. Entries in square brackets denote matches played in RWC Finals.

Abercrombie, C H (United Services) 1910 I, E, 1911 F, W, 1913 F, W
Abercrombie, J G (Edinburgh U) 1949 F, W, I, 1950 F, W, I, E
Agnew, W C C (Stewart's Coll FP) 1930 W, I
Ainslie, R (Edinburgh Inst FP) 1879 I, E, 1880 I, E, 1881 E, 1882 I, E
Ainslie, T (Edinburgh Inst FP) 1881 E, 1882 I, E, 1883 W, I, E, 1884 W, I, E, 1885 W, I 1,2
Aitchison, G R (Edinburgh Wands) 1883 I
Aitchison, T G (Gala) 1929 W, I, E
Aitken, A I (Edinburgh Inst FP) 1889 I
Aitken, G G (Oxford U) 1924 W, I, E, 1925 F, W, I, E, 1929 F
Aitken, J (Gala) 1977 E, I, F, 1981 F, W, E, I, NZ 1,2, R, A, 1982 E, I, F, W, 1983 F, W, E, NZ, 1984 W, E, I, F, R
Aitken, R (London Scottish) 1947 W
Allan, B (Glasgow Acads) 1881 I
Allan, J (Edinburgh Acads) 1990 NZ 1, 1991, W, I, R, [J, I, WS, E, NZ]
Allan, J L (Melrose) 1952 F, W, I, 1953 W
Allan, J L F (Cambridge U) 1957 I, E
Allan, J W (Melrose) 1927 F, 1928 I, 1929 F, W, I, E, 1930 F, E, 1931 F, W, I, E, 1932 SA, W, I, 1934 I, E
Allan, R C (Hutchesons' GSFP) 1969 I
Allardice, W D (Aberdeen GSFP) 1947 A, 1948 F, W, I, 1949 F, W, I, E
Allen, H W (Glasgow Acads) 1873 E
Anderson, A H (Glasgow Acads) 1894 I
Anderson, D G (London Scottish) 1889 I, 1890 W, I, E, 1891 W, E, 1892 W, E
Anderson, E (Stewart's Coll FP) 1947 I, E
Anderson, J W (W of Scotland) 1872 E
Anderson, T (Merchiston) 1882 I
Angus, A W (Watsonians) 1909 W, 1910 F, W, E, 1911 W, I, 1912 F, W, I, E, SA, 1913 F, W, 1914 E, 1920 F, W, I, E
Anton, P A (St Andrew's U) 1873 E
Armstrong, G (Jedforest, Newcastle) 1988 A, 1989 W, E, I, F, Fj, R, 1990 I, F, W, E, NZ 1,2, Arg, 1991 F, W, E, I, R, [J, I, WS, E, NZ], 1993 I, F, W, E, 1994 E, I, 1996 NZ, 1,2, A, 1997 W, SA (R), 1998 It, I, F, W, E, SA (R), 1999 W, E, I, F, Arg, R, [SA, U, Sm, NZ]
Arneil, R J (Edinburgh Acads, Leicester and Northampton) 1968 I, E, A, 1969 F, W, I, E, SA, 1970 F, W, I, E, A, 1971 F, W, I, E (2[1C]), 1972 F, W, E, NZ
Arthur, A (Glasgow Acads) 1875 E, 1876 E
Arthur, J W (Glasgow Acads) 1871 E, 1872 E
Asher, A G G (Oxford U) 1882 I, 1884 W, I, E, 1885 W, 1886 I, E
Auld, W (W of Scotland) 1889 W, 1890 W
Auldjo, L J (Abertay) 1878 E

Bain, D McL (Oxford U) 1911 E, 1912 F, W, E, SA, 1913 F, W, I, E, 1914 W, I
Baird, G R T (Kelso) 1981 A, 1982 E, I, F, W, A 1,2, 1983 I, F, W, E, NZ, 1984 W, E, I, F, A, 1985 I, W, E, 1986 F, W, E, I, R, 1987 E, 1988 I
Balfour, A (Watsonians) 1896 W, I, E, 1897 E
Balfour, L M (Edinburgh Acads) 1872 E
Bannerman, E M (Edinburgh Acads) 1872 E, 1873 E
Bannerman, J M (Glasgow HSFP) 1921 F, W, I, E, 1922 F, W, I, E, 1923 F, W, I, E, 1924 F, W, I, E, 1925 F, W, I, E, 1926 F, W, I, E, 1927 F, W, I, E, A, 1928 F, W, I, E, 1929 F, W, I, E
Barclay, J A (Glasgow) 2007 [NZ]
Barnes, I A (Hawick) 1972 W, 1974 F (R), 1975 E (R), NZ, 1977 I, F, W
Barrie, R W (Hawick) 1936 E
Bearne, K R F (Cambridge U, London Scottish) 1960 F, W
Beattie, J A (Hawick) 1929 F, W, 1930 W, 1931 F, W, I, E, 1932 SA, W, I, E, 1933 W, E, I, 1934 I, E, 1935 W, I, E, NZ, 1936 W, I, E
Beattie, J R (Glasgow Acads) 1980 I, F, W, E, 1981 F, W, E, I, 1983 F, W, E, NZ, 1984 E (R), R, A, 1985 I, 1986 F, W, E, I, R, 1987 I, F, W, E
Beattie, J W (Glasgow) 2006 R,PI, 2007 F
Beattie, R S (Newcastle, Bristol) 2000 NZ 1,2(R), Sm (R), 2003 E(R), It(R), I 2, [J(R),US,Fj]
Bedell-Sivright, D R (Cambridge U, Edinburgh U) 1900 W, 1901 W, I, E, 1902 W, I, E, 1903 W, I, 1904 W, I, E, 1905 NZ, 1906 W, I, E, SA, 1907 W, I, E, 1908 W, I
Bedell-Sivright, J V (Cambridge U) 1902 W
Begbie, T A (Edinburgh Wands) 1881 I, E
Bell, D L (Watsonians) 1975 I, F, W, E
Bell, J A (Clydesdale) 1901 W, I, E, 1902 W, I, E
Bell, L H I (Edinburgh Acads) 1900 E, 1904 W, I
Berkeley, W V (Oxford U) 1926 F, 1929 F, W, I
Berry, C W (Fettesian-Lorettonians) 1884 I, E, 1885 W, I 1, 1887 I, W, E, 1888 W, I
Bertram, D M (Watsonians) 1922 F, W, I, E, 1923 F, W, I, E, 1924 W, I, E
Beveridge, G (Glasgow) 2000 NZ 2(R), US (R), Sm (R), 2002 Fj(R), 2003 W 2, 2005 R(R)
Biggar, A G (London Scottish) 1969 SA, 1970 F, I, E, A, 1971 F, W, I, E (2[1C]), 1972 F, W
Biggar, M A (London Scottish) 1975 I, F, W, E, 1976 W, E, I, 1977 I, F, W, 1978 I, F, W, E, NZ, 1979 W, E, I, F, NZ, 1980 I, F, W, E
Birkett, G A (Harlequins, London Scottish) 1975 NZ
Bishop, J M (Glasgow Acads) 1893 I
Bisset, A A (RIE Coll) 1904 W
Black, A W (Edinburgh U) 1947 F, W, 1948 E, 1950 W, I, E
Black, W P (Glasgow HSFP) 1948 F, W, I, E, 1951 E
Blackadder, W F (W of Scotland) 1938 E
Blaikie, C F (Heriot's FP) 1963 I, E, 1966 E, 1968 A, 1969 F, W, I, E
Blair, M R L (Edinburgh) 2002 C, US, 2003 F(t+R), W 1(R), SA 2(R), It 2, I 2, [US], 2004 W(R),E(R),It(R),F(R),I(R),Sm(R),A1(R), 3(R),J(R),A4(R),SA(R),2005 I(t&R),It(R),W(R),E,R,Arg, Sm(R), NZ(R), 2006 F,W,E,I,It(R),SA 1,2,R,PI(R),A, 2007 I2,SA, [Pt,R, It,Arg]
Blair, P C B (Cambridge U) 1912 SA, 1913 F, W, I, E
Bolton, W H (W of Scotland) 1876 E
Borthwick, J B (Stewart's Coll FP) 1938 W, I
Bos, F H ten (Oxford U, London Scottish) 1959 E, 1960 F, W, SA, 1961 F, SA, W, I, E, 1962 F, W, I, E, 1963 F, W, I, E
Boswell, J D (W of Scotland) 1889 W, I, 1890 W, I, E, 1891 W, I, E, 1892 W, I, E, 1893 I, E, 1894 I, E
Bowie, T C (Watsonians) 1913 I, E, 1914 I, E
Boyd, G M (Glasgow HSFP) 1926 E
Boyd, J L (United Services) 1912 E, SA
Boyle, A C W (London Scottish) 1963 F, W, I
Boyle, A H W (St Thomas's Hospital, London Scottish) 1966 A, 1967 F, NZ, 1968 F, W, I
Brash, J C (Cambridge U) 1961 E

Breakey, R W (Gosforth) 1978 E
Brewis, N T (Edinburgh Inst FP) 1876 E, 1878 E, 1879 I, E, 1880 I, E
Brewster, A K (Stewart's-Melville FP) 1977 E, 1980 I, F, 1986 E, I, R
Brotherstone, S J (Melrose, Brive, Newcastle) 1999 I (R), 2000 F, W, E, US, A, Sm, 2002 C (R)
Brown, A H (Heriot's FP) 1928 E, 1929 F, W
Brown, A R (Gala) 1971 E (2[1C]), 1972 F, W, E
Brown, C H C (Dunfermline) 1929 E
Brown, D I (Cambridge U) 1933 W, E, I
Brown, G L (W of Scotland) 1969 SA, 1970 F, W (R), I, E, A, 1971 F, W, I, E (2[1C]), 1972 F, W, E, NZ, 1973 E (R), P, 1974 W, E, I, F, 1975 I, F, W, E, A, 1976 F, W, E, I
Brown, J A (Glasgow Acads) 1908 W, I
Brown, J B (Glasgow Acads) 1879 I, E, 1880 I, E, 1881 I, E, 1882 I, E, 1883 W, I, E, 1884 W, I, E, 1885 I 1,2, 1886 W, I, E
Brown, K D R (Borders, Glasgow) 2005 R,Sm(R),NZ(R), 2006 SA 1(R),2(R),R,PI,A, 2007 E,W,It,I1,2(R),SA,[Pt(R),R(R),NZ, It(R),Arg(R)]
Brown, P C (W of Scotland, Gala) 1964 F, NZ, W, I, E, 1965 I, E, SA, 1966 A, 1969 I, E, 1970 W, E, 1971 F, W, I, E (2[1C]), 1972 F, W, E, NZ, 1973 F, W, I, E, P
Brown, T G (Heriot's FP) 1929 W
Brown, W D (Glasgow Acads) 1871 E, 1872 E, 1873 E, 1874 E, 1875 E
Brown, W S (Edinburgh Inst FP) 1880 I, E, 1882 I, E, 1883 W, E
Browning, A (Glasgow HSFP) 1920 I, 1922 F, W, I, 1923 W, I, E
Bruce, C R (Glasgow Acads) 1947 F, W, I, E, 1949 F, W, I, E
Bruce, N S (Blackheath, Army and London Scottish) 1958 F, A, I, E, 1959 F, W, I, E, 1960 F, W, I, E, SA, 1961 F, SA, W, I, E, 1962 F, W, I, E, 1963 F, W, I, E, 1964 F, NZ, W, I, E
Bruce, R M (Gordonians) 1947 A, 1948 F, W, I
Bruce-Lockhart, J H (London Scottish) 1913 W, 1920 E
Bruce-Lockhart, L (London Scottish) 1948 E, 1950 F, W, 1953 I, E
Bruce-Lockhart, R B (Cambridge U and London Scottish) 1937 I, 1939 I, E
Bryce, C C (Glasgow Acads) 1873 E, 1874 E
Bryce, R D H (W of Scotland) 1973 I (R)
Bryce, W E (Selkirk) 1922 W, I, E, 1923 F, W, I, E, 1924 F, W, I, E
Brydon, W R C (Heriot's FP) 1939 W
Buchanan, A (Royal HSFP) 1871 E
Buchanan, F G (Kelvinside Acads and Oxford U) 1910 F, 1911 F, W
Buchanan, J C R (Stewart's Coll FP) 1921 W, I, E, 1922 W, I, E, 1923 F, W, I, E, 1924 F, W, I, E, 1925 F, I
Buchanan-Smith, G A E (London Scottish, Heriot's FP) 1989 Fj (R), 1990 Arg
Bucher, A M (Edinburgh Acads) 1897 E
Budge, G M (Edinburgh Wands) 1950 F, W, I, E
Bullmore, H H (Edinburgh U) 1902 I
Bulloch, A J (Glasgow) 2000 US, A, Sm, 2001 F (t+R), E
Bulloch, G C (West of Scotland, Glasgow) 1997 SA, 1998 It, I, F, W, E, Fj, A 1, SA, 1999 W, E, It, I, F, Arg, [SA, U, Sm, NZ], 2000 It, I, W (R), NZ 1,2, A (R), Sm (R), 2001 F, W, E, It, I, Tg, Arg, NZ, 2002 E, It, I, F, W, C, US, R, SA, Fj, 2003 I 1, F, W 1, E, It 1, SA 1,2, It 2(R), W2, I 2, [US,F,Fj,A], 2004 W,E,It,F,I,Sm,A1,2,3,J,A4,SA, 2005 F,I,It,W,E
Burnell, A P (London Scottish, Montferrand) 1989 E, I, F, Fj, R, 1990 I, F, W, E, Arg, 1991 F, W, E, I, R, [J, Z, I, WS, E, NZ], 1992 E, I, F, W, 1993 I, F, W, E, NZ, 1994 W, E, I, F, Arg 1,2, SA, 1995 [Iv, Tg (R), F (R)], WS, 1998 E, SA, 1999 W, E, It, I, F, Arg, [Sp, Sm (R), NZ]
Burnet, P J (London Scottish and Edinburgh Acads) 1960 SA
Burnet, W (Hawick) 1912 E
Burnet, W A (W of Scotland) 1934 W, 1935 W, I, E, NZ, 1936 W, I, E
Burnett, J N (Heriot's FP) 1980 I, F, W, E
Burns, G G (Watsonians, Edinburgh) 1999 It (R), 2001 Tg (R), NZ (R), 2002 US (R)
Burrell, G (Gala) 1950 F, W, I, 1951 SA

Cairns, A G (Watsonians) 1903 W, I, E, 1904 W, I, E, 1905 W, I, E, 1906 W, I, E
Calder, F (Stewart's-Melville FP) 1986 F, W, E, I, R, 1987 I, F, W, E, [F, Z, R, NZ], 1988 I, F, W, E, 1989 W, E, I, F, R, 1990 I, F, W, E, NZ 1,2, 1991 R, [J, I, WS, E, NZ]
Calder, J H (Stewart's-Melville FP) 1981 F, W, E, I, NZ 1,2, R, A, 1982 E, I, F, W, A 1,2, 1983 I, F, W, E, NZ, 1984 W, E, I, F, A, 1985 I, F, W
Callam, D A (Edinburgh) 2006 R(R),PI(R),A, 2007 E,W,It,I1,F(R),SA, [NZ]
Callander, G J (Kelso) 1984 R, 1988 I, F, W, E, A
Cameron, A (Glasgow HSFP) 1948 W, 1950 I, E, 1951 F, W, I, E, SA, 1953 I, E, 1955 F, W, I, E, 1956 F, W, I
Cameron, A D (Hillhead HSFP) 1951 F, 1954 F, W
Cameron, A W (Watsonians) 1887 W, 1893 W, 1894 I
Cameron, D (Glasgow HSFP) 1953 I, E, 1954 F, NZ, I, E
Cameron, N W (Glasgow U) 1952 E, 1953 F, W
Campbell, A J (Hawick) 1984 I, F, R, 1985 I, F, W, E, 1986 F, W, E, I, R, 1988 F, W, A
Campbell, G T (London Scottish) 1892 W, I, E, 1893 I, E, 1894 W, I, E, 1895 W, I, E, 1896 W, I, E, 1897 I, 1899 I, 1900 E
Campbell, H H (Cambridge U, London Scottish) 1947 I, E, 1948 I, E
Campbell, J A (W of Scotland) 1878 E, 1879 I, E, 1881 I, E
Campbell, J A (Cambridge U) 1900 I
Campbell, N M (London Scottish) 1956 F, W
Campbell, S J (Dundee HSFP) 1995 C, I, F, W, E, R, [Iv, NZ (R)], WS (t), 1996 I, F, W, E, 1997 A, SA, 1998 Fj (R), A 2(R)
Campbell-Lamerton, J R E (London Scottish) 1986 F, 1987 [Z, R(R)]
Campbell-Lamerton, M J (Halifax, Army, London Scottish) 1961 F, SA, W, I, 1962 F, W, I, E, 1963 F, W, I, E, 1964 I, E, 1965 F, W, I, E, SA, 1966 F, W, I, E
Carmichael, A B (W of Scotland) 1967 I, NZ, 1968 F, W, I, E, A, 1969 F, W, I, E, SA, 1970 F, W, I, E, A, 1971 F, W, I, E (2[1C]), 1972 F, W, E, NZ, 1973 F, W, I, E, P, 1974 W, E, I, F, 1975 I, F, W, E, NZ, A, 1976 F, W, E, I, 1977 E, I (R), F, W, 1978 I
Carmichael, J H (Watsonians) 1921 F, W, I
Carrick, J S (Glasgow Acads) 1876 E, 1877 E
Cassels, D Y (W of Scotland) 1880 E, 1881 I, 1882 I, E, 1883 W, I, E
Cathcart, C W (Edinburgh U) 1872 E, 1873 E, 1876 E
Cawkwell, G L (Oxford U) 1947 F
Chalmers, C M (Melrose) 1989 W, E, I, F, Fj, 1990 I, F, W, E, NZ 1,2, Arg, 1991 F, W, E, I, R, [J, Z (R), I, WS, E, NZ], 1992 E, I, F, W, A 1,2, 1993 I, F, W, E, NZ, 1994 W, SA, 1995 C, I, F, W, E, R, [Iv, Tg, F, NZ], WS, 1996 A, It, 1997 W, I, F, A (R), SA, 1998 It, I, F, W, E, 1999 Arg (R)
Chalmers, T (Glasgow Acads) 1871 E, 1872 E, 1873 E, 1874 E, 1875 E, 1876 E
Chambers, H F T (Edinburgh U) 1888 W, I, 1889 W, I
Charters, R G (Hawick) 1955 W, I, E
Chisholm, D H (Melrose) 1964 I, E, 1965 E, SA, 1966 F, I, E, A, 1967 F, W, NZ, 1968 F, W, I
Chisholm, R W T (Melrose) 1955 I, E, 1956 F, W, I, E, 1958 F, W, A, I, 1960 SA
Church, W C (Glasgow Acads) 1906 W
Clark, R L (Edinburgh Wands, Royal Navy) 1972 F, W, E, NZ, 1973 F, W, I, E, P
Clauss, P R A (Oxford U) 1891 W, I, E, 1892 W, E, 1895 I
Clay, A T (Edinburgh Acads) 1886 W, I, E, 1887 I, W, E, 1888 W
Clunies-Ross, A (St Andrew's U) 1871 E
Coltman, S (Hawick) 1948 I, 1949 F, W, I, E
Colville, A G (Merchistonians, Blackheath) 1871 E, 1872 E
Connell, G C (Trinity Acads and London Scottish) 1968 E, A, 1969 F, E, 1970 F
Cooper, M McG (Oxford U) 1936 W, I
Corcoran, I (Gala) 1992 A 1(R)
Cordial, I F (Edinburgh Wands) 1952 F, W, I, E
Cotter, J L (Hillhead HSFP) 1934 I, E
Cottington, G S (Kelso) 1934 I, E, 1935 W, I, 1936 E
Coughtrie, S (Edinburgh Acads) 1959 F, W, I, E, 1962 W, I, E, 1963 F, W, I, E
Couper, J H (W of Scotland) 1896 W, I, 1899 I
Coutts, F H (Melrose, Army) 1947 W, I, E
Coutts, I D F (Old Alleynians) 1951 F, 1952 E
Cowan, R C (Selkirk) 1961 F, 1962 F, W, I, E
Cowie, W L K (Edinburgh Wands) 1953 E
Cownie, W B (Watsonians) 1893 W, I, E, 1894 W, I, E, 1895 W, I, E

Crabbie, G E (Edinburgh Acads) 1904 W
Crabbie, J E (Edinburgh Acads, Oxford U) 1900 W, 1902 I, 1903 W, I, 1904 E, 1905 W
Craig, A (Orrell, Glasgow) 2002 C, US, R, SA, Fj, 2003 I 1, F(R), W 1(R), E, It 1, SA 1,2, W 2, I 2, [J,US,F], 2004 A3(R), 2005 F,I,It,W,E
Craig, J B (Heriot's FP) 1939 W
Craig, J M (West of Scotland, Glasgow) 1997 A, 2001 W (R), E (R), It
Cramb, R I (Harlequins) 1987 [R(R)], 1988 I, F, A
Cranston, A G (Hawick) 1976 W, E, I, 1977 E, W, 1978 F (R), W, E, NZ, 1981 NZ 1,2
Crawford, J A (Army, London Scottish) 1934 I
Crawford, W H (United Services, RN) 1938 W, I, E, 1939 W, E
Crichton-Miller, D (Gloucester) 1931 W, I, E
Crole, G B (Oxford U) 1920 F, W, I, E
Cronin, D F (Bath, London Scottish, Bourges, Wasps) 1988 I, F, W, E, A, 1989 W, E, I, F, Fj, R, 1990 I, F, W, E, NZ 1,2, 1991 F, W, E, I, R, [Z], 1992 A 2, 1993 I, F, W, E, NZ, 1995 C, I, F, [Tg, F, NZ], WS, 1996 NZ 1,2, A, It, 1997 F (R), 1998 I, F, W, E
Cross, M (Merchistonians) 1875 E, 1876 E, 1877 I, E, 1878 E, 1879 I, E, 1880 I, E
Cross, W (Merchistonians) 1871 E, 1872 E
Cumming, R S (Aberdeen U) 1921 F, W
Cunningham, G (Oxford U) 1908 W, I, 1909 W, E, 1910 F, I, E, 1911 E
Cunningham, R F (Gala) 1978 NZ, 1979 W, E
Currie, L R (Dunfermline) 1947 A, 1948 F, W, I, 1949 F, W, I, E
Cusiter, C P (Borders, Perpignan) 2004 W,E,It,F,I,Sm,A1,2,3, J,A4,SA,2005 F,I,It,W,Arg(R),Sm,NZ, 2006 F(R),W(R),E(R),I(R), It,R(R),PI, 2007 E,W,It,I1,F(R),I2(R), [R(R),NZ,It(R),Arg(R)]
Cuthbertson, W (Kilmarnock, Harlequins) 1980 I, 1981 W, E, I, NZ 1,2, R, A, 1982 E, I, F, W, A 1,2, 1983 I, F, W, NZ, 1984 W, E, A

Dalgleish, A (Gala) 1890 W, E, 1891 W, I, 1892 W, 1893 W, 1894 W, I
Dalgleish, K J (Edinburgh Wands, Cambridge U) 1951 I, E, 1953 F, W
Dall, A K (Edinburgh) 2003 W 2(R)
Dallas, J D (Watsonians) 1903 E
Danielli, S C J (Bath, Borders)) 2003 It 2, W 2, [J(R),US,Fj,A], 2004 W, E,It,F,I,2005 F,I
Davidson, J A (London Scottish, Edinburgh Wands) 1959 E, 1960 I, E
Davidson, J N G (Edinburgh U) 1952 F, W, I, E, 1953 F, W, 1954 F
Davidson, J P (RIE Coll) 1873 E, 1874 E
Davidson, R S (Royal HSFP) 1893 E
Davies, D S (Hawick) 1922 F, W, I, E, 1923 F, W, I, E, 1924 F, E, 1925 W, I, E, 1926 F, W, I, E, 1927 F, W, I
Dawson, J C (Glasgow Acads) 1947 A, 1948 F, W, 1949 F, W, I, 1950 F, W, I, E, 1951 F, W, I, E, SA, 1952 F, W, I, E, 1953 E
Deans, C T (Hawick) 1978 F, W, E, NZ, 1979 W, E, I, F, NZ, 1980 I, F, 1981 F, W, E, I, NZ 1,2, R, A, 1982 E, I, F, W, A 1,2, 1983 I, F, W, E, NZ, 1984 W, E, I, F, A, 1985 I, F, W, E, 1986 F, W, E, I, R, 1987 I, F, W, E, [F, Z, R, NZ]
Deans, D T (Hawick) 1968 E
Deas, D W (Heriot's FP) 1947 F, W
Dewey, R E (Edinburgh, Ulster) 2006 R, 2007 E(R),W,It,I1,F,I2,SA, [Pt,R,NZ(R),It,Arg]
Dick, L G (Loughborough Colls, Jordanhill, Swansea) 1972 W (R), E, 1974 W, E, I, F, 1975 I, F, W, E, NZ, A, 1976 F, 1977 E
Dick, R C S (Cambridge U, Guy's Hospital) 1934 W, I, E, 1935 W, I, E, NZ, 1936 W, I, E, 1937 W, 1938 W, I, E
Dickinson, A (Gloucester) 2007 [NZ]
Dickson, G (Gala) 1978 NZ, 1979 W, E, I, F, NZ, 1980 W, 1981 F, 1982 W (R)
Dickson, M R (Edinburgh U) 1905 I
Dickson, W M (Blackheath, Oxford U) 1912 F, W, E, SA, 1913 F, W, I
Di Rollo, M P (Edinburgh) 2002 US (R), 2005 R,Arg,Sm,NZ, 2006 F,E,I,It,SA 1,2, R,PI,A, 2007 E,W,It,I1,F(R), [Pt,NZ]
Dobson, J (Glasgow Acads) 1911 E, 1912 F, W, I, E, SA
Dobson, J D (Glasgow Acads) 1910 I
Dobson, W G (Heriot's FP) 1922 W, I, E
Docherty, J T (Glasgow HSFP) 1955 F, W, 1956 E, 1958 F, W, A, I, E
Dods, F P (Edinburgh Acads) 1901 I
Dods, J H (Edinburgh Acads) 1895 W, I, E, 1896 W, I, E, 1897 I, E
Dods, M (Gala, Northampton) 1994 I (t), Arg 1,2, 1995 WS, 1996 I, F, W, E
Dods, P W (Gala) 1983 I, F, W, E, NZ, 1984 W, E, I, F, R, A, 1985 I, F, W, E, 1989 W, E, I, F, 1991 I (R), R, [Z, NZ (R)]
Donald, D G (Oxford U) 1914 W, I
Donald, R L H (Glasgow HSFP) 1921 W, I, E
Donaldson, W P (Oxford U, W of Scotland) 1893 I, 1894 I, 1895 E, 1896 I, E, 1899 I
Don-Wauchope, A R (Fettesian-Lorettonians) 1881 E, 1882 E, 1883 W, 1884 W, I, E, 1885 W, I 1,2, 1886 W, I, E, 1888 I
Don-Wauchope, P H (Fettesian-Lorettonians) 1885 I 1,2, 1886 W, 1887 I, W, E
Dorward, A F (Cambridge U, Gala) 1950 F, 1951 SA, 1952 W, I, E, 1953 F, W, E, 1955 F, 1956 I, E, 1957 F, W, I, E
Dorward, T F (Gala) 1938 W, I, E, 1939 I, E
Douglas, B A F (Borders) 2002 R, SA, Fj, 2003 I 1, F, W 1, E, It 1, SA 1,2, It 2, W 2, [J,US(t&R),F(R),Fj,A], 2004 W,E,It,F,I,Sm,A1,2,3,A4(R),SA(R),2005 F(R),I(R),It(R),W(R),E(R),R,Arg, NZ, 2006 F,W,E,I,It,SA 1,2(R)
Douglas, G (Jedforest) 1921 W
Douglas, J (Stewart's Coll FP) 1961 F, SA, W, I, E, 1962 F, W, I, E, 1963 F, W, I
Douty, P S (London Scottish) 1927 A, 1928 F, W
Drew, D (Glasgow Acads) 1871 E, 1876 E
Druitt, W A H (London Scottish) 1936 W, I, E
Drummond, A H (Kelvinside Acads) 1938 W, I
Drummond, C W (Melrose) 1947 F, W, I, E, 1948 F, I, E, 1950 F, W, I, E
Drybrough, A S (Edinburgh Wands, Merchistonians) 1902 I, 1903 I
Dryden, R H (Watsonians) 1937 E
Drysdale, D (Heriot's FP) 1923 F, W, I, E, 1924 F, W, I, E, 1925 F, W, I, E, 1926 F, W, I, E, 1927 F, W, I, E, A, 1928 F, W, I, E, 1929 F
Duff, P L (Glasgow Acads) 1936 W, I, 1938 W, I, E, 1939 W
Duffy, H (Jedforest) 1955 F
Duke, A (Royal HSFP) 1888 W, I, 1889 W, I, 1890 W, I
Dunbar, J P A (Leeds) 2005 F(R), It(R)
Duncan, A W (Edinburgh U) 1901 W, I, E, 1902 W, I, E
Duncan, D D (Oxford U) 1920 F, W, I, E
Duncan, M D F (W of Scotland) 1986 F, W, E, R, 1987 I, F, W, E, [F, Z, R, NZ], 1988 I, F, W, E, A, 1989 W
Duncan, M M (Fettesian-Lorettonians) 1888 W
Dunlop, J W (W of Scotland) 1875 E
Dunlop, Q (W of Scotland) 1971 E (2[1C])
Dykes, A S (Glasgow Acads) 1932 E
Dykes, J C (Glasgow Acads) 1922 F, E, 1924 I, 1925 F, W, I, 1926 F, W, I, E, 1927 F, W, I, E, A, 1928 F, I, 1929 F, W, I
Dykes, J M (Clydesdale, Glasgow HSFP) 1898 I, E, 1899 W, E, 1900 W, I, 1901 W, I, E, 1902 E

Edwards, D B (Heriot's FP) 1960 I, E, SA
Edwards, N G B (Harlequins, Northampton) 1992 E, I, F, W, A 1, 1994 W
Elgie, M K (London Scottish) 1954 NZ, I, E, W, 1955 F, W, I, E
Elliot, C (Langholm) 1958 E, 1959 F, 1960 F, 1963 E, 1964 F, NZ, W, I, E, 1965 F, W, I
Elliot, M (Hawick) 1895 W, 1896 E, 1897 I, E, 1898 I, E
Elliot, T (Gala) 1905 E
Elliot, T (Gala) 1955 W, I, E, 1956 F, W, I, E, 1957 F, W, I, E, 1958 W, A, I
Elliot, T G (Langholm) 1968 W, A, 1969 F, W, 1970 E
Elliot, W I D (Edinburgh Acads) 1947 F, W, E, A, 1948 F, W, I, E, 1949 F, W, I, E, 1950 F, W, I, E, 1951 F, W, I, E, SA, 1952 F, W, I, E, 1954 NZ, I, E, W
Ellis, D G (Currie) 1997 W, E, I, F
Emslie, W D (Royal HSFP) 1930 F, 1932 I
Eriksson, B R S (London Scottish) 1996 NZ 1, A, 1997 E
Evans, H L (Edinburgh U) 1885 I 1,2
Ewart, E N (Glasgow Acads) 1879 E, 1880 I, E

Fahmy, Dr E C (Abertillery) 1920 F, W, I, E
Fairley, I T (Kelso, Edinburgh) 1999 It, I (R), [Sp (R)]

Fasson, F H (London Scottish, Edinburgh Wands) 1900 W, 1901 W, I, 1902 W, E
Fell, A N (Edinburgh U) 1901 W, I, E, 1902 W, E, 1903 W, E
Ferguson, J H (Gala) 1928 W
Ferguson, W G (Royal HSFP) 1927 A, 1928 F, W, I, E
Fergusson, E A J (Oxford U) 1954 F, NZ, I, E, W
Finlay, A B (Edinburgh Acads) 1875 E
Finlay, J F (Edinburgh Acads) 1871 E, 1872 E, 1874 E, 1875 E
Finlay, N J (Edinburgh Acads) 1875 E, 1876 E, 1878 E, 1879 I, E, 1880 I, E, 1881 I, E
Finlay, R (Watsonians) 1948 E
Fisher, A T (Waterloo, Watsonians) 1947 I, E
Fisher, C D (Waterloo) 1975 NZ, A, 1976 W, E, I
Fisher, D (W of Scotland) 1893 I
Fisher, J P (Royal HSFP, London Scottish) 1963 E, 1964 F, NZ, W, I, E, 1965 F, W, I, E, SA, 1966 F, W, I, E, A, 1967 F, W, I, E, NZ, 1968 F, W, I, E
Fleming, C J N (Edinburgh Wands) 1896 I, E, 1897 I
Fleming, G R (Glasgow Acads) 1875 E, 1876 E
Fletcher, H N (Edinburgh U) 1904 E, 1905 W
Flett, A B (Edinburgh U) 1901 W, I, E, 1902 W, I
Forbes, J L (Watsonians) 1905 W, 1906 I, E
Ford, D St C (United Services, RN) 1930 I, E, 1931 E, 1932 W, I
Ford, J R (Gala) 1893 I
Ford, R W (Borders, Glasgow) 2004 A3(R), 2006 W(R),E(R),PI(R),A(R), 2007 E(R),W(R),It(R),I1(R),F,I2,SA, [Pt(R),R,It,Arg]
Forrest, J E (Glasgow Acads) 1932 SA, 1935 E, NZ
Forrest, J G S (Cambridge U) 1938 W, I, E
Forrest, W T (Hawick) 1903 W, I, E, 1904 W, I, E, 1905 W, I
Forsayth, H H (Oxford U) 1921 F, W, I, E, 1922 W, I, E
Forsyth, I W (Stewart's Coll FP) 1972 NZ, 1973 F, W, I, E, P
Forsyth, J (Edinburgh U) 1871 E
Foster, R A (Hawick) 1930 W, 1932 SA, I, E
Fox, J (Gala) 1952 F, W, I, E
Frame, J N M (Edinburgh U, Gala) 1967 NZ, 1968 F, W, I, E, 1969 W, I, E, SA, 1970 F, W, I, E, A, 1971 F, W, I, E (2[1C]), 1972 F, W, E, 1973 P (R)
France, C (Kelvinside Acads) 1903 I
Fraser, C F P (Glasgow U) 1888 W, 1889 W
Fraser, J W (Edinburgh Inst FP) 1881 E
Fraser, R (Cambridge U) 1911 F, W, I, E
French, J (Glasgow Acads) 1886 W, 1887 I, W, E
Frew, A (Edinburgh U) 1901 W, I, E
Frew, G M (Glasgow HSFP) 1906 SA, 1907 W, I, E, 1908 W, I, E, 1909 W, I, E, 1910 F, W, I, 1911 I, E
Friebe, J P (Glasgow HSFP) 1952 E
Fullarton, I A (Edinburgh) 2000 NZ 1(R),2, 2001 NZ (R), 2003 It 2(R), I 2(t), 2004 Sm(R), A1(R),2
Fulton, A K (Edinburgh U, Dollar Acads) 1952 F, 1954 F
Fyfe, K C (Cambridge U, Sale, London Scottish) 1933 W, E, 1934 E, 1935 W, I, E, NZ, 1936 W, E, 1939 I

Gallie, G H (Edinburgh Acads) 1939 W
Gallie, R A (Glasgow Acads) 1920 F, W, I, E, 1921 F, W, I, E
Gammell, W B B (Edinburgh Wands) 1977 I, F, W, 1978 W, E
Geddes, I C (London Scottish) 1906 SA, 1907 W, I, E, 1908 W, E
Geddes, K I (London Scottish) 1947 F, W, I, E
Gedge, H T S (Oxford U, London Scottish, Edinburgh Wands) 1894 W, I, E, 1896 E, 1899 W, E
Gedge, P M S (Edinburgh Wands) 1933 I
Gemmill, R (Glasgow HSFP) 1950 F, W, I, E, 1951 F, W, I
Gibson, W R (Royal HSFP) 1891 I, E, 1892 W, I, E, 1893 W, I, E, 1894 W, I, E, 1895 W, I, E
Gilbert-Smith, D S (London Scottish) 1952 E
Gilchrist, J (Glasgow Acads) 1925 F
Gill, A D (Gala) 1973 P, 1974 W, E, I, F
Gillespie, J I (Edinburgh Acads) 1899 E, 1900 W, E, 1901 W, I, E, 1902 W, I, 1904 I, E
Gillies, A C (Watsonians) 1924 W, I, E, 1925 F, W, E, 1926 F, W, 1927 F, W, I, E
Gilmour, H R (Heriot's FP) 1998 Fj
Gilray, C M (Oxford U, London Scottish) 1908 E, 1909 W, E, 1912 I
Glasgow, I C (Heriot's FP) 1997 F (R)
Glasgow, R J C (Dunfermline) 1962 F, W, I, E, 1963 I, E, 1964 I, E, 1965 W, I
Glen, W S (Edinburgh Wands) 1955 W
Gloag, L G (Cambridge U) 1949 F, W, I, E
Godman, P J (Edinburgh) 2005 R(R),Sm(R),NZ(R), 2006 R,PI(R),A(t&R), 2007 W,It
Goodfellow, J (Langholm) 1928 W, I, E
Goodhue, F W J (London Scottish) 1890 W, I, E, 1891 W, I, E, 1892 W, I, E
Gordon, R (Edinburgh Wands) 1951 W, 1952 F, W, I, E, 1953 W
Gordon, R E (Royal Artillery) 1913 F, W, I
Gordon, R J (London Scottish) 1982 A 1,2
Gore, A C (London Scottish) 1882 I
Gossman, B M (W of Scotland) 1980 W, 1983 F, W
Gossman, J S (W of Scotland) 1980 E (R)
Gowans, J J (Cambridge U, London Scottish) 1893 W, 1894 W, E, 1895 W, I, E, 1896 I, E
Gowland, G C (London Scottish) 1908 W, 1909 W, E, 1910 F, W, I, E
Gracie, A L (Harlequins) 1921 F, W, I, E, 1922 F, W, I, E, 1923 F, W, I, E, 1924 F
Graham, G (Newcastle) 1997 A (R), SA (R), 1998 I, F (R), W (R), 1999 F (R), Arg (R), R, [SA, U, Sm, NZ (R)], 2000 I (R), US, A, Sm, 2001 I (R), Tg (R), Arg (R), NZ (R), 2002 E (R), It (R), I (R), F (R), W (R)
Graham, I N (Edinburgh Acads) 1939 I, E
Graham, J (Kelso) 1926 I, E, 1927 F, W, I, E, A, 1928 F, W, I, E, 1930 I, E, 1932 SA, W
Graham, J H S (Edinburgh Acads) 1876 E, 1877 I, E, 1878 E, 1879 I, E, 1880 I, E, 1881 I, E
Grant, D (Hawick) 1965 F, E, SA, 1966 F, W, I, E, A, 1967 F, W, I, E, NZ, 1968 F
Grant, D M (East Midlands) 1911 W, I
Grant, M L (Harlequins) 1955 F, 1956 F, W, 1957 F
Grant, T O (Hawick) 1960 I, E, SA, 1964 F, NZ, W
Grant, W St C (Craigmount) 1873 E, 1874 E
Gray, C A (Nottingham) 1989 W, E, I, F, Fj, R, 1990 I, F, W, E, NZ 1,2, Arg, 1991 F, W, E, I, [J, I, WS, E, NZ]
Gray, D (W of Scotland) 1978 E, 1979 I, F, NZ, 1980 I, F, W, E, 1981 F
Gray, G L (Gala) 1935 NZ, 1937 W, I, E
Gray, S D (Borders) 2004 A3
Gray, T (Northampton, Heriot's FP) 1950 E, 1951 F, E
Greenlees, H D (Leicester) 1927 A, 1928 F, W, 1929 I, E, 1930 E
Greenlees, J R C (Cambridge U, Kelvinside Acads) 1900 I, 1902 W, I, E, 1903 W, I, E
Greenwood, J T (Dunfermline and Perthshire Acads) 1952 F, 1955 F, W, I, E, 1956 F, W, I, E, 1957 F, W, E, 1958 F, W, A, I, E, 1959 F, W, I
Greig, A (Glasgow HSFP) 1911 I
Greig, L L (Glasgow Acads, United Services) 1905 NZ, 1906 SA, 1907 W, 1908 W, I
Greig, R C (Glasgow Acads) 1893 W, 1897 I
Grieve, C F (Oxford U) 1935 W, 1936 E
Grieve, R M (Kelso) 1935 W, I, E, NZ, 1936 W, I, E
Grimes, S B (Watsonians, Newcastle) 1997 A (t+R), 1998 I (R), F (R), W (R), E (R), Fj, A 1, 2, 1999 W (R), E, It, I, F, Arg, R, [SA, U, Sm (R), NZ (R)], 2000 It, I, F (R), W, US, A, Sm (R), 2001 F (R), W (R), E (R), It, I (R), Tg, Arg, NZ, 2002 E, It, I, F (R), W (R), C, US, R, SA, Fj, 2003 I 1, F, W 1, E(R), It 1(R), W 2, I 2, [J,US,F,Fj,A], 2004 W,E,It,F,I,Sm,A1,J,A4,SA, 2005 F,I,It,W,E(R)
Gunn, A W (Royal HSFP) 1912 F, W, I, SA, 1913 F

Hall, A J A (Glasgow) 2002 US (R)
Hall, D W H (Edinburgh) 2003 W 2(R), 2005 R(R),Arg,Sm(R), NZ(R), 2006 F,E,I,It(R),SA 1(R),2,R,PI,A, 2007 E,W,It,I1,F(R)
Hamilton, A S (Headingley) 1914 W, 1920 F
Hamilton, C P (Newcastle) 2004 A2(R), 2005 R,Arg,Sm,NZ
Hamilton, H M (W of Scotland) 1874 E, 1875 E
Hamilton, J L (Leicester) 2006 R(R),A(R), 2007 E,W,It(R),I1(R),F(R),I2,SA, [R,NZ(R),It,Arg]
Hannah, R S M (W of Scotland) 1971 I
Harrower, P R (London Scottish) 1885 W
Hart, J G M (London Scottish) 1951 SA
Hart, T M (Glasgow U) 1930 W, I
Hart, W (Melrose) 1960 SA
Harvey, L (Greenock Wands) 1899 I
Hastie, A J (Melrose) 1961 W, I, E, 1964 I, E, 1965 E, SA, 1966 F, W, I, E, A, 1967 F, W, I, NZ, 1968 F, W

Hastie, I R (Kelso) 1955 F, 1958 F, E, 1959 F, W, I
Hastie, J D H (Melrose) 1938 W, I, E
Hastings, A G (Cambridge U, Watsonians, London Scottish) 1986 F, W, E, I, R, 1987 I, F, W, E, [F, Z, R, NZ], 1988 I, F, W, E, A, 1989 Fj, R, 1990 I, F, W, E, NZ 1,2, Arg, 1991 F, W, E, I, [J, I, WS, E, NZ], 1992 E, I, F, W, A 1, 1993 I, F, W, E, NZ, 1994 W, E, I, F, SA, 1995 C, I, F, W, E, R, [Iv, Tg, F, NZ]
Hastings, S (Watsonians) 1986 F, W, E, I, R, 1987 I, F, W, [R], 1988 I, F, W, A, 1989 W, E, I, F, Fj, R, 1990 I, F, W, E, NZ 1,2, Arg, 1991 F, W, E, I, [J, Z, I, WS, E, NZ], 1992 E, I, F, W, A 1,2, 1993 I, F, W, E, NZ, 1994 E, I, F, SA, 1995 W, E, R (R), [Tg, F, NZ], 1996 I, F, W, E, NZ 2, It, 1997 W, E (R)
Hay, B H (Boroughmuir) 1975 NZ, A, 1976 F, 1978 I, F, W, E, NZ, 1979 W, E, I, F, NZ, 1980 I, F, W, E, 1981 F, W, E, I, NZ 1,2
Hay, J A (Hawick) 1995 WS
Hay-Gordon, J R (Edinburgh Acads) 1875 E, 1877 I, E
Hegarty, C B (Hawick) 1978 I, F, W, E
Hegarty, J J (Hawick) 1951 F, 1953 F, W, I, E, 1955 F
Henderson, A R (Glasgow) 2001 I (R), Tg (R), NZ (R), 2002 It, I, US (R), 2003 SA 1,2, It 2, I 2, [US,F,Fj,A], 2004 W,E(t&R),It(R),F,I,Sm,A1,2,3,J,A4,SA, 2005 W(R),R, Arg,Sm, NZ, 2006 F,W,E,I,It,SA 1,2,PI,A, 2007 E,It(R),I1(R),F,I2,SA, [NZ,It(R),Arg(R)]
Henderson, B C (Edinburgh Wands) 1963 E, 1964 F, I, E, 1965 F, W, I, E, 1966 F, W, I, E
Henderson, F W (London Scottish) 1900 W, I
Henderson, I C (Edinburgh Acads) 1939 I, E, 1947 F, W, E, A, 1948 I, E
Henderson, J H (Oxford U, Richmond) 1953 F, W, I, E, 1954 F, NZ, I, E, W
Henderson, J M (Edinburgh Acads) 1933 W, E, I
Henderson, J Y M (Watsonians) 1911 E
Henderson, M M (Dunfermline) 1937 W, I, E
Henderson, N F (London Scottish) 1892 I
Henderson, R G (Newcastle Northern) 1924 I, E
Hendrie, K G P (Heriot's FP) 1924 F, W, I
Hendry, T L (Clydesdale) 1893 W, I, E, 1895 I
Henriksen, E H (Royal HSFP) 1953 I
Hepburn, D P (Woodford) 1947 A, 1948 F, W, I, E, 1949 F, W, I, E
Heron, G (Glasgow Acads) 1874 E, 1875 E
Hill, C C P (St Andrew's U) 1912 F, I
Hilton, D I W (Bath, Glasgow) 1995 C, I, F, W, E, R, [Tg, F, NZ], WS, 1996 I, F, W, E, NZ 1,2, A, It, 1997 W, A, SA, 1998 It, I (R), F, W, E, A 1,2, SA (R), 1999 W (R), E (R), It (R), I (R), F, R (R), [SA (R), U (R), Sp], 2000 It (R), F (R), W (R), 2002 SA(R)
Hines, N J (Edinburgh, Glasgow, Perpignan) 2000 NZ 2(R), 2002 C, US, R(R), SA(R), Fj(R), 2003 W 1(R), E, It 1, SA 1,2, It 2, W 2(R), I 2, [US,F(R),Fj,A], 2004 E(R),It(R),F(R), I(R),A3,J,A4,SA,2005 F(R),I(R),It(R),W(R),E, 2006 E(R),I,It,SA 1,2,R,PI, 2007 W(R),It,I1,F,I2,SA, [Pt,R,It,Arg]
Hinshelwood, A J W (London Scottish) 1966 F, W, I, E, A, 1967 F, W, I, E, NZ, 1968 F, W, I, E, A, 1969 F, W, I, SA, 1970 F, W
Hinshelwood, B G (Worcester) 2002 C (R), R(R), SA(R), Fj, 2003 It 2, [J,US(R),Fj(R),A(R)], 2004 W,E,It,Sm,A1,2,J,A4,SA, 2005 It(R)
Hodge D W (Watsonians, Edinburgh) 1997 F (R), A, SA (t+R), 1998 A 2(R), SA, 1999 W, Arg, R, [Sp, Sm (R)], 2000 F (R), W, E, NZ 1,2, US (R), Sm (R), 2001 F (R), W, E, It, I (R), 2002 E, W (R), C, US
Hodgson, C G (London Scottish) 1968 I, E
Hogg, A (Edinburgh) 2004 W,E(R),It,F(R),I,Sm,A1,2,3,J,A4,SA, 2005 F,I,It,W,E,R,Arg,Sm,NZ, 2006 F,W,E,I,It,SA 1,2, 2007 E(R),W(R),It(R),I1(R),F,I2,SA(t&R), [Pt,R,It,Arg]
Hogg, C D (Melrose) 1992 A 1,2, 1993 NZ (R), 1994 Arg 1,2
Hogg, C G (Boroughmuir) 1978 F (R), W (R)
Holmes, S D (London Scottish) 1998 It, I, F
Holms, W F (RIE Coll) 1886 W, E, 1887 I, E, 1889 W, I
Horsburgh, G B (London Scottish) 1937 W, I, E, 1938 W, I, E, 1939 W, I, E
Howie, D D (Kirkcaldy) 1912 F, W, I, E, SA, 1913 F, W
Howie, R A (Kirkcaldy) 1924 F, W, I, E, 1925 W, I, E
Hoyer-Millar, G C (Oxford U) 1953 I
Huggan, J L (London Scottish) 1914 E
Hume, J (Royal HSFP) 1912 F, 1920 F, 1921 F, W, I, E, 1922 F
Hume, J W G (Oxford U, Edinburgh Wands) 1928 I, 1930 F
Hunter, F (Edinburgh U) 1882 I
Hunter, I G (Selkirk) 1984 I (R), 1985 F (R), W, E
Hunter, J M (Cambridge U) 1947 F
Hunter, M D (Glasgow High) 1974 F
Hunter, W J (Hawick) 1964 F, NZ, W, 1967 F, W, I, E
Hutchison, W R (Glasgow HSFP) 1911 E
Hutton, A H M (Dunfermline) 1932 I
Hutton, J E (Harlequins) 1930 E, 1931 F

Inglis, H M (Edinburgh Acads) 1951 F, W, I, E, SA, 1952 W, I
Inglis, J M (Selkirk) 1952 E
Inglis, W M (Cambridge U, Royal Engineers) 1937 W, I, E, 1938 W, I, E
Innes, J R S (Aberdeen GSFP) 1939 W, I, E, 1947 A, 1948 F, W, I, E
Ireland, J C H (Glasgow HSFP) 1925 W, I, E, 1926 F, W, I, E, 1927 F, W, I, E
Irvine, A R (Heriot's FP) 1972 NZ, 1973 F, W, I, E, P, 1974 W, E, I, F, 1975 I, F, W, E, NZ, A, 1976 F, W, E, I, 1977 E, I, F, W, 1978 I, F, E, NZ, 1979 W, E, I, F, NZ, 1980 I, F, W, E, 1981 F, W, E, I, NZ 1,2, R, A, 1982 E, I, F, W, A 1,2
Irvine, D R (Edinburgh Acads) 1878 E, 1879 I, E
Irvine, R W (Edinburgh Acads) 1871 E, 1872 E, 1873 E, 1874 E, 1875 E, 1876 E, 1877 I, E, 1878 E, 1879 I, E, 1880 I, E
Irvine T W (Edinburgh Acads) 1885 I 1,2, 1886 W, I, E, 1887 I, W, E, 1888 W, I, 1889 I

Jackson, K L T (Oxford U) 1933 W, E, I, 1934 W
Jackson, T G H (Army) 1947 F, W, E, A, 1948 F, W, I, E, 1949 F, W, I, E
Jackson, W D (Hawick) 1964 I, 1965 E, SA, 1968 A, 1969 F, W, I, E
Jacobsen, A F (Edinburgh) 2002 C (R), US, 2003 I 2, 2004 It,F,I,A3,J,A4,SA, 2005 R,Arg(R),Sm, 2006 R(R),PI(R),A(R), 2007 E(R),W(R),It(t&R),I1(R),F(R),I2,SA(R), [Pt]
Jamieson, J (W of Scotland) 1883 W, I, E, 1884 W, I, E, 1885 W, I 1,2
Jardine, I C (Stirling County) 1993 NZ, 1994 W, E (R), Arg 1,2, 1995 C, I, F, [Tg, F (t & R), NZ (R)], 1996 I, F, W, E, NZ 1,2, 1998 Fj
Jeffrey, J (Kelso) 1984 A, 1985 I, E, 1986 F, W, E, I, R, 1987 I, F, W, E, [F, Z, R], 1988 I, W, A, 1989 W, E, I, F, Fj, R, 1990 I, F, W, E, NZ 1,2, Arg, 1991 F, W, E, I, [J, I, WS, E, NZ]
Johnston, D I (Watsonians) 1979 NZ, 1980 I, F, W, E, 1981 R, A, 1982 E, I, F, W, A 1,2, 1983 I, F, W, NZ, 1984 W, E, I, F, R, 1986 F, W, E, I, R
Johnston, H H (Edinburgh Collegian FP) 1877 I, E
Johnston, J (Melrose) 1951 SA, 1952 F, W, I, E
Johnston, W C (Glasgow HSFP) 1922 F
Johnston, W G S (Cambridge U) 1935 W, I, 1937 W, I, E
Joiner, C A (Melrose, Leicester) 1994 Arg 1,2, 1995 C, I, F, W, E, R, [Iv, Tg, F, NZ], 1996 I, F, W, E, NZ 1, 1997 SA, 1998 It, I, A 2(R), 2000 NZ 1(R),2, US (R)
Jones, P M (Gloucester) 1992 W (R)
Junor, J E (Glasgow Acads) 1876 E, 1877 I, E, 1878 E, 1879 E, 1881 I

Keddie, R R (Watsonians) 1967 NZ
Keith, G J (Wasps) 1968 F, W
Keller, D H (London Scottish) 1949 F, W, I, E, 1950 F, W, I
Kellock, A D (Edinburgh, Glasgow) 2004 A3(t&R), 2005 R(R),Arg(R),Sm(R),NZ(R), 2006 F,W,E,It(R),SA 1(R),2,PI(R),A, 2007 E
Kelly, R F (Watsonians) 1927 A, 1928 F, W, E
Kemp, J W Y (Glasgow HSFP) 1954 W, 1955 F, W, I, E, 1956 F, W, I, E, 1957 F, W, I, E, 1958 F, W, A, I, E, 1959 F, W, I, E, 1960 F, W, I, E, SA
Kennedy, A E (Watsonians) 1983 NZ, 1984 W, E, A
Kennedy, F (Stewart's Coll FP) 1920 F, W, I, E, 1921 E
Kennedy, N (W of Scotland) 1903 W, I, E
Ker, A B M (Kelso) 1988 W, E
Ker, H T (Glasgow Acads) 1887 I, W, E, 1888 I, 1889 W, 1890 I, E
Kerr, D S (Heriot's FP) 1923 F, W, 1924 F, 1926 I, E, 1927 W, I, E, 1928 I, E
Kerr, G (Leeds, Borders, Glasgow) 2003 I 1(R), F(R), W 1(R), E(R), SA 1,2, W 2, [J(R),US,F], 2004 W(R),E(R),It(R),F(R),I(R), J,A4,SA, 2005 F,I,It,W,E,Arg,Sm(R), NZ, 2006 F,W,E,I,It,SA 1,2,R,PI,A, 2007 E,W,It,I1,F,SA, [Pt(R),R,NZ(R),It,Arg]

Kerr, G C (Old Dunelmians, Edinburgh Wands) 1898 I, E, 1899 I, W, E, 1900 W, I, E
Kerr, J M (Heriot's FP) 1935 NZ, 1936 I, E, 1937 W, I
Kerr, R C (Glasgow) 2002 C, US, 2003 W 2
Kerr, W (London Scottish) 1953 E
Kidston, D W (Glasgow Acads) 1883 W, E
Kidston, W H (W of Scotland) 1874 E
Kilgour, I J (RMC Sandhurst) 1921 F
King, J H F (Selkirk) 1953 F, W, E, 1954 E
Kininmonth, P W (Oxford U, Richmond) 1949 F, W, I, E, 1950 F, W, I, E, 1951 F, W, I, E, SA, 1952 F, W, I, 1954 F, NZ, I, E, W
Kinnear, R M (Heriot's FP) 1926 F, W, I
Knox, J (Kelvinside Acads) 1903 W, I, E
Kyle, W E (Hawick) 1902 W, I, E, 1903 W, I, E, 1904 W, I, E, 1905 W, I, E, NZ, 1906 W, I, E, 1908 E, 1909 W, I, E, 1910 W

Laidlaw, A S (Hawick) 1897 I
Laidlaw, F A L (Melrose) 1965 F, W, I, E, SA, 1966 F, W, I, E, A, 1967 F, W, I, E, NZ, 1968 F, W, I, A, 1969 F, W, I, E, SA, 1970 F, W, I, E, A, 1971 F, W, I
Laidlaw, R J (Jedforest) 1980 I, F, W, E, 1981 F, W, E, I, NZ 1,2, R, A, 1982 E, I, F, W, A 1,2, 1983 I, F, W, E, NZ, 1984 W, E, I, F, R, A, 1985 I, F, W, E, 1986 F, W, E, I, R, 1987 I, F, W, E, [F, R, NZ], 1988 I, F, W, E
Laing, A D (Royal HSFP) 1914 W, I, E, 1920 F, W, I, 1921 F
Lambie, I K (Watsonians) 1978 NZ (R), 1979 W, E, NZ
Lambie, L B (Glasgow HSFP) 1934 W, I, E, 1935 W, I, E, NZ
Lamond, G A W (Kelvinside Acads) 1899 W, E, 1905 E
Lamont, R P (Glasgow, Sale) 2005 W,E,R,Arg,Sm, 2007 E(R),I1(R),F(R),I2,SA, [Pt,R,It,Arg]
Lamont, S F (Glasgow, Northampton) 2004 Sm,A1,2,3,J,A4,SA, 2005 F,I,It,W,E,R,Arg,Sm,NZ, 2006 F,W,E,I,It,SA1,R,PI,A, 2007 E,W,It,I1,F,I2, [Pt,R,It,Arg]
Laney, B J (Edinburgh) 2001 NZ, 2002 E, It, I, F, W, C, US, R, SA, Fj, 2003 I 1, F, SA 2(R), It 2(R), W 2, 2004 W,E,It,I(R)
Lang, D (Paisley) 1876 E, 1877 I
Langrish, R W (London Scottish) 1930 F, 1931 F, W, I
Lauder, W (Neath) 1969 I, E, SA, 1970 F, W, I, A, 1973 F, 1974 W, E, I, F, 1975 I, F, NZ, A, 1976 F, 1977 E
Laughland, I H P (London Scottish) 1959 F, 1960 F, W, I, E, 1961 SA, W, I, E, 1962 F, W, I, E, 1963 F, W, I, 1964 F, NZ, W, I, E, 1965 F, W, I, E, SA, 1966 F, W, I, E, 1967 E
Lawrie, J R (Melrose) 1922 F, W, I, E, 1923 F, W, I, E, 1924 W, I, E
Lawrie, K G (Gala) 1980 F (R), W, E
Lawson, A J M (Edinburgh Wands, London Scottish) 1972 F (R), E, 1973 F, 1974 W, E, 1976 E, I, 1977 E, 1978 NZ, 1979 W, E, I, F, NZ, 1980 W (R)
Lawson, R G M (Gloucester) 2006 A(R), 2007 E(R),W(R),It(R),I1(R),F,SA(R), [Pt(R),NZ(R)]
Lawson, S (Glasgow, Sale) 2005 R,Arg(R),Sm,NZ, 2006 F(R),W,I(R),It,SA 1,2(R),R(R), 2007 [Pt,R(R),NZ,Arg(R)]
Lawther, T H B (Old Millhillians) 1932 SA, W
Ledingham, G A (Aberdeen GSFP) 1913 F
Lee, D J (London Scottish, Edinburgh) 1998 I (R), F, W, E, Fj, A 1,2, SA, 2001 Arg, 2004 It(R),F,I(R)
Lees, J B (Gala) 1947 I, A, 1948 F, W, E
Leggatt, H T O (Watsonians) 1891 W, I, E, 1892 W, I, 1893 W, E, 1894 I, E
Lely, W G (Cambridge U, London Scottish) 1909 I
Leslie, D G (Dundee HSFP, W of Scotland, Gala) 1975 I, F, W, E, NZ, A, 1976 F, W, E, I, 1978 NZ, 1980 E, 1981 W, E, I, NZ 1,2, R, A, 1982 E, 1983 I, F, W, E, 1984 W, E, I, F, R, 1985 F, W, E
Leslie, J A (Glasgow, Northampton) 1998 SA, 1999 W, E, It, I, F, [SA], 2000 It, F, W, US, A, Sm, 2001 F, W, E, It, I, Tg, Arg, NZ, 2002 F, W
Leslie, M D (Glasgow, Edinburgh) 1998 SA (R), 1999 W, E, It, I, F, R, [SA, U, Sm, NZ], 2000 It, I, F, W, E, NZ 1,2, 2001 F, W, E, It, 2002 It (R), I (R), F, W, R, SA, Fj(R), 2003 I 1, F, SA 1(R), 2 (R), It 2(R), W 2, [J(R),US(R)]
Liddell, E H (Edinburgh U) 1922 F, W, I, 1923 F, W, I, E
Lind, H (Dunfermline) 1928 I, 1931 F, W, I, E, 1932 SA, W, E, 1933 W, E, I, 1934 W, I, E, 1935 I, 1936 E
Lindsay, A B (London Hospital) 1910 I, 1911 I
Lindsay, G C (London Scottish) 1884 W, 1885 I 1, 1887 W, E
Lindsay-Watson, R H (Hawick) 1909 I
Lineen, S R P (Boroughmuir) 1989 W, E, I, F, Fj, R, 1990 I, F, W, E, NZ 1,2, Arg, 1991 F, W, E, I, R, [J, Z, I, E, NZ], 1992 E, I, F, W, A 1,2
Little, A W (Hawick) 1905 W
Logan, K M (Stirling County, Wasps) 1992 A 2, 1993 E (R), NZ (t), 1994 W, E, I, F, Arg 1,2, SA, 1995 C, I, F, W, E, R, [Iv, Tg, F, NZ], WS, 1996 W (R), NZ 1,2, A, It, 1997 W, E, I, F, A, 1998 I, F, SA (R), 1999 W, E, It, I, F, Arg, R, [SA, U, Sm, NZ], 2000 It, I, F, Sm, 2001 F, W, E, It, 2002 I (R), F (R), W, 2003 I 1, F, W 1, E, It 1, SA 1,2, It 2, I 2, [J,US(R),F,Fj,A]
Logan, W R (Edinburgh U, Edinburgh Wands) 1931 E, 1932 SA, W, I, 1933 W, E, I, 1934 W, I, E, 1935 W, I, E, NZ, 1936 W, I, E, 1937 W, I, E
Longstaff, S L (Dundee HSFP, Glasgow) 1998 F (R), W, E, Fj, A 1,2 1999 It (R), I (R), Arg (R), R, [U (R), Sp], 2000 It, I, NZ 1
Lorraine, H D B (Oxford U) 1933 W, E, I
Loudoun-Shand, E G (Oxford U) 1913 E
Lowe, J D (Heriot's FP) 1934 W
Lumsden, I J M (Bath, Watsonians) 1947 F, W, A, 1949 F, W, I, E
Lyall, G G (Gala) 1947 A, 1948 F, W, I, E
Lyall, W J C (Edinburgh Acads) 1871 E

Mabon, J T (Jedforest) 1898 I, E, 1899 I, 1900 I
Macarthur, J P (Waterloo) 1932 E
MacCallum, J C (Watsonians) 1905 E, NZ, 1906 W, I, E, SA, 1907 W, I, E, 1908 W, I, E, 1909 W, I, E, 1910 F, W, I, E, 1911 F, I, E, 1912 F, W, I, E
McClung, T (Edinburgh Acads) 1956 I, E, 1957 W, I, E, 1959 F, W, I, 1960 W
McClure, G B (W of Scotland) 1873 E
McClure, J H (W of Scotland) 1872 E
McCowan, D (W of Scotland) 1880 I, E, 1881 I, E, 1882 I, E, 1883 I, E, 1884 I, E
McCowat, R H (Glasgow Acads) 1905 I
McCrae, I G (Gordonians) 1967 E, 1968 I, 1969 F (R), W, 1972 F, NZ
McCrow, J W S (Edinburgh Acads) 1921 I
Macdonald, A E D (Heriot's FP) 1993 NZ
McDonald, C (Jedforest) 1947 A
Macdonald, D C (Edinburgh U) 1953 F, W, 1958 I, E
Macdonald, D S M (Oxford U, London Scottish, W of Scotland) 1977 E, I, F, W, 1978 I, W, E
Macdonald, J D (London Scottish, Army) 1966 F, W, I, E, 1967 F, W, I, E
Macdonald, J M (Edinburgh Wands) 1911 W
Macdonald, J S (Edinburgh U) 1903 E, 1904 W, I, E, 1905 W
Macdonald, K R (Stewart's Coll FP) 1956 F, W, I, 1957 W, I, E
Macdonald, R (Edinburgh U) 1950 F, W, I, E
McDonald, W A (Glasgow U) 1889 W, 1892 I, E
Macdonald, W G (London Scottish) 1969 I (R)
MacDougall, B (Borders) 2006 W, SA2(R)
Macdougall, J B (Greenock Wands, Wakefield) 1913 F, 1914 I, 1921 F, I, E
McEwan, M C (Edinburgh Acads) 1886 E, 1887 I, W, E, 1888 W, I, 1889 W, I, 1890 W, I, E, 1891 W, I, E, 1892 E
MacEwan, N A (Gala, Highland) 1971 F, W, I, E (2[1C]), 1972 F, W, E, NZ, 1973 F, W, I, E, P, 1974 W, E, I, F, 1975 W, E
McEwan, W M C (Edinburgh Acads) 1894 W, E, 1895 W, E, 1896 W, I, E, 1897 I, E, 1898 I, E, 1899 I, W, E, 1900 W, E
MacEwen, R K G (Cambridge U, London Scottish) 1954 F, NZ, I, W, 1956 F, W, I, E, 1957 F, W, I, E, 1958 W
Macfadyen, D J H (Glasgow) 2002 C (R), US, 2004 Sm,A1,2,3,J,A4,SA, 2006 SA 1,2(R)
Macfarlan, D J (London Scottish) 1883 W, 1884 W, I, E, 1886 W, I, 1887 I, 1888 I
McFarlane, J L H (Edinburgh U) 1871 E, 1872 E, 1873 E
McGaughey, S K (Hawick) 1984 R
McGeechan, I R (Headingley) 1972 NZ, 1973 F, W, I, E, P, 1974 W, E, I, F, 1975 I, F, W, E, NZ, A, 1976 F, W, E, I, 1977 E, I, F, W, 1978 I, F, W, NZ, 1979 W, E, I, F
McGlashan, T P L (Royal HSFP) 1947 F, I, E, 1954 F, NZ, I, E, W
MacGregor, D G (Watsonians, Pontypridd) 1907 W, I, E
MacGregor, G (Cambridge U) 1890 W, I, E, 1891 W, I, E, 1893 W, I, E, 1894 W, I, E, 1896 E
MacGregor, I A A (Hillhead HSFP, Llanelli) 1955 I, E, 1956 F, W, I, E, 1957 F, W, I

MacGregor, J R (Edinburgh U) 1909 I
McGuinness, G M (W of Scotland) 1982 A 1,2, 1983 I, 1985 I, F, W, E
McHarg, A F (W of Scotland, London Scottish) 1968 I, E, A, 1969 F, W, I, E, 1971 F, W, I, E (2[1C]), 1972 F, E, NZ, 1973 F, W, I, E, P, 1974 W, E, I, F, 1975 I, F, W, E, NZ, A, 1976 F, W, E, I, 1977 E, I, F, W, 1978 I, F, W, NZ, 1979 W, E
McIlwham, G R (Glasgow Hawks, Glasgow, Bordeaux-Bègles) 1998 Fj, A 2(R), 2000 E (R), NZ 2(R), US (R), A (R), Sm (R), 2001 F (R), W (R), E (R), It (R), 2003 SA 2(R), It 2(R), W 2(R), I 2, [A(R)]
McIndoe, F (Glasgow Acads) 1886 W, I
MacIntyre, I (Edinburgh Wands) 1890 W, I, E, 1891 W, I, E
McIvor, D J (Edinburgh Acads) 1992 E, I, F, W, 1993 NZ, 1994 SA
Mackay, E B (Glasgow Acads) 1920 W, 1922 E
McKeating, E (Heriot's FP) 1957 F, W, 1961 SA, W, I, E
McKelvey, G (Watsonians) 1997 A
McKendrick, J G (W of Scotland) 1889 I
Mackenzie, A D G (Selkirk) 1984 A
Mackenzie, C J G (United Services) 1921 E
Mackenzie, D D (Edinburgh U) 1947 W, I, E, 1948 F, W, I
Mackenzie, D K A (Edinburgh Wands) 1939 I, E
Mackenzie, J M (Edinburgh U) 1905 NZ, 1909 W, I, E, 1910 W, I, E, 1911 W, I
McKenzie, K D (Stirling County) 1994 Arg 1,2, 1995 R, [Iv], 1996 I, F, W, E, NZ 1,2, A, It, 1998 A 1(R), 2
Mackenzie, R C (Glasgow Acads) 1877 I, E, 1881 I, E
Mackie, G Y (Highland) 1975 A, 1976 F, W, 1978 F
MacKinnon, A (London Scottish) 1898 I, E, 1899 I, W, E, 1900 E
Mackintosh, C E W C (London Scottish) 1924 F
Mackintosh, H S (Glasgow U, W of Scotland) 1929 F, W, I, E, 1930 F, W, I, E, 1931 F, W, I, E, 1932 SA, W, I, E
MacLachlan, L P (Oxford U, London Scottish) 1954 NZ, I, E, W
Maclagan, W E (Edinburgh Acads) 1878 E, 1879 I, E, 1880 I, E, 1881 I, E, 1882 I, E, 1883 W, I, E, 1884 W, I, E, 1885 W, I 1,2, 1887 I, W, E, 1888 W, I, 1890 W, I, E
McLaren, A (Durham County) 1931 F
McLaren, E (London Scottish, Royal HSFP) 1923 F, W, I, E, 1924 F
McLaren, J G (Bourgoin, Glasgow, Bordeaux-Bègles, Castres) 1999 Arg, R, [Sp, Sm], 2000 It (R), F, E, NZ 1, 2001 F, W, E (R), I, Tg, Arg, NZ, 2002 E, It, I, F, W, 2003 W 1, E, It 1, SA 1(R), It 2, I 2(R), [J,F(R),Fj(t&R),A(R)]
McLauchlan, J (Jordanhill) 1969 E, SA, 1970 F, W, 1971 F, W, I, E (2[1C]), 1972 F, W, E, NZ, 1973 F, W, I, E, P, 1974 W, E, I, F, 1975 I, F, W, E, NZ, A, 1976 F, W, E, I, 1977 W, 1978 I, F, W, E, NZ, 1979 W, E, I, F, NZ
McLean, D I (Royal HSFP) 1947 I, E
Maclennan, W D (Watsonians) 1947 F, I
MacLeod, D A (Glasgow U) 1886 I, E
MacLeod, G (Edinburgh Acads) 1878 E, 1882 I
McLeod, H F (Hawick) 1954 F, NZ, I, E, W, 1955 F, W, I, E, 1956 F, W, I, E, 1957 F, W, I, E, 1958 F, W, A, I, E, 1959 F, W, I, E, 1960 F, W, I, E, SA, 1961 F, SA, W, I, E, 1962 F, W, I, E
MacLeod, K G (Cambridge U) 1905 NZ, 1906 W, I, E, SA,1907 W, I, E, 1908 I, E
MacLeod, L M (Cambridge U) 1904 W, I, E, 1905 W, I, NZ
MacLeod, S J (Borders, Llanelli Scarlets) 2004 A3,J(t&R),A4(R),SA(R), 2006 F(R),W(R),E,SA2(R), 2007 I2(R), [Pt(R),R(R),NZ,It(R),Arg(R)]
Macleod, W M (Fettesian-Lorettonians, Edinburgh Wands) 1886 W, I
McMillan, K H D (Sale) 1953 F, W, I, E
MacMillan, R G (London Scottish) 1887 W, I, E, 1890 W, I, E, 1891 W, E, 1892 W, I, E, 1893 W, E, 1894 W, I, E, 1895 W, I, E, 1897 I, E
MacMyn, D J (Cambridge U, London Scottish) 1925 F, W, I, E, 1926 F, W, I, E, 1927 E, A, 1928 F
McNeil, A S B (Watsonians) 1935 I
McPartlin, J J (Harlequins, Oxford U) 1960 F, W, 1962 F, W, I, E
Macphail, J A R (Edinburgh Acads) 1949 E, 1951 SA
Macpherson, D G (London Hospital) 1910 I, E
Macpherson, G P S (Oxford U, Edinburgh Acads) 1922 F, W, I, E, 1924 W, E, 1925 F, W, E, 1927 F, W, I, E, 1928 F, W, E, 1929 I, E, 1930 F, W, I, E, 1931 W, E, 1932 SA, E
Macpherson, N C (Newport) 1920 W, I, E, 1921 F, E, 1923 I, E
McQueen, S B (Waterloo) 1923 F, W, I, E
Macrae, D J (St Andrew's U) 1937 W, I, E, 1938 W, I, E, 1939 W, I, E
Madsen, D F (Gosforth) 1974 W, E, I, F, 1975 I, F, W, E, 1976 F, 1977 E, I, F, W, 1978 I
Mair, N G R (Edinburgh U) 1951 F, W, I, E
Maitland, G (Edinburgh Inst FP) 1885 W, I 2
Maitland, R (Edinburgh Inst FP) 1881 E, 1882 I, E, 1884 W, 1885 W
Maitland, R P (Royal Artillery) 1872 E
Malcolm, A G (Glasgow U) 1888 I
Manson, J J (Dundee HSFP) 1995 E (R)
Marsh, J (Edinburgh Inst FP) 1889 W, I
Marshall, A (Edinburgh Acads) 1875 E
Marshall, G R (Selkirk) 1988 A (R), 1989 Fj, 1990 Arg, 1991 [Z]
Marshall, J C (London Scottish) 1954 F, NZ, I, E, W
Marshall, K W (Edinburgh Acads) 1934 W, I, E, 1935 W, I, E, 1936 W, 1937 E
Marshall, T R (Edinburgh Acads) 1871 E, 1872 E, 1873 E, 1874 E
Marshall, W (Edinburgh Acads) 1872 E
Martin, H (Edinburgh Acads, Oxford U) 1908 W, I, E, 1909 W, E
Masters, W H (Edinburgh Inst FP) 1879 I, 1880 I, E
Mather, C G (Edinburgh, Glasgow) 1999 R (R), [Sp, Sm (R)], 2000 F (t), 2003 [F,Fj,A], 2004 W,E,F
Maxwell, F T (Royal Engineers) 1872 E
Maxwell, G H H P (Edinburgh Acads, RAF, London Scottish) 1913 I, E, 1914 W, I, E, 1920 W, E, 1921 F, W, I, E, 1922 F, E
Maxwell, J M (Langholm) 1957 I
Mayer, M J M (Watsonians, Edinburgh) 1998 SA, 1999 [SA (R), U, Sp, Sm, NZ], 2000 It, I
Mein, J (Edinburgh Acads) 1871 E, 1872 E, 1873 E, 1874 E, 1875 E
Melville, C L (Army) 1937 W, I, E
Menzies, H F (W of Scotland) 1893 W, I, 1894 W, E
Metcalfe, G H (Glasgow Hawks, Glasgow) 1998 A 1,2, 1999 W, E, It, I, F, Arg, R, [SA, U, Sm, NZ], 2000 It, I, F, W, E, 2001 I, Tg, 2002 E, It, I, F, W (R), C, US, 2003 I 1, F, W 1, E, It 1, SA 1,2, W 2, I 2, [US,F,Fj,A]
Metcalfe, R (Northampton, Edinburgh) 2000 E, NZ 1,2, US (R), A (R), Sm, 2001 F, W, E
Methuen, A (London Scottish) 1889 W, I
Michie, E J S (Aberdeen U, Aberdeen GSFP) 1954 F, NZ, I, E, 1955 W, I, E, 1956 F, W, I, E, 1957 F, W, I, E
Millar, J N (W of Scotland) 1892 W, I, E, 1893 W, 1895 I, E
Millar, R K (London Scottish) 1924 I
Millican, J G (Edinburgh U) 1973 W, I, E
Milne, C J B (Fettesian-Lorettonians, W of Scotland) 1886 W, I, E
Milne, D F (Heriot's FP) 1991 [J(R)]
Milne, I G (Heriot's FP, Harlequins) 1979 I, F, NZ, 1980 I, F, 1981 NZ 1,2, R, A, 1982 E, I, F, W, A 1,2, 1983 I, F, W, E, NZ, 1984 W, E, I, F, A, 1985 F, W, E, 1986 F, W, E, I, R, 1987 I, F, W, E, [F, Z, NZ], 1988 A, 1989 W, 1990 NZ 1,2
Milne, K S (Heriot's FP) 1989 W, E, I, F, Fj, R, 1990 I, F, W, E, NZ 2, Arg, 1991 F, W (R), E, [Z], 1992 E, I, F, W, A 1, 1993 I, F, W, E, NZ, 1994 W, E, I, F, SA, 1995 C, I, F, W, E, [Tg, F, NZ]
Milne, W M (Glasgow Acads) 1904 I, E, 1905 W, I
Milroy, E (Watsonians) 1910 W, 1911 E, 1912 W, I, E, SA, 1913 F, W, I, E, 1914 I, E
Mitchell, G W E (Edinburgh Wands) 1967 NZ, 1968 F, W
Mitchell, J G (W of Scotland) 1885 W, I 1,2
Moffat, J S D (Edinburgh, Borders) 2002 R, SA, Fj(R), 2004 A3
Moir, C C (Northampton) 2000 W, E, NZ 1
Moncreiff, F J (Edinburgh Acads) 1871 E, 1872 E, 1873 E
Monteith, H G (Cambridge U, London Scottish) 1905 E, 1906 W, I, E, SA, 1907 W, I, 1908 E
Monypenny, D B (London Scottish) 1899 I, W, E
Moodie, A R (St Andrew's U) 1909 E, 1910 F, 1911 F
Moore, A (Edinburgh Acads) 1990 NZ 2, Arg, 1991 F, W, E
Morgan, D W (Stewart's-Melville FP) 1973 W, I, E, P, 1974 I, F, 1975 I, F, W, E, NZ, A, 1976 F, W, 1977 I, F, W, 1978 I, F, W, E

Morrison, G A (Glasgow) 2004 A1(R),2(R),3,J(R),A4(R),SA(R)
Morrison, I R (London Scottish) 1993 I, F, W, E, 1994 W, SA, 1995 C, I, F, W, E, R, [Tg, F, NZ]
Morrison, M C (Royal HSFP) 1896 W, I, E, 1897 I, E, 1898 I, E, 1899 I, W, E, 1900 W, E, 1901 W, I, E, 1902 W, I, E, 1903 W, I, 1904 W, I, E
Morrison, R H (Edinburgh U) 1886 W, I, E
Morrison, W H (Edinburgh Acads) 1900 W
Morton, D S (W of Scotland) 1887 I, W, E, 1888 W, I, 1889 W, I, 1890 I, E
Mowat, J G (Glasgow Acads) 1883 W, E
Mower, A L (Newcastle) 2001 Tg, Arg, NZ, 2002 It, 2003 I 1, F, W 1, E, It 1, SA 1,2, W 2, I 2
Muir, D E (Heriot's FP) 1950 F, W, I, E, 1952 W, I, E
Munnoch, N M (Watsonians) 1952 F, W, I
Munro, D S (Glasgow High Kelvinside) 1994 W, E, I, F, Arg 1,2, 1997 W (R)
Munro, P (Oxford U, London Scottish) 1905 W, I, E, NZ, 1906 W, I, E, SA, 1907 I, E, 1911 F, W, I
Munro, R (St Andrew's U) 1871 E
Munro, S (Ayr, W of Scotland) 1980 I, F, 1981 F, W, E, I, NZ 1,2, R, 1984 W
Munro, W H (Glasgow HSFP) 1947 I, E
Murdoch, W C W (Hillhead HSFP) 1935 E, NZ, 1936 W, I, 1939 E, 1948 F, W, I, E
Murray, C A (Hawick, Edinburgh) 1998 E (R), Fj, A 1,2, SA, 1999 W, E, It, I, F, Arg, [SA, U, Sp, Sm, NZ], 2000 NZ 2, US, A, Sm, 2001 F, W, E, It (R), Tg, Arg
Murray, E A (Glasgow, Northampton) 2005 R(R), 2006 R,PI,A, 2007 E,W,It,I1,F,I2,SA, [Pt,R,It,Arg]
Murray, G M (Glasgow Acads) 1921 I, 1926 W
Murray, H M (Glasgow U) 1936 W, I
Murray, K T (Hawick) 1985 I, F, W
Murray, R O (Cambridge U) 1935 W, E
Murray, S (Bedford, Saracens, Edinburgh) 1997 A, SA, 1998 It, Fj, A 1,2, SA, 1999 W, E, It, I, F, Arg, R, [SA, U, Sm, NZ], 2000 It, I, F, W, E, NZ 1, US, A, Sm, 2001 F, W, E, It, I, Tg, Arg, NZ, 2002 E, It, I, F, W, R, SA, 2003 I 1, F, W 1, E, It 1, SA 1,2, It 2, W 2, [J,F,A(R)], 2004 W,E,It,F,I,Sm,A1,2, 2005 F,I,It,W,E,R,Arg,Sm,NZ, 2006 F,W,I,It,SA1,R,PI,A, 2007 E(t&R),W,It,I1,F,SA(R),[Pt,NZ]
Murray, W A K (London Scottish) 1920 F, I, 1921 F

Napier, H M (W of Scotland) 1877 I, E, 1878 E, 1879 I, E
Neill, J B (Edinburgh Acads) 1963 E, 1964 F, NZ, W, I, E, 1965 F
Neill, R M (Edinburgh Acads) 1901 E, 1902 I
Neilson, G T (W of Scotland) 1891 W, I, E, 1892 W, E, 1893 W, 1894 W, I, 1895 W, I, E, 1896 W, I, E
Neilson, J A (Glasgow Acads) 1878 E, 1879 E
Neilson, R T (W of Scotland) 1898 I, E, 1899 I, W, 1900 I, E
Neilson, T (W of Scotland) 1874 E
Neilson, W (Merchiston, Cambridge U, London Scottish) 1891 W, E, 1892 W, I, E, 1893 I, E, 1894 E, 1895 W, I, E, 1896 I, 1897 I, E
Neilson, W G (Merchistonians) 1894 E
Nelson, J B (Glasgow Acads) 1925 F, W, I, E, 1926 F, W, I, E, 1927 F, W, I, E, 1928 I, E, 1929 F, W, I, E, 1930 F, W, I, E, 1931 F, W, I
Nelson, T A (Oxford U) 1898 E
Nichol, J A (Royal HSFP) 1955 W, I, E
Nichol, S A (Selkirk) 1994 Arg 2(R)
Nicol, A D (Dundee HSFP, Bath, Glasgow) 1992 E, I, F, W, A 1,2, 1993 NZ, 1994 W, 1997 A, SA, 2000 I (R), F, W, E, NZ 1,2, 2001 F, W, E, I (R), Tg, Arg, NZ
Nimmo, C S (Watsonians) 1920 E

Ogilvy, C (Hawick) 1911 I, E, 1912 I
Oliver, G H (Hawick) 1987 [Z], 1990 NZ 2(R), 1991 [Z]
Oliver, G K (Gala) 1970 A
Orr, C E (W of Scotland) 1887 I, E, W, 1888 W, I, 1889 W, I, 1890 W, I, E, 1891 W, I, E, 1892 W, I, E
Orr, H J (London Scottish) 1903 W, I, E, 1904 W, I
Orr, J E (W of Scotland) 1889 I, 1890 W, I, E, 1891 W, I, E, 1892 W, I, E, 1893 I, E
Orr, J H (Edinburgh City Police) 1947 F, W
Osler, F L (Edinburgh U) 1911 F, W

Park, J (Royal HSFP) 1934 W
Parks, D A (Glasgow) 2004 W(R),E(R),F(R),I, Sm (t&R),A1,2,3,J,A4,SA, 2005 F,I,It, W,R,Arg,Sm,NZ, 2006 F,W,E,I,It(R),SA1,PI,A, 2007 E,I1,F,I2(R),SA(R), [Pt,R,NZ(R), It,Arg]
Paterson, C D (Edinburgh) 1999 [Sp], 2000 F, W, E, NZ 1,2, US, A, Sm, 2001 F, W, E, It, I, NZ, 2002 E, It, I, F, W, C, US, R, SA, Fj, 2003 I 1, F, W 1, E, It 1, SA 1,2, It 2(R), W 2(R), I 2, [J,US,F,Fj,A], 2004 W,E,It,F,I,Sm,A3,J,A4,SA,2005 F,I,It,W,E,R,Arg,Sm,NZ, 2006 F,W,E,I,It,SA 1,2,R(R),PI,A, 2007 E,W,It,I1,F,I2,SA, [Pt(R),R,NZ,It,Arg]
Paterson, D S (Gala) 1969 SA, 1970 I, E, A, 1971 F, W, I, E (2[1C]), 1972 W
Paterson, G Q (Edinburgh Acads) 1876 E
Paterson, J R (Birkenhead Park) 1925 F, W, I, E, 1926 F, W, I, E, 1927 F, W, I, E, A, 1928 F, W, I, E, 1929 F, W, I, E
Patterson, D (Hawick) 1896 W
Patterson, D W (West Hartlepool) 1994 SA, 1995 [Tg]
Pattullo, G L (Panmure) 1920 F, W, I, E
Paxton, I A M (Selkirk) 1981 NZ 1,2, R, A, 1982 E, I, F, W, A 1,2, 1983 I, E, NZ, 1984 W, E, I, F, 1985 I (R), F, W, E, 1986 W, E, I, R, 1987 I, F, W, E, [F, Z, R, NZ], 1988 I, E, A
Paxton, R E (Kelso) 1982 I, A 2(R)
Pearson, J (Watsonians) 1909 I, E, 1910 F, W, I, E, 1911 F, 1912 F, W, SA, 1913 I, E
Pender, I M (London Scottish) 1914 E
Pender, N E K (Hawick) 1977 I, 1978 F, W, E
Penman, W M (RAF) 1939 I
Peterkin, W A (Edinburgh U) 1881 E, 1883 I, 1884 W, I, E, 1885 W, I 1,2
Peters, E W (Bath) 1995 C, I, F, W, E, R, [Tg, F, NZ], 1996 I, F, W, E, NZ 1,2, A, It, 1997 A, SA, 1998 W, E, Fj, A 1,2, SA, 1999 W, E, It, I
Petrie, A G (Royal HSFP) 1873 E, 1874 E, 1875 E, 1876 E, 1877 I, E, 1878 E, 1879 I, E, 1880 I, E
Petrie, J M (Glasgow) 2000 NZ 2, US, A, Sm, 2001 F, W, It (R), I (R), Tg, Arg, 2002 F (t), W (R), C, R(R), Fj, 2003 F(t+R), W 1(R), SA 1(R), 2 (R), It 2, W 2, I 2(R), [J,US,F(t&R),A(R)], 2004 It(R),I(R),Sm(R),A1(R),2(t&R),3(R),J,A4,SA(R), 2005 F,I,It,W,E(R),R, 2006 F(R), W(R),I(R),SA 2
Philip, T K (Edinburgh) 2004 W,E,It,F,I
Philp, A (Edinburgh Inst FP) 1882 E
Pinder, S J (Glasgow) 2006 SA 1(R),2(R)
Pocock, E I (Edinburgh Wands) 1877 I, E
Pollock, J A (Gosforth) 1982 W, 1983 E, NZ, 1984 E (R), I, F, R, 1985 F
Polson, A H (Gala) 1930 E
Pountney, A C (Northhampton) 1998 SA, 1999 W (t+R), E (R), It (t+R), I (R), F, Arg, [SA, U, Sm, NZ], 2000 It, I, F, W, E, US,A, Sm, 2001 F, W, E, It, I, 2002 E, I, F, W, R, SA, Fj
Proudfoot, M C (Melrose, Glasgow) 1998 Fj, A 1,2, 2003 I 2(R)
Purdie, W (Jedforest) 1939 W, I, E
Purves, A B H L (London Scottish) 1906 W, I, E, SA, 1907 W, I, E, 1908 W, I, E
Purves, W D C L (London Scottish) 1912 F, W, I, SA, 1913 I, E

Rea, C W W (W of Scotland, Headingley) 1968 A, 1969 F, W, I, SA, 1970 F, W, I, A, 1971 F, W, E (2[1C])
Redpath, B W (Melrose, Narbonne, Sale) 1993 NZ (t), 1994 E (t), F, Arg 1,2, 1995 C, I, F, W, E, R, [Iv, F, NZ], WS, 1996 I, F, W, E. A (R), It, 1997 E, I, F, 1998 Fj, A 1,2, SA, 1999 R (R), [U (R), Sp], 2000 It, I, US, A, Sm, 2001 F (R), E (R), It, I, 2002 E, It, I, F, W, R, SA, Fj, 2003 I 1, F, W 1, E, It 1, SA 1,2, [J,US(R),F,Fj,A]
Reed, A I (Bath, Wasps) 1993 I, F, W, E, 1994 E, I, F, Arg 1,2, SA, 1996 It, 1997 W, E, I, F, 1999 It (R), F (R), [Sp]
Reid, C (Edinburgh Acads) 1881 I, E, 1882 I, E, 1883 W, I, E, 1884 W, I, E, 1885 W, I 1,2, 1886 W, I, E, 1887 I, W, E, 1888 W, I
Reid, J (Edinburgh Wands) 1874 E, 1875 E, 1876 E, 1877 I, E
Reid, J M (Edinburgh Acads) 1898 I, E, 1899 I
Reid, M F (Loretto) 1883 I, E
Reid, R E (Glasgow) 2001 Tg (R), Arg
Reid, S J (Boroughmuir, Leeds, Narbonne) 1995 WS, 1999 F, Arg, [Sp], 2000 It (t), F, W, E (t)
Reid-Kerr, J (Greenock Wand) 1909 E
Relph, W K L (Stewart's Coll FP) 1955 F, W, I, E
Renny-Tailyour, H W (Royal Engineers) 1872 E
Renwick, J M (Hawick) 1972 F, W, E, NZ, 1973 F, 1974 W, E, I, F, 1975 I, F, W, E, NZ, A, 1976 F, W, E (R), 1977 I, F, W,

1978 I, F, W, E, NZ, 1979 W, E, I, F, NZ, 1980 I, F, W, E, 1981 F, W, E, I, NZ 1,2, R, A, 1982 E, I, F, W, 1983 I, F, W, E, 1984 R
Renwick, W L (London Scottish) 1989 R
Renwick, W N (London Scottish, Edinburgh Wands) 1938 E, 1939 W
Richardson, J F (Edinburgh Acads) 1994 SA
Ritchie, G (Merchistonians) 1871 E
Ritchie, G F (Dundee HSFP) 1932 E
Ritchie, J M (Watsonians) 1933 W, E, I, 1934 W, I, E
Ritchie, W T (Cambridge U) 1905 I, E
Robb, G H (Glasgow U) 1881 I, 1885 W
Roberts, G (Watsonians) 1938 W, I, E, 1939 W, E
Robertson, A H (W of Scotland) 1871 E
Robertson, A W (Edinburgh Acads) 1897 E
Robertson, D (Edinburgh Acads) 1875 E
Robertson, D D (Cambridge U) 1893 W
Robertson, I (London Scottish, Watsonians) 1968 E, 1969 E, SA, 1970 F, W, I, E, A
Robertson, I P M (Watsonians) 1910 F
Robertson, J (Clydesdale) 1908 E
Robertson, K W (Melrose) 1978 NZ, 1979 W, E, I, F, NZ, 1980 W, E, 1981 F, W, E, I, R, A, 1982 E, I, F, A 1,2, 1983 I, F, W, E, 1984 E, I, F, R, A, 1985 I, F, W, E, 1986 I, 1987 F (R), W, E, [F, Z, NZ], 1988 E, A, 1989 E, I, F
Robertson, L (London Scottish United Services) 1908 E, 1911 W, 1912 W, I, E, SA, 1913 W, I, E
Robertson, M A (Gala) 1958 F
Robertson, R D (London Scottish) 1912 F
Robson, A (Hawick) 1954 F, 1955 F, W, I, E, 1956 F, W, I, E, 1957 F, W, I, E, 1958 W, A, I, E, 1959 F, W, I, E, 1960 F
Rodd, J A T (United Services, RN, London Scottish) 1958 F, W, A, I, E, 1960 F, W, 1962 F, 1964 F, NZ, W, 1965 F, W, I
Rogerson, J (Kelvinside Acads) 1894 W
Roland, E T (Edinburgh Acads) 1884 I, E
Rollo, D M D (Howe of Fife) 1959 E, 1960 F, W, I, E, SA, 1961 F, SA, W, I, E, 1962 F, W, E, 1963 F, W, I, E, 1964 F, NZ, W, I, E, 1965 F, W, I, E, SA, 1966 F, W, I, E, A, 1967 F, W, E, NZ, 1968 F, W, I
Rose, D M (Jedforest) 1951 F, W, I, E, SA, 1953 F, W
Ross, A (Kilmarnock) 1924 F, W
Ross, A (Royal HSFP) 1905 W, I, E, 1909 W, I
Ross, A R (Edinburgh U) 1911 W, 1914 W, I, E
Ross, E J (London Scottish) 1904 W
Ross, G (Edinburgh, Leeds) 2001 Tg, 2002 R, SA, Fj(R), 2003 I 1, W 1(R), SA 2(R), It 2, I 2, [J], 2004 Sm,A1(R), 2(R),J(R), SA(R),2005 It(R),W(R),E, 2006 F(R),W(R),E(R),I(R),It, SA 1(R),2
Ross, G T (Watsonians) 1954 NZ, I, E, W
Ross, I A (Hillhead HSFP) 1951 F, W, I, E
Ross, J (London Scottish) 1901 W, I, E, 1902 W, 1903 E
Ross, K I (Boroughmuir FP) 1961 SA, W, I, E, 1962 F, W, I, E, 1963 F, W, E
Ross, W A (Hillhead HSFP) 1937 W, E
Rottenburg, H (Cambridge U, London Scottish) 1899 W, E, 1900 W, I, E
Roughead, W N (Edinburgh Acads, London Scottish) 1927 A, 1928 F, W, I, E, 1930 I, E, 1931 F, W, I, E, 1932 W
Rowan, N A (Boroughmuir) 1980 W, E, 1981 F, W, E, I, 1984 R, 1985 I, 1987 [R], 1988 I, F, W, E
Rowand, R (Glasgow HSFP) 1930 F, W, 1932 E, 1933 W, E, I, 1934 W
Roxburgh, A J (Kelso) 1997 A, 1998 It, F (R), W, E, Fj, A 1(R),2(R)
Roy, A (Waterloo) 1938 W, I, E, 1939 W, I, E
Russell, R R (Saracens, London Irish) 1999 R, [U (R), Sp, Sm (R), NZ (R)], 2000 I (R), 2001 F (R), 2002 F (R), W (R), 2003 W 1(R), It 1(R), SA 1 (R), 2 (R), It 2, I 2(R), [J,F(R),Fj(t),A(R)] , 2004 W(R),E(R),F(R),I(R),J(R),A4(R),SA(R), 2005 It(R)
Russell, W L (Glasgow Acads) 1905 NZ, 1906 W, I, E
Rutherford, J Y (Selkirk) 1979 W, E, I, F, NZ, 1980 I, F, E, 1981 F, W, E, I, NZ 1,2, A, 1982 E, I, F, W, A 1,2, 1983 E, NZ, 1984 W, E, I, F, R, 1985 I, F, W, E, 1986 F, W, E, I, R, 1987 I, F, W, E, [F]

Sampson, R W F (London Scottish) 1939 W, 1947 W
Sanderson, G A (Royal HSFP) 1907 W, I, E, 1908 I
Sanderson, J L P (Edinburgh Acads) 1873 E
Schulze, D G (London Scottish) 1905 E, 1907 I, E, 1908 W, I, E, 1909 W, I, E, 1910 W, I, E, 1911 W
Scobie, R M (Royal Military Coll) 1914 W, I, E
Scotland, K J F (Heriot's FP, Cambridge U, Leicester) 1957 F, W, I, E, 1958 E, 1959 F, W, I, E, 1960 F, W, I, E, 1961 F, SA, W, I, E, 1962 F, W, I, E, 1963 F, W, I, E, 1965 F
Scott, D M (Langholm, Watsonians) 1950 I, E, 1951 W, I, E, SA, 1952 F, W, I, 1953 F
Scott, J M B (Edinburgh Acads) 1907 E, 1908 W, I, E, 1909 W, I, E, 1910 F, W, I, E, 1911 F, W, I, 1912 W, I, E, SA, 1913 W, I, E
Scott, J S (St Andrew's U) 1950 E
Scott, J W (Stewart's Coll FP) 1925 F, W, I, E, 1926 F, W, I, E, 1927 F, W, I, E, A, 1928 F, W, E, 1929 E, 1930 F
Scott, M (Dunfermline) 1992 A 2
Scott, R (Hawick) 1898 I, 1900 I, E
Scott, S (Edinburgh, Borders) 2000 NZ 2 (R), US (t+R), 2001 It (R), I (R), Tg (R), NZ (R), 2002 US (R), R(R), Fj(R), 2004 Sm(R), A1(R)
Scott, T (Langholm, Hawick) 1896 W, 1897 I, E, 1898 I, E, 1899 I, W, E, 1900 W, I, E
Scott, T M (Hawick) 1893 E, 1895 W, I, E, 1896 W, E, 1897 I, E, 1898 I, E, 1900 W, I
Scott, W P (W of Scotland) 1900 I, E, 1902 I, E, 1903 W, I, E, 1904 W, I, E, 1905 W, I, E, NZ, 1906 W, I, E, SA, 1907 W, I, E
Scoular, J G (Cambridge U) 1905 NZ, 1906 W, I, E, SA
Selby, J A R (Watsonians) 1920 W, I
Shackleton, J A P (London Scottish) 1959 E, 1963 F, W, 1964 NZ, W, 1965 I, SA
Sharp, A V (Bristol) 1994 E, I, F, Arg 1,2 SA
Sharp, G (Stewart's FP, Army) 1960 F, 1964 F, NZ, W
Shaw, G D (Sale) 1935 NZ, 1936 W, 1937 W, I, E, 1939 I
Shaw, I (Glasgow HSFP) 1937 I
Shaw, J N (Edinburgh Acads) 1921 W, I
Shaw, R W (Glasgow HSFP) 1934 W, I, E, 1935 W, I, E, NZ, 1936 W, I, E, 1937 W, I, E, 1938 W, I, E, 1939 W, I, E
Shedden, D (W of Scotland) 1972 NZ, 1973 F, W, I, E, P, 1976 W, E, I, 1977 I, F, W, 1978 I, F, W
Shepherd, R J S (Melrose) 1995 WS, 1996 I, F, W, E, NZ 1,2, A, It, 1997 W, E, I, F, SA, 1998 It, I, W (R), Fj (t), A 1,2
Shiel, A G (Melrose, Edinburgh) 1991 [I (R), WS], 1993 I, F, W, E, NZ, 1994 Arg 1,2, SA, 1995 R, [Iv, F, NZ], WS, 2000 I, NZ 1(R),2
Shillinglaw, R B (Gala, Army) 1960 I, E, SA, 1961 F, SA
Simmers, B M (Glasgow Acads) 1965 F, W, 1966 A, 1967 F, W, I, 1971 F (R)
Simmers, W M (Glasgow Acads) 1926 W, I, E, 1927 F, W, I, E, A, 1928 F, W, I, E, 1929 F, W, I, E, 1930 F, W, I, E, 1931 F, W, I, E, 1932 SA, W, I, E
Simpson, G L (Kirkcaldy, Glasgow) 1998 A 1,2, 1999 Arg (R), R, [SA, U, Sm, NZ], 2000 It, I, NZ 1(R), 2001 I, Tg (R), Arg (R), NZ
Simpson, J W (Royal HSFP) 1893 I, E, 1894 W, I, E, 1895 W, I, E, 1896 W, I, 1897 E, 1899 W, E
Simpson, R S (Glasgow Acads) 1923 I
Simson, E D (Edinburgh U, London Scottish) 1902 E, 1903 W, I, E, 1904 W, I, E, 1905 W, I, E, NZ, 1906 W, I, E, 1907 W, I, E
Simson, J T (Watsonians) 1905 NZ, 1909 W, I, E, 1910 F, W, 1911 I
Simson, R F (London Scottish) 1911 E
Sloan, A T (Edinburgh Acads) 1914 W, 1920 F, W, I, E, 1921 F, W, I, E
Sloan, D A (Edinburgh Acads, London Scottish) 1950 F, W, E, 1951 W, I, E, 1953 F
Sloan, T (Glasgow Acads, Oxford U) 1905 NZ, 1906 W, SA, 1907 W, E, 1908 W, 1909 I
Smeaton, P W (Edinburgh Acads) 1881 I, 1883 I, E
Smith, A R (Oxford U) 1895 W, I, E, 1896 W, I, 1897 I, E, 1898 I, E, 1900 I, E
Smith, A R (Cambridge U, Gosforth, Ebbw Vale, Edinburgh Wands) 1955 W, I, E, 1956 F, W, I, E, 1957 F, W, I, E, 1958 F, W, A, I, 1959 F, W, I, E, 1960 F, W, I, E, SA, 1961 F, SA, W, I, E, 1962 F, W, I, E
Smith, C J (Edinburgh) 2002 C, US (R), 2004 Sm(t&R),A1(R),2(R),3(R),J(R), 2005 Arg(R),Sm,NZ(R), 2006 F(R),W(R),E(R), I(R),It(R),SA 1(R),2,R(R), 2007 I2(R), [R(R),NZ,It(R),Arg(R)]
Smith, D W C (London Scottish) 1949 F, W, I, E, 1950 F, W, I, 1953 I

Smith, E R (Edinburgh Acads) 1879 I
Smith, G K (Kelso) 1957 I, E, 1958 F, W, A, 1959 F, W, I, E, 1960 F, W, I, E, 1961 F, SA, W, I, E
Smith, H O (Watsonians) 1895 W, 1896 W, I, E, 1898 I, E, 1899 W, I, E, 1900 E, 1902 E
Smith, I R (Gloucester, Moseley) 1992 E, I, W, A 1,2, 1994 E (R), I, F, Arg 1,2, 1995 [Iv], WS, 1996 I, F, W, E, NZ 1,2, A, It, 1997 E, I, F, A, SA
Smith, I S (Oxford U, Edinburgh U) 1924 W, I, E, 1925 F, W, I, E, 1926 F, W, I, E, 1927 F, I, E, 1929 F, W, I, E, 1930 F, W, I, 1931 F, W, I, E, 1932 SA, W, I, E, 1933 W, E, I
Smith I S G (London Scottish) 1969 SA, 1970 F, W, I, E, 1971 F, W, I
Smith, M A (London Scottish) 1970 W, I, E, A
Smith, R T (Kelso) 1929 F, W, I, E, 1930 F, W, I
Smith, S H (Glasgow Acads) 1877 I, 1878 E
Smith, T J (Gala) 1983 E, NZ, 1985 I, F
Smith T J (Watsonians, Dundee HSFP, Glasgow, Brive, Northampton) 1997 E, I, F, 1998 SA, 1999 W, E, It, I, Arg, R, [SA, U, Sm, NZ], 2000 It, I, F, W, E, NZ 1,2, US, A, Sm, 2001 F, W, E, It, I, Tg, Arg, NZ, 2002 E, It, I, F, W, R, SA, Fj, 2003 I 1, F, W 1, E, It 1,2, [J,US,F,Fj,A], 2004 W,E,Sm,A1,2,2005 F,I,It,W,E
Sole, D M B (Bath, Edinburgh Acads) 1986 F, W, 1987 I, F, W, E, [F, Z, R, NZ], 1988 I, F, W, E, A, 1989 W, E, I, F, Fj, R, 1990 I, F, W, E, NZ 1,2, Arg, 1991 F, W, E, I, R, [J, I, WS, E, NZ], 1992 E, I, F, W, A 1,2
Somerville, D (Edinburgh Inst FP) 1879 I, 1882 I, 1883 W, I, E, 1884 W
Southwell, H F G (Edinburgh) 2004 Sm(t&R),A1,2,3(R), J,A4,SA,2005 F,I,It,W,E,R(R),Arg(R),Sm(R),NZ, 2006 F,W,E,I,It, SA 1,2, 2006 R,PI(t&R),A(R), 2007 E,W,It,I1,SA(R), [Pt(R),R(R), NZ,It(R),Arg(R)]
Speirs, L M (Watsonians) 1906 SA, 1907 W, I, E, 1908 W, I, E, 1910 F, W, E
Spence, K M (Oxford U) 1953 I
Spencer, E (Clydesdale) 1898 I
Stagg, P K (Sale) 1965 F, W, E, SA, 1966 F, W, I, E, A, 1967 F, W, I, E, NZ, 1968 F, W, I, E, A, 1969 F, W, I (R), SA, 1970 F, W, I, E, A
Stanger, A G (Hawick) 1989 Fj, R, 1990 I, F, W, E, NZ 1,2, Arg, 1991 F, W, E, I, R, [J, Z, I, WS, E, NZ], 1992 E, I, F, W, A 1,2, 1993 I, F, W, E, NZ, 1994 W, E, I, F, SA, 1995 R, [Iv], 1996 NZ 2, A, It, 1997 W, E, I, F, A, SA, 1998 It, I (R), F, W, E
Stark, D A (Boroughmuir, Melrose, Glasgow Hawks) 1993 I, F, W, E, 1996 NZ 2(R), It (R), 1997 W (R), E, SA
Steel, J F (Glasgow) 2000 US, A, 2001 I, Tg, NZ
Steele, W C C (Langholm, Bedford, RAF, London Scottish) 1969 E, 1971 F, W, I, E (2[1C]), 1972 F, W, E, NZ, 1973 F, W, I, E, 1975 I, F, W, E, NZ (R), 1976 W, E, I, 1977 E
Stephen, A E (W of Scotland) 1885 W, 1886 I
Steven, P D (Heriot's FP) 1984 A, 1985 F, W, E
Steven, R (Edinburgh Wands) 1962 I
Stevenson, A K (Glasgow Acads) 1922 F, 1923 F, W, E
Stevenson, A M (Glasgow U) 1911 F
Stevenson, G D (Hawick) 1956 E, 1957 F, 1958 F, W, A, I, E, 1959 W, I, E, 1960 W, I, E, SA, 1961 F, SA, W, I, E, 1963 F, W, I, 1964 E, 1965 F
Stevenson, H J (Edinburgh Acads) 1888 W, I, 1889 W, I, 1890 W, I, E, 1891 W, I, E, 1892 W, I, E, 1893 I, E
Stevenson, L E (Edinburgh U) 1888 W
Stevenson, R C (London Scottish) 1897 I, E, 1898 E, 1899 I, W, E
Stevenson, R C (St Andrew's U) 1910 F, I, E, 1911 F, W, I
Stevenson, W H (Glasgow Acads) 1925 F
Stewart, A K (Edinburgh U) 1874 E, 1876 E
Stewart, A M (Edinburgh Acads) 1914 W
Stewart, B D (Edinburgh Acads, Edinburgh) 1996 NZ 2, A, 2000 NZ 1,2
Stewart, C A R (W of Scotland) 1880 I, E
Stewart, C E B (Kelso) 1960 W, 1961 F
Stewart, J (Glasgow HSFP) 1930 F
Stewart, J L (Edinburgh Acads) 1921 I
Stewart M J (Northampton) 1996 It, 1997 W, E, I, F, A, SA, 1998 It, I, F, W, Fj (R), 2000 It, I, F, W, E, NZ 1(R), 2001 F, W, E, It, I, Tg, Arg, NZ, 2002 E, It, I, F, W, C, US, R(R)
Stewart, M S (Stewart's Coll FP) 1932 SA, W, I, 1933 W, E, I, 1934 W, I, E
Stewart, W A (London Hospital) 1913 F, W, I, 1914 W
Steyn, S S L (Oxford U) 1911 E, 1912 I
Strachan, G M (Jordanhill) 1971 E (C) (R), 1973 W, I, E, P
Strokosch, A K (Edinburgh) 2006 A(R)
Stronach, R S (Glasgow Acads) 1901 W, E, 1905 W, I, E
Stuart, C D (W of Scotland) 1909 I, 1910 F, W, I, E, 1911 I, E
Stuart, L M (Glasgow HSFP) 1923 F, W, I, E, 1924 F, 1928 E, 1930 I, E
Suddon, N (Hawick) 1965 W, I, E, SA, 1966 A, 1968 E, A, 1969 F, W, I, 1970 I, E, A
Sutherland, W R (Hawick) 1910 W, E, 1911 F, E, 1912 F, W, E, SA, 1913 F, W, I, E, 1914 W
Swan, J S (Army, London Scottish, Leicester) 1953 E, 1954 F, NZ, I, E, W, 1955 F, W, I, E, 1956 F, W, I, E, 1957 F, W, 1958 F
Swan, M W (Oxford U, London Scottish) 1958 F, W, A, I, E, 1959 F, W, I
Sweet, J B (Glasgow HSFP) 1913 E, 1914 I
Symington, A W (Cambridge U) 1914 W, E

Tait, A V (Kelso, Newcastle, Edinburgh) 1987 [F(R), Z, R, NZ], 1988 I, F, W, E, 1997 I, F, A, 1998 It, I, F, W, E, SA, 1999 W (R), E, It, I, F, Arg, R, [A, U, NZ]
Tait, J G (Edinburgh Acads) 1880 I, 1885 I 2
Tait, P W (Royal HSFP) 1935 E
Taylor, E G (Oxford U) 1927 W, A
Taylor, R C (Kelvinside-West) 1951 W, I, E, SA
Taylor, S M (Edinburgh, Stade Français) 2000 US, A, 2001 E, It, I, NZ (R), 2002 E, It, I, F, W, C, US, R, SA, Fj, 2003 I 1, F, W 1, E, It 1, SA 1,2, It 2, I 2, [J,US,F,Fj,A], 2004 W,E,It,F,I, 2005 It,W,E,Arg,Sm,NZ, 2006 F,W,E,I,It,PI,A, 2007 E,W,It,I1,F,I2, [Pt,R,It,Arg]
Telfer, C M (Hawick) 1968 A, 1969 F, W, I, E, 1972 F, W, E, 1973 W, I, E, P, 1974 W, E, I, 1975 A, 1976 F
Telfer, J W (Melrose) 1964 F, NZ, W, I, E, 1965 F, W, I, 1966 F, W, I, E, 1967 W, I, E, 1968 E, A, 1969 F, W, I, E, SA, 1970 F, W, I
Tennent, J M (W of Scotland) 1909 W, I, E, 1910 F, W, E
Thom, D A (London Scottish) 1934 W, 1935 W, I, E, NZ
Thom, G (Kirkcaldy) 1920 F, W, I, E
Thom, J R (Watsonians) 1933 W, E, I
Thomson, A E (United Services) 1921 F, W, E
Thomson, A M (St Andrew's U) 1949 I
Thomson, B E (Oxford U) 1953 F, W, I
Thomson, F M A (Glasgow) 2007 I2(t&R),SA(R), [NZ(R)]
Thomson, I H M (Heriot's FP, Army) 1951 W, I, 1952 F, W, I, 1953 I, E
Thomson, J S (Glasgow Acads) 1871 E
Thomson, R H (London Scottish, PUC) 1960 I, E, SA, 1961 F, SA, W, I, E, 1963 F, W, I, E, 1964 F, NZ, W
Thomson, W H (W of Scotland) 1906 SA
Thomson, W J (W of Scotland) 1899 W, E, 1900 W
Timms, A B (Edinburgh U, Edinburgh Wands) 1896 W, 1900 W, I, 1901 W, I, E, 1902 W, E, 1903 W, E, 1904 I, E, 1905 I, E
Tod, H B (Gala) 1911 F
Tod, J (Watsonians) 1884 W, I, E, 1885 W, I 1,2, 1886 W, I, E
Todd, J K (Glasgow Acads) 1874 E, 1875 E
Tolmie, J M (Glasgow HSFP) 1922 E
Tomes, A J (Hawick) 1976 E, I, 1977 E, 1978 I, F, W, E, NZ, 1979 W, E, I, F, NZ, 1980 F, W, E, 1981 F, W, E, I, NZ 1,2, R, A, 1982 E, I, F, W, A 1,2, 1983 I, F, W, 1984 W, E, I, F, R, A, 1985 W, E, 1987 I, F, E (R), [F, Z, R, NZ]
Torrie, T J (Edinburgh Acads) 1877 E
Townsend, G P J (Gala, Northampton, Brive, Castres, Borders) 1993 E (R), 1994 W, E, I, F, Arg 1,2, 1995 C, I, F, W, E, WS, 1996 I, F, W, E, NZ 1,2, A, It, 1997 W, E, I, F, A, SA, 1998 It, I, F, W, E, Fj, A 1,2, SA (R), 1999 W, E, It, I, F, [SA, U, Sp (R), Sm, NZ], 2000 It, I, F, W, E, NZ 1,2, US, A, Sm, 2001 F, It, I, Arg, NZ, 2002 E, It, I, F, W, R(R), SA(R), Fj, 2003 I 1(R), F, W 1, E, It 1, SA 1,2, W 2, [J(R),US,F,Fj,A]
Tukalo, I (Selkirk) 1985 I, 1987 I, F, W, E, [F, Z, R, NZ], 1988 F, W, E, A, 1989 W, E, I, F, Fj, 1990 I, F, W, E, NZ 1, 1991 I, R, [J, Z, I, WS, E, NZ], 1992 E, I, F, W, A 1,2
Turk, A S (Langholm) 1971 E (R)
Turnbull, D J (Hawick) 1987 [NZ], 1988 F, E, 1990 E (R), 1991 F, W, E, I, R, [Z], 1993 I, F, W, E, 1994 W
Turnbull, F O (Kelso) 1951 F, SA
Turnbull, G O (W of Scotland) 1896 I, E, 1897 I, E, 1904 W
Turnbull, P (Edinburgh Acads) 1901 W, I, E, 1902 W, I, E
Turner, F H (Oxford U, Liverpool) 1911 F, W, I, E, 1912 F, W, I, E, SA, 1913 F, W, I, E, 1914 I, E

Turner, J W C (Gala) 1966 W, A, 1967 F, W, I, E, NZ, 1968 F, W, I, E, A, 1969 F, 1970 E, A, 1971 F, W, I, E (2[1C])

Usher, C M (United Services, Edinburgh Wands) 1912 E, 1913 F, W, I, E, 1914 E, 1920 F, W, I, E, 1921 W, E, 1922 F, W, I, E
Utterson, K N (Borders) 2003 F, W 1, E(R)

Valentine, A R (RNAS, Anthorn) 1953 F, W, I
Valentine, D D (Hawick) 1947 I, E
Veitch, J P (Royal HSFP) 1882 E, 1883 I, 1884 W, I, E, 1885 I 1,2, 1886 E
Villar, C (Edinburgh Wands) 1876 E, 1877 I, E

Waddell, G H (London Scottish, Cambridge U) 1957 E, 1958 F, W, A, I, E, 1959 F, W, I, E, 1960 I, E, SA, 1961 F, 1962 F, W, I, E
Waddell, H (Glasgow Acads) 1924 F, W, I, E, 1925 I, E, 1926 F, W, I, E, 1927 F, W, I, E, 1930 W
Wade, A L (London Scottish) 1908 E
Wainwright, R I (Edinburgh Acads, West Hartlepool, Watsonians, Army, Dundee HSFP) 1992 I (R), F, A 1,2, 1993 NZ, 1994 W, E, 1995 C, I, F, W, E, R, [Iv, Tg, F, NZ], WS, 1996 I, F, W, E, NZ 1,2, 1997 W, E, I, F, SA, 1998 It, I, F, W, E, Fj, A 1,2
Walker, A (W of Scotland) 1881 I, 1882 E, 1883 W, I, E
Walker, A W (Cambridge U, Birkenhead Park) 1931 F, W, I, E, 1932 I
Walker, J G (W of Scotland) 1882 E, 1883 W
Walker, M (Oxford U) 1952 F
Walker, N (Borders, Ospreys) 2002 R, SA, Fj, 2007 W(R),It(R),F,I2(R),SA, [R(R),NZ]
Wallace, A C (Oxford U) 1923 F, 1924 F, W, E, 1925 F, W, I, E, 1926 F
Wallace, W M (Cambridge U) 1913 E, 1914 W, I, E
Wallace, M I (Glasgow High Kelvinside) 1996 A, It, 1997 W
Walls, W A (Glasgow Acads) 1882 E, 1883 W, I, E, 1884 W, I, E, 1886 W, I, E
Walter, M W (London Scottish) 1906 I, E, SA, 1907 W, I, 1908 W, I, 1910 I
Walton, P (Northampton, Newcastle) 1994 E, I, F, Arg 1,2, 1995 [Iv], 1997 W, E, I, F, SA (R), 1998 I, F, SA, 1999 W, E, It, I, F (R), Arg, R, [SA (R), U (R), Sp]
Warren, J R (Glasgow Acads) 1914 I
Warren, R C (Glasgow Acads) 1922 W, I, 1930 W, I, E
Waters, F H (Cambridge U, London Scottish) 1930 F, W, I, E, 1932 SA, W, I
Waters, J A (Selkirk) 1933 W, E, I, 1934 W, I, E, 1935 W, I, E, NZ, 1936 W, I, E, 1937 W, I, E
Waters, J B (Cambridge U) 1904 I, E
Watherston, J G (Edinburgh Wands) 1934 I, E
Watherston, W R A (London Scottish) 1963 F, W, I
Watson, D H (Glasgow Acads) 1876 E, 1877 I, E
Watson, W S (Boroughmuir) 1974 W, E, I, F, 1975 NZ, 1977 I, F, W, 1979 I, F
Watt, A G J (Glasgow High Kelvinside) 1991 [Z], 1993 I, NZ, 1994 Arg 2(t & R)
Watt, A G M (Edinburgh Acads) 1947 F, W, I, A, 1948 F, W
Weatherstone, T G (Stewart's Coll FP) 1952 E, 1953 I, E, 1954 F, NZ, I, E, W, 1955 F, 1958 W, A, I, E, 1959 W, I, E
Webster, S L (Edinburgh) 2003 I 2(R), 2004 W(R),E,It, F,I,Sm,A1,2, 2005 It,NZ(R), 2006 F(R), W(R), E(R), I(R),It(R),SA 1(R),2,R,PI,A, 2007 W(R),I2,SA, [Pt,R,NZ,It,Arg]
Weir, G W (Melrose, Newcastle) 1990 Arg, 1991 R, [J, Z, I, WS, E, NZ], 1992 E, I, F, W, A 1,2, 1993 I, F, W, E, NZ, 1994 W (R), E, I, F, SA, 1995 F (R), W, E, R, [Iv, Tg, F, NZ], WS, 1996 I, F, W, E, NZ 1,2, A, It (R), 1997 W, E, I, F, 1998 It, I, F, W, E, SA, 1999 W, Arg (R), R (R), [SA (R), Sp, Sm, NZ], 2000 It (R), I (R), F
Welsh, R (Watsonians) 1895 W, I, E, 1896 W
Welsh, R B (Hawick) 1967 I, E
Welsh, W B (Hawick) 1927 A, 1928 F, W, I, 1929 I, E, 1930 F, W, I, E, 1931 F, W, I, E, 1932 SA, W, I, E, 1933 W, E, I
Welsh, W H (Edinburgh U) 1900 I, E, 1901 W, I, E, 1902 W, I, E
Wemyss, A (Gala, Edinburgh Wands) 1914 W, I, 1920 F, E, 1922 F, W, I
West, L (Edinburgh U, West Hartlepool) 1903 W, I, E, 1905 I, E, NZ, 1906 W, I, E
Weston, V G (Kelvinside Acads) 1936 I, E
White, D B (Gala, London Scottish) 1982 F, W, A 1,2, 1987 W, E, [F, R, NZ], 1988 I, F, W, E, A, 1989 W, E, I, F, Fj, R, 1990 I, F, W, E, NZ 1,2, 1991 F, W, E, I, R, [J, Z, I, WS, E, NZ], 1992 E, I, F, W
White, D M (Kelvinside Acads) 1963 F, W, I, E
White, J P R (Glasgow, Sale) 2000 E, NZ 1,2, US (R), A (R), Sm, 2001 F (R), I, Tg, Arg, NZ, 2002 E, It, I, F, W, C, US, SA(R), Fj, 2003 F(R), W 1, E, It 1, SA 1,2, It 2, [J,US(R),F,Fj(R),A], 2004 W(R),E,It,F,I,Sm,A1,2,J(R),A4(R),SA,2005 F,I,E,Arg,Sm,NZ, 2006 F,W,E,I,It,SA 1,2,R, 2007 I2,SA, [Pt,R,It,Arg]
White, T B (Edinburgh Acads) 1888 W, I, 1889 W
Whittington, T P (Merchistonians) 1873 E
Whitworth, R J E (London Scottish) 1936 I
Whyte, D J (Edinburgh Wands) 1965 W, I, E, SA, 1966 F, W, I, E, A, 1967 F, W, I, E
Will, J G (Cambridge U) 1912 F, W, I, E, 1914 W, I, E
Wilson, A W (Dunfermline) 1931 F, I, E
Wilson, A W (Glasgow) 2005 R(R)
Wilson, G A (Oxford U) 1949 F, W, E
Wilson, G R (Royal HSFP) 1886 E, 1890 W, I, E, 1891 I
Wilson, J H (Watsonians) 1953 I
Wilson, J S (St Andrew's U) 1931 F, W, I, E, 1932 E
Wilson, J S (United Services, London Scottish) 1908 I, 1909 W
Wilson, R (London Scottish) 1976 E, I, 1977 E, I, F, 1978 I, F, 1981 R, 1983 I
Wilson, R L (Gala) 1951 F, W, I, E, SA, 1953 F, W, E
Wilson, R W (W of Scotland) 1873 E, 1874 E
Wilson, S (Oxford U, London Scottish) 1964 F, NZ, W, I, E, 1965 W, I, E, SA, 1966 F, W, I, A, 1967 F, W, I, E, NZ, 1968 F, W, I, E
Wood, A (Royal HSFP) 1873 E, 1874 E, 1875 E
Wood, G (Gala) 1931 W, I, 1932 W, I, E
Woodburn, J C (Kelvinside Acads) 1892 I
Woodrow, A N (Glasgow Acads) 1887 I, W, E
Wotherspoon, W (W of Scotland) 1891 I, 1892 I, 1893 W, E, 1894 W, I, E
Wright, F A (Edinburgh Acads) 1932 E
Wright, H B (Watsonians) 1894 W
Wright, K M (London Scottish) 1929 F, W, I, E
Wright, P H (Boroughmuir) 1992 A 1,2, 1993 F, W, E, 1994 W, 1995 C, I, F, W, E, R, [Iv, Tg, F, NZ], 1996 W, E, NZ 1
Wright, R W J (Edinburgh Wands) 1973 F
Wright, S T H (Stewart's Coll FP) 1949 E
Wright, T (Hawick) 1947 A
Wyllie, D S (Stewart's-Melville FP) 1984 A, 1985 W (R), E, 1987 I, F, [F, Z, R, NZ], 1989 R, 1991 R, [J (R), Z], 1993 NZ (R), 1994 W (R), E, I, F

Young, A H (Edinburgh Acads) 1874 E
Young, E T (Glasgow Acads) 1914 E
Young, R G (Watsonians) 1970 W
Young, T E B (Durham) 1911 F
Young, W B (Cambridge U, London Scottish) 1937 W, I, E, 1938 W, I, E, 1939 W, I, E, 1948 E

SCOTLAND DOMESTIC 2006–07
BACK FROM THE BRINK

Scottish club rugby produced one of the most exciting title races in recent memory as Currie ended Glasgow Hawks' three-year reign as BT Premiership One champions and became top-flight league winners for the first time in the club's 36-year history.

The Edinburgh outfit, which nearly folded three years ago under the weight of their financial problems, finished a staggering 37 points behind the Hawks in 2005–06 but set the Premiership pace throughout the campaign to defy pre-season predictions and end Glasgow's recent dominance of the competition.

Despite a brief crisis of confidence just as the season reached its climax, Currie secured the title two days before Christmas in their penultimate game against Heriots to ensure the festive period went with a bang.

"There are a whole host of emotions going on, with relief amongst them," said Currie coach and former player Ally Donaldson as his team were confirmed as champions.

"We were under a lot of pressure this season, so obviously there is a lot of satisfaction and pride in these players. We have worked very hard and have played well for about one year now.

"To win something for this club after being there for so long means a lot to me. It means that at least we will have a happy Christmas."

Currie began the campaign in August in fine form while the Hawks looked a shadow of the side that had claimed the title the previous season and it soon became clear it would be Ayr and Watsonians rather than the defending champions who would provide the real challenge.

Donaldson's side began with six straight wins – averaging over 35 points a game – while the Hawks could muster a mere two victories over the same period. Ayr, coached by Craig Redpath, briefly wobbled with three defeats but Watsonians established themselves as genuine contenders with six wins out of seven.

The first sign of any Currie weakness came in October when they travelled to Anniesland to face Glasgow. The Hawks' poor form did not suggest an upset was on the cards but the visitors were caught cold by the fired-up champions, who scored six tries to record a resounding 42–5 win.

The result temporarily dented Currie's confidence and seven days later they suffered their second defeat of the season, losing 32–15 to Heriots at Malleny Park. The Edinburgh club's title charge seemed to be coming off the rails and with Ayr and Cammy Mather's Watsonians both continuing to maintain the pressure, the title race was wide open.

The following week Currie went to Myreside to face Watsonians in a top of the table clash that they had to win and to Donaldson's relief, his side rediscovered their form to record an impressive 22–5 win.

Self-belief restored, Currie embarked on a five match winning streak – including a 51–0 mauling of Dundee HSFP and a 88–17 demolition of Boroughmuir – and although Ayr were also unbeaten over the same period, they were now within touching distance of the title.

December's clash with Ayr at Millbrae would have all but ended the battle but the home side were determined to take the title race to the wire and twice came back from a 10 point deficit to take the match 30–26.

"The lads showed great heart to get a win like that," said Ayr captain Scott Lines. "Now we have to hope that Watsonians and Currie slip up and we have to be ready to pounce."

The following week Lines' hopes were realised. Glasgow completed a double over Currie at Malleny Park while Watsonians went down at Dundee HSFP. In contrast, Ayr sneaked a crucial win at Melrose and the Premiership season remained in the balance.

Currie, however, were not to be denied and two days before Christmas finally confirmed themselves as champions. Donaldson's team played their part by beating Heriot's in a 39–26 thriller at Goldenacre in which they scored five tries for a priceless bonus point but they still had to wait for the result from the later kick-off between Glasgow and Ayr at Old Anniesland before they could begin the celebrations.

When news of the Hawks' 11–8 victory came in, Currie were officially Premiership One champions.

In the BT Cup, however, last season's beaten finalists Currie failed to translate their league form into more silverware and fell in the fifth round to Edinburgh Academical, paving the way for the Accies to face Glasgow Hawks in the final at Murrayfield.

The Premiership Two underdogs were hoping to pull off a major shock but the Hawks were determined to put their disappointing league campaign behind them and tries from John Fitzpatrick and Ally Maclay, plus four penalties an a conversion from Mike Adamson, steered them to a 24–13 win that went some way to salvaging their season.

"This gives us a real platform to start next season with some confidence," said Hawks coach Davie Wilson. "It was a really tough afternoon's work, but I felt we matched them up front and eventually that gave us the opportunity to perform from the back. It was a great performance and everybody played a part."

Elsewhere, the Scottish RFU unveiled a new tournament – the Scottish Hydro Electric Super Cup – featuring the 10 Premiership clubs in a tournament that rugby fans and administrators beyond Scotland watched with avid interest.

The Super Cup was chosen by the IRB as a vehicle to trial new experimental laws designed to make rugby easier to understand, easier to play and to take out the subjectivity from refereeing decisions. Originally trialed at Stellenbosch University in South Africa in 2006, the new laws were particularly focused on speeding up the tackle and post tackle phases of the game.

Watsonians and Boroughmuir battled through to the inaugural final at the Myreside Stadium at the end of March and the nine tries the two sides produced – Watsonians emerging 35–29 winners – certainly suggested the new laws had some effect.

"The game was faster than under the present laws and I think if you were to analyse it, the ball was in play more than would be the average," said Bill Nolan, the chairman of the IRB's Laws Project Group.

"When players saw the opportunity to apply the experimental laws they did so, sometimes to great advantage."

BT PREMIERSHIP ONE 2006–07 RESULTS

26 August, 2006: **Hawick** 20 **Boroughmuir** 34, **Dundee HSFP** 17 **Melrose** 14, **Aberdeen GSFP** 19 **Currie** 29, **Watsonians** 8 **Ayr** 0, **Heriots** 41 **Glasgow Hawks** 22. 2 September, 2006: **Boroughmuir** 10 **Dundee HSFP** 16, **Glasgow Hawks** 7 **Watsonians** 21, **Heriots** 12 **Melrose** 14, **Ayr** 26 **Aberdeen GSFP** 14, **Currie** 51 **Hawick** 20. 9 September, 2006: **Hawick** 13 **Ayr** 14, **Aberdeen GSFP** 14 **Glasgow Hawks** 35, **Melrose** 21 **Boroughmuir** 23, **Watsonians** 21 **Heriots** 16, **Dundee HSFP** 22 **Currie** 44. 16 September, 2006: **Boroughmuir** 20 **Currie** 32, **Melrose** 23 **Watsonians** 17, **Dundee HSFP** 26 **Ayr** 27, **Hawick** 10 **Glasgow Hawks** 7, **Aberdeen GSFP** 19 **Heriots** 35. 23 September, 2006: **Glasgow Hawks** 28 **Dundee HSFP** 5, **Ayr** 20 **Boroughmuir** 22, **Currie** 42 **Melrose** 13, **Watsonians** 52 **Aberdeen GSFP** 17, **Heriots** 29 **Hawick** 0. 30 September, 2006: **Dundee HSFP** 34 **Heriots** 19, **Hawick** 10 **Watsonians** 41, **Currie** 16 **Ayr** 11, **Melrose** 38 **Aberdeen GSFP** 16, **Boroughmuir** 51 **Glasgow Hawks** 21. 7 October, 2006: **Heriots** 10 **Boroughmuir** 27, **Ayr** 40 **Melrose** 10, **Glasgow Hawks** 42 **Currie** 5, **Aberdeen GSFP** 16 **Hawick** 10, **Watsonians** 29 **Dundee HSFP** 17. 14 October, 2006: **Dundee HSFP** 34 **Aberdeen GSFP** 11, **Ayr** 23 **Glasgow Hawks**

20, **Melrose** 25 **Hawick** 20, **Currie** 15 **Heriots** 32, **Boroughmuir** 39 **Watsonians** 26. 21 October, 2006: **Heriots** 13 **Ayr** 6, **Hawick** 22 **Dundee HSFP** 23, **Aberdeen GSFP** 41 **Boroughmuir** 34, **Glasgow Hawks** 39 **Melrose** 10, **Watsonians** 5 **Currie** 22. 28 October, 2006: **Ayr** 15 **Watsonians** 8, **Boroughmuir** 10 **Hawick** 20, **Currie** 30 **Aberdeen GSFP** 20, **Glasgow Hawks** 15 **Heriots** 22, **Melrose** 34 **Dundee HSFP** 10. 4 November, 2006: **Aberdeen GSFP** 18 **Ayr** 36, **Dundee HSFP** 26 **Boroughmuir** 7, **Hawick** 7 **Currie** 27, **Melrose** 18 **Heriots** 59, **Watsonians** 39 **Glasgow Hawks** 37. 11 November, 2006: **Ayr** 40 **Hawick** 8, **Boroughmuir** 23 **Melrose** 27, **Currie** 51 **Dundee HSFP** 0, **Glasgow Hawks** 34 **Aberdeen GSFP** 7, **Heriots** 6 **Watsonians** 24. 18 November, 2006: **Ayr** 34 **Dundee HSFP** 3, **Currie** 88 **Boroughmuir** 17, **Glasgow Hawks** 27 **Hawick** 17, **Heriots** 31 **Aberdeen GSFP** 13, **Watsonians** 33 **Melrose** 24. 2 December, 2006: **Aberdeen GSFP** 21 **Watsonians** 24, **Boroughmuir** 20 **Ayr** 20, **Dundee HSFP** 12 **Glasgow Hawks** 19, **Hawick** 11 **Heriots** 7, **Melrose** 12 **Currie** 15. 9 December, 2006: **Aberdeen GSFP** 16 **Melrose** 19, **Ayr** 30 **Currie** 26, **Glasgow Hawks** 15 **Boroughmuir** 14, **Heriots** 32 **Dundee HSFP** 18, **Watsonians** 52 **Hawick** 6. 16 December, 2006: **Boroughmuir** 37 **Heriots** 48, **Currie** 22 **Glasgow Hawks** 27, **Dundee HSFP** 31 **Watsonians** 11, **Hawick** 26 **Aberdeen GSFP** 7, **Melrose** 16 **Ayr** 20. 23 December, 2006: **Glasgow Hawks** 11 **Ayr** 8, **Hawick** 17 **Melrose** 27, **Heriots** 26 **Currie** 39, **Watsonians** 45 **Boroughmuir** 22. 13 January, 2007: **Ayr** 20 **Heriots** 3, **Boroughmuir** 54 **Aberdeen GSFP** 5, **Currie** 12 **Watsonians** 10, **Dundee HSFP** 13 **Hawick** 14, **Melrose** 12 **Glasgow Hawks** 8. 21 April, 2006: **Aberdeen GSFP** 18 **Dundee HSFP** 52

FINAL TABLE

	P	W	D	L	For	A	PD	Pts
Currie	18	14	0	4	566	333	233	67
Ayr	18	12	1	5	390	255	135	61
Watsonians	18	12	0	6	466	325	141	58
Heriots	18	10	0	8	441	353	88	52
Glasgow H	18	10	0	8	414	333	81	51
Boroughmuir	18	7	1	10	464	501	-37	42
Melrose	18	9	0	9	357	427	-70	42
Dundee HSFP	18	8	0	10	359	424	-65	39
Hawick	18	5	0	13	251	450	-199	26
Aberdeen GSFP	18	2	0	16	292	599	-307	11

QUARTER-FINALS

7 April, 2007	
Stewart's Melville FP 31 **Glasgow Hawks** 89	**Aberdeen GSFP** 20 **Boroughmuir** 34
West of Scotland FC 23 **Dundee HSFP** 15	**Edinburgh Academical FC** 18 **Hawick** 11

SEMI-FINALS

21 April, 2007	
West of Scotland FC 17 **Glasgow Hawks** 19	**Edinburgh Academical FC** 38 **Boroughmuir** 14

FINAL

5 May, Murrayfield, Edinburgh

GLASGOW HAWKS 24 (1G, 4PG, 1T)
EDINBURGH ACADEMICAL FC 13 (2T, 1DG)

GLASGOW HAWKS: M Strang; S Gordon, R Munday, S Duffy (captain), R Kerr; M Adamson, K Sinclair; N Cox, D Malcolm, G Mories, A Dale, S Warnock, N Caddell, J Fitzpatrick, A Maclay Substitutions: G MacFadyen for Cox (26 mins); S Smith for Duffy (32 mins); J MacLay for Malcolm (48 mins); G Francis for Calddell (60 mins)

SCORERS *Tries:* Fitzpatrick, Maclay *Conversion*: Adamson *Penalty Goals*: Adamson (4)

EDINBURGH ACCIES: R Browne; J Howison, L McCann, P Loudon, D Rattray; G Douglas, M Campbell; P Burns, J Edwards, A Marsh, E Stuart, N Pike, D Teague (captain), J Parker, G Campbell Substitutions: D MacLeod for Burns (57 mins); E Stott for Marsh (57 mins); C Kinloch for Browne (70 mins); S Walker for Doulgas (70 mins); S Paterson for Pike (70 mins)

SCORERS *Tries:* Teague, Stewart *Drop Goal*: Douglas

REFEREE P Allan (Watsonians)

Getty Images

South Africa crowned an incredible four years by lifting the Webb Ellis Cup in 2007.

SOUTH AFRICA

SOUTH AFRICA'S 2006–07 TEST RECORD

OPPONENTS	DATE	VENUE	RESULT
Ireland	11 November	A	**Lost** 15–32
England	18 November	A	**Lost** 21–23
England	25 November	A	**Won** 25–14
England	26 May	H	**Won** 58–10
England	2 June	H	**Won** 55–22
Samoa	9 June	H	**Won** 35–8
Australia	16 June	H	**Won** 22–19
New Zealand	23 June	H	**Lost** 21–26
Australia	7 July	A	**Lost** 17–25
New Zealand	14 July	A	**Lost** 6–33
Namibia	15 August	H	**Won** 105–13
Samoa	9 September	N	**Won** 59–7 (WC)
England	14 September	N	**Won** 36–0 (WC)
Tonga	22 September	N	**Won** 30–25 (WC)
USA	30 September	N	**Won** 64–15 (WC)
Fiji	7 October	N	**Won** 37–20 (WC)
Argentina	14 October	N	**Won** 37–13 (WC)
England	20 October	N	**Won** 15–6 (WC)

JOY UNBOUNDED FOR THE SPRINGBOKS

South Africa dethroned England as world champions to lift the Webb Ellis Cup in Paris and maintain the southern hemisphere's virtual monopoly on the Rugby World Cup. The Springboks' hard-fought 15–6 victory in the Stade de France made it five out of six triumphs for the Tri-Nations triumvirate since the inaugural tournament in 1987 and ended English dreams of becoming the first side to successfully defend their title.

In the process, Jake White's side emulated the achievements of the 1995 Springboks who famously lifted the cup in Johannesburg and although 12 years later it was incumbent president Thabo Mbeki rather than Nelson Mandela celebrating with the players after the final whistle, the sense of symmetry was inescapable. South Africa were world champions once again.

"To see the president of our country sitting on the players' shoulders, it doesn't get much better than that," White said after the final. "People ask why we take the World Cup so seriously. It's much bigger than any other event, what it did to us as a nation. We've now won a World Cup away from home. We had our president sitting in the changing room. He was saying how proud he was of being a South African."

The final itself was not a classic of running rugby but what it lacked in panache – or tries – it more than made up for in terms of drama and tension as South Africa ceded territory and possession to England but scored their points at pivotal times.

A Percy Montgomery penalty after six minutes gave the Springboks an early lead which they were never to surrender and two more from the full-back's boot before the break gave White's team a 9–3 advantage.

The turning point of the match came minutes into the second-half. England centre Mathew Tait pierced the Springbok midfield and the ball was worked to Mark Cueto on the wing. Danie Rossouw made a despairing tackle as Cueto dived for the line and after three agonising minutes, the TMO ruled the Englishman had been forced into touch. South Africa had escaped and a fourth penalty from Montgomery five minutes later and long-range effort from Francois Steyn form half-way secured a famous victory.

"I'm sitting here and trying not to cry," said Springbok skipper John Smit. "It's a feeling you can't put into words. Twelve years ago, I sat watching the final at Ellis Park and wondered whether it was possible to do it again. Dreams come true."

The Springboks' Rugby World Cup opener against Samoa at the Parc

Dave Rogers\Getty Images

It's Ours! The Webb Ellis Cup and the victorious South African team.

des Princes was an opportunity for White's side to lay down a marker for the rest of the tournament and although they initially had to subdue a predictably physical Samoan challenge, they eventually ran out handsome winners.

The Pacific Islanders trailed by just two points at one stage in the first-half but Bryan Habana scored the first of his four tries and the Springboks eased away and at full time they were 59–7 victors.

"You could see a lot of nerves out there from both sides early on but all credit to our boys," White said after his side's eight-try romp. "The way they finished it off in the second half is a huge positive for us going forward in the competition."

The eagerly-anticipated clash with the English in Saint-Denis five days later was widely expected to settle the issue of which side would claim top spot in Pool A but if South Africa were expecting a titanic struggle for forward supremacy and a cagey battle between the kickers, they were mistaken.

The Springboks destroyed the defending champions in the Stade de France and once flanker Juan Smith had crashed over in the sixth minute, there was only going to be one winner. Two tries from JP Pietersen and the metronomic boot of Percy Montgomery rubbed further salt into the English wounds and South Africa recorded a crushing 36–0 win.

"We are obviously delighted," White said. "To get a result like that was obviously pleasing and this is one of the biggest victories we've had as a group of people. When the World Cup draw was made, we always knew this would be a tough game for us."

The South Africans had produced a performance that proved they were capable of reaching the final but any sense of complacency that could have engendered by their humiliation of England was quickly displaced in their next game against Tonga in Lens.

With the quarter-finals seemingly on the horizon, White decided to rest 11 of his starting line-up from the England game but the Tongans were in no mood to give the Springbok second string a gentle run out and led 10–7 early in the second-half. White brought on the cavalry in the shape of Habana, Francois Steyn, Victor Matfield, BJ Botha and John Smit to rescue the situation and the raft of substitutions initially seemed to do the trick. Two quick tries saw the Springboks move 27–10 in front but Tonga were not finished and two scores of their own set up a nervous climax. The South African sighs of relief at full-time with the score 30–25 in their favour were almost audible.

There were however no similar scares in the final group games against the USA in Montpellier and their 64–15 win wrapped up top spot for the 1995 champions and set up a quarter-final clash with the cavalier Fijians, one of the tournament's surprise packages.

The clash in Marseille was billed as a classic contrast of styles between abrasive South African forward power and Fiji's natural, uninhibited flair and so it proved in the Stade Velodrome as the two sides produced an absorbing encounter.

Initially, the Springbok pack ruled the roost and provided the platform for White's side to cruise into a 20–6 lead but the South Sea Islanders refused to be bowed and had the crowd on their feet with two stunning second-half tries from the irrepressible Vilimoni Delasau and Sireli Bobo that levelled the match at 20–20. South Africa were reeling and they duly reverted to a 10-man game to subdue Fiji and late tries from Juan Smith and Butch James secured a 37–20 victory. The South Africans had been given a major scare but were through to the last four.

"We are quite happy we got out alive today," admitted skipper John Smit. "The priority was to get through but we made life difficult for ourselves. We knew Fiji were solid and well organised, with a couple of great runners. Their skills are top-class. They came out at us and at 20–20, I thought I didn't want to be in that position with only a couple of minutes to go."

Argentina were the semi-final opponents and many anticipated a bruising encounter. The Pumas pack were expected to stand up to the Springbok forwards and for the first time in the tournament, South Africa could not simply outmuscle the opposition up front.

The Argentinean front row did indeed give Smit and his front five colleagues food for thought in the Stade de France but it was actually out wide where the match was won and lost. The Pumas had taken the tournament by storm but they looked uncharacteristically nervous against South Africa and made crucial mistakes at pivotal times.

An interception try for Fourie du Preez was the Springboks' first gift of the day and when Schalk Burger stole Argentinean ball, Habana was away for the second try. A third soft try before half-time – Danie Rossouw cantering over after Juan Martin Hernandez spilled the ball – effectively ended the game as contest and Habana's second score after the break sealed a 37–13 win and set-up the rematch with England in Paris in the final.

"We have won the last four games against England but World Cup finals are different," cautioned White after the semi-final victory. England have a lot of players who have played in a World Cup final. That experience is a massive advantage. We have achieved nothing so far. We are really proud of our achievement but it is meaningless if we don't get a win next weekend."

There was precious little in South Africa's results earlier in the season to suggest they were capable of mounting a sustained World Cup bid. The annual journey north in the Autumn saw the Springboks side beaten on successive weekends by Ireland and England and although White's side restored a degree of pride in the second Test with England – winning 25–14 at Twickenham – it was not a particularly happy or indeed fruitful pre-Christmas visit.

The summer saw England arrive for a two-Test series and although, on paper, South Africa's 58–10 win in Bloemfontein and 55–22 triumph in Pretoria a week later seemed encouraging, England's squad was missing a raft of first-choice players and it was difficult to gauge how good the Springboks' performances had actually been.

The Tri-Nations began with a morale-boosting 22–19 win over the Wallabies in Cape Town courtesy of Francois Steyn's two late drop goals but the All Blacks snatched victory from the jaws of defeat a week later in Durban to bring the Springboks' abruptly back down to earth.

White decided to rest his key players for the two away games in Australia and New Zealand and although his second string proved surprisingly resilient, they were beaten twice and South Africa finished bottom of the Tri-Nations for a second successive season.

The World Cup was less than two months away and the Springboks' build-up had raised more questions about their prospects than they'd answered. White's side would have to do their talking at the tournament itself.

SOUTH AFRICA INTERNATIONAL STATISTICS

MATCH RECORDS UP TO 31ST OCTOBER 2007

MOST CONSECUTIVE TEST WINS

17 1997 A2,It, F 1,2, E,S, 1998 I 1,2,W 1,E 1, A 1,NZ 1,2, A 2, W 2, S, I 3

15 1994 Arg 1,2, S, W 1995 WS, A, R, C, WS, F, NZ, W, It, E, 1996 Fj

MOST CONSECUTIVE TESTS WITHOUT DEFEAT

Matches	Wins	Draws	Periods
17	17	0	1997 to 1998
16	15	1	1994 to 1996
15	12	3	1960 to 1963

MOST POINTS IN A MATCH

BY THE TEAM

Pts.	Opponent	Venue	Year
134	Uruguay	E London	2005
105	Namibia	Cape Town	2007
101	Italy	Durban	1999
96	Wales	Pretoria	1998
74	Tonga	Cape Town	1997
74	Italy	Port Elizabeth	1999
72	Uruguay	Perth	2003
68	Scotland	Murrayfield	1997
64	USA	Montpellier	2007
62	Italy	Bologna	1997
61	Australia	Pretoria	1997

BY A PLAYER

Pts.	Player	Opponent	Venue	Year
35	P C Montgomery	Namibia	Cape Town	2007
34	J H de Beer	England	Paris	1999
31	P C Montgomery	Wales	Pretoria	1998
30	T Chavhanga	Uruguay	E London	2005
29	G S du Toit	Italy	Port Elizabeth	1999
29	P C Montgomery	Samoa	Paris	2007
28	G K Johnson	W Samoa	Johannesburg	1995
26	J H de Beer	Australia	Pretoria	1997
26	P C Montgomery	Scotland	Murrayfield	1997
25	J T Stransky	Australia	Bloemfontein	1996
25	C S Terblanche	Italy	Durban	1999

MOST TRIES IN A MATCH

BY THE TEAM

Tries	Opponent	Venue	Year
21	Uruguay	E London	2005
15	Wales	Pretoria	1998
15	Italy	Durban	1999
15	Namibia	Cape Town	2007
12	Tonga	Cape Town	1997
12	Uruguay	Perth	2003
11	Italy	Port Elizabeth	1999
10	Ireland	Dublin	1912
10	Scotland	Murrayfield	1997

BY A PLAYER

Tries	Player	Opponent	Venue	Year
6	T Chavhanga	Uruguay	E London	2005
5	C S Terblanche	Italy	Durban	1999
4	C M Williams	W Samoa	Johannesburg	1995
4	P W G Rossouw	France	Parc des Princes	1997
4	C S Terblanche	Ireland	Bloemfontein	1998
4	B G Habana	Samoa	Paris	2007

MOST CONVERSIONS IN A MATCH

BY THE TEAM

Cons	Opponent	Venue	Year
13	Italy	Durban	1999
13	Uruguay	E London	2005
12	Namibia	Cape Town	2007
9	Scotland	Murrayfield	1997
9	Wales	Pretoria	1998
8	Italy	Port Elizabeth	1999
8	USA	Montpellier	2007
7	Scotland	Murrayfield	1951
7	Tonga	Cape Town	1997
7	Italy	Bologna	1997
7	France	Parc des Princes	1997
7	Italy	Genoa	2001
7	Samoa	Pretoria	2002
7	Samoa	Brisbane	2003
7	England	Bloemfontein	2007

BY A PLAYER

Cons	Player	Opponent	Venue	Year
12	P C Montgomery	Namibia	Cape Town	2007
9	P C Montgomery	Wales	Pretoria	1998
8	P C Montgomery	Scotland	Murrayfield	1997
8	G S du Toit	Italy	Port Elizabeth	1999
8	G S du Toit	Italy	Durban	1999
7	A O Geffin	Scotland	Murrayfield	1951
7	J M F Lubbe	Tonga	Cape Town	1997
7	H W Honiball	Italy	Bologna	1997
7	H W Honiball	France	Parc des Princes	1997
7	A S Pretorius	Samoa	Pretoria	2002
7	J N B van der Westhuyzen	Uruguay	E London	2005
7	P C Montgomery	England	Bloemfontein	2007

MOST PENALTIES IN A MATCH

BY THE TEAM

Pens	Opponent	Venue	Year
8	Scotland	Port Elizabeth	2006
7	France	Pretoria	1975
7	France	Cape Town	2006
6	Australia	Bloemfontein	1996
6	Australia	Twickenham	1999
6	England	Pretoria	2000
6	Australia	Durban	2000
6	France	Johannesburg	2001
6	Scotland	Johannesburg	2003

BY A PLAYER

Pens	Player	Opponent	Venue	Year
7	P C Montgomery	Scotland	Port Elizabeth	2006
7	P C Montgomery	France	Cape Town	2006
6	G R Bosch	France	Pretoria	1975
6	J T Stransky	Australia	Bloemfontein	1996
6	J H de Beer	Australia	Twickenham	1999
6	A J J van Straaten	England	Pretoria	2000
6	A J J van Straaten	Australia	Durban	2000
6	P C Montgomery	France	Johannesburg	2001
6	L J Koen	Scotland	Johannesburg	2003

MOST DROPPED GOALS IN A MATCH

BY THE TEAM

Drops	Opponent	Venue	Year
5	England	Paris	1999
4	England	Twickenham	2006
3	S America	Durban	1980
3	Ireland	Durban	1981
3	Scotland	Murrayfield	2004

BY A PLAYER

Drops	Player	Opponent	Venue	Year
5	J H de Beer	England	Paris	1999
4	A S Pretorius	England	Twickenham	2006
3	H E Botha	S America	Durban	1980
3	H E Botha	Ireland	Durban	1981
3	J N B van der Westhuyzen	Scotland	Murrayfield	2004
2	B L Osler	N Zealand	Durban	1928
2	H E Botha	NZ Cavaliers	Cape Town	1986
2	J T Stransky	N Zealand	Johannesburg	1995
2	J H de Beer	N Zealand	Johannesburg	1997
2	P C Montgomery	N Zealand	Cardiff	1999
2	F P L Steyn	Australia	Cape Town	2007

MOST CAPPED PLAYERS

Caps	Player	Career Span
94	P C Montgomery	1997 to 2007
89	J H van der Westhuizen	1993 to 2003
80	J P du Randt	1994 to 2007
77	M G Andrews	1994 to 2001
74	J W Smit	2000 to 2007
67	V Matfield	2001 to 2007
66	A G Venter	1996 to 2001
64	B J Paulse	1999 to 2007
54	A-H le Roux	1994 to 2002
50	P A van den Berg	1999 to 2007
47	J T Small	1992 to 1997
47	C J van der Linde	2002 to 2007
46	J C van Niekerk	2001 to 2006
44	J P Botha	2002 to 2007
43	J Dalton	1994 to 2002
43	P W G Rossouw	1997 to 2003
42	G H Teichmann	1995 to 1999
42	R B Skinstad	1997 to 2007
41	J H Smith	2003 to 2007
39	D W Barry	2000 to 2006
39	C P J Krige	1999 to 2003
38	F C H du Preez	1961 to 1971
38	J H Ellis	1965 to 1976
38	K Otto	1995 to 2000
38	A H Snyman	1996 to 2006
38	P F du Preez	2004 to 2007
38	S W P Burger	2003 to 2007

MOST CONSECUTIVE TESTS

Tests	Player	Span
46	J W Smit	2003 to 2007
39	G H Teichmann	1996 to 1999
26	A H Snyman	1996 to 1998
26	A N Vos	1999 to 2001
25	S H Nomis	1967 to 1972
25	A G Venter	1997 to 1999
25	A-H le Roux	1998 to 1999

MOST TESTS AS CAPTAIN

Tests	Captain	Span
48	J W Smit	2003 to 2007
36	G H Teichmann	1996 to 1999
29	J F Pienaar	1993 to 1996
22	D J de Villiers	1965 to 1970
18	C P J Krigé	1999 to 2003
16	A N Vos	1999 to 2001
15	M du Plessis	1975 to 1980
12	R B Skinstad	2001 to 2007
11	J F K Marais	1971 to 1974

MOST POINTS IN TESTS

Pts	Player	Tests	Career
873	P C Montgomery	94	1997 to 2007
312	H E Botha	28	1980 to 1992
240	J T Stransky	22	1993 to 1996
221	A J J van Straaten	21	1999 to 2001
190	J H van der Westhuizen	89	1993 to 2003
181	J H de Beer	13	1997 to 1999
165	A S Pretorius	30	2002 to 2007
156	H W Honiball	35	1993 to 1999
150	B G Habana	35	2004 to 2007
145	L J Koen	15	2000 to 2003
135*	B J Paulse	64	1999 to 2007
130	P J Visagie	25	1967 to 1971

* includes a penalty try

MOST TRIES IN TESTS

Tries	Player	Tests	Career
38	J H van der Westhuizen	89	1993 to 2003
30	B G Habana	35	2004 to 2007
27*	B J Paulse	64	1999 to 2007
24	P C Montgomery	94	1997 to 2007
21	P W G Rossouw	43	1997 to 2003
20	J T Small	47	1992 to 1997
20	J Fourie	37	2003 to 2007
19	D M Gerber	24	1980 to 1992
19	C S Terblanche	37	1998 to 2003
14	C M Williams	27	1993 to 2000

* includes a penalty try

MOST CONVERSIONS IN TESTS

Cons	Player	Tests	Career
150	P C Montgomery	94	1997 to 2007
50	H E Botha	28	1980 to 1992
38	H W Honiball	35	1993 to 1999
33	J H de Beer	13	1997 to 1999
30	J T Stransky	22	1993 to 1996
28	A S Pretorius	30	2002 to 2007
25	G S du Toit	14	1998 to 2006
23	A J J van Straaten	21	1999 to 2001
23	L J Koen	15	2000 to 2003
20	P J Visagie	25	1967 to 1971

MOST PENALTY GOALS IN TESTS

Pens	Player	Tests	Career
145	P C Montgomery	94	1997 to 2007
55	A J J van Straaten	21	1999 to 2001
50	H E Botha	28	1980 to 1992
47	J T Stransky	22	1993 to 1996
31	L J Koen	15	2000 to 2003
27	J H de Beer	13	1997 to 1999
25	H W Honiball	35	1993 to 1999
25	A S Pretorius	30	2002 to 2007
23	G R Bosch	9	1974 to 1976
19	P J Visagie	25	1967 to 1971

MOST DROPPED GOALS IN TESTS

Drops	Player	Tests	Career
18	H E Botha	28	1980 to 1992
8	J H de Beer	13	1997 to 1999
8	A S Pretorius	30	2002 to 2007
6	P C Montgomery	94	1997 to 2007
5	J D Brewis	10	1949 to 1953
5	P J Visagie	25	1967 to 1971
4	B L Osler	17	1924 to 1933

TRI NATIONS RECORDS

RECORD	DETAIL		SET
Most points in season	148	in four matches	1997
Most tries in season	18	in four matches	1997
Highest Score	61	61-22 v Australia (h)	1997
Biggest win	39	61-22 v Australia (h)	1997
Highest score conceded	55	35-55 v N Zealand (a)	1997
Biggest defeat	49	0-49 v Australia (a)	2006
Most points in matches	195	P C Montgomery	1997 to 2007
Most points in season	64	J H de Beer	1997
Most points in match	26	J H de Beer	v Australia (h),1997
Most tries in matches	7	B J Paulse	1999 to 2007
Most tries in season	3	P C Montgomery	1997
	3	M C Joubert	2002
	3	M C Joubert	2004
	3	J de Villiers	2004
	3	B G Habana	2005
	3	J Fourie	2006
	3	P F du Preez	2006
Most tries in match	3	M C Joubert	v New Zealand (h) 2004
Most cons in matches	23	P C Montgomery	1997 to 2007
Most cons in season	12	J H de Beer	1997
Most cons in match	6	J H de Beer	v Australia (h),1997
Most pens in matches	40	P C Montgomery	1997 to 2007
Most pens in season	13	A J J van Straaten	2000
	13	A J J van Straaten	2001
Most pens in match	6	J T Stransky	v Australia (h),1996
	6	A J J van Straaten	v Australia (h),2000

MISCELLANEOUS RECORDS

RECORD	HOLDER	DETAIL
Longest Test Career	J P du Randt	1994–2007
Youngest Test Cap	A J Hartley	18 yrs 18 days in 1891
Oldest Test Cap	J N Ackermann	37 yrs 34 days in 2007

CAREER RECORDS OF SOUTH AFRICA INTERNATIONAL PLAYERS (UP TO 31 OCTOBER 2007)

PLAYER	DEBUT	CAPS	T	C	P	D	PTS
BACKS							
T Chavhanga	2005 v U	2	6	0	0	0	30
M Claassens	2004 v W	8	0	0	0	0	0
J de Villiers	2002 v F	33	13	0	0	0	65
P F du Preez	2004 v I	38	9	0	0	0	45
B A Fortuin	2006 v I	2	0	0	0	0	0
J Fourie	2003 v U	37	20	0	0	0	100
P J Grant	2007 v A	2	0	0	0	0	0
B G Habana	2004 v E	35	30	0	0	0	150
D J Hougaard	2003 v U	8	2	13	10	1	69
A D James	2001 v F	26	3	5	12	0	61
E R Januarie	2005 v U	21	3	0	0	0	15
W Julies	1999 v Sp	11	2	0	0	0	10
P C Montgomery	1997 v BI	94	24	150	145	6	873
W M Murray	2007 v Sm	3	0	0	0	0	0
A Z Ndungane	2006 v A	10	1	0	0	0	5
W Olivier	2006 v S	20	0	0	0	0	0
B J Paulse	1999 v It	64	27*	0	0	0	135
R Pienaar	2006 v NZ	18	3	0	1	0	18
J-P R Pietersen	2006 v A	15	6	0	0	0	30
A S Pretorius	2002 v W	30	2	28	25	8	165
J C Pretorius	2006 v I	2	0	0	0	0	0
F P L Steyn	2006 v I	16	4	0	4	3	41
A K Willemse	2003 v S	19	4	0	0	0	20
FORWARDS							
J N Ackermann	1996 v Fj	13	0	0	0	0	0
E P Andrews	2004 v I	23	0	0	0	0	0
B J Botha	2006 v NZ	16	0	0	0	0	0
G van G Botha	2005 v A	12	0	0	0	0	0
J P Botha	2002 v F	44	7	0	0	0	35
G J J Britz	2004 v I	13	0	0	0	0	0
S W P Burger	2003 v Gg	38	10	0	0	0	50

P D Carstens	2002 v S	7	0	0	0	0	0
J Cronjé	2004 v I	32	4	0	0	0	20
B W du Plessis	2007 v A	9	1	0	0	0	5
J N du Plessis	2007 v A	4	0	0	0	0	0
J P du Randt	1994 v Arg	80	5	0	0	0	25
L Floors	2006 v E	1	0	0	0	0	0
H Lobberts	2006 v E	2	0	0	0	0	0
V Matfield	2001 v It	67	5	0	0	0	25
G J Muller	2006 v S	21	0	0	0	0	0
M C Ralepelle	2006 v NZ	2	0	0	0	0	0
D J Rossouw	2003 v U	31	6	0	0	0	30
L D Sephaka	2001 v US	24	0	0	0	0	0
R B Skinstad	1997 v E	42	11	0	0	0	55
J W Smit	2000 v C	74	4	0	0	0	20
J H Smith	2003 v S	41	9	0	0	0	45
P J Spies	2006 v A	9	2	0	0	0	10
G G Steenkamp	2004 v S	13	1	0	0	0	5
P A van den Berg	1999 v It	50	4	0	0	0	20
C J van der Linde	2002 v S	47	4	0	0	0	20
J L van Heerden	2003 v S	14	1	0	0	0	5
P J Wannenburg	2002 v F	20	3	0	0	0	15
L A Watson	2007 v Sm	1	0	0	0	0	0

* Paulse's figures include a penalty try awarded against Wales in 2002

SOUTH AFRICAN INTERNATIONAL PLAYERS (UP TO 31 OCTOBER 2007)

Entries in square brackets denote matches played in RWC Finals.

Ackermann, D S P (WP) 1955 BI 2,3,4, 1956 A 1, 2, NZ 1, 3, 1958 F 2
Ackermann, J N (NT, BB, N) 1996 Fj, A 1, NZ 1, A 2, 2001 F 2(R), It 1, NZ 1(R), A 1, 2006 I, E1, 2, 2007 Sm, A2
Aitken, A D (WP) 1997 F 2(R), E, 1998 I 2(R), W 1(R), NZ 1,2(R), A 2(R)
Albertyn, P K (SWD) 1924 BI 1,2,3,4
Alexander, F A (GW) 1891 BI 1,2
Allan, J (N) 1993 A 1(R), Arg 1,2(R), 1994 E 1,2, NZ 1,2,3, 1996 Fj, A 1, NZ 1, A 2, NZ 2
Allen, P B (EP) 1960 S
Allport, P H (WP) 1910 BI 2,3
Anderson, J W (WP) 1903 BI 3
Anderson, J H (WP) 1896 BI 1,3,4
Andrew, J B (Tvl) 1896 BI 2
Andrews, E P (WP) 2004 I1, 2, W1(t&R), PI, NZ1, A1, NZ2, A2, W2, I3, E, 2005 F1, A2, NZ2(t), Arg(R), F3(R), 2006 S1, 2,F,A1(R),NZ1(t), 2007 A2(R),NZ2(R)
Andrews, K S (WP) 1992 E, 1993 F 1,2, A 1(R), 2,3, Arg 1(R), 2, 1994 NZ 3
Andrews, M G (N) 1994 E 2, NZ 1,2,3, Arg 1,2, S, W, 1995 WS, [A, WS, F, NZ], W, It, E, 1996 Fj, A 1, NZ 1, A 2, NZ 2,3,4,5, Arg 1,2, F 1,2, W, 1997 Tg (R), BI 1,2, NZ 1, A 1, NZ 2, A 2, It, F 1,2, E, S, 1998 I 1,2, W 1, E 1, A 1, NZ 1,2, A 2, W 2, S, I 3, E 2, 1999 NZ 1,2(R), A 2(R), [S, U, E, A 3, NZ 3], 2000 A 2, NZ 2, A 3, Arg, I, W, E 3, 2001 F 1,2, It 1, NZ 1, A 1,2, NZ 2, F 3, E
Antelme, J G M (Tvl) 1960 NZ 1,2,3,4, 1961 F
Apsey, J T (WP) 1933 A 4,5, 1938 BI 2
Ashley, S (WP) 1903 BI 2
Aston, F T D (Tvl) 1896 BI 1,2,3,4
Atherton, S (N) 1993 Arg 1,2, 1994 E 1,2, NZ 1,2,3, 1996 NZ 2
Aucamp, J (WT) 1924 BI 1,2

Baard, A P (WP) 1960 I
Babrow, L (WP) 1937 A 1,2, NZ 1,2,3
Badenhorst, C (OFS) 1994 Arg 2, 1995 WS (R)
Bands, R E (BB) 2003 S 1,2, Arg (R), A 1, NZ 1, A 2, NZ 2, [U,E,Sm(R),NZ(R)]
Barnard, A S (EP) 1984 S Am 1,2, 1986 Cv 1,2
Barnard, J H (Tvl) 1965 S, A 1,2, NZ 3,4
Barnard, R W (Tvl) 1970 NZ 2(R)
Barnard, W H M (NT) 1949 NZ 4, 1951 W
Barry, D W (WP) 2000 C, E 1,2, A 1(R), NZ 1, A 2, 2001 F 1,2, US (R), 2002 W 2, Arg, Sm, NZ 1, A 1, NZ 2, A 2, 2003 A 1, NZ 1, A 2, [U,E,Sm,NZ], 2004 PI, NZ1, A1, NZ2, A2, W2, I3,E, Arg(t), 2005 F1,2,A1,NZ2,W(R),F3(R), 2006 F
Barry, J (WP) 1903 BI 1,2,3
Bartmann, W J (Tvl, N) 1986 Cv 1,2,3,4, 1992 NZ, A, F, 1,2
Bastard, W E (N) 1937 A 1, NZ 1,2,3, 1938 BI 1,3
Bates, A J (WT) 1969 E, 1970 NZ 1,2, 1972 E
Bayvel, P C R (Tvl) 1974 BI 2,4, F 1,2, 1975 F 1,2, 1976 NZ 1,2,3,4
Beck, J J (WP) 1981 NZ 2(R), 3(R), US
Bedford, T P (N) 1963 A 1,2,3,4, 1964 W, F, 1965 I, A 1,2, 1968 BI 1,2,3,4, F 1,2, 1969 A 1,2,3,4, S, E, 1970 I, W, 1971 F 1,2
Bekker, H J (WP) 1981 NZ 1,3
Bekker, H P J (NT) 1952 E, F, 1953 A 1,2,3,4, 1955 BI 2,3,4, 1956 A 1,2, NZ 1,2,3,4
Bekker, M J (NT) 1960 S
Bekker, R P (NT) 1953 A 3,4
Bekker, S (NT) 1997 A 2(t)
Bennett, R G (Border) 1997 Tg (R), BI 1(R), 3, NZ 1, A 1, NZ 2
Bergh, W F (SWD) 1931 W, I, 1932 E, S, 1933 A 1,2,3,4,5, 1937 A 1,2, NZ 1,2,3, 1938 BI 1,2,3
Bestbier, A (OFS) 1974 F 2(R)
Bester, J J N (WP) 1924 BI 2,4
Bester, J L A (WP) 1938 BI 2,3
Beswick, A M (Bor) 1896 BI 2,3,4
Bezuidenhout, C E (NT) 1962 BI 2,3,4
Bezuidenhout, C J (MP) 2003 NZ 2(R), [E,Sm,NZ]
Bezuidenhout, N S E (NT) 1972 E, 1974 BI 2,3,4, F 1,2, 1975 F 1,2, 1977 Wld
Bierman, J N (Tvl) 1931 I
Bisset, W M (WP) 1891 BI 1,3
Blair, R (WP) 1977 Wld
Bobo, G (GL) 2003 S 2(R), Arg, A 1(R), NZ 2, 2004 S(R)
Boome, C S (WP) 1999 It 1,2, W, NZ 1(R), A 1, NZ 2, A 2, 2000 C, E 1,2, 2003 S 1(R),2(R), Arg (R), A 1(R), NZ 1(R), A 2, NZ 2(R), [U(R),Gg,NZ(R)]
Bosch, G R (Tvl) 1974 BI 2, F 1,2, 1975 F 1,2, 1976 NZ 1,2,3,4
Bosman, H M (FS) 2005 W,F3, 2006 A1(R)
Bosman, N J S (Tvl) 1924 BI 2,3,4
Botha, B J (N) 2006 NZ2(R),3,A3, I(R),E1,2, 2007 E1,Sm,A1,NZ1,Nm(R),S(t&R), [Sm(R),E1,Tg(R),US]
Botha, D S (NT) 1981 NZ 1
Botha, G van G (BB) 2005 A3(R), F3(R), 2007 E1(R),2(R),Sm(R),A1(R),NZ1,A2, NZ2(R),Nm,S, [Tg]
Botha, H E (NT) 1980 S Am 1,2, BI 1,2,3,4, S Am 3,4, F, 1981 I 1,2, NZ 1,2,3, US, 1982 S Am 1,2, 1986 Cv 1,2,3,4, 1989 Wld 1,2, 1992 NZ, A, F 1,2, E
Botha, J A (Tvl) 1903 BI 3
Botha, J P (BB) 2002 F, 2003 S 1,2, A 1, NZ 1, A 2(R), [U,E,Gg,Sm,NZ], 2004 I1,PI, NZ1, A1, NZ2, A2, W2, I3, E, S, Arg, 2005 A1, 2, 3, NZ1, A4, NZ2, Arg, W, F3, 2007 E1,2,A1, NZ1,Nm,S, [Sm, E1, Tg, US(R), Fj, Arg,E2]
Botha, J P F (NT) 1962 BI 2,3,4
Botha, P H (Tvl) 1965 A 1,2
Boyes, H C (GW) 1891 BI 1,2
Brand, G H (WP) 1928 NZ 2,3, 1931 W, I, 1932 E, S, 1933 A 1,2,3,4,5, 1937 A 1,2, NZ 2,3, 1938 BI 1
Bredenkamp, M J (GW) 1896 BI 1,3
Breedt, J C (Tvl) 1986 Cv 1,2,3,4, 1989 Wld 1,2, 1992 NZ, A
Brewis, J D (NT) 1949 NZ 1,2,3,4, 1951 S, I, W, 1952 E, F, 1953 A 1
Briers, T P D (WP) 1955 BI 1,2,3,4, 1956 NZ 2,3,4
Brink D J (WP) 1906 S, W, E
Brink, R (WP) 1995 [R, C]
Britz, G J J (FS, WP) 2004 I1(R), 2(R), W1(R), PI, A1, NZ2, A2(R), I3(t), S(t&R),Arg(R), 2005 U, 2006 E2(R), 2007 NZ2(R)
Britz, W K (N) 2002 W 1
Brooks, D (Bor) 1906 S

Brosnihan, W (GL, N) 1997 A 2, 2000 NZ 1(t+R), A 2(t+R), NZ 2(R), A 3(R), E 3(R)
Brown, C B (WP) 1903 BI 1,2,3
Brynard, G S (WP) 1965 A 1, NZ 1,2,3,4, 1968 BI 3,4
Buchler, J U (Tvl) 1951 S, I, W, 1952 E, F, 1953 A 1,2,3,4, 1956 A 2
Burdett, A F (WP) 1906 S, I
Burger, J M (WP) 1989 Wld 1,2
Burger, M B (NT) 1980 BI 2(R), S Am 3, 1981 US (R)
Burger, S W P (WP) 1984 E 1,2, 1986 Cv 1,2,3,4
Burger, S W P (WP) 2003 [Gg(R),Sm(R),NZ(R)], 2004 I1,2,W1,PI,NZ1,A1,NZ2,A2, W2,I3,E, 2005 F1, 2, A1, 2(R), 3(R), NZ1, A4, NZ2,Arg(R),W,F3, 2006 S1,2, 2007 E1,2, A1,NZ1,Nm,S, [Sm,US,Fj,Arg,E2]
Burger, W A G (Bor) 1906 S, I, W, 1910 BI 2

Carelse, G (EP) 1964 W, F, 1965 I, S, 1967 F 1,2,3, 1968 F 1,2, 1969 A 1,2,3,4, S
Carlson, R A (WP) 1972 E
Carolin, H W (WP) 1903 BI 3, 1906 S, I
Carstens, P D (N) 2002 S, E, 2006 E1(t&R),2(R), 2007 E1,2(t&R),Sm(R)
Castens, H H (WP) 1891 BI 1
Chavhanga, T (WP) 2005 U, 2007 NZ2(R)
Chignell, T W (WP) 1891 BI 3
Cilliers, G D (OFS) 1963 A 1,3,4
Cilliers, N V (WP) 1996 NZ 3(t)
Claassen, J T (WT) 1955 BI 1,2,3,4, 1956 A 1,2, NZ 1,2,3,4, 1958 F 1,2, 1960 S, NZ 1,2,3, W, I, 1961 E, S, F, I, A 1,2, 1962 BI 1,2,3,4
Claassen, W (N) 1981 I 1,2, NZ 2,3, US, 1982 S Am 1,2
Claassens, M (FS) 2004 W2(R),S(R),Arg(R), 2005 Arg(R), W,F3, 2007 A2(R),NZ2(R)
Clark, W H G (Tvl) 1933 A 3
Clarkson, W A (N) 1921 NZ 1,2, 1924 BI 1
Cloete, H A (WP) 1896 BI 4
Cockrell, C H (WP) 1969 S, 1970 I, W
Cockrell, R J (WP) 1974 F 1,2, 1975 F 1,2, 1976 NZ 1,2, 1977 Wld, 1981 NZ 1,2(R), 3, US
Coetzee, D (BB) 2002 Sm, 2003 S 1,2, Arg, A 1, NZ 1, A 2, NZ 2, [U,E,Sm(R),NZ(R)], 2004 S(R),Arg(R), 2006 A1(R)
Coetzee, J H H (WP) 1974 BI 1, 1975 F 2(R), 1976 NZ 1,2,3,4
Conradie, J H (WP) 2002 W 1,2, Arg (R), Sm, NZ 1, A 1, NZ 2(R), A 2(R), S, E, 2004 W1(R),PI,NZ2,A2, 2005 Arg
Cope, D K (Tvl) 1896 BI 2
Cotty, W (GW) 1896 BI 3
Crampton, G (GW) 1903 BI 2
Craven, D H (WP) 1931 W, I, 1932 S, 1933 A 1,2,3,4,5, 1937 A 1,2, NZ 1,2,3, 1938 BI 1,2,3,
Cronjé, G (BB) 2003 NZ 2, 2004 I2(R),W1(R)
Cronjé, J (BB, GL) 2004 I1, 2, W1, PI, NZ1, A1, NZ2(R), A2(t&R), S(t&R), Arg, 2005 U, F1, 2, A1, 3, NZ1(R), 2(t), Arg, W, F3, 2006 S2(R), F(R), A1(t&R), NZ1, A2, NZ2, A3(R), I(R),E1, 2007 A2(R),NZ2,Nm
Cronje, P A (Tvl) 1971 F 1,2, A 1,2,3, 1974 BI 3,4
Crosby, J H (Tvl) 1896 BI 2
Crosby, N J (Tvl) 1910 BI 1,3
Currie, C (GW) 1903 BI 2

D'Alton, G (WP) 1933 A 1
Dalton, J (Tvl, GL, Falcons) 1994 Arg 1(R), 1995 [A, C], W, It, E, 1996 NZ 4(R),5, Arg 1,2, F 1,2, W, 1997 Tg (R), BI 3, NZ 2, A 2, It, F 1,2, E, S, 1998 I 1,2, W 1, E 1, A 1, NZ 1,2, A 2, W 2, S, I 3, E 2, 2002 W 1,2, Arg, NZ 1, A 1, NZ 2, A 2, F, E
Daneel, G M (WP) 1928 NZ 1,2,3,4, 1931 W, I, 1932 E, S
Daneel, H J (WP) 1906 S, I, W, E
Davidson, C D (N) 2002 W 2(R), Arg, 2003 Arg, NZ 1(R), A 2
Davids, Q (WP) 2002 W 2, Arg (R), Sm (R), 2003 Arg, 2004 I1(R),2,W1,PI(t&R), NZ1(R)
Davison, P M (EP) 1910 BI 1
De Beer, J H (OFS) 1997 BI 3, NZ 1, A 1, NZ 2, A 2, F 2(R), S, 1999 A 2, [S, Sp, U, E, A 3]
De Bruyn, J (OFS) 1974 BI 3

De Jongh, H P K (WP) 1928 NZ 3
De Klerk, I J (Tvl) 1969 E, 1970 I, W
De Klerk, K B H (Tvl) 1974 BI 1,2,3(R), 1975 F 1,2, 1976 NZ 2(R), 3,4, 1980 S Am 1,2, BI 2, 1981 I 1,2
De Kock, A N (GW) 1891 BI 2
De Kock, D (Falcons) 2001 It 2(R), US
De Kock, J S (WP) 1921 NZ 3, 1924 BI 3
De Kock, N A (WP) 2001 It 1, 2002 Sm (R), NZ 1(R),2, A 2, F, 2003 [U(R),Gg,Sm(R), NZ(R)]
Delport, G M (GL, Worcester) 2000 C (R), E 1(t+R), A 1, NZ 1, A 2, NZ 2, A 3, Arg, I, W, 2001 F 2, It 1, 2003 A 1, NZ 2, [U,E,Sm,NZ]
Delport, W H (EP) 1951 S, I, W, 1952 E, F, 1953 A 1,2,3,4
De Melker, S C (GW) 1903 BI 2, 1906 E
Devenish, C E (GW) 1896 BI 2
Devenish, G St L (Tvl) 1896 BI 2
Devenish, G E (Tvl) 1891 BI 1
De Villiers, D I (Tvl) 1910 BI 1,2,3
De Villiers, D J (WP, Bol) 1962 BI 2,3, 1965 I, NZ 1,3,4, 1967 F 1,2,3,4, 1968 BI 1,2,3,4, F 1,2, 1969 A 1,4, E, 1970 I, W, NZ 1,2,3,4
De Villiers, H A (WP) 1906 S, W, E
De Villiers, H O (WP) 1967 F 1,2,3,4, 1968 F 1,2, 1969 A 1,2,3,4, S, E, 1970 I, W
De Villiers, J (WP) 2002 F, 2004 PI,NZ1,A1,NZ2,A2,W2(R),E, 2005 U,F1,2,A1,2,3, NZ1,A4,NZ2,Arg,W,F3, 2006 S1,NZ2,3,A3,I,E1,2, 2007 E1,2,A1,NZ1,Nm, [Sm]
De Villiers, P du P (WP) 1928 NZ 1,3,4, 1932 E, 1933 A 4, 1937 A 1,2, NZ 1
Devine, D (Tvl) 1924 BI 3, 1928 NZ 2
De Vos, D J J (WP) 1965 S, 1969 A 3, S
De Waal, A N (WP) 1967 F 1,2,3,4
De Waal, P J (WP) 1896 BI 4
De Wet, A E (WP) 1969 A 3,4, E
De Wet, P J (WP) 1938 BI 1,2,3
Dinkelmann, E E (NT) 1951 S, I, 1952 E, F, 1953 A 1, 2
Dirksen, C W (NT) 1963 A 4, 1964 W, 1965 I, S, 1967 F 1,2,3,4, 1968 BI 1,2
Dlulane, V T (MP) 2004 W2(R)
Dobbin, F J (GW) 1903 BI 1,2, 1906 S, W, E, 1910 BI 1, 1912 S, I, W
Dobie, J A R (Tvl) 1928 NZ 2
Dormehl, P J (WP) 1896 BI 3,4
Douglass, F W (EP) 1896 BI 1
Drotské, A E (OFS) 1993 Arg 2, 1995 [WS (R)], 1996 A 1(R), 1997 Tg, BI 1,2,3(R), NZ 1, A 1, NZ 2(R), 1998 I 2(R), W 1(R), I 3(R), 1999 It 1,2, W, NZ 1, A 1, NZ 2, A 2, [S, Sp (R), U, E, A 3, NZ 3]
Dryburgh, R G (WP) 1955 BI 2,3,4, 1956 A 2, NZ 1,4, 1960 NZ 1,2
Duff, B R (WP) 1891 BI 1,2,3
Duffy, B A (Bor) 1928 NZ 1
Du Plessis, B W (N) 2007 A2(t&R),NZ2,Nm(R), S(R), [Sm(R), E1(R), US(R), Arg(R), E2(t)]
Du Plessis, C J (WP) 1982 S Am 1,2, 1984 E 1,2, S Am 1,2, 1986 Cv 1,2,3,4, 1989 Wld 1,2
Du Plessis, D C (NT) 1977 Wld, 1980 S Am 2
Du Plessis, F (Tvl) 1949 NZ 1,2,3
Du Plessis, J N (FS) 2007 A2,NZ2, [Fj,Arg(t&R)]
Du Plessis, M (WP) 1971 A 1,2,3, 1974 BI 1,2, F 1,2, 1975 F 1,2, 1976 NZ 1,2,3,4, 1977 Wld, 1980 S Am 1,2, BI 1,2,3,4, S Am 4, F
Du Plessis, M J (WP) 1984 S Am 1,2, 1986 Cv 1,2,3,4, 1989 Wld 1,2
Du Plessis, N J (WT) 1921 NZ 2,3, 1924 BI 1,2,3
Du Plessis, P G (NT) 1972 E
Du Plessis, T D (NT) 1980 S Am 1,2
Du Plessis, W (WP) 1980 S Am 1,2, BI 1,2,3,4, S Am 3,4, F, 1981 NZ 1,2,3, 1982 S Am 1,2
Du Plooy, A J J (EP) 1955 BI 1
Du Preez, F C H (NT) 1961 E, S, A 1,2, 1962 BI 1, 2, 3, 4, 1963 A 1, 1964 W, F, 1965 A 1,2, NZ 1,2,3,4, 1967 F 4, 1968 BI 1,2,3,4, F 1,2, 1969 A 1,2, S, 1970 I, W, NZ 1,2,3,4, 1971 F 1,2, A 1,2,3
Du Preez, G J D (GL) 2002 Sm (R), A 1(R)

Du Preez, J G H (WP) 1956 NZ 1
Du Preez, P F (BB) 2004 I1, 2, W1, PI(R), NZ1, A1, NZ2(R), A2(R), W2, I3, E, S, Arg, 2005 U(R), F1, 2(R), A1(R), 2(R), 3, NZ1(R), A4(R), 2006 S1, 2, F, A1(R), NZ1, A2, NZ2,3,A3, 2007 Nm,S, [Sm, E1, US, Fj, Arg, E2]
Du Preez, R J (N) 1992 NZ, A, 1993 F 1,2, A 1,2,3
Du Rand, J A (R, NT) 1949 NZ 2,3, 1951 S, I, W, 1952 E, F, 1953 A 1,2,3,4, 1955 BI 1,2,3,4, 1956 A 1, 2, NZ 1, 2, 3, 4
Du Randt, J P (OFS, FS) 1994 Arg 1,2, S, W, 1995 WS, [A, WS, F, NZ], 1996 Fj, A 1, NZ 1, A 2, NZ 2,3,4, 1997 Tg, BI 1,2,3, NZ 1, A 1, NZ 2, A 2, It, F 1,2, E, S, 1999 NZ 1, A 1, NZ 2, A 2, [S, Sp (R), U, E, A 3, NZ 3], 2004 I1, 2, W1, PI, NZ1,A1,NZ2,A2,W2,I3,E, S(R), Arg(R), 2005 U(R),F1,A1,NZ1,A4,NZ2,Arg, W(R), F3, 2006 S1, 2, F, A1, NZ1, A2, NZ2,3,A3, 2007 Sm, NZ1, Nm, S, [Sm, E1, US, Fj, Arg, E2]
Du Toit, A F (WP) 1928 NZ 3,4
Du Toit, B A (Tvl) 1938 BI 1,2,3
Du Toit, G S (GW, WP) 1998 I 1, 1999 It 1,2, W (R), NZ 1,2, 2004 I1,W1(R),A1(R), S(R),Arg, 2006 S1(R), 2(R), F(R)
Du Toit, P A (NT) 1949 NZ 2,3,4, 1951 S, I, W, 1952 E, F
Du Toit, P G (WP) 1981 NZ 1, 1982 S Am 1,2, 1984 E 1,2
Du Toit, P S (WP) 1958 F 1,2, 1960 NZ 1,2,3,4, W, I, 1961 E, S, F, I, A 1,2
Duvenhage, F P (GW) 1949 NZ 1,3

Edwards, P (NT) 1980 S Am 1,2
Ellis, J H (SWA) 1965 NZ 1,2,3,4, 1967 F 1,2,3,4, 1968 BI 1,2,3,4, F 1,2, 1969 A 1,2,3,4, S, 1970 I, W, NZ 1,2,3,4, 1971 F 1,2, A 1,2,3, 1972 E, 1974 BI 1,2,3,4, F 1,2, 1976 NZ 1
Ellis, M C (Tvl) 1921 NZ 2,3, 1924 BI 1,2,3,4
Els, W W (OFS) 1997 A 2(R)
Engelbrecht, J P (WP) 1960 S, W, I, 1961 E, S, F, A 1,2, 1962 BI 2,3,4, 1963 A 2,3, 1964 W, F, 1965 I, S, A 1,2, NZ 1,2,3,4, 1967 F 1,2,3,4, 1968 BI 1,2, F 1,2, 1969 A 1,2
Erasmus, F S (NT, EP) 1986 Cv 3,4, 1989 Wld 2
Erasmus, J C (OFS, GL) 1997 BI 3, A 2, It, F 1,2, S, 1998 I 1,2, W 1, E 1, A 1, NZ 2, A 2, S, W 2, I 3, E 2, 1999 It 1,2, W, A 1, NZ 2, A 2, [S, U, E, A 3, NZ 3], 2000 C, E 1, A 1, NZ 1,2, A 3, 2001 F 1,2
Esterhuizen, G (GL) 2000 NZ 1(R),2, A 3, Arg, I, W (R), E 3(t)
Etlinger, T E (WP) 1896 BI 4

Ferreira, C (OFS) 1986 Cv 1,2
Ferreira, P S (WP) 1984 S Am 1,2
Ferris, H H (Tvl) 1903 BI 3
Fleck R F (WP) 1999 It 1,2, NZ 1(R), A 1, NZ 2(R), A 2, [S, U, E, A 3, NZ 3], 2000 C, E 1,2, A 1, NZ 1, A 2, NZ 2, A 3, Arg, I, W, E 3, 2001 F 1(R),2, It 1, NZ 1, A 1,2, 2002 S, E
Floors, L (FS) 2006 E2
Forbes, H H (Tvl) 1896 BI 2
Fortuin, B A (FS) 2006 I, 2007 A2
Fourie, C (EP) 1974 F 1,2, 1975 F 1,2
Fourie, J (GL) 2003 [U,Gg,Sm(R),NZ(R)], 2004 I2,E(R),S,Arg, 2005 U(R),F2(R),A1(R), 2, 3, NZ1, A4, NZ2, Arg, W,F3, 2006 S1,A1,NZ1,A2,NZ2,3,A3, 2007 Sm(R),A1,NZ1,Nm, S, [Sm,E1,US,Fj,Arg,E2]
Fourie, T T (SET) 1974 BI 3
Fourie, W L (SWA) 1958 F 1,2
Francis, J A J (Tvl) 1912 S, I, W, 1913 E, F
Frederickson, C A (Tvl) 1974 BI 2, 1980 S Am 1,2
Frew, A (Tvl) 1903 BI 1
Froneman, D C (OFS) 1977 Wld
Froneman, I L (Bor) 1933 A 1
Fuls, H T (Tvl, EP) 1992 NZ (R), 1993 F 1,2, A 1,2,3, Arg 1,2
Fry, S P (WP) 1951 S, I, W, 1952 E, F, 1953 A 1,2,3,4, 1955 BI 1,2,3,4
Fynn, E E (N) 2001 F 1, It 1(R)
Fyvie, W (N) 1996 NZ 4(t & R), 5(R), Arg 2(R)

Gage, J H (OFS) 1933 A 1
Gainsford, J L (WP) 1960 S, NZ 1,2,3,4, W, I, 1961 E, S, F, A 1,2, 1962 BI 1,2,3,4, 1963 A 1,2,3,4, 1964 W, F, 1965 I, S, A 1,2, NZ 1,2,3,4, 1967 F 1,2,3
Garvey, A C (N) 1996 Arg 1,2, F 1,2, W, 1997 Tg, BI 1,2,3(R), A 1(t), It, F 1,2, E, S, 1998 I 1,2, W 1, E1, A 1, NZ 1,2 A 2, W 2, S, I 3, E 2, 1999 [Sp]
Geel, P J (OFS) 1949 NZ 3
Geere, V (Tvl) 1933 A 1,2,3,4,5
Geffin, A O (Tvl) 1949 NZ 1,2,3,4, 1951 S, I, W
Geldenhuys, A (EP) 1992 NZ, A, F 1,2
Geldenhuys, S B (NT) 1981 NZ 2,3, US, 1982 S Am 1,2, 1989 Wld 1,2
Gentles, T A (WP) 1955 BI 1,2,4, 1956 NZ 2,3, 1958 F 2
Geraghty, E M (Bor) 1949 NZ 4
Gerber, D M (EP, WP) 1980 S Am 3,4, F, 1981 I 1,2, NZ 1,2,3, US, 1982 S Am 1,2, 1984 E 1,2, S Am 1,2, 1986 Cv 1,2,3,4, 1992 NZ, A, F 1,2, E
Gerber, H J (WP) 2003 S 1,2
Gerber, M C (EP) 1958 F 1,2, 1960 S
Gericke, F W (Tvl) 1960 S
Germishuys, J S (OFS, Tvl) 1974 BI 2, 1976 NZ 1, 2, 3, 4, 1977 Wld, 1980 S Am 1,2, BI 1,2,3,4, S Am 3,4, F, 1981 I 1,2, NZ 2,3, US
Gibbs, B (GW) 1903 BI 2
Goosen, C P (OFS) 1965 NZ 2
Gorton, H C (Tvl) 1896 BI 1
Gould, R L (N) 1968 BI 1,2,3,4
Grant, P J (WP) 2007 A2(R),NZ2(R)
Gray, B G (WP) 1931 W, 1932 E, S, 1933 A 5
Greeff, W W (WP) 2002 Arg (R), Sm, NZ 1, A 1, NZ 2, A 2, F, S, E, 2003 [U,Gg]
Greenwood, C M (WP) 1961 I
Greyling, P J F (OFS) 1967 F 1,2,3,4, 1968 BI 1, F 1,2, 1969 A 1,2,3,4, S, E, 1970 I, W, NZ 1,2,3,4, 1971 F 1,2, A 1,2,3, 1972 E
Grobler, C J (OFS) 1974 BI 4, 1975 F 1,2
Guthrie, F H (WP) 1891 BI 1,3, 1896 BI 1

Habana, B G (GL, BB) 2004 E(R),S,Arg, 2005 U,F1,2,A1,2,3,NZ1,A4,NZ2,Arg,W,F3, 2006 S2,F,A1,NZ1,A2,NZ2,3, I, E1,2, 2007 E1,2, S, [Sm,E1,Tg(R),US,Fj,Arg,E2]
Hahn, C H L (Tvl) 1910 BI 1,2,3
Hall, D B (GL) 2001 F 1,2, NZ 1, A 1,2, NZ 2, It 2, E, US, 2002 Sm, NZ 1,2, A 2
Halstead, T M (N) 2001 F 3, It 2, E, US (R), 2003 S 1,2
Hamilton, F (EP) 1891 BI 1
Harris, T A (Tvl) 1937 NZ 2,3, 1938 BI 1,2,3
Hartley, A J (WP) 1891 BI 3
Hattingh, H (NT) 1992 A (R), F 2(R), E, 1994 Arg 1,2
Hattingh, L B (OFS) 1933 A 2
Heatlie, B H (WP) 1891 BI 2,3, 1896 BI 1,4, 1903 BI 1,3
Hendricks, M (Bol) 1998 I 2(R), W 1(R)
Hendriks, P (Tvl) 1992 NZ, A, 1994 S, W, 1995 [A, R, C], 1996 A 1, NZ 1, A 2, NZ 2,3,4,5
Hepburn, T B (WP) 1896 BI 4
Heunis, J W (NT) 1981 NZ 3(R), US, 1982 S Am 1,2, 1984 E 1,2, S Am 1,2, 1986 Cv 1,2,3,4, 1989 Wld 1,2
Hill, R A (R) 1960 W, I, 1961 I, A 1,2, 1962 BI 4, 1963 A 3
Hills, W G (NT) 1992 F 1,2, E, 1993 F 1,2, A 1
Hirsch, J G (EP) 1906 I, 1910 BI 1
Hobson, T E C (WP) 1903 BI 3
Hoffman, R S (Bol) 1953 A 3
Holton, D N (EP) 1960 S
Honiball, H W (N) 1993 A 3(R), Arg 2, 1995 WS (R), 1996 Fj, A 1, NZ 5, Arg 1,2, F 1,2, W, 1997 Tg, BI 1,2,3(R), NZ 1(R), A 1(R), NZ 2, A 2, It, F 1,2, E, 1998 W 1(R), E 1, A 1, NZ 1,2, A 2, W 2, S, I 3, E 2, 1999 [A 3(R), NZ 3]
Hopwood, D J (WP) 1960 S, NZ 3,4, W, 1961 E, S, F, I, A 1,2, 1962 BI 1,2,3,4, 1963 A 1,2,4, 1964 W, F, 1965 S, NZ 3,4

Hougaard, D J (BB) 2003 [U(R),E(R),Gg,Sm,NZ], 2007 Sm,A2,NZ2
Howe, B F (Bor) 1956 NZ 1,4
Howe-Browne, N R F G (WP) 1910 BI 1,2,3
Hugo, D P (WP) 1989 Wld 1,2
Human, D C F (WP) 2002 W 1,2, Arg (R), Sm (R)
Hurter, M H (NT) 1995 [R, C], W, 1996 Fj, A 1, NZ 1,2,3,4,5, 1997 NZ 1,2, A 2

Immelman, J H (WP) 1913 F

Jackson, D C (WP) 1906 I, W, E
Jackson, J S (WP) 1903 BI 2
Jacobs, A A (Falcons) 2001 It 2(R), US, 2002 W 1(R), Arg, Sm (R), NZ 1(t+R), A 1(R), F, S, E (R)
James, A D (N) 2001 F 1,2, NZ 1, A 1,2, NZ 2, 2002 F (R), S, E, 2006 NZ1,A2,NZ2,3(R),E1, 2007 E1,2,A1,NZ1,Nm,S, [Sm,E1,US,Fj,Arg,E2]
Jansen, E (OFS) 1981 NZ 1
Jansen, J S (OFS) 1970 NZ 1,2,3,4, 1971 F 1,2, A 1,2,3, 1972 E
Jantjes, C A (GL) 2001 It 1, A 1,2, NZ 2, F 3, It 2, E, US, 2005 Arg,W
Januarie, E R (GL) 2005 U,F2,A1,2,3(R),NZ1,A4,NZ2, 2006 S1(R),2(R),F(R),A1, I,E1, 2, 2007 E1,2,Sm, Nm(R), [Sm(R),Tg]
Jennings, C B (Bor) 1937 NZ 1
Johnson, G K (Tvl) 1993 Arg 2, 1994 NZ 3, Arg 1, 1995 WS, [R, C, WS]
Johnstone, P G A (WP) 1951 S, I, W, 1952 E, F, 1956 A 1, NZ 1,2,4
Jones, C H (Tvl) 1903 BI 1,2
Jones, P S B (WP) 1896 BI 1,3,4
Jordaan, N (BB) 2002 E (R)
Jordaan, R P (NT) 1949 NZ 1,2,3,4
Joubert, A J (OFS, N) 1989 Wld 1(R), 1993 A 3, Arg 1, 1994 E 1,2, NZ 1,2(R), 3, Arg 2, S, W, 1995 [A, C, WS, F, NZ], W, It, E, 1996 Fj, A 1, NZ 1,3,4,5, Arg 1,2, F 1,2, W, 1997 Tg, BI 1,2, A 2
Joubert, M C (Bol, WP) 2001 NZ 1, 2002 W 1,2, Arg (R), Sm, NZ 1, A1, NZ 2, A 2, F (R), 2003 S 2, Arg, A 1, 2004 I1,2,W1,PI,NZ1,A1,NZ2,A2,W2,I3,E,S,Arg, 2005 U,F1,2, A1
Joubert, S J (WP) 1906 I, W, E
Julies, W (Bol, SWD, GL) 1999 [Sp], 2004 I1, 2, W1, S, Arg, 2005 A2(R),3(t), 2006 F(R), 2007 Sm, [Tg]

Kahts, W J H (NT) 1980 BI 1,2,3, S Am 3,4, F, 1981 I 1,2, NZ 2, 1982 S Am 1,2
Kaminer, J (Tvl) 1958 F 2
Kayser, D J (EP, N) 1999 It 2(R), A 1(R), NZ 2, A 2, [S, Sp (R), U, E, A 3], 2001 It 1(R), NZ 1(R), A 2(R), NZ 2(R)
Kebble, G R (N) 1993 Arg 1,2, 1994 NZ 1(R), 2
Kelly, E W (GW) 1896 BI 3
Kempson, R B (N, WP, Ulster) 1998 I 2(R), W 1, E 1, A 1, NZ 1,2 A 2, W 2, S, I 3, E 2, 1999 It 1,2, W, 2000 C, E 1,2, A 1, NZ 1, A 2,3, Arg, I, W, E 3, 2001 F 1,2(R), NZ 1, A 1,2, NZ 2, 2003 S 1(R),2(R), Arg, A 1(R), NZ 1(R), A 2
Kenyon, B J (Bor) 1949 NZ 4
Kipling, H G (GW) 1931 W, I, 1932 E, S, 1933 A 1,2,3,4,5
Kirkpatrick, A I (GW) 1953 A 2, 1956 NZ 2, 1958 F 1, 1960 S, NZ 1,2,3,4, W, I, 1961 E, S, F
Knight, A S (Tvl) 1912 S, I, W, 1913 E, F
Knoetze, F (WP) 1989 Wld 1,2
Koch, A C (Bol) 1949 NZ 2,3,4, 1951 S, I, W, 1952 E, F, 1953 A 1,2,4, 1955 BI 1,2,3,4, 1956 A 1, NZ 2,3, 1958 F 1,2, 1960 NZ 1,2
Koch, H V (WP) 1949 NZ 1,2,3,4
Koen, L J (GL, BB) 2000 A 1, 2001 It 2, E, US, 2003 S 1,2, Arg, A 1, NZ 1, A 2, NZ 2, [U,E,Sm(R),NZ(R)]
Kotze, G J M (WP) 1967 F 1,2,3,4
Krantz, E F W (OFS) 1976 NZ 1, 1981 I 1,
Krige, C P J (WP) 1999 It 2, W, NZ 1, 2000 C (R), E 1(R),2, A 1(R), NZ 1, A 2, NZ 2, A 3, Arg, I, W, E 3, 2001 F 1,2, It 1(R), A 1(t+R), It 2(R), E (R), 2002 W 2, Arg, Sm, NZ 1, A 1, NZ 2, A 2, F, S, E, 2003 Arg, A 1, NZ 1, A 2, NZ 2, [E,Sm,NZ]
Krige, J D (WP) 1903 BI 1,3, 1906 S, I, W
Kritzinger, J L (Tvl) 1974 BI 3,4, F 1,2, 1975 F 1,2, 1976 NZ 4
Kroon, C M (EP) 1955 BI 1
Kruger, P E (Tvl) 1986 Cv 3,4
Kruger, R J (NT, BB) 1993 Arg 1,2, 1994 S, W, 1995 WS, [A, R, WS, F, NZ], W, It, E, 1996 Fj, A 1, NZ 1, A 2, NZ 2,3,4,5, Arg 1,2, F 1,2, W, 1997 Tg, BI 1,2, NZ 1, A 1, NZ 2, 1999 NZ 2, A 2(R), [Sp, NZ 3(R)]
Kruger, T L (Tvl) 1921 NZ 1,2, 1924 BI 1,2,3,4, 1928 NZ 1,2
Kuhn, S P (Tvl) 1960 NZ 3,4, W, I, 1961 E, S, F, I, A 1,2, 1962 BI 1,2,3,4, 1963 A 1,2,3, 1965 I, S

Labuschagne, J J (GL) 2000 NZ 1(R), 2002 W 1,2, Arg, NZ 1, A 1, NZ 2, A2, F, S, E
La Grange, J B (WP) 1924 BI 3,4
Larard, A (Tvl) 1896 BI 2,4
Lategan, M T (WP) 1949 NZ 1,2,3,4, 1951 S, I, W, 1952 E, F, 1953 A 1,2
Laubscher, T G (WP) 1994 Arg 1,2, S, W, 1995 It, E
Lawless, M J (WP) 1964 F, 1969 E (R), 1970 I, W
Ledger, S H (GW) 1912 S, I, 1913 E, F
Leonard, A (WP, SWD) 1999 A 1, [Sp]
Le Roux, A H (OFS, N) 1994 E 1, 1998 I 1,2, W 1(R), E 1(R), A 1(R), NZ 1(R),2(R), A 2(R), W 2(R), S (R), I 3(R), E 2(t+R), 1999 It 1(R),2(R), W (R), NZ 1(R), A 1(R), NZ 2(R), A 2(R), [S(R), Sp, U (R), E (R), A 3(R), NZ 3(R)], 2000 E 1(t+R),2(R), A 1(R),2(R), NZ 2, A 3(R), Arg (R), I (t), W (R), E 3(R), 2001 F 1(R),2, It 1, NZ 1(R), A 1(R), 2(R), NZ 2(R), F 3, It 2, E, US (R), 2002 W 1(R), 2(R), Arg, NZ 1(R), A 1(R), NZ 2(R), A 2(R)
Le Roux, H P (Tvl) 1993 F 1,2, 1994 E 1,2, NZ 1,2,3, Arg 2, S, W, 1995 WS [A, R, C (R), WS, F, NZ], W, It, E, 1996 Fj, NZ 2, Arg 1,2, F 1,2, W
Le Roux, J H S (Tvl) 1994 E 2, NZ 1,2
Le Roux, M (OFS) 1980 BI 1,2,3,4, S Am 3,4, F, 1981 I 1
Le Roux, P A (WP) 1906 I, W, E
Little, E M (GW) 1891 BI 1,3
Lobberts, H (BB) 2006 E1(R), 2007 NZ2(R)
Lochner, G P (WP) 1955 BI 3, 1956 A 1,2, NZ 1,2,3,4, 1958 F 1,2
Lochner, G P (EP) 1937 NZ 3, 1938 BI 1,2
Lockyear, R J (GW) 1960 NZ 1,2,3,4, 1960 I, 1961 F
Lombard, A C (EP) 1910 BI 2
Lombard, F (FS) 2002 S, E
Lötter, D (Tvl) 1993 F 2, A 1,2
Lotz, J W (Tvl) 1937 A 1,2, NZ 1,2,3, 1938 BI 1,2,3
Loubscher, R I P (EP, N) 2002 W 1, 2003 S 1, [U(R),Gg]
Loubser, J A (WP) 1903 BI 3, 1906 S, I, W, E, 1910 BI 1,3
Lourens, M J (NT) 1968 BI 2,3,4
Louw, F H (WP) 2002 W 2(R), Arg, Sm
Louw, J S (Tvl) 1891 BI 1,2,3
Louw, M J (Tvl) 1971 A 2,3
Louw, M M (WP) 1928 NZ 3,4, 1931 W, I, 1932 E, S, 1933 A 1,2,3,4,5, 1937 A 1,2, NZ 2,3, 1938 BI 1,2,3
Louw, R J (WP) 1980 S Am 1,2, BI 1,2,3,4 S Am 3,4, F, 1981 I 1,2, NZ 1,3, 1982 S Am 1,2, 1984 E 1,2, S Am 1,2
Louw, S C (WP) 1933 A 1,2,3,4,5, 1937 A 1, NZ 1,2,3, 1938 BI 1,2,3
Lubbe, E (GW) 1997 Tg, BI 1
Luyt, F P (WP) 1910 BI 1,2,3, 1912 S, I, W, 1913 E
Luyt, J D (EP) 1912 S, W, 1913 E, F
Luyt, R R (W P) 1910 BI 2,3, 1912 S, I, W, 1913 E, F
Lyons, D J (EP) 1896 BI 1
Lyster, P J (N) 1933 A 2,5, 1937 NZ 1

McCallum, I D (WP) 1970 NZ 1,2,3,4, 1971 F 1,2, A 1,2,3, 1974 BI 1,2
McCallum, R J (WP) 1974 BI 1
McCulloch, J D (GW) 1913 E, F

MacDonald, A W (R) 1965 A 1, NZ 1,2,3,4
Macdonald, D A (WP) 1974 BI 2
Macdonald, I (Tvl) 1992 NZ, A, 1993 F 1, A 3, 1994 E 2, 1995 WS (R)
McDonald, J A J (WP) 1931 W, I, 1932 E, S
McEwan, W M C (Tvl) 1903 BI 1,3
McHardy, E E (OFS) 1912 S, I, W, 1913 E, F
McKendrick, J A (WP) 1891 BI 3
Malan, A S (Tvl) 1960 NZ 1,2,3,4, W, I, 1961 E, S, F, 1962 BI 1, 1963 A 1,2,3, 1964 W, 1965 I, S
Malan, A W (NT) 1989 Wld 1,2, 1992 NZ, A, F 1,2, E
Malan, E (NT) 1980 BI 3(R), 4
Malan, G F (WP) 1958 F 2, 1960 NZ 1,3,4, 1961 E, S, F, 1962 BI 1,2,3, 1963 A 1,2,4, 1964 W, 1965 A 1,2, NZ 1,2
Malan, P (Tvl) 1949 NZ 4
Mallett, N V H (WP) 1984 S Am 1,2
Malotana K (Bor) 1999 [Sp]
Mans, W J (WP) 1965 I, S
Marais, C F (WP) 1999 It 1(R),2(R), 2000 C, E 1,2, A 1, NZ 1, A 2, NZ 2, A 3, Arg (R), W (R)
Marais, F P (Bol) 1949 NZ 1,2, 1951 S, 1953 A 1,2
Marais, J F K (WP) 1963 A 3, 1964 W, F, 1965 I, S, A 2, 1968 BI, 1,2,3,4, F 1,2, 1969 A 1,2,3,4, S, E, 1970 I, W, NZ 1,2,3,4, 1971 F 1,2, A 1,2,3, 1974 BI 1,2,3,4, F 1,2
Maré, D S (Tvl) 1906 S
Marsberg, A F W (GW) 1906 S, W, E
Marsberg, P A (GW) 1910 BI 1
Martheze, W C (GW) 1903 BI 2, 1906 I, W
Martin, H J (Tvl) 1937 A 2
Matfield, V (BB) 2001 It 1(R), NZ 1, A 2, NZ 2, F 3, It 2, E, US, 2002 W 1, Sm, NZ 1, A 1, NZ 2(R), 2003 S 1,2, Arg, A 1, NZ 1, A 2, NZ 2, [U,E,Sm,NZ], 2004 I1,2,W1,NZ2, A2,W2,I3,E,S,Arg, 2005 F1, 2, A1, 2, 3, NZ1, A4, NZ2, Arg, W,F3, 2006 S1, 2, F, A1, NZ1, A2, NZ2,3,A3, 2007 E1,2,A1,NZ1,Nm,S, [Sm,E1,Tg(R),US,Fj,Arg,E2]
Mellet, T B (GW) 1896 BI 2
Mellish, F W (WP) 1921 NZ 1,3, 1924 BI 1,2,3,4
Mentz, H (N) 2004 I1,W1(R)
Merry, J (EP) 1891 BI 1
Metcalf, H D (Bor) 1903 BI 2
Meyer, C du P (WP) 1921 NZ 1,2,3
Meyer, P J (GW) 1896 BI 1
Meyer, W (OFS, GL) 1997 S (R), 1999 It 2, NZ 1(R), A 1(R), 2000 C (R), E 1, NZ 1(R),2(R), Arg, I, W, E 3, 2001 F 1(R),2, It 1, F 3(R), It 2, E, US (t+R), 2002 W 1,2, Arg, NZ 1,2, A 2, F
Michau, J M (Tvl) 1921 NZ 1
Michau, J P (WP) 1921 NZ 1,2,3
Millar, W A (WP) 1906 E, 1910 BI 2,3, 1912 I, W, 1913 F
Mills, W J (WP) 1910 BI 2
Moll, T (Tvl) 1910 BI 2
Montini, P E (WP) 1956 A 1,2
Montgomery, P C (WP, Newport, N) 1997 BI 2,3, NZ 1, A 1, NZ 2, A 2, F 1,2, E, S, 1998 I 1,2, W 1, E 1, A 1, NZ 1,2, A 2, W 2, S, I 3, E 2, 1999 It 1,2, W, NZ 1, A 1, NZ 2, A 2, [S, U, E, A 3, NZ 3], 2000 C, E 1,2, A 1, NZ 1, A 2(R), Arg, I, W, E 3, 2001 F 1, 2(t), It 1, NZ 1, F 3(R), It 2(R), 2004 I2, W1, PI, NZ1, A1, NZ2, A2, W2,I3,E,S, 2005 U,F1,2, A1, 2, 3, NZ1, A4, NZ2, Arg, W, F3, 2006 S1,2,F,A1,NZ1,A2,NZ2, 2007 E1,2,Sm(R), A1, NZ1, Nm,S, [Sm, E1,Tg(R),US,Fj,Arg,E2]
Moolman, L C (NT) 1977 Wld, 1980 S Am 1,2, BI 1,2,3,4, S Am 3,4, F, 1981 I 1,2, NZ 1,2,3, US, 1982 S Am 1,2, 1984 S Am 1,2, 1986 Cv 1,2,3,4
Mordt, R H (Z-R, NT) 1980 S Am 1,2, BI 1,2,3,4, S Am 3,4, F, 1981 I 2, NZ 1,2,3, US, 1982 S Am 1,2, 1984 S Am 1,2
Morkel, D A (Tvl) 1903 BI 1
Morkel, D F T (Tvl) 1906 I, E, 1910 BI 1,3, 1912 S, I, W, 1913 E, F
Morkel, H J (WP) 1921 NZ 1
Morkel, H W (WP) 1921 NZ 1,2
Morkel, J A (WP) 1921 NZ 2,3
Morkel, J W H (WP) 1912 S, I, W, 1913 E, F
Morkel, P G (WP) 1912 S, I, W, 1913 E, F, 1921 NZ 1,2,3
Morkel, P K (WP) 1928 NZ 4
Morkel, W H (WP) 1910 BI 3, 1912 S, I, W, 1913 E, F, 1921 NZ 1,2,3
Morkel, W S (Tvl) 1906 S, I, W, E
Moss, C (N) 1949 NZ 1,2,3,4
Mostert, P J (WP) 1921 NZ 1,2,3, 1924 BI 1,2,4, 1928 NZ 1,2,3,4, 1931 W, I, 1932 E, S
Muir, D J (WP) 1997 It, F 1,2, E, S
Mulder, J C (Tvl, GL) 1994 NZ 2,3, S, W, 1995 WS, [A, WS, F, NZ], W, It, E, 1996 Fj, A 1, NZ 1, A 2, NZ 2,5, Arg 1,2, F 1,2, W, 1997 Tg, BI 1, 1999 It 1(R),2, W, NZ 1, 2000 C(R), A 1, E 3, 2001 F 1, It 1
Muller, G H (WP) 1969 A 3,4, S, 1970 W, NZ 1,2,3,4, 1971 F 1,2, 1972 E, 1974 BI 1,3,4
Muller, G J (N) 2006 S1(R),NZ1(R),A2,NZ2,3,A3, I(R), E1,2, 2007 E1(R),2(R),Sm(R), A1(R),NZ1(R),A2, NZ2,Nm(R) , [Sm(R),E1(R),Fj(t&R),Arg(t&R)]
Muller, G P (GL) 2003 A 2, NZ 2, [E,Gg(R),Sm,NZ]
Muller, H L (OFS) 1986 Cv 4(R), 1989 Wld 1(R)
Muller, H S V (Tvl) 1949 NZ 1,2,3,4, 1951 S, I, W, 1952 E, F, 1953 A 1,2,3,4
Muller, L J J (N) 1992 NZ, A
Muller, P G (N) 1992 NZ, A, F 1,2, E, 1993 F 1,2, A 1,2,3, Arg 1,2, 1994 E 1,2, NZ 1, S, W, 1998 I 1,2, W 1, E 1, A 1, NZ 1,2, A 2, 1999 It 1, W, NZ 1, A 1, [Sp, E, A 3, NZ 3]
Murray, W M (N) 2007 Sm,A2,NZ2
Myburgh, F R (EP) 1896 BI 1
Myburgh, J L (NT) 1962 BI 1, 1963 A 4, 1964 W, F, 1968 BI 1,2,3, F 1,2, 1969 A 1,2,3,4, E, 1970 I, W, NZ 3, 4
Myburgh, W H (WT) 1924 BI 1

Naude, J P (WP) 1963 A 4, 1965 A 1,2, NZ 1,3,4, 1967 F 1,2,3,4, 1968 BI 1,2,3,4
Ndungane, A Z (BB) 2006 A1,2,NZ2,3,A3, E1,2, 2007 E2,Nm(R), [US]
Neethling, J B (WP) 1967 F 1,2,3,4, 1968 BI 4, 1969 S, 1970 NZ 1,2
Nel, J A (Tvl) 1960 NZ 1,2, 1963 A 1,2, 1965 A 2, NZ 1,2,3,4, 1970 NZ 3,4
Nel, J J (WP) 1956 A 1,2, NZ 1,2,3,4, 1958 F 1,2
Nel, P A R O (Tvl) 1903 BI 1,2,3
Nel, P J (N) 1928 NZ 1,2,3,4, 1931 W, I, 1932 E, S, 1933 A 1,3,4,5, 1937 A 1,2, NZ 2,3
Nimb, C F (WP) 1961 I
Nomis, S H (Tvl) 1967 F 4, 1968 BI 1,2,3,4, F 1,2, 1969 A 1,2,3,4, S, E, 1970 I, W, NZ 1,2,3,4, 1971 F 1,2, A 1,2,3, 1972 E
Nykamp, J L (Tvl) 1933 A 2

Ochse, J K (WP) 1951 I, W, 1952 E, F, 1953 A 1,2,4
Oelofse, J S A (Tvl) 1953 A 1,2,3,4
Oliver, J F (Tvl) 1928 NZ 3,4
Olivier, E (WP) 1967 F 1,2,3,4, 1968 BI 1,2,3,4, F 1,2, 1969 A 1,2,3,4, S, E
Olivier, J (NT) 1992 F 1,2, E, 1993 F 1,2 A 1,2,3, Arg 1, 1995 W, It (R), E, 1996 Arg 1,2, F 1,2, W
Olivier, W (BB) 2006 S1(R),2,F,A1,NZ1,A2,NZ2(R),3,A3, I(R), E1,2, 2007 E1,2, NZ1(R),A2,NZ2, [E1(R),Tg,Arg(R)]
Olver, E (EP) 1896 BI 1
Oosthuizen, J J (WP) 1974 BI 1, F 1,2, 1975 F 1,2, 1976 NZ 1,2,3,4
Oosthuizen, O W (NT, Tvl) 1981 I 1(R), 2, NZ 2,3, US, 1982 S Am 1,2, 1984 E 1,2
Osler, B L (WP) 1924 BI 1,2,3,4, 1928 NZ 1,2,3,4, 1931 W, I, 1932 E, S, 1933 A 1,2,3,4,5
Osler, S G (WP) 1928 NZ 1
Otto, K (NT, BB) 1995 [R, C (R), WS (R)], 1997 BI 3, NZ 1, A 1, NZ 2, It, F 1,2, E, S, 1998 I 1,2, W 1, E 1, A 1, NZ 1,2, A 2, W 2, S, I 3, E 2, 1999 It 1, W, NZ 1, A 1, [S (R), Sp, U, E, A 3, NZ 3], 2000 C, E 1,2, A 1
Oxlee, K (N) 1960 NZ 1,2,3,4, W, I, 1961 S, A 1,2, 1962 BI 1,2,3,4, 1963 A 1,2,4, 1964 W, 1965 NZ 1,2

Pagel, G L (WP) 1995 [A (R), R, C, NZ (R)], 1996 NZ 5(R)
Parker, W H (EP) 1965 A 1,2
Partridge, J E C (Tvl) 1903 BI 1
Paulse, B J (WP) 1999 It 1,2, NZ 1, A 1,2(R), [S (R), Sp, NZ 3], 2000 C, E 1,2, A 1, NZ 1, A 2, NZ 2, A 3, Arg, W, E 3, 2001 F 1,2, It 1, NZ 1, A 1,2, NZ 2, F 3, It 2, E, 2002 W 1,2, Arg, Sm (R), A 1, NZ 2, A 2, F, S, E, 2003 [Gg], 2004 I1, 2, W1, PI, NZ1, A1, NZ2, A2, W2,I3,E, 2005 A2,3,NZ1,A4,F3, 2006 S1, 2, A1(R), NZ1, 3(R),A3(R), 2007 A2,NZ2
Payn, C (N) 1924 BI 1,2
Pelser, H J M (Tvl) 1958 F 1, 1960 NZ 1,2,3,4, W, I, 1961 F, I, A 1,2
Pfaff, B D (WP) 1956 A 1
Pickard, J A J (WP) 1953 A 3,4, 1956 NZ 2, 1958 F 2
Pienaar, J F (Tvl) 1993 F 1,2, A 1,2,3, Arg 1,2, 1994 E 1,2, NZ 2,3, Arg 1,2, S, W, 1995 WS, [A, C, WS, F, NZ], W, It, E, 1996 Fj, A 1, NZ 1, A 2, NZ 2
Pienaar, R (N) 2006 NZ2(R),3(R),A3(R), I(t), E1(R), 2007 E1(R),2(R),Sm(R),A1,NZ1, A2,NZ2,Nm(R),S(R), [E1(t&R),Tg,US(R),Arg(R)]
Pienaar, Z M J (OFS) 1980 S Am 2(R), BI 1,2,3,4, S Am 3,4, F, 1981 I 1,2, NZ 1,2,3
Pietersen, J-P R (N) 2006 A3, 2007 Sm,A1,NZ1,A2,NZ2,Nm,S, [Sm,E1,Tg,US(R),Fj, Arg,E2]
Pitzer, G (NT) 1967 F 1,2,3,4, 1968 BI 1,2,3,4, F 1,2, 1969 A 3,4
Pope, C F (WP) 1974 BI 1,2,3,4, 1975 F 1,2, 1976 NZ 2,3,4
Potgieter, H J (OFS) 1928 NZ 1,2
Potgieter, H L (OFS) 1977 Wld
Powell, A W (GW) 1896 BI 3
Powell, J M (GW) 1891 BI 2, 1896 BI 3, 1903 BI 1,2
Prentis, R B (Tvl) 1980 S Am 1,2, BI 1,2,3,4, S Am 3,4, F, 1981 I 1,2
Pretorius, A S (GL) 2002 W 1,2, Arg, Sm, NZ 1, A 1, NZ 2, F, S (R), E, 2003 NZ 1(R), A 1, 2005 A2,3,NZ1,A4,NZ2,Arg, 2006 NZ2(R),3,A3, I, E1(t&R),2, 2007 S(R) , [Sm(R), E1(R),Tg,US(R),Arg(R)]
Pretorius, J C (GL) 2006 I, 2007 NZ2
Pretorius, N F (Tvl) 1928 NZ 1,2,3,4
Prinsloo, J (Tvl) 1958 F 1,2
Prinsloo, J (NT) 1963 A 3
Prinsloo, J P (Tvl) 1928 NZ 1
Putter, D J (WT) 1963 A 1,2,4

Raaff, J W E (GW) 1903 BI 1,2, 1906 S, W, E, 1910 BI 1
Ralepelle, M C (BB) 2006 NZ2(R), E2(R)
Ras, W J de Wet (OFS) 1976 NZ 1(R), 1980 S Am 2(R)
Rautenbach, S J (WP) 2002 W 1(R),2(t+R), Arg (R), Sm, NZ 1(R), A 1, NZ 2(R), A 2(R), 2003 [U(R),Gg,Sm,NZ], 2004 W1,NZ1(R)
Reece-Edwards, H (N) 1992 F 1,2, 1993 A 2
Reid, A (WP) 1903 BI 3
Reid, B C (Bor) 1933 A 4
Reinach, J (OFS) 1986 Cv 1,2,3,4
Rens, I J (Tvl) 1953 A 3,4
Retief, D F (NT) 1955 BI 1,2,4, 1956 A 1,2, NZ 1,2,3,4
Reyneke, H J (WP) 1910 BI 3
Richards, A R (WP) 1891 BI 1,2,3
Richter, A (NT) 1992 F 1,2, E, 1994 E 2, NZ 1,2,3, 1995 [R, C, WS (R)]
Riley, N M (ET) 1963 A 3
Riordan, C A (Tvl) 1910 BI 1,2
Robertson, I W (R) 1974 F 1,2, 1976 NZ 1,2,4
Rodgers, P H (NT, Tvl) 1989 Wld 1,2, 1992 NZ, F 1,2
Rogers, C D (Tvl) 1984 E 1,2, S Am 1,2
Roos, G D (WP) 1910 BI 2,3
Roos, P J (WP) 1903 BI 3, 1906 I, W, E
Rosenberg, W (Tvl) 1955 BI 2,3,4, 1956 NZ 3, 1958 F 1
Rossouw, C L C (Tvl, N) 1995 WS, [R, WS, F, NZ], 1999 NZ 2(R), A 2(t), [Sp, NZ 3(R)]
Rossouw, D H (WP) 1953 A 3, 4
Rossouw, D J (BB) 2003 [U,Gg,Sm(R),NZ], 2004 E(R),S,Arg, 2005 U,F1,2,A1,W(R), F3(R), 2006 S1,2,F,A1,I,E1,2, 2007 E1,Sm,A1(R),NZ1,S, [Sm,E1,Tg,Fj,Arg,E2]
Rossouw, P W G (WP) 1997 BI 2,3, NZ 1, A 1, NZ 2(R), A 2(R), It, F 1,2, E, S, 1998 I 1,2, W 1, E 1, A 1, NZ 1,2, A 2, W 2, S, I 3, E 2, 1999 It 1, W, NZ 1, A 1(R), NZ 2, A 2, [S, U, E, A 3], 2000 C, E 1,2, A 2, Arg (R), I, W, 2001 F 3, US, 2003 Arg
Rousseau, W P (WP) 1928 NZ 3,4
Roux, F du T (WP) 1960 W, 1961 A 1,2, 1962 BI 1,2,3,4, 1963 A 2, 1965 A 1,2, NZ 1,2,3,4, 1968 BI 3,4, F 1,2 1969 A 1,2,3,4, 1970 I, NZ 1,2,3,4
Roux, J P (Tvl) 1994 E 2, NZ 1,2,3, Arg 1, 1995 [R, C, F (R)], 1996 A 1(R), NZ 1, A 2, NZ 3
Roux, O A (NT) 1969 S, E, 1970 I, W, 1972 E, 1974 BI 3,4
Roux, W G (BB) 2002 F (R), S, E
Russell, R B (MP, N) 2002 W 1(R),2, Arg, A 1(R), NZ 2(R), A 2, F, E (R), 2003 Arg (R), A 1(R), NZ 1, A 2(R), 2004 I2(t&R),W1,NZ1(R),W2(R),Arg(R), 2005 U(R),F2(R), A1(t),Arg(R),W(R), 2006 F

Samuels, T A (GW) 1896 BI 2,3,4
Santon, D (Bol) 2003 A 1(R), NZ 1(R), A 2(t), [Gg(R)]
Sauermann, J T (Tvl) 1971 F 1,2, A 1, 1972 E, 1974 BI 1
Schlebusch, J J J (OFS) 1974 BI 3,4, 1975 F 2
Schmidt, L U (NT) 1958 F 2, 1962 BI 2
Schmidt, U L (NT, Tvl) 1986 Cv 1,2,3,4, 1989 Wld 1, 2, 1992 NZ, A, 1993 F 1,2, A 1,2,3, 1994 Arg 1, 2, S, W
Schoeman, J (WP) 1963 A 3,4, 1965 I, S, A 1, NZ 1,2
Scholtz, C P (WP, Tvl) 1994 Arg 1, 1995 [R, C, WS]
Scholtz, H (FS) 2002 A 1(R), NZ 2(R), A 2(R), 2003 [U(R),Gg]
Scholtz, H H (WP) 1921 NZ 1,2
Schutte, P J W (Tvl) 1994 S, W
Scott, P A (Tvl) 1896 BI 1,2,3,4
Sendin, W D (GW) 1921 NZ 2
Sephaka, L D (GL) 2001 US, 2002 Sm, NZ 1, A 1, NZ 2, A 2, F, 2003 S 1,2, A 1, NZ 1, A 2(t+R), NZ 2, [U,E(t&R),Gg], 2005 F2,A1,2(R),W, 2006 S1(R), NZ3(t&R), A3(R), I
Serfontein, D J (WP) 1980 BI 1,2,3,4, S Am 3,4, F, 1981 I 1,2, NZ 1,2,3, US, 1982 S Am 1,2, 1984 E 1,2, S Am 1,2
Shand, R (GW) 1891 BI 2,3
Sheriff, A R (Tvl) 1938 BI 1,2,3
Shimange, M H (FS, WP) 2004 W1(R), NZ2(R), A2(R), W2(R), 2005 U(R),A1(R),2(R), Arg(R), 2006 S1(R)
Shum, E H (Tvl) 1913 E
Sinclair, D J (Tvl) 1955 BI 1,2,3,4
Sinclair, J H (Tvl) 1903 BI 1
Skene, A L (WP) 1958 F 2
Skinstad, R B (WP, GL, N) 1997 E (t), 1998 W 1(R), E 1(t), NZ 1(R),2(R), A 2(R), W 2(R), S, I 3, E 2, 1999 [S, Sp (R), U, E, A 3], 2001 F 1(R),2(R), It 1, NZ 1, A 1,2, NZ 2, F 3, It 2, E, 2002 W 1,2, Arg, Sm, NZ 1, A 1, NZ 2, A 2, 2003 Arg (R), 2007 E2(t&R), Sm,NZ1,A2, [E1(R),Tg,US(R),Arg(R)]
Slater, J T (EP) 1924 BI 3,4, 1928 NZ 1
Smal, G P (WP) 1986 Cv 1,2,3,4, 1989 Wld 1,2
Small, J T (Tvl, N, WP) 1992 NZ, A, F 1,2, E, 1993 F 1,2, A 1,2,3, Arg 1,2, 1994 E 1,2, NZ 1,2,3(t), Arg 1, 1995 WS, [A, R, F, NZ], W, It, E (R), 1996 Fj, A 1, NZ 1, A 2, NZ 2, Arg 1,2, F 1,2, W, 1997 Tg, BI 1, NZ 1(R), A 1(R), NZ 2, A 2, It, F 1,2, E, S
Smit, F C (WP) 1992 E
Smit, J W (N) 2000 C (t), A 1(R), NZ 1(t+R), A 2(R), NZ 2(R), A 3(R), Arg, I, W, E 3, 2001 F 1,2, It 1, NZ 1(R), A 1(R),2(R), NZ 2(R), F 3(R), It 2, E, US (R), [U(R), E(t&R), Gg,Sm,NZ], 2004 I1, 2, W1, PI, NZ1, A1, NZ2, A2, W2, I3, E, S, Arg, 2005 U,F1,2,A1,2,3, NZ1, A4, NZ2, Arg, W, F3, 2006 S1, 2, F, A1, NZ1, A2, NZ2, 3, A3, I, E1, 2, 2007 E1,2,Sm,A1, [Sm, E1, Tg(R), US, Fj, Arg, E2]
Smith, C M (OFS) 1963 A 3,4, 1964 W, F, 1965 A 1,2, NZ 2
Smith, C W (GW) 1891 BI 2, 1896 BI 2,3

Smith, D (GW) 1891 BI 2
Smith D J (Z-R) 1980 BI 1,2,3,4
Smith, G A C (EP) 1938 BI 3
Smith, J H (FS) 2003 S 1(R),2(R), A 1, NZ 1, A 2, NZ 2, [U,E,Sm,NZ], 2004 W2, 2005 U(R), F2(R), A2, 3, NZ1, A4, NZ2, Arg, W,F3, 2006 S1,2,F,A1,NZ1,A2, I, E2, 2007 E1,2, A1,Nm,S, [Sm,E1,Tg(t&R),US,Fj,Arg,E2]
Smith, P F (GW) 1997 S (R), 1998 I 1(t),2, W 1, NZ 1(R),2(R), A 2(R), W 2, 1999 NZ 2
Smollan, F C (Tvl) 1933 A 3,4,5
Snedden, R C D (GW) 1891 BI 2
Snyman, A H (NT, BB, N) 1996 NZ 3,4, Arg 2(R), W (R), 1997 Tg, BI 1,2,3, NZ 1, A 1, NZ 2, A 2, It, F 1,2, E, S, 1998 I 1,2, W 1, E 1, A 1, NZ 1,2, A 2, W 2, S, I 3, E 2, 1999 NZ 2, 2001 NZ 2, F 3, US, 2002 W 1, 2003 S 1, NZ 1, 2006 S1,2
Snyman, D S L (WP) 1972 E, 1974 BI 1,2(R), F 1,2, 1975 F 1,2, 1976 NZ 2,3, 1977 Wld
Snyman, J C P (OFS) 1974 BI 2,3,4
Sonnekus, G H H (OFS) 1974 BI 3, 1984 E 1,2
Sowerby, R S (N) 2002 Sm (R)
Spies, J J (NT) 1970 NZ 1,2,3,4
Spies, P J (BB) 2006 A1,NZ2,3,A3, I, E1, 2007 E1(R), 2, A1
Stander, J C J (OFS) 1974 BI 4(R), 1976 NZ 1,2,3,4
Stapelberg, W P (NT) 1974 F 1,2
Starke, J J (WP) 1956 NZ 4
Starke, K T (WP) 1924 BI 1,2,3,4
Steenkamp, G G (FS) 2004 S,Arg, 2005 U,F2(R), A2,3, NZ1(R), A4(R), 2007 E1(R), 2, A1, [Tg,Fj(R)]
Steenekamp, J G A (Tvl) 1958 F 1
Stegmann, A C (WP) 1906 S, I
Stegmann, J A (Tvl) 1912 S, I, W, 1913 E, F
Stewart, C (WP) 1998 S, I 3, E 2
Stewart, D A (WP) 1960 S, 1961 E, S, F, I, 1963 A 1, 3, 4, 1964 W, F, 1965 I
Steyn, F P L (N) 2006 I,E1,2, 2007 E1(R), 2(R), Sm, A1(R),NZ1(R),S, [Sm(R),E1,Tg(R), US,Fj,Arg,E2]
Stofberg, M T S (OFS, NT, WP) 1976 NZ 2,3, 1977 Wld, 1980 S Am 1,2, BI 1,2,3,4, S Am 3,4, F, 1981 I 1,2, NZ 1,2, US, 1982 S Am 1,2, 1984 E 1,2
Strachan, L C (Tvl) 1932 E, S, 1937 A 1,2, NZ 1,2,3, 1938 BI 1,2,3
Stransky, J (N, WP) 1993 A 1,2,3, Arg 1, 1994 Arg 1,2, 1995 WS, [A, R (t), C, F, NZ], W, It, E, 1996 Fj (R), NZ 1, A 2, NZ 2,3,4,5(R)
Straeuli, R A W (Tvl) 1994 NZ 1, Arg 1,2, S, W, 1995 WS, [A, WS, NZ (R)], E (R)
Strauss, C P (WP) 1992 F 1,2, E, 1993 F 1,2, A 1,2,3, Arg 1,2, 1994 E 1, NZ 1,2, Arg 1,2
Strauss, J A (WP) 1984 S Am 1,2
Strauss, J H P (Tvl) 1976 NZ 3,4, 1980 S Am 1
Strauss, S S F (GW) 1921 NZ 3
Strydom, C F (OFS) 1955 BI 3, 1956 A 1,2, NZ 1,4, 1958 F 1,
Strydom, J J (Tvl, GL) 1993 F 2, A 1,2,3, Arg 1,2, 1994 E 1, 1995 [A, C, F, NZ], 1996 A 2(R), NZ 2(R), 3,4, W (R), 1997 Tg, BI 1,2,3, A 2
Strydom, L J (NT) 1949 NZ 1,2
Styger, J J (OFS) 1992 NZ (R), A, F 1,2, E, 1993 F 2(R), A 3(R)
Suter, M R (N) 1965 I, S
Swanepoel, W (OFS, GL) 1997 BI 3(R), A 2(R), F 1(R), 2, E, S, 1998 I 2(R), W 1(R), E 2(R), 1999 It 1,2(R), W, A 1, [Sp, NZ 3(t)], 2000 A 1, NZ 1, A 2, NZ 2, A 3
Swart, J (WP) 1996 Fj, NZ 1(R), A 2, NZ 2,3,4,5, 1997 BI 3(R), It, S (R)
Swart, J J N (SWA) 1955 BI 1
Swart, I S (Tvl) 1993 A 1,2,3, Arg 1, 1994 E 1,2, NZ 1,3, Arg 2(R), 1995 WS, [A, WS, F, NZ], W, 1996 A 2

Taberer, W S (GW) 1896 BI 2
Taylor, O B (N) 1962 BI 1
Terblanche, C S (Bol, N) 1998 I 1,2, W 1, E 1, A 1, NZ 1,2, A 2, W 2, S, I 3, E 2, 1999 It 1(R),2, W, A 1, NZ 2(R), [Sp, E (R), A 3(R), NZ 3], 2000 E 3, 2002 W 1,2, Arg, Sm, NZ 1, A 1,2(R), 2003 S 1,2, Arg, A 1, NZ 1, A 2, NZ 2, [Gg]
Teichmann, G H (N) 1995 W, 1996 Fj, A 1, NZ 1, A 2, NZ 2,3,4,5, Arg 1,2, F 1,2, W, 1997 Tg, BI 1,2,3, NZ 1, A 1, NZ 2, A 2, It, F 1,2 E, S, 1998 I 1,2, W 1, E 1, A 1, NZ 1,2, A 2, W 2, S, I 3, E 2, 1999 It 1, W, NZ 1
Theron, D F (GW) 1996 A 2(R), NZ 2(R), 5, Arg 1,2, F 1,2, W, 1997 BI 2(R), 3, NZ 1(R), A 1, NZ 2(R)
Theunissen, D J (GW) 1896 BI 3
Thompson, G (WP) 1912 S, I, W
Tindall, J C (WP) 1924 BI 1, 1928 NZ 1,2,3,4
Tobias, E G (SARF, Bol) 1981 I 1,2, 1984 E 1,2, S Am 1, 2
Tod, N S (N) 1928 NZ 2
Townsend, W H (N) 1921 NZ 1
Trenery, W E (GW) 1891 BI 2
Tromp, H (NT) 1996 NZ3,4, Arg 2(R), F 1(R)
Truter, D R (WP) 1924 BI 2,4
Truter, J T (N) 1963 A 1, 1964 F, 1965 A 2
Turner, F G (EP) 1933 A 1,2,3, 1937 A 1,2, NZ 1,2,3, 1938 BI 1,2,3
Twigge, R J (NT) 1960 S
Tyibilika, S (N) 2004 S,Arg, 2005 U,A2,Arg, 2006 NZ1,A2,NZ2

Ulyate, C A (Tvl) 1955 BI 1,2,3,4, 1956 NZ 1,2,3
Uys, P de W (NT) 1960 W, 1961 E, S, I, A 1,2, 1962 BI 1,4, 1963 A 1,2, 1969 A 1(R), 2
Uys, P J (Pumas) 2002 S

Van Aswegen, H J (WP) 1981 NZ 1, 1982 S Am 2(R)
Van Biljon, L (N) 2001 It 1(R), NZ 1, A 1,2, NZ 2, F 3, It 2(R), E (R), US, 2002 F (R), S, E (R), 2003 NZ 2(R)
Van Broekhuizen, H D (WP) 1896 BI 4
Van Buuren, M C (Tvl) 1891 BI 1
Van de Vyver, D F (WP) 1937 A 2
Van den Berg, D S (N) 1975 F 1,2, 1976 NZ 1,2
Van den Berg, M A (WP) 1937 A 1, NZ 1,2,3
Van den Berg, P A (WP, GW, N) 1999 It 1(R),2, NZ 2, A 2, [S, U (t+R), E (R), A 3(R), NZ 3(R)], 2000 E 1(R), A 1, NZ 1, A 2, NZ 2(R), A 3(t+R), Arg, I, W, E 3, 2001 F 1(R),2, A 2(R), NZ 2(R), US, 2004 NZ1, 2005 U, F1, 2, A1(R), 2(R), 3(R), 4(R), Arg(R), F3(R), 2006 S2(R), A1(R), NZ1, A2(R), NZ2(R), A3(R), I, E1(R),2(R), 2007 Sm,A2(R), NZ2,Nm(t&R),S(R), [Tg,US]
Van den Bergh, E (EP) 1994 Arg 2(t & R)
Van der Linde, A (WP) 1995 It, E, 1996 Arg 1(R), 2(R), F 1(R), W (R), 2001 F 3(R)
Van der Linde, C J (FS) 2002 S (R), E(R), 2004 I1(R), 2(R), PI(R), A1(R), NZ2(t&R), A2(R), W2(R), I3(R), E(t&R), S,Arg, 2005 U,F1(R), 2,A1(R), 3, NZ1, A4, NZ2, Arg, W,F3, 2006 S2(R), F(R), A1, NZ1, A2, NZ2, I, E1, 2, 2007 E1(R), 2, A1(R), NZ1(R), A2, NZ2, Nm,S, [Sm,E1(R),Tg,US(R),Arg,E2]
Van der Merwe, A J (Bol) 1955 BI 2,3,4, 1956 A 1,2, NZ 1,2,3,4, 1958 F 1, 1960 S, NZ 2
Van der Merwe, A V (WP) 1931 W
Van der Merwe, B S (NT) 1949 NZ 1
Van der Merwe, H S (NT) 1960 NZ 4, 1963 A 2,3,4, 1964 F
Van der Merwe, J P (WP) 1970 W
Van der Merwe, P R (SWD, WT, GW) 1981 NZ 2,3, US, 1986 Cv 1,2, 1989 Wld 1
Vanderplank, B E (N) 1924 BI 3,4
Van der Schyff, J H (GW) 1949 NZ 1,2,3,4, 1955 BI 1
Van der Watt, A E (WP) 1969 S (R), E, 1970 I
Van der Westhuizen, J C (WP) 1928 NZ 2,3,4, 1931 I
Van der Westhuizen, J H (WP) 1931 I, 1932 E, S
Van der Westhuizen, J H (NT, BB) 1993 Arg 1,2, 1994 E 1,2(R), Arg 2, S, W, 1995 WS, [A, C (R), WS, F, NZ], W, It, E, 1996 Fj, A 1,2(R), NZ 2,3(R), 4,5, Arg 1,2, F 1,2, W, 1997 Tg, BI 1,2,3, NZ 1, A 1, NZ 2, A 2, It, F 1, 1998 I 1,2, W 1, E 1, A 1, NZ 1,2, A 2, W 2, S, I 3, E 2, 1999 NZ 2, A 2, [S, Sp (R), U, E, A 3, NZ 3], 2000 C, E 1,2, A 1(R), NZ 1(R), A 2(R), Arg, I, W, E 3, 2001 F 1,2, It 1(R), NZ 1, A 1,2,

NZ 2, F 3, It 2, E, US (R), 2003 S 1,2, A 1, NZ 1, A 2(R), NZ 2, [U,E,Sm,NZ]
Van der Westhuyzen, J N B (MP, BB) 2000 NZ 2(R), 2001 It 1(R), 2003 S 1(R),2, Arg, A 1, 2003 [E,Sm,NZ], 2004 I1, 2, W1, Pl, NZ1, A1, NZ2, A2, W2, I3, E, S, Arg, 2005 U,F1,2, A1,4(R),NZ2(R), 2006 S1, 2,F,A1
Van Druten, N J V (Tvl) 1924 Bl 1,2,3,4, 1928 NZ 1,2,3,4
Van Heerden, A J (Tvl) 1921 NZ 1,3
Van Heerden, F J (WP) 1994 E 1,2(R), NZ 3, 1995 It, E, 1996 NZ 5(R), Arg 1(R),2(R), 1997 Tg, Bl 2(t+R), 3(R), NZ 1(R),2(R), 1999 [Sp]
Van Heerden, J L (NT, Tvl) 1974 Bl 3,4, F 1,2, 1975 F 1, 2, 1976 NZ 1,2,3,4, 1977 Wld, 1980 Bl 1,3,4, S Am 3,4, F
Van Heerden, J L (BB) 2003 S 1,2, A 1, NZ 1, A 2(t), 2007 A2,NZ2,S(R), [Sm(R),E1,Tg, US,Fj(R),E2(R)]
Van Jaarsveld, C J (Tvl) 1949 NZ 1
Van Jaarsveldt, D C (R) 1960 S
Van Niekerk, J A (WP) 1928 NZ 4
Van Niekerk, J C (GL, WP) 2001 NZ 1(R), A 1(R), NZ 2(t+R), F 3(R), It2, US, 2002 W 1(R),2(R), Arg (R), Sm, NZ 1, A 1, NZ 2, A 2, F, S, E, 2003 A 2, NZ 2, [U,E,Gg,Sm], 2004 NZ1(R), A1(t), NZ2, A2, W2, I3, E, S, Arg(R), 2005 U(R),F2(R),A1(R),2,3,NZ1,A4, NZ2, 2006 S1,2,F,A1,NZ1(R),A2(R)
Van Reenen, G L (WP) 1937 A 2, NZ 1
Van Renen, C G (WP) 1891 Bl 3, 1896 Bl 1,4
Van Renen, W (WP) 1903 Bl 1,3
Van Rensburg, J T J (Tvl) 1992 NZ, A, E, 1993 F 1,2, A 1, 1994 NZ 2
Van Rooyen, G W (Tvl) 1921 NZ 2,3
Van Ryneveld, R C B (WP) 1910 Bl 2,3
Van Schalkwyk, D (NT) 1996 Fj (R), NZ 3,4,5, 1997 Bl 2,3, NZ 1, A 1
Van Schoor, R A M (R) 1949 NZ 2,3,4, 1951 S, I, W, 1952 E, F, 1953 A 1,2,3,4
Van Straaten, A J J (WP) 1999 It 2(R), W, NZ 1(R), A 1, 2000 C, E 1,2, NZ 1, A 2, NZ 2, A 3, Arg (R), I (R), W, E 3, 2001 A 1,2, NZ 2, F 3, It 2, E
Van Vollenhoven, K T (NT) 1955 Bl 1,2,3,4, 1956 A 1,2, NZ 3
Van Vuuren, T F (EP) 1912 S, I, W, 1913 E, F
Van Wyk, C J (Tvl) 1951 S, I, W, 1952 E, F, 1953 A 1,2,3,4, 1955 Bl 1
Van Wyk, J F B (NT) 1970 NZ 1,2,3,4, 1971 F 1,2, A 1,2,3, 1972 E, 1974 Bl 1,3,4, 1976 NZ 3,4
Van Wyk, S P (WP) 1928 NZ 1,2
Van Zyl, B P (WP) 1961 I
Van Zyl, C G P (OFS) 1965 NZ 1,2,3,4
Van Zyl, D J (WP) 2000 E 3(R)
Van Zyl, G H (WP) 1958 F 1, 1960 S, NZ 1,2,3,4, W, I, 1961 E, S, F, I, A 1,2, 1962 Bl 1,3,4
Van Zyl, H J (Tvl) 1960 NZ 1,2,3,4, I, 1961 E, S, I, A 1,2
Van Zyl, P J (Bol) 1961 I
Veldsman, P E (WP) 1977 Wld
Venter, A G (OFS) 1996 NZ 3,4,5, Arg 1,2, F 1,2, W, 1997 Tg, Bl 1,2,3, NZ 1, A 1, NZ 2, It, F 1,2, E, S, 1998 I 1,2, W 1, E 1, A 1, NZ 1,2, A 2, W 2, S (R), I 3(R), E 2(R), 1999 It 1,2(R), W (R), NZ 1, A 1, NZ 2, A 2, [S, U, E, A 3, NZ 3], 2000 C, E 1,2, A 1, NZ 1, A 2, NZ 2, A 3, Arg, I, W, E 3, 2001 F 1, It 1, NZ 1, A 1,2, NZ 2, F 3(R), It 2(R), E (t+R), US (R)
Venter, A J (N) 2000 W (R), E 3(R), 2001 F 3, It 2, E, US, 2002 W 1,2, Arg, NZ 1(R),2, A 2, F, S (R), E, 2003 Arg, 2004 Pl,NZ1,A1,NZ2(R),A2,I3,E, 2006 NZ3,A3
Venter, B (OFS) 1994 E 1,2, NZ 1,2,3, Arg 1,2, 1995 [R, C, WS (R), NZ (R)], 1996 A 1, NZ 1, A 2, 1999 A 2, [S, U]
Venter, F D (Tvl) 1931 W, 1932 S, 1933 A 3
Versfeld, C (WP) 1891 Bl 3
Versfeld, M (WP) 1891 Bl 1,2,3
Vigne, J T (Tvl) 1891 Bl 1,2,3
Viljoen, J F (GW) 1971 F 1,2, A 1,2,3, 1972 E
Viljoen, J T (N) 1971 A 1,2,3
Villet, J V (WP) 1984 E 1,2
Visagie, I J (WP) 1999 It 1, W, NZ 1, A 1, NZ 2, A 2, [S, U, E, A 3, NZ 3], 2000 C, E 2, A 1, NZ 1, A 2, NZ 2, A 3, 2001 NZ 1, A 1,2, NZ 2, F 3, It 2(R), E (t+R), US, 2003 S 1(R),2(R), Arg
Visagie, P J (GW) 1967 F 1,2,3,4, 1968 Bl 1,2,3,4, F 1,2, 1969 A 1,2,3,4, S, E, 1970 NZ 1,2,3,4, 1971 F 1,2, A 1,2,3
Visagie, R G (OFS, N) 1984 E 1,2, S Am 1,2, 1993 F 1
Visser, J de V (WP) 1981 NZ 2, US
Visser, M (WP) 1995 WS (R)
Visser, P J (Tvl) 1933 A 2
Viviers, S S (OFS) 1956 A 1,2, NZ 2,3,4
Vogel, M L (OFS) 1974 Bl 2(R)
Von Hoesslin, D J B (GW) 1999 It 1(R),2, W (R), NZ 1, A 1(R)
Vos, A N (GL) 1999 It 1(t+R),2, NZ 1(R),2(R), A 2, [S (R), Sp, E (R), A 3(R), NZ 3], 2000 C, E 1,2, A 1, NZ 1, A 2, NZ 2, A 3, Arg, I, W, E 3, 2001 F 1,2, It 1, NZ 1, A 1,2, NZ 2, F 3, It 2, E, US

Wagenaar, C (NT) 1977 Wld
Wahl, J J (WP) 1949 NZ 1
Walker, A P (N) 1921 NZ 1,3, 1924 Bl 1,2,3,4
Walker, H N (OFS) 1953 A 3, 1956 A 2, NZ 1,4
Walker, H W (Tvl) 1910 Bl 1,2,3
Walton, D C (N) 1964 F, 1965 I, S, NZ 3,4, 1969 A 1,2, E
Wannenburg, P J (BB) 2002 F (R), E, 2003 S 1,2, Arg, A 1(t+R), NZ 1(R), 2004 I1,2, W1,Pl(R), 2006 S1(R), F,NZ2(R), 3, A3, 2007 Sm(R),NZ1(R),A2,NZ2
Waring, F W (WP) 1931 I, 1932 E, 1933 A 1,2,3,4,5
Watson, L A (WP) 2007 Sm
Wegner, N (WP) 1993 F 2, A 1,2,3
Wentzel, M van Z (Pumas) 2002 F (R), S
Wessels, J J (WP) 1896 Bl 1,2,3
Whipp, P J M (WP) 1974 Bl 1,2, 1975 F 1, 1976 NZ 1,3,4, 1980 S Am 1,2
White, J (Bor) 1931 W, 1933 A 1,2,3,4,5, 1937 A 1,2, NZ 1,2
Wiese, J J (Tvl) 1993 F 1, 1995 WS, [R, C, WS, F, NZ], W, It, E, 1996 NZ 3(R), 4(R), 5, Arg 1,2, F 1,2, W
Willemse, A K (GL) 2003 S 1,2, NZ 1, A 2, NZ 2, [U,E,Sm,NZ], 2004 W2,I3, 2007 E1, 2(R), Sm, A1,NZ1,Nm,S(R), [Tg]
Williams, A E (GW) 1910 Bl 1
Williams, A P (WP) 1984 E 1,2
Williams, C M (WP, GL) 1993 Arg 2, 1994 E 1,2, NZ 1,2,3, Arg 1,2, S, W, 1995 WS, [WS, F, NZ], It, E, 1998 A 1(t), NZ 1(t), 2000 C (R), E 1(t),2(R), A 1(R), NZ 2, A 3, Arg, I, W (R)
Williams, D O (WP) 1937 A 1,2, NZ 1,2,3, 1938 Bl 1,2,3
Williams, J G (NT) 1971 F 1,2, A 1,2,3, 1972 E, 1974 Bl 1,2,4, F 1,2, 1976 NZ 1,2
Wilson, L G (WP) 1960 NZ 3,4, W, I, 1961 E, F, I, A 1,2, 1962 Bl 1,2,3,4, 1963 A 1,2,3,4, 1964 W, F, 1965 I, S, A 1,2, NZ 1,2,3,4
Wolmarans, B J (OFS) 1977 Wld
Wright, G D (EP, Tvl) 1986 Cv 3,4, 1989 Wld 1,2, 1992 F 1,2, E
Wyness, M R K (WP) 1962 Bl 1,2,3,4, 1963 A 2

Zeller, W C (N) 1921 NZ 2,3
Zimerman, M (WP) 1931 W, I, 1932 E, S

CURRIE CUP 2007

CHEETAHS CLAW THEIR WAY BACK

By Iain Spragg

Free State got both hands firmly on the 2007 Currie Cup after a dramatic comeback in the final against the Golden Lions in Bloemfontein. The Cheetahs had been forced to share the trophy a year earlier after a 28–28 stalemate with the Blue Bulls but 12 months later they were able to claim sole ownership of the silverware.

The Cheetahs trailed the Bulls 18–6 in the Vodacom Park with 15 minutes on the clock but a try from substitute Mattheus de Bruyn four minutes from time and a crucial Willem de Waal conversion completed a remarkable fightback and sealed their 20–18 triumph.

Victory gave Free State their third consecutive title while defeat for the Lions extended their wait to lift the Currie Cup once again to eight years following their 1999 success.

"When we were 6–18 down I didn't think, at that stage, that we could come back," admitted Cheetahs coach Naka Drotske after lifting the trophy. "I was delighted with the way that we got back into the game. I think in the first half we played really well and we kept the momentum going. Hats off to the Lions, that they came back like they did in the early part of the second half."

Tries early in the second-half from Frederik Wepener and Jano Vermaak seemed to have established a winning platform for the Lions but they were ultimately unable to weather Free State's late charge.

"We put in a brave performance but unfortunately brave just isn't good enough," conceded Lions coach Eugene Eloff. "When you're ahead 18–6 you really should knock the opposition out of the game. However, I would like to compliment my team on one hell of an effort. We played to the death and in the end it just didn't go our way. I though the Cheetahs showed a lot of character to come back like that."

Victory in the final was, in truth, no more than Drotske's side deserved after an outstanding campaign in which they were the dominant force from day one. The Sharks clung onto their coat tails through the regular season but the Cheetahs were unquestionably the best team in the tournament.

The campaign began in late June and Free State laid down an ominous marker to their Currie Cup rivals in their opener against Boland Kavaliers at the Vodacom Park with a devastating 91–3 romp. Gavin Passens and Richardt Strauss each helped themselves to a hat-trick in a 12-try demolition and it was evident in week one the Cheetahs would be the team to beat.

A comprehensive 51–10 rout of the Wildeklawer Griquas followed a fortnight later to maintain the momentum and although the Lions pushed them close at Ellis Park in week three, there was still no stopping Free State. The home side had their chances but fly-half Louis Strydom missed five of his seven kicks at goal while de Waal, his opposite number, was in inspired form and set up all three of his side's tries in a 27–11 win.

Western Province and the Sharks were both powerless to stop the Cheetahs juggernaut and it was not until September that Drotske's troops were finally beaten. The venue was Newlands and it was Western Province who were to exact revenge for their own earlier defeat.

It seemed business as usual in Cape Town when de Waal slotted a drop goal in the opening seconds but Free State went on to produce an uncharacteristically scrappy and indisciplined performance and Western Province pounced. A try from Francois van der Merwe on the half hour mark set the tone and further scores from Breyton Paulse and Cornelis Uys edged the home side closer to victory. Second-half yellow cards for Cheetahs' duo Marius Joubert and Andre-Henri le Roux hampered their attempts to cut the deficit and Western Province emerged 34–20 victors.

"The players need all the credit they can get for this," said victorious coach Gary Gold. "All we really do is create an environment and let them be the decision-makers and the masters of their own destiny. When we lose it is frustrating from a management team point of view because there is nothing you can do, but when they play like that, they deserve all the credit. They really do."

Defeat for the Cheetahs, however, was to prove merely a minor setback. With two league games remaining, their place in the play-offs was already assured but they shook off the disappointment of surrendering their unbeaten record with victories against the Sharks and the Bulls to finish top of the table with just one defeat in 14.

The first of the semi-finals pitted the Sharks against the Lions at the Absa Stadium in Durban but the home side's hopes of reaching the final were shattered by Lions centre Jaco Pretorius, who scored either side of half-time to inspire his side to a 19–12 victory. Two penalties from scrum-half Rory Kockett gave the Sharks an early advantage but Pretorius' first try a minute before the break cut the deficit and his second six minutes into the second period established a lead that the Lions were not to relinquish.

"We played pretty much all the ruby, we just didn't convert our opportunities," he explained. "We made plenty of line-breaks, but it was that last pass. It's hard to believe we lost. I was really happy at half-time and with 40 minutes to go, I thought we just had to keep going, tidy up in a couple areas.

"But credit to the Lions, their defensive ability was very good, they scrambled well and they slowed ball down when they needed to. In the end, they kept us out and when we needed to finish, we didn't."

The second semi-final saw the Cheetahs entertain the Blue Bulls in

Bloemfontein and although the home side were hot favourites, the visitors pushed them all the way in a tense, low-scoring encounter.

Fly-half Derick Hougaard scored the Bulls' first points of the game with an eighth-minute penalty but de Waal hit back four minutes later with three points.

The two kickers traded another penalty apiece and at half-time, the two teams were locked at 6–6. The decisive point in the game came just four minutes after the break when wing Edrick Fredericks provided the finish to a sweeping Free State counter attack for the first and only try of the clash. The conversion was missed by de Waal but there were no more scores before the final whistle and the Cheetahs emerged 11–6 winners.

"The Cheetahs deserve to go to the final," said Bulls captain Derick Kuun. "We didn't play to our structures in the second half. It was heartbreaking. We were on the verge of scoring but it was a turnover and they capitalised to score the try."

The final a fortnight later was no less dramatic as Free State and the Lions produced an enthralling encounter worthy of the final.

The Cheetahs drew first blood with a de Wall penalty after six minutes but Strydom levelled two minutes later. A second de Waal three-pointer made it 6–3 to the Cheetahs at half-time but both sides were saving the real fireworks for the second period.

Free State number eight Darron Nell was sin binned early in the second-half and the Lions took advantage of their numerical advantage to score the first try through Frederik Wepener. A second score from Jano Vermaak on the hour put the visitors firmly in the driving seat and when wing Edrick Fredericks became the second Cheetahs player to see yellow, the odds were heavily stacked in the Lions favour.

Free State, however, had other ideas and Heinrich Brussow's 67th minute try gave them hope. A yellow card for Lions wing Ryno Benjamin gave Drotske's side further encouragement and two minutes after the sin-binning they were level after Mattheus de Bruyn crashed over. The scores were tied at 18–18 but after having been forced to share the trophy with the Bulls 12 months earlier, the Cheetahs were desperate to avoid a repeat and de Waal stepped forward to calmly slot the all-important conversion. Free State were 20–18 victors and the outright champions.

"It's still a young team and I think that they have a big future," Drotske said after the final. "The guys spread it wide at times and sometimes they kept it tight, making it a good game to watch. Both teams did their homework and I think we put them under a lot of pressure and they also put us under pressure – typical final stuff. I thought that overall it was a great final."

At the other end of the table Valke, who lost all 14 of their league games, preserved their Currie Cup Premier Division status when they beat the South Western Districts Eagles 21–11 in the second leg of their play-off clash to wrap up a 43–28 aggregate win.

CURRIE CUP 2007 RESULTS

22 June: **Free State Cheetahs** 91 **Boland Kavaliers** 3, **Blue Bulls** 43 **Valke** 26. 23 June: **Western Province** 18 **Golden Lions** 13. 29 June: **Valke** 11 **Free State Cheetahs** 45. 30 June: **Boland Kavaliers** 15 **Western Province** 10, **Wildeklawer Griquas** 26 **Blue Bulls** 8, **Golden Lions** 14 **Sharks** 7. 6 July: **Valke** 33 **Boland Kavaliers** 39, **Sharks** 32 **Western Province** 16. 7 July: **Free State Cheetahs** 51 **Wildeklawer Griquas** 10, **Blue Bulls** 25 **Golden Lions** 11. 14 July: **Sharks** 43 **Wildeklawer Griquas** 20. 20 July: **Wildeklawer Griquas** 63 **Valke** 10. 21 July: **Golden Lions** 11 **Free State Cheetahs** 27, **Boland Kavaliers** 12 **Sharks** 26, **Western Province** 17 **Blue Bulls** 26. 27 July: **Valke** 5 **Golden Lions** 62. 28 July: **Free State Cheetahs** 45 **Western Province** 13, **Wildeklawer Griquas** 43 **Boland Kavaliers** 32, **Sharks** 29 **Blue Bulls** 10. 3 August: **Blue Bulls** 36 **Boland Kavaliers** 12. 4 August: **Golden Lions** 45 **Wildeklawer Griquas** 24, **Western Province** 47 **Valke** 18, **Sharks** 22 **Free State Cheetahs** 42.10 August: **Valke** 22 **Sharks** 45. 11 August: **Boland Kavaliers** 10 **Golden Lions** 15, **Wildeklawer Griquas** 25 **Western Province** 30, **Free State Cheetahs** 44 **Blue Bulls** 18. 17 August: **Valke** 7 **Blue Bulls** 48. 18 August: **Wildeklawer Griquas** 14 **Sharks** 24, **Boland Kavaliers** 20 **Free State Cheetahs** 22, **Golden Lions** 19 **Western Province** 16. 31 August: **Free State Cheetahs** 80 **Valke** 33. 1 September: **Blue Bulls** 46 **Wildeklawer Griquas** 3, **Western Province** 62 **Boland Kavaliers** 10, **Sharks** 21 **Golden Lions** 3. 7 September: **Boland Kavaliers** 24 **Valke** 20. 8 September: **Wildeklawer Griquas** 17 **Free State Cheetahs** 21, **Golden Lions** 27 **Blue Bulls** 22, **Western Province** 22 **Sharks** 19. 14 September: **Sharks** 50 **Boland Kavaliers** 25. 15 September: **Valke** 25 **Wildeklawer Griquas** 65, **Free State Cheetahs** 24 **Golden Lions** 19, **Blue Bulls** 35 **Western Province** 10. 21 September: **Blue Bulls** 18 **Sharks** 26. 22 September: **Golden Lions** 61 **Valke** 10, **Boland Kavaliers** 22 **Wildeklawer Griquas** 57, **Western Province** 34 **Free State Cheetahs** 20. 28 September: **Valke** 23 **Western Province** 46. 29 September: **Wildeklawer Griquas** 0 **Golden Lions** 28, **Boland Kavaliers** 15 **Blue Bulls** 62, **Free State Cheetahs** 25 **Sharks** 23. 5 October: **Blue Bulls** 17 **Free State Cheetahs** 29. 6 October: **Golden Lions** 75 **Boland Kavaliers** 0, **Sharks** 43 **Valke** 29, **Western Province** 37 **Wildeklawer Griquas** 7.

FINAL TABLE

	P	W	D	L	F	A	BP	Pts
Cheetahs	14	13	0	1	566	251	8	60
Sharks	14	10	0	4	410	272	11	51
Lions	14	9	0	5	403	229	6	42
Bulls	14	8	0	6	424	282	7	39
WP	14	8	0	6	378	307	7	39
Griquas	14	5	0	9	374	432	7	27
Kavaliers	14	3	0	11	239	602	6	18
Valke	14	0	0	14	292	711	5	5

SEMI-FINALS

SHARKS 12 (4PG) GOLDEN LIONS 19 (2G, 1T)

FREE STATE CHEETAHS 11 (2PG, 1T) BLUE BULLS 6 (2PG)

FINAL

27 October, Vodacom Park, Bloemfontein

FREE STATE CHEETAHS 20 (2G, 2PG) GOLDEN LIONS 18 (1G, 2PG, 1T)

FREE STATE CHEETAHS: A Hollenbach; E Fredericks, M Joubert, H Meyer, G Passens; W de Waal, N Oelschig; W du Preez, C Strauss, J Calldo, R Duncan (captain), C van Zyl, H Scholtz, D Vermeulen, D Nell Substitutions: M de Bruyn for Hollenbach (16 mins), J du Plessis for Calldo (51 mins), B Pieterse for Duncan (57 mins), H Brussow for Scholtz (57 mins), L Floors for Nell (61 mins), H Bosman for Meyer (62 mins)

SCORERS *Tries:* Brussow, de Bruyn *Conversions:* de Waal (2) *Penalty Goals:* de Waal (2)

GOLDEN LIONS: L Ludik; J Boshoff, J Pretorius, W Venter, R Benjamin; L Strydom, J Vermaak; H van der Merwe, F Wepener, L Sephaka, A van Zyl, F van der Merwe, P Grobbelaar, E Joubert (captain), J Cronje Substitutions: E Rose for Strydom (49 mins), W Koch for Cronje (68 mins), W Human for Pretorius (72 mins), E Reynecke for Wepener (73 mins), J van Rensburg for Sephaka (77 mins), J van Zyl for Vermaak (79 mins)

SCORERS *Tries:* Wepener, Vermaak *Conversion:* Rose *Penalty Goals:* Rose, Strydom

REFEREE M Lawrence (South Africa)

YELLOW CARDS Nell (48 mins), Fredericks (63 mins), Benjamin (74 mins)

TONGA

TONGA'S 2006–07 TEST RECORD

OPPONENTS	DATE	VENUE	RESULT
Korea	10 Feb	N	**Won** 83–3
Australia A	25 May	A	**Lost** 15–60
Japan	2 June	N	**Lost** 17–20
Junior All Blacks	9 June	H	**Lost** 13–39
Fiji	16 June	H	**Won** 21–15
Samoa	23 June	A	**Lost** 3–50
USA	12 Sept	N	**Won** 25–15 (WC)
Samoa	16 Sept	N	**Won** 19–15 (WC)
South Africa	22 Sept	N	**Lost** 25–30 (WC)
England	28 Sept	N	**Lost** 20–36 (WC)

WALKING IN WONDERLAND

By Frankie Deges

The fact that Tonga arrived at their last match of the 2007 Rugby World Cup with many pundits believing they could dethrone defending champions England and advance to the quarter-finals – for the first time – was a clear statement of how the Pacific Island nation managed to turn the tables and escape its own past at this World Cup.

On the wet and humid Parisian night, they were beaten by a solid England team that although never in doubt of victory had to work hard for every piece of ball and every bit of possession. But it was the Tongans – the biggest success of the 2007 World Cup – that were clapped off the Parc des Princes after a farewell lap of honour.

So, Tonga, who played in all but one Rugby World Cup to date and had only managed two wins before this one, returned to Nuku'alofa with their heads held high and were feted like heroes. The tournament was on television back in Tonga and the country stopped whenever their team played. This squad, with players based in as many as six countries, will now have to find ways to ensure their commitment for the tournament is back when they go back to international rugby next year.

This 2007 tournament was by far the best by the 'Ikale Tahi' (Sea Eagles). Victories against USA and Samoa doubled their previous count from four previous tournaments. The fact they ran South Africa close, very close, and arrived to their last game with a real chance of gate crashing the tournament was proof of this.

They not only had players that stood out – Nili Latu, the captain was one of the best flankers in the first part of the tournament and Finau Maka – the one with the most memorable hairstyle in this World Cup – another great performer, as Tonga managed to qualify directly for next World Cup, in 2011 for the first time.

Tonga's route to the finals normally involves them losing their South Sea qualifying tournament to Fiji and Samoa, before beating another side (usually Korea) in the repechage round. This time they can start planning for the 2011 event – in New Zealand – immediately!

Coach Quddus Fielea, a player in the Tongan side at the inaugural World Cup, 20 years ago, came to the job pretty late in their pre-World Cup campaign. Tonga had failed to qualify directly, finishing third of three in the Pacific final qualifying rounds needing to travel to Auckland in February to beat Korea and book their place in this World Cup via one of the two repechage places – the other went to Portugal.

Having done that, the preparation got underway under Australian-born

Adam Leach. He would make it to World Cup, but assisting Portugal. Leach was instrumental in getting Tonga to work as a professional team, with structure to its at times lose game style. It was after disagreements with the Tongan Rugby Union that Leach resigned, allowing the arrival of Fielea who in turn took the team to even higher highs.

Arriving in France, the Tongans were talking the talk in saying they were aiming for a quarter-final spot. They came close and in failing at least managed to qualify for the next Rugby World Cup, in neighbouring New Zealand, by finishing third in their pool.

As much as some people believe that this team is full of *fly-ins*, only one of the 30 players in France 2007 was born outside of Tonga (yet of direct Tongan descent); it is understandable that the large majority of them are actually based overseas, only three of them still play in the island.

Their skipper Nili Latu said: "We are proud, and are trying to make people change their opinions on Tongan rugby. We are trying to change the face of rugby in the country. We are playing for the livelihood of Tongan rugby. We don't have the facilities but we have each other."

His team played with the heart that is needed at this level, starting with a solid and hard-earned win against the USA Eagles. With a 13–0 lead after 26 minutes, the plucky Americans never gave up and it took all the Tongans had in them to beat their opposition. In the end, Tonga fly-half Pierre Hola kept a cool head and managed to control the game whilst in the process scoring ten points to go with the three tries scored by Finau Maka, Joseph Vaka and Viliami Vaki.

Next up were the cousins from Samoa. And what a game it was! In ending a nine-match losing streak against Samoa, not only did they manage to beat the auld enemy 19–15, but grew in self esteem in a way that few teams did in the tournament. Both teams had met three months earlier when Tonga travelled to Apia where they lost 50–3.

The match was a torrid affair as anyone would expect from one between these two proud nations, but the fact that the Tongans managed to control the more experienced Samoans with a sending off (of Hale T Pole) and two sin-bins only spoke volumes of their hunger. In the words of inspirational Latu, "we wanted it more than them."

The nerve wracking five final minutes had the winners down to 13 men and defending their line with every ounce of their sapping strength. Samoa desperately threw everything at them, but the final whistle saw the Tongans celebrating.

Played on a Sunday, the very religious Tongan side had faced a conundrum, but it was resolved thanks to the power of prayer. "Sunday is a day of rest, but a special service for the team on the morning of the match ensured that they were convinced of what they were doing. We had this prayer and dedicated the game to the Almighty God," explained coach Fielea.

Next came South Africa who chose to rest a few of its star players, a decision they were almost made to regret. It came close to becoming an embarrassment for the Springboks who in their only previous encounter against the Tongans in 1997 had won 74–10. In a sunny afternoon in Lens, had it not been for SA coach Jake White using his bench wisely, the 30–25 win could have been a loss.

The Tongans were leading early into the second half 10–7, and South Africa only drew level with a penalty in the 54th minute. This left 26 minutes of real action in which a further 35 points were scored. A bonus point for Tonga was achieved with a penalty, but it was a victory in itself for the friendly Tongans who by then had become one of the surprises of the tournament.

Six days later, they were confident enough to tackle the English. It was to be a match too far for Fielea's team. Again, their previous encounter in the 1999 World Cup had ended in a 101–10 drubbing. Leaving the Parc des Princes, the scoreboard read England 36 Tonga 20.

Coach Fielea added: "It is important for us to take home the certainty of already knowing we will go to the next tournament. I am very satisfied with what has been achieved. One of our goals was reaching the quarter-finals, but I want to thank the boys for doing such a wonderful job for our nation. It is a very big step forward for Tongan rugby. What we have achieved is a milestone for us, and our supporters are over the moon with what has happened."

He continued: "We need help in the Islands. The International Rugby Board is putting funds in for academies, which is great, but the only time we get to play top tier teams is at the World Cup. We don't get the main ideas of the game because it has moved on and we need to keep up."

The future is now for Tonga and in a way they have to help themselves. The IRB Pacific Nations Cup has brought a much needed fixture list not only for Tonga but also for Samoa, Fiji and Japan. The investment made by the International Rugby Board is huge and confirms that they fully support the Islands.

The IRB's investment in Tonga over the past 12 months was expanded to provide greater assistance to the administrative structures of the Union. In May, KPMG undertook a review of the financial and administrative structures of the Union. The report identified a number of key areas to be addressed by the TRFU and the IRB – the most significant of which was the employment of a Finance Manager, which the IRB has agreed to part-fund.

The employment of a High Performance Manager in the second half of 2007, was a welcome addition and the temporary Licensed Training Centre in Nuku'alofa is fully operational and land for a permanent facility (40 acres) was recently handed over to the TRFU.

The IRB believes that Fiji, Tonga and Samoa have the potential to make the step up from Tier 2 to Tier 1 and the implementation of specific high performance programmes together with new competitions is providing the platform for this. Fiji broke into the quarter-finals for the second time in their history and Tonga came close. Samoa was on the same pool as Tonga and failed in their intention of breaking out of pool stage.

TONGA INTERNATIONAL RECORDS

UP TO 31ST OCTOBER 2007

WINNING MARGIN

Date	Opponent	Result	Winning Margin
21/03/2003	Korea	119–0	**119**
08/07/2006	Cook Islands	90–0	**90**
01/01/1979	Solomon Islands	92–3	**89**
10/02/2007	Korea	83–3	**80**
15/03/2003	Korea	75–0	**75**

MOST POINTS IN A MATCH

BY THE TEAM

Date	Opponent	Result	Pts.
21/03/2003	Korea	119–0	**119**
01/01/1979	Solomon Islands	92–3	**92**
08/07/2006	Cook Islands	90–0	**90**
06/12/2002	Papua New Guinea	84–12	**84**
10/02/2007	Korea	83–3	**83**

MOST TRIES IN A MATCH

BY THE TEAM

Date	Opponent	Result	Tries
21/03/2003	Korea	119–0	**17**
08/07/2006	Cook Islands	90–0	**14**
10/02/2007	Korea	83–3	**13**
24/06/2006	Cook Islands	77–10	**13**

MOST CONVERSIONS IN A MATCH

BY THE TEAM

Date	Opponent	Result	Cons
21/03/2003	Korea	119–0	**17**
08/07/2006	Cook Islands	90–0	**10**

MOST PENALTIES IN A MATCH

BY THE TEAM

Date	Opponent	Result	Pens
10/11/2001	Scotland	20–43	**5**

MOST DROP GOALS IN A MATCH

BY THE TEAM

1 on 8 Occasions

MOST POINTS IN A MATCH

BY A PLAYER

Date	Player	Opponent	Pts.
21/03/2003	Pierre Hola	Korea	**39**
10/02/2007	Fangatapu Apikotoa	Korea	**28**
04/05/1999	Sateki Tu'ipulotu	Korea	**27**
21/03/2003	Benhur Kivalu	Korea	**25**
06/12/2002	Pierre Hola	Papua New Guinea	**24**

MOST TRIES IN A MATCH

BY A PLAYER

Date	Player	Opponent	Tries
21/03/2003	Benhur Kivalu	Korea	**5**
24/06/2006	Viliami Hakalo	Cook Islands	**3**
08/07/2006	Tevita Vaikona	Cook Islands	**3**
05/07/1997	Siua Taumalolo	Cook Islands	**3**
28/03/1999	Siua Taumalolo	Georgia	**3**
04/05/1999	Jonny Koloi	Korea	**3**

MOST CONVERSIONS IN A MATCH

BY A PLAYER

Date	Player	Opponent	Cons
21/03/2003	Pierre Hola	Korea	17
08/07/2006	Fangatapu Apikotoa	Cook Islands	9
10/02/2007	Fangatapu Apikotoa	Korea	9
06/12/2002	Pierre Hola	Papua New Guinea	9
05/07/1997	Kusitafu Tonga	Cook Islands	9

MOST PENALTIES IN A MATCH

BY A PLAYER

Date	Player	Opponent	Pens
25/05/2001	Kusitafu Tonga	Fiji	4
10/11/2001	Sateki Tu'ipulotu	Scotland	4
19/02/1995	Sateki Tu'ipulotu	Japan	4
23/07/2005	Fangatapu Apikotoa	Samoa	4
16/09/2007	Pierre Hola	Samoa	4

MOST DROP GOALS IN A MATCH

BY A PLAYER

1 on 8 Occasions

MOST CAPPED PLAYERS

Name	Caps
'Elisi Vunipola	41
Benhur Kivalu	38
Manu Vunipola	34
Fe'ao Vunipola	32

LEADING TRY SCORERS

Name	Tries
Siua Taumalolo	12
Fepikou Tatafu	11
Benhur Kivalu	10

LEADING CONVERSIONS SCORERS

Name	Cons
Pierre Hola	60
Sateki Tu'ipulotu	33
Fangatapu 'Apikotoa	29
Kusitafu Tonga	25

LEADING PENALTY SCORERS

Name	Pens
Sateki Tu'ipulotu	32
Pierre Hola	27
Siua Taumalolo	12
Tomasi Lovo	12

LEADING DROP GOAL SCORERS

Name	DGs
Pierre Hola	3

LEADING POINTS SCORERS

Name	Pts.
Pierre Hola	255
Sateki Tu'ipulotu	190
Siua Taumalolo	108
Fangatapu 'Apikotoa	97

USA

USA'S 2006–07 TEST RECORD

OPPONENTS	DATE	VENUE	RESULT
England Saxons	18 May	A	**Lost** 3–51
Scotland A	23 May	N	**Lost** 9–13
Canada	2 June	N	**Lost** 10–52
England	8 Sept	N	**Lost** 10–28 (WC)
Tonga	12 Sept	N	**Lost** 15–25 (WC)
Samoa	26 Sept	N	**Lost** 21–25 (WC)
South Africa	30 Sept	N	**Lost** 15–64 (WC)

THE ONLY WAY IS UP

By Alex Goff

For American rugby the massive changes of the previous two years – head coach and Chief Executive stepping down, a complete revamp of the Board, and a massive influx of IRB cash – weren't done by the time 2007 rolled around.

By late 2006 the new Board had named a new Chief Executive and a new Director of Rugby Operations, and interestingly, decided the same man should fulfill both roles.

Former England captain Nigel Melville did just that, moved his family to the United States and despite having his job start officially on January 1 was seen all over the country at meetings and clinics talking about the game.

Melville's first job was to get some money behind a national team that had undergone huge personnel changes over the past year, and get them ready for a World Cup. And he and his staff delivered, signing on Setanta and Sony Bravia, among others, to help fund USA programs.

Head coach Peter Thorburn had waded through a bushel of players trying to find the right ones, and it appeared when his team beat Uruguay handily the previous Autumn that he had done just that.

But injuries to his starting half-back combination of Mike Hercus (Gwent Dragons) and Chad Erskine (Waterloo) forced him to spend the Churchill Cup experimenting again – putting young Nese Malifa (Belmont Shore) in at outside-half, and then full-back Francois Viljoen (also of Belmont Shore).

The Eagles started the Churchill Cup poorly, mauled by the England Saxons 51–3, and while they looked a shade more competitive against Scotland A 13–9, the loss against Canada shook them to the core.

The USA measures itself against Canada at every opportunity. From the youth levels on up the Can-Am games carry with them great passion and intensity. So for the USA to have lost their World Cup qualifier to the Canadians 56–7 the previous year was unacceptable. In this year's game at Twickenham, Leeds prop Mike MacDonald touched down for the team's first try of the season and the lead, but after that it was all Canada as the USA defensive line fell apart. 52–10 for the Northerners, and much, much to do.

From June 2 to August 26 the USA had no more games to play, and yet the squad was far from being set. Thorburn looked to use the North American 4 (NA4) competition for game time for his players. The initial plan of this IRB-funded cross-border competition was to blood the next generation of internationals. But in 2007 there was no tomorrow, the USA players needed tough competition. Thorburn put assistants Marty Wiggins and Adam Friend in charge of the two USA teams – the Falcons and the Hawks – and several regular national team players got on the field.

During the NA4 some young talent did indeed emerge – Thretton Palamo, Malifa and John van der Geissen all got a shot.

Among the stars of the NA4 were Viljoen at fly-half and full-back, and fly-half/center Scott Peterson. Those two had faced off at the pivot in the Super League final – Peterson leading the underdog Chicago Lions, and Viljoen nursing a hamstring injury in a valiant attempt to get a championship for Belmont Shore.

Both men played well in that final, but it was Viljoen's inspirational leadership and 19 points that brought victory for Belmont Shore.

Thorburn threw a few curveballs (or, since he's a New Zealander, off-breaks) and named a squad that did not include regular national team players such as scrum-half Kimball Kjar, or prop Mike French.

It was time for new blood, said Thorburn, as he took a few flyers – 18-year-old Palamo one of them, Zimbabwe-born 7s speed merchant Takudzwa "Zee" Ngwenya another.

Ngwenya had emerged in Sevens, which is an important part of the US development.

In 2007 the USA participated in only three IRB Sevens World Series events, with the knowledge that they had to show improvement if they wanted to get more. Head coach Al Caravelli took his team to two warmup tournaments in late 2006 – Bangkok, which the Eagles won, and Singapore and used it to look at players like Ngwenya and Chris Wyles, who both showed well later in France.

In the IRB Sevens World Series the US did do better. They lost all five in Wellington, but led every game at halftime. In San Diego, they finished 3–3 and won the Shield, and were unlucky not to make the Cup round.

San Diego's leg of the Series remains the biggest rugby party in the USA, and with a new home in PETCO Park, and a new five-year commitment to holding the tournament in the States, there was plenty to celebrate.

Six weeks later the Eagles finished their Sevens season in Hong Kong, in possibly the most important tournament for the USA 7s team in several years. There they beat France in the crucial opener and made the Cup quarter-finals, earning IRB Sevens World Series points for the first time in five years. The reward was two more tournaments in the coming Sevens season.

But before the Rugby World Cup finals started the USA received another big blow when the highly-respected Viljoen tore his ACL in training.

Everything pointed to a massive victory by England in Lens in their World Cup opener. But what happened instead was a gritty performance that rapidly pulled the partisan English crowd to their side.

The USA lost, but scored a try and garnered almost all the compliments. The downside on the day was Paul Emerick's dangerous tackle on Olly Barkley. The offence got him a yellow card, and then a five-week suspension for the team's best back.

That all had to be put aside, because the USA had another game against Tonga four days and 500 miles later in Montpellier.

Against Tonga the Eagles allowed a try and a penalty in the first five minutes, and chased the game for the rest of the day. Repeated protestations about ball-killing went unheeded, but with almost two-thirds of the ball and territory, the USA had only themselves to blame for scoring just two tries as they lost 25–15.

Two weeks off didn't shake off the flat start as the USA looked at sea against Samoa in St. Etienne. But in the second half they poured it on. Ngwenya showed why he can be a star with a brilliant solo try that sparked a comeback that just fell short.

And to the final game. South Africa would win that one easily, 67–14. The USA would slowly start to wilt under the stress and pressure of a tense season. But they wouldn't do it before turning in one more piece of magic. Flanker Todd Clever intercepting a pass, handing off Butch James, and linking with lock Alec Parker and Hercus before Ngwenya got the ball again. He only had the lightning quick Bryan Habana to beat, which he did with an in-and-out and a burst of the jets that had everyone talking.

"I guess the rugby world considers Bryan the fastest guy around. Well Takudzwa put his hand up today," boasted Hercus.

The USA's World Cup ended and so did the tenure of Peter Thorburn, who returns to New Zealand. Immediately Melville was on the job to find not only a head coach, but other coaches to head up the NA4 teams and the High Performance programs he and John Broker are putting together.

Despite no wins in 2007 the Eagles did show flashes of what could be. They need funds and the right structure to develop their players, and these days it looks like they might be getting there.

National Championship season is a busy time for USA Rugby as there are 22 official and unofficial titles handed out, from girls U19 to men's Super League and All-Star.

In the 18-team Super League while the presence of the Chicago Lions in their first final perhaps heralded a power shift in the league, it was Belmont Shore, in their sixth straight final, who won.

At the All-Star level the Midwest finally won the men's title they had so often come close to claiming, and with their women's team made it a double.

At the college level Cal-Berkeley were once again champions, for the 16th time in 17 years. BYU, Army, Navy and Penn State all had their licks, but Cal was rarely challenged. Utah's Highland was hardly less dominant in the high school championships, winning their 15th out of the last 19, this time before a home crowd that topped 5,000.

USA INTERNATIONAL RECORDS

UP TO 31ST OCTOBER 2007

WINNING MARGIN

Date	Opponent	Result	Winning Margin
01/07/2006	Barbados	91–0	**91**
06/07/1996	Japan	74–5	**69**
07/11/1989	Uruguay	60–3	**57**
12/03/1994	Bermuda	60–3	**57**

MOST POINTS IN A MATCH

BY THE TEAM

Date	Opponent	Result	Pts.
01/07/2006	Barbados	91–0	**91**
06/07/1996	Japan	74–5	**74**
17/05/2003	Japan	69–27	**69**
12/04/2003	Spain	62–13	**62**
08/04/1998	Portugal	61–5	**61**

MOST TRIES IN A MATCH

BY THE TEAM

Date	Opponent	Result	Tries
01/07/2006	Barbados	91–0	**13**
17/05/2003	Japan	69–27	**11**
07/11/1989	Uruguay	60–3	**11**
06/07/1996	Japan	74–5	**11**

MOST CONVERSIONS IN A MATCH

BY THE TEAM

Date	Opponent	Result	Cons
01/07/2006	Barbados	91–0	**13**
07/11/1989	Uruguay	60–3	**8**
06/07/1996	Japan	74–5	**8**

MOST PENALTIES IN A MATCH

BY THE TEAM

Date	Opponent	Result	Pens
18/09/1996	Canada	18–23	**6**

MOST DROP GOALS IN A MATCH

BY THE TEAM

1 on 14 Occasions

MOST POINTS IN A MATCH

BY A PLAYER

Date	Player	Opponent	Pts.
07/11/1989	Chris O'Brien	Uruguay	**26**
31/05/2004	Mike Hercus	Russia	**26**
01/07/2006	Mike Hercus	Barbados	**26**
12/03/1994	Chris O'Brien	Bermuda	**25**
06/07/1996	Matt Alexander	Japan	**24**

MOST TRIES IN A MATCH

BY A PLAYER

Date	Player	Opponent	Tries
06/07/1996	Vaea Anitoni	Japan	**4**
07/06/1997	Brian Hightower	Japan	**4**
08/04/1998	Vaea Anitoni	Portugal	**4**

MOST CONVERSIONS IN A MATCH

BY A PLAYER

Date	Player	Opponent	Cons
01/07/2006	Mike Hercus	Barbados	**13**
06/07/1996	Matt Alexander	Japan	**8**
07/11/1989	Chris O'Brien	Uruguay	**7**
17/05/2003	Mike Hercus	Japan	**7**
27/04/2003	Mike Hercus	Spain	**6**
12/03/1994	Chris O'Brien	Bermuda	**6**

MOST PENALTIES IN A MATCH

BY A PLAYER

Date	Player	Opponent	Pens
18/09/1996	Matt Alexander	Canada	6
21/09/1996	Matt Alexander	Uruguay	5
02/10/1993	Chris O'Brien	Australia	5
20/10/2003	Mike Hercus	Scotland	5
22/05/1999	Kevin Dalzell	Fiji	5
09/06/1984	Ray Nelson	Canada	5

MOST DROP GOALS IN A MATCH

BY A PLAYER

1 on 14 Occasions

MOST CAPPED PLAYERS

Name	Caps
Luke Gross	62
Dave Hodges	53
Alec Parker	50
Mike MacDonald	47

LEADING TRY SCORERS

Name	Tries
Vaea Anitoni	26
Philip Eloff	10
Riaan van Zyl	10
Mike Hercus	9

LEADING CONVERSIONS SCORERS

Name	Cons
Mike Hercus	75
Matt Alexander	45
Chris O'Brien	24
Grant Wells	14

LEADING PENALTY SCORERS

Name	Pens
Mike Hercus	59
Matt Alexander	55
Mark Williams	35

LEADING DROP GOAL SCORERS

Name	DGs
Mike Hercus	3

LEADING POINTS SCORERS

Name	Pts.
Mike Hercus	381
Matt Alexander	286
Chris O'Brien	144
Mark Williams	143
Vaea Anitoni	130

WALES

WALES' 2006–07 TEST RECORD

OPPONENTS	DATE	VENUE	RESULT
Australia	4 November	H	**Drew** 29–29
Pacific Islands	11 November	H	**Won** 38–20
Canada	17 November	H	**Won** 61–26
New Zealand	25 November	H	**Lost** 10–45
Ireland	4 February	H	**Lost** 9–19
Scotland	10 February	A	**Lost** 9–21
France	24 February	A	**Lost** 21–32
Italy	10 March	A	**Lost** 20–23
England	17 March	H	**Won** 27–18
Australia	26 May	A	**Lost** 23–29
Australia	2 June	A	**Lost** 0–31
England	4 August	A	**Lost** 5–62
Argentina	18 August	H	**Won** 27–20
France	26 August	H	**Lost** 7–34
Canada	9 September	N	**Won** 42–17 (WC)
Australia	15 September	N	**Lost** 20–32 (WC)
Japan	20 September	N	**Won** 72–18 (WC)
Fiji	29 September	N	**Lost** 34–38 (WC)

AGONY INFLICTED ON WALES

By Iain Spragg

David Rogers/Getty Images

Wales were left shattered after losing to Fiji in Nantes and going out of the World Cup.

"**Hurricane Catastrophe has been** hurtling towards Welsh rugby since the beginning of the year," ran the stinging editorial in *The Western Mail*. "And we finally felt its full, devastating force with the final whistle on Saturday. This is one of the bleakest moments in the history of our national sport."

Wales' 38–34 World Cup defeat to Fiji in Nantes was certainly a body blow to the people of the Principality, a result arguably as bleak as their infamous reverse against Western Samoa in Cardiff 16 years earlier. Both results ensured Wales' early exit from the respective tournaments and the scars from the game in the Stade de la Beaujoire against the Fijians will probably take as long to heal as those suffered in the wake of the Samoan debacle. Wales' World Cup challenge had imploded.

The repercussions were certainly swift and brutal. Despite his public assertion he wanted to remain in the job, Gareth Jenkins was sacked as the coach by the WRU the day after the match after just 16 months in charge and six wins in 20 outings. The process of rebuilding was to start immediately.

Warren Little/Getty Images

Shane Williams was on great form in 2007, scoring a spectacular try against Fiji in the World Cup.

"It is all about results and winning and we have fallen short," WRU chief executive Roger Lewis said when Jenkins' fate was confirmed. "It is a huge disappointment for us all. All of Welsh rugby needs to look at itself and ask itself the tough questions.

"Sixteen months is a tough call but Gareth has always said 'judge me on the World Cup'. When we are at this level it is about winning. There is a collective responsibility for where we have arrived at today and there is a collective desire to ensure we don't arrive at this position in 2011."

Wales began the World Cup with Fiji very much on their mind. Drawn in Pool B with Canada, Australia, Japan and the South Sea islanders, Jenkins and his team knew that unless they could topple the Wallabies in Cardiff, their hopes of progressing to the quarter-finals would probably hinge on the final game against the Fijians. And so it proved.

They began the tournament against Canada in Nantes and although their final 42–17 winning margin appeared comfortable enough, the match was not without tension for Jenkins' evidently rusty side. The Canucks led 17–9 early in the second-half and it needed the introduction of Stephen Jones and Gareth Thomas from the bench to spark the team into life and precipitate a flurry of face-saving tries. Wales were up and running but had been far from convincing.

Six days later they were in the familiar surroundings of the Millennium Stadium for the Australia game. Although the Wallabies had failed to

Dave Rogers/Getty Images

Wales finished a disappointing Six Nations with a 27–18 win over England.

win on their previous two visits to Cardiff, they were the pre-match favourites and the Welsh camp were happy to play down expectations in the build-up.

"I wouldn't say it is make-or-break at this early stage but it's a huge game for us," admitted fly-half and captain Stephen Jones. "We are up against a good side who are in form, so for us it is going to be a challenge. We have set standards against Canada, but against Australia we have to raise the bar again."

In truth, Wales were never really at the races, although the final 32–20 scoreline suggests a much closer contest than it ever was in Cardiff. The Wallabies effectively won the game in the first half with a brand of physical and dynamic rugby to which the home side had no answer. Stirling Mortlock, Matt Giteau and Chris Latham all crossed in the opening 40 minutes and the visitors were virtually home and dry at 25–3 at the break.

There was a fleeting moment of hope in the second-half when Jon Thomas crashed over but thoughts of an epic fight back were crushed by Latham's second try of the game and although Shane Williams helped himself to a late consolation, the match was done and dusted and Fiji were beginning to loom large on the horizon.

First, however, Wales had to despatch Japan and did so emphatically with an 11-try romp and 72–18 victory at the Millennium Stadium. It was a timely boost so soon after the disappointment of the Australia game but the coach was under no illusions that his team were still not at their peak.

"We are not entirely satisfied," Jenkins said after the match. "There were still aspects of the game that we were disappointed with. There was good stuff there tonight but there was stuff that we were frustrated with as well."

The adventurous, free-running Fijians would certainly provide a far sterner test.

The tension as the two sides took to the field in Nantes was palpable. For Wales, defeat was unthinkable while Fiji were on the verge of reaching the quarter-finals for the first time since 1987.

Sometimes such high stakes can inhibit teams but here the opposite was true and although it was ultimately no consolation for Jenkins and his players, the two sides proceeded to produce a true World Cup classic of nerve-jangling, drama-strewn rugby.

An early penalty from Stephen Jones was merely the appetiser and the first of the game's eight tries went to the Fijians. James Hook lost possession after a big hit from Seru Rabeni, Fiji broke and flanker Akapusi Qera went over. The irrepressible Vilimoni Delasau added the second after a fine chip and chase and Wales knew they were in a match. Two penalties from Nicky Little and a third try from Kele Leawere ominously extended the lead.

Wales hit back when Alex Popham went over from a scrum and further cut the Fijian advantage early in the second-half with a dazzling long-range run from Shane Williams that had the crowd on their feet. Wales were now in the ascendancy and further tries from Gareth Thomas – the 40th of his international career on his 100th appearance – and Mark Jones put them 29–25 in front.

Some expected Fiji to wilt in the face of the Welsh revival but two further Little penalties steadied the nerves and the game was headed for a dramatic climax. Martyn Williams looked to have sealed it with a long-range interception but there was to be one more twist in the tale as the impressive Delasau was hauled down inches short only for Graham Dewes to wriggle over from close range and break Welsh hearts after the decision was referred to television match official. Wales trooped off disconsolately while Fiji's players began their wild celebrations in the middle of the pitch.

"I accept and understand the decision that has been taken and I leave the post with sadness but no regrets," Jenkins in the wake of the defeat and his inevitable dismissal. "I have worked with a tremendous team of coaches, administrators and players and I leave in the full knowledge that we have given it our all."

The omens for a successful World Cup campaign had not been good. Wales began the 2006–07 season with an entertaining 29–29 draw with Australia in Cardiff and after they had seen off a combined Pacific Islands team at the Millennium Stadium seven days later, it seemed Jenkins had a platform on which to build.

New Zealand put a major if not fatal dent in Welsh expectations a fortnight later with a 45–10 victory in the Principality but there remained cautious optimism in the camp going into the Six Nations.

The first game against Ireland in Cardiff, however, was to set the tone for the rest of the tournament. Brian O'Driscoll blocked Stephen Jones' attempted clearance, Rory Best collected the loose ball to score after just 46 seconds and Eddie O'Sullivan's side went on to win 19–9.

Defeats in Paris and Edinburgh followed and there was further embarrassment at the Stadio Flaminio in Rome against Italy. Outscored three tries to two by an inspired Azzurri side, Wales had a chance to snatch a share of the spoils in the Italian capital when they were awarded a last-minute penalty which, if successful, would transform their 23–20 deficit into a 23–23 draw. But thinking they had enough time to kick for touch, win the resulting lineout and go for a match-winning try, James Hook put the ball out only for referee Chris White to blow for full time. Wales had controversially thrown away a chance for their first points of the competition and with England the visitors at the Millennium Stadium in the final fixture, they were facing the dreaded prospect of the Wooden Spoon.

In normal circumstances, any victory over the English would excuse a multitude of other sins but even after they had beaten the old enemy 27–18 in Cardiff, avoiding a Six Nations whitewash in the process, the alarm bells were still ringing. Four defeats in five outings was no sort of preparation for an assault on the World Cup.

Jenkins took his team Down Under in the summer and although they pushed the Wallabies close in the first Test in Sydney and were only denied a first victory in Australia since 1969 when Stephen Hoiles scored with the last move of the game, they were demolished in the second Test in Brisbane and returned home with more questions than answers.

Two warm-up defeats to England and France in August sandwiched a decent win over Argentina in Cardiff but Jenkins must have known his side were still on the back foot heading into the World Cup. The disastrous defeat to Fiji only served to confirm the growing suspicion that Wales were heading in the wrong direction.

WALES INTERNATIONAL STATISTICS

MATCH RECORDS UP TO 31ST OCTOBER 2007

MOST CONSECUTIVE TEST WINS

11 1907 1908 E,S,F,I,A, 1909 E,S,F,I, 1910 F
10 1999 F1,It,E,Arg 1,2,SA,C,F2,Arg 3,J
8 1970 F, 1971 E,S,I,F, 1972 E,S,F
8 2004 J, 2005 E,It,F,S,I,US,C

MOST CONSECUTIVE TESTS WITHOUT DEFEAT

Matches	Wins	Draws	Periods
11	11	0	1907 to 1910
10	10	0	1999 to 1999
8	8	0	1970 to 1972
8	8	0	2004 to 2005

MOST POINTS IN A MATCH

BY THE TEAM

Pts.	Opponent	Venue	Year
102	Portugal	Lisbon	1994
98	Japan	Cardiff	2004
81	Romania	Cardiff	2001
77	U S A	Hartford	2005
72	Japan	Cardiff	2007
70	Romania	Wrexham	1997
66	Romania	Cardiff	2004
64	Japan	Cardiff	1999
64	Japan	Osaka	2001
61	Canada	Cardiff	2006
60	Italy	Treviso	1999
60	Canada	Toronto	2005
58	Fiji	Cardiff	2002
57	Japan	Bloemfontein	1995
55	Japan	Cardiff	1993

BY A PLAYER

Pts.	Player	Opponent	Venue	Year
30	N R Jenkins	Italy	Treviso	1999
29	N R Jenkins	France	Cardiff	1999
28	N R Jenkins	Canada	Cardiff	1999
28	N R Jenkins	France	Paris	2001
28	G L Henson	Japan	Cardiff	2004
27	N R Jenkins	Italy	Cardiff	2000
27	C Sweeney	U S A	Hartford	2005
26	S M Jones	Romania	Cardiff	2001
24	N R Jenkins	Canada	Cardiff	1993
24	N R Jenkins	Italy	Cardiff	1994
24	G L Henson	Romania	Wrexham	2003
23	A C Thomas	Romania	Wrexham	1997
23	N R Jenkins	Argentina	Llanelli	1998
23	N R Jenkins	Scotland	Murrayfield	2001
22	N R Jenkins	Portugal	Lisbon	1994
22	N R Jenkins	Japan	Bloemfontein	1995
22	N R Jenkins	England	Wembley	1999
22	S M Jones	Canada	Cardiff	2002
22	J Hook	England	Cardiff	2007

MOST TRIES IN A MATCH

BY THE TEAM

Tries	Opponent	Venue	Year
16	Portugal	Lisbon	1994
14	Japan	Cardiff	2004
11	France	Paris	1909
11	Romania	Wrexham	1997
11	Romania	Cardiff	2001
11	U S A	Hartford	2005
11	Japan	Cardiff	2007
10	France	Swansea	1910
10	Japan	Osaka	2001
10	Romania	Cardiff	2004
9	France	Cardiff	1908
9	Japan	Cardiff	1993
9	Japan	Cardiff	1999
9	Japan	Tokyo	2001
9	Canada	Toronto	2005
9	Canada	Cardiff	2006

BY A PLAYER

Tries	Player	Opponent	Venue	Year
4	W Llewellyn	England	Swansea	1899
4	R A Gibbs	France	Cardiff	1908
4	M C R Richards	England	Cardiff	1969
4	I C Evans	Canada	Invercargill	1987
4	N Walker	Portugal	Lisbon	1994
4	G Thomas	Italy	Treviso	1999
4	S M Williams	Japan	Osaka	2001
4	T G L Shanklin	Romania	Cardiff	2004
4	C L Charvis	Japan	Cardiff	2004

MOST CONVERSIONS IN A MATCH

BY THE TEAM

Cons	Opponent	Venue	Year
14	Japan	Cardiff	2004
11	Portugal	Lisbon	1994
11	U S A	Hartford	2005
10	Romania	Cardiff	2001
8	France	Swansea	1910
8	Japan	Cardiff	1999
8	Romania	Cardiff	2004
8	Canada	Cardiff	2006
7	France	Paris	1909
7	Japan	Osaka	2001
7	Japan	Cardiff	2007

BY A PLAYER

Cons	Player	Opponent	Venue	Year
14	G L Henson	Japan	Cardiff	2004
11	N R Jenkins	Portugal	Lisbon	1994
11	C Sweeney	U S A	Hartford	2005
10	S M Jones	Romania	Cardiff	2001
8	J Bancroft	France	Swansea	1910
8	N R Jenkins	Japan	Cardiff	1999
8	J Hook	Canada	Cardiff	2006
7	S M Jones	Japan	Osaka	2001
7	S M Jones	Romania	Cardiff	2004
6	J Bancroft	France	Paris	1909
6	G L Henson	Romania	Wrexham	2003
6	C Sweeney	Canada	Toronto	2005

MOST PENALTIES IN A MATCH

BY THE TEAM

Pens	Opponent	Venue	Year
9	France	Cardiff	1999
8	Canada	Cardiff	1993
7	Italy	Cardiff	1994
7	Canada	Cardiff	1999
7	Italy	Cardiff	2000
6	France	Cardiff	1982
6	Tonga	Nuku'alofa	1994
6	England	Wembley	1999
6	Canada	Cardiff	2002

BY A PLAYER

Pens	Player	Opponent	Venue	Year
9	N R Jenkins	France	Cardiff	1999
8	N R Jenkins	Canada	Cardiff	1993
7	N R Jenkins	Italy	Cardiff	1994
7	N R Jenkins	Canada	Cardiff	1999
7	N R Jenkins	Italy	Cardiff	2000
6	G Evans	France	Cardiff	1982
6	N R Jenkins	Tonga	Nuku'alofa	1994
6	N R Jenkins	England	Wembley	1999
6	S M Jones	Canada	Cardiff	2002

MOST DROP GOALS IN A MATCH

BY THE TEAM

Drops	Opponent	Venue	Year
3	Scotland	Murrayfield	2001
2	Scotland	Swansea	1912
2	Scotland	Cardiff	1914
2	England	Swansea	1920
2	Scotland	Swansea	1921
2	France	Paris	1930
2	England	Cardiff	1971
2	France	Cardiff	1978
2	England	Twickenham	1984
2	Ireland	Wellington	1987
2	Scotland	Cardiff	1988
2	France	Paris	2001

BY A PLAYER

Drops	Player	Opponent	Venue	Year
3	N R Jenkins	Scotland	Murrayfield	2001
2	J Shea	England	Swansea	1920
2	A Jenkins	Scotland	Swansea	1921
2	B John	England	Cardiff	1971
2	M Dacey	England	Twickenham	1984
2	J Davies	Ireland	Wellington	1987
2	J Davies	Scotland	Cardiff	1988
2	N R Jenkins	France	Paris	2001

MOST CAPPED PLAYERS

Caps	Player	Career Span
100	Gareth Thomas	1995 to 2007
93	C L Charvis	1996 to 2007
92	G O Llewellyn	1989 to 2004
87	N R Jenkins	1991 to 2002
76	M E Williams	1996 to 2007
72	I C Evans	1987 to 1998
66	S M Jones	1998 to 2007
59	R Howley	1996 to 2002
58	G R Jenkins	1991 to 2000
58	D J Peel	2001 to 2007
55	J P R Williams	1969 to 1981
54	R N Jones	1986 to 1995
53	G O Edwards	1967 to 1978
53	I S Gibbs	1991 to 2001
52	L S Quinnell	1993 to 2002
52	G D Jenkins	2002 to 2007
51	D Young	1987 to 2001
51	S M Williams	2000 to 2007
48	D R James	1996 to 2007
48	K A Morgan	1997 to 2007
46	T G L Shanklin	2001 to 2007
46	T G R Davies	1966 to 1978
46	P T Davies	1985 to 1995
45	I M Gough	1998 to 2007

MOST CONSECUTIVE TESTS

Tests	Player	Career span
53	G O Edwards	1967 to 1978
43	K J Jones	1947 to 1956
39	G Price	1975 to 1983
38	T M Davies	1969 to 1976
33	W J Bancroft	1890 to 1901

MOST TESTS AS CAPTAIN

Tests	Player	Career span
28	I C Evans	1991 to 1995
22	R Howley	1998 to 1999
22	C L Charvis	2002 to 2004
21	Gareth Thomas	2003 to 2007
19	J M Humphreys	1995 to 2003
18	A J Gould	1889 to 1897
14	D C T Rowlands	1963 to 1965
14	W J Trew	1907 to 1913

MOST DROP GOALS IN TESTS

Drops	Player	Tests	Career
13	J Davies	32	1985 to 1997
10	N R Jenkins	87	1991 to 2002
8	B John	25	1966 to 1972
7	W G Davies	21	1978 to 1985

MOST TRIES IN TESTS

Tries	Player	Tests	Career
40	Gareth Thomas	100	1995 to 2007
35	S M Williams	51	2000 to 2007
33	I C Evans	72	1987 to 1998
21	C L Charvis	93	1996 to 2007
20	G O Edwards	53	1967 to 1978
20	T G R Davies	46	1966 to 1978
18	G R Williams	44	2000 to 2005
17	R A Gibbs	16	1906 to 1911
17	J L Williams	17	1906 to 1911
17	K J Jones	44	1947 to 1957
17	T G L Shanklin	46	2001 to 2007

MOST CONVERSIONS IN TESTS

Cons	Player	Tests	Career
130	N R Jenkins	87	1991 to 2002
106	S M Jones	66	1998 to 2007
43	P H Thorburn	37	1985 to 1991
38	J Bancroft	18	1909 to 1914
30	A C Thomas	23	1996 to 2000
29	G L Henson	22	2001 to 2007
25	C Sweeney	34	2003 to 2007
24	J Hook	19	2006 to 2007
20	W J Bancroft	33	1890 to 1901
20	I R Harris	25	2001 to 2004

MOST PENALTY GOALS IN TESTS

Penalties	Player	Tests	Career
235	N R Jenkins	87	1991 to 2002
106	S M Jones	66	1998 to 2007
70	P H Thorburn	37	1985 to 1991
36	P Bennett	29	1969 to 1978
35	S P Fenwick	30	1975 to 1981
32	A C Thomas	23	1996 to 2000
22	G Evans	10	1981 to 1983

MOST POINTS IN TESTS

Points	Player	Tests	Career
1049	N R Jenkins	87	1991 to 2002
569	S M Jones	66	1998 to 2007
304	P H Thorburn	37	1985 to 1991
211	A C Thomas	23	1996 to 2000
200	Gareth Thomas	100	1995 to 2007
175	S M Williams	51	2000 to 2007
166	P Bennett	29	1969 to 1978
157	I C Evans	72	1987 to 1998

INTERNATIONAL CHAMPIONSHIP RECORDS

RECORD	DETAIL		SET
Most points in season	151	in five matches	2005
Most tries in season	21	in four matches	1910
Highest Score	49	49-14 v France	1910
Biggest win	35	49-14 v France	1910
Highest score conceded	60	26-60 v England	1998
Biggest defeat	51	0-51 v France	1998
Most appearances	45	G O Edwards	1967 - 1978
Most points in matches	406	N R Jenkins	1991 - 2001
Most points in season	74	N R Jenkins	2001
Most points in match	28	N R Jenkins	v France, 2001
Most tries in matches	18	G O Edwards	1967 - 1978
Most tries in season	6	M C R Richards	1969
Most tries in match	4	W Llewellyn	v England, 1899
	4	M C R Richards	v England, 1969
Most cons in matches	50	S M Jones	2000 - 2007
Most cons in season	12	S M Jones	2005
Most cons in match	8	J Bancroft	v France, 1910
Most pens in matches	93	N R Jenkins	1991 - 2001
Most pens in season	16	P H Thorburn	1986
	16	N R Jenkins	1999
Most pens in match	7	N R Jenkins	v Italy, 2000
Most drops in matches	8	J Davies	1985 - 1997
Most drops in season	5	N R Jenkins	2001
Most drops in match	3	N R Jenkins	v Scotland, 2001

RECORD	HOLDER	DETAIL
Longest Test Career	G O Llewellyn	1989 to 2004
Youngest Test Cap	N Biggs	18 yrs 49 days in 1888
Oldest Test Cap	T H Vile	38 yrs 152 days in 1921

CAREER RECORDS OF WALES INTERNATIONAL PLAYERS (UP TO 31 OCTOBER 2007)

PLAYER	DEBUT	CAPS	T	C	P	D	PTS
BACKS							
A Brew	2007 v I	3	0	0	0	0	0
L M Byrne	2005 v NZ	14	2	0	0	0	10
G J Cooper	2001 v F	35	7	0	0	0	35
C D Czekaj	2005 v C	6	1	0	0	0	5
Gavin Evans	2006 v PI	1	0	0	0	0	0
G L Henson	2001 v J	22	3	29	18	1	130
J Hook	2006 v Arg	19	5	24	19	2	136
D R James	1996 v A	48	15	0	0	0	75
T James	2007 v E	1	0	0	0	0	0
M A Jones	2001 v E	34	12	0	0	0	60
S M Jones	1998 v SA	66	6	106	106	3	569
H N Luscombe	2003 v S	16	2	0	0	0	10
K A Morgan	1997 v US	48	12	0	0	0	60
S T Parker	2002 v R	26	6	0	0	0	30
D J Peel	2001 v J	58	5	0	0	0	25
M Phillips	2003 v R	27	3	0	0	0	15
J P Robinson	2001 v J	23	7	0	0	0	35
T G L Shanklin	2001 v J	46	17	0	0	0	85
C Sweeney	2003 v It	34	4	25	5	1	88
Gareth Thomas	1995 v J	100	40	0	0	0	200
A Williams	2003 v R	5	0	0	0	0	0
S M Williams	2000 v F	51	35	0	0	0	175
FORWARDS							
H Bennett	2003 v I	13	0	0	0	0	0
C L Charvis	1996 v A	93	21	0	0	0	105
B J Cockbain	2003 v R	24	1	0	0	0	5
Mefin Davies	2002 v SA	38	2	0	0	0	10
Ian Evans	2006 v Arg	7	1	0	0	0	5
I M Gough	1998 v SA	45	1	0	0	0	5
R Hibbard	2006 v Arg	4	0	0	0	0	0
C L Horsman	2005 v NZ	14	1	0	0	0	5
W James	2007 v E	4	0	0	0	0	0
G D Jenkins	2002 v R	52	3	0	0	0	15
A R Jones	2003 v E	44	1	0	0	0	5
A-W Jones	2006 v Arg	17	3	0	0	0	15

Ceri Jones	2007 v A	2	0	0	0	0	0
Duncan Jones	2001 v A	44	0	0	0	0	0
R P Jones	2004 v SA	16	2*	0	0	0	10
S Morgan	2007 v A	1	0	0	0	0	0
M J Owen	2002 v SA	41	2	0	0	0	10
A J Popham	2003 v A	31	4	0	0	0	20
M Rees	2005 v US	16	2	0	0	0	10
R A Sidoli	2002 v SA	42	2	0	0	0	10
R Sowden-Taylor	2005 v It	4	0	0	0	0	0
G V Thomas	2001 v J	22	4	0	0	0	20
D Thomas	2000 v Sm	33	1†	0	0	0	5
J Thomas	2003 v A	38	7	0	0	0	35
Rhys Thomas	2006 v Arg	2	0	0	0	0	0
T R Thomas	2005 v US	25	1	0	0	0	5
M E Williams	1996 v Bb	76	13	0	0	1	68

* Iestyn Thomas's figures include a penalty try awarded against Fiji in 2002

† Ryan Jones's figures include a penalty try awarded against Canada in 2006

WALES INTERNATIONAL PLAYERS

UP TO 31ST OCTOBER 2007

Note: Years given for International Championship matches are for second half of season; eg 1972 means season 1971–72. Years for all other matches refer to the actual year of the match. Entries in square brackets denote matches played in RWC Finals.

Ackerman, R A (Newport, London Welsh) 1980 NZ, 1981 E, S, A, 1982 I, F, E, S, 1983 S, I, F, R, 1984 S, I, F, E, A, 1985 S, I, F, E, Fj
Alexander, E P (Llandovery Coll, Cambridge U) 1885 S, 1886 E, S, 1887 E, I
Alexander, W H (Llwynypia) 1898 I, E, 1899 E, S, I, 1901 S, I
Allen, A G (Newbridge) 1990 F, E, I
Allen, C P (Oxford U, Beaumaris) 1884 E, S
Andrews, F (Pontypool) 1912 SA, 1913 E, S, I
Andrews, F G (Swansea) 1884 E, S
Andrews, G E (Newport) 1926 E, S, 1927 E, F, I
Anthony, C T (Swansea, Newport, Gwent Dragons) 1997 US 1(R),2(R), C (R), Tg (R), 1998 SA 2, Arg, 1999 S, I (R), 2001 J 1,2, I (R), 2002 I, F, It, E, S, 2003 R (R)
Anthony, L (Neath) 1948 E, S, F
Appleyard, R C (Swansea) 1997 C, R, Tg, NZ, 1998 It, E (R), S, I, F
Arnold, P (Swansea) 1990 Nm 1, 2, Bb, 1991 E, S, I, F 1, A, [Arg, A], 1993 F (R), Z 2, 1994 Sp, Fj, 1995 SA, 1996 Bb (R)
Arnold, W R (Swansea) 1903 S
Arthur, C S (Cardiff) 1888 I, M, 1891 E
Arthur, T (Neath) 1927 S, F, I, 1929 E, S, F, I, 1930 E, S, I, F, 1931 E, S, F, I, SA, 1933 E, S
Ashton, C (Aberavon) 1959 E, S, I, 1960 E, S, I, 1962 I
Attewell, S L (Newport) 1921 E, S, F

Back, M J (Bridgend) 1995 F (R), E (R), S, I
Badger, O (Llanelli) 1895 E, S, I, 1896 E
Baker, A (Neath) 1921 I, 1923 E, S, F, I
Baker, A M (Newport) 1909 S, F, 1910 S
Bancroft, J (Swansea) 1909 E, S, F, I, 1910 F, E, S, I, 1911 E, F, I, 1912 E, S, I, 1913 I, 1914 E, S, F
Bancroft, W J (Swansea) 1890 S, E, I, 1891 E, S, I, 1892 E, S, I, 1893 E, S, I, 1894 E, S, I, 1895 E, S, I, 1896 E, S, I, 1897 E, 1898 I, E, 1899 E, S, I, 1900 E, S, I, 1901 E, S, I
Barlow, T M (Cardiff) 1884 I
Barrell, R J (Cardiff) 1929 S, F, I, 1933 I
Bartlett, J D (Llanelli) 1927 S, 1928 E, S
Bassett, A (Cardiff) 1934 I, 1935 E, S, I, 1938 E, S
Bassett, J A (Penarth) 1929 E, S, F, I, 1930 E, S, I, 1931 E, S, F, I, SA, 1932 E, S, I
Bateman, A G (Neath, Richmond, Northampton) 1990 S, I, Nm 1,2, 1996 SA, 1997 US, S, F, E, R, NZ, 1998 It, E, S, I, 1999 S, Arg 1,2, SA, C, [J, A (R)], 2000 It, E, S, I, Sm, US, SA, 2001 E (R), It (t), R, I, Art (R), Tg
Bater, J (Ospreys) 2003 R (R)
Bayliss, G (Pontypool) 1933 S
Bebb, D I E (Carmarthen TC, Swansea) 1959 E, S, I, F, 1960 E, S, I, F, SA, 1961 E, S, I, F, 1962 E, S, F, I, 1963 E, F, NZ, 1964 E, S, F, SA, 1965 E, S, I, F, 1966 F, A, 1967 S, I, F, E
Beckingham, G (Cardiff) 1953 E, S, 1958 F
Bennett, A M (Cardiff) 1995 [NZ] SA, Fj
Bennett, H (Ospreys) 2003 I 2(R), S 2(R), [C(R),Tg(R)], 2004 S(R),F(R),Arg 1(R),2, SA1(R), 2006 Arg 2,PI(R), 2007 E2, [J(R)]
Bennett, I (Aberavon) 1937 I
Bennett, P (Cardiff Harlequins) 1891 E, S, 1892 S, I
Bennett, P (Llanelli) 1969 F (R), 1970 SA, S, F, 1972 S (R), NZ, 1973 E, S, I, F, A, 1974 S, I, F, E, 1975 S (R), I, 1976 E, S, I, F, 1977 I, F, E, S, 1978 E, S, I, F
Bergiers, R T E (Cardiff Coll of Ed, Llanelli) 1972 E, S, F, NZ, 1973 E, S, I, F, A, 1974 E, 1975 I
Bevan, G W (Llanelli) 1947 E
Bevan, J A (Cambridge U) 1881 E
Bevan, J C (Cardiff, Cardiff Coll of Ed) 1971 E, S, I, F, 1972 E, S, F, NZ, 1973 E, S
Bevan, J D (Aberavon) 1975 F, E, S, A
Bevan, S (Swansea) 1904 I
Beynon, B (Swansea) 1920 E, S
Beynon, G E (Swansea) 1925 F, I
Bidgood, R A (Newport) 1992 S, 1993 Z 1,2, Nm, J (R)
Biggs, N W (Cardiff) 1888 M, 1889 I, 1892 I, 1893 E, S, I, 1894 E, I
Biggs, S H (Cardiff) 1895 E, S, 1896 S, 1897 E, 1898 I, E, 1899 S, I, 1900 I
Birch, J (Neath) 1911 S, F
Birt, F W (Newport) 1911 E, S, 1912 E, S, I, SA, 1913 E
Bishop, D J (Pontypool) 1984 A
Bishop, E H (Swansea) 1889 S
Blackmore, J H (Abertillery) 1909 E
Blackmore, S W (Cardiff) 1987 I, [Tg (R), C, A]
Blake, J (Cardiff) 1899 E, S, I, 1900 E, S, I, 1901 E, S, I
Blakemore, R E (Newport) 1947 E
Bland, A F (Cardiff) 1887 E, S, I, 1888 S, I, M, 1890 S, E, I
Blyth, L (Swansea) 1951 SA, 1952 E, S
Blyth, W R (Swansea) 1974 E, 1975 S (R), 1980 F, E, S, I
Boobyer, N (Llanelli) 1993 Z 1(R),2, Nm, 1994 Fj, Tg, 1998 F, 1999 It (R)
Boon, R W (Cardiff) 1930 S, F, 1931 E, S, F, I, SA, 1932 E, S, I, 1933 E, I
Booth, J (Pontymister) 1898 I
Boots, J G (Newport) 1898 I, E, 1899 I, 1900 E, S, I, 1901 E, S, I, 1902 E, S, I, 1903 E, S, I, 1904 E
Boucher, A W (Newport) 1892 E, S, I, 1893 E, S, I, 1894 E, 1895 E, S, I, 1896 E, I, 1897 E
Bowcott, H M (Cardiff, Cambridge U) 1929 S, F, I, 1930 E, 1931 E, S, 1933 E, I
Bowdler, F A (Cross Keys) 1927 A, 1928 E, S, I, F, 1929 E, S, F, I, 1930 E, 1931 SA, 1932 E, S, I, 1933 I
Bowen, B (S Wales Police, Swansea) 1983 R, 1984 S, I, F, E, 1985 Fj, 1986 E, S, I, F, Fj, Tg, WS, 1987 [C, E, NZ], US, 1988 E, S, I, F, WS, 1989 S, I
Bowen, C A (Llanelli) 1896 E, S, I, 1897 E
Bowen, D H (Llanelli) 1883 E, 1886 E, S, 1887 E
Bowen, G E (Swansea) 1887 S, I, 1888 S, I
Bowen, W (Swansea) 1921 S, F, 1922 E, S, I, F
Bowen, Wm A (Swansea) 1886 E, S, 1887 E, S, I, 1888 M, 1889 S, I, 1890 S, E, I, 1891 E, S
Brace, D O (Llanelli, Oxford U) 1956 E, S, I, F, 1957 E, 1960 S, I, F, 1961 I
Braddock, K J (Newbridge) 1966 A, 1967 S, I
Bradshaw, K (Bridgend) 1964 E, S, I, F, SA, 1966 E, S, I, F
Brew, A (Newport Gwent Dragons, Ospreys) 2007 I(R),A2,E2
Brew, N R (Gwent Dragons) 2003 R
Brewer, T J (Newport) 1950 E, 1955 E, S
Brice, A B (Aberavon) 1899 E, S, I, 1900 E, S, I, 1901 E, S, I, 1902 E, S, I, 1903 E, S, I, 1904 E, S, I
Bridges, C J (Neath) 1990 Nm 1,2, Bb, 1991 E (R), I, F 1, A
Bridie, R H (Newport) 1882 I

Britton, G R (Newport) 1961 S
Broster, B G J (Saracens) 2005 US(R),C
Broughton, A S (Treorchy) 1927 A, 1929 S
Brown, A (Newport) 1921 I
Brown, J (Cardiff) 1925 I
Brown, J A (Cardiff) 1907 E, S, I, 1908 E, S, F, 1909 E
Brown, M (Pontypool) 1983 R, 1986 E, S, Fj (R), Tg, WS
Bryant, D J (Bridgend) 1988 NZ 1,2, WS, R, 1989 S, I, F, E
Bryant, J (Celtic Warriors) 2003 R (R)
Buchanan, A (Llanelli) 1987 [Tg, E, NZ, A], 1988 I
Buckett, I M (Swansea) 1994 Tg, 1997 US 2, C
Budgett, N J (Ebbw Vale, Bridgend) 2000 S, I, Sm (R), US, SA, 2001 J 1(R),2, 2002 I, F, It, E, S
Burcher, D H (Newport) 1977 I, F, E, S
Burgess, R C (Ebbw Vale) 1977 I, F, E, S, 1981 I, F, 1982 F, E, S
Burnett, R (Newport) 1953 E
Burns, J (Cardiff) 1927 F, I
Bush, P F (Cardiff) 1905 NZ, 1906 E, SA, 1907 I, 1908 E, S, 1910 S, I
Butler, E T (Pontypool) 1980 F, E, S, I, NZ (R), 1982 S, 1983 E, S, I, F, R, 1984 S, I, F, E, A
Byrne, L M (Llanelli Scarlets, Ospreys) 2005 NZ(R),Fj,SA, 2006 E(t&R),S(t&R),I,It,F,Arg 1,2, PI, 2007 F1,A1,E2

Cale, W R (Newbridge, Pontypool) 1949 E, S, I, 1950 E, S, I, F
Cardey, M D (Llanelli) 2000 S
Carter, A J (Newport) 1991 E, S
Cattell, A (Llanelli) 1883 E, S
Challinor, C (Neath) 1939 E
Charteris, L C (Newport Gwent Dragons) 2004 SA2(R),R, 2005 US,C,NZ(R),Fj
Charvis, C L (Swansea, Tarbes, Newcastle, Newport Gwent Dragons) 1996 A 3(R), SA, 1997 US, S, I, F, 1998 It (R), E, S, I, F, Z (R), SA 1,2, Arg, 1999 S, I, F 1, It, E, Arg 1, SA, F 2, [Arg 3, A], 2000 F, It (R), E, S, I, Sm, US, SA, 2001 E, S, F, It, R, I, Arg, Tg, A, 2002 E (R), S, SA 1,2, R, Fj, C, NZ, 2003 It, E 1(R), S 1(R), I 1, F,A, NZ, E 2, S 2, [C,Tg,It,NZ,E], 2004 S,F,E,It,Arg 1,2,SA1,2,R,NZ,J, 2005 US,C,NZ,SA,A, 2006 E,S,I,It, 2007 A1,2,E2,Arg(R),F2(R), [C(t&R),A,J,Fj]
Clapp, T J S (Newport) 1882 I, 1883 E, S, 1884 E, S, I, 1885 E, S, 1886 S, 1887 E, S, I, 1888 S, I
Clare, J (Cardiff) 1883 E
Clark, S S (Neath) 1882 I, 1887 I
Cleaver, W B (Cardiff) 1947 E, S, F, I, A, 1948 E, S, F, I, 1949 I, 1950 E, S, I, F
Clegg, B G (Swansea) 1979 F
Clement, A (Swansea) 1987 US (R), 1988 E, NZ 1, WS (R), R, 1989 NZ, 1990 S (R), I (R), Nm 1,2, 1991 S (R), A (R), F 2, [WS, A], 1992 I, F, E, S, 1993 I (R), F, J, C, 1994 S, I, F, Sp, C (R), Tg, WS, It, SA, 1995 F, E, [J, NZ, I]
Clement, W H (Llanelli) 1937 E, S, I, 1938 E, S, I
Cobner, T J (Pontypool) 1974 S, I, F, E, 1975 F, E, S, I, A, 1976 E, S, 1977 F, E, S, 1978 E, S, I, F, A 1
Cockbain, B J (Celtic Warriors, Ospreys) 2003 R, [C,It,NZ,E], 2004 S,I,F,E,Arg 1,2,SA2,NZ, 2005 E,It,F,S,I,US,C(R),NZ,Fj, 2007 F1(t&R),A1
Coldrick, A P (Newport) 1911 E, S, I, 1912 E, S, F
Coleman, E (Newport) 1949 E, S, I
Coles, F C (Pontypool) 1960 S, I, F
Collins, J (Aberavon) 1958 A, E, S, F, 1959 E, S, I, F, 1960 E, 1961 F
Collins, R G (S Wales Police, Cardiff, Pontypridd) 1987 E (R), I, [I, E, NZ], US, 1988 E, S, I, F, R, 1990 E, S, I, 1991 A, F 2, [WS], 1994 C, Fj, Tg, WS, R, It, SA, 1995 F, E, S, I
Collins, T (Mountain Ash) 1923 I
Conway-Rees, J (Llanelli) 1892 S, 1893 E, 1894 E
Cook, T (Cardiff) 1949 S, I
Cooper, G J (Bath, Celtic Warriors, Newport Gwent Dragons, Gloucester) 2001 F, J 1,2, 2003 E 1, S 1, I 1, F(R), A, NZ, E 2, [C,Tg,It(t&R),NZ,E], 2004 S,I,F,E,It,R(R),NZ(R),J, 2005 E(R), It(R),F(R),NZ(R),Fj,SA,A, 2006 E(R),PI(R), 2007 A1(R),E2, [J(R)]
Cooper, V L (Llanelli) 2002 C, 2003 I 2(R), S 2
Cope, W (Cardiff, Blackheath) 1896 S
Copsey, A H (Llanelli) 1992 I, F, E, S, A, 1993 E, S, I, J, C, 1994 E (R), Pt, Sp (R), Fj, Tg, WS (R)
Cornish, F H (Cardiff) 1897 E, 1898 I, E, 1899 I
Cornish, R A (Cardiff) 1923 E, S, 1924 E, 1925 E, S, F, 1926 E, S, I, F
Coslett, K (Aberavon) 1962 E, S, F
Cowey, B T V (Welch Regt, Newport) 1934 E, S, I, 1935 E
Cresswell, B (Newport) 1960 E, S, I, F
Cummins, W (Treorchy) 1922 E, S, I, F
Cunningham, L J (Aberavon) 1960 E, S, I, F, 1962 E, S, F, I, 1963 NZ, 1964 E, S, I, F, SA
Czekaj, C D (Cardiff Blues) 2005 C, 2006 Arg 1(R), 2007 I,S,A1,22007 I,S,A1,2

Dacey, M (Swansea) 1983 E, S, I, F, R, 1984 S, I, F, E, A, 1986 Fj, Tg, WS, 1987 F (R), [Tg]
Daniel, D J (Llanelli) 1891 S, 1894 E, S, I, 1898 I, E, 1899 E, I
Daniel, L T D (Newport) 1970 S
Daniels, P C T (Cardiff) 1981 A, 1982 I
Darbishire, G (Bangor) 1881 E
Dauncey, F H (Newport) 1896 E, S, I
Davey, C (Swansea) 1930 F, 1931 E, S, F, I, SA, 1932 E, S, I, 1933 E, S, 1934 E, S, I, 1935 E, S, I, NZ, 1936 S, 1937 E, I, 1938 E, I
David, R J (Cardiff) 1907 I
David, T P (Llanelli, Pontypridd) 1973 F, A, 1976 I, F
Davidge, G D (Newport) 1959 F, 1960 S, I, F, SA, 1961 E, S, I, 1962 F
Davies, A (Cambridge U, Neath, Cardiff) 1990 Bb (R), 1991 A, 1993 Z 1,2, J, C, 1994 Fj, 1995 [J, I]
Davies, A C (London Welsh) 1889 I
Davies, A E (Llanelli) 1984 A
Davies, B (Llanelli) 1895 E, 1896 E
Davies, B (Llanelli Scarlets) 2006 I(R)
Davies, C (Cardiff) 1947 S, F, I, A, 1948 E, S, F, I, 1949 F, 1950 E, S, I, F, 1951 E, S, I
Davies, C (Llanelli) 1988 WS, 1989 S, I (R), F
Davies, C H A (Llanelli, Cardiff) 1957 I, 1958 A, E, S, I, 1960 SA, 1961 E
Davies, C L (Cardiff) 1956 E, S, I
Davies, C R (Bedford, RAF) 1934 E
Davies, D (Bridgend) 1921 I, 1925 I
Davies, D B (Llanelli) 1907 E
Davies, D B (Llanelli) 1962 I, 1963 E, S
Davies, D G (Cardiff) 1923 E, S
Davies, D H (Neath) 1904 S
Davies, D H (Aberavon) 1924 E
Davies, D I (Swansea) 1939 E
Davies, D J (Neath) 1962 I
Davies, D M (Somerset Police) 1950 E, S, I, F, 1951 E, S, I, F, SA, 1952 E, S, I, F, 1953 I, F, NZ, 1954 E
Davies, E (Aberavon) 1947 A, 1948 I
Davies, E (Maesteg) 1919 NZA
Davies, E G (Cardiff) 1912 E, F
Davies, E G (Cardiff) 1928 F, 1929 E, 1930 S
Davies, G (Swansea) 1900 E, S, I, 1901 E, S, I, 1905 E, S, I
Davies, G (Cambridge U, Pontypridd) 1947 S, A, 1948 E, S, F, I, 1949 E, S, F, 1951 E, S
Davies, G (Llanelli) 1921 F, I, 1925 F
Davies, H (Swansea) 1898 I, E, 1901 S, I
Davies, H (Swansea, Llanelli) 1939 S, I, 1947 E, S, F, I
Davies, H (Neath) 1912 E, S
Davies, H (Bridgend) 1984 S, I, F, E
Davies, H J (Cambridge U, Aberavon) 1959 E, S
Davies, H J (Newport) 1924 S
Davies, I T (Llanelli) 1914 S, F, I
Davies, J (Neath, Llanelli, Cardiff) 1985 E, Fj, 1986 E, S, I, F, Fj, Tg, WS, 1987 F, E, S, I, [I, Tg (R), C, E, NZ, A], 1988 E, S, I, F, NZ 1,2, WS, R, 1996 A 3, 1997 US (t), S (R), F (R), E
Davies, Rev J A (Swansea) 1913 S, F, I, 1914 E, S, F, I
Davies, J D (Neath, Richmond) 1991 I, F 1, 1993 F (R), Z 2, J, C, 1994 S, I, F, E, Pt, Sp, C, WS, R, It, SA, 1995 F, E, [J, NZ, I] SA, 1996 It, E, S, I, F 1, A 1, Bb, F 2, It, 1998 Z, SA 1
Davies, J H (Aberavon) 1923 I
Davies, L (Swansea) 1939 S, I
Davies, L (Bridgend) 1966 E, S, I
Davies, L B (Neath, Cardiff, Llanelli) 1996 It, E, S, I, F 1, A 1, Bb, F 2, It (R), 1997 US 1,2, C, R, Tg, NZ (R), 1998 E (R), I, F, 1999 C, 2001 I, 2003 It

Davies, L M (Llanelli) 1954 F, S, 1955 I
Davies, M (Swansea) 1981 A, 1982 I, 1985 Fj
Davies, Mefin (Pontypridd, Celtic Warriors, Gloucester) 2002 SA 2(R), R, Fj, 2003 It, S 1(R), I 1(R), F, A(R), NZ(R), I 2, R, [Tg,NZ(R),E(R)], 2004 S,F,It(R),Arg 1,2(R),SA1,2(R),R,NZ,J, 2005 E,It,F,S,I,C(R),NZ,SA(R),A(t), 2006 S(R),I(R),It(R),F(R), 2007 A2
Davies, M J (Blackheath) 1939 S, I
Davies, N G (London Welsh) 1955 E
Davies, N G (Llanelli) 1988 NZ 2, WS, 1989 S, I, 1993 F, 1994 S, I, E, Pt, Sp, C, Fj, Tg (R), WS, R, It, 1995 E, S, I, Fj, 1996 E, S, I, F 1, A 1,2, Bb, F 2, 1997 E
Davies, P T (Llanelli) 1985 E, Fj, 1986 E, S, I, F, Fj, Tg, WS, 1987 F, E, I, [Tg, C, NZ], 1988 WS, R, 1989 S, I, F, E, NZ, 1990 F, E, S, 1991 I, F 1, A, F 2, [WS, Arg, A], 1993 F, Z 1, Nm, 1994 S, I, F, E, C, Fj (R), WS, R, It, 1995 F, I
Davies, R H (Oxford U, London Welsh) 1957 S, I, F, 1958 A, 1962 E, S
Davies, S (Treherbert) 1923 I
Davies, S (Swansea) 1992 I, F, E, S, A, 1993 E, S, I, Z 1(R),2, Nm, J, 1995 F, [J, I], 1998 I (R), F
Davies, T G R (Cardiff, London Welsh) 1966 A, 1967 S, I, F, E, 1968 E, S, 1969 S, I, F, NZ 1,2, A, 1971 E, S, I, F, 1972 E, S, F, NZ, 1973 E, S, I, F, A, 1974 S, F, E, 1975 F, E, S, I, 1976 E, S, I, F, 1977 I, F, E, S, 1978 E, S, I, A 1,2
Davies, T J (Devonport Services, Swansea, Llanelli) 1953 E, S, I, F, 1957 E, S, I, F, 1958 A, E, S, F, 1959 E, S, I, F, 1960 E, SA, 1961 E, S, F
Davies, T M (London Welsh, Swansea) 1969 S, I, F, E, NZ 1,2, A, 1970 SA, S, E, I, F, 1971 E, S, I, F, 1972 E, S, F, NZ, 1973 E, S, I, F, A, 1974 S, I, F, E, 1975 F, E, S, I, A, 1976 E, S, I, F
Davies, W (Cardiff) 1896 S
Davies, W (Swansea) 1931 SA, 1932 E, S, I
Davies, W A (Aberavon) 1912 S, I
Davies, W G (Cardiff) 1978 A 1,2, NZ, 1979 S, I, F, E, 1980 F, E, S, NZ, 1981 E, S, A, 1982 I, F, E, S, 1985 S, I, F
Davies, W T H (Swansea) 1936 I, 1937 E, I, 1939 E, S, I
Davis, C E (Newbridge) 1978 A 2, 1981 E, S
Davis, M (Newport) 1991 A
Davis, W E N (Cardiff) 1939 E, S, I
Dawes, S J (London Welsh) 1964 I, F, SA, 1965 E, S, I, F, 1966 A, 1968 I, F, 1969 E, NZ 2, A, 1970 SA, S, E, I, F, 1971 E, S, I, F
Day, H C (Newport) 1930 S, I, F, 1931 E, S
Day, H T (Newport) 1892 I, 1893 E, S, 1894 S, I
Day, T B (Swansea) 1931 E, S, F, I, SA, 1932 E, S, I, 1934 S, I, 1935 E, S, I
Deacon, J T (Swansea) 1891 I, 1892 E, S, I
Delahay, W J (Bridgend) 1922 E, S, I, F, 1923 E, S, F, I, 1924 NZ, 1925 E, S, F, I, 1926 E, S, I, F, 1927 S
Delaney, L (Llanelli) 1989 I, F, E, 1990 E, 1991 F 2, [WS, Arg, A], 1992 I, F, E
Delve, G L (Bath) 2006 S(R),I(R),Arg 1(R),2(R)
Devereux, D (Neath) 1958 A, E, S
Devereux, J A (S Glamorgan Inst, Bridgend) 1986 E, S, I, F, Fj, Tg, WS, 1987 F, E, S, I, [I, C, E, NZ, A], 1988 NZ 1,2, R, 1989 S, I
Diplock, R (Bridgend) 1988 R
Dobson, G (Cardiff) 1900 S
Dobson, T (Cardiff) 1898 I, E, 1899 E, S
Donovan, A J (Swansea) 1978 A 2, 1981 I (R), A, 1982 E, S
Donovan, R (S Wales Police) 1983 F (R)
Douglas, M H J (Llanelli) 1984 S, I, F
Douglas, W M (Cardiff) 1886 E, S, 1887 E, S
Dowell, W H (Newport) 1907 E, S, I, 1908 E, S, F, I
Durston, A (Bridgend) 2001 J 1,2
Dyke, J C M (Penarth) 1906 SA
Dyke, L M (Penarth, Cardiff) 1910 I, 1911 S, F, I

Edmunds, D A (Neath) 1990 I (R), Bb
Edwards, A B (London Welsh, Army) 1955 E, S
Edwards, B O (Newport) 1951 I
Edwards, D (Glynneath) 1921 E
Edwards, G O (Cardiff, Cardiff Coll of Ed) 1967 F, E, NZ, 1968 E, S, I, F, 1969 S, I, F, E, NZ 1,2, A, 1970 SA, S, E, I, F, 1971 E, S, I, F, 1972 E, S, F, NZ, 1973 E, S, I, F, A, 1974 S, I, F, E, 1975 F, E, S, I, A, 1976 E, S, I, F, 1977 I, F, E, S, 1978 E, S, I, F
Eidman, I H (Cardiff) 1983 S, R, 1984 I, F, E, A, 1985 S, I, Fj, 1986 E, S, I, F
Elliott, J E (Cardiff) 1894 I, 1898 I, E
Elsey, W J (Cardiff) 1895 E
Emyr, Arthur (Swansea) 1989 E, NZ, 1990 F, E, S, I, Nm 1,2, 1991 F 1,2, [WS, Arg, A]
Evans, A (Pontypool) 1924 E, I, F
Evans, B (Swansea) 1933 S
Evans, B (Llanelli) 1933 E, S, 1936 E, S, I, 1937 E
Evans, B R (Swansea, Cardiff Blues) 1998 SA 2(R), 1999 F 1, It, E, Arg 1,2, C, [J (R), Sm (R), A (R)], 2000 Sm, US, 2001 J 1(R), 2002 SA 1,2, R(R), Fj, C, NZ, 2003 It, E 1, S 1, I 2, R, 2004 F(R),E(t),It(R)
Evans, B S (Llanelli) 1920 E, 1922 E, S, I, F
Evans, C (Pontypool) 1960 E
Evans, D (Penygraig) 1896 S, I, 1897 E, 1898 E
Evans, D B (Swansea) 1926 E
Evans, D D (Cheshire, Cardiff U) 1934 E
Evans, D P (Llanelli) 1960 SA
Evans, D W (Cardiff) 1889 S, I, 1890 E, I, 1891 E
Evans, D W (Oxford U, Cardiff, Treorchy) 1989 F, E, NZ, 1990 F, E, S, I, Bb, 1991 A (R), F 2(R), [A (R)], 1995 [J (R)]
Evans, E (Llanelli) 1937 E, 1939 S, I
Evans, F (Llanelli) 1921 S
Evans, G (Cardiff) 1947 E, S, F, I, A, 1948 E, S, F, I, 1949 E, S, I
Evans, G (Maesteg) 1981 S (R), I, F, A, 1982 I, F, E, S, 1983 F, R
Evans, Gavin (Llanelli Scarlets) 2006 PI(R)
Evans, G L (Newport) 1977 F (R), 1978 F, A 2(R)
Evans, G R (Llanelli) 1998 SA 1, 2003 I 2, S 2, [NZ]
Evans, Ian (Ospreys) 2006 Arg 1,2,A,C,NZ, 2007 [J(R),Fj]
Evans, I (London Welsh) 1934 S, I
Evans, I (Swansea) 1922 E, S, I, F
Evans, I C (Llanelli, Bath) 1987 F, E, S, I, [I, C, E, NZ, A], 1988 E, S, I, F, NZ 1,2, 1989 I, F, E, 1991 E, S, I, F 1, A, F 2, [WS, Arg, A], 1992 I, F, E, S, A, 1993 E, S, I, F, J, C, 1994 S, I, E, Pt, Sp, C, Fj, Tg, WS, R, 1995 E, S, I, [J, NZ, I], SA, Fj, 1996 It, E, S, I, F 1, A 1,2, Bb, F 2, A 3, SA, 1997 US, S, I, F, 1998 It
Evans, I L (Llanelli) 1991 F 2(R)
Evans, J (Llanelli) 1896 S, I, 1897 E
Evans, J (Blaina) 1904 E
Evans, J (Pontypool) 1907 E, S, I
Evans, J D (Cardiff) 1958 I, F
Evans, J E (Llanelli) 1924 S
Evans, J R (Newport) 1934 E
Evans, O J (Cardiff) 1887 E, S, 1888 S, I
Evans, P D (Llanelli) 1951 E, F
Evans, R (Cardiff) 1889 S
Evans, R (Bridgend) 1963 S, I, F
Evans, R L (Llanelli) 1993 E, S, I, F, 1994 S, I, F, E, Pt, Sp, C, Fj, WS, R, It, SA, 1995 F, [NZ, I (R)]
Evans, R T (Newport) 1947 F, I, 1950 E, S, I, F, 1951 E, S, I, F
Evans, S (Swansea, Neath) 1985 F, E, 1986 Fj, Tg, WS, 1987 F, E, [I, Tg]
Evans, T (Swansea) 1924 I
Evans, T G (London Welsh) 1970 SA, S, E, I, 1972 E, S, F
Evans, T H (Llanelli) 1906 I, 1907 E, S, I, 1908 I, A, 1909 E, S, F, I, 1910 F, E, S, I, 1911 E, S, F, I
Evans, T P (Swansea) 1975 F, E, S, I, A, 1976 E, S, I, F, 1977 I
Evans, V (Neath) 1954 I, F, S
Evans, W (Llanelli) 1958 A
Evans, W F (Rhymney) 1882 I, 1883 S
Evans, W G (Brynmawr) 1911 I
Evans, W H (Llwynypia) 1914 E, S, F, I
Evans, W J (Pontypool) 1947 S
Evans, W R (Bridgend) 1958 A, E, S, I, F, 1960 SA, 1961 E, S, I, F, 1962 E, S, I
Everson, W A (Newport) 1926 S

Faulkner, A G (Pontypool) 1975 F, E, S, I, A, 1976 E, S, I, F, 1978 E, S, I, F, A 1,2, NZ, 1979 S, I, F
Faull, J (Swansea) 1957 I, F, 1958 A, E, S, I, F, 1959 E, S, I, 1960 E, F

Fauvel, T J (Aberavon) 1988 NZ 1(R)
Fear, A G (Newport) 1934 S, I, 1935 S, I
Fender, N H (Cardiff) 1930 I, F, 1931 E, S, F, I
Fenwick, S P (Bridgend) 1975 F, E, S, A, 1976 E, S, I, F, 1977 I, F, E, S, 1978 E, S, I, F, A 1,2, NZ, 1979 S, I, F, E, 1980 F, E, S, I, NZ, 1981 E, S
Finch, E (Llanelli) 1924 F, NZ, 1925 F, I, 1926 F, 1927 A, 1928 I
Finlayson, A A J (Cardiff) 1974 I, F, E
Fitzgerald, D (Cardiff) 1894 S, I
Ford, F J V (Welch Regt, Newport) 1939 E
Ford, I (Newport) 1959 E, S
Ford, S P (Cardiff) 1990 I, Nm 1,2, Bb, 1991 E, S, I, A
Forster, J A (Newport Gwent Dragons) 2004 Arg 1
Forward, A (Pontypool, Mon Police) 1951 S, SA, 1952 E, S, I, F
Fowler, I J (Llanelli) 1919 NZA
Francis, D G (Llanelli) 1919 NZA, 1924 S
Francis, P (Maesteg) 1987 S
Funnell, J S (Ebbw Vale) 1998 Z (R), SA 1

Gabe, R T (Cardiff, Llanelli) 1901 I, 1902 E, S, I, 1903 E, S, I, 1904 E, S, I, 1905 E, S, I, NZ, 1906 E, I, SA, 1907 E, S, I, 1908 E, S, F, I
Gale, N R (Swansea, Llanelli) 1960 I, 1963 E, S, I, NZ, 1964 E, S, I, F, SA, 1965 E, S, I, F, 1966 E, S, I, F, A, 1967 E, NZ, 1968 E, 1969 NZ 1(R),2, A
Gallacher, I S (Llanelli) 1970 F
Garrett, R M (Penarth) 1888 M, 1889 S, 1890 S, E, I, 1891 S, I, 1892 E
Geen, W P (Oxford U, Newport) 1912 SA, 1913 E, I
George, E E (Pontypridd, Cardiff) 1895 S, I, 1896 E
George, G M (Newport) 1991 E, S
Gething, G I (Neath) 1913 F
Gibbs, A (Newbridge) 1995 I, SA, 1996 A 2, 1997 US 1,2, C
Gibbs, I S (Neath, Swansea) 1991 E, S, I, F 1, A, F 2, [WS, Arg, A], 1992 I, F, E, S, A, 1993 E, S, I, F, J, C, 1996 It, A 3, SA, 1997 US, S, I, F, Tg, NZ, 1998 It, E, S, SA 2, Arg, 1999 S, I, F 1, It, E, C, F 2, [Arg 3, J, Sm, A], 2000 I, Sm, US, SA, 2001 E, S, F, It
Gibbs, R A (Cardiff) 1906 S, I, 1907 E, S, 1908 E, S, F, I, 1910 F, E, S, I, 1911 E, S, F, I
Giles, R (Aberavon) 1983 R, 1985 Fj (R), 1987 [C]
Girling, B E (Cardiff) 1881 E
Goldsworthy, S J (Swansea) 1884 I, 1885 E, S
Gore, J H (Blaina) 1924 I, F, NZ, 1925 E
Gore, W (Newbridge) 1947 S, F, I
Gough, I M (Newport, Pontypridd, Newport Gwent Dragons, Ospreys) 1998 SA 1, 1999 S, 2000 F, It (R), E (R), S, I, Sm, US, SA, 2001 E, S, F, It, Tg, A, 2002 I (R), F (R), It, S, 2003 R, 2005 It(R),US(R),SA,A, 2006 E,S,I,It,F,Arg 1,2,A,C,NZ, 2007 I,S(R),F1,It,E1,Arg,F2, [C,A,Fj(R)]
Gould, A J (Newport) 1885 E, S, 1886 E, S, 1887 E, S, I, 1888 S, 1889 I, 1890 S, E, I, 1892 E, S, I, 1893 E, S, I, 1894 E, S, 1895 E, S, I, 1896 E, S, I, 1897 E
Gould, G H (Newport) 1892 I, 1893 S, I
Gould, R (Newport) 1882 I, 1883 E, S, 1884 E, S, I, 1885 E, S, 1886 E, 1887 E, S
Graham, T C (Newport) 1890 I, 1891 S, I, 1892 E, S, 1893 E, S, I, 1894 E, S, 1895 E, S
Gravell, R W R (Llanelli) 1975 F, E, S, I, A, 1976 E, S, I, F, 1978 E, S, I, F, A 1,2, NZ, 1979 S, I, 1981 I, F, 1982 F, E, S
Gray, A J (London Welsh) 1968 E, S
Greenslade, D (Newport) 1962 S
Greville, H G (Llanelli) 1947 A
Griffin, Dr J (Edinburgh U) 1883 S
Griffiths, C (Llanelli) 1979 E (R)
Griffiths, D (Llanelli) 1888 M, 1889 I
Griffiths, G (Llanelli) 1889 I
Griffiths, G M (Cardiff) 1953 E, S, I, F, NZ, 1954 I, F, S, 1955 I, F, 1957 E, S
Griffiths, J (Swansea) 2000 Sm (R)
Griffiths, J L (Llanelli) 1988 NZ 2, 1989 S
Griffiths, M (Bridgend, Cardiff, Pontypridd) 1988 WS, R, 1989 S, I, F, E, NZ, 1990 F, E, Nm 1,2, Bb, 1991 I, F 1,2, [WS, Arg, A], 1992 I, F, E, S, A, 1993 Z 1,2, Nm, J, C, 1995 F (R), E, S, I, [J, I], 1998 SA 1
Griffiths, V M (Newport) 1924 S, I, F
Gronow, B (Bridgend) 1910 F, E, S, I
Gwilliam, J A (Cambridge U, Newport) 1947 A, 1948 I, 1949 E, S, I, F, 1950 E, S, I, F, 1951 E, S, I, SA, 1952 E, S, I, F, 1953 E, I, F, NZ, 1954 E
Gwynn, D (Swansea) 1883 E, 1887 S, 1890 E, I, 1891 E, S
Gwynn, W H (Swansea) 1884 E, S, I, 1885 E, S

Hadley, A M (Cardiff) 1983 R, 1984 S, I, F, E, 1985 F, E, Fj, 1986 E, S, I, F, Fj, Tg, 1987 S (R), I, [I, Tg, C, E, NZ, A], US, 1988 E, S, I, F
Hall, I (Aberavon) 1967 NZ, 1970 SA, S, E, 1971 S, 1974 S, I, F
Hall, M R (Cambridge U, Bridgend, Cardiff) 1988 NZ 1(R),2, WS, R, 1989 S, I, F, E, NZ, 1990 F, E, S, 1991 A, F 2, [WS, Arg, A], 1992 I, F, E, S, A, 1993 E, S, I, 1994 S, I, F, E, Pt, Sp, C, Tg, R, It, SA, 1995 F, S, I, [J, NZ, I]
Hall, W H (Bridgend) 1988 WS
Hancock, F E (Cardiff) 1884 I, 1885 E, S, 1886 S
Hannan, J (Newport) 1888 M, 1889 S, I, 1890 S, E, I, 1891 E, 1892 E, S, I, 1893 E, S, I, 1894 E, S, I, 1895 E, S, I
Harding, A F (London Welsh) 1902 E, S, I, 1903 E, S, I, 1904 E, S, I, 1905 E, S, I, NZ, 1906 E, S, I, SA, 1907 I, 1908 E, S
Harding, G F (Newport) 1881 E, 1882 I, 1883 E, S
Harding, R (Swansea, Cambridge U) 1923 E, S, F, I, 1924 I, F, NZ, 1925 F, I, 1926 E, I, F, 1927 E, S, F, I, 1928 E
Harding, T (Newport) 1888 M, 1889 S, I
Harris, C A (Aberavon) 1927 A
Harris, D J E (Pontypridd, Cardiff) 1959 I, F, 1960 S, I, F, SA, 1961 E, S
Harris, I R (Cardiff) 2001 Arg, Tg, A, 2002 I, It (R), E, S (R), Fj(R), C(R), NZ(R), 2003 It, E 1(R), S 1(R), I 1(R), F, I 2, S 2, [C,Tg,It,E], 2004 S,I,F,It
Hathway, G F (Newport) 1924 I, F
Havard, Rev W T (Llanelli) 1919 NZA
Hawkins, F (Pontypridd) 1912 I, F
Hayward, B I (Ebbw Vale) 1998 Z (R), SA 1
Hayward, D (Newbridge) 1949 E, F, 1950 E, S, I, F, 1951 E, S, I, F, SA, 1952 E, S, I, F
Hayward, D J (Cardiff) 1963 E, NZ, 1964 S, I, F, SA
Hayward, G (Swansea) 1908 S, F, I, A, 1909 E
Hellings, R (Llwynypia) 1897 E, 1898 I, E, 1899 S, I, 1900 E, I, 1901 E, S
Henson, G L (Swansea, Ospreys) 2001 J 1(R), R, 2003 NZ(R), R, 2004 Arg 1,2,SA1,2,R,NZ,J, 2005 E,It,F,S,I, 2006 I(R),F(R),A,NZ(R), 2007 A1(t&R),2(R)
Herrerá·, R C (Cross Keys) 1925 S, F, I, 1926 E, S, I, F, 1927 E
Hiams, H (Swansea) 1912 I, F
Hibbard, R (Ospreys) 2006 Arg 1(R),2(R), 2007 A1(R),2(R)
Hickman, A (Neath) 1930 E, 1933 S
Hiddlestone, D D (Neath) 1922 E, S, I, F, 1924 NZ
Hill, A F (Cardiff) 1885 S, 1886 E, S, 1888 S, I, M, 1889 S, 1890 S, I, 1893 E, S, I, 1894 E, S, I
Hill, S D (Cardiff) 1993 Z 1,2, Nm, 1994 I (R), F, SA, 1995 F, SA, 1996 A 2, F 2(R), It, 1997 E
Hinam, S (Cardiff) 1925 I, 1926 E, S, I, F
Hinton, J T (Cardiff) 1884 I
Hirst, G L (Newport) 1912 S, 1913 S, 1914 E, S, F, I
Hodder, W (Pontypool) 1921 E, S, F
Hodges, J J (Newport) 1899 E, S, I, 1900 E, S, I, 1901 E, S, 1902 E, S, I, 1903 E, S, I, 1904 E, S, 1905 E, S, I, NZ, 1906 E, S, I
Hodgson, G T R (Neath) 1962 I, 1963 E, S, I, F, NZ, 1964 E, S, I, F, SA, 1966 S, I, F, 1967 I
Hollingdale, H (Swansea) 1912 SA, 1913 E
Hollingdale, T H (Neath) 1927 A, 1928 E, S, I, F, 1930 E
Holmes, T D (Cardiff) 1978 A 2, NZ, 1979 S, I, F, E, 1980 F, E, S, I, NZ, 1981 A, 1982 I, F, E, 1983 E, S, I, F, 1984 E, 1985 S, I, F, E, Fj
Hook, J (Ospreys) 2006 Arg 1(R),2,A(R),PI, C,NZ(R), 2007 I,S,F1,It,E1,A1,2,Arg,F2, [C,A(R),J,Fj]
Hopkin, W H (Newport) 1937 S
Hopkins, K (Cardiff, Swansea) 1985 E, 1987 F, E, S, [Tg, C (R)], US
Hopkins, P L (Swansea) 1908 A, 1909 E, I, 1910 E
Hopkins, R (Maesteg) 1970 E (R)
Hopkins, T (Swansea) 1926 E, S, I, F
Hopkins, W J (Aberavon) 1925 E, S

Horsman, C L (Worcester) 2005 NZ(R),Fj,SA,A, 2006 Pl, 2007 I,F1,It,E1,A2(R),E2,F2, [J,Fj]
Howarth, S P (Sale, Newport) 1998 SA 2, Arg, 1999 S, I, F 1, It, E, Arg 1,2, SA, C, F 2, [Arg 3, J, Sm, A], 2000 F, It, E
Howells, B (Llanelli) 1934 E
Howells, W G (Llanelli) 1957 E, S, I, F
Howells, W H (Swansea) 1888 S, I
Howley, R (Bridgend, Cardiff) 1996 E, S, I, F 1, A 1,2, Bb, F 2, It, A 3, SA, 1997 US, S, I, F, E, Tg (R), NZ, 1998 It, E, S, I, F, Z, SA 2, Arg, 1999 S, I, F 1, It, E, Arg 1,2, SA, C, F 2, [Arg 3, J, Sm, A], 2000 F, It, E, Sm, US, SA, 2001 E, S, F, R, I, Arg, Tg, A, 2002 I, F, It, E, S
Hughes, D (Newbridge) 1967 NZ, 1969 NZ 2, 1970 SA, S, E, I
Hughes, G (Penarth) 1934 E, S, I
Hughes, H (Cardiff) 1887 S, 1889 S
Hughes, K (Cambridge U, London Welsh) 1970 I, 1973 A, 1974 S
Hullin, W (Cardiff) 1967 S
Humphreys, J M (Cardiff, Bath) 1995 [NZ, I], SA, Fj, 1996 It, E, S, I, F 1, A 1,2, Bb, It, A 3, SA, 1997 S, I, F, E, Tg (R), NZ (R), 1998 It (R), E (R), S (R), I (R), F (R), SA 2, Arg, 1999 S, Arg 2(R), SA (R), C, [J (R)], 2003 E 1, I 1
Hurrell, J (Newport) 1959 F
Hutchinson, F (Neath) 1894 I, 1896 S, I
Huxtable, R (Swansea) 1920 F, I
Huzzey, H V P (Cardiff) 1898 I, E, 1899 E, S, I
Hybart, A J (Cardiff) 1887 E

Ingledew, H M (Cardiff) 1890 I, 1891 E, S
Isaacs, I (Cardiff) 1933 E, S

Jackson, T H (Swansea) 1895 E
James, B (Bridgend) 1968 E
James, C R (Llanelli) 1958 A, F
James, D (Swansea) 1891 I, 1892 S, I, 1899 E
James, D R (Treorchy) 1931 F, I
James, D R (Bridgend, Pontypridd, Llanelli Scarlets) 1996 A 2(R), It, A 3, SA, 1997 I, Tg (R), 1998 F (R), Z, SA 1,2, Arg, 1999 S, I, F 1, It, E, Arg 1,2, SA, F 2, [Arg 3, Sm, A], 2000 F, It (R), I (R), Sm (R), US, SA, 2001 E, S, F, It, R, I, 2002 I, F, It, E, S (R), NZ(R), 2005 SA,A, 2006 I,F, 2007 E2,Arg, [J]
James, E (Swansea) 1890 S, 1891 I, 1892 S, I, 1899 E
James, M (Cardiff) 1947 A, 1948 E, S, F, I
James, P (Ospreys) 2003 R
James, T (Cardiff Blues) 2007 E2(R)
James, T O (Aberavon) 1935 I, 1937 S
James, W (Gloucester) 2007 E2,Arg(R),F2(R), [J]
James, W J (Aberavon) 1983 E, S, I, F, R, 1984 S, 1985 S, I, F, E, Fj, 1986 E, S, I, F, Fj, Tg, WS, 1987 E, S, I
James, W P (Aberavon) 1925 E, S
Jarman, H (Newport) 1910 E, S, I, 1911 E
Jarrett, K S (Newport) 1967 E, 1968 E, S, 1969 S, I, F, E, NZ 1,2, A
Jarvis, L (Cardiff) 1997 R (R)
Jeffery, J J (Cardiff Coll of Ed, Newport) 1967 NZ
Jenkin, A M (Swansea) 1895 I, 1896 E
Jenkins, A (Llanelli) 1920 E, S, F, I, 1921 S, F, 1922 F, 1923 E, S, F, I, 1924 NZ, 1928 S, I
Jenkins, D M (Treorchy) 1926 E, S, I, F
Jenkins, D R (Swansea) 1927 A, 1929 E
Jenkins, E (Newport) 1910 S, I
Jenkins, E M (Aberavon) 1927 S, F, I, A, 1928 E, S, I, F, 1929 F, 1930 E, S, I, F, 1931 E, S, F, I, SA, 1932 E, S, I
Jenkins, G D (Pontypridd, Celtic Warriors, Cardiff Blues) 2002 R, NZ(R), 2003 E 1(R), S 1(R), I 1, F, A, NZ, I 2(R), E 2, [C,Tg,It(R),NZ(R),E(R)], 2004 S(R),I(R),F,E,It,Arg 1(R),2(R),SA1,2(R),R,NZ,J, 2005 E,It,F,S,I, 2006 E(R),S(R),I(R),It(R),F(R),A,C,NZ(R), 2007 I,S(R),F1,It,E1,2(R),Arg(R),F2(R), [C,A,J(R),Fj]
Jenkins, G R (Pontypool, Swansea) 1991 F 2, [WS (R), Arg, A], 1992 I, F, E, S, A, 1993 C, 1994 S, I, F, E, Pt, Sp, C, Tg, WS, R, It, SA, 1995 F, E, S, I, [J], SA (R), Fj (t), 1996 E (R), 1997 US, US 1, C, 1998 S, I, F, Z, SA 1(R), 1999 I (R), F 1, It, E, Arg 1,2, SA, F 2, [Arg 3, J, Sm, A], 2000 F, It, E, S, I, Sm, US, SA
Jenkins, J C (London Welsh) 1906 SA
Jenkins, J L (Aberavon) 1923 S, F
Jenkins, L H (Mon TC, Newport) 1954 I, 1956 E, S, I, F
Jenkins, N R (Pontypridd, Cardiff) 1991 E, S, I, F 1, 1992 I, F, E, S, 1993 E, S, I, F, Z 1,2, Nm, J, C, 1994 S, I, F, E, Pt, Sp, C, Tg, WS, R, It, SA, 1995 F, E, S, I, [J, NZ, I], SA, Fj, 1996 F 1, A 1,2, Bb, F 2, It, A 3(R), SA, 1997 S, I, F, E, Tg, NZ, 1998 It, E, S, I, F, SA 2, Arg, 1999 S, I, F 1, It, E, Arg 1,2, SA, C, F 2, [Arg 3, J, Sm, A], 2000 F, It, E, I (R), Sm (R), US (R), SA, 2001 E, S, F, It, 2002 SA 1(R),2(R), R
Jenkins, V G J (Oxford U, Bridgend, London Welsh) 1933 E, I, 1934 S, I, 1935 E, S, NZ, 1936 E, S, I, 1937 E, 1938 E, S, 1939 E
Jenkins, W (Cardiff) 1912 I, F, 1913 S, I
John, B (Llanelli, Cardiff) 1966 A, 1967 S, NZ, 1968 E, S, I, F, 1969 S, I, F, E, NZ 1,2, A, 1970 SA, S, E, I, 1971 E, S, I, F, 1972 E, S, F
John, D A (Llanelli) 1925 I, 1928 E, S, I
John, D E (Llanelli) 1923 F, I, 1928 E, S, I
John, E R (Neath) 1950 E, S, I, F, 1951 E, S, I, F, SA, 1952 E, S, I, F, 1953 E, S, I, F, NZ, 1954 E
John G (St Luke's Coll, Exeter) 1954 E, F
John, J H (Swansea) 1926 E, S, I, F, 1927 E, S, F, I
John, P (Pontypridd) 1994 Tg, 1996 Bb (t), 1997 US (R), US 1,2, C, R, Tg, 1998 Z (R), SA 1
John, S C (Llanelli, Cardiff) 1995 S, I, 1997 E (R), Tg, NZ (R), 2000 F (R), It (R), E (R), Sm (R), SA (R), 2001 E (R), S (R), Tg (R), A, 2002 I, F, It (R), S (R)
Johnson, T A (Cardiff) 1921 E, F, I, 1923 E, S, F, 1924 E, S, NZ, 1925 E, S, F
Johnson, W D (Swansea) 1953 E
Jones, A H (Cardiff) 1933 E, S
Jones, A M (Llanelli Scarlets) 2006 E(t&R),S(R)
Jones, A R (Ospreys) 2003 E 2(R), S 2, [C(R),Tg(R),It,NZ,E], 2004 S,I,Arg 1,2,SA1,2,R,NZ,J(t&R), 2005 E,It,F,S,I,US,NZ,Fj(R),SA(t&R),A(R), 2006 E,S,I,It,F,Arg 1,2, A,Pl(R),C,NZ, 2007 S,It(R),E1(R),A1,Arg, [C,A]
Jones, A-W (Ospreys) 2006 Arg 1,2,Pl,C(R),NZ(R), 2007 I,S,F1,It,E1,2,Arg,F2, [C,A,J,Fj]
Jones, B (Abertillery) 1914 E, S, F, I
Jones, Bert (Llanelli) 1934 S, I
Jones, Bob (Llwynypia) 1901 I
Jones, B J (Newport) 1960 I, F
Jones, B Lewis (Devonport Services, Llanelli) 1950 E, S, I, F, 1951 E, S, SA, 1952 E, I, F
Jones, Ceri (Harlequins) 2007 A1(R),2
Jones, C W (Cambridge U, Cardiff) 1934 E, S, I, 1935 E, S, I, NZ, 1936 E, S, I, 1938 E, S, I
Jones, C W (Bridgend) 1920 E, S, F
Jones, D (Neath) 1927 A
Jones, D (Aberavon) 1897 E
Jones, D (Swansea) 1947 E, F, I, 1949 E, S, I, F
Jones, D (Treherbert) 1902 E, S, I, 1903 E, S, I, 1905 E, S, I, NZ, 1906 E, S, SA
Jones, D (Newport) 1926 E, S, I, F, 1927 E
Jones, D (Llanelli) 1948 E
Jones, D (Cardiff) 1994 SA, 1995 F, E, S, [J, NZ, I], SA, Fj, 1996 It, E, S, I, F 1, A 1,2, Bb, It, A 3
Jones, D A R (Llanelli Scarlets) 2002 Fj, C, NZ, 2003 It(R), E 1, S 1, I 1, F, NZ, E 2, [C,Tg,It,NZ(R),E], 2004 S,I,F,E,It,Arg 2,SA1,2,R,NZ,J, 2005 E,Fj, 2006 F(R)
Jones, D J (Neath, Ospreys) 2001 A (R), 2002 I (R), F (R), 2003 I 2, S 2,[C,It], 2004 S,E,It,Arg1,2,SA1(R),2,R(R),NZ(t&R),J, 2005 US,C,NZ,SA,A, 2006 E,S,I,It,F,Arg 1,2, A(R),Pl,C(R),NZ, 2007 I(R),S,F1(R),It(R),E1(R),Arg,F2, [C(R),A(R),J,Fj(R)]
Jones, D K (Llanelli, Cardiff) 1962 E, S, F, I, 1963 E, F, NZ, 1964 E, S, SA, 1966 E, S, I, F
Jones, D L (Ebbw Vale, Celtic Warriors, Cardiff Blues) 2000 Sm, 2003 R (R), 2004 SA1
Jones, D P (Pontypool) 1907 I
Jones, E H (Neath) 1929 E, S
Jones, E L (Llanelli) 1930 F, 1933 E, S, I, 1935 E
Jones, Elvet L (Llanelli) 1939 S
Jones, G (Ebbw Vale) 1963 S, I, F
Jones, G (Llanelli) 1988 NZ 2, 1989 F, E, NZ, 1990 F
Jones, G G (Cardiff) 1930 S, 1933 I
Jones, G H (Bridgend) 1995 SA
Jones, H (Penygraig) 1902 S, I
Jones, H (Neath) 1904 I
Jones, H (Swansea) 1930 I, F

Jones, Iorwerth (Llanelli) 1927 A, 1928 E, S, I, F
Jones, I C (London Welsh) 1968 I
Jones, Ivor E (Llanelli) 1924 E, S, 1927 S, F, I, A, 1928 E, S, I, F, 1929 E, S, F, I, 1930 E, S
Jones, J (Aberavon) 1901 E
Jones, J (Swansea) 1924 F
Jones, Jim (Aberavon) 1919 NZA, 1920 E, S, 1921 S, F, I
Jones, J A (Cardiff) 1883 S
Jones, J P (Tuan) (Pontypool) 1913 S
Jones, J P (Pontypool) 1908 A, 1909 E, S, F, I, 1910 F, E, 1912 E, F, 1913 F, I, 1920 F, I, 1921 E
Jones, K D (Cardiff) 1960 SA, 1961 E, S, I, 1962 E, F, 1963 E, S, I, NZ
Jones, K J (Newport) 1947 E, S, F, I, A, 1948 E, S, F, I, 1949 E, S, I, F, 1950 E, S, I, F, 1951 E, S, I, F, SA, 1952 E, S, I, F, 1953 E, S, I, F, NZ, 1954 E, I, F, S, 1955 E, S, I, F, 1956 E, S, I, F, 1957 S
Jones, K P (Ebbw Vale) 1996 Bb, F 2, It, A 3, 1997 I (R), E, 1998 S, I, F (R), SA 1
Jones, K W J (Oxford U, London Welsh) 1934 E
Jones, Matthew (Ospreys) 2005 C(R)
Jones, M A (Neath, Ebbw Vale) 1987 S, 1988 NZ 2(R), 1989 S, I, F, E, NZ, 1990 F, E, S, I, Nm 1,2, Bb, 1998 Z
Jones, M A (Llanelli Scarlets) 2001 E (R), S, J 1, 2002 R, Fj, C, NZ, 2003 It, I 1, A, NZ, E 2, [C,Tg,It,E], 2006 E,S,I,It,Arg 1,2,PI,C,NZ, 2007 S,F1,It,E1,Arg,F2, [C,A,Fj]
Jones, P (Newport) 1912 SA, 1913 E, S, F, 1914 E, S, F, I
Jones, P B (Newport) 1921 S
Jones, R (Swansea) 1901 I, 1902 E, 1904 E, S, I, 1905 E, 1908 F, I, A, 1909 E, S, F, I, 1910 F, E
Jones, R (London Welsh) 1929 E
Jones, R (Northampton) 1926 E, S, F
Jones, R (Swansea) 1927 A, 1928 F
Jones, R B (Cambridge U) 1933 E, S
Jones, R E (Coventry) 1967 F, E, 1968 S, I, F
Jones, R G (Llanelli, Cardiff) 1996 It, E, S, I, F 1, A 1, 1997 US (R), S (R), US 1,2, R, Tg, NZ
Jones, R L (Llanelli) 1993 Z 1,2, Nm, J, C
Jones, R N (Swansea) 1986 E, S, I, F, Fj, Tg, WS, 1987 F, E, S, I, [I, Tg, E, NZ, A], US, 1988 E, S, I, F, NZ 1, WS, R, 1989 I, F, E, NZ, 1990 F, E, S, I, 1991 E, S, F 2, [WS, Arg, A], 1992 I, F, E, S, A, 1993 E, S, I, 1994 I (R), Pt, 1995 F, E, S, I, [NZ, I]
Jones, R P (Ospreys) 2004 SA2,NZ(R),J, 2005 E(R),F,S,I,US, 2006 A,C,NZ, 2007 I,S,F1,It,E1
Jones, S (Neath, Newport Gwent Dragons) 2001 J 1(R), 2004 SA2,R(R),NZ(R),J(R)
Jones, S M (Llanelli Scarlets, Clermont Auvergne) 1998 SA 1(R), 1999 C (R), [J (R)], 2000 It (R), S, I, 2001 E, F (R), J 1,2, R, I, Arg, Tg, A, 2002 I, F, It, S, SA 1,2, R(R), Fj, C, NZ, 2003 S 1, I 1, F, A, NZ, E 2, [Tg,It(R),NZ,E], 2004 S,I,F,E,It,SA2,R,NZ, 2005 E,It,F,S,I,NZ,SA,A, 2006 E,S,I,It,F,A,NZ, 2007 I,S,F1,It, [C(R),A,J,Fj]
Jones, S T (Pontypool) 1983 S, I, F, R, 1984 S, 1988 E, S, F, NZ 1,2
Jones, Tom (Newport) 1922 E, S, I, F, 1924 E, S
Jones, T B (Newport) 1882 I, 1883 E, S, 1884 S, 1885 E, S
Jones, W (Cardiff) 1898 I, E
Jones, W (Mountain Ash) 1905 I
Jones, W I (Llanelli, Cambridge U) 1925 E, S, F, I
Jones, W J (Llanelli) 1924 I
Jones, W K (Cardiff) 1967 NZ, 1968 E, S, I, F
Jones-Davies, T E (London Welsh) 1930 E, I, 1931 E, S
Jones-Hughes, J (Newport) 1999 [Arg 3(R), J], 2000 F
Jordan, H M (Newport) 1885 E, S, 1889 S
Joseph, W (Swansea) 1902 E, S, I, 1903 E, S, I, 1904 E, S, 1905 E, S, I, NZ, 1906 E, S, I, SA
Jowett, W F (Swansea) 1903 E
Judd, S (Cardiff) 1953 E, S, I, F, NZ, 1954 E, F, S, 1955 E, S
Judson, J H (Llanelli) 1883 E, S

Kedzlie, Q D (Cardiff) 1888 S, I
Keen, L (Aberavon) 1980 F, E, S, I
Knight, P (Pontypridd) 1990 Nm 1,2, Bb (R), 1991 E, S
Knill, F M D (Cardiff) 1976 F (R)

Lamerton, A E H (Llanelli) 1993 F, Z 1,2, Nm, J
Lane, S M (Cardiff) 1978 A 1(R),2, 1979 I (R), 1980 S, I
Lang, J (Llanelli) 1931 F, I, 1934 S, I, 1935 E, S, I, NZ, 1936 E, S, I, 1937 E
Lawrence, S (Bridgend) 1925 S, I, 1926 S, I, F, 1927 E
Law, V J (Newport) 1939 I
Legge, W S G (Newport) 1937 I, 1938 I
Leleu, J (London Welsh, Swansea) 1959 E, S, 1960 F, SA
Lemon, A (Neath) 1929 I, 1930 S, I, F, 1931 E, S, F, I, SA, 1932 E, S, I, 1933 I
Lewis, A J L (Ebbw Vale) 1970 F, 1971 E, I, F, 1972 E, S, F, 1973 E, S, I, F
Lewis, A L P (Cardiff) 1996 It, E, S, I, A 2(t), 1998 It, E, S, I, F, SA 2, Arg, 1999 F 1(R), E (R), Arg 1(R),2(R), SA (R), C (R), [J (R), Sm (R), A (R)], 2000 Sm (R), US (R), SA (R), 2001 F (R), J 1,2, 2002 R(R)
Lewis, A R (Abertillery) 1966 E, S, I, F, A, 1967 I
Lewis, B R (Swansea, Cambridge U) 1912 I, 1913 I
Lewis, C P (Llandovery Coll) 1882 I, 1883 E, S, 1884 E, S
Lewis, D H (Cardiff) 1886 E, S
Lewis, E J (Llandovery) 1881 E
Lewis, E W (Llanelli, Cardiff) 1991 I, F 1, A, F 2, [WS, Arg, A], 1992 I, F, S, A, 1993 E, S, I, F, Z 1,2, Nm, J, C, 1994 S, I, F, E, Pt, Sp, Fj, WS, R, It, SA, 1995 E, S, I, [J, I], 1996 It, E, S, I, F 1
Lewis, G (Pontypridd, Swansea) 1998 SA 1(R), 1999 It (R), Arg 2, C, [J], 2000 F (R), It, S, I, Sm, US (t+R), 2001 F (R), J 1,2, R, I
Lewis, G W (Richmond) 1960 E, S
Lewis, H (Swansea) 1913 S, F, I, 1914 E
Lewis, J G (Llanelli) 1887 I
Lewis, J M C (Cardiff, Cambridge U) 1912 E, 1913 S, F, I, 1914 E, S, F, I, 1921 I, 1923 E, S
Lewis, J R (S Glam Inst, Cardiff) 1981 E, S, I, F, 1982 F, E, S
Lewis, M (Treorchy) 1913 F
Lewis, P I (Llanelli) 1984 A, 1985 S, I, F, E, 1986 E, S, I
Lewis, T W (Cardiff) 1926 E, 1927 E, S
Lewis, W (Llanelli) 1925 F
Lewis, W H (London Welsh, Cambridge U) 1926 I, 1927 E, F, I, A, 1928 F
Llewellyn, D S (Ebbw Vale, Newport) 1998 SA 1(R), 1999 F 1(R), It (R), [J (R)]
Llewellyn, G D (Neath) 1990 Nm 1,2, Bb, 1991 E, S, I, F 1, A, F 2
Llewellyn, G O (Neath, Harlequins, Ospreys, Narbonne) 1989 NZ, 1990 E, S, I, 1991 E, S, A (R), 1992 I, F, E, S, A, 1993 E, S, I, F, Z 1,2, Nm, J, C, 1994 S, I, F, E, Pt, Sp, C, Tg, WS, R, It, SA, 1995 F, E, S, I, [J, NZ, I], 1996 It, E, S, I, F 1, A 1,2, Bb, F 2, It, A 3, SA, 1997 US, S, I, F, E, US 1,2, NZ, 1998 It, E, 1999 C (R), [Sm], 2002 E (R), SA 1,2, R(R), Fj, C, NZ, 2003 E 1(R), S 1(R), I 1, F, A, NZ, I 2, S 2(R), [C,Tg,It,E(R)], 2004 S,F(R),E(R),It,Arg 1,2,SA1,R,NZ
Llewellyn, P D (Swansea) 1973 I, F, A, 1974 S, E
Llewellyn, W (Llwynypia) 1899 E, S, I, 1900 E, S, I, 1901 E, S, I, 1902 E, S, I, 1903 I, 1904 E, S, I, 1905 E, S, I, NZ
Llewelyn, D B (Newport, Llanelli) 1970 SA, S, E, I, F, 1971 E, S, I, F, 1972 E, S, F, NZ
Lloyd, A (Bath) 2001 J 1
Lloyd, D J (Bridgend) 1966 E, S, I, F, A, 1967 S, I, F, E, 1968 S, I, F, 1969 S, I, F, E, NZ 1, A, 1970 F, 1972 E, S, F, 1973 E, S
Lloyd, E (Llanelli) 1895 S
Lloyd, G L (Newport) 1896 I, 1899 S, I, 1900 E, S, 1901 E, S, 1902 S, I, 1903 E, S, I
Lloyd, P (Llanelli) 1890 S, E, 1891 E, I
Lloyd, R A (Pontypool) 1913 S, F, I, 1914 E, S, F, I
Lloyd, T (Maesteg) 1953 I, F
Lloyd, T C (Neath) 1909 F, 1913 F, I, 1914 E, S, F, I
Loader, C D (Swansea) 1995 SA, Fj, 1996 F 1, A 1,2, Bb, F 2, It, A 3, SA, 1997 US, S, I, F, E, US 1, R, Tg, NZ
Lockwood, T W (Newport) 1887 E, S, I
Long, E C (Swansea) 1936 E, S, I, 1937 E, S, 1939 S, I
Luscombe, H N (Newport Gwent Dragons, Harlequins) 2003 S 2(R), 2004 Arg 1,2,SA1,2,R,J, 2005 E,It,S(t&R), 2006 E,S,I,It,F, 2007 I
Lyne, H S (Newport) 1883 S, 1884 E, S, I, 1885 E

McBryde, R C (Swansea, Llanelli, Neath, Llanelli Scarlets) 1994 Fj, SA (t), 1997 US 2, 2000 I (R), 2001 E, S, F, It, R, I, Arg, Tg, A, 2002 I, F, It, E, S (R), SA 1,2, C, NZ, 2003 A, NZ, E 2, S 2, [C,It,NZ,E], 2004 I,E,It, 2005 It(R),F(R),S(R),I(R)
McCall, B E W (Welch Regt, Newport) 1936 E, S, I

McCarley, A (Neath) 1938 E, S, I
McCutcheon, W M (Swansea) 1891 S, 1892 E, S, 1893 E, S, I, 1894 E
McIntosh, D L M (Pontypridd) 1996 SA, 1997 E (R)
Madden, M (Llanelli) 2002 SA 1(R), R, Fj(R), 2003 I 1(R), F(R)
Maddock, H T (London Welsh) 1906 E, S, I, 1907 E, S, 1910 F
Maddocks, K (Neath) 1957 E
Main, D R (London Welsh) 1959 E, S, I, F
Mainwaring, H J (Swansea) 1961 F
Mainwaring, W T (Aberavon) 1967 S, I, F, E, NZ, 1968 E
Major, W C (Maesteg) 1949 F, 1950 S
Male, B O (Cardiff) 1921 F, 1923 S, 1924 S, I, 1927 E, S, F, I, 1928 S, I, F
Manfield, L (Mountain Ash, Cardiff) 1939 S, I, 1947 A, 1948 E, S, F, I
Mann, B B (Cardiff) 1881 E
Mantle, J T (Loughborough Colls, Newport) 1964 E, SA
Margrave, F L (Llanelli) 1884 E, S
Marinos, A W N (Newport, Gwent Dragons)) 2002 I (R), F, It, E, S, SA 1,2, 2003 R
Marsden-Jones, D (Cardiff) 1921 E, 1924 NZ
Martin, A J (Aberavon) 1973 A, 1974 S, I, 1975 F, E, S, I, A, 1976 E, S, I, F, 1977 I, F, E, S, 1978 E, S, I, F, A 1,2, NZ, 1979 S, I, F, E, 1980 F, E, S, I, NZ, 1981 I, F
Martin, W J (Newport) 1912 I, F, 1919 NZA
Mason, J (Pontypridd) 1988 NZ 2(R)
Mathews, Rev A A (Lampeter) 1886 S
Mathias, R (Llanelli) 1970 F
Matthews, C (Bridgend) 1939 I
Matthews, J (Cardiff), 1947 E, A, 1948 E, S, F, 1949 E, S, I, F, 1950 E, S, I, F, 1951 E, S, I, F
May, P S (Llanelli) 1988 E, S, I, F, NZ 1,2, 1991 [WS]
Meek, N N (Pontypool) 1993 E, S, I
Meredith, A (Devonport Services) 1949 E, S, I
Meredith, B V (St Luke's Coll, London Welsh, Newport) 1954 I, F, S, 1955 E, S, I, F, 1956 E, S, I, F, 1957 E, S, I, F, 1958 A, E, S, I, 1959 E, S, I, F, 1960 E, S, F, SA, 1961 E, S, I, 1962 E, S, F, I
Meredith, C C (Neath) 1953 S, NZ, 1954 E, I, F, S, 1955 E, S, I, F, 1956 E, I, 1957 E, S
Meredith, J (Swansea) 1888 S, I, 1890 S, E
Merry, A E (Pill Harriers) 1912 I, F
Michael, G (Swansea) 1923 E, S, F
Michaelson, R C B (Aberavon, Cambridge U) 1963 E
Miller, F (Mountain Ash) 1896 I, 1900 E, S, I, 1901 E, S, I
Mills, F M (Swansea, Cardiff) 1892 E, S, I, 1893 E, S, I, 1894 E, S, I, 1895 E, S, I, 1896 E
Moon, R H StJ B (Llanelli) 1993 F, Z 1,2, Nm, J, C, 1994 S, I, F, E, Sp, C, Fj, WS, R, It, SA, 1995 E (R), 2000 S, I, Sm (R), US (R), 2001 E (R), S (R)
Moore, A P (Cardiff) 1995 [J], SA, Fj, 1996 It
Moore, A P (Swansea) 1995 SA (R), Fj, 1998 S, I, F, Z, SA 1, 1999 C, 2000 S, I, US (R), 2001 E (R), S, F, It, J 1,2, R, I, Arg, Tg, A, 2002 F, It, E, S
Moore, S J (Swansea, Moseley) 1997 C, R, Tg
Moore, W J (Bridgend) 1933 I
Morgan, C H (Llanelli) 1957 I, F
Morgan, C I (Cardiff) 1951 I, F, SA, 1952 E, S, I, 1953 S, I, F, NZ, 1954 E, I, S, 1955 E, S, I, F, 1956 E, S, I, F, 1957 E, S, I, F, 1958 E, S, I, F
Morgan, C S (Cardiff Blues) 2002 I, F, It, E, S, SA 1,2, R(R), 2003 F, 2005 US
Morgan, D (Swansea) 1885 S, 1886 E, S, 1887 E, S, I, 1889 I
Morgan, D (Llanelli) 1895 I, 1896 E
Morgan, D R R (Llanelli) 1962 E, S, F, I, 1963 E, S, I, F, NZ
Morgan, E (Llanelli) 1920 I, 1921 E, S, F
Morgan, Edgar (Swansea) 1914 E, S, F, I
Morgan, E T (London Welsh) 1902 E, S, I, 1903 I, 1904 E, S, I, 1905 E, S, I, NZ, 1906 E, S, I, SA, 1908 F
Morgan, F L (Llanelli) 1938 E, S, I, 1939 E
Morgan, H J (Abertillery) 1958 E, S, I, F, 1959 I, F, 1960 E, 1961 E, S, I, F, 1962 E, S, F, I, 1963 S, I, F, 1965 E, S, I, F, 1966 E, S, I, F, A
Morgan, H P (Newport) 1956 E, S, I, F
Morgan, I (Swansea) 1908 A, 1909 E, S, F, I, 1910 F, E, S, I, 1911 E, F, I, 1912 S
Morgan, J L (Llanelli) 1912 SA, 1913 E
Morgan, K A (Pontypridd, Swansea, Newport Gwent Dragons) 1997 US 1,2, C, R, NZ, 1998 S, I, F, 2001 J 1,2, R, I, Arg, Tg, A, 2002 I, F, It, E, S, SA 1,2, 2003 E 1, S 1, [C,It], 2004 J(R), 2005 E(R),It(R),F,S,I,US,C,NZ,Fj, 2006 A,Pl, NZ, 2007 I,S,It,E1,Arg,F2, [C,A(R),J]
Morgan, M E (Swansea) 1938 E, S, I, 1939 E
Morgan, N (Newport) 1960 S, I, F
Morgan, P E J (Aberavon) 1961 E, S, F
Morgan, P J (Llanelli) 1980 S (R), I, NZ (R), 1981 I
Morgan, R (Newport) 1984 S
Morgan, S (Cardiff Blues) 2007 A2(R)
Morgan, T (Llanelli) 1889 I
Morgan, W G (Cambridge U) 1927 F, I, 1929 E, S, F, I, 1930 I, F
Morgan, W L (Cardiff) 1910 S
Moriarty, R D (Swansea) 1981 A, 1982 I, F, E, S, 1983 E, 1984 S, I, F, E, 1985 S, I, F, 1986 Fj, Tg, WS, 1987 [I, Tg, C (R), E, NZ, A]
Moriarty, W P (Swansea) 1986 I, F, Fj, Tg, WS, 1987 F, E, S, I, [I, Tg, C, E, NZ, A], US, 1988 E, S, I, F, NZ 1
Morley, J C (Newport) 1929 E, S, F, I, 1930 E, I, 1931 E, S, F, I, SA, 1932 E, S, I
Morris, D R (Neath, Swansea, Leicester) 1998 Z, SA 1(R),2(R), 1999 S, I, It (R), 2000 US, SA, 2001 E, S, F, It, Arg, Tg, A, 2004 Arg 1(R),2(R),SA1(R)
Morris, G L (Swansea) 1882 I, 1883 E, S, 1884 E, S
Morris, H T (Cardiff) 1951 F, 1955 I, F
Morris, J I T (Swansea) 1924 E, S
Morris, M S (S Wales Police, Neath) 1985 S, I, F, 1990 I, Nm 1,2, Bb, 1991 I, F 1, [WS (R)], 1992 E
Morris, R R (Swansea, Bristol) 1933 S, 1937 S
Morris, S (Cross Keys) 1920 E, S, F, I, 1922 E, S, I, F, 1923 E, S, F, I, 1924 E, S, F, NZ, 1925 E, S, F
Morris, W (Abertillery) 1919 NZA, 1920 F, 1921 I
Morris, W (Llanelli) 1896 S, I, 1897 E
Morris, W D (Neath) 1967 F, E, 1968 E, S, I, F, 1969 S, I, F, E, NZ 1,2, A, 1970 SA, S, E, I, F, 1971 E, S, I, F, 1972 E, S, F, NZ, 1973 E, S, I, A, 1974 S, I, F, E
Morris, W J (Newport) 1965 S, 1966 F
Morris, W J (Pontypool) 1963 S, I
Moseley, K (Pontypool, Newport) 1988 NZ 2, R, 1989 S, I, 1990 F, 1991 F 2, [WS, Arg, A]
Murphy, C D (Cross Keys) 1935 E, S, I
Mustoe, L (Cardiff) 1995 Fj, 1996 A 1(R),2, 1997 US 1,2, C, R (R), 1998 E (R), I (R), F (R)

Nash, D (Ebbw Vale) 1960 SA, 1961 E, S, I, F, 1962 F
Newman, C H (Newport) 1881 E, 1882 I, 1883 E, S, 1884 E, S, 1885 E, S, 1886 E, 1887 E
Nicholas, D L (Llanelli) 1981 E, S, I, F
Nicholas, T J (Cardiff) 1919 NZA
Nicholl, C B (Cambridge U, Llanelli) 1891 I, 1892 E, S, I, 1893 E, S, I, 1894 E, S, 1895 E, S, I, 1896 E, S, I
Nicholl, D W (Llanelli) 1894 I
Nicholls, E G (Cardiff) 1896 S, I, 1897 E, 1898 I, E, 1899 E, S, I, 1900 S, I, 1901 E, S, I, 1902 E, S, I, 1903 I, 1904 E, 1905 I, NZ, 1906 E, S, I, SA
Nicholls, F E (Cardiff Harlequins) 1892 I
Nicholls, H (Cardiff) 1958 I
Nicholls, S H (Cardiff) 1888 M, 1889 S, I, 1891 S
Norris, C H (Cardiff) 1963 F, 1966 F
Norster, R L (Cardiff) 1982 S, 1983 E, S, I, F, 1984 S, I, F, E, A, 1985 S, I, F, E, Fj, 1986 Fj, Tg, WS, 1987 F, E, S, I, [I, C, E], US, 1988 E, S, I, F, NZ 1, WS, 1989 F, E
Norton, W B (Cardiff) 1882 I, 1883 E, S, 1884 E, S, I

Oakley, R L (Gwent Dragons) 2003 I 2, S 2(R)
O'Connor, A (Aberavon) 1960 SA, 1961 E, S, 1962 F, I
O'Connor, R (Aberavon) 1957 E
O'Neill, W (Cardiff) 1904 S, I, 1905 E, S, I, 1907 E, I, 1908 E, S, F, I
O'Shea, J P (Cardiff) 1967 S, I, 1968 S, I, F
Oliver, G (Pontypool) 1920 E, S, F, I
Osborne, W T (Mountain Ash) 1902 E, S, I, 1903 E, S, I
Ould, W J (Cardiff) 1924 E, S
Owen, A (Swansea) 1924 E

Owen, G D (Newport) 1955 I, F, 1956 E, S, I, F
Owen, M J (Pontypridd, Newport Gwent Dragons) 2002 SA 1,2, R, C(R), NZ(R), 2003 It, I 2, S 2, 2004 S(R),I(R),F,E,It,Arg 1,2,SA2,R,NZ,J, 2005 E,It,F,S,I,NZ,Fj,SA,A, 2006 E,S,I,It,F,Pl, 2007 A1(R),2,E2, [C(R),A(R),J(R),Fj(R)]
Owen, R M (Swansea) 1901 I, 1902 E, S, I, 1903 E, S, I, 1904 E, S, I, 1905 E, S, I, NZ, 1906 E, S, I, SA, 1907 E, S, 1908 F, I, A, 1909 E, S, F, I, 1910 F, E, 1911 E, S, F, I, 1912 E, S

Packer, H (Newport) 1891 E, 1895 S, I, 1896 E, S, I, 1897 E
Palmer, F (Swansea) 1922 E, S, I
Parfitt, F C (Newport) 1893 E, S, I, 1894 E, S, I, 1895 S, 1896 S, I
Parfitt, S A (Swansea) 1990 Nm 1(R), Bb
Parker, D S (Swansea) 1924 I, F, NZ, 1925 E, S, F, I, 1929 F, I, 1930 E
Parker, S T (Pontypridd, Celtic Warriors, Newport Gwent Dragons, Ospreys) 2002 R, Fj, C, NZ, 2003 E 2, [C,It,NZ], 2004 S,I,Arg 1,2,SA1,2,NZ, 2005 Fj,SA,A, 2006 Pl,C,NZ, 2007 A1,2,F2(t&R), [C,A]
Parker, T (Swansea) 1919 NZA, 1920 E, S, I, 1921 E, S, F, I, 1922 E, S, I, F, 1923 E, S, F
Parker, W (Swansea) 1899 E, S
Parks, R D (Pontypridd, Celtic Warriors) 2002 SA 1(R), Fj(R), 2003 I 2, S 2
Parsons, G W (Newport) 1947 E
Pascoe, D (Bridgend) 1923 F, I
Pask, A E I (Abertillery) 1961 F, 1962 E, S, F, I, 1963 E, S, I, F, NZ, 1964 E, S, I, F, SA, 1965 E, S, I, F, 1966 E, S, I, F, A, 1967 S, I
Payne, G W (Army, Pontypridd) 1960 E, S, I
Payne, H (Swansea) 1935 NZ
Peacock, H (Newport) 1929 S, F, I, 1930 S, I, F
Peake, E (Chepstow) 1881 E
Pearce, G P (Bridgend) 1981 I, F, 1982 I (R)
Pearson, T W (Cardiff, Newport) 1891 E, I, 1892 E, S, 1894 S, I, 1895 E, S, I, 1897 E, 1898 I, E, 1903 E
Peel, D J (Llanelli Scarlets) 2001 J 2(R), R (R), Tg (R), 2002 I (R), It (R), E (R), S (R), SA 1,2, R, Fj, C, NZ, 2003 It, S 1(R), I 1(R), F, NZ(R), I 2, S 2, [C(R),Tg(R),It,NZ(R),E(R)], 2004 S(R),I(R),F(R),E(R),It(R),Arg 1,2,SA1,2,R,NZ, 2005 E,It,F,S,I, 2006 E,S,I,It,A,C,NZ, 2007 I,S,F1,It,E1,Arg,F2, [C,A,Fj]
Pegge, E V (Neath) 1891 E
Perego, M A (Llanelli) 1990 S, 1993 F, Z 1, Nm (R), 1994 S, I, F, E, Sp
Perkins, S J (Pontypool) 1983 S, I, F, R, 1984 S, I, F, E, A, 1985 S, I, F, E, Fj, 1986 E, S, I, F
Perrett, F L (Neath) 1912 SA, 1913 E, S, F, I
Perrins, V C (Newport) 1970 SA, S
Perry, W (Neath) 1911 E
Phillips, A J (Cardiff) 1979 E, 1980 F, E, S, I, NZ, 1981 E, S, I, F, A, 1982 I, F, E, S, 1987 [C, E, A]
Phillips, B (Aberavon) 1925 E, S, F, I, 1926 E
Phillips, D H (Swansea) 1952 F
Phillips, H P (Newport) 1892 E, 1893 E, S, I, 1894 E, S
Phillips, H T (Newport) 1927 E, S, F, I, A, 1928 E, S, I, F
Phillips, K H (Neath) 1987 F, [I, Tg, NZ], US, 1988 E, NZ 1, 1989 NZ, 1990 F, E, S, I, Nm 1,2, Bb, 1991 E, S, I, F 1, A
Phillips, L A (Newport) 1900 E, S, I, 1901 S
Phillips, M (Llanelli Scarlets, Cardiff Blues, Ospreys) 2003 R, 2004 Arg 1(R),2(R),J(R), 2005 US,C,NZ,Fj(R),SA(R), 2006 S(R),It(R),F,Arg 1,2,Pl,C(R),NZ(R), 2007 I(R),F1(R),E1(R),A1,2,F2(R), [C(R),A(R),J,Fj(R)]
Phillips, R (Neath) 1987 US, 1988 E, S, I, F, NZ 1,2, WS, 1989 S, I
Phillips, W D (Cardiff) 1881 E, 1882 I, 1884 E, S, I
Pickering, D F (Llanelli) 1983 E, S, I, F, R, 1984 S, I, F, E, A, 1985 S, I, F, E, Fj, 1986 E, S, I, F, Fj, 1987 F, E, S
Plummer, R C S (Newport) 1912 S, I, F, SA, 1913 E
Pook, T (Newport) 1895 S
Popham, A J (Leeds, Llanelli Scarlets) 2003 A (R), I 2, R, S 2, [Tg,NZ], 2004 I(R),It(R),SA1,J(R), 2005 C,Fj(R), 2006 E(R),It(R),F,Arg 1,2,Pl,NZ(R), 2007 I,S,F1,It,E1,2(R),Arg,F2, [C,A(t),J,Fj]
Powell, G (Ebbw Vale) 1957 I, F
Powell, J (Cardiff) 1906 I
Powell, J (Cardiff) 1923 I
Powell, R D (Cardiff) 2002 SA 1(R),2(R), C(R)
Powell, R W (Newport) 1888 S, I
Powell, W C (London Welsh) 1926 S, I, F, 1927 E, F, I, 1928 S, I, F, 1929 E, S, F, I, 1930 S, I, F, 1931 E, S, F, I, SA, 1932 E, S, I, 1935 E, S, I
Powell, W J (Cardiff) 1920 E, S, F, I
Price, B (Newport) 1961 I, F, 1962 E, S, 1963 E, S, F, NZ, 1964 E, S, I, F, SA, 1965 E, S, I, F, 1966 E, S, I, F, A, 1967 S, I, F, E, 1969 S, I, F, NZ 1,2, A
Price, G (Pontypool) 1975 F, E, S, I, A, 1976 E, S, I, F, 1977 I, F, E, S, 1978 E, S, I, F, A 1,2, NZ, 1979 S, I, F, E, 1980 F, E, S, I, NZ, 1981 E, S, I, F, A, 1982 I, F, E, S, 1983 E, I, F
Price, M J (Pontypool, RAF) 1959 E, S, I, F, 1960 E, S, I, F, 1962 E
Price, R E (Weston-s-Mare) 1939 S, I
Price, T G (Llanelli) 1965 E, S, I, F, 1966 E, A, 1967 S, F
Priday, A J (Cardiff) 1958 I, 1961 I
Pritchard, C (Pontypool) 1928 E, S, I, F, 1929 E, S, F, I
Pritchard, C C (Newport, Pontypool) 1904 S, I, 1905 NZ, 1906 E, S
Pritchard, C M (Newport) 1904 I, 1905 E, S, NZ, 1906 E, S, I, SA, 1907 E, S, I, 1908 E, 1910 F, E
Proctor, W T (Llanelli) 1992 A, 1993 E, S, Z 1,2, Nm, C, 1994 I, C, Fj, WS, R, It, SA, 1995 S, I, [NZ], Fj, 1996 It, E, S, I, A 1,2, Bb, F 2, It, A 3, 1997 E(R), US 1,2, C, R, 1998 E (R), S, I, F, Z, 2001 A
Prosser, D R (Neath) 1934 S, I
Prosser, G (Neath) 1934 E, S, I, 1935 NZ
Prosser, G (Pontypridd) 1995 [NZ]
Prosser, J (Cardiff) 1921 I
Prosser, T R (Pontypool) 1956 S, F, 1957 E, S, I, F, 1958 A, E, S, I, F, 1959 E, S, I, F, 1960 E, S, I, F, SA, 1961 I, F
Prothero, G J (Bridgend) 1964 S, I, F, 1965 E, S, I, F, 1966 E, S, I, F
Pryce-Jenkins, T J (London Welsh) 1888 S, I
Pugh, C (Maesteg) 1924 E, S, I, F, NZ, 1925 E, S
Pugh, J D (Neath) 1987 US, 1988 S (R), 1990 S
Pugh, P (Neath) 1989 NZ
Pugh, R (Ospreys) 2005 US(R)
Pugsley, J (Cardiff) 1910 E, S, I, 1911 E, S, F, I
Pullman, J J (Neath) 1910 F
Purdon, F T (Newport) 1881 E, 1882 I, 1883 E, S

Quinnell, D L (Llanelli) 1972 F (R), NZ, 1973 E, S, A, 1974 S, F, 1975 E (R), 1977 I (R), F, E, S, 1978 E, S, I, F, A 1, NZ, 1979 S, I, F, E, 1980 NZ
Quinnell, J C (Llanelli, Richmond, Cardiff) 1995 Fj, 1996 A 3(R), 1997 US (R), S (R), I (R), E (R), 1998 SA 2, Arg, 1999 I, F 1, It, E, Arg 1,2, SA, C, F 2, [Arg 3, J, A], 2000 It, E, 2001 S (R), F (R), It (R), J 1,2, R (R), I (R), Arg, 2002 I, F
Quinnell, L S (Llanelli, Richmond) 1993 C, 1994 S, I, F, E, Pt, Sp, C, WS, 1997 US, S, I, F, E, 1998 It, E, S (R), Z, SA 2, Arg, 1999 S, I, F 1, It, E, Arg 1,2, SA, C, F 2, [Arg 3, Sm, A], 2000 F, It, E, Sm, US, SA, 2001 E, S, F, It, Arg, Tg, A, 2002 I, F, It, E, R, C(R)

Radford, W J (Newport) 1923 I
Ralph, A R (Newport) 1931 F, I, SA, 1932 E, S, I
Ramsey, S H (Treorchy) 1896 E, 1904 E
Randell, R (Aberavon) 1924 I, F
Raybould, W H (London Welsh, Cambridge U, Newport) 1967 S, I, F, E, NZ, 1968 I, F, 1970 SA, E, I, F (R)
Rayer, M A (Cardiff) 1991 [WS (R), Arg, A (R)], 1992 E (R), A, 1993 E, S, I, Z 1, Nm, J (R), 1994 S (R), I (R), F, E, Pt, C, Fj, WS, R, It
Rees, Aaron (Maesteg) 1919 NZA
Rees, Alan (Maesteg) 1962 E, S, F
Rees, A M (London Welsh) 1934 E, 1935 E, S, I, NZ, 1936 E, S, I, 1937 E, S, I, 1938 E, S
Rees, B I (London Welsh) 1967 S, I, F
Rees, C F W (London Welsh) 1974 I, 1975 A, 1978 NZ, 1981 F, A, 1982 I, F, E, S, 1983 E, S, I, F
Rees, D (Swansea) 1968 S, I, F
Rees, Dan (Swansea) 1900 E, 1903 E, S, 1905 E, S
Rees, E B (Swansea) 1919 NZA
Rees, H (Cardiff) 1937 S, I, 1938 E, S, I
Rees, H E (Neath) 1979 S, I, F, E, 1980 F, E, S, I, NZ, 1983 E, S, I, F

Rees, J (Swansea) 1920 E, S, F, I, 1921 E, S, I, 1922 E, 1923 E, F, I, 1924 E
Rees, J I (Swansea) 1934 E, S, I, 1935 S, NZ, 1936 E, S, I, 1937 E, S, I, 1938 E, S, I
Rees, L M (Cardiff) 1933 I
Rees, M (Llanelli Scarlets) 2005 US, 2006 Arg 1,A,C,NZ(R), 2007 I(R),S(t&R),F1,It,E1,A1,Arg,F2, [C,A,Fj]
Rees, P (Llanelli) 1947 F, I
Rees, P M (Newport) 1961 E, S, I, 1964 I
Rees, R (Swansea) 1998 Z
Rees, T (Newport) 1935 S, I, NZ, 1936 E, S, I, 1937 E, S
Rees, T A (Llandovery) 1881 E
Rees, T E (London Welsh) 1926 I, F, 1927 A, 1928 E
Rees-Jones, G R (Oxford U, London Welsh) 1934 E, S, 1935 I, NZ, 1936 E
Reeves, F (Cross Keys) 1920 F, I, 1921 E
Reynolds, A (Swansea) 1990 Nm 1,2(R), 1992 A (R)
Rhapps, J (Penygraig) 1897 E
Rice-Evans, W (Swansea) 1890 S, 1891 E, S
Richards, B (Swansea)1960 F
Richards, C (Pontypool) 1922 E, S, I, F, 1924 I
Richards, D S (Swansea) 1979 F, E, 1980 F, E, S, I, NZ, 1981 E, S, I, F, 1982 I, F, 1983 E, S, I, R (R)
Richards, E G (Cardiff) 1927 S
Richards, E S (Swansea) 1885 E, 1887 S
Richards, H D (Neath) 1986 Tg (R), 1987 [Tg, E (R), NZ]
Richards, I (Cardiff) 1925 E, S, F
Richards, K H L (Bridgend) 1960 SA, 1961 E, S, I, F
Richards, M C R (Cardiff) 1968 I, F, 1969 S, I, F, E, NZ 1,2, A
Richards, R (Aberavon) 1913 S, F, I
Richards, R (Cross Keys) 1956 F
Richards, T L (Maesteg) 1923 I
Richardson, S J (Aberavon) 1978 A 2(R), 1979 E
Rickards, A R (Cardiff) 1924 F
Ring, J (Aberavon) 1921 E
Ring, M G (Cardiff, Pontypool) 1983 E, 1984 A, 1985 S, I, F, 1987 I, [I, Tg, A], US, 1988 E, S, I, F, NZ 1,2, 1989 NZ, 1990 F, E, S, I, Nm 1,2, Bb, 1991 E, S, I, F 1,2, [WS, Arg, A]
Ringer, J (Bridgend) 2001 J 1(R),2(R)
Ringer, P (Ebbw Vale, Llanelli) 1978 NZ, 1979 S, I, F, E, 1980 F, E, NZ
Roberts, C (Neath) 1958 I, F
Roberts, D E A (London Welsh) 1930 E
Roberts, E (Llanelli) 1886 E, 1887 I
Roberts, E J (Llanelli) 1888 S, I, 1889 I
Roberts, G J (Cardiff) 1985 F (R), E, 1987 [I, Tg, C, E, A]
Roberts, H M (Cardiff) 1960 SA, 1961 E, S, I, F, 1962 S, F, 1963 I
Roberts, J (Cardiff) 1927 E, S, F, I, A, 1928 E, S, I, F, 1929 E, S, F, I
Roberts, M G (London Welsh) 1971 E, S, I, F, 1973 I, F, 1975 S, 1979 E
Roberts, T (Newport, Risca) 1921 S, F, I, 1922 E, S, I, F, 1923 E, S
Roberts, W (Cardiff) 1929 E
Robins, J D (Birkenhead Park) 1950 E, S, I, F, 1951 E, S, I, F, 1953 E, I, F
Robins, R J (Pontypridd) 1953 S, 1954 F, S, 1955 E, S, I, F, 1956 E, F, 1957 E, S, I, F
Robinson, I R (Cardiff) 1974 F, E
Robinson, J P (Cardiff Blues) 2001 J 1(R),2(R), Arg (R), Tg (R), A, 2002 I, Fj(R), C, NZ, 2003 A, NZ, I 2, S 2, 2006 Arg 1,2, 2007 I,S,F1(R),A1,2,Arg(t&R),F2,[J]
Robinson, M F D (Swansea) 1999 S, I, F 1, Arg 1
Robinson, N J (Cardiff Blues) 2003 I 2, R, 2004 Arg 1(R),2,SA1, 2005 US,C,NZ(R),Fj, 2006 S(R),Arg 1,2
Rocyn-Jones, D N (Cambridge U) 1925 I
Roderick, W B (Llanelli) 1884 I
Rogers, P J D (London Irish, Newport, Cardiff) 1999 F 1, It, E, Arg 1,2, SA, C, F 2, [Arg 3, J, Sm, A], 2000 F, It, E, S, I, SA
Rosser, M A (Penarth) 1924 S, F
Rowland, E M (Lampeter) 1885 E
Rowlands, C F (Aberavon) 1926 I
Rowlands, D C T (Pontypool) 1963 E, S, I, F, NZ, 1964 E, S, I, F, SA, 1965 E, S, I, F
Rowlands, G (RAF, Cardiff) 1953 NZ, 1954 E, F, 1956 F
Rowlands, K A (Cardiff) 1962 F, I, 1963 I, 1965 I, F
Rowles, G R (Penarth) 1892 E
Rowley, M (Pontypridd) 1996 SA, 1997 US, S, I, F, R
Roy, W S (Cardiff) 1995 [J (R)]
Russell, S (London Welsh) 1987 US

Samuel, D (Swansea) 1891 I, 1893 I
Samuel, F (Mountain Ash) 1922 S, I, F
Samuel, J (Swansea) 1891 I
Scourfield, T (Torquay) 1930 F
Scrine, G F (Swansea) 1899 E, S, 1901 I
Selley, T J (Llanelli Scarlets) 2005 US(R)
Shanklin, J L (London Welsh) 1970 F, 1972 NZ, 1973 I, F
Shanklin, T G L (Saracens, Cardiff Blues) 2001 J 2, 2002 F, It, SA 1(R),2(R),R, Fj, 2003 It, E 1, S 1, I 1, F(t+R), A, NZ, S 2, [Tg,NZ], 2004 I(R),F(R),E,It(R),Arg 1(R),2, SA1,2(R),R,NZ,J, 2005 E,It,F,S,I, 2006 A,C,NZ, 2007 S(R),F1,It,E1,2,Arg, [C,A,J(R),Fj]
Shaw, G (Neath) 1972 NZ, 1973 E, S, I, F, A, 1974 S, I, F, E, 1977 I, F
Shaw, T W (Newbridge) 1983 R
Shea, J (Newport) 1919 NZA, 1920 E, S, 1921 E
Shell, R C (Aberavon) 1973 A (R)
Sidoli, R A (Pontypridd, Celtic Warriors, Cardiff Blues) 2002 SA 1(R),2(R),R, Fj, NZ, 2003 It, E 1, S 1, I 1, F, A, NZ, E 2, [C(R),Tg,It(R),NZ,E], 2004 I,It(R), 2005 E,It,F,S,I,C,NZ,Fj(R),SA,A, 2006 E,S,I,It,F,Pl,C(R), 2007 I(t&R),S,A1,2,E2
Simpson, H J (Cardiff) 1884 E, S, I
Sinkinson, B D (Neath) 1999 F 1, It, E, Arg 1,2, SA, F 2, [Arg 3, J, Sm, A], 2000 F, It, E, 2001 R (R), I, Arg (R), Tg, A, 2002 It (R)
Skrimshire, R T (Newport) 1899 E, S, I
Skym, A (Llanelli) 1928 E, S, I, F, 1930 E, S, I, F, 1931 E, S, F, I, SA, 1932 E, S, I, 1933 E, S, I, 1935 E
Smith, J S (Cardiff) 1884 E, I, 1885 E
Smith, R (Ebbw Vale) 2000 F (R)
Sowden-Taylor, R (Cardiff Blues) 2005 It(R),C(R),NZ(R), 2007 A2(R)
Sparks, B (Neath) 1954 I, 1955 E, F, 1956 E, S, I, 1957 S
Spiller, W J (Cardiff) 1910 S, I, 1911 E, S, F, I, 1912 E, F, SA, 1913 E
Squire, J (Newport, Pontypool) 1977 I, F, 1978 E, S, I, F, A 1, NZ, 1979 S, I, F, E, 1980 F, E, S, I, NZ, 1981 E, S, I, F, A, 1982 I, F, E, 1983 E, S, I, F
Stadden, W J W (Cardiff) 1884 I, 1886 E, S, 1887 I, 1888 S, M, 1890 S, E
Stephens, C (Bridgend) 1998 E (R), 2001 J 2(R)
Stephens, C J (Llanelli) 1992 I, F, E, A
Stephens, G (Neath) 1912 E, S, I, F, SA, 1913 E, S, F, I, 1919 NZA
Stephens, I (Bridgend) 1981 E, S, I, F, A, 1982 I, F, E, S, 1984 I, F, E, A
Stephens, Rev J G (Llanelli) 1922 E, S, I, F
Stephens, J R G (Neath) 1947 E, S, F, I, 1948 I, 1949 S, I, F, 1951 F, SA, 1952 E, S, I, F, 1953 E, S, I, F, NZ, 1954 E, I, 1955 E, S, I, F, 1956 S, I, F, 1957 E, S, I, F
Stock, A (Newport) 1924 F, NZ, 1926 E, S
Stone, P (Llanelli) 1949 F
Strand-Jones, J (Llanelli) 1902 E, S, I, 1903 E, S
Sullivan, A C (Cardiff) 2001 Arg, Tg
Summers, R H B (Haverfordwest) 1881 E
Sutton, S (Pontypool, S Wales Police) 1982 F, E, 1987 F, E, S, I, [C, NZ (R), A]
Sweeney, C (Pontypridd, Celtic Warriors, Newport Gwent Dragons) 2003 It(R), E 1, NZ(R), I 2, S 2, [C,It,NZ(t&R),E(t)], 2004 I(R),F(R),E(R),It(R),Arg 1,SA1(R),2(R),R(R),J, 2005 It(R),F(t),S(R),US,C,NZ,Fj(R),SA(t&R),A(R), 2006 Pl,C(R), 2007 S(t),A2(R),E2,F2(R), [J(R)]
Sweet-Escott, R B (Cardiff) 1891 S, 1894 I, 1895 I

Tamplin, W E (Cardiff) 1947 S, F, I, A, 1948 E, S, F
Tanner, H (Swansea, Cardiff) 1935 NZ, 1936 E, S, I, 1937 E, S, I, 1938 E, S, I, 1939 E, S, I, 1947 E, S, F, I, 1948 E, S, F, I, 1949 E, S, I, F
Tarr, D J (Swansea, Royal Navy) 1935 NZ
Taylor, A R (Cross Keys) 1937 I, 1938 I, 1939 E
Taylor, C G (Ruabon) 1884 E, S, I, 1885 E, S, 1886 E, S, 1887 E, I
Taylor, H T (Cardiff) 1994 Pt, C, Fj, Tg, WS (R), R, It, SA, 1995 E, S, [J, NZ, I], SA, Fj, 1996 It, E, S, I, F 1, A 1,2, It, A 3

Taylor, J (London Welsh) 1967 S, I, F, E, NZ, 1968 I, F, 1969 S, I, F, E, NZ 1, A, 1970 F, 1971 E, S, I, F, 1972 E, S, F, NZ, 1973 E, S, I, F

Taylor, M (Pontypool, Swansea, Llanelli Scarlets, Sale) 1994 SA, 1995 F, E, SA (R), 1998 Z, SA 1,2, Arg, 1999 I, F 1, It, E, Arg 1,2, SA, F 2, [Arg 3, J, Sm, A], 2000 F, It, E, S, Sm, US, 2001 E, S, F, It, 2002 S, SA 1,2, 2003 E 1, S 1, I 1, F, A, NZ, E 2, [C(R),Tg,NZ,E], 2004 F,E,It,R(R), 2005 I,US,C,NZ

Thomas, A (Newport) 1963 NZ, 1964 E

Thomas, A C (Bristol, Swansea) 1996 It, E, S, I, F 2(R), SA, 1997 US, S, I, F, US 1,2, C, R, NZ (t), 1998 It, E, S (R), Z, SA 1, 2000 Sm, US, SA (R)

Thomas, A G (Swansea, Cardiff) 1952 E, S, I, F, 1953 S, I, F, 1954 E, I, F, 1955 S, I, F

Thomas, Bob (Swansea) 1900 E, S, I, 1901 E

Thomas, Brian (Neath, Cambridge U) 1963 E, S, I, F, NZ, 1964 E, S, I, F, SA, 1965 E, 1966 E, S, I, 1967 NZ, 1969 S, I, F, E, NZ 1,2

Thomas, C (Bridgend) 1925 E, S

Thomas, C J (Newport) 1888 I, M, 1889 S, I, 1890 S, E, I, 1891 E, I

Thomas, D (Aberavon) 1961 I

Thomas, Dick (Mountain Ash) 1906 SA, 1908 F, I, 1909 S

Thomas, D J (Swansea) 1904 E, 1908 A, 1910 E, S, I, 1911 E, S, F, I, 1912 E

Thomas, D J (Swansea) 1930 S, I, 1932 E, S, I, 1933 E, S, 1934 E, 1935 E, S, I

Thomas, D L (Neath) 1937 E

Thomas, E (Newport) 1904 S, I, 1909 S, F, I, 1910 F

Thomas, G (Llanelli) 1923 E, S, F, I

Thomas, G (Newport) 1888 M, 1890 I, 1891 S

Thomas, G (Bridgend, Cardiff, Celtic Warriors, Toulouse, Cardiff Blues) 1995 [J, NZ, I], SA, Fj, 1996 F 1, A 1,2, Bb, F 2, It, A 3, 1997 US, S, I, F, E, US 1,2, C, R, Tg, NZ, 1998 It, E, S, I, F, SA 2, Arg, 1999 F 1(R), It, E, Arg 2, SA, F 2, [Arg 3, J (R), Sm, A], 2000 F, It, E, S, I, US (R), SA, 2001 E, F, It, J 1,2, R, Arg, Tg, A, 2002 E, R, Fj, C, NZ, 2003 It, E 1, S 1, I 1, F, I 2, E 2, [C,It,NZ(R),E], 2004 S,I,F,E,It,SA2,R,NZ, 2005 E,It,F,NZ,SA,A, 2006 E,S,A,C, 2007 It(t&R),E1,A1,2,E2,Arg,F2, [C(R),A,Fj]

Thomas, G V (Bath, Ospreys, Llanelli Scarlets) 2001 J 1,2, R, I (R), Arg, Tg (R), A (R), 2002 S (R), SA 2(R),R(R), 2003 It(R), E 1, S 1, F, E 2(R), R, 2006 Arg 1,2,Pl, 2007 I(t&R),A1,2

Thomas, H (Llanelli) 1912 F

Thomas, H (Neath) 1936 E, S, I, 1937 E, S, I

Thomas, H W (Swansea) 1912 SA, 1913 E

Thomas, I (Bryncethin) 1924 E

Thomas, I D (Ebbw Vale, Llanelli Scarlets) 2000 Sm, US (R), SA (R), 2001 J 1,2, R, I, Arg (R), Tg, 2002 It, E, S, SA 1,2, Fj, C, NZ, 2003 It, E 1, S 1, I 1, F, A, NZ, E 2, [Tg,NZ,E], 2004 I,F, 2007 A1,2,E2

Thomas, J (Swansea, Ospreys) 2003 A, NZ(R), E 2(R), R, [It(R),NZ,E], 2004 S(t&R),I, F,E,Arg 2(R),SA1(R),R(t&R),J, 2005 E(R),It,F(R),S(R),US,C,NZ, 2006 It(R),F(R),A,Pl(R),C,NZ, 2007 S(R),F1(R),It(R),E1(R),A1,2,Arg,F2, [C,A]

Thomas, J D (Llanelli) 1954 I

Thomas, L C (Cardiff) 1885 E, S

Thomas, M C (Newport, Devonport Services) 1949 F, 1950 E, S, I, F, 1951 E, S, I, F, SA, 1952 E, S, I, F, 1953 E, 1956 E, S, I, F, 1957 E, S, 1958 E, S, I, F, 1959 I, F

Thomas, M G (St Bart's Hospital) 1919 NZA, 1921 S, F, I, 1923 F, 1924 E

Thomas, N (Bath) 1996 SA (R), 1997 US 1(R),2, C (R), R, Tg, NZ, 1998 Z, SA 1

Thomas, R (Pontypool) 1909 F, I, 1911 S, F, 1912 E, S, SA, 1913 E

Thomas, Rhys (Newport Gwent Dragons) 2006 Arg 2(R), 2007 E2(R)

Thomas, R C C (Swansea) 1949 F, 1952 I, F, 1953 S, I, F, NZ, 1954 E, I, F, S, 1955 S, I, 1956 E, S, I, 1957 E, 1958 A, E, S, I, F, 1959 E, S, I, F

Thomas, R L (London Welsh) 1889 S, I, 1890 I, 1891 E, S, I, 1892 E

Thomas, S (Llanelli) 1890 S, E, 1891 I

Thomas, T R (Cardiff Blues) 2005 US(R),C,NZ(R),Fj,SA,A, 2006 E,S,I,It,F,Pl,C(R),NZ, 2007 I,S,F1(R),It(R),E1(R),2(R),F2(R), [C(R),A(R),J,Fj(R)]

Thomas, W D (Llanelli) 1966 A, 1968 S, I, F, 1969 E, NZ 2, A, 1970 SA, S, E, I, F, 1971 E, S, I, F, 1972 E, S, F, NZ, 1973 E, S, I, F, 1974 E

Thomas, W G (Llanelli, Waterloo, Swansea) 1927 E, S, F, I, 1929 E, 1931 E, S, SA, 1932 E, S, I, 1933 E, S, I

Thomas, W H (Llandovery Coll, Cambridge U) 1885 S, 1886 E, S, 1887 E, S, 1888 S, I, 1890 E, I, 1891 S, I

Thomas, W J (Cardiff) 1961 F, 1963 F

Thomas, W J L (Llanelli, Cardiff) 1995 SA, Fj, 1996 It, E, S, I, F 1, 1996 Bb (R), 1997 US

Thomas, W L (Newport) 1894 S, 1895 E, I

Thomas, W T (Abertillery) 1930 E

Thompson, J F (Cross Keys) 1923 E

Thorburn, P H (Neath) 1985 F, E, Fj, 1986 E, S, I, F, 1987 F, [I, Tg, C, E, NZ, A], US, 1988 S, I, F, WS, R (R), 1989 S, I, F, E, NZ, 1990 F, E, S, I, Nm 1,2, Bb, 1991 E, S, I, F 1, A

Titley, M H (Bridgend, Swansea) 1983 R, 1984 S, I, F, E, A, 1985 S, I, Fj, 1986 F, Fj, Tg, WS, 1990 F, E

Towers, W H (Swansea) 1887 I, 1888 M

Travers, G (Pill Harriers, Newport) 1903 E, S, I, 1905 E, S, I, NZ, 1906 E, S, I, SA, 1907 E, S, I, 1908 E, S, F, I, A, 1909 E, S, I, 1911 S, F, I

Travers, W H (Newport) 1937 S, I, 1938 E, S, I, 1939 E, S, I, 1949 E, S, I, F

Treharne, E (Pontypridd) 1881 E, 1883 E

Trew, W J (Swansea) 1900 E, S, I, 1901 E, S, 1903 S, 1905 S, 1906 S, 1907 E, S, 1908 E, S, F, I, A, 1909 E, S, F, I, 1910 F, E, S, 1911 E, S, F, I, 1912 S, 1913 S, F

Trott, R F (Cardiff) 1948 E, S, F, I, 1949 E, S, I, F

Truman, W H (Llanelli) 1934 E, 1935 E

Trump, L C (Newport) 1912 E, S, I, F

Turnbull, B R (Cardiff) 1925 I, 1927 E, S, 1928 E, F, 1930 S

Turnbull, M J L (Cardiff) 1933 E, I

Turner, P (Newbridge) 1989 I (R), F, E

Uzzell, H (Newport) 1912 E, S, I, F, 1913 S, F, I, 1914 E, S, F, I, 1920 E, S, F, I

Uzzell, J R (Newport) 1963 NZ, 1965 E, S, I, F

Vickery, W E (Aberavon) 1938 E, S, I, 1939 E

Vile, T H (Newport) 1908 E, S, 1910 I, 1912 I, F, SA, 1913 E, 1921 S

Vincent, H C (Bangor) 1882 I

Voyle, M J (Newport, Llanelli, Cardiff) 1996 A 1(t), F 2, 1997 E, US 1,2, C, Tg, NZ, 1998 It, E, S, I, F, Arg (R), 1999 S (R), I (t), It (R), SA (R), F 2(R), [J, A (R)], 2000 F (R)

Wakeford, J D M (S Wales Police) 1988 WS, R

Waldron, R (Neath) 1965 E, S, I, F

Walker, N (Cardiff) 1993 I, F, J, 1994 S, F, E, Pt, Sp, 1995 F, E, 1997 US 1,2, C, R (R), Tg, NZ, 1998 E

Waller, P D (Newport) 1908 A, 1909 E, S, F, I, 1910 F

Walne, N J (Richmond, Cardiff) 1999 It (R), E (R), C

Walters, N (Llanelli) 1902 E

Wanbon, R (Aberavon) 1968 E

Ward, W S (Cross Keys) 1934 S, I

Warlow, J (Llanelli) 1962 I

Waters, D R (Newport) 1986 E, S, I, F

Waters, K (Newbridge) 1991 [WS]

Watkins, D (Newport) 1963 E, S, I, F, NZ, 1964 E, S, I, F, SA, 1965 E, S, I, F, 1966 E, S, I, F, 1967 I, F, E

Watkins, E (Neath) 1924 E, S, I, F

Watkins, E (Blaina) 1926 S, I, F

Watkins, E (Cardiff) 1935 NZ, 1937 S, I, 1938 E, S, I, 1939 E, S

Watkins, H (Llanelli) 1904 S, I, 1905 E, S, I, 1906 E

Watkins, I J (Ebbw Vale) 1988 E (R), S, I, F, NZ 2, R, 1989 S, I, F, E

Watkins, L (Oxford U, Llandaff) 1881 E

Watkins, M J (Newport) 1984 I, F, E, A

Watkins, M J (Llanelli Scarlets) 2003 It(R), E 1(R), S 1(R), I 1(R), R, S 2, 2005 US(R),C(R),Fj,SA(R),A, 2006 E,S,I,It,F,Arg 1,2(R)

Watkins, S J (Newport, Cardiff) 1964 S, I, F, 1965 E, S, I, F, 1966 E, S, I, F, A, 1967 S, I, F, E, NZ, 1968 E, S, 1969 S, I, F, E, NZ 1, 1970 E, I

Watkins, W R (Newport) 1959 F

Watts, D (Maesteg) 1914 E, S, F, I

Watts, J (Llanelli) 1907 E, S, I, 1908 E, S, F, I, A, 1909 S, F, I

Watts, W (Llanelli) 1914 E

Watts, W H (Newport) 1892 E, S, I, 1893 E, S, I, 1894 E, S, I, 1895 E, I, 1896 E
Weatherley, D J (Swansea) 1998 Z
Weaver, D (Swansea) 1964 E
Webb, J (Abertillery) 1907 S, 1908 E, S, F, I, A, 1909 E, S, F, I, 1910 F, E, S, I, 1911 E, S, F, I, 1912 E, S
Webb, J E (Newport) 1888 M, 1889 S
Webbe, G M C (Bridgend) 1986 Tg (R), WS, 1987 F, E, S, [Tg], US, 1988 F (R), NZ 1, R
Webster, R E (Swansea) 1987 [A], 1990 Bb, 1991 [Arg, A], 1992 I, F, E, S, A, 1993 E, S, I, F
Wells, G T (Cardiff) 1955 E, S, 1957 I, F, 1958 A, E, S
Westacott, D (Cardiff) 1906 I
Wetter, H (Newport) 1912 SA, 1913 E
Wetter, J J (Newport) 1914 S, F, I, 1920 E, S, F, I, 1921 E, 1924 I, NZ
Wheel, G A D (Swansea) 1974 I, E (R), 1975 F, E, I, A, 1976 E, S, I, F, 1977 I, E, S, 1978 E, S, I, F, A 1,2, NZ, 1979 S, I, 1980 F, E, S, I, 1981 E, S, I, F, A, 1982 I
Wheeler, P J (Aberavon) 1967 NZ, 1968 E
Whitefoot, J (Cardiff) 1984 A (R), 1985 S, I, F, E, Fj, 1986 E, S, I, F, Fj, Tg, WS, 1987 F, E, S, I, [I, C]
Whitfield, J (Newport) 1919 NZA, 1920 E, S, F, I, 1921 E, 1922 E, S, I, F, 1924 S, I
Whitson, G K (Newport) 1956 F, 1960 S, I
Wilkins, G (Bridgend) 1994 Tg
Williams, A (Bridgend, Swansea) 1990 Nm 2(R), 1995 Fj (R)
Williams, A (Ospreys, Bath) 2003 R (R), 2005 v US(R),C(R), 2006 Arg 2(R), 2007 A2(R)
Williams, B (Llanelli) 1920 S, F, I
Williams, B H (Neath, Richmond, Bristol) 1996 F 2, 1997 R, Tg, NZ, 1998 It, E, Z (R), SA 1, Arg (R), 1999 S (R), I, It (R), 2000 F (R), It (R), E (t+R), 2001 R (R), I (R), Tg (R), A (R), 2002 I (R), F (R), It (R), E (R), S
Williams, B L (Cardiff) 1947 E, S, F, I, A, 1948 E, S, F, I, 1949 E, S, I, 1951 I, SA, 1952 S, 1953 E, S, I, F, NZ, 1954 S, 1955 E
Williams, B R (Neath) 1990 S, I, Bb, 1991 E, S
Williams, C (Llanelli) 1924 NZ, 1925 E
Williams, C (Aberavon, Swansea) 1977 E, S, 1980 F, E, S, I, NZ, 1983 E
Williams, C D (Cardiff, Neath) 1955 F, 1956 F
Williams, D (Llanelli) 1998 SA 1(R)
Williams, D (Ebbw Vale) 1963 E, S, I, F, 1964 E, S, I, F, SA, 1965 E, S, I, F, 1966 E, S, I, A, 1967 F, E, NZ, 1968 E, 1969 S, I, F, E, NZ 1,2, A, 1970 SA, S, E, I, 1971 E, S, I, F
Williams, D B (Newport, Swansea) 1978 A 1, 1981 E, S
Williams, E (Neath) 1924 NZ, 1925 F
Williams, E (Aberavon) 1925 E, S
Williams, F L (Cardiff) 1929 S, F, I, 1930 E, S, I, F, 1931 F, I, SA, 1932 E, S, I, 1933 I
Williams, G (Aberavon) 1936 E, S, I
Williams, G (London Welsh) 1950 I, F, 1951 E, S, I, F, SA, 1952 E, S, I, F, 1953 NZ, 1954 E
Williams, G (Bridgend) 1981 I, F, 1982 E (R), S
Williams, G J (Bridgend, Cardiff) 2003 It(R), E 1(R), S 1, F(R), E 2(R)
Williams, G P (Bridgend) 1980 NZ, 1981 E, S, A, 1982 I
Williams, G R (Cardiff Blues) 2000 I, Sm, US, SA, 2001 S, F, It, R (R), I (R), Arg, Tg (R), A (R), 2002 F (R), It (R), E (R), S, SA 1,2, R, Fj, C, NZ, 2003 It, E 1, S 1, I 1, F, A, NZ, E 2, [Tg,It(R)], 2004 S,I,F,E,It,Arg1,R,J, 2005 F(R),S,US,C
Williams, J (Blaina) 1920 E, S, F, I, 1921 S, F, I
Williams, J F (London Welsh) 1905 I, NZ, 1906 S, SA
Williams, J J (Llanelli) 1973 F (R), A, 1974 S, I, F, E, 1975 F, E, S, I, A, 1976 E, S, I, F, 1977 I, F, E, S, 1978 E, S, I, F, A 1,2, NZ, 1979 S, I, F, E
Williams, J L (Cardiff) 1906 SA, 1907 E, S, I, 1908 E, S, I, A, 1909 E, S, F, I, 1910 I, 1911 E, S, F, I
Williams, J P R (London Welsh, Bridgend) 1969 S, I, F, E, NZ 1,2, A, 1970 SA, S, E, I, F, 1971 E, S, I, F, 1972 E, S, F, NZ, 1973 E, S, I, F, A, 1974 S, I, F, 1975 F, E, S, I, A, 1976 E, S, I, F, 1977 I, F, E, S, 1978 E, S, I, F, A 1,2, NZ, 1979 S, I, F, E, 1980 NZ, 1981 E, S
Williams, L (Llanelli, Cardiff) 1947 E, S, F, I, A, 1948 I, 1949 E
Williams, L H (Cardiff) 1957 S, I, F, 1958 E, S, I, F, 1959 E, S, I, 1961 F, 1962 E, S
Williams, M (Newport) 1923 F
Williams, M E (Pontypridd, Cardiff Blues) 1996 Bb, F 2, It (t), 1998 It, E, Z, SA 2, Arg, 1999 S, I, C, J, [Sm], 2000 E (R), 2001 E, S, F, It, 2002 I, F, It, E, S, SA 1,2, Fj, C, NZ, 2003 It, E 1, S 1, I 1, F, A, NZ, E 2, [C,Tg(R),It,E(R)], 2004 S,I, F(t&R),E(R),It,SA2(t&R),R(R),NZ(R),J(R), 2005 E,It,F,S,I,Fj,SA,A, 2006 E,S,I,It,F,A,C,NZ, 2007 I,S,F1,It,E1,Arg,F2, [C,A,J,Fj]
Williams, O (Bridgend) 1990 Nm 2
Williams, O (Llanelli) 1947 E, S, A, 1948 E, S, F, I
Williams, R (Llanelli) 1954 S, 1957 F, 1958 A
Williams, R D G (Newport) 1881 E
Williams, R F (Cardiff) 1912 SA, 1913 E, S, 1914 I
Williams, R H (Llanelli) 1954 I, F, S, 1955 S, I, F, 1956 E, S, I, 1957 E, S, I, F, 1958 A, E, S, I, F, 1959 E, S, I, F, 1960 E
Williams, S (Llanelli) 1947 E, S, F, I, 1948 S, F
Williams, S A (Aberavon) 1939 E, S, I
Williams, S M (Neath, Cardiff, Northampton) 1994 Tg, 1996 E (t), A 1,2, Bb, F 2, It, A 3, SA, 1997 US, S, I, F, E, US 1,2(R), C, R (R), Tg (R), NZ (t+R), 2002 SA 1,2, R, Fj(R), 2003 It, E 1, S 1, F(R)
Williams, S M (Neath, Ospreys) 2000 F (R), It, E, S, I, Sm, SA (R), 2001 J 1,2, I, 2003 R, [NZ,E], 2004 S,I,F,E,It,Arg 1,2,SA1,2,NZ,J, 2005 E,It,F,S,I,NZ,Fj,SA,A, 2006 E,S,It,F,Arg 1,2,A,Pl(R),C,NZ, 2007 F1,It,E1,F2, [C,A,J,Fj]
Williams, T (Pontypridd) 1882 I
Williams, T (Swansea) 1888 S, I
Williams, T (Swansea) 1912 I, 1913 F, 1914 E, S, F, I
Williams, Tudor (Swansea) 1921 F
Williams, T G (Cross Keys) 1935 S, I, NZ, 1936 E, S, I, 1937 S, I
Williams, W A (Crumlin) 1927 E, S, F, I
Williams, W A (Newport) 1952 I, F, 1953 E
Williams, W E O (Cardiff) 1887 S, I, 1889 S, 1890 S, E
Williams, W H (Pontymister) 1900 E, S, I, 1901 E
Williams, W O G (Swansea, Devonport Services) 1951 F, SA, 1952 E, S, I, F, 1953 E, S, I, F, NZ, 1954 E, I, F, S, 1955 E, S, I, F, 1956 E, S, I
Williams, W P J (Neath) 1974 I, F
Williams-Jones, H (S Wales Police, Llanelli) 1989 S (R), 1990 F (R), I, 1991 A, 1992 S, A, 1993 E, S, I, F, Z 1, Nm, 1994 Fj, Tg, WS (R), It (t), 1995 E (R)
Willis, W R (Cardiff) 1950 E, S, I, F, 1951 E, S, I, F, SA, 1952 E, S, 1953 S, NZ, 1954 E, I, F, S, 1955 E, S, I, F
Wiltshire, M L (Aberavon) 1967 NZ, 1968 E, S, F
Windsor, R W (Pontypool) 1973 A, 1974 S, I, F, E, 1975 F, E, S, I, A, 1976 E, S, I, F, 1977 I, F, E, S, 1978 E, S, I, F, A 1,2, NZ, 1979 S, I, F
Winfield, H B (Cardiff) 1903 I, 1904 E, S, I, 1905 NZ, 1906 E, S, I, 1907 S, I, 1908 E, S, F, I, A
Winmill, S (Cross Keys) 1921 E, S, F, I
Wintle, M E (Llanelli) 1996 It
Wintle, R V (London Welsh) 1988 WS (R)
Wooller, W (Sale, Cambridge U, Cardiff) 1933 E, S, I, 1935 E, S, I, NZ, 1936 E, S, I, 1937 E, S, I, 1938 S, I, 1939 E, S, I
Wyatt, C P (Llanelli) 1998 Z (R), SA 1(R),2, Arg, 1999 S, I, F 1, It, E, Arg 1,2, SA, C (R), F 2, [Arg 3, J (R), Sm, A], 2000 F, It, E, US, SA, 2001 E, R, I, Arg (R), Tg (R), A (R), 2002 I, It (R), E, S (R), 2003 A(R), NZ(t+R), E 2, [Tg(R),NZ(R)]
Wyatt, G (Pontypridd, Celtic Warriors) 1997 Tg, 2003 R (R)
Wyatt, M A (Swansea) 1983 E, S, I, F, 1984 A, 1985 S, I, 1987 E, S, I

Yapp, J (Cardiff Blues) 2005 E(R),It(R),F(R),S(R),I(R),C(R),Fj, 2006 Arg 1(R)
Young, D (Swansea, Cardiff) 1987 [E, NZ], US, 1988 E, S, I, F, NZ 1,2, WS, R, 1989 S, NZ, 1990 F, 1996 A 3, SA, 1997 US, S, I, F, E, R, NZ, 1998 It, E, S, I, F, 1999 I, E (R), Arg 1(R),2(R), SA, C (R), F 2, [Arg 3, J, Sm, A], 2000 F, It, E, S, I, 2001 E, S, F, It, R, I, Arg
Young, G A (Cardiff) 1886 E, S
Young, J (Harrogate, RAF, London Welsh) 1968 S, I, F, 1969 S, I, F, E, NZ 1, 1970 E, I, F, 1971 E, S, I, F, 1972 E, S, F, NZ, 1973 E, S, I, F
Young, P (Gwent Dragons) 2003 R (R)

WALES: DOMESTIC 2006–07

HAT-TRICK TIME FOR ALL BLACKS

Neath maintained their dominance of the semi-professional game in Wales with a third successive Principality Premiership crown – although Rowland Phillips' side the were made to work significantly harder for the silverware than in previous seasons.

The Welsh All Blacks romped to the title in 2006, finishing 15 points clear of second-place Bridgend, but had to endure a far more tense campaign in 2006–07 as both Ebbw Vale and Newport pushed them all the way.

In fact, such was the concerted challenge from both the Steelmen, who had topped the table for much of the season, and the Black And Ambers that the destination of the title remained in doubt until all three sides' final league fixtures.

Neath finished their campaign seven days before their two main rivals with a crucial 20–18 win at Pontypridd, a result which left Newport needing to score an unlikely 15 tries at home to Pontypridd a week later to overhaul them. The miracle result failed to materialise – Newport actually lost 28–25 at Rodney Parade – and the Welsh All Blacks could begin celebrating a hat-trick of Premiership triumphs, while Ebbw Vale's victory over Llanelli at Eugene Cross Park saw Alex Codling's team snatch second place from the Black and Ambers.

"There is no doubt the quality of the Premiership has increased over the past few seasons," said Neath captain Steve Martin after the dramatic conclusion of the season. "Our playing record shows that – winning the title this season has been harder than any other. Any side can beat anyone else now.

"You can never have enough success and at Neath we always want more. Everyone works very hard at the club and there is a desire to kick on and raise the bar again next season."

It was obvious from the early stages of the campaign that Neath would not have things all their own way. A narrow 33–30 opening day defeat against Glamorgan Wanderers at the Memorial Ground suggested Phillips' team were not quite in the all-conquering form of previous years and although they bounced back the following weekend with a comprehensive 57–17 mauling of Pontypridd, a 23–23 draw with Ebbw Vale in week three proved they were not going to ease away from the pack without a fight.

Newport, meanwhile, recovered from their own surprise opening day loss to Aberavon at Rodney Parade to string together a four-match winning run that confirmed it would be a three-horse race for honours.

It initially seemed that it would be the Steelmen who would last the distance. The side's tense 15–11 win over Cross Keys at Pandy Park at the end of September sparked a seven-match winning run that extended through to December. In contrast, both Neath and Newport struggled for any kind of consistency. December, in particular, proved a disastrous month for the defending champions with defeats to Newport and Llanelli, as well as a 23–23 draw with Vale.

The New Year, however, signalled a change in fortunes for all three title contenders. Ebbw Vale began to stutter while Neath gathered momentum and produced an impressive run of results which would eventually clinch the Premiership crown.

The Black and Ambers began their charge in earnest in January with victory over Wanderers. Five further victories followed to suggest the silverware would be staying at The Gnoll. The run was briefly interrupted at the end of March with a 25–21 defeat at Cardiff but it was to be Neath's only league defeat in 2007. Victory over Newport in the penultimate game of the season proved crucial and the Black and Ambers were champions once again.

"It's been sweeter this time round as we've had to work harder for the title," said head coach Rowland Phillips, who has been at the helm for all three of Neath's title triumphs. "Last year we won with three games to play but we had to fight to succeed this season.

"We have a backs-to-the-wall attitude that brings out the best in us when we fight for success rather than accepting situations. I want to keep that going."

At the other end of the table, Llandovery finished rock bottom with a mere seven wins in their 24 league outings but were spared the heartache of relegation because none of the sides from the lower divisions were able to satisfy the Welsh Rugby Union's criteria for top-flight rugby.

But if their Premiership campaign was a huge disappointment for the Drovers and their supporters, they found more than a little solace in the Konica Minolta Cup, pulling off a fairytale victory over Cardiff in the final of the competition to lift the trophy for the first time in the club's history.

The clash between the two clubs at the Millennium Stadium was widely expected to see Cardiff emerge victorious for an eighth time but Llandovery clearly had other ideas and made their intentions clear as early as the third minute when left wing Viv Jenkins went over for the first score of the match, which was converted.

Drovers fly-half Howard Thomas traded penalties with his opposite number Craig Evans but two second-half drop goals from the Cardiff number ten – the second coming with in the sixth minute of injury time – gave his team a 18–13 lead and Llandovery seemed down and out.

But there was still time for more drama and a minute later substitute prop Endaf Howells bulldozed his way over to level the scores. With two tries to Cardiff's none and the scores level at 18–18, Llandovery already had one hand on the trophy but Thomas removed all doubt with the conversion and the Drovers players and supporters began their celebrations.

"The fans were absolutely phenomenal on Saturday and we could hear them singing right the way through the game and it really helped us," said Drovers prop Andrew Jones, who retired at the end of the season after 21 years of service for the club.

"When we came back after the game, people were lining the streets with banners and flags, it was incredible. I saw people that I haven't seen for years and it seemed as though everyone from the town was there."

PRINCIPALITY PREMIERSHIP 2006–07 RESULTS

2 September, 2006: **Bedwas** 18 **Cross Keys** 3, **Bridgend** 7 **Ebbw Vale** 16, **Cardiff** 30 **Swansea** 36, **Llanelli** 17 **Maesteg** 16, **Newport** 16 **Aberavon** 19, **Pontypridd** 13 **Llandovery** 33, **Wanderers** 33 **Neath** 30. 9 September, 2006: **Bridgend** 35 **Cross Keys** 13, **Cardiff** 36 **Llanelli** 24, **Ebbw Vale** 7 **Newport** 12, **Llandovery** 13 **Aberavon** 32, **Maesteg** 29 **Bedwas** 15, **Neath** 57 **Pontypridd** 17, **Swansea** 33 **Wanderers** 29. 16 September, 2006: **Aberavon** 12 **Pontypridd** 33, **Bedwas** 33 **Swansea** 25, **Cardiff** 24 **Bridgend** 21, **Cross Keys** 43 **Llandovery** 17, **Ebbw Vale** 23 **Neath** 23, **Llanelli** 18 **Wanderers** 25, **Newport** 37 **Maesteg** 18. 23 September, 2006: **Aberavon** 30 **Cardiff** 21, **Llandovery** 28 **Bedwas** 12, **Maesteg** 37 **Ebbw Vale** 23, **Neath** 24 **Llanelli** 22, **Newport** 29 **Bridgend** 11, **Pontypridd** 40 **Swansea** 15, **Wanderers** 25 **Cross Keys** 32. 30 September, 2006: **Aberavon** 19 **Maesteg** 18, **Bedwas** 9 **Newport** 27, **Bridgend** 37 **Wanderers** 12, **Cross Keys** 11 **Ebbw Vale** 15, **Llandovery** 21 **Llanelli** 6, **Pontypridd** 20 **Cardiff** 18, **Swansea** 19 **Neath** 42. 7 October, 2006: **Cross Keys** 39 **Pontypridd** 6, **Ebbw Vale** 27 **Aberavon** 25, **Llandovery** 14 **Cardiff** 23, **Llanelli** 64 **Bridgend** 22, **Neath** 34 **Maesteg** 13, **Swansea** 33 **Newport** 13, **Wanderers** 13 **Bedwas** 19. 14 October, 2006: **Bridgend** 18 **Neath** 13, **Cardiff** 44 **Cross Keys** 26, **Ebbw Vale** 24 **Swansea** 13, **Llanelli** 24 **Aberavon** 22, **Maesteg** 23 **Wanderers** 11, **Newport** 68 **Llandovery** 15, **Pontypridd**

24 **Bedwas** 10. 21 October, 2006: **Aberavon** 23 **Bridgend** 22, **Bedwas** 16 **Ebbw Vale** 19, **Cardiff** 26 **Wanderers** 11, **Cross Keys** 18 **Llanelli** 18, **Llandovery** 13 **Neath** 27, **Pontypridd** 14 **Newport** 22, **Swansea** 6 **Maesteg** 16. 28 October, 2006: **Bridgend** 25 **Swansea** 0, **Ebbw Vale** 23 **Pontypridd** 13, Glamorgan **Wanderers** 20 **Aberavon** 20, **Llanelli** 28 **Bedwas** 19, **Maesteg** 22 **Llandovery** 12, **Neath** 6 **Cross Keys** 10, **Newport** 18 **Cardiff** 18. 8 November, 2006: **Wanderers** 11 **Newport** 23. 10 November, 2006: **Llandovery** 28 **Bridgend** 29, **Llanelli** 37 **Pontypridd** 7, **Cardiff** 19 **Ebbw Vale** 21, **Bedwas** 20 **Neath** 18, **Aberavon** 33 **Swansea** 12. 18 November, 2006: **Bedwas** 15 **Bridgend** 11, **Ebbw Vale** 39 **Wanderers** 22, **Llanelli** 27 **Newport** 13, **Neath** 27 **Cardiff** 19, **Pontypridd** 32 **Maesteg** 17, **Swansea** 15 **Llandovery** 10. 2 December, 2006: **Aberavon** 21 **Bedwas** 12, **Bridgend** 7 **Pontypridd** 9, **Cross Keys** 15 **Swansea** 11, **Llanelli** 17 **Ebbw Vale** 13, **Maesteg** 19 **Cardiff** 31, **Newport** 25 **Neath** 21, **Wanderers** 57 **Llandovery** 35. 9 December, 2006: **Bridgend** 14 **Cardiff** 5, **Llandovery** 22 **Cross Keys** 16, **Maesteg** 18 **Newport** 40, **Neath** 23 **Ebbw Vale** 23, **Pontypridd** 37 **Aberavon** 8, **Swansea** 17 **Bedwas** 3, **Wanderers** 13 **Llanelli** 22. 16 December, 2006: **Bedwas** 13 **Llandovery** 9, **Bridgend** 27 **Newport** 18, **Cardiff** 28 **Aberavon** 23, **Cross Keys** 23 **Wanderers** 24, **Ebbw Vale** 18 **Maesteg** 15, **Llanelli** 31 **Neath** 11, **Swansea** 10 **Pontypridd** 14. 23 December, 2006: **Swansea** 3 **Llanelli** 37. 26 December, 2006: **Bedwas** 12 **Cardiff** 20, **Aberavon** 22 **Neath** 24, **Bridgend** 20 **Maesteg** 15, **Cross Keys** 13 **Newport** 13, **Llandovery** 9 **Ebbw Vale** 13, **Pontypridd** 29 **Wanderers** 6. 30 December, 2006: **Ebbw Vale** 21 **Cross Keys** 3, **Neath** 29 **Swansea** 5, **Newport** 39 **Bedwas** 11, **Wanderers** 15 **Bridgend** 3, **Cardiff** 6 **Pontypridd** 13. 6 January, 2007: **Ebbw Vale** 37 **Bridgend** 23, **Llandovery** 19 **Pontypridd** 27, **Maesteg** 33 **Llanelli** 21, **Neath** 36 **Wanderers** 20, **Swansea** 23 **Cardiff** 22. 13 January, 2007: **Aberavon** 39 **Ebbw Vale** 19, **Bedwas** 10 **Wanderers** 11, **Bridgend** 14 **Llanelli** 8, **Cardiff** 42 **Llandovery** 21, **Maesteg** 9 **Neath** 18, **Newport** 22 **Swansea** 10, **Pontypridd** 22 **Cross Keys** 12. 20 January, 2007: **Aberavon** 34 **Llanelli** 34, **Bedwas** 27 **Pontypridd** 27, **Cross Keys** 12 **Cardiff** 8, **Llandovery** 25 **Newport** 13, **Neath** 27 **Bridgend** 17, **Swansea** 18 **Ebbw Vale** 23, **Wanderers** 21 **Maesteg** 10. 3 February, 2007: **Bridgend** 16 **Aberavon** 24, **Ebbw Vale** 25 **Bedwas** 19, **Llanelli** 24 **Cross Keys** 27, **Maesteg** 11 **Swansea** 14, **Neath** 48 **Llandovery** 13, **Wanderers** 31 **Cardiff** 34. 24 February, 2007: **Cross Keys** 16 **Aberavon** 10. 3 March, 2007: **Aberavon** 9 **Wanderers** 35, **Bedwas** 21 **Llanelli** 16, **Cardiff** 19 **Newport** 29, **Llandovery** 31 **Maesteg** 17, **Pontypridd** 31 **Ebbw Vale** 22, **Swansea** 20 **Bridgend** 6. 9 March, 2007: **Cross Keys** 7 **Bedwas** 10, **Newport** 17 **Wanderers** 34. 14 March, 2007: **Ebbw Vale** 22 **Cardiff** 27. 16 March, 2007: **Bridgend** 8 **Llandovery** 14, **Maesteg** 25 **Cross Keys** 13, **Neath** 34 **Bedwas** 14, **Pontypridd** 17 **Llanelli** 11, **Swansea** 26 **Aberavon** 20. 24 March, 2007: **Cross Keys** 13 **Neath** 22, **Newport** 22 **Ebbw Vale** 11. 31 March, 2007: **Aberavon** 29 **Cross Keys** 27, **Bridgend** 19 **Bedwas** 10, **Cardiff** 25 **Neath** 21, **Llandovery** 16 **Swansea** 19, **Maesteg** 21 **Pontypridd** 16, **Wanderers** 26 **Ebbw Vale** 26. 1 April, 2007: **Newport** 18 **Llanelli** 13. 7 April, 2007: **Cardiff** 30 **Bedwas** 32, **Ebbw Vale** 28 **Llandovery** 21, **Llanelli** 23 **Swansea** 36, **Maesteg** 26 **Bridgend** 16, **Newport** 20 **Cross Keys** 17, **Wanderers** 10 **Pontypridd** 8. 8 April, 2007: **Neath** 39 **Aberavon** 19. 14 April, 2007: **Bedwas** 20 **Aberavon** 7, **Neath** 30 **Newport** 12, **Swansea** 41 **Cross Keys** 29. 18 April, 2007: **Cardiff** 16 **Maesteg** 23, **Wanderers** 44 **Swansea** 27. 20 April, 2007: **Llanelli** 38 **Llandovery** 17. 21 April, 2007: **Aberavon** 21 **Newport** 28, **Cross Keys** 32 **Maesteg** 25, **Pontypridd** 18 **Neath** 20. 25 April, 2007: **Bedwas** 46 **Maesteg** 20. 28 April, 2007: **Cross Keys** 15 **Bridgend** 17, **Ebbw Vale** 19 **Llanelli** 12, **Maesteg** 35 **Aberavon** 37, **Newport** 25 **Pontypridd** 28. 2 May, 2007: **Aberavon** 45 **Llandovery** 13, **Llanelli** 37 **Cardiff** 10. 5 May, 2007: **Llandovery** 13 **Wanderers** 18, **Pontypridd** 28 **Bridgend** 17.

FINAL TABLE 2006–07

	P	W	D	L	For	A	Pts
Neath	26	17	2	7	704	473	53
Ebbw Vale	26	16	3	7	557	503	51
Newport	26	16	2	8	619	480	50
Pontypridd	26	16	1	9	543	504	49
Llanelli	26	12	2	12	629	509	38
Glam Wanderers	26	12	2	12	577	602	38
Aberavon	26	12	2	12	603	615	38
Cardiff	26	12	1	13	601	580	37
Swansea	26	12	0	14	487	609	36
Bedwas	26	11	1	14	446	524	34
Bridgend	26	11	0	15	459	508	33
Maesteg	26	10	0	16	531	596	30
Cross Keys	26	9	2	15	485	528	29
Llandovery	26	7	0	19	482	692	21

ASDA ONE EAST

Winners: Beddau

ASDA ONE WEST

Winners: Bonymaen

ASDA TWO EAST

Winners: Llantrisant

ASDA TWO WEST

Winners: Tonmawr

ASDA THREE EAST

Winners: Penallta

ASDA THREE SOUTH EAST

Winners: Pencoed

ASDA THREE SOUTH WEST

Winners: Mumbles

ASDA THREE WEST

Winners: Tumble

ASDA FOUR EAST

Winners: Garndiffaith

ASDA FOUR SOUTH EAST

Winners: Bedlinog

ASDA FOUR SOUTH WEST

Winners: BP R.F.C (Llandarcy)

ASDA FOUR WEST

Winners: Llanybydder

ASDA FOUR NORTH

Winners: Mold

ASDA FIVE EAST

Winners: Abertillery / Blaenau Gwent

ASDA FIVE SOUTH EAST

Winners: Rhiwbina

ASDA FIVE SOUTH CENTRAL

Winners: Glyncorrwg

ASDA FIVE SOUTH WEST

Winners: Neath Athletic

ASDA FIVE WEST

Winners: Tycroes

ASDA FIVE NORTH

Winners: Dolgellau

QUARTER-FINALS

24–25 March, 2007

Aberavon 19 **Bridgend** 20

Llanelli 37 **Pontypridd** 30

Bedwas 14 **Llandovery** 21

Swansea 8 **Cardiff** 39

SEMI-FINALS

14–15 April, 2007

Llandovery 20 **Llanelli** 19

Cardiff 23 **Bridgend** 16

FINAL

28 April, Millennium Stadium, Cardiff

LLANDOVERY 20 (2G, 2PG)
CARDIFF 18 (4PG, 2DG)

LLANDOVERY: I Davies; O Rowlands, M Jones, J Lewis, V Jenkins; H Thomas, R Walters; P John, E Phillips, A B Jones, T Walker, A Davies (captain), E Gwynne, J Mills, G Williams Substitutions: D Allinson for Isaacs (45 mins); M Amos for Down (68 mins); N Hampson for Lucas (70 mins)

SCORERS *Tries:* Jenkins, Howells *Conversions*: H Thomas (2) *Penalty Goals*: H Thomas (2)

CARDIFF: J Roberts; E Jones, R Davies, R Jones, L Andrews; C Evans, T Isaacs; R Gill, R Johnston, S Roberts, C Stamatakis, J Down, G Lucas, A Powell, G Gravell (captain) Substitutions: A R Jones for Phillips (temp 10 to 18 mins); G Bennett for Gwynne (temp 48 to 60 mins); Jones for Phillips (68 mins); E Howells for A B Jones (72 mins); Bennett for Gwynne (83 mins)

SCORERS *Penalty Goals:* Evans (4) *Drop Goals*: Evans (2)

REFEREE H Watkins (Maesteg)

Yellow cards Lucas (31 mins) G Williams (33 mins)

BRITISH & IRISH LIONS

THOSE FAMOUS MEN IN RED

By Iain Spragg

The history of the British & Irish Lions did not make for encouraging reading for the 2005 squad as they prepared to tackle the All Blacks. The Lions had ventured to New Zealand eight times before and only once – in 1971 – had they returned home victorious.

In fact, since the first Lions squad to be selected from all four Home Unions in 1910 set off for South Africa, only six had recorded series victories in 23 attempts against the three southern hemisphere powers. The 2005 vintage knew the odds, not to mention history, were against them.

Not that the Lions left for New Zealand under prepared. Head coach Clive Woodward included a staggering 45 players in his squad (many of them stalwarts from England's World Cup campaign two years earlier) and was supported by a record 26–strong backroom staff. A pre-tour match against Argentina at the Millennium Stadium was arranged, a precedent designed to allow Woodward to assess his resources before getting on the plane.

It was an experimental side missing many of the anticipated Test team that took the field in Cardiff in May, but inexperience could only partly explain a lacklustre performance against an under-strength Argentina. The match was drawn 25–25 and the Lions had stumbled at the first hurdle.

The tour proper, however, began brightly. The Bay of Plenty and Taranaki were dispatched without any major problems but the alarm bells began to ring for the first wave of the estimated 30,000 Lions fans who eventually made the trip when New Zealand Maori pulled off a famous 19–13 victory in Waikato. Woodward's side had proved fallible.

Wellington, Otago and Southland provided the final opposition in the build-up to the first Test in Christchurch and although the Lions won all three, the doubts about their ability to beat the All Blacks had grown. The tourists were up against it.

The first Test started badly and got worse. Captain Brian O'Driscoll was ruled out of the tour after only two minutes after a double tackle by his opposite number Tana Umaga and Keven Mealamu resulted in

Shaun Botterill/Getty Images

Sir Clive Woodward led the last Lions tour – in 2005 – but who will be in charge when they embark on their trip to South Africa in 2009?

a dislocated shoulder. The legality of the tackle hung like a black cloud over the rest of the tour.

The Lions never recovered from losing their skipper, their lineout disintegrated and the All Blacks made light of the atrocious conditions, outclassing their opponents (as well as outscoring them two tries to nil) in a 21–3 victory.

"Our set piece was superb, our tight five superb and we were able to place them under pressure," All Black coach Graham Henry said after the match. "The tight five deserve a huge amount of credit and that was the basis for the win. They were dominant around the field and made a lot of tackles. The loose forwards could function and that gave the backs a platform."

A week later the two sides crossed swords again in Wellington but the Lions fans hoping for a series-saving reverse were to be disappointed.

The match started well for the tourists when Gareth Thomas, replacing O'Driscoll as captain, scored after just two minutes but it proved a false dawn as the All Blacks, inspired by Daniel Carter at fly-half, came storming back to crush the visitors 48–18 and seal the series It was the Lions heaviest defeat in their history and Carter's 33-point personal haul, including two of New Zealand's five tries, was also a record.

"We lost some key players but started really well and looked sharp, but things drifted away after 10 minutes," a dejected Woodward said after the final whistle put the Lions of their misery. "They scored some great tries at the end and we struggled to defend. I don't intend to defend myself. We are what we are. I was put in charge and made the decisions and I just want to pat everyone on the back."

Woodward chopped and changed his side for the third Test in Auckland – the tour party had now grown to 51 strong because of injury – but it made little different to the Lions fortunes and the All Blacks emerged 38–19 victors to complete a series whitewash.

"They were tenacious, never gave up and played like true Lions," said Umaga, who scored two of his side's five tries. "It has been a tough week. The way they performed today said a lot about the Lions. They battered us."

In truth, not even Umaga's generous praise could disguise the gulf in class between the two sides. The Lions had expected to dominate New Zealand up front through the series and failed, while the All Blacks back line was infinitely more potent than anything the tourists could aspire to. The Lions had been comprehensively outplayed in all three Tests.

Woodward was predictably determined to remain positive. "We are disappointed – we came out to win the Test series so we have failed," he said. "It's actually been a successful tour, and has been a great experience. The people who say we took too many players are totally wrong.

Phil Walter/Getty Images

The 2005 Lions were robbed of captain Brian O'Driscoll (above) and key man Richard Hill within 15 minutes of the start of the First Test and lost Lawrence Dallaglio in the first game.

It's been a very professional tour. Most of the people criticising are from the amateur era."

The British and New Zealand press, however, were united in their disagreement with the Lions coach. "From start to finish the tour was a bit of a mess," wrote Richard Loe in the New Zealand Herald on Sunday. "This team has been poorly conceived, selected and poorly managed and they have played poorly. If you look at the forwards, none of them can run, pass and catch. Woodward brought over 50 players and, as far as I can see, about 90 per cent of them have been buggered up on this tour."

His views were echoed by Paul Ackford in the Sunday Telegraph. "Salute the bravery and the spirit of the 2005 Lions by all means, but the humiliation is complete," Ackford wrote. "The Lions were honest, well-intentioned, but nowhere near good enough under Woodward. He must carry the can for that. But they probably wouldn't have been appreciably better under anyone else."

Shaun Botterill/Getty Images

South African fans will give the Lions a big welcome in 2009!

2005 TOUR RESULTS

23 May, Millennium Stadium, Cardiff

LIONS 25 (1G, 6PG) ARGENTINA 25 (1G, 6PG)

LIONS: G E A Murphy; D A Hickie, O J Smith, G W D'Arcy, S M Williams; J P Wilkinson, G J Cooper; C G Rowntree, J S Byrne, J J Hayes, D F O'Callaghan, D J Grewcock, M E Corry, L W Moody, M J Owen (captain) Substitutions: S P Horgan for Smith (62 mins); C P Cusiter for Cooper (60 mins); S G Thompson for Byrne (71 mins); J M White for Hayes (55 mins); B J Kay for Grewcock (71 mins)

SCORERS TRY: Smith Conversions: Wilkinson Penalty Goals: Wilkinson (6)

ARGENTINA: B Stortoni; J N Piossek, L Arbizu, F Contepomi (captain) F Leonell; F Todeschini, N F Miranda; F Mendez, M Ledesma, M Reggiardo, P Bouza, M Sambucetti, F Genoud, M Schusterman, J M Leguizamon Substitution: L L Fleming for Todeschini (72 mins)

SCORERS TRY: Piossek Conversion: Todeschini Penalty Goals: Todeschini (6)

REFEREE S Dickinson (Australia)

4 June, Rotorua International Stadium

Bay of Plenty 20 **Lions** 34

8 June, Yarrow Stadium, New Plymouth

Taranaki 14 **Lions** 36

11 June, Waikato Stadium, Hamilton

New Zealand Maori 19 **Lions** 13

15 June, Westpac Stadium, Wellington

Wellington 6 **Lions** 23

18 June, Carisbrook, Dunedin

Otago 19 **Lions** 30

21 June, Rugby Park, Invercargill

Southland 16 **Lions** 26

First Test, 25 June, Jade Stadium, Christchurch

NEW ZEALAND 21 (1G, 3PG, 1T) LIONS 3 (1PG)

NEW ZEALAND: L MacDonald; D Howlett, T Umaga (captain), A Mauger, S Sivivatu; D Carter, J Marshall; T Woodcock, K Mealamu, C Hayman, C Jack, A Williams, J Collins, R McCaw, R So'oialo Substitutions: M Muliaina for MacDonald (69 mins); R Gear for Umaga (75 mins); B Kelleher for Marshall (67 mins); G Somerville for Woodcock (67 mins); D Witcombe for Mealamu (75 mins); S Lauaki for Collins (77 mins)

SCORERS Tries: Williams, Sivivatu Conversion: Carter Penalty Goals: Carter (3)

LIONS: J T Robinson; O J Lewsey, B G O'Driscoll (captain), J P Wilkinson, G Thomas; S M Jones, D J Peel; G D Jenkins, J S Byrne, J M White, P J O'Connell, B J Kay, R A Hill, N A Back, M E Corry Substitutions: S P Horgan for Robinson (57 mins); W J H Greenwood for O'Driscoll (2 mins); M J S Dawson for Peel (74 mins); S G Thompson for Byrne (57 mins); D J Grewcock for Kay (57 mins); R P Jones for Hill (18 mins)

SCORER PENALTY GOAL: Wilkinson

YELLOW CARD O'Connell (11 mins)

REFEREE J Jutge (France)

28 June, Arena Manawatu, Palmerston North

Manawatu 6 **Lions** 109

Second Test, 2 July, Westpac Stadium, Wellington

NEW ZEALAND 48 (4G, 5PG, 1T) LIONS 18 (1G, 2PG, 1T)

NEW ZEALAND: M Muliaina; R Gear, T Umaga (captain), A Mauger, S Sivivatu; D Carter, B Kelleher; T Woodcock, K Mealamu, G Somerville, C Jack, A Williams, J Collins, R McCaw, R So'oialo Substiutions: L MacDonald for Mauger (38 mins); M Nonu for Sivivatu (73 mins); J Marshall for Kelleher (66 mins); C Johnstone for Woodcock (78 mins); D Witcombe for Mealamu (70 mins); J Gibbes for Jack (74 mins); S Lauaki for Collins (66 mins)

SCORERS Tries: Carter (2) Umaga, Sivivatu, McCaw Conversions: Carter (4) Penalty Goals: Carter (5)

LIONS: O J Lewsey; J T Robinson, G Thomas (captain), G L Henson, S M Williams; J P Wilkinson, D J Peel; G D Jenkins, S G Thompson, J M White, P J O'Connell, D F O'Callaghan, S H Easterby, L W Moody, R P Jones Subsitutions: S P Horgan for Henson (70 mins); S M Jones for Wilkinson (60 mins); C G Rowntree for Jenkins (60 mins); M E Corry for O'Callaghan (73 mins); J S Byrne for Thompson (78 mins)

SCORERS TRIES: Thomas, Easterby Conversion: Wilkinson Penalty Goals: Wilkinson (2)

REFEREE A Cole (Australia)

5 July, Eden Park, Auckland

Auckland 13 **Lions** 17

Third Test, 9 July, Eden Park, Auckland

NEW ZEALAND 38 (5G, 1PG) LIONS 19 (1G, 4PG)

NEW ZEALAND: M Muliaina; R Gear, C Smith, T Umaga (captain), S Sivivatu; L McAlister, B Kelleher; T Woodcock, K Mealamu, G Somerville, C Jack, A Williams, J Collins, R So'oialo, S Lauaki Substitutions: J Marshall for Kelleher (46 mins); C Johnstone for Woodcock (44 mins); J Ryan for Jack (77 mins); M Holah for Lauaki (40 mins)

SCORERS Tries: Umaga (2), Smith, Williams, Gear Conversions: McAlister (5) Penalty Goal: McAlister

YELLOW CARDS Umaga (8 mins) Collins (54 mins).

LIONS: G E A Murphy; M J Cueto, W J H Greenwood, G Thomas (captain), O J Lewsey; S M Jones, D J Peel; G D Jenkins, J S Byrne, J M White, D F O'Callaghan, P J O'Connell, S H Easterby, L W Moody, R P Jones Substitutions: S P Horgan for Thomas (51 mins); R J R O'Gara for Murphy (66 mins); M J S Dawson for Peel (48 mins); C G Rowntree for Jenkins (48 mins); G C Bulloch for Byrne (70 mins), M E Williams for Moody (76 mins); M E Corry for R P Jones (68 mins)

SCORERS TRY: Moody Conversion: S M Jones Penalty Goals: S M Jones (4)

REFEREE J Kaplan (South Africa)

Dave Rogers/Getty Images

All Blacks captain Tana Umaga (left) managed to score two tries and get yellow-carded in the final Test victory.

BRITISH/IRISH LIONS INTERNATIONAL STATISTICS

AFTER THE 2005 TOUR

MATCH RECORDS

MOST CONSECUTIVE TEST WINS

6	1891	SA 1,2,3,	1896	SA 1,2,3
3	1899	A 2,3,4		
3	1904	A 1,2,3		
3	1950	A 1,2,	1955	SA 1
3	1974	SA 1,2,3		

MOST CONSECUTIVE TESTS WITHOUT DEFEAT

Matches	Wins	Draws	Periods
6	6	0	1891 to 1896
6	4	2	1971 to 1974

MOST POINTS IN A MATCH

BY THE TEAM

Pts.	Opponent	Venue	Year
31	Australia	Brisbane	1966
29	Australia	Brisbane	2001
28	S Africa	Pretoria	1974
26	S Africa	Port Elizabeth	1974
25	S Africa	Cape Town	1997
24	Australia	Sydney	1950
24	Australia	Sydney	1959

BY A PLAYER

Pts.	Player	Opponent	Venue	Year
18	A J P Ward	S Africa	Cape Town	1980
18	A G Hastings	N Zealand	Christchurch	1993
18	J P Wilkinson	Australia	Sydney	2001
17	T J Kiernan	S Africa	Pretoria	1968
16	B L Jones	Australia	Brisbane	1950

MOST TRIES IN A MATCH

BY THE TEAM

Tries	Opponent	Venue	Year
5	Australia	Sydney	1950
5	S Africa	Johannesburg	1955
5	Australia	Sydney	1959
5	Australia	Brisbane	1966
5	S Africa	Pretoria	1974

BY A PLAYER

Tries	Player	Opponent	Venue	Year
2	A M Bucher	Australia	Sydney	1899
2	W Llewellyn	Australia	Sydney	1904
2	C D Aarvold	N Zealand	Christchurch	1930
2	J E Nelson	Australia	Sydney	1950
2	M J Price	Australia	Sydney	1959
2	M J Price	N Zealand	Dunedin	1959
2	D K Jones	Australia	Brisbane	1966
2	T G R Davies	N Zealand	Christchurch	1971
2	J J Williams	S Africa	Pretoria	1974
2	J J Williams	S Africa	Port Elizabeth	1974

MOST CONVERSIONS IN A MATCH

BY THE TEAM

Cons	Opponent	Venue	Year
5	Australia	Brisbane	1966
4	S Africa	Johannesburg	1955
3	Australia	Sydney	1950
3	Australia	Sydney	1959
3	Australia	Brisbane	2001

BY A PLAYER

Cons	Player	Opponent	Venue	Year
5	S Wilson	Australia	Brisbane	1966
4	A Cameron	S Africa	Johannesburg	1955
3	J P Wilkinson	Australia	Brisbane	2001

MOST PENALTIES IN A MATCH

BY THE TEAM

Pens	Opponent	Venue	Year
6	N Zealand	Christchurch	1993
5	S Africa	Pretoria	1968
5	S Africa	Cape Town	1980
5	Australia	Sydney	1989
5	S Africa	Cape Town	1997
5	S Africa	Durban	1997

BY A PLAYER

Pens	Player	Opponent	Venue	Year
6	A G Hastings	N Zealand	Christchurch	1993
5	T J Kiernan	S Africa	Pretoria	1968
5	A J P Ward	S Africa	Cape Town	1980
5	A G Hastings	Australia	Sydney	1989
5	N R Jenkins	S Africa	Cape Town	1997
5	N R Jenkins	S Africa	Durban	1997

MOST DROP GOALS IN A MATCH

BY THE TEAM

Pens	Opponent	Venue	Year
2	S Africa	Port Elizabeth	1974

BY A PLAYER

Pens	Player	Opponent	Venue	Year
2	P Bennett	S Africa	Port Elizabeth	1974

CAREER RECORDS

MOST CAPPED PLAYERS

Caps	Player	Career Span
17	W J McBride	1962 to 1974
13	R E G Jeeps	1955 to 1962
12	C M H Gibson	1966 to 1971
12	G Price	1977 to 1983
10	A J F O'Reilly	1955 to 1959
10	R H Williams	1955 to 1959
10	G O Edwards	1968 to 1974

MOST CONSECUTIVE TESTS

Tests	Player	Span
15	W J McBride	1966 to 1974
12	C M H Gibson	1966 to 1971
12	G Price	1977 to 1983

MOST TESTS AS CAPTAIN

Tests	Captain	Span
6	A R Dawson	1959
6	M O Johnson	1997 to 2001

MOST TESTS IN INDIVIDUAL POSITIONS

Position	Player	Tests	Span
Full-back	J P R Williams	8	1971 to 1974
Wing	A J F O'Reilly	9	1955 to 1959
Centre	C M H Gibson	8	1966 to 1971
	J C Guscott	8	1989 to 1997
Fly-half	P Bennett	8	1974 to 1977
Scrum-half	R E G Jeeps	13	1955 to 1962
Prop	G Price	12	1977 to 1983
Hooker	B V Meredith	8	1955 to 1962
Lock	W J McBride	17	1962 to 1974
Flanker	N A A Murphy	8	1959 to 1966
No 8	T M Davies	8	1971 to 1974

MOST POINTS IN TESTS

Points	Player	Tests	Career
66	A G Hastings	6	1989 to 1993
47	J P Wilkinson	5	2001 to 2005
44	P Bennett	8	1974 to 1977
41	N R Jenkins	4	1997 to 2001
35	T J Kiernan	5	1962 to 1968
30	S Wilson	5	1966
30	B John	5	1968 to 1971

MOST TRIES IN TESTS

Tries	Player	Tests	Career
6	A J F O'Reilly	10	1955 to 1959
5	J J Williams	7	1974 to 1977
4	W Llewellyn	4	1904
4	M J Price	5	1959

MOST CONVERSIONS IN TESTS

Cons	Player	Tests	Career
6	S Wilson	5	1966
6	J P Wilkinson	5	2001 to 2005
4	J F Byrne	4	1896
4	C Y Adamson	4	1899
4	B L Jones	3	1950
4	A Cameron	2	1955

MOST PENALTY GOALS IN TESTS

Penalties	Player	Tests	Career
20	A G Hastings	6	1989 to 1993
13	N R Jenkins	4	1997 to 2001
11	T J Kiernan	5	1962 to 1968
10	P Bennett	8	1974 to 1977
10	J P Wilkinson	5	2001 to 2005
7	S O Campbell	7	1980 to 1983

MOST DROP GOALS IN TESTS

Drops	Player	Tests	Career
2	P F Bush	4	1904
2	D Watkins	6	1966
2	B John	5	1968 to 1971
2	P Bennett	8	1974 to 1977
2	C R Andrew	5	1989 to 1993

SERIES RECORDS

RECORD	HOLDER	DETAIL
Most team points		79 in S Africa 1974
Most team tries		10 in S Africa 1955 & 1974
Most points by player	N R Jenkins	41 in S Africa 1997
Most tries by player	W Llewellyn	4 in Australia 1904
	J J Williams	4 in S Africa 1974

MAJOR TOUR RECORDS

RECORD	DETAIL	YEAR	PLACE
Most team points	842	1959	Australia, NZ & Canada
Most team tries	165	1959	Australia, NZ & Canada
Highest score & biggest win	116–10	2001	v W Australia President's XV
Most individual points	188 by B John	1971	Australia & N Zealand
Most individual tries	22 by A J F O'Reilly	1959	Australia, NZ & Canada
Most points in match	37 by A G B Old	1974 v SW Districts	Mossel Bay, S Africa
Most tries in match	6 by D J Duckham	1971 v W Coast/Buller	Greymouth, N Zealand
	6 by J J Williams	1974 v SW Districts	Mossel Bay, S Africa

MISCELLANEOUS RECORDS

RECORD	HOLDER	DETAIL
Longest Test Career	W J McBride	13 seasons, 1962–1974
Youngest Test Cap	A J F O'Reilly	19 yrs 91 days in 1955
Oldest Test Cap	N A Back	36 yrs 160 days in 2005

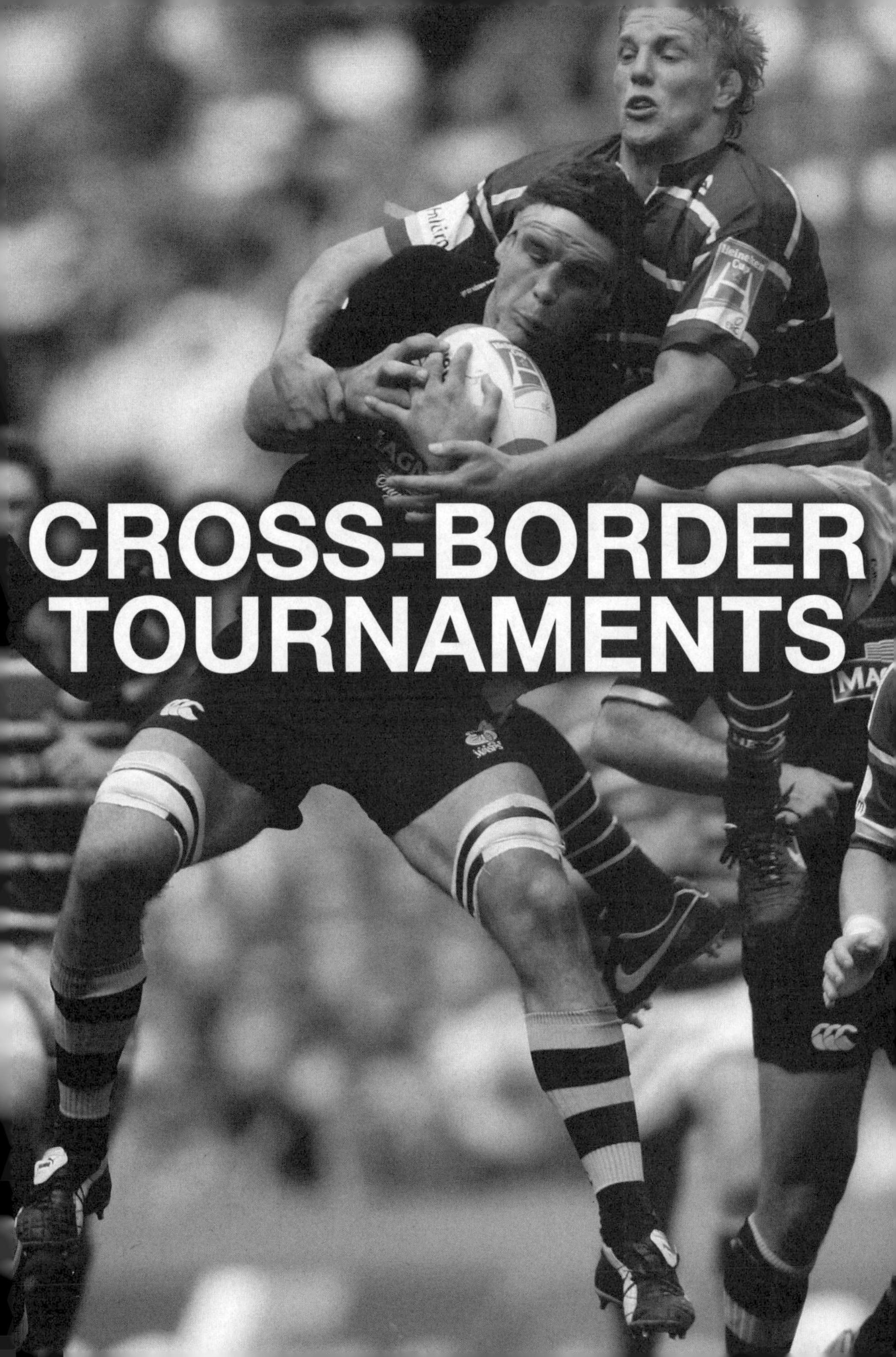

CROSS-BORDER TOURNAMENTS

AN ENGLISH MONOPOLY

By Iain Spragg

Stu Forster/Getty Images

Wasps captained by Lawrence Dallaglio (centre) won the first all-English final.

The Heineken Cup final was supposed to be a thoroughly English affair. After all, it was the first final in the 12-year history of the competition to be contested by two Premiership teams and the hostilities were to be conducted at Twickenham, the spiritual home of the English game.

The fact the two protagonists were Leicester and Wasps, the perennial rivals of the professional era in England, only served to add to the sense of drama. Anglo Saxon club rugby really had never had it so good.

Ironic then, that it was actually a Frenchman – Wasps' gnarled, veteran hooker Raphael Ibanez – who was to have the greatest say on proceedings.

Individuals rarely win matches single-handedly but Ibanez certainly did his Gallic best to be remembered as Wasps' hero on the day in a titanic struggle that eventually saw the London side crowned the champions of Europe for a second time in front of a record 81,076 supporters.

There were only two tries at Twickenham for the crowd to cheer but the Dax-born number two was at the heart of both, providing the scoring pass from a lineout for the first for scrum-half Eoin Reddan and crashing over himself for the second. The Frenchman, with a little help from the rest of the magnificent Wasps pack, had crushed Leicester's dream of an unprecedented Treble.

"We couldn't let Leicester get too much supremacy over us in the professional era," said Wasps skipper Lawrence Dallaglio after his team had defied the pre-match predictions of a Tigers' victory. "They've had a fantastic season, have won two trophies and are worthy champions, but today was all about Wasps.

"You've got to feel for them because they come into this game having won two titles and everyone is talking about them walking away with the Heineken Cup. Yet they're playing a club with the pedigree of Wasps who know how to win on the big stage."

Leicester had returned to Twickenham just eight days after they had mauled Gloucester to secure the Guinness Premiership. The EDF Energy Cup was already safely sitting in the Welford Road trophy cabinet but the clean sweep of all three trophies eluded them as Ibanez and his fellow forwards refused to take a backward step in the brutal exchanges up front.

"Wasps deserved their victory," said Pat Howard, coaching Leicester for the final time before returning to his native Australia. "We weren't allowed to play and consequently we lost.

"They're a very physical side and it was a physical battle. We lost our composure a bit. There were two well-taken tries but we had chances and didn't take them. The Treble can be done but there's lots of things that have to go right."

The group stages of the competition however did not augur well for an all English final and it was the performances of Llanelli and Biarritz that caught the eye as both sides swept all before them en route to the last eight.

The Scarlets were drawn in Pool Five with Toulouse, Ulster and London Irish and were clearly determined to avoid a repeat of their failure to make the quarter-finals the previous season. Their opener at London Irish proved their mettle as they survived a second-half fight

Dave Rogers/Getty Images

The Welsh challenge ended in the semi-finals this time when Llanelli were unable to live with Leicester.

back from the Exiles to claim a 32-25 victory and their 21-15 win over Ulster at Stradey Park in the next game confirmed that Phil Davies' side would be a force to be reckoned with.

Three more wins followed and when Llanelli beat the Exiles in the return fixture in January, they were confirmed as group winners with a 100 per cent record.

"I am very proud of what we have achieved in this competition so far," Davies said. "I was pleased with the win and the fact that we have got a home quarter-final."

It was a similar story for Biarritz, the 2006 Heineken Cup runners-up, in Pool Six. Faced by Northampton, Borders and Parma, the reigning French champions side were rarely troubled en route to six wins from six and their pre-tournament billing as favourites appeared more than justified.

In the other groups, Wasps' progress from Pool One was relatively serene and the only blemish on their otherwise perfect record was a 19-12 defeat in Perpignan in October while Leinster were Pool Two winners ahead of Agen with four wins from six.

Pool Three was tight between Stade Francais and the Ospreys but it was ultimately the Parisians who clinched a place in the last eight. The crucial fixture came in the penultimate round of matches in January when Stade visited the Liberty Stadium and came away with a 22-22 draw courtesy of Lionel Beauxis' late penalty. It was a result that left Stade in top spot and the Ospreys' hopes of reaching the quarter-finals hanging by a thread and although Lyn Jones' side beat Sale in their final game, they failed to secure the bonus point required to clinch one of the best runners-up places.

But if Pool Three was tense, Pool Four was an indisputable cliffhanger as Leicester and defending champions Munster slugged it out in a heavyweight battle that ebbed and flowed until the last.

Munster drew first blood in the opening pool fixture at Welford Road courtesy of late penalty from Ronan O'Gara for a 21-19 victory. Both clubs then swept aside Cardiff and Bourgoin home and away to set up a mouth-watering clash in Ireland that would decide the group winners. Leicester would have to become the first side in Heineken Cup history to win at Thomond Park to guarantee their passage into the knockout stages.

Unsurprisingly it was a titanic battle but tries either side of the break from Geordan Murphy and Ollie Smith were enough to give the Tigers a historic 18-6 win and, courtesy of their superior points difference, top spot in the group.

"It is obviously hugely disappointing for us, but the better team won," O'Gara conceded after the defeat. "They talked it up but they walked the walk. Leicester were hugely dominant up front - their pack performance was terrific."

The first quarter saw Munster travel to Llanelli but any hopes the 2006 champions had that their reverse to the Tigers was merely a blip were dispelled by first-half tries at Stradey Park from Dafydd James and Gavin Thomas. The early scores proved pivotal and the Scarlets held for a 24-15 triumph.

Ireland's other surviving representative – Leinster – were also to fall at the first knockout hurdle after a 35-13 mauling by Wasps at Adams Park. The London side scored twice while skipper Lawrence Dallaglio was in the sin bin and Michael Cheika's side were out.

The real shock came in the Estadio Anoeta in San Sebastien where in-form Biarritz were the hosts and Northampton, heading for relegation from the Premiership, the visitors.

Not even ardent Saints supporters could have believed their side had a genuine chance of success but the home side produced an error-strewn display and when centre Robbie Kydd intercepted a loose pass in the second-half to score, the fairytale became a reality. The Saints were unlikely 7-6 winners and Heineken Cup semi-finalists.

"I think we were 100-1 in a two-horse race - quite big odds, but that's what sport is all about," said incredulous Saints coach Paul Grayson. "In the big picture, we didn't really think about getting a win because on paper, Biarritz should have won. But you never know when you are going to get something like an intercept to turn the game."

Leicester completed the semi-final line-up after beating Stade Francais 21-20 at Welford Road and the stage was set for the battle for a place at Twickenham.

Neither last-four clash however was to match the drama of the quarter-finals.

Llanelli were hoping to make it to the final after two previous semi-final defeats but it was not to prove third time lucky for the Welshmen against Leicester at the Walkers Stadium as fly-half Andy Goode took control of proceedings, scored 23 points and steered his team to a comfortable 33-17 win.

The second, all English semi-final was also to finish without great incident as Wasps ended Northampton's hopes at the Ricoh Arena. The Saints briefly threatened to stage another upset when they raced into a 13-0 first-half lead but Wasps kept their cool and scored 30 unanswered points, including a brace from wing Paul Sackey, to ease into the final.

"It was a jolt to go behind, but nobody panicked," Wasps director of rugby Ian McGeechan admitted. "Once we started to get our basics going and then built momentum, it was a case of just remaining patient and waiting for the opportunities to come."

The pre-match build up to the final was all about Leicester. Eight days before their date with Wasps, the Tigers had mercilessly mauled Gloucester to claim the Premiership title - while Wasps had failed to even make the play-offs - and many confidently predicted Howard's team would repeat the trick against the Londoners.

The reality was altogether different. From the first brutal exchanges, it was obvious the Wasps forwards would not go the same way of their Gloucester counterparts the previous week and their willingness to take on Leicester up front laid the platform for their hard-fought victory.

But it was Ibanez who was to provide the two, match-turning moments of brilliance that ultimately separated the two sides. The first came in the 14th minute when the Leicester pack ambled towards a lineout and Ibanez took the gilt-edged chance to throw short to Reddan, who scampered over unmolested.

The second came in the second quarter of the first half and proved the Tigers had yet to learn their lesson. Ibanez again took a quick throw-in at a lineout to Simon Shaw, who deftly returned the ball to his hooker and the Frenchman was in at the corner. Leicester had been sucker punched twice.

Alex King kept Wasps' noses in front with four penalties to three from Goode and the Londoners were home and dry to clinch their second European title in four seasons.

HEINEKEN CUP 2006–07 RESULTS

ROUND ONE

October 20, 2006

Reivers 35 **Overmach Parma** 3

London Irish 25 **Llanelli** 32

Ospreys 17 **Sale** 16

Agen 19 **Edinburgh** 17

October 21, 2006

Ulster 30 **Toulouse** 3

Bourgoin 5 **Cardiff** 13

Treviso 10 **Perpignan** 25

Leinster 37 **Gloucester** 20

Calvisano 10 **Stade Francais** 45

October 22, 2006

Wasps 19 **Castres** 13

Biarritz 22 **Northampton** 10

Leicester 19 **Munster** 21

ROUND TWO

October 27, 2006

Llanelli 21 **Ulster** 15

Castres 41 **Treviso** 22

Sale 67 **Calvisano** 11

October 28, 2006

Overmach Parma 7 **Biarritz** 50

Northampton 37 **Reivers** 13

Stade Francais 27 **Ospreys** 14

Perpignan 19 **Wasps** 12

Gloucester 26 **Agen** 32

Munster 41 **Bourgoin** 23

October 29, 2006

Edinburgh 25 **Leinster** 24

Toulouse 37 **London Irish** 17

Cardiff 17 **Leicester** 21

ROUND THREE

December 8, 2006	
Bourgoin 13 **Leicester** 28	
December 9, 2006	
Reivers 0 **Biarritz** 25	**Llanelli** 20 **Toulouse** 19
Calvisano 27 **Ospreys** 50	**London Irish** 29 **Ulster** 13
Overmach Parma 21 **Northampton** 68	**Castres** 36 **Perpignan** 28
Gloucester 38 **Edinburgh** 22	**Leinster** 26 **Agen** 10
December 10, 2006	
Cardiff 12 **Munster** 22	**Stade Francais** 27 **Sale** 16
Wasps 55 **Treviso** 0	

ROUND FOUR

December 15, 2006	
Ospreys 26 **Calvisano** 9	**Perpignan** 30 **Castres** 3
Ulster 29 **London Irish** 13	
December 16, 2006	
Toulouse 34 **Llanelli** 41	**Northampton** 36 **Overmach Parma** 0
Leicester 57 **Bourgoin** 3	**Agen** 13 **Leinster** 25
Treviso 5 **Wasps** 71	**Munster** 32 **Cardiff** 18
December 17, 2006	
Edinburgh 14 **Gloucester** 31	**Sale** 12 **Stade Francais** 6
Biarritz 27 **Reivers** 17	

ROUND FIVE

January 12, 2007	
Agen 26 **Gloucester** 18	**Biarritz** 45 **Overmach Parma** 3
January 13, 2007	
London Irish 24 **Toulouse** 26	**Leicester** 34 **Cardiff** 0
Ulster 11 **Llanelli** 35	**Wasps** 22 **Perpignan** 14
Calvisano 11 **Sale** 29	**Leinster** 49 **Edinburgh** 10
Treviso 21 **Castres** 40	
January 14, 2007	
Bourgoin 27 **Munster** 30	**Reivers** 19 **Northampton** 29
Ospreys 22 **Stade Francais** 22	

ROUND SIX

January 19, 2007	
Edinburgh 7 **Agen** 19	**Gloucester** 19 **Leinster** 13
January 20, 2007	
Castres 13 **Wasps** 16	**Stade Francais** 47 **Calvisano** 6
Perpignan 45 **Treviso** 25	**Cardiff** 27 **Bourgoin** 24
Sale 7 **Ospreys** 18	**Munster** 6 **Leicester** 13
January 21, 2007	
Llanelli 20 **London Irish** 16	**Northampton** 8 **Biarritz** 17
Toulouse 28 **Ulster** 13	**Overmach Parma** 45 **Reivers** 37

GROUP TABLES

POOL ONE

	P	W	D	L	For	A	Pts
Wasps	6	5	0	1	195	64	23
Perpignan	6	4	0	2	161	108	18
Castres	6	3	0	3	146	136	16
Treviso	6	0	0	6	83	277	0

POOL FOUR

	P	W	D	L	For	A	Pts
Leicester	6	5	0	1	172	60	23
Munster	6	5	0	1	152	112	23
Cardiff	6	2	0	4	87	138	9
Bourgoin	6	0	0	6	95	196	4

POOL TWO

	P	W	D	L	For	A	Pts
Leinster	6	4	0	2	174	97	21
Agen	6	4	0	2	119	119	17
Gloucester	6	3	0	3	152	144	15
Edinburgh	6	1	0	5	95	180	5

POOL FIVE

	P	W	D	L	For	A	Pts
Llanelli	6	6	0	0	169	120	27
Toulouse	6	3	0	3	147	145	17
Ulster	6	2	0	4	111	129	10
L Irish	6	1	0	5	124	157	9

POOL THREE

	P	W	D	L	For	A	Pts
Stade	6	4	1	1	174	80	22
Ospreys	6	4	1	1	147	108	20
Sale	6	3	0	3	147	90	15
Calvisano	6	0	0	6	74	264	0

POOL SIX

	P	W	D	L	For	A	Pts
Biarritz	6	6	0	0	186	45	29
Saints	6	4	0	2	188	92	20
Borders	6	1	0	5	121	166	6
Parma	6	1	0	5	79	271	5

QUARTER-FINALS

March 30, 2007	
Llanelli 24 **Munster** 15	
March 31, 2007	
Wasps 35 **Leinster** 13	
April 1, 2007	
Biarritz 6 **Northampton** 7	**Leicester** 21 **Stade Francais** 20

SEMI-FINALS

21 April, Walkers Stadium, Leicester

LEICESTER 33 (3G, 4PG)
LLANELLI 17 (2G, 1PG)

LEICESTER: G Murphy; T Varndell, D Hipkiss, D Gibson, A Tuilagi; A Goode, H Ellis; A Moreno, G Chuter, J White, L Deacon, B Kay, L Moody, S Jennings, M Corry (captain) Substitutions: B Deacon for Corry (temp 27 to 33 mins); S Vesty for Gibson (40 mins); L Cullen for Kay (64 mins); M Holford for Moreno (68 mins); B Deacon for Jennings (84 mins)

SCORERS *Tries:* Goode, Jennings, L Deacon Conversions: Goode (3) Penalty Goals: Goode (4)

LLANELLI: B Davies; D James, R King, G Evans, M Jones; S Jones, D Peel; I Thomas, M Rees, D Manu, V Cooper, S MacLeod, S Easterby (captain), G Thomas, A Popham Substitutions: I Afeaki for Cooper (76 mins); N Thomas for Popham (76 mins)

SCORERS *Tries:* M Jones, Rees Conversions: S Jones (2) Penalty Goal: S Jones

REFEREE A Rolland (Ireland)

YELLOW CARDS Murphy (13 mins), Moreno (45 mins), Manu (45 mins)

22 April, Ricoh Arena, Coventry

WASPS 30 (2G, 2PG, 2T)
NORTHAMPTON 13 (1G, 2PG)

WASPS: M van Gisbergen; P Sackey, F Waters, D Waldouck, T Voyce; D Cipriani, E Reddan; P Vickery, R Ibanez, P Bracken, S Shaw, T Palmer, J Worsley, T Rees, L Dallaglio (captain) Substitutions: N Adams for Bracken (47 mins); J Haskell for Dallaglio (58 mins); J Ward for Ibanez (68 mins); J Lewsey for Cipriani (72 mins); D Leo for Worsley (78 mins); M McMillan for Reddan (79 mins)

SCORERS *Tries:* Sackey (2), Haskell, Lewsey Conversions: van Gisbergen (2) Penalty Goals: van Gisbergen (2)

NORTHAMPTON: B Reihana (captain); S Lamont, J Clarke, R Kydd, B Cohen; C Spencer, M Robinson; T Smith, M Cortese, J Brooks, D Browne, C Short, P Tupai, B Lewitt, D Browne

Substitutions: D Gerard for D Browne (60 mins); C Labit for D Browne (61 mins); S Tonga'uiha for Smith (73 mins); P Diggin for Clarke (76 mins); J Howard for Robinson (78 mins)

SCORERS *Try:* Reihana Conversion: Reihana Penalty Goals: Reihana (2)

REFEREE A Lewis (Ireland)

YELLOW CARD Lewitt (49 mins)

FINAL

20 May, Twickenham, London

LEICESTER 9 (3PG)
WASPS 25 (4PG, 2T, 1DG)

LEICESTER: G Murphy; S Rabeni, D Hipkiss, D Gibson, A Tuilagi; A Goode, F Murphy; M Ayerza, G Chuter, J White, L Deacon, B Kay, L Moody, S Jennings, M Corry (captain) Substitutions: L Cullen for L Deacon (temp 46 to 51 mins); O Smith for Gibson (51 mins); Cullen for Kay (54 mins); I Humphreys for Goode (63 mins); A Moreno for Ayerza (74 mins); S Vesty for G Murphy (77 mins); J Buckland for Chuter (78 mins); B Deacon for Moody (78 mins)

SCORERS *Penalty Goals:* Goode (3)

WASPS: D Cipriani; P Sackey, F Waters, J Lewsey, T Voyce; A King, E Reddan; T French, R Ibanez, P Vickery, S Shaw, T Palmer, J Worsley, T Rees, L Dallaglio (captain) Substitutions: J Haskell for Dallaglio (51 mins); D Leo for Shaw (55 mins); J Ward for Leo (temp 64 to 70 mins); M van Gisbergen for King (74 mins); P Bracken for Vickery (75 mins); D Waldouck for Waters (77 mins); Ward for Ibanez (77 mins); M McMillan for Reddan (79 mins)

SCORERS *Tries:* Reddan, Ibanez Penalty Goals: King (4) Drop Goal: King

REFEREE A Lewis (Ireland)

FRENCH SIDES HIT BACK

Christopher Lee/Getty Images

Clermont captain, Aurelien Rougerie beats his team-mates to get his hands on the European Challenge Cup.

France finally reclaimed the Challenge Cup from the English for the first time in seven seasons as Clermont Auvergne beat Bath to triumph in Europe's second-tier competition, rugby's equivalent of the UEFA Cup.

The Premiership's dominance of the tournament dated back to 2001 when NEC Harlequins' victory over Narbonne had ushered in an era of six successive English victories but Clermont became the fifth French side to lift the trophy in May after outplaying Bath at the Twickenham Stoop.

The last Top 14 club to be crowned champions were Pau in 2000 and despite a late rally from Steve Meehan's west country side, Clermont were always in control of the final and eventually ran out worthy 22-16 winners.

"It was a game of real intensity and my players are very tired," said Clermont coach Vern Cotter, the New Zealander in his first season in France after leaving Bay of Plenty in the summer.

"All credit to Bath, they are a proud side who kept going to the final whistle. After we went 22-6 ahead, they simply ran harder and faster at us.

"They got a try and a penalty to bring themselves back into it, and I have to admit I had my eyes closed when they were driving that final lineout. But our defence was superb and I think we deserved it in the end."

For Bath, defeat marked a ninth season without silverware. The once all-conquering side last lifted a trophy in 1998 when they won the Heineken Cup and captain Steve Borthwick was clearly mindful of the club's barren run as he spoke in the immediate aftermath of the Clermont defeat.

"We've got a group of players who are incredibly ambitious," Borthwick said. "What we need to see over the summer is Bath matching the players' ambition. The players are asking why we are not making signings. We see other clubs with fantastic training facilities, but where are ours? Where is the investment in our club?"

Clermont's progress from the group stages, which began in October, was relatively serene. Drawn in Group Five alongside Worcester, Italian side Viadana and Top 14 rivals Albi, Cotter's side were unbeaten in their six qualifying games, accumulating four bonus points in the process to finish nine points clear of the second-placed Warriors.

Bath's route to the final began in Group Four and pitted them against Harlequins, Connacht and Montpellier. The Irish and French challenge failed to materialise and Bath strolled into the last eight courtesy of crucial home and away victories over Harlequins.

The most keenly-contested battle for a quarter-final place came in Group One as the Dragons and Bristol slugged it out. Bucharest and Bayonne offered little resistance to either team and although Bristol beat the Welshmen 11-7 at the Memorial Stadium, the Dragons returned the favour 17-11 at Rodney Parade. Both sides won their final group games to finish level on points but it was the Principality side who went through as winners after scoring one more try in the head-to-head meeting between the two clubs.

"It wasn't a great performance and we were staring down the

barrel," said Dragons coach Paul Turner after his side won 32-15 in Bayonne to secure the bonus point they needed. "But we turned it around and won comfortably at the end. The boys don't like to do things easily."

There was, however, some consolation for Bristol who still joined the five group winners in the quarter-finals as one of the three best runners-up.

Group Two was also a closely-contested affair as Saracens and Glasgow fought a tight Anglo-Scottish battle for top spot. The two sides met at Vicarage Road in the opening round of games with the London team narrowly claiming the spoils (28-23) but home and away victories for both clubs against Narbonne and Parma set up a mouth-watering final group game clash at Hughenden.

Atrocious conditions in Glasgow dashed any hopes of a free-flowing game but there was drama aplenty as the two teams fought out a 6-6 draw courtesy of two penalties apiece from Dan Parks and Glen Jackson. The result confirmed Saracens as group winners but there was also cause for celebration for the Warriors, who went through as runners-up.

"It doesn't matter who we play, we're in the quarter-finals," said Glasgow coach Sean Lineen. "It wasn't pretty, there were mistakes. I thought the set-piece was unbelievable and our forward pack really stood up to them, so I'm very proud."

In Group Three it was a two-horse race for qualification as Brive, the 1997 Heineken Cup champions, and Newcastle vied for top spot. The crucial fixture proved to be the Falcons visit to the Parc Municipal, which the French side won 41-12 and although the Falcons gained revenge (24-17) in the return game, it was Brive who won the group with Newcastle also progressing.

The quarter-finals saw handsome victories for Bath over Bristol (51-12) and the Dragons over Brive (39-17) while Newcastle pushed Clermont all the way at the Stade Marcel Michelin before going down 24-19. Glasgow were also close to pulling off a surprise away win against Saracens at Vicarage Road but paid the price for a poor first-half display and eventually lost 23-19.

"I have to give Glasgow credit," said Saracens director of rugby Alan Gaffney. "They played some exceptional rugby and could have stolen the game. We went 13-0 in front and thought we were in a sevens game. The more we opened the game up, the more it suited Glasgow. It took a lot to hold out."

The first of the semi-finals in April pitted Clermont at home to the Dragons with the French side firm favourites to make it to the final. The early exchanges, however, suggested an upset could be on the cards when Aled Brew crashed over for Turner's team but the home side recovered and the writing was on the wall when captain Aurelien Rougerie crossed. The try was followed by two more from Clermont and although the Dragons had scored five tries of their own by the final whistle, the Frenchman had six and a 46-29 victory.

"We knew it would be tough and we gave our all, but the first 20 minutes let us down," Turner said. "With such a small squad it's hard for us and that was exposed at times out there against a strong French side."

There was significantly more drama in the second semi-final between Saracens and Bath at the Vicarage Road and the West Country side made it through to face Clermont by the skin of their teeth.

The visitors started the stronger leading 28-18 at half-time but rallied after the break with two Dan Scarbrough tries to leave themselves just one point adrift. Bath, however, clung on and when the final whistle blew they were 31-30 victors.

"It was a show of desire at wanting to be in the final," admitted coach Meehan. "Saracens executed very well and put us under a lot of pressure but the guys scrambled and worked really hard for each other. It was one of those games where defence wins you matches."

The final at the Stoop in May was expected to go Clermont's way after their performances earlier in the tournament and Bath's indifferent Premiership form

The first-half was a nervous one as both sides probed and parried and after 40 minutes, Bath enjoyed a slender 6-3 advantage thanks to two Olly Barkley penalties to one from Clermont fly-half Brock James.

But it was a significantly different story in the second period as the Frenchmen suddenly cut loose and scored three tries from Julien Malzieu, Tony Marsh and James in the space of 18 minutes to transform the complexion of the match.

Bath gave themselves hope when Joe Maddock scored a dazzling solo try on 63 minutes, which Barkley converted, to cut their arrears to 22-13 but despite another penalty and some agonising near-misses, they could not reel Clermont back in and the Challenge Cup was on its way to France.

We were probably lucky to come away with a win, to be honest," said Clermont's New Zealand centre Marsh. "There was desperate defending there at the end."

Defeat for Bath was a double blow because it also cost the club a place in the Heineken Cup next season.

"I feel for the players," admitted Meehan. "They gave it everything in the competition and I am very disappointed for them. We have quality players and we showed that today. I think you could expect Bath to up their game next season."

CHALLENGE CUP RESULTS

ROUND ONE	
Connacht 18 **Harlequins** 19	**Montauban** 13 **Brive** 26
Dragons 50 **Bayonne** 3	**Montpellier** 14 **Bath** 21
Newcastle 50 **Padova** 5	**Parma** 16 **Narbonne** 19
Bucharest 3 **Bristol** 27	**Worcester** 25 **Viadana** 7
Albi 21 **Auvergne** 30	**Saracens** 28 **Glasgow** 23
ROUND TWO	
Glasgow 69 **Parma** 7	**Bristol** 11 **Dragons** 7
Viadana 26 **Albi** 13	**Bucharest** 32 **Bayonne** 27
Bath 21 **Connacht** 19	**Auvergne** 29 **Worcester** 23
Brive 41 **Newcastle** 12	**Harlequins** 57 **Montpellier** 10
Padova 5 **Montauban** 53	**Narbonne** 20 **Saracens** 37
ROUND THREE	
Connacht 26 **Montpellier** 13	**Montauban** 16 **Newcastle** 10
Bayonne 17 **Bristol** 38	**Dragons** 66 **Bucharest** 10
Glasgow 51 **Narbonne** 7	**Brive** 78 **Padova** 18
Harlequins 18 **Bath** 24	**Worcester** 29 **Albi** 0
Viadana 9 **Auvergne** 14	**Saracens** 71 **Parma** 16
ROUND FOUR	
Montpellier 35 **Connacht** 22	**Bristol** 48 **Bayonne** 6
Bucharest 29 **Dragons** 39	**Bath** 20 **Harlequins** 14
Parma 16 **Saracens** 36	**Auvergne** 57 **Viadana** 29
Padova 6 **Brive** 48	**Albi** 12 **Worcester** 23
Narbonne 7 **Glasgow** 8	**Newcastle** 35 **Montauban** 0
ROUND FIVE	
Connacht 24 **Bath** 36	**Montauban** 19 **Padova** 7
Bayonne 38 **Bucharest** 31	**Dragons** 17 **Bristol** 11
Montpellier 27 **Harlequins** 37	**Newcastle** 24 **Brive** 17
Parma 17 **Glasgow** 47	**Worcester** 22 **Auvergne** 35
Albi 17 **Viadana** 27	**Saracens** 47 **Narbonne** 20
ROUND SIX	
Bristol 33 **Bucharest** 19	**Glasgow** 6 **Saracens** 6
Bayonne 15 **Dragons** 32	**Bath** 42 **Montpellier** 17
Harlequins 26 **Connacht** 10	**Auvergne** 45 **Albi** 3
Brive 15 **Montauban** 6	**Padova** 6 **Newcastle** 50
Viadana 16 **Worcester** 19	**Narbonne** 54 **Parma** 12

FINAL GROUP TABLES

GROUP ONE

	P	W	D	L	For	A	BP	Pts
Dragons	6	5	0	1	208	79	5	25
Bristol	6	5	0	1	168	69	5	25
Bucuresti	6	1	0	5	124	230	4	8
Bayonne	6	1	0	5	106	228	3	7

GROUP TWO

	P	W	D	L	For	A	BP	Pts
Saracens	6	5	1	0	225	101	4	26
Glasgow	6	4	1	1	204	72	4	22
Narbonne	6	2	0	4	127	171	2	10
Parma	6	0	0	6	84	296	1	1

GROUP THREE

	P	W	D	L	For	A	BP	Pts
Brive	6	5	0	1	225	79	4	24
Newcastle	6	4	0	2	181	85	5	21
Montauban	6	3	0	3	107	98	1	13
Petrarca	6	0	0	6	47	298	0	0

GROUP FOUR

	P	W	D	L	For	A	BP	Pts
Bath	6	6	0	0	164	106	2	26
Harlequins	6	4	0	2	171	109	5	21
Connacht	6	1	0	5	119	150	4	8
Montpellier	6	1	0	5	116	205	1	5

GROUP FIVE

	P	W	D	L	For	A	BP	Pts
Clermont	6	6	0	0	210	107	4	28
Worcester	6	4	0	2	141	99	3	19
Viadanna	6	2	0	4	114	145	3	11
Albi	6	0	0	6	66	180	0	0

QUARTER-FINALS

30 March, 2007	
Auvergne 24 **Newcastle** 19	
31 March, 2007	
Bath 51 **Bristol** 12	**Dragons** 39 **Brive** 17
1 April, 2007	
Saracens 23 **Glasgow** 19	

SEMI-FINALS

21 April, Stade Marcel Michelin, Clermont-Ferrand

CLERMONT AUVERGNE 46 (5G, 2PG, 1T) THE DRAGONS 29 (3G, 3T)

CLERMONT AUVERGNE: A Peclier; A Rougerie (captain), G Esterhuizen, T Marsh, V Delasau; B James, P Mignoni; T Domingo, B Miguel, D Zirakashvili, D Barrier, T Privat, M Dieude, M Etien, G Longo Substitutions: A Floch for Peclier (40 mins); M Scelzo for Domingo (44 mins); J Cudmore for Barrier (48 mins); E Vermeulen for Dieude (51 mins); R Chanal for Marsh (55 mins); A Pic for Mignoni (73 mins)

Yellow card: Etien (37 mins)

SCORERS *Tries*: Rougerie, Longo, Domingo, Marsh, Miguel, Mignoni Conversions: James (5) Penalty Goals: James (2)

Dragons: K Morgan (captain); G Wyatt, P Emerick, N Brew, A Brew; C Sweeney, G Cooper; A Black, S Jones, R Thomas, I Gough, L Charteris, J Bearman, J Ringer, M Owen Substitutions: P Dollman for N Brew (37 mins); B Daly for Jones (56 mins); A Hall for Gough (63 mins); N Fitisemanu for Bearman (68 mins); A Walker for Cooper (71 mins); A Thomas for Sweeney (71 mins); J Corsi for R Thomas (75 mins)

YELLOW CARD: Ringer (23 mins), Scorers Tries: A Brew (2), Black, Gough, Dollman Conversions: Sweeney (2)

REFEREE D Pearson (England)

22 April, Vicarage Road, Watford

SARACENS 30 (2G, 2PG, 2T)
BATH 31 (4G, 1PG)

SARACENS: T Castaignede; D Scarbrough, K Sorrell, A Farrell, R Penney; G Jackson, N de Kock; N Lloyd, S Byrne, C Visagie, H Vyvyan, S Raiwalui (captain), K Chesney, R Hill, B Skirving Substitutions: A Dickens for de Kock (40 mins); C Johnston for Visagie (47 mins); D Seymour for Hill (57 mins); I Fullarton for Raiwalui (65 mins); M Cairns for Byrne (67 mins); Visagie for Lloyd (79 mins)

SCORERS *Tries* Penney (2), Scarbrough (2) Conversions Jackson (2) Penalties: Jackson (2)

Bath: J Maddock; T Cheeseman, E Fuimaono-Sapolu, O Barkley, D Bory; S Berne, N Walshe; D Barnes, L Mears, M Stevens, S Borthwick (captain), D Grewcock, A Beattie, M Lipman, I Feau'nati Substitutions: P Short for Beattie (67 mins); P Dixon for Mears (71 mins); C Goodman for Feau'nati (71 mins); C Walker for Maddock (79 mins)

SCORERS *Tries*: Beattie, Grewcock, Bory, Berne Conversions: Barkley (4) Penalty Goals: Barkley

Referee N Owens (Wales)

FINAL

19 May, Twickenham Stoop, London

CLERMONT AUVERGNE 22 (2G, 1PG, 1T)
BATH 16 (1G, 3PG)

CLERMONT AUVERGNE: A Floch; A Rougerie (captain), G Esterhuizen, T Marsh, J Malzieu; B James, P Mignoni; L Emmanuelli, M Ledesma, M Scelzo, J Cudmore, T Privat, M Dieude, S Broomhall, E Vermeulen Substitutions: S Baikeinuku for Marsh (temp 2 to 13 mins); L Jacquet for Privat (47 mins); G Longo for Dieude (51 mins); Baikeinuku for Esterhuizen (60 mins); B Miguel for Ledesma (64 mins); G Shvelidze for Scelzo (67 mins)

SCORERS *Tries*: Malzieu, Marsh, James Conversions: James (2) Penalty Goal: James

BATH: N Abendanon; J Maddock, E Fuimaono-Sapolu, O Barkley, D Bory; S Berne, N Walshe; D Barnes, L Mears, M Stevens, S Borthwick (captain), D Grewcock, A Beattie, M Lipman, I Feaunati Substitutions: T Cheeseman for Fuimaono-Sapolu (temp 41 to 52 mins); C Malone for Bory (45 mins); A Williams for Walshe (60 mins); J Scaysbrook for Feaunati (60 mins); P Dixon for Mears (62 mins); P Short for Beattie (62 mins), Cheeseman for Berne (65 mins)

SCORERS *Try:* Maddock Conversion: Barkley Penalty Goals: Barkley (3)

REFEREE N Owens (Wales)

LEICESTER'S CUP RUNNETH OVER

Dave Rogers/Getty Images

Yes! The Tigers' five-year wait is over.

The five barren years in which Leicester had failed to get their hands on a single piece of silverware were finally consigned to history as the Tigers lifted the inaugural EDF Energy Cup at Twickenham and in the process completed the first instalment of what would have been an unprecedented trophy treble.

The Tigers had last tasted success in 2002 when they claimed their second successive Heineken Cup but Pat Howard's side finally returned to winning ways in a classic EDF final against the Ospreys that had threatened to degenerate into a Leicester procession but witnessed a dramatic Welsh fightback and a nerve-jangling finish.

The Englishmen found themselves 28 points to six to the good at

Twickenham inside the first half hour and apparently heading for a handsome victory. But the Ospreys steeled themselves after the break and their fluid, counter-attacking brand of rugby almost saw them snatch victory from the jaws of defeat. The Tigers eventually clung on for a 41–35 win to emulate Wasps – 26–10 victors over Llanelli in the final the previous season – and claim Anglo-Welsh bragging rights.

"Fair play to Ospreys, that was a hell of a comeback," admitted Leicester captain Martin Corry. "We felt we had them, grinding them down, but we spilled the ball, they scored from 80 metres and made it a hell of a game.

"We are disappointed we let the lead slip but we got the trophy at the end and that is what counts. Trophies matter, of course they do. Year on year we judge ourselves on that, nothing else. We have been in a few finals in the last few years and never clinched it, so hopefully this is the start for us."

For the Ospreys, it was a deeply disappointing climax to a competition they were unbeaten in until their Twickenham reverse but took some solace from a second-half revival which enthralled the 60,000 strong crowd in London.

"We weren't in the game in the first half and that was through our own errors, two or three from myself," said former All Blacks scrum-half Justin Marshall.

"Sometimes you just seem to slip deeper into a hole the harder you try. But in the second half we showed we deserved to be here. We put on a show, made a game of it and we can be proud of our efforts."

The two Twickenham protagonists enjoyed contrasting passages through to the final as the four, four-team groups – featuring all 12 Guinness Premiership sides and the four professional Welsh outfits – entered the fray in September.

Lyn Jones' Ospreys were the first in action, entertaining Gloucester at the Liberty Stadium. The Cherry and Whites were unbeaten in the Premiership but came badly unstuck in the Principality as the home side ran in six tries, including a brace from Sonny Parker, to wrap up a commanding 49–19 victory and a bonus point.

Cardiff followed the Ospreys' lead in the their own high-profile Anglo-Welsh skirmish with a 36–20 victory over the holders Wasps at the Arms Park. Locked at 17– 17 at the break, the Blues pulled clear in the second-half courtesy of a try from wing Mosese Luveitasau and a faultless kicking display from full-back Ben Blair to get their campaign off to a winning start.

"There are very few games whereby you have an opportunity to change people's perception of you," said Cardiff coach Dai Young. "We have had a lot of lean years, but I wanted the players to make a statement today that we are on our way back."

The English challenge was led by Leicester – 41–17 victors over the Dragons at Welford Road – and Premiership champions Sale, who were too strong for Newcastle (28–5) at Edgeley Park.

The second round of matches saw all four group leaders victorious again. Cardiff scored an impressive 40–29 win at Saracens, the Ospreys returned from the West Country with 31–24 win over Bath under their belts while the Tigers travelled to Worcester to record a 35–20 triumph.

Sale, however, were less convincing. The Sharks led 20–15 at half-time in their clash with Harlequins at the Stoop and although the lead changed hands twice in the second period, the home side seemed to have snatched the game with Tom Williams' injury-time try. Unfortunately for Quins, Adrian Jarvis missed the conversion to take the spoils and Sale emerged 28–27 winners.

"We've come here and changed a lot of players, a lot of young kids played and we looked OK when we had the ball," said Sharks director of rugby Philippe Saint-Andre. "When you change nine or 10 players it's difficult and the defence was sometimes shaky, but I'm pleased with the character of my team. I can't say it was a very good performance but I was very pleased with the young guys. There were a lot of positive things today."

The final round of group games in December saw comfortable wins for the Ospreys, Cardiff and Sale but Leicester suffered a surprise 18–5 reverse against Northampton at Franklin's Gardens after Pat Howard decided to blood a number of young players. Worcester's win over the Dragons could have threatened the Tigers' progress to the semi-finals but Leicester's two bonus points to the Warriors' none ensured their place in the knockout stage.

The stage was set for the semi-finals and, perhaps fittingly, two games that would ensure the Anglo-Welsh competition would feature an Anglo-Welsh final as the Ospreys tackled Cardiff and Sale faced Leicester.

The first game between the Sharks and the Tigers – a rerun of last season's Guinness Premiership final that Sale won convincingly – may have failed to live up to pre-match expectations in the Millennium Stadium but Leicester supporters were hardly complaining as their side barged their way to a 29–19 win.

Although both sides crossed the line twice in Cardiff, crucially it was the Tigers who scored first through the impressive Alesana Tuilagi and they never looked back. Ignacio Fernandez Lobbe's try for Sale 10 minutes from time may have frayed a few Tigers nerves but in truth Leicester were always in command and worthy winners.

"We are on course for the treble and that is our goal," said Pat Howard. "It's not easy but we are going to try and fight on all three fronts because we are a big club and we want to have goals that are very high. That is where we stand."

The second, all Welsh semi-final was a more one-side affair as the Ospreys swept aside Cardiff's challenge. It may have been a more keenly fought contest had the Blues not seen three players – Scott Morgan, Deiniol Jones and Robert Sidoli – all banished to the sin bin in a fiery first half but the damage was done and the Ospreys crossed twice through Sonny Parker and Lee Byrne while Cardiff were below strength. James Hook added 17 points with the boot and the Blues were beaten 27–10 to set up an Ospreys showdown with Leicester.

"We played 160 minutes of rugby against them [Leicester] last season, and I thought we were the better team for about 140 of those minutes," said Lyn Jones after the game. "But Leicester won both games, and they are not in the top two of the Premiership for nothing.

"They also want to play, and they are a pretty positive side, so we might have a cracker of a final on our hands at Twickenham."

The supporters who made the journey to London for the final in April must have initially been sceptical about Jones' predictions. Two early penalties from Hook proved to be a false dawn for the Welshmen as the Tigers embarked on a rampant scoring spree that seemed to have ended the match as a meaningful contest.

Tom Varndell's 12th minute try was the catalyst and Tom Croft, Ben Kay and Tuilagi all followed his lead to establish a 28–9 lead for the Tigers at half-time.

The Ospreys were in real danger of a terrible mauling but Jones' rallied his troops in the dressing room and they emerged for the second-half with a real sense of purpose. Lee Byrne began the fightback and when Shane Williams scored twice, an unlikely escape act genuinely looked on the cards as the Twickenham crowd revelled in the tension and drama.

But just as the Ospreys appeared to have taken the upper hand, Leicester hit back with a second score from Varndell and although the Welsh side kept in touch with a late try from Nikki Walker, it was just too little too late. The Tigers had survived and secured the first part of what they hoped would be a historic domestic and European hat-trick.

"That was an amazing game and for us it was so important to lift the trophy, to get the monkey off our backs after five empty years," said a relieved Howard. "For the neutral it was a fantastic game. For us it was a bit nail biting at the end. I am extremely happy with the victory."

GROUP STANDINGS

POOL A

	P	W	D	L	F	A	BP	Pts
Ospreys	3	3	0	0	114	46	2	14
Gloucester	3	2	0	1	112	86	2	10
Bristol	3	1	0	2	50	112	0	4
Bath	3	0	0	3	51	83	2	2

POOL C

	P	W	D	L	F	A	BP	Pts
Sale	3	3	0	0	77	37	0	12
Newcastle	3	2	0	1	51	55	0	8
Llanelli	3	1	0	2	40	53	1	5
Harlequins	3	0	0	3	52	75	3	3

POOL B

	P	W	D	L	F	A	BP	Pts
Cardiff	3	3	0	0	107	56	1	13
Irish	3	1	0	2	56	78	1	5
Saracens	3	1	0	2	79	91	0	4
Wasps	3	1	0	2	58	75	0	4

POOL D

	P	W	D	L	F	A	BP	Pts
Leicester	3	2	0	1	81	55	2	10
Worcester	3	2	0	1	67	57	0	8
Dragons	3	1	0	2	53	71	0	4
Saints	3	1	0	2	37	55	0	4

SEMI-FINALS

24 March, Millennium Stadium, Cardiff

Sale 19 (3PG, 2T) Leicester 29 (2G, 5PG)

SALE: J Laharrague; J Robinson (captain), E Seveali'i, C Bell, O Ripol; D Larrechea, R Wigglesworth; A Sheridan, S Bruno, S Turner, C Jones, D Schofield, J Fernandez-Lobbe, S Chabal, M Lund Substitutions: L Thomas for Larrechea (43 mins); I Fernandez-Lobbe for Schofield (59 mins); B Evans for Sheridan (65 mins); B Foden for Wigglesworth (69 mins); S Cox for Chabal (69 mins); C Mayor for Bell (70 mins); A Titterrell for Bruno (74 mins)

SCORERS *Tries*: Chabal, I Fernandez-Lobbe *Penalty Goals*: Larrechea, Thomas (2)

LEICESTER: G Murphy; T Varndell, D Hipkiss, D Gibson, A Tuilagi; P Burke, H Ellis; M Ayerza, G Chuter, M Holford, L Deacon, B Kay, S Jennings, M Corry (captain); L Moody Substitutions: B Deacon for Corry (24 mins); A Moreno for Holford (46 mins); A Goode for Burke (47 mins); S Rabeni for Varndell (62 mins); F Murphy for Ellis (68 mins)

SCORERS *Tries*: Tuilagi, Hipkiss *Conversions*: Goode (2) *Penalty Goals*: Burke (2), Goode (3)

REFEREE N Owens (Wales)

YELLOW CARD Sheridan (37 mins), Moody (61 mins)

24 March, Millennium Stadium, Cardiff

OSPREYS 27 (1G, 4PG, 1T, 1DG)
CARDIFF BLUES 10 (1G, 1PG)

OSPREYS: L Byrne; S Williams, S Parker, A Bishop, N Walker; J Hook, J Marshall; D Jones (captain), H Bennett, A Jones, B Cockbain, AW Jones, R Jones, F Tiatia, J Thomas Substitutions: B Williams for Bennett (temp 12 to 14 mins); R Pugh for Tiatia (72 mins); B Williams for Bennett (73 mins); P James for A Jones (75 mins); (S Terblanche for Byrne (78 mins); S Connor for Hook (78 mins); J Spice for Marshall (78 mins)

SCORERS *Tries*: Parker, Byrne *Conversion*: Hook *Penalty Goals*: Hook (4) *Drop Goal*: Hook

CARDIFF BLUES: B Blair; T James, J Robinson, M Stcherbina, C Czekaj; N Robinson, M Phillips; T Filise, R Thomas, G Powell, D Jones, R Sidoli, S Morgan, X Rush (captain), M Williams Substitutions: B Davies for Jones (57 mins); M Lewis for Morgan (68 mins); G Williams for Thomas (71 mins); N MacLeod for Robinson (73 mins); S Roberts for Filise (75 mins)

SCORERS *Try*: Blair *Conversion*: Blair *Penalty Goal*: Blair

REFEREE W Barnes (England)

YELLOW CARDS Morgan (21 mins), D Jones (29 mins), Sidoli (38 mins)

FINAL

15 April, Twickenham, London

LEICESTER 41 (5G, 2PG)
OSPREYS 35 (3G, 3PG, 1T)

LEICESTER: S Vesty; T Varndell, D Hipkiss, D Gibson, A Tuilagi; P Burke, H Ellis; M Castrogiovanni, G Chuter, J White, L Cullen, B Kay, T Croft, S Jennings, M Corry (captain) Substitutions: A Goode for Burke (40 mins); F Murphy for Ellis (temp 42 to 51 mins); B Deacon for Croft (51 mins); L Deacon for Cullen (67 mins); A Moreno for Castrogiovanni (78 mins)

SCORERS *Tries*: Varndell (2), Croft, Kay, Tuilagi *Conversions*: Burke (4), Goode *Penalty Goals*: Goode (2)

OSPREYS: L Byrne; S Williams, S Parker, A Bishop, N Walker; J Hook, J Marshall; D Jones (captain), H Bennett, A Jones, B Cockbain, A W Jones, R Jones, J Thomas, F Tiatia Substitutions: P James for A Jones (57 mins); R Pugh for Tiatia (71 mins); B Williams for Bennett (71 mins); S Terblanche for Byrne (74 mins); J Spice for Marshall (74 mins); S Connor for Bishop (80 mins); M Powell for Cockbain (80 mins)

SCORERS *Tries*: Byrne, Williams (2), Walker *Conversions*: Hook (3) *Penalty Goals*: Hook (3)

REFEREE A Lewis (Ireland)

BOKS BREAK THE DOMINATION

By John Eales

Getty Images

The Bulls celebrate becoming Super 14 champions.

The second season of Super 14 rugby was a fascinating one that had much to recommend it, not least a superb final that kept everyone guessing until the last. From my own Australian perspective, there were more disappointments than triumphs over the four months of the tournament but, looking at it from a neutral point of view, I thought it was a great advert overall for southern hemisphere rugby.

There's no argument that the Bulls' dramatic victory in the final over the Sharks, making them South Africa's first ever Super 12 or 14 winners, gave the competition a shot in the arm. I don't go along with the argument that New Zealand's dominance over the years in the shape of the Crusaders and the Blues has been necessarily bad for the tournament but conversely I do think the Bulls' first success will give the Super 14 extra spice next season and beyond. It never hurts to see the silverware shared around.

But you can't please all of the people all of the time and the competition did once again have its detractors. Not for the first time, the chief criticism was the perception that defences have become too strong and the average number of points per game was somehow below par or not good enough.

I've argued before that the theory that a deluge of points in some way equates to a good game, even a good spectacle, is flawed. I accept that the 2007 Super 14 had some pretty uninspiring clashes but I still can't see how fewer tries automatically equates with poor rugby. I thought this year some of the game between the top sides – the Bulls, the Sharks, the Crusaders and the Blues – were top notch encounters that had a bit of everything for everybody. I'm sure I'm not the only one who can appreciate a game featuring some world class tactical kicking, even if that means ambitious, attacking rugby might be at a premium in that particular match. No-one wants to see kicking all game, every game but just like a strong defence or an astute territorial game, it has its place.

Of course, the spectre of the World Cup loomed large on the horizon for Super 14 spectators and players alike. It has become such a big tournament that I think that these days it is inevitable that it will cast a shadow and it's not only the Super 14 that has to try and go about its business in a World Cup year. I'm sure it was exactly the same for the Six Nations in 2007, with players, fans and those who write about the game always having one eye on how events would unfold in September and October.

I don't agree with the argument that the World Cup particularly detracted from the Super 14. Yes, it's on peoples' minds but it's ridiculous to suggest the players out on the pitch are thinking about how hard to go into a tackle during the heat of a match, worrying about making this or that World Cup squad.

What did happen was the decision by New Zealand – or more accurately Graham Henry – to hold back the All Blacks' top 22 players for the first half of the tournament. It was a move that angered some people but even though I agree it did undermine the competition somewhat, I don't think you can blame Henry. His priority is to the New Zealand team and not the Super 14 and from a purely pragmatic point of view, it was definitely the right decision.

Ironically, the decision didn't actually have the results many people predicted. The argument went that the Kiwi sides, particularly the Crusaders, would suffer without their star players in the first half of the competition and then come storming back once the big names returned.

The opposite was true. The Crusaders were in touch at the top of the table from the start of the campaign and then welcomed back the big boys like Richie McCaw, Dan Carter, Chris Jack, Leon MacDonald and Reuben Thorne, yet they still lost two of their last three games. Similarly, the Blues were happy to see their All Black contingent return for the second phase of the tournament and lost three of their last four. Both sides' late slip-ups cost them home advantage in the semi-finals and arguably a place in the final.

Hindsight is a wonderful thing but I really wasn't that surprised to see some of the rested Kiwis fail to hit the ground running. It's tempting to believe world class players can have three months good training but no competitive games and then simply come back into the side and pick up where they left off. Rugby is as much about rhythm, grooving your technique week after week, as strength, fitness and even innate talent and it was always going to be a big ask for the rested Kiwis to just sail back into their respective sides and suddenly set the world alight.

Looking at the Super 14 on a country-by-country basis and starting with South Africa, it was obviously a great year and a long time coming. Although it was the Bulls who ultimately took the plaudits, I thought the standard of the five South African sides improved across the board, particularly on the road, which has been their traditional Achilles Heel. In the past, the South Africans have failed to add a dimension to their acknowledged brute power but this year I thought all their teams executed the basics very well and exploited the blistering speed some of them have out wide.

As the dramatic final proved, there was very little to choose between the Sharks and the Bulls right until the death. It was an edge-of-your-seat match that twisted and turned and in the end it took a dramatic late intervention from Bryan Habana, who is without doubt the fastest man I have seen on a rugby pitch for many years, to separate them. I'm sure the Sharks were dismayed to lose in that way but they can console themselves with the knowledge that in JP Pietersen and Francois Steyn, they have two of the most exciting young backs in world rugby.

As I said at the start, it was a disappointing season for the Australians. Some would argue the introduction of the fourth franchise – the Force – in 2006 has weakened the overall challenge but I would counter with 'no pain, no gain'. The new team has given rugby union a platform in

Western Australia and that can only be good for the future. The Force finished a creditable seventh in only their second season in the competition and the big-name signings of Matt Giteau and Drew Mitchell both came off. I think the management had even higher ambitions at the start of the season but it was still an encouraging year.

The Brumbies, boasting the experience of George Gregan, Stephen Larkham and Stirling Mortlock, will have been disappointed not to have made the semi-finals for a third year running but the emergence of youngster Adam Ashley-Cooper was a positive. The Reds finished bottom of the pile, which was a fair reflection of the performances, but they suffered more than most with injuries and probably didn't have enough old heads to guide some exciting youngsters like Quade Cooper and Berrick Barnes. The Waratahs also had more than fair share of injuries but wing Lachlan Turner's performances were certainly a positive.

From a New Zealand perspective, the tournament must have been a disappointment by their own high standards and like many, I was surprised that the Crusaders and the Blues finished so poorly. For the Crusaders, Stephen Brett enhanced his reputation deputising for Dan Carter but a first ever semi-final loss for the side will have been a shock to the system.

The Hurricanes were again something of an enigma, capable of threatening the best teams one week and then pretty average the next but I was still a little surprised not to see them challenging for a top four finish.

The Highlanders were a team without stars, concentrating on developing their young talent and they relied heavily on their front five while the Chiefs probably suffered more than most at the start with the withdrawal of their All Black contingent. They lost a lot of games by small margins and I felt they were perhaps unlucky not to make the top four. The Blues started the tournament on fire but stumbled towards the end and paid a heavy price, losing to the Sharks in the semi-final.

Overall, the 2007 Super 14 won't down go as a vintage year but it will be remembered as the year the Bulls finally broke South Africa's duck. I think the competition is in rude health, despite some arguments to the contrary, and it is still providing the best young players with a platform to showcase their talents, which is crucial.

SUPER 14 2007 RESULTS

February 2: **Blues** 34 **Crusaders** 25, **Force** 7 **Highlanders** 8, **Lions** 16 **Waratahs** 25. February 3: **Chiefs** 15 **Brumbies** 21, **Reds** 25 **Hurricanes** 16, **Sharks** 17 **Bulls** 3, **Cheetahs** 27 **Stormers** 9. February 9: **Chiefs** 32 **Hurricanes** 39, **Stormers** 3 **Force** 22, **Sharks** 22 **Waratahs** 9. February 10: **Crusaders** 33 **Reds** 22, **Brumbies** 15 **Blues** 17, **Bulls** 24 **Cheetahs** 20, **Lions** 11 **Highlanders** 6. February 16: **Stormers** 21 **Chiefs** 16, **Bulls** 27 **Force** 30. February 17: **Reds** 3 **Brumbies** 6, **Hurricanes** 23 **Blues** 22, **Cheetahs** 30 **Waratahs** 26, **Lions** 9 **Crusaders** 3, **Sharks** 23 **Highlanders** 16. February 23: **Hurricanes** 11 **Brumbies** 10. February 24: **Highlanders** 35 **Stormers** 24, **Blues** 38 **Reds** 13, **Force** 24 **Lions** 25, **Bulls** 30 **Chiefs** 27, **Cheetahs** 28 **Crusaders** 49. March 2: **Blues** 28 **Highlanders** 9, **Waratahs** 16 **Force** 16, **Cheetahs** 22 **Chiefs** 22. March 3: **Hurricanes** 17 **Stormers** 30, **Brumbies** 7 **Bulls** 19, **Reds** 20 **Lions** 26, **Sharks** 27 **Crusaders** 26. March 9: **Highlanders** 33 **Reds** 17, **Brumbies** 26 **Stormers** 13, **Force** 18 **Hurricanes** 17. March 10: **Blues** 41 **Lions** 14, **Waratahs** 19 **Bulls** 32, **Cheetahs** 14 **Sharks** 30. March 16: **Chiefs** 34 **Lions** 7, **Force** 38 **Reds** 3. March 17: **Crusaders** 32 **Bulls** 10, **Waratahs** 10 **Stormers** 16, **Cheetahs** 38 **Brumbies** 20, **Sharks** 27 **Hurricanes** 14. March 23: **Blues** 34 **Waratahs** 6. March 24: **Highlanders** 13 **Bulls** 22, **Crusaders** 36 **Stormers** 11, **Reds** 19 **Chiefs** 21, **Sharks** 10 **Brumbies** 21, **Lions** 30 **Hurricanes** 7. March 30: **Highlanders** 21 **Cheetahs** 17, **Force** 22 **Sharks** 12. March 31: **Hurricanes** 17 **Bulls** 9, **Chiefs** 11 **Blues** 18, **Waratahs** 33 **Crusaders** 34, **Lions** 9 **Brumbies** 14. April 6: **Blues** 26 **Cheetahs** 8. April 7: **Highlanders** 34 **Chiefs** 38, **Crusaders** 53 **Force** 0, **Reds** 16 **Sharks** 59, **Stormers** 30 **Lions** 8, **Brumbies** 36 **Waratahs** 10. April 13: **Hurricanes** 37 **Cheetahs** 15. April 14: **Chiefs** 64 **Force** 36, **Highlanders** 3 **Crusaders** 38, **Blues** 25 **Sharks** 32, **Waratahs** 26 **Reds** 13, **Bulls** 49 **Stormers** 12. April 20: **Crusaders** 23 **Hurricanes** 13, **Brumbies** 14 **Force** 12. April 21: **Reds** 23 **Cheetahs** 13, **Chiefs** 35 **Sharks** 27, **Waratahs** 25 **Highlanders** 26, **Lions** 7 **Bulls** 31, **Stormers** 33 **Blues** 20. April 27: **Hurricanes** 22 Wellington 21, **Waratahs** 23 **Chiefs** 28, **Force** 45 **Cheetahs** 17, **Bulls** 40 **Blues** 19. April 28: **Brumbies** 15 **Crusaders** 6, **Sharks** 33 **Lions** 3, **Stormers** 37 **Reds** 34. May 4: **Crusaders** 24 **Chiefs** 30, **Force** 6 **Blues** 33. May 5: **Highlanders** 10 **Brumbies** 29, **Hurricanes** 14 **Waratahs** 38, **Lions** 10 **Cheetahs** 16, **Stormers** 10 **Sharks** 36, **Bulls** 92 **Reds** 3

FINAL TABLE

	P	W	D	L	For	A	BP	Pts
Sharks	13	10	0	3	355	214	5	45
Bulls	13	9	0	4	388	223	6	42
Crusaders	13	8	0	5	382	235	10	42
Blues	13	9	0	4	355	235	6	42
Brumbies	13	9	0	4	234	173	4	40
Chiefs	13	7	1	5	373	321	10	40
Force	13	6	1	6	276	292	6	32
Hurricanes	13	6	0	7	247	300	3	27
Highlanders	13	5	0	8	235	301	7	27
Stormers	13	6	0	7	249	326	3	27
Cheetahs	13	4	1	8	265	342	4	22
Lions	13	5	0	8	175	284	2	22
Waratahs	13	3	1	9	266	317	7	21
Reds	13	2	0	11	201	438	3	11

SEMI-FINALS

12 May, Asba Stadium, Durban

SHARKS 34 (2G, 4PG, 1DG, 1T)
BLUES 18 (1G, 2PG, 1T)

SHARKS: P Montgomery; F Steyn, W Murray, B Barritt, JP Pietersen; B James, R Pienaar; D Carstens, J Smit (captain), BJ Botha, J Ackermann, J Muller, J Botes, AJ Venter, R Kankowski Substitutes: B du Plessis, T Mtawarira, A van den Berg, W Britz, B Skinstad, R Kockott, A Jacobs

SCORERS *Tries*: Muller, James, Murray Conversions: Montgomery (2) Penalty Goals: Montgomery (4) Drop Goal: James

BLUES: G Pisi; D Howlett, A Tuitavake, I Toeava, R Wulff; I Nacewa, S Devine; T Woodcock, D Witcombe, J Afoa, G Rawlinson, T Flavell (captain), J Kaino, D Braid, N Williams Substitutes: K Mealamu, N White, A MacDonald, J Collins, T Moa, D Holwell, B Atiga

SCORERS: Wulf, Nacewa Conversion: Nacewa Penalty Goals: Nacewa (2)

REFEREE S Dickinson (Australia)

12 May, Loftus Versfeld, Pretoria

BULLS 27 (8PG, 1DG)
CRUSADERS 12 (4PG)

BULLS: J Roets; A Ndungane, JP Nel, W Olivier, B Habana; D Hougaard, H Adams; G Steenkamp, G Botha, R Gerber, D Rossouw, V Matfield (captain), P Wannenburg, W van Heerden, P Spies Substitutes: J Engels, D Thiart, B Botha, D Kuun, N Eyre, M Steyn, J van der Westhuyzen

SCORERS *Penalty Goals*: Hougaard (8) Drop Goal: Hougaard

CRUSADERS: L MacDonald; R Gear, C Laulala, A Mauger, C Ralph; D Carter, K Senio; B Franks, C Flynn, C Johnstone, C Jack, R Filipo, R Thorne, R McCaw (captain), M Tuiali'i Substitutes: T Paulo, W Crockett, M Paterson, K Read, A Ellis, S Brett, J Leo'o

SCORERS *Penalty Goals*: Carter (4)

REFEREE: Matt Goddard (Australia)

FINAL

19 May, Asba Stadium, Durban

SHARKS 19 (3PG, 2T)
BULLS 20 (2G, 2PG)

SHARKS: P Montgomery; F Steyn, W Murray, B Barrett, J P Pietersen; B James, R Pienaar; D Carstens, J Smit (captain), B Botha, J Ackermann, J Muller, J Notes, R Kankowski, A Venter

SUBSTITUTES: B du Plessis, T Mtawarira, A van den Berg, W Britz, B Skinstad, R Kockott, A Jacobs

SCORERS *Tries*: Pietersen, van den Berg Penalty Goals: Montgomery (3)

BULLS: J Roets; A Ndungane, J P Nel, W Olivier, B Habana; D Hougaard, F du Preez; G Steenkamp, G Botha, R Gerber, B Botha, V Matfield (captain), P Wannenberg, P Spies, W van Heerden

SUBSTITUTES: J Engels, D Thiart, D Rossouw, D Kuün, H Adams, M Steyn, J van der Westhuyzen

SCORERS *Tries*: Spies, Habana Conversions: Hougaard (2) Penalty Goals: Hougaard (2)

REFEREE S Walsh (New Zealand)

OSPREYS SOAR TO ANOTHER TITLE

Huw Evans Agency

Opsrey's flanker Ryan Jones gets his hands on the first Magners League trophy.

The Celtic League was claimed by the Ospreys for a second time in three seasons as the battle between Wales, Ireland and Scotland's finest once again produced a dramatic denouement that left the destination of the title in doubt until the final round of games.

The 2005-06 campaign had seen Ulster clinch the honours in the 78th minute of their final match against the Ospreys courtesy of a nerveless David Humphreys' drop goal but a year on it was the Welsh side's turn to experience the joy of a last-gasp victory to be crowned champions.

Rebranded the Magners League, the tournament headed into the final weekend of fixtures in May with the Ospreys, Cardiff and Leinster –

the side denied by Ulster's late, late show – all still in contention. The Blues ended Irish hopes with a 27-11 win over Leinster at the Arms Park on Friday night to move into top spot but the Ospreys, playing on Saturday, knew a victory over the Borders at Netherdale would see them leapfrog their Principality rivals and become the first side to win the title for a second time.

The clash was not only the Borders' last ever game before being disbanded by the Scottish RFU due to financial problems, but also Gregor Townsend's last match before retirement, and on an emotional day Steve Bates' side came close to producing a major upset. The Ospreys, however, were not to be denied and despite a nervy display, they hung on for a crucial 24-16 victory.

"Naturally we are thrilled but it is hard to celebrate when the team we faced are going out of existence," said Ospreys coach Lyn Jones. "Borders produced a really brave performance, as we knew they would, and we feel for them. The feeling is more of relief than anything else. We have lost twice recently at this venue, so we took nothing for granted."

The Ospreys' elation was in stark contrast to Leinster's heartbreak, who once again had to settle for being runners-up having gone into the final round of matches in pole position.

"It's two years in a row now we've lost the title on the last weekend and it's very disappointing," admitted Leinster coach Michael Cheika after his side's defeat to Cardiff. "We weren't good enough tonight, it's pretty clear, although we tried very hard and there was a lot of commitment.

"But it didn't flow for us, we made a few mistakes and that took the pressure off them despite us having a lot of the ball."

The season began in early September, mercifully free of the political wranglings that had threatened to derail the previous campaign, and the early exchanges soon suggested that the Irish provinces would not have things all their own way as they did the year before.

Munster were downed in Cardiff (22-13) on the opening day, Leinster were beaten by Edinburgh (20-14) at Murrayfield while defending champions Ulster were also seen off by the Gunners (20-15) in the Scottish capital.

The first major clash of the campaign saw Cardiff make the short trip to the Liberty Stadium to face the Ospreys. A full house of points from Blues fly-half Nick Robinson appeared to have sealed victory for Dai Young's side but the number ten turned from hero to villain when a loose kick late on was seized on by substitute flanker Ritchie Pugh, who raced over to give the Ospreys an 18-16 win.

Of the genuine title contenders, it was Llanelli who made the most convincing of starts. Beaten on the opening day by Ulster at Ravenhill, the Scarlets dusted themselves off and embarked on a six match winning run – including a narrow 23-22 triumph over the Dragons at Rodney Parade – and with Cardiff, the Ospreys and Leinster all losing twice over the same period, it was Phil Davies' side who had the momentum with them.

Until, that is, their Boxing Day clash with the Ospreys at Liberty Stadium, a 20,500 sell-out in Swansea and a record attendance for a Welsh region in the Celtic League.

The Ospreys were licking their wounds after losing 30-24 to Cardiff three days earlier but shrugged off their disappointment and inspired by 23 points from the boot of Wales fly-half James Hook, they stormed to a timely 50-24 win. The title race was wide open again.

"We'd had an awful start against the Blues last week, but this time the Scarlets looked like they hadn't played for a while," said Lyn Jones. "But we were too strong for them and deserved to win.

"Every time you face the Scarlets in a local derby like this there's a lot of spirit in the game and you have to be happy with scoring that number of points and getting that sort of result."

The result sparked a dreadful sequence for the Scarlets – they lost four more games in succession to severely dent their title ambitions – but neither Cardiff nor Leinster were capable of taking full advantage.

The Blues were edged out 14-13 by the Dragons at Rodney Parade while Leinster were left to rue dropping vital points against provincial rivals Ulster and then Munster in December.

The clash with Ulster at a wind-swept Ravenhill was a fierce but scrappy contest that ended in a 6-6 stalemate while the showdown with Munster, the reigning Heineken Cup champions, at Thomond Park produced more points but an even more disappointing result as Ronan O'Gara landed five second-half penalties in a 25-11 win.

"There wasn't a whole lot of space out there and we just managed to pick off our chances," said Munster coach Declan Kidney. "It's a measure of the team that they had the patience to turn things around. We gave away some penalties but we kept our discipline generally and it was a day when penalties were being given away."

The jockeying for position between the leading sides continued through the early months of 2007 but it was the Ospreys who surged ahead with six wins on the bounce – including what were to prove pivotal triumphs over the Scarlets (19-6) and Leinster (19-7) – and the stage was set for the grand finale of what had already proved to be a rollercoaster campaign.

The build-up to the final round of games in early May saw Leinster narrowly at the top of the table, one point clear of the Ospreys and three clear of Cardiff and a crunch clash between the Irish province and the Blues at Arms Park beckoned.

The game itself was not as close as many had predicted in wet conditions in Cardiff and tries from Robin Sowden-Taylor, Gareth Williams, Rhys Williams and Marc Stcherbina sealed a convincing 27-11 win for the home side, who also wrapped up a bonus point. Cardiff were now two points clear and only the Ospreys could snatch the title from Dai Young's side.

"We've done as much as we can do," Young said. "The focus was to win the game and I thought we did that very well. The players went out from the word go and really performed. Hopefully it will be enough, but it's out of our hands now. Hopefully, the Borders can do us a favour."

Cardiff's sense of hope was to be short-lived and less than 24 hours later the Ospreys had recorded the victory in Scotland that they knew they needed.

It was not, however, a victory without nerves and tension.

The Ospreys began in what seemed commanding form at Netherdale with tries from Filo Tiatia and Sonny Parker early on and when Parker scored his second after half-time, the result – and the destination of the Magners League title – appeared in little doubt. But the Borders were clearly determined not to be consigned to history without a fight and hit back with a try from Ed Kalman and a penalty from the boot of Calum MacRae to drag them to within five points of the visitors. In the end, the Ospreys were forced to rely on a long-range penalty from James Hook to finally subdue the Reivers recovery and send them above Cardiff in the table by a solitary point.

It was the third time in six years the Celtic crown was bound for Wales and a sad but dignified end to the Borders' five-year stint as a professional outfit.

"We have to concentrate on getting the professional game right in Scotland because, if you don't do that, we might as well give up on running an international team," said Gregor Townsend as he brought his 12-year professional career to an end.

"If there is a way of getting back up to three and then four teams, then we have to do that. In two years I can see Welsh rugby streaking past Irish rugby. Two Welsh teams finished top of the Magners League this year, so it is going in that direction. It is a rugby nation and they have finally got their heads around professional rugby."

MAGNERS LEAGUE RESULTS

September 1: **Border Reivers** 15 **Connacht** 29, **Cardiff** 22 **Munster** 13, **Glasgow** 23 **Dragons** 24. September 2: **Ospreys** 17 **Edinburgh** 11, **Ulster** 31 **Llanelli** 16. September 8: **Connacht** 15 **Ospreys** 10, **Edinburgh** 20 **Leinster** 14, **Llanelli** 31 **Glasgow** 17. September 9: **Munster** 9 **Border Reivers** 8, **Dragons** 25 **Ulster** 32. September 12: **Dragons** 22 **Llanelli** 23. September 13: **Ospreys** 18 **Cardiff** 16. September 15: **Connacht** 15 **Llanelli** 37, **Edinburgh** 20 **Ulster** 15, **Glasgow** 24 **Munster** 13, **Ospreys** 30 **Border Reivers** 13. September 16: **Leinster** 16 **Cardiff** 9. September 22: **Border Reivers** 8 **Dragons** 20, **Cardiff** 27 **Glasgow** 9, **Connacht** 22 **Edinburgh** 22, **Ulster** 43 **Ospreys** 7. September 23: **Llanelli** 33 **Leinster** 21. September 29: **Connacht** 16 **Leinster** 31, **Edinburgh** 14 **Glasgow** 9. September 30: **Munster** 21 **Ulster** 13. October 6: **Connacht** 17 **Ulster** 24, **Glasgow** 25 **Border Reivers** 0, **Leinster** 27 **Munster** 20. October 13: **Border Reivers** 22 **Leinster** 19, **Connacht** 16 **Dragons** 9, **Munster** 10 **Edinburgh** 21, **Ospreys** 26 **Glasgow** 9. October 14: **Ulster** 32 **Cardiff** 12. November 3: **Edinburgh** 13 **Cardiff** 23, **Glasgow** 39 **Connacht** 34, **Ulster** 32 **Border Reivers** 8. November 4: **Leinster** 35 **Dragons** 13. November 5: **Llanelli** 25 **Munster** 12. November 10: **Border Reivers** 13 **Llanelli** 19, **Leinster** 38 **Glasgow** 23, **Dragons** 17 **Edinburgh** 10. November 18: **Cardiff** 15 **Connacht** 13. November 25: **Munster** 25 **Ospreys** 20. December 1: **Edinburgh** 17 **Border Reivers** 3. December 2: **Ulster** 6 **Leinster** 6. December 3: **Munster** 13 **Connacht** 0. December 22: **Glasgow** 34 **Edinburgh** 27. December 23: **Cardiff** 30 **Ospreys** 24. December 26: **Ospreys** 50 **Llanelli** 24, **Ulster** 20 **Connacht** 10. December 27: **Dragons** 14 **Cardiff** 13, **Munster** 25 **Leinster** 11. December 29: **Border Reivers** 19 **Glasgow** 20. December 31: **Connacht** 8 **Munster** 14, **Leinster** 20 **Ulster** 12, **Ospreys** 12 **Dragons** 6. January 1: **Cardiff** 29 **Llanelli** 10. January 5: **Dragons** 19 **Munster** 12, **Edinburgh** 24 **Llanelli** 14. January 6: **Cardiff** 36 **Border Reivers** 15, **Glasgow** 8 **Ulster** 19, **Leinster** 45 **Ospreys** 22. January 26: **Dragons** 48 **Border Reivers** 0, **Edinburgh** 49 **Connacht** 31, **Glasgow** 22 **Cardiff** 3, **Leinster** 44 **Llanelli** 34. January 27: **Ospreys** 29 **Ulster** 22. February 16: **Border Reivers** 0 **Munster** 36, **Glasgow** 30 **Llanelli** 14, **Leinster** 13 **Edinburgh** 6, **Ulster** 14 **Dragons** 7. February 17: **Ospreys** 31 **Connacht** 10. March 2: **Connacht** 20 **Border Reivers** 17, **Dragons** 13 **Glasgow** 3, **Edinburgh** 12 **Ospreys** 30, **Munster** 12 **Cardiff** 19. March 3: **Llanelli** 17 **Ulster** 11. March 23: **Llanelli** 35 **Dragons** 11, **Border Reivers** 10 **Edinburgh** 3, **Ulster** 21 **Munster** 24. March 24: **Leinster** 30 **Connacht** 21. April 6: **Llanelli** 53 **Border Reivers** 11, **Edinburgh** 30 Newport 20, **Glasgow** 26 **Leinster** 20. April 7: **Connacht** 16 **Cardiff** 16, **Ospreys** 20 **Munster** 12. April 13: **Connacht** 23 **Glasgow** 40, Newport 22 **Leinster** 23, **Border Reivers** 9 **Ulster** 33. April 14: **Cardiff** 48 **Edinburgh** 0, **Munster** 20 **Llanelli** 0. April 20: **Cardiff** 20 **Ulster** 17. April 24: **Llanelli** 6 **Ospreys** 19. April 27: **Ospreys** 19 **Leinster** 17, **Border Reivers** 14 **Cardiff** 41, **Ulster** 10 **Glasgow** 24. April 28: **Munster** 15 **Dragons** 7. April 29: **Llanelli** 42 **Edinburgh** 17. May 1: **Cardiff** 31 **Dragons** 20. May 4: **Dragons** 23 **Connacht** 0, **Edinburgh** 9 **Munster** 35, **Glasgow** 29 **Ospreys** 26. May 5: **Llanelli** 38 **Cardiff** 10, **Leinster** 31 **Border Reivers** 0. May 8: **Dragons** 13 **Ospreys** 27. May 11: **Cardiff** 27 **Leinster** 11, **Llanelli** 19 **Connacht** 10, **Ulster** 16 **Edinburgh** 10. May 12: **Border Reivers** 16 **Ospreys** 24, **Munster** 38 **Glasgow** 20

FINAL TABLE

	P	W	D	L	For	A	BP	Pts
Ospreys	20	14	0	6	461	374	8	64
Cardiff	20	13	1	6	447	327	9	63
Leinster	20	12	1	7	472	376	11	61
Llanelli	20	12	0	8	490	417	9	57
Ulster	20	11	1	8	423	310	9	55
Munster	20	12	0	8	379	294	6	54
Glasgow	20	11	0	9	434	419	5	49
Edinburgh	20	8	1	11	335	423	8	42
Dragons	20	8	0	12	353	362	7	39
Connacht	20	4	2	14	326	474	6	26
Borders	20	2	0	18	201	545	4	12

Getty Images

David Humphreys headed the Magners (Celtic) League scoring charts at the end of the 2006–07 with 797 career points for Ulster.

ALL BLACKS STAY ON TOP

By Dominic Rumbles

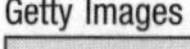
Getty Images

The Junior All Blacks celebrate their second successive crown.

The Junior All Blacks retained the IRB Pacific Nations Cup trophy with an undefeated defence of the title. However, unlike their 2006 campaign, when they cruised serenely to the title, New Zealand's second string had to contend with the inclusion of a strong Australia A side and the emergence of a significant challenge from the much-improved Pacific Island nations.

Ian Foster's side effectively wrapped up the title with a 50-0 thrashing of Australia A in the penultimate round of the competition. The result meant that the New Zealanders could not be overhauled and that the trophy would remain in Kiwi hands.

Few could have predicted the demolition that was to unfold as Australia A, in the Pacific Nations Cup for the first time, also entered the match undefeated. However, tries from Stephen Donald, Tom

Donnelly, Sione Lauaki and Scott Hamilton within the opening half an hour killed off the Australian challenge.

The victory, achieved during a Rugby World Cup year, certainly delighted the New Zealand management. "We are fortunate to have such top quality players available in this country and to play in a tournament that benefits New Zealand and Pacific Island rugby in particular," said Junior All Blacks coach Ian Foster. "The competition provides a tough testing ground for players to show they have what it takes to make the Rugby World Cup squad."

Indeed within a multitude of impressive performances two players in particular showed that they had what it takes with Graham Henry naming young talents Andrew Ellis and Sione Lauaki within his 30-man RWC squad.

The second Pacific Nations Cup tournament - one element of the International Rugby Board's US$50 million global strategic investment programme that was launched in August 2005 to increase the competitiveness of the global game – may have had an expanded format with the addition of Australia A, but the opening round had a familiar look to it as the Junior All Blacks opened in style with a 31-10 victory over Samoa in what was the second match for the Samoans (they had previously defeated Fiji 8-3 in a match owing to test scheduling). There were also victories for debutants Australia A and Fiji.

All six teams were up and running, but it was clear that the two A sides were the pick of the bunch. However, round two was to prove historic as Japan, having made clear improvements under former All Black John Kirwan, produced the upset of the tournament, defeating Tonga 20-17 in the first match in an entertaining double-header at Coffs Harbour. The emphatic jubilation of the Japan squad showed just how much it meant to a team that had never previously won in the tournament, while proving that Kirwan is developing the pack to match more physical sides.

"It is a great day for Japanese rugby," said a jubilant Kirwan. "It is important that this team believes in itself and today we proved that we can compete, we can win. All Japanese Rugby fans should be proud of what has been achieved."

The second match at the Harbour was no less exciting as home side Australia A held off a spirited comeback by Samoa to win 27-15 to secure second place in the standings. Trailing by 15 points early in the second half the Samoans pulled the scores back to 20-15 before the Australians finally killed off the game.

Just two matches were played in round three owing to the rescheduled Samoa v Fiji match, but the weekend further enhanced the domination of the Tier 1 A sides, who both recorded comfortable victories. The Junior All Blacks racked up their third successive bonus point win with a 39-13 win over Tonga, while Australia A showed improvement to cruise past Japan 71-10. The result set up a mouth-watering clash against the New Zealand side where one team would surrender its one hundred percent record.

Both sides went into the match rightly full of confidence, but any thoughts of a titanic tussle were dismissed in the space of thirty first half minutes as the Junior All Blacks ripped apart Laurie Fisher's side with an exquisite performance bristling with pace, power and cutting edge. While the result prompted a few red faces within the Australian camp, few could argue that the Junior All Blacks were the class of 2007.

The other two matches were no less significant. Japan buoyed by their first victory caused Samoa a scare, leading 3-0 at half time and dominating the forward exchanges before being edged out 15-3 thanks to a try from Lome Fa'atau. Tonga, on the back of an encouraging performance against the Junior All Blacks downed rivals Fiji 21-15 at Churchill Park to keep hopes alive of a third place finish.

With the destination of the silverware decided and Australia A safe in second place there was still plenty to play for entering the final round of matches, with the battle for third intense as the four Island Unions looked to claim the bragging rights in the Pacific. That mantle went to Samoa who thrashed Tonga 50-3 in Apia to round off their campaign in style. On what was an emotional day for veteran wing Brian Lima, playing his final match on home soil after an illustrious international career, the Samoans scored seven tries including a brace for Lima's friend and Bristol team mate David Lemi.

Japan, improving with every outing under Kirwan, continued to impress and despite eventually being outclassed 50-3 by the champions in Tokyo, had the better of the opening exchanges and caused their opponents sufficient problems in the set piece to suggest that they would be competitive during Rugby World Cup. Fiji also signed off with an encouraging display holding Australia A to a 14-14 draw in Suva in a match they ought to have won. Indeed it took a late moment of brilliance from wing Lachlan Turner who dotted down at the death to save the Australian's blushes.

Despite the dominance of the Junior All Blacks once again, the IRB Pacific Nations Cup demonstrated the significant progress that is being made within each of the Pacific Island Unions. The IRB funded High Performance Units in Fiji, Samoa and Tonga unearthed a number of talented local players who booked Rugby World Cup squad places on the back of their performances during the tournament, while the increased competitiveness of each team suggested that the IRB Pacific Nations Cup, coupled with the IRB Pacific Cup is the perfect development vehicle to take Pacific Island Rugby to new levels.

FINAL TABLE

	P	W	D	L	F	A	PD	Bonus 4 tries	Points <7 loss	Pts
Junior All Blacks	5	5	0	0	228	34	194	5	0	25
Australia A	5	3	1	1	172	104	68	2	0	16
Samoa	5	3	0	2	96	67	29	1	0	13
Fiji	5	1	1	3	70	115	-45	1	2	9
Tonga	5	1	0	4	69	184	-115	0	1	5
Japan	5	1	0	4	51	182	-131	0	0	4

Results		
Samoa 8	**Fiji** 3	**Apia**
Tonga15	**Australia A** 60	**Sydney**
Fiji 30	**Japan**15	**Lautoka**
Samoa 10	**Junior All Blacks** 31	**Apia**
Fiji 8	**Junior All Blacks** 57	**Suva**
Tonga 17	**Japan** 20	**Coffs Harbour**
Australia A 27	**Samoa** 15	**Coffs Harbour**
Tonga 13	**Junior All Blacks** 39	**Nuku'alofa**
Australia A 71	**Japan** 10	**Townsville**
Japan 3	**Samoa** 13	**Sendai**
Fiji 15	**Tonga** 21	**Lautoka**
Junior All Blacks 50	**Australia A** 0	**Dunedin**
Samoa 50	**Tonga** 3	**Apia**
Fiji 14	**Australia A** 14	**Suva**
Japan 3	**Junior All Blacks** 51	**Tokyo**

UPOLU CONTINUE SAMOAN DOMINANCE

By Dominic Rumbles

Uplou Samoa proud to be crowned champions.

Upolu Samoa maintained the Samoan stranglehold on the IRB Pacific Rugby Cup with a convincing victory over Tau'uta Reds in an entertaining Grand Final in Tonga. Selefuti Patu's side defeated the Reds 35-15 courtesy of two Lagolasi Fonoti second half tries to secure Upolu's first piece of silverware and extend Samoa's dominance of the competition.

Following the resounding success of the inaugural competition last year, it was difficult to see how the competition could reach new heights. However, the 2007 IRB Pacific Rugby Cup proved to be even better, attracting large crowds and producing five rounds of scintillating action with no fewer than eight of the 15 matches in the round robin stage decided by three points or less.

The competition is just one element of the IRB's US$50 million global strategic investment programme that was launched in August 2005 and is the first of its kind in the Pacific. The IRB is committed to increasing the competitiveness of the global Game and by offering more opportunities to develop players, a pathway is being created to ensure that more and more nations will, in the future, be competitive at the highest level.

"I would say that the Pacific Rugby Cup is a lifeline for players in the Islands," explained Manu Samoa's head coach Michael Jones. "It is a key vehicle for Pacific Islands Rugby to bridge that gap in the competition pathway from club or provincial level to full test rugby and it has proven pivotal in both player development and selection for the national team and is a very significant step forward for Pacific Islands Rugby,"

The former All Black flanker had plenty to rave about. Not only did the Samoan sides fair well, with Upolu claiming the crown, but the competition also proved to be an invaluable selection tool ahead of the Rugby World Cup, with a number of the competition's rising stars graduating to represent Samoa at the Tournament in France.

Once again the Pacific Rugby Cup was typical Pacific Rugby, tough and uncompromising with a liberal dose of attacking flair. However, there was one noticeable difference from the competition's debut season – there was more structure, while the standard of Rugby was higher, highlighting the excellent work of the High Performance Units that have been established by the IRB in each country, to aid with local player development.

Following Savai'i's success in the inaugural competition in 2006 all eyes were on the defending champions to see whether they could repeat their feat. However, the opening round was to go against the 2006 form book as Fiji Barbarians defeated Tautahi Gold 20-18 and Tau'uta Reds despatched 2006 runners-up Fiji Warriors 23-20. However, it was Upolu Samoa who recorded the shock of the day, with Timoteo Iosua scoring a last minute converted try to shock reigning champions Savai'i Samoa 14-13 at a packed Apia Stadium. The result ensured that the honours were evenly spread across the three Unions.

If the opening round was close, Round two was no less dramatic. Upolu picked up where they left off with yet another one point victory – this time edging past Fiji Barbarians 26-25 in Apia thanks to an injury time Timoteo Iosua penalty. While Upolu were enjoying life unbeaten in the competition the champions were stuttering. A second successive defeat, this time at the hands of Fiji Warriors in Suva, left Savai'i wondering where it had all gone wrong. In the all Tongan affair the Reds outlined their title credentials with a relatively comfortable 21-13 victory over Gold. It was to be the biggest margin of victory in the competition to date.

By Round three just two sides remained unbeaten, but in the top of the table clash it was the Reds who emerged unscathed from a physical encounter to take the spoils by just one point. In a highly entertaining match, it looked as though Upolu would come out on top on home soil, but full back Mesui Kailea kicked a 40 metre penalty deep in injury time to steal the spoils for the visitors. Another kick at the death was to decide the match between Fiji Barbarians and Savai'i Samoa in Sigatoka as Jo Tora inflicted yet more misery on the Samoan side. It was a result that left the champions stranded at the bottom of the table as Tautahi Gold saw off 2006 finalists Fiji Barbarians 13-10 to record their opening win of the campaign.

Needing a victory to confirm their place in the Grand Final, Tau'uta Reds entered their round four match against winless Savai'i Samoa in high spirits. Yet, in the shock of the competition, Savai'i showed some of the class that earned them the title in 2006 to beat the leaders 25-12 to throw wide open the race to the title. Upolu failed to capitalise though as Tautahi Gold scored a try at the death to continue their upsurge in form, while the Fiji Warriors put in a much improved performance to win the Fijian derby 20-14. The results meant that four teams; Fiji Barbarians, Upolu Samoa, Fiji Warriors and Tautahi Gold had all registered two wins in the chase to haul back the leaders and qualify for the grand final.

The scene was set for a dramatic final round of matches and the Pacific Rugby Cup once again lived up to expectations. The Reds, needing a win to secure a home draw in the final, defeated Fiji Barbarians 21-14 to become the first Tongan side ever to contest a PRC final, while Joshua Keil's injury time penalty secured a 29-27 victory over a plucky Warriors side in Fiji to confirm their place in the final. The final match of the weekend, effectively a dead rubber, saw Savai'i Samoa continue their rehabilitation, seeing off Tautahi Gold 22-34, but it was a case of too little too late for the champions.

The final itself was fitting of a competition that had entertained every minute of the way. A crowd of more than 3000 crammed into Nuku'alofa's Teufaiva Stadium to see the best sides in the PRC go head to head and they were not to be disappointed as the two teams served up a high-quality feast of Rugby. However, despite vociferous home support, the Reds were unable to repeat their round three success over Upolu and struggled to match the Samoan side's strength in the set piece as the impressive Joshua Keil contributed 15 points to help Upolu to a 35-15 victory.

Speaking after the final whistle Michael Jones could barely control his delighted as he watched a Samoan side lift the Pacific Rugby Cup for the second time in succession. "This really is a fantastic result for Samoan Rugby," said Jones. "For Upolu to emulate Savai'i's feat last year is a significant accomplishment and as head coach of the national side I feel that the PRC teams have set a high benchmark for selection ahead of the IRB Pacific Nations Cup test series."

Yet again the IRB Pacific Rugby Cup not only proved that it is a worthy addition to the international rugby calendar, but it also proved to be the closest and most fiercely competitive tournament of the year. It also achieved its core aim of completing a defined competition pathway for locally-based players on the Islands as several players graduated from the competition to compete in the IRB Pacific Nations Cup and secure a place in their respective Rugby World Cup 2007 squads.

FINAL TABLE

	P	W	D	L	F	A	PD	Bonus Points 4 tries	Bonus Points <7 loss	Pts
Tau'uta Reds	5	4	0	1	108	102	6	1	0	17
Upolu Samoa	5	3	0	2	112	114	-2	1	2	15
Savaii Samoa	5	2	0	3	106	88	18	1	3	12
Fiji Barbarians	5	2	0	3	97	108	-11	1	3	12
Fiji Warriors	5	2	0	3	93	90	3	0	3	11
Tautahi Gold	5	2	0	3	84	98	-14	1	1	10

IRB Pacific Rugby Cup Final – 5 April, Teufaiva Stadium, Tonga

UPOLU SAMOA 35
TAU'UTA REDS 15

TAU'UTA REDS: V Poteki, U Kailea, H Tonga'uiha (captain), O Takai, S Tu'akoi, M Aholelei, E Taufa, L 'Ilolahia, R Mahe, O Fifita, I Fine, T Tanginoa, S Mata'u, S Etimoni Poteki, T Fonua

SUBSTITUTES: A Hu'akau, T Toke, K Halafihi, T Takai, S Kapeli, T Sikalele, T Na'a

SCORERS *Tries*: R Mahe, S Poteki, M 'Aholelei

UPOLU SAMOA: D Tausili, G Sitia, P Toelupe, S Moala, L Fonoti, J Keil, D Gabriel, M Magele, A Cortz, M Solofuti, T Fitiao, O Pipili, D Kerslake, M Salanoa, S Tavita

SUBSTITUTES: A Williams, T Moala, A Utumapu, S Sila, N Tauafao, O Keil, M Schuster

SCORERS: M Salanoa, M Solofuti, L Fonoti (2), Conversions: J Keil (3), Penalties J Keil (3)

BACK-TO-BACK TRIUMPHS

By Karen Bond

Getty Images

Canada fans were able to celebrate another title in North America.

Canada West retained the IRB North America 4 title with a comfortable 43–11 defeat of the USA Falcons, out-scoring their main rivals by six tries to one at the Rotary Stadium in Abbotsford, British Columbia, in what was a repeat of the inaugural final 12 months earlier. On that occasion only 11 points had separated the two teams, and few would have predicted such a huge victory given they had met only four days earlier in Burnaby Lake when Canada West came from behind to sneak a 13–11 win in round five.

There had been little sign of a runaway victory at half time, when West led only 17–6 having played into the wind for the opening 40 minutes, but 24 unanswered points – including tries for forwards David Biddle, Nanyak Dala and Scott Franklin – put the game beyond reach before

Takudzwa Ngwenya scored a consolation try for the Falcons in what was their third straight defeat in the competition. It was, perhaps, fitting that West retained their crown, having topped the standings with four wins and one defeat – by the Falcons in round three – to reach the final.

The silverware remaining in Canada will have delighted national coach Ric Suggitt, but the emergence of a number of home-based players also gave him a headache when it came to selecting his squad for the Rugby World Cup, albeit a welcome one as the North America 4 lived up to its intentions of creating an opportunity for players in Canada and the USA to showcase their talents at a higher level and greater intensity than club rugby, making them better equipped to make the transition to Test rugby in the future.

A prime example of a player seizing the opportunity presented by the North America 4 was teenager Nathan Hirayama, who had captained Canada to the Division B final at the IRB Under 19 World Championship in Northern Ireland in April. Fast forward three months and the fly half had played for the senior national team in the Barclays Churchill Cup, toured New Zealand and impressed for Canada West in the latter stages of the NA4 – kicking 13 points in the final – to earn a place in Suggitt's extended 32-man training squad for the Rugby World Cup.

"The NA4 brought out good performances by certain individuals. You had the youngsters like Nathan Hirayama, who is just a 19-year-old and went to the Under 19 World Cup," admitted Geraint John, Rugby Canada's High Performance Director. "Then he showed great maturity in the NA4 final as an outside half as well, so that was pleasing to see and he is a player that we believe has got a great, great future ahead of him. I think people didn't think he would get to the World Cup, but you never know."

There would be no double for Canadian rugby to savour though, with Canada East having lost a dramatic third place playoff 34–29 to the USA Hawks in the first game of the concluding double header. The lead changed hand six times during the match, the last time in the dying seconds when the Hawks completed their recovery from 29–15 down with a second try by replacement Jone Naqica following an interception by Nese Malifa, another find of the competition for USA Eagles head coach Peter Thorburn.

The victory by the Hawks not only avenged their loss at the same stage last year, but also proved the only win for an American team in the second part of the competition, which was played on Canadian soil after a seven-week break for the Barclays Churchill Cup and Canada's tour of New Zealand. The 'home' victory proved to be a trait throughout the 2007 event with West the only Canadian team to win a match on the American leg of the tournament with their 32–20 defeat of the Hawks in round two.

The second North America 4 tournament – one element of the International Rugby Board's US$50 million global strategic investment programme that was launched in August 2005 to increase the competitiveness of the global game – had followed a similar form guide to the inaugural competition with USA Falcons and Canada West quickly emerging as the title contenders with victories in the all-American and all-Canadian affairs of the opening round in early April, even if West only scraped a 26–24 win over East in Vancouver in comparison to the Falcons' 48–17 victory over the Hawks in San Diego.

All four representative teams then converged on Stanford, California, a month later for back-to-back double headers over a four-day period with the Falcons-West encounter in round three the undoubted highlight. Both sides went into the match with a 2–0 record, the Falcons having beaten Canada East 20–5 with national captain Mike Hercus pulling the strings before two Carl Pocock tries helped the defending champions triumph over the Hawks, Malifa having scored all the latter's points with two converted tries and two penalties in an impressive NA4 debut.

Only a point separated the teams at half time – the Falcons lead 12–11 – but tries from scrum half Chad Erskine and full back Andrew Osborne in the 10 minutes after the break stretched that advantage and, while West fought back with a try for prop Hubert Buydens, it was the Americans who held on for victory with a last minute score by Osborne sealing the 29–16 win. The victory also secured the first 'double' with USA Hawks coming out on top in the battle of the winless teams with a 36–23 win in a match which saw three yellow cards and six tries, three by each side with fly half Jason Kelly kicking 21 points for the victors.

The Falcons therefore topped the standings with an unbeaten record from West, Hawks and the winless East as attention turned to the national sides at the Barclays Churchill Cup in England, a tournament which yielded another convincing win for Canada [52–10] over their North America rivals to see the sides swap places in the IRB World Rankings and provided a confidence boost for West and East when the North America 4 resumed on home soil in British Columbia.

Fortunes could not have been more different in the opening match, the Falcons unbeaten and East yet to record a victory, but the Canadians had set themselves a target of winning three in a row to finish the competition on a high. Few would have predicted a shock though, even with the Falcons having lost 10 of their original squad by the resumption, but that is exactly what unfolded at the Brockton Oval with number 8 Aaron Carpenter capping a dominant display with East's fifth try in a 33–22 victory that took them off the bottom of the standings.

The Falcons still topped these, albeit only on point differential after

West defied a brief hailstorm and persistent heavy rain to beat USA Hawks 35–7 with Hirayama belying his tender age with a controlled display in difficult conditions. So to the penultimate round to determine who would top the table, the teams already knowing who would contest the final and third place playoff and therefore seeking a psychological blow over the side they would face again in those showdowns.

Those blows were struck by the Canadians with West coming from behind to beat the Falcons thanks to Bryn Keys' conversion of James Potter's try with half an hour remaining in the match at Burnaby Lake. However while this match proved a tense affair, the East continued their revival with a 29–13 defeat of the Hawks, although they did make hard work of it having been given a dream start with three converted tries in the opening 15 minutes. The reality was, as Hawks captain Mike French admitted, their "silly mistakes made it too much to come back from". Fortunately for French, the Hawks were able to turn the tables on their conquerors four days later to finish third overall.

RESULTS

ROUND ONE

7 April – Little Qualcomm Rugby Complex, San Diego	**USA Falcons** 48 – 17 **USA Hawks**
7 April – Thunderbird Stadium, Vancouver, British Columbia	**Canada West** 26 – 24 **Canada East**

ROUND TWO

9 May – Steuber Rugby Stadium, Stanford, California	**USA Falcons** 20 – 5 **Canada East**
Canada West 32 – 20 **USA Hawks**	

ROUND THREE

12 May – Steuber Rugby Stadium, Stanford, California	**USA Hawks** 36 – 23 **Canada East**
USA Falcons 29 – 16 **Canada West**	

ROUND FOUR

29 June – Brockton Oval, Vancouver, British Columbia	**Canada East** 33 – 22 **USA Falcons**
Canada West 35 – 7 **USA Hawks**	

ROUND FIVE

3 July – Burnaby Sports Complex, Burnaby Lake, British Columbia	**Canada East** 29 – 13 **USA Hawks**
Canada West 13 – 11 **USA Falcons**	

THIRD PLACE PLAY-OFF

7 July – Rotary Stadium, Abbotsford, British Columbia **USA Hawks** 34 – 29 **Canada East**

FINAL TABLE

	P	W	D	L	F	A	PD	Bonus Points 4 tries	Bonus Points <7 loss	Pts
Canada West	5	4	0	1	122	91	31	2	0	18
USA Falcons	5	3	0	2	130	84	46	2	1	15
Canada East	5	2	0	3	114	117	-3	2	1	11
US Hawks	5	1	0	4	93	167	-74	0	0	4

NORTH AMERICA 4 FINAL

7 July, Rotary Stadium, Abbotsford, British Columbia

WEST 43 (5G, 1PG, 1T)
USA FALCONS 11 (2PG, 1T)

CANADA WEST: P Desaulles, M Lawson, Scott Franklin, T Healy, T Hotson, N Dala A Kleeberger, D Biddle, J Buchanan, N Hirayama, T La Carte, N Trenkel, C Culpan, S Mercier, DTH van der Merwe.

REPLACEMENTS: H Buydens, E Christensen, M Perizzolo, A Buan, N Meechan, T McKeen, J Potter.

SCORERS:*Tries:* Desaulles, Trenkel, Buan, Biddle, Dala, Franklin *Conversions:* Hirayama (5) *Penalties:* Hirayama.

USA FALCONS: C Moreno, B Burdette, C Osentowski, M Mangan, L Gross, M Aylor, R Pretorius, T Meidinger, M Petri, J Kelly, T Ngwenya, V Esikia, T Palamo, S Sika, T Osborne.

REPLACEMENTS: O Lentz, B Olmes, H Mexted, L Puloka, D Haynes, S Peterson, T Meek.

SCORERS: *Try:* Ngwenya *Penalties:* Kelly (2).

REFEREE: Kris Draper (USA)

BOKS BREAK NEW GROUND

By Dominic Rumbles

IRB

The IRB Nations Cup reached new heights in 2007 with an expanded tournament that provided both a competitive feast of quality rugby and put the game back on the map in Romania.

The competition was deservedly won by a powerful Emerging Springboks side bristling with Rugby World Cup hopefuls and talented youngsters, who held off the challenge of reigning champions Argentina A to claim the title for the first time.

However, away from the debutant's jubilation there was further reason

IRB

to celebrate, as the IRB would have been extremely pleased with the impact of the tournament.

Having invested heavily in the tournament as a key initiative of the unprecedented three-year US$50 million global strategic investment programme, the game's governing body hoped that new tournament's such as the IRB Nations Cup would provide a high level of competition for Tier 1 Test sides while offering an expanded match calendar for Tier 2 and 3 Test sides, promoting greater competitiveness within the international game.

The 2007 tournament delivered on all fronts. It put Romanian Rugby back on the map, played a large part in developing players across all six participating unions while also providing valuable World Cup preparation time for the three test sides; Georgia, Namibia and hosts Romania.

Not only was the historic city of Bucharest a welcoming host, the Romanian public warmed to the tournament and it's triple-header match days and the thousands that turned up to the Arcul de Triumf were rewarded with three highly-competitive match days.

Indeed it was not until the very last match on the final match day that the Emerging Boks were crowned champions after recording a 24–10 victory over defending champions Argentina A.

For jubilant Emerging Boks centre Jaco Pretorius winning the title was a special moment, especially considering the level of competition.

"It was a tough tournament," said the former South Africa Sevens captain, Pretorius.

"Georgia actually shocked us quite a bit, a lot of people expected that we were going to give them 50 points and it definitely didn't happen. They were very physical and they definitely stepped up a level as the tournament progressed. I think every participating team gained something positive from the Nations Cup and I hope that the Boks get the opportunity to compete again next year."

Round one opened with three intriguing fixtures. The pre-tournament hype surrounded Romania and whether they would be competitive on home soil?

Hosting a major tournament for the first time since the 1930s added to the pressure. It could have not started more disastrously for Sorin Socol's out of sorts team, who were despatched 61–7 by the Springboks.

"We have been cut down to size, and we must take stock and do something about it," said an obviously frustrated Manager Robert Antonin, who pointed out that he was struggling to find any balance to the squad.

In the second match of the tournament the two Rugby World Cup 2007 qualifiers Namibia and Georgia produced an entertaining spectacle, but it was the Georgians who dealt the psychological blow ahead of their pool D match, running out 26–18 winners thanks to a phenomenal performance from the pack, a victory they were able to repeat at the World Cup.

The third match was a repeat of the 2006 final with champions Argentina A taking on Italy A. The result was also a repeat as the Argentineans won an entertaining match 27–20 thanks to 12 points from the boot of Santiago Fernandez.

Argentina A and the Emerging Springboks both remained unbeaten after picking up victories over Namibia and Georgia respectively in round two. The defending champions were first up against Namibia with Gonzalo Camacho scoring two of their seven tries in a 47–13 victory over a much improved Namibian outfit at the 'Arcul de Triumf' stadium.

Then it was the turn of the Emerging Springboks, although they were made to work very hard by an impressive Georgia defence for a 24–7 victory with centre Marius Delport scoring a hat-trick of tries.

The final match of the day saw Romania claim their first victory of the competition, beating Italy A 19–8 to the delight of the home crowd with a much improved performance from their opener against the Emerging Springboks.

The third and final round was well worth the wait. Ever improving Georgia, benefiting from IRB assistance in terms of coaching and management support, faced 2006 runners-up Italy A, Namibia faced Romania and in a perfectly scripted finale, undefeated sides Argentina A and the Emerging Springboks clashed in a winner-takes-all match.

All three matches were exciting. Georgia picked up their second win of the tournament with a narrow 22–20 victory, leaving a buoyant side in positive mood ahead of a second Rugby World Cup campaign.

The day's second match was no less competitive. Thousands of fans packed into the national stadium to watch Romania's last game. After a disappointing start to the tournament, Socol's side had demonstrated significant improvements, highlighting the importance of the competition, and duly signed-off in style, defeating Namibia 28–16 and leaving Namibia winless.

The final match was a tough affair, pitting two hugely physical sides against each other. Defending champions Argentina A fought valiantly throughout, but an impressive display of power, pace and skill and a brace of tries by winger Tonderai Chavanga saw the Emerging Springboks emerge victorious to claim the IRB Nations Cup trophy at the first time of asking.

Once again the IRB Nations Cup had proven it's tremendous worth as a major competition on the international Rugby calendar. While ultimately each participating side was focused on winning, the tournament provided an invaluable opportunity for the likes of Georgia, Romania and Namibia to put into practice a number of high performance and coaching practices ahead of Rugby World Cup. Indeed their performances during the tournament in France suggested that each Union had made significant strides.

IRB NATIONS CUP – FINAL TOURNAMENT STANDINGS

	P	W	L	D	PF	PA	BP	PTS
1 EMERGING BOKS	3	3	0	0	109	24	1	13
2 ARGENTINA A	3	2	1	0	84	57	1	9
3 GEORGIA	3	2	1	0	55	62	0	8
4 ROMANIA	3	2	1	0	54	85	0	8
5 ITALY A	3	0	3	0	48	68	2	2
6 NAMIBIA	3	0	3	0	47	101	0	0

RESULTS

05/06/2007	Argentina A	27–20	Italy A
05/06/2007	Romania	8–61	Emerging Springboks
05/06/2007	Georgia	26–18	Namibia
10/06/2007	Namibia	13–47	Argentina A
10/06/2007	Romania	19–8	Italy A
10/06/2007	Emerging Springboks	24–12	Georgia
16/06/2007	Romania	28–16	Namibia
16/06/2007	Emerging Springboks	24–10	Argentina A
16/06/2007	Italy A	20–22	Georgia

LEADING POINT SCORERS

Player	Team	PTS
Peter Grant	Emerging Boks	44
Luciano Orquera	Italy A	30
Valentin Calafeteanu	Romania	29
Santiago Fernández	Argentina A	29
Tertius Losper	Namibia	21

Dave Rogers/Getty Images

Australia kicked off their Autumn 2006 tour to Europe with a thrilling 29–29 draw against Wales.

MAJOR RUGBY TOURS 2006-07

By Chris Rhys

AUSTRALIA TO EUROPE 2006

Tour party

FULL BACKS: CE Latham (Queensland Reds)
THREE QUARTERS: C Rathbone (ACT Brumbies), L Tuqiri (Queensland Reds), SA Mortlock (ACT Brumbies), CB Shepherd (Western Force), MA Gerrard (ACT Brumbies), SNG Staniforth (Western Force)
HALFBACKS: SJ Larkham (ACT Brumbies), MS Rogers (NSW Waratahs), MJ Giteau (Western Force), JJ Valentine (NSW Waratahs)
FORWARDS: AKE Baxter (NSW Waratahs), RC Blake (Queensland Reds), GT Shepherdson (ACT Brumbies), NJ Henderson (ACT Brumbies), BA Robinson (NSW Waratahs), ST Moore (Queensland Reds), TP McIsaac (Western Force), BJ Cannon (Western Force), T Polota-Nau (NSW Waratahs), NC Sharpe (Western Force), DJ Vickerman (Western Force), AM Campbell (ACT Brumbies), RD Elsom (NSW Waratahs), PR Waugh (NSW Waratahs), WL Palu (NSW Waratahs), SA Hoiles (ACT Brumbies), MD Chisholm (ACT Brumbies)
MANAGER: P Thomson **COACH:** J Connelly **ASSISTANT COACHES:** S Johnson, M Foley, J Muggleton

Match 1, 4 November, Millennium Stadium, Cardiff
Wales 29 (2G 5PG) Australia 29 (3G 1PG 1T)

WALES: KA Morgan (Dragons); G Thomas (Stade Toulousain), TGL Shanklin (Blues), GL Henson (Ospreys), SM Williams (Ospreys); SM Jones (Scarlets)(capt), DJ Peel (Scarlets); GD Jenkins (Blues), M Rees (Scarlets), AR Jones (Ospreys), IM Gough (Dragons), I Evans (Ospreys), J Thomas (Ospreys), RP Jones (Ospreys), ME Williams (Blues)
SUBSTITUTIONS: J Hook (Ospreys) for SM Jones (23 mins), D Jones (Ospreys) for AR Jones (66 mins)
SCORERS *Tries:* SM Williams, ME Williams *Conversions:* Hook (2) *Penalty goals:* SM Jones, Henson, Hook (3)
AUSTRALIA: Latham; Rathbone, Tuqiri, Larkham, Shepherd; Rogers, Giteau; Baxter, McIsaac, Blake, Sharpe, Vickerman, Elsom, Palu, Waugh (capt)
SUBSTITUTIONS: Cannon for McIsaac (35 mins), Hoiles for Palu (54 mins), Valentine for Larkham (57 mins), Chisholm for Vickerman (58 mins)
SCORERS: *Tries:* Shepherd (2), Giteau, Latham *Conversions:* Giteau (3) *Penalty goal:* Giteau
REFEREE: SR Walsh (New Zealand)

Match 2, 11 November, Stadio Flaminio, Rome
Italy 18 (6PG) Australia 25 (2G 2PG 1T)

ITALY: G Peens (L'Aquila); K Robertson (Viadana), G-J Canale (Clermont-Auvergne), Mirco Bergamasco (Stade Francais), P Canavosio (Castres Olympique); R Pez (Bayonne), P Griffen (Calvisano); A lo Cicero (L'Aquila), C Festuccia (Parma Rugby), M-L Castrogiovanni (Leicester Tigers), S Dellape (Biarritz Olympique), M Bortolami (Gloucester Rugby)(capt), A Zanni, (Calvisano) S Parisse (Stade Francais), Mauro Bergamasco (Stade Francais)

SUBSTITUTIONS: J Sole (Viadana) for Zanni (53 mins), C Nieto (Gloucester Rugby) for Castrogiovanni (53 mins)

SCORER: *Penalty goals:* Pez (6)

AUSTRALIA: Latham; Rathbone, Mortlock (capt), Larkham, Tuqiri; Rogers, Giteau, Baxter, Cannon, Shepherdson, Sharpe, Chisholm, Elsom, Palu, Smith

SUBSTITUTIONS: Moore for Palu (temporary 8-14 mins), Henderson for Shepherdson (75 mins), Campbell for Chisholm (75 mins)

SCORERS: *Tries:* Rogers, Shepherdson, Mortlock *Conversions:* Mortlock (2) *Penalty goals:* Mortlock (2)

REFEREE: N Owens (Wales)

Match 3, 19 November, Lansdowne Road, Dublin
Ireland 21 (1G 3PG 1T) Australia 6 (2PG)

IRELAND: GEA Murphy (Leicester Tigers); SP Horgan (Leinster), BG O'Driscoll (Leinster)(capt), GMD D'Arcy (Leinster), DA Hickie (Leinster); RJR O'Gara (Munster), IJ Boss (Ulster); BG Young (Ulster), R Best (Ulster), JJ Hayes (Munster), DP O'Callaghan (Munster), PJ O'Connell (Munster) NA Best (Munster), DP Leamy (Munster), DP Wallace (Munster)

SUBSTITUTIONS: SH Easterby (Scarlets) for NA Best (60 mins), MJ Horan (Munster) for Young (60 mins), PA Stringer (Munster) for Boss (69 mins), ME O'Kelly (Leinster) for O'Connell (69 mins), FJ Sheahan (Munster) for R Best (69 mins), GT Dempsey (Leinster) for Murphy (74 mins)

SCORERS: *Tries:* Hickie, Murphy *Conversion:* O'Gara *Penalty goals:* O'Gara (3)

AUSTRALIA: Latham; Rathbone, Tuqiri, Mortlock (capt), Gerrard; Larkham, Giteau; Baxter, McIsaac, Shepherdson, Sharpe, Chisholm, Elsom, Palu, Waugh

SUBSTITUTIONS: Rogers for Larkham (27 mins), Robinson for Baxter (40 mins), Smith for Palu (51 mins), Moore for McIsaac (55 mins), Staniforth for Rathbone (63 mins), Campbell for Chisholm (71 mins), Valentine for Giteau (76 mins)

SCORER: *Penalty goals:* Mortlock (2)

REFEREE: M Jonker (South Africa)

Match 4, 25 November, Murrayfield
Scotland 15 (1G 1PG 1T) Australia 44 (5G 3PG)

SCOTLAND: CD Paterson (Edinburgh Rugby)(capt); SF Lamont (Northampton Saints), MP di Rollo (Edinburgh Rugby), AR Henderson (Glasgow Warriors), SL Webster (Edinburgh Rugby); DA Parks (Glasgow Warriors), MRL Blair (Edinburgh Rugby); G Kerr (Border Reivers), DWH Hall (Edinburgh Rugby), EA Murray (Glasgow Warriors), AD Kellock (Edinburgh Rugby), S Murray (Edinburgh Rugby), SM Taylor (Edinburgh Rugby) , DA Callam (Edinburgh Rugby), KDR Brown (Border Reivers)

SUBSTITUTIONS: HGF Southwell (Edinburgh Rugby) for Webster (8 mins), AF Jacobsen (Edinburgh Rugby) for Kerr (48 mins), PJ Godman (Edinburgh Rugby) for Di Rollo (temporary 47-56 mins) and for Parks (56 mins), RW Ford (Glasgow Warriors) for Hall (56 mins), AK Strokosch (Edinburgh Rugby) for Brown (68 mins), JL Hamilton (Leicester Tigers) for S Murray (68 mins), RGM Lawson (Gloucester Rugby) for Blair (70 mins)

SCORERS: *Tries:* Webster, SF Lamont *Conversion:* Paterson *Penalty goal:* Paterson

AUSTRALIA: Latham; Gerrard, Mortlock (capt), Staniforth, Tuqiri; Larkham, Giteau; Robinson, Moore, Shepherdson, Sharpe, Campbell, Elsom, Lyons, Smith

SUBSTITUTIONS: Waugh for Smith (59 mins), Palu for Lyons (59 mins), Polota-Nau for Moore (73 mins), Rogers for Staniforth (73 mins), Baxter for Robinson (75 mins), Chisholm for Elsom (temporary 67-75 mins) and for Campbell (75 mins), Valentine for Larkham (79 mins)

SCORERS: *Tries:* Gerrard (2), Larkham, Moore, Latham *Conversions:* Mortlock (5) *Penalty goals:* Mortlock (3)

REFEREE: DM Courtney (Ireland)

NEW ZEALAND TO EUROPE 2006

Tour party

FULL BACKS: JM Muliaina (Waikato & Chiefs), LR MacDonald (Canterbury & Crusaders)

THREE QUARTERS: RL Gear (Tasman & Crusaders), JT Rokocoko (Auckland & Blues), SW Sivivatu (Waikato & Chiefs), MA Nonu (Wellington & Hurricanes), AJD Mauger (Canterbury & Crusaders), CG Smith (Wellington & Hurricanes)

HALF BACKS: DW Carter (Canterbury & Crusaders), CL McAlister (North Harbour & Blues), NJ Evans (Otago & Highlanders), BT Kelleher (Waikato & Chiefs), AM Ellis (Canterbury & Crusaders), PAT Weepu (Wellington & Hurricanes)

FORWARDS: TD Woodcock (North Harbour & Blues), CJ Hayman (Otago & Highlanders), CD Dermody (Southland & Highlanders), JF Afoa (Auckland & Blues), NS Tialata (Wellington & Hurricanes), FK Mealamu (Auckland & Blues), AK Hore (Taranaki & Highlanders), AD Oliver (Otago & Highlanders), JAC Ryan (Otago & Highlanders), AJ Williams (Auckland & Blues), CR Jack (Tasman & Crusaders), KJ Robinson (Waikato & Chiefs), RD Thorne (Canterbury & Crusaders), JJ Eaton (Taranaki & Hurricanes), MC Masoe (Wellington & Hurricanes), RH McCaw (Canterbury & Crusaders), J Collins (Wellington & Hurricanes), R So'oialo (Wellington & Hurricanes)

MANAGER: D Shand **COACH:** G Henry Assistant **COACHES:** S Hansen, W Smith

CAPTAIN: RH McCaw

Match 1, 5 November, Twickenham
England 20 (1G 1PG 2T) New Zealand 41 (3G 5PG 1T)

ENGLAND: IR Balshaw (Gloucester Rugby); PH Sackey (London Wasps), JD Noon (Newcastle Falcons), A Allen (Gloucester Rugby), BC Cohen (Northampton Saints); CC Hodgson (Sale Sharks), S Perry (Bristol Rugby); AJ Sheridan (Sale Sharks), GS Chuter (Leicester Tigers), JM White (Leicester Tigers), DJ Grewcock (Bath Rugby), BJ Kay (Leicester Tigers), ME Corry (Leicester Tigers) (capt), PH Sanderson (Worcester Warriors), LW Moody (Leicester Tigers)

SUBSTITUTIONS: MB Lund (Sale Sharks) for Sanderson (59 mins), PC Richards (Gloucester Rugby) for Perry (65 mins), LA Mears (Bath Rugby) for Chuter (74 mins)

SCORERS: *Tries:* Noon, Cohen, Perry *Conversion:* Hodgson *Penalty goal:* Hodgson

NEW ZEALAND: Muliaina; Gear, Nonu, Mauger, Rokocoko; Carter, Kelleher; Woodcock, Mealamu, Hayman, Jack, Robinson, Thorne, Masoe, McCaw (capt)

SUBSTITUTIONS: Ellis for Kelleher (67 mins), Sivivatu for Gear (69 mins), So'oialo for Thorne (70 mins), Dermody for Woodcock (70 mins), Hore for Mealamu (74 mins), Afoa for Hayman (74 mins)

SCORERS: *Tries:* Mauger, Rokocoko, Hayman, Carter *Conversions:* Carter (3) *Penalty goals:* Carter (5)

REFEREE: J Jutge (France)

Match 2, 11 November, Stade Gerland, Lyon
France 3 (1DG) New Zealand 47 (3G 2PG 4T)

FRANCE: J Laharrague (USA Perpignan); A Rougerie (Clermont Auvergne), F Fritz (Stade Toulousain), Y Jauzion (Stade Toulousain), C Dominici (Stade Francais); D Traille (Biarritz Olympique), D Yachvili (Biarritz Olympique); S Marconnet (Stade Francais), D Szarzewski (Stade Francais), P de Villiers (Stade Francais), F Pelous (Stade Toulousain)(capt), P Pape (Castres Olympique), T Dusautoir (Stade Toulousain), E Vermeulen (Clermont Auvergne), J Bonnaire (CS Bourgoin Jallieu)

SUBSTITUTIONS: R Ibanez (London Wasps) for Szarzewski (46 mins), O Milloud (CS Bourgoin Jallieu) for Marconnet (46 mins), L Nallet (Castres Olympique) for Pelous (51 mins), R Martin (Stade Francais) for Dusautoir (64 mins), D Marty (USA Perpignan) for Fritz (69 mins), J-B Elissalde (Stade Toulousain) for Yachvili (75 mins)

SCORER: *Dropped goal:* Fritz

NEW ZEALAND: MacDonald; Rokocoko, Smith, McAlister, Sivivatu; Carter, Weepu; Woodcock, Oliver, Hayman, Ryan, Williams, Collins, So'oialo, McCaw (capt)

SUBSTITUTIONS: Mealamu for Oliver (49 mins), Kelleher for Weepu (55 mins), Eaton for McCaw (58 mins), Nonu for Carter (60 mins), Tialata for Woodcock (67 mins), Muliaina for MacDonald (73 mins)

SCORERS: *Tries:* Sivivatu (2), McCaw, Carter, Smith, Rokocoko, McAlister *Conversions:* Carter (3) *Penalty goals:* Carter (2)

REFEREE: SJ Dickinson (Australia)

Match 3, 18 November, Stade de France, Paris
France 11 (2PG 1T) New Zealand 23 (2G 3PG)

FRANCE: P Elhorga (SU Agen); A Rougerie (Clermont-Auvergne), F Fritz (Stade Toulousain), Y Jauzion (Stade Toulousain), C Heymans (Stade Toulousain); D Traille (Biarritz Olympique), J-B Elissalde (Stade Toulousain); O Milloud (CS Bourgoin Jallieu), R Ibanez (London Wasps)(capt), P de Villiers (Stade Francais), L Nallet (Castres Olympique), P Pape (Castres Olympique), J Bonnaire (CS Bourgoin Jallieu), E Vermeulen (Clermont-Auvergne), R Martin (Stade Francais)

SUBSTITUTIONS: D Yachvili (Biarritz Olympique) for Elissalde (26 mins), S Betsen (Biarritz Olympique) for Martin (56 mins), S Marconnet (Stade Francais) for De Villiers (56 mins), D Szarzewski (Stade Francais) for Ibanez (56 mins), C Dominici (Stade Francais) for Elhorga (69 mins), L Jacquet (Clermont-Auvergne) for Pape (69 mins)

SCORERS: *Try:* Heymans *Penalty goals:* Yachvili (2)

NEW ZEALAND: MacDonald; Rokocoko, Muliaina, Nonu, Sivivatu; Carter, Kelleher; Woodcock, Mealamu, Hayman, Jack, Williams, Collins, So'oialo, McCaw (capt)

SUBSTITUTIONS: Tialata for Woodcock (58 mins), Eaton for Jack (60 mins), Masoe for So'oialo (69 mins), Evans for Carter (73 mins), Ellis for Kelleher (73 mins), Hore for Mealamu (73 mins)

SCORERS: *Tries:* Rokocoko, Nonu *Conversions:* Carter (2) *Penalty goals:* Carter (3)

REFEREE: C White (England)

Match 4, 25 November, Millennium Stadium, Cardiff
Wales 10 (1G 1PG) New Zealand 45 (4G 4PG 1T)

WALES: KA Morgan (Dragons); MA Jones (Scarlets), TGL Shanklin (Blues), ST Parker (Ospreys), SM Williams (Ospreys); SM Jones (Scarlets)(capt), DJ Peel (Scarlets); D Jones (Ospreys), TR Thomas (Blues), AR Jones (Ospreys), IM Gough (Dragons), I Evans (Ospreys), J Thomas (Ospreys), RP Jones (Ospreys), ME Williams (Blues)

SUBSTITUTIONS: AJ Popham (Scarlets) for RP Jones (46 mins), J Hook (Ospreys) for Shanklin (46 mins), GD Jenkins (Blues) for D Jones (46 mins), A-W Jones (Ospreys) for Evans (55 mins), M Phillips (Blues) for Peel (62 mins), M Rees (Scarlets) for TR Thomas (71 mins), GL Henson (Ospreys) for Parker (72 mins)

SCORERS: *Try:* ME Williams Conversion; Hook *Penalty goal:* SM Jones

NEW ZEALAND: Muliaina; Gear, Smith, McAlister, Sivivatu; Carter, Kelleher; Tialata, Oliver, Hayman, Robinson, Williams, Collins, So'oialo, McCaw (capt)

SUBSTITUTIONS: Woodcock for Tialata (34 mins), Hore for Oliver (48 mins), Weepu for Kelleher (48 mins), Ryan for Williams (62 mins), Evans for Carter (62 mins), Thorne for So'oialo (62 mins), Nonu for Sivivatu (75 mins)

SCORERS: *Tries:* Sivivatu (3), McAlister, Penalty try *Conversions:* Carter (2), Evans (2) *Penalty goals:* Carter (4)

REFEREE: D Pearson (England)

ARGENTINA TO EUROPE 2006

Tour party

FULL BACKS: J-M Hernandez (Stade Francais)

THREE QUARTERS: J-M Nunez Piossek (Bayonne), P Gomez Cora (CA Lomas), H Agulla (Hindu), G-P Tiesi (London Irish), M Avramovic (Worcester Warriors), I Corleto (Stade Francais), H Senillosa (Hindu), M Contepomi (Rovigo), F Leonelli (Glasgow Warriors)

HALF BACKS: F Contepomi (Leinster), F Todeschini (Montpellier-Herault), A Pichot (Stade Francais), N Fernandez Miranda (Hindu), N Vergallo (Jockey Club, Rosario)

FORWARDS: M Ayerza (Leicester Tigers), OJ Hasan (Stade Toulousain), M Scelzo (Clermont-Auvergne), JF Gomez (Los Matreros), A Vernet Basualdo (Alumni), ME Ledesma (Clermont Auvergne), P Gamberini* (CASI), CI Fernandez Lobbe (Sale Sharks), P Albacete (Stade Toulousain), E Lozada (CASI), R Alvarez (USA Perpignan), J Arocena* (Alumni), J-M Leguizamon (London Irish), J-M Fernandez Lobbe (Sale Sharks), M Durand (Montpellier-Herault), M Schusterman (Leeds Tykes), G Longo (Clermont Auvergne)

MANAGER: JL Rolandi **COACH:** M Loffreda Assistant **COACHES:** D Baetti, L Cusworth, DM Cash **CAPTAIN:** A Pichot

* Replacement on tour

Match 1, 11 November, Twickenham
England 18 (1G 2PG 1T) Argentina 25 (1G 6PG)

ENGLAND: IR Balshaw (Gloucester Rugby); PH Sackey (London Wasps), JD Noon (Newcastle Falcons), A Allen (Gloucester Rugby), BC Cohen (Northampton Saints); CC Hodgson (Sale Sharks), S Perry (Bristol Rugby); PT Freshwater (USA Perpignan), GS Chuter (Leicester Tigers), JM White (Leicester Tigers), DJ Grewcock (Bath Rugby), BJ Kay (Leicester Tigers), ME Corry (Leicester Tigers)(capt), PH Sanderson (Worcester Warriors), LW Moody (Leicester Tigers)

SUBSTITUTIONS: PC Richards (Gloucester Rugby) for Perry (47 mins), T Palmer (London Wasps) for Grewcock (50 mins), T Flood (Newcastle Falcons) for Hodgson (52 mins), OJ Lewsey (London Wasps) for Sackey (53 mins), LA Mears (Bath Rugby) for Chuter (69 mins), MB Lund (Sale Sharks) for Sanderson (temporary 7-11 mins, 70 mins)

SCORERS: *Tries:* Sackey, Balshaw *Conversion:* Hodgson *Penalty goals:* Hodgson, Flood

ARGENTINA: Hernandez; Nunez Piossek, Tiesi, Avramovic, Gomez Cora; F Contepomi, Pichot (capt); Ayerza, Ledesma, Hasan, CI Fernandez Lobbe, Albacete, Leguizamon, Longo, J-M Fernandez Lobbe

SUBSTITUTIONS: Todeschini for Tiesi (21 mins), Agulla for Avramovic (56 mins), Lozada for CI Fernandez Lobbe (temporary 56-60 mins), Scelzo for Hasan (65 mins), Schusterman for Leguizamon (67 mins)

SCORERS: *Try:* Todeschini *Conversion:* Todeschini *Penalty goals:* Todeschini (5), F Contepomi

REFEREE: KM Deaker (New Zealand)

Match 2, 25 November, Stade de France, Paris
France 27 (3G 2PG) Argentina 26 (2G 4PG)

FRANCE: P Elhorga (SU Agen); C Dominici (Stade Francais), F Fritz (Stade Toulousain), Y Jauzion (Stade Toulousain), C Heymans (Stade Toulousain); D Traille (Biarritz Olympique), D Yachvili (Biarritz Olympique); O Milloud (CS Bourgoin Jallieu), R Ibanez (London Wasps)(capt), P de Villiers (Stade Francais), L Nallet (Castres Olympique), L Jacquet (Clermont-Auvergne), J Bonnaire (CS Bourgoin Jallieu), E Vermeulen (Clermont-Auvergne), R Martin (Stade Francais)

SUBSTITUTIONS: S Betsen (Biarritz Olympique) for Martin (32 mins), D Szarzewski (Stade Francais) for Ibanez (62 mins), S Marconnet (Stade Francais) for Milloud (62 mins), D Marty (USA Perpignan) for Jauzion (77 mins)

SCORERS: *Tries:* Dominci (2), Fritz *Conversions:* Yachvili (3) *Penalty goals:* Yachvili (2)

ARGENTINA: Hernandez; Nunez Piossek, M Contepomi, F Contepomi, Corleto; Todeschini, Pichot (capt); Scelzo, Ledesma, Hasan, Cl Fernandez Lobbe, Albacete, Durand, Longo, J-M Fernandez Lobbe

SUBSTITUTIONS: Senillosa for Todeschini (24 mins), Leguizamon for Durand (53 mins), Ayerza for Hasan (57 mins)

SCORERS: *Tries:* Longo, Hernandez *Conversions:* F Contepomi (2) *Penalty goals:* F Contepomi (2), Todeschini (2)

REFEREE: AJ Spreadbury (England)

PACIFIC ISLANDERS TO EUROPE 2006

Tour party

FULL BACKS: N Ligairi (Fiji), L Crichton (Samoa), J Taumololo (Tonga)

THREE QUARTERS: L Fa'atau (Samoa), S Tagicakibau (Samoa), K Ratuvou (Fiji), S Rabeni (Fiji), S Mapusua (Samoa), S Bai (Fiji), E Seveali'I (Samoa), R Caucaunibuca (Fiji), T Lavea (Samoa), Alesana Tuilagi (Samoa)

HALF BACKS: T Pisi (Samoa), M Rauluni (Fiji), J Polu(leuligaga)(Samoa)

FORWARDS: J Va'a (Samoa), T Taumoepeau (Tonga), C Johnston (Samoa), T Filise (Tonga), M Schwalger (Samoa), A Lutui (Tonga), S Raiwalui (Fiji), D Leo (Samoa), M Molitika (Tonga), S Sititi (Samoa), N Latu (Tonga), V Vaki (Tonga), H T-Pole (Tonga), E Taione (Tonga), I Domalailai (Fiji), A Ratouva (Fiji)

MANAGER J Browne Coach P Lam Assistant **COACHES:** SP Howarth, M Casey **CAPTAIN** S Rawalui

Match 1, 11 November, Millennium Stadium, Cardiff
Wales 38 (5G 1PG) Pacific Islanders 20 (1G 1PG 2T)

WALES: KA Morgan (Dragons); LM Byrne (Ospreys), ST Parker (Ospreys), J Hook (Ospreys), MA Jones (Scarlets); C Sweeney (Dragons), M Phillips (Blues); D Jones (Ospreys)(capt), TR Thomas (Blues), CL Horsman (Worcester Warriors), MJ Owen (Dragons), RA Sidoli (Blues), A-W Jones (Ospreys), AJ Popham (Scarlets), GV Thomas (Scarlets)

SUBSTITUTIONS: SM Williams (Ospreys) for MA Jones (52 mins), AR Jones (Ospreys) for Horsman (55 mins), G Evans (Scarlets) for Byrne (60 mins), GJ Cooper (Dragons) for Phillips (70 mins), H Bennett (Ospreys) for TR Thomas (70 mins), J Thomas (Ospreys) for Owen (70 mins)

SCORERS: *Tries:* MA Jones, Hook, Morgan, Byrne, Sweeney *Conversions:* Sweeney (5), *Penalty goal:* Sweeney

PACIFIC ISLANDERS: Ligairi; Fa'atau, Rabeni, Mapusua, Tagicakibau; Pisi, M Rauluni; Va'a, Schwalger, Taumoepeau, Raiwalui (capt), Leo, Sititi, T-Pole, Latu

SUBSTITUTIONS: Ratuvou for Tagicakibau (16 mins), Taione for T-Pole (50 mins), Lutui for

Schwalger (56 mins), Molitika for Leo (65 mins), Johnston for Taumoepeau (66 mins), Bai for Mapusua (66 mins), Polu for Rauluni (72 mins)

SCORERS: *Tries:* Va'a, Mapusua, Ratuvou *Conversion:* Pisi *Penalty goal:* Pisi

REFEREE: W Barnes (England)

Match 2, 18 November, Murrayfield
Scotland 34 (4G 1PG 1DG) Pacific Islanders 22 (1G 3T)

SCOTLAND: CD Paterson (Edinburgh Rugby)(capt); SF Lamont (Northampton Saints), MP di Rollo (Edinburgh Rugby), AR Henderson (Glasgow Warriors), SL Webster (Edinburgh Rugby); DA Parks (Glasgow Warriors), CP Cusiter (Border Reivers); G Kerr (Border Reivers), DWH Hall (Edinburgh Rugby), EA Murray (Glasgow Warriors), NJ Hines (USA Perpignan), S Murray (Edinburgh Rugby), SM Taylor (Edinburgh Rugby), JW Beattie (Glasgow Warriors), KDR Brown (Glasgow Warriors)

SUBSTITUTIONS: DA Callam (Edinburgh Rugby) for Beattie (6 mins), MRL Blair (Edinburgh Rugby) for Cusiter (11 mins), RW Ford (Glasgow Warriors) for Hall (57 mins), AF Jacobsen (Edinburgh Rugby) for Kerr (57 mins), AD Kellock (Edinburgh Rugby) for Taylor (65 mins), PJ Godman (Edinburgh Rugby) for Parks (73 mins), HFG Southwell (Edinburgh Rugby) for SF Lamont (temporary 62-64 mins) and for Paterson (77 mins)

SCORERS: *Tries:* Di Rollo, Callam, Brown, Henderson *Conversions:* Paterson (4) *Penalty goal:* Patterson *Dropped goal:* Di Rollo

PACIFIC ISLANDERS: Ligairi; Fa'atau, Ratuvou, Seveali'i, Caucaunibuca; Pisi, M Rauluni; Filise, Schwalger, Taumoepeau, Raiwalui (capt), Leo, Vaki, Taione, Latu

SUBSTITUTIONS: Lutui for Schwalger (30 mins), Rabeni for Caucaunibuca (53 mins), Molitika for Vaki (53 mins), Sititi for Taione (53 mins), Va'a for Filise (65 mins), Bai for Seveali'i (65 mins)

SCORERS: *Tries:* Ratuvou (2), Caucaunibuca, Leo *Conversion:* Pisi

REFEREE: BJ Lawrence (New Zealand)

Match 3, 26 November, Lansdowne Road, Dublin
Ireland 61 (6G 3PG 2T) Pacific Islanders 17 (1G 2T)

IRELAND: GT Dempsey (Leinster); L Fitzgerald (Leinster), BG O'Driscoll (Leinster)(capt), SP Horgan (Leinster), DA Hickie (Leinster); P Wallace (Ulster), PA Stringer (Munster); BG Young (Ulster), FJ Sheahan (Munster), JJ Hayes (Munster), ME O'Kelly (Leinster), PJ O'Connell (Munster), SH Easterby (Scarlets), JPR Heaslip (Leinster), S Ferris (Ulster)

SUBSTITUTIONS: GMD D'Arcy (Leinster) for Dempsey (41 mins), IJ Boss (Ulster) for O'Driscoll (60 mins), SJ Best (Ulster) for Hayes (62 mins), DP Leamy (Munster) for Heaslip (74 mins), R Best (Ulster) for Sheahan (74 mins), DP O'Callaghan (Munster) for O'Kelly (74 mins), RJR O'Gara (Munster) for Fitzgerald (78 mins)

SCORERS: *Tries:* SH Easterby (2), Hickie, P Wallace, O'Kelly, Horgan, R Best, O'Connell *Conversions:* P Wallace (6) *Penalty goals:* P Wallace (3)

PACIFIC ISLANDERS: Ligairi; Fa'atau, Rabeni, Seveali'i, Ratuvou; Pisi, M Rauluni; Va'a, Lutui, Taumoepeau, Raiwalaui (capt), Leo, Molitika, T-Pole, Latu

SUBSTITUTIONS: Polu for Rauluni (30 mins), Mapusua for Seveali'i (38 mins), Alesana Tuilagi for Ligairi (41 mins), Taione for T-Pole (48 mins), A Ratuva for Latu (59 mins), Filise for Va'a (temporary 30-40 mins, and 59 mins), Schwalger for Tuilagi (77 mins)

SCORERS: *Tries:* Pisi, Rabeni, Fa'atau *Conversion:* Pisi

REFEREE: C Berdos (France)

ROMANIA TO SCOTLAND 2006

11 November 2006, Murrayfield
Scotland 48 (5G 1PG 2T) Romania 6 (2PG)

SCOTLAND: HGF Southwell (Edinburgh Rugby); SF Lamont (Northampton Saints), MP di Rollo (Edinburgh Rugby), RE Dewey (Edinburgh Rugby), SL Webster (Edinburgh Rugby); PJ Godman (Edinburgh Rugby), MRL Blair (Edinburgh Rugby); G Kerr (Border Reivers), DWH Hall (Edinburgh Rugby), EA Murray (Glasgow Warriors), NJ Hines (USA Perpignan), S Murray (Edinburgh Rugby), JPR White (Sale Sharks)(capt), JW Beattie (Glasgow Warriors), KDR Brown (Glasgow Warriors)

SUBSTITUTIONS: DA Callam (Edinburgh Rugby) for White (38 mins), AF Jacobsen (Edinburgh Rugby) for Kerr (50 mins), CJ Smith (Edinburgh Rugby) for EA Murray (54 mins), JL Hamilton (Leicester Tigers) for Hines (54 mins), CP Cusiter (Border Reivers) for Blair (60 mins), CD Paterson (Edinburgh Rugby) for Southwell (66 mins), S Lawson (Glasgow Warriors) for Hall (70 mins)

SCORERS: *Tries:* Southwell (2), Beattie, Dewey, Godman, Hall, Cusiter *Conversions:* Godman (5) *Penalty goal:* Godman

ROMANIA: F Vlaicu (Steaua Bucharest); G Brezoianu (Unattached), C Dascalu (Steaua Bucharest), R Gontineac (RC Aurillac), I Teodorescu (Arad); I Dimofte (Arad), V Calafeteanu (Dinamo Bucharest); P Balan (Biarritz Olympique), M Tincu (USA Perpignan), B Balan (RC Montauban), S Socol (Pau)(capt), C Petre (AS Beziers), F Corodeanu (RC Grenoble), O Tonita (USA Perpignan), C Ratiu (Dinamo Bucharest)

SUBSTITUTIONS: P Ion (Bath Rugby) for B Balan (45 mins), C Gal (Steaua Bucharest) for Dascalu (53 mins), V Ursache (Arad) for Corodeanu (62 mins), C Popescu (SU Agen) for P Balan (64 mins), I Tofan (RC Limoges) for Gontineac (69 mins), R Mavrodin (Pau) for Tincu (71 mins), A Lupu (Steaua Bucharest) for Calafeteanu (72 mins)

SCORER: *Penalty goals:* Vlaicu (2)

REFEREE: M Goddard (Australia)

SOUTH AFRICA TO EUROPE 2006

Tour party

FULL BACKS: BA Fortuin (Cheetahs)

THREE QUARTERS: JC Pretorius (Cats), BG Habana (Bulls), AZ Ndungane (Bulls) J de Villiers (Stormers), FPL Steyn (Sharks), W Olivier (Bulls), J-P R Pietersen (Sharks)

HALF BACKS: AS Pretorius (Cats), AD James (Sharks), ER Januarie (Cats), R Pienaar (Sharks)

FORWARDS: LD Sephaka (Cats), CJ van der Linde (Cheetahs), BJ Botha (Sharks), PD Carstens (Sharks), JW Smit (Sharks), G van G Botha (Bulls), MC Ralepelle (Bulls), JN Ackermann (Sharks), PA van den Berg (Sharks), GJ Muller (Sharks), DJ Rossouw (Bulls), JH Smith (Cheetahs), H Lobberts (Bulls), PJ Spies (Bulls), J Cronje (Bulls), LK Floors* (Cheetahs), GJJ Britz* (Stormers)

MANAGER: Z Yeye **COACH:** J White Assistant **COACHES:** G Smal, A Coetzee **CAPTAIN:** JW Smit

* Replacement on tour

Match 1, 11 November, Lansdowne Road, Dublin
Ireland 32 (3G 2PG 1T) South Africa 15 (1G 1PG 1T)

IRELAND: GT Dempsey (Leinster); SP Horgan (Leinster), BG O'Driscoll (Leinster)(capt), GMD D'Arcy (Leinster), AD Trimble (Ulster); RJR O'Gara (Munster), PA Stringer (Munster); MJ Horan (Munster), R Best (Ulster), JJ Hayes (Munster), DP O'Callaghan (Munster), PJ O'Connell (Munster), NA Best (Ulster), DP Leamy (Munster) , DP Wallace (Munster)

SUBSTITUTIONS: SH Easterby (Scarlets) for NA Best (60 mins), GEA Murphy (Leicester Tigers) for Trimble (66 mins), BG Young (Ulster) for Horan (66 mins), IJ Boss (Ulster) for Stringer (74 mins), FJ Sheahan (Munster) for R Best (77 mins), P Wallace (Ulster) for O'Gara (77 mins), ME O'Kelly (Leinster) for O'Connell (77 mins)

SCORERS: *Tries:* Trimble, D Wallace, Horan, Horgan *Conversions:* O'Gara (3) *Penalty goals:* O'Gara (2)

SOUTH AFRICA: Fortuin; J Pretorius, Habana, De Villiers, Steyn; A Pretorius, Januarie; Sephaka, Smit (capt), Van der Linde, Ackermann, Van den Berg, Rossouw, Spies, Smith

SUBSTITUTIONS: Pienaar for Januarie (temporary 3-9 mins), BJ Botha for Sephaka (40 mins), Muller for Ackermann (52 mins), Cronje for Rossouw (72 mins), Olivier for J Pretorius (72 mins)

SCORERS: *Tries:* Steyn, Habana *Conversion:* A Pretorius *Penalty goal:* A Pretorius

REFEREE: PJ Honiss (New Zealand)

Match 2, 18 November, Twickenham
England 23 (2G 3PG) South Africa 21 (1G 2PG 1DG 1T)

ENGLAND: OJ Lewsey (London Wasps); MJ Cueto (Sale Sharks), M Tait (Newcastle Falcons), JD Noon (Newcastle Falcons), BC Cohen (Northampton Saints); CC Hodgson (Sale Sharks), PC Richards (Gloucester Rugby); AJ Sheridan (Sale Sharks), GS Chuter (Leicester Tigers), JM White (Leicester Tigers), T Palmer (London Wasps), BJ Kay (Leicester Tigers), JPR Worsley (London Wasps), ME Corry (Leicester Tigers) (capt), PH Sanderson (Worcester Warriors)

SUBSTITUTIONS: AJ Goode (Leicester Tigers) for Hodgson (38 mins), PJ Vickery (London Wasps) for Sheridan (48 mins), LA Mears (Bath Rugby) for Chuter (56 mins), LW Moody (Leicester Tigers) for P Sanderson (56 mins), CM Jones (Sale Sharks) for Kay (56 mins), S Perry (Bristol Rugby) for Richards (68 mins)

SCORERS: *Tries:* Cueto, Vickery *Conversions:* Goode (2) *Penalty goals:* Hodgson (2), Goode

SOUTH AFRICA: Steyn; Ndungane, Olivier, De Villiers, Habana; James, Januarie; Van der Linde, Smit (capt), BJ Botha, Ackermann, Muller, Spies, J Cronje, Rossouw

SUBSTITUTIONS: Lobberts for Cronje (40 mins), A Pretorius for James (temporary 38-40 mins) and for De Villiers (56 mins), Carstens for Van der Linde (temporary 20-30 mins, and 68 mins), Pienaar for Januarie (73 mins), Van den Berg for Ackermann (76 mins)

SCORERS: *Tries:* James, Ndungane *Conversion:* James *Penalty goals:* James (2) *Dropped goal:* Steyn

REFEREE: SR Walsh (New Zealand)

Match 3, 25 November, Twickenham
England 14 (3PG 1T) South Africa 25 (1G 2PG 4DG)

ENGLAND: OJ Lewsey (London Wasps); MJ Cueto (Sale Sharks), M Tait (Newcastle Falcons), JD Noon (Newcastle Falcons), BC Cohen (Northampton Saints); AJ Goode (Leicester Tigers), PC Richards (Gloucester Rugby); PJ Vickery (London Wasps), LA Mears (Bath Rugby), JM White (Leicester Tigers), T Palmer (London Wasps), CM Jones (Sale Sharks), JPR Worsley (London Wasps), ME Corry (Leicester Tigers) (capt), PH Sanderson (Worcester Warriors)

SUBSTITUTIONS: LW Moody (Leicester Tigers) for Sanderson (48 mins), BJ Kay (Leicester Tigers) for Palmer (48 mins), S Perry (Bristol Rugby) for Richards (48 mins), GS Chuter (Leicester Tigers) for Mears (67 mins), T Flood (Newcastle Falcons) for Goode (76 mins)

SCORERS: *Try:* Cueto *Penalty goals:* Goode (3)

SOUTH AFRICA: Steyn; Ndungane, Olivier, De Villiers, Habana; A Pretorius, Januarie; Van der Linde, Smit (capt), BJ Botha, Ackermann, Muller, Floors, Rossouw, Smith

SUBSTITUTIONS: Carstens for Van der Linde (66 mins), Britz for Floors (67 mins), Van den Berg for Smith (70 mins), Ralepelle for Muller (79 mins)

SCORERS: *Try:* Van der Linde *Conversion:* A Pretorius *Penalty goals:* A Pretorius (2) *Dropped goals:* A Pretorius (4)

REFEREE: A Lewis (Ireland)

CANADA TO EUROPE 2006

Tour party

FULL BACKS: E Fairhurst (Cornish Pirates), DTH Van der Merwe (James Bay AA)
THREE QUARTERS: M Pyke (RC Montauban), J Mensah-Coker (RC Albi), J Pritchard (Bedford), R Smith (RC Montauban), D Spicer (RC Auch), D van Camp (Aurora Barbarians)
HALF BACKS: D Daypuck (Castaway Wanderers), A Monro (Edinburgh Rugby), M Williams (RC Albi)
FORWARDS: K Tkachuk (Glasgow Warriors), F Gainer (RC Albi), M Pletch (Oakville Crusaders), D Pletch (Oakville Crusaders) M Lawson (Velox-Valhallians), P Riordan (Burnaby Lake), L Tait (Overmach Parma), M Burak (Pau), S Ault (Barrhaven Scottish), M Webb (Vancouver Rowing Club), S McKeen (Cornish Pirates), S-M Stephen (AS Beziers), A Carpenter (Brantford Harlequins), A Abrams (Castaway Wanderers), A Kleeberger (Victoria University) O Atkinson (Stade Bordelais)
MANAGER: R McGeein Coach R Suggitt Assistant coaches G Ella, J Tait, K Wirachowski
CAPTAIN: M Williams

Match 1, 17 November, Millennium Stadium, Cardiff
Wales 61 (8G 1T) Canada 26 (2G 3PG 1DG)

WALES: G Thomas (Stade Toulousain)(capt); MA Jones (Scarlets), TGL Shanklin (Blues), ST Parker (Ospreys), SM Williams (Ospreys); J Hook (Ospreys), DJ Peel (Scarlets); GD Jenkins (Blues), M Rees (Scarlets), AR Jones (Ospreys), IM Gough (Dragons), I Evans (Ospreys), J Thomas (Ospreys), RP Jones (Ospreys), ME Williams (Blues)
SUBSTITUTIONS: TR Thomas (Blues) for Rees (52 mins), D Jones (Ospreys) for Jenkins (52 mins), M Phillips (Blues) for Peel (58 mins), C Sweeney (Dragons) for Parker (58 mins), RA Sidoli (Blues) for Evans (63 mins), A-W Jones (Ospreys) for ME Williams (69 mins)
SCORERS: *Tries:* J Thomas (2), G Thomas, SM Williams, Rees, Penalty try, Peel, Sweeney, Shanklin *Conversions:* Hook (8)
CANADA: Fairhurst; Pritchard, Smith, Spicer, Pyke; Daypuck, Williams (capt); Tkachuk, Lawson, Gainer, Tait, Burak, Webb, Stephen, McKeen
SUBSTITUTIONS: Ault for Tait (temporary 26-32 mins), Monro for Spicer (40 mins), M Pletch for Gainer (42 mins), Riordan for Lawson (49 mins), D Pletch for Tkachuk (49 mins), Carpenter for Stephen (55 mins), Mensah-Coker for Williams (66 mins)
SCORERS: *Tries:* D Pletch, Pyke *Conversions:* Pritchard (2) *Penalty goals:* Pritchard (3) *Dropped goal:* Daypuck
REFEREE: AJ Spreadbury (England)

Match 2, 25 November, Stadio Comprerensoriale, Fontanafredda
Italy 41 (5G 2PG) Canada 6 (2PG)

ITALY: D Bortolussi (Montpellier-Herault), W Spragg (Calvisano), Mirco Bergamasco (Stade Francais), W Pozzebon (Bristol Rugby), M Stanojevic (Bristol Rugby); A Scanavacca (Calvisano), P Griffen (Calvisano); A lo Cicero (L'Aquila), F Ongaro (Saracens), C Nieto (Gloucester Rugby), S Dellape (Biarritz Olympique), M Bortolami (Gloucester Rugby)(capt), J Sole (Viadana), S Parisse (Stade Francais), Mauro Bergamasco (Stade Francais)
SUBSTITUTIONS: G-J Canale (Clermont-Auvergne) for Pozzebon (50 mins), A Zanni (Calvisano) for Dellape (50 mins), M-L Castrogiovanni (Leicester Tigers) for Lo Cicero 50 mins), C Festuccia (Rugby Parma) for Ongaro (54 mins), S Picone (Treviso) for Griffen (58 mins), M Zaffiri (Calvisano) for Mauro Bergamasco (78 mins)
SCORERS: *Tries:* Stanojevic (2), Bortolami, Zanni, Castrogiovanni *Conversions:* Bortolussi (5) *Penalty goals:* Bortolussi (2)
CANADA: Fairhurst; Pyke, Smith, Daypuck, Mensah-Coker; Monro, Williams (capt); D Pletch, Riordan, Gainer, Tait, Atkinson, Webb, Carpenter, McKeen
SUBSTITUTIONS: Van Camp for Monro (52 mins), Van der Merwe for Mensah-Coker (58

mins), Abrams for Riordan (61 mins), Tkachuk for D Pletch (65 mins), M Pletch for Gainer (65 mins), Kleeberger for McKeen (74 mins), Ault for Atkinson (76 mins)

SCORER: *Penalty goals:* Monro (2)

REFEREE: M Jonker (South Africa)

WALES TO AUSTRALIA 2007

Tour party

FULL BACKS: LM Byrne (Ospreys), G Thomas (Blues)

THREE QUARTERS: A Brew (Dragons), CD Czekaj (Blues), JP Robinson (Blues), ST Parker (Ospreys), GL Henson (Ospreys), T James (Blues)

HALF BACKS: J Hook (Ospreys), C Sweeney (Dragons), M Phillips (Blues), GJ Cooper (Dragons), A Williams (Bath Rugby)

FORWARDS: CL Horsman (Worcester Warriors), ID Thomas (Scarlets), AR Jones (Ospreys), Ceri Jones (NEC Harlequins), J Corsi (Dragons), S Roberts (Blues), TR Thomas (Blues), R Hibbard (Ospreys), M Rees (Scarlets), G Williams (Blues), BJ Cockbain (Ospreys), RA Sidoli (Blues), S Morgan (Blues), CL Charvis (Dragons), J Thomas (Ospreys), GV Thomas (Scarlets), R Sowden-Taylor (Blues), MJ Owen (Dragons)

MANAGER: A Phillips **COACH:** G Jenkins Assistant **COACHES:** R McBryde, N Jenkins, N Davies, R Phillips **CAPTAIN:** G Thomas

Match 1, 26 May, Telstra Stadium, Sydney
Australia 29 (3G 1PG 1T) Wales 23 (2G 2PG 1DG)

AUSTRALIA: JL Huxley (ACT Brumbies); MA Gerrard (ACT Brumbies), SA Mortlock (ACT Brumbies), AP Ashley-Cooper (ACT Brumbies), DA Mitchell (Western Force); SH Norton-Knight (NSW Waratahs), MJ Giteau (Western Force); MJ Dunning (NSW Waratahs), ST Moore (Queensland Reds), GT Shepherdson (ACT Brumbies), NC Sharpe (Western Force), MD Chisholm (ACT Brumbies), RD Elsom (NSW Waratahs), WL Palu (NSW Waratahs), PR Waugh (NSW Waratahs)(capt)

SUBSTITUTIONS: GB Smith (ACT Brumbies) for Waugh (52 mins), BA Robinson (NSW Waratahs) for Dunning (52 mins), GM Gregan (ACT Brumbies) for Ashley-Cooper (65 mins), DJ Vickerman (NSW Waratahs) for Chisholm (66 mins), SA Hoiles (ACT Brumbies) for Palu (71 mins), AL Freier (NSW Waratahs) for Moore (71 mins)

SCORERS: *Tries:* Palu, Giteau, Sharpe, Hoiles *Conversions:* Mortlock (3) *Penalty goal:* Mortlock

WALES: Byrne; G Thomas (capt), JP Robinson, Parker, Czekaj; Hook, Phillips; ID Thomas, Rees, AR Jones, Cockbain, Sidoli; Charvis, J Thomas, GV Thomas

SUBSTITUTIONS: Owen for Cockbain (34 mins), Henson for G Thomas (temporary 23-29 mins) and for J Robinson (66 mins), Cooper for Phillips (71 mins), Ceri Jones for ID Thomas (71 mins), Hibbard for Rees (74 mins)

SCORERS: *Tries:* J Robinson, G Thomas *Conversions:* Hook (2) *Penalty goals:* Hook (2) *Dropped goal:* Hook

REFEREE: JI Kaplan (South Africa)

Match 2, 2 June, Suncorp Stadium, Brisbane
Australia 31 (2G 4PG 1T) Wales 0

AUSTRALIA: JL Huxley (ACT Brumbies); DBN Ioane (Queensland Reds), SA Mortlock (ACT Brumbies)(capt), AP Ashley-Cooper (ACT Brumbies), DA Mitchell (Western Force); SJ Larkham (ACT Brumbies), MJ Giteau (Western Force); BA Robinson (NSW Waratahs), ST Moore (Queensland Reds), GT Sheperdson (ACT Brumbies), NC Sharpe (Western Force), DJ Vickerman (NSW Waratahs), RD Elsom (NSW Waratahs), WL Palu (NSW Waratahs), GB Smith (ACT Brumbies)

SUBSTITUTIONS: GM Gregan (ACT Brumbies) for Ashley-Cooper (40 mins), AL Freier (NSW Waratahs) for Moore (40 mins), MJ Dunning (NSW Waratahs) for Robinson (50 mins), PR Waugh (NSW Waratahs) for Smith (58 mins), MD Chisholm (ACT Brumbies) for Sharpe (50 mins), MA Gerrard (ACT Brumbies) for Giteau (65 mins), SA Hoiles (ACT Brumbies) for Palu (69 mins)

SCORERS: *Tries:* Ioane, Mitchell, Huxley *Conversions:* Mortlock (2) *Penalty goals:* Mortlock (4)

WALES: G Thomas (capt); A Brew, JP Robinson, Parker, Czekaj; Hook, Phillips; ID Thomas, M Davies, Ceri Jones, Owen, Sidoli, Charvis, J Thomas, GV Thomas

SUBSTITUTIONS: Henson for Czekaj (21 mins), Sweeney for JP Robinson (29 mins), Horsman for ID Thomas (50 mins), Hibbard for M Davies (58 mins), S Morgan for Sidoli (60 mins), R Sowden-Taylor for GV Thomas (69 mins), A Williams for Phillips (74 mins)

REFEREE: PG Honiss (New Zealand)

ENGLAND TO SOUTH AFRICA 2007

Tour party

FULL BACKS: M Brown (NEC Harlequins), N Abendanon* (Bath Rugby)

THREE QUARTERS: JT Robinson (Sale Sharks), IR Balshaw (Gloucester Rugby), JD Simpson-Daniel (Gloucester Rugby), D Strettle (NEC Harlequins), DGR Scarborough (Saracens), JD Noon (Newcastle Falcons), M Tait (Newcastle Falcons), A Allen (Gloucester Rugby), A Farrell (Saracens), T Ojo (London Irish)

HALF BACKS: T Flood (Newcastle Falcons), JP Wilkinson (Newcastle Falcons), ACT Gomarsall (NEC Harlequins), S Perry (Bristol Rugby)

FORWARDS: KP Yates (Saracens), SC Turner (Sale Sharks), DE Crompton (Bristol Rugby), N Wood (Gloucester Rugby), MJH Stevens* (Bath Rugby), MI Cairns (Saracens), MP Regan (Bristol Rugby), AJ Titterell (Sale Sharks), D Schofield (Sale Sharks), A Brown (Gloucester Rugby), RA Winters (Bristol Rugby), CM Jones (Sale Sharks), AR Hazell (Gloucester Rugby), PH Sanderson (Worcester Warriors), N Easter (NEC Harlequins), B Skirving (Saracens), MB Lund (Sale Sharks), P Buxton (Gloucester Rugby)

MANAGER V Brown **COACH:** B Ashton Assistant **COACHES:** M Ford, J Wells **CAPTAIN:** JT Robinson

* Replacement on tour

Match 1, 26 May, Vodacom Park, Free State Stadium, Bloemfontein
South Africa 58 (7G 3PG) England 10 (1G 1PG)

SOUTH AFRICA: PC Montgomery (Sharks); AK Willemse (Cats), W Olivier (Bulls), J de Villiers (Stormers), BG Habana (Bulls); AD James (Sharks), ER Januarie (Lions); PD Carstens (Sharks), JW Smit (Sharks)(capt), BJ Botha (Sharks), JP Botha (Bulls), V Matfield (Bulls), JH Smith (Cheetahs), DJ Rossouw (Bulls), SWP Burger (Stormers)

SUBSTITUTIONS: CJ van der Linde (Cheetahs) for BJ Botha (40 mins), GJ Muller (Sharks) for JP Botha (40 mins), GG Steenkamp (Bulls) for Carstens (47 mins), FPL Steyn (Sharks) for Willemse (52 mins), PJ Spies (Bulls) for Rossouw (54 mins), R Pienaar (Sharks) for De Villiers (63 mins), G van G Botha (Bulls) for Smit (70 mins)

SCORERS: *Tries:* Habana (2), Willemse, De Villiers, Burger, Steyn, Van der Linde *Conversions:* Montgomery (7) *Penalty goals:* Montgomery (3)

ENGLAND: M Brown; Balshaw, Tait, Flood, Robinson (capt); Wilkinson, Gomarsall; Yates, Regan, Turner, Schofield, A Brown, Jones, Easter, Hazell

SUBSTITUTIONS: Sanderson for Hazell (40 mins), Crompton for Turner (52 mins), Winters for Jones (54 mins), Simpson-Daniel for Balshaw (57 mins), Perry for Wilkinson (72 mins), Cairns for Regan (74 mins)

SCORERS: *Try:* Simpson-Daniel *Conversion:* Wilkinson *Penalty goal:* Wilkinson

REFEREE: SR Walsh (New Zealand)

Match 2, 2 June, Loftus Versveld, Pretoria
South Africa 55 (6G 1PG 2T) England 22 (1G 5PG)

SOUTH AFRICA: PC Montgomery (Sharks); AZ Ndungane (Bulls), W Olivier (Bulls), J de Villiers (Stormers), BG Habana (Bulls); AD James (Sharks), ER Januarie (Lions); GG Steenkamp (Bulls), JW Smit (Sharks) (capt), CJ van der Linde (Cheetahs), JP Botha (Bulls), V Matfield (Bulls), JH Smith (Cheetahs), PJ Spies (Bulls), SWP Burger (Stormers)

SUBSTITUTIONS: AK Willemse (Lions) for Ndungane (51 mins), GJ Muller (Sharks) for JP Botha (63 mins), PD Carstens (Sharks) for Van der Linde (temporary 56-66 mins) and for Steenkamp (66 mins), G van G Botha (Bulls) for Smit (69 mins), R Pienaar (Sharks) for Januarie (69 mins), FPL Steyn (Sharks) for Montgomery (69 mins), RB Skinstad (Sharks) for Smith (temporary 9-16 and 72-77 mins) and for Habana (77 mins)

SCORERS: *Tries:* Spies (2), Habana (2), Januarie, Burger, JP Botha, Montgomery *Conversions:* Montgomery (5), James *Penalty goal:* Montgomery

ENGLAND: M Brown; Scarborough, Tait, Flood, Noon; Wilkinson (capt), Gomarsall; Yates, Regan, Stevens, Winters, A Brown, Easter, Skirving, Lund

SUBSTITUTIONS: Perry for Gomarsall (54 mins), Turner for Yates (57 mins), Abendanon for M Brown (62 mins), Jones for A Brown (62 mins), Titterell for Regan (69 mins), Schofield for Winters (72 mins)

SCORERS: *Try:* Scarborough *Conversion:* Wilkinson *Penalty goals:* Wilkinson (5)

REFEREE: J Jutge (France)

IRELAND TO ARGENTINA 2007

Tour party

FULL BACKS: GW Duffy (Connacht), GEA Murphy (Leicester Tigers)

THREE QUARTERS: BB Carney (Munster), AD Trimble (Ulster), TJ Bowe (Ulster), KP Lewis (Leinster), TG O'Leary (Munster), BJ Murphy (Munster), RDJ Kearney (Leinster), L Fitzgerald (Leinster)

HALF BACKS: P Wallace (Ulster), JW Staunton (London Wasps), IJ Boss (Ulster), EG Reddan (London Wasps)

FORWARDS: BG Young (Ulster), SJ Best (Ulster), TD Buckley (Munster), FJ Sheahan (Munster), P Bracken (London Wasps), BJ Jackman (Leinster), JP Flannery (Munster), T Hogan (Leinster), ME O'Kelly (Leinster), MR O'Driscoll (Munster), LFM Cullen (Leicester Tigers), AN Quinlan (Munster), S Ferris (Ulster), NA Best (Ulster), JPR Heaslip (Leinster), KD Gleeson (Leinster), S Jennings (Leicester Tigers)

MANAGER: G Carmody **COACH:** E O'Sullivan Assistant **COACH:** N O'Donovan **CAPTAIN:** SJ Best

Match 1, 26 May, Estadio Brigadier Estanislao Lopez, Santa Fe
Argentina 22 (1G 4PG 1DG) Ireland 20 (2G 2PG)

ARGENTINA: BM Stortoni (Bristol Rugby); T de Vedia (Saracens), H Senillosa (Hindu), M Avramovic (Worcester Warriors), FJ Leonelli (Glasgow Warriors); F Contepomi (Leinster)(capt), N Vergallo (Jockey Club, Rosario); MI Ayerza (Leicester Tigers), A Vernet Basualdo (Alumni), SG Bonorino (Capitolina), E Lozada (CASI), P Bouza (Leeds Carnegie), M Durand (Montpellier-Herault), J-M Leguizamon (London Irish), J-M Fernandez Lobbe (Sale Sharks)

SUBSTITUTIONS: G Fessia (Cordoba Athletic) for Durand (71 mins), P Cardinali (CS Bourgoin Jallieu) for Bonorino (75 mins)

SCORERS: *Try:* Senillosa *Conversion:* F Contepomi *Penalty goals:* F Contepomi (4) *Dropped goal:* F Contepomi

IRELAND: Duffy; Carney, Trimble, Lewis, Bowe; P Wallace, Boss; Young, Flannery, SJ Best (capt), Hogan, O'Kelly, NA Best, Heaslip, Gleeson

SUBSTITUTIONS: GEA Murphy for Duffy (temporary 15-22) and Wallace (62 mins), Buckley for Young (65 mins), MR O'Driscoll for Hogan (temporary 22-26 and 60 mins), Ferris for Gleeson (71 mins), Jackman for Flannery (78 mins), O'Leary for Lewis (78 mins), BJ Murphy for Bowe (80 mins)

SCORERS: *Tries:* Carney, Penalty try *Conversions:* P Wallace (2) *Penalty goals:* P Wallace, Duffy

REFEREE: LE Bray (New Zealand)

Match 2, 2 June, Velez Sarsfield Stadium, Buenos Aires
Argentina 16 (1G 3PG) Ireland 0

ARGENTINA: F Serra Miras (SIC); T de Vedia (Saracens), H Senillosa (Hindu), M Contepomi (Rovigo), FJ Leonelli (Glasgow Warriors); F Todeschini (Montpellier-Herault), N Vergallo (Jockey Club, Rosario); MI Ayerza (Leicester Tigers), P Gambarini (CASI) SG Bonorino (Capitolina), E Lozada (CASI), R Alvarez (USA Perpignan), M Durand (Montpellier-Herault)(capt), J-M Leguizamon (London Irish), J-M Fernandez Lobbe (Sale Sharks)

SUBSTITUTIONS: E Guinazu (SU Agen) for Bonorino (65 mins), P Bouza (Leeds Carnegie) for Lozada (68 mins), M Schusterman (Leeds Carnegie) for Durand (74 mins)

SCORERS: *Try:* M Contepomi *Conversion:* Todeschini *Penalty goals:* Todeschini (3)

IRELAND: GEA Murphy; Carney, BJ Murphy, Duffy, Kearney; Staunton, Reddan; Young, Sheahan, SJ Best (capt), Cullen, MR O'Driscoll, Quinlan, Ferris, Jennings

SUBSTITUTIONS: NA Best for Ferris (47 mins), O'Kelly for MR O'Driscoll (53 mins), Lewis for BJ Murphy (66 mins), Jackman for Sheahan (74 mins), Buckley for Young (74 mins), Fitzgerald for GEA Murphy (78 mins)

REFEREE: KM Deaker (New Zealand)

FRANCE TO NEW ZEALAND 2007

Tour party

FULL BACKS: T Castaignede (Saracens), J Laharrague (Sale Sharks)

THREE QUARTERS: N Laharrague (USA Perpignan), B Thiery (Bayonne), J-F Coux (CS Bourgoin Jallieu), A Mignardi (SU Agen), J-P Grandclaude (USA Perpignan), L Valbon (CA Brive), M Forest (CS Bourgoin Jallieu), L Mazars (RC Narbonne)

HALF BACKS: B Boyet (CS Bourgoin Jallieu), N Durand (USA Perpignan)

FORWARDS: C Califano (Gloucester Rugby), N Mas (USA Perpignan), F Montanella (Auch), O Sourgens (CS Bourgoin Jallieu), S Bruno (Sale Sharks), R Ibanez (London Wasps), P Pape (Castres Olympique), J Pierre (CS Bourgoin Jallieu), O Olibeau (USA Perpignan), G le Corvec (USA Perpignan), D Chouly (CA Brive), S Chabal (Sale Sharks), O Magne (London Irish), F Ouedraogo (Montpellier-Herault)

MANAGER J Dunyach, J Maso **COACH:** B Laporte **ASSISTANT COACHES:** B Vivies, D Ellis, J Brunel

Match 1, 2 June, Eden Park, Auckland
New Zealand 42 (4G 3PG 1T) France 11 (2PG 1T)

NEW ZEALAND: LR MacDonald (Crusaders); JT Rokocoko (Blues), I Toeava (Blues), AJD Mauger (Crusaders), SW Sivivatu (Chiefs); DW Carter (Crusaders), PAT Weepu (Hurricanes); TD Woodcock (Blues), KF Mealamu (Blues), CJ Hayman (Highlanders), CR Jack (Crusaders), AJ Williams (Blues), RD Thorne (Crusaders), MC Masoe (Hurricanes), RH McCaw (Crusaders)(capt)

SUBSTITUTIONS: NJ Evans (Highlanders) for Carter (40 mins), R So'oialo (Hurricanes) for McCaw (40 mins), BG Leonard (Chiefs) for Weepu (63 mins), AK Hore (Highlanders) for Mealamu (63 mins), MA Nonu (Hurricanes) for Sivivatu (73 mins), TV Flavell (Blues) for Jack (73 mins), NS Tialata (Hurricanes) for Hayman (73 mins)

SCORERS: *Tries:* Mauger (2), Sivivatu (2), So'oialo *Conversions:* Evans (2), Carter, Weepu *Penalty goals:* Carter, Weepu, Evans

FRANCE: Castaignede; Thiery, Mignardi, Grandclaude, Coux; Boyet, Durand, Califano, Bruno, Mas, Pape (capt), Pierre, Le Corvec, Chabal, Magne

SUBSTITUTIONS: Valbon for Grandclaude (16 mins), Olibeau for Pierre (56 mins), Montanella for Mas (56 mins), Chouly for Le Corvec (63 mins), Ibanez for Pape (74 mins), Forest for Coux (74 mins), J Laharrague for Thiery (76 mins)

SCORERS: *Try:* Coux *Penalty goals:* Boyet (2)

REFEREE: SJ Dickinson (Australia)

Match 2, 9 June, WestPac Stadium, Wellington
New Zealand 61 (5G 2PG 4T) France 10 (1G 1PG)

NEW ZEALAND: LR MacDonald (Crusaders); JT Rokocoko (Blues), I Toeava (Blues), CL McAlister (Blues), SW Sivivatu (Chiefs); NJ Evans (Highlanders), BT Kelleher (Chiefs); TD Woodcock (Blues), AD Oliver (Highlanders), CJ Hayman (Highlanders), CR Jack (Crusaders), AJ Williams (Blues), J Collins (Hurricanes), R So'oialo (Hurricanes), RH McCaw (Crusaders)(capt)

SUBSTITUTIONS: TV Flavell (Blues) for Williams (24 mins), BG Leonard (Chiefs) for Kelleher (48 mins), NS Tialata (Hurricanes) for Woodcock (59 mins), MC Masoe (Hurricanes) for McCaw (59 mins), DC Howlett (Blues) for MacDonald (59 mins), KF Mealamu (Blues) for Oliver (61 mins), MA Nonu (Hurricanes) for Toeava (67 mins)

SCORERS: *Tries:* Rokocoko (2), Oliver, Kelleher, MacDonald, Toeava, Collins, Mealamu, Evans *Conversions:* McAlister (5) *Penalty goals:* McAlister (2)

FRANCE: Castaignede: J Laharrague, Mignardi, Mazars, Coux; Boyet, Durand; Califano, Bruno, Sourgens, Pape (capt), Pierre, Chouly, Chabal, Magne

SUBSTITUTIONS: Thiery for Mazars (24 mins), Olibeau for Pape (34 mins), Ouedraogo for Chabal (54 mins), Mas for Sourgens (47 mins), N Laharrague for Boyet (61 mins), Forest for Durand (67 mins), Ibanez for Mignardi (74 mins)

SCORERS: *Try:* J Laharrague *Conversion:* Boyet *Penalty goal:* Boyet

REFEREE: C Joubert (South Africa)

ITALY TO SOUTH AMERICA 2007

Tour party

FULL BACKS: D Bortolussi (Montpellier-Herault)

THREE QUARTERS: A Galante (Rugby Parma), E Galon (Overmach Parma), E Patrizio (Padova), M Pratichetti (Calvisano), K Robertson (Viadana), M Stanojevic (Bristol Rugby), A Stoica (Montpellier-Herault)

HALF BACKS: R de Marigny (Calvisano), C Burton (RC Orleans), P Canavosio (Castres Olympique), P Griffen (Calvisano)

FORWARDS: A Lo Cicero (L'Aquila), C Nieto (Gloucester Rugby), M Aguero (Viadana), F Staibano (Overmach Parma), F Ongaro (Saracens), C Festuccia (Rugby Parma), CA Del Fava (CS Bourgoin Jallieu), V Bernabo (Calvisano), R Barbieri (Overmach Parma), A Pavanello (Treviso), R Mandelli (Rugby Parma), S Orlando (Treviso), J Sole (Viadana), A Zanni (Calvisano)

MANAGER C Checchinato **COACH:** P Berbizier Assistant **COACHES:** C Orlandi, J-P Cariat **CAPTAIN:** Lo Cicero

Match 1, 2 June, Gran Parque Central, Montevideo
Uruguay 5 (1T) Italy 29 (3G 1PG 1T)

URUGUAY: Arocena; Morales, Llovet, Pastore, Bulanti; M Crosa, Labat; Sanchez, Arboleya, Sagario, Alzueta, Protasi, Giuria, Lussich, Conti (capt)

SUBSTITUTIONS: Szabo for Arboleya (41 mins), Levaggi for Sagario (60 mins), Ariano for Alzueta (66 mins), Posse for Giuria 66 mins)

SCORER: *Try:* Arocena

ITALY: Burton; Robertson, Patrizio, Stoica, Pratichetti; De Marigny, Griffen; Lo Cicero (capt), Festuccia, Staibano, Del Fava, Bernabo, Sole, Zanni, Barbieri

SUBSTITUTIONS: Orlando for Zanni (43 mins), Aguero for Staibano (45 mins), Galante for Patrizio (47 mins), Galon for Robertson (temporary 56-58 mins), Bortolussi for De Marigny (61 mins), Ongaro for Festuccia (61 mins)

SCORERS: *Tries:* Pratichetti (3), Aguero *Conversions:* Burton (3) *Penalty goal:* Burton

REFEREE: R Debney (England)

Match 2, 9 June, Esatdio Malvinas Argentinas, Mendoza
Argentina 24 (1G 4PG 1T) Italy 6 (2PG)

ARGENTINA: F Serra Miras (SIC) ; H Agulla (Hindu), M Gaitan (Biarritz Olympique), M Contepomi (Rovigo), FJ Leonelli (Glasgow Warriors) M Bosch (Biarritz Olympique), N Fernandez Miranda (Bayonne); P Henn (RC Montauban), P Gamberini (CASI), O Hasan (Stade Toulousain), CI Fernandez Lobbe (Sale Sharks), M Carizza (Biarritz Olympique), M Durand (Montpellier-Herault)(capt), JM Leguizamon (London Irish), JM Fernandez Lobbe (Sale Sharks)

SUBSTITUTIONS: E Guinazu (SU Agen) for Henn (47 mins), M Schusterman (Leeds Carnegie) for Durand (62 mins), J Fernandez Miranda (Hindu) for Bosch (67 mins), SG Bonorino (Capitolina) for Hasan (71 mins), R Alvarez (USA Perpignan) for Carizza (71 mins)

SCORERS: *Tries:* Leonelli, Serra Miras *Conversion:* Serra Miras *Penalty goals:* Serra Miras (4)

ITALY: Bortolussi; Robertson, Galante, Stoica, Pratichetti; Burton, Canavosio; Lo Cicero (capt), Ongaro, Nieto, De Fava, Bernabo, Sole, Barbieri, Mandelli

SUBSTITUTIONS: Griffen for Canavosio (29 mins), Festuccia for Ongaro (45 mins), Orlando for Mandelli (53 mins), Staibano for Nieto (53 mins), Aguero for Barbieri (68 mins), Pavanello for Bernabo (71 mins), Galon for Galante (78 mins)

SCORER: *Penalty goals:* Bortolussi (2)

REFEREE: LC Bray (New Zealand)

FIJI TO AUSTRALIA 2007

9 June, Subiaco Oval, Perth
Australia 49 (3G 1PG 5T) Fiji 0

AUSTRALIA: JL Huxley (ACT Brumbies) ; LD Tuqiri (NSW Waratahs), AP Ashley-Cooper (ACT Brumbies), SNG Staniforth (Western Force), DA Mitchell (Western Force); SJ Larkham (ACT Brumbies), GM Gregan (ACT Brumbies); MJ Dunning (NSW Waratahs), AL Freier (NSW Waratahs), AKE Baxter (NSW Waratahs), JE Horwill (Queensland Reds), DJ Vickerman (NSW Waratahs), MD Chisholm (ACT Brumbies), DJ Lyons (NSW Waratahs), PR Waugh (NSW Waratahs)(capt)

SUBSTITUTIONS: SH Norton-Knight (NSW Waratahs) for Larkham (55 mins), ST Moore (Queensland Reds) for Freier (58 mins), SA Hoiles (ACT Brumbies) for Lyons (60 mins), GB Smith (ACT Brumbies) for Waugh (68 mins), BA Robinson (NSW Waratahs) for Dunning (68 mins), SJ Cordingley (Queensland Reds) for Gregan (68 mins), SA Mortlock (ACT Brumbies) for Huxley (73 mins)

SCORERS: *Tries:* Staniforth (2), Tuqiri (2), Huxley, Larkham, Norton-Knight, Ashley-Cooper *Conversions:* Huxley (3) *Penalty goal:* Huxley

FIJI: M Vakacegu (Suva); M Luveitasau (Suva), V Goneva (Nadi), G Lovobalavu (Suva), I Neivua (Nadroga); J Prasad (Suva), M Rauluni (Saracens); G Dewes (Marist, NZ), S Koto (Suva), H Qiodravu (RC Orleans), K Leawere (Hino Motors), I Rawaqa (World), A Satala (Suva), A Doviverata (Yamaha)(capt)

SUBSTITUTIONS: T Rawaqa (Lautoka) for Vakacegu (52 mins), W Lewaravu (Naitasiri) for Rawaqa (60 mins), A Turukawa (Nadroga) for Satala (temporary 37-47) and for Qiodravu

(60 mins), V Buatava (Western Force) for Prasad (70 mins), W Gadolo (Suva) for Koto (70 mins), T Soqeta (Taranaki) for Doviverata (70 mins), V Rauluni (Morrinsville, NZ) for Leveitasau (75 mins)

REFEREE: BJ Lawrence (New Zealand)

SAMOA TO SOUTH AFRICA 2007

9 June, Ellis Park, Johannesburg
South Africa 35 (2G 2PG 3T) Samoa 8 (1PG 1T)

SOUTH AFRICA: FPL Steyn (Sharks); AK Willemse (Lions), WM Murray (Sharks), W Julies (Bulls), J-PR Pietersen (Sharks); DJ Hougaard (Bulls) , ER Januarie (Lions); JP du Randt (Cheetahs), JW Smit (Sharks)(capt), BJ Botha (Sharks), JN Ackermann (Sharks), PA Van den Berg (Sharks), LA Watson (Stormers), RB Skinstad (Sharks), DJ Rossouw (Bulls)

SUBSTITUTIONS: J Fourie (Lions) for Willemse (43 mins), R Pienaar (Sharks) for Januarie (44 mins), G van G Botha (Bulls) for Smit (50 mins), PJ Wannenburg (Bulls) for Watson (50 mins), PD Carstens (Sharks) for Du Randt (52 mins), PC Montgomery (Sharks) for Julies (55 mins), GJ Muller (Sharks) for Ackermann (60 mins)

SCORERS: *Tries:* Smit, Pietersen, Steyn, Wannenburg, Montgomery *Conversions:* Hougaard, Montgomery *Penalty goals:* Hougaard (2)

SAMOA: G Williams (Connacht); L Fa'atau (Glasgow Warriors), Anitelea Tuilagi, (Leicester Tigers) S Mapusua (London Irish), Alesana Tuilagi (Leicester Tigers); L Crichton (Worcester Warriors), S So'oialo (NEC Harlequins); J Va'a (Glasgow Warriors), M Schwalger (Hurricanes), C Johnston (Saracens), F Levi (Ricoh), K Thompson (Highlanders) D Leo (London Wasps), S Sititi (NTT)(capt), J Purdie (Wellington)

SUBSTITUTIONS: A To'oala (Bristol Rugby) for Purdie (54 mins), I Tekori (Waitakere) for Levi (56 mins), E Seveali'I (Sale Sharks) for Mapusua (61 mins), J Polu (North Harbour) for So'oialo (62 mins), M Salanoa (Scopa) for Schwalger (62 mins), DA Kerslake (Upolu) for Va'a (temporary 41-48 and from 68 mins), D Lemi (Bristol Rugby) for Fa'atau (68 mins)

SCORERS: *Try:* Anitelea Tuilagi *Penalty goal:* Williams

REFEREE: D Changleng (Scotland)

CANADA TO NEW ZEALAND 2007

Tour party

FULL BACKS: M Pyke (RC Montauban), DTH van der Merwe (James Bay AA)

THREE QUARTERS: J Mensah-Coker (RC Albi), J Pritchard (Bedford), C Culpan (Meraloma), D Spicer (Victoria University), D van Camp (Aurora Barbarians) E Fairhurst (Cornish Pirates). N Dala (Wild Oats, Saskatoon), N Trenkel (Capilano)

HALF BACKS: R Smith (RC Montauban), N Hirayama (Victoria University), A Monro (Waterloo), M Williams (RC Albi)

FORWARDS: K Tkchuk (Glasgow Warriors) S Franklin (Castaway Wanderers), D Pletch (Oakville Crusaders), M Pletch (Oakville Crusaders), P Riordan (Burnaby Lake), A Carpenter (Brantford Harlequins), J Jackson (Stade Bordeaux-Begles), L Tait (Overmach Parma), M Burak (Pau), C Yukes (SU Agen), S McKeen (Cornish Pirates), A Kleeberger (Victoria University), S-M Stephen (AS Beziers), M Perizzolo (Burnaby Lake)

MANAGER R McGeein Coach R Suggitt Assistant coaches G Ella, J Tait, K Wirachowski

Match 1, 16 June, Waikato Stadium, Rugby Park, Hamilton
New Zealand 64 (7G 3T) Canada 13 (1G 2PG)

NEW ZEALAND: JM Muliaina (Chiefs); DC Howlett (Blues), CL McAlister (Blues), AJD Mauger (Crusaders), SW Sivivatu (Chiefs); DW Carter (Crusaders), BT Kelleher (Chiefs); JE Schwalger (Hurricanes), AK Hore (Highlanders), NS Tialata (Hurricanes), TV Flavell (Blues), RA Filipo (Crusaders), RD Thorne (Crusaders)(capt), J Collins (Hurricanes), MC Masoe (Hurricanes)
SUBSTITUTIONS: RH McCaw (Crusaders) for Flavell (45 mins), PAT Weepu (Hurricanes) for Kelleher (47 mins), RL Gear (Crusaders) for McAlister (47 mins), LR MacDonald (Crusaders) for Muliaina (58 mins)
SCORERS: *Tries:* Carter (3), Sivivatu, McAlister, Schwalger, Hore, Masoe, Howlett, Gear *Conversions:* Carter (7)
CANADA: Pyke; Mensah-Coker, Culpan, Spicer, Pritchard; Smith, Williams (capt); Tkachuk, Riordan, Franklin, Tait, Burak, Yukes, Stephen, McKeen
SUBSTITUTIONS: Van Camp for Spicer (40 mins), Carpenter for Yukes (55 mins), Jackson for Tait (57 mins), M Pletch for Franklin (61 mins), Fairhurst for Van Camp (66 mins), Kleeberger for McKeen (temporary 31–40 mins) and for Stephen (72 mins), D Pletch for Tkchuk (74 mins)
SCORERS: *Try:* Pyke *Conversion:* Pritchard *Penalty goals:* Pritchard (2)
REFEREE: C Berdos (France)

Match 2, 21 June, Rotorua Stadium
New Zealand U21 13 (1G 2PG) Canada XV 16 (2PG 2T)

New Zealand U21 **SCORERS:** *Try:* B Smith *Conversion:* L Munro *Penalty goals:* C Slade, L Munro
Canada XV **SCORERS:** *Tries:* Webb, Tkachuk *Penalty goals:* Monro, Pritchard

SUMMER SERIES 2007

4 August, Twickenham
England 62 (7G 1PG 2T) Wales (1T)

ENGLAND: M Tait (Newcastle Falcons); D Strettle (NEC Harlequins), D Hipkiss (Leicester Tigers), A Farrell (Saracens) JT Robinson (Unattached); JP Wilkinson (Newcastle Falcons), S Perry (Bristol Rugby); AJ Sheridan (Sale Sharks), MP Regan (Bristol Rugby), PJ Vickery (London Wasps)(capt), SD Shaw (London Wasps), SW Borthwick (Bath Rugby), ME Corry (Leicester Tigers), N Easter (NEC Harlequins) JPR Worsley (London Wasps)
SUBSTITUTIONS: MJH Stevens (Bath Rugby) for Vickery (40 mins), GS Chuter (Leicester Tigers) for Regan (55 mins), LBN Dallaglio (London Wasps) for Easter (57 mins), LW Moody (Leicester Tigers) for Corry (69 mins), T Flood (Newcastle Falcons) for Farrell (temporary)
SCORERS: *Tries:* Easter (4), Borthwick, Perry, Dallaglio, Robinson, Tait *Conversions:* Wilkinson (7) *Penalty goal:* Wilkinson
WALES: LM Byrne (Ospreys); DR James (Scarlets), TGL Shanklin (Blues), G Thomas (Blues)(capt), A Brew (Ospreys); C Sweeney (Dragons), GJ Cooper (Gloucester Rugby); ID Thomas (Scarlets), H Bennett (Ospreys), CL Horsman (Worcester Warriors), W James (Gloucester Rugby), RA Sidoli (Blues), A-W Jones (Ospreys), MJ Owen (Dragons), CL Charvis (Dragons)
SUBSTITUTIONS: TR Thomas (Blues) for Bennett (51 mins), AJ Popham (Scarlets) for Owen (51 mins), R Thomas (Dragons) for Horsman (51 mins), GD Jenkins (Blues) for ID Thomas (54 mins), T James (Blues) for Shanklin (77 mins)
SCORER: *Try:* DR James
REFEREE: J Jutge (France)

11 August, Murrayfield
Scotland 31 (3G 2T) Ireland 21 (1G 3PG 1T)

SCOTLAND: RP Lamont (Sale Sharks); SF Lamont (Northampton Saints), RE Dewey (Ulster), AR Henderson (Glasgow Warriors), SL Webster (Edinburgh Rugby); CD Paterson (Gloucester Rugby), MRL Blair (Edinburgh Rugby); AF Jacobsen (Edinburgh Rugby), RW Ford (Glasgow Warriors), EA Murray (Northampton Saints), NJ Hines (USA Perpignan), JL Hamilton (Leicester Tigers), JPR White (Sale Sharks)(capt), SM Taylor (Stade Francais), A Hogg (Edinburgh Rugby)

SUBSTITUTIONS: KDR Brown (Glasgow Warriors) for Taylor (38 mins), SJ MacLeod (Scarlets) for White (56 mins), CJ Smith (Edinburgh Rugby) for EA Murray (56 mins), N Walker (Ospreys) for Dewey (59 mins), CP Cusiter (USA Perpignan) for Blair (60 mins), DA Parks (Glasgow Warriors) for Paterson (60 mins), FMA Thomson (Glasgow Warriors) for Ford (temporary 39-43 mins, 67-78 mins) and Hamilton (78 mins)

SCORERS: *Tries:* Henderson (3), Hogg, EA Murray *Conversions:* Paterson (2), Parks

IRELAND: GEA Murphy (Leicester Tigers); BB Carney (Munster), BG O'Driscoll (Leinster)(capt), GW Duffy (Connacht), TJ Bowe (Ulster); P Wallace (Ulster), IJ Boss (Ulster); BG Young (Ulster), JP Flannery (Munster), SJ Best (Ulster), ME O'Kelly (Leinster), PJ O'Connell (Munster), NA Best (Ulster), JPR Heaslip (Leinster), S Ferris (Ulster)

SUBSTITUTIONS: AD Trimble (Ulster) for Duffy (26 mins), AN Quinlan (Munster) for O'Kelly (temporary 8-11, 23-32 and 40 mins), KD Gleeson (Leinster) for NA Best (64 mins), RJR O'Gara (Munster) for O'Driscoll (66 mins), JJ Hayes (Munster) for Young (70 mins), R Best (Ulster) for Flannery (74 mins), EG Reddan (London Wasps) for Boss (74 mins)

SCORERS: *Tries:* Boss, Trimble *Conversion:* P Wallace *Penalty goals:* P Wallace (2), Murphy

REFEREE: AJ Spreadbury (England)

11 August, Twickenham
England 15 (4PG 1DG) France 21 (1G 3PG 1T)

ENGLAND: N Abendanon (Bath Rugby); PH Sackey (London Wasps), JD Noon (Newcastle Falcons), MJ Catt (London Irish)(capt), OJ Lewsey (London Wasps); OJ Barkley (Bath Rugby), S Perry (Bristol Rugby); AJ Sheridan (Sale Sharks), MP Regan (Bristol Rugby), MJH Stevens (Bath Rugby), SD Shaw (London Wasps), BJ Kay (Leicester Tigers), J Haskell (London Wasps), LBN Dallaglio (London Wasps), JPR Worsley (London Wasps)

SUBSTITUTIONS: LA Mears (Bath Rugby) for Regan (49 mins), ACT Gomarsall (NEC Harlequins) for Perry (49 mins), PJ Vickery (London Wasps) for Stevens (56 mins), ME Corry (Leicester Tigers) for Shaw (56 mins), JP Wilkinson (Newcastle Falcons) for Catt (77 mins)

SCORERS: *Penalty goals:* Barkley (4) *Dropped goal:* Gomarsall

FRANCE: C Poitrenaud (Stade Toulousain); A Rougerie (Clermont-Auvergne), D Marty (USA Perpignan), D Traille (Biarritz Olympique), V Clerc (Stade Toulousain); D Skrela (Stade Francais), P Mignoni (Clermont-Auvergne) O Milloud (CS Bourgoin Jallieu), R Ibanez (London Wasps)(capt), J-B Poux (Stade Toulousain), F Pelous (Stade Toulousain), J Thion (Biarritz Olympique), S Betsen (Biarritz Olympique), J Bonnaire (CS Bourgoin Jallieu), R Martin (Stade Francais)

SUBSTITUTIONS: J-B Elissalde (Stade Toulousain) for Mignoni (43 mins), D Szarzewski (Stade Francais) for Ibanez (51 mins), Y Nyanga (Stade Toulousain) for Betsen (56 mins), S Chabal (Sale Sharks) for Pelous (56 mins), F Michalak (Stade Toulousain) for Traille (56 mins), N Mas (USA Perpignan) for Poux (65 mins)

SCORERS: *Tries:* Pelous, Chabal *Conversion:* Elissalde *Penalty goals:* Skrela (2), Elissalde

REFEREE: A Lewis (Ireland)

15 August, Newlands, Cape Town
South Africa 105 (12G 2PG 3T) Namibia 13 (1G 2PG)

SOUTH AFRICA: PC Montgomery (Sharks); AK Willemse (Lions), J Fourie (Lions), J de Villiers (Stormers), J-PR Pietersen (Sharks); AD James (Sharks), PF du Preez (Bulls); JP du Randt (Cheetahs), G van G Botha (Bulls), CJ van der Linde (Cheetahs), JP Botha (Bulls), V Matfield (Bulls)(capt), JH Smith (Cheetahs), J Cronje (Lions), SWP Burger (Stormers)

SUBSTITUTIONS: R Pienaar (Sharks) for James (62 mins), BW du Plessis (Sharks) for G Botha (62 mins), BJ Botha (Sharks) for Van der Linde (62 mins), ER Januarie (Lions) for Du Preez (62 mins), AZ Ndungane (Bulls) for Willemse (71 mins), GJ Muller (Sharks) for JP Botha (71 mins), PA Van den Berg (Sharks) for Burger (temporary 8-20 mins) and Matfield (74 mins)

SCORERS: *Tries:* Burger (3), Smith (3) De Villiers, Pietersen, Fourie, Du Randt, Montgomery, Willemse, B du Plessis, Pienaar, van der Linde *Conversions:* Montgomery (12) *Penalty goals:* Montgomery (2)

NAMIBIA: JH Bock (Reho Falcons); BC Langenhoven (North West University), L-W Botes (University of Johannesburg), WP Van Zyl (Boland), MJ Africa (Reho Falcons); E Wessels (Maties), JH van Tonder (United); G Lensing (Sharks)(capt), H Horn (Border), M Visser (Border), U Kazombiaze (Western Suburbs), N Esterhuyse (Maties), J Niewenhuis (Reho Falcons), J Burger (Griqualand West), T du Plessis (Maties)

SUBSTITUTIONS: JH Redelinghuys (Griqualand West) for Visser (36 mins), TC Losper (Griqualand West) for Bock (40 mins), JA du Toit (Western Province) for Lensing (62 mins), HD Lintvelt (United) for Burger (temporary 25-28 mins) and for T du Plessis (64 mins), Du P Grobler (United) for Wessels (64 mins), EA Jantjies (Western Suburbs) for Van Tonder (67 mins), JM Meyer (Wanderers) for Burger (28-30 mins) and Horn (74 mins)

SCORERS: *Tries:* Langenhoven *Conversion:* Wessels *Penalty goals:* Wessels (2)

REFEREE: JI Kaplan (South Africa)

18 August, Millennium Stadium, Cardiff
Wales 27 (3G 2PG) Argentina 20 (2G 2PG)

WALES: KA Morgan (Dragons); DR James (Scarlets), TGL Shanklin (Blues), G Thomas (Blues)(capt), MA Jones (Scarlets); J Hook (Ospreys), DJ Peel (Scarlets); D Jones (Ospreys), M Rees (Scarlets), AR Jones (Ospreys), IM Gough (Ospreys), A-W Jones (Ospreys), J Thomas (Ospreys), AJ Popham (Scarlets), ME Williams (Blues)

SUBSTITUTIONS: GD Jenkins (Blues) for D Jones (57 mins), W James (Gloucester Rugby) for Gough (60 mins), CL Charvis (Dragons) for ME Williams (67 mins), JP Robinson (Blues) for G Thomas (65-72 mins) and for MA Jones (74 mins)

SCORERS: *Tries:* G Thomas, A-W Jones, MA Jones *Conversions:* Hook (3) *Penalty goals:* Hook (2)

ARGENTINA: F Serra Miras (SIC); L Borges (Stade Francais), M Gaitan (Biarritz Olympique), F Contepomi (Leinster), I Corleto (Stade Francais); F Todeschini (Montpellier-Herault), A Pichot (Stade Francais)(capt); R Roncero (Stade Francais), ME Ledesma (Clermont-Auvergne), M Scelzo (Clermont-Auvergne), CI Fernandez-Lobbe (Sale Sharks), P Albacete (Stade Toulousain), JM Leguizamon (London Irish), G Longo (Clermont-Auvergne), JM Fernandez-Lobbe (Sale Sharks)

SUBSTITUTIONS: M Durand (Montpellier-Herault) for Leguizamon (60 mins), R Alvarez (USA Perpignan) for CI Fernandez-Lobbe (60 mins), SG Bonorino (Capitolino) for Scelzo (60 mins), M Contepomi (Newman) for F Contepomi (79 mins)

SCORERS: *Tries:* Corleto (2) *Conversions:* Todeschini (2) *Penalty goals:* Todeschini (2)

REFEREE: C White (England)

18 August, Stade Velodrome, Marseille
France 22 (1G 5PG) England 9 (3PG)

FRANCE: C Poitrenaud (Stade Toulousain); C Dominici (Stade Francais), Y Jauzion (Stade Toulousain), D Traille (Biarritz Olympique), C Heymans (Stade Toulousain); F Michalak (Stade Toulousain), J-B Elissalde (Stade Toulousain); O Milloud (CS Bourgoin Jallieu), R Ibanez (London Wasps)(capt), J-B Poux (Stade Toulousain), F Pelous (Stade Toulousain), J Thion (Biarritz Olympique), Y Nyanga (Stade Toulousain), I Harinordoquy (Biarritz Olympique), T Dusautoir (Stade Toulousain)

SUBSTITUTIONS: S Bruno (Sale Sharks) for Ibanez (57 mins), L Nallet (Castres Olympique) for Pelous (57 mins), J Bonnaire (CS Bourgoin Jallieu) for Nyanga (59 mins), N Mas (USA Perpignan) for Poux (63 mins), P Mignoni (Clermont-Auvergne) for Elissalde (67 mins), D Skrela (Stade Francais) for Traille (71 mins)

SCORERS: *Try:* Jauzion *Conversion:* Elissalde *Penalty goals:* Elissalde (4), Michalak

ENGLAND: MJ Cueto (Sale Sharks); OJ Lewsey (London Wasps), D Hipkiss (Leicester Tigers), A Farrell (Saracens) JT Robinson (Unattached) ; JP Wilkinson (Newcastle Falcons), S Perry (Bristol Rugby); PT Freshwater (USA Perpignan), MP Regan (Bristol Rugby), PJ Vickery (London Wasps)(capt), SD Shaw (London Wasps), SW Borthwick (Bath Rugby), ME Corry (Leicester Tigers), N Easter (NEC Harlequins), T Rees (London Wasps)

SUBSTITUTIONS: MJH Stevens (Bath Rugby) for Vickery (40 mins), LBN Dallaglio (London Wasps) for Easter (50 mins), LA Mears (Bath Rugby) for Regan (50 mins), PH Sackey (London Wasps) for Lewsey (61 mins), JPR Worsley (London Wasps) for Rees (62 mins), OJ Barkley (Bath Rugby) for Corry (71 mins), ACT Gomarsall (NEC Harlequins) for Perry (77 mins)

SCORER: *Penalty goals:* Wilkinson (3)

REFEREE: AC Rolland (Ireland)

18 August, Stadio Perucca, Saint Vincent, Aosta
Italy 36 (4G 1PG 1T) Japan 12 (1G 1T)

ITALY: D Bortolussi (Montpellier-Herault); K Robertson (Viadana), G-J Canale (Clermont-Auvergne), Mirco Bergamasco (Stade Francais), M Stanojevic (Bristol Rugby); R Pez (Bayonne), A Troncon (Clermont-Auvergne); A lo Cicero (L'Aquila), C Festuccia (Rugby Parma), M-L Castrogiovanni (Leicester Tigers), S Dellape (Biarritz Olympique), M Bortolami (Gloucester Rugby)(capt), J Sole (Viadana), S Parisse (Stade Francais), Mauro Bergamasco (Stade Francais)

SUBSTITUTIONS: S Perugini (Stade Toulousain) for Lo Cicero (41 mins), A Masi (Biarritz Olympique) for Canale (41 mins), V Bernabo (CA Brive) for Dellape (59 mins), M Vosawai (Overmach Parma) for Sole (59 mins), R de Marigny (Calvisano) for Pez (66 mins), P Canavosio (Castres Olympique) for Troncon (72 mins), L Ghiraldini (Calvisano) for Festuccia (72 mins)

SCORERS: *Tries:* Stanojevic (2), Robertson, Lo Cicero, Mauro Bergamasco *Conversions:* Bortolussi (4) *Penalty goal:* Bortolussi

JAPAN: B Robins (Ricoh); K Endo (Toyota), Y Imamura (Kobe), S Onishi (Yamaha) C Loamanu (Saitama); E Ando (NEC), T Yoshida (Toshiba); T Nishiura (Coca Cola), Y Matsuraba (Kobe), T Soma (Sanyo), H Ono (Toshiba), L Thompson (Kintetsu), H Makiri (Fukuoka), T Miuchi (NEC)(capt), P O'Reilly (Sanyo)

SUBSTITUTIONS: LS Vatuvei (Kintetsu) for H Ono (45 mins), R Yamamura (Yamaha) for Soma (55 mins), R Asano (NEC) for O'Reilly (60 mins), G Aruga (Suntory) for Loamanu (65 mins), K Ono (Fukuoka) for Robins (77 mins)

SCORERS: *Tries:* Nishiura, Makiri *Conversion:* Ando

REFEREE: D Pearson (England)

24 August, Ravenhill, Belfast
Ireland 23 (2G 2PG 1DG) Italy 20 (2G 1PG 1DG)

IRELAND: GT Dempsey (Leinster); GEA Murphy (Leicester Tigers), AD Trimble (Ulster), GMD D'Arcy (Leinster), DA Hickie (Leinster); RJR O'Gara (Munster), PA Stringer (Munster); MJ Horan (Munster), R Best (Ulster), JJ Hayes (Munster), DF O'Callaghan (Munster), PJ O'Connell (Munster)(capt), SH Easterby (Scarlets), DP Leamy (Munster), NA Best (Ulster)

SUBSTITUTIONS: SJ Best (Ulster) for Hayes (66 mins), ME O'Kelly (Leinster) for O'Connell (68 mins), JP Flannery (Munster) for R Best (75 mins), IJ Boss (Ulster) for Stringer (78 mins), BB Carney (Munster) for Hickie (78 mins)

SCORERS: *Tries:* Trimble, O'Gara *Conversions:* O'Gara (2) *Penalty goals:* O'Gara (2) *Dropped goal:* O'Gara

ITALY: D Bortolussi (Montpellier-Herault); K Robertson (Viadana), G-J Canale (Clermont-Auvergne), Mirco Bergamasco (Stade Francais), M Pratchetti (Calvisano); R de Marigny (Calvisano), A Troncon (Clermont-Auvergne); S Perugini (Stade Toulousain), F Ongaro (Saracens), M-L Castrogiovanni (Leicester Tigers), V Bernabo (CA Brive), M Bortolami (Gloucester Rugby)(capt), R Barbieri (Treviso), S Parisse (Stade Francais) A Zanni (Calvisano)

SUBSTITUTIONS: M Vosawai (Overmach Parma) for Barbieri (40 mins), E Galon (Overmach Parma) for Bortolussi (47 mins), M Aguero (Viadana) for Perugini (50 mins), J Sole (Viadana) for Vosawai (64 mins), P Griffen (Calvisano) for Canale (66 mins), P Canavosio (castres Olympique) for Mirco Bergamasco (75 mins)

SCORERS: *Tries:* Troncon, Pratichetti *Conversions:* Bortolussi, De Marigny *Penalty goal:* Bortolussi *Dropped goal:* Bortolussi

REFEREE: N Owens (Wales)

25 August, Murrayfield
Scotland 3 (1PG) South Africa 27 (3G 2PG)

SCOTLAND: RP Lamont (Sale Sharks); N Walker (Ospreys), RE Dewey (Ulster), AR Henderson (Glasgow Warriors), SL Webster (Edinburgh Rugby); CD Paterson (Gloucester Rugby), MRL Blair (Edinburgh Rugby); G Kerr (Unattached), RW Ford (Glasgow Warriors), EA Murray (Northampton Saints), NJ Hines (USA Perpignan), JL Hamilton (Leicester Tigers), JPR White (Sale Sharks)(capt), DA Callam (Edinburgh Rugby), KDR Brown (Glasgow Warriors)

SUBSTITUTIONS: AF Jacobsen (Edinburgh Rugby) for Kerr (28 mins), HGF Southwell (Edinburgh Rugby) for Henderson (45 mins), S Murray (RC Montauban) for Hamilton (45 mins), DA Parks (Glasgow Warriors) for Paterson (54 mins), A Hogg (Edinburgh Rugby) for White (temporary 30-40 mins) and for Callam (62 mins), FMA Thomson (Glasgow Warriors) for Ford (66 mins), RGM Lawson (Gloucester Rugby) for Blair (66 mins)

SCORER: *Penalty goal:* Paterson

SOUTH AFRICA: PC Montgomery (Sharks); J-PR Pietersen (Sharks), J Fourie (Lions), FPL Steyn (Sharks), BG Habana (Bulls); AD James (Sharks), PF du Preez (Bulls); JP du Randt (Cheetahs), G van G Botha (Bulls), CJ van der Linde (Cheetahs), JP Botha (Bulls), V Matfield (Bulls)(capt), JH Smith (Cheetahs), DJ Rossouw (Bulls), SWP Burger (Stormers)

SUBSTITUTIONS: JL van Heerden (Bulls) for Rossouw (55 mins), AS Pretorius (Lions) for Steyn (55 mins), BJ Botha (Sharks) for Du Randt (temporary 30-40 mins and from 61 mins), R Pienaar (Sharks) for Montgomery (61 mins), BW du Plessis (Sharks) for G Botha (61 mins), PA van den Berg (Sharks) for JP Botha (61 mins), AK Willemse (Lions) for Pietersen (72 mins)

SCORERS: *Tries:* Habana, Fourie, Du Preez *Conversions:* Montgomery (3) *Penalty goals:* Montgomery (2)

REFEREE: C Berdos (France)

26 August, Millennium Stadium, Cardiff
Wales 7 (1G) France 34 (4G 2PG)

WALES: KA Morgan (Dragons); MA Jones (Scarlets), JP Robinson (Blues), G Thomas (Blues)(capt), SM Williams (Ospreys); J Hook (Ospreys), DJ Peel (Scarlets); D Jones (Ospreys), M Rees (Scarlets), CL Horsman (Worcester Warriors), IM Gough (Ospreys), A-W Jones (Ospreys), J Thomas (Ospreys), AJ Popham (Scarlets), ME Williams (Blues)

SUBSTITUTIONS: M Phillips (Ospreys) for Peel (40 mins), GD Jenkins (Blues) for D Jones (40 mins), TR Thomas (Blues) for Rees (45 mins), CL Charvis (Dragons) for ME Williams (51 mins), ST Parker (Ospreys) for G Thomas (temporary 15-20, 44-52 mins) and for Morgan (60 mins), W James (Gloucester Rugby) for A-W Jones (62 mins), C Sweeney (Dragons) for Hook (69 mins)

SCORER: *Try:* Hook *Conversion:* Hook

FRANCE: C Heymans (Stade Toulousain); A Rougerie (Clermont-Auvergne), Y Jauzion (Stade Toulousain), D Skrela (Stade Francais), V Clerc (Stade Toulousain); L Beauxis (Stade Francais), P Mignoni (Clermot Auvergne); N Mas (USA Perpignan), D Szarzewski (Stade Francais), P de Villiers (Stade Francais), S Chabal (Sale Sharks), J Thion (Biarritz Olympique), S Betsen (Biarritz Olympique)(capt), I Harinordoquy (Biarritz Olympique), R Martin (Stade Francais)

SUBSTITUTIONS: F Pelous (Stade Toulousain) for Thion (40 mins), S Bruno (Sale Sharks) for Szarzewski (40 mins), J-B Elissalde (Stade Toulousain) for Mignoni (40 mins), T Dusautoir (Stade Toulousain) for Harinordoquy (47 mins), J-B Poux (Stade Toulousain) for De Villiers (53 mins), D Traille (Biarritz Olympique) for Skrela (62 mins), C Dominici (Stade Francais) for Rougerie (72 mins)

SCORERS: *Tries:* Thion, Mignoni, Rougerie, Bruno *Conversions:* Beauxis (3), Elissalde *Penalty goals:* Beauxis (2)

REFEREE: W Barnes (England)

REFEREES' SIGNALS

PENALTY KICK
Shoulders parallel with the touchline. Arm angled up, pointing towards non-offending team.

FREE KICK
Shoulders parallel with touchline. Arm bent square at elbow, upper arm pointing towards non-offending team.

TRY AND PENALTY TRY
Referee's back to dead ball line. Arm raised vertically.

ADVANTAGE
Arm outstretched, waist high, towards non-offending team, for a period of approximately five seconds.

SCRUM AWARDED

Shoulders parallel with touchline. Arm horizontal, pointing towards team to throw in the ball.

FORMING A SCRUM

Elbows bent, hands above head, fingers touching.

THROW FORWARD/FORWARD PASS

Hands gesture as if passing an imaginary ball forward.

KNOCK ON

Arm out-stretched with open hand above head, and moves backwards and forwards.

NOT RELEASING BALL IMMEDIATELY IN THE TACKLE

Both hands are close to the chest as if holding an imaginary ball.

TACKLER NOT RELEASING TACKLED PLAYER

Arms brought together as if grasping a player and then opening as if releasing a player.

TACKLER OR TACKLED PLAYER NOT ROLLING AWAY

A circular movement with the finger and arm moving away from the body.

ENTERING TACKLE FROM THE WRONG DIRECTION

Arm held horizontal then sweep of the arm in a semi-circle.

INTENTIONALLY FALLING OVER ON A PLAYER
Curved arm makes gesture to imitate action of falling player. Signal is made in direction in which offending player fell.

DIVING TO GROUND NEAR TACKLE Straight arm gesture, pointing downwards to imitate diving action.

UNPLAYABLE BALL IN RUCK OR TACKLE
Award of scrum to team moving forward at time of stoppage. Shoulders parallel with the touchline, arm horizontal pointing towards the team to throw in the ball, then pointing the arm and hand towards the other team's goal line whilst moving it backwards and forwards.

UNPLAYABLE BALL IN MAUL
Arm out to award scrummage to side not in possession at maul commencement. Other arm out as if signalling advantage and then swing it across body with hand ending on opposite shoulder..

JOINING A RUCK OR A MAUL IN FRONT OF THE BACK FOOT AND FROM THE SIDE
The hand and arms are held horizontally. Moving sideways.

INTENTIONALLY COLLAPSING RUCK OR MAUL
Both arms at shoulder height as if bound around opponent. Upper body is lowered and twisted as if pulling down opponent who is on top.

PROP PULLING DOWN OPPONENT
Clenched fist and arm bent. Gesture imitates pulling opponent down.

PROP PULLING OPPONENT ON
Clenched fist and arm straight at shoulder height. Gesture imitates pulling opponent on.

WHEELING SCRUM MORE THAN 90 DEGREES
Rotating index finger above the head.

FOOT UP BY FRONT ROW PLAYER
Foot raised, foot touched.

THROW IN AT SCRUM NOT STRAIGHT
Hands at knee level imitating throw not straight.

FAILURE TO BIND FULLY
One arm out-stretched as if binding. Other hand moves up and down arm to indicate the extent of a full bind.

HANDLING BALL IN RUCK OR SCRUM
Hand at ground level, making sweeping action, as if handling the ball.

THROW IN AT LINEOUT NOT STRAIGHT
Shoulders parallel with touchline. Hand above head indicates the path of the ball, not straight.

CLOSING GAP IN LINEOUT
Both hands at eye level, pointing up, palms inward. Hands meet in squeezing action.

BARGING IN LINEOUT
Arm horizontal, elbow pointing out. Arm and shoulder move outwards as if barging opponent.

LEANING ON PLAYER IN LINEOUT
Arm horizontal, bent at elbow, palm down. Downward gesture.

PUSHING OPPONENT IN LINEOUT
Both hands at shoulder level, with palms outward, making pushing gesture.

EARLY LIFTING AND LIFTING IN LINEOUT
Both fists clenched in front, at waist level, making lifting gesture.

OFFSIDE AT LINEOUT
Hand and arm move horizontally across chest, towards offence.

OBSTRUCTION IN GENERAL PLAY
Arms crossed in front of chest at right angles to each other, like open scissors.

OFFSIDE AT SCRUM, RUCK OR MAUL
Shoulders parallel with touchline. Arm hanging straight down, swings in arc along offside line.

OFFSIDE CHOICE: PENALTY KICK OR SCRUM
One arm is for penalty kick. Other arm points to place where scrum may be taken instead of a kick.

OFFSIDE UNDER 10-METRE LAW OR NOT 10 METRES AT PENALTY AND FREE KICKS
Both hands held open above head.

HIGH TACKLE (FOUL PLAY)
Hand moves horizontally in front of neck.

STAMPING (FOUL PLAY: ILLEGAL USE OF BOOT)
Stamping action or similar gesture to indicate the offence..

PUNCHING (FOUL PLAY)
Clenches fist punches open palm.

DISSENT (DISPUTING REFEREE'S DECISION)
Outstretched arm with hand opening and closing to imitate talking.

AWARD OF DROP-OUT ON 22-METRE LINE
Arm points to centre of 22-metre line.

BALL HELD UP IN IN-GOAL
Space between hands indicates that the ball was not grounded.

PHYSIOTHERAPIST NEEDED
One arm raised indicates physiotherapist is needed for injured player.

TIMEKEEPER TO STOP AND START WATCH
Arm held up in the air and whistle blown when watch should be stopped or started

DISMISSALS IN MAJOR INTERNATIONAL MATCHES

Up to 31 October 2007. These cover all matches for which the eight senior members of the International Board have awarded caps, and also all matches played in Rugby World Cup final stages.

A E Freethy	sent off	C J Brownlie (NZ)	E v NZ	1925
K D Kelleher	sent off	C E Meads (NZ)	S v NZ	1967
R T Burnett	sent off	M A Burton (E)	A v E	1975
W M Cooney	sent off	J Sovau (Fj)	A v Fj	1976
N R Sanson	sent off	G A D Wheel (W)	W v I	1977
N R Sanson	sent off	W P Duggan (I)	W v I	1977
D I H Burnett	sent off	P Ringer (W)	E v W	1980
C Norling	sent off	J-P Garuet (F)	F v I	1984
K V J Fitzgerald	sent off	H D Richards (W)	NZ v W	*1987
F A Howard	sent off	D Codey (A)	A v W	*1987
K V J Fitzgerald	sent off	M Taga (Fj)	Fj v E	1988
O E Doyle	sent off	A Lorieux (F)	Arg v F	1988
B W Stirling	sent off	T Vonolagi (Fj)	E v Fj	1989
B W Stirling	sent off	N Nadruku (Fj)	E v Fj	1989
F A Howard	sent off	K Moseley (W)	W v F	1990
F A Howard	sent off	A Carminati (F)	S v F	1990
F A Howard	sent off	A Stoop (Nm)	Nm v W	1990
A J Spreadbury	sent off	A Benazzi (F)	A v F	1990
C Norling	sent off	P Gallart (F)	A v F	1990
C J Hawke	sent off	F E Mendez (Arg)	E v Arg	1990
E F Morrison	sent off	C Cojocariu (R)	R v F	1991
J M Fleming	sent off	P L Sporleder (Arg)	WS v Arg	*1991
J M Fleming	sent off	M G Keenan (WS)	WS v Arg	*1991
S R Hilditch	sent off	G Lascubé (F)	F v E	1992
S R Hilditch	sent off	V Moscato (F)	F v E	1992
D J Bishop	sent off	O Roumat (Wld)	NZ v Wld	1992
E F Morrison	sent off	J T Small (SA)	A v SA	1993
I Rogers	sent off	M E Cardinal (C)	C v F	1994
I Rogers	sent off	P Sella (F)	C v F	1994
D Mené	sent off	J D Davies (W)	W v E	1995
S Lander	sent off	F Mahoni (Tg)	F v Tg	*1995
D T M McHugh	sent off	J Dalton (SA)	SA v C	*1995
D T M McHugh	sent off	R G A Snow (C)	SA v C	*1995
D T M McHugh	sent off	G L Rees (C)	SA v C	*1995
J Dumé	sent off	G R Jenkins (W)	SA v W	1995
W J Erickson	sent off	V B Cavubati (Fj)	NZ v Fj	1997
W D Bevan	sent off	A G Venter (SA)	NZ v SA	1997
C Giacomel	sent off	R Travaglini (Arg)	F v Arg	1997
W J Erickson	sent off	D J Grewcock (E)	NZ v E	1998
S R Walsh	sent off	J Sitoa (Tg)	A v Tg	1998

R G Davies	sent off	M Giovanelli (It)	S v It	1999
C Thomas	sent off	T Leota (Sm)	Sm v F	1999
C Thomas	sent off	G Leaupepe (Sm)	Sm v F	1999
S Dickinson	sent off	J-J Crenca (F)	NZ v F	1999
E F Morrison	sent off	M Vunibaka (Fj)	Fj v C	*1999
A Cole	sent off	D R Baugh (C)	C v Nm	*1999
W J Erickson	sent off	N Ta'ufo'ou (Tg)	E v Tg	*1999
P Marshall	sent off	B D Venter (SA)	SA v U	*1999
P C Deluca	sent off	W Cristofoletto (It)	F v It	2000
J I Kaplan	sent off	A Troncon (It)	It v I	2001
R Dickson	sent off	G Leger (Tg)	W v Tg	2001
P C Deluca	sent off	N J Hines (S)	US v S	2002
P D O'Brien	sent off	M C Joubert (SA)	SA v A	2002
P D O'Brien	sent off	J J Labuschagne (SA)	E v SA	2002
S R Walsh	sent off	V Ma'asi (Tg)	Tg v I	2003
N Williams	sent off	S D Shaw (E)	NZ v E	2004
S J Dickinson	sent off	P C Montgomery (SA)	W v SA	2005
S M Lawrence	sent off	L W Moody (E)	E v Sm	2005
S M Lawrence	sent off	A Tuilagi (Sm)	E v Sm	2005
S R Walsh	sent off	S Murray (S)	W v S	2006
S M Lawrence	sent off	A Tuilagi (Sm)	E v Sm	2005
S R Walsh	sent off	S Murray (S)	W v S	2006
J I Kaplan	sent off	H T-Pole (Tg)	Sm v Tg	*2007
A C Rolland	sent off	J Nieuwenhuis (Nm)	F v Nm	*2007

* Matches in World Cup final stages

THE DIRECTORY

UNIONS IN MEMBERSHIP OF THE IRB

ANDORRA - FEDERACIÓ ANDORRANA DE RUGBY
Region: FIRA-AER
Founded: 1986
IRB Member: 1991
www.vpcrugby.org
Phone: +37 682 2232
FAX: +376864564
Add: Baixada del Moli
No.31 Casal de L'Esport del MICG, Andorra La Vella
AD 500, ANDORRA

ARABIAN GULF - ARABIAN GULF R.F.U.
Region: ARFU
Founded: 1984
IRB Member: 1990
www.agrfu.com
Phone: +971 434 52677
FAX: +971 434 52688
PO Box 65785
Office 2066, Dune centre
Al Diyafa Street, Satwa, Dubai
United Arab Emirates
ARABIAN GULF

ARGENTINA - UNION ARGENTINA DE RUGBY
Region: CONSUR
Founded: 1899
IRB Member: 1987
www.uar.com.ar
Phone: +541 1 4383 2211
FAX: +541 1 4383 2211102
Avda Rivadavia 1227 EP
Buenos Aires, Capital Federal, 1033
ARGENTINA

AUSTRALIA - AUSTRALIAN R.U.
Region: FORU
Founded: 1949
IRB Member: 1949
www.rugby.com.au
Phone: +61 2 99563444
FAX: +61299553299
Level 30, 2 Park Street
Sydney, NSW2060, AUSTRALIA

AUSTRIA - OSTERREICHISCHER RUGBY VERBAND
Región: FIRA-AER
Founded: 1990
IRB Member: 1992
www.rugby-austria.at
Phone: 43 1 92 58 21 27
FAX: 43 1 492 58 21 43
Schneiders Vienna
Koppstrassee 27/29
Vienna
A-1160
AUSTRIA

BAHAMAS - BAHAMAS R.U
Region: NAWIRA
Founded: 1973
IRB Member: 1996
www.rugbybahamas.com
Phone: +1242 323 2165
FAX: +12423937451
Bahamas Rugby Football Union
PO Box N-7213
Nassau, BAHAMAS

BARBADOS - BARBADOS R.F.U
Region: NAWIRA
Founded: 1965
IRB Member: 1995
www.rugbybarbados.com
Phone: +1 246 437 3836
FAX: +12464373838
The Plantation Complex
St Laurence Main Road
Christ Church
Barbados (W.I.), BARBADOS

BELGUIM - FÉDÉRATION BELGE DE RUGBY
Region: FIRA-AER
Founded: 1931
IRB Member: 1988
www.rugby.be
Phone: 00 32 2 479 9332
FAX: 00 32 2 476 2282
Avenue de Marathon 135C
Boite 5, Brussels
B-1020, BELGIUM

BERMUDA - BERMUDA R.F.U
Region: NAWIRA
Founded: 1964
IRB Member: 1992
www.bermudarfu.com
Phone: +1 441 2950071
FAX: +14412924649
P.O Box HM 1909
Hamilton, HM BX, BERMUDA

BOSNIA AND HERZEGOVINA - R.F.U. OF BOSNIA & HERZEGOVINA
Region: FIRA-AER
Founded: 1992
IRB Member: 1996
Phone: +387 32 41 6323
FAX: +387 32 41 6323
Ragbi Savez Bosne I Hercegovine
Bulevar Kralja Tvrtka 1 7200 Zenica, Bosnia & Herzegovina
BOSNIA & HERZEGOVINA

BOTSWANA - BOTSWANA R.U.
Region: CAR
Founded: 1992
IRB Member: 1994
Phone: 00267 360 4272
FAX: 00267 390 7410
P.O BOX 1920
GABORONE, BOTSWANA

BRAZIL - ASSOCIAÇÃO BRASILEIRA DE RUGBY
Region: CONSUR
Founded: 1972
IRB Member: 1995
www.brasilrugby.com.br
Phone: +55 11 3864 1336
FAX: +551138681703
R. Da Germaine Burchard
451 - s.53 - Agua Branca
Sao Paulo
CEP: 05002-62, BRAZIL

BULGARIA - BULGARIAN RUGBY FEDERATION
Region: FIRA-AER
Founded: 1962
IRB Member: 1992
Phone: 00 359 2 958 5847/62
FAX: 00 359 2 958 0137
Bulgarian Rugby Federation
75 Vassil Levski Blvd
Sofia, BULGARIA

CAMEROON - FÉDÉRATION CAMEROUNAISE DE RUGBY - (FECARUGBY)
Region: CAR
Founded: 1997
IRB Member: 1999
Phone: +2379913267
FAX: +2372205594
BP 15464
Yaoundé, CAMEROON

CANADA - RUGBY CANADA
Region: NAWIRA
Founded: 1965
IRB Member: 1987
www.rugbycanada.ca
Phone: +1 905 780 8998
FAX: +14163521243
Toronto Office
40 Vogell Road Ontario
Richmond Hill
L4B 3N6, CANADA

CAYMAN ISLANDS - CAYMAN R.U.
Region: NAWIRA
Founded: 1971
IRB Member: 1977
www.caymanrugby.com
Phone: +1 345 949 7960
FAX: +1 345 946 5786
PO Box 1161 GT
Grand Cayman British West Indies
Cayman Islands ,CAYMAN

CHILE - FEDERACIÓN DE RUGBY DE CHILE
Region: CONSUR
Founded: 1935
IRB Member: 1991
www.feruchi.cl
Phone: +562 275 9314
FAX: +5622751248
Av. Larrain 11. 095,La Reina
Santiago, CHILE

CHINA - CHINA R.U. **Region:** ARFU
Founded: 1996
IRB Member: 1997
Phone: +86 10 671 450 78
FAX: +86 10 671 62 993
N°9 Tiyuguan Road
Chongwen District, Beijing
100763, CHINA

CHINESE TAPEI - CHINESE TAIPEI R.F.U.
Region: ARFU
Founded: 1946
IRB Member: 1986
Phone: +886 2877 22 159/167
FAX: +886 2877 22 171
Chinese Taipei Rugby Football Union
Room 808 8F N020, Chu Lun Street
Taipei, 104, CHINESE TAIPEI

COLUMBIA - PRO FEDERACIÓN COLOMBIANA DE RUGBY
Region: CONSUR
IRB Member: 1999
scorpions.**simplement**.com/
columbia.htm
Phone: +571 520 5236
FAX: +571 525 235
Transversal 15 # 126a - 81 Apto 102, Bogota,
COLOMBIA

COOK ISLANDS - COOK ISLANDS RU
Region: FORU
Founded: 1989
IRB Member: 1995
www.**rugby**.co.ck
Phone: +682 25854
FAX: 68225853
P.O. Box 898
Rarotonga, COOK ISLANDS

CROATIA - HRVATSKI RAGBIJASKI SAVEZ
Region: FIRA-AER
Founded: 1962
IRB Member: 1992
www.**rugby**.hr
Phone: +385 1 365 0250
FAX: +38513092921
Trg Kresimira Cosica 11, Zagreb
10000, CROATIA

CZECH REPUBLIC - CESKA RUGBYOVA UNIE
Region: FIRA-AER
Founded: 1926
IRB Member: 1988
www.**rugbyunion**.cz
Phone: +42 02 33351 341
FAX: +420233351341
Mezi Stadiony PS 40
Praha 6, 160 17
CZECH REPUBLIC

DENMARK - DANSK R.U.
Region: FIRA-AER
Founded: 1950
IRB Member: 1988
www.**rugby**.dk
Phone: +4543262800
FAX: +4543262801
Idraettens Hus
Brondby Stadion 20
Brondby, DK-2605 - Brondby
DENMARK

ENGLAND - THE RUGBY FOOTBALL UNION
Region: FIRA-AER
Founded: 1871
IRB Member: 1890
www.**rfu**.com
Phone: +44 208 8922000
FAX: +442088913814
Rugby House, Rugby Road
Twickenham, TWI IDS
ENGLAND

FIJI - FIJI R.U.
Region: FORU
Founded: 1913
IRB Member: 1987
www.**fijirugbyunion**.com
Phone: +679 3302 787
FAX: +679 3300 936
35 Gordon Street PO Box 1234
Suva, FIJI

FINLAND - SUOMEN RUGBY - LITTO
Region: FIRA-AER
Founded: 1968
IRB Member: 2001
www.**rugbyfinland**.com
Phone: 00 358 40 732 5436
Spjutvagen 7
Borga/Porvoo
06150, FINLAND

FRANCE - FÉDÉRATION FRANÇAISE DE RUGBY
Region: FIRA-AER
Founded: 1919
IRB Member: 1978
www.**ffr**.fr
Phone: 331 5321 1515
FAX: 0033144919109
Fédération française de rugby
9 Rue de Liège
Paris, 75009, FRANCE

GEORGIA - GEORGIA RUGBY UNION
Region: FIRA-AER
Founded: 1961
IRB Member: 1992
www.**rugby**.ge
Phone: 00 995 32 294 754
FAX: 00 995 32 294 763
49A Chavchavadze Ave
Sports Department, Tbilisi
0162, GEORGIA

GERMANY - DEUTSCHER RUGBY VERBAND
Region: FIRA-AER
Founded: 1900
IRB Member: 1988
www.**rugby**.de
Phone: +49 511 14763
FAX: +495111610206
P.O. Box 1566
Lower Saxony, Hannover
30015, GERMANY

GUAM - GUAM RUGBY FOOTBALL UNION
Region: ARFU
Founded: 1997
IRB Member: 1998
www.**rugbyonguam**.com
Phone: +1 671 477 7250
FAX: +16714721264
Guam Rugby Football Union
Po Box 7246 Tamuning, Guam
96931, GUAM

GUYANA - GUYANA R.F.U.
Region: NAWIRA
Founded: 1920
IRB Member: 1995
Phone: +592 623-8186
FAX: +592 226 0240
Guyana Rugby Football Union
P.O. Box 101730
Georgetown, GUYANA

HONG KONG - HONG-KONG R.F.U.
Region: ARFU
Founded: 1953
IRB Member: 1988
www.**hkrugby**.com
Phone: 00 852 2504 8311
FAX: 00 852 2576 7237
Rooms 2001, Olympic House, 1 Stadium Path
So Kon Po Causeway Bay
Causeway Bay, HONG KONG

HUNGARY - MAGYAR ROGBI SZOVETSEG
Region: FIRA-AER
Founded: 1990
IRB Member: 1991
www.**rugby**.hu
Phone: +36 1 460 6887
FAX: 0036 1 460 6888
Magyar Rogbi Szovetseg
Istvanmezei ut 1-3, Budapest
H -1146, HUNGARY

INDIA - INDIAN R.F.U.
Region: ARFU
Founded: 1968
IRB Member: 2001
www.**irfu**.org
Phone: +9122 2209 6357
FAX: +912222091822
2nd Flr Nawab House
M. Karve 63 M K Road - Marine Lines, Mumbai
400002, INDIA

IRELAND - IRISH RUGBY FOOTBALL UNION
Region: FIRA-AER
Founded: 1874
IRB Member: 1886
www.**irishrugby**.ie
Phone: +353 1 647 3800
FAX: 016473801
Irish Rugby Football Union
62 Lansdowne Road Ballsbridge
Dublin 4, IRELAND

ISRAEL - ISRAEL RU
Region: FIRA-AER
Founded: 1971
IRB Member: 1988
www.**israel-rugby**.org.il
Phone: +972 9 7422 062
FAX: +97297422062
Israel Rugby Football Union
PO Box 560, Raanana
43104, ISRAEL

ITALY-FEDERAZIONE ITALIANA RUGBY
Region: FIRA-AER
Founded: 1928
IRB Member: 1987
www.**federugby**.it
Phone: +3906452131 02 /37
FAX: +39 06 452131.76
Federazione Italiana Rugby
Stadio Olimpico Curva Nord
Roma, 00194, ITALY

IVORY COAST - D'IVORIE COTE
Region: CAR
Founded: 1961
IRB Member: 1988
Phone: +225 20 21 2083
FAX: +225 20347 107
Federation Ivoirienne de Rugby
01 BP 2357 Abidjan
01 Cote d'Ivorie, IVORY COAST

JAMAICA
Region: NAWIRA
Founded: 1946
IRB Member: 1996
Phone: +1 876 925 6703
FAX: +18769311743
Jamaica Rugby Union,
PO Box 144
Kingston 5, JAMAICA

JAPAN - JAPAN RUGBY FOOTBALL UNION
Region: ARFU
Founded: 1926
IRB Member: 1987
www.rugby-japan.jp
Phone: +813 3401 3323
FAX: +81354105523
Japan Rugby Football Union
2-8-35 Kitaaoyama Minato-Ku
Tokyo, 107-0061, JAPAN

KAZAKHSTAN - KAZAKHSTAN R.U.
Region: ARFU
Founded: 1993
IRB Member: 1997
Phone: 00 7 333 236 7079
FAX: +73272507357
Kazakhstan Rugby Football Union
Apt. 4 7 Kashgarskaya Street
Almaty, 480083, KAZAKHSTAN

KENYA - KENYA R.F.U.
Region: CAR
Founded: 1923
IRB Member: 1990
www.kenyarfu.com
Phone: +254203876438
FAX: + 2542574425
RFUEA Grounds
Ngong Road P.O. Box 48322
Nairobi, KENYA

KOREA - KORÉA R.U.
Region: ARFU
Founded: 1945
IRB Member: 1988
rugby.sports.or.kr
Phone: +822 420 4244
FAX: +8224204246
Korea Rugby Union
Olympic Building 88 Oryun-Dong, Songpa-Gu,
KOREA

LATVIA - LATVIAN RUGBY FEDERATION
Region: FIRA-AER
Founded: 1960
IRB Member: 1991
Phone: +371 722 0320
FAX: +3717320180
Pulkv.Brieza Str.19/1, RIGA
LV-1010, LATVIA

LITHUANIA - LITHUANIAN RUGBY UNION
Region: FIRA-AER
Founded: 1961
IRB Member: 1992
www.litrugby.lt
Phone: 003752335474
FAX: +3752335474
6 rue Zemaites, Vilnius Lithuania
2600, LITHUANIA

LUXEMBOURG - FÉDÉRATION LUXEMBOURGEOISE DE RUGBY
Region: FIRA-AER
Founded: 1974
IRB Member: 1991
www.rugby.lu
Phone: +352 29 7598
FAX: +352 29 7598
Boite Postale 1965
L-1019 LUXEMBOURG-GARE
LUXEMBOURG

MADAGASCAR - FÉDÉRATION MALAGASY DE RUGBY
Region: CAR
Founded: 1963
IRB Member: 1998
Phone: 00 261 202268869
FAX: 00 261 202268869
Fédération Malagasy de Rugby
Lot VE 50 Ambatonakanga
Antananarivo, 101
MADAGASCAR

MALAYSIA-MALAYSIAN R.U.
Region: ARFU
Founded: 1927
IRB Member: 1988
www.mru.org.my
Phone: +603 2031 8336
FAX: +60320788336
Malaysian Rugby Union
Suite 1.12 Wisma OCM
Kuala Lumpar, 50150, MALAYSIA

MALTA - MALTA RFU
Region: FIRA-AER
Founded: 1991
IRB Member: 2000
www.maltarugby.com
Phone: +356 99495966
FAX: +35621317743
Malta Rugby Football Union
241 Tower Road Sliema SLM 05
Gzira, Malta, MALTA

MOLDOVA - FEDERATION OF RUGBY MOLDOVA
Region: FIRA-AER
Founded: 1992
IRB Member: 1994
Phone: +3 73 22222 674
FAX: +37322222674
Str Columna 106, Chisinau
MD 2012, MOLDOVA

MONACO - FÉDÉRATION MONÉGASQUE DE RUGBY
Region: FIRA-AER
Founded: 1996
IRB Member: 1998
www.monaco-rugby.com
Phone: +377 97 77 1568
FAX: 08658143426
"le Formentor", 27 avenue Princesse Grace,
Monaco
98000, MONACO

MOROCCO - FÉDÉRATION ROYALE MAROCAINE DE RUGBY
Region: CAR
Founded: 1956
IRB Member: 1988
Phone: +212 22 94 82 47
FAX: +21222369060
Federation Royale Marocaine de Rugby
Complexe Sportif Mohamed V Porte 9, Casablanca,
MOROCCO

NAMIBIA - NAMIBIA RU
Region: CAR
Founded: 1990
IRB Member: 1990
www.geocities.com/VNamRugby
Phone: +264 61251 775
FAX: +26461251028
Namibia Rugby Union PO Box 138
Lichtenstein Street Olympia
Windhoek, NAMIBIA

NETHERLANDS - NETHERLANDS RUGBY BOARD
Region: FIRA-AER
Founded: 1932
IRB Member: 1988
www.rugby.nl
Phone: 0031 (0) 20 48 08 100
FAX: 0031 (0) 20 48 08 101
Nederlandse Rugby Bond
Bok de Korverweg 6, Amsterdam
1067 HR, NETHERLANDS

NEW ZEALAND - NEW ZEALAND R.F.U.
Region: FORU
Founded: 1892
IRB Member: 1949
www.allblacks.com
Phone: +644 499 4995
FAX: 006444994224
New Zealand Rugby Football Union
1 Hinemoa Street Centre Port
Wellington, NEW ZEALAND

NIGERIA - NIGERIA RUGBY FOOTBALL FEDERATION
Region: CAR
Founded: 1998
IRB Member: 2001
Phone: +234 01 585 0529
FAX: 00234015850530
Federal Ministry Of Sports & Social Development
National Stadium PO Box 1381 Marina, Lagos,
NIGERIA

NIUE ISLANDS - NIUE RU
Region: FORU
Founded: 1952
IRB Member: 1999
nru.virtualave.net
Phone: +683 4153
FAX: +683 4322
Niue Rugby Football Union
PO Box 11 Alofi
Niue Island, NIUE ISLANDS

NORWAY - NORWEGIAN R U
Region: FIRA-AER
Founded: 1982
IRB Member: 1993
www.rugby.no
Phone: +47 21 02 98 45
FAX: +47 21 02 98 46
Serviceboks 1 Ullevaal Stadion
Oslo, N-0840, NORWAY

PAPUA NEW GUINEA
Region: FORU
Founded: 1963
IRB Member: 1993
Phone: +675 323 4212
FAX: +6753234211
Papua New Guinea Rugby Football Union
Shop Front 2, Gateway Hotel Morea-Tobo
RoadP.O. Box 864
Port Moresby
PAPUA NEW GUINEA

PARAGUAY - UNION DE RUGBY DEL PARAGUAY
Region: CONSUR
Founded: 1970
IRB Member: 1989
Phone: +595 21 496 390
FAX: +59521496390
Union de Rugby del Paraguay
Independencia Nacional 250 casi Palma 1er Piso
Asuncion, PARAGUAY

PERU - FEDERACION RUGBY DE PERU
Region: CONSUR
Founded: 1997
IRB Member: 1999
Phone: +51 1 241 2349
Union Peruana de Rugby
Av. Miguel Dasso 126 ofic. 305
Lima, 27, PERU

POLAND - POLISH R.U.
Region: FIRA-AER
Founded: 1957
IRB Member: 1988
www.pzrugby.pl
Phone: 48 22 835 3587
FAX: 0048228651046
Polski Zwiazek Rugby
Marymoncka 34, Warszawa
01-813, POLAND

PORTUGAL - FEDERAÇÃO PORTUGUESA DE RUGBY
Region: FIRA-AER
Founded: 1926
IRB Member: 1988
www.fpr.pt
Phone: 00 351 21 799 1690
FAX: 00 351 21 793 6135
Federacao Portuguesa de Rugby
Rua Julieta Ferrao NR12-3rd Floor
Lisboa, 1600-131, PORTUGAL

ROMANIA - ROMANIAN RUGBY FEDERATION
Region: FIRA-AER
Founded: 1931
IRB Member: 1997
www.rugby.ro
Phone: +40 2 1 224 54 82
FAX: 0040213192449
Federatia Romana de Rugby
Bd. Marasti No. 18-20
Bucharest, ROMANIA

RUSSIA - R.U. OF RUSSIA
Region: FIRA-AER
Founded: 1936
IRB Member: 1990
www.rugby.ru
Phone: 007 495 6370003
FAX: 00 7095 725 4680
Rugby Union of Russia
8 Luzhneckaya Naberezhnaya
Moscow, 119992, RUSSIA

SAMOA - SAMOA RUGBY FOOTBALL UNION
Region: FORU
Founded: 1924
IRB Member: 1988
www.manusamoa.com.ws
Phone: 00685 26 792
FAX: 0068525009
Samoa Rugby Football Union
Cross Island Road
Malifa, SAMOA

SCOTLAND - SCOTTISH R.U.
Region: FIRA-AER
Founded: 1873
IRB Member: 1886
www.sru.org.uk
Phone: 44 131 346 5000
FAX: +441313465001
Scottish Rugby Union
Murrayfield, Edinburgh
EH12 5PJ, SCOTLAND

SENEGAL - FÉDÉRATION SÉNÉGALAISE DE RUGBY
Region: CAR
Founded: 1960
IRB Member: 1999
Phone: 221 821 5858
FAX: 002218218651
Fédération Sénégalaise De Rugby
73 rue Amadou Ndoye
Dakar, SENEGAL

SERBIA AND MONTENEGRO - RUGBY UNION OF SERBIA AND MONTENEGRO
Region: FIRA-AER
Founded: 1954
IRB Member: 1988
Phone: +381 11 324 5743
FAX: +381113245743
Rugby Union of Serbia and Montenegro Terazije
Terazije 35/111 PO Box 1013
Belgrade
SERBIA AND MONTENEGRO

SINGAPORE - SINGAPORE R.U.
Region: ARFU
Founded: 1948
IRB Member: 1989
www.**sru**.org.sg
Phone: 00 656 4694038
FAX: 00 656 467 0283
Singapore Rugby Union
301 Toa Payoh Lor.6 Toa Payoh Swimming Complex
319 392, SINGAPORE

SLOVENIA - RUGBY ZVEZA SLOVENIJE
Region: FIRA-AER
Founded: 1989
IRB Member: 1996
Phone: +386 1 230 2322
FAX: +386 1 232 1154
Rugby Zveza Slovenije
c/o Studio Mi
Linhartova 8 - 1000 Ljubljana
SLOVENIA

SOLOMON ISLANDS - SOLOMON ISLANDS R.U. FEDERATION
Region: FORU
Founded: 1963
IRB Member: 1999
Phone: 00 677 215 95
FAX: 00 677 215 96
Solomon Islands Rugby Union Federation, PO Box 642
Honaria, SOLOMON ISLANDS

SOUTH AFRICA - SOUTH AFRICA R.F.U.
Region: CAR
Founded: 1889
IRB Member: 1949
www.**sarugby**.co.za
Phone: 00 27 21 659 6700
FAX: 00 27 21 686 3907
5th Floor, Sports Science Institute
Boundary Road PO Box 99 Newlands 7725
Newlands, 7700, SOUTH AFRICA

SPAIN - FEDERACION ESPANOLA DE RUGBY
Region: FIRA-AER
Founded: 1923
IRB Member: 1988
www.**ferugby**.com
Phone: 00 34 91 541 49 78/88
FAX: 00 34 91 559 09 86
Federacion Espanola de Rugby
Ferraz 16-4, Madrid
28008, SPAIN

SRI LANKA - SRI LANKA R.F.U.
Region: ARFU
Founded: 1908
IRB Member: 1988
www.**srilankarugby**.com
Phone: +9411 266 73 21
FAX: +9411 2667320
7 A Reid Avenue
Colombo, 07, SRI LANKA

ST. LUCIA - ST. LUCIA R.F.U.
Region: NAWIRA
Founded: 1996
IRB Member: 1996
Phone: 00 1 758 45 03896
FAX: 00 1 758 452 4794
St. Lucia Rugby Football Union
Hill Top PO Box 614
Castries, ST. LUCIA

ST. VINCENT AND GRANADA - ST. VINCENT AND THE GRENADINES R.U.
Region: NAWIRA
Founded: 1998
IRB Member: 2003
Phone: 1 784 457 5135
FAX: 1 784 457 4396
PO BOX 1034
Kingstown
St. Vincent & the Grenadines
ST. VINCENT & THE GRENADINES

SWAZILAND - SWAZILAND R.U.
Region: CAR
Founded: 1995
IRB Member: 1998
www.swazilandrugb.com
Phone: +268 505 2886
FAX: +2685052886
Swaziland Rugby Union
c/o Homecentre 8 Mhlakuvane Street Manzini,
Mbabane, SWAZILAND

SWEDEN - SVENSKA RUGBY FORBUNDET
Region: FIRA-AER
Founded: 1932
IRB Member: 1988
www.rugby.se
Phone: 004686996524
FAX: 004686996527
Idrottens Hus
S-114 73 Stockholm, Stockholm, 114 73, SWEDEN

SWITZERLAND - FÉDÉRATION SUISSE DE RUGBY
Region: FIRA-AER
Founded: 1972
IRB Member: 1988
www.rugby.ch
Phone: 00 41 31 301 23 88
FAX: 0041 31 301 23 88
Swiss Rugby Union
Pavillonweg 3, 3012 Bern
PO Box 7705 - 3001 Berb, SWITZERLAND

TAHITI - FÉDÉRATION TAHITIENNE DE RUGBY DE POLYNESIE FRANCAISE
Region: FORU
Founded: 1989
IRB Member: 1994
Phone: 689 48 12 28/689 42 04 10
FAX: N/A
Federation Tahitienne de Rugby de Polynesie Francaise
(Tahiti Rugby Union) B.P. 650 Papeete
PapeeteTahiti 98714
French Polynesia, TAHITI

THAILAND - THAI R.U.
Region: ARFU
Founded: 1938
IRB Member: 1989
www.thai-tru.com
Phone: 662 215 3839
FAX: 006622141712
Thai Rugby Union
Thephasdin Stadium Rama 1 Rd.
Bangkok, 10330, THAILAND

TONGA - TONGA RFU
Region: FORU
Founded: 1923
IRB Member: 1987
Phone: 676 26 045
FAX: 676 26 044
Tonga Rugby Football Union
P.O. Box 369 Nuku'alofa, TONGA

TRINIDAD AND TOBAGO - TRINIDAD AND TOBAGO R.F.U.
Region: NAWIRA
Founded: 1928
IRB Member: 1992
www.ttrfu.com
Phone: 1 868 628 9048
FAX: 1 868 628 9049
Trinidad and Tobago Rugby Football Union
PO Box 5090 Tragarete Road Post Office
Woodbrook, Trinidad and Tobago,
TRINIDAD & TOBAGO

FÉDÉRATION TUNISIENNE DE RUGBY
Region: CAR
Founded: 1972
IRB Member: 1988
Phone: 00 216 71 755 066/517
FAX: 00 216 71 751 737
Federation Tunisienne de Rugby
Boite Postale 318 - 1004 El Menzah, Tunis,
TUNISIA

UGANDA - UGANDA R.F.U.
Region: CAR
Founded: 1955
IRB Member: 1977
www.urfu.org
Phone: +256 41 259 280
FAX: +25641259280
Uganda Rugby Union
PO Box 22108
Kampala, UGANDA

UKRAINE - NATIONAL RUGBY FEDERATION OF UKRAINE
Region: FIRA-AER
Founded: 1991
IRB Member: 1992
www.rugby.org.ua
Phone: 00 380 44 2896748
FAX: 00 380 44 2891494
National Rugby Federation of Ukraine105 st
Frunze2nd Floor of the Spartak Stadium
42 Rue Esplanadna str.
Kiev, 01023, UKRAINE

URUGUAY - UNION DE RUGBY DEL URUGUAY
Region: CONSUR
Founded: 1951
IRB Member: 1989
www.uru.org.uy
Phone: +5982 712 3826/3648
FAX: +59827106082
Union de Rugby del Uruguay
Bulevard Artigas 420
Montevideo, 11300, URUGUAY

USA - UNITED STATES OF AMERICA RUGBY
Region: NAWIRA
Founded: 1975
IRB Member: 1987
www.usarugby.org
Phone: +1 303 539 0300
FAX: +13035390311
USA Rugby Football Union
1033 Walnut Street, Ste.200
Boulder, CO 80302, USA

VANUATU - VANUATU R.F.U.
Region: FORU
Founded: 1980
IRB Member: 1999
Phone: +678 424 93
FAX: +67823529
Vanuatu Rugby Football Union
PO Box 284 / 1584
Port Vila, VANUATU

VENEZUELA-FEDERACIÓN VENEZOLANA DE RUGBY
Region: CONSUR
Founded: 1991
IRB Member: 1998
Phone: 00584168087366
FAX: +582129767575
Carretera hacia Fila de Mariches
Centro de Servicios La Florencia, allado del Restauante
Riskos via Urbanizacion , Miranda, 1070, VENEZUELA

WALES - WELSH R.U.
Region: FIRA-AER
Founded: 1881
IRB Member: 1886
www.wru.co.uk
Phone: +44 8700138600
FAX: +442920822474
Welsh Rugby Union
1st Floor Golate House 101 St. Mary's Street, Cardiff
CF10 1GE, WALES

ZAMBIA - ZAMBIA R.F.U.
Region: CAR
Founded: 1975
IRB Member: 1995
Phone: 00 260 223 1604
FAX: 00 260 223 1604
Zambia Rugby Football Union
Room 116 1st Floor Sanlam Building, Kitwe, ZAMBIA

ZIMBABWE - ZIMBABWE R.U.
Region: CAR
Founded: 1895
IRB Member: 1987
www.zimsevensrugby.com
Phone: 00263 4740 562
FAX: 00263 4778 242
The National Sports Stadium
Bay 26, Office Y105 Harare, Harare
Y105, ZIMBABWE

AMERICAN SAMOA – AMERICAN SAMOA R.F.U
Region: FORU
IRB Associate Member: 2005

ARMENIA - ARMENIA R.F.U
Region: FIRA-AER
IRB Associate Member: 2004
Phone: 0037 42 553671
FAX: 003742151090
9 Abovian str,
Yerevan, 375001, ARMENIA

AZERBAIJAN - AZERBAIJAN R.U
Region: FIRA-AER
IRB Associate Member: 2004
Phone: 00994502122704
FAX: 00994124973745
c/o Amerada Hess ACG Ltd
10-33 Izmir Str, Hyatt Tower II, 5th Floor, AZ
1004 BAKU, Azerbijan, AZERBAIJAN

BRITISH VIRGIN ISLANDS
Region: NAWIRA
IRB Associate Member: 2001
Phone: 00 1 284 494 4388
FAX: 00 1 284 494 3088
C/o Smith-Hughes Raworth and McKenzin, BOX
173 Road Town, Tortola

BURUNDI - BURUNDI RFU
Region: CAR
IRB Associate Member: 2004
Place de Independance
BP 1103, Bujumbuna, BURUNDI

CAMBODIA - CAMBODIA FEDERATION OF RUGBY
Region: ARFU
IRB Associate Member: 2004
Cambodian Federation of Rugby
74 Boulevard Preah Sihanouk
CAMBODIA

GHANA - GHANA RUGBY UNION
Region: CAR
IRB Associate Member: 2004
Phone: 0023321661058
FAX: 0023321689789
PO Box GP 1272
ACCRA Ghana, GHANA

KRYGYZSTAN - KRYGYZSTAN RUGBY UNION
Region: ARFU
IRB Associate Member: 2004
Phone: 0073272334992
FAX: 0073272507357
7 Kashgarskaya Street
Àpt 4 Almaty Kazakhstan 480083, Kazakhstan
480083, KYRGYZSTAN

LAO - LAO RUGBY UNION
Region: ARFU
IRB Associate Member: 2004
Lao Rugby Union
c/o- Sodetour 086 Phonexay Street, Ban Fay
Vientiane, Lao P.D.R, LAO

MALI - MALI RFU
Region: CAR
IRB Associate Member: 2004
PO Box 91, Stade Omnisports
Modibo Keita, MALI

MAURITANIA - FÉDÉRATION MAURITANIENNE DE RUGBY
Region: CAR
IRB Associate Member: 2003
Phone: 0022 26 433617
FAX: 0022 26 430028
BP 3201 Nouakchott
Mauritania, MAURITANIA

MAURITIUS - RUGBY UNION MAURITIUS
Region: CAR
IRB Associate Member: 2004
www.mauritiusrugby.mu
Phone: 002304835471
FAX: 002304835471
Lot. DG01, Ruisseau Créole
Rivière Noire, MAURITIUS

MEXICO - FEDERACIÓN MEXICANA DE RUGBY A.C
Region: NAWIRA
Founded: 1972
IRB Member: 2003
www.mexrugby.com
Phone: 00525552764439
FAX: 00525552764439
Villahermosa 21 – B
Colonia Condesa, Mexico
06100, MEXICO

MONGOLIA - MONGOLIA RUGBY UNION
Region: ARFU
IRB Associate Member: 2004
Phone: 0097611343625
FAX: 0097611343817
Khan Uul District
Chinggis Avenue Erel Complex
MONGOLIA

PAKISTAN - PAKISTAN RUGBY UNION
Region: ARFU
IRB Associate Member: 2004
www.pakistanrugby.com
Phone: 0092425751999
FAX: 0092425712109
Servis House
2 Main Gulberg
Lahore
54662
PAKISTAN

PHILIPPINES - PHILIPPINES RUGBY FOOTBALL UNION
Region: ARFU
Founded: 1998
IRB Member: 2004
www.prfu.com
Phone: +632 8528171
c/o The PRFU Secretariat
12 Sunset Drive Los Tamaraos Village NAIA Rd
Paranaque
Metro Manila
PHILLIPINES

RWANDA - RWANDA RUGBY FEDERATION
Region: CAR
IRB Associate Member: 2004
Phone: 00250503481
FAX: 00250503478
Rwanda P.BOX 3264
Kigali RWANDA

TANZANIA - TANZANIA RUGBY UNION
Region: CAR
IRB Associate Member: 2004
IRB Member: 2004
Phone: 00255272508917
FAX: 00255272508434
PO Box 1182
Arusha
TANZANIA

TOGO - FÉDÉRATION TOGOLAISE DE RUGBY
Region: CAR
Founded: 2001
IRB Member: 2004
Phone: +228 2227513
FAX: +228 2227369
BP 7512, Lomé, TOGO

UZBEKISTAN - UZBEKISTAN RUGBY FOOTBALL UNION
Region: ARFU
IRB Associate Member: 2004
Phone: (+998 712) 97-97-49
FAX: (+998 712) 97-97-49
1,Lisunova Str, h.119 apartment 27, Tashkent,
700204, UZBEKISTAN

REGIONAL ASSOCIATIONS

ARFU (ASIA)
Asian Rugby Football Union
Flat 40C, Tower 6 Sorrento, Union Square
No. 1 Austin Road, Kowloon
Hong Kong, ARFU

CAR (AFRICA)
C/O Aziz Bougja
116 rue Damremont 75018 Paris
Paris, CAR

CONSUR (SOUTH AMERICA)
c/o Union Argentina de Rugby
Rivadavia 1227, entre piso 1033 Capital Federal
Buenos Aires, Argentina

FIRA-AER (EUROPE)
9 Rue de Liege
75009 Paris, Paris, France

FORU (OCEANIA)
c/o Andy Conway
Level 7 Rugby House
Rugby House
181 Miller Street, North Sydney NSW 2060

NAWIRA (NORTH AMERICA AND THE WEST INDIES)
C/O Legacy Financial
Suite 104, Savannah Court 10B Queens Park West
Port of Spain, Trinidad, NAWIRA

KEY FIXTURES FOR 2008

KICK OFFS ARE UK & IRELAND TIMES

RBS SIX NATIONS

*All games live on BBC

Sat 2 February
Ireland v **Italy**
Croke Park, 2pm

Sat 2 February
England v **Wales**
Twickenham, 4.30pm

Sun 3 February
Scotland v **France**
Murrayfield, 3pm

Sat 9 February
Wales v **Scotland**
Millennium Stadium, 2pm

Sat 9 February
France v **Ireland**
Stade de France, 4pm

Sun 10 February
Italy v **England**
Stadio Flaminio, 2.30pm

Sat 23 February
Wales v **Italy**
Millennium Stadium, 3pm

Sat 23 February
Ireland v **Scotland**
Croke Park, 5pm

Sat 23 February
France v **England**
Stade de France, 8pm

Saturday 8 March
Ireland v **Wales**
Croke Park, 1.15pm

Saturday 8 March
Scotland v **England**
Murrayfield, 3.15pm

Sunday 9 March
France v **Italy**
Stade de France, 3pm

Saturday 15 March
Italy v **Scotland**
Stadio Flaminio, 1pm

Saturday 15 March
England v **Ireland**
Twickenham, 3pm

Saturday 15 March
Wales v **France**
Millennium Stadium, 5pm